Intelligent Information Systems – Vol. 3

REASONING ABOUT FUZZY TEMPORAL
AND
SPATIAL INFORMATION FROM THE WEB

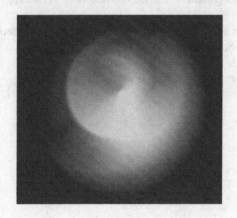

INTELLIGENT INFORMATION SYSTEMS

Series Editors: Da Ruan *(Belgian Nuclear Research Centre (SCK.CEN) &*
Ghent University, Belgium)
Jie Lu *(University of Technology, Sdyney, Australia)*

Vol. 1   Advances in Artificial Intelligence for Privacy Protection and Security
edited by Agusti Solanas & Antoni Martínez-Ballesté (Rovira i
Virgili University, Spain)

Vol. 2   E-Business in the 21st Century: Realities, Challenges and Outlook
by Jun Xu (Southern Cross University, Australia) &
Mohammed Quaddus (Curtin University of Technology, Australia)

Vol. 3   Reasoning about Fuzzy Temporal and Spatial Information from the Web
by Steven Schockaert (Ghent University, Belgium),
Martine De Cock (Ghent University, Belgium) &
Etienne Kerre (Ghent University, Belgium)

Intelligent Information Systems – Vol. 3

REASONING ABOUT FUZZY TEMPORAL
AND
SPATIAL INFORMATION FROM THE WEB

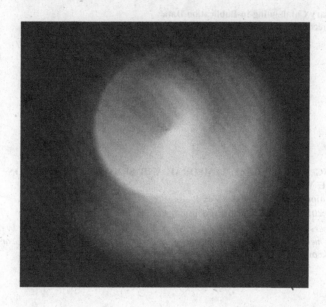

Steven Schockaert • Martine De Cock • Etienne Kerre

Ghent University, Belgium

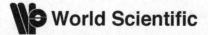

World Scientific

NEW JERSEY • LONDON • SINGAPORE • BEIJING • SHANGHAI • HONG KONG • TAIPEI • CHENNAI

Published by

World Scientific Publishing Co. Pte. Ltd.

5 Toh Tuck Link, Singapore 596224

USA office: 27 Warren Street, Suite 401-402, Hackensack, NJ 07601

UK office: 57 Shelton Street, Covent Garden, London WC2H 9HE

British Library Cataloguing-in-Publication Data
A catalogue record for this book is available from the British Library.

REASONING ABOUT FUZZY TEMPORAL AND SPATIAL INFORMATION FROM THE WEB
Intelligent Information Systems — Vol. 3

Copyright © 2010 by World Scientific Publishing Co. Pte. Ltd.

ISBN-13 978-981-4307-89-5
ISBN-10 981-4307-89-0

Printed in Singapore by World Scientific Printers.

Preface

Traditionally, research in artificial intelligence (AI) has centered around formal representations of information, with the main focus lying on the expressivity of different knowledge representation languages, their computational complexity, and the development of sound and complete reasoners. In information retrieval (IR), on the other hand, the key notion has been manipulating numbers of occurrences of terms, for instance to find statistical evidence that a given text document is relevant to a given textual query, and the most important focus has been on scalability, robustness and the precision-recall trade-off of different retrieval models. Due to a significant progress in domains such as information extraction and natural language processing, however, hybrid approaches have recently emerged, which try to apply symbolic reasoning on information that has been automatically extracted from natural language text. This observation is related to the more general trend of trying to endow search engines with more intelligence by restricting search engine results to what is actually needed to meet the user's information need (focused information access), rather than simply providing a list of possibly relevant documents.

Symbolic reasoning in IR has among others been studied for the analysis of news stories and for building question answering systems, two areas in which temporal information is prevalent. Indeed, temporal relations and events appear to be fundamental both in natural language processing and artificial intelligence, and if automated reasoning from natural language is to be successful, a thorough understanding of the temporal structure of the underlying discourse is required. When moving from news stories to information from the web, however, traditional symbolic reasoning seems not applicable anymore, due to the informal nature of the language, and of the topics that are discussed. For example, while most people would think of the Cold War as something which has happened after the Second World War, many historians date the beginning of the Cold War as early as the end of the 1917 Russian Revolution. The existence of such types of disagreement on the temporal boundaries of events calls for extensions of classical formalisms

Disagreement on the boundaries of categories is most naturally modeled using fuzzy set theory, and various models for representing fuzzy event boundaries have already been proposed. In this existing work, however, only the modeling aspect has been studied, and reasoning with fuzzy temporal information has hardly been covered at all. Thus there seems to be a gap between what has been done on temporal reasoning in AI, focusing on efficiency and reasoning, and what has been done in the context of fuzzy set theory, focusing on expressivity and modeling. It is precisely this missing link between AI and fuzzy set theory that seems crucial to allow reasoning about the kind of informal information we find on the web.

This book is an attempt to find this missing link in the temporal and spatial domains. After three introductory chapters, also introducing the required technical background, fuzzy temporal information processing is studied from three different angles in Chapters 4–6: modeling fuzzy temporal information in Chapter 4 (fuzzy set theory), reasoning with fuzzy temporal information in chapter 5 (AI) and applying fuzzy temporal information on web information in Chapter 6 (IR). As such, our focus is both on obtaining new theoretical insights, and on applying and evaluating them in a practical setting. Subsequently, we also look at fuzzy spatial information from the same three angles in Chapter 7–9. In studying both temporal and spatial information, we discover many parallels, but at the same time, we also lay bare a number of surprising differences between how fuzzy temporal and spatial information behaves.

This book originated from the doctoral thesis of the first author, which was successfully defended in April 2008. Encouraged by the enthusiastic reports of the committee members, and by two awards that have been given to this thesis (the ECCAI Artificial Intelligence Dissertation Award, and the FWO/IBM Belgium Prize for Computer Science), we have decided to publish this book, and make the obtained results available to a larger audience. We are grateful to Alia Abdelmoty, David Ahn, Chris Cornelis, Maarten de Rijke, Christopher Jones, Philip Smart, and Florian Twaroch for many fruitful discussions, and their comments and suggestions which have clearly influenced the results in this work. We also would like to thank the external members of the reading committee, Anthony Cohn,

Didier Dubois, and Dirk Vermeir, for their useful suggestions on the first version of the thesis, and Da Ruan for his help with the publication of this book. Finally, we would like to thank the Research Foundation – Flanders (FWO) for the financial support.

Contents

Preface   v

1. Introduction   1

   1.1   Document Retrieval   1

   1.2   Intelligent Information Access   5

   1.3   Recent Trends   7

       1.3.1   Object Retrieval   7

       1.3.2   Web 2.0   9

       1.3.3   Semantic Web 11

   1.4   The Role of Time and Space 12

   1.5   Overview 14

2. Preliminaries from Fuzzy Set Theory   17

   2.1   Vagueness 17

   2.2   Fuzzy Logic Connectives 21

   2.3   Fuzzy Sets 28

       2.3.1   Definitions 28

       2.3.2   Fuzzy Sets in $\mathbb{R}$ 32

   2.4   Fuzzy Relations 36

   2.5   Criticism of Fuzzy Set Theory 41

3. Relatedness of Fuzzy Sets   47

   3.1   Introduction 47

   3.2   Definition 49

   3.3   Properties 52

       3.3.1   Basic Properties 52

        3.3.2   Interaction 60

        3.3.3   Transitivity 68

    3.4   Proof of the Transitivity Table 70

4.   Representing Fuzzy Temporal Information   87

    4.1   Introduction 87

    4.2   Temporal Relations 91

        4.2.1   Crisp Temporal Relations 91

        4.2.2   Fuzzification of Temporal Relations 96

    4.3   Definitions Based on Relatedness Measures 98

        4.3.1   Generalizing Constraints between Boundary Points 99

        4.3.2   The Case for the Łukasiewicz Connectives 101

        4.3.3   Fuzzy Allen Relations 105

    4.4   Properties 108

        4.4.1   Properties of the Generalized Boundary Constraints 108

        4.4.2   Properties of the Fuzzy Allen Relations 112

    4.5   Evaluating the Fuzzy Temporal Relations 122

        4.5.1   Characterization for Linear Fuzzy Sets 122

        4.5.2   Characterization for Piecewise Linear Fuzzy Time

                 Intervals 139

        4.5.3   Alternative Characterizations for $\beta = 0$ 148

5.   Reasoning about Fuzzy Temporal Information   155

    5.1   Introduction 155

    5.2   Temporal Reasoning 157

    5.3   Complete Reasoning about Fuzzy Time Spans 160

        5.3.1   FI–Satisfiability 162

        5.3.2   Computational Complexity 173

        5.3.3   Entailment 183

        5.3.4   Implementation of a Fuzzy Temporal Reasoner . . 194

    5.4   Efficient Reasoning about Fuzzy Time Spans 200

        5.4.1   2–Consistency 205

        5.4.2   Transitivity of Fuzzy Temporal Relations 215

        5.4.3   Experimental Results 222

6.   Event–based Information Retrieval   229

    6.1   Introduction 229

    6.2   Temporal Information Extraction 231

    6.3   Extracting Time spans 233

        6.3.1   Crisp Time Spans 233

        6.3.2   Fuzzy Time Spans 235

    6.4   Extracting Qualitative Relations 242

        6.4.1   Co–occurring Dates 245

        6.4.2   Document Structure 250

    6.5   Fuzzy Temporal Reasoning 252

        6.5.1   Constructing a Knowledge Base 252

        6.5.2   Reasoning 257

        6.5.3   Event Retrieval 262

    6.6   Experimental Results 267

7. Representing Fuzzy Spatial Information   273

    7.1   Introduction 273

    7.2   Spatial Relations 276

        7.2.1   Crisp Spatial Relations 276

        7.2.2   Fuzzification of Spatial Relations 281

    7.3   Definitions Based on Relatedness Measures 284

        7.3.1   Fuzzy Spatial Relations between Points 285

        7.3.2   Fuzzy Spatial Relations between Vague Regions . 288

        7.3.3   Composing Fuzzy Spatial Relations 294

    7.4   Fuzzifying the RCC 317

        7.4.1   Fuzzy RCC Relations 320

        7.4.2   Properties 322

        7.4.3   Transitivity 326

    7.5   Interpretation of Fuzzy RCC Relations 337

        7.5.1   Resemblance Relations 338

        7.5.2   Semantics of the Fuzzy RCC Relations 342

8. Reasoning about Fuzzy Spatial Information   353

    8.1   Introduction 353

    8.2   Spatial Reasoning 360

    8.3   Satisfiability of Fuzzy Topological Information 362

        8.3.1   Definitions 362

        8.3.2   Satisfiability 366

        8.3.3   Other Reasoning Tasks 377

    8.4   Properties 381

        8.4.1   Reduction to the RCC 382

8.4.2   Relationship with the Egg–Yolk Calculus   392
8.4.3   Realizability in Any Dimension   398

9. Geographic Information Retrieval   409

9.1   Introduction   409
9.2   Acquisition of Geographical Knowledge   412
9.3   Location Approximation and Local Search   414
        9.3.1   Collecting Data   414
        9.3.2   Representing Vague Geographical Information   . .   417
        9.3.3   Location Approximation   427
        9.3.4   Experimental Results   430
9.4   Establishing Fuzzy Footprints   434
        9.4.1   Weighting the Input Data   434
        9.4.2   Defining Neighbourhoods   436
        9.4.3   Analyzing the Fuzzy Footprints   439
        9.4.4   Experimental Results   440
9.5   Modelling the Neighbourhoods of Cardiff: A Case Study .   445
        9.5.1   Containment Relations   446
        9.5.2   Adjacency Relations   452
        9.5.3   Fuzzy Spatial Reasoning   453

Conclusions   459

Appendix A   Proof of Proposition ??   467

Appendix B   Proof of Proposition ??   487

B.1 $\delta_1 = \delta_2 = 0$ 487
        B.1.1   Restrictions for $be^{\preccurlyeq}(A,C)$ and $eb^{\preccurlyeq}(A,C)$ 487
        B.1.2   Restrictions for $bb^{\preccurlyeq}(A,C)$ and $ee^{\preccurlyeq}(A,C)$ 489
B.2 $\delta_1 = 0, \delta_2 > 0$ 491
        B.2.1   Restriction for $be^{\preccurlyeq}(A,C)$ 491
        B.2.2   Restrictions for $bb^{\preccurlyeq}(A,C)$ and $ee^{\preccurlyeq}(A,C)$ 495
        B.2.3   Restriction for $eb^{\preccurlyeq}(A,C)$ 502
B.3 $\delta_1 > 0, \delta_2 = 0$ 504
        B.3.1   Restriction for $be^{\preccurlyeq}(A,C)$ 504
        B.3.2   Restrictions for $bb^{\preccurlyeq}(A,C)$ and $ee^{\preccurlyeq}(A,C)$ 507
        B.3.3   Restriction for $eb^{\preccurlyeq}(A,C)$ 514
B.4 $\delta_1 > 0, \delta_2 > 0$ 515
        B.4.1   Restrictions for $bb^{\preccurlyeq}(A,C)$ and $ee^{\preccurlyeq}(A,C)$ 516

B.4.2   Restrictions for $be^{\preceq}(A,C)$ and $eb^{\preceq}(A,C)$ 518

Appendix C   Proof of Proposition ?? 523

C.1   Lemmas 524

C.2   Connection 536

C.3   Overlap 540

C.4   Part of 546

C.5   Non–Tangential Part of 555

Bibliography 575

Chapter 1

Introduction

Although the central focus of this book is not on information retrieval (IR), it is in this domain that the main motivation for our work is rooted. In this introductory chapter, we provide a glimpse at the field of IR, highlighting how research is increasingly moving towards more "intelligent" techniques and a more thorough use of semantics. In the first section, we focus on the classical paradigm of document retrieval, which has initially been developed in the 1970s and 1980s, but received a tremendous boost in the 1990s with the advent of the web. The next section sketches a number of more advanced information access paradigms, adopting linguistic processing as the main vehicle for achieving intelligence. Subsequently, in Section 1.3, a number of recent trends are discussed, focusing on semantic approaches for retrieving objects, rather than documents. In a final section, we argue that the tendency towards more semantics in IR goes hand in hand with an increased need for appropriate models of time and space. We furthermore emphasize the informal nature of available temporal and spatial information and the resulting need to explicitly deal with vagueness. To conclude, we provide an overview of how these issues will be addressed in the remainder of this book.

1.1 Document Retrieval

The field IR, in general, is concerned with assisting users in acquiring information of interest. By far the most dominant IR paradigm is based on users formulating keyword queries such as *Norway hiking national parks* to express information needs (e.g., Would Norway be an appropriate holiday destination for me?). These queries are subsequently used by the system to estimate the relevance of each document in the collection of interest.

Finally, the most relevant documents are presented to the user in the form of a ranked list. Although an abundance of mathematical models exists for estimating the degree of relevance of a document, they are virtually always based on the same two principles:

(1) the higher the number of occurrences of the query terms in a document, the more likely it is relevant;
(2) the fewer documents a particular query term appears in, the more weight should be given to it.

Thus, documents are essentially reduced to bags of words, as calculations only depend on the number of times a given term appears in a given document. Note, however, that this basic model has been extended along various lines and state–of–the–art systems additionally incorporate features such as the proximity of query terms in a document, allow the use of phrases in queries, etc. Nonetheless, the techniques employed seem surprisingly simple: documents are selected and ranked without any attempt to grasp the semantics of either the query or the documents.

A wide array of more "intelligent" techniques have been proposed to improve the performance of document retrieval systems, albeit with mixed success. A recurring theme is the semantic gap between the query terms and the actual terms used in the document. In particular, most words in English, and many other languages, can have different meanings in different contexts (polysemy), and different words can still have the same meaning (synonymy). A significant increase in performance can therefore be expected when document and query terms are mapped to unambiguous concepts (word sense disambiguation). As different synonyms are mapped to the same concept, more relevant documents should be found. Moreover, as polysemous words are mapped to different concepts in different contexts, less irrelevant documents should be returned: only if the polysemous word is used in the same sense in both query and document, the document will be considered relevant. Experimental results along these lines have been largely disappointing, however [Sanderson (2000); Smeaton (1999); Voorhees (1999)]. The main conclusion drawn in [Voorhees (1999)] is that linguistic techniques have to be essentially perfect to be helpful, which they are not. For example, if the algorithm for disambiguating polysemous words is too error–prone, more relevant documents are missed because of these errors than discovered because of using concepts. In particular, it turns out to be extremely difficult to disambiguate the query terms, as only very little context is available to this end, viz., the other query terms. Along similar lines, in [Mihalcea and Moldovan (2001)] it is proposed to apply a named entity (NE) recognizer to recognize entities such as persons, locations and organizations in documents. This information could help to locate relevant documents if it is known, in advance, that the desired information is concerned with, e.g., a person. Similar considerations as for word sense disambiguation apply. For example, in [Chu-Carroll and Prager (2007)], an experimental study is conducted to analyse the relationship between the accuracy of the NE recognizer and the effect on retrieval performance, i.e., how good an NE recognizer should be in order to be helpful. Other natural language processing (NLP) techniques that have been applied to IR are part–of–speech tagging (e.g., [Kraaij and Pohlmann (1996)]), following an assumption that nouns in documents should influence the degree of relevance more than verbs or adjectives, and noun phrase chunking (e.g., [Evans and Zhai (1996)]), following an assumption that linguistically motivated phrases are better suited for estimating a document's relevance score than statistically motivated phrases. Again, experimental results are mixed, revealing positive effects in some cases and negative effects in others. This seems to suggest that NLP is not as paramount in information retrieval as was originally thought. Note, however, that some simple linguistically oriented techniques are nevertheless fundamental in current IR systems, in particular the removal of stop words (i.e., non–content words such as "and", "he", "are", etc.) and stemming (i.e., removing certain suffices from words). The use of more advanced techniques seems to be impeded by the current state–of–the–art in NLP. Another generally accepted explanation for the disappointing results of NLP techniques is the observation that the statistical techniques utilized in IR implicitly capture more linguistic meaning than intuition would suggest.

A strategy which is closely related to NLP is the use of machine readable dictionaries, or thesauri, to bridge the semantic gap. The main hypothesis here, as for word sense disambiguation, is that many relevant documents are missed because the query terms are not exactly the same as the terms that occur in some relevant documents. Documents might use synonyms, but also hypernyms (i.e., more general terms) or hyponyms (i.e., more specific terms) of the query terms. In particular, it is assumed that by automatically expanding the user's query with terms that are related to it, performance will increase. Clearly, the success of such techniques is closely tied to the quality of the thesaurus used. Various experimental results have shown that using general–purpose hand–crafted thesauri, such as WordNet, is usually not successful, even when manually disambiguating word senses (e.g., [Smeaton and Berrut (1996)]). In general, such thesauri tend to be too shallow and broad to be useful. On the other hand, in domain–specific contexts, using a thesaurus that closely corresponds to the language use in the document collection of interest can significantly improve retrieval performance, but such thesauri are expensive to build and only available for a limited number of domains. As an alternative, it has been proposed to automatically build thesauri using the targeted document collection. The general idea is that term co–occurrence is a reasonable indication of semantic relatedness: terms which often occur in the same document (e.g., "service" and "tie–break") are likely related to the same concept (e.g., tennis). The main advantages of this method are that thesauri can be constructed without any cost, and, moreover, that the thesauri obtained are guaranteed to correspond closely to the document collection (e.g., contain the most significant terms from the collection). In [Qiu and Frei (1993)], an improvement of 20% was witnessed using such automatically constructed thesauri on a relatively small document collection; for larger collections, smaller improvements are usually found. However, the use of thesauri for query expansion is in practice heavily outperformed by a much simpler technique called relevance feedback [Billerbeck and Zobel (2004)]. This technique attempts to expand queries without the need for a thesaurus at all. Specifically, using the original query, a number of relevant documents are selected (e.g., the first 10 ranked documents). To expand the initial query, terms from these top–ranked documents are selected according to some criterion (i.e., terms occurring often in the top–ranked documents and relatively seldom in the document collection as a whole).

Finally, when moving to web search, a number of fundamental extensions to the general document retrieval model are needed. While using the web gives rise to a number of interesting opportunities, e.g., due to the existence of hyperlinks and standards such as HTML, at the same time it brings about new difficulties. For example, there is no quality control on the web: everybody can essentially publish anything. As a consequence, the relevance of a web document is not exclusively determined by its topic anymore, as in standard document retrieval models, but also by its quality or reliability. Therefore, search engines on the web combine scores for the topical relevance of a web page with scores estimating its quality. The best–known algorithm for estimating the quality of a web page is the PageRank algorithm [Brin and Page (1998); Page *et al.* (1998)], which uses hyperlinks to this end. The underlying assumption is that the more high quality web pages refer to a given page p, the more likely p is of high quality as well. Hyperlinks can also be effectively used to better estimate the topical relevance of a web page. Specifically, the anchor text of a hyperlink from page p to page q, i.e., the text which can be clicked to follow the hyperlink, provides a useful description of the content of page q. Various studies have demonstrated the tremendous positive effect of using anchor text in this way [Craswell *et al.* (2001); Westerveld *et al.* (2002)]. Another opportunity for improving document retrieval models in web search is based on the more or less uniform structure of web pages as HTML documents. From these documents, various fields can be extracted, which can be given different weights, e.g., terms occurring in titles should have a greater impact than terms occurring in the body of some section [Hu *et al.* (2005)].

1.2 Intelligent Information Access

Clearly, the standard model for document retrieval, as developed in the 1970s and 1980s, can be significantly improved along various lines. Few of these techniques, however, appear truly intelligent. On the contrary, applying more advanced techniques often results in degraded, rather than improved effectiveness. This observation has led many researchers to believe that the very nature of document retrieval is, to some extent, responsible for this. After all, providing a user with a list of possibly relevant documents is in itself not often perceived as a convincing display of intelligence. A greater impact of intelligent techniques can be expected when more challenging retrieval paradigms are being considered. In particular, a number of paradigms have been explored in which the burden of acquiring information is placed on the machine to a much larger extent. If only a ranked list of documents is returned, the user still needs to sift through the search results and often needs to read large bodies of text. While this may be acceptable when users are looking for general information about a broad topic, better paradigms can be conceived to deal with situations where users have a very specific information need.

One example are question answering (QA) systems. QA systems differ from document retrieval systems in two fundamental ways: natural language questions are used to convey an information need, rather than keyword queries, and the system responds by providing an exact answer, rather than a list of relevant documents. The difficulty in implementing a QA system is largely tied to the complexity of the question types considered. The easiest questions are factoid questions, requiring short fact–based answers (e.g., "How many calories are there in a Big Mac" [Dang *et al.* (2007)]). An essential ingredient of QA systems is their ability to recognize (named) entities. If a question starts with "Who was", the answer should be a person (or organization), if it starts with "Where was", it should be a location and if it starts with "How many" it should be a number. State–of–the–art QA systems involve complex question analysis to infer the implied answer type, and adopt techniques to recognize fine–grained named entities. Typically, a considerable amount of linguistic processing is performed, in addition, to determine if a particular entity of the desired type is indeed the answer to the question. For example, the best performing system at TREC 2007, the main evaluation forum for QA systems, utilized advanced techniques for recognizing and normalizing temporal expressions, and for identifying temporal relations among different events and between events and time references [Moldovan *et al.* (2007)]. Among others, it correctly found the answer to the question *How many grants does the Fulbright Program award each year?* from the following fragment

> The program named after the former Senator J. William Fulbright awards approximately 4,500 new grants annually.

thus recognizing that "each year" corresponds to "annually", and found the answer to *In what year did Kurt Weill die?* from

> Today's Birthdays: Bedrich Smetana, Bohemian composer (1824-1884); ... Kurt Weill, German-born American composer (1900-1950);

At the other side of the question spectrum, complex relationship questions occur, such as [Dang *et al.* (2007)]

> The analyst would like to know of efforts to curtail the transport of drugs from Mexico to the U.S. Specifically, the analyst would like to know of the success of the efforts by local or international authorities.

Clearly, an appropriate answer to such a question comprises more than a single fact. Rather, a summary of the most important information from the most relevant documents should be given. To help systems understand the question, currently, at TREC, an additional summary of the question is provided, following a small number of fixed templates:

> What evidence is there for transport of [drugs] from [Mexico] to [the U.S.]?

In addition to question answering, a number of other intelligent methods for information access have been investigated. For example, while QA systems are useful to obtain very specific information, users are often confronted with a much more general information need. When a user's goal is to learn more about a given topic in general, reading large bodies of text may be exactly what is wanted. To improve on general document retrieval models in these contexts, techniques such as novelty detection can be applied [Allan *et al.* (2003)]. The resulting systems proceed by scanning possibly relevant documents for relevant sentences. The goal is to provide a ranking of sentences, rather than a ranking of documents, such that the user only needs to read the relevant parts from the relevant documents. Moreover, the system attempts to eliminate redundancy by filtering out sentences containing only information that is expressed by higher ranked sentences as well. A related area is topic detection and tracking (TDT), focusing in particular on summarizing and organizing news stories. Evaluation tasks of interest in TDT include segmenting a continuous stream of news stories by topic, identifying stories discussing the same topic, finding which story was the first to report on a given topic, and monitoring a news stream for follow–up information on a specified topic [Lavrenko *et al.* (2002)].

1.3 Recent Trends

1.3.1 *Object Retrieval*

While there is a considerable amount of intelligence in the information access techniques described in the previous section, this intelligence mainly results from linguistic processing. In particular, there is almost no semantic knowledge involved: systems recognize that something is the answer to a given question, but have no real understanding of what is going on. Illustrating this point, [Jijkoun *et al.* (2003)] reports on a system which returned "frogs" as the answer to the question "Who built the Berlin wall". While we have no trouble recognizing that this answer is wrong — even without knowing the correct answer Erich Honecker — this is not at all obvious to a retrieval system. Formalizing the common–sense knowledge to recognize such "clearly" wrong answers (e.g., frogs do not generally build walls) is a difficult and open–ended endeavour. Nevertheless, current research in IR is increasingly aiming at bringing more semantics into the retrieval process. One important witness of this process is the tendency to move from retrieval of documents (or sentences, paragraphs, answers) to retrieval of objects. Typically, search engines following this trend are capable of retrieving one type of objects only; examples include Google Scholar[1] (scientific publications), Google Maps[2] (businesses), Google Code Search[3] (program code), Live Products Search[4] (commercial products), Last.fm[5] (music), YouTube[6] (video), Flickr[7] (images) and Upcoming[8] (local events). To obtain object-level search results, information discovered on different web pages often needs to be merged, as the values of different attributes are found in different contexts. For example, Google Scholar is based on bibliographical information about scientific articles, where attributes such as title, author names and publication year may be extracted from a different web page than the corresponding citation information and PDF file. In [Nie *et al.* (2007)], models are introduced to estimate the degree of relevance of an object w.r.t. a given query, thereby extending classical relevance models for documents. Whereas the reliability and relevance of a document in classical IR stands by itself, for object retrieval, the accuracy and relevancy of the object extraction phase needs to be additionally taken into account.

By limiting the number of supported object types, more intelligent techniques can be employed, adapted to the different requirements of different object types. For example, in [Balog *et al.* (2007)], various strategies are implemented to find people that have expertise in a given topic. To achieve this goal, in addition to standard techniques based on statistical language models, advantage is taken of specific characteristics of the underlying domain. For example, knowledge about the organizational unit of a person in a company is used as context information, while semantic relationships between different topics are used to deal with terminological diversity. Another example are retrieval systems for multimedia, such as image, audio and video. One possibility to implement a search engine for images, for instance, is to analyze all images of interest to obtain certain visual features, and to use these features in deciding to what degree an image satisfies a given query [Rui *et al.* (1999)]. While this is a reasonable approach in some contexts (e.g., databases of finger prints), it is difficult to implement an open–domain image retrieval system by only looking at visual features. As an alternative, textual cues are often employed. Images in HTML docu-

---

[1]http://scholar.google.be/
[2]http://maps.google.com/
[3]http://www.google.com/codesearch
[4]http://products.live.com/
[5]http://www.last.fm/
[6]http://www.youtube.com/
[7]http://www.flickr.com/
[8]http://upcoming.yahoo.com/

ments, for instance, are frequently accompanied by textual descriptions, either as an explicit image caption, or in the surrounding text. Also the combination of these strategies, utilizing both visual and textual cues, is sometimes considered [Kherfi *et al.* (2004)]. In that case, textual features are usually considered first, resulting in a first set of relevant images. From these images, visual features are extracted, which are subsequently compared to the visual features in the image database to retrieve additional relevant images, thus using some form of relevance feedback.

1.3.2   *Web 2.0*

In recent years, the way users experience the world wide web has drastically changed, from a medium merely intended to obtain information to a medium in which they can actively participate. This novel way of using web technology is often referred to as the Web 2.0, suggesting an improvement over the original web or Web 1.0. Typical witnesses of this change are weblogs (blogs), which allow users to express their opinion about certain topics, but also collaborative efforts such as Wikipedia[9], an online encyclopedia exclusively containing articles written by users. Other examples are web sites such as Flickr, YouTube and del.icio.us[10], where users provide tags describing certain objects (resp. photographs, videos and bookmarks).

This change in web usage also implies a change in how information should be searched, providing new opportunities, but also new challenges. Blogs, for instance, contain a wealth of information that was previously often inaccessible, but their informal language usage makes it hard to use NLP techniques, while their variable quality calls for new relevance models. Typical IR tasks for blogs include recognizing spam blogs (splogs), retrieving blog postings about a certain named entity (person, event, place, etc.), and retrieving opinions from blogs [Macdonald and Ounis (2006)]. Next, user–specified tags can effectively be used to improve the quality of retrieval systems. As the tags associated to an image, audio or video fragment, bookmark, etc. tend to be good descriptors, comparing query terms to tags yields surprisingly effective retrieval performance. Taking image retrieval as an example, assume we are interested in pictures of bananas. If a sufficient number of tags are provided for each image, the chances of an image containing bananas being tagged with "banana" or "bananas" is extremely high. The problem of creating an image retrieval system then

---

[9]http://www.wikipedia.org
[10]http://del.icio.us/

reduces to acquiring high–quality tags for images. On web sites such as Flickr, many users — somewhat surprisingly — spontaneously provide an abundance of tags, both for their own photographs and for photographs of others. To acquire tags for images on the web in general, the ESP game has been conceived [von Ahn and Dabbish (2004)]. In this game, users, often unaware of this side–effect, provide image tags while playing a game. Specifically, two randomly paired users are shown the same image. They can score points by guessing what word the other player has used to describe the image. As the image is the only thing connecting the two players, their guesses reflect what is depicted on the image. Each guess is therefore recorded as a tag for the image and can subsequently be used in image retrieval systems. The game instantly became a wide success and by now[11] over 33 million tags have thus been collected. Because of its success, this idea has been borrowed in other systems as well, including Google Image Labeler[12].

The sudden availability of tags is a rich and somewhat unexpected source of information for multimedia retrieval systems. To take maximal benefit of these tags, useful ranking schemes are needed: if 100 images are tagged "banana" there is no obvious way of choosing the most relevant image of a banana. In [Hotho *et al.* (2006)], ideas inspired by the PageRank algorithm are proposed to this end, favouring images that have been tagged with many important tags, provided by many important users. Similarly, a tag is important if it has been often used by important users for important images and a user is important if he has frequently used important tags to tag important images. Somewhat along the same lines, [Bao *et al.* (2007)] discusses techniques to improve document retrieval by looking at tagged bookmarks.

Finally, Wikipedia is increasingly used to support intelligent information access. One of the most important advantages of Wikipedia is its size — currently over 9 million articles[13] — and its semi–structured nature. Every article on Wikipedia roughly corresponds to a concept and links between Wikipedia pages (wiki links) suggest useful semantic relationships. Moreover, articles are often assigned user–defined categories. Exploiting this structure, it has been proposed to use Wikipedia as a thesaurus for query expansion, as it is both open–domain and reasonably comprehensive (compared to, e.g., WordNet), yielding interesting results [Milne *et al.*

---

[11]See http://www.espgame.org/, accessed January 29, 2008.
[12]http://images.google.com/imagelabeler/
[13]See http://en.wikipedia.org/wiki/Wikipedia, accessed January 31, 2008.

(2007)]. Other efforts have focused on automatically generating Wikipedia infoboxes [Wu and Weld (2007)], thus obtaining a structured knowledge base from the semi–structured Wikipedia articles, as well as discovering missing links between Wikipedia articles [Adafre and de Rijke (2005)] and linking terms in arbitrary documents to their corresponding Wikipedia page whenever appropriate [Mihalcea and Csomai (2007)].

1.3.3 *Semantic Web*

In [Berners-Lee *et al.* (2001)], Tim Berners–Lee, known as the inventor of the world wide web, outlines a number of ideas about how the web in its current form should develop to a web of semantics. The central idea of this Semantic Web (SW) is the use of standardized formalisms to semantically annotate resources, and an extensive use of ontologies to provide meaning for these annotations. While to some extent resembling the characteristics of the Web 2.0, a number of fundamental differences exist. First of all, while the Web 2.0 mainly reflects a different usage of existing technologies, the SW relies on a wide variety of new technologies and standards. Furthermore, while tags in Web 2.0 applications are generated by users, the SW requires formalised semantic annotations, adhering to centrally defined standards and terminology. These differences entail both the main advantages and drawbacks of the SW approach. Its main advantage lies in the possibility to use specialised reasoners which are capable of proving whether a particular object is relevant to a particular query. As no natural language processing is needed anymore, and references to the same object or concept are made explicit, information from different sources can "straightforwardly" be combined to obtain information that could not have been derived from one source only. The main drawback is that currently, the required semantic annotations and ontologies are too sparse to yield applications of practical significance. As argued in [Shadbolt *et al.* (2006)], in some domains, the efforts and costs of creating ontologies and semantically annotating resources are worthwhile. Examples include the biomedical domain and some commercial applications where an immediate benefit from using semantics is intuitively clear. For most domains, however, this is not the case. The success of relying on user communities, like tagging–based approaches, is moreover questionable. Creating ontologies requires both significant expertise in the domain being modelled and the enabling SW technologies. Attaching semantic annotations to resources furthermore requires a certain degree of familiarity with the ontologies to select appropriate concepts. In [Fensel *et al.* (2000)], two additional problems have been identified: the scalability of SW reasoners when moving to knowledge bases containing millions of facts, and the limited flexibility of current querying mechanisms on the SW. Finally, note that although the SW has not yet lived up to the initial expectations, substantial contributions have been made in particular domains, the biomedical domain probably being the most–well known (e.g., [De Roure and Hendler (2004); Sougata (2005); Zhao *et al.* (2004)]).

1.4   The Role of Time and Space

The concepts of time and space are paramount in our perception of the world. Everything we experience takes place at a certain time and a certain place. In [Freksa (1997)], it is argued that exactly this omnipresence is responsible for the fact that temporal and spatial phenomena are more often than not neglected in knowledge representation, by exclusively focusing on the notions of truth and falsity. A similar observation can be made regarding IR, where traditionally the emphasis has mostly been on the topical relevance of documents, ignoring their spatial and temporal scope. However, the relevance of a document may very well be influenced by the geographical context: a web page about a tennis club in Ghent may be extremely relevant to a user in Ghent, but is probably of no interest to a user in Fiji. Also the temporal context frequently influences relevancy: an opinion article about today's political situation may be of little value next year. To deal with geographical context in IR, it has been proposed to geo-reference documents, i.e., associate geographical coordinates to documents describing their geographical scope [Jones *et al.* (2001); Larson (1996); Silva *et al.* (2006)]. The geographical scope of the documents considered for retrieval can then be compared with the geographic context of the user, or with explicitly formulated geographical constraints. The georeferencing process itself relies heavily on gazetteers, i.e., geographical knowledge bases containing, among others, the coordinates of different place names. More recently, similar approaches to deal with temporal context have been proposed, attaching a temporal scope to documents [Alonso *et al.* (2007); Mckay and Cunningham (2000)]. Rather than using external knowledge sources, these approaches rely on techniques for recognizing dates and time expressions in documents and for normalising them to a standard format, resolving, for example, expressions such as "last Friday" to the actual date they refer to.

Furthermore, the need to explicitly deal with temporal and spatial information generally increases as more semantics are used. State–of–the–art QA systems, for instance, rely heavily on gazetteers to deal with place names [Ko *et al.* (2007); Leidner *et al.* (2003)], as well as on specialised modules for processing time expressions in natural language [Harabagiu and Bejan (2005); Moldovan *et al.* (2007)]. Next, both geographic and temporal information are paramount in analysing blogs. For example, in [Lin and Halavais (2004)], geographic references in blog posts are used to analyse and compare blogging behaviour in different parts of America. Thus, among others, useful information can be obtained about how opinions on certain topics differ between different cities, states or countries. Temporal features are central in most types of blog analyses, focusing on events or changing trends [Glance *et al.* (2004); Kumar *et al.* (2005)]. Moreover, sometimes geographical and temporal information are used together to collect information from blogs. For example, [Dalli (2006)] is concerned with identifying the places in the world that receive most attention at a given time. Similarly, [Kurashima *et al.* (2006)] adopts a combination of temporal and geographical information to mine user experiences about sightseeing spots from blogs. Finally, for the retrieval of objects, often geographic and temporal features are useful. Local search services such as Google Maps allow users to find businesses satisfying a given geographical constraint, whereas temporal constraints can be used in Google Scholar to find relevant publications. When searching for people, locations are sometimes used to disambiguate different people with the same name [Lefever *et al.* (2007)].

Whether or not the needed temporal and spatial awareness can be implemented often depends on the availability of suitable knowledge bases. Spatial awareness, for example, is made possible because of the widespread use of gazetteers. These geographical knowledge bases contain coordinates of cities, boundaries of administrative regions, etc. On a smaller scale, however, useful geographic knowledge is seldom available. The exact locations of landmarks and the boundaries of city neighbourhoods, for instance, are usually not available to the system. This imposes a severe restriction on further development in GIR systems. Moreover, the nature of many tasks, including blog analyses, entails the use of informal language. The place names people use in everyday communication (i.e., vernacular place names) are not always officially defined. This has two important practical implications for GIR: many place names do not occur in gazetteers, and accurate representations of their spatial extent are not readily available. Next, to implement temporal awareness in retrieval systems, often only dates and time expressions are utilized. A significant fraction of temporal information in texts, however, is expressed through event names. By analogy with geographical gazetteers, structured knowledge bases containing the time spans of events would be useful to process this temporal information. Such event gazetteers do unfortunately not exist for most types of events. Hence, there is a clear need for techniques to harvest spatial knowledge about places and temporal knowledge about events in an automated way from the web. Note that such a strategy, if successfully realized, would not only result in information about officially defined place names and events, but also about, for instance, vernacular place names.

Most of the spatial and temporal information in texts, however, is of a qualitative nature: place p is said to be north of place q, p is said to be within region R, event e is said to be during event f, etc. Nonetheless, by mining such qualitative relations, useful knowledge can be obtained. On one hand, such qualitative relations can sometimes help to build approximate quantitative models. For example, if we know some places that are located in region R and some places that are located just outside R, useful, approximate boundaries for R can often be derived. On the other hand, qualitative descriptions may be useful in their own right as well, to verify whether a given event or place satisfies an imposed temporal or spatial constraint. This latter scenario often involves temporal or spatial reasoning to derive relations that have not explicitly been discovered in texts. For example, if we find that event e happened during event f and f happened before event g, we can infer that e also happened before g. A central issue in implementing this strategy, however, is the vagueness of most real–world events and (non–administrative) places. When exactly did the Cold War begin, for instance? Where exactly are the boundaries of Ghent's city centre? Moreover, the vagueness of events and places implies that qualitative relations between them may be vague as well: is the Sint–Pietersnieuwstraat inside or outside Ghent's city centre? Was the end of World War II at the same time, before, or after the beginning of the Cold War? As will be explained in detail throughout this book, because of this vagueness, classical frameworks for temporal and spatial reasoning cannot be used anymore. The principal aim of our work is therefore to extend these classical frameworks and make them suitable in a context where vagueness is the rule, rather than an exception.

1.5 Overview

The structure of this book is as follows. In the next chapter, we recall some necessary preliminaries from the theory of fuzzy sets, which we will use as the main mathematical vehicle to represent vagueness. In Chapter 3, we introduce a general framework for modelling relatedness between fuzzy sets. In particular, we introduce a number of measures which leverage a fuzzy relation between individual objects to a fuzzy relation between fuzzy sets of these objects. The following three chapters all discuss temporal information, but from three different perspectives. First, in Chapter 4, we show how fuzzy temporal relations between vague events can be defined, and which properties of their crisp counterparts are thus preserved. To define these fuzzy temporal relations, the measures of relatedness from Chapter 3 are used to obtain a generalization of the well–known interval algebra for temporal reasoning. Next, in Chapter 5, we look at fuzzy temporal information from an artificial intelligence angle: when is a knowledge base containing fuzzy temporal relations consistent, what logical consequences can be derived from it, and what is the computational complexity of the underlying reasoning tasks. In Chapter 6, we return to our original motivation and explore practical applications of fuzzy temporal reasoning in IR. The last part of this book deals with spatial information, following roughly the same pattern of three different chapters and three different perspectives. Chapter 7 is concerned with modelling fuzzy spatial relations. After going in some detail about fuzzy nearness and orientation relations, again using the relatedness measures from Chapter 3, we introduce a generalization of the well–known RCC calculus for topological reasoning. In Chapter 8, we demonstrate how the main reasoning tasks in our fuzzy RCC can be solved, focusing, among others, on deciding when a knowledge base is consistent and deriving logical consequences. Finally, in Chapter 9, we explore applications in IR, demonstrating in particular the applicability of fuzzy spatial relations and fuzzy spatial models in general.

The notations and concepts introduced in Chapter 2 are fundamental to understand the remainder of the book, although readers with experience in fuzzy set theory can probably skim through it rather quickly. Also a basic understanding of the relatedness measures introduced in Chapter 3 is essential. However, Chapters 4–6, dealing with temporal information, can be read independently from Chapters 7–9, dealing with spatial information. Finally, note that some of the results in this book have already been published elsewhere:

Chapter 4 A study of how Allen relations could be generalized was presented in [Schockaert *et al.* (2008c)] (©2008, with kind permission from IEEE). Subsequently, techniques for the efficient evaluation of fuzzy temporal relations, in particular for piecewise–linear fuzzy time intervals, were discussed in [Schockaert *et al.* (2006)] (©2006, with kind permission from IEEE).

Chapter 5 In [Schockaert and De Cock (2008)] (©2008, with kind permission from Elsevier), we investigated fundamental reasoning properties of our fuzzy temporal relations. Algorithms for efficient fuzzy temporal reasoning based on algebraic closure algorithms were presented in [Schockaert and De Cock (2009)] (©2009, with kind permission from IEEE).

Chapter 6 An extensive evaluation of how fuzzy temporal reasoning could be applied to information retrieval was presented in [Schockaert *et al.* (to appear)] (©2009, with kind permission of Springer Science+Business Media).

Chapter 7 Our fuzzification of the RCC was first presented in [Schockaert *et al.* (2008b)] (©2008, with kind permission from Elsevier) and [Schockaert *et al.* (2008a)] (©2008, with kind permission from Elsevier). In [Schockaert *et al.* (2008e)] (©2008, with kind permission from IEEE), we discussed the propagation of nearness and cardinal direction between points, as well as the use of relatedness measures to model fuzzy spatial relations between fuzzy regions.

Chapter 8 In [Schockaert *et al.* (2009)] (©2009, with kind permission from Elsevier) we addressed the main reasoning tasks in our fuzzy RCC, and we identified a link with the original calculus.

Chapter 9 In [Schockaert *et al.* (2008d)] (©2008, with kind permission from Taylor & Francis Ltd), we examined the idea of approximating the location of places using natural language hints. Modelling the spatial extent of vague regions by harvesting information from the web was first explored in [Schockaert *et al.* (2005)] (©2005, with kind permission from Springer Science+Business Media) for large–scale regions, and later in [Schockaert and De Cock (2007)] (©2007, with kind permission from the Association for Computing Machinery, Inc.) for city neighbourhoods. In [Schockaert *et al.* (2008f)], we focused on the problem of mining topological spatial relations from web documents (©2008, with kind permission from Springer Science+Business Media).

Chapter 2

Preliminaries from Fuzzy Set Theory

2.1 Vagueness

To deal with the complexities of the real world, human reasoning makes use of concepts to group objects that are in some sense similar. Rather than thinking of small greenish amphibians which are characterized by long hind legs, a short body, webbed digits, protruding eyes and the absence of a tail[1], we think of frogs. We furthermore extrapolate from earlier experiences with individual objects to gain insight about the characteristics of these concepts as a whole, as well as about their relationships with other concepts. Note that such abstractions are fundamental in human intelligence: it organizes our thought processes and allows for efficient communication. At the same time, however, it is often difficult, if not impossible, to specify exactly how a concept is defined, i.e., to provide the exact criteria that need to be satisfied for an object to be an instance of a given concept. Usually, it is easy to give examples of objects that clearly belong to a concept (prototypes), and examples of objects that clearly do not. More often than not, however, human concepts are affected by vagueness and for some objects, it is particularly hard to tell whether or not they belong to a given concept. It has even been suggested that except for some artificially defined concepts (as they occur in mathematics, for example), all human concepts are in fact vague [Russell (1923)]. At first glance, we might be inclined to think that a concept such as frog is well–defined, as biologists surely can classify every living animal as being a frog or not being a frog. Going back in the evolution, however, we find ancestors of our current frogs which would not be classified as frogs at all, and in between, there have been animals which increasingly resembled frogs. The vagueness of concepts is further

---

[1] http://en.wikipedia.org/wiki/Frog, accessed Feb. 2, 2008.

illustrated in the following fragment from [Varzi (2001b)] (adapted from [Bellow (1964)]):

> Remember the story of the most–most? It's the story of that club in New York where people are the most of every type. There is the hairiest bald man and the baldest hairy man; the shortest giant and the tallest dwarf; the smartest idiot and the stupidest wise man. They are all there, including honest thieves and crippled acrobats. On Saturday night they have a party, eat, drink, dance. Then they have a contest. "And if you can tell the hairiest bald man from the baldest hairy man – we are told – you get a prize."

Whether or not a person is bald obviously depends on the number of hairs on his head. Clearly, a person with only 10 hairs is bald and John Lennon was not, but where exactly do we draw the boundary? Is there a number n such that people with less than n hairs are bald, and the others are not, and if so, can we determine the value of this particular number n? Intuitively, we might feel that no such n can possibly exist, as it contradicts the following, seemingly irrefutable rule:

> R1: If somebody with n hairs is bald, then somebody with $n + 1$ hairs is bald as well.

On the other hand, if we choose to accept this rule, we have no choice but to conclude that everybody is bald (even John Lennon). Indeed, since somebody with no hairs is bald, we can prove for any natural number m that somebody with m hairs is bald as well, by m consecutive applications of the rule above. This paradox is a variant to the well–known sorites paradox, and different solutions to it have already been proposed, corresponding to different computational models of vagueness. Some attempts have been inspired by three–valued logics. For example, in [Gentilhomme (1968)], it is proposed to represent concepts like bald using a pair of sets $(\underline{A}, \overline{A})$ rather than a single set, where $\underline{A} \subseteq \overline{A}$. The set $\underline{A}$ contains the objects that definitely belong to the concept being modelled, whereas $\overline{A} \setminus \underline{A}$ contains the borderline cases; the pair $(\underline{A}, \overline{A})$ is called a flou set. Returning to our example of baldness, this solution essentially corresponds to the existence of two well–defined numbers, n_1 and n_2 such that everybody with less than n_1 hairs is clearly bald, everybody with more than n_2 hairs is clearly not, and everybody else is considered to be a borderline case. This provides us with an argument for rejecting rule R1 and thus a way out of the aforementioned paradox. Unfortunately, it is easy to construct similar paradoxes for this three–values case. Indeed, we could easily argue that

R2: If somebody with n hairs is *clearly* bald, then somebody with $n + 1$ hairs is *clearly* bald as well.

In other words, the same problems still occur as there apparently is vagueness about the values of n_1 and n_2, in the same way that there was vagueness about the value of n. We could, therefore add two new classes, in addition to clearly bald people, borderline cases and people who are clearly not bald. These two new classes would correspond to people who are on the boundary between clearly bald people and borderline cases, and people who are on the boundary between people who are clearly not bald and borderline cases. In accordance, we would then need to define four values n_1, n_2, n_3, n_4 that separate these five classes of people. This however does not solve the core problem either: adding more classes means introducing more numbers, each of which is essentially ill–defined. Opponents of the multi–valued approach have therefore argued that introducing more classes makes the problem worse, rather than solving it [Varzi (2001b)]:

> Multiplying the number of relevant boundaries amounts to making an even stronger commitment to precision than that of the members of the most–most club.

A popular solution to the abruptness of the boundaries between different classes was proposed by Zadeh in [Zadeh (1965)]. The central idea is to utilize a continuum of different degrees of belonging to a certain concept (e.g., being bald). Specifically, Zadeh proposed to model a vague concept such as bald as a mapping A from a suitable universe X to the unit interval $[0, 1]$. For an object x in X, $A(x)$ is called the membership degree of x in A; it reflects the degree to which x belongs to the concept modelled by A. For the ease of presentation, we will often use A at the same time to refer to this mapping and to refer to the associated vague concept. The mapping A is called a fuzzy set, or, sometimes, the membership function of the vague concept. An example of a fuzzy set modelling bald is depicted in Figure 2.1. The set of real numbers could be an appropriate universe here (adopting the view that somebody can have half a hair, or three quarters of a hair[2]). Note that again there are particular numbers n_1 and n_2, corresponding to the transition from begin bald to degree 1 and being bald to a degree in $]0, 1[$, and the transition to being bald to degree 0. However, the situation here is fundamentally different from multi–valued approaches, as the difference in membership degrees in a sufficiently small neighbourhood around n_1 and

---

[2]When something is considered a full hair, half a hair, etc., is of course again subject to vagueness, but this does not affect the current discussion.

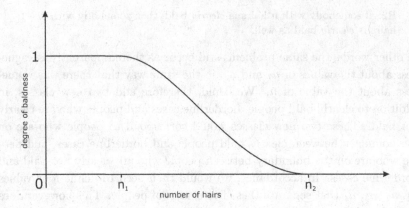

Fig. 2.1   Modelling baldness as a fuzzy set.

n_2 can be assumed arbitrarily small. Essential in the fuzzy set approach is the inherently gradual nature of the transition from being bald to not being bald.

A fundamentally different approach to deal with vague concepts are supervaluation semantics [Fine (1975)]. Their central hypothesis is that vagueness results from under–determinacy: when we use a term like bald, we refer in fact to a crisp concept, but we are vague about what specific crisp concept we have in mind. As such, there can be truth value gaps, i.e., propositions which are not assigned any truth value at all. The possible crisp concepts corresponding to a vague term t are called precisifications of t. A statement involving a vague term can be true in some precisifications and false in other precisifications. If a statement is true (resp. false) in all possible precisifications, it is called supertrue (resp. superfalse). Returning to our example about baldness, the supervaluation approach assumes that there exists a number n that marks the transition from being bald to not being bald, but that we cannot determine the exact value of n. Instead, it is assumed that n might be any number between some value n_1 and some value n_2. The statement "Bob is bald" is supertrue if Bob has less than n_1 hairs, superfalse if Bob has more than n_2 hairs. If the number of hairs on Bob's head is between n_1 and n_2, "Bob is bald" may be true or false. The main advantage of supervaluation semantics is that the framework of classical logic can still be used in the presence of vagueness. As a consequence, for instance, the law of the excluded middle remains satisfied. Indeed, the statement "Bob is bald *or* Bob is not bald" is true in every precisification of bald, and therefore supertrue.

What technique tackles the problem of vagueness in the best way has been the subject of much philosophical debate. Supervaluation semantics are appealing because of their conformity to the laws of classical logic. On the other hand, they are not endowed with the same level of expressivity as fuzzy set based approaches. After all, claiming that Bob and Alice may both be bald or not bald, depending on the view taken, is less informative than claiming that Bob is bald to degree 0.9 and Alice is bald to degree 0.3. The expressivity resulting from membership degrees often proves to be crucial in practical applications, but is, at the same time, the cause for much philosophical controversy. We briefly discuss some of the criticism on the use of degrees of truth in Section 2.5. Note, however, that the principles underlying supervaluation semantics, are not "supertrue" either. For example, [Collins and Varzi (2000)] presents an interesting case against the assumption that all vague terms can in principle be made precise. Finally, multi–valued approaches such as flou sets may provide an appropriate trade–off between expressive power and computational efficiency, notwithstanding their theoretical issues of artificial class boundaries. Intuitively, we could argue that the more borderline classes are introduced, the less critical a correct classification of every object becomes. In other words, although multi–valued approaches increase the number of artificial boundaries, the individual boundaries themselves become less important. There is a useful analogy here[3]: although we cannot model a circle using a finite number of straight lines, with, say, 50 straight lines, an approximation can be obtained that is sufficient for most practical applications. However, as multi–valued approaches can be regarded as a special case of the fuzzy set approach, we will not consider them separately henceforth.

2.2 Fuzzy Logic Connectives

The cornerstone in fuzzy set theory and fuzzy logic is the notion of a truth degree. It is assumed that a particular statement p can not only be true or false, like in classical logics, but can additionally take intermediate degrees of truth. Typically, the unit interval $[0, 1]$ is used to represent such truth degrees, where 1 corresponds to the classical notion of true, and 0 corresponds to false. Note, however, that this is not the only possibility. An important question then is how to generalize logical connectives such

---

[3]This example is taken from the Stanford Encylopedia of Philosophy, available from http://plato.stanford.edu/entries/vagueness/, accessed Feb. 4, 2008.

Table 2.1   Popular choices of t–norms and t–conorms.

t–norm	t–conorm
$T_M(a, b) = \min(a, b)$	$S_M(a, b) = \max(a, b)$
$T_P(a, b) = ab$	$S_P(a, b) = a + b - ab$
$T_W(a, b) = \max(0, a + b - 1)$	$S_W(a, b) = \min(1, a + b)$

as conjunction, disjunction, negation and implication: if p is true to degree 0.4 and q is true to degree 0.7, what should be the truth degree of "p and q"? It seems obvious to define these fuzzy logic connectives such that, when applied to the classical truth degrees 0 and 1, they behave as their classical counterparts. Logical negation is most frequently modelled by the complement w.r.t. 1. For example, if p is true to degree 0.4, then "not p" is assumed to be true to degree $1 - 0.4 = 0.6$. Next, fuzzy conjunction is usually modelled by a t–norm (triangular norm).

Definition 2.1 (t–norm). *[Klement* et al. *(2002)] A t–norm, or triangular norm, is a mapping T from $[0, 1]^2$ to $[0, 1]$ such that for all a, b and c in $[0, 1]$*

$$T(a, 1) = a \tag{2.1}$$

$$T(a, b) = T(b, a) \tag{2.2}$$

$$T(T(a, b), c) = T(a, T(b, c)) \tag{2.3}$$

$$a \leq b \Rightarrow T(a, c) \leq T(b, c) \tag{2.4}$$

From the boundary condition (2.1), we find that $T(0, 1) = 0$ and $T(1, 1) = 1$; from the symmetry condition (2.2) we furthermore find $T(1, 0) = T(0, 1) = 0$; and from the fact that T is increasing, (2.4), we have $T(0, 0) \leq T(0, 1) = 0$. In other words, when restricted to 0 and 1, every t–norm behaves as a classical conjunction operator. In the first column of Table 2.1, a number of particularly popular t–norms are given; T_M, T_P and T_W are called the minimum, product and Łukasiewicz t–norm respectively. In different applications, different t–norms are most appropriate. The main reason is that in generalizing logical conjunction to fuzzy truth degrees, not all its properties can be preserved. For example, it can be shown that the minimum T_M is the only t–norm satisfying idempotency (i.e., $T_M(a, a) = a$ for all a in $[0, 1]$; [Klement *et al.* (2002)]). On the other hand, of the three t–norms in Table 2.1, only T_W satisfies the law of contradiction: $T_W(a, 1 - a) = 0$ for all a in $[0, 1]$. Which t–norm should be used in a given application therefore depends on the properties of logical conjunction that are considered to be most crucial in the given context. We refer to [Kerre (1993)] for a thorough discussion of the logical properties that remain valid when respectively T_M, T_P and T_W are used. It is possible to define an ordering relation $\leq$ on t–norms as follows.

Definition 2.2. [Klement *et al.* (2002)] Let T_1 and T_2 be t–norms. If $T_1(a, b) \leq T_2(a, b)$ for all a and b in $[0, 1]$, we say that T_1 is weaker than T_2, written $T_1 \leq T_2$.

It is easy to show that $T_W \leq T_P \leq T_M$. Furthermore, for any t–norm T, it holds that $T \leq T_M$ [Klement *et al.* (2002)]. Certain additional properties for t–norms are of special interest, resulting in particular classes of t–norms. Note, for example, that no form of continuity is imposed by the definition of a t–norm. In practice, however, it may be desirable that small variations in the arguments a and b result in small changes in the value of $T(a, b)$. Imposing continuity also leads to a number of interesting theoretical properties, as will become clear below. Note, however, that from a theoretical perspective, it is usually sufficient that T is left–continuous, i.e., that the partial mappings of T are left–continuous. For example, let J be an arbitrary index set, and let $(a_j)_{j \in J}$ and $(b_j)_{j \in J}$ be families in $[0, 1]$. For an arbitrary t–norm T, it holds that

$$T(\sup_{j \in J} a_j, b) \geq \sup_{j \in J} T(a_j, b) \tag{2.5}$$

$$T(\inf_{j \in J} a_j, b) \leq \inf_{j \in J} T(a_j, b) \tag{2.6}$$

which follows easily from the definitions of supremum and infimum and the fact that the partial mappings of T are increasing, i.e., (2.4). If, however, T is left–continuous, we have (see, e.g., [Turunen (1999)])

$$T(\sup_{j \in J} a_j, b) = \sup_{j \in J} T(a_j, b) \tag{2.7}$$

and if T is continuous, we also have

$$T(\inf_{j \in J} a_j, b) = \inf_{j \in J} T(a_j, b) \tag{2.8}$$

The following two definitions provide additional ways of discriminating between t–norms.

Definition 2.3 (Archimedean). *[Klement* et al. *(2002)] A t–norm T is called Archimedean if for every a in $[0, 1]$, it holds that $T(a, a) < a$.*

Definition 2.4 (nilpotent). *[Klement* et al. *(2002)] A t–norm T is called nilpotent if there exist a and b in $]0, 1]$ such that $T(a, b) = 0$. Values a and b meeting this requirement are called zero–divisors of T.*

For example, T_P and T_W are Archimedean, whereas T_M is not. Of the t–norms from Table 2.1, only T_W is nilpotent; all a and b in $]0, 1]$ satisfying $a + b \leq 1$ are zero–divisors. The following two lemmas provide important characterizations of continuous Archimedean t–norms.

Lemma 2.1. *[Klement et al. (2002)] If T is a continuous Archimedean t–norm, there exists a strictly decreasing continuous $[0, 1] - [0, +\infty]$ function f such that $f(1) = 0$ and*

$$T(x, y) = f^{(-1)}(f(x) + f(y))$$

where

$$f^{(-1)}(x) = \begin{cases} f^{-1}(x) & \text{if } x \leq f(0) \\ 0 & \text{otherwise} \end{cases}$$

Lemma 2.2. *[Klement et al. (2002)] If T is a continuous, Archimedean, nilpotent t–norm, there exists a strictly increasing continuous bijection ϕ of $[0, 1]$ such that*

$$T(a, b) = \phi^{-1}(T_W(\phi(a), \phi(b)))$$

for all a and b in $[0, 1]$.

Note that, for the ease of presentation, we will sometimes write $T(a_1, a_2, \ldots, a_n)$ instead of $T(a_1, T(a_2, \ldots, T(a_{n-1}, a_n) \ldots))$; this can be done without cause for confusion due to the associativity of t–norms.

To generalize logical disjunction, we can proceed in a similar way as for conjunction. In particular, logical disjunction is usually generalized using t–conorms (triangular conorms).

Definition 2.5 (t–conorm). *[Klement et al. (2002)] A t–conorm, or triangular conorm, is a mapping S from $[0, 1]^2$ to $[0, 1]$ such that for all a, b and c in $[0, 1]$*

$$S(a, 0) = a \tag{2.9}$$

$$S(a, b) = S(b, a) \tag{2.10}$$

$$S(S(a, b), c) = S(a, S(b, c)) \tag{2.11}$$

$$a \leq b \Rightarrow S(a, c) \leq S(b, c) \tag{2.12}$$

One can easily verify that the behaviour of any t–conorm S corresponds to that of the classical disjunction, when restricted to the values 0 and 1. Again there are a wide class of t–conorms available, each preserving different logical properties; the most common choices are presented in the second column of Table 2.1. Note, however, that the t–norm T and t–conorm S are usually not chosen independent from each other in applications. For example, when T and S are taken from the same line of Table 2.1, the laws of De Morgan are satisfied, i.e.

$$S(a, b) = 1 - T(1 - a, 1 - b) \tag{2.13}$$

$$T(a, b) = 1 - S(1 - a, 1 - b) \tag{2.14}$$

for all a and b in $[0, 1]$. Next, it can be shown that for every t–conorm S and all a and b in $[0, 1]$, it holds that $S(a, b) \geq S_M(a, b)$. We also have the following lemma.

Lemma 2.3. *Let S be a t–conorm. For all a, b and c in $[0, 1]$, it holds that*

$$S(\min(a, b), \min(a, c)) \geq \min(a, S(b, c))$$

Proof. If $a \leq b$, we immediately have

$$S(\min(a, b), \min(a, c)) = S(a, \min(a, c))$$
$$\geq \max(a, \min(a, c))$$
$$\geq a$$
$$\geq \min(a, S(b, c))$$

and similar if $a \leq c$. On the other hand, if $a > b$ and $a > c$, we have

$$S(\min(a, b), \min(a, c)) = S(b, c) \geq \min(a, S(b, c))$$

$\square$

Finally, to generalize logical implication, a number of different possibilities exist. We will only focus on the two most popular choices: S–implicators and residual implicators (or R–implicators).

Definition 2.6. Let S be a t–conorm. The mapping I_S defined for all a and b in $[0, 1]$ by

$$I_S(a, b) = S(1 - a, b)$$

is called an S–implicator.

Definition 2.7. Let T be a left–continuous t–norm. The mapping I_T defined for all a and b in $[0, 1]$ by

$$I_T(a, b) = \sup\{\lambda | \lambda \in [0, 1] \text{ and } T(a, \lambda) \leq b\}$$

is called a residual implicator (or R–implicator).

Table 2.2   Popular choices of implicators.

S–implicator	R–implicator
$I_{S_M}(a, b) = \max(1 - a, b)$	$I_{T_M}(a, b) = \begin{cases} 1 & \text{if } a \leq b \\ b & \text{otherwise} \end{cases}$
$I_{S_P}(a, b) = 1 - a + ab$	$I_{T_P}(a, b) = \begin{cases} 1 & \text{if } a \leq b \\ \frac{b}{a} & \text{otherwise} \end{cases}$
$I_{S_W}(a, b) = \min(1, 1 - a + b)$	$I_{T_W}(a, b) = \min(1, 1 - a + b)$

It is easy to see that the behaviour of any S–implicator and any residual implicator corresponds to that of the classical implication, when restricted to the values 0 and 1. The S–implicators and residual implicators corresponding to the connectives from Table 2.1 are presented in Table 2.2. Note in particular that $I_{S_W} = I_{T_W}$. In general, when we refer to implicators, we mean every $[0, 1]^2 - [0, 1]$ mapping I which is decreasing in its first argument, increasing in its second argument, and which behaves like the classical implication for the values 0 and 1, i.e., $I(0, 0) = I(0, 1) = I(1, 1) = 1$ and $I(1, 0) = 0$. It can be verified that all S–implicators and residual implicators satisfy these requirements [De Cock (2002)]. We find from the definitions of infimum and supremum that for every implicator I

$$I(\sup_{j \in J} a_j, b) \leq \inf_{j \in J} I(a_j, b) \tag{2.15}$$

$$I(a, \inf_{j \in J} b_j) \leq \inf_{j \in J} I(a, b_j) \tag{2.16}$$

$$I(\inf_{j \in J} a_j, b) \geq \sup_{j \in J} I(a_j, b) \tag{2.17}$$

$$I(a, \sup_{j \in J} b_j) \geq \sup_{j \in J} I(a, b_j) \tag{2.18}$$

where J is an arbitrary index set, and $(a_j)_{j \in J}$ and $(b_j)_{j \in J}$ are families in $[0, 1]$. If, moreover, T is a left–continuous t–norm, we also have for the residual implicator I_T that

$$I_T(\sup_{j \in J} a_j, b) = \inf_{j \in J} I_T(a_j, b) \tag{2.19}$$

$$I_T(a, \inf_{j \in J} b_j) = \inf_{j \in J} I_T(a, b_j) \tag{2.20}$$

Clearly, S–implicators are the more intuitive of the two, as they straightforwardly generalize the classical definition of implication: $p \Rightarrow q \equiv \neg p \lor q$. On the other hand, residual implicators tend to conform better to the notion of a generalized implication, preserving more important properties of classical implication such as transitivity and shunting. Of central importance is the following residuation principle, which holds for any left–continuous t–norm T and its corresponding residual implicator I_T [Klement *et al.* (2002)]:

$$T(a,b) \leq c \Leftrightarrow a \leq I_T(b,c) \tag{2.21}$$

for all a, b and c in $[0,1]$. This property is sometimes also called Galois correspondence or adjunction property. The following lemma reveals a number of additional logical properties that are preserved by residual implicators.

Lemma 2.4. *If T is a left–continuous t–norm, it holds that*

$$I_T(1,a) = a \tag{2.22}$$

$$a \leq b \Leftrightarrow I_T(a,b) = 1 \tag{2.23}$$

$$T(I_T(a,b),c) \leq I_T(a,T(b,c)) \tag{2.24}$$

$$T(a,I_T(a,b)) \leq b \tag{2.25}$$

$$I_T(T(a,b),c) = I_T(a,I_T(b,c)) \tag{2.26}$$

$$I_T(a,I_T(b,c)) = I_T(b,I_T(a,c)) \tag{2.27}$$

$$T(I_T(a,b),I_T(b,c)) \leq I_T(a,c) \tag{2.28}$$

$$T(I_T(a,b),I_T(c,d)) \leq I_T(T(a,c),T(b,d)) \tag{2.29}$$

$$T(a,I_T(b,c)) \leq I_T(I_T(a,b),c) \tag{2.30}$$

Proof. Most of these properties are well–known. For example, (2.22), (2.23), (2.26) and (2.27) are shown in [Turunen (1999)]; (2.25) is shown in [Novák *et al.* (1999)]; (2.28) is shown in [Fodor and Roubens (1994)]; and (2.24) and (2.30) are shown in [De Cock (2002)]. Hence, we only need to show (2.29). By applying (2.24) (twice) and (2.26), we find

$$
\begin{aligned}
T(I_T(a,b),I_T(c,d)) &\leq I_T(a,T(b,I_T(c,d))) \\
&\leq I_T(a,I_T(c,T(b,d))) \\
&= I_T(T(a,c),T(b,d)) \quad\quad \square
\end{aligned}
$$

Lemma 2.5. *[Klement* et al. *(2002)] If T is a continuous t–norm, it holds that*

$$T(a,I_T(a,b)) = \min(a,b) \tag{2.31}$$

The following lemma relates the ordering of t-norms to an ordering of their corresponding residual implicators.

Lemma 2.6. *Let T_1 and T_2 be two t-norms satisfying $T_1 \leq T_2$. For every a and b in $[0,1]$, it holds that*

$$I_{T_1}(a,b) \geq I_{T_2}(a,b) \tag{2.32}$$

Proof.   Let a and b be elements of $[0,1]$. Because $T_1 \leq T_2$, we have that for any $\lambda \in [0,1]$, it holds that

$$T_2(a,\lambda) \leq b \Rightarrow T_1(a,\lambda) \leq b$$

Hence

$$\{\lambda | \lambda \in [0,1] \text{ and } T_2(a,\lambda) \leq b\} \subseteq \{\lambda | \lambda \in [0,1] \text{ and } T_1(a,\lambda) \leq b\}$$

From the monotonicity of the supremum, we conclude

$$\sup\{\lambda | \lambda \in [0,1] \text{ and } T_2(a,\lambda) \leq b\} \leq \sup\{\lambda | \lambda \in [0,1] \text{ and } T_1(a,\lambda) \leq b\}$$

which is equivalent to (2.32) by the definition of a residual implicator. $\square$

In this book, we will mainly use residual implicators. For the ease of presentation, we will therefore write I_M, I_P and I_W instead of I_{T_M}, I_{T_P} and I_{T_W}. Each of these implicators satisfies properties that are not shared by the others. This is particularly true for I_W as it is an S–implicator, in addition to being a residual implicator. To conclude this section, we summarize some of the more interesting properties of the Łukasiewicz connectives T_W, S_W and I_W, which are not satisfied in general for left–continuous t–norms and their corresponding t–conorms and residual implicators. For a and b in $[0,1]$, it holds that

$$I_W(a,b) = I_W(1-b,1-a) \tag{2.33}$$

$$S_W(1-a,b) = I_W(a,b) \tag{2.34}$$

$$1 - I_W(a,b) = T_W(a,1-b) \tag{2.35}$$

$$T_W(a,1-a) = 0 \tag{2.36}$$

$$S_W(a,1-a) = 1 \tag{2.37}$$

2.3   Fuzzy Sets

2.3.1   *Definitions*

As explained in the introduction, a fuzzy set is defined as a membership function, i.e., a mapping from a universe X to the unit interval $[0,1]$. As such, fuzzy sets can be seen as a generalization of the characteristic function χ_A of a set A, defined for all x in X as

$$\chi_A(x) = \begin{cases} 1 & \text{if } x \in A \\ 0 & \text{otherwise} \end{cases}$$

The notation $\mathcal{F}(X)$ is used to denote the class of all fuzzy sets in the universe X. We use expressions such as $\{a_1/\lambda_1, a_2/\lambda_2, \ldots, a_n/\lambda_n\}$ to denote the fuzzy set A defined for each x in X as $(a, b, c \in X)$

$$A(x) = \begin{cases} \lambda_1 & \text{if } x = a_1 \\ \lambda_2 & \text{if } x = a_2 \\ \ldots \\ \lambda_n & \text{if } x = a_n \\ 0 & \text{otherwise} \end{cases}$$

Slightly abusing notation, we will sometimes, for the ease of presentation, use an expression of the form $\{a_1, a_2, \ldots, a_n\}$ to denote the fuzzy set $\{a_1/1, a_2/1, \ldots, a_n/1\}$, thereby identifying sets with their characteristic function. To denote fuzzy sets in $\mathbb{R}$, we will, moreover, use expressions such as

$$\{[p_1, p_2[/\lambda_1, [p_2, p_3[/\lambda_2, \ldots, [p_k, p_{k+1}]/\lambda_k, \ldots,]p_{n-1}, p_n]/\lambda_{n-1}\}$$

to denote the fuzzy set A in $\mathbb{R}$ defined as $(\lambda_1, \lambda_2, \ldots, \lambda_{n-1} \in [0, 1]$, and $p_1 < p_2 < \cdots < p_n)$

$$A(p) = \begin{cases} \lambda_1 & \text{if } p \in [p_1, p_2[\\ \lambda_2 & \text{if } p \in [p_2, p_3[\\ \ldots \\ \lambda_k & \text{if } p \in [p_k, p_{k+1}] \\ \ldots \\ \lambda_{n-1} & \text{if } p \in]p_{n-1}, p_n] \\ 0 & \text{otherwise} \end{cases}$$

for all p in $\mathbb{R}$. Given a fuzzy set A in X, various related crisp sets in X can be defined. In particular, we define the support $supp(A)$, the kernel $ker(A)$, and the α–level sets A_α $(\alpha \in]0, 1])$ of A as

$$supp(A) = \{x | x \in X \text{ and } A(x) > 0\}$$
$$ker(A) = \{x | x \in X \text{ and } A(x) = 1\}$$
$$A_\alpha = \{x | x \in X \text{ and } A(x) \geq \alpha\}$$

For α in $[0, 1[$, the strict α–level sets $A_{\overline{\alpha}}$ of A are defined as

$$A_{\overline{\alpha}} = \{x | x \in X \text{ and } A(x) > \alpha\}$$

If $ker(A) \neq \emptyset$, A is called normalised, and every x in $ker(A)$ is called a modal value of A. In general, the height $hgt(A)$ and plinth $plt(A)$ of A are defined as

$$hgt(A) = \sup_{x \in X} A(x)$$

$$plt(A) = \inf_{x \in X} A(x)$$

Note that if A is normalised, then $hgt(A) = 1$, although the converse does not necessarily hold. For example, let the fuzzy set A in $\mathbb{R}$ be defined as follows

$$A(p) = \begin{cases} 1 - \frac{1}{p} & \text{if } p \geq 1 \\ 0 & \text{otherwise} \end{cases}$$

for all p in $\mathbb{R}$. Then $hgt(A) = 1$ while $ker(A) = \emptyset$.

The fuzzy logic operators defined in the previous section can be used to generalize set operations such as intersection, union and complement to fuzzy sets. In particular, let T be a t–norm, S a t–conorm, and A and B fuzzy sets in a universe X. For all x in X, we define

$$(A \cap_T B)(x) = T(A(x), B(x)) \tag{2.38}$$

$$(A \cup_S B)(x) = S(A(x), B(x)) \tag{2.39}$$

$$(coA)(x) = 1 - A(x) \tag{2.40}$$

If $T = T_M$, we usually write $A \cap B$ instead of $A \cap_T B$, and similarly, for $S = S_M$, we write $A \cup B$ instead of $A \cup_S B$. Set inclusion is typically generalized to fuzzy sets as follows:

$$A \subseteq B \equiv (\forall x \in X)(A(x) \leq B(x)) \tag{2.41}$$

From the monotonicity of the supremum and infimum, we immediately obtain the following lemma.

Lemma 2.7 (monotonicity). *Let A and B be fuzzy sets in X such that $A \subseteq B$. It holds that*

$$hgt(A) \leq hgt(B)$$

$$plt(A) \leq plt(B)$$

Note that inclusion of fuzzy sets is defined in (2.41) as a crisp relation: either A is included in B or it is not. On the other hand, the degree of overlap and the degree of inclusion are two frequently used, graded measures for comparing fuzzy sets. Specifically, the degree of overlap $overl(A, B)$ between two fuzzy sets A and B in X is defined as [Kerre (1993)]

$$overl(A, B) = \sup_{x \in X} T(A(x), B(x)) \tag{2.42}$$

modelling the degree to which there exists an element of X that is contained both in A and in B. In the same way, the degree of inclusion $incl(A, B)$ of A in B is defined as [Kerre (1993)]

$$incl(A, B) = \inf_{x \in X} I_T(A(x), B(x)) \tag{2.43}$$

modelling the degree to which all elements of X that are contained in A, are also contained in B.

Besides representing vague concepts, we sometimes need to process uncertainty resulting from the use of these vague concepts. Fuzzy sets are interpreted in this context as flexible restrictions and the resulting theory is called possibility theory [Zadeh (1978)]. For example, knowing that Bob is tall, the values of Bob's length are constrained. Clearly, it is not possible, given this knowledge, that Bob is only 1m40, while 1m95 would be perfectly compatible. However, there are also borderline cases. For example, is it still possible that Bob is 1m75, 1m80, 1m85? The solution offered by possibility theory is to associate a possibility distribution π with Bob's length, such that for every length l, $\pi(l)$ reflects the degree to which it is possible that Bob's length is l. Knowing only that Bob is tall, [Zadeh (1978)] proposes to define π for every length l as $\pi(l) = Tall(l)$, i.e., the degree to which it is possible that Bob has length l is defined as the degree to which l can be considered tall. The possibility measure Π and the necessity measure N are defined from a possibility distribution π as follows:

$$\Pi(A) = \sup_{x \in A} \pi(x)$$
$$N(A) = 1 - \Pi(X \setminus A)$$

where $A \subseteq X$ and, in this example, X is the universe of all lengths. Note that $\Pi(A)$ reflects the possibility that the length of Bob is contained in the set A, whereas $N(A)$ reflects the degree to which Bob's length is necessarily contained in A. Possibility theory is easily confused with fuzzy logic and with probability theory, which are, however, both fundamentally different. For example, fuzzy logics deal with degrees of truth, which makes their truth–functionality a reasonable assumption. Possibility theory, on the other hand, deals with degrees of belief, which requires that dependencies between different propositions be taken into account. Furthermore, although probability and possibility theory both deal with uncertainty, different aspects of uncertainty are highlighted. A detailed account of the differences between fuzzy logics, possibility theory and probability theory is given in [Dubois and Prade (2001)].

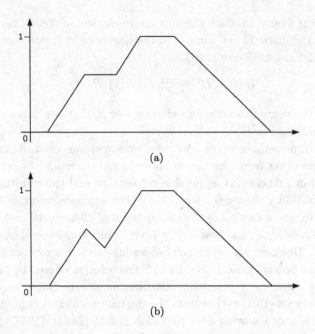

Fig. 2.2   Example of a fuzzy set which is (a) convex, (b) not convex.

2.3.2   *Fuzzy Sets in* $\mathbb{R}$

To represent temporal concepts, fuzzy sets in $\mathbb{R}$ will play a central role. Often, additional properties are required of such fuzzy sets, including convexity and various forms of continuity.

Definition 2.8 (convexity). *[Kerre (1993)] A fuzzy set A in $\mathbb{R}$ is called convex iff*

$$(\forall(p,q) \in \mathbb{R}^2)(\forall\lambda \in [0,1])(A(\lambda p + (1 - \lambda)q) \geq \min(A(p), A(q)))$$

Note, however, that this notion of convexity is sometimes also called quasi–convexity, reserving the term convexity for a stronger property [Chen *et al.* (2004)]. Intuitively, a fuzzy set in $\mathbb{R}$ is convex if it is monotone (i.e., increasing or decreasing), or if it consists of an increasing part followed by a decreasing part. In Figure 2.2, an example is given of a convex fuzzy set, as well as a non–convex fuzzy set. The following characterization of convexity is often useful in practice.

Lemma 2.8. *[Kerre and Van Schooten (1988)] A fuzzy set A in $\mathbb{R}$ is convex iff for all α in $]0,1]$, A_α is convex, i.e., an interval.*

Although continuity is often an interesting property to have, it is not always necessary. In practice, it is therefore common to only impose a weaker form of continuity on fuzzy sets in $\mathbb{R}$ called semi–continuity.

Definition 2.9 (semi–continuity). *[Chen et al. (2004)] Let X be a subset of $\mathbb{R}$. A mapping f from X to $\mathbb{R}$ is called upper semi–continuous in a point x from X if*

$$(\forall \varepsilon > 0)(\exists \delta > 0)(\forall y \in X)(|x - y| < \delta \Rightarrow f(y) < f(x) + \varepsilon)$$

Similarly, f is called lower semi–continuous in x if

$$(\forall \varepsilon > 0)(\exists \delta > 0)(\forall y \in X)(|x - y| < \delta \Rightarrow f(y) > f(x) - \varepsilon)$$

Clearly f is continuous in x iff f is both upper and lower semi–continuous in x. It is possible to derive an interesting characterization of upper and lower semi–continuity for fuzzy sets. First, recall that the inverse image $f^{-1}(D)$ of an $\mathbb{R} - [0, 1]$ mapping f under the set D is defined by ($D \subseteq [0, 1]$)

$$f^{-1}(D) = \{p | p \in \mathbb{R} \text{ and } f(p) \in D\}$$

Next, let $\tau_{|.|}$ be the natural topology on $\mathbb{R}$ induced by the absolute value metric, i.e., for $X \subseteq \mathbb{R}$, we have that $X \in \tau_{|.|}$ iff X is the union of a collection of open intervals.

Lemma 2.9 (semi–continuity). *[Kerre (1993)] A fuzzy set A in $\mathbb{R}$ is upper semi–continuous iff*

$$(\forall \alpha \in]0, 1])(A^{-1}([0, \alpha[) \in \tau_{|.|})$$

and lower semi–continuous iff

$$(\forall \alpha \in [0, 1[)(A^{-1}(]\alpha, 1]) \in \tau_{|.|})$$

Intuitively an upper semi–continuous fuzzy set is right–continuous in its increasing parts and left–continuous in its decreasing parts. Figure 2.3 displays examples of fuzzy sets which are upper semi–continuous, lower semi–continuous and not semi–continuous (i.e., neither upper nor lower semi–continuous). Note that $A^{-1}(]\alpha, 1]) = A_{\overline{\alpha}}$ and $A^{-1}([0, \alpha[) = \mathbb{R} \setminus A_\alpha$. This immediately leads to the following characterization of semi–continuity for fuzzy sets.

Lemma 2.10. *A fuzzy set A in $\mathbb{R}$ is upper semi–continuous iff for all α in $]0, 1]$, A_α is closed. Furthermore, A is lower semi–continuous if for all α in $[0, 1[$, $A_{\overline{\alpha}}$ is open.*

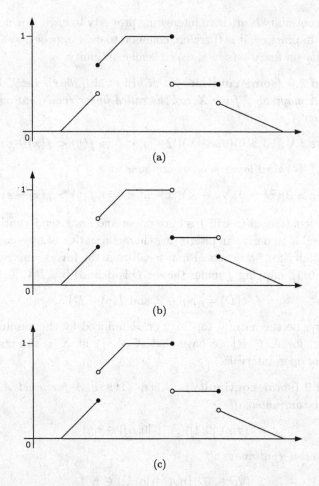

Fig. 2.3   Example of a fuzzy set which is (a) upper semi–continuous, (b) lower semi–continuous, (c) not semi–continuous.

Combining Lemma 2.8 and Lemma 2.10, we find that a fuzzy set A in $\mathbb{R}$ is upper semi–continuous and convex iff all α–level sets A_α ($\alpha \in]0, 1]$) are closed intervals. The next well–known lemma reveals an important advantage of working with upper or lower semi–continuous fuzzy sets.

Lemma 2.11. *[Douglas (1933)] Let A be a fuzzy set in $\mathbb{R}$ and let X be a non–empty, compact (i.e., closed and bounded) subset of $\mathbb{R}$. If A is upper semi–continuous, then A has a maximum over X, i.e., there exists an x_0*

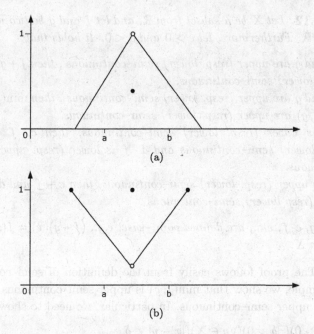

Fig. 2.4 Example of a fuzzy set which is (a) lower semi–continuous and does not have a maximum over $[a, b]$, (b) upper semi–continuous and does not have a minimum over $[a, b]$.

in X such that

$$\sup_{x \in X} A(x) = \max_{x \in X} A(x) = A(x_0)$$

Likewise, if A is lower semi–continuous, then A has a minimum over X, i.e., there exists an x_0 in X such that

$$\inf_{x \in X} A(x) = \min_{x \in X} A(x) = A(x_0)$$

This lemma often simplifies proofs involving semi–continuous fuzzy sets considerably. Note that a lower (resp. upper) semi–continuous fuzzy set does not necessarily have a maximum (resp. minimum) over a non–empty compact set. As a counterexample, Figure 2.4 depicts a lower semi–continuous fuzzy set which does not have a maximum over $[a, b]$, as well as an upper semi–continuous fuzzy set which does not have a minimum over $[a, b]$. Finally, we provide a lemma which allows us to derive, for instance, that $A \cap_{T_W} B$ is upper semi–continuous when both A and B are upper semi–continuous (A and B being fuzzy sets in $\mathbb{R}$).

Lemma 2.12. *Let X be a subset from $\mathbb{R}$, and let f and g be two mappings from X to $\mathbb{R}$. Furthermore, let $c > 0$ and $d < 0$. It holds that*

(1) If f and g are upper (resp. lower) semi–continuous , then $f + g$ is upper (resp. lower) semi–continuous.

(2) If f and g are upper (resp. lower) semi–continuous , then $\min(f, g)$ and $\max(f, g)$ are upper (resp. lower) semi–continuous.

(3) If f is upper (resp. lower) semi–continuous, then $c \cdot f$ is upper (resp lower) semi–continuous and $d \cdot f$ is lower (resp. upper) semi–continuous.

(4) If f is upper (resp. lower) semi–continuous, then $c + f$ and $d + f$ are upper (resp lower) semi–continuous

where $f + g$, $c \cdot f$, etc., are defined point–wise, e.g., $(f + g)(x) = f(x) + g(x)$ for all x in X.

Proof.   The proof follows easily from the definition of semi–continuity. As an example, we show that $\min(f, g)$ is upper semi–continuous if f and g are both upper semi–continuous. In particular, we need to show that

$$(\forall \varepsilon > 0)(\exists \delta > 0)(\forall y \in X)(|x - y| < \delta$$
$$\Rightarrow \min(f(y), g(y)) < \min(f(x), g(x)) + \varepsilon)$$

Let $\varepsilon > 0$. From the upper semi–continuity of f and g, we know that there exists a $\delta_1 > 0$ and a $\delta_2 > 0$ such that

$$|x - y| < \delta_1 \Rightarrow f(y) < f(x) + \varepsilon$$
$$|x - y| < \delta_2 \Rightarrow g(y) < g(x) + \varepsilon$$

For $|x - y| < \min(\delta_1, \delta_2)$ we therefore have

$$\min(f(y), g(y)) < \min(f(x) + \varepsilon, g(x) + \varepsilon) = \min(f(x), g(x)) + \varepsilon \qquad \Box$$

2.4   Fuzzy Relations

In classical set theory, a relation from a set X to a set Y is formally defined as a subset of the Cartesian product $X \times Y$. Accordingly, a fuzzy relation R from a universe X to a universe Y is defined as a fuzzy set in the universe $X \times Y$. For x in X and y in Y, $R(x, y)$ represents the degree to which x stands in relation R with y. For example, let X be the universe of all people and Y be the universe of all research topics. A fuzzy relation R from X to Y could then be used to model the degree to which each person x is an expert on topic y. A fuzzy relation from X to X is simply called a fuzzy relation in X. A fuzzy relation R in X is called (T being a t–norm)

(1) reflexive   iff $R(x,x) = 1$ for all x in X
(2) irreflexive   iff $R(x,x) = 0$ for all x in X
(3) symmetric   iff $R(x,y) = R(y,x)$ for all x and y in X
(4) T–asymmetric   iff $T(R(x,y), R(y,x)) = 0$ for all x and y in X
(5) T–transitive   iff $T(R(x,y), R(y,z)) \leq R(x,z)$ for all x, y, z in X

A fuzzy relation which is at same time reflexive, symmetric and T–transitive is called a fuzzy T–equivalence relation. Next, note that because fuzzy relations are defined as fuzzy sets, operators from fuzzy set theory can be used to define, for example, the intersection, union and complement of fuzzy relations. However, the notion of a relation also gives rise to a number of important additional operations. For example, the inverse of a fuzzy relation R from X to Y is the fuzzy relation R^{-1} from Y to X, defined for all y in Y and x in X as

$$R^{-1}(y,x) = R(x,y)$$

Another important example is the composition of fuzzy relations. Let T be a t–norm, R a fuzzy relation from X to Y and S a fuzzy relation from Y to Z. The sup–T composition of R and S is the fuzzy relation $R \circ_T S$ from X to Z, defined as

$$(R \circ_T S)(x,z) = \sup_{y \in Y} T(R(x,y), S(y,z))$$

for all x in X and z in Z. When it is clear from the context which t–norm is used, we sometimes write $R \circ S$ instead of $R \circ_T S$. Note that $R \circ_T S$ generalizes the composition of crisp relations, defined as

$$x(R \circ S)z \equiv (\exists y \in Y)(xRy \wedge ySz)$$

In [Bandler and Kohout (1980)], two different types of compositions are introduced, often called the Bandler–Kohout compositions. Specifically, for all x in X and z in Z, the superproduct $R \rhd_I S$ and subproduct $R \lhd_I S$ are defined as

$$R \rhd_I S(x,z) = \inf_{y \in Y} I(S(y,z), R(x,y))$$

$$R \lhd_I S(x,z) = \inf_{y \in Y} I(R(x,y), S(y,z))$$

where I is an implicator. It is easy to see that

$$(R^{-1} \circ_T S^{-1})^{-1} = S \circ_T R \tag{2.44}$$

$$(R^{-1} \lhd_I S^{-1})^{-1} = S \rhd_I R \tag{2.45}$$

$$(R^{-1} \rhd_I S^{-1})^{-1} = S \lhd_I R \tag{2.46}$$

Furthermore, various forms of associativity can be shown for the composition of fuzzy relations, as illustrated by the following two lemmas.

Lemma 2.13. *Let T be a left–continuous t–norm and let R be a fuzzy relation from X to Y, S a fuzzy relation from Y to Z and W a fuzzy relation from Z to U. It holds that*

$$(R \circ_T S) \circ_T W = R \circ_T (S \circ_T W)$$

Proof. From (2.7) and the associativity of T, we find for all x in X and u in U

$$
\begin{aligned}
((R \circ_T S) \circ_T W)(x,u) &= \sup_{z \in Z} T((R \circ_T S)(x,z), W(z,u)) \\
&= \sup_{z \in Z} T(\sup_{y \in Y} T(R(x,y), S(y,z)), W(z,u)) \\
&= \sup_{z \in Z} \sup_{y \in Y} T(T(R(x,y), S(y,z)), W(z,u)) \\
&= \sup_{z \in Z} \sup_{y \in Y} T(R(x,y), T(S(y,z), W(z,u))) \\
&= \sup_{y \in Y} T(R(x,y), \sup_{z \in Z} T(S(y,z), W(z,u))) \\
&= \sup_{y \in Y} T(R(x,y), (S \circ_T W)(y,u)) \\
&= (R \circ_T (S \circ_T W))(x,u) \qquad \square
\end{aligned}
$$

Lemma 2.14. *Let T be a left–continuous t–norm, I_T its residual implicator, R a fuzzy relation from X to Y, S a fuzzy relation from Y to Z and W a fuzzy relation from Z to U. It holds that*

$$(R \lhd_{I_T} S) \rhd_{I_T} W = R \lhd_{I_T} (S \rhd_{I_T} W)$$

Proof. Using (2.20) and (2.27), we find for all x in X and u in U

$$
\begin{aligned}
((R \lhd_{I_T} S) \rhd_{I_T} W)(x,u) &= \inf_{z \in Z} I_T(W(z,u), (R \lhd_{I_T} S)(x,z)) \\
&= \inf_{z \in Z} I_T(W(z,u), \inf_{y \in Y} I_T(R(x,y), S(y,z))) \\
&= \inf_{z \in Z} \inf_{y \in Y} I_T(W(z,u), I_T(R(x,y), S(y,z))) \\
&= \inf_{z \in Z} \inf_{y \in Y} I_T(R(x,y), I_T(W(z,u), S(y,z))) \\
&= \inf_{y \in Y} I_T(R(x,y), \inf_{z \in Z} I_T(W(z,u), S(y,z))) \\
&= \inf_{y \in Y} I_T(R(x,y), (S \rhd_{I_T} W)(y,u)) \\
&= (R \lhd_{I_T} (S \rhd_{I_T} W))(x,u) \qquad \square
\end{aligned}
$$

The direct image $R{\uparrow}_T A$ and the superdirect image $R{\downarrow}_I A$ of a fuzzy set A in X under a fuzzy relation R in X are the fuzzy sets in X defined by (T being a t–norm and I an implicator; [Kerre (1992)])

$$(R{\uparrow}_T A)(y) = \sup_{x \in X} T(R(x, y), A(x)) \qquad (2.47)$$

$$(R{\downarrow}_I A)(y) = \inf_{x \in X} I(R(x, y), A(x)) \qquad (2.48)$$

for all y in X. If the t–norm or implicator used is clear from the context, we sometimes write $R{\uparrow}A$ and $R{\downarrow}A$ instead of $R{\uparrow}_T A$ and $R{\downarrow}_I A$. For notational convenience, we furthermore introduce the following abbreviations:

$$R{\uparrow}{\uparrow}A = R{\uparrow}(R{\uparrow}A)$$
$$R{\downarrow}{\downarrow}A = R{\downarrow}(R{\downarrow}A)$$
$$R{\uparrow}{\downarrow}A = R{\uparrow}(R{\downarrow}A)$$
$$R{\downarrow}{\uparrow}A = R{\downarrow}(R{\uparrow}A)$$

We will also refer to fuzzy sets like $R{\uparrow}{\uparrow}{\downarrow}A$, which are defined analogously. In general, we write $R{\uparrow}^n A$ and $R{\downarrow}^n A$ to denote the result of n consecutive applications on A of $R \uparrow$ and $R \downarrow$ respectively. Direct and superdirect images have proven useful in various contexts, including image processing, fuzzy rough set theory, and the study of linguistic modifiers such as "very" and "more or less" [Nachtegael *et al.* (2002)]. Another example is the compositional rule of inference [Zadeh (1973)]. Recall the example from the end of Section 2.3.1 where we used the information that "Bob is tall" to define a possibility distribution on the possible lengths of Bob. Now assume that, instead of knowing that "Bob is tall", we know that "Alice is rather tall" and "Bob is much taller than Alice". The compositional rule of inference then suggests to restrict the possible lengths of Bob as $MTT \uparrow RT$, where RT is a fuzzy set modelling "rather tall" and MTT is a fuzzy relation modelling "much taller than".

In [Bodenhofer (2003)], it is shown that $R{\downarrow}{\uparrow}A$ and $R{\uparrow}{\downarrow}A$ bear close similarity to the concepts of closure and interior from classical topology. A fuzzy set A is called R-closed iff $R{\downarrow}{\uparrow}A = A$ and R–open iff $R{\uparrow}{\downarrow}A = A$ [Bodenhofer (2003)]. The fuzzy set $R{\downarrow}{\uparrow}A$ is sometimes called the R–closure of A. We conclude this section with a number of lemmas, revealing useful properties about the direct and superdirect image. A first important observation is that for a fuzzy T–equivalence relation R, repeatedly applying different images does not alter the result of the first application; this is formalised in the next lemma.

Lemma 2.15. *[Bodenhofer (2003)] Let R be a fuzzy T-equivalence relation in X, A a fuzzy set in X and T a left-continuous t-norm. It holds that*

$$R{\downarrow}_{I_T}{\uparrow}_T A = R{\uparrow}_T{\uparrow}_T A = R{\uparrow}_T A$$
$$R{\uparrow}_T{\downarrow}_{I_T} A = R{\downarrow}_{I_T}{\downarrow}_{I_T} A = R{\downarrow}_{I_T} A$$

For an arbitrary fuzzy relation R, this result does not hold anymore. However, if R is symmetric, the following, weaker properties can be shown.

Lemma 2.16. *[Bodenhofer (2003)] Let R be a symmetric fuzzy relation in X, A a fuzzy set in X and T a left-continuous t-norm. It holds that*

$$R{\uparrow}_T{\downarrow}_{I_T}{\uparrow}_T A = R{\uparrow}_T A \tag{2.49}$$
$$R{\downarrow}_{I_T}{\uparrow}_T{\downarrow}_{I_T} A = R{\downarrow}_{I_T} A \tag{2.50}$$

Corollary 2.1. *Under the assumptions of Lemma 2.16, it holds that*

$$R{\uparrow}_T{\downarrow}_{I_T}{\uparrow}_T{\downarrow}_{I_T} A = R{\uparrow}_T{\downarrow}_{I_T} A \tag{2.51}$$
$$R{\downarrow}_{I_T}{\uparrow}_T{\downarrow}_{I_T}{\uparrow}_T A = R{\downarrow}_{I_T}{\uparrow}_T A \tag{2.52}$$

The following lemma reveals an important relationship between the various fuzzy relational images.

Lemma 2.17. *[Bodenhofer (2003)] Let R be a reflexive and symmetric fuzzy relation in X, A a fuzzy set in X and T a left-continuous t-norm. It holds that*

$$R{\downarrow}_{I_T} A \subseteq R{\uparrow}_T{\downarrow}_{I_T} A \subseteq A \subseteq R{\downarrow}_{I_T}{\uparrow}_T A \subseteq R{\uparrow}_T A \tag{2.53}$$

Finally, we present a number of properties regarding the interaction between the fuzzy relational images and fuzzy set operations.

Lemma 2.18 (interaction with $\cup$ and $\cap$). *[Bodenhofer (2003)] Let R be an arbitrary fuzzy relation in X, A and B fuzzy sets in X and T a left-continuous t-norm. It holds that*

$$R{\uparrow}_T(A \cup B) = (R{\uparrow}_T A) \cup (R{\uparrow}_T B) \tag{2.54}$$
$$R{\uparrow}_T(A \cap B) \subseteq (R{\uparrow}_T A) \cap (R{\uparrow}_T B) \tag{2.55}$$
$$R{\downarrow}_{I_T}(A \cap B) = (R{\downarrow}_{I_T} A) \cap (R{\downarrow}_{I_T} B) \tag{2.56}$$
$$R{\downarrow}_{I_T}(A \cup B) \supseteq (R{\downarrow}_{I_T} A) \cup (R{\downarrow}_{I_T} B) \tag{2.57}$$

Corollary 2.2. *Under the assumptions of Lemma 2.18, it holds that*

$$R{\downarrow}_{I_T}{\uparrow}_T(A \cup B) \supseteq (R{\downarrow}_{I_T}{\uparrow}_T A) \cup (R{\downarrow}_{I_T}{\uparrow}_T B) \tag{2.58}$$

$$R{\uparrow}_{I_T}{\downarrow}_T(A \cup B) \supseteq (R{\uparrow}_{I_T}{\downarrow}_T A) \cup (R{\uparrow}_{I_T}{\downarrow}_T B) \tag{2.59}$$

$$R{\downarrow}_{I_T}{\uparrow}_T(A \cap B) \subseteq (R{\downarrow}_{I_T}{\uparrow}_T A) \cap (R{\downarrow}_{I_T}{\uparrow}_T B) \tag{2.60}$$

$$R{\uparrow}_{I_T}{\downarrow}_T(A \cap B) \subseteq (R{\uparrow}_{I_T}{\downarrow}_T A) \cap (R{\uparrow}_{I_T}{\downarrow}_T B) \tag{2.61}$$

Lemma 2.19 (interaction with $\subseteq$). *[Bodenhofer (2003)] Let R be an arbitrary fuzzy relation in X, A and B fuzzy sets in X and T a left-continuous t-norm. It holds that*

$$A \subseteq B \Rightarrow R{\uparrow}_T A \subseteq R{\uparrow}_T B \tag{2.62}$$

$$A \subseteq B \Rightarrow R{\downarrow}_{I_T} A \subseteq R{\downarrow}_{I_T} B \tag{2.63}$$

Lemma 2.20 (interaction with *incl*). *Let R be a symmetric fuzzy relation in X, let A and B be fuzzy sets in X, and let T a left-continuous t-norm. It holds that*

$$incl(R{\uparrow}_T A, B) = incl(A, R{\downarrow}_{I_T} B) \tag{2.64}$$

$$incl(R{\uparrow}_T A, R{\uparrow}_T B) = incl(R{\downarrow}_{I_T}{\uparrow}_T A, R{\downarrow}_{I_T}{\uparrow}_T B) \tag{2.65}$$

Proof. First, note that (2.65) follows immediately from (2.49) and (2.64). Therefore, we only need to show (2.64):

$$incl(R{\uparrow}_T A, B) = \inf_{x \in X} I_T(\sup_{y \in X} T(R(y, x), A(y)), B(x))$$

By (2.19) and (2.26), we obtain

$$= \inf_{x \in X} \inf_{y \in X} I_T(T(R(y, x), A(y)), B(x))$$

$$= \inf_{x \in X} \inf_{y \in X} I_T(A(y), I_T(R(y, x), B(x)))$$

and finally by (2.20)

$$= \inf_{y \in X} I_T(A(y), \inf_{x \in X} I_T(R(y, x), B(x)))$$

$$= \inf_{y \in X} I_T(A(y), (R{\downarrow}_{I_T} B)(y))$$

$$= incl(A, R{\downarrow}_{I_T} B)$$

$\square$

2.5   Criticism of Fuzzy Set Theory

As we already hinted at in the introduction of this chapter, the theory of fuzzy sets has been the subject of considerable debate. Ever since its introduction, opponents of the theory have been trying to reveal fundamental flaws (e.g., [Keefe (1998)]), resulting each time in a range of counter-arguments by proponents of the theory (e.g., [Smith (2003)]), subsequently being refuted by opponents (e.g., [Keefe (2003)]), etc. Of central importance in most of the discussion is the meaning of a degree of truth. In contrast to probabilities, for example, truth degrees are not endowed with any formal definition, i.e., fuzzy set theory does not provide the means to obtain the truth degrees, only the tools to manipulate them. In consequence, truth degrees are often criticized for being over–specific: why do we call somebody bald to degree 0.648 and not to degree 0.649? This over–specificity results in membership functions which are to some extent arbitrary, and are therefore, it is argued, meaningless [Keefe (1998)]. A classical response is that the exact membership degrees are not important at all, numbers are only used as a means to define an ordering on the objects of interest. As such, the unit interval $[0, 1]$ can, in principle be replaced by other bounded, linear ordering relations [Dubois *et al.* (2005)]:

> Contrary to what the terminology (vague, fuzzy) may suggest, gradual predicates allow for a refined model of categories, more expressive than the Boolean setting, and reflecting the common usage of some words as underlying preferred meanings or default typicality orderings of situations they refer to. Membership functions are just convenient context-dependent numerical representations of this ordering.

Even more generally, arbitrary pre–order relations can be used to define truth degrees [Dubois *et al.* (2005)], although usually, only those pre–order relations that constitute a bounded lattice are considered [Goguen (1967)]. When non–linear pre–order relations are used, degrees of truth may be incomparable with each other, modelling that, e.g., p is not more true than q, but at the same time q is not more true than p. Such behaviour may be useful for concepts that are defined from multiple attributes in non–trivial ways, e.g., the concept of an intelligent person (e.g., how do you compare mathematicians with philosophers).

While the view of membership degrees as only defining an ordering relation convincingly solves the problem of over–specificity if vague concepts are treated independently from each other, it becomes problematic when membership degrees from different concepts need to be combined. For example, assume there are three objects of interest a, b and c and we want to assess the degree to which they are large, as well as the degree to which they are red. Using a pre–order relation $<$, we may define

$$Red(a) < Red(b) < Red(c)$$
$$Large(c) < Large(b) < Large(a)$$

meaning that, for example, it is more true that c is red than that b is red, and it is more true that b is large than that c is large. Now, consider the statement "b is both red and large". Is this true to a larger extent than "c is large", than "a is red", than "a is red and large"? Clearly, we cannot seriously answer these questions without additional knowledge. This, however, stands in contrast with the typical view of fuzzy logic as being truth–functional. When we use t–norms to generalize logical conjunction, for example, we implicitly assume that the truth degree of "p and q" only depends on the truth degrees of "p" and "q". Unfortunately, on the unit interval, similar problems arise when truth–functionality is assumed together with the view of membership degrees as only defining an ordering. Specifically, Keefe [Keefe (1998)] argues that if the actual truth degrees were unimportant, it should be possible to define a $[0, 1] - [0, 1]$ mapping f which is non–trivial (i.e., $f(a) \neq a$ for at least one a in $[0, 1]$) and which preserves the relative ordering of the truth degrees. However, it is shown that, when truth–functionality is assumed, this is not the case. For example, assume that the statements "p" and "q" are true to degree 0.3 and 0.8 respectively, and assume, for simplicity, that we are only interested in p and q. Adopting the standard negation, we find that "not p" is true to degree 0.7, in other words, "not p" is less true than "q". If a slightly different assignment of the membership degrees is used, i.e., "p" is true to degree 0.2 and "q" is true to degree 0.7, this is no longer the case. Indeed, we then have that "not p" is true to degree 0.8, and therefore more true than "q". Hence, the truth functionality of the negation imposes specific requirements on the mappings f that can be allowed. The other connectives impose further requirements, leading (for some choices of connectives) to $f(a) = a$ as the only mapping that does not alter any relative ordering. This observation leads Keefe [Keefe (1998)] to the conclusion that knowledge about the exact membership degrees is fundamental and that, since in practice these degrees are always to some extent arbitrary, approaches such as fuzzy set theory are inherently flawed.

The conclusion from Keefe is based on two premises, however: truth–functionality and the central importance of the relative order of the membership degrees. While rejecting the truth–functionality of fuzzy logics would solve most theoretical and philosophical problems, it is not an acceptable solution from a practical point of view. The second premise also seems hard to reject, but is, in principle, not critical at all. Smith [Smith (2003)] argues that from "x is taller than y", we should not conclude that "x is tall" is more true than "y is tall" (thus refuting the claim from [Keefe (1998)] that a fuzzy set representing tall people is nothing more than a measure of length). Rather than taking relative order as the main principle governing truth degrees, Smith [Smith (2005)] suggests to adopt the following view:

> If a and b are very close in F–relevant respects, then $F(a)$ and $F(b)$ are very close in respect of truth

Of key importance here is that the converse is not imposed, i.e., if $F(a)$ and $F(b)$ are very close in respect of truth, it is not required that a and b are very close in F–relevant respects. For example, we should be prepared to accept that both somebody of 1m80 and somebody of 1m70 could be tall to degree 0.7, while somebody of 1m75 is considered tall to degree 0.71. In other words, the view of membership degrees as defining an ordering relation is too strict, at least from a philosophical point of view. On the other hand, the membership functions defined by an expert will effectively induce a meaningful ordering relation. Whether or not this ordering relation remains meaningful regarding derived concepts (e.g., the intersection of two fuzzy sets), however, depends entirely on the application and the specific methodology that has been followed to arrive at the initial membership degrees. Note however that, in practice, this will often be the case, which could accommodate for the fact that the relative order of the membership degrees is often considered paramount.

Another case against the truth–functionality of graded approaches to vagueness has been presented in [Fine (1975)]. The central issue here is that, according to Fine, a theory of vagueness should be able to deal with penumbral connection, i.e., the possibility that logical relations hold among indefinite propositions. Taking three–valued logic as an example, Fine considers an object x that is a borderline case of the vague concepts pink, red and small, i.e., the truth values of "x is pink", "x is red" and "x is small" are indefinite. Fine argues that the truth value of "x is pink and red" should be false, as pink and red are mutually exclusive properties, whereas the truth value of "x is pink and small" should be indefinite. However, this argument is based on an intuition that is not universally accepted. For example, we could as well argue that the truth value of "x is pink and red" should be indefinite, as neither of the propositions "x is pink" and "x is red" is false. For a more thorough discussion about these and other philosophical issues regarding graded approaches to vagueness, we refer to [Vásconez (2006)].

In addition to philosophical objections against fuzzy set theory, its practical value for AI systems has been questioned as well. A typical example is [Elkan (1994b)], where Elkan identifies fuzzy control as the only area in which the theory of fuzzy sets has achieved significant practical applications. Since, moreover, it is argued, the success of fuzzy control has little to do with the use of fuzzy sets, the theory should be abandoned altogether. To further support this latter claim, a theorem is shown which attempts to demonstrate that fuzzy logic collapses to two–valued logic. The theorem, however, builds from the premise that if two propositions p and q are equivalent in two–valued logic, they should have the same truth degree in a fuzzy logic. Since this premise is too strict to capture fuzzy logics in general, the resulting conclusion is typically not taken as a serious threat for fuzzy set theory (e.g., [Dubois and Prade (2001); Freksa (1994)]). A second critique from Elkan is on fuzzy rule–based systems, where he argues against the use of fuzzy set theory by demonstrating that truth–functionality does not always make sense in this context. As explained in detail in [Dubois and Prade (2001)], this critique is not justified because it confuses degrees of truth with degrees of belief. As the counterexamples given are based on degrees of belief, possibility theory should have been adopted, which would effectively solve the problems identified by Elkan. The critique of fuzzy control, on the other hand, appears more fundamental. In [Dubois and Prade (1997)], a related observation is made concerning the use of fuzzy set theory to approximate functions, e.g., within the realm of control applications:

> It is questionable whether the present trend in fuzzy engineering, that immerses fuzzy logic inside the jungle of function approximation methods will produce path breaking results that puts fuzzy–based systems well over already existing tools. It is not clear either that it will accelerate the recognition of fuzzy set theory, since there is a clear trend to keep the name "fuzzy" and forget the contents of the theory.

Elkan, however, generalizes from observations about fuzzy control theory and fuzzy rule–based systems to the application of fuzzy set theory in AI in general. For example, in [Elkan (1994a)], he claims about the distinction between probabilities and degrees of truth:

It appears to me that the AI community has not forgotten this very binary distinction, but rather the community has implicitly rejected the claim that it is a uniquely important distinction.

This over–generalization has been countered by various authors, advocating the use of fuzzy set theory in AI. For example, [Dubois and Prade (1997)] stresses the importance of fuzzy set theory in bridging the gap between numerical processing and symbolic computation. The limited success of fuzzy set based techniques in AI systems — Elkan's main argument for rejecting fuzzy set theory — is explained from the observation that many fuzzy logic advocates tend to reject symbolic AI for not being capable of dealing with real complex systems. Therefore, it is argued that more effort is needed to fuse symbolic AI and fuzzy set theory beyond fuzzy rule–based systems, thus putting the blame on practitioners of fuzzy set theory rather than on the theory itself. Along similar lines, [Freksa (1994)] defends the use of fuzzy sets in AI from their ability to summarize complex descriptions by abstracting from details. Among others, [Freksa (1994)] suggests to represent complex systems such as weather prediction on a coarser level than the most primitive, using fuzzy sets, and thereby rendering an intractable problem tractable. Our motivation for employing fuzzy set theory in representing vague temporal and spatial phenomena will be further clarified in the following chapters.

Chapter 3

Relatedness of Fuzzy Sets

3.1 Introduction

Fuzzy relations are a widely–used vehicle for representing relatedness between objects. Sometimes, these objects can, in turn, be regarded as fuzzy sets on a universe of more atomic objects. More specifically, let ρ be a fuzzy relation from $\mathcal{F}(U)$ to $\mathcal{F}(V)$, i.e., for a fuzzy set A in a universe U and a fuzzy set B in a universe V, $\rho(A, B)$ expresses the degree to which A is related to B according to some criterion. Many studies have already examined techniques to define a degree of relatedness between fuzzy sets, expressing, for example, a degree of similarity (e.g., [De Baets *et al.* (2001); Janssens (2006); Tsiporkova and Zimmermann (1998); Zwick *et al.* (1973)]) or a degree of inclusion (e.g., [De Baets *et al.* (2002); Sinha and Dougherty (1993); Young (1996)]). We are specifically interested, however, in the situation where ρ can be defined in terms of a more primitive fuzzy relation R from U to V.

Example 3.1. As a running example throughout this chapter, we let P be the universe of people, including $p_1, p_2, \ldots, p_5$ and K the universe of keywords, including ONT (ontologies), DB (databases), DM (data mining), AI (artificial intelligence), ML (machine learning), IR (information retrieval), IE (information extraction) and NLP (natural language processing). A fuzzy set of persons is assumed to represent a community of researchers; clearly, a researcher can belong to different communities in varying degrees. A fuzzy set of keywords is assumed to represent the topics of interest of a particular workshop, conference or journal. Furthermore, we assume that a fuzzy relation R from P to K is given, expressing for each person p and each keyword k to what extent p is interested in research about k:

47

R	ONT	DB	DM	AI	ML	IR	IE	NLP
p_1	0.2	0	0.8	1	0.9	0.6	0.4	0.4
p_2	0.7	1	0.9	0.2	0	0.5	0	0.2
p_3	1	0.6	0	0.6	0.4	0.4	0.8	0.6
p_4	0.6	0.2	0	0.6	0.9	1	0.9	0.8
p_5	0	0	0.3	0.8	0.6	0.1	0.4	1

Let $A = \{p_3/0.9, p_4/1, p_5/0.2\}$ and $B = \{ONT/0.7, IE/1\}$. Now we want to leverage R to a fuzzy relation ρ from $\mathcal{F}(P)$ to $\mathcal{F}(K)$ such that $\rho(A, B)$ represents the degree to which the topics of conference B are of interest to community A. One possibility is to define $\rho(A, B)$ as the degree to which at least one person in A is interested in at least one topic from B, e.g.,

$$\rho(A, B) = \sup_{p \in P} \sup_{k \in K} \min(A(p), B(k), R(p, k))$$

$$= \max(\min(A(p_3), B(ONT), R(p_3, ONT)),$$
$$\min(A(p_3), B(IE), R(p_3, IE)),$$
$$\min(A(p_4), B(ONT), R(p_4, ONT)),$$
$$\min(A(p_4), B(IE), R(p_4, IE)),$$
$$\min(A(p_5), B(ONT), R(p_5, ONT)),$$
$$\min(A(p_5), B(IE), R(p_5, IE)))$$

$$= \max(\min(0.9, 0.7, 1), \min(0.9, 1, 0.8), \min(1, 0.7, 0.6),$$
$$\min(1, 1, 0.9), \min(0.2, 0.7, 0), \min(0.2, 1, 0.4))$$

$$= 0.9$$

In this chapter, we discuss a number of alternative ways to define relatedness measures for fuzzy sets by evaluating the relatedness of their elements. These measures will play a central role in the remainder of this book, as we will use them to define temporal and spatial relations between vague time periods and regions respectively. Thus, the formal properties of the relatedness measures which are discussed in this chapter, such as transitivity or reflexivity, will naturally carry over to the temporal and spatial reasoning frameworks introduced in the following chapters.

3.2 Definition

Throughout this chapter, we assume that T is a left–continuous t–norm and I_T its residual implicator. As before, let A be a fuzzy set in U, R a fuzzy relation from U to V and B a fuzzy set in V. Furthermore, let $\overleftarrow{A}$ and $\overrightarrow{B}$ be the fuzzy relations in U and V respectively, defined by

$$\overleftarrow{A}(u_1, u_2) = A(u_2)$$
$$\overrightarrow{B}(v_1, v_2) = B(v_1)$$

for all u_1 and u_2 in U and all v_1 and v_2 in V. Since $\overleftarrow{A}$ is a fuzzy relation from U to U, the sup–T composition $\overleftarrow{A} \circ_T R$ is a fuzzy relation from U to V, and since $\overrightarrow{B}$ is a fuzzy relation from V to V, the composition $(\overleftarrow{A} \circ_T R) \circ_T \overrightarrow{B}$ is a fuzzy relation from U to V as well. It holds that $(\overleftarrow{A} \circ_T R) \circ_T \overrightarrow{B}$ is a constant mapping in $U \times V$. Indeed, for any (u_1, v_1) in $U \times V$, we obtain

$$((\overleftarrow{A} \circ_T R) \circ_T \overrightarrow{B})(u_1, v_1) = \sup_{v \in V} T((\overleftarrow{A} \circ_T R)(u_1, v), \overrightarrow{B}(v, v_1))$$
$$= \sup_{v \in V} T(\sup_{u \in U} T(\overleftarrow{A}(u_1, u), R(u, v)), \overrightarrow{B}(v, v_1))$$
$$= \sup_{v \in V} T(\sup_{u \in U} T(A(u), R(u, v)), B(v))$$

which does not depend on the specific element (u_1, v_1) in which $((\overleftarrow{A} \circ_T R) \circ_T \overrightarrow{B})$ was evaluated. Note that, due to the associativity of the sup–T product (Lemma 2.13), we have that

$$(\overleftarrow{A} \circ_T R) \circ_T \overrightarrow{B} = \overleftarrow{A} \circ_T (R \circ_T \overrightarrow{B})$$

This idea of using fuzzy relational composition to define relatedness of fuzzy sets was introduced in [Goguen (1967)], where $((\overleftarrow{A} \circ_T R) \circ_T \overrightarrow{B})$ was called the (fuzzy relational) double image of A and B. The value of $((\overleftarrow{A} \circ_T R) \circ_T \overrightarrow{B})$ in an arbitrary point (u, v) of $U \times V$ expresses the degree to which some element of A is related (w.r.t. R) to some element of B. For notational convenience, we will denote this value by $A \circ_T R \circ_T B$. Note that the traditional degree of overlap *overl* is a special case of this relatedness measure as for $U = V$

$$overl(A, B) = A \circ_{T_M} E \circ_{T_M} B$$

where E is the identity relation in U, defined for (u, v) in U^2 by $E(u, v) = 1$ if $u = v$ and $E(u, v) = 0$ otherwise.

By composing the fuzzy relations $\overleftarrow{A}$, R and $\overrightarrow{B}$ using different types of compositions, in particular the sub- and superproduct, we obtain alternative measures of relatedness between A and B. For example, for (u_1, v_1) in $U \times V$, we find

$$((\overleftarrow{A} \lhd_{I_T} R) \rhd_{I_T} \overrightarrow{B})(u_1, v_1) = \inf_{v \in V} I_T(\overrightarrow{B}(v, v_1), (\overleftarrow{A} \lhd_{I_T} R)(u_1, v))$$

$$= \inf_{v \in V} I_T(\overrightarrow{B}(v, v_1), \inf_{u \in U} I_T(\overleftarrow{A}(u_1, u), R(u, v)))$$

$$= \inf_{v \in V} I_T(B(v), \inf_{u \in U} I_T(A(u), R(u, v)))$$

By Lemma 2.14, we find that

$$(\overleftarrow{A} \lhd_{I_T} R) \rhd_{I_T} \overrightarrow{B} = \overleftarrow{A} \lhd_{I_T} (R \rhd_{I_T} \overrightarrow{B})$$

The value of $(\overleftarrow{A} \lhd_{I_T} R) \rhd_{I_T} \overrightarrow{B}$ in an arbitrary point (u, v) of $U \times V$ expresses the degree to which every element of A is related to every element of B. We will denote this value by $A \lhd_{I_T} R \rhd_{I_T} B$. In a similar way, we obtain the following relatedness measures by using various combinations of the sup–T-, sub- and superproduct:

(1) The degree to which every element of A is only related to elements of B:

$$A \lhd_{I_T} (R \lhd_{I_T} B) = \inf_{u \in U} I_T(A(u), \inf_{v \in V} I_T(R(u, v), B(v))) \qquad (3.1)$$

(2) The degree to which every element of B is only related to elements of A:

$$(A \rhd_{I_T} R) \rhd_{I_T} B = \inf_{v \in V} I_T(B(v), \inf_{u \in U} I_T(R(u, v), A(u))) \qquad (3.2)$$

(3) The degree to which some element of B is related to every element of A:

$$(A \lhd_{I_T} R) \circ_T B = \sup_{v \in V} T(\inf_{u \in U} I_T(A(u), R(u, v)), B(v)) \qquad (3.3)$$

(4) The degree to which every element of A is related to some element of B:

$$A \lhd_{I_T} (R \circ_T B) = \inf_{u \in U} I_T(A(u), \sup_{v \in V} T(R(u, v), B(v))) \qquad (3.4)$$

(5) The degree to which every element of B is related to some element of A:

$$(A \circ_T R) \rhd_{I_T} B = \inf_{v \in V} I_T(B(v), \sup_{u \in U} T(A(u), R(u, v))) \qquad (3.5)$$

(6) The degree to which some element of A is related to every element of B:

$$A \circ_T (R \rhd_{I_T} B) = \sup_{u \in U} T(A(u), \inf_{v \in V} I_T(B(v), R(u,v))) \qquad (3.6)$$

(7) The degree to which some element of A is only related to elements of B:

$$A \circ_T (R \lhd_{I_T} B) = \sup_{u \in U} T(A(u), \inf_{v \in V} I_T(R(u,v), B(v))) \qquad (3.7)$$

(8) The degree to which some element of B is only related to elements of A:

$$(A \rhd_{I_T} R) \circ_T B = \sup_{v \in V} T(\inf_{u \in U} I_T(R(u,v), A(u)), B(v)) \qquad (3.8)$$

In practice we will often omit the subscript T and I_T in $\circ_T$, $\lhd_{I_T}$ and $\rhd_{I_T}$ when it is clear from the context which t-norm is used. Note that $A \lhd_{I_T} (R \circ_T B)$ and $(A \circ_T R) \rhd_{I_T} B$ generalize the well–known degree of inclusion *incl* between A and B, i.e., for $U = V$ and E the identity relation in U it holds that

$$A \lhd_{I_T} (E \circ_T B) = incl(A, B)$$

Also note that we will not explore all possible combinations of the sup–T-, sub- and superproduct. For example, we will not discuss the relatedness measure defined by

$$(A \lhd_{I_T} R) \lhd_{I_T} B = \inf_{v \in V} I_T(\inf_{u \in U} I_T(A(u), R(u,v)), B(v))$$

The reason for this is that the applicability of these measures — at least in the context of temporal and spatial reasoning — seems limited. However, the relatedness measure defined by

$$(A \circ_T R) \lhd_{I_T} B = \inf_{v \in V} I_T(\sup_{u \in U} T(A(u), R(u,v)), B(v))$$

is equal to $A \lhd_{I_T} (R \lhd_{I_T} B)$, which can easily be shown using (2.26), (2.19) and (2.20). Similarly, it holds that $A \rhd_{I_T} (R \circ_T B)$, defined analogously as the other measures, equals $(A \rhd_{I_T} R) \rhd_{I_T} B$.

We conclude this section by illustrating the semantics of some of the relatedness measures with an example.

Example 3.2. Consider again the fuzzy relation R and the fuzzy sets A and B from Example 3.1, and assume $T = T_M$. Different relatedness measures allow us to assess the relevance of conference B to community A

in different ways. For example, the degree to which every topic from B is of interest to every person in A is 0, since

$$A \lhd R \rhd B \leq I_M(A(p_5), I_M(B(ONT), R(p_5, ONT)))$$
$$= I_M(0.2, I_M(0.7, 0))$$
$$= 0$$

Similarly, the degree $A \lhd (R \lhd B)$ to which conference B addresses all the research interests of the people in community A is 0:

$$(A \lhd (R \lhd B)) \leq I_M(A(p_5), I_M(R(p_5, NLP), B(NLP)))$$
$$= I_M(0.2, I_M(1, 0))$$
$$= 0$$

On the other hand, the degree $A \lhd (R \circ B)$ to which every person in A is at least interested in one topic of B is given by:

$$A \lhd (R \circ B) = \inf_{p \in P} I_M(A(p), \sup_{k \in K} T_M(R(p, k), B(k)))$$
$$= \min(I_M(A(p_3), \max(T_M(R(p_3, ONT), B(ONT)),$$
$$T_M(R(p_3, IE), B(IE)))),$$
$$I_M(A(p_4), \max(T_M(R(p_4, ONT), B(ONT)),$$
$$T_M(R(p_4, IE), B(IE)))),$$
$$I_M(A(p_5), \max(T_M(R(p_5, ONT), B(ONT)),$$
$$T_M(R(p_5, IE), B(IE)))))$$
$$= \min(I_M(0.9, \max(T_M(1, 0.7), T_M(0.8, 1))),$$
$$I_M(1, \max(T_M(0.6, 0.7), T_M(0.9, 1))),$$
$$I_M(0.2, \max(T_M(0, 0.7), T_M(0.4, 1))))$$
$$= \min(I_M(0.9, 0.8), I_M(1, 0.9), I_M(0.2, 0.4))$$
$$= \min(0.8, 0.9, 1)$$
$$= 0.8$$

3.3 Properties

3.3.1 *Basic Properties*

The relatedness measures introduced in Section 3.2 are a very general notion which may be used in a wide range of applications. Nevertheless, even in a general setting, a number of interesting properties can be derived. For example, it is easy to see that the measures are not completely independent of each other:

$$(A \triangleleft_{I_T} R) \circ_T B = B \circ_T (R^{-1} \triangleright_{I_T} A) \tag{3.9}$$

$$A \triangleleft_{I_T} (R \circ_T B) = (B \circ_T R^{-1}) \triangleright_{I_T} A \tag{3.10}$$

$$A \circ_T (R \triangleleft_{I_T} B) = (B \triangleright_{I_T} R^{-1}) \circ_T A \tag{3.11}$$

$$A \triangleleft_{I_T} (R \triangleleft_{I_T} B) = (B \triangleright_{I_T} R^{-1}) \triangleright_{I_T} A \tag{3.12}$$

Furthermore, as stated in the next proposition, they obey the ordering depicted in Figure 3.1, provided some natural requirements are met.

Proposition 3.1. *Let A and B be fuzzy sets in U and V respectively, and R a fuzzy relation from U to V. It holds that*

$$A \circ_T (R \triangleright_{I_T} B) \leq (A \circ_T R) \triangleright_{I_T} B \tag{3.13}$$

$$(A \triangleleft_{I_T} R) \circ_T B \leq A \triangleleft_{I_T} (R \circ_T B) \tag{3.14}$$

If A and B are normalised, it holds that

$$(A \circ_T R) \triangleright_{I_T} B \leq A \circ_T R \circ_T B \tag{3.15}$$

$$A \triangleleft_{I_T} (R \circ_T B) \leq A \circ_T R \circ_T B \tag{3.16}$$

$$(A \triangleright_{I_T} R) \triangleright_{I_T} B \leq (A \triangleright_{I_T} R) \circ_T B \tag{3.17}$$

$$A \triangleleft_{I_T} (R \triangleleft_{I_T} B) \leq A \circ_T (R \triangleleft_{I_T} B) \tag{3.18}$$

$$A \triangleleft_{I_T} R \triangleright_{I_T} B \leq (A \triangleleft_{I_T} R) \circ_T B \tag{3.19}$$

$$A \triangleleft_{I_T} R \triangleright_{I_T} B \leq A \circ_T (R \triangleright_{I_T} B) \tag{3.20}$$

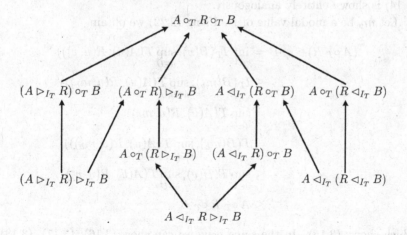

Fig. 3.1   Ordering of relatedness measures (under the conditions of Proposition 3.1).

If for every v in V, the partial mapping $R(., v)$ is a normalised fuzzy set in U, it holds that

$$(A \rhd_{I_T} R) \circ_T B \leq A \circ_T R \circ_T B \tag{3.21}$$

$$(A \rhd_{I_T} R) \rhd_{I_T} B \leq (A \circ_T R) \rhd_{I_T} B \tag{3.22}$$

If for every u in U, the partial mapping $R(u, .)$ is a normalised fuzzy set in V, it holds that

$$A \circ_T (R \lhd_{I_T} B) \leq A \circ_T R \circ_T B \tag{3.23}$$

$$A \lhd_{I_T} (R \lhd_{I_T} B) \leq A \lhd_{I_T} (R \circ_T B) \tag{3.24}$$

Proof.   To show (3.13), we find using (2.6), (2.24) and (2.18)

$$
\begin{aligned}
A \circ_T (R \rhd_{I_T} B) &= \sup_{u \in U} T(A(u), \inf_{v \in V} I_T(B(v), R(u,v))) \\
&\leq \sup_{u \in U} \inf_{v \in V} T(A(u), I_T(B(v), R(u,v))) \\
&\leq \sup_{u \in U} \inf_{v \in V} I_T(B(v), T(A(u), R(u,v))) \\
&\leq \inf_{v \in V} \sup_{u \in U} I_T(B(v), T(A(u), R(u,v))) \\
&\leq \inf_{v \in V} I_T(B(v), \sup_{u \in U} T(A(u), R(u,v))) \\
&= (A \circ_T R) \rhd_{I_T} B
\end{aligned}
$$

(3.14) is shown entirely analogously.

Let m_b be a modal value of B. Using (2.22) we obtain

$$
\begin{aligned}
(A \circ_T R) \rhd_{I_T} B &= \inf_{v \in V} I_T(B(v), \sup_{u \in U} T(A(u), R(u,v))) \\
&\leq I_T(B(m_b), \sup_{u \in U} T(A(u), R(u, m_b))) \\
&= \sup_{u \in U} T(A(u), R(u, m_b)) \\
&= T(B(m_b), \sup_{u \in U} T(A(u), R(u, m_b))) \\
&\leq \sup_{v \in V} T(B(v), \sup_{u \in U} T(A(u), R(u,v))) \\
&\leq A \circ_T R \circ_T B
\end{aligned}
$$

which shows (3.15). In the same way, we can show (3.16), (3.17), (3.18), (3.19) and (3.20).

Assume that for every v in V, there exists a u_v in U such that $R(u_v, v) = 1$. We obtain using (2.22)

$$
\begin{aligned}
(A \rhd_{I_T} R) \circ_T B &= \sup_{v \in V} T(B(v), \inf_{u \in U} I_T(R(u,v), A(u))) \\
&\leq \sup_{v \in V} T(B(v), I_T(R(u_v, v), A(u_v))) \\
&= \sup_{v \in V} T(B(v), A(u_v)) \\
&= \sup_{v \in V} T(B(v), T(R(u_v, v), A(u_v))) \\
&\leq \sup_{v \in V} T(B(v), \sup_{u \in U} T(R(u,v), A(u))) \\
&= A \circ_T R \circ_T B
\end{aligned}
$$

showing (3.21). The proof of (3.22), (3.23) and (3.24) is analogous. $\quad\square$

Note that the condition that the partial mappings $R(., v)$ and $R(u, .)$ be normalised is easily met in practice: if $U = V$, for instance, it is sufficient that R is reflexive.

When A and B are fuzzy sets in the same universe U (i.e., $U = V$), the fuzzy relation R may exhibit properties like reflexivity, irreflexivity or symmetry. The following propositions reveal for which relatedness measures such properties of R carry over.

Proposition 3.2 (Reflexivity). *If A is a fuzzy set in U and R is a reflexive fuzzy relation in U then*

$$A \lhd_{I_T} (R \circ_T A) = 1 \tag{3.25}$$

$$(A \circ_T R) \rhd_I A = 1 \tag{3.26}$$

If A is normalised, it holds that

$$A \circ_T R \circ_T A = 1 \tag{3.27}$$

Proof. As an example we prove (3.25).

$$
\begin{aligned}
A \lhd_{I_T} (R \circ_T A) &= \inf_{u \in U} I_T(A(u), \sup_{v \in U} T(R(u,v), A(v))) \\
&\geq \inf_{u \in U} I_T(A(u), T(R(u,u), A(u))) \\
&= \inf_{u \in U} I_T(A(u), A(u))
\end{aligned}
$$

By (2.23) we verify that the latter is 1. The proof of (3.26) is analogous. Finally, (3.27) follows straightforwardly from (3.25) by Proposition 3.1. $\quad\square$

Proposition 3.3 (Irreflexivity). *If A is a fuzzy set in U and R is an irreflexive fuzzy relation in U then*

$$A \circ_T (R \rhd_{I_T} A) = 0 \tag{3.28}$$

$$(A \lhd_{I_T} R) \circ_T A = 0 \tag{3.29}$$

$$\tag{3.30}$$

If A is normalised, it holds that

$$A \lhd_{I_T} R \rhd_{I_T} A = 0 \tag{3.31}$$

Proof. As an example we prove (3.28).

$$
\begin{aligned}
A \circ_T (R \rhd_{I_T} A) &= \sup_{u \in U} T(A(u), \inf_{v \in U} I_T(A(v), R(u,v))) \\
&\leq \sup_{u \in U} T(A(u), I_T(A(u), R(u,u))) \\
&= \sup_{u \in U} T(A(u), I_T(A(u), 0))
\end{aligned}
$$

By (2.25) we verify that the latter equals 0. The proof of (3.29) is analogous, while (3.31) immediately follows from (3.28) by Proposition 3.1. □

Note that the reflexivity or irreflexivity of R does not carry over to the measures (3.1), (3.2), (3.7) and (3.8), which corresponds to what we would intuitively expect. For example, let A be the crisp set $\{1, 2, 3\}$ and R let be defined by $R(p,q) = 1$ if $p \leq q$ and $R(p,q) = 0$ otherwise ($p, q \in \mathbb{R}$). Then clearly R is reflexive, while each element of A is related to real numbers which are not contained in A, hence

$$A \circ_T (R \lhd_{I_T} A) = (A \rhd_{I_T} R) \circ_T A = 0$$

On the other hand, if we define R such that $R(p,q) = 1$ if $p = 1$ and $q = 2$, and $R(p,q) = 0$ otherwise, then R is irreflexive, while each element of A is only related to other elements of A, hence

$$A \lhd_{I_T} (R \lhd_{I_T} A) = (A \rhd_{I_T} R) \rhd_{I_T} A = 1$$

Example 3.3. As before, let K be the universe of keywords, and let B be the fuzzy set of keywords defined in Example 3.1. Furthermore, let S^{RT} be the fuzzy relation in K defined as

S^{RT}	ONT	DB	DM	AI	ML	IR	IE	NLP
ONT	1	0.6	0	0.5	0	0.3	0.4	0
DB	0.6	1	0.8	0	0	0	0.2	0
DM	0	0.8	1	0	0.3	0	0	0
AI	0.5	0	0	1	0.7	0	0.2	0.4
ML	0	0	0.3	0.7	1	0.2	0.8	0.7
IR	0.3	0	0	0	0.2	1	0.7	0.3
IE	0.4	0.2	0	0.2	0.8	0.7	1	0.5
NLP	0	0	0	0.4	0.7	0.3	0.5	1

The fuzzy relation S^{RT} expresses to what degree two keywords have a related meaning. It is reflexive and symmetric. From Proposition 3.2 we know that $B \triangleleft_{I_M} (S^{RT} \circ_{T_M} B) = 1$; in other words, every keyword belonging to the fuzzy set B is related to at least one keyword from the same fuzzy set B to degree 1. However, this does not imply that there is a keyword in B which is related to any other keyword from B to degree 1:

$$(B \triangleleft_{I_M} S^{RT}) \circ_{T_M} B$$
$$= \max(T_M(B(ONT), \min(I_M(B(ONT), S^{RT}(ONT, ONT)),$$
$$I_M(B(IE), S^{RT}(IE, ONT)))),$$
$$T_M(B(IE), \min(I_M(B(ONT), S^{RT}(ONT, IE)),$$
$$I_M(B(IE), S^{RT}(IE, IE))))))$$
$$= \max(T_M(0.7, \min(I_M(0.7, 1), I_M(1, 0.4))),$$
$$T_M(1, \min(I_M(0.7, 0.4), I_M(1, 1))))$$
$$= \max(T_M(0.7, 0.4), T_M(1, 0.4))$$
$$= 0.4$$

Next, we define an irreflexive and T_M–asymmetric fuzzy relation of keywords S^{NT}:

S^{NT}	ONT	DB	DM	AI	ML	IR	IE	NLP
ONT	0	0.7	0	0.3	0	0.4	0	0
DB	0	0	0	0	0	0	0	0
DM	0	0.8	0	0	0	0	0	0
AI	0	0	0	0	0	0	0	0
ML	0	0	0.3	0.8	0	0	0	0
IR	0	0	0	0	0	0	0	0
IE	0	0	0	0.3	0.3	0.6	0	0.8
NLP	0	0	0	0.9	0.4	0	0	0

For two keywords k_1 and k_2, $S^{NT}(k_1, k_2)$ reflects the extent to which k_1 is a subfield of k_2. Proposition 3.3 implies that $(B \triangleleft_{I_M} S^{NT}) \circ_{T_M} B = 0$, i.e., keywords belonging to B to some degree cannot be more general than all keywords in B to a strictly positive degree, since no keyword can be more general than itself.

Lemma 3.1. *If A and B are fuzzy sets in U and R is a fuzzy relation in U then*

$$A \triangleleft_{I_T} R \triangleright_{I_T} B = B \triangleleft_{I_T} R^{-1} \triangleright_{I_T} A \qquad (3.32)$$

$$A \circ_T R \circ_T B = A \circ_T R^{-1} \circ_T B \qquad (3.33)$$

Proof.   As an example we prove (3.32). The proof of (3.33) is analogous. Using (2.20) and (2.27), we find

$$
\begin{aligned}
A \triangleleft_{I_T} R \triangleright_{I_T} B &= \inf_{u \in U} I_T(A(u), \inf_{v \in U} I_T(B(v), R(u, v))) \\
&= \inf_{u \in U} \inf_{v \in U} I_T(A(u), I_T(B(v), R(u, v))) \\
&= \inf_{u \in U} \inf_{v \in U} I_T(B(v), I_T(A(u), R(u, v))) \\
&= \inf_{v \in U} \inf_{u \in U} I_T(B(v), I_T(A(u), R(u, v))) \\
&= \inf_{v \in U} I_T(B(v), \inf_{u \in U} I_T(A(u), R(u, v))) \\
&= \inf_{v \in U} I_T(B(v), \inf_{u \in U} I_T(A(u), R^{-1}(v, u))) \\
&= B \triangleleft_{I_T} R^{-1} \triangleright_{I_T} A \qquad \qquad \square
\end{aligned}
$$

Proposition 3.4 (Symmetry). *If A and B are fuzzy sets in U and R is a symmetric fuzzy relation in U then*

$$A \triangleleft_{I_T} R \triangleright_{I_T} B = B \triangleleft_{I_T} R \triangleright_{I_T} A \qquad (3.34)$$

$$A \circ_T R \circ_T B = B \circ_T R \circ_T A \qquad (3.35)$$

Proof.   The proof follows immediately from Lemma 3.1 and the fact that $R^{-1} = R$. $\qquad \square$

Proposition 3.5 (Asymmetry). *Let A and B be fuzzy sets in U, and let R be a T–asymmetric fuzzy relation in U. It holds that*

$$T(A \circ_T (R \triangleright_{I_T} B), B \circ_T (R \triangleright_{I_T} A)) = 0 \qquad (3.36)$$

$$T((A \triangleleft_{I_T} R) \circ_T B, (B \triangleleft_{I_T} R) \circ_T A) = 0 \qquad (3.37)$$

If A and B are normalised, it holds that

$$T(A \triangleleft_{I_T} R \triangleright_{I_T} B, B \triangleleft_{I_T} R \triangleright_{I_T} A) = 0 \qquad (3.38)$$

Proof. To show (3.36), we obtain using (2.7) and (2.25)

$$T(A \circ_T (R \rhd_{I_T} B), B \circ_T (R \rhd_{I_T} A))$$

$$= T(\sup_{u \in U} T(A(u), \inf_{v \in U} I_T(B(v), R(u, v))),$$

$$\sup_{w \in U} T(B(w), \inf_{x \in U} I_T(A(x), R(w, x))))$$

$$= \sup_{u \in U} \sup_{w \in U} T(A(u), \inf_{v \in U} I_T(B(v), R(u, v)), B(w), \inf_{x \in U} I_T(A(x), R(w, x)))$$

$$\leq \sup_{u \in U} \sup_{w \in U} T(A(u), I_T(B(w), R(u, w)), B(w), I_T(A(u), R(w, u)))$$

$$\leq \sup_{u \in U} \sup_{w \in U} T(R(u, w), R(w, u))$$

Due to the T–asymmetry of R, the latter expression equals 0. In the same way, we can show (3.37). Finally, (3.38) follows straightforwardly from (3.36) using Proposition 3.1. $\qquad\square$

Note that most relatedness measures are neither symmetric or T–asymmetric when R exhibits these properties. As for (ir)reflexivity, this corresponds to what we would intuitively expect.

Example 3.4. Let B and S^{NT} be defined as in Example 3.4 and let $C = \{DB/1, IR/0.8\}$. It holds that

$$B \circ_{T_M} (S^{NT} \rhd_{I_M} C)$$

$$= \max(T_M(B(ONT), \min(I_M(C(DB), S^{NT}(ONT, DB))),$$
$$I_M(C(IR), S^{NT}(ONT, IR)))),$$
$$T_M(B(IE), \min(I_M(C(DB), S^{NT}(IE, DB))),$$
$$I_M(C(IR), S^{NT}(IE, IR)))))$$

$$= \max(T_M(0.7, \min(I_M(1, 0.7), I_M(0.8, 0.4))),$$
$$T_M(1, \min(I_M(1, 0), I_M(0.8, 0.6)))))$$

$$= \max(\min(0.7, 0.4), \min(1, 0))$$

$$= 0.4$$

Since $B \circ_{T_M} (S^{NT} \rhd_{I_M} C) > 0$ and S^{NT} is T_M–asymmetric, we know from Proposition 3.5 that $C \circ_{T_M} (S^{NT} \rhd_{I_M} B) = 0$. Intuitively, as there is a topic which belongs to B to some extent, and which is to some extent more specific than all topics from C, there can be no topic in C which is more specific than all topics from B to a strictly positive degree.

3.3.2 *Interaction*

Next, we derive some properties concerning the interaction between the relatedness measures and the union, intersection and complement of fuzzy sets.

Proposition 3.6 (Interaction with $\cup$). *Let A, A_1 and A_2 be fuzzy sets in U, B, B_1 and B_2 fuzzy sets in V, and R, R_1 and R_2 fuzzy relations from U to V. It holds that*

$$(A_1 \cup A_2) \circ_T R \circ_T B = \max(A_1 \circ_T R \circ_T B, A_2 \circ_T R \circ_T B) \tag{3.39}$$

$$A \circ_T R \circ_T (B_1 \cup B_2) = \max(A \circ_T R \circ_T B_1, A \circ_T R \circ_T B_2) \tag{3.40}$$

$$A \circ_T (R_1 \cup R_2) \circ_T B = \max(A \circ_T R_1 \circ_T B, A \circ_T R_2 \circ_T B) \tag{3.41}$$

$$(A_1 \cup A_2) \lhd_{I_T} R \rhd_{I_T} B = \min(A_1 \lhd_{I_T} R \rhd_{I_T} B, A_2 \lhd_{I_T} R \rhd_{I_T} B) \tag{3.42}$$

$$A \lhd_{I_T} R \rhd_{I_T} (B_1 \cup B_2) = \min(A \lhd_{I_T} R \rhd_{I_T} B_1, A \lhd_{I_T} R \rhd_{I_T} B_2) \tag{3.43}$$

$$A \lhd_{I_T} (R_1 \cup R_2) \rhd_{I_T} B \geq \max(A \lhd_{I_T} R_1 \rhd_{I_T} B, A \lhd_{I_T} R_2 \rhd_{I_T} B) \tag{3.44}$$

$$(A_1 \cup A_2) \lhd_{I_T} (R \lhd_{I_T} B) = \min(A_1 \lhd_{I_T} (R \lhd_{I_T} B), A_2 \lhd_{I_T} (R \lhd_{I_T} B)) \tag{3.45}$$

$$A \lhd_{I_T} (R \lhd_{I_T} (B_1 \cup B_2)) \geq \max(A \lhd_{I_T} (R \lhd_{I_T} B_1), A \lhd_{I_T} (R \lhd_{I_T} B_2)) \tag{3.46}$$

$$A \lhd_{I_T} ((R_1 \cup R_2) \lhd_{I_T} B) = \min(A \lhd_{I_T} (R_1 \lhd_{I_T} B), A \lhd_{I_T} (R_2 \lhd_{I_T} B)) \tag{3.47}$$

$$((A_1 \cup A_2) \rhd_{I_T} R) \rhd_{I_T} B \geq \max((A_1 \rhd_{I_T} R) \rhd_{I_T} B, (A_2 \rhd_{I_T} R) \rhd_{I_T} B) \tag{3.48}$$

$$(A \rhd_{I_T} R) \rhd_{I_T} (B_1 \cup B_2) = \min((A \rhd_{I_T} R) \rhd_{I_T} B_1, (A \rhd_{I_T} R) \rhd_{I_T} B_2) \tag{3.49}$$

$$(A \rhd_{I_T} (R_1 \cup R_2)) \rhd_{I_T} B = \min((A \rhd_{I_T} R_1) \rhd_{I_T} B, (A \rhd_{I_T} R_2) \rhd_{I_T} B) \tag{3.50}$$

$$((A_1 \cup A_2) \lhd_{I_T} R) \circ_T B \leq \min((A_1 \lhd_{I_T} R) \circ_T B, (A_2 \lhd_{I_T} R) \circ_T B) \tag{3.51}$$

$$(A \lhd_{I_T} R) \circ_T (B_1 \cup B_2) = \max((A \lhd_{I_T} R) \circ_T B_1, (A \lhd_{I_T} R) \circ_T B_2) \tag{3.52}$$

$$(A \lhd_{I_T} (R_1 \cup R_2)) \circ_T B \geq \max((A \lhd_{I_T} R_1) \circ_T B, (A \lhd_{I_T} R_2) \circ_T B) \tag{3.53}$$

$$(A_1 \cup A_2) \lhd_{I_T} (R \circ_T B) = \min(A_1 \lhd_{I_T} (R \circ_T B), A_2 \lhd_{I_T} (R \circ_T B))$$
$$(3.54)$$

$$A \lhd_{I_T} (R \circ_T (B_1 \cup B_2)) \geq \max(A \lhd_{I_T} (R \circ_T B_1), A \lhd_{I_T} (R \circ_T B_2))$$
$$(3.55)$$

$$A \lhd_{I_T} ((R_1 \cup R_2) \circ_T B) \geq \max(A \lhd_{I_T} (R_1 \circ_T B), A \lhd_{I_T} (R_2 \circ_T B))$$
$$(3.56)$$

$$((A_1 \cup A_2) \circ_T R) \rhd_{I_T} B \geq \max((A_1 \circ_T R) \rhd_{I_T} B, (A_2 \circ_T R) \rhd_{I_T} B)$$
$$(3.57)$$

$$(A \circ_T R) \rhd_{I_T} (B_1 \cup B_2) = \min((A \circ_T R) \rhd_{I_T} B_1, (A \circ_T R) \rhd_{I_T} B_2)$$
$$(3.58)$$

$$(A \circ_T (R_1 \cup R_2)) \rhd_{I_T} B \geq \max((A \circ_T R_1) \rhd_{I_T} B, (A \circ_T R_2) \rhd_{I_T} B)$$
$$(3.59)$$

$$(A_1 \cup A_2) \circ_T (R \rhd_{I_T} B) = \max(A_1 \circ_T (R \rhd_{I_T} B), A_2 \circ_T (R \rhd_{I_T} B))$$
$$(3.60)$$

$$A \circ_T (R \rhd_{I_T} (B_1 \cup B_2)) \leq \min(A \circ_T (R \rhd_{I_T} B_1), A \circ_T (R \rhd_{I_T} B_2))$$
$$(3.61)$$

$$A \circ_T ((R_1 \cup R_2) \rhd_{I_T} B) \geq \max(A \circ_T (R_1 \rhd_{I_T} B), A \circ_T (R_2 \rhd_{I_T} B))$$
$$(3.62)$$

$$(A_1 \cup A_2) \circ_T (R \lhd_{I_T} B) = \max(A_1 \circ_T (R \lhd_{I_T} B), A_2 \circ_T (R \lhd_{I_T} B))$$
$$(3.63)$$

$$A \circ_T (R \lhd_{I_T} (B_1 \cup B_2)) \geq \max(A \circ_T (R \lhd_{I_T} B_1), A \circ_T (R \lhd_{I_T} B_2))$$
$$(3.64)$$

$$A \circ_T ((R_1 \cup R_2) \lhd_{I_T} B) \leq \min(A \circ_T (R_1 \lhd_{I_T} B), A \circ_T (R_2 \lhd_{I_T} B))$$
$$(3.65)$$

$$((A_1 \cup A_2) \rhd_{I_T} R) \circ_T B \geq \max((A_1 \rhd_{I_T} R) \circ_T B, (A_2 \rhd_{I_T} R) \circ_T B)$$
$$(3.66)$$

$$(A \rhd_{I_T} R) \circ_T (B_1 \cup B_2) = \max((A \rhd_{I_T} R) \circ_T B_1, (A \rhd_{I_T} R) \circ_T B_2)$$
$$(3.67)$$

$$(A \rhd_{I_T} (R_1 \cup R_2)) \circ_T B \leq \min((A \rhd_{I_T} R_1) \circ_T B, (A \rhd_{I_T} R_2) \circ_T B)$$
$$(3.68)$$

Proof. To show (3.39), we find

$$(A_1 \cup A_2) \circ_T R \circ_T B$$
$$= \sup_{u \in U} T((A_1 \cup A_2)(u), \sup_{v \in V} T(R(u,v), B(v)))$$

$$= \sup_{u \in U} T(\max(A_1(u), A_2(u)), \sup_{v \in V} T(R(u,v), B(v)))$$

$$= \sup_{u \in U} \max(T(A_1(u), \sup_{v \in V} T(R(u,v), B(v))),$$

$$T(A_2(u), \sup_{v \in V} T(R(u,v), B(v))))$$

$$= \max(\sup_{u \in U} T(A_1(u), \sup_{v \in V} T(R(u,v), B(v))),$$

$$\sup_{u \in U} T(A_2(u), \sup_{v \in V} T(R(u,v), B(v))))$$

$$= \max(A_1 \circ_T R \circ_T B, A_2 \circ_T R \circ_T B)$$

In the same way, we can show (3.40), (3.41), (3.52), (3.60), (3.63) and (3.67).

For (3.42), we obtain

$$(A_1 \cup A_2) \triangleleft_{I_T} R \triangleright_{I_T} B$$

$$= \inf_{u \in U} I_T((A_1 \cup A_2)(u), \inf_{v \in V} I_T(B(v), R(u,v)))$$

$$= \inf_{u \in U} I_T(\max(A_1(u), A_2(u)), \inf_{v \in V} I_T(B(v), R(u,v)))$$

$$= \inf_{u \in U} \min(I_T(A_1(u), \inf_{v \in V} I_T(B(v), R(u,v))),$$

$$I_T(A_2(u), \inf_{v \in V} I_T(B(v), R(u,v))))$$

$$= \min(\inf_{u \in U} I_T(A_1(u), \inf_{v \in V} I_T(B(v), R(u,v))),$$

$$\inf_{u \in U} I_T(A_2(u), \inf_{v \in V} I_T(B(v), R(u,v))))$$

$$= \min(A_1 \triangleleft_{I_T} R \triangleright_{I_T} B, A_2 \triangleleft_{I_T} R \triangleright_{I_T} B)$$

In the same way, we can show (3.43), (3.45), (3.54) and (3.58).

To show (3.44), we find

$$A \triangleleft_{I_T} (R_1 \cup R_2) \triangleright_{I_T} B$$

$$= \inf_{u \in U} I_T(A(u), \inf_{v \in V} I_T(B(v), (R_1 \cup R_2)(u,v)))$$

$$= \inf_{u \in U} I_T(A(u), \inf_{v \in V} I_T(B(v), \max(R_1(u,v), R_2(u,v))))$$

$$= \inf_{u \in U} I_T(A(u), \inf_{v \in V} \max(I_T(B(v), R_1(u,v)), I_T(B(v), R_2(u,v))))$$

$$\geq \inf_{u \in U} I_T(A(u), \max(\inf_{v \in V} I_T(B(v), R_1(u,v)), \inf_{v \in V} I_T(B(v), R_2(u,v))))$$

$$= \inf_{u \in U} \max(I_T(A(u), \inf_{v \in V} I_T(B(v), R_1(u,v))),$$

$$I_T(A(u), \inf_{v \in V} I_T(B(v), R_2(u,v))))$$

$$\geq \max(\inf_{u \in U} I_T(A(u), \inf_{v \in V} I_T(B(v), R_1(u,v))),$$

$$\inf_{u \in U} I_T(A(u), \inf_{v \in V} I_T(B(v), R_2(u,v)))))$$

$$= \max(A \lhd_{I_T} R_1 \rhd_{I_T} B, A \lhd_{I_T} R_2 \rhd_{I_T} B)$$

In the same way, we can show (3.46) and (3.48)

For (3.51), we obtain

$$((A_1 \cup A_2) \lhd_{I_T} R) \circ_T B$$

$$= \sup_{v \in V} T(B(v), \inf_{u \in U} I_T((A_1 \cup A_2)(u), R(u,v)))$$

$$= \sup_{v \in V} T(B(v), \inf_{u \in U} I_T(\max(A_1(u), A_2(u)), R(u,v)))$$

$$= \sup_{v \in V} T(B(v), \inf_{u \in U} \min(I_T(A_1(u), R(u,v)), I_T(A_2(u), R(u,v))))$$

$$= \sup_{v \in V} T(B(v), \min(\inf_{u \in U} I_T(A_1(u), R(u,v)), \inf_{u \in U} I_T(A_2(u), R(u,v))))$$

$$= \sup_{v \in V} \min(T(B(v), \inf_{u \in U} I_T(A_1(u), R(u,v))),$$

$$T(B(v), \inf_{u \in U} I_T(A_2(u), R(u,v))))$$

$$\leq \min(\sup_{v \in V} T(B(v), \inf_{u \in U} I_T(A_1(u), R(u,v))),$$

$$\sup_{v \in V} T(B(v), \inf_{u \in U} I_T(A_2(u), R(u,v))))$$

$$= \min((A_1 \lhd_{I_T} R) \circ_T B, (A_2 \lhd_{I_T} R) \circ_T B)$$

In the same way, we can show (3.51), (3.61), (3.65) and (3.68). The remaining cases are all analogous to the four cases discussed. $\qquad \square$

Proposition 3.7 (Interaction with $\cap$). *Let A, A_1 and A_2 be fuzzy sets in U, B, B_1 and B_2 fuzzy sets in V, and R, R_1 and R_2 fuzzy relations from U to V. It holds that*

$$(A_1 \cap A_2) \circ_T R \circ_T B \leq \min(A_1 \circ_T R \circ_T B, A_2 \circ_T R \circ_T B) \qquad (3.69)$$

$$A \circ_T R \circ_T (B_1 \cap B_2) \leq \min(A \circ_T R \circ_T B_1, A \circ_T R \circ_T B_2) \qquad (3.70)$$

$$A \circ_T (R_1 \cap R_2) \circ_T B \leq \min(A \circ_T R_1 \circ_T B, A \circ_T R_2 \circ_T B) \qquad (3.71)$$

$$(A_1 \cap A_2) \lhd_{I_T} R \rhd_{I_T} B \geq \max(A_1 \lhd_{I_T} R \rhd_{I_T} B, A_2 \lhd_{I_T} R \rhd_{I_T} B)$$
$$(3.72)$$

$$A \lhd_{I_T} R \rhd_{I_T} (B_1 \cap B_2) \geq \max(A \lhd_{I_T} R \rhd_{I_T} B_1, A \lhd_{I_T} R \rhd_{I_T} B_2)$$
$$(3.73)$$

$$A \triangleleft_{I_T} (R_1 \cap R_2) \triangleright_{I_T} B = \min(A \triangleleft_{I_T} R_1 \triangleright_{I_T} B, A \triangleleft_{I_T} R_2 \triangleright_{I_T} B) \tag{3.74}$$

$$(A_1 \cap A_2) \triangleleft_{I_T} (R \triangleleft_{I_T} B) \geq \max(A_1 \triangleleft_{I_T} (R \triangleleft_{I_T} B), A_2 \triangleleft_{I_T} (R \triangleleft_{I_T} B)) \tag{3.75}$$

$$A \triangleleft_{I_T} (R \triangleleft_{I_T} (B_1 \cap B_2)) = \min(A \triangleleft_{I_T} (R \triangleleft_{I_T} B_1), A \triangleleft_{I_T} (R \triangleleft_{I_T} B_2)) \tag{3.76}$$

$$A \triangleleft_{I_T} ((R_1 \cap R_2) \triangleleft_{I_T} B) \geq \max(A \triangleleft_{I_T} (R_1 \triangleleft_{I_T} B), A \triangleleft_{I_T} (R_2 \triangleleft_{I_T} B)) \tag{3.77}$$

$$((A_1 \cap A_2) \triangleright_{I_T} R) \triangleright_{I_T} B = \min((A_1 \triangleright_{I_T} R) \triangleright_{I_T} B, (A_2 \triangleright_{I_T} R) \triangleright_{I_T} B) \tag{3.78}$$

$$(A \triangleright_{I_T} R) \triangleright_{I_T} (B_1 \cap B_2) \geq \max((A \triangleright_{I_T} R) \triangleright_{I_T} B_1, (A \triangleright_{I_T} R) \triangleright_{I_T} B_2) \tag{3.79}$$

$$(A \triangleright_{I_T} (R_1 \cap R_2)) \triangleright_{I_T} B \geq \max((A \triangleright_{I_T} R_1) \triangleright_{I_T} B, (A \triangleright_{I_T} R_2) \triangleright_{I_T} B) \tag{3.80}$$

$$((A_1 \cap A_2) \triangleleft_{I_T} R) \circ_T B \geq \max((A_1 \triangleleft_{I_T} R) \circ_T B, (A_2 \triangleleft_{I_T} R) \circ_T B) \tag{3.81}$$

$$(A \triangleleft_{I_T} R) \circ_T (B_1 \cap B_2) \leq \min((A \triangleleft_{I_T} R) \circ_T B_1, (A \triangleleft_{I_T} R) \circ_T B_2) \tag{3.82}$$

$$(A \triangleleft_{I_T} (R_1 \cap R_2)) \circ_T B \leq \min((A \triangleleft_{I_T} R_1) \circ_T B, (A \triangleleft_{I_T} R_2) \circ_T B) \tag{3.83}$$

$$(A_1 \cap A_2) \triangleleft_{I_T} (R \circ_T B) \geq \max(A_1 \triangleleft_{I_T} (R \circ_T B), A_2 \triangleleft_{I_T} (R \circ_T B)) \tag{3.84}$$

$$A \triangleleft_{I_T} (R \circ_T (B_1 \cap B_2)) \leq \min(A \triangleleft_{I_T} (R \circ_T B_1), A \triangleleft_{I_T} (R \circ_T B_2)) \tag{3.85}$$

$$A \triangleleft_{I_T} ((R_1 \cap R_2) \circ_T B) \leq \min(A \triangleleft_{I_T} (R_1 \circ_T B), A \triangleleft_{I_T} (R_2 \circ_T B)) \tag{3.86}$$

$$((A_1 \cap A_2) \circ_T R) \triangleright_{I_T} B \leq \min((A_1 \circ_T R) \triangleright_{I_T} B, (A_2 \circ_T R) \triangleright_{I_T} B) \tag{3.87}$$

$$(A \circ_T R) \triangleright_{I_T} (B_1 \cap B_2) \geq \max((A \circ_T R) \triangleright_{I_T} B_1, (A \circ_T R) \triangleright_{I_T} B_2) \tag{3.88}$$

$$(A \circ_T (R_1 \cap R_2)) \triangleright_{I_T} B \leq \min((A \circ_T R_1) \triangleright_{I_T} B, (A \circ_T R_2) \triangleright_{I_T} B) \tag{3.89}$$

$$(A_1 \cap A_2) \circ_T (R \triangleright_{I_T} B) \leq \min(A_1 \circ_T (R \triangleright_{I_T} B), A_2 \circ_T (R \triangleright_{I_T} B)) \tag{3.90}$$

$$A \circ_T (R \rhd_{I_T} (B_1 \cap B_2)) \geq \max(A \circ_T (R \rhd_{I_T} B_1), A \circ_T (R \rhd_{I_T} B_2)) \tag{3.91}$$

$$A \circ_T ((R_1 \cap R_2) \rhd_{I_T} B) \leq \min(A \circ_T (R_1 \rhd_{I_T} B), A \circ_T (R_2 \rhd_{I_T} B)) \tag{3.92}$$

$$(A_1 \cap A_2) \circ_T (R \lhd_{I_T} B) \leq \min(A_1 \circ_T (R \lhd_{I_T} B), A_2 \circ_T (R \lhd_{I_T} B)) \tag{3.93}$$

$$A \circ_T (R \lhd_{I_T} (B_1 \cap B_2)) \leq \min(A \circ_T (R \lhd_{I_T} B_1), A \circ_T (R \lhd_{I_T} B_2)) \tag{3.94}$$

$$A \circ_T ((R_1 \cap R_2) \lhd_{I_T} B) \geq \max(A \circ_T (R_1 \lhd_{I_T} B), A \circ_T (R_2 \lhd_{I_T} B)) \tag{3.95}$$

$$((A_1 \cap A_2) \rhd_{I_T} R) \circ_T B \leq \min((A_1 \rhd_{I_T} R) \circ_T B, (A_2 \rhd_{I_T} R) \circ_T B) \tag{3.96}$$

$$(A \rhd_{I_T} R) \circ_T (B_1 \cap B_2) \leq \min((A \rhd_{I_T} R) \circ_T B_1, (A \rhd_{I_T} R) \circ_T B_2) \tag{3.97}$$

$$(A \rhd_{I_T} (R_1 \cap R_2)) \circ_T B \geq \max((A \rhd_{I_T} R_1) \circ_T B, (A \rhd_{I_T} R_2) \circ_T B) \tag{3.98}$$

Proof. The proof is analogous to the proof of Proposition 3.6. □

Proposition 3.8 (Interaction with $\subseteq$). *Let A, A_1 and A_2 be fuzzy sets in U, B, B_1 and B_2 fuzzy sets in V, and R, R_1 and R_2 fuzzy relations from U to V such that $A_1 \subseteq A_2$, $B_1 \subseteq B_2$ and $R_1 \subseteq R_2$. It holds that*

$$A_1 \circ_T R \circ_T B \leq A_2 \circ_T R \circ_T B \tag{3.99}$$

$$A \circ_T R \circ_T B_1 \leq A \circ_T R \circ_T B_2 \tag{3.100}$$

$$A \circ_T R_1 \circ_T B \leq A \circ_T R_2 \circ_T B \tag{3.101}$$

$$A_1 \lhd_{I_T} R \rhd_{I_T} B \geq A_2 \lhd_{I_T} R \rhd_{I_T} B \tag{3.102}$$

$$A \lhd_{I_T} R \rhd_{I_T} B_1 \geq A \lhd_{I_T} R \rhd_{I_T} B_2 \tag{3.103}$$

$$A \lhd_{I_T} R_1 \rhd_{I_T} B \leq A \lhd_{I_T} R_2 \rhd_{I_T} B \tag{3.104}$$

$$A_1 \lhd_{I_T} (R \lhd_{I_T} B) \geq A_2 \lhd_{I_T} (R \lhd_{I_T} B) \tag{3.105}$$

$$A \lhd_{I_T} (R \lhd_{I_T} B_1) \leq A \lhd_{I_T} (R \lhd_{I_T} B_2) \tag{3.106}$$

$$A \lhd_{I_T} (R_1 \lhd_{I_T} B) \geq A \lhd_{I_T} (R_2 \lhd_{I_T} B) \tag{3.107}$$

$$(A_1 \rhd_{I_T} R) \rhd_{I_T} B \leq (A_2 \rhd_{I_T} R) \rhd_{I_T} B \tag{3.108}$$

$$(A \rhd_{I_T} R) \rhd_{I_T} B_1 \geq (A \rhd_{I_T} R) \rhd_{I_T} B_2 \tag{3.109}$$

$$(A \rhd_{I_T} R_1) \rhd_{I_T} B \geq (A \rhd_{I_T} R_2) \rhd_{I_T} B \tag{3.110}$$

$$(A_1 \lhd_{I_T} R) \circ_T B \geq (A_2 \lhd_{I_T} R) \circ_T B \tag{3.111}$$

$$(A \lhd_{I_T} R) \circ_T B_1 \leq (A \lhd_{I_T} R) \circ_T B_2 \tag{3.112}$$

$$(A \lhd_{I_T} R_1) \circ_T B \leq (A \lhd_{I_T} R_2) \circ_T B \tag{3.113}$$

$$A_1 \lhd_{I_T} (R \circ_T B) \geq A_2 \lhd_{I_T} (R \circ_T B) \tag{3.114}$$

$$A \lhd_{I_T} (R \circ_T B_1) \leq A \lhd_{I_T} (R \circ_T B_2) \tag{3.115}$$

$$A \lhd_{I_T} (R_1 \circ_T B) \leq A \lhd_{I_T} (R_2 \circ_T B) \tag{3.116}$$

$$(A_1 \circ_T R) \rhd_{I_T} B \leq (A_2 \circ_T R) \rhd_{I_T} B \tag{3.117}$$

$$(A \circ_T R) \rhd_{I_T} B_1 \geq (A \circ_T R) \rhd_{I_T} B_2 \tag{3.118}$$

$$(A \circ_T R_1) \rhd_{I_T} B \leq (A \circ_T R_2) \rhd_{I_T} B \tag{3.119}$$

$$A_1 \circ_T (R \rhd_{I_T} B) \leq A_2 \circ_T (R \rhd_{I_T} B) \tag{3.120}$$

$$A \circ_T (R \rhd_{I_T} B_1) \geq A \circ_T (R \rhd_{I_T} B_2) \tag{3.121}$$

$$A \circ_T (R_1 \rhd_{I_T} B) \leq A \circ_T (R_2 \rhd_{I_T} B) \tag{3.122}$$

$$A_1 \circ_T (R \lhd_{I_T} B) \leq A_2 \circ_T (R \lhd_{I_T} B) \tag{3.123}$$

$$A \circ_T (R \lhd_{I_T} B_1) \leq A \circ_T (R \lhd_{I_T} B_2) \tag{3.124}$$

$$A \circ_T (R_1 \lhd_{I_T} B) \geq A \circ_T (R_2 \lhd_{I_T} B) \tag{3.125}$$

$$(A_1 \rhd_{I_T} R) \circ_T B \leq (A_2 \rhd_{I_T} R) \circ_T B \tag{3.126}$$

$$(A \rhd_{I_T} R) \circ_T B_1 \leq (A \rhd_{I_T} R) \circ_T B_2 \tag{3.127}$$

$$(A \rhd_{I_T} R_1) \circ_T B \geq (A \rhd_{I_T} R_2) \circ_T B \tag{3.128}$$

Proof. The proof follows straightforwardly from Lemma 2.7, the fact that the partial mappings of T and second partial mappings of I_T are increasing, and the fact that the first partial mappings of I_T are decreasing.   □

Proposition 3.9 (Interaction with complement). *Let A be a fuzzy set in U, B a fuzzy set in V and R a fuzzy relation from U to V. It holds that*

$$1 - A \circ_{T_W} (R \rhd_{I_W} B) = A \lhd_{I_W} ((coR) \circ_{T_W} B) \tag{3.129}$$

$$1 - A \lhd_{I_W} (R \circ_{T_W} B) = A \circ_{T_W} ((coR) \rhd_{I_W} B) \tag{3.130}$$

$$1 - (A \lhd_{I_W} R) \circ_{T_W} B = (A \circ_{T_W} (coR)) \rhd_{I_W} B \tag{3.131}$$

$$1 - (A \circ_{T_W} R) \rhd_{I_W} B = (A \lhd_{I_W} (coR)) \circ_{T_W} B \tag{3.132}$$

$$1 - A \circ_{T_W} R \circ_{T_W} B = A \lhd_{I_W} (coR) \rhd_{I_W} B \tag{3.133}$$

$$1 - A \lhd_{I_W} R \rhd_{I_W} B = A \circ_{T_W} (coR) \circ_{T_W} B \tag{3.134}$$

$$1 - A \lhd_{I_W} (R \lhd_{I_W} B) = A \circ_{T_W} R \circ_{T_W} (coB) \tag{3.135}$$

$$1 - (A \rhd_{I_W} R) \rhd_{I_W} B = (coA) \circ_{T_W} R \circ_{T_W} B \tag{3.136}$$

$$1 - A \circ_{T_W} (R \triangleleft_{I_W} B) = A \triangleleft_{I_W} (R \circ_{T_W} (coB)) \qquad (3.137)$$

$$1 - (A \triangleright_{I_W} R) \circ_{T_W} B = ((coA) \circ_{T_W} R) \triangleright_{I_W} B) \qquad (3.138)$$

Proof. To prove (3.129), we find using (2.35)

$$1 - A \circ_{T_W} (R \triangleright_{I_W} B)$$

$$= 1 - \sup_{u \in U} T_W(A(u), \inf_{v \in V} I_W(B(v), R(u,v)))$$

$$= \inf_{u \in U} 1 - T_W(A(u), \inf_{v \in V} I_W(B(v), R(u,v)))$$

$$= \inf_{u \in U} I_W(A(u), 1 - \inf_{v \in V} I_W(B(v), R(u,v)))$$

$$= \inf_{u \in U} I_W(A(u), \sup_{v \in V} 1 - I_W(B(v), R(u,v)))$$

$$= \inf_{u \in U} I_W(A(u), \sup_{v \in V} T_W(B(v), 1 - R(u,v)))$$

$$= \inf_{u \in U} I_W(A(u), \sup_{v \in V} T_W(B(v), (coR)(u,v)))$$

$$= A \triangleleft_{I_W} ((coR) \circ_{T_W} B)$$

Note that (3.130) follows immediately from (3.129) using the fact that $co(coR) = R$. In a similar way, we can show (3.131)–(3.138). $\qquad \square$

The proof of Proposition 3.9 is based on the observation that

$$(\forall a, b \in [0,1])(I_W(a,b) = 1 - T_W(a, 1 - b)) \qquad (3.139)$$

It is easy to see that (3.139) is a necessary condition, i.e., for any t-norm T not satisfying (3.139), Proposition 3.9 cannot hold. Indeed, let a and b be arbitrary elements from $[0,1]$ and let $A = \{u_1\}$, $B = \{v_1/a\}$ and $R = \{(u_1, v_1)/b\}$; we have that

$$1 - A \circ_T (R \triangleright_{I_T} B)$$

$$= 1 - \sup_{u \in U} T(A(u), \inf_{v \in V} I_T(B(v), R(u,v)))$$

$$= 1 - \inf_{v \in V} I_T(B(v), R(u_1, v))$$

$$= 1 - I_T(B(v_1), R(u_1, v_1))$$

$$= 1 - I_T(a, b)$$

Similarly, we find that $A \triangleleft_{I_W} (coR \circ_{T_W} B) = T(a, 1 - b)$. Hence, (3.129) can only hold in general iff $I_T(a,b) = 1 - T(a, 1 - b)$ for all a and b in $[0,1]$.

3.3.3 Transitivity

Frequently, we need to establish information about the relatedness of A and C, given (only) information about the relatedness of A and B, as well as information about the relatedness of B and C. As we will show in this section, the relatedness measures allow such kind of inferences. Specifically, we will derive transitivity rules of the form $T(\alpha, \beta) \leq \gamma$ for appropriate expressions α, β and γ. These transitivity rules are summarized in Table 3.1, where the entry on the row for $A \circ R \circ B$ and the column for $B \lhd S \rhd C$, for instance, should be interpreted as

$$T(A \circ_T R \circ_T B, B \lhd_{I_T} S \rhd_{I_T} C) \leq A \circ_T ((R \circ_T S) \rhd_{I_T} C) \qquad (3.140)$$

where T is a left–continuous t–norm, A, B and C are normalised fuzzy sets in the universes U, V and W respectively, R is a fuzzy relation from U to V and S is a fuzzy relation from V to W. The proof of these transitivity rules is presented in Section 3.4. In applications, such transitivity rules are often useful for making common–sense inferences. This is illustrated in the next example.

Example 3.5. Assume that we know that there is a person in community A who is interested in at least one topic from conference B to degree 0.7, and that for every topic k in conference B, there is a topic in conference C that is, at least to degree 0.8, more general than k, i.e.:

$$A \circ R \circ B = 0.7$$
$$B \lhd (S^{NT} \circ C) \geq 0.8$$

where R is defined as in Example 3.1 and S^{NT} as in Example 3.3. Intuitively, given the information about A, B and C, we would expect that at least one of the topics in C encompasses one of the research interests of a person in A to some degree. Using the transitivity table, we can derive a lower bound for this degree:

$$A \circ (R \circ S^{NT}) \circ C \geq T(A \circ R \circ B, B \lhd (S^{NT} \circ C)) \geq T(0.7, 0.8)$$

where the sup–T composition $R \circ S^{NT}$ of the fuzzy relations R and S^{NT} is given by

$R \circ S^{NT}$	ONT	DB	DM	AI	ML	IR	IE	NLP
p_1	0	0.8	0.3	0.8	0.4	0.4	0	0.4
p_2	0	0.8	0	0.3	0.2	0.4	0	0
p_3	0	0.7	0.3	0.6	0.4	0.6	0	0.8
p_4	0	0.6	0.3	0.8	0.4	0.6	0	0.8
p_5	0	0.3	0.3	0.9	0.4	0.4	0	0.4

Table 3.1 Transitivity table for relatedness measures.

	$B \circ S \circ C$	$B \circ S \triangle C$	$(B \triangle S) \circ C$	$B \triangle S \circ C$	$B \triangle (S \circ C)$	$(B \circ S) \triangle C$
$A \circ R \circ B$	1	$A \circ ((R \circ S)) \triangle C$	$A \circ (R \circ S) \circ C$	$A \circ (R \circ S) \circ C$	$A \circ (R \circ S) \circ C$	1
$A \triangle R \triangle B$	$(A \triangle (R \circ S)) \circ C$	$A \triangle (R \circ S) \triangle C$	$(A \triangle (R \circ S)) \circ C$	$(A \triangle (R \circ S)) \circ C$	$A \circ (R \circ S) \circ C$	$A \triangle (R \circ S) \triangle C$
$(A \triangle R) \circ B$	1	$A \triangle (R \circ S) \triangle C$	$A \triangle (R \circ S) \circ C$	$A \triangle (R \circ S) \circ C$	$A \circ (R \circ S) \circ C$	1
$A \triangle (R \circ B)$	1	$A \triangle (R \circ S) \triangle C$	$A \triangle (R \circ S) \circ C$	$A \triangle (R \circ S) \circ C$	$A \circ ((R \circ S)) \circ C$	1
$(A \circ R) \triangle B$	$A \circ (R \circ S) \circ C$	$A \circ (R \circ S) \triangle C$	$A \circ (R \circ S) \circ C$	$A \circ (R \circ S) \circ C$	$A \circ (R \circ S) \circ C$	$(A \circ (R \circ S)) \triangle C$
$A \circ (R \triangle B)$	$A \circ (R \circ S) \circ C$	$A \circ (R \circ S) \triangle C$	$A \circ (R \circ S) \circ C$	$A \circ (R \circ S) \circ C$	$A \circ (R \circ S) \circ C$	$A \circ ((R \circ S)) \triangle C$
$(A \triangle R) \circ B$	1	$(A \triangle (R \triangle S)) \triangle C$	$(A \triangle (R \triangle S)) \circ C$	$A \circ (R \triangle S) \circ C$	$(A \triangle (R \triangle S)) \circ C$	1
$A \triangle (R \triangle B)$	$A \circ ((R \triangle S)) \circ C$	$A \circ (R \triangle S) \triangle C$	$A \circ (R \triangle S) \circ C$	$A \circ (R \triangle S) \circ C$	$A \circ (R \triangle S) \circ C$	1
$(A \triangle R) \triangle B$	$(A \triangle (R \triangle S)) \circ C$	$(A \triangle (R \triangle S)) \triangle C$	$(A \triangle (R \triangle S)) \circ C$	$(A \triangle (R \triangle S)) \circ C$	$(A \triangle (R \triangle S)) \circ C$	$(A \triangle (R \triangle S)) \triangle C$
$A \triangle (R \triangle B)$	$(A \triangle (R \triangle S)) \circ C$	$A \triangle (R \triangle S) \triangle C$	$A \triangle (R \triangle S) \circ C$	$A \triangle (R \triangle S) \circ C$	$(A \triangle (R \triangle S)) \circ C$	1

	$B \circ (S \triangle C)$	$(B \triangle S) \triangle C$	$B \triangle (S \triangle C)$
$A \circ R \circ B$		1	
$A \triangle R \triangle B$	$A \triangle (R \circ S) \triangle C$	$A \triangle ((R \triangle S) \triangle C)$	$A \triangle ((R \triangle S) \triangle C)$
$(A \triangle R) \circ B$		1	$A \triangle ((R \triangle S) \triangle C)$
$A \triangle (R \circ B)$		1	$A \triangle ((R \triangle S) \triangle C)$
$(A \circ R) \triangle B$	$A \circ ((R \triangle S) \triangle C)$	1	$A \circ ((R \triangle S) \triangle C)$
$A \circ (R \triangle B)$	$A \circ ((R \triangle S) \triangle C)$	$A \circ (R \triangle S) \triangle C$	$A \circ ((R \triangle S) \triangle C)$
$(A \triangle R) \circ B$		1	1
$A \triangle (R \triangle B)$		1	$A \triangle (R \circ S) \triangle C$
$(A \triangle R) \triangle B$	$(A \triangle (R \triangle S)) \triangle C$	1	1
$A \triangle (R \triangle B)$		1	$A \triangle ((R \circ S) \triangle C)$

For a person p and a keyword k, $(R \circ S^{NT})(p, k)$ reflects to what degree k encompasses one of the research interests of p.

Recall that we have made the assumption that A, B and C are normalised fuzzy sets. However, we have not required that the partial mappings of R and S are normalised. When this additional condition holds, first applying (3.21)–(3.24) may lead to stronger conclusions than those mentioned in the transitivity table. For example, given that $(A \rhd_{I_T} R) \circ_T B = 0.6$ and $B \lhd_{I_T} S \rhd_{I_T} C = 0.7$, Table 3.1 allows us to deduce that

$$(A \rhd_{I_T} (R \rhd_{I_T} S)) \rhd_{I_T} C \geq T((A \rhd_{I_T} R) \circ_T B, B \lhd_{I_T} S \rhd_{I_T} C)$$
$$= T(0.6, 0.7)$$

On the other hand, by first applying (3.21), assuming the partial mappings of R are normalised, we obtain

$$A \circ_T ((R \circ_T S) \rhd_{I_T} C) \geq T(A \circ_T R \circ_T B, B \lhd_{I_T} S \rhd_{I_T} C)$$
$$\geq T((A \rhd_{I_T} R) \circ_T B, B \lhd_{I_T} S \rhd_{I_T} C)$$
$$= T(0.6, 0.7)$$

Which of these two conclusions is the stronger conclusion depends on whether $(A \rhd_{I_T} (R \rhd_{I_T} S)) \rhd_{I_T} C$ is greater or less than $A \circ_T ((R \circ_T S) \rhd_{I_T} C)$, which in turn depends on the specific definition of R and S.

Note that, in contrast, applying (3.13)–(3.20) will never lead to stronger conclusions.

3.4   Proof of the Transitivity Table

Throughout this section, let R be a fuzzy relation from U to V and S a fuzzy relation from V to W. Furthermore, let A be a normalised fuzzy set in U, B a normalised fuzzy set in V and C a normalised fuzzy set in W.

Proposition 3.10.

$$T(A \lhd_{I_T} R \rhd_{I_T} B, B \circ_T S \circ_T C) \leq (A \lhd_{I_T} (R \circ_T S)) \circ_T C \tag{3.141}$$

$$T(A \lhd_{I_T} R \rhd_{I_T} B, (B \lhd_{I_T} S) \circ_T C) \leq (A \lhd_{I_T} (R \circ_T S)) \circ_T C \tag{3.142}$$

$$T(A \lhd_{I_T} R \rhd_{I_T} B, B \lhd_{I_T} (S \circ_T C)) \leq (A \lhd_{I_T} (R \circ_T S)) \circ_T C \tag{3.143}$$

$$T(A \circ_T R \circ_T B, B \lhd_{I_T} S \rhd_{I_T} C) \leq A \circ_T ((R \circ_T S) \rhd_{I_T} C) \tag{3.144}$$

$$T((A \circ_T R) \rhd_{I_T} B, B \lhd_{I_T} S \rhd_{I_T} C) \leq A \circ_T ((R \circ_T S) \rhd_{I_T} C) \tag{3.145}$$

$$T(A \circ_T (R \rhd_{I_T} B), B \lhd_{I_T} S \rhd_{I_T} C) \leq A \circ_T ((R \circ_T S) \rhd_{I_T} C) \tag{3.146}$$

Proof. By using (2.7) we obtain

$$T(A \triangleleft_{I_T} R \triangleright_{I_T} B, B \circ_T S \circ_T C)$$

$$= T(\inf_{v' \in V} I_T(B(v'), \inf_{u \in U} I_T(A(u), R(u, v'))),$$

$$\sup_{w \in W} T(C(w), \sup_{v \in V} T(B(v), S(v, w))))$$

$$= \sup_{v \in V} \sup_{w \in W} T(\inf_{v' \in V} I_T(B(v'), \inf_{u \in U} I_T(A(u), R(u, v'))),$$

$$C(w), B(v), S(v, w))$$

$$\leq \sup_{v \in V} \sup_{w \in W} T(I_T(B(v), \inf_{u \in U} I_T(A(u), R(u, v))), C(w), B(v), S(v, w))$$

By (2.25), we have

$$\leq \sup_{v \in V} \sup_{w \in W} T(\inf_{u \in U} I_T(A(u), R(u, v)), C(w), S(v, w))$$

$$= \sup_{v \in V} \sup_{w \in W} T(T(\inf_{u \in U} I_T(A(u), R(u, v)), S(v, w)), C(w))$$

and by (2.6) and (2.24)

$$\leq \sup_{v \in V} \sup_{w \in W} T(\inf_{u \in U} T(I_T(A(u), R(u, v)), S(v, w)), C(w))$$

$$\leq \sup_{v \in V} \sup_{w \in W} T(\inf_{u \in U} I_T(A(u), T(R(u, v), S(v, w))), C(w))$$

and finally by (2.7) and (2.18)

$$= \sup_{v \in V} T(\sup_{w \in W} \inf_{u \in U} I_T(A(u), T(R(u, v), S(v, w))), C(w))$$

$$\leq \sup_{w \in W} T(\inf_{u \in U} \sup_{v \in V} I_T(A(u), T(R(u, v), S(v, w))), C(w))$$

$$\leq \sup_{w \in W} T(\inf_{u \in U} I_T(A(u), \sup_{v \in V} T(R(u, v), S(v, w))), C(w))$$

$$= (A \triangleleft_{I_T} (R \circ_T S)) \circ_T C$$

Thus we have shown that (3.141) holds; (3.142) and (3.143) follow from (3.141) by Proposition 3.1. For example, to show (3.142), we find using (3.14) and (3.16)

$$T(A \triangleleft_{I_T} R \triangleright_{I_T} B, (B \triangleleft_{I_T} S) \circ_T C) \leq T(A \triangleleft_{I_T} R \triangleright_{I_T} B, B \triangleleft_{I_T} (S \circ_T C))$$

$$\leq T(A \triangleleft_{I_T} R \triangleright_{I_T} B, B \circ_T S \circ_T C)$$

Furthermore, (3.144) follows from (3.141) using (3.33), (3.32) and (3.9). Specifically, we know by (3.141) that

$$T(C \triangleleft_{I_T} S^{-1} \triangleright_{I_T} B, B \circ_T R^{-1} \circ_T A) \leq (C \triangleleft_{I_T} (S^{-1} \circ_T R^{-1})) \circ_T A$$

which is equivalent to

$$T(B \lhd_{I_T} S \rhd_{I_T} C, A \circ_T R \circ_T B) \leq A \circ_T ((S^{-1} \circ_T R^{-1})^{-1} \rhd_{I_T} C)$$

by (3.33), (3.32) and (3.9). This last inequality is equivalent to (3.144) because of (2.44). Similarly, (3.145) follows from (3.143) using (3.32), (3.10) and (3.9); and (3.146) follows from (3.142) using (3.32) and (3.9).   □

Proposition 3.11.

$$T((A \circ_T R) \rhd_{I_T} B, B \circ_T S \circ_T C) \leq A \circ_T (R \circ_T S) \circ_T C \qquad (3.147)$$

$$T(A \circ_T (R \rhd_{I_T} B), B \circ_T S \circ_T C) \leq A \circ_T (R \circ_T S) \circ_T C \qquad (3.148)$$

$$T((A \circ_T R) \rhd_{I_T} B, (B \lhd_{I_T} S) \circ_T C) \leq A \circ_T (R \circ_T S) \circ_T C \qquad (3.149)$$

$$T(A \circ_T (R \rhd_{I_T} B), (B \lhd_{I_T} S) \circ_T C) \leq A \circ_T (R \circ_T S) \circ_T C \qquad (3.150)$$

$$T((A \circ_T R) \rhd_{I_T} B, B \lhd_{I_T} (S \circ_T C)) \leq A \circ_T (R \circ_T S) \circ_T C \qquad (3.151)$$

$$T(A \circ_T (R \rhd_{I_T} B), B \lhd_{I_T} (S \circ_T C)) \leq A \circ_T (R \circ_T S) \circ_T C \qquad (3.152)$$

$$T(A \circ_T R \circ_T B, (B \lhd_{I_T} S) \circ_T C) \leq A \circ_T (R \circ_T S) \circ_T C \qquad (3.153)$$

$$T(A \circ_T R \circ_T B, B \lhd_{I_T} (S \circ_T C)) \leq A \circ_T (R \circ_T S) \circ_T C \qquad (3.154)$$

Proof.   Using (2.7) we have

$$T((A \circ_T R) \rhd_{I_T} B, B \circ_T S \circ_T C)$$

$$= T(\inf_{v \in V} I_T(B(v), \sup_{u \in U} T(A(u), R(u, v))),$$

$$\sup_{w \in W} T(C(w), \sup_{v \in V} T(B(v), S(v, w))))$$

$$= \sup_{v \in V} \sup_{w \in W} T(\inf_{v' \in V} I_T(B(v'), \sup_{u \in U} T(A(u), R(u, v'))), C(w), B(v), S(v, w))$$

$$\leq \sup_{v \in V} \sup_{w \in W} T(I_T(B(v), \sup_{u \in U} T(A(u), R(u, v))), C(w), B(v), S(v, w))$$

and by (2.25) and (2.7)

$$\leq \sup_{v \in V} \sup_{w \in W} T(\sup_{u \in U} T(A(u), R(u, v)), C(w), S(v, w))$$

$$\leq \sup_{u \in U} T(A(u), \sup_{w \in W} T(C(w), \sup_{v \in V} T(R(u, v), S(u, v))))$$

$$= A \circ_T (R \circ_T S) \circ_T C$$

which proves (3.147); (3.148)-(3.152) follow from (3.147) by Proposition 3.1. Furthermore, (3.153) follows from (3.148) using (3.33) and (3.9), while (3.154) follows from (3.147) using (3.33) and (3.10).   □

Proposition 3.12.

$$T(A \triangleleft_{I_T} R \triangleright_{I_T} B, B \triangleleft_{I_T} S \triangleright_{I_T} C) \leq A \triangleleft_{I_T} (R \circ_T S) \triangleright_{I_T} C \quad (3.155)$$

$$T((A \triangleleft_{I_T} R) \circ_T B, B \triangleleft_{I_T} S \triangleright_{I_T} C) \leq A \triangleleft_{I_T} (R \circ_T S) \triangleright_{I_T} C \quad (3.156)$$

$$T(A \triangleleft_{I_T} (R \circ_T B), B \triangleleft_{I_T} S \triangleright_{I_T} C) \leq A \triangleleft_{I_T} (R \circ_T S) \triangleright_{I_T} C \quad (3.157)$$

$$T(A \triangleleft_{I_T} R \triangleright_{I_T} B, (B \circ_T S) \triangleright_{I_T} C) \leq A \triangleleft_{I_T} (R \circ_T S) \triangleright_{I_T} C \quad (3.158)$$

$$T(A \triangleleft_{I_T} R \triangleright_{I_T} B, B \circ_T (S \triangleright_{I_T} C)) \leq A \triangleleft_{I_T} (R \circ_T S) \triangleright_{I_T} C \quad (3.159)$$

Proof. By (2.6), (2.29) and (2.7), we have

$$T(A \triangleleft_{I_T} (R \circ_T B), B \triangleleft_{I_T} S \triangleright_{I_T} C)$$

$$= T(\inf_{u \in U} I_T(A(u), \sup_{v \in V} T(B(v), R(u,v))),$$

$$\inf_{w \in W} I_T(C(w), \inf_{v \in V} I_T(B(v), S(v,w))))$$

$$\leq \inf_{u \in U} \inf_{w \in W} T(I_T(A(u), \sup_{v \in V} T(B(v), R(u,v))),$$

$$I_T(C(w), \inf_{v \in V} I_T(B(v), S(v,w))))$$

$$\leq \inf_{u \in U} \inf_{w \in W} I_T(T(A(u), C(w)),$$

$$T(\sup_{v \in V} T(B(v), R(u,v)), \inf_{v \in V} I_T(B(v), S(v,w))))$$

$$= \inf_{u \in U} \inf_{w \in W} I_T(T(A(u), C(w)),$$

$$\sup_{v \in V} T(B(v), R(u,v), \inf_{v' \in V} I_T(B(v'), S(v',w))))$$

$$\leq \inf_{u \in U} \inf_{w \in W} I_T(T(A(u), C(w)), \sup_{v \in V} T(B(v), R(u,v), I_T(B(v), S(v,w))))$$

and by (2.25), (2.26) and (2.20) we have

$$\leq \inf_{u \in U} \inf_{w \in W} I_T(T(A(u), C(w)), \sup_{v \in V} T(R(u,v), S(v,w)))$$

$$= \inf_{u \in U} \inf_{w \in W} I_T(A(u), I_T(C(w), \sup_{v \in V} T(R(u,v), S(v,w))))$$

$$= \inf_{u \in U} I_T(A(u), \inf_{w \in W} I_T(C(w), \sup_{v \in V} T(R(u,v), S(v,w))))$$

$$= A \triangleleft_{I_T} (R \circ_T S) \triangleright_{I_T} C$$

showing (3.157); (3.155) and (3.156) follow from (3.157) by Proposition 3.1. Furthermore, (3.158) follows from (3.157) using (3.32) and (3.10), while and (3.159) follows from (3.156) using (3.32) and (3.9). □

Proposition 3.13.

$$T((A \lhd_{I_T} R) \circ_T B, (B \lhd_{I_T} S) \circ_T C) \leq (A \lhd_{I_T} (R \circ_T S)) \circ_T C \quad (3.160)$$

$$T(A \lhd_{I_T} (R \circ_T B), (B \lhd_{I_T} S) \circ_T C) \leq (A \lhd_{I_T} (R \circ_T S)) \circ_T C \quad (3.161)$$

$$T((A \lhd_{I_T} R) \circ_T B, B \lhd_{I_T} (S \circ_T C)) \leq (A \lhd_{I_T} (R \circ_T S)) \circ_T C \quad (3.162)$$

$$T(A \circ_T (R \rhd_{I_T} B), B \circ_T (S \rhd_{I_T} C)) \leq A \circ_T ((R \circ_T S) \rhd_{I_T} C) \quad (3.163)$$

$$T((A \circ_T R) \rhd_{I_T} B, B \circ_T (S \rhd_{I_T} C)) \leq A \circ_T ((R \circ_T S) \rhd_{I_T} C) \quad (3.164)$$

$$T(A \circ_T (R \rhd_{I_T} B), (B \circ_T S) \rhd_{I_T} C) \leq A \circ_T ((R \circ_T S) \rhd_{I_T} C) \quad (3.165)$$

Proof. By (2.7) and (2.6) we obtain

$$T(A \lhd_{I_T} (R \circ_T B), (B \lhd_{I_T} S) \circ_T C)$$

$$= T(\inf_{u \in U} I_T(A(u), \sup_{v \in V} T(B(v), R(u, v))),$$

$$\sup_{w \in W} T(C(w), \inf_{v \in V} I_T(B(v), S(v, w))))$$

$$= \sup_{w \in W} T(\inf_{u \in U} I_T(A(u), \sup_{v \in V} T(B(v), R(u, v))),$$

$$C(w), \inf_{v \in V} I_T(B(v), S(v, w)))$$

$$= \sup_{w \in W} T(C(w), T(\inf_{u \in U} I_T(A(u), \sup_{v \in V} T(B(v), R(u, v))),$$

$$\inf_{v \in V} I_T(B(v), S(v, w))))$$

$$\leq \sup_{w \in W} T(C(w), \inf_{u \in U} T(I_T(A(u), \sup_{v \in V} T(B(v), R(u, v))),$$

$$\inf_{v \in V} I_T(B(v), S(v, w))))$$

By (2.24) and (2.7) we obtain

$$\leq \sup_{w \in W} T(C(w), \inf_{u \in U} I_T(A(u), T(\sup_{v \in V} T(B(v), R(u, v)),$$

$$\inf_{v \in V} I_T(B(v), S(v, w)))))$$

$$= \sup_{w \in W} T(C(w), \inf_{u \in U} I_T(A(u), \sup_{v \in V} T(T(B(v), R(u, v)),$$

$$\inf_{v' \in V} I_T(B(v'), S(v', w)))))$$

$$\leq \sup_{w \in W} T(C(w), \inf_{u \in U} I_T(A(u), \sup_{v \in V} T(B(v), R(u, v), I_T(B(v), S(v, w))))))$$

and by (2.25)

$$\leq \sup_{w \in W} T(C(w), \inf_{u \in U} I_T(A(u), \sup_{v \in V} T(R(u, v), S(v, w))))$$

$$= (A \lhd_{I_T} (R \circ_T S)) \circ_T C$$

which shows (3.161). The proof of (3.162) is analogous. Furthermore (3.160) follows from (3.161) by Proposition 3.1. Finally, (3.163) follows from (3.160) using (3.9); (3.164) follows from (3.162) using (3.10) and (3.9)); and (3.165) follows from (3.161) using (3.10) and (3.9). □

Proposition 3.14.

$$T(A \lhd_{I_T} (R \circ_T B), B \lhd_{I_T} (S \circ_T C)) \leq A \lhd_{I_T} ((R \circ_T S) \circ_T C) \quad (3.166)$$

$$T((A \circ_T R) \rhd_{I_T} B, (B \circ_T S) \rhd_{I_T} C) \leq (A \circ_T (R \circ_T S)) \rhd_{I_T} C \quad (3.167)$$

Proof. By (2.6) we have

$$T(A \lhd_{I_T} (R \circ_T B), B \lhd_{I_T} (S \circ_T C))$$

$$= T(\inf_{u \in U} I_T(A(u), \sup_{v \in V} T(B(v), R(u, v))),$$

$$\inf_{v \in V} I_T(B(v), \sup_{w \in W} T(C(w), S(v, w))))$$

$$\leq \inf_{u \in U} T(I_T(A(u), \sup_{v \in V} T(B(v), R(u, v))),$$

$$\inf_{v \in V} I_T(B(v), \sup_{w \in W} T(C(w), S(v, w))))$$

By (2.24) and (2.7) we obtain

$$\leq \inf_{u \in U} I_T(A(u), T(\sup_{v \in V} T(B(v), R(u, v)),$$

$$\inf_{v \in V} I_T(B(v), \sup_{w \in W} T(C(w), S(v, w)))))$$

$$= \inf_{u \in U} I_T(A(u), \sup_{v \in V} T(B(v), R(u, v)),$$

$$\inf_{v' \in V} I_T(B(v'), \sup_{w \in W} T(C(w), S(v', w)))))$$

$$\leq \inf_{u \in U} I_T(A(u), \sup_{v \in V} T(B(v), R(u, v), I_T(B(v), \sup_{w \in W} T(C(w), S(v, w))))))$$

and by (2.25) and (2.7)

$$\leq \inf_{u \in U} I_T(A(u), \sup_{v \in V} T(R(u, v), \sup_{w \in W} T(C(w), S(v, w))))$$

$$= \inf_{u \in U} I_T(A(u), \sup_{v \in V} \sup_{w \in W} T(R(u, v), T(C(w), S(v, w))))$$

$$= \inf_{u \in U} I_T(A(u), \sup_{w \in W} T(C(w), \sup_{v \in V} T(R(u, v), S(v, w))))$$

$$= A \lhd_{I_T} ((R \circ_T S) \circ_T C)$$

which completes the proof of (3.166); (3.167) follows by applying (3.10).□

Proposition 3.15.

$$T(A \circ_T R \circ_T B, B \lhd_{I_T} (S \lhd_{I_T} C)) \leq A \circ_T ((R \lhd_{I_T} S) \lhd_{I_T} C) \quad (3.168)$$

$$T(A \circ_T (R \rhd_{I_T} B), B \lhd_{I_T} (S \lhd_{I_T} C)) \leq A \circ_T ((R \lhd_{I_T} S) \lhd_{I_T} C) \quad (3.169)$$

$$T((A \rhd_{I_T} R) \rhd_{I_T} B, B \circ_T S \circ_T C) \leq (A \rhd_{I_T} (R \rhd_{I_T} S)) \circ_T C \quad (3.170)$$

$$T((A \rhd_{I_T} R) \rhd_{I_T} B, (B \lhd_{I_T} S) \circ_T C) \leq (A \rhd_{I_T} (R \rhd_{I_T} S)) \circ_T C \quad (3.171)$$

Proof. We obtain using (2.7)

$$T(A \circ_T R \circ_T B, B \lhd_{I_T} (S \lhd_{I_T} C))$$

$$= T(\sup_{v \in V} T(B(v), \sup_{u \in U} T(A(u), R(u,v))),$$

$$\inf_{v \in V} I_T(B(v), \inf_{w \in W} I_T(S(v,w), C(w))))$$

$$= \sup_{v \in V} T(B(v), \sup_{u \in U} T(A(u), R(u,v)),$$

$$\inf_{v' \in V} I_T(B(v'), \inf_{w \in W} I_T(S(v',w), C(w))))$$

$$\leq \sup_{v \in V} T(B(v), \sup_{u \in U} T(A(u), R(u,v)), I_T(B(v), \inf_{w \in W} I_T(S(v,w), C(w))))$$

By (2.25), (2.7) and (2.6) we find

$$\leq \sup_{v \in V} T(\sup_{u \in U} T(A(u), R(u,v)), \inf_{w \in W} I_T(S(v,w), C(w)))$$

$$= \sup_{v \in V} \sup_{u \in U} T(A(u), T(R(u,v), \inf_{w \in W} I_T(S(v,w), C(w))))$$

$$\leq \sup_{v \in V} \sup_{u \in U} T(A(u), \inf_{w \in W} T(R(u,v), I_T(S(v,w), C(w))))$$

and by (2.30), (2.7) and (2.17)

$$\leq \sup_{v \in V} \sup_{u \in U} T(A(u), \inf_{w \in W} I_T(I_T(R(u,v), S(v,w)), C(w)))$$

$$= \sup_{u \in U} T(A(u), \sup_{v \in V} \inf_{w \in W} I_T(I_T(R(u,v), S(v,w)), C(w)))$$

$$\leq \sup_{u \in U} T(A(u), \inf_{w \in W} \sup_{v \in V} I_T(I_T(R(u,v), S(v,w)), C(w)))$$

$$\leq \sup_{u \in U} T(A(u), \inf_{w \in W} I_T(\inf_{v \in V} I_T(R(u,v), S(v,w)), C(w)))$$

$$= A \circ_T ((R \lhd_{I_T} S) \lhd_{I_T} C)$$

which already shows (3.168). The proof of (3.170) follows easily from (3.168) using (3.33), (3.12) and (3.11). Next, (3.169) follows from (3.168) by Proposition 3.1. Finally, (3.171) follows from (3.169) using (3.9), (3.12) and (3.11). □

Proposition 3.16.

$$T(A \circ_T (R \lhd_{I_T} B), B \lhd_{I_T} S \rhd_{I_T} C) \leq A \circ_T ((R \lhd_{I_T} S) \rhd_{I_T} C) \qquad (3.172)$$

$$T(A \lhd_{I_T} R \rhd_{I_T} B, (B \rhd_{I_T} S) \circ_T C) \leq (A \lhd_{I_T} (R \rhd_{I_T} S)) \circ_T C \qquad (3.173)$$

Proof. We find by (2.7) and (2.6)

$$T(A \circ_T (R \lhd_{I_T} B), B \lhd_{I_T} S \rhd_{I_T} C)$$

$$= T(\sup_{u \in U} T(A(u), \inf_{v \in V} I_T(R(u,v), B(v))),$$

$$\inf_{v \in V} I_T(B(v), \inf_{w \in W} I_T(C(w), S(v,w))))$$

$$= \sup_{u \in U} T(A(u), \inf_{v \in V} I_T(R(u,v), B(v))),$$

$$\inf_{v \in V} I_T(B(v), \inf_{w \in W} I_T(C(w), S(v,w))))$$

$$= \sup_{u \in U} T(A(u), T(\inf_{v \in V} I_T(R(u,v), B(v))),$$

$$\inf_{v \in V} I_T(B(v), \inf_{w \in W} I_T(C(w), S(v,w)))))$$

$$\leq \sup_{u \in U} T(A(u), \inf_{v \in V} T(\inf_{v' \in V} I_T(R(u,v'), B(v'))),$$

$$I_T(B(v), \inf_{w \in W} I_T(C(w), S(v,w))))))$$

$$\leq \sup_{u \in U} T(A(u), \inf_{v \in V} T(I_T(R(u,v), B(v))),$$

$$I_T(B(v), \inf_{w \in W} I_T(C(w), S(v,w))))))$$

and by (2.28), (2.20) and (2.27)

$$\leq \sup_{u \in U} T(A(u), \inf_{v \in V} I_T(R(u,v), \inf_{w \in W} I_T(C(w), S(v,w))))$$

$$= \sup_{u \in U} T(A(u), \inf_{v \in V} \inf_{w \in W} I_T(R(u,v), I_T(C(w), S(v,w))))$$

$$= \sup_{u \in U} T(A(u), \inf_{v \in V} \inf_{w \in W} I_T(C(w), I_T(R(u,v), S(v,w))))$$

$$= \sup_{u \in U} T(A(u), \inf_{w \in W} I_T(C(w), \inf_{v \in V} I_T(R(u,v), S(v,w))))$$

$$= A \circ_T ((R \lhd_{I_T} S) \rhd_{I_T} C)$$

showing (3.172). Applying (3.11), (3.32) and (3.9) yields (3.173). $\square$

Proposition 3.17.

$$T(A \lhd_{I_T} R \rhd_{I_T} B, B \circ_T (S \lhd_{I_T} C)) \leq A \lhd_{I_T} ((R \lhd_{I_T} S) \lhd_{I_T} C) \quad (3.174)$$

$$T(A \lhd_{I_T} R \rhd_{I_T} B, B \lhd_{I_T} (S \lhd_{I_T} C)) \leq A \lhd_{I_T} ((R \lhd_{I_T} S) \lhd_{I_T} C) \quad (3.175)$$

$$T((A \rhd_{I_T} R) \circ B, B \lhd_{I_T} S \rhd_{I_T} C) \leq (A \rhd_{I_T} (R \rhd_{I_T} S)) \rhd_{I_T} C \quad (3.176)$$

$$T((A \rhd_{I_T} R) \rhd B, B \lhd_{I_T} S \rhd_{I_T} C) \leq (A \rhd_{I_T} (R \rhd_{I_T} S)) \rhd_{I_T} C \quad (3.177)$$

Proof.   We find using (2.7), (2.25) and (2.6)

$$T(A \lhd_{I_T} R \rhd_{I_T} B, B \circ_T (S \lhd_{I_T} C)))$$

$$= T(\inf_{v \in V} I_T(B(v), \inf_{u \in U} I_T(A(u), R(u,v))),$$

$$\sup_{v \in V} T(B(v), \inf_{w \in W} I_T(S(v,w), C(w))))$$

$$= \sup_{v \in V} T(\inf_{v' \in V} I_T(B(v'), \inf_{u \in U} I_T(A(u), R(v',u))),$$

$$T(B(v), \inf_{w \in W} I_T(S(v,w), C(w))))$$

$$\leq \sup_{v \in V} T(I_T(B(v), \inf_{u \in U} I_T(A(u), R(u,v))),$$

$$T(B(v), \inf_{w \in W} I_T(S(v,w), C(w))))$$

$$= \sup_{v \in V} T(\inf_{u \in U} I_T(A(u), R(u,v)), \inf_{w \in W} I_T(S(v,w), C(w)))$$

$$\leq \sup_{v \in V} \inf_{u \in U} T(I_T(A(u), R(u,v)), \inf_{w \in W} I_T(S(v,w), C(w)))$$

and by (2.24), (2.6) and (2.30)

$$\leq \sup_{v \in V} \inf_{u \in U} I_T(A(u), T(R(u,v), \inf_{w \in W} I_T(S(v,w), C(w))))$$

$$\leq \sup_{v \in V} \inf_{u \in U} I_T(A(u), \inf_{w \in W} T(R(u,v), I_T(S(v,w), C(w))))$$

$$\leq \sup_{v \in V} \inf_{u \in U} I_T(A(u), \inf_{w \in W} I_T(I_T(R(u,v), S(v,w)), C(w)))$$

$$\leq \inf_{u \in U} \sup_{v \in V} I_T(A(u), \inf_{w \in W} I_T(I_T(R(u,v), S(v,w)), C(w)))$$

and finally by (2.18) and (2.17)

$$\leq \inf_{u \in U} I_T(A(u), \sup_{v \in V} \inf_{w \in W} I_T(I_T(R(u,v), S(v,w)), C(w)))$$

$$\leq \inf_{u \in U} I_T(A(u), \inf_{w \in W} \sup_{v \in V} I_T(I_T(R(u,v), S(v,w)), C(w)))$$

$$\leq \inf_{u \in U} I_T(A(u), \inf_{w \in W} I_T(\inf_{v \in V} I_T(R(u,v), S(v,w)), C(w)))$$

$$= A \lhd_{I_T} ((R \lhd_{I_T} S) \lhd_{I_T} C)$$

proving (3.174). Next, (3.176) follows from (3.174) by using (3.32), (3.11) and (3.12), while (3.175) follows from (3.174) by Proposition 3.1. Finally, (3.177) follows from (3.175) by (3.32) and (3.12). $\qquad\square$

Proposition 3.18.

$$T(A \lhd_{I_T} (R \lhd_{I_T} B), B \lhd_{I_T} S \rhd_{I_T} C) \leq A \lhd_{I_T} (R \lhd_{I_T} S) \rhd_{I_T} C \quad (3.178)$$

$$T(A \lhd_{I_T} R \rhd_{I_T} B, (B \rhd_{I_T} S) \rhd_{I_T} C) \leq A \lhd_{I_T} (R \rhd_{I_T} S) \rhd_{I_T} C \quad (3.179)$$

Proof. We find using (2.6) and (2.26)

$$T(A \lhd_{I_T} (R \lhd_{I_T} B), B \lhd_{I_T} S \rhd_{I_T} C)$$

$$= T(\inf_{u \in U} I_T(A(u), \inf_{v \in V} I_T(R(u,v), B(v))),$$

$$\inf_{v \in V} I_T(B(v), \inf_{w \in W} I_T(C(w), S(v,w))))$$

$$\leq \inf_{v \in V} T(\inf_{u \in U} I_T(A(u), \inf_{v'} I_T(R(u,v'), B(v'))),$$

$$I_T(B(v), \inf_{w \in W} I_T(C(w), S(v,w))))$$

$$\leq \inf_{v \in V} T(\inf_{u \in U} I_T(A(u), I_T(R(u,v), B(v))),$$

$$I_T(B(v), \inf_{w \in W} I_T(C(w), S(v,w))))$$

$$\leq \inf_{v \in V} \inf_{u \in U} T(I_T(A(u), I_T(R(u,v), B(v))),$$

$$I_T(B(v), \inf_{w \in W} I_T(C(w), S(v,w))))$$

$$= \inf_{v \in V} \inf_{u \in U} T(I_T(T(A(u), R(u,v)), B(v)),$$

$$I_T(B(v), \inf_{w \in W} I_T(C(w), S(v,w))))$$

and using (2.28), (2.20) and (2.26)

$$\leq \inf_{v \in V} \inf_{u \in U} I_T(T(A(u), R(u,v)), \inf_{w \in W} I_T(C(w), S(v,w)))$$

$$= \inf_{v \in V} \inf_{u \in U} \inf_{w \in W} I_T(T(A(u), R(u,v)), I_T(C(w), S(v,w)))$$

$$= \inf_{v \in V} \inf_{u \in U} \inf_{w \in W} I_T(T(A(u), R(u,v), C(w)), S(v,w))$$

$$= \inf_{v \in V} \inf_{u \in U} \inf_{w \in W} I_T(T(A(u), C(w)), I_T(R(u,v), S(v,w)))$$

$$= \inf_{u \in U} \inf_{w \in W} I_T(T(A(u), C(w)), \inf_{v \in V} I_T(R(u,v), S(v,w)))$$

$$= \inf_{u \in U} \inf_{w \in W} I_T(A(u), I_T(C(w), \inf_{v \in V} I_T(R(u,v), S(v,w))))$$

$$= \inf_{u \in U} I_T(A(u), \inf_{w \in W} I_T(C(w), \inf_{v \in V} I_T(R(u,v), S(v,w))))$$

$$= A \lhd_{I_T} (R \lhd_{I_T} S) \rhd_{I_T} C$$

which shows (3.178); (3.179) follows by (3.12) and (3.32).   □

Proposition 3.19.

$$T(A \lhd_{I_T} (R \circ_T B), B \lhd_{I_T} (S \lhd_{I_T} C)) \leq A \lhd_{I_T} ((R \lhd_{I_T} S) \lhd_{I_T} C)$$
$$(3.180)$$

$$T((A \lhd_{I_T} R) \circ_T B, B \lhd_{I_T} (S \lhd_{I_T} C)) \leq A \lhd_{I_T} ((R \lhd_{I_T} S) \lhd_{I_T} C)$$
$$(3.181)$$

$$T((A \rhd_{I_T} R) \rhd_{I_T} B, (B \circ_T S) \rhd_{I_T} C) \leq (A \rhd_{I_T} (R \rhd_{I_T} S)) \rhd_{I_T} C$$
$$(3.182)$$

$$T((A \rhd_{I_T} R) \rhd_{I_T} B, B \circ_T (S \rhd_{I_T} C)) \leq (A \rhd_{I_T} (R \rhd_{I_T} S)) \rhd_{I_T} C$$
$$(3.183)$$

Proof.   We find using (2.6), (2.24) and (2.7)

$$T(A \lhd_{I_T} (R \circ_T B), B \lhd_{I_T} (S \lhd_{I_T} C)))$$
$$= T(\inf_{u \in U} I_T(A(u), \sup_{v \in V} T(R(u,v), B(v))),$$
$$\inf_{v \in V} I_T(B(v), \inf_{w \in W} I_T(S(v,w), C(w))))$$
$$\leq \inf_{u \in U} T(I_T(A(u), \sup_{v \in V} T(R(u,v), B(v))),$$
$$\inf_{v \in V} I_T(B(v), \inf_{w \in W} I_T(S(v,w), C(w))))$$
$$\leq \inf_{u \in U} I_T(A(u), T(\sup_{v \in V} T(R(u,v), B(v)),$$
$$\inf_{v \in V} I_T(B(v), \inf_{w \in W} I_T(S(v,w), C(w)))))$$
$$= \inf_{u \in U} I_T(A(u), \sup_{v \in V} T(R(u,v), B(v),$$
$$\inf_{v' \in V} I_T(B(v'), \inf_{w \in W} I_T(S(v',w), C(w))))))$$
$$\leq \inf_{u \in U} I_T(A(u), \sup_{v \in V} T(R(u,v), B(v), I_T(B(v), \inf_{w \in W} I_T(S(v,w), C(w))))))$$

and by (2.25), (2.6), (2.30) and (2.17)

$$\leq \inf_{u \in U} I_T(A(u), \sup_{v \in V} T(R(u,v), \inf_{w \in W} I_T(S(v,w), C(w))))$$
$$\leq \inf_{u \in U} I_T(A(u), \sup_{v \in V} \inf_{w \in W} T(R(u,v), I_T(S(v,w), C(w))))$$
$$\leq \inf_{u \in U} I_T(A(u), \sup_{v \in V} \inf_{w \in W} I_T(I_T(R(u,v), S(v,w)), C(w)))$$
$$\leq \inf_{u \in U} I_T(A(u), \inf_{w \in W} \sup_{v \in V} I_T(I_T(R(u,v), S(v,w)), C(w)))$$

$$\leq \inf_{u \in U} I_T(A(u), \inf_{w \in W} I_T(\inf_{v \in V} I_T(R(u,v), S(v,w)), C(w)))$$

$$= A \lhd_{I_T} ((R \lhd_{I_T} S) \lhd_{I_T} C)$$

proving (3.180). Next, (3.182) follows from (3.180) by using (3.10) and (3.12), while (3.181) follows from (3.180) by Proposition 3.1. Finally, (3.183) follows from (3.181) by (3.9) and (3.12). □

Proposition 3.20.

$$T((A \circ_T R) \rhd_{I_T} B, B \circ_T (S \lhd_{I_T} C)) \leq A \circ_T ((R \lhd_{I_T} S) \lhd_{I_T} C) \quad (3.184)$$

$$T(A \circ_T (R \rhd_{I_T} B), B \circ_T (S \lhd_{I_T} C)) \leq A \circ_T ((R \lhd_{I_T} S) \lhd_{I_T} C) \quad (3.185)$$

$$T((A \circ_T R) \rhd_{I_T} B, B \lhd_{I_T} (S \lhd_{I_T} C)) \leq A \circ_T ((R \lhd_{I_T} S) \lhd_{I_T} C) \quad (3.186)$$

$$T((A \rhd_{I_T} R) \circ_T B, B \lhd_{I_T} (S \circ_T C)) \leq (A \rhd_{I_T} (R \rhd_{I_T} S)) \circ_T C \quad (3.187)$$

$$T((A \rhd_{I_T} R) \circ_T B, (B \lhd_{I_T} S) \circ_T C) \leq (A \rhd_{I_T} (R \rhd_{I_T} S)) \circ_T C \quad (3.188)$$

$$T((A \rhd_{I_T} R) \rhd_{I_T} B, B \lhd_{I_T} (S \circ_T C)) \leq (A \rhd_{I_T} (R \rhd_{I_T} S)) \circ_T C \quad (3.189)$$

Proof. Using (2.7), (2.25) and (2.6), we find

$$T((A \circ_T R) \rhd_{I_T} B, B \circ_T (S \lhd_{I_T} C))$$

$$= T(\inf_{v \in V} I_T(B(v), \sup_{u \in U} T(A(u), R(u,v))),$$

$$\sup_{v \in V} T(B(v), \inf_{w \in W} I_T(S(v,w), C(w))))$$

$$= \sup_{v \in V} T(\inf_{v' \in V} I_T(B(v'), \sup_{u \in U} T(A(u), R(u,v'))), B(v),$$

$$\inf_{w \in W} I_T(S(v,w), C(w)))$$

$$\leq \sup_{v \in V} T(I_T(B(v), \sup_{u \in U} T(A(u), R(u,v))), B(v), \inf_{w \in W} I_T(S(v,w), C(w)))$$

$$\leq \sup_{v \in V} T(\sup_{u \in U} T(A(u), R(u,v)), \inf_{w \in W} I_T(S(v,w), C(w)))$$

$$= \sup_{v \in V} \sup_{u \in U} T(A(u), R(u,v), \inf_{w \in W} I_T(S(v,w), C(w)))$$

$$\leq \sup_{v \in V} \sup_{u \in U} T(A(u), \inf_{w \in W} T(R(u,v), I_T(S(v,w), C(w))))$$

and using (2.30), (2.7) and (2.17)

$$\leq \sup_{v \in V} \sup_{u \in U} T(A(u), \inf_{w \in W} I_T(I_T(R(u,v), S(v,w)), C(w)))$$

$$= \sup_{u \in U} T(A(u), \sup_{v \in V} \inf_{w \in W} I_T(I_T(R(u,v), S(v,w)), C(w)))$$

$$\leq \sup_{u \in U} T(A(u), \inf_{w \in W} \sup_{v \in V} I_T(I_T(R(u,v), S(v,w)), C(w)))$$

$$\leq \sup_{u \in U} T(A(u), \inf_{w \in W} I_T(\inf_{v \in V} I_T(R(u,v), S(v,w)), C(w)))$$

$$= A \circ_T ((R \lhd_{I_T} S) \lhd_{I_T} C)$$

which proves (3.184). Using Proposition 3.1 we can also verify (3.185) and (3.186). Next, (3.187) follows from (3.184) using (3.10) and (3.11), while (3.188) follows from (3.185) using (3.9) and (3.11). Finally, (3.189) follows from (3.186) by (3.10), (3.12) and (3.11). □

Proposition 3.21.

$$T(A \circ_T (R \rhd_{I_T} B), (B \rhd_{I_T} S) \circ_T C) \leq A \circ_T (R \rhd_{I_T} S) \circ_T C \quad (3.190)$$

$$T(A \circ_T (R \lhd_{I_T} B), (B \lhd_{I_T} S) \circ_T C) \leq A \circ_T (R \lhd_{I_T} S) \circ_T C \quad (3.191)$$

Proof.   Using (2.7), (2.6) and (2.28) yields

$$T(A \circ_T (R \rhd_{I_T} B), (B \rhd_{I_T} S) \circ_T C)$$

$$= T(\sup_{u \in U} T(A(u), \inf_{v \in V} I_T(B(v), R(u,v))),$$

$$\sup_{w \in W} T(C(w), \inf_{v \in V} I_T(S(v,w), B(v))))$$

$$= \sup_{u \in U} T(A(u), \inf_{v \in V} I_T(B(v), R(u,v)),$$

$$\sup_{w \in W} T(C(w), \inf_{v \in V} I_T(S(v,w), B(v))))$$

$$= \sup_{u \in U} T(A(u), \sup_{w \in W} T(C(w), \inf_{v \in V} I_T(B(v), R(u,v)),$$

$$\inf_{v \in V} I_T(S(v,w), B(v))))$$

$$\leq \sup_{u \in U} T(A(u), \sup_{w \in W} T(C(w), \inf_{v \in V} T(I_T(B(v), R(u,v)),$$

$$\inf_{v' \in V} I_T(S(v',w), B(v')))))$$

$$\leq \sup_{u \in U} T(A(u), \sup_{w \in W} T(C(w), \inf_{v \in V} T(I_T(B(v), R(u,v)), I_T(S(v,w), B(v)))))$$

$$\leq \sup_{u \in U} T(A(u), \sup_{w \in W} T(C(w), \inf_{v \in V} I_T(S(v,w), R(u,v))))$$

$$= A \circ_T (R \rhd_{I_T} S) \circ_T C$$

proving (3.190); (3.191) follows by (3.9), (3.11) and (3.33). □

Proposition 3.22.

$$T(A \circ_T (R \rhd_{I_T} B), (B \rhd_{I_T} S) \rhd_{I_T} C) \leq A \circ_T ((R \rhd_{I_T} S) \rhd_{I_T} C) \quad (3.192)$$

$$T(A \lhd_{I_T} (R \lhd_{I_T} B), (B \lhd_{I_T} S) \circ_T C) \leq (A \lhd_{I_T} (R \lhd_{I_T} S)) \circ_T C \quad (3.193)$$

Proof. Using (2.7), (2.6) and (2.24), we find

$$T(A \circ_T (R \triangleright_{I_T} B), (B \triangleright_{I_T} S) \triangleright_{I_T} C)$$

$$= T(\sup_{u \in U} T(A(u), \inf_{v \in V} I_T(B(v), R(u,v))),$$

$$\inf_{w \in W} I_T(C(w), \inf_{v \in V} I_T(S(v,w), B(v))))$$

$$= \sup_{u \in U} T(A(u), \inf_{v \in V} I_T(B(v), R(u,v))),$$

$$\inf_{w \in W} I_T(C(w), \inf_{v \in V} I_T(S(v,w), B(v))))$$

$$\leq \sup_{u \in U} T(A(u), \inf_{w \in W} T(\inf_{v \in V} I_T(B(v), R(u,v)),$$

$$I_T(C(w), \inf_{v \in V} I_T(S(v,w), B(v)))))$$

$$\leq \sup_{u \in U} T(A(u), \inf_{w \in W} I_T(C(w), T(\inf_{v \in V} I_T(B(v), R(u,v)),$$

$$\inf_{v \in V} I_T(S(v,w), B(v)))))$$

and using (2.6) and (2.28)

$$\leq \sup_{u \in U} T(A(u), \inf_{w \in W} I_T(C(w), \inf_{v \in V} T(I_T(B(v), R(u,v)),$$

$$\inf_{v' \in V} I_T(S(v',w), B(v')))))$$

$$\leq \sup_{u \in U} T(A(u), \inf_{w \in W} I_T(C(w), \inf_{v \in V} T(I_T(B(v), R(u,v)),$$

$$I_T(S(v,w), B(v)))))$$

$$\leq \sup_{u \in U} T(A(u), \inf_{w \in W} I_T(C(w), \inf_{v \in V} I_T(S(v,w), R(u,v))))$$

$$= A \circ_T ((R \triangleright_{I_T} S) \triangleright_{I_T} C)$$

proving (3.192); (3.193) follows by (3.9) and (3.12). □

Proposition 3.23.

$$T(A \circ_T (R \triangleleft_{I_T} B), B \triangleleft_{I_T} (S \triangleleft_{I_T} C)) \leq A \circ_T ((R \circ_T S) \triangleleft_{I_T} C) \quad (3.194)$$

$$T((A \triangleright_{I_T} R) \triangleright_{I_T} B, (B \triangleright_{I_T} S) \circ_T C) \leq (A \triangleright_{I_T} (R \circ_T S)) \circ_T C \quad (3.195)$$

Proof. Using (2.7), (2.6) and (2.28)

$$T(A \circ_T (R \lhd_{I_T} B), B \lhd_{I_T} (S \lhd_{I_T} C))$$

$$= T(\sup_{u \in U} T(A(u), \inf_{v \in V} I_T(R(u,v), B(v))),$$

$$\inf_{v \in V} I_T(B(v), \inf_{w \in W} I_T(S(v,w), C(w))))$$

$$= \sup_{u \in U} T(A(u), \inf_{v \in V} I_T(R(u,v), B(v))),$$

$$\inf_{v \in V} I_T(B(v), \inf_{w \in W} I_T(S(v,w), C(w))))$$

$$\leq \sup_{u \in U} T(A(u), \inf_{v \in V} T(\inf_{v'} I_T(R(u,v'), B(v')),$$

$$I_T(B(v), \inf_{w \in W} I_T(S(v,w), C(w)))))$$

$$\leq \sup_{u \in U} T(A(u), \inf_{v \in V} T(I_T(R(u,v), B(v)),$$

$$I_T(B(v), \inf_{w \in W} I_T(S(v,w), C(w)))))$$

$$\leq \sup_{u \in U} T(A(u), \inf_{v \in V} I_T(R(u,v), \inf_{w \in W} I_T(S(v,w), C(w))))$$

and using (2.20), (2.26) and (2.17)

$$= \sup_{u \in U} T(A(u), \inf_{v \in V} \inf_{w \in W} I_T(R(u,v), I_T(S(v,w), C(w))))$$

$$= \sup_{u \in U} T(A(u), \inf_{v \in V} \inf_{w \in W} I_T(T(R(u,v), S(v,w)), C(w)))$$

$$\leq \sup_{u \in U} T(A(u), \inf_{w \in W} I_T(\sup_{v \in V} T(R(u,v), S(v,w)), C(w)))$$

$$= A \circ_T ((R \circ_T S) \lhd_{I_T} C)$$

which proves (3.194). From (3.11) and (3.12) we also obtain (3.195). □

Proposition 3.24.

$$T(A \lhd_{I_T} (R \lhd_{I_T} B), B \lhd_{I_T} (S \lhd_{I_T} C)) \leq A \lhd_{I_T} ((R \circ_T S) \lhd_{I_T} C) \tag{3.196}$$

$$T((A \rhd_{I_T} R) \rhd_{I_T} B, (B \rhd_{I_T} S) \rhd_{I_T} C) \leq (A \rhd_{I_T} ((R \circ_T S)) \rhd_{I_T} C \tag{3.197}$$

Proof. Using (2.20), (2.26) and (2.6) we find

$$T(A \lhd_{I_T} (R \lhd_{I_T} B), B \lhd_{I_T} (S \lhd_{I_T} C))$$
$$= T(\inf_{u \in U} I_T(A(u), \inf_{v \in V} I_T(R(u,v), B(v))),$$
$$\inf_{v \in V} I_T(B(v), \inf_{w \in W} I_T(S(v,w), C(w))))$$
$$= T(\inf_{u \in U} \inf_{v \in V} I_T(A(u), I_T(R(u,v), B(v))),$$
$$\inf_{v \in V} I_T(B(v), \inf_{w \in W} I_T(S(v,w), C(w))))$$
$$= T(\inf_{u \in U} \inf_{v \in V} I_T(T(A(u), R(u,v)), B(v)),$$
$$\inf_{v \in V} I_T(B(v), \inf_{w \in W} I_T(S(v,w), C(w))))$$
$$\leq \inf_{u \in U} \inf_{v \in V} T(I_T(T(A(u), R(u,v)), B(v)),$$
$$\inf_{v'} I_T(B(v'), \inf_{w \in W} I_T(S(v',w), C(w))))$$
$$\leq \inf_{u \in U} \inf_{v \in V} T(I_T(T(A(u), R(u,v)), B(v)),$$
$$I_T(B(v), \inf_{w \in W} I_T(S(v,w), C(w))))$$

and using (2.28), (2.20), (2.26)

$$\leq \inf_{u \in U} \inf_{v \in V} I_T(T(A(u), R(u,v)), \inf_{w \in W} I_T(S(v,w), C(w)))$$
$$= \inf_{v \in V} \inf_{u \in U} \inf_{w \in W} I_T(T(A(u), R(u,v)), I_T(S(v,w), C(w)))$$
$$= \inf_{v \in V} \inf_{u \in U} \inf_{w \in W} I_T(T(S(v,w), A(u), R(u,v)), C(w))$$
$$= \inf_{v \in V} \inf_{u \in U} \inf_{w \in W} I_T(A(u), I_T(T(R(u,v), S(v,w)), C(w)))$$
$$= \inf_{u \in U} I_T(A(u), \inf_{v \in V} \inf_{w \in W} I_T(T(R(u,v), S(v,w)), C(w)))$$

and finally using (2.17)

$$\leq \inf_{u \in U} I_T(A(u), \inf_{w \in W} I_T(\sup_{v \in V} T(R(u,v), S(v,w)), C(w)))$$
$$= A \lhd_{I_T} ((R \circ_T S) \lhd_{I_T} C)$$

showing (3.196). By (3.12) we also obtain (3.197). $\qquad\square$

Chapter 4

Representing Fuzzy Temporal Information

4.1 Introduction

While it is customary to talk about events and time periods like World War II, the Great Depression or the Age of Enlightenment, identifying appropriate beginning and ending dates for them is difficult, if not impossible [Chan (1978); Freksa (1997); Nagypál and Motik (2003); Ohlbach (2004); Borghini and Varzi (2006)]. First, many events and time periods have an inherently gradual onset or ending, making it hard to pinpoint exact temporal boundaries. Examples include the Cold War, the Renaissance, Impressionism, the Dotcom Bubble, or the Great Depression. Other events are vague because they are an ill–defined aggregation of smaller–scale events. World War II, for instance, is a name which is used to refer to a number of battles, invasions, sieges, etc. around the early 1940s. Many of these small–scale military conflicts are clearly a part of World War II (e.g., the Battle of the Bulge in 1944), or clearly not a part of World War II (e.g., the First Battle of Ypres in 1914). About other conflicts, however, one can take different views: the Japanese invasion of China in 1937, the Soviet-Japanese Border War of 1939, the German annexation of Czechoslovakia in 1939. All these events are strongly related to World War II, but it is unclear whether we should consider them as belonging to or as preceding the war. Note that this vagueness of events and time periods is fundamentally different from the uncertainty that exists among historians about, for example, the time period during which the Mona Lisa was painted. Furthermore, it does not only pertain to large–scale events: when exactly does the event of sleeping begin, or falling down a flight of stairs? In fact, one can argue that at an appropriately fine–grained level of granularity, all events are characterized by a time span which is ill–defined (e.g. [Borghini and Varzi (2006); Russell

87

(1923)]). Finally, vague temporal markers are frequently found in natural language to convey underspecified temporal information: early summer, during his childhood, in the evening.

A formal definition of the notion of an event is difficult to provide. Clearly, an event is something that happens at a particular time and a particular place (e.g., World War II); it can have parts (e.g., the Battle of the Bulge), it can belong to a certain category (e.g., Military Conflict) and it can have consequences (e.g., the Cold War) [Zacks and Tversky (2001)]. We will, however, abstract away from any particular formalization of events, and focus on their temporal dimension only. As such, we will conceptually make no difference between time periods and events.

Vague time periods and time spans of vague events are naturally represented as fuzzy sets of real numbers, i.e., time instants. For a time instant t ($t \in \mathbb{R}$), $A(t)$ expresses to what extent t belongs to time span A. When A is a crisp time period, for all t in $\mathbb{R}$, $A(t)$ is either 0 (perfect non-membership) or 1 (perfect membership). When A is a vague time period, on the other hand, A will typically be gradually increasing over an interval $[t_1, t_2]$ and gradually decreasing over an interval $[t_3, t_4]$, where $A(t) = 1$ for t in $[t_2, t_3]$ and $A(t) = 0$ for $t < t_1$ and $t > t_4$. As an example, consider Picasso's Blue, Rose and Cubist period. Regarding the definition of the Rose period, for example, we find[1]

> So 1904 is a transitional year and belongs neither truly to the blue period,
> nor to the rose period.

Similarly, the ending of the Rose period, as well as the beginning and ending of the Cubist period are inherently gradual. Figure 4.1 depicts a possible definition of Picasso's Rose period, as well as the ending of his Blue period and the beginning of his Cubist period. These definitions reflect the gradual transition to the Rose period during 1904, as well as Picasso's experiments with new styles from 1906 and especially from 1907, eventually leading to his Cubist period.

Clearly, the definition of a fuzzy set representing a vague time period is to some extent subjective. In fact, there is no real reason why January 1, 1907 should belong to the Rose period to degree 0.8 and not to degree 0.75 or 0.85. What is most important is the qualitative ordering the membership degrees impose, e.g., June 1, 1907 is more compatible with the Rose period than the with Cubist period; March 15, 1904 is less compatible with the Rose period than June 1, 1907, etc. In some applications,

---

[1]http://pablo-picasso.paintings.name/rose-period/, accessed May 21, 2007

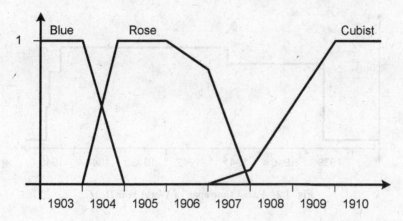

Fig. 4.1 Fuzzy sets defining the vague time span of Picasso's Blue, Rose, and Cubist period.

we may intuitively look at the actual values of the membership degree at a given instant t, as an estimation of the percentage of people who would consider t to be during the time span under consideration, while in other applications, membership degrees rather reflect the personal opinion of an individual expert. As another example, Figure 4.2 displays a possible definition of the time span of World War II. Increases and decreases in the membership function correspond to small–scale events such as the German invasion of Poland (September 1, 1939), the British and French declaration of war against Germany (September 3, 1939), the attack on Pearl Harbor (December 7, 1941), the unconditional surrender of Germany (May 7, 1945), and the unconditional surrender of Japan (August 15, 1945). The amount by which the membership function increases or decreases at a particular instant reflects the importance of the corresponding event. Intuitively, the more people regard the German invasion of Poland as the real beginning of World War II, the more the membership function will increase at September 1, 1939. Thus, fuzzy sets allow to model time spans of vague events much more naturally than crisp intervals, which are traditionally used to model time spans. In particular, the fuzzy set model explicitly acknowledges that there may be different views about the temporal boundaries of a vague event, some of which may be more important than others. However, it is important to keep in mind that the fuzzy set model is still an abstraction, necessarily failing to capture some subtleties about the temporal dimension of events. For example, for a vague event with two possible beginning dates, the fuzzy set model does not distinguish between the case where

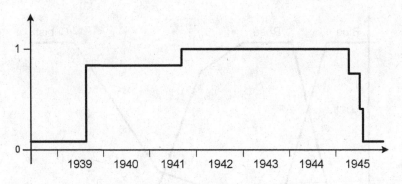

Fig. 4.2   Fuzzy time span of World War II.

(1) there are two groups of people (e.g., different parties in a war), each group having their own crisp interpretation about the beginning date.
(2) everybody agrees on the fact that both of the dates mark the beginning of the event to some extent.

Nonetheless, we are convinced that fuzzy sets provide a reasonable compromise between expressivity and computational feasibility. After all, in most application domains, distinguishing between the two cases above will not even be possible given the information available.

While (fuzzy) time spans provide explicit temporal knowledge about events, they may not always be available. This is particularly true for systems which rely on information extracted from natural language texts, which may lack any explicit time information about the events of interest, while, at the same time, face an abundance of implicit temporal information. It may be known that event A happened during B and after C, that A lasted for about three weeks and was shortly followed by an event D. One important question is what the semantics are of such temporal relations when the participating events are vague. Did the Cold War begin strictly before World War II, during World War II, strictly after World War II? The answer depends on our point of view of the Cold War and World War II. Historians sometimes think of 1917 — the end of the Russian revolution — as the real start of the Cold War, thereby implying that World War II happened during the Cold War. Most commonly, however, the end of the 1940s is considered as the beginning of the Cold War. Accordingly, World War II is generally considered to be before the Cold War, so temporal relations between vague events can be vague as well. While it seems evident to model vague temporal relations as fuzzy relations, in light of the fuzzy set model for time spans, it is not at all obvious how to define these fuzzy relations. As for fuzzy time spans, the membership degrees of the fuzzy relations should reflect a degree of compatibility, e.g., World War II should be before the Cold War to a higher degree than during the Cold War. Moreover, these degrees should only depend on the (fuzzy) time spans of the participating events. Finally, it is paramount that fuzzy temporal relations are defined such that they behave similar to their traditional, crisp counterparts. People talk about temporal relations between vague events as if they were well–defined, e.g., if someone expresses that A is before B and B is before C, one intuitively thinks of A as being before C. When A, B and C are vague events, however, the assertions that A is before B and B is before C may only be true to some degree, and, depending on how the fuzzy temporal relations are defined, it may or may not be possible to infer that A is before C to some particular degree. In our view, fuzzy temporal relations should allow for such inferences by satisfying generalized properties about transitivity, symmetry, reflexivity, etc.

In this chapter we define such fuzzy temporal relations using the relatedness measures from Chapter 3. We show that, unlike previous definitions, the resulting fuzzy relations satisfy many interesting properties. We furthermore argue that in this context, the Łukasiewicz connectives are the best choice for the fuzzy logic connectives in the definition of the relatedness measures. Finally, we investigate how the fuzzy temporal relations can be evaluated (efficiently) in practical applications, and how they can be characterized in a way that is convenient in theoretical contexts (e.g., in terms of α–level sets).

4.2 Temporal Relations

4.2.1 *Crisp Temporal Relations*

While humans essentially perceive temporal information quantitatively, the vast majority of this information is implicitly reduced to its relevant qualities [Freksa (1997)]. For example, when we learn that a movie lasts 150 minutes, we realize that its length is considerably longer than that of an average movie and act accordingly (e.g., postpone watching the movie until the weekend). As such, qualitative knowledge about time plays a much more fundamental role in cognitive processes than quantitative information. Hence, it should come as no surprise that qualitative information abounds

Table 4.1   Allen's thirteen temporal interval relations between intervals $A = [a^-, a^+]$ and $B = [b^-, b^+]$ (©2008 IEEE).

Name	Definition	
before	$b(A, B)$	$\equiv$ $a^+ < b^-$
overlaps	$o(A, B)$	$\equiv$ $a^- < b^-$ and $b^- < a^+$ and $a^+ < b^+$
during	$d(A, B)$	$\equiv$ $b^- < a^-$ and $a^+ < b^+$
meets	$m(A, B)$	$\equiv$ $a^+ = b^-$
starts	$s(A, B)$	$\equiv$ $a^- = b^-$ and $a^+ < b^+$
finishes	$f(A, B)$	$\equiv$ $a^+ = b^+$ and $b^- < a^-$
equals	$e(A, B)$	$\equiv$ $a^- = b^-$ and $a^+ = b^+$
after	$bi(A, B)$	$\equiv$ $b(B, A)$
overlapped-by	$oi(A, B)$	$\equiv$ $o(B, A)$
contains	$di(A, B)$	$\equiv$ $d(B, A)$
met–by	$mi(A, B)$	$\equiv$ $m(B, A)$
started–by	$si(A, B)$	$\equiv$ $s(B, A)$
finished–by	$fi(A, B)$	$\equiv$ $f(B, A)$

in natural language, either explicitly (e.g., After he came back from work, he immediately drank a glass of water.), by the careful use of different tenses (He drank a glass of water; it had been a warm day at work.), or implicitly through the ordering of sentences in a text.

This omnipresence of qualitative information is also reflected in the temporal representation and reasoning literature, initiated by Allen's seminal work on qualitative interval relations [Allen (1983)]. Allen defined a set of 13 qualitative relations that may hold between two compact intervals $A = [a^-, a^+]$ and $B = [b^-, b^+]$. The definitions of these temporal relations are presented in Table 4.1. Note that the 13 relations are jointly exhaustive and pairwise disjoint (JEPD): for any pair of intervals, exactly one of the relations is satisfied. These 13 relations are called the basic relations; other relations can be defined by considering unions of basic relations, resulting in a total number of $2^{13} = 8192$ possible temporal relations between two intervals. Unions of basic relations are used to represent incomplete information (e.g., either A is before B or B is before A). The resulting framework is called the Interval Algebra (IA).

Allen envisaged a scenario in which all available temporal information is given in the form of such temporal relations. We might know, for instance, that $b(x, y)$, $o(x, z)$ and $m(z, y)$ without having any information about the exact boundary points of the intervals x, y and z. Thus, x, y and z can be considered as variables whose possible values are intervals. To avoid confusion, we will use lower case letters to denote variables and upper case letters to denote specific intervals. Given a knowledge base like $\{b(x, y), m(x, z), o(w, y), (b \cup m \cup d \cup di)(w, z)\}$, we might be interested in checking its satisfiability (or consistency), i.e., do there actually exist intervals by which we can substitute the variables such that all temporal relations are satisfied? If the knowledge base is indeed satisfiable, is it possible to infer new information, e.g., does it follow that $b(x,w)$? To (partially) answer such questions, Allen devised an algorithm based on transitivity rules like

if $o(x,y)$ and $d(y,z)$ **then** $(o \cup d \cup s)(x,z)$

Table 4.2 displays these transitivity rules for all pairs of basic relations, except e (as transitivity rules involving e are obviously trivial). Note that sometimes transitivity rules are needed which contain non–basic temporal relations in the antecedent. For example, given $(o \cup mi)(x,y)$ and $d(y,z)$, what can we infer about the temporal relation between x and z? We know that either $o(x,y)$ and $d(y,z)$ or $mi(x,y)$ and $d(y,z)$. In the former case, it holds that $(o \cup d \cup s)(x,z)$ while in the latter case $(oi \cup d \cup f)(x,z)$. Hence, we always have that $(o \cup oi \cup d \cup s \cup f)(x,z)$. In this way, transitivity rules for non–basic temporal relations can easily be obtained from those for basic temporal relations. Allen's algorithm proceeds by applying transitivity rules until no new information is obtained anymore. It can be shown that this process takes $O(n^3)$ time, where n is the number of variables in the initial knowledge base [Vilain *et al.* (1989)].

Example 4.1. Assume that we initially know that $\{b(x,y), m(x,z),$ $o(w,y), (b \cup m \cup d \cup di)(w,z)\}$. Note that, due to the correspondence between b and bi, m and mi, o and oi, and d and di, this is equivalent to $\{bi(y,x), mi(z,x), oi(y,w), (bi \cup mi \cup di \cup d)(z,w)\}$. From $b(x,y)$ and $oi(y,w)$, we derive, using the transitivity table, that $(b \cup o \cup m \cup d \cup s)(x,w)$, or $(bi \cup oi \cup mi \cup di \cup si)(w,x)$. From $(bi \cup oi \cup mi \cup di \cup si)(w,x)$ and $m(x,z)$ we find $(bi \cup o \cup oi \cup mi \cup d \cup di \cup f \cup fi \cup s \cup si \cup e)(w,z)$. Since we already know that $(b \cup m \cup d \cup di)(w,z)$, this implies $(d \cup di)(w,z)$. In the same way, we find from $bi(y,x)$ and $m(x,z)$ that $(bi \cup oi \cup mi \cup d \cup f)(y,z)$. Finally, from $m(x,z)$ and $(d \cup di)(z,w)$ we find $(o \cup d \cup s \cup b)(x,w)$, which is stronger than our earlier conclusion that $(b \cup o \cup m \cup d \cup s)(x,w)$. No further information can be derived by the transitivity rules.

Note that Allen's algorithm is not complete; some conclusions cannot be revealed by only applying transitivity rules. An example of such a scenario can be found in [Allen (1983)]. Moreover, reasoning in the IA was shown to be NP–complete in general [Vilain *et al.* (1989)]. We will come back to this in Chapter 5.

Table 4.2 Transitivity table for basic Allen relations, where 1 stands for the union of all 13 basic relations (©2008 IEEE).

	b	bi	d	di	o	oi	m	mi	s	si	f	fi
b	b	1	b,o,m,d,s	b	b	b,o,m,d,s	b	b,o,m,d,s	b	b	b,o,m,d,s	b
bi	1	bi	bi,oi,mi,d,f	bi	bi,oi,mi,d,f	bi	bi,oi,mi,d,f	bi	bi,oi,mi,d,f	bi	bi	bi
d	b	bi	d	1	b,o,m,d,s	bi,oi,mi,d,f	b	bi	d	bi,oi,mi,d,f	d	b,o,m,d,s
di	b,o,m,di,fi	bi,oi,di,mi,si	o,oi,d,s,f,di,si,fi,e	di	b,o,m,di,fi	oi,di,si	o,di,fi	oi,di,si	di,fi,o	di	di,si,oi	di
o	b	bi,oi,di,mi,si	o,d,s	b,o,m,di,fi	b,o,m	o,oi,d,s,f,di,si,fi,e	b	oi,di,si	o	di,fi,o	d,s,o	b,o,m
oi	b,o,m,di,fi	bi	oi,d,f	bi,oi,mi,di,si	o,oi,d,s,f,di,si,fi,e	bi,oi,mi	o,di,fi	bi	oi,d,f	oi,bi,mi	oi	oi,di,si
m	b	bi,oi,mi,di,si	o,d,s	b	b	o,d,s	b	f,fi,e	m	m	d,s,o	b
mi	b,o,m,di,fi	bi	oi,d,f	bi	oi,d,f	bi	s,si,e	bi	d,f,oi	bi	mi	mi
s	b	bi	d	b,o,m,di,fi	b,o,m	oi,d,f	b	mi	s	s,si,e	d	b,m,o
si	b,o,m,di,fi	bi	oi,d,f	di	o,di,fi	oi	o,di,fi	mi	s,si,e	si	oi	di
f	b	bi,oi,mi,di,si	d	bi,oi,mi,di,si	o,d,s	bi,oi,mi	m	bi	d	bi,oi,mi	f	f,fi,e
fi	b	bi,oi,mi,di,si	o,d,s	di	o	oi,di,si	m	si,oi,di	o	di	f,fi,e	fi

Another line of research has focused on quantitative temporal reasoning, or temporal reasoning with metric constraints. In [Dechter *et al.* (1991)], Temporal Constraint Problems (TCPs) are introduced. In this framework, a temporal relation between two variables x and y takes the form of

$$(a_1 \leq y - x \leq b_1) \vee (a_2 \leq y - x \leq b_2) \vee \cdots \vee (a_k \leq y - x \leq b_k)$$

where the intervals of real numbers $[a_1, b_1], [a_2, b_2], \ldots [a_k, b_k]$ are assumed to be pairwise disjoint, and variables such as x and y correspond to real numbers (time instants). Temporal constraints in this case express information like "A happened either between 2 and 4 days after B, or between 10 and 12 days before B". When none of the temporal constraints contains disjunctions (i.e., $k = 1$), a TCP is called a Simple TCP (STCP). Also unary constraints can be encoded:

$$(a_1 \leq x \leq b_1) \vee (a_2 \leq x \leq b_2) \vee \cdots \vee (a_k \leq x \leq b_k)$$

expressing information like "A happened between July 12 and July 16, 1946". Combinations of Allen relations and metric constraints have also been considered, first in [Kautz and Ladkin (1991)] by iteratively solving the quantitative and qualitative subproblems independently of each other and appropriately propagating constraints between both subproblems, and later in [Meiri (1996)], using a more elegant and uniform representation.

Finally, in [Jonsson and Bäckström (1998)] and [Koubarakis (2001)], arbitrary disjunctions of linear inequalities, called linear constraints, are considered. Specifically, an atomic linear constraint over a set of variables X is an expression of the form $a_1 x_1 + a_2 x_2 + \cdots + a_n x_n \Delta b$ where $a_1, a_2, \ldots, a_n, b \in \mathbb{R}$, $x_1, x_2, \ldots, x_n \in X$, and Δ is $<, \leq, >, \geq, =$ or $\neq$. If $\phi_1, \phi_2, \ldots, \phi_m$ are atomic linear constraints over X, $\phi_1 \vee \phi_2 \vee \cdots \vee \phi_m$ is called a linear constraint over X. If $m > 1$, the linear constraint is called disjunctive. The framework of linear constraints subsumes most other frameworks for temporal reasoning, including all frameworks discussed so far. Moreover, many new kinds of constraints can be specified, e.g., interval $[a^-, a^+]$ is longer than interval $[b^-, b^+]$ can be specified as $a^+ - a^- > b^+ - b^-$. However, reasoning with arbitrary disjunctive linear constraints is NP–complete [Sontag (1985)]. Optimized reasoners are also much more difficult to implement, since they can take less advantage of prior knowledge about the temporal constraints being used (e.g. transitivity tables). Therefore, research generally continues to focus on more restricted formalisms in which more efficient reasoning can be performed. One example is [A.K. Pujari (1999)] in which temporal relations involving points, intervals and durations are investigated.

4.2.2   *Fuzzification of Temporal Relations*

Vagueness has many faces, requiring different techniques in different contexts. Most work on modelling vague temporal information deals with situations where events have precise boundaries, but where our knowledge about them is vague, e.g., "*A* started in the *early summer* of 2004", or "*A* happened *about* 3 hours after *B*". This kind of vagueness, which is purely epistemic, is usually modelled using possibility theory. For example, in [Dubois and Prade (1989)] possibility theory is employed to represent vague dates (e.g., early summer), and vague temporal constraints (e.g., *A* happened about 2 months before *B*). Based on this possibilistic approach, [Barro *et al.* (1994)] introduced fuzzy temporal constraint networks, a generalization of STCPs. Rather than restricting the possible values of $y - x$ for a pair of variables (x, y) by an interval, a (convex) fuzzy set in $\mathbb{R}$ is used to this end. Such fuzzy restrictions on the time difference between variables can be used to encode more flexible constraints. For example, while statements like "*y* occurs between two and four days after *x*" are naturally modelled in STCPs, statements like "*y* occurs a few days after *x*" are not. Sound and complete reasoning procedures were provided in [Marín *et al.* (1994)]. Disjunctions of such fuzzy temporal restrictions were considered in [Bosch *et al.* (2002)], thus obtaining a fuzzification of arbitrary TCPs. In [Dubois *et al.* (2003)], an extension of the IA is introduced to cope with statements like "*A* happened *long* before *B*", where again *A* and *B* are crisp intervals.

A different line of research has focused on fuzzy extensions of classical temporal reasoning calculi to encode preferences. For example, [Khatib *et al.* (2001)] discusses a generalization of TCPs in which a preference value is attached to each temporal constraint. When a given set of temporal constraints is inconsistent, the preference values are used to determine which constraints should be ignored. Similarly, [Badaloni and Giacomin (2006)] introduces the framework IA^{fuz} in which preference values are attached to basic Allen relations. A relation in IA^{fuz} can thus be regarded as a fuzzy set of basic Allen relations. Fuzzy sets of basic Allen relations have also been considered in [Guesgen *et al.* (1994)], where the adequate modelling of temporal expressions in natural language was the main motivation, rather than encoding preferences.

In the approaches mentioned above, events are still assumed to begin and end at well–defined instants of time. On the other hand, as we discussed in the introduction of this chapter, many real–world events and time periods are genuinely vague. The corresponding vague time spans can, in principle, be modelled in several ways. For example, [Pianesi and Varzi (1996)] proposes definitions of temporal relations which do not explicitly refer to time, somewhat similar in spirit to the well–known region connection calculus for spatial reasoning [Randell *et al.* (1992)]. In such an approach, however, temporal relations between vague events are crisp relations, which may be counterintuitive in many situations. In [Bittner (2002)], rough sets are used to represent time spans of events. Temporal relations are then defined by specifying an upper bound of relations that possibly hold between two events, and a lower bound of relations that are guaranteed to hold. Most commonly, however, fuzzy sets are used to represent the time span of vague events, and temporal relations are defined as fuzzy relations. The definitions of these fuzzy temporal relations are typically inspired by measures for comparing and ranking fuzzy numbers (e.g., [Bodenhofer (1999)] and [Dubois and Prade (1983)]).

A key problem in generalizing temporal relations to cope with fuzzy time spans is that traditionally, temporal relations have been defined as constraints on boundary points of intervals. Because such well–defined boundary points are absent in fuzzy time intervals, alternative ways of looking at temporal relations are required. Nagypál and Motik [Nagypál and Motik (2003)] start from the observation that several sets of time points can be associated with each interval $A = [a^-, a^+]$, viz. the semi–intervals $A^{<-} =]-\infty, a^-[$, $A^{\leq-} =]-\infty, a^-]$, $A^{<+} =]-\infty, a^+[$, $A^{\leq+} =]-\infty, a^+]$, $A^{>-} =]a^-, +\infty[$, $A^{\geq-} = [a^-, +\infty[$, $A^{>+} =]a^+, +\infty[$ and $A^{\geq+} = [a^+, +\infty[$. Qualitative constraints on the boundary points of two intervals $A = [a^-, a^+]$ and $B = [b^-, b^+]$ can be translated into set operations on the corresponding semi–intervals. For example, $m(A, B)$ holds iff $a^+ = b^-$, which can be expressed as $A^{>+} \cap B^{<-} = \emptyset \wedge A^{<+} \cap B^{>-} = \emptyset$. To define qualitative temporal relations between fuzzy time spans, Nagypál and Motik define $A^{<-}, A^{\leq-}, A^{<+}, A^{\leq+}, A^{>-}, A^{\geq-}, A^{>+}, A^{\geq+}$ for a fuzzy set A as:

$$A^{>-}(p) = \sup_{q<p} A(q) \qquad A^{\leq-}(p) = 1 - A^{>-}(p)$$

$$A^{\geq-}(p) = \sup_{q\leq p} A(q) \qquad A^{<-}(p) = 1 - A^{\geq-}(p)$$

$$A^{<+}(p) = \sup_{q>p} A(q) \qquad A^{\geq+}(p) = 1 - A^{<+}(p)$$

$$A^{\leq+}(p) = \sup_{q\geq p} A(q) \qquad A^{>+}(p) = 1 - A^{\leq+}(p)$$

The degree to which $m(A, B)$ is satisfied, for instance, is then defined as

$$m(A, B)$$

$$= \min(1 - \sup_{p \in \mathbb{R}} \min(A^{>+}(p), B^{<-}(p)), 1 - \sup_{p \in \mathbb{R}} \min(A^{<+}(p), B^{>-}(p)))$$

$$= \min(\inf_{p \in \mathbb{R}} \max(1 - A^{>+}(p), 1 - B^{<-}(p)),$$

$$\inf_{p \in \mathbb{R}} \max(1 - A^{<+}(p), 1 - B^{>-}(p)))$$

$$= \min(\inf_{p \in \mathbb{R}} \max(A^{\leq+}(p), B^{\geq-}(p)), \inf_{p \in \mathbb{R}} \max(A^{\geq+}(p), B^{\leq-}(p)))$$

Although this approach has a certain appeal — our own definitions will be based on a similar technique — the resulting fuzzy temporal relations do not always behave intuitively. For example, for crisp intervals the equals relation is reflexive, while starts, finishes and during are irreflexive. Taking into account this intended meaning, we would expect that for fuzzy time spans $e(A, A) = 1$ and $s(A, A) = f(A, A) = d(A, A) = 0$, or at least, that $e(A, A) > \max(s(A, A), f(A, A), d(A, A))$. However, using the definitions proposed by Nagypál and Motik, if A is a continuous fuzzy set in $\mathbb{R}$, it holds that $e(A, A) = s(A, A) = f(A, A) = d(A, A) = 0.5$. The reason for this anomaly lies in the definition of the fuzzy sets $A^{<-}, A^{\leq-}, \ldots, A^{\geq+}$. While these definitions do correspond to their intended meaning when A is a crisp interval, for a continuous fuzzy set A in $\mathbb{R}$, we have the undesirable property that $A^{>-} = A^{\geq-}$, $A^{<-} = A^{\leq-}$, $A^{>+} = A^{\geq+}$ and $A^{<+} = A^{\leq+}$.

In [Ohlbach (2004)], a fundamentally different approach to modelling temporal relations between fuzzy time spans is taken. The starting point is that even for crisp intervals A and B, relations like before can hold to some degree. For example, if $A = [0, 50]$ and $B = [45, 100]$, we may intuitively think of A as being before B, instead of overlapping with B, because most of A is before the beginning of B. In [Ohlbach (2004)], the degree to which $b(A, B)$ holds is therefore defined based on which fraction of A is before the beginning of B, where A and B may be crisp or fuzzy time spans. When temporal relations are defined in this way, we (deliberately) lose the original meaning of Allen's relations. Although such definitions may definitely be useful in many domains (e.g., querying temporal databases), they are not suitable as a basis for fuzzy temporal reasoning.

4.3 Definitions Based on Relatedness Measures

Our goal in defining fuzzy temporal relations is twofold. First, we want to define generalizations of Allen's relations which are similar in spirit to the definitions of Nagypál and Motik, but without the shortcomings discussed above. Second, we want to combine these qualitative fuzzy temporal relations with (vague) quantitative information like "the end of A is 4 minutes before the beginning of B", or "the end of A is *long* before the beginning of B". The definitions should behave intuitively, and be suitable as a basis for fuzzy temporal reasoning.

As motivated in the introduction, we will represent ill–defined time spans as fuzzy sets in $\mathbb{R}$. However, not all fuzzy sets in $\mathbb{R}$ are suitable for modelling time spans.

Definition 4.1 (Fuzzy time interval). *A fuzzy (time) interval is a normalised fuzzy set in $\mathbb{R}$ with bounded support, such that for every α in $]0, 1]$, A_α is a closed interval.*

The condition that fuzzy time intervals are normalised appears quite natural. Furthermore, we require that they have a bounded support to adequately generalize the notion of a bounded interval, and that all α–levels are closed to adequately generalize the notion of a closed interval. In some applications, we may, moreover, wish to exclude the case that A_α is a singleton.

Definition 4.2 (Nondegenerate fuzzy time interval). *A fuzzy (time) interval is called nondegenerate iff A_1 is a nondegenerate interval.*

Note that every fuzzy time interval is convex and upper semi–continuous, by Lemma 2.10 and Lemma 2.8.

4.3.1 *Generalizing Constraints between Boundary Points*

Like Nagypál and Motik we seek to transform constraints between boundary points of intervals into a form that does not explicitly refer to these boundary points. Rather than set–operations, however, we will use first–order expressions, corresponding to both quantitative and qualitative constraints. For example, for crisp intervals $A = [a^-, a^+]$ and $B = [b^-, b^+]$, it is easy to see that $(d \in \mathbb{R})$

$$a^- < b^- - d \Leftrightarrow (\exists p \in \mathbb{R})(p \in A \land (\forall q \in \mathbb{R})(q \in B \Rightarrow p < q - d)) \quad (4.1)$$

Generalizing the right–hand side in (4.1), we define the degree $bb_d^{\lessgtr}(A, B)$ to which the beginning of A is more than d time units before the beginning of B, A and B being fuzzy time intervals, as

$$bb_d^{\lll}(A, B) = \sup_{p \in \mathbb{R}} T(A(p), \inf_{q \in \mathbb{R}} I_T(B(q), L_d^{\lll}(p, q)))$$

$$= A \circ (L_d^{\lll} \rhd B)$$

where $L_d^{\lll}(p, q) = 1$ if $p < q - d$ and $L_d^{\lll}(p, q) = 0$ otherwise. Note how relatedness measures are used here to lift the relation $L_d^{\lll}$ between time points to a fuzzy relation between fuzzy sets. Taking this idea one step further, we define the fuzzy relation $L_{(\alpha,\beta)}^{\lll}$ between time points as follows ($\alpha \in \mathbb{R}$, $\beta \geq 0$):

$$L_{(\alpha,\beta)}^{\lll}(p, q) = \begin{cases} 1 & \text{if } q - p > \alpha + \beta \\ 0 & \text{if } q - p \leq \alpha \\ \frac{q-p-\alpha}{\beta} & \text{otherwise} \end{cases} \quad (4.2)$$

for each p and q in $\mathbb{R}$. $L_{(\alpha,\beta)}^{\lll}$ models a flexible metric constraint between time points. Intuitively, $L_{(\alpha,\beta)}^{\lll}(p, q)$ could be seen as the degree to which p is about α time units before q, where β reflects the degree of tolerance. The higher the value of β, the more flexible the constraint becomes; for $\beta = 0$, $L_{(\alpha,\beta)}^{\lll} = L_\alpha^{\lll}$. For appropriate values of α and β, within a given context, $L_{(\alpha,\beta)}^{\lll}(p, q)$ can also be seen as the degree to which p is long before q. The fuzzy relation $L_{(\alpha,\beta)}^{\lll}$ is depicted in Figure 4.3. For reasons which will become clear below, we will use the Łukasiewicz t–norm T_W to define fuzzy temporal relations. The degree $bb_{(\alpha,\beta)}^{\lll}(A, B)$ to which the beginning of A is long (or, approximately α time units) before the beginning of B is then defined as

$$bb_{(\alpha,\beta)}^{\lll}(A, B) = A \circ_{T_W} (L_{(\alpha,\beta)}^{\lll} \rhd_{I_W} B)$$

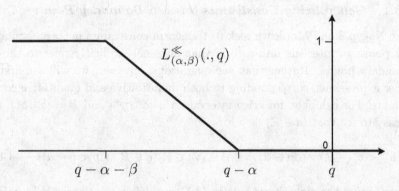

Fig. 4.3 $L_{(\alpha,\beta)}^{\lll}(.,q)$: fuzzy set of time points long before q (©2008 IEEE).

Using other relatedness measures, we obtain other kinds of fuzzy temporal relations, in particular the degree $ee^{\ll}_{(\alpha,\beta)}(A,B)$ to which the end of A is (long) before the end of B, the degree $be^{\ll}_{(\alpha,\beta)}(A,B)$ to which the beginning of A is (long) before the end of B and the degree $eb^{\ll}_{(\alpha,\beta)}(A,B)$ to which the end of A is (long) before the beginning of B:

$$ee^{\ll}_{(\alpha,\beta)}(A,B) = (A \lhd_{I_W} L^{\ll}_{(\alpha,\beta)}) \circ_{T_W} B$$

$$be^{\ll}_{(\alpha,\beta)}(A,B) = A \circ_{T_W} L^{\ll}_{(\alpha,\beta)} \circ_{T_W} B$$

$$eb^{\ll}_{(\alpha,\beta)}(A,B) = A \lhd_{I_W} L^{\ll}_{(\alpha,\beta)} \rhd_{I_W} B$$

Finally, in addition to generalizing strict inequalities like $a^- < b^-$, we also want to generalize constraints such as $a^- \leq b^-$. We define the degree $bb^{\preccurlyeq}_{(\alpha,\beta)}(A,B)$ to which the beginning of A is before or at approximately the same time as the beginning of B as

$$bb^{\preccurlyeq}_{(\alpha,\beta)}(A,B) = 1 - bb^{\ll}_{(\alpha,\beta)}(B,A) \tag{4.3}$$

generalizing the fact that $p \leq q \Leftrightarrow \neg(q < p)$ for p and q in $\mathbb{R}$. Similarly we define $ee^{\preccurlyeq}_{(\alpha,\beta)}$, $be^{\preccurlyeq}_{(\alpha,\beta)}$ and $eb^{\preccurlyeq}_{(\alpha,\beta)}$:

$$ee^{\preccurlyeq}_{(\alpha,\beta)}(A,B) = 1 - ee^{\ll}_{(\alpha,\beta)}(B,A) \tag{4.4}$$

$$be^{\preccurlyeq}_{(\alpha,\beta)}(A,B) = 1 - eb^{\ll}_{(\alpha,\beta)}(B,A) \tag{4.5}$$

$$eb^{\preccurlyeq}_{(\alpha,\beta)}(A,B) = 1 - be^{\ll}_{(\alpha,\beta)}(B,A) \tag{4.6}$$

Similar as for $bb^{\ll}_{(\alpha,0)}$, we will sometimes write $ee^{\ll}_{(\alpha,0)}$, $be^{\ll}_{(\alpha,0)}$, $\ldots,eb^{\preccurlyeq}_{(\alpha,0)}$ as $ee^{\ll}_\alpha$, $be^{\ll}_\alpha$, $\ldots,eb^{\preccurlyeq}_\alpha$. Furthermore, we will sometimes write $bb^{\ll}_0$, $ee^{\ll}_0$, $\ldots,eb^{\preccurlyeq}_0$ as $bb^{\ll}$, $ee^{\ll}$, $\ldots,eb^{\preccurlyeq}$. In the same fashion, we sometimes write $L^{\ll}$ and $L^{\preccurlyeq}$ instead of $L^{\ll}_0$ and $L^{\preccurlyeq}_0$.

4.3.2 *The Case for the Łukasiewicz Connectives*

One obvious reason for committing ourselves to the Łukasiewicz connectives is given by Proposition 3.9, which allows us to directly express the fuzzy temporal relations $bb^{\preccurlyeq}_{(\alpha,\beta)}$, $ee^{\preccurlyeq}_{(\alpha,\beta)}$, $be^{\preccurlyeq}_{(\alpha,\beta)}$ and $eb^{\preccurlyeq}_{(\alpha,\beta)}$ by relatedness measures. Specifically, let the fuzzy relation $L^{\preccurlyeq}_{(\alpha,\beta)}$ be defined as

$$L^{\preccurlyeq}_{(\alpha,\beta)} = (coL^{\ll}_{(\alpha,\beta)})^{-1} \tag{4.7}$$

For p and q in $\mathbb{R}$, $L^{\preccurlyeq}_{(\alpha,\beta)}(p,q)$ expresses the degree to which p is not more than approximately α time units after q. For appropriate α and β, within a given context, $L^{\preccurlyeq}_{(\alpha,\beta)}(p,q)$ can be interpreted as the degree to which p is more or less before q, or, the degree to which p is before or at approximately the same time as q. The fuzzy relation $L^{\preccurlyeq}_{(\alpha,\beta)}$ is depicted in Figure 4.4. It is easy to see that

$$L^{\preccurlyeq}_{(\alpha,\beta)}(p,q) = \begin{cases} 1 & \text{if } q - p \geq -\alpha \\ 0 & \text{if } q - p < -\alpha - \beta \\ \frac{q-p+\alpha+\beta}{\beta} & \text{otherwise} \end{cases} \tag{4.8}$$

Moreover, if $\beta > 0$, it holds that

$$L^{\lll}_{(\alpha,\beta)} = L^{\preccurlyeq}_{(-\alpha-\beta,\beta)} \tag{4.9}$$

From Proposition 3.9, Lemma 3.1 and (3.9)–(3.10), we find that

$$bb^{\preccurlyeq}_{(\alpha,\beta)}(A,B) = (A \circ_{Tw} L^{\preccurlyeq}_{(\alpha,\beta)}) \rhd_{Iw} B$$

$$ee^{\preccurlyeq}_{(\alpha,\beta)}(A,B) = A \lhd_{Iw} (L^{\preccurlyeq}_{(\alpha,\beta)} \circ_{Tw} B)$$

$$be^{\preccurlyeq}_{(\alpha,\beta)}(A,B) = A \circ_{Tw} L^{\preccurlyeq}_{(\alpha,\beta)} \circ_{Tw} B$$

$$eb^{\preccurlyeq}_{(\alpha,\beta)}(A,B) = A \lhd_{Iw} L^{\preccurlyeq}_{(\alpha,\beta)} \rhd_{Iw} B$$

The definitions of the fuzzy temporal relations, in terms of relatedness measures, as well as their correspondence with crisp constraints are presented in Table 4.3. As a consequence of this characterization of $bb^{\preccurlyeq}_{(\alpha,\beta)}$, $ee^{\preccurlyeq}_{(\alpha,\beta)}$, $be^{\preccurlyeq}_{(\alpha,\beta)}$ and $eb^{\preccurlyeq}_{(\alpha,\beta)}$ in terms or relatedness measures, we know that the fuzzy temporal relations satisfy a number of desirable transitivity properties, such as:

$$T_W(bb^{\preccurlyeq}(A,B), bb^{\preccurlyeq}(B,C)) \leq bb^{\preccurlyeq}(A,C) \tag{4.10}$$

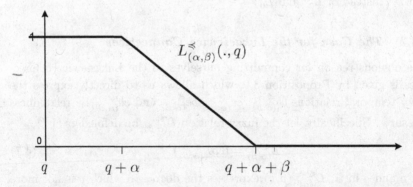

Fig. 4.4 $L^{\preccurlyeq}_{(\alpha,\beta)}(.,q)$: fuzzy set of time points before or at approximately the same time as q (©2008 IEEE).

Table 4.3 Definition of the fuzzy temporal relations between fuzzy time intervals A and B, and their correspondence with the classical definitions when $A = [a^-, a^+]$ and $B = [b^-, b^+]$ are crisp intervals (©2008 IEEE).

Crisp intervals	Fuzzy time intervals
$a^- < b^- \Leftrightarrow (\exists p)(p \in A \wedge (\forall q)(q \in B \Rightarrow p < q))$	$bb_{(\alpha,\beta)}^{\ll}(A, B) = A \circ (L_{(\alpha,\beta)}^{\ll} \triangleright B)$
$a^- \leq b^- \Leftrightarrow (\forall q)(q \in B \Rightarrow (\exists x)(p \in A \wedge p \leq q))$	$bb_{(\alpha,\beta)}^{\lessdot}(A, B) = (A \circ L_{(\alpha,\beta)}^{\lessdot}) \triangleright B$
$a^+ < b^+ \Leftrightarrow (\exists q)(q \in B \wedge (\forall p)(p \in A \Rightarrow p < q))$	$ee_{(\alpha,\beta)}^{\ll}(A, B) = (A \triangleleft L_{(\alpha,\beta)}^{\ll}) \circ B$
$a^+ \leq b^+ \Leftrightarrow (\forall p)(p \in A \Rightarrow (\exists q)(q \in B \wedge p \leq q))$	$ee_{(\alpha,\beta)}^{\lessdot}(A, B) = A \triangleleft (L_{(\alpha,\beta)}^{\lessdot} \circ B)$
$a^- < b^+ \Leftrightarrow (\exists p)(\exists q)(p \in A \wedge q \in B \wedge p < q)$	$be_{(\alpha,\beta)}^{\ll}(A, B) = A \circ L_{(\alpha,\beta)}^{\ll} \circ B$
$a^- \leq b^+ \Leftrightarrow (\exists p)(\exists q)(p \in A \wedge q \in B \wedge p \leq q)$	$be_{(\alpha,\beta)}^{\lessdot}(A, B) = A \circ L_{(\alpha,\beta)}^{\lessdot} \circ B$
$a^+ < b^- \Leftrightarrow (\forall p)(\forall q)(p \in A \wedge q \in B \Rightarrow p < q)$	$eb_{(\alpha,\beta)}^{\ll}(A, B) = A \triangleleft L_{(\alpha,\beta)}^{\ll} \triangleright B$
$a^+ \leq b^- \Leftrightarrow (\forall p)(\forall q)(p \in A \wedge q \in B \Rightarrow p \leq q)$	$eb_{(\alpha,\beta)}^{\lessdot}(A, B) = A \triangleleft L_{(\alpha,\beta)}^{\lessdot} \triangleright B$

generalizing the fact that if the beginning of a crisp interval A is before the beginning of a crisp interval B, and the beginning of B is before the beginning of a crisp interval C, then also the beginning of A is before the beginning of C. Note that (4.10) can be verified by the transitivity rules for relatedness measures (Table 3.1), and the fact that $L^{\lessdot} \circ L^{\lessdot} = L^{\lessdot}$ (see Proposition 4.1 below). On the other hand, such transitivity properties are not shared by definitions using other popular choices of t–norms such as T_M or T_P. For example, let A, B and C be defined as in Figure 4.5. Regardless of whether T is T_M, T_P or T_W, it holds that

$$A \circ_T (L^{\ll} \triangleright_{I_T} B) = B \circ_T (L^{\ll} \triangleright_{I_T} C) = 0.5$$
$$A \circ_T (L^{\ll} \triangleright_{I_T} C) = 1$$

In other words, the beginning of A (resp. B) is before the beginning of B (resp. C) to degree 0.5, whereas the beginning of A is before the beginning of C to degree 1. This implies that if we had used T_M in the definitions of

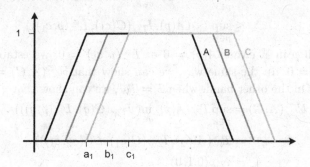

Fig. 4.5 The transitivity property (4.10) may be violated when T_M or T_P is used.

the fuzzy temporal relations, it would hold that

$$T_M(bb^{\preceq}(C,B), bb^{\preceq}(B,A)) = \min(1 - bb^{\ll}(B,C), 1 - bb^{\ll}(A,B))$$
$$= 0.5$$

while $bb^{\preceq}(C,A) = 1 - bb^{\ll}(A,C) = 0$, violating (4.10). In the same way, we would find

$$T_P(bb^{\preceq}(C,B), bb^{\preceq}(B,A)) = 0.25 > 0 = bb^{\preceq}(C,A)$$

when T_P had been used in the definitions of the fuzzy temporal relations. Although we could, in principle, define $bb^{\preceq}_{(\alpha,\beta)}$, $ee^{\preceq}_{(\alpha,\beta)}$, $be^{\preceq}_{(\alpha,\beta)}$ and $eb^{\preceq}_{(\alpha,\beta)}$ directly in terms of relatedness measures, we would then lose the important property that $bb^{\ll}_{(\alpha,\beta)}(A,B) = 1 - bb^{\preceq}_{(\alpha,\beta)}(B,A)$, $ee^{\ll}_{(\alpha,\beta)}(A,B) = 1 - ee^{\preceq}_{(\alpha,\beta)}(B,A)$, etc.

Another advantage of the Łukasiewicz connectives is that I_W is continuous whereas I_M and I_P are not. Clearly, it is desirable that small changes in the definitions of the fuzzy time intervals A and B result in small changes of the values of $bb^{\ll}_{(\alpha,\beta)}(A,B)$, $ee^{\ll}_{(\alpha,\beta)}(A,B)$, $be^{\ll}_{(\alpha,\beta)}(A,B)$ and $eb^{\ll}_{(\alpha,\beta)}(A,B)$. This is particularly true in applications where fuzzy time intervals are constructed automatically from, for example, web documents, as in such applications, small variations in membership degrees may be due to noise (e.g., incorrect information on web pages, errors introduced by the information extraction technique that is used, etc.). Consider the fuzzy time intervals A, B and C depicted in Figure 4.6. Because B and C are very similar, we would like to have that the value of $bb^{\ll}(A,B)$ is close to the value of $bb^{\ll}(A,C)$. Irrespective of the t–norm T being used, it holds that $bb^{\ll}(A,B) = 1$, i.e., the beginning of A is strictly before the beginning of B to degree 1. When using T_M, however, we would have that

$$bb^{\ll}(A,C) = \sup_{p \in \mathbb{R}} T_M(A(p), \inf_{q \in \mathbb{R}} I_{T_M}(C(q), L^{\ll}(p,q)))$$

$$\leq \sup_{p \in \mathbb{R}} T_M(A(p), I_{T_M}(C(c_1), L^{\ll}(p,c_1)))$$

As for each p in $\mathbb{R}$ either $A(p) = 0$ or $L^{\ll}(p,c_1) = 0$, we establish that $bb^{\ll}(A,C) = 0$. In the same way, we can show that $bb^{\ll}(A,C) = 0$ when using T_P. On the other hand, when $T = T_W$, we can show that

$$bb^{\ll}(A,C) = \sup_{p \in \mathbb{R}} T_W(A(p), \inf_{q \in \mathbb{R}} I_{T_W}(C(q), L^{\ll}(p,q)))$$

$$= T_W(A(a_2), I_{T_W}(C(c_1), L^{\ll}(a_2,c_1)))$$

$$= I_{T_W}(0.1, 0)$$

$$= 0.9$$

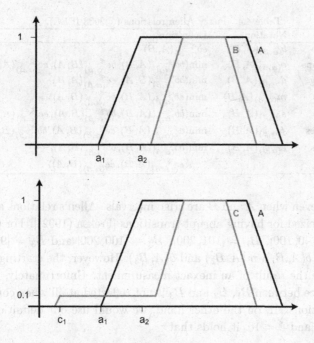

Fig. 4.6 Since the definition of the fuzzy time intervals B and C are similar, it is desirable that $|bb^{\ll}(A, B) - bb^{\ll}(A, C)|$ is small.

4.3.3 *Fuzzy Allen Relations*

Once we know how to generalize constraints between boundary points of fuzzy time intervals, it is relatively straightforward to generalize Allen's interval relations. We use the minimum to combine different constraints, thus obtaining the generalized definitions in Table 4.4. Due to its idempotency, using the minimum to combine different generalized boundary constraints feels much more natural than, for example, using the Łukasiewicz t–norm. Moreover, it turns out that this choice of the minimum is a prerequisite for some interesting properties which will be introduced below. Note that the definitions in Table 4.4 coincide with Allen's original definitions if each α_i and β_i equals 0, and A and B are crisp sets. We will sometimes write b_α instead of $b_{(\alpha,0)}$ and b instead of $b_{(0,0)}$, and similar for the other fuzzy Allen relations.

In dealing with fuzzy Allen relations, we are mainly interested in modelling qualitative information, hence, in principle, it may be sufficient to consider the case where $\alpha = \beta = 0$ only. Nonetheless, values of α and β different from 0 may be useful to introduce a notion of tolerance in Allen's

Table 4.4   Fuzzy Allen relations (©2008 IEEE).

Name	Notation	Definition
before	$b_{(\alpha,\beta)}(A,B)$	$eb^{\ll}_{(\alpha,\beta)}(A,B)$
overlaps	$o_{(\alpha,\beta)}(A,B)$	$\min(bb^{\ll}_{(\alpha,\beta)}(A,B), be^{\ll}_{(\alpha,\beta)}(B,A), ee^{\ll}_{(\alpha,\beta)}(A,B))$
during	$d_{(\alpha,\beta)}(A,B)$	$\min(bb^{\ll}_{(\alpha,\beta)}(B,A), ee^{\ll}_{(\alpha,\beta)}(A,B))$
meets	$m_{(\alpha,\beta)}(A,B)$	$\min(eb^{\lessgtr}_{(\alpha,\beta)}(A,B), be^{\lessgtr}_{(\alpha,\beta)}(B,A))$
starts	$s_{(\alpha,\beta)}(A,B)$	$\min(bb^{\lessgtr}_{(\alpha,\beta)}(A,B), bb^{\lessgtr}_{(\alpha,\beta)}(B,A), ee^{\ll}_{(\alpha,\beta)}(A,B))$
finishes	$f_{(\alpha,\beta)}(A,B)$	$\min(ee^{\lessgtr}_{(\alpha,\beta)}(A,B), ee^{\lessgtr}_{(\alpha,\beta)}(B,A), bb^{\ll}_{(\alpha,\beta)}(B,A))$
equals	$e_{(\alpha,\beta)}(A,B)$	$\min(bb^{\lessgtr}_{(\alpha,\beta)}(A,B), bb^{\lessgtr}_{(\alpha,\beta)}(B,A),$
		$ee^{\lessgtr}_{(\alpha,\beta)}(A,B), ee^{\lessgtr}_{(\alpha,\beta)}(B,A))$

relations, even when A and B are crisp intervals. Allen's relations are sometimes criticized for having abrupt transitions [Freksa (1992)]. For example, when $A = [0, 100]$, $B_1 = [101, 200]$, $B_2 = [100, 200]$ and $B_3 = [99, 200]$ it holds that $b(A, B_1)$, $m(A, B_2)$ and $o(A, B_3)$. However, the starting point of B_i may be the result of an inexact measurement. Unfortunately, the close resemblance between B_1, B_2 and B_3 is not reflected at all when considering Allen relations. If, on the other hand, we would use our definitions with, say, $\alpha = 0$ and $\beta = 10$, it holds that

$$bb^{\ll}_{(0,10)}(A, B_1) = 1 \qquad bb^{\ll}_{(0,10)}(A, B_2) = 1 \qquad bb^{\ll}_{(0,10)}(A, B_3) = 1$$
$$ee^{\ll}_{(0,10)}(A, B_1) = 1 \qquad ee^{\ll}_{(0,10)}(A, B_2) = 1 \qquad ee^{\ll}_{(0,10)}(A, B_3) = 1$$
$$eb^{\ll}_{(0,10)}(A, B_1) = 0.1 \qquad eb^{\ll}_{(0,10)}(A, B_2) = 0 \qquad eb^{\ll}_{(0,10)}(A, B_3) = 0$$
$$be^{\ll}_{(0,10)}(B_1, A) = 0 \qquad be^{\ll}_{(0,10)}(B_2, A) = 0 \qquad be^{\ll}_{(0,10)}(B_3, A) = 0.1$$
$$eb^{\lessgtr}_{(0,10)}(A, B_1) = 1 \qquad eb^{\lessgtr}_{(0,10)}(A, B_2) = 1 \qquad eb^{\lessgtr}_{(0,10)}(A, B_3) = 0.9$$
$$be^{\lessgtr}_{(0,10)}(B_1, A) = 0.9 \qquad be^{\lessgtr}_{(0,10)}(B_2, A) = 1 \qquad be^{\lessgtr}_{(0,10)}(B_3, A) = 1$$

which leads to

$$b_{(0,10)}(A, B_1) = 0.1 \qquad b_{(0,10)}(A, B_2) = 0 \qquad b_{(0,10)}(A, B_3) = 0$$
$$m_{(0,10)}(A, B_1) = 0.9 \qquad m_{(0,10)}(A, B_2) = 1 \qquad m_{(0,10)}(A, B_3) = 0.9$$
$$o_{(0,10)}(A, B_1) = 0 \qquad o_{(0,10)}(A, B_2) = 0 \qquad o_{(0,10)}(A, B_3) = 0.1$$

Note how A is considered to meet with B_1, B_2 and B_3 to a high degree because the end of A is located close to the end of B. For $b_{(0,10)}(A, B_1)$ to hold to a higher degree, the beginning of B_1 would have to be longer after the end of A. Also note how $b_{(0,10)}(A, B_i) + m_{(0,10)}(A, B_i) + o_{(0,10)}(A, B_i) = 1$; as we will see below, this is not a coincidence. In [Dubois *et al.* (2003)], fuzzy relations between crisp intervals are introduced for a similar purpose.

Table 4.5   Freksa's conceptual neighbourhoods [Freksa (1992)] (©2008 IEEE).

Name	Definition
precedes	$pr(A, B) \equiv a^+ \leq b^-$
succeeds	$sd(A, B) \equiv b^+ \leq a^-$
older	$ol(A, B) \equiv a^- < b^-$
head to head with	$hh(A, B) \equiv a^- = b^-$
younger	$yo(A, B) \equiv b^- < a^-$
survived by	$sb(A, B) \equiv a^+ < b^+$
tail to tail with	$tt(A, B) \equiv a^+ = b^+$
survives	$sv(A, B) \equiv b^+ < a^+$
born before death of	$bd(A, B) \equiv a^- < b^+$
contemporary of	$ct(A, B) \equiv a^- < b^+$ and $b^- < a^+$
died after birth of	$db(A, B) \equiv b^- < a^+$
older & survived by	$ob(A, B) \equiv a^- < b^-$ and $a^+ < b^+$
older contemporary of	$oc(A, B) \equiv a^- < b^-$ and $b^- < a^+$
surviving contemporary of	$sc(A, B) \equiv a^- < b^+$ and $b^+ < a^+$
survived by contemporary of	$bc(A, B) \equiv b^- < a^+$ and $a^+ < b^+$
younger contemporary of	$yc(A, B) \equiv b^- < a^-$ and $a^- < b^+$
younger & survives	$ys(A, B) \equiv b^- < a^-$ and $b^+ < a^+$

On the other hand, [Freksa (1992)] proposes to solve this problem by using coarser temporal relations (e.g., the union of o, m and b). A similar technique, based on fuzzy sets of basic Allen relations is suggested in [Guesgen *et al.* (1994)]. Our definitions, on the other hand, have the clear advantage that they are also suitable for fuzzy time intervals.

Many entries in Table 4.2 contain unions of Allen relations. Moreover, most of these unions appear more than once. Freksa [Freksa (1992)] observed that such unions of Allen relations correspond to coarser temporal relations, called conceptual neighbourhoods. The definitions of the relevant conceptual neighbourhoods are shown in Table 4.5. Generalizing these definitions to cope with fuzzy time intervals and imprecise temporal relations is straightforward, again using relatedness measures. For example the degree to which $ct_{(\alpha,\beta)}(A, B)$ holds for fuzzy time intervals A and B, $\alpha \in \mathbb{R}$ and $\beta \geq 0$, is defined as

$$ct_{(\alpha,\beta)}(A, B) = \min(be^{\ll}_{(\alpha,\beta)}(A, B), be^{\ll}_{(\alpha,\beta)}(B, A))$$

For crisp intervals A and B, it holds that

$$ct = o \cup oi \cup d \cup s \cup f \cup di \cup si \cup fi \cup e$$

On the other hand, when A and B are fuzzy time intervals, this equality does not necessarily hold anymore. We will come back to this when discussing generalized transitivity rules.

4.4   Properties

In this section, we will demonstrate that our fuzzy temporal relations based on relatedness measures are a sound generalization of Allen's relations, unaffected by anomalies of the kind discussed in Section 4.2.2. To arrive at this conclusion, we will show that our definitions satisfy important generalizations of properties such as transitivity, (ir)reflexivity and (a)symmetry.

4.4.1   *Properties of the Generalized Boundary Constraints*

For the generalized constraints between boundary points $bb^{\lll}_{(\alpha,\beta)}$, $ee^{\lll}_{(\alpha,\beta)}$, $\ldots$, $eb^{\preccurlyeq}_{(\alpha,\beta)}$, relevant properties follow straightforwardly from those of the relatedness measures, as discussed in Chapter 3, and some properties of the fuzzy relations $L^{\lll}_{(\alpha,\beta)}$ and $L^{\preccurlyeq}_{(\alpha,\beta)}$. For example, when $\alpha \geq 0$ it is easy to see that $L^{\lll}_{(\alpha,\beta)}$ is irreflexive and $L^{\preccurlyeq}_{(\alpha,\beta)}$ is reflexive. As an immediate consequence, we find using Proposition 3.3 that $bb^{\lll}_{(\alpha,\beta)}$, $ee^{\lll}_{(\alpha,\beta)}$ and $eb^{\lll}_{(\alpha,\beta)}$ are irreflexive, and using Proposition 3.2 that $bb^{\preccurlyeq}_{(\alpha,\beta)}$, $ee^{\preccurlyeq}_{(\alpha,\beta)}$ and $be^{\preccurlyeq}_{(\alpha,\beta)}$ are reflexive. Next, to formulate transitivity rules for these generalized boundary constraints, we present a characterization of the sup–T compositions between $L^{\lll}_{(\alpha,\beta)}$ and $L^{\preccurlyeq}_{(\alpha,\beta)}$. First, we need to show the following three lemmas.

Lemma 4.1. *Let $\alpha_1, \alpha_2 \in \mathbb{R}$ and $\beta \geq 0$; it holds that*

$$L^{\lll}_{(\alpha_1+\alpha_2,\beta)}(p,q) = L^{\lll}_{(\alpha_1,\beta)}(p+\alpha_2,q) \tag{4.11}$$

$$L^{\lll}_{(\alpha_1+\alpha_2,\beta)}(p,q) = L^{\lll}_{(\alpha_1,\beta)}(p,q-\alpha_2) \tag{4.12}$$

$$L^{\preccurlyeq}_{(\alpha_1+\alpha_2,\beta)}(p,q) = L^{\preccurlyeq}_{(\alpha_1,\beta)}(p-\alpha_2,q) \tag{4.13}$$

$$L^{\preccurlyeq}_{(\alpha_1+\alpha_2,\beta)}(p,q) = L^{\preccurlyeq}_{(\alpha_1,\beta)}(p,q+\alpha_2) \tag{4.14}$$

for all p and q in $\mathbb{R}$.

Proof.   trivial   □

Lemma 4.2. *Let $\alpha \in \mathbb{R}$ and $\beta_1, \beta_2 \geq 0$; it holds that*

$$L^{\lll}_{(\alpha+\beta_2,\beta_1)}(p,q) \leq L^{\lll}_{(\alpha+\min(\beta_1,\beta_2),\max(\beta_1,\beta_2))}(p,q) \tag{4.15}$$

for all p and q in $\mathbb{R}$.

Proof.   If $\beta_1 \geq \beta_2$, the proof is trivial; therefore assume that $\beta_1 < \beta_2$. For $q - p \leq \alpha + \beta_2$ and for $q - p > \alpha + \beta_1 + \beta_2$ (4.15) trivially holds, since

in the former case the left–hand side of (4.15) equals 0, while in the latter
case the right–hand side equals 1. Hence, we only need to consider the case
where $\beta_1 > 0$ and $\alpha + \beta_2 < q - p \leq \alpha + \beta_1 + \beta_2$; it holds that

$$\frac{q - p - \alpha - \beta_2}{\beta_1} \leq \frac{q - p - \alpha - \beta_1}{\beta_2}$$
$$\Leftrightarrow (q - p - \alpha)\beta_2 - \beta_2^2 \leq (q - p - \alpha)\beta_1 - \beta_1^2$$
$$\Leftrightarrow (q - p - \alpha)(\beta_2 - \beta_1) \leq \beta_2^2 - \beta_1^2$$

Since $\beta_2 - \beta_1 > 0$ we obtain

$$\Leftrightarrow q - p \leq \alpha + \beta_1 + \beta_2$$

which completes the proof. $\square$

Lemma 4.3. *Let* $\alpha_1, \alpha_2 \in \mathbb{R}$ *and* $\beta_1, \beta_2 \geq 0$; *it holds that*

$$T_W(L^{\lll}_{(\alpha_1,\beta_1)}(p,q), L^{\lll}_{(\alpha_2,\beta_2)}(q,r)) \leq L^{\lll}_{(\alpha_1+\alpha_2+\min(\beta_1,\beta_2),\max(\beta_1,\beta_2))}(p,r) \tag{4.16}$$

$$T_W(L^{\prec}_{(\alpha_1,\beta_1)}(p,q), L^{\prec}_{(\alpha_2,\beta_2)}(q,r)) \leq L^{\prec}_{(\alpha_1+\alpha_2,\max(\beta_1,\beta_2))}(p,r) \tag{4.17}$$

$$T_W(L^{\prec}_{(\alpha_1,\beta_1)}(p,q), L^{\lll}_{(\alpha_2,\beta_2)}(q,r)) \leq L^{\lll}_{(\alpha_2-\alpha_1+\min(\beta_1,\beta_2)-\beta_1,\max(\beta_1,\beta_2))}(p,r) \tag{4.18}$$

$$T_W(L^{\lll}_{(\alpha_1,\beta_1)}(p,q), L^{\prec}_{(\alpha_2,\beta_2)}(q,r)) \leq L^{\lll}_{(\alpha_1-\alpha_2+\min(\beta_1,\beta_2)-\beta_2,\max(\beta_1,\beta_2))}(p,r) \tag{4.19}$$

for all p, q *and* r *in* $\mathbb{R}$.

Proof. First we prove (4.16). When $q - p \leq \alpha_1$ or $r - q \leq \alpha_2$ (4.16)
obviously holds since the left–hand side equals 0. When $q - p > \alpha_1 + \beta_1$ we
have

$$T_W(L^{\lll}_{(\alpha_1,\beta_1)}(p,q), L^{\lll}_{(\alpha_2,\beta_2)}(q,r)) = L^{\lll}_{(\alpha_2,\beta_2)}(q,r)$$

Because the first partial mappings of $L^{\lll}_{(\alpha_2,\beta_2)}$ are decreasing, and by using
the assumption $q - p > \alpha_1 + \beta_1$ we obtain

$$L^{\lll}_{(\alpha_2,\beta_2)}(q,r) \leq L^{\lll}_{(\alpha_2,\beta_2)}(p + \alpha_1 + \beta_1, r)$$

and by (4.11)

$$L^{\lll}_{(\alpha_2,\beta_2)}(p + \alpha_1 + \beta_1, r) = L^{\lll}_{(\alpha_1+\alpha_2+\beta_1,\beta_2)}(p, r)$$

and by Lemma 4.2

$$L^{\lll}_{(\alpha_1+\alpha_2+\beta_1,\beta_2)}(p, r) \leq L^{\lll}_{(\alpha_1+\alpha_2+\min(\beta_1,\beta_2),\max(\beta_1,\beta_2))}(p, r)$$

In the same way, we can prove (4.16) when $r - q > \alpha_2 + \beta_2$. Finally, assume $\alpha_1 < q - p \leq \alpha_1 + \beta_1$ and $\alpha_2 < r - q \leq \alpha_2 + \beta_2$ (hence $\beta_1 > 0$ and $\beta_2 > 0$). For $\beta_1 \leq \beta_2$ we obtain

$$T_W(L^{\lll}_{(\alpha_1,\beta_1)}(p,q), L^{\lll}_{(\alpha_2,\beta_2)}(q,r)) = \max(0, L^{\lll}_{(\alpha_1,\beta_1)}(p,q) + L^{\lll}_{(\alpha_2,\beta_2)}(q,r) - 1)$$

$$= \max(0, \frac{q - p - \alpha_1}{\beta_1} + \frac{r - q - \alpha_2}{\beta_2} - 1)$$

$$= \max(0, \frac{q - p - \alpha_1 - \beta_1}{\beta_1} + \frac{r - q - \alpha_2}{\beta_2})$$

Since $q - p - \alpha_1 - \beta_1 \leq 0$ and $\beta_1 \leq \beta_2$, we have

$$\leq \max(0, \frac{q - p - \alpha_1 - \beta_1}{\beta_2} + \frac{r - q - \alpha_2}{\beta_2})$$

$$= \max(0, \frac{r - p - \alpha_1 - \alpha_2 - \beta_1}{\beta_2})$$

$$= L^{\lll}_{(\alpha_1 + \alpha_2 + \beta_1, \beta_2)}(p, r)$$

For $\beta_1 > \beta_2$ the proof is entirely analogous.

Next, we prove (4.17). When $\beta_1 = 0$ and $q - p < -\alpha_1$, (4.17) is trivially satisfied as the left–hand side equals 0. When $\beta_1 = 0$ and $q - p \geq -\alpha_1$, we find

$$T_W(L^{\preccurlyeq}_{(\alpha_1,\beta_1)}(p,q), L^{\preccurlyeq}_{(\alpha_2,\beta_2)}(q,r)) = L^{\preccurlyeq}_{(\alpha_2,\beta_2)}(q,r)$$

Using the fact that the first partial mappings of $L^{\preccurlyeq}_{(\alpha_2,\beta_2)}$ are decreasing, we obtain

$$L^{\preccurlyeq}_{(\alpha_2,\beta_2)}(q,r) \leq L^{\preccurlyeq}_{(\alpha_2,\beta_2)}(p - \alpha_1, r)$$

and by (4.13)

$$L^{\preccurlyeq}_{(\alpha_2,\beta_2)}(p - \alpha_1, r) = L^{\preccurlyeq}_{(\alpha_1 + \alpha_2, \beta_2)}(p, r)$$

showing (4.17). In entirely the same fashion, we can show (4.17) when $\beta_2 = 0$. Finally, assume $\beta_1 > 0$ and $\beta_2 > 0$. By (4.9), we find

$$T_W(L^{\preccurlyeq}_{(\alpha_1,\beta_1)}(p,q), L^{\preccurlyeq}_{(\alpha_2,\beta_2)}(q,r))$$

$$= T_W(L^{\lll}_{(-\alpha_1 - \beta_1, \beta_1)}(p,q), L^{\lll}_{(-\alpha_2 - \beta_2, \beta_2)}(q,r))$$

By (4.16), we obtain

$$\leq L^{\lll}_{(-\alpha_1 - \alpha_2 - \beta_1 - \beta_2 + \min(\beta_1,\beta_2), \max(\beta_1,\beta_2))}(p, r)$$

$$= L^{\lll}_{(-\alpha_1 - \alpha_2 - \max(\beta_1,\beta_2), \max(\beta_1,\beta_2))}(p, r)$$

and finally by (4.9)

$$= L^{\preccurlyeq}_{(\alpha_1 + \alpha_2, \max(\beta_1,\beta_2))}(p, r)$$

The proof of (4.18) and (4.19) is analogous. $\square$

Proposition 4.1 (Composition). *Let* $\alpha_1, \alpha_2 \in \mathbb{R}$ *and* $\beta_1, \beta_2 \geq 0$; *it holds that*

$$L_{(\alpha_1,\beta_1)}^{\lll} \circ_{T_W} L_{(\alpha_2,\beta_2)}^{\lll} = L_{(\alpha_1+\alpha_2+\min(\beta_1,\beta_2),\max(\beta_1,\beta_2))}^{\lll} \tag{4.20}$$

$$L_{(\alpha_1,\beta_1)}^{\prec} \circ_{T_W} L_{(\alpha_2,\beta_2)}^{\prec} = L_{(\alpha_1+\alpha_2,\max(\beta_1,\beta_2))}^{\prec} \tag{4.21}$$

$$L_{(\alpha_1,\beta_1)}^{\prec} \circ_{T_W} L_{(\alpha_2,\beta_2)}^{\lll} = L_{(\alpha_2-\alpha_1+\min(\beta_1,\beta_2)-\beta_1,\max(\beta_1,\beta_2))}^{\lll} \tag{4.22}$$

$$L_{(\alpha_1,\beta_1)}^{\lll} \circ_{T_W} L_{(\alpha_2,\beta_2)}^{\prec} = L_{(\alpha_1-\alpha_2+\min(\beta_1,\beta_2)-\beta_2,\max(\beta_1,\beta_2))}^{\lll} \tag{4.23}$$

Proof. We prove (4.20) as an example; the proof of (4.21)–(4.23) is analogous. By (4.16) we already have

$$(L_{(\alpha_1,\beta_1)}^{\lll} \circ_{T_W} L_{(\alpha_2,\beta_2)}^{\lll})(p,r) \leq L_{(\alpha_1+\alpha_2+\min(\beta_1,\beta_2),\max(\beta_1,\beta_2))}^{\lll}(p,r)$$

for arbitrary p and r in $\mathbb{R}$. Conversely, for $\beta_1 \leq \beta_2$ we have

$$\sup_{q \in \mathbb{R}} T_W(L_{(\alpha_1,\beta_1)}^{\lll}(p,q), L_{(\alpha_2,\beta_2)}^{\lll}(q,r))$$

$$\geq \sup_{\varepsilon > 0} T_W(L_{(\alpha_1,\beta_1)}^{\lll}(p,p+\alpha_1+\beta_1+\varepsilon), L_{(\alpha_2,\beta_2)}^{\lll}(p+\alpha_1+\beta_1+\varepsilon,r))$$

$$= \sup_{\varepsilon > 0} T_W(1, L_{(\alpha_2,\beta_2)}^{\lll}(p+\alpha_1+\beta_1+\varepsilon,r))$$

$$= \sup_{\varepsilon > 0} L_{(\alpha_2,\beta_2)}^{\lll}(p+\alpha_1+\beta_1+\varepsilon,r)$$

Taking into account that the first partial mappings of $L_{(\alpha_2,\beta_2)}^{\lll}$ are decreasing and right–continuous, we obtain

$$\sup_{b \in \mathbb{R}} T_W(L_{(\alpha_1,\beta_1)}^{\lll}(p,q), L_{(\alpha_2,\beta_2)}^{\lll}(q,r)) \geq L_{(\alpha_2,\beta_2)}^{\lll}(p+\alpha_1+\beta_1,r)$$

and by (4.11)

$$L_{(\alpha_2,\beta_2)}^{\lll}(p+\alpha_1+\beta_1,r) = L_{(\alpha_1+\alpha_2+\beta_1,\beta_2)}^{\lll}(p,r)$$

For $\beta_1 > \beta_2$ the proof is entirely analogous. $\qquad\square$

In particular, for $\alpha = 0$ and $\beta_1 = \beta_2 = \beta$, Proposition 4.1 reveals that

$$T_W(L_{(0,\beta)}^{\lll}(p,q), L_{(0,\beta)}^{\lll}(q,r)) \leq L_{(0,\beta)}^{\lll}(p,r) \tag{4.24}$$

$$T_W(L_{(0,\beta)}^{\prec}(p,q), L_{(0,\beta)}^{\prec}(q,r)) \leq L_{(0,\beta)}^{\prec}(p,r) \tag{4.25}$$

$$T_W(L_{(0,\beta)}^{\prec}(p,q), L_{(0,\beta)}^{\lll}(q,r)) \leq L_{(0,\beta)}^{\lll}(p,r) \tag{4.26}$$

$$T_W(L_{(0,\beta)}^{\lll}(p,q), L_{(0,\beta)}^{\prec}(q,r)) \leq L_{(0,\beta)}^{\lll}(p,r) \tag{4.27}$$

From (4.24) and (4.25), we learn that $L_{(0,\beta)}^{\lll}$ and $L_{(0,\beta)}^{\prec}$ are T_W–transitive. Furthermore, (4.26) and (4.27) express a mixed transitivity between $L_{(0,\beta)}^{\lll}$ and $L_{(0,\beta)}^{\prec}$, generalizing that from $p \leq q$ and $q < r$ we can infer $p < r$, and similarly, that from $p < q$ and $q \leq r$ we can infer $p < r$.

4.4.2   Properties of the Fuzzy Allen Relations

4.4.2.1   Basic properties

As we will show in this section, our generalization of Allen's relations preserves many interesting properties. First of all, recall that the 13 interval relations are jointly exhaustive, which means that between any two time intervals at least one of the relations holds. For fuzzy time intervals we obtain the following generalization.

Proposition 4.2 (Exhaustivity). *Let A and B be fuzzy time intervals. It holds that ($\alpha \in \mathbb{R}$, $\beta \geq 0$)*

$$S_W(b_{(\alpha,\beta)}(A,B), bi_{(\alpha,\beta)}(A,B), o_{(\alpha,\beta)}(A,B), oi_{(\alpha,\beta)}(A,B), d_{(\alpha,\beta)}(A,B),$$
$$di_{(\alpha,\beta)}(A,B), m_{(\alpha,\beta)}(A,B), mi_{(\alpha,\beta)}(A,B), s_{(\alpha,\beta)}(A,B), si_{(\alpha,\beta)}(A,B),$$
$$f_{(\alpha,\beta)}(A,B), fi_{(\alpha,\beta)}(A,B), e_{(\alpha,\beta)}(A,B))$$
$$= 1$$

Proof. We have

$$S_W(s_{(\alpha,\beta)}(A,B), si_{(\alpha,\beta)}(A,B), e_{(\alpha,\beta)}(A,B))$$
$$= S_W(\min((A \circ L^{\preceq}_{(\alpha,\beta)}) \rhd B, (B \circ L^{\preceq}_{(\alpha,\beta)}) \rhd A, (A \lhd L^{\ll}_{(\alpha,\beta)}) \circ B),$$
$$\min((B \circ L^{\preceq}_{(\alpha,\beta)}) \rhd A, (A \circ L^{\preceq}_{(\alpha,\beta)}) \rhd B, (B \lhd L^{\ll}_{(\alpha,\beta)}) \circ A),$$
$$\min((A \circ L^{\preceq}_{(\alpha,\beta)}) \rhd B, (B \circ L^{\preceq}_{(\alpha,\beta)}) \rhd A,$$
$$A \lhd (L^{\preceq}_{(\alpha,\beta)} \circ B), B \lhd (L^{\preceq}_{(\alpha,\beta)} \circ A)))$$

By twice applying (2.15) we obtain that

$$S_W(\min(a,b_1), \min(a,b_2), \min(a,b_3)) \geq \min(a, S_W(b_1,b_2,b_3))$$

for all a, b_1, b_2 and b_3 in $[0,1]$. Substituting

$$a := \min((A \circ L^{\preceq}_{(\alpha,\beta)}) \rhd B, (B \circ L^{\preceq}_{(\alpha,\beta)}) \rhd A)$$
$$b_1 := (A \lhd L^{\ll}_{(\alpha,\beta)}) \circ B$$
$$b_2 := (B \lhd L^{\ll}_{(\alpha,\beta)}) \circ A$$
$$b_3 := \min(A \lhd (L^{\preceq}_{(\alpha,\beta)} \circ B), B \lhd (L^{\preceq}_{(\alpha,\beta)} \circ A))$$

we obtain

$$S_W(s_{(\alpha,\beta)}(A,B), si_{(\alpha,\beta)}(A,B), e_{(\alpha,\beta)}(A,B))$$
$$\geq \min((A \circ L_{(\alpha,\beta)}^{\vec{\ll}}) \rhd B, (B \circ L_{(\alpha,\beta)}^{\vec{\ll}}) \rhd A,$$
$$S_W((A \lhd L_{(\alpha,\beta)}^{\ll}) \circ B, (B \lhd L_{(\alpha,\beta)}^{\ll}) \circ A,$$
$$\min(A \lhd (L_{(\alpha,\beta)}^{\vec{\ll}} \circ B), B \lhd (L_{(\alpha,\beta)}^{\vec{\ll}} \circ A))))$$
$$= \min((A \circ L_{(\alpha,\beta)}^{\vec{\ll}}) \rhd B, (B \circ L_{(\alpha,\beta)}^{\vec{\ll}}) \rhd A,$$
$$S_W((A \lhd L_{(\alpha,\beta)}^{\ll}) \circ B, (B \lhd L_{(\alpha,\beta)}^{\ll}) \circ A, A \lhd (L_{(\alpha,\beta)}^{\vec{\ll}} \circ B)),$$
$$S_W((A \lhd L_{(\alpha,\beta)}^{\ll}) \circ B, (B \lhd L_{(\alpha,\beta)}^{\ll}) \circ A, B \lhd (L_{(\alpha,\beta)}^{\vec{\ll}} \circ A)))$$

By (3.132),(3.10) and (4.7) we know that $(B \lhd L_{(\alpha,\beta)}^{\ll}) \circ A = 1 - A \lhd (L_{(\alpha,\beta)}^{\vec{\ll}} \circ B)$ and therefore $S_W((B \lhd L_{(\alpha,\beta)}^{\ll}) \circ A, A \lhd (L_{(\alpha,\beta)}^{\vec{\ll}} \circ B)) = 1$; in the same way, we find $S_W((A \lhd L_{(\alpha,\beta)}^{\ll}) \circ B, B \lhd (L_{(\alpha,\beta)}^{\vec{\ll}} \circ A)) = 1$. We obtain

$$= \min((A \circ L_{(\alpha,\beta)}^{\vec{\ll}}) \rhd B, (B \circ L_{(\alpha,\beta)}^{\vec{\ll}}) \rhd A)$$
$$= hh_{(\alpha,\beta)}(A,B)$$

We can show analogously that

$$S_W(o_{(\alpha,\beta)}(A,B), fi_{(\alpha,\beta)}(A,B), di_{(\alpha,\beta)}(A,B))$$
$$\geq \min(A \circ (L_{(\alpha,\beta)}^{\ll} \rhd B), B \circ L_{(\alpha,\beta)}^{\ll} \circ A) = oc_{(\alpha,\beta)}(A,B)$$

$$S_W(oi_{(\alpha,\beta)}(A,B), f_{(\alpha,\beta)}(A,B), d_{(\alpha,\beta)}(A,B))$$
$$\geq \min(B \circ (L_{(\alpha,\beta)}^{\ll} \rhd A), A \circ L_{(\alpha,\beta)}^{\ll} \circ B) = yc_{(\alpha,\beta)}(A,B)$$

$$S_W(b_{(\alpha,\beta)}(A,B), m_{(\alpha,\beta)}(A,B)) \geq A \lhd L_{(\alpha,\beta)}^{\vec{\ll}} \rhd B = pr_{(\alpha,\beta)}(A,B)$$

$$S_W(bi_{(\alpha,\beta)}(A,B), mi_{(\alpha,\beta)}(A,B)) \geq B \lhd L_{(\alpha,\beta)}^{\vec{\ll}} \rhd A = sd_{(\alpha,\beta)}(A,B)$$

$$S_W(hh_{(\alpha,\beta)}(A,B), yc_{(\alpha,\beta)}(A,B), oc_{(\alpha,\beta)}(A,B))$$
$$\geq \min(A \circ L_{(\alpha,\beta)}^{\ll} \circ B, B \circ L_{(\alpha,\beta)}^{\ll} \circ A) = ct_{(\alpha,\beta)}(A,B)$$

$$S_W(ct_{(\alpha,\beta)}(A,B), pr_{(\alpha,\beta)}(A,B), sd_{(\alpha,\beta)}(A,B)) = 1$$

which completes the proof. $\qquad\square$

For nondegenerate time intervals, i.e., time intervals $[a^-, a^+]$ with $a^- < a^+$, Allen's relations are pairwise disjoint. This means that at most one of the 13 relations holds between two given nondegenerate time intervals, and hence precisely one.

Definition 4.3. Let $\alpha \geq 0$ and $\beta \geq 0$. A fuzzy time interval A is called nondegenerate w.r.t. (α, β) iff $be_{(\alpha,\beta)}^{\ll}(A,A) = 1$, i.e., if the beginning of A is (long) before the end of A to degree 1.

Note that the notion of being nondegenerate w.r.t. $(0,0)$ coincides with our earlier definition of a nondegenerate fuzzy time interval (Definition 4.2). By restricting ourselves to nondegenerate fuzzy time intervals, we obtain a generalization of the pairwise disjointness of Allen's relations:

Proposition 4.3 (Pairwise disjointness). *Let A and B be nondegenerate fuzzy time intervals w.r.t. $(2\alpha, \beta)$. Moreover, let R and S be fuzzy Allen relations, defined w.r.t. (α, β) (e.g., $b_{(\alpha,\beta)}$). If $\alpha \geq 0$, $\beta \geq 0$ and $R \neq S$, it holds that*

$$T_W(R(A,B), S(A,B)) = 0$$

Proof.   To prove the pairwise disjointness of the fuzzy temporal relations, $\frac{13 \times 12}{2} = 78$ cases have to be considered. Here, as an example, we provide a proof for two of these cases. First, we show that

$$T_W(d_{(\alpha,\beta)}(A,B), m_{(\alpha,\beta)}(A,B)) = 0$$

We find

$$T_W(d_{(\alpha,\beta)}(A,B), m_{(\alpha,\beta)}(A,B))$$
$$= T_W(\min(bb^{\lll}_{(\alpha,\beta)}(B,A), ee^{\lll}_{(\alpha,\beta)}(A,B)), \min(eb^{\prec}_{(\alpha,\beta)}(A,B), be^{\prec}_{(\alpha,\beta)}(B,A)))$$
$$= T_W(\min(B \circ (L^{\lll}_{(\alpha,\beta)} \rhd A), (A \lhd L^{\lll}_{(\alpha,\beta)}) \circ B),$$
$$\quad \min(A \lhd L^{\prec}_{(\alpha,\beta)} \rhd B, B \circ L^{\prec}_{(\alpha,\beta)} \circ A))$$
$$\leq T_W(B \circ (L^{\lll}_{(\alpha,\beta)} \rhd A), A \lhd L^{\prec}_{(\alpha,\beta)} \rhd B)$$

From the transitivity table for relatedness measures (Table 3.1), we find

$$T_W(B \circ (L^{\lll}_{(\alpha,\beta)} \rhd A), A \lhd L^{\prec}_{(\alpha,\beta)} \rhd B) \leq B \circ ((L^{\lll}_{(\alpha,\beta)} \circ L^{\prec}_{(\alpha,\beta)}) \rhd B)$$

By (4.23) we obtain

$$B \circ ((L^{\lll}_{(\alpha,\beta)} \circ L^{\prec}_{(\alpha,\beta)}) \rhd B) = B \circ (L^{\lll}_{(0,\beta)} \rhd B)$$

As for $\alpha \geq 0$, $L^{\lll}_{(\alpha,\beta)}$ is an irreflexive fuzzy relation, Proposition 3.3 entails that

$$B \circ (L^{\lll}_{(0,\beta)} \rhd B) = 0$$

As a second example, we show that

$$T_W(s_{(\alpha,\beta)}(A,B), m_{(\alpha,\beta)}(A,B)) = 0$$

Since A is nondegenerate w.r.t. $(2\alpha, \beta)$, we obtain using Table 3.1 and (4.22)

$$(B \circ L^{\prec}_{(\alpha,\beta)}) \rhd A = T_W((B \circ L^{\prec}_{(\alpha,\beta)}) \rhd A, A \circ L^{\lll}_{(2\alpha,\beta)} \circ A)$$
$$\leq B \circ (L^{\prec}_{(\alpha,\beta)} \circ L^{\lll}_{(2\alpha,\beta)}) \circ A$$
$$= B \circ L^{\lll}_{(\alpha,\beta)} \circ A$$

Using this observation, as well as Table 3.1 and (4.23), we find

$$T_W(s_{(\alpha,\beta)}(A,B), m_{(\alpha,\beta)}(A,B))$$
$$= T_W(\min(bb^{\preccurlyeq}_{(\alpha,\beta)}(A,B), bb^{\preccurlyeq}_{(\alpha,\beta)}(B,A), ee^{\lll}_{(\alpha,\beta)}(A,B)),$$
$$\qquad \min(eb^{\preccurlyeq}_{(\alpha,\beta)}(A,B), be^{\preccurlyeq}_{(\alpha,\beta)}(B,A)))$$
$$= T_W(\min((A \circ L^{\preccurlyeq}_{(\alpha,\beta)}) \rhd B, (B \circ L^{\preccurlyeq}_{(\alpha,\beta)}) \rhd A, (A \lhd L^{\lll}_{(\alpha,\beta)}) \circ B),$$
$$\qquad \min(A \lhd L^{\preccurlyeq}_{(\alpha,\beta)} \rhd B, B \circ L^{\preccurlyeq}_{(\alpha,\beta)} \circ A))$$
$$\leq T_W((B \circ L^{\preccurlyeq}_{(\alpha,\beta)}) \rhd A, A \lhd L^{\preccurlyeq}_{(\alpha,\beta)} \rhd B)$$
$$\leq T_W(B \circ L^{\lll}_{(\alpha,\beta)} \circ A, A \lhd L^{\preccurlyeq}_{(\alpha,\beta)} \rhd B)$$
$$\leq B \circ ((L^{\lll}_{(\alpha,\beta)} \circ L^{\preccurlyeq}_{(\alpha,\beta)}) \rhd B)$$
$$= B \circ (L^{\lll}_{(0,\beta)} \rhd B)$$

which equals 0 by Proposition 3.3. □

The condition that A and B should be nondegenerate fuzzy time intervals is only needed when R or S is $m_{(\alpha,\beta)}$ or $mi_{(\alpha,\beta)}$. This is not different from the traditional crisp case. For example, using Allen's definitions we have for two crisp intervals $A = [a, b]$ and $B = [b, c]$ that $m(A, B)$ holds. However, if $a = b$ and $b < c$, we also have that $s(A, B)$ holds. Likewise, if $b = c$ and $a < b$, we have that $fi(A, B)$ holds. As the next two propositions show, our definitions also satisfy generalizations of the (a)symmetry and the (ir)reflexivity properties of Allen's relations.

Proposition 4.4 ((A)symmetry). *Let $\alpha \geq 0$ and $\beta \geq 0$. The fuzzy relations $b_{(\alpha,\beta)}$, $bi_{(\alpha,\beta)}$, $o_{(\alpha,\beta)}$, $oi_{(\alpha,\beta)}$, $d_{(\alpha,\beta)}$, $di_{(\alpha,\beta)}$, $s_{(\alpha,\beta)}$, $si_{(\alpha,\beta)}$, $f_{(\alpha,\beta)}$ and $fi_{(\alpha,\beta)}$ are T_W-asymmetric, i.e., let R be one of the aforementioned fuzzy relations and let A and B be fuzzy time intervals. It holds that*

$$T_W(R(A,B), R(B,A)) = 0 \tag{4.28}$$

Furthermore, it holds that

$$e_{\gamma_{12}}(A, B) = e_{\gamma_{12}}(B, A) \tag{4.29}$$

If A and B are nondegenerate fuzzy time intervals w.r.t. (α, β), it holds that

$$T_W(m_{(\alpha,\beta)}(A,B), m_{(\alpha,\beta)}(B,A)) = 0 \tag{4.30}$$
$$T_W(mi_{(\alpha,\beta)}(A,B), mi_{(\alpha,\beta)}(B,A)) = 0 \tag{4.31}$$

Proof.   As an example, we show that

$$T_W(d_{(\alpha,\beta)}(A,B), d_{(\alpha,\beta)}(B,A)) = 0$$

By using Table 3.1 and (4.20) we obtain

$$
\begin{aligned}
&T_W(d_{(\alpha,\beta)}(A,B), d_{(\alpha,\beta)}(B,A)) \\
&= T_W(\min(ee^{\lll}_{(\alpha,\beta)}(A,B), bb^{\lll}_{(\alpha,\beta)}(B,A)), \min(ee^{\lll}_{(\alpha,\beta)}(B,A), bb^{\lll}_{(\alpha,\beta)}(A,B))) \\
&= T_W(\min((A \vartriangleleft L^{\lll}_{(\alpha,\beta)}) \circ B, B \circ (L^{\lll}_{(\alpha,\beta)} \vartriangleright A)), \\
&\qquad \min((B \vartriangleleft L^{\lll}_{(\alpha,\beta)}) \circ A, A \circ (L^{\lll}_{(\alpha,\beta)} \vartriangleright B))) \\
&\leq T_W((A \vartriangleleft L^{\lll}_{(\alpha,\beta)}) \circ B, (B \vartriangleleft L^{\lll}_{(\alpha,\beta)}) \circ A) \\
&\leq (A \vartriangleleft (L^{\lll}_{(\alpha,\beta)} \circ L^{\lll}_{(\alpha,\beta)})) \circ A \\
&= (A \vartriangleleft L^{\lll}_{(2\alpha+\beta,\beta)}) \circ A
\end{aligned}
$$

which equals 0 by Proposition 3.3, since for $\alpha \geq 0$, $L^{\lll}_{(\alpha,\beta)}$ is an irreflexive fuzzy relation.

As another example, we show that

$$T_W(m_{(\alpha,\beta)}(A,B), m_{(\alpha,\beta)}(B,A)) = 0$$

provided A and B are nondegenerate fuzzy time intervals w.r.t. (α,β). We obtain

$$
\begin{aligned}
&T_W(m_{(\alpha,\beta)}(A,B), m_{(\alpha,\beta)}(B,A)) \\
&= T_W(\min(eb^{\prec}_{(\alpha,\beta)}(A,B), be^{\prec}_{(\alpha,\beta)}(B,A)), \min(eb^{\prec}_{(\alpha,\beta)}(B,A), be^{\prec}_{(\alpha,\beta)}(A,B))) \\
&= T_W(\min(A \vartriangleleft L^{\prec}_{(\alpha,\beta)} \vartriangleright B, B \circ L^{\prec}_{(\alpha,\beta)} \circ A), \\
&\qquad \min(B \vartriangleleft L^{\prec}_{(\alpha,\beta)} \vartriangleright A, A \circ L^{\prec}_{(\alpha,\beta)} \circ B)) \\
&\leq T_W(A \vartriangleleft L^{\prec}_{(\alpha,\beta)} \vartriangleright B, B \vartriangleleft L^{\prec}_{(\alpha,\beta)} \vartriangleright A)
\end{aligned}
$$

Since A is nondegenerate, we have by Table 3.1 and (4.23) that

$$
\begin{aligned}
A \vartriangleleft L^{\prec}_{(\alpha,\beta)} \vartriangleright B &= T_W(A \circ L^{\lll}_{(\alpha,\beta)} \circ A, A \vartriangleleft L^{\prec}_{(\alpha,\beta)} \vartriangleright B) \\
&\leq A \circ ((L^{\lll}_{(\alpha,\beta)} \circ L^{\prec}_{(\alpha,\beta)}) \vartriangleright B) \\
&= A \circ (L^{\lll}_{(0,\beta)} \vartriangleright B)
\end{aligned}
$$

In the same way, since B is nondegenerate, we obtain

$$B \vartriangleleft L^{\prec}_{(\alpha,\beta)} \vartriangleright A \leq B \circ (L^{\lll}_{(0,\beta)} \vartriangleright A)$$

Hence we already have

$$T_W(m_{(\alpha,\beta)}(A,B), m_{(\alpha,\beta)}(B,A)) \le T_W(A \circ (L_{(0,\beta)}^{\lll} \rhd B), B \circ (L_{(0,\beta)}^{\lll} \rhd A))$$

and by Table 3.1 and (4.20)

$$\le A \circ ((L_{(0,\beta)}^{\lll} \circ L_{(0,\beta)}^{\lll}) \rhd A)$$
$$= A \circ (L_{(\beta,\beta)}^{\lll} \rhd A)$$

which equals 0 by Proposition 3.3. □

Proposition 4.5 ((Ir)reflexivity). *Let* $\alpha \ge 0$ *and* $\beta \ge 0$. *The fuzzy relations* $b_{(\alpha,\beta)}$, $bi_{(\alpha,\beta)}$, $o_{(\alpha,\beta)}$, $oi_{(\alpha,\beta)}$, $d_{(\alpha,\beta)}$, $di_{(\alpha,\beta)}$, $s_{(\alpha,\beta)}$, $si_{(\alpha,\beta)}$, $f_{(\alpha,\beta)}$ *and* $fi_{(\alpha,\beta)}$ *are irreflexive, i.e., let* R *be one of the aforementioned fuzzy relations and let* A *be a fuzzy time interval. It holds that*

$$R(A,A) = 0 \qquad (4.32)$$

Furthermore, it holds that

$$e_{(\alpha,\beta)}(A,A) = 1 \qquad (4.33)$$

If A *is a nondegenerate fuzzy time interval w.r.t.* (α,β), *it holds that*

$$m_{(\alpha,\beta)}(A,A) = mi_{(\alpha,\beta)}(A,A) = 0 \qquad (4.34)$$

Proof. We will only show that $m_{(\alpha,\beta)}(A,A) = 0$, provided A is a non-degenerate fuzzy time interval w.r.t. (α,β), as the other equalities follow straightforwardly from Proposition 3.2 and Proposition 3.3. We obtain

$$m_{(\alpha,\beta)}(A,A) = \min(A \lhd L_{(\alpha,\beta)}^{\prec} \rhd A, A \circ L_{(\alpha,\beta)}^{\prec} \circ A) \le A \lhd L_{(\alpha,\beta)}^{\prec} \rhd A$$

Since A is nondegenerate w.r.t. (α,β) we have by Table 3.1 and (4.22)

$$m_{(\alpha,\beta)}(A,A) \le T_W(A \lhd L_{(\alpha,\beta)}^{\prec} \rhd A, A \circ L_{(\alpha,\beta)}^{\lll} \circ A)$$
$$\le (A \lhd (L_{(\alpha,\beta)}^{\prec} \circ L_{(\alpha,\beta)}^{\lll})) \circ A$$
$$= (A \lhd L_{(0,\beta)}^{\lll}) \circ A$$

which equals 0 by Proposition 3.3. □

In Proposition 4.2–4.5, fuzzy relations of the form $L_{(\alpha,\beta)}^{\lll}$ and $L_{(\alpha,\beta)}^{\prec}$ are used to express the concepts 'long before' and 'more or less before'. In principle, more general classes of fuzzy relations could be used to this end, i.e., fuzzy relations that cannot be written as either $L_{(\alpha,\beta)}^{\lll}$ or $L_{(\alpha,\beta)}^{\prec}$. As can easily be seen from their proofs, these propositions remain valid when other fuzzy relations are used, provided some weak assumptions are satisfied. For example, let R and S be arbitrary fuzzy relations in $\mathbb{R}$ which are used to express the concepts 'long before' and 'more or less before' respectively. Then, Proposition 4.2 remains valid as soon as $R(x, y) = 1 - S(y, x)$ for all x and y in $\mathbb{R}$. For Proposition 4.3–4.5 to hold, we also have to assume, among others, that the fuzzy relations R, $R \circ S$, $R \circ S \circ S$, etc. are irreflexive. However, using fuzzy relations of the form $L_{(\alpha,\beta)}^{\lll}$ and $L_{(\alpha,\beta)}^{\prec}$ to express fuzzy orderings of time points has a number of important advantages. As shown in Section 4.4.1, these fuzzy relations satisfy many desirable properties, and their sup–T_W composition can be conveniently characterized (Proposition 4.1), which is important for reasoning with fuzzy temporal relations. Moreover, in Section 4.5.2, we will show how using $L_{(\alpha,\beta)}^{\lll}$ and $L_{(\alpha,\beta)}^{\prec}$ leads to an efficient characterization of the fuzzy temporal relations when applied to piecewise linear fuzzy time intervals.

4.4.2.2   *Transitivity*

Allen's transitivity table (Table 4.2) provides a means to draw useful inferences. When $A = [a^-, a^+]$, $B = [b^-, b^+]$ and $C = [c^-, c^+]$ are crisp intervals, we can deduce, for example, from $d(A, B)$ and $m(B, C)$ that $b(A, C)$ holds. Indeed by $d(A, B)$ we have $a^+ < b^+$ and by $m(B, C)$ we have $b^+ = c^-$; from $a^+ < b^+$ and $b^+ = c^-$ we conclude $a^+ < c^-$, or, in other words, $b(A, C)$. When A, B and C are fuzzy time intervals, we would like to make similar deductions. In particular, we are interested in generalized transitivity rules of the form

$$T_W(d_{(\alpha_1,\beta_1)}(A, B), m_{(\alpha_2,\beta_2)}(B, C)) \leq b_{(\alpha_3,\beta_3)}(A, C)$$

for suitable values of α_3 and β_3. Such inferences can easily be made, employing the transitivity rules for relatedness measures:

$$
\begin{aligned}
&T_W(d_{(\alpha_1,\beta_1)}(A, B), m_{(\alpha_2,\beta_2)}(B, C)) \\
&= T_W(\min(B \circ (L_{(\alpha_1,\beta_1)}^{\lll} \rhd A), (A \lhd L_{(\alpha_1,\beta_1)}^{\lll}) \circ B), \\
&\qquad \min(B \lhd L_{(\alpha_2,\beta_2)}^{\prec} \rhd C, C \circ L_{(\alpha_2,\beta_2)}^{\prec} \circ B)) \\
&= \min(T_W(B \circ (L_{(\alpha_1,\beta_1)}^{\lll} \rhd A), B \lhd L_{(\alpha_2,\beta_2)}^{\prec} \rhd C), \\
&\qquad\quad T_W(B \circ (L_{(\alpha_1,\beta_1)}^{\lll} \rhd A), C \circ L_{(\alpha_2,\beta_2)}^{\prec} \circ B), \\
&\qquad\quad T_W((A \lhd L_{(\alpha_1,\beta_1)}^{\lll}) \circ B, B \lhd L_{(\alpha_2,\beta_2)}^{\prec} \rhd C), \\
&\qquad\quad T_W((A \lhd L_{(\alpha_1,\beta_1)}^{\lll}) \circ B, C \circ L_{(\alpha_2,\beta_2)}^{\prec} \circ B)) \\
&\leq T_W((A \lhd L_{(\alpha_1,\beta_1)}^{\lll}) \circ B, B \lhd L_{(\alpha_2,\beta_2)}^{\prec} \rhd C)
\end{aligned}
$$

Using the transitivity table for relatedness measures (Table 3.1) and (4.23), we obtain

$$\leq A \lhd (L^{\lll}_{(\alpha_1,\beta_1)} \circ L^{\prec}_{(\alpha_2,\beta_2)}) \rhd C$$

$$= A \lhd L^{\lll}_{(\alpha_1-\alpha_2+\min(\beta_1,\beta_2)-\beta_2,\max(\beta_1,\beta_2))} \rhd C$$

$$= b_{(\alpha_1-\alpha_2+\min(\beta_1,\beta_2)-\beta_2,\max(\beta_1,\beta_2))}(A,C)$$

In particular, if $\alpha_1 = \alpha_2 = 0$ and $\beta_1 = \beta_2 = \beta$, we obtain

$$T_W(d_{(0,\beta)}(A,B), m_{(0,\beta)}(B,C)) \leq b_{(0,\beta)}(A,C)$$

As another example, for crisp intervals A, B and C, we can establish from $m(A,B)$ and $m(B,C)$ that $b(A,C)$ holds, under the assumption that B is a nondegenerate interval. For fuzzy time intervals A, B and C, we find (again assuming $\alpha_1 = \alpha_2 = 0$ and $\beta_1 = \beta_2 = \beta$)

$$T_W(m_{(0,\beta)}(A,B), m_{(0,\beta)}(B,C))$$

$$= T_W(\min(A \lhd L^{\prec}_{(0,\beta)} \rhd B, B \circ L^{\prec}_{(0,\beta)} \circ A),$$

$$\min(B \lhd L^{\prec}_{(0,\beta)} \rhd C, C \circ L^{\prec}_{(0,\beta)} \circ B))$$

$$\leq T_W(A \lhd L^{\prec}_{(0,\beta)} \rhd B, B \lhd L^{\prec}_{(0,\beta)} \rhd C)$$

Assuming that B is nondegenerate w.r.t. $(0,\beta)$, i.e., that $B \circ L^{\lll}_{(0,\beta)} \circ B = 1$, and using Table 3.1 and (4.22), we obtain

$$A \lhd L^{\prec}_{(0,\beta)} \rhd B = T_W(A \lhd L^{\prec}_{(0,\beta)} \rhd B, B \circ L^{\lll}_{(0,\beta)} \circ B)$$

$$\leq (A \lhd (L^{\prec}_{(0,\beta)} \circ L^{\lll}_{(0,\beta)})) \circ B$$

$$= (A \lhd L^{\lll}_{(0,\beta)}) \circ B$$

and thus, using Table 3.1 and (4.23),

$$T_W(A \lhd L^{\prec}_{(0,\beta)} \rhd B, B \lhd L^{\prec}_{(0,\beta)} \rhd C)$$

$$\leq T_W((A \lhd L^{\lll}_{(0,\beta)}) \circ B, B \lhd L^{\prec}_{(0,\beta)} \rhd C)$$

$$\leq A \lhd (L^{\lll}_{(0,\beta)} \circ L^{\prec}_{(0,\beta)}) \rhd C$$

$$= A \lhd L^{\lll}_{(0,\beta)} \rhd C$$

$$= b_{(0,\beta)}(A,C)$$

Such kind of deductions can easily be made in an automated way for various values of the parameters α_1, α_2, β_1 and β_2. In the majority of the applications, however, $\alpha_1 = \alpha_2 = \beta_1 = \beta_2 = 0$ will hold, i.e., the available temporal information is completely qualitative. In this case, the parameters α_3 and β_3 in the conclusion of the generalized transitivity rule will be

0 as well. Hence, we can formulate a transitivity table that is deductively closed. Such a transitivity table is presented in Table 4.6. Let R_3 be the entry in this table on the row corresponding with R_1 and the column corresponding with R_2. For nondegenerate fuzzy time intervals A, B and C w.r.t. $(0,0)$, it holds that $T_W(R_1(A,B), R_2(B,C)) \leq R_3(A,C)$. One can verify that for crisp intervals, Table 4.6 coincides with Freksa's transitivity table, and, as a consequence, by restricting Table 4.6 to the first 13 rows and the first 13 columns, we obtain a sound generalization of Allen's transitivity table. Note, however, that while Allen's transitivity table explicitly contains unions of basic Allen relations, our generalized transitivity table (as well as Freksa's transitivity table) contains (generalized) conceptual neighbourhoods instead. While for crisp intervals, using unions of Allen relations is equivalent to using conceptual neighbourhoods, this does not hold anymore for fuzzy time intervals. For example, when A, B and C are crisp intervals, it holds that

$$tt(A,B) = \max(f(A,B), fi(A,B), e(A,B))$$

However, when A, B and C are fuzzy time intervals, we only have that

$$tt(A,B) \geq \max(f(A,B), fi(A,B), e(A,B))$$

For example, let the fuzzy time intervals A and B be defined as

$$A(p) = \begin{cases} 1 & \text{if } p \in [10,20] \\ 0 & \text{otherwise} \end{cases} \qquad B(p) = \begin{cases} 1 & \text{if } p \in [15,20] \\ 0.5 & \text{if } p \in [5,15[\\ 0 & \text{otherwise} \end{cases}$$

for all p in $\mathbb{R}$. It holds that

$$ee^{\prec}(A,B) = ee^{\prec}(B,A) = 1$$
$$bb^{\ll}(A,B) = bb^{\ll}(B,A) = bb^{\prec}(A,B) = bb^{\prec}(B,A) = 0.5$$

and

$$tt(A,B) = \min(ee^{\prec}(A,B), ee^{\prec}(B,A)) = 1$$
$$f(A,B) = \min(bb^{\ll}(B,A), tt(A,B)) = 0.5$$
$$fi(A,B) = \min(bb^{\ll}(A,B), tt(A,B)) = 0.5$$
$$e(A,B) = \min(b^{\prec}(A,B), b^{\prec}(B,A), tt(A,B)) = 0.5$$

Hence, in this case

$$tt(A,B) > \max(f(A,B), fi(A,B), e(A,B))$$

Table 4.6 Transitivity table for fuzzy temporal interval relations (©2008 IEEE).

	b	m	o	fi	di	si	e	s	d	f	oi	mi	bi	ob	oc	hh	yc	bc	tt	sc	ys	yo	sb	sv	ct	bd	db
b	b	b	b	b	b	b	b	b	b	b	b	b	1	b	b	m	b	sb	sb	sb	1	b	sb	1	sb	sb	1
m	b	b	b	ob	ol	ol	b	ob	s	bc	yc	yc	1	b	ol	m	yc	bc	tt	sc	1	b	sb	1	bd	bd	1
o	b	b	b	fi	di	di	o	s	d	bc	yc	yc	bi	ob	oc	oc	yc	bc	sc	sc	ys	yo	sb	sv	bd	bd	db
fi	b	b	o	fi	di	di	fi	s	oc	bc	mi	mi	bi	ob	oc	oc	yc	bc	sc	sc	ys	yo	sb	sv	bd	bd	db
di	ol	ol	ol	di	di	di	di	oc	oc	bd	bi	bi	bi	ol	ol	oc	db	db	bd	bd	1	db	bd	db	db	db	db
si	ol	ol	di	di	di	si	si	d	d	bd	bi	bi	bi	ol	ol	hh	db	db	bd	sc	ys	ol	bd	sv	bd	bd	db
e	b	m	o	fi	di	si	e	s	d	f	oi	mi	bi	ob	oc	hh	yc	bc	tt	sc	ys	yo	sb	sv	ct	bd	db
s	b	b	o	si	si	si	s	s	d	d	yc	yc	bi	sb	sb	hh	yc	bc	sc	sc	ys	yo	sb	sv	ct	bd	db
d	b	b	d	d	d	d	d	d	d	d	bi	bi	bi	bd	bd	bd	yo	yo	bd	bd	bd	1	db	sv	bd	bd	db
f	b	b	d	d	oc	oc	f	d	d	f	bi	bi	bi	bd	bd	bd	yc	bc	tt	sc	bd	1	db	sv	bd	bd	db
oi	ol	ol	yc	mi	mi	oi	oi	yc	bi	bi	bi	bi	bi	ol	ol	oc	yo	yo	bd	bd	bd	1	db	sv	bd	bd	db
mi	ol	ol	yc	mi	mi	mi	mi	yc	bi	bi	bi	bi	bi	ol	ol	hh	yo	yo	bd	bd	bd	1	db	sv	bd	bd	db
bi	1	1	yo	yo	yo	bi	bi	bi	bi	bi	bi	bi	bi	1	1	yo	db	db	bd	bd	bd	1	db	sv	bd	bd	db
ob	b	b	ob	ob	ol	ol	ob	ob	d	bc	yc	yc	bi	ob	ol	hh	yc	bc	sc	sc	ys	yo	sb	sv	bd	bd	db
oc	ol	ol	oc	oc	ol	ol	oc	oc	d	bc	yc	yc	bi	ol	ol	oc	bc	bc	sc	sc	ys	yo	sb	sv	bd	bd	db
hh	ol	ol	oc	oc	ol	hh	hh	oc	d	bc	yc	yc	bi	ol	ol	hh	yc	bc	sc	sc	ys	yo	sb	sv	bd	bd	db
yc	ol	ol	yc	yc	ol	ol	yc	yc	bi	bi	bi	bi	bi	ol	ol	oc	yo	yo	bd	bd	bd	1	db	sv	bd	bd	db
bc	b	b	bc	bc	oc	oc	bc	bc	d	f	bi	bi	bi	bd	bd	bd	yc	bc	tt	sc	bd	1	db	sv	bd	bd	db
tt	sb	sb	sc	sc	sc	tt	tt	sc	bd	bd	bi	bi	bi	sb	sb	sb	sv	sv	tt	sc	ys	yo	sb	sv	ct	bd	db
sc	sb	sb	sc	sc	sc	sc	sc	sc	bd	bd	bi	bi	bi	sb	sb	sb	sv	sv	sc	sc	ys	yo	sb	sv	ct	bd	db
ys	1	1	yo	yo	yo	ys	ys	yo	bd	bd	bi	bi	bi	1	1	yo	db	db	bd	bd	ys	yo	sb	sv	ct	bd	db
ol	b	b	yo	yo	yo	ol	ol	yo	bd	bd	bi	bi	bi	1	1	ol	db	db	bd	bd	bd	1	db	sv	db	bd	db
yo	b	b	yo	yo	yo	yo	yo	yo	bd	bd	bi	bi	bi	1	1	yo	db	db	bd	bd	bd	1	db	sv	db	bd	db
sb	sb	sb	sb	sb	db	db	sb	sb	db	db	db	db	db	sb	sb	sb	db	db	db	db	db	db	sb	db	db	bd	db
sv	1	1	sv	sv	sv	sv	sv	sv	db	db	db	db	db	sv	sv	sv	db	db	db	db	db	db	sv	sv	db	bd	db
ct	sb	sb	ct	ct	ct	ct	ct	ct	bd	bd	bi	bi	bi	sb	sb	sb	sv	sv	ct	sc	ys	yo	sb	sv	ct	bd	db
bd	1	1	db	db	db	db	bd	bd	bd	bd	bd	bd	bd	1	1	db	db	db	bd	bd	bd	1	db	sv	db	bd	db
db	1	1	db	db	db	db	db	db	db	db	db	db	db	1	1	db	db	db	db	db	db	db	db	db	db	db	db

4.5   Evaluating the Fuzzy Temporal Relations

Due to the suprema and infima involved, it is often unclear how to evaluate the fuzzy temporal relations for particular values of α and β, and particular fuzzy time intervals A and B. The most obvious solution is to apply discretization techniques, but these are computationally expensive and only provide an approximated value. Assume, for example, that we somehow choose n points x_i and n points y_j $(1 \leq i, j \leq n)$ such that

$$\max_{i=1}^{n} T_W(A(x_i), \max_{j=1}^{n} T_W(B(y_j), L_{(\alpha,\beta)}^{\preccurlyeq}(x_i, x_j))) \tag{4.35}$$

is a reasonable approximation of $be_{(\alpha,\beta)}^{\preccurlyeq}(A, B)$. Evaluating (4.35) still requires $\Theta(n^2)$ basic arithmetic operations, which may be prohibitively high in applications requiring high precision, and therefore high values of n. On the other hand, applications may only need to evaluate fuzzy temporal relations between certain classes of fuzzy time intervals. In particular, many applications only deal with piecewise linear fuzzy time intervals. In this section, we provide a characterization of the fuzzy temporal relations for such fuzzy time intervals. Using this characterization, the fuzzy temporal relations can be evaluated much more efficiently, compared to using discretization, and, moreover, the result is always exact. First, in Section 4.5.1 we consider linear fuzzy sets. Subsequently, in Section 4.5.2 we show how evaluating fuzzy temporal relations for piecewise linear fuzzy intervals can be reduced to evaluating the fuzzy relations for linear fuzzy sets. Finally, in Section 4.5.3, we provide a number of other characterizations of the fuzzy temporal relations for the special case where $\beta = 0$. Besides their practical value, these characterizations are also useful in theoretical contexts. In the next chapter, for instance, we will apply them to obtain reasoning procedures.

4.5.1   *Characterization for Linear Fuzzy Sets*

4.5.1.1   *Evaluating* $be_{(\alpha,\beta)}^{\lll}$, $be_{(\alpha,\beta)}^{\preccurlyeq}$, $eb_{(\alpha,\beta)}^{\lll}$ *and* $eb_{(\alpha,\beta)}^{\preccurlyeq}$

Let A and B be linear fuzzy sets in $\mathbb{R}$, i.e., for all p in $\mathbb{R}$, it holds that

$$A(p) = \begin{cases} \lambda_0^a + (p - a_0)\frac{\lambda_1^a - \lambda_0^a}{a_1 - a_0} & \text{if } a_0 \leq p < a_1 \\ \lambda_1^a & \text{if } p = a_1 \\ 0 & \text{otherwise} \end{cases} \tag{4.36}$$

$$B(p) = \begin{cases} \lambda_0^b + (p - b_0)\frac{\lambda_1^b - \lambda_0^b}{b_1 - b_0} & \text{if } b_0 \leq p < b_1 \\ \lambda_1^b & \text{if } p = b_1 \\ 0 & \text{otherwise} \end{cases} \quad (4.37)$$

where $\lambda_0^a, \lambda_1^a, \lambda_0^b, \lambda_1^b \in [0,1]$, $a_0, a_1, b_0, b_1 \in \mathbb{R}$, $a_0 \leq a_1$ and $b_0 \leq b_1$. First, we will focus on a characterization of $be_{(\alpha,\beta)}^{\ll}(A, B)$ and $be_{(\alpha,\beta)}^{\prec}(A, B)$. Our starting point is the observation that if $\lambda_0^a < \lambda_1^a$, $A(p) = L_{(0,\Delta_a)}^{\ll}(a^-, p)$ for every p in $[a_0, a_1]$, where

$$\Delta_a = \frac{a_1 - a_0}{\lambda_1^a - \lambda_0^a}$$

$$a^- = a_0 - \Delta_a \lambda_0^a$$

Similarly, if $\lambda_0^b > \lambda_1^b$, $B(p) = 1 - L_{(0,\Delta_b)}^{\ll}(b^-, p) = L_{(0,\Delta_b)}^{\prec}(p, b^-)$ for every p in $[b_0, b_1]$, where

$$\Delta_b = \frac{b_1 - b_0}{\lambda_0^b - \lambda_1^b}$$

$$b^- = b_0 - \Delta_b(1 - \lambda_0^b)$$

This correspondence is illustrated in Figure 4.7. Thus we find that

$$be_{(\alpha,\beta)}^{\ll}(A, B)$$
$$= \sup_{p \in \mathbb{R}} T_W(A(p), \sup_{q \in \mathbb{R}} T_W(L_{(\alpha,\beta)}^{\ll}(p, q), B(q)))$$
$$= \sup_{p \in [a_0, a_1]} T_W(L_{(0,\Delta_a)}^{\ll}(a^-, p), \sup_{q \in [b_0, b_1]} T_W(L_{(\alpha,\beta)}^{\ll}(p, q), L_{(0,\Delta_b)}^{\prec}(q, b^-)))$$

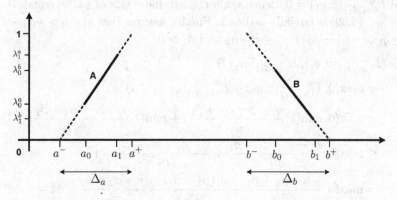

Fig. 4.7   Relationship between the linear fuzzy set A (resp. B) and $L_{(0,\Delta_a)}^{\prec}(a^-, .)$ (resp. $L_{(0,\Delta_b)}^{\prec}(., b^-)$) (©2008 IEEE).

The following lemmas are concerned with a characterization of expressions such as

$$\sup_{q\in[q_0,q_1]} T_W(L^{\preccurlyeq}_{(\alpha_1,\beta_1)}(p,q), L^{\preccurlyeq}_{(\alpha_2,\beta_2)}(q,r)) \tag{4.38}$$

In particular, after a technical lemma (Lemma 4.4), we first consider a similar characterization for the case where the supremum ranges over $]-\infty, q_1]$ (Lemma 4.5) and over $[q_0, +\infty[$ (Lemma 4.6). Subsequently, these two characterizations are used to find a characterization for (4.38) (Lemma 4.7). Finally, we discuss how this characterization can be employed for evaluating expressions like $be^{\preccurlyeq}_{(\alpha,\beta)}(A, B)$.

Lemma 4.4. Let $\beta_1, \beta_2 \geq 0$ and $\alpha_1, \alpha_2 \in \mathbb{R}$. If $\beta_1 \leq \beta_2$, $q_1 \leq q_2$ and $q_2 - p \leq -\alpha_1$, it holds that

$$T_W(L^{\preccurlyeq}_{(\alpha_1,\beta_1)}(p,q_1), L^{\preccurlyeq}_{(\alpha_2,\beta_2)}(q_1,r)) \leq T_W(L^{\preccurlyeq}_{(\alpha_1,\beta_1)}(p,q_2), L^{\preccurlyeq}_{(\alpha_2,\beta_2)}(q_2,r)) \tag{4.39}$$

If $\beta_1 \geq \beta_2$, $q_1 \leq q_2$ and $r - q_2 \leq -\alpha_2$, it holds that

$$T_W(L^{\preccurlyeq}_{(\alpha_1,\beta_1)}(p,q_1), L^{\preccurlyeq}_{(\alpha_2,\beta_2)}(q_1,r)) \geq T_W(L^{\preccurlyeq}_{(\alpha_1,\beta_1)}(p,q_2), L^{\preccurlyeq}_{(\alpha_2,\beta_2)}(q_2,r)) \tag{4.40}$$

Proof. As an example, we show (4.39); the proof of (4.40) is entirely analogous. If $q_1 - p \leq -\alpha_1 - \beta_1$ or $r - q_1 \leq -\alpha_2 - \beta_2$, (4.39) is trivially satisfied as its left–hand side equals 0. If $r - q_2 \geq -\alpha_2$, it holds that $L^{\preccurlyeq}_{(\alpha_2,\beta_2)}(q_2,r) = 1$; (4.39) follows from $L^{\preccurlyeq}_{(\alpha_1,\beta_1)}(p,q_1) \leq L^{\preccurlyeq}_{(\alpha_1,\beta_1)}(p,q_2)$. If $\beta_1 = 0$ and $q_1 < q_2$, the assumption $q_2 - p \leq -\alpha_1$ implies $q_1 - p < -\alpha_1$ and $L^{\preccurlyeq}_{(\alpha_1,\beta_1)}(p,q_1) = 0$, hence again the left–hand side of (4.39) equals 0. If $q_1 = q_2$, (4.39) is trivially satisfied. Finally, assume that $q_1 - p > -\alpha_1 - \beta_1$, $r - q_1 > -\alpha_2 - \beta_2$, $r - q_2 < -\alpha_2$ and $\beta_1 > 0$

$$T_W(L^{\preccurlyeq}_{(\alpha_1,\beta_1)}(p,q_1), L^{\preccurlyeq}_{(\alpha_2,\beta_2)}(q_1,r))$$

$$= \max(0, L^{\preccurlyeq}_{(\alpha_1,\beta_1)}(p,q_1) + L^{\preccurlyeq}_{(\alpha_2,\beta_2)}(q_1,r) - 1)$$

$$= \max(0, \min(1, \frac{q_1 - p + \alpha_1 + \beta_1}{\beta_1}) + \min(1, \frac{r - q_1 + \alpha_2 + \beta_2}{\beta_2}) - 1)$$

$$\leq \max(0, \frac{q_1 - p + \alpha_1 + \beta_1}{\beta_1} + \frac{r - q_1 + \alpha_2 + \beta_2}{\beta_2} - 1)$$

$$= \max(0, \frac{-p + \alpha_1 + \beta_1}{\beta_1} + \frac{q_1(\beta_2 - \beta_1)}{\beta_2\beta_1} + \frac{r + \alpha_2 + \beta_2}{\beta_2} - 1)$$

$$\leq \max(0, \frac{-p + \alpha_1 + \beta_1}{\beta_1} + \frac{q_2(\beta_2 - \beta_1)}{\beta_2\beta_1} + \frac{r + \alpha_2 + \beta_2}{\beta_2} - 1)$$

$$= \max(0, \frac{q_2 - p + \alpha_1 + \beta_1}{\beta_1} + \frac{r - q_2 + \alpha_2 + \beta_2}{\beta_2} - 1)$$

$$\leq \max(0, \max(0, \frac{q_2 - p + \alpha_1 + \beta_1}{\beta_1}) + \max(0, \frac{r - q_2 + \alpha_2 + \beta_2}{\beta_2}) - 1)$$

Since $q_2 - p \leq -\alpha_1$ and $r - q_2 < -\alpha_2$, we find

$$= \max(0, \max(0, \min(1, \frac{q_2 - p + \alpha_1 + \beta_1}{\beta_1}))$$

$$+ \max(0, \min(1, \frac{r - q_2 + \alpha_2 + \beta_2}{\beta_2})) - 1)$$

$$= T_W(L_{(\alpha_1,\beta_1)}^{\preccurlyeq}(p, q_2), L_{(\alpha_2,\beta_2)}^{\preccurlyeq}(q_2, r))$$

$\qquad\qquad\qquad\qquad\qquad\qquad\qquad\qquad\qquad\qquad\qquad$ □

Lemma 4.5. *Let $\beta_1, \beta_2 \geq 0$ and $\alpha_1, \alpha_2 \in \mathbb{R}$. It holds that*

$$\sup_{q \leq q_0} T_W(L_{(\alpha_1,\beta_1)}^{\preccurlyeq}(p, q), L_{(\alpha_2,\beta_2)}^{\preccurlyeq}(q, r))$$

$$= T_W(L_{(\alpha_1,\beta_1)}^{\preccurlyeq}(p, q_0), L_{(\alpha_2,\max(\beta_1,\beta_2))}^{\preccurlyeq}(\min(p - \alpha_1, q_0), r)) \quad (4.41)$$

Proof. We provide separate proofs for the case where $\beta_1 \leq \beta_2$ and the case where $\beta_1 > \beta_2$.

(1) If $\beta_1 \leq \beta_2$, we find

$$\sup_{q \leq q_0} T_W(L_{(\alpha_1,\beta_1)}^{\preccurlyeq}(p, q), L_{(\alpha_2,\beta_2)}^{\preccurlyeq}(q, r))$$

$$\geq T_W(L_{(\alpha_1,\beta_1)}^{\preccurlyeq}(p, \min(p - \alpha_1, q_0)), L_{(\alpha_2,\beta_2)}^{\preccurlyeq}(\min(p - \alpha_1, q_0), r))$$

$$= \min(T_W(L_{(\alpha_1,\beta_1)}^{\preccurlyeq}(p, p - \alpha_1), L_{(\alpha_2,\beta_2)}^{\preccurlyeq}(\min(p - \alpha_1, q_0), r)),$$

$$T_W(L_{(\alpha_1,\beta_1)}^{\preccurlyeq}(p, q_0), L_{(\alpha_2,\beta_2)}^{\preccurlyeq}(\min(p - \alpha_1, q_0), r)))$$

$$= \min(L_{(\alpha_2,\beta_2)}^{\preccurlyeq}(\min(p - \alpha_1, q_0), r),$$

$$T_W(L_{(\alpha_1,\beta_1)}^{\preccurlyeq}(p, q_0), L_{(\alpha_2,\beta_2)}^{\preccurlyeq}(\min(p - \alpha_1, q_0), r)))$$

$$= T_W(L_{(\alpha_1,\beta_1)}^{\preccurlyeq}(p, q_0), L_{(\alpha_2,\beta_2)}^{\preccurlyeq}(\min(p - \alpha_1, q_0), r))$$

Conversely, we show that for every $q \leq q_0$

$$T_W(L_{(\alpha_1,\beta_1)}^{\preccurlyeq}(p, q), L_{(\alpha_2,\beta_2)}^{\preccurlyeq}(q, r))$$

$$\leq T_W(L_{(\alpha_1,\beta_1)}^{\preccurlyeq}(p, q_0), L_{(\alpha_2,\beta_2)}^{\preccurlyeq}(\min(p - \alpha_1, q_0), r))$$

For $q_0-p \leq -\alpha_1$, this follows immediately from (4.39). For $q_0-p > -\alpha_1$ we find using Lemma 4.3 and (4.13)

$$T_W(L^{\preccurlyeq}_{(\alpha_1,\beta_1)}(p,q), L^{\preccurlyeq}_{(\alpha_2,\beta_2)}(q,r))$$
$$\leq L^{\preccurlyeq}_{(\alpha_1+\alpha_2,\beta_2)}(p,r)$$
$$= L^{\preccurlyeq}_{(\alpha_2,\beta_2)}(p-\alpha_1,r)$$

From $p - \alpha_1 < q_0$, we furthermore obtain

$$= L^{\preccurlyeq}_{(\alpha_2,\beta_2)}(\min(p-\alpha_1,q_0),r)$$
$$= T_W(L^{\preccurlyeq}_{(\alpha_1,\beta_1)}(p,p-\alpha_1), L^{\preccurlyeq}_{(\alpha_2,\beta_2)}(\min(p-\alpha_1,q_0),r))$$

and using the fact that $L^{\preccurlyeq}_{(\alpha_1,\beta_1)}$ is increasing in the second argument, we obtain

$$\leq T_W(L^{\preccurlyeq}_{(\alpha_1,\beta_1)}(p,q_0), L^{\preccurlyeq}_{(\alpha_2,\beta_2)}(\min(p-\alpha_1,q_0),r))$$

(2) If $\beta_2 < \beta_1$, we obtain, using the fact that $L^{\preccurlyeq}_{(0,0)}(q,q_0) = 1$ if $q \leq q_0$ and $L^{\preccurlyeq}_{(0,0)}(q,q_0) = 0$ otherwise

$$\sup_{q\leq q_0} T_W(L^{\preccurlyeq}_{(\alpha_1,\beta_1)}(p,q), L^{\preccurlyeq}_{(\alpha_2,\beta_2)}(q,r))$$
$$= \sup_{q\in\mathbb{R}} T_W(L^{\preccurlyeq}_{(\alpha_1,\beta_1)}(p,q), \min(L^{\preccurlyeq}_{(0,0)}(q,q_0), L^{\preccurlyeq}_{(\alpha_2,\beta_2)}(q,r)))$$
$$\leq \min(\sup_{q\in\mathbb{R}} T_W(L^{\preccurlyeq}_{(\alpha_1,\beta_1)}(p,q), L^{\preccurlyeq}_{(0,0)}(q,q_0)),$$
$$\sup_{q\in\mathbb{R}} T_W(L^{\preccurlyeq}_{(\alpha_1,\beta_1)}(p,q), L^{\preccurlyeq}_{(\alpha_2,\beta_2)}(q,r)))$$

From Proposition 4.1, we find that the latter expression equals

$$\min(L^{\preccurlyeq}_{(\alpha_1,\beta_1)}(p,q_0), L^{\preccurlyeq}_{(\alpha_1+\alpha_2,\beta_1)}(p,r))$$

Conversely, we find

$$\sup_{q\leq q_0} T_W(L^{\preccurlyeq}_{(\alpha_1,\beta_1)}(p,q), L^{\preccurlyeq}_{(\alpha_2,\beta_2)}(q,r))$$
$$\geq T_W(L^{\preccurlyeq}_{(\alpha_1,\beta_1)}(p,\min(q_0,r+\alpha_2)), L^{\preccurlyeq}_{(\alpha_2,\beta_2)}(\min(q_0,r+\alpha_2),r))$$
$$= L^{\preccurlyeq}_{(\alpha_1,\beta_1)}(p,\min(q_0,r+\alpha_2))$$

Using the fact that the second partial mappings of $L^{\preccurlyeq}_{(\alpha_1,\beta_1)}$ are increasing and (4.14), we find

$$= \min(L^{\preccurlyeq}_{(\alpha_1,\beta_1)}(p,q_0), L^{\preccurlyeq}_{(\alpha_1,\beta_1)}(p,r+\alpha_2))$$
$$= \min(L^{\preccurlyeq}_{(\alpha_1,\beta_1)}(p,q_0), L^{\preccurlyeq}_{(\alpha_1+\alpha_2,\beta_1)}(p,r))$$

Thus, it remains to be shown that

$$\min(L^{\preccurlyeq}_{(\alpha_1,\beta_1)}(p,q_0), L^{\preccurlyeq}_{(\alpha_1+\alpha_2,\beta_1)}(p,r))$$
$$= T_W(L^{\preccurlyeq}_{(\alpha_1,\beta_1)}(p,q_0), L^{\preccurlyeq}_{(\alpha_2,\beta_1)}(\min(p-\alpha_1,q_0),r))$$

(a) If $p - \alpha_1 \leq q_0$, we obtain using the fact that $L^{\preccurlyeq}_{(\alpha_1,\beta_1)}(p,q_0) = 1$ and (4.13)

$$T_W(L^{\preccurlyeq}_{(\alpha_1,\beta_1)}(p,q_0), L^{\preccurlyeq}_{(\alpha_2,\beta_1)}(p-\alpha_1,r))$$
$$= L^{\preccurlyeq}_{(\alpha_2,\beta_1)}(p-\alpha_1,r)$$
$$= L^{\preccurlyeq}_{(\alpha_1+\alpha_2,\beta_1)}(p,r)$$
$$= \min(L^{\preccurlyeq}_{(\alpha_1,\beta_1)}(p,q_0), L^{\preccurlyeq}_{(\alpha_1+\alpha_2,\beta_1)})(p,r))$$

(b) If $p - \alpha_1 > q_0$ and $r - q_0 \geq -\alpha_2$, we obtain using the fact that $L^{\preccurlyeq}_{(\alpha_2,\beta_1)}(q_0,r) = 1$, $L^{\preccurlyeq}_{(\alpha_1,\beta_1)}(p,q_0) \leq L^{\preccurlyeq}_{(\alpha_1,\beta_1)}(p,r+\alpha_2)$ and (4.14)

$$T_W(L^{\preccurlyeq}_{(\alpha_1,\beta_1)}(p,q_0), L^{\preccurlyeq}_{(\alpha_2,\beta_1)}(q_0,r))$$
$$= L^{\preccurlyeq}_{(\alpha_1,\beta_1)}(p,q_0)$$
$$= \min(L^{\preccurlyeq}_{(\alpha_1,\beta_1)}(p,q_0), L^{\preccurlyeq}_{(\alpha_1,\beta_1)}(p,r+\alpha_2))$$
$$= \min(L^{\preccurlyeq}_{(\alpha_1,\beta_1)}(p,q_0), L^{\preccurlyeq}_{(\alpha_1+\alpha_2,\beta_1)}(p,r))$$

(c) Finally, if $p - \alpha_1 > q_0$ and $r - q_0 < -\alpha_2$, we know using (4.14) that $L^{\preccurlyeq}_{(\alpha_1,\beta_1)}(p,q_0) \geq L^{\preccurlyeq}_{(\alpha_1,\beta_1)}(p,r+\alpha_2) = L^{\preccurlyeq}_{(\alpha_1+\alpha_2,\beta_1)}(p,r)$. Together with (4.17), this yields

$$T_W(L^{\preccurlyeq}_{(\alpha_1,\beta_1)}(p,q_0), L^{\preccurlyeq}_{(\alpha_2,\beta_1)}(q_0,r))$$
$$\leq L^{\preccurlyeq}_{(\alpha_1+\alpha_2,\beta_1)}(p,r)$$
$$= \min(L^{\preccurlyeq}_{(\alpha_1,\beta_1)}(p,q_0), L^{\preccurlyeq}_{(\alpha_1+\alpha_2,\beta_1)}(p,r))$$

Conversely, we find from (4.39) and (4.14)

$$T_W(L^{\preccurlyeq}_{(\alpha_1,\beta_1)}(p,q_0), L^{\preccurlyeq}_{(\alpha_2,\beta_1)}(q_0,r))$$
$$\geq T_W(L^{\preccurlyeq}_{(\alpha_1,\beta_1)}(p,r+\alpha_2), L^{\preccurlyeq}_{(\alpha_2,\beta_1)}(r+\alpha_2,r))$$
$$= L^{\preccurlyeq}_{(\alpha_1,\beta_1)}(p,r+\alpha_2)$$
$$= L^{\preccurlyeq}_{(\alpha_1+\alpha_2,\beta_1)}(p,r)$$
$$= \min(L^{\preccurlyeq}_{(\alpha_1,\beta_1)}(p,q_0), L^{\preccurlyeq}_{(\alpha_1+\alpha_2,\beta_1)}(p,r))$$

$\square$

Note that no suprema or infima occur in the right–hand side of (4.41), which can therefore be evaluated in constant time.

Lemma 4.6. *Let* $\beta_1, \beta_2 \geq 0$ *and* $\alpha_1, \alpha_2 \in \mathbb{R}$. *It holds that*

$$\sup_{q \geq q_0} T_W(L^{\preceq}_{(\alpha_1,\beta_1)}(p,q), L^{\preceq}_{(\alpha_2,\beta_2)}(q,r))$$

$$= T_W(L^{\preceq}_{(\alpha_1,\max(\beta_1,\beta_2))}(p, \max(r+\alpha_2, q_0)), L^{\preceq}_{(\alpha_2,\beta_2)}(q_0, r))$$

Proof.   The proof is entirely analogous to the proof of Lemma 4.5.   □

Lemma 4.7. *Let* $\beta_1, \beta_2 \geq 0$, $\alpha_1, \alpha_2 \in \mathbb{R}$ *and* $q_0 \leq q_1$. *If* $\beta_1 \leq \beta_2$, *it holds that*

$$\sup_{q \in [q_0, q_1]} T_W(L^{\preceq}_{(\alpha_1,\beta_1)}(p,q), L^{\preceq}_{(\alpha_2,\beta_2)}(q,r))$$

$$= T_W(L^{\preceq}_{(\alpha_1,\beta_1)}(p,q_1), L^{\preceq}_{(\alpha_2,\beta_2)}(\min(q_1, \max(q_0, p-\alpha_1)), r)) \tag{4.42}$$

If $\beta_1 \geq \beta_2$, *it holds that*

$$\sup_{q \in [q_0, q_1]} T_W(L^{\preceq}_{(\alpha_1,\beta_1)}(p,q), L^{\preceq}_{(\alpha_2,\beta_2)}(q,r))$$

$$= T_W(L^{\preceq}_{(\alpha_1,\beta_1)}(p, \min(q_1, \max(q_0, r+\alpha_2))), L^{\preceq}_{(\alpha_2,\beta_2)}(q_0, r)) \tag{4.43}$$

Proof.   As an example, we show (4.42); let $\beta_1 \leq \beta_2$.

(1) Assume that $p - \alpha_1 \geq q_0$. Using the fact that $L^{\preceq}_{(0,0)}(q_0, q)$ equals 1 if $q_0 \leq q$ and 0 otherwise, we find

$$\sup_{q \in [q_0, q_1]} T_W(L^{\preceq}_{(\alpha_1,\beta_1)}(p,q), L^{\preceq}_{(\alpha_2,\beta_2)}(q,r))$$

$$= \sup_{q \leq q_1} T_W(\min(L^{\preceq}_{(0,0)}(q_0, q), L^{\preceq}_{(\alpha_1,\beta_1)}(p,q)), L^{\preceq}_{(\alpha_2,\beta_2)}(q,r))$$

$$\leq \min(\sup_{q \leq q_1} T_W(L^{\preceq}_{(0,0)}(q_0, q), L^{\preceq}_{(\alpha_2,\beta_2)}(q,r)),$$

$$\sup_{q \leq q_1} T_W(L^{\preceq}_{(\alpha_1,\beta_1)}(p,q), L^{\preceq}_{(\alpha_2,\beta_2)}(q,r)))$$

Using Lemma 4.5, we find

$$= \min(T_W(L^{\preceq}_{(0,0)}(q_0, q_1), L^{\preceq}_{(\alpha_2,\beta_2)}(\min(q_0, q_1), r)),$$

$$T_W(L^{\preceq}_{(\alpha_1,\beta_1)}(p, q_1), L^{\preceq}_{(\alpha_2,\beta_2)}(\min(p-\alpha_1, q_1), r)))$$

and using $q_0 \leq q_1$ and $p - \alpha_1 \geq q_0$

$$= \min(L^{\preceq}_{(\alpha_2,\beta_2)}(q_0,r), T_W(L^{\preceq}_{(\alpha_1,\beta_1)}(p,q_1), L^{\preceq}_{(\alpha_2,\beta_2)}(\min(p-\alpha_1,q_1),r)))$$

$$= \min(L^{\preceq}_{(\alpha_2,\beta_2)}(q_0,r), T_W(L^{\preceq}_{(\alpha_1,\beta_1)}(p,q_1),$$
$$L^{\preceq}_{(\alpha_2,\beta_2)}(\min(\max(p-\alpha_1,q_0),q_1),r)))$$

Since $q_0 \leq \min(\max(p-\alpha_1,q_0),q_1)$, we obtain $L^{\preceq}_{(\alpha_2,\beta_2)}(q_0,r) \geq L^{\preceq}_{(\alpha_2,\beta_2)}(\min(\max(p-\alpha_1,q_0),q_1),r)$ and thus

$$= T_W(L^{\preceq}_{(\alpha_1,\beta_1)}(p,q_1), L^{\preceq}_{(\alpha_2,\beta_2)}(\min(\max(p-\alpha_1,q_0),q_1),r))$$

Conversely, we find

$$T_W(L^{\preceq}_{(\alpha_1,\beta_1)}(p,q_1), L^{\preceq}_{(\alpha_2,\beta_2)}(\min(\max(p-\alpha_1,q_0),q_1),r))$$

$$= T_W(\min(L^{\preceq}_{(\alpha_1,\beta_1)}(p,p-\alpha_1), L^{\preceq}_{(\alpha_1,\beta_1)}(p,q_1)),$$
$$L^{\preceq}_{(\alpha_2,\beta_2)}(\min(\max(p-\alpha_1,q_0),q_1),r))$$

$$= T_W(L^{\preceq}_{(\alpha_1,\beta_1)}(p,\min(q_1,p-\alpha_1)),$$
$$L^{\preceq}_{(\alpha_2,\beta_2)}(\min(\max(p-\alpha_1,q_0),q_1),r))$$

And, finally, using $p - \alpha_1 \geq q_0$

$$= T_W(L^{\preceq}_{(\alpha_1,\beta_1)}(p,\min(q_1,\max(q_0,p-\alpha_1))),$$
$$L^{\preceq}_{(\alpha_2,\beta_2)}(\min(\max(p-\alpha_1,q_0),q_1),r))$$

$$\leq \sup_{q \in [q_0,q_1]} T_W(L^{\preceq}_{(\alpha_1,\beta_1)}(p,q), L^{\preceq}_{(\alpha_2,\beta_2)}(q,r))$$

(2) If $p - \alpha_1 < q_0$, then for all q in $[q_0,q_1]$ it holds that $q - p > -\alpha_1$, hence $L^{\preceq}_{(\alpha_1,\beta_1)}(p,q) = 1$. To prove (4.42), we therefore need to show that

$$\sup_{q \in [q_0,q_1]} L^{\preceq}_{(\alpha_2,\beta_2)}(q,r) = L^{\preceq}_{(\alpha_2,\beta_2)}(\min(q_1,\max(q_0,p-\alpha_1)),r)$$

From $\min(q_1,\max(q_0,p-\alpha_1))$ in $[q_0,q_1]$, we already know that

$$\sup_{q \in [q_0,q_1]} L^{\preceq}_{(\alpha_2,\beta_2)}(q,r) \geq L^{\preceq}_{(\alpha_2,\beta_2)}(\min(q_1,\max(q_0,p-\alpha_1)),r)$$

Conversely, we find

$$\sup_{q \in [q_0,q_1]} L^{\preceq}_{(\alpha_2,\beta_2)}(q,r) = L^{\preceq}_{(\alpha_2,\beta_2)}(q_0,r)$$

$$= L^{\preceq}_{(\alpha_2,\beta_2)}(\max(q_0,p-\alpha_1),r)$$

and, since $L^{\preceq}_{(\alpha_2,\beta_2)}$ is decreasing in its first argument

$$\leq L^{\preceq}_{(\alpha_2,\beta_2)}(\min(q_1,\max(q_0,p-\alpha_1)),r)$$

$$\square$$

Corollary 4.1. *Let* $\beta_1, \beta_2 \geq 0$ *and* $\alpha_1, \alpha_2 \in \mathbb{R}$. *If* $0 < \beta_1 \leq \beta_2$, *it holds that*

$$\sup_{q \in [q_0, q_1]} T_W(L^{\ll}_{(\alpha_1, \beta_1)}(p, q), L^{\preceq}_{(\alpha_2, \beta_2)}(q, r)) \tag{4.44}$$

$$= T_W(L^{\ll}_{(\alpha_1, \beta_1)}(p, q_1), L^{\preceq}_{(\alpha_2, \beta_2)}(\min(q_1, \max(q_0, p + \alpha_1 + \beta_1)), r))$$

$$\sup_{q \in [q_0, q_1]} T_W(L^{\preceq}_{(\alpha_1, \beta_1)}(p, q), L^{\preceq}_{(\alpha_2, \beta_2)}(q, r)) \tag{4.45}$$

$$= T_W(L^{\preceq}_{(\alpha_1, \beta_1)}(p, q_1), L^{\preceq}_{(\alpha_2, \beta_2)}(\min(q_1, \max(q_0, p - \alpha_1)), r))$$

$$\sup_{q \in [q_0, q_1]} T_W(L^{\ll}_{(\alpha_1, \beta_1)}(p, q), L^{\ll}_{(\alpha_2, \beta_2)}(q, r)) \tag{4.46}$$

$$= T_W(L^{\ll}_{(\alpha_1, \beta_1)}(p, q_1), L^{\ll}_{(\alpha_2, \beta_2)}(\min(q_1, \max(q_0, p + \alpha_1 + \beta_1)), r))$$

If $0 < \beta_2 \leq \beta_1$, *it holds that*

$$\sup_{q \in [q_0, q_1]} T_W(L^{\ll}_{(\alpha_1, \beta_1)}(p, q), L^{\preceq}_{(\alpha_2, \beta_2)}(q, r)) \tag{4.47}$$

$$= T_W(L^{\ll}_{(\alpha_1, \beta_1)}(p, \min(q_1, \max(q_0, r + \alpha_2))), L^{\preceq}_{(\alpha_2, \beta_2)}(q_0, r))$$

$$\sup_{q \in [q_0, q_1]} T_W(L^{\preceq}_{(\alpha_1, \beta_1)}(p, q), L^{\ll}_{(\alpha_2, \beta_2)}(q, r)) \tag{4.48}$$

$$= T_W(L^{\preceq}_{(\alpha_1, \beta_1)}(p, \min(q_1, \max(q_0, r - \alpha_2 - \beta_2))), L^{\ll}_{(\alpha_2, \beta_2)}(q_0, r))$$

$$\sup_{q \in [q_0, q_1]} T_W(L^{\ll}_{(\alpha_1, \beta_1)}(p, q), L^{\ll}_{(\alpha_2, \beta_2)}(q, r)) \tag{4.49}$$

$$= T_W(L^{\ll}_{(\alpha_1, \beta_1)}(p, \min(q_1, \max(q_0, r - \alpha_2 - \beta_2))), L^{\ll}_{(\alpha_2, \beta_2)}(q_0, r))$$

Proof. (4.44)–(4.49) follow staightforwardly from (4.42) and (4.43) using (4.9). $\square$

Recall that we need to evaluate expressions like

$$\sup_{p \in [a_0, a_1]} T_W(L^{\ll}_{(0, \Delta_a)}(a^-, p), \sup_{q \in [b_0, b_1]} T_W(L^{\ll}_{(\alpha, \beta)}(p, q), L^{\preceq}_{(0, \Delta_b)}(q, b^-))) \tag{4.50}$$

This can always be accomplished using the characterizations (4.42)–(4.49). First, we will illustrate this with an example.

Example 4.2. Let A and B be defined as in (4.36)–(4.37), where

$$
\begin{array}{llll}
a_0 = 5 & a_1 = 10 & b_0 = 15 & b_1 = 31 \\
\lambda_0^a = 0.2 & \lambda_1^a = 0.8 & \lambda_0^b = 0.9 & \lambda_1^b = 0.5
\end{array}
$$

We find

$$\Delta_a = \frac{10-5}{0.8-0.2} = \frac{25}{3}$$

$$\Delta_b = \frac{31-15}{0.9-0.5} = 40$$

$$a^- = 5 - 0.2\frac{25}{3} = \frac{10}{3}$$

$$b^- = 15 - (1-0.9)40 = 11$$

Furthermore, let $\alpha = 5$ and $\beta = 20$. We find using (4.44)

$$\sup_{q\in[15,31]} T_W(L^{\ll}_{(5,20)}(p,q), L^{\prec}_{(0,40)}(q,11))$$

$$= T_W(L^{\ll}_{(5,20)}(p,31), L^{\prec}_{(0,40)}(\min(31,\max(15,p+5+20)),11))$$

For $p \in [5,6[$, we find using (4.13)

$$T_W(L^{\ll}_{(5,20)}(p,31), L^{\prec}_{(0,40)}(\min(31,\max(15,p+5+20)),11))$$

$$= T_W(1, L^{\prec}_{(0,40)}(p+5+20,11))$$

$$= L^{\prec}_{(0,40)}(p+5+20,11)$$

$$= L^{\prec}_{(-25,40)}(p,11)$$

while for $p \in [6,10]$, we obtain $p + 5 + 20 \geq 31$; hence

$$T_W(L^{\ll}_{(5,20)}(p,31), L^{\prec}_{(0,40)}(\min(31,\max(15,p+5+20)),11))$$

$$= T_W(L^{\ll}_{(5,20)}(p,31), L^{\prec}_{(0,40)}(31,11))$$

$$= T_W(L^{\ll}_{(5,20)}(p,31), \frac{1}{2})$$

This yields, using (2.7), (4.44) and (4.46)

$$be^{\ll}_{(\alpha,\beta)}(A,B)$$

$$= \sup_{p\in[5,10]} T_W(L^{\ll}_{(0,\frac{25}{3})}(\frac{10}{3},p), \sup_{q\in[15,31]} T_W(L^{\ll}_{(5,20)}(p,q), L^{\prec}_{(0,40)}(q,11)))$$

$$= \max(\sup_{p\in[5,6[} T_W(L^{\ll}_{(0,\frac{25}{3})}(\frac{10}{3},p), L^{\prec}_{(-25,40)}(p,11)),$$

$$\sup_{p\in[6,10]} T_W(L^{\ll}_{(0,\frac{25}{3})}(\frac{10}{3},p), L^{\ll}_{(5,20)}(p,31), \frac{1}{2}))$$

$$= \max(\sup_{p\in[5,6[} T_W(L^{\ll}_{(0,\frac{25}{3})}(\frac{10}{3},p), L^{\prec}_{(-25,40)}(p,11)),$$

$$T_W(\frac{1}{2}, \sup_{p\in[6,10]} T_W(L^{\ll}_{(0,\frac{25}{3})}(\frac{10}{3},p), L^{\ll}_{(5,20)}(p,31))))$$

$$= \max(\lim_{\substack{\varepsilon \to 0 \\ >}} \sup_{p \in [5, 6-\varepsilon]} T_W(L^{\ll}_{(0,\frac{25}{3})}(\frac{10}{3}, p), L^{\preccurlyeq}_{(-25,40)}(p, 11)),$$

$$T_W(\frac{1}{2}, \sup_{p \in [6,10]} T_W(L^{\ll}_{(0,\frac{25}{3})}(\frac{10}{3}, p), L^{\ll}_{(5,20)}(p, 31))))$$

$$= \max(\lim_{\substack{\varepsilon \to 0 \\ >}} T_W(L^{\ll}_{(0,\frac{25}{3})}(\frac{10}{3}, 6 - \varepsilon),$$

$$L^{\preccurlyeq}_{(-25,40)}(\max(5, \min(6 - \varepsilon, \frac{10}{3} + \frac{25}{3})), 11)),$$

$$T_W(\frac{1}{2}, L^{\ll}_{(0,\frac{25}{3})}(\frac{10}{3}, 10), L^{\ll}_{(5,20)}(\max(6, \min(10, \frac{10}{3} + \frac{25}{3})), 31)))$$

As $L^{\ll}_{(0,\frac{25}{3})}$ and $L^{\preccurlyeq}_{(-25,40)}$ are continuous, we find

$$= \max(T_W(L^{\ll}_{(0,\frac{25}{3})}(\frac{10}{3}, 6), L^{\preccurlyeq}_{(-25,40)}(6, 11)),$$

$$T_W(\frac{1}{2}, L^{\ll}_{(0,\frac{25}{3})}(\frac{10}{3}, 10), L^{\ll}_{(5,20)}(10, 31)))$$

$$= \max(T_W(\frac{6 - \frac{10}{3}}{\frac{25}{3}}, \frac{11 - 6 - 25 + 40}{40}), T_W(\frac{1}{2}, \frac{10 - \frac{10}{3}}{\frac{25}{3}}, \frac{31 - 10 - 5}{20}))$$

$$= \max(T_W(\frac{8}{25}, \frac{1}{2}), T_W(\frac{1}{2}, \frac{4}{5}, \frac{4}{5}))$$

$$= \max(0, 0.1)$$

$$= 0.1$$

When applying (4.44) for the first time in the example above, we obtain an expression of the form $T_W(L^{\ll}_{(\alpha,\beta)}(p, b_1), L^{\preccurlyeq}_{(0,\Delta_b)}(\min(b_1, \max(b_0, p + \alpha + \beta)), b^-))$. The second application of (4.44) and the application of (4.46) in this example are made possible by the fact that either $L^{\ll}_{(\alpha,\beta)}(p, b_1)$ or $L^{\preccurlyeq}_{(0,\Delta_b)}(\min(b_1, \max(b_0, p + \alpha + \beta)), b^-)$ is constant. Indeed, either $b_1 - p > \alpha + \beta$, implying $L^{\ll}_{(\alpha,\beta)}(p, b_1) = 1$, or $b_1 - p \leq \alpha + \beta$, implying $\min(b_1, \max(b_0, p + \alpha + \beta)) = b_1$. Therefore, we have that the value of $be^{\ll}_{(\alpha_1,\beta_1)}(A, B)$ or $be^{\preccurlyeq}_{(\alpha_2,\beta_2)}(A, B)$ can always be found by repeatedly applying Corollary 4.1, provided $\beta_1 > 0$, $\beta_2 > 0$, $\lambda^a_0 < \lambda^a_1$ and $\lambda^b_0 > \lambda^b_1$. The following two lemmas reveal that similar characterizations can be used when $\beta_1 = 0$ or $\beta_2 = 0$.

Lemma 4.8. *Let* $\alpha_1, \alpha_2 \in \mathbb{R}$. *If* $\beta_2 > 0$, *it holds that*

$$\sup_{q \in [q_0, q_1]} T_W(L^{\lll}_{(\alpha_1, 0)}(p, q), L^{\prec}_{(\alpha_2, \beta_2)}(q, r))$$

$$= T_W(L^{\lll}_{(\alpha_1, 0)}(p, q_1), L^{\prec}_{(\alpha_2, \beta_2)}(\min(q_1, \max(q_0, p + \alpha_1)), r)) \quad (4.51)$$

$$\sup_{q \in [q_0, q_1]} T_W(L^{\prec}_{(\alpha_1, 0)}(p, q), L^{\lll}_{(\alpha_2, \beta_2)}(q, r))$$

$$= T_W(L^{\prec}_{(\alpha_1, 0)}(p, q_1), L^{\lll}_{(\alpha_2, \beta_2)}(\min(q_1, \max(q_0, p - \alpha_1)), r)) \quad (4.52)$$

$$\sup_{q \in [q_0, q_1]} T_W(L^{\lll}_{(\alpha_1, 0)}(p, q), L^{\lll}_{(\alpha_2, \beta_2)}(q, r))$$

$$= T_W(L^{\lll}_{(\alpha_1, 0)}(p, q_1), L^{\lll}_{(\alpha_2, \beta_2)}(\min(q_1, \max(q_0, p + \alpha_1)), r)) \quad (4.53)$$

If $\beta_1 > 0$, *it holds that*

$$\sup_{q \in [q_0, q_1]} T_W(L^{\lll}_{(\alpha_1, \beta_1)}(p, q), L^{\prec}_{(\alpha_2, 0)}(q, r))$$

$$= T_W(L^{\lll}_{(\alpha_1, \beta_1)}(p, \min(q_1, \max(q_0, r + \alpha_2))), L^{\prec}_{(\alpha_2, 0)}(q_0, r)) \quad (4.54)$$

$$\sup_{q \in [q_0, q_1]} T_W(L^{\prec}_{(\alpha_1, \beta_1)}(p, q), L^{\lll}_{(\alpha_2, 0)}(q, r))$$

$$= T_W(L^{\prec}_{(\alpha_1, \beta_1)}(p, \min(q_1, \max(q_0, r - \alpha_2))), L^{\lll}_{(\alpha_2, 0)}(q_0, r)) \quad (4.55)$$

$$\sup_{q \in [q_0, q_1]} T_W(L^{\lll}_{(\alpha_1, \beta_1)}(p, q), L^{\lll}_{(\alpha_2, 0)}(q, r))$$

$$= T_W(L^{\lll}_{(\alpha_1, \beta_1)}(p, \min(q_1, \max(q_0, r - \alpha_2))), L^{\lll}_{(\alpha_2, 0)}(q_0, r)) \quad (4.56)$$

Proof. First we show (4.51). It holds that $L^{\lll}_{(\alpha_1, 0)}(p, q) = 1$ if $q > p + \alpha_1$ and $L^{\lll}_{(\alpha_1, 0)}(p, q) = 0$ otherwise. As the first partial mapping of $L^{\prec}_{(\alpha_2, \beta_2)}$ is decreasing, the supremum in (4.51) is attained for the lowest value in $[q_0, q_1]$ which is still (strictly) greater than $p + \alpha_1$ (if any). Hence, we find

$$\sup_{q \in [q_0, q_1]} T_W(L^{\lll}_{(\alpha_1, 0)}(p, q), L^{\prec}_{(\alpha_2, \beta_2)}(q, r))$$

$$= \sup_{\varepsilon > 0} T_W(L^{\lll}_{(\alpha_1, 0)}(p, \min(q_1, \max(q_0, p + \alpha_1 + \varepsilon))),$$

$$L^{\prec}_{(\alpha_2, \beta_2)}(\min(q_1, \max(q_0, p + \alpha_1 + \varepsilon)), r))$$

$$= \sup_{\varepsilon > 0} T_W(\min(L^{\lll}_{(\alpha_1, 0)}(p, q_1), L^{\lll}_{(\alpha_1, 0)}(p, \max(q_0, p + \alpha_1 + \varepsilon))),$$

$$L^{\prec}_{(\alpha_2, \beta_2)}(\min(q_1, \max(q_0, p + \alpha_1 + \varepsilon)), r))$$

It holds that $L^{\lll}_{(\alpha_1, 0)}(p, \max(q_0, p + \alpha_1 + \varepsilon)) \geq L^{\lll}_{(\alpha_1, 0)}(p, p + \alpha_1 + \varepsilon) = 1$ for every $\varepsilon > 0$. We thus obtain

$$= \sup_{\varepsilon > 0} T_W(L^{\lll}_{(\alpha_1, 0)}(p, q_1), L^{\prec}_{(\alpha_2, \beta_2)}(\min(q_1, \max(q_0, p + \alpha_1 + \varepsilon)), r)) \quad (4.57)$$

Since $\beta_2 > 0$, the partial mappings of $L^{\preccurlyeq}_{(\alpha_2,\beta_2)}$ are continuous; hence, the latter expression equals the right–hand side of (4.51).

To show (4.52), we proceed in a similar way. The supremum is attained for the lowest value in $[q_0, q_1]$ which is still greater than or equal to $p - \alpha_1$ (if any):

$$\sup_{q \in [q_0, q_1]} T_W(L^{\preccurlyeq}_{(\alpha_1,0)}(p,q), L^{\lll}_{(\alpha_2,\beta_2)}(q,r))$$

$$= T_W(L^{\preccurlyeq}_{(\alpha_1,0)}(p, \min(q_1, \max(q_0, p - \alpha_1))),$$
$$L^{\lll}_{(\alpha_2,\beta_2)}(\min(q_1, \max(q_0, p - \alpha_1)), r))$$

Since $L^{\preccurlyeq}_{(\alpha_1,0)}(p, \max(q_0, p - \alpha_1)) \geq L^{\preccurlyeq}_{(\alpha_1,0)}(p, p - \alpha_1) = 1$, the latter expression is equal to the right–hand side of (4.52).

Next, (4.53) follows immediately from (4.51) using the fact that $L^{\lll}_{(\alpha_2,\beta_2)} = L^{\preccurlyeq}_{(-\alpha_2-\beta_2,\beta_2)}$. Finally, the proof of (4.54)–(4.56) is entirely analogous.   □

Lemma 4.9. *Let* $\alpha_1, \alpha_2 \in \mathbb{R}$. *It holds that*

$$\sup_{q \in [q_0, q_1]} T_W(L^{\lll}_{(\alpha_1,0)}(p,q), L^{\preccurlyeq}_{(\alpha_2,0)}(q,r))$$

$$= \begin{cases} 1 & \text{if } q_1 > p + \alpha_1, \ q_0 \leq r + \alpha_2 \text{ and } r > p + \alpha_1 - \alpha_2 \\ 0 & \text{otherwise} \end{cases}$$

(4.58)

$$\sup_{q \in [q_0, q_1]} T_W(L^{\preccurlyeq}_{(\alpha_1,0)}(p,q), L^{\lll}_{(\alpha_2,0)}(q,r))$$

$$= \begin{cases} 1 & \text{if } q_1 \geq p - \alpha_1, \ q_0 < r - \alpha_2 \text{ and } r > p - \alpha_1 + \alpha_2 \\ 0 & \text{otherwise} \end{cases}$$

(4.59)

$$\sup_{q \in [q_0, q_1]} T_W(L^{\lll}_{(\alpha_1,0)}(p,q), L^{\lll}_{(\alpha_2,0)}(q,r))$$

$$= \begin{cases} 1 & \text{if } q_1 > p + \alpha_1, \ q_0 < r - \alpha_2 \text{ and } r > p + \alpha_1 + \alpha_2 \\ 0 & \text{otherwise} \end{cases}$$

(4.60)

Proof.   As an example, we show (4.58). The left–hand side of (4.58) is 1 iff there exists a q such that

$$q \in [q_0, q_1] \text{ and } L^{\lll}_{(\alpha,0)}(p,q) = 1 \text{ and } L^{\preccurlyeq}_{(\alpha_2,0)}(q,r) = 1$$

or

$$q_0 \leq q \leq q_1 \text{ and } p + \alpha_1 < q \text{ and } q \leq r + \alpha_2$$

In other words, iff the intersection of $[q_0, q_1]$ and $]p + \alpha_1, r + \alpha_2]$ is not empty, which is the case exactly when

$$p + \alpha_1 < r + \alpha_2 \text{ and } q_0 \leq r + \alpha_2 \text{ and } q_1 > p + \alpha_1 \qquad \square$$

As described above, Lemma 4.7–4.9 and Corollary 4.1 can be used to find the value of $be_{(\alpha,\beta)}^{\ll}(A, B)$ and $be_{(\alpha,\beta)}^{\prec}(A, B)$ when $\lambda_0^a < \lambda_1^a$ and $\lambda_0^b > \lambda_1^b$, i.e., when A is an increasing and B is a decreasing linear fuzzy set. We now consider the case where $\lambda_0^a \geq \lambda_1^a$ or $\lambda_0^b \leq \lambda_1^b$. First, assume that both $\lambda_0^a \geq \lambda_1^a$ and $\lambda_0^b \leq \lambda_1^b$. It holds that

$$be_{(\alpha,\beta)}^{\prec}(A, B) = \sup_{p \in \mathbb{R}} T_W(A(p), \sup_{q \in \mathbb{R}} T_W(L_{(\alpha,\beta)}^{\prec}(p, q), B(q)))$$

$$= T_W(A(a_0), T_W(L_{(\alpha,\beta)}^{\prec}(a_0, b_1), B(b_1)))$$

since A is decreasing over $[a_0, a_1]$, B is increasing over $[b_0, b_1]$, and the first (resp. second) partial mappings of $L_{(\alpha,\beta)}^{\prec}$ are decreasing (resp. increasing). Similarly, if $\lambda_0^a \geq \lambda_1^a$ and $\lambda_0^b > \lambda_1^b$, we find

$$be_{(\alpha,\beta)}^{\prec}(A, B)$$

$$= \sup_{p \in \mathbb{R}} T_W(A(p), \sup_{q \in \mathbb{R}} T_W(L_{(\alpha,\beta)}^{\prec}(p, q), B(q)))$$

$$= T_W(A(a_0), \sup_{q \in [b_0, b_1]} T_W(L_{(\alpha,\beta)}^{\prec}(a_0, q), L_{(0,\Delta_b)}^{\prec}(q, b^-)))$$

The latter expression can be evaluated using Lemma 4.7. Finally, if $\lambda_0^a < \lambda_1^a$ and $\lambda_0^b \leq \lambda_1^b$, we find

$$be_{(\alpha,\beta)}^{\prec}(A, B)$$

$$= \sup_{p \in \mathbb{R}} T_W(A(p), \sup_{q \in \mathbb{R}} T_W(L_{(\alpha,\beta)}^{\prec}(p, q), B(q)))$$

$$= \sup_{p \in [a_0, a_1]} T_W(L_{(0,\Delta_a)}^{\ll}(a^-, p), T_W(L_{(\alpha,\beta)}^{\prec}(p, b_1), B(b_1)))$$

$$= T_W(\sup_{p \in [a_0, a_1]} T_W(L_{(0,\Delta_a)}^{\ll}(a^-, p), L_{(\alpha,\beta)}^{\prec}(p, b_1)), B(b_1))$$

which can be evaluated using Corollary 4.1 (if $\beta > 0$) or Lemma 4.8 (if $\beta = 0$). Finally, note that using (4.5)–(4.6), the values of $eb_{(\alpha,\beta)}^{\ll}(A, B)$ and $eb_{(\alpha,\beta)}^{\prec}(A, B)$ can be found by first evaluating, respectively, $be_{(\alpha,\beta)}^{\prec}(B, A)$ and $be_{(\alpha,\beta)}^{\ll}(B, A)$.

4.5.1.2 Evaluating $bb^{\lll}_{(\alpha,\beta)}$, $bb^{\prec}_{(\alpha,\beta)}$, $ee^{\lll}_{(\alpha,\beta)}$ and $ee^{\prec}_{(\alpha,\beta)}$

Next, we show how $bb^{\prec}_{(\alpha,\beta)}(A,B)$ can be evaluated. Let A and B be defined by (4.36) and (4.37). If $\lambda_0^a < \lambda_1^a$ and $\lambda_0^b < \lambda_1^b$, it holds that $A(p) = L^{\lll}_{(0,\Delta_a)}(a^-,p)$ for all $p \in [a_0, a_1]$ and $B(p) = L^{\lll}_{(0,\Delta_b)}(b^-,p)$ for all $p \in [b_0, b_1]$, where

$$\Delta_a = \frac{a_1 - a_0}{\lambda_1^a - \lambda_0^a} \quad \Delta_b = \frac{b_1 - b_0}{\lambda_1^b - \lambda_0^b} \quad a^- = a_0 - \Delta_a(\lambda_0^a) \quad b^- = b_0 - \Delta_b(\lambda_0^b)$$

We thereby find

$$bb^{\prec}_{(\alpha,\beta)}(A,B)$$
$$= \inf_{q \in \mathbb{R}} I_W(B(q), \sup_{p \in \mathbb{R}} T_W(A(p), L^{\prec}_{(\alpha,\beta)}(p,q)))$$
$$= \inf_{q \in [b_0,b_1]} I_W(L^{\lll}_{(0,\Delta_b)}(b^-,q), \sup_{p \in [a_0,a_1]} T_W(L^{\lll}_{(0,\Delta_a)}(a^-,p), L^{\prec}_{(\alpha,\beta)}(p,q)))$$

To find the value of $bb^{\prec}_{(\alpha,\beta)}(A,B)$, we will need the following lemma.

Lemma 4.10. *Let $\alpha \in \mathbb{R}$, $\beta \geq 0$, $p,q \in \mathbb{R}$ and $\lambda \in [0,1]$. It holds that*

$$T_W(\lambda, L^{\lll}_{(\alpha,\beta)}(p,q)) = \min(\lambda, L^{\lll}_{(\alpha+\beta(1-\lambda),\beta)}(p,q)) \qquad (4.61)$$

$$T_W(\lambda, L^{\prec}_{(\alpha,\beta)}(p,q)) = \min(\lambda, L^{\prec}_{(\alpha-\beta(1-\lambda),\beta)}(p,q)) \qquad (4.62)$$

Proof. For $\beta = 0$, (4.61) and (4.62) become trivial as both the left–hand side and right–hand side of (4.61) and (4.62) are either λ or 0. Therefore, assume $\beta > 0$. If $p \geq q - \alpha$, $L^{\lll}_{(\alpha+\beta(1-\lambda),\beta)}(p,q) \leq L^{\lll}_{(\alpha,\beta)}(p,q) = 0$, showing (4.61). If $p < q - \alpha$, we have $\frac{q-p-\alpha}{\beta} > 0$, hence

$$T_W(\lambda, L^{\lll}_{(\alpha,\beta)}(p,q)) = \max(0, \lambda + L^{\lll}_{(\alpha,\beta)}(p,q) - 1)$$
$$= \max(0, \lambda + \min(1, \frac{q-p-\alpha}{\beta}) - 1)$$
$$= \max(0, \min(\lambda, \lambda - 1 + \frac{q-p-\alpha}{\beta}))$$
$$= \max(0, \min(\lambda, \frac{q-p-\alpha-\beta(1-\lambda)}{\beta}))$$
$$= \max(0, \min(\lambda, \min(1, \frac{q-p-\alpha-\beta(1-\lambda)}{\beta})))$$
$$= \min(\lambda, \max(0, \min(1, \frac{q-p-\alpha-\beta(1-\lambda)}{\beta})))$$
$$= \min(\lambda, L^{\lll}_{(\alpha+\beta(1-\lambda),\beta)}(p,q))$$

Using the assumption that $\beta > 0$, (4.62) follows easily from (4.61) by (4.9):

$$T_W(\lambda, L^{\preceq}_{(\alpha,\beta)}(p,q)) = T_W(\lambda, L^{\lll}_{(-\alpha-\beta,\beta)}(p,q))$$
$$= \min(\lambda, L^{\lll}_{(-\alpha-\beta+\beta(1-\lambda),\beta)}(p,q))$$
$$= \min(\lambda, L^{\lll}_{(-\alpha-\lambda\beta,\beta)}(p,q))$$
$$= \min(\lambda, L^{\preceq}_{(\alpha-\beta(1-\lambda),\beta)}(p,q))$$

□

Example 4.3. Let A and B be defined as in (4.36)–(4.37), where

$$a_0 = 15 \qquad a_1 = 25 \qquad b_0 = 5 \qquad b_1 = 10$$
$$\lambda_0^a = 0.3 \qquad \lambda_1^a = 0.8 \qquad \lambda_0^b = 0.4 \qquad \lambda_1^b = 0.6$$

We find

$$\Delta_a = \frac{25 - 15}{0.8 - 0.3} = 20$$
$$\Delta_b = \frac{10 - 5}{0.6 - 0.4} = 25$$
$$a^- = 15 - 0.3 \cdot 20 = 9$$
$$b^- = 5 - 0.4 \cdot 25 = -5$$

Furthermore, let $\alpha = 5$ and $\beta = 10$. We find using (4.47)

$$\sup_{p \in \mathbb{R}} T_W(A(p), L^{\preceq}_{(5,10)}(p,q))$$
$$= \sup_{p \in [15,25]} T_W(L^{\lll}_{(0,20)}(9,p), L^{\preceq}_{(5,10)}(p,q))$$
$$= T_W(L^{\lll}_{(0,20)}(9, \min(25, \max(15, q+5))), L^{\preceq}_{(5,10)}(15,q))$$

For $q \in [5,10]$, we find

$$= T_W(L^{\lll}_{(0,20)}(9,15), L^{\preceq}_{(5,10)}(15,q))$$
$$= T_W(\frac{15-9}{20}, L^{\preceq}_{(5,10)}(15,q))$$
$$= T_W(0.3, L^{\preceq}_{(5,10)}(15,q))$$

and using (4.62)

$$= \min(0.3, L^{\preceq}_{(5-10(1-0.3),10)}(15,q))$$
$$= \min(0.3, L^{\preceq}_{(-2,10)}(15,q))$$

We obtain

$$bb^{\preccurlyeq}_{(5,10)}(A,B)$$

$$= \inf_{q \in \mathbb{R}} I_W(B(q), \sup_{p \in \mathbb{R}} T_W(A(p), L^{\preccurlyeq}_{(5,10)}(p,q)))$$

$$= \inf_{q \in [5,10]} I_W(L^{\lll}_{(0,25)}(-5,q), \min(0.3, L^{\preccurlyeq}_{(-2,10)}(15,q)))$$

$$= \min(\inf_{q \in [5,10]} I_W(L^{\lll}_{(0,25)}(-5,q), 0.3),$$

$$\qquad \inf_{q \in [5,10]} I_W(L^{\lll}_{(0,25)}(-5,q), L^{\preccurlyeq}_{(-2,10)}(15,q)))$$

$$= \min(I_W(L^{\lll}_{(0,25)}(-5,10), 0.3), \inf_{q \in [5,10]} I_W(L^{\lll}_{(0,25)}(-5,q), L^{\preccurlyeq}_{(-2,10)}(15,q)))$$

$$= \min(I_W(\frac{15}{25}, 0.3), \inf_{q \in [5,10]} I_W(L^{\lll}_{(0,25)}(-5,q), L^{\preccurlyeq}_{(-2,10)}(15,q)))$$

$$= \min(0.7, \inf_{q \in [5,10]} I_W(L^{\lll}_{(0,25)}(-5,q), L^{\preccurlyeq}_{(-2,10)}(15,q)))$$

Using (2.35), (4.7) and (4.49), we find

$$= \min(0.7, 1 - \sup_{q \in [5,10]} T_W(L^{\lll}_{(0,25)}(-5,q), 1 - L^{\preccurlyeq}_{(-2,10)}(15,q)))$$

$$= \min(0.7, 1 - \sup_{q \in [5,10]} T_W(L^{\lll}_{(0,25)}(-5,q), L^{\lll}_{(-2,10)}(q,15)))$$

$$= \min(0.7, 1 - T_W(L^{\lll}_{(0,25)}(-5, \min(10, \max(5, 15+2-10))),$$

$$\qquad\qquad L^{\lll}_{(-2,10)}(5,15)))$$

$$= \min(0.7, 1 - T_W(L^{\lll}_{(0,25)}(-5,7), L^{\lll}_{(-2,10)}(5,15)))$$

$$= \min(0.7, 1 - T_W(\frac{12}{25}, 1))$$

$$= \min(0.7, \frac{13}{25})$$

$$= \min(0.7, 0.52)$$

$$= 0.52$$

Note how Lemma 4.10 is used in this example to make a second application of Lemma 4.7 possible, whereas this was not necessary in example 4.2 due to the use of (2.7). If $\lambda^a_0 \geq \lambda^a_1$ or $\lambda^b_0 \geq \lambda^b_1$, we can proceed in a similar way.

Specifically, if both $\lambda_0^a \geq \lambda_1^a$ and $\lambda_0^b \geq \lambda_1^b$, we have

$$bb_{(\alpha,\beta)}^{\prec}(A,B) = \inf_{q\in\mathbb{R}} I_W(B(q), \sup_{p\in\mathbb{R}} T_W(A(p), L_{(\alpha,\beta)}^{\prec}(p,q)))$$

$$= I_W(B(b_0), T_W(A(a_0), L_{(\alpha,\beta)}^{\prec}(a_0,b_0)))$$

If $\lambda_0^a \geq \lambda_1^a$ and $\lambda_0^b < \lambda_1^b$, we have

$$bb_{(\alpha,\beta)}^{\prec}(A,B)$$

$$= \inf_{q\in\mathbb{R}} I_W(B(q), \sup_{p\in\mathbb{R}} T_W(A(p), L_{(\alpha,\beta)}^{\prec}(p,q)))$$

$$= \inf_{q\in[b_0,b_1]} I_W(L_{(0,\Delta_b)}^{\ll}(b^-,q), T_W(\lambda_0^a, L_{(\alpha,\beta)}^{\prec}(a_0,q)))$$

$$= \inf_{q\in[b_0,b_1]} I_W(L_{(0,\Delta_b)}^{\ll}(b^-,q), \min(\lambda_0^a, L_{(\alpha-\beta(1-\lambda_0^a),\beta)}^{\prec}(a_0,q)))$$

$$= \min(\inf_{q\in[b_0,b_1]} I_W(L_{(0,\Delta_b)}^{\ll}(b^-,q), \lambda_0^a),$$

$$\inf_{q\in[b_0,b_1]} I_W(L_{(0,\Delta_b)}^{\ll}(b^-,q), L_{(\alpha-\beta(1-\lambda_0^a),\beta)}^{\prec}(a_0,q)))$$

$$= \min(I_W(L_{(0,\Delta_b)}^{\ll}(b^-,b_1), \lambda_0^a),$$

$$1 - \sup_{q\in[b_0,b_1]} T_W(L_{(0,\Delta_b)}^{\ll}(b^-,q), L_{(\alpha-\beta(1-\lambda_0^a),\beta)}^{\ll}(q,a_0)))$$

The last expression can be evaluated using Corollary 4.1 (if $\beta > 0$) or Lemma 4.8 (if $\beta = 0$). Finally, if $\lambda_0^a < \lambda_1^a$ and $\lambda_0^b \geq \lambda_1^b$, we have

$$bb_{(\alpha,\beta)}^{\prec}(A,B) = \inf_{q\in\mathbb{R}} I_W(B(q), \sup_{p\in\mathbb{R}} T_W(A(p), L_{(\alpha,\beta)}^{\prec}(p,q)))$$

$$= I_W(B(b_0), \sup_{p\in\mathbb{R}} T_W(L_{(0,\Delta_a)}^{\ll}(a^-,p), L_{(\alpha,\beta)}^{\prec}(p,b_0)))$$

which can again be evaluated using Corollary 4.1 or Lemma 4.8. To evaluate $ee_{(\alpha,\beta)}^{\prec}(A,B)$, we can proceed in an entirely similar manner. Finally, using (4.3)–(4.4), the values of $bb_{(\alpha,\beta)}^{\ll}(A,B)$ and $ee_{(\alpha,\beta)}^{\ll}(A,B)$ can be found by first evaluating, respectively, $bb_{(\alpha,\beta)}^{\prec}(B,A)$ and $ee_{(\alpha,\beta)}^{\prec}(B,A)$.

4.5.2 Characterization for Piecewise Linear Fuzzy Time Intervals

We define a piecewise linear fuzzy time interval as a fuzzy time interval which can be written as the union of a finite number of linear fuzzy sets. The next proposition shows how the value of $eb_{(\alpha,\beta)}^{\ll}(A,B)$, $eb_{(\alpha,\beta)}^{\prec}(A,B)$,

$be^{\ll}_{(\alpha,\beta)}(A,B)$ and $be^{\preccurlyeq}_{(\alpha,\beta)}(A,B)$ can easily be found using the characterizations for linear fuzzy sets.

Proposition 4.6. *Let $A = \bigcup_{i=1}^{n} A_i$, $B = \bigcup_{j=1}^{m} B_j$, where A_i and B_j are linear fuzzy sets in $\mathbb{R}$ $(1 \le i \le n$ and $1 \le j \le m)$. It holds that*

$$eb^{\ll}_{(\alpha,\beta)}(A,B) = \min_{i=1}^{n} \min_{j=1}^{m} eb^{\ll}_{(\alpha,\beta)}(A_i,B_j) \tag{4.63}$$

$$eb^{\preccurlyeq}_{(\alpha,\beta)}(A,B) = \min_{i=1}^{n} \min_{j=1}^{m} eb^{\preccurlyeq}_{(\alpha,\beta)}(A_i,B_j) \tag{4.64}$$

$$be^{\ll}_{(\alpha,\beta)}(A,B) = \max_{i=1}^{n} \max_{j=1}^{m} be^{\ll}_{(\alpha,\beta)}(A_i,B_j) \tag{4.65}$$

$$be^{\preccurlyeq}_{(\alpha,\beta)}(A,B) = \max_{i=1}^{n} \max_{j=1}^{m} be^{\preccurlyeq}_{(\alpha,\beta)}(A_i,B_j) \tag{4.66}$$

Proof.   This proposition follows trivially from Proposition 3.6. $\square$

Unfortunately, a similar characterization for $bb^{\ll}_{(\alpha,\beta)}(A,B)$, $bb^{\preccurlyeq}_{(\alpha,\beta)}(A,B)$, $ee^{\ll}_{(\alpha,\beta)}(A,B)$, and $ee^{\preccurlyeq}_{(\alpha,\beta)}(A,B)$ cannot be found.   For example, $bb^{\preccurlyeq}_{(\alpha,\beta)}(A,B) = \min_{j=1}^{m} \max_{i=1}^{n} bb^{\preccurlyeq}_{(\alpha,\beta)}(A_i,B_j)$ does not hold in general due to the inequality in (3.57). However, it holds that

$$bb^{\preccurlyeq}_{(\alpha,\beta)}(A,B) = \inf_{q\in\mathbb{R}} I_W(B(q), \sup_{p\in\mathbb{R}} T_W(A(p), L^{\preccurlyeq}_{(\alpha,\beta)}(p,q)))$$

$$= \inf_{q\in\mathbb{R}} I_W(\max_{j=1}^{m} B_j(q), \sup_{p\in\mathbb{R}} T_W(\max_{i=1}^{n} A_i(p), L^{\preccurlyeq}_{(\alpha,\beta)}(p,q)))$$

$$= \inf_{q\in\mathbb{R}} \min_{j=1}^{m} I_W(B_j(q), \sup_{p\in\mathbb{R}} \max_{i=1}^{n} T_W(A_i(p), L^{\preccurlyeq}_{(\alpha,\beta)}(p,q)))$$

$$= \min_{j=1}^{m} \inf_{q\in\mathbb{R}} I_W(B_j(q), \max_{i=1}^{n} \sup_{p\in\mathbb{R}} T_W(A_i(p), L^{\preccurlyeq}_{(\alpha,\beta)}(p,q)))$$

Since A and B are fuzzy time intervals — and therefore convex — they consist of an increasing part, being the union of a number of increasing linear fuzzy sets, and a decreasing part, being the union of a number of decreasing linear fuzzy sets. In particular, let A^{inc}, B^{inc}, A^{dec} and B^{dec} be the increasing and decreasing parts of A and B; note that $A = A^{inc} \cup A^{dec}$ and $B = B^{inc} \cup B^{dec}$. Due to the convexity of A, we can assume that the greatest element m_a of $supp(A^{inc})$ is the same as the smallest element of $supp(A^{dec})$, and that, moreover, $A^{inc}(m_a) = A^{dec}(m_a) = 1$. Note that an arbitrary element from the core of A can be chosen as m_a. Similar considerations apply for B. As $L^{\preccurlyeq}_{(\alpha,\beta)}$ is decreasing in its first argument, it holds that

$$T_W(A(p), L^{\preccurlyeq}_{(\alpha,\beta)}(p,q)) \le T_W(A(m_a), L^{\preccurlyeq}_{(\alpha,\beta)}(m_a,q))$$

for every $p \geq m_a$. Hence

$$\sup_{p \in \mathbb{R}} T_W(A(p), L^{\preccurlyeq}_{(\alpha,\beta)}(p,q)) = \sup_{p \in \mathbb{R}} T_W(A^{inc}(p), L^{\preccurlyeq}_{(\alpha,\beta)}(p,q))$$

Similarly, we find that

$$\inf_{q \in \mathbb{R}} I_W(B(q), \sup_{p \in \mathbb{R}} T_W(A^{inc}(p), L^{\preccurlyeq}_{(\alpha,\beta)}(p,q)))$$

$$= \inf_{q \in \mathbb{R}} I_W(B^{inc}(q), \sup_{p \in \mathbb{R}} T_W(A^{inc}(p), L^{\preccurlyeq}_{(\alpha,\beta)}(p,q)))$$

In other words

$$bb^{\preccurlyeq}_{(\alpha,\beta)}(A,B) = bb^{\preccurlyeq}_{(\alpha,\beta)}(A^{inc}, B^{inc})$$

Therefore, we can assume without loss of generality that A and B are unions of increasing linear fuzzy sets only, i.e., $A = A^{inc}$ and $B = B^{inc}$.

Since both A_i and the partial mappings of $L^{\preccurlyeq}_{(\alpha,\beta)}$ are piecewise linear, the fuzzy set C defined for all q in $\mathbb{R}$ by

$$C(q) = \max_{i=1}^{n} \sup_{p \in \mathbb{R}} T_W(A_i(p), L^{\preccurlyeq}_{(\alpha,\beta)}(p,q)) \tag{4.67}$$

is a piecewise linear fuzzy set. Moreover, using the characterizations discussed in Section (4.5.1), we can obtain an explicit definition of this fuzzy set, which is needed to obtain the value of $bb^{\preccurlyeq}_{(\alpha,\beta)}(A,B)$.

Example 4.4. Let $A = A_1 \cup A_2 \cup A_3 \cup A_4$ and $B = B_1 \cup B_2 \cup B_3$ be defined as in Figure 4.8(a). A first observation is that

$$\max_{i=1}^{4} \sup_{p \in \mathbb{R}} T_W(A_i(p), L^{\preccurlyeq}_{(\alpha,\beta)}(p,q)) = \max_{i=1}^{2} \sup_{p \in \mathbb{R}} T_W(A_i(p), L^{\preccurlyeq}_{(\alpha,\beta)}(p,q))$$

since $(A_3 \cup A_4)(p) \leq A_2(80)$ for any p in $[80, 120]$. Let $\alpha = \beta = 20$ and

$$\Delta_{a_1} = \frac{50}{0.4} = 125$$

$$\Delta_{a_2} = \frac{10}{0.6} = \frac{50}{3}$$

$$a_1^- = 20$$

$$a_2^- = 70 - 0.4\frac{50}{3} = \frac{190}{3}$$

We obtain using (4.47)

$$\sup_{p \in \mathbb{R}} T_W(A_1(p), L^{\preccurlyeq}_{(20,20)}(p,q))$$

$$= \sup_{p \in [20,70]} T_W(L^{\ll}_{(0,125)}(20,p), L^{\preccurlyeq}_{(20,20)}(p,q))$$

$$= T_W(L^{\ll}_{(0,125)}(20, \min(70, \max(20, q+20))), L^{\preccurlyeq}_{(20,20)}(20,q))$$

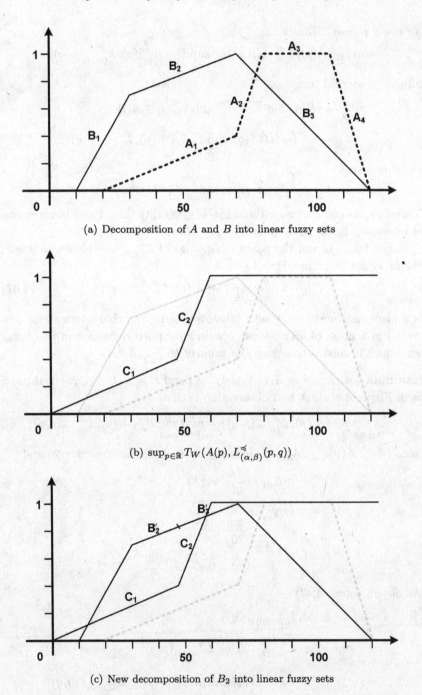

(a) Decomposition of A and B into linear fuzzy sets

(b) $\sup_{p \in \mathbb{R}} T_W(A(p), L^{\preccurlyeq}_{(\alpha,\beta)}(p,q))$

(c) New decomposition of B_2 into linear fuzzy sets

Fig. 4.8   Evaluation of $bb^{\preccurlyeq}_{(\alpha,\beta)}$ for piecewise linear fuzzy time intervals (©2008 IEEE).

For $q \leq 0$, we find

$$\sup_{p\in\mathbb{R}} T_W(A_1(p), L^{\preccurlyeq}_{(20,20)}(p,q)) \leq L^{\ll}_{(0,125)}(20,20) = 0$$

For $q \geq 50$, we have

$$\sup_{p\in\mathbb{R}} T_W(A_1(p), L^{\preccurlyeq}_{(20,20)}(p,q)) = L^{\ll}_{(0,125)}(20,70) = \frac{2}{5}$$

and for $q \in]0,50[$

$$\sup_{p\in\mathbb{R}} T_W(A_1(p), L^{\preccurlyeq}_{(20,20)}(p,q)) = L^{\ll}_{(0,125)}(20,q+20) = \frac{q}{125}$$

Turning now to A_2, we find using (4.44)

$$\sup_{p\in\mathbb{R}} T_W(A_2(p), L^{\preccurlyeq}_{(20,20)}(p,q))$$

$$= \sup_{p\in[70,80]} T_W(L^{\ll}_{(0,\frac{50}{3})}(\frac{190}{3},p), L^{\preccurlyeq}_{(20,20)}(p,q))$$

$$= T_W(L^{\ll}_{(0,\frac{50}{3})}(\frac{190}{3},80), L^{\preccurlyeq}_{(20,20)}(\min(80,\max(70,\frac{190}{3}+\frac{50}{3})),q))$$

$$= L^{\preccurlyeq}_{(20,20)}(80,q)$$

$$= \begin{cases} 0 & \text{if } q \leq 40 \\ 1 & \text{if } q \geq 60 \\ \frac{q-40}{20} & \text{otherwise} \end{cases}$$

Together, we obtain

$$C(q) = \max_{i=1}^{2} \sup_{p\in\mathbb{R}} T_W(A_i(p), L^{\preccurlyeq}_{(\alpha,\beta)}(p,q)) = \begin{cases} 0 & \text{if } q \leq 0 \\ \frac{q}{125} & \text{if } q \in]0,\frac{1000}{21}] \\ \frac{q-40}{20} & \text{if } q \in]\frac{1000}{21},60[\\ 1 & \text{if } q \geq 60 \end{cases}$$

where we used the fact that $\frac{q}{125} \geq \frac{q-40}{20}$ iff $q \leq \frac{40\cdot125}{125-20} = \frac{1000}{21}$. We let C_1 and C_2 denote the linear fuzzy sets defined for each q in $\mathbb{R}$ by

$$C_1(q) = \begin{cases} \frac{q}{125} & \text{if } q \in [0,\frac{1000}{21}] \\ 0 & \text{otherwise} \end{cases} \qquad C_2(q) = \begin{cases} \frac{q-40}{20} & \text{if } q \in [\frac{1000}{21},60] \\ 0 & \text{otherwise} \end{cases}$$

The linear fuzzy sets C_1 and C_2 are depicted in Figure 4.8(b). We can conclude that

$$bb^{\preccurlyeq}_{(20,20)}(A,B) = \min_{j=1}^{2} \inf_{q\in\mathbb{R}} I_W(B_j(q), \max_{k=1}^{2} C_k(q))$$

In general, we can evaluate $bb^{\preccurlyeq}_{(\alpha,\beta)}(A, B)$ by first identifying linear fuzzy sets C_k ($k \in \{1, 2, \dots, s\}$) such that

$$bb^{\preccurlyeq}_{(\alpha,\beta)}(A, B) = \min_{j=1}^{m} \inf_{q \in \mathbb{R}} I_W(B_j(q), \max_{k=1}^{s} C_k(q)) \qquad (4.68)$$

as illustrated in Example 4.4. An expression of the form $\inf_{q \in \mathbb{R}} I_W(B_j(q), C_k(q))$, for B_j and C_k linear fuzzy sets, can be evaluated using the characterizations from Section 4.5.1. We therefore attempt to transform the right-hand side of (4.68) in this direction. The following lemma allows to simplify the consequent of an implication while preserving its value.

Lemma 4.11. *Let A and B be fuzzy sets in $\mathbb{R}$, and let B' be the fuzzy set in $\mathbb{R}$ defined for every p in $\mathbb{R}$ by*

$$B'(p) = B \cap supp(A)$$

It holds that

$$I_W(A(p), B'(p)) = I_W(A(p), B(p)) \qquad (4.69)$$

Proof.   For $p \in \mathbb{R}$ we find

$$I_W(A(p), B'(p)) = I_W(A(p), \min(B(p), supp(A)(p)))$$
$$= \min(I_W(A(p), B(p)), I_W(A(p), supp(A)(p)))$$

Whenever $A(p) > 0$, it holds that $supp(A)(p) = 1$, hence we have $I_W(A(p), supp(A)(p)) = 1$ and

$$\min(I_W(A(p), B(p)), I_W(A(p), supp(A)(p))) = I_W(A(p), B(p)) \qquad \square$$

Applying Lemma 4.11 to $I_W(B_j(q), \max_{k=1}^{s} C_k(q))$ yields

$$I_W(B_j(q), (\bigcup_{k=1}^{s} C_k \cap supp(B_j))(q))$$

Since $\bigcup_{k=1}^{s} C_k$ is an increasing piecewise linear fuzzy set, we can assume without loss of generality that $supp(C_k) = [c_k, c_{k+1}]$ for k in $\{2, \dots, s\}$ and $supp(C_1) =]c_1, c_2]$ or $supp(C_1) = [c_1, c_2]$. Moreover, all C_k are increasing, i.e., $C_k(c_k) \leq C_k(c_{k+1}) \leq C_{k+1}(c_{k+1}) \leq C_{k+1}(c_{k+2})$ for k in $\{1, \dots, s-1\}$. Hence, for all q in $[c_{k_0}, c_{k_0+1}[$, we obtain $(\bigcup_{k=1}^{s} C_k)(q) = C_{k_0}(q)$ while $(\bigcup_{k=1}^{s} C_k)(c_{k_0+1}) = C_{k_0+1}(c_{k_0+1})$. For each j in $\{1, \dots, m\}$, we can furthermore assume that the support of B_j is of the form $[b_j^-, b_j^+]$ or $]b_j^-, b_j^+]$ such that for each k in $\{1, 2, \dots, s+1\}$, $c_k \notin]b_j^-, b_j^+[$. Indeed, if this were not the case for some k_0, we could decompose B_j into the linear fuzzy sets B_j^1 and B_j^2, defined by

$$B_j^1(q) = \begin{cases} B_j(q) & \text{if } q \leq c_{k_0} \\ 0 & \text{otherwise} \end{cases} \qquad B_j^2(q) = \begin{cases} B_j(q) & \text{if } q \geq c_{k_0} \\ 0 & \text{otherwise} \end{cases}$$

for every q in $\mathbb{R}$. This implies that for each j in $\{1, \ldots, m\}$ there exists a k_1 in $\{1, \ldots, s\}$ such that $supp(B_j) \subseteq [c_{k_1}, c_{k_1+1}]$. If $b_j^+ \neq c_{k_1+1}$ then $\max_{k=1}^s C_k(q) = C_{k_1}(q)$ for every q in $supp(B_j)$. From Lemma 4.11, we then know that

$$\inf_{q \in \mathbb{R}} I_W(B_j(q), \max_{k=1}^s C_k(q)) = \inf_{q \in \mathbb{R}} I_W(B_j(q), C_{k_1}(q))$$

The right-hand side of this equality can be evaluated using the characterizations from Section 4.5.1. On the other hand, if $b_j^+ = c_{k_1+1}$, we find $\max_{k=1}^s C_k(q) = C_{k_1}(q)$ for every q in $[b_j^-, b_j^+[$ and $\max_{k=1}^s C_k(b_j^+) = C_{k_1+1}(b_j^+) \geq C_{k_1}(b_j^+)$. We obtain

$$\inf_{q \in \mathbb{R}} I_W(B_j(q), \max_{k=1}^s C_k(q))$$

$$= \inf_{q \in [b_j^-, b_j^+]} I_W(B_j(q), (C_{k_1} \cup C_{k_1+1})(q))$$

$$= \min(\inf_{q \in [b_j^-, b_j^+[} I_W(B_j(q), C_{k_1}(q)), I_W(B_j(b_j^+), C_{k_1+1}(b_j^+)))$$

Since B_j and C_{k_1} are left-continuous in b_j^+, we find

$$= \min(\inf_{q \in [b_j^-, b_j^+]} I_W(B_j(q), C_{k_1}(q)), I_W(B_j(b_j^+), C_{k_1+1}(b_j^+)))$$

$$= \inf_{q \in [b_j^-, b_j^+]} I_W(B_j(q), C_{k_1}(q))$$

where the last equality follows from $C_{k+1}(b_j^+) \geq C_k(b_j^+)$. Again, the latter expression can be evaluated using the characterizations from Section 4.5.1.

Example 4.5. Let $A = A_1 \cup A_2 \cup A_3 \cup A_4$, $B = B_1 \cup B_2 \cup B_3$, C_1 and C_2 be defined as in Example 4.4. From Example 4.4, we already know that

$$bb_{(20,20)}^{\preceq}(A, B) = \min_{j=1}^2 \inf_{q \in \mathbb{R}} I_W(B_j(q), \max_{k=1}^2 C_k(q))$$

where $supp(C_1) =]0, \frac{1000}{21}]$, $supp(C_2) = [\frac{1000}{21}, 60]$, $supp(B_1) =]10, 30]$ and $supp(B_2) = [30, 70]$. Because $\frac{1000}{21} \in]30, 70[$, we need to decompose B_2 into the two linear fuzzy sets B_2' and B_3', defined for each q in $\mathbb{R}$ by

$$B_2'(q) = \begin{cases} B_2(q) & \text{if } q \leq \frac{1000}{21} \\ 0 & \text{otherwise} \end{cases} \qquad B_3'(q) = \begin{cases} B_2(q) & \text{if } q \geq \frac{1000}{21} \\ 0 & \text{otherwise} \end{cases}$$

Figure 4.8(c) illustrates the definition of B_2' and B_3'. We find

$$\Delta_{b_1} = \frac{20}{0.7} = \frac{200}{7}.$$

$$\Delta_{b_2} = \frac{40}{0.3} = \frac{400}{3}$$

$$\Delta_{c_1} = \frac{\frac{1000}{21}}{\frac{1000}{21}} = 125$$

$$\Delta_{c_2} = \frac{60 - \frac{1000}{21}}{1 - \frac{\frac{1000}{21} - 40}{20}} = \frac{\frac{260}{21}}{\frac{13}{21}} = 20$$

$$b_1^- = 10$$

$$b_2^- = 30 - 0.7 \cdot \frac{400}{3} = -\frac{190}{3}$$

$$c_1^- = 0$$

$$c_2^- = \frac{1000}{21} - 20\frac{\frac{1000}{21} - 40}{20} = 40$$

We obtain using (4.69), (2.35), (4.7) and (4.44)

$$\inf_{q \in \mathbb{R}} I_W(B_1(q), \max_{k=1}^{2} C_k(q))$$

$$= \inf_{q \in \mathbb{R}} I_W(B_1(q), C_1(q))$$

$$= \inf_{q \in [10,30]} I_W(L^{\lll}_{(0, \frac{200}{7})}(10, q), L^{\lll}_{(0,125)}(0, q))$$

$$= 1 - \sup_{q \in [10,30]} T_W(L^{\lll}_{(0, \frac{200}{7})}(10, q), L^{\preccurlyeq}_{(0,125)}(q, 0))$$

$$= 1 - T_W(L^{\lll}_{(0, \frac{200}{7})}(10, 30), L^{\preccurlyeq}_{(0,125)}(\min(30, \max(10, 10 + \frac{200}{7})), 0))$$

$$= 1 - T_W(L^{\lll}_{(0, \frac{200}{7})}(10, 30), L^{\preccurlyeq}_{(0,125)}(30, 0))$$

$$= 1 - T_W(\frac{20}{\frac{200}{7}}, \frac{125 - 30}{125})$$

$$= 1 - T_W(\frac{7}{10}, \frac{19}{25})$$

$$= \frac{27}{50}$$

and using (4.69), (2.35), (4.7) and (4.47)

$$\inf_{q \in \mathbb{R}} I_W(B_2'(q), \max_{k=1}^{2} C_k(q))$$

$$= \inf_{q \in \mathbb{R}} I_W(B_2'(q), C_1(q))$$

$$= \inf_{q \in [30, \frac{1000}{21}]} I_W(L^{\ll}_{(0, \frac{400}{3})}(-\frac{190}{3}, q), L^{\ll}_{(0,125)}(0, q))$$

$$= 1 - \sup_{q \in [30, \frac{1000}{21}]} T_W(L^{\ll}_{(0, \frac{400}{3})}(-\frac{190}{3}, q), L^{\preccurlyeq}_{(0,125)}(q, 0))$$

$$= 1 - T_W(L^{\ll}_{(0, \frac{400}{3})}(-\frac{190}{3}, \min(\frac{1000}{21}, \max(30, 0))), L^{\preccurlyeq}_{(0,125)}(30, 0))$$

$$= 1 - T_W(L^{\ll}_{(0, \frac{400}{3})}(-\frac{190}{3}, 30), L^{\preccurlyeq}_{(0,125)}(30, 0))$$

$$= 1 - T_W(\frac{\frac{280}{3}}{\frac{400}{3}}, \frac{125 - 30}{125})$$

$$= 1 - T_W(\frac{7}{10}, \frac{19}{25})$$

$$= \frac{27}{50}$$

and finally, again using (4.69), (2.35), (4.7) and (4.47)

$$\inf_{q \in \mathbb{R}} I_W(B'_3(q), \max_{k=1}^{2} C_k(q))$$

$$= \inf_{q \in \mathbb{R}} I_W(B'_3(q), C_2(q))$$

$$= \inf_{q \in [\frac{1000}{21}, 70]} I_W(L^{\ll}_{(0, \frac{400}{3})}(-\frac{190}{3}, q), L^{\ll}_{(0,20)}(40, q))$$

$$= 1 - \sup_{q \in [\frac{1000}{21}, 70]} T_W(L^{\ll}_{(0, \frac{400}{3})}(-\frac{190}{3}, q), L^{\preccurlyeq}_{(0,20)}(q, 40))$$

$$= 1 - T_W(L^{\ll}_{(0, \frac{400}{3})}(-\frac{190}{3}, \min(70, \max(\frac{1000}{21}, 40))), L^{\preccurlyeq}_{(0,20)}(\frac{1000}{21}, 40))$$

$$= 1 - T_W(L^{\ll}_{(0, \frac{400}{3})}(-\frac{190}{3}, \frac{1000}{21}), L^{\preccurlyeq}_{(0,20)}(\frac{1000}{21}, 40))$$

$$= 1 - T_W(\frac{\frac{2330}{21}}{\frac{400}{3}}, \frac{60 - \frac{1000}{21}}{20})$$

$$= 1 - T_W(\frac{233}{280}, \frac{13}{21})$$

$$= \frac{461}{840}$$

We conclude

$$bb^{\preccurlyeq}_{(20,20)}(A, B) = \min(bb^{\preccurlyeq}_{(20,20)}(A, B_1), bb^{\preccurlyeq}_{(20,20)}(A, B'_2), bb^{\preccurlyeq}_{(20,20)}(A, B'_3))$$

$$= \min(\frac{27}{50}, \frac{461}{840})$$

$$= \frac{27}{50}$$

In a similar fashion, we can evaluate expressions like $ee^{\prec}_{(\alpha,\beta)}(A,B)$. Finally, the values of $bb^{\ll}_{(\alpha,\beta)}(A,B)$ and $ee^{\ll}_{(\alpha,\beta)}(A,B)$ can be found by first evaluating $bb^{\prec}_{(\alpha,\beta)}(B,A)$ and $ee^{\prec}_{(\alpha,\beta)}(B,A)$, respectively, making use of (4.3) and (4.4).

4.5.3 *Alternative Characterizations for $\beta = 0$*

In many situations, we only need to deal with the case where $\beta = 0$ in $L^{\ll}_{(\alpha,\beta)}$ or $L^{\prec}_{(\alpha,\beta)}$, i.e., either temporal information is purely qualitative (and $\alpha = 0$) or the metric constraints are all well-defined. To simplify the discussion, we will therefore restrict ourselves to this special case in the next chapter. It is then possible to obtain a number of interesting characterizations, which are — although of some practical significance — mainly useful in theoretical discussions. The next lemma shows how fuzzy temporal relations can be characterized by crisp temporal relations on their α–level sets (recall that, for instance, $bb^{\ll}_d = bb^{\ll}_{(d,0)}$).

Lemma 4.12. *Let A and B be fuzzy time intervals, $l \in{]}0,1]$ and $k \in [0,1[$. It holds that*

$$bb^{\ll}_d(A,B) \geq l \Leftrightarrow (\forall \varepsilon \in{]}0,l])(\exists \lambda \in{]}l-\varepsilon,1])(bb^{\ll}_d(A_\lambda, B_{\lambda+\varepsilon-l})) \qquad (4.70)$$

$$bb^{\ll}_d(A,B) \leq k \Leftrightarrow (\forall \lambda \in{]}k,1])(bb^{\prec}_d(B_{\lambda-k}, A_\lambda)) \qquad (4.71)$$

$$ee^{\ll}_d(A,B) \geq l \Leftrightarrow (\forall \varepsilon \in{]}0,l])(\exists \lambda \in{]}l-\varepsilon,1])(ee^{\ll}_d(A_{\lambda+\varepsilon-l}, B_\lambda)) \qquad (4.72)$$

$$ee^{\ll}_d(A,B) \leq k \Leftrightarrow (\forall \lambda \in{]}k,1])(ee^{\prec}_d(B_\lambda, A_{\lambda-k})) \qquad (4.73)$$

$$be^{\ll}_d(A,B) \geq l \Leftrightarrow (\forall \varepsilon \in{]}0,l[)(\exists \lambda \in [l-\varepsilon,1])(be^{\ll}_d(A_\lambda, B_{1-\lambda-\varepsilon+l})) \qquad (4.74)$$

$$be^{\ll}_d(A,B) \leq k \Leftrightarrow (\forall \varepsilon \in{]}0,1-k[)(\forall \lambda \in [k+\varepsilon,1])(eb^{\prec}_d(B_{1-\lambda+\varepsilon+k}, A_\lambda)) \qquad (4.75)$$

$$eb^{\ll}_d(A,B) \geq l \Leftrightarrow (\forall \varepsilon \in{]}0,l])(\forall \lambda \in [1-l+\varepsilon,1])(eb^{\ll}_d(A_{1-\lambda+\varepsilon+1-l}, B_\lambda)) \qquad (4.76)$$

$$eb^{\ll}_d(A,B) \leq k \Leftrightarrow (\exists \lambda \in [1-k,1])(be^{\prec}_d(B_\lambda, A_{2-\lambda-k})) \qquad (4.77)$$

Proof. First we consider (4.70):

$$bb^{\ll}_d(A,B) \geq l$$

$$\Leftrightarrow \sup_{p\in\mathbb{R}} T_W(A(p), \inf_{q\in\mathbb{R}} I_W(B(q), L^{\ll}_d(p,q))) \geq l$$

$$\Leftrightarrow (\forall \varepsilon \in{]}0,l])(\sup_{p\in\mathbb{R}} T_W(A(p), \inf_{q\in\mathbb{R}} I_W(B(q), L^{\ll}_d(p,q))) > l-\varepsilon)$$

$$\Leftrightarrow (\forall \varepsilon \in]0,l])(\exists p \in \mathbb{R})(T_W(A(p), \inf_{q \in \mathbb{R}} I_W(B(q), L_d^{\ll}(p,q)))) > l - \varepsilon)$$

If $A(p) = 0$, it holds that $T(A(p), \inf_{q \in \mathbb{R}} I_T(B(q), L_d^{\ll}(p,q))) = 0$. Therefore, we can assume that $A(p) > 0$. Hence, there must exist a λ in $]0,1]$ such that $\lambda = A(p)$ and thus $p \in A_\lambda$:

$$\Leftrightarrow (\forall \varepsilon \in]0,l])(\exists \lambda \in]0,1])(\exists p \in A_\lambda)(T_W(\lambda, \inf_{q \in \mathbb{R}} I_W(B(q), L_d^{\ll}(p,q)))) > l - \varepsilon)$$

$$\Leftrightarrow (\forall \varepsilon \in]0,l])(\exists \lambda \in]0,1])(\exists p \in A_\lambda)(\lambda + \inf_{q \in \mathbb{R}} I_W(B(q), L_d^{\ll}(p,q)) - 1 > l - \varepsilon)$$

$$\Leftrightarrow (\forall \varepsilon \in]0,l])(\exists \lambda \in]0,1])(\exists p \in A_\lambda)(\inf_{q \in \mathbb{R}} I_W(B(q), L_d^{\ll}(p,q)) > l + 1 - \lambda - \varepsilon)$$

As any fuzzy time interval is upper semi–continuous, the mapping defined by $1 - B(q)$ for each q in $\mathbb{R}$ is lower semi–continuous. Moreover, as $L_d^{\ll}(p,q)$ is lower semi–continuous, the mapping defined by $I_W(B(q), L_d^{\ll}(p,q))$ for each q in $\mathbb{R}$ is lower semi–continuous as well. Hence, the infimum $\inf_{q \in \mathbb{R}} I_W(B(q), L_d^{\ll}(p,q))$ is attained for some q in $\mathbb{R}$. We therefore find

$$\Leftrightarrow (\forall \varepsilon \in]0,l])(\exists \lambda \in]0,1])(\exists p \in A_\lambda)(\forall q \in \mathbb{R})$$
$$(I_W(B(q), L_d^{\ll}(p,q)) > l + 1 - \lambda - \varepsilon)$$

For $\lambda \leq l - \varepsilon$, $I_W(B(q), L_d^{\ll}(p,q)) > l + 1 - \lambda - \varepsilon$ can never be satisfied, hence

$$\Leftrightarrow (\forall \varepsilon \in]0,l])(\exists \lambda \in]l - \varepsilon, 1])(\exists p \in A_\lambda)(\forall q \in \mathbb{R})$$
$$(I_W(B(q), L_d^{\ll}(p,q)) > l + 1 - \lambda - \varepsilon)$$

If $L_d^{\ll}(p,q) = 1$, then $I_W(B(q), L_d^{\ll}(p,q)) = 1$, while $I_W(B(q), L_d^{\ll}(p,q)) = 1 - B(q)$ if $L_d^{\ll}(p,q) = 0$. We thereby obtain

$$\Leftrightarrow (\forall \varepsilon \in]0,l])(\exists \lambda \in]l - \varepsilon, 1])(\exists p \in A_\lambda)(\forall q \in \mathbb{R})$$
$$(L_d^{\ll}(p,q) = 1 \vee 1 - B(q) > l + 1 - \lambda - \varepsilon)$$

$$\Leftrightarrow (\forall \varepsilon \in]0,l])(\exists \lambda \in]l - \varepsilon, 1])(\exists p \in A_\lambda)(\forall q \in \mathbb{R})$$
$$(L_d^{\ll}(p,q) = 1 \vee \neg(B(q) \geq \lambda + \varepsilon - l))$$

$$\Leftrightarrow (\forall \varepsilon \in]0,l])(\exists \lambda \in]l - \varepsilon, 1])(\exists p \in A_\lambda)(\forall q \in \mathbb{R})$$
$$(L_d^{\ll}(p,q) = 1 \vee \neg(q \in B_{\lambda + \varepsilon - l}))$$

$$\Leftrightarrow (\forall \varepsilon \in]0,l])(\exists \lambda \in]l - \varepsilon, 1])(\exists p \in A_\lambda)(\forall q \in \mathbb{R})$$
$$(q \in B_{\lambda + \varepsilon - l} \Rightarrow L_d^{\ll}(p,q) = 1)$$

$$\Leftrightarrow (\forall \varepsilon \in]0,l])(\exists \lambda \in]l - \varepsilon, 1])(bb_d^{\ll}(A_\lambda, B_{\lambda + \varepsilon - l}))$$

proving (4.70).

Turning now to (4.71), we find

$$bb_d^{\lll}(A, B) \leq k$$

$$\Leftrightarrow \sup_{p \in \mathbb{R}} T_W(A(p), \inf_{q \in \mathbb{R}} I_W(B(q), L_d^{\lll}(p, q))) \leq k$$

$$\Leftrightarrow (\forall p \in \mathbb{R})(T_W(A(p), \inf_{q \in \mathbb{R}} I_W(B(q), L_d^{\lll}(p, q))) \leq k) \qquad (4.78)$$

If $A(p) = 0$, then $T_W(A(p), \inf_{q \in \mathbb{R}} I_W(B(q), L_d^{\lll}(p, q))) \leq k$ is satisfied. Consequently, it is sufficient to show that for every p satisfying $A(p) > 0$, it holds that

$$T_W(A(p), \inf_{q \in \mathbb{R}} I_W(B(q), L_d^{\lll}(p, q))) \leq k \qquad (4.79)$$

or equivalently, to show that (4.79) holds for every $\lambda \in]0, 1]$ and every p in A_λ:

$$\Leftrightarrow (\forall \lambda \in]0, 1])(\forall p \in A_\lambda)(T_W(A(p), \inf_{q \in \mathbb{R}} I_W(B(q), L_d^{\lll}(p, q))) \leq k) \quad (4.80)$$

which implies

$$(\forall \lambda \in]0, 1])(\forall p \in A_\lambda)(T_W(\lambda, \inf_{q \in \mathbb{R}} I_W(B(q), L_d^{\lll}(p, q))) \leq k) \qquad (4.81)$$

since $p \in A_\lambda$ means that $A(p) \geq \lambda$. Conversely, we also have that (4.81) implies (4.80). Indeed, if (4.80) is violated, i.e., $T_W(A(p_0), \inf_{q \in \mathbb{R}} I_W(B(q), L_d^{\lll}(p_0, q))) > k$ for some $\lambda_0 \in]0, 1]$ and some $p_0 \in A_{\lambda_0}$, then (4.81) is violated for $\lambda = A(p_0)$ and $p = p_0$. We conclude that (4.78) is equivalent to (4.81). We furthermore obtain

$$(\forall \lambda \in]0, 1])(\forall p \in A_\lambda)(T_W(\lambda, \inf_{q \in \mathbb{R}} I_W(B(q), L_d^{\lll}(p, q))) \leq k)$$

$$\Leftrightarrow (\forall \lambda \in]0, 1])(\forall p \in A_\lambda)(\lambda + \inf_{q \in \mathbb{R}} I_W(B(q), L_d^{\lll}(p, q)) - 1 \leq k)$$

$$\Leftrightarrow (\forall \lambda \in]0, 1])(\forall p \in A_\lambda)(\inf_{q \in \mathbb{R}} I_W(B(q), L_d^{\lll}(p, q)) \leq 1 - \lambda + k)$$

If $\lambda \leq k$, then $I_W(B(q), L_d^{\lll}(p, q)) \leq 1 - \lambda + k$ is satisfied. Therefore, we have

$$\Leftrightarrow (\forall \lambda \in]k, 1])(\forall p \in A_\lambda)(\inf_{q \in \mathbb{R}} I_W(B(q), L_d^{\lll}(p, q)) \leq 1 - \lambda + k)$$

$$\Leftrightarrow (\forall \lambda \in]k, 1])(\forall p \in A_\lambda)(\exists q \in \mathbb{R})(I_W(B(q), L_d^{\lll}(p, q)) \leq 1 - \lambda + k)$$

$$\Leftrightarrow (\forall \lambda \in]k, 1])(\forall p \in A_\lambda)(\exists q \in \mathbb{R})(L_d^{\lll}(p, q) = 0 \wedge B(q) \geq \lambda - k)$$

$$\Leftrightarrow (\forall \lambda \in]k, 1])(\forall p \in A_\lambda)(\exists q \in \mathbb{R})(L_d^{\lll}(p, q) = 0 \wedge q \in B_{\lambda-k})$$

$$\Leftrightarrow (\forall \lambda \in]k, 1])(\forall p \in A_\lambda)(\exists q \in B_{\lambda-k})(L_d^{\lll}(p, q) = 0)$$

$$\Leftrightarrow (\forall \lambda \in]k, 1])(\forall p \in A_\lambda)(\exists q \in B_{\lambda-k})(\neg(L_d^{\lll}(p, q) = 1))$$

$$\Leftrightarrow (\forall \lambda \in]k, 1])(\neg(\exists p \in A_\lambda)(\forall q \in B_{\lambda-k})(L_d^{\lll}(p, q) = 1))$$

$$\Leftrightarrow (\forall \lambda \in]k, 1])(\neg bb_d^{\lll}(A_\lambda, B_{\lambda-k}))$$

$$\Leftrightarrow (\forall \lambda \in]k, 1])(bb_d^{\lessgtr}(B_{\lambda-k}, A_\lambda))$$

which proves (4.71). The characterizations (4.72)–(4.77) can be shown in the same way as (4.70) or (4.71). □

If the fuzzy time intervals A and B only take a finite number of different membership degrees, only a finite number of α–level sets needs to be considered. This observation is used in the following proposition, where a technique is identified to assess whether, e.g., $bb_d^{\lll}(A, B) \leq k$ holds.

Proposition 4.7. *Let A and B be fuzzy time intervals that only take membership degrees from a set $M = \{0, \Delta, 2\Delta, \ldots, 1\}$, $\Delta \in]0, 1[$, $k \in M \setminus \{1\}$ and $l \in M \setminus \{0\}$. It holds that:*

$$bb_d^{\lll}(A, B) \geq l \tag{4.82}$$
$$\Leftrightarrow A_l^- < B_\Delta^- - d \vee A_{l+\Delta}^- < B_{2\Delta}^- - d \vee \cdots \vee A_1^- < B_{1-l+\Delta}^- - d$$

$$bb_d^{\lll}(A, B) \leq k \tag{4.83}$$
$$\Leftrightarrow B_\Delta^- \leq A_{k+\Delta}^- + d \wedge B_{2\Delta}^- \leq A_{k+2\Delta}^- + d \wedge \cdots \wedge B_{1-k}^- \leq A_1^- + d$$

$$ee_d^{\lll}(A, B) \geq l \tag{4.84}$$
$$\Leftrightarrow A_\Delta^+ < B_l^+ - d \vee A_{2\Delta}^+ < B_{l+\Delta}^+ - d \vee \cdots \vee A_{1-l+\Delta}^+ < B_1^+ - d$$

$$ee_d^{\lll}(A, B) \leq k \tag{4.85}$$
$$\Leftrightarrow B_{k+\Delta}^+ \leq A_\Delta^+ + d \wedge B_{k+2\Delta}^+ \leq A_{2\Delta}^+ + d \wedge \cdots \wedge B_1^+ \leq A_{1-k}^+ + d$$

$$be_d^{\lll}(A, B) \geq l \tag{4.86}$$
$$\Leftrightarrow A_l^- < B_1^+ - d \vee A_{l+\Delta}^- < B_{1-\Delta}^+ - d \vee \cdots \vee A_1^- < B_l^+ - d$$

$$be_d^{\lll}(A, B) \leq k \tag{4.87}$$
$$\Leftrightarrow B_1^+ \leq A_{k+\Delta}^- + d \wedge B_{1-\Delta}^+ \leq A_{k+2\Delta}^- + d \wedge \cdots \wedge B_{k+\Delta}^+ \leq A_1^- + d$$

$$eb_d^{\lll}(A, B) \geq l \tag{4.88}$$
$$\Leftrightarrow A_1^+ < B_{1-l+\Delta}^- - d \wedge A_{1-\Delta}^+ < B_{1-l+2\Delta}^- - d \wedge \cdots \wedge A_{1-l+\Delta}^+ < B_1^- - d$$

$$eb_d^{\lll}(A, B) \leq k \tag{4.89}$$
$$\Leftrightarrow B_{1-k}^- \leq A_1^+ + d \vee B_{1-k+\Delta}^- \leq A_{1-\Delta}^+ + d \vee \cdots \vee B_1^- \leq A_{1-k}^+ + d$$

Proof. As an example, we show (4.82). From Lemma 4.12 we already know that

$$bb_d^{\lll}(A, B) \geq l \Leftrightarrow (\forall \varepsilon \in]0, l])(\exists \lambda \in]l - \varepsilon, 1])(bb_d^{\lll}(A_\lambda, B_{\lambda+\varepsilon-l}))$$

First note that if $\varepsilon_1 < \varepsilon_2$, then $B_{\lambda+\varepsilon_1-l}^- \lesseqgtr B_{\lambda+\varepsilon_2-l}^-$ and therefore

$$bb_d^{\lll}(A_\lambda, B_{\lambda+\varepsilon_1-l}) \Rightarrow bb_d^{\lll}(A_\lambda, B_{\lambda+\varepsilon_2-l})$$

We thus obtain

$$bb_d^{\lll}(A, B) \geq l \Leftrightarrow (\forall \varepsilon \in]0, \Delta[)(\exists \lambda \in]l - \varepsilon, 1])(bb_d^{\lll}(A_\lambda, B_{\lambda+\varepsilon-l}))$$

Let $\varepsilon \in]0, \Delta[$ and let λ in $]l - \varepsilon, 1]$ be such that $bb_d^{\lll}(A_\lambda, B_{\lambda+\varepsilon-l})$. We first show that there must exist some λ' in $\{l, l + \Delta, \ldots, 1\}$ such that $bb_d^{\lll}(A_{\lambda'}, B_{\lambda'+\varepsilon-l})$. If $\lambda \in]l-\varepsilon, l[$, then $A_\lambda = A_l$ as A only takes membership degrees from M. Moreover, $B_{\lambda+\varepsilon-l}^- \leq B_{l+\varepsilon-l}^-$, hence from $bb_d^{\lll}(A_\lambda, B_{\lambda+\varepsilon-l})$ we establish $bb_d^{\lll}(A_l, B_{l+\varepsilon-l})$, i.e., we can choose $\lambda' = l$. Similarly, if $\lambda \in]i\Delta, (i + 1)\Delta[$ ($i \in \mathbb{N}$, $l \leq i\Delta < (i + 1)\Delta \leq 1$), we have that $bb_d^{\lll}(A_\lambda, B_{\lambda+\varepsilon-l})$ implies $bb_d^{\lll}(A_{(i+1)\Delta}, B_{(i+1)\Delta+\varepsilon-l})$, and we can choose $\lambda' = (i+1)\Delta$. This yields

$$bb_d^{\lll}(A, B) \geq l \Leftrightarrow (\forall \varepsilon \in]0, \Delta[)(\exists \lambda \in \{l, l + \Delta, \ldots, 1\})(bb_d^{\lll}(A_\lambda, B_{\lambda+\varepsilon-l}))$$

Since now $\lambda \in M$ and $\varepsilon \in]0, \Delta[$, we have that $B_{\lambda+\varepsilon-l} = B_{\lambda+\Delta-l}$:

$$bb_d^{\lll}(A, B) \geq l \Leftrightarrow (\forall \varepsilon \in]0, \Delta[)(\exists \lambda \in \{l, l + \Delta, \ldots, 1\})(bb_d^{\lll}(A_\lambda, B_{\lambda+\Delta-l}))$$
$$\Leftrightarrow (\exists \lambda \in \{l, l + \Delta, \ldots, 1\})(bb_d^{\lll}(A_\lambda, B_{\lambda+\Delta-l}))$$

proving (4.82). $\qquad \square$

When A and B only take a finite number of different membership degrees, the value of $be^{\prec}(A, B)$, $bb^{\prec}(A, B)$, etc., can easily be found. If $\alpha = \beta = 0$, we obtain the following lemma.

Lemma 4.13. *Let A and B be fuzzy time intervals which are constant over $]p_1, p_2[,]p_2, p_3[, \ldots]p_{n-1}, p_n[$. Assume, moreover, that the support of A and B is contained in $[p_1, p_n]$, and that p_a and p_b are modal values of A and B respectively $(1 \leq a, b \leq n)$. It holds that*

$$be^{\prec}(A, B) = \max_{i \in \{1, 2, \ldots, a\}} T_W(A(p_i), B(\max(p_i, p_b))) \tag{4.90}$$

$$bb^{\prec}(A, B) = \min_{i \in \{1, \ldots, \min(a,b)\}} I_W(B(p_i), A(p_i)) \tag{4.91}$$

$$ee^{\prec}(A, B) = \min_{i \in \{\max(a,b), \ldots, n\}} I_W(A(p_i), B(p_i)) \tag{4.92}$$

$$eb^{\prec}(A, B) = \min_{i \in \{a, a+1, \ldots, n\}} (1 - T_W(A(p_i), B(\min(p_{i-1}, p_b)))) \tag{4.93}$$

$$be^{\lll}(A, B) = \max_{i \in \{b, b+1, \ldots, n\}} T_W(B(p_i), A(\min(p_{i-1}, p_a))) \tag{4.94}$$

$$bb^{\lll}(A, B) = \max_{i \in \{1, \ldots, \min(a,b)\}} T_W(A(p_i), 1 - B(p_i)) \tag{4.95}$$

$$ee^{\lll}(A, B) = \max_{i \in \{\max(a,b), \ldots, n\}} T_W(B(p_i), 1 - A(p_i)) \tag{4.96}$$

$$eb^{\lll}(A, B) = \min_{i \in \{1, 2, \ldots, b\}} (1 - T_W(B(p_i), A(\max(p_i, p_a)))) \tag{4.97}$$

where $p_0 < p_1 \leq p_2 \leq \cdots \leq p_n$ such that $A(p_0) = B(p_0) = 0$.

Proof. As an example, we show (4.90). The proof of (4.91)–(4.93) is analogous. Note that (4.94)–(4.97) follow straightforwardly from (4.90)–(4.93) by (4.3)–(4.6), (2.34) and (2.13)–(2.14).

Let the $\mathbb{R} - \mathbb{R}$ mappings l and r be defined as

$$l(p) = \begin{cases} p & \text{if } p < p_1 \\ \max\{p_i | i \in \{1,2,\ldots,n\} \wedge p_i \leq p\} & \text{otherwise} \end{cases}$$

$$r(p) = \begin{cases} p & \text{if } p > p_n \\ \min\{p_i | i \in \{1,2,\ldots,n\} \wedge p_i \geq p\} & \text{otherwise} \end{cases}$$

for all p in $\mathbb{R}$. Since A (resp. B) is increasing for values smaller than p_a (resp. p_b) and decreasing for values greater than p_a (resp. p_b), we have

$$be^{\preccurlyeq}(A,B) = \sup_{p \in \mathbb{R}} T_W(A(p), \sup_{q \in \mathbb{R}} T_W(B(q), L^{\preccurlyeq}(p,q)))$$

$$= \sup_{p \leq m_a} T_W(A(p), \sup_{q \geq m_b} T_W(B(q), L^{\preccurlyeq}(p,q)))$$

$$= \sup_{p \leq m_a} T_W(A(p), \sup_{q \geq m_b, p \leq q} B(q))$$

$$= \sup_{p \leq m_a} \sup_{q \geq m_b, p \leq q} T_W(A(p), B(q))$$

By definition of a fuzzy time interval, if $p \leq m_a$, $A(l(p)) = A(p)$, and if $p \geq m_b$, $B(r(p)) = B(p)$. Based in this observation, we obtain

$$\sup_{p \leq m_a} \sup_{q \geq m_b, p \leq q} T_W(A(p), B(q))$$

$$= \sup_{p \leq m_a} \sup_{q \geq m_b, p \leq q} T_W(A(l(p)), B(r(q)))$$

$$= \max_{i \in \{1,2,\ldots,a\}} \max_{\substack{j \in \{b,b+1,\ldots,n\} \\ i \leq j}} T_W(A(p_i), B(p_j))$$

As B is decreasing for values greater than p_b, the maximum for j is attained by the smallest value in $\{b, b+1, \ldots, n\}$ satisfying $i \leq j$, i.e., $\max(b,i)$. □

Finally, we can show the following characterization of $bb_d^{\ll}$ and $ee_d^{\ll}$.

Lemma 4.14. *Let A and B be normalised and convex fuzzy sets in $\mathbb{R}$. Furthermore, let m_a and m_b be arbitrary modal values of A and B respectively. It holds that*

$$bb_d^{\ll}(A,B) = \sup_{p+d<m_b, p \leq m_a} T_W(A(p), 1 - B(p+d)) \qquad (4.98)$$

$$ee_d^{\ll}(A,B) = \sup_{p-d>m_a, p \geq m_b} T_W(B(p), 1 - A(p-d)) \qquad (4.99)$$

Proof. By definition of $bb_d^{\lll}$, we obtain

$$bb_d^{\lll}(A,B) = \sup_{p\in\mathbb{R}} T_W(A(p), \inf_{q\in\mathbb{R}} I_W(B(q), L_d^{\lll}(p,q)))$$

$$= \max(\sup_{p\geq m_b-d} T_W(A(p), \inf_{q\in\mathbb{R}} I_W(B(q), L_d^{\lll}(p,q))),$$

$$\sup_{p<m_b-d} T_W(A(p), \inf_{q\in\mathbb{R}} I_W(B(q), L_d^{\lll}(p,q))))$$

From the convexity of B, we establish that B is increasing for values smaller than m_b and decreasing for values greater than m_b. Hence, we obtain

$$\inf_{q\in\mathbb{R}} I_W(B(q), L_d^{\lll}(p,q)) = \begin{cases} I_W(B(p+d), L_d^{\lll}(p,p+d)) & \text{if } p < m_b - d \\ I_W(B(m_b), L_d^{\lll}(p,m_b)) & \text{if } p \geq m_b - d \end{cases}$$

We thus find

$$\max(\sup_{p\geq m_b-d} T_W(A(p), \inf_{q\in\mathbb{R}} I_W(B(q), L_d^{\lll}(p,q))),$$

$$\sup_{p<m_b-d} T_W(A(p), \inf_{q\in\mathbb{R}} I_W(B(q), L_d^{\lll}(p,q))))$$

$$= \max(\sup_{p\geq m_b-d} T_W(A(p), I_W(B(m_b), L_d^{\lll}(p,m_b))),$$

$$\sup_{p<m_b-d} T_W(A(p), I_W(B(p+d), L_d^{\lll}(p,p+d))))$$

$$= \max(\sup_{p\geq m_b-d} T_W(A(p), I_W(1,0)), \sup_{p<m_b-d} T_W(A(p), I_W(B(p+d),0)))$$

$$= \max(\sup_{p\geq m_b-d} T_W(A(p),0), \sup_{p<m_b-d} T_W(A(p), 1-B(p+d)))$$

$$= \sup_{p<m_b-d} T_W(A(p), 1-B(p+d))$$

Due to its convexity, A is increasing for values smaller than m_a and decreasing for values greater than m_a. Hence if $p < m_b - d$ and $p > m_a$, it holds that $T_W(A(p), 1-B(p+d))) \leq T_W(A(m_a), 1-B(m_a+d))$. Therefore, we have that

$$\sup_{p<m_b-d} T_W(A(p), 1-B(p+d)) = \sup_{p<m_b-d, p\leq m_a} T_W(A(p), 1-B(p+d))$$

proving (4.98). Eq. (4.99) is shown entirely analogously. $\qquad\square$

Chapter 5

Reasoning about Fuzzy Temporal Information

5.1 Introduction

The temporal information conveyed by natural language texts is predominantly of a qualitative nature. Besides quantitative information, such as (fuzzy) time spans, we may, for example, find that the Battle of France *happened before* the Battle of Britain, or that Voltaire *lived during* the Age of Enlightenment. Many applications can exploit qualitative temporal information as a surrogate for missing dates and time spans. Examples are multi–document summarization, where a chronological ordering of events occurring in different documents is needed to obtain a fluent narrative, and temporal question answering, where detailed temporal knowledge is used to find answers to questions satisfying a temporal restriction imposed by the user (e.g., Which paintings did Salvator Dali create before his Surrealist period?). In such scenarios, however, applications based on classical temporal reasoning algorithms often fail to work correctly when the events or time periods involved are vague. For example, when extracting information about the life and work of Picasso from web documents, inconsistencies quickly arise:

(1) Bread and Fruit Dish on a Table (1909) marks the beginning of Picasso's "Analytical" Cubism ... [1]
(2) The first stage of Picasso's cubism is known as analytical cubism. It began in 1908 and ended in 1912, ... [2]
(3) The 'Demoiselles d'Avignon' of 1907 mark the beginning of his [Picasso's] Cubist period in which he exceeded the classical form. [3]

[1] http://www.abcgallery.com/P/picasso/picassobio.html, accessed May 21, 2007
[2] http://www.pokemonultimate.wanadoo.co.uk/picasso.html, accessed May 21, 2007
[3] http://www.kettererkunst.com/details-e.php?obnr=410702527&anummer=315, ac-

155

The most common solution to the problem of inconsistencies is discarding the least reliable information until a consistent knowledge base is attained, provided we can differentiate between the reliability of the available information. The underlying assumption is that inconsistencies are caused by the inclusion of incorrect statements in the knowledge base. On the other hand, in the example above, none of the three statements is completely false; inconsistencies result from different viewpoints about the beginning of Picasso's Cubist period. Therefore, a more realistic approach is to acknowledge that some of the temporal relations are only true to some extent: the beginning of Picasso's Analytical Cubism coincides with the beginning of cubism to some degree λ_1, Picasso's Cubist period began with "Demoiselles d'Avignon" in 1907 to some degree λ_2, Picasso's Analytical Cubism began in 1908 to some degree λ_3, Picasso's Analytical Cubism began with "Bread and Fruit Dish on a Table" in 1909 to some degree λ_4. Rather than completely rejecting some information, we can then weaken the original interpretations of some, or even all statements by finding appropriate values of $\lambda_1, \lambda_2, \lambda_3, \lambda_4$, leading to a consistent interpretation of the sentences above.

In this chapter, we discuss reasoning tasks that are based on upper and lower bounds of fuzzy temporal relations between unknown fuzzy time intervals. For example, knowing that x, y, and z are fuzzy time intervals, is it possible that simultaneously $bb_3^{\lll}(x,y) \geq 0.6$, $bb_4^{\lll}(y,z) \leq 0.5$, $be_2^{\lll}(y,z) \leq 0.8$, and $ee_8^{\lll}(x,z) \geq 0.3$? From the available knowledge, what can be said about the possible values of $be_9^{\lll}(x,z)$? Our primary objective is to obtain a temporal reasoning framework that is suitable for temporal reasoning about vague events in applications such as multi–document summarization, event–based retrieval or question answering. After providing some background information on existing temporal reasoning frameworks, we discuss sound and complete algorithms for reasoning tasks such as satisfiability checking, entailment checking and finding the best truth–value bound. We furthermore demonstrate that reasoning about fuzzy time intervals is — like its crisp counterpart — NP–complete. Finally, we introduce techniques for efficient, but incomplete reasoning. Such techniques are of key importance for applications dealing with a large number of events, in which completeness is not a critical issue. Starting from a generalization of Allen's $O(n^3)$ algorithm, we investigate how more inconsistencies can be detected and more conclusions can be established, while keeping the $O(n^3)$

time complexity.

5.2 Temporal Reasoning

In Chapter 4, we briefly discussed Allen's algorithm for reasoning in the interval algebra. This efficient polynomial–time algorithm correctly finds a number of conclusions from a given set of assertions. Moreover, if the initial knowledge base contains only basic Allen relations, it is complete [Valdés-Pérez (1987)], i.e., it finds all consequences that follow from the available information. In particular, this means that it can be used to check the satisfiability of such a knowledge base. However, as was already explained in [Allen (1983)], this result does not hold in general; when non–basic relations occur, some conclusions cannot be found by only applying transitivity rules. In general, it can be shown that the satisfiability checking problem in the IA is NP–complete [Vilain *et al.* (1989)]. Motivated by this observation, a considerable amount of research has been directed towards identifying larger sets of temporal relations for which satisfiability checking, and other reasoning tasks of interest, can be solved in polynomial time. Such sets of Allen relations are called tractable subfragments of the IA.

The NP–completeness is caused by the disjunctive nature of non–basic Allen relations. However, many unions of basic Allen relations can be expressed as non–disjunctive constraints on the boundary points of the intervals involved. For example, $\Theta = \{(b \cup m)(x, y), (s \cup e \cup si)(y, z), o(z, x)\}$ can be reduced to the following set of linear equalities and inequalities:

$$x^- < x^+ \qquad y^- < y^+ \qquad z^- < z^+ \qquad x^+ \leq y^-$$
$$y^- = z^- \qquad z^- < x^- \qquad z^+ > x^- \qquad z^+ < x^+$$

where x^- and x^+ correspond to the (unknown) beginning and ending of the interval x, and similar for y and z. Clearly, if there exist real numbers which we can assign to the variables x^-, x^+, y^-, y^+, z^- and z^+ such that the linear inequalities are satisfied, the set Θ is satisfiable and vice versa. Since the satisfiability of these linear constraints can be checked in polynomial time, the corresponding subfragment of the IA is tractable; it is called SA. In total, 188 temporal relations are contained in SA [van Beek and Cohen (1990)]. Moreover, Allen's $O(n^3)$ algorithm can still be used for satisfiability checking when (only) relations from SA are used. However, if we are interested in finding the strongest temporal relation between each pair of variables entailed by a given knowledge base — a problem known as minimal labeling — Allen's algorithm is only complete if none of the corresponding inequalities involve $\neq$, which is the case for 83 of the 188 relations from SA. An $O(n^4)$ algorithm which always finds the minimal labeling entailed by a knowledge base of SA relations is presented in [van Beek and Cohen (1990)]. In [Nebel and Bürckert (1995)], a much larger tractable subfragment of the IA, called the ORD–Horn subfragment, has been identified. It contains 868 temporal relations, including all relations from SA. Furthermore, it was shown that this tractable subfragment is maximal, i.e., it is not possible to add more relations without losing the tractability[4]. In [Drakengren and Jonsson (1997a)], eight more tractable subfragments of the IA were identified, and another nine were identified in [Drakengren and Jonsson (1997b)]. Finally, in [Krokhin *et al.* (2003)] it was shown that all tractable subfragments of the IA are subsets of these 18 maximal tractable subfragments. This implies that there can be no other maximal tractable subfragments, i.e., the boundary between tractable and intractable subfragments has been completely characterized. Note that the ORD–Horn subfragment is the only maximal tractable subfragment containing all basic Allen relations.

Tractable subfragments are interesting because they allow for efficient, polynomial–time reasoning when the available information can be expressed without using the full expressivity of the IA. In some applications, however, the expressivity of the tractable subfragments is too limited and algorithms with an exponential worst–time complexity are required. Complete reasoning about arbitrary Allen relations can be done by backtracking over all disjunctive relations [Allen (1983)]. In particular, let Θ be a set of assertions of the form $r(x_i, x_j)$ where x_i and x_j are variables and r is an Allen relation, and let $r_1, r_2, \ldots, r_n$ be basic Allen relations. It is easy to see that $\Theta \cup \{(r_1 \cup r_2 \cup \cdots \cup r_n)(x_1, x_2)\}$ is satisfiable iff $\Theta \cup \{r_1(x_1, x_2)\}$ is satisfiable or $\Theta \cup \{r_2(x_1, x_2)\}$ is satisfiable, or $\ldots$, or $\Theta \cup \{r_n(x_1, x_2)\}$ is satisfiable. If Θ contains other disjunctive relations, we can repeat this argument until we arrive at sets of assertions involving only basic relations. Finally, we can apply Allen's algorithm to these sets of assertions to verify whether at least one of them is satisfiable. The efficiency of this rather naive backtracking approach can be improved considerably by using Allen's algorithm for forward checking [Ladkin and Reinefeld (1993)]. The idea is to apply Allen's algorithm in all intermediate steps of the backtracking process. Recall that Allen's algorithm is sound, hence if it discovers an inconsistency we know

---

[4]Throughout this book, we implicitly assume that $P \neq NP$.

that the backtracking search needs not be continued. Moreover, in applying Allen's algorithm many of the remaining disjuncts will be eliminated, thereby pruning the search tree significantly. A further optimization, using the tractable ORD–Horn subfragment is introduced in [Nebel (1997)]. Rather than splitting $(r_1 \cup r_2 \cup \cdots \cup r_n)(x_1, x_2)$ into assertions involving basic Allen relations, we can split it into assertions involving relations from the ORD–Horn fragment. At the leaves of the search tree, we then find sets of assertions involving only ORD–Horn relations, whose satisfiability can again be decided using Allen's algorithm. It can be expected that the average branching factor of the search tree is drastically reduced in this way. This is indeed confirmed by experimental evidence in [Nebel (1997)], albeit only for very hard problem instances.

Also reasoning about metric temporal information in the form of TCPs is NP–complete [Dechter *et al.* (1991)]. Therefore, TCPs which only contain one disjunct per constraint are sometimes considered. Such problems are called Simple TCPs (STCPs) and can be solved in $O(n^3)$, n being the number of variables [Dechter *et al.* (1991)]. Various ways to extend the expressivity of STCPs have been explored which keep the polynomial time complexity, including STCPs with strict inequalities [Gerevini and Cristani (1997)] and with inequations [Koubarakis (1992)]. As the disjunctive nature of general TCPs is often unavoidable in real–world problems, several highly optimized backtracking procedures for reasoning about TCPs, and disjunctions of temporal constraints in general, have been developed [Stergiou and Koubarakis (2000); Tsamardinos and Pollack (2003)]. In addition to forward checking, it has been proposed to speed up backtracking by applying conflict–directed backjumping, semantic branching, no–good recording and removal of subsumed variables. We will come back to these techniques in Section 5.3.4, where they will be adopted to optimize our fuzzy temporal reasoner.

While reasoning about non–atomic linear constraints is NP–complete, a particularly interesting tractable subfragment has been identified, subsuming, among others, the ORD–Horn subfragment of the IA. The central idea is to allow only disjunctions with inequations. Specifically, the linear constraint $\phi_1 \vee \phi_2 \vee \cdots \vee \phi_m$ is called Horn if at least $m - 1$ of the disjuncts ϕ_i correspond to $\neq$. All atomic linear constraints are Horn, as well as, for example, $3x + 4y \leq 6 \vee x \neq 8 \vee y \neq 7 \vee x + 3y \neq 12$. On the other hand, a linear constraint like $3x + 4y \leq 6 \vee x \geq 8$ is not Horn. It has been shown independently in [Jonsson and Bäckström (1998)] and [Koubarakis (2001)] that reasoning about Horn linear constraints is tractable.

Fuzzy temporal reasoning has mainly been investigated in the context of fuzzy temporal constraint networks. In [Marín *et al.* (1994)], it has been shown that reasoning with fuzzy temporal constraint networks is tractable, provided all fuzzy restrictions are convex fuzzy sets in $\mathbb{R}$. Efficient techniques for backtracking over disjunctions of such fuzzy constraints have been investigated in [Bosch *et al.* (2002)]. Finally, also the reasoning properties of fuzzy temporal reasoning frameworks for encoding preferences have been thoroughly investigated. For example, it is shown in [Badaloni and Giacomin (2006)] that reasoning in IA^{fuz} is in the same complexity class as reasoning in the IA. Furthermore, a generalization of the ORD–Horn subfragment of the IA is identified which allows for tractable reasoning, and which is maximal in this respect. To the best of our knowledge, however, the issue of temporal reasoning about fuzzy time intervals has previously not been addressed.

5.3   Complete Reasoning about Fuzzy Time Spans

Our aim is to identify procedures to verify whether it is possible, for example, that simultaneously $bb_3^{\lll}(x, y) \geq 0.6$, $bb_4^{\lll}(y, z) \leq 0.5$, $be_2^{\lll}(y, z) \leq 0.8$, and $ee_8^{\lll}(x, z) \geq 0.3$ hold, given that x, y and z are fuzzy time intervals. This problem is usually called satisfiability (or consistency) checking. Traditionally, most reasoning tasks of interest can be reduced to satisfiability checking. An important example is entailment checking, i.e., checking whether it is necessarily the case that some given assertion γ holds, given that a set of assertions Θ is satisfied. Another important reasoning task is finding a consistent scenario (or solution), e.g., knowing that the set $\{bb_3^{\lll}(x, y) \geq 0.6, bb_4^{\lll}(y, z) \leq 0.5, be_2^{\lll}(y, z) \leq 0.8, ee_8^{\lll}(x, z) \geq 0.3\}$ is satisfiable, can we explicitly construct fuzzy time intervals corresponding to x, y and z which satisfy these assertions. Throughout this chapter, we assume that all upper and lower bounds are taken from a fixed, finite set $M = \{0, \Delta, 2\Delta, \ldots, 1\}$, where $\Delta = \frac{1}{\rho}$ for some $\rho \in \mathbb{N} \setminus \{0\}$. For convenience, we write M_0 for $M \setminus \{0\}$ and M_1 for $M \setminus \{1\}$. Also note that we will not consider vague metric constraints, i.e., while we will deal with expressions like $bb_4^{\lll}(y, z)$, we will not deal with expressions like $bb_{(4,10)}^{\lll}(y, z)$. Generalizing the discussion below to allow for vague metric constraints is an open problem left for future work.

Our reasoning procedures reduce the problem of reasoning about fuzzy time intervals to crisp temporal reasoning with linear constraints. Consequently, we will need to talk about, for example, satisfiability of assertions about fuzzy time intervals as well as assertions about time points. To avoid confusion, we will therefore differentiate between FI–satisfiability (satisfiability for assertions about fuzzy time intervals) and P–satisfiability (satisfiability for assertions about time points), FI–interpretations and P–interpretations, etc.

Definition 5.1 (Atomic FI–formula). *An atomic FI–formula over a set of variables X is an expression of the form $r(x, y) \geq l$ or $r(x, y) \leq k$, where $l \in M_0$, $k \in M_1$, $(x, y) \in X^2$ and r is $bb_d^{\lll}$, $ee_d^{\lll}$, $be_d^{\lll}$ or $eb_d^{\lll}$ $(d \in \mathbb{R})$.*

Note that we will not consider atomic FI–formulas like $bb_d^{\lessgtr}(x, y) \geq l$. Such expressions can be omitted from the discussion without loss of generality because of their correspondence to atomic FI–formulas involving $bb_d^{\lll}$, $ee_d^{\lll}$, $be_d^{\lll}$ or $eb_d^{\lll}$. In applications, however, it may be convenient to use $bb_d^{\lessgtr}(x, y) \geq l$ as a notational alternative to $bb_d^{\lll}(y, x) \leq 1 - l$.

Definition 5.2 (FI–formula). *An FI–formula over a set of variables X is an expression of the form*

$$\phi_1 \vee \phi_2 \vee \cdots \vee \phi_n$$

where ϕ_1, ϕ_2, ..., ϕ_n are atomic FI–formulas over X. If $n > 1$, the FI–formula is called disjunctive.

Definition 5.3 (FI–interpretation). *An FI–interpretation over a set of variables X is a mapping that assigns a fuzzy interval to each variable in X. An FI_M–interpretation over X is an FI–interpretation that maps every variable from X to a fuzzy interval which takes only membership degrees from M.*

Definition 5.4 (P–interpretation). *A P–interpretation over a set of variables X is a mapping that assigns a real number to each variable in X.*

The interpretation $\mathcal{I}(x)$ of a variable x, corresponding to an FI–interpretation or P–interpretation $\mathcal{I}$, will also be written as $x^{\mathcal{I}}$. An FI–interpretation $\mathcal{I}$ over X satisfies the FI–formula $bb_d^{\lll}(x, y) \geq l$ ($x, y \in X$, $l \in M_0$, $d \in \mathbb{R}$) iff $bb_d^{\lll}(x^{\mathcal{I}}, y^{\mathcal{I}}) \geq l$, and similar for other types of atomic FI–formulas. Likewise, an atomic linear constraint $a_1 x_1 + a_2 x_2 + \cdots + a_n x_n \, \Delta \, b$ is satisfied by a P–interpretation $\mathcal{I}$ iff $a_1 x_1^{\mathcal{I}} + a_2 x_2^{\mathcal{I}} + \cdots + a_n x_n^{\mathcal{I}} \, \Delta \, b$, where Δ is $<, \leq, >, \geq, =$ or $\neq$. Furthermore, if $\mathcal{I}$ is an FI–interpretation (resp.

P–interpretation) and $\phi_1, \phi_2, \ldots, \phi_n$ are atomic FI–formulas (resp. atomic linear constraints), $\mathcal{I}$ satisfies $\phi_1 \vee \phi_2 \vee \cdots \vee \phi_n$ iff $\mathcal{I}$ satisfies ϕ_1 or $\mathcal{I}$ satisfies ϕ_2 or ... or $\mathcal{I}$ satisfies ϕ_n.

Definition 5.5 (FI–satisfiable). *A set Θ of FI–formulas over a set of variables X is said to be FI–satisfiable (resp. FI_M–satisfiable) iff there exists an FI–interpretation (resp. FI_M–interpretation) over X which satisfies every FI–formula in Θ. An FI–interpretation (resp. FI_M–interpretation) meeting this requirement is called an FI–model (resp. FI_M–model) of Θ.*

Definition 5.6 (P–satisfiable). *A set Ψ of linear constraints over a set of variables X is said to be P–satisfiable iff there exists a P–interpretation over X which satisfies every linear constraint in Ψ. A P–interpretation meeting this requirement is called a P–model of Ψ.*

5.3.1 FI–Satisfiability

One of the most important temporal reasoning tasks consists of checking whether a given knowledge base is consistent. Here, this corresponds to checking the FI–satisfiability of a set of FI–formulas Θ. To solve this problem, we will show how a set Ψ of linear constraints can be constructed which is P–satisfiable iff Θ is FI–satisfiable. In this way, existing, highly optimized reasoners for temporal problems can be reused to reason about vague temporal information. This reduction from FI–satisfiability to P–satisfiability is made possible by virtue of the following proposition, stating that because the upper and lower bounds in a set of FI–formulas are taken from the set M, as defined above, we can restrict ourselves to fuzzy intervals that only take membership degrees from M.

Proposition 5.1. *Let Θ be a set of FI–formulas over X. It holds that Θ is FI–satisfiable iff Θ is FI_M–satisfiable.*

Proof. Clearly, if Θ is FI_M–satisfiable then Θ is also FI–satisfiable. Conversely, we show that given an FI–model $\mathcal{I}$ of Θ, it is always possible to construct an FI_M–model $\mathcal{I}^*$ of Θ.

Let $\mathcal{I}$ be an FI–model of Θ, and let the $[0,1] - [0,1]$ mappings l and u be defined for y_0 in $[0,1]$ as

$$l(y_0) = \max\{y | y \in M \text{ and } y \leq y_0\}$$
$$u(y_0) = \min\{y | y \in M \text{ and } y \geq y_0\}$$

From the definition of fuzzy time interval (Definition 4.1), we establish that for each x in X, there exists an m_x in $\mathbb{R}$ such that $x^{\mathcal{I}}(m_x) = 1$. We now define $\mathcal{I}'$ as a mapping from X to the class of fuzzy sets in $\mathbb{R}$:

$$x^{\mathcal{I}'}(p) = \begin{cases} l(x^{\mathcal{I}}(p)) & \text{if } p \leq m_x \\ u(x^{\mathcal{I}}(p)) & \text{if } p > m_x \end{cases}$$

for all x in X and p in $\mathbb{R}$. Figure 5.1 depicts the relationship between $\mathcal{I}$ and $\mathcal{I}'$. Although for x in X, the fuzzy set $x^{\mathcal{I}'}$ only takes membership degrees from M, $\mathcal{I}'$ is not an FI_M–interpretation as the α–level sets of $x^{\mathcal{I}'}$ do not necessarily correspond to closed intervals ($\alpha \in]0,1]$, $x \in X$). However, from $\mathcal{I}'$, we can construct an FI_M–interpretation $\mathcal{I}^*$ as follows. Let P be the (finite) set of points in which $x^{\mathcal{I}'}$ is discontinuous for at least one x in X ($P \subseteq \mathbb{R}$), and let P_s^x be the set of points in which $x^{\mathcal{I}'}$ is not upper semi–continuous ($P_s^x \subseteq P$), i.e., P_s^x contains the endpoints of α–level sets of $x^{\mathcal{I}'}$ which do not correspond to closed intervals. Furthermore, let D be the set of distances d occurring in the FI–formulas from Θ ($D \subseteq \mathbb{R}$).

The FI_M–interpretation $\mathcal{I}^*$ is defined as

$$x^{\mathcal{I}^*}(p) = \begin{cases} \min_{q \in [p, p+\varepsilon[} x^{\mathcal{I}'}(q) & \text{if } (\exists q \in P_s^x)(q \in]p, p+\varepsilon[) \\ x^{\mathcal{I}'}(p) & \text{otherwise} \end{cases}$$

for all x in X and p in $\mathbb{R}$, where ε denotes an arbitrary, fixed element from $]0, \min\{|p+d-q| : p,q \in P \land d \in D \cup \{0\} \land p+d \neq q\}[$. The definition of $x^{\mathcal{I}^*}$ is illustrated in Figure 5.1(c). To prove that $\mathcal{I}^*(x)$ satisfies all FI–formulas from Θ, we first show that for d in $\mathbb{R}$, x and y in X, and m in M, it holds that

$$bb_d^{\ll}(x^{\mathcal{I}}, y^{\mathcal{I}}) \leq m \Rightarrow bb_d^{\ll}(x^{\mathcal{I}'}, y^{\mathcal{I}'}) \leq m \tag{5.1}$$

$$bb_d^{\ll}(x^{\mathcal{I}}, y^{\mathcal{I}}) \geq m \Rightarrow bb_d^{\ll}(x^{\mathcal{I}'}, y^{\mathcal{I}'}) \geq m \tag{5.2}$$

$$ee_d^{\ll}(x^{\mathcal{I}}, y^{\mathcal{I}}) \leq m \Rightarrow ee_d^{\ll}(x^{\mathcal{I}'}, y^{\mathcal{I}'}) \leq m \tag{5.3}$$

$$ee_d^{\ll}(x^{\mathcal{I}}, y^{\mathcal{I}}) \geq m \Rightarrow ee_d^{\ll}(x^{\mathcal{I}'}, y^{\mathcal{I}'}) \geq m \tag{5.4}$$

$$be_d^{\ll}(x^{\mathcal{I}}, y^{\mathcal{I}}) \leq m \Rightarrow be_d^{\ll}(x^{\mathcal{I}'}, y^{\mathcal{I}'}) \leq m \tag{5.5}$$

$$be_d^{\ll}(x^{\mathcal{I}}, y^{\mathcal{I}}) \geq m \Rightarrow be_d^{\ll}(x^{\mathcal{I}'}, y^{\mathcal{I}'}) \geq m \tag{5.6}$$

$$eb_d^{\ll}(x^{\mathcal{I}}, y^{\mathcal{I}}) \leq m \Rightarrow eb_d^{\ll}(x^{\mathcal{I}'}, y^{\mathcal{I}'}) \leq m \tag{5.7}$$

$$eb_d^{\ll}(x^{\mathcal{I}}, y^{\mathcal{I}}) \geq m \Rightarrow eb_d^{\ll}(x^{\mathcal{I}'}, y^{\mathcal{I}'}) \geq m \tag{5.8}$$

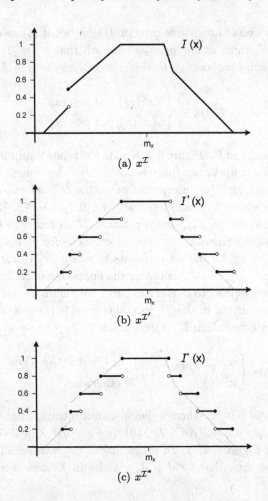

Fig. 5.1   Relationship between the FI–interpretation $\mathcal{I}$, the mapping $\mathcal{I}'$ and the FI$_M$–interpretation $\mathcal{I}^*$

To show (5.1) and (5.2), we obtain by (4.98)

$$bb_d^{\ll}(x^{\mathcal{I}'}, y^{\mathcal{I}'}) = \sup_{p+d<m_y, p\leq m_x} T_W(x^{\mathcal{I}'}(p), 1 - y^{\mathcal{I}'}(p+d))$$

$$= \sup_{p+d<m_y, p\leq m_x} T_W(x^{\mathcal{I}}(p) - (x^{\mathcal{I}}(p) - x^{\mathcal{I}'}(p)),$$

$$1 - y^{\mathcal{I}}(p+d) + (y^{\mathcal{I}}(p+d) - y^{\mathcal{I}'}(p+d)))$$

From the definition of $\mathcal{I}'$, it follows that $(x^{\mathcal{I}}(p) - x^{\mathcal{I}'}(p)) \in [0, \Delta[$ and $(y^{\mathcal{I}}(p+d) - y^{\mathcal{I}'}(p+d)) \in [0, \Delta[$, for $p+d < m_y$ and $p \leq m_x$. Hence, we have

$$\leq \sup_{p+d<m_y, p\leq m_x} T_W(x^\mathcal{I}(p), 1 - y^\mathcal{I}(p+d) + (y^\mathcal{I}(p+d) - y^{\mathcal{I}'}(p+d)))$$

$$\leq \sup_{p+d<m_y, p\leq m_x} T_W(x^\mathcal{I}(p), 1 - y^\mathcal{I}(p+d)) + (y^\mathcal{I}(p+d) - y^{\mathcal{I}'}(p+d))$$

$$< \sup_{p+d<m_y, p\leq m_x} T_W(x^\mathcal{I}(p), 1 - y^\mathcal{I}(p+d)) + \Delta$$

$$= bb_d^\lll(x^\mathcal{I}, y^\mathcal{I}) + \Delta$$

Similarly, we can show that

$$bb_d^\lll(x^{\mathcal{I}'}, y^{\mathcal{I}'}) > bb_d^\lll(x^\mathcal{I}, y^\mathcal{I}) - \Delta$$

Hence

$$bb_d^\lll(x^{\mathcal{I}'}, y^{\mathcal{I}'}) - bb_d^\lll(x^\mathcal{I}, y^\mathcal{I}) \in]-\Delta, \Delta[\tag{5.9}$$

Assume that $bb_d^\lll(x^{\mathcal{I}'}, y^{\mathcal{I}'}) > m$ would hold. Since both $bb_d^\lll(x^{\mathcal{I}'}, y^{\mathcal{I}'})$ and m are contained in M, this implies that $bb_d^\lll(x^{\mathcal{I}'}, y^{\mathcal{I}'}) \geq m+\Delta$. Using (5.9) we establish that $bb_d^\lll(x^\mathcal{I}, y^\mathcal{I}) > m$ also holds, proving (5.1) by contraposition. In the same way, it follows from $bb_d^\lll(x^{\mathcal{I}'}, y^{\mathcal{I}'}) < m$ that $bb_d^\lll(x^{\mathcal{I}'}, y^{\mathcal{I}'}) \leq m - \Delta$ and thus $bb_d^\lll(x^\mathcal{I}, y^\mathcal{I}) < m$, proving (5.2). The implications (5.3)–(5.8) can be shown entirely analogously.

Next, we show that

$$bb_d^\lll(x^{\mathcal{I}'}, y^{\mathcal{I}'}) = bb_d^\lll(x^{\mathcal{I}^*}, y^{\mathcal{I}^*}) \tag{5.10}$$

$$ee_d^\lll(x^{\mathcal{I}'}, y^{\mathcal{I}'}) = ee_d^\lll(x^{\mathcal{I}^*}, y^{\mathcal{I}^*}) \tag{5.11}$$

$$be_d^\lll(x^{\mathcal{I}'}, y^{\mathcal{I}'}) = be_d^\lll(x^{\mathcal{I}^*}, y^{\mathcal{I}^*}) \tag{5.12}$$

$$eb_d^\lll(x^{\mathcal{I}'}, y^{\mathcal{I}'}) = eb_d^\lll(x^{\mathcal{I}^*}, y^{\mathcal{I}^*}) \tag{5.13}$$

First note that (5.10) immediately follows from the definition of $\mathcal{I}^*$ by (4.98), as for each p satisfying $p \leq m_x$ and $p + d < m_y$, $x^{\mathcal{I}^*}(p) = x^{\mathcal{I}'}(p)$ and $y^{\mathcal{I}^*}(p+d) = y^{\mathcal{I}'}(p+d)$. Turning now to (5.11), we find using (4.99) that

$$ee_d^\lll(x^{\mathcal{I}'}, y^{\mathcal{I}'}) = \sup_{p-d>m_x, p\geq m_y} T_W(y^{\mathcal{I}'}(p), 1 - x^{\mathcal{I}'}(p-d)) \tag{5.14}$$

$$ee_d^\lll(x^{\mathcal{I}^*}, y^{\mathcal{I}^*}) = \sup_{p-d>m_x, p\geq m_y} T_W(y^{\mathcal{I}^*}(p), 1 - x^{\mathcal{I}^*}(p-d)) \tag{5.15}$$

where m_x and m_y are the smallest modal values of $x^{\mathcal{I}'}$ and $y^{\mathcal{I}'}$, or, equivalently, of $x^{\mathcal{I}^*}$ and $y^{\mathcal{I}^*}$. First, we show that for every p_1 satisfying $p_1 - d > m_x$ and $p_1 \geq m_y$ there exists a p_2 satisfying $p_2 - d > m_x$ and $p_2 \geq m_y$ such that

$$T_W(y^{\mathcal{I}'}(p_1), 1 - x^{\mathcal{I}'}(p_1 - d)) = T_W(y^{\mathcal{I}^*}(p_2), 1 - x^{\mathcal{I}^*}(p_2 - d)) \tag{5.16}$$

which already proves $ee_d^{\ll}(x^{\mathcal{I}'}, y^{\mathcal{I}'}) \leq ee_d^{\ll}(x^{\mathcal{I}^*}, y^{\mathcal{I}^*})$. If $y^{\mathcal{I}'}(p_1) = y^{\mathcal{I}^*}(p_1)$ and $x^{\mathcal{I}'}(p_1 - d) = x^{\mathcal{I}^*}(p_1 - d)$ we can choose $p_2 = p_1$. Next, assume that $y^{\mathcal{I}'}(p_1) > y^{\mathcal{I}^*}(p_1)$ and $x^{\mathcal{I}'}(p_1 - d) > x^{\mathcal{I}^*}(p_1 - d)$. This means that there is a q_1 in P_s^y and q_2 in P_s^x such that $q_1 \in]p_1, p_1 + \varepsilon[$ and $q_2 \in]p_1 - d, p_1 - d + \varepsilon[$. The latter implies that $q_2 + d \in]p_1, p_1 + \varepsilon[$ which, combined with the former, yields $|q_2 + d - q_1| < \varepsilon$. By definition of ε, this is only possible if $q_2 = q_1 - d$, since for $q_2 + d \neq q_1$, the definition of ε would imply $\varepsilon < |q_2 + d - q_1|$. We show that (5.16) is satisfied for $p_2 = q_1 - \varepsilon$. Note that $m_x, m_y \in P$ but $m_x \notin P_s^x$ and $m_y \notin P_s^y$, hence $m_x \neq q_2$ and $m_y \neq q_1$, and even $m_x < q_2$ and $m_y < q_1$. The definition of ε implies that $\varepsilon < q_1 + 0 - m_y$ and $\varepsilon < q_2 + 0 - m_x$. Since $q_2 = q_1 - d$ and $p_2 = q_1 - \varepsilon$, this entails $p_2 \geq m_y$ and $p_2 - d > m_x$. Since $y^{\mathcal{I}'}$ is constant over $[q_1 - \varepsilon, q_1[$, by definition of ε, it holds that $y^{\mathcal{I}^*}(q_1 - \varepsilon) = y^{\mathcal{I}'}(q_1 - \varepsilon)$, or $y^{\mathcal{I}^*}(p_2) = y^{\mathcal{I}'}(p_2)$. As $p_1 \in]q_1 - \varepsilon, q_1[$, it holds that $y^{\mathcal{I}'}$ is constant over $[p_2, p_1]$, hence $y^{\mathcal{I}'}(p_2) = y^{\mathcal{I}'}(p_1)$. In the same way, we establish $x^{\mathcal{I}^*}(p_2 - d) = x^{\mathcal{I}'}(p_1 - d)$.

If $y^{\mathcal{I}'}(p_1) > y^{\mathcal{I}^*}(p_1)$ and $x^{\mathcal{I}'}(p_1 - d) = x^{\mathcal{I}^*}(p_1 - d)$, there is a q_1 in P_s^y such that $q_1 \in]p_1, p_1 + \varepsilon[$. We show that (5.16) is satisfied for $p_2 = q_1 - \varepsilon$. As in the previous case, the definition of ε implies that $\varepsilon < q_1 + 0 - m_y$, hence $p_2 \geq m_y$. Again, we have that $y^{\mathcal{I}^*}(p_2) = y^{\mathcal{I}^*}(q_1 - \varepsilon) = y^{\mathcal{I}'}(q_1 - \varepsilon) = y^{\mathcal{I}'}(p_2)$, and $y^{\mathcal{I}'}(p_2) = y^{\mathcal{I}'}(p_1)$. Note that $x^{\mathcal{I}'}$ is continuous in $[q_1 - d - \varepsilon, q_1 - d[$. Indeed, if $x^{\mathcal{I}'}$ were discontinuous in a point q_2 from $[q_1 - d - \varepsilon, q_1 - d[$, it would hold that $0 < |q_2 - q_1 + d| \leq \varepsilon$, which is impossible by definition of ε. Since $p_1 - d > m_x$ and there are no discontinuities in $[q_1 - d - \varepsilon, p_1 - d]$, we know that $q_1 - d - \varepsilon > m_x$ (recall that m_x is the smallest modal value of $x^{\mathcal{I}'}$). The continuity of $x^{\mathcal{I}'}$ in $[q_1 - d - \varepsilon, q_1 - d[$ furthermore implies that $x^{\mathcal{I}^*}(q_1 - d - \varepsilon) = x^{\mathcal{I}'}(q_1 - d - \varepsilon)$, and, since $p_1 - d < q_1 - d$, $x^{\mathcal{I}'}(q_1 - d - \varepsilon) = x^{\mathcal{I}'}(p_1 - d)$. From $p_2 = q_1 - \varepsilon$ we can conclude that $x^{\mathcal{I}^*}(p_2 - d) = x^{\mathcal{I}'}(p_1 - d)$

The case where $y^{\mathcal{I}'}(p_1) = y^{\mathcal{I}^*}(p_1)$ and $x^{\mathcal{I}'}(p_1 - d) > x^{\mathcal{I}^*}(p_1 - d)$ is shown entirely analogously.

Conversely, we show that for every p_2 satisfying $p_2 - d > m_x$ and $p_2 \geq m_y$ there exists a p_1 satisfying $p_1 - d > m_x$ and $p_1 \geq m_y$ such that (5.16) is satisfied. If $y^{\mathcal{I}'}(p_2) = y^{\mathcal{I}^*}(p_2)$ and $x^{\mathcal{I}'}(p_2 - d) = x^{\mathcal{I}^*}(p_2 - d)$ we can choose $p_1 = p_2$. If $y^{\mathcal{I}'}(p_2) > y^{\mathcal{I}^*}(p_2)$ and $x^{\mathcal{I}'}(p_2 - d) > x^{\mathcal{I}^*}(p_2 - d)$ there is a q_1 in P_s^y and q_2 in P_s^x such that $q_1 \in]p_2, p_2 + \varepsilon[$ and $q_2 \in]p_2 - d, p_2 - d + \varepsilon[$. We show that (5.16) is satisfied for $p_1 = q_1$. Again, this is only possible if $q_2 = q_1 - d$ by definition of ε. First note that $p_1 = q_1$, $q_1 \in]p_2, p_2 + \varepsilon[$ and $p_2 \geq m_y$ entail $p_1 \geq m_y$, while $p_1 = q_1$, $q_1 - d \in]p_2 - d, p_2 + \varepsilon - d[$ and $p_2 - d > m_x$ entail $p_1 - d > m_x$. As $q_1 \in P_s^y$, we know that $y^{\mathcal{I}'}$

is lower semi–continuous in q_1. Since $y^{\mathcal{I}'}$ is decreasing in q_1, this means that $y^{\mathcal{I}'}$ is right–continuous in q_1. Furthermore, by definition of ε we know that $y^{\mathcal{I}'}$ is continuous over $[q_1 - \varepsilon, q_1[$ and over $]q_1, q_1 + \varepsilon]$. Together with $p_2 \in]q_1 - \varepsilon, q_1[$, this yields $y^{\mathcal{I}^*}(p_2) = y^{\mathcal{I}'}(q_1) = y^{\mathcal{I}'}(p_1)$. Similarly, we can show that $x^{\mathcal{I}^*}(p_2 - d) = x^{\mathcal{I}'}(q_1 - d)$.

If $y^{\mathcal{I}'}(p_2) > y^{\mathcal{I}^*}(p_2)$ and $x^{\mathcal{I}'}(p_2 - d) = x^{\mathcal{I}^*}(p_2 - d)$ there is a q_1 in P_s^y such that $q_1 \in]p_2, p_2 + \varepsilon[$. We show that (5.16) is satisfied for $p_1 = q_1$. As before, we have that $p_1 \geq m_y$, $p_1 - d > m_x$, and $y^{\mathcal{I}^*}(p_2) = y^{\mathcal{I}'}(q_1)$. Note that $x^{\mathcal{I}'}$ is continuous in $[q_1 - d - \varepsilon, q_1 - d[\cup]q_1 - d, q_1 - d + \varepsilon]$. Indeed, for every q_2 in $[q_1 - d - \varepsilon, q_1 - d + \varepsilon] \setminus \{q_1 - d\}$, it holds that $0 < |q_2 - q_1 + d| \leq \varepsilon$, which implies $q_2 \notin P$, using the definition of ε. If $x^{\mathcal{I}'}$ is also continuous in $q_1 - d$, then obviously $x^{\mathcal{I}^*}(p_2 - d) = x^{\mathcal{I}'}(q_1 - d)$. If $x^{\mathcal{I}'}$ is upper semi–continuous in $q_1 - d$ then $x^{\mathcal{I}'}$ is also left–continuous (as $x^{\mathcal{I}'}$ is decreasing in $q_1 - d$), hence $x^{\mathcal{I}'}(q_1 - d) = x^{\mathcal{I}'}(p_2 - d) = x^{\mathcal{I}^*}(p_2 - d)$. Finally, we show that $x^{\mathcal{I}'}$ cannot be lower semi–continuous in $q_1 - d$. Indeed, this would imply that $q_1 - d \in P_s^x$ and thus $x^{\mathcal{I}'}(p_2 - d) > x^{\mathcal{I}^*}(p_2 - d)$, which contradicts the assumption that $x^{\mathcal{I}'}(p_2 - d) = x^{\mathcal{I}^*}(p_2 - d)$.

The case where $y^{\mathcal{I}'}(p_1) = y^{\mathcal{I}^*}(p_1)$ and $x^{\mathcal{I}'}(p_1 - d) > x^{\mathcal{I}^*}(p_1 - d)$ is shown in the same way.

Finally, (5.12) and (5.13) can be shown analogously. $\qquad\square$

Clearly, $\Theta \cup \{r_1 \vee r_2\}$ is FI–satisfiable iff either $\Theta \cup \{r_1\}$ is FI–satisfiable or $\Theta \cup \{r_2\}$ is FI–satisfiable. Therefore, we only consider sets of atomic FI–formulas in the procedure described below. Given a set of atomic FI–formulas Θ over a set of variables X, we construct a set of variables X' and a set of linear constraints Ψ over X' such that Θ is FI–satisfiable iff Ψ is P–satisfiable. From Proposition 5.1, we know that we can restrict ourselves to fuzzy intervals that only take membership degrees from M. Proposition 4.7 furthermore reveals that checking whether an FI_M interpretation satisfies an FI–formula can be done by evaluating a constant number of linear inequalities. This suggests the following procedure for constructing X' and Ψ.

Let X' and Ψ initially be the empty set. For each variable x in X, we add the new variables $x_\Delta^-, x_{2\Delta}^-, \ldots, x_1^-, x_1^+, \ldots, x_{2\Delta}^+$ and x_Δ^+ to X'. Intuitively, these new variables correspond to the beginning and ending points of α–level sets of the fuzzy interval corresponding with x. By adding the following linear constraints to Ψ, for each m in $M_1 \setminus \{0\}$, we ensure that in every P–model $\mathcal{I}$ of Ψ, these new variables can indeed be interpreted as beginning and ending points of α–level sets of a fuzzy interval:

$$x_1^- \leq x_1^+ \tag{5.17}$$

$$x_m^- \leq x_{m+\Delta}^- \tag{5.18}$$

$$x_{m+\Delta}^+ \leq x_m^+ \tag{5.19}$$

In this way, every P–model $\mathcal{I}$ of Ψ corresponds to an FI_M–interpretation $\mathcal{I}'$ of Θ in which $x^{\mathcal{I}'}$ is the fuzzy interval taking only membership degrees from M, defined through its α–level sets by $(\mathcal{I}'(x))_m = [\mathcal{I}(x_m^-), \mathcal{I}(x_m^+)]$ for all $m \in M_0$.

Finally, for each FI–formula in Θ, we add a particular set of linear constraints to Ψ, based on the equivalences of Proposition 4.7. For example, if Θ contains the FI–formula $bb_d^{\lll}(x, y) \leq k$, we add the following linear constraint:

$$y_\Delta^- \leq x_{k+\Delta}^- + d, y_{2\Delta}^- \leq x_{k+2\Delta}^- + d, \ldots, y_{1-k}^- \leq x_1^- + d \tag{5.20}$$

Similarly, if Θ contains the FI–formula $bb_d^{\lll}(x, y) \geq l$, we add the following linear constraint:

$$x_l^- < y_\Delta^- - d \vee x_{l+\Delta}^- < y_{2\Delta}^- - d \vee \cdots \vee x_1^- < y_{1-l+\Delta}^- - d \tag{5.21}$$

Note that disjunctive FI–formulas correspond to (sets of) linear constraints as well, hence this procedure is not inherently restricted to sets of atomic FI–formulas. However, the number of linear constraints can be exponential in the number of disjuncts in the FI–formulas.

As expressed by the following proposition, the set of linear constraints Ψ is P–satisfiable iff Θ is FI–satisfiable.

Proposition 5.2. *Let Θ be a finite set of atomic FI–formulas over X, and let Ψ be the corresponding set of linear constraints, obtained by the procedure outlined above. It holds that Θ is FI–satisfiable iff Ψ is P–satisfiable.*

Proof. Assume that Θ is FI–satisfiable. Then there exists an FI_M–model $\mathcal{I}$ of Θ by Proposition 5.1. We define the P–interpretation $\mathcal{I}'$ for all variables $x_{i\Delta}^-$ and $x_{i\Delta}^+$ as ($i \in \mathbb{N}$, $\Delta \leq i\Delta \leq 1$):

$$\mathcal{I}'(x_{i\Delta}^-) = (x^{\mathcal{I}})_{i\Delta}^- \tag{5.22}$$

$$\mathcal{I}'(x_{i\Delta}^+) = (x^{\mathcal{I}})_{i\Delta}^+ \tag{5.23}$$

In other words, $\mathcal{I}'(x_{i\Delta}^-)$ and $\mathcal{I}'(x_{i\Delta}^+)$ correspond to the beginning and ending of the $i\Delta$–level set of the fuzzy time interval $x^{\mathcal{I}}$. Figure 5.2 illustrates the relationship between $\mathcal{I}$ and $\mathcal{I}'$. Clearly, $\mathcal{I}'$ satisfies (5.17)–(5.19). By

Proposition 4.7, we also have that all (sets of) linear constraints like (5.20) and (5.21) are satisfied. Hence, $\mathcal{I}$ is a P–model of Ψ.

Conversely, assume that Ψ is P–satisfiable. Then there exists a P–model $\mathcal{I}'$ of Ψ. We define the FI_M–interpretation $\mathcal{I}$ from $\mathcal{I}'$ as

$$x^{\mathcal{I}}(r) = \begin{cases} \max\{\lambda | \lambda \in M \wedge r \in [\mathcal{I}'(x_\lambda^-), \mathcal{I}'(x_\lambda^+)]\} & \text{if } r \in [\mathcal{I}'(x_\Delta)^-, \mathcal{I}'(x_\Delta)^+] \\ 0 & \text{otherwise} \end{cases}$$

(5.24)

for each x in X and r in $\mathbb{R}$. By construction of Ψ, we have that $x^{\mathcal{I}}$ is a fuzzy time interval. Moreover, by Proposition 4.7, we establish that $\mathcal{I}$ satisfies every FI–formula in Θ. □

Interestingly, by reducing FI–satisfiability to P–satisfiability of a set of linear constraints, we can impose additional constraints on the variables involved. For example, we can express that a given variable x corresponds to a crisp interval, rather than a fuzzy interval, by adding the linear constraints $x_\Delta^- = x_{2\Delta}^-, x_{2\Delta}^- = x_{3\Delta}^-, \ldots, x_{1-\Delta}^- = x_1^-, x_1^+ = x_{1-\Delta}^+, \ldots, x_{2\Delta}^+ = x_\Delta^+$ to Ψ. By additionally adding $x_1^- = x_1^+$, we can even ensure that x is always interpreted as an instant (time point). Similarly, we can add $x_1^- < x_1^+$ to express that x should never be interpreted as a time point. If we know that the beginning of x is inherently gradual, we can even impose $\{x_\Delta^- < x_{2\Delta}^-, x_{2\Delta}^- < x_{3\Delta}^-, \ldots, x_{1-\Delta}^- < x_1^-\}$. Such additional constraints can be very useful if it is a priori known which variables correspond to (possibly) vague events, crisp events, and instants. Moreover, adding such constraints does not change the computational complexity of the algorithm.

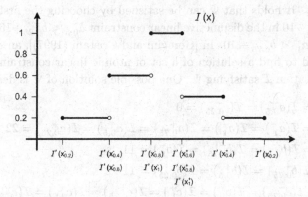

Fig. 5.2   There exists an FI_M–interpretation $\mathcal{I}$ for a set of FI–formulas Θ iff there exists a P–interpretation $\mathcal{I}'$ for the corresponding set Ψ of linear constraints.

Another important advantage of the reduction to P–satisfiability is that existing, optimized algorithms for reasoning about linear constraints can be used. Existing algorithms can not only be used for checking FI–satisfiability, but also to find FI–models (or consistent scenarios) of FI–satisfiable sets of FI–formulas. This technique is illustrated in the following example.

Example 5.1. Let $\Theta = \{bb_{10}^{\leqslant}(a, b) \geq 0.5, eb_5^{\leqslant}(c, a) \geq 0.5, eb_5^{\leqslant}(b, c) \geq 0.75\}$. We can choose $\Delta = 0.25$, and thus $M = \{0, 0.25, 0.5, 0.75, 1\}$. The linear constraints of the form (5.17)–(5.19) are given by

$$\Psi_1 = \{a_{0.25}^- \leq a_{0.5}^-, a_{0.5}^- \leq a_{0.75}^-, a_{0.75}^- \leq a_1^-, a_1^- \leq a_1^+,$$
$$a_1^+ \leq a_{0.75}^+, a_{0.75}^+ \leq a_{0.5}^+, a_{0.5}^+ \leq a_{0.25}^+,$$
$$b_{0.25}^- \leq b_{0.5}^-, b_{0.5}^- \leq b_{0.75}^-, b_{0.75}^- \leq b_1^-, b_1^- \leq b_1^+,$$
$$b_1^+ \leq b_{0.75}^+, b_{0.75}^+ \leq b_{0.5}^+, b_{0.5}^+ \leq b_{0.25}^+,$$
$$c_{0.25}^- \leq c_{0.5}^-, c_{0.5}^- \leq c_{0.75}^-, c_{0.75}^- \leq c_1^-, c_1^- \leq c_1^+,$$
$$c_1^+ \leq c_{0.75}^+, c_{0.75}^+ \leq c_{0.5}^+, c_{0.5}^+ \leq c_{0.25}^+\}$$

The additional linear constraints corresponding to the FI–formulas in Θ are given by

$$\Psi_2 = \{a_{0.5}^- < b_{0.25}^- - 10 \vee a_{0.75}^- < b_{0.5}^- - 10 \vee a_1^- < b_{0.75}^- - 10,$$
$$c_1^+ < a_{0.75}^- - 5, c_{0.75}^+ < a_1^- - 5,$$
$$b_1^+ < c_{0.5}^- - 5, b_{0.75}^+ < c_{0.75}^- - 5, b_{0.5}^+ < c_1^- - 5\}$$

The set Ψ of all linear constraints corresponding with Θ is then given by $\Psi_1 \cup \Psi_2$. It holds that Ψ can be satisfied by choosing the first disjunct $a_{0.5}^- < b_{0.25}^- - 10$ in the disjunctive linear constraint $a_{0.5}^- < b_{0.25}^- - 10 \vee a_{0.75}^- < b_{0.5}^- - 10 \vee a_1^- < b_{0.75}^- - 10$. In [Gerevini and Cristani (1997)], an algorithm is presented to find a solution of a set of atomic linear constraints, i.e., a P–interpretation $\mathcal{I}$ satisfying Ψ. One possible solution of Ψ is defined by

$$\mathcal{I}(a_{0.25}^-) = \mathcal{I}(a_{0.5}^-) = \mathcal{I}(c_{0.25}^-) = 0$$
$$\mathcal{I}(a_{0.75}^-) = \mathcal{I}(a_1^-) = \mathcal{I}(a_1^+) = \mathcal{I}(a_{0.75}^+) = \mathcal{I}(a_{0.5}^+) = \mathcal{I}(a_{0.25}^+) = 22$$
$$\mathcal{I}(b_{0.25}^-) = \mathcal{I}(b_{0.5}^-) = \mathcal{I}(b_{0.75}^-) = \mathcal{I}(b_1^-) = 11$$
$$\mathcal{I}(b_1^+) = \mathcal{I}(b_{0.75}^+) = \mathcal{I}(b_{0.5}^+) = \mathcal{I}(b_{0.25}^+) = 11$$
$$\mathcal{I}(c_{0.5}^-) = \mathcal{I}(c_{0.75}^-) = \mathcal{I}(c_1^-) = \mathcal{I}(c_1^+) = \mathcal{I}(c_{0.75}^+) = \mathcal{I}(c_{0.5}^+) = \mathcal{I}(c_{0.25}^+) = 16$$

As explained above, the P–model $\mathcal{I}$ of Ψ defines an FI_M–model $\mathcal{I}'$ of Θ.

In applications, we usually need to find an FI–satisfiable set of FI–formulas, corresponding to some given (natural language) description, rather than checking the FI–satisfiability of a given set of FI–formulas. Typically, in this context, the information provided may be inconsistent when interpreted as classical, crisp temporal relations. The goal is then to weaken information such as *A happened before B* to *A happened before B at least to degree 0.8*. The various lower and upper bounds introduced in this way (e.g., 0.8) should be the strongest possible, w.r.t. a given precision Δ. The next example illustrates this process.

Example 5.2. Consider again the example about Picasso's work from the introduction. To allow for a concise description, we use the following abbreviations to refer to the relevant events and periods:

BFT Picasso creates Bread and Fruit Dish on a Table
DMA Picasso creates the Demoiselles d'Avignon
AC Picasso's Analytical Cubism period
C Picasso's Cubism period

The information that Bread and Fruit Dish on a Table marks the beginning of Picasso's Analytical Cubism can be represented as

$$bb^{\preccurlyeq}(BFT, AC) \geq \lambda_1 \tag{5.25}$$
$$bb^{\preccurlyeq}(AC, BFT) \geq \lambda_2 \tag{5.26}$$
$$ee^{\ll}(BFT, AC) \geq \lambda_3 \tag{5.27}$$

where initially λ_1, λ_2 and λ_3 are assumed to be 1. Values lower than 1 are only considered when inconsistencies arise. Similarly, the information that the Demoiselles d'Avignon marks the beginning of Picasso's Cubist period can be represented as

$$bb^{\preccurlyeq}(DMA, C) \geq \lambda_4 \tag{5.28}$$
$$bb^{\preccurlyeq}(C, DMA) \geq \lambda_5 \tag{5.29}$$
$$ee^{\ll}(DMA, C) \geq \lambda_6 \tag{5.30}$$

Next, the information that Analytical Cubism is the first stage of Picasso's Cubism can be represented by

$$bb^{\preccurlyeq}(AC, C) \geq \lambda_7 \tag{5.31}$$
$$bb^{\preccurlyeq}(C, AC) \geq \lambda_8 \tag{5.32}$$
$$ee^{\ll}(AC, C) \geq \lambda_9 \tag{5.33}$$

In addition to this qualitative description, we also have some quantitative information. In particular, we know that Bread and Fruit Dish on a Table was created in 1909, the Demoiselles d'Avignon was created in 1907 and Analytical Cubism lasted from somewhere in 1908 to somewhere in 1912. We can encode this information using metric constraints by referring to an artificial time point Z, for instance, corresponding to the beginning of the year 1900:

$$bb_8^{\preccurlyeq}(Z, AC) \geq \lambda_{10} \qquad\qquad bb_{-9}^{\preccurlyeq}(AC, Z) \geq \lambda_{11} \qquad (5.34)$$

$$ee_{12}^{\preccurlyeq}(Z, AC) \geq \lambda_{12} \qquad\qquad ee_{-13}^{\preccurlyeq}(AC, Z) \geq \lambda_{13} \qquad (5.35)$$

$$bb_9^{\preccurlyeq}(Z, BFT) \geq \lambda_{14} \qquad\qquad ee_{-10}^{\preccurlyeq}(BFT, Z) \geq \lambda_{15} \qquad (5.36)$$

$$bb_7^{\preccurlyeq}(Z, DMA) \geq \lambda_{16} \qquad\qquad ee_{-8}^{\preccurlyeq}(DMA, Z) \geq \lambda_{17} \qquad (5.37)$$

When checking the FI–satisfiability of this representation for various values of the lower bounds λ_i, we need to ensure that Z is a time point. As discussed above, this can be done by adding the constraint $Z_{\Delta}^{-} = Z_{2\Delta}^{-} = \cdots = Z_1^{-} = Z_1^{+} = \cdots = Z_{\Delta}^{+}$ to the corresponding set of linear constraints. From available domain knowledge, we may moreover find out that creating a painting is a crisp event[5], and therefore impose that DMA and BFT are crisp intervals in a similar way.

For $\lambda_1 = \lambda_2 = \cdots = \lambda_{17} = 1$, the description above is not FI–satisfiable. Hence, we need to weaken one or more of the lower bounds, i.e., we let some of the λ_i correspond to values from M lower than 1. Different sets of lower bounds may be weakened to obtain an FI–satisfiable representation. Moreover, the actual strategy adopted to decide how to arrive at such a representation may differ from application to application, as well as depend on additional background information (e.g., degrees of confidence in each of the original natural language statements). In the example at hand, we may impose that $\lambda_{14} = \lambda_{15} = \lambda_{16} = \lambda_{17} = 1$, as Z, BFT and DMA all refer to crisp events. Furthermore, we may initially require that $\lambda_1 = \lambda_2 = \cdots = \lambda_{13}$, as we lack any further background knowledge for differentiating between the FI–formulas. Assuming $\Delta = 0.25$, we first try $\lambda_1 = \cdots = \lambda_{13} = 0.75$, which is not FI–satisfiable, and next $\lambda_1 = \cdots = \lambda_{13} = 0.5$, which turns out to be FI–satisfiable. Although we have now arrived at an FI–satisfiable interpretation of the natural language statements, it is not necessarily *maximally* FI–satisfiable, i.e., it may be the

---

[5]Although the assumption made in this example is reasonable in most contexts, creating a painting could be seen as a vague event as well, assuming, for instance, that related studies and sketches made prior to the actual painting belong to the creation to varying degrees.

case that not all of the λ_i's ($i \in \{1, 2, \ldots, 13\}$) need to be weakened to 0.5. Therefore, we subsequently try to strengthen the λ_i's again, one by one. For example, when $\lambda_2 = 0.75$ or even $\lambda_2 = 1$, the resulting representation remains FI–satisfiable. On the other hand, strengthening λ_1 to 0.75 leads to a representation which is not FI–satisfiable anymore (even when $\lambda_2 = 0.5$). Thus, after a linear number of FI–satisfiability checks, we obtain the following maximally FI–satisfiable representation:

$$\lambda_{14} = \lambda_{15} = \lambda_{16} = \lambda_{17} = 1$$
$$\lambda_2 = \lambda_3 = \lambda_4 = \lambda_6 = \lambda_7 = \lambda_8 = \lambda_9 = \lambda_{10} = \lambda_{12} = \lambda_{13} = 1$$
$$\lambda_1 = \lambda_5 = \lambda_{11} = 0.5$$

A corresponding FI–interpretation is depicted in Figure 5.3, illustrating that the inconsistencies in the original natural language statements are caused by the vagueness of the Analytical Cubism and Cubism periods. In this FI–interpretation, both periods are assumed to have started in 1907 to degree 0.5, and to have started completely in 1909.

5.3.2 *Computational Complexity*

Let $\mathcal{A}$ be a subset of $\mathcal{F}_X$, the set of all FI–formulas over a set of variables X. In the following discussion, we assume that X contains a sufficiently large, or infinite number of different variables. We call FISAT($\mathcal{A}$) the problem of deciding whether a finite set of FI–formulas from $\mathcal{A}$ is FI–

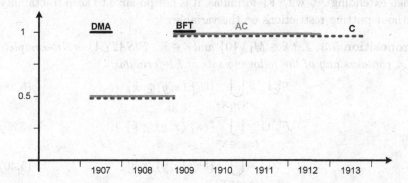

Fig. 5.3 FI–interpretation of events corresponding to the creation of Bread and Fruit Dish on a Table (*BFT*) and the Demoiselles d'Avignon (*DMA*), as well as Picasso's Analytical Cubism (*AC*) and Cubism (*C*) periods.

satisfiable. Deciding the P–satisfiability of an arbitrary set of linear constraints is NP–complete [Sontag (1985)]. To decide whether a set Θ of FI–formulas is FI–satisfiable, we can guess which disjuncts can be satisfied for all disjunctive FI–formulas, resulting in a set of atomic FI–formulas Θ'. Checking if Θ' is FI–satisfiable can be polynomially reduced to checking the P–satisfiability of a set of linear constraints, as explained above. We thus find that FISAT($\mathcal{A}$) is in NP for every $\mathcal{A} \subseteq \mathcal{F}_X$. As will become clear below, FISAT($\mathcal{F}_X$) is also NP–hard and thereby NP–complete. However, checking the P–satisfiability of a set of linear constraints without disjunctions is tractable [Jonsson and Bäckström (1998); Koubarakis (2001)]. From Proposition 4.7, it follows that a significant subset of the FI–formulas do not lead to disjunctive linear constraints. We will refer to this subset as $\mathcal{F}_X^t$:

$$\mathcal{F}_X^t = \bigcup_{(x,y) \in X^2} \bigcup_{d \in \mathbb{R}} \left(\{bb_d^\ll(x,y) \leq k | k \in M_1\} \cup \{ee_d^\ll(x,y) \leq k | k \in M_1\} \right.$$
$$\cup \{be_d^\ll(x,y) \leq k | k \in M_1\} \cup \{eb_d^\ll(x,y) \geq l | l \in M_0\}$$
$$\left. \cup \{bb_d^\ll(x,y) \geq 1, ee_d^\ll(x,y) \geq 1, be_d^\ll(x,y) \geq 1, eb_d^\ll(x,y) \leq 0\} \right)$$

Clearly FISAT($\mathcal{F}_X^t$) is tractable. Note, however, that the procedure described above for deciding FISAT($\mathcal{F}_X^t$) is only weakly polynomial, as it depends on the value of $\frac{1}{\Delta} = \rho$.

To support efficient reasoning, it is of interest to identify maximally tractable subsets of $\mathcal{F}_X$, i.e., sets of FI–formulas $\mathcal{A} \subseteq \mathcal{F}_X$ such that FISAT($\mathcal{A}$) is tractable and for any proper superset $\mathcal{A}'$ of $\mathcal{A}$, it holds that FISAT($\mathcal{A}'$) is NP–complete. As we show in the following two propositions, when extending $\mathcal{F}_X^t$ with FI–formulas, it is not possible to keep tractability without putting restrictions on the variables.

Proposition 5.3. *Let $k \in M_1 \setminus \{0\}$ and $d \in \mathbb{R}$. FISAT($\mathcal{A}$) is NP–complete if $\mathcal{A}$ contains any of the following sets of FI–formulas:*

$$\mathcal{F}_X^t \cup \bigcup_{(x,y) \in X^2} \{bb_d^\ll(x,y) \geq k\} \tag{5.38}$$

$$\mathcal{F}_X^t \cup \bigcup_{(x,y) \in X^2} \{ee_d^\ll(x,y) \geq k\} \tag{5.39}$$

$$\mathcal{F}_X^t \cup \bigcup_{(x,y) \in X^2} \{be_d^\ll(x,y) \geq k\} \tag{5.40}$$

$$\mathcal{F}_X^t \cup \bigcup_{(x,y) \in X^2} \{eb_d^\ll(x,y) \leq k\} \tag{5.41}$$

Proof. As an example, we show (5.38) for $d = 0$. The proof for (5.39)–(5.41) and $d \neq 0$ is entirely analogous.

Since $\text{FISAT}(\mathcal{F}_X)$ is in NP, we already have that $\text{FISAT}(\mathcal{A})$ is in NP. To establish the NP–hardness of $\text{FISAT}(\mathcal{A})$, we will show that 3SAT can be polynomially reduced to it. The proof is inspired by [Nebel and Bürckert (1995)], where a similar reduction is made to prove NP–hardness for the satisfiability problem in a subfragment of the Interval Algebra.

Let $\mathcal{D} = \{C_1, C_2, \ldots, C_n\}$, where C_i denotes a clause of the form $l_{i1} \vee l_{i2} \vee l_{i3}$, containing exactly three disjuncts. Each literal l_{ij} is either an atomic proposition or the negation of an atomic proposition. 3SAT is the problem of deciding whether $\mathcal{D}$ is satisfiable, i.e., deciding if there exists a truth assignment of the atomic propositions that makes all clauses from $\mathcal{D}$ true. To prove (5.38), we will construct a set Θ of FI–formulas from $\mathcal{A}$ which is FI–satisfiable iff $\mathcal{D}$ is satisfiable, thereby reducing 3SAT to $\text{FISAT}(\mathcal{A})$.

For each i in $\{1, \ldots, n\}$ and j in $\{1, 2, 3\}$, we add the following FI–formulas to Θ:

$$bb^{\ll}(a_{ij}, b_{ij}) \geq k \tag{5.42}$$
$$bb^{\ll}(c_{ij}, b_{ij}) \leq k - \Delta \tag{5.43}$$

where a_{ij}, b_{ij} and c_{ij} are different variables from X.

These FI–formulas correspond to the following linear constraints:

$$(a_{ij})_k^- < (b_{ij})_\Delta^- \vee (a_{ij})_{k+\Delta}^- < (b_{ij})_{2\Delta}^- \vee \cdots \vee (a_{ij})_1^- < (b_{ij})_{1-k+\Delta}^- \tag{5.44}$$
$$\{(b_{ij})_\Delta^- \leq (c_{ij})_k^-, (b_{ij})_{2\Delta}^- \leq (c_{ij})_{k+\Delta}^-, \ldots, (b_{ij})_{1-k+\Delta}^- \leq (c_{ij})_1^-\} \tag{5.45}$$

Linear constraints can be depicted as a graph in which nodes correspond to variables, and edges labeled with $<$ or $\leq$ are added between two nodes if $<$ or $\leq$ is imposed on the corresponding variables. Figure 5.4 shows the graph corresponding to (5.44)–(5.45). Linear constraints with disjunctions are displayed as dotted lines, as only one of several possible edges needs to be satisfied in this case. Furthermore, we add the following FI–formulas to Θ:

$$bb^{\ll}(c_{i1}, d_{i1}) \geq 1 \qquad\qquad bb^{\ll}(a_{i2}, d_{i1}) \leq 1 - \Delta$$
$$bb^{\ll}(c_{i2}, d_{i2}) \geq 1 \qquad\qquad bb^{\ll}(a_{i3}, d_{i2}) \leq 1 - \Delta$$
$$bb^{\ll}(c_{i3}, d_{i3}) \geq 1 \qquad\qquad bb^{\ll}(a_{i1}, d_{i3}) \leq 1 - \Delta$$

The corresponding linear constraints are given by

$$(c_{i1})_1^- < (d_{i1})_\Delta^- \qquad\qquad (d_{i1})_\Delta^- \leq (a_{i2})_1^- \tag{5.46}$$
$$(c_{i2})_1^- < (d_{i2})_\Delta^- \qquad\qquad (d_{i2})_\Delta^- \leq (a_{i3})_1^- \tag{5.47}$$
$$(c_{i3})_1^- < (d_{i3})_\Delta^- \qquad\qquad (d_{i3})_\Delta^- \leq (a_{i1})_1^- \tag{5.48}$$

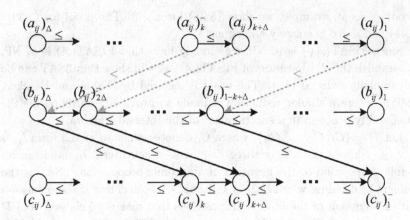

Fig. 5.4   Linear constraints (5.44)–(5.45).

Figure 5.5 contains a graph corresponding to Figure 5.4 for a_{i1}, b_{i1} and c_{i1}, as well as the graph for a_{i2}, b_{i2} and c_{i2}, and the graph for a_{i3}, b_{i3} and c_{i3}. For clarity, the nodes for the b_{ij}–variables are omitted. Furthermore, these three subgraphs are linked together by the constraints (5.46)–(5.48). If $(a_{i1})_1^- < (c_{i1})_1^-$, $(a_{i2})_1^- < (c_{i2})_1^-$ and $(a_{i3})_1^- < (c_{i3})_1^-$ would hold, we obtain $(a_{i1})_1^- < (c_{i1})_1^- < (a_{i2})_1^- < (c_{i2})_1^- < (a_{i3})_1^- < (c_{i3})_1^- < (a_{i1})_1^-$, and thus $(a_{i1})_1^- < (a_{i1})_1^-$ which cannot be satisfied. Hence, every FI–model of Θ corresponds to a P–model in which at least one of $(a_{i1})_1^- \geq (c_{i1})_1^-$, $(a_{i2})_1^- \geq (c_{i2})_1^-$ and $(a_{i3})_1^- \geq (c_{i3})_1^-$ holds. A truth assignment that makes l_{ij} true if $(a_{ij})_1^- \geq (c_{ij})_1^-$ will therefore make all clauses in $\mathcal{D}$ true. To ensure that such a truth assignment indeed exists, what remains is to make sure that an atomic proposition l_{ij} and its negation, denoted below by l_{rs}, are not made true simultaneously. If we want to define a correspondence between Θ and $\mathcal{D}$, we therefore need to encode that one of $(a_{ij})_1^- < (c_{ij})_1^-$ or $(a_{rs})_1^- < (c_{rs})_1^-$ must hold. This can be accomplished by adding the following FI–formulas to Θ:

$$bb^{\ll}(e_{ijrs}, c_{ij}) \leq \Delta \qquad (5.49)$$

$$bb^{\ll}(e_{ijrs}, f_{ijrs}) \geq 1 \qquad (5.50)$$

$$bb^{\ll}(a_{rs}, f_{ijrs}) \leq k - \Delta \qquad (5.51)$$

$$bb^{\ll}(e_{rsij}, c_{rs}) \leq \Delta \qquad (5.52)$$

$$bb^{\ll}(e_{rsij}, f_{rsij}) \geq 1 \qquad (5.53)$$

$$bb^{\ll}(a_{ij}, f_{rsij}) \leq k - \Delta \qquad (5.54)$$

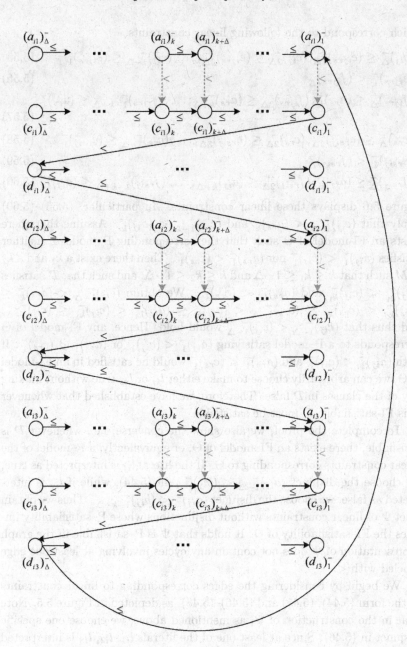

Fig. 5.5   Linear constraints (5.46)–(5.48).

which correspond to the following linear constraints

$$(c_{ij})_{\overline{\Delta}} \le (e_{ijrs})_{\overline{2\Delta}}, (c_{ij})_{\overline{2\Delta}} \le (e_{ijrs})_{\overline{3\Delta}}, \ldots, (c_{ij})_{\overline{1-\Delta}} \le (e_{ijrs})_{\overline{1}} \qquad (5.55)$$

$$(e_{ijrs})_{\overline{1}} < (f_{ijrs})_{\overline{\Delta}} \qquad (5.56)$$

$$(f_{ijrs})_{\overline{\Delta}} \le (a_{rs})_{\overline{k}}, (f_{ijrs})_{\overline{2\Delta}} \le (a_{rs})_{\overline{k+\Delta}}, \ldots, (f_{ijrs})_{\overline{1-k+\Delta}} \le (a_{rs})_{\overline{1}} \qquad (5.57)$$

$$(c_{rs})_{\overline{\Delta}} \le (e_{rsij})_{\overline{2\Delta}}, (c_{rs})_{\overline{2\Delta}} \le (e_{rsij})_{\overline{3\Delta}}, \ldots, (c_{rs})_{\overline{1-\Delta}} \le (e_{rsij})_{\overline{1}} \qquad (5.58)$$

$$(e_{rsij})_{\overline{1}} < (f_{rsij})_{\overline{\Delta}} \qquad (5.59)$$

$$(f_{rsij})_{\overline{\Delta}} \le (a_{ij})_{\overline{k}}, (f_{rsij})_{\overline{2\Delta}} \le (a_{ij})_{\overline{k+\Delta}}, \ldots, (f_{rsij})_{\overline{1-k+\Delta}} \le (a_{ij})_{\overline{1}} \quad (5.60)$$

Figure 5.6 displays these linear constraints. In particular, (5.55)–(5.60) imply that $(c_{ij})_{\overline{1-\Delta}} < (a_{rs})_{\overline{k}}$ and $(c_{rs})_{\overline{1-\Delta}} < (a_{ij})_{\overline{k}}$. Assume that there exists an FI-model of Θ such that the corresponding P–model $\mathcal{I}'$ neither satisfies $(a_{ij})_{\overline{1}} < (c_{ij})_{\overline{1}}$ nor $(a_{rs})_{\overline{1}} < (c_{rs})_{\overline{1}}$. Then there exist a k_1 and a k_2 in M such that $k \le k_1 \le 1-\Delta$ and $k \le k_2 \le 1-\Delta$, and such that $\mathcal{I}'$ satisfies $(a_{ij})_{\overline{k_1}} < (c_{ij})_{\overline{k_1}}$ and $(a_{rs})_{\overline{k_2}} < (c_{rs})_{\overline{k_2}}$. We obtain $(c_{ij})_{\overline{1-\Delta}} < (a_{rs})_{\overline{k}} \le (a_{rs})_{\overline{k_2}} < (c_{rs})_{\overline{k_2}} \le (c_{rs})_{\overline{1-\Delta}} < (a_{ij})_{\overline{k}} \le (a_{ij})_{\overline{k_1}} < (c_{ij})_{\overline{k_1}} \le (c_{ij})_{\overline{1-\Delta}}$, and thus that $(c_{ij})_{\overline{1-\Delta}} < (c_{ij})_{\overline{1-\Delta}}$ would hold. Hence, any FI-model of Θ corresponds to a P–model satisfying $(a_{ij})_{\overline{1}} < (c_{ij})_{\overline{1}}$ or $(a_{rs})_{\overline{1}} < (c_{rs})_{\overline{1}}$. If both $(a_{ij})_{\overline{1}} < (c_{ij})_{\overline{1}}$ and $(a_{rs})_{\overline{1}} < (c_{rs})_{\overline{1}}$ would be satisfied in an FI-model of Θ, we can arbitrarily choose to make either l_{ij} or l_{rs} true without making any of the clauses in $\mathcal{D}$ false. Therefore, we have established that whenever Θ is FI-satisfiable, $\mathcal{D}$ must be satisfiable.

To complete the proof, we also show the converse, i.e., whenever $\mathcal{D}$ is satisfiable, there exists an FI–model of Θ, or equivalently, a P–model of the linear constraints corresponding to Θ. If the literal l_{ij} is interpreted as true, we choose the disjunct $(a_{ij})_{\overline{1-\Delta}} < (b_{ij})_{\overline{1-k}}$ in (5.44), while if l_{ij} is interpreted as false, we choose the disjunct $(a_{ij})_{\overline{1}} < (b_{ij})_{\overline{1-k+\Delta}}$. Thus we obtain a set Ψ of linear constraints without disjunctions whose P–satisfiability implies the FI–satisfiability of Θ. It holds that Ψ is P–satisfiable iff the graph representation of Ψ does not contain any cycles involving at least one edge labeled with $<$.

We begin by considering the edges corresponding to linear constraints of the form (5.44), (5.45) and (5.46)–(5.48), as depicted in Figure 5.5. Note that in the construction of Ψ, as mentioned above, we choose one specific disjunct in (5.46). Since at least one of the literals l_{i1}, l_{i2}, l_{i3} is interpreted as true, for at least one j in $\{1, 2, 3\}$, we choose the disjunct $(a_{ij})_{\overline{1-\Delta}} < (b_{ij})_{\overline{1-k}}$, resulting in $(a_{ij})_{\overline{1-\Delta}} < (c_{ij})_{\overline{1-\Delta}}$ instead of $(a_{ij})_{\overline{1}} < (c_{ij})_{\overline{1}}$. For a cycle, however, we would need $(a_{i1})_{\overline{1}} < (c_{i1})_{\overline{1}}$, $(a_{i2})_{\overline{1}} < (c_{i2})_{\overline{1}}$ and

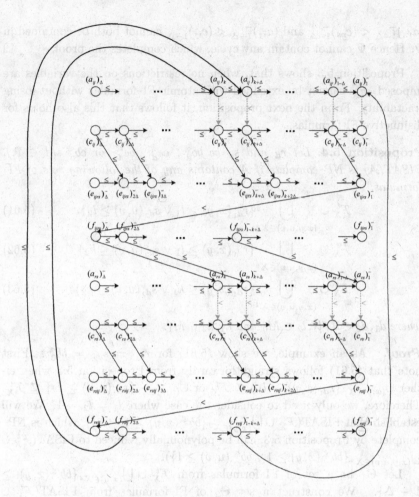

Fig. 5.6   Linear constraints (5.55)–(5.60).

$(a_{i3})_1^- < (c_{i3})_1^-$. From this we conclude that the constraints of the form (5.44), (5.45) and (5.46)–(5.48) alone do not lead to cycles in the graph representation of Ψ.

Any cycle would therefore have to include at least one edge corresponding to a linear constraint of the form (5.55)–(5.60). Such a cycle can only occur if for some i, j, r, s in $\{1, 2, \ldots, n\}$, we have that $(c_{ij})_{1-\Delta}^- < (a_{rs})_k^-$, $(a_{rs})_{1-\Delta}^- < (c_{rs})_{1-\Delta}^-$, $(c_{rs})_{1-\Delta}^- < (a_{ij})_k^-$ and $(a_{ij})_{1-\Delta}^- < (c_{ij})_{1-\Delta}^-$. By construction, $(c_{ij})_{1-\Delta}^- < (a_{rs})_k^-$ and $(c_{rs})_{1-\Delta}^- < (a_{ij})_k^-$ are only implied by Ψ iff $l_{ij} \equiv \neg l_{rs}$. However, if this is the case, either l_{ij} or l_{rs} is false, and

$(a_{rs})^-_{1-\Delta} < (c_{rs})^-_{1-\Delta}$ and $(a_{ij})^-_{1-\Delta} < (c_{ij})^-_{1-\Delta}$ cannot both be contained in Ψ. Hence Ψ cannot contain any cycle, which completes the proof. $\square$

Proposition 5.3 shows that, when no restrictions on the variables are imposed, $\mathcal{F}^t_X$ cannot be extended with atomic FI–formulas without losing tractability. From the next proposition, it follows that this also holds for disjunctive FI-formulas.

Proposition 5.4. *Let r_d and s_d be $bb^{\lll}_d$, $ee^{\lll}_d$, $be^{\lll}_d$ or $eb^{\lll}_d$ $(d \in \mathbb{R})$. FISAT($\mathcal{A}$) is NP–complete if $\mathcal{A}$ contains any of the following sets of FI–formulas:*

$$\mathcal{F}^t_X \cup \bigcup_{(x,y,u,v) \in X^4} \{r_{d_1}(x,y) \geq l_1 \vee s_{d_2}(u,v) \geq l_2\} \qquad (5.61)$$

$$\mathcal{F}^t_X \cup \bigcup_{(x,y,u,v) \in X^4} \{r_{d_1}(x,y) \geq l_1 \vee s_{d_2}(u,v) \leq k_2\} \qquad (5.62)$$

$$\mathcal{F}^t_X \cup \bigcup_{(x,y,u,v) \in X^4} \{r_{d_1}(x,y) \leq k_1 \vee s_{d_2}(u,v) \leq k_2\} \qquad (5.63)$$

where $d_1, d_2 \in \mathbb{R}$, $l_1, l_2 \in M_0$ and $k_1, k_2 \in M_1$.

Proof. As an example, we show (5.61) for $r_{d_1} = s_{d_2} = bb^{\lll}_0$. First note that (5.61) follows straightforwardly from Proposition 5.3 when either $\bigcup_{(x,y) \in X^2} \{r_{d_1}(x,y) \geq l_1\} \not\subseteq \mathcal{F}^t_X$ or $\bigcup_{(u,v) \in X^2} \{s_{d_2}(u,v) \geq l_2\} \not\subseteq \mathcal{F}^t_X$. Therefore, we only need to consider the case where $l_1 = l_2 = 1$. We will establish that FISAT($\mathcal{F}^t_X \cup \bigcup_{(x,y) \in X^2} \{bb^{\lll}(x,y) \geq 1 - \Delta\}$), which is NP–complete by Proposition 5.3, can be polynomially reduced to FISAT($\mathcal{F}^t_X \cup \bigcup_{(x,y,u,v) \in X^4} \{bb^{\lll}(x,y) \geq 1 \vee bb^{\lll}(u,v) \geq 1\}$).

Let Θ_1 be a set of FI–formulas from $\mathcal{F}^t_X \cup \bigcup_{(x,y) \in X^2} \{bb^{\lll}(x,y) \geq 1 - \Delta\}$. We construct a set Θ_2 of FI–formulas from FISAT($\mathcal{F}^t_X \cup \bigcup_{(x,y,u,v) \in X^4} \{bb^{\lll}(x,y) \geq 1 \vee bb^{\lll}(u,v) \geq 1\}$) by replacing every FI–formula in Θ_1 of the form $bb^{\lll}(x,y) \geq 1 - \Delta$ by the following FI–formulas

$$bb^{\lll}(x,v) \geq 1 \vee bb^{\lll}(u,y) \geq 1$$
$$bb^{\lll}(u,x) \leq \Delta$$
$$bb^{\lll}(y,v) \leq \Delta$$

giving rise to the following linear constraints:

$$x^-_1 < v^-_\Delta \vee u^-_1 < y^-_\Delta \qquad (5.64)$$

$$\{x^-_\Delta \leq u^-_{2\Delta}, x^-_{2\Delta} \leq u^-_{3\Delta}, \ldots, x^-_{1-\Delta} \leq u^-_1\} \qquad (5.65)$$

$$\{v^-_\Delta \leq y^-_{2\Delta}, v^-_{2\Delta} \leq y^-_{3\Delta}, \ldots, v^-_{1-\Delta} \leq y^-_1\} \qquad (5.66)$$

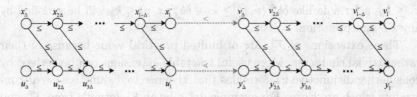

Fig. 5.7   Linear constraints (5.64)–(5.66).

These linear constraints are depicted in Figure 5.7. On the other hand, the corresponding FI–formula $bb^{\ll}(x,y) \geq 1 - \Delta$ from Θ_1 gives rise to

$$x_{1-\Delta}^- < y_\Delta^- \vee x_1^- < y_{2\Delta}^-$$

Let Ψ_1 and Ψ_2 be the sets of linear constraints corresponding to Θ_1 and Θ_2 respectively. By Proposition 5.2, it suffices to show that Ψ_1 is P–satisfiable iff Ψ_2 is P–satisfiable. Clearly, if $\mathcal{I}$ is a P–model of Ψ_2, $\mathcal{I}$ is also a P–model of Ψ_1. Conversely, we show that if $\mathcal{I}$ is a P–model of Ψ_1, there exists a P–model $\mathcal{I}'$ of Ψ_2. For all variables a occurring in Ψ_1, we define $\mathcal{I}'(a) = \mathcal{I}(a)$. Moreover, for additional variables occurring in (5.64)–(5.66), $\mathcal{I}'$ is defined as follows. For each k in $\{2\Delta, 3\Delta, \ldots, 1\}$, we define

$$\mathcal{I}'(u_k^-) = \mathcal{I}(x_{k-\Delta}^-)$$

while for each k in $\{\Delta, \ldots, 1-2\Delta, 1-\Delta\}$, we define

$$\mathcal{I}'(v_k^-) = \mathcal{I}(y_{k+\Delta}^-)$$

Finally, we define

$$\mathcal{I}'(u_\Delta^-) = \mathcal{I}'(u_{2\Delta}^-)$$
$$\mathcal{I}'(v_1^-) = \mathcal{I}'(v_{1-\Delta}^-)$$

Note that $\mathcal{I}'(x_{1-\Delta}^-) < \mathcal{I}'(y_\Delta^-) \vee \mathcal{I}'(x_1^-) < \mathcal{I}'(y_{2\Delta}^-)$ implies that $\mathcal{I}'$ satisfies (5.64), as $\mathcal{I}'(x_{1-\Delta}^-) = \mathcal{I}'(u_1^-)$ and $\mathcal{I}'(v_\Delta^-) = \mathcal{I}'(y_{2\Delta}^-)$. Clearly, $\mathcal{I}'$ also satisfies (5.65) and (5.66), hence $\mathcal{I}'$ is a P–model of Ψ_2.   □

To find tractable sets of FI–formulas that are larger than $\mathcal{F}_X^t$, we can impose restrictions on the variables in the FI–formulas. For example, it can be shown that $bb_d^{\ll}(x,x) = ee_d^{\ll}(x,x) = eb_d^{\ll}(x,x) = 0$ for any $d \geq 0$. Hence, for example, $bb_d^{\ll}(x,x) \leq k$ is satisfied by any FI–interpretation for every $k \in M_1$, while no FI–interpretation can satisfy $bb_d^{\ll}(x,x) \geq l$ for $l \in M_0$. Therefore, if ϕ is an FI–formula from $\mathcal{F}_X^t$, FISAT$(\mathcal{F}_X^t \cup \{\phi \vee bb_d^{\ll}(x,x) \leq k_1 \vee ee_d^{\ll}(x,x) \leq k_2 \vee bb_d^{\ll}(z,z) \geq l_1\})$ is still tractable. In the same way, if

$k_1 \leq k_2$, a formula like $bb_d^{\lll}(x, y) \geq k_1 \vee bb_d^{\lll}(x, y) \leq k_2$ will be satisfied by any FI–interpretation.

These extensions of $\mathcal{F}_X^t$ are of limited practical value because of their rather trivial character. More useful tractable extensions can be derived by considering disjunctive FI–formulas that give rise to disjunctive linear constraints which are Horn. For example, let ϕ be an FI–formula from $\mathcal{F}_X^t$ and let the corresponding set of linear constraints be given by $\{\rho_1, \rho_2, \ldots, \rho_s\}$. An FI–formula like $\phi \vee bb_d^{\lll}(x, y) \geq \Delta \vee bb_{-d}^{\lll}(y, x) \geq \Delta$ gives rise to the set of linear constraints $\{\alpha_1, \alpha_2, \ldots, \alpha_s\}$, where

$$\alpha_i = \rho_i \vee x_\Delta^- < y_\Delta^- - d \vee x_{2\Delta}^- < y_{2\Delta}^- - d \vee \cdots \vee x_1^- < y_1^- - d$$
$$\vee \, y_\Delta^- - d < x_\Delta^- \vee y_{2\Delta}^- - d < x_{2\Delta}^- \vee \cdots \vee y_1^- - d < x_1^-$$
$$= \rho_i \vee x_\Delta^- \neq y_\Delta^- - d \vee x_{2\Delta}^- \neq y_{2\Delta}^- - d \vee \cdots \vee x_1^- \neq y_1^- - d \quad.$$

In other words, each α_i is a Horn linear constraint ($i \in \{1, 2, \ldots, s\}$), hence $\text{FISAT}(\mathcal{F}_X^t \cup \{\phi \vee bb_d^{\lll}(x, y) \geq \Delta \vee bb_d^{\lll}(y, x) \geq \Delta\})$ is tractable.

More generally, let the set $\mathcal{G}_X$ of FI–formulas be defined as follows:

$$\mathcal{G}_X = \bigcup_{(x,y) \in X^2} \bigcup_{d \in \mathbb{R}} \{bb_d^{\lll}(x, y) \geq \Delta \vee bb_{-d}^{\lll}(y, x) \geq \Delta,$$

$$ee_d^{\lll}(x, y) \geq \Delta \vee ee_{-d}^{\lll}(y, x) \geq \Delta,$$

$$be_d^{\lll}(x, y) \geq 1 \vee be_{-d}^{\lll}(y, x) \geq 1\}$$

Furthermore, let $\mathcal{H}_X$ be recursively defined as follows

(1) If $\phi \in \mathcal{F}_X^t$, then $\phi \in \mathcal{H}_X$
(2) If $\phi_1 \in \mathcal{H}_X$ and $\phi_2 \in \mathcal{G}_X$, then $(\phi_1 \vee \phi_2) \in \mathcal{H}_X$
(3) $\mathcal{H}_X$ contains no other elements

As any FI–formula in $\mathcal{H}_X$ corresponds to a Horn linear constraint, or a set of Horn linear constraints, we have that $\text{FISAT}(\mathcal{H}_X)$ is tractable.

When $\Delta = 1$ (i.e., $M = \{0, 1\}$), we know by Proposition 5.1 that a set of FI–formulas is FI–satisfiable iff there exists an interpretation that assigns a crisp interval to every variable. The set of FI–formulas $\mathcal{H}_X$ is then exactly equal to the set of all Horn linear constraints involving the endpoints of these crisp intervals. Hence, for $\Delta = 1$, our (tractable) fuzzy temporal reasoning framework degenerates to reasoning about (Horn) linear constraints. By decreasing the value of Δ to $\frac{1}{2}, \frac{1}{3}, \frac{1}{4}, \frac{1}{5}, \ldots$, an increasingly higher expressiveness is achieved.

5.3.3 Entailment

Let Θ be a set of FI–formulas over X, and γ an FI–formula over X. We say that Θ entails γ, written $\Theta \models \gamma$, iff every FI–model of Θ is also an FI–model of $\{\gamma\}$. The notion of entailment is important for applications, because it allows to draw conclusions that are not explicitly contained in an initial set of assertions. Obviously, $\Theta \models \gamma$ if Θ and the negation of γ can never be satisfied at the same time. For example, $\Theta \models bb_d^{\ll}(x,y) \leq k$ iff $\Theta \cup \{bb_d^{\ll}(x,y) > k\}$ is not FI–satisfiable. Unfortunately, our procedure for checking FI–satisfiability cannot be applied for strict inequalities like $bb_d^{\ll}(x,y) > k$. However, for every FI_M–interpretation $\mathcal{I}$, we have that $bb_d^{\ll}(x^{\mathcal{I}},y^{\mathcal{I}}) > k$ iff $bb_d^{\ll}(x^{\mathcal{I}},y^{\mathcal{I}}) \geq k + \Delta$. Inspired by this observation, we say that Θ weakly entails γ (w.r.t. M), written $\Theta \models_M \gamma$ iff every FI_M–model of Θ is also an FI_M–model of $\{\gamma\}$. Checking weak entailment can straightforwardly be reduced to checking FI–satisfiability.

Proposition 5.5. *Let Θ be a set of FI–formulas and let $r(x,y)$ be one of $bb_d^{\ll}(x,y)$, $ee_d^{\ll}(x,y)$, $be_d^{\ll}(x,y)$ and $eb_d^{\ll}(x,y)$ $(d \in \mathbb{R}, (x,y) \in X^2)$. For k in M_1 and l in M_0 it holds that*

(1) $\Theta \models_M r(x,y) \geq l$ iff $\Theta \cup \{r(x,y) \leq l - \Delta\}$ is not FI–satisfiable.
(2) $\Theta \models_M r(x,y) \leq k$ iff $\Theta \cup \{r(x,y) \geq k + \Delta\}$ is not FI–satisfiable.

Proof. The proof follows trivially from the fact that for any FI_M–interpretation $\mathcal{I}$, $r(x^{\mathcal{I}},y^{\mathcal{I}}) < l$ implies $r(x^{\mathcal{I}},y^{\mathcal{I}}) \leq l - \Delta$ and $r(x^{\mathcal{I}},y^{\mathcal{I}}) > k$ implies $r(x^{\mathcal{I}},y^{\mathcal{I}}) \geq k + \Delta$. $\qquad\square$

As the name already suggests, weak entailment is a weaker notion than entailment, i.e., $(\Theta \models \gamma) \Rightarrow (\Theta \models_M \gamma)$. Nonetheless, weak entailment can still be used in applications to derive sound conclusions, by virtue of the following proposition.

Proposition 5.6. *Let Θ be a set of FI–formulas and let $r(x,y)$ be one of $bb_d^{\ll}(x,y)$, $ee_d^{\ll}(x,y)$, $be_d^{\ll}(x,y)$ and $eb_d^{\ll}(x,y)$ $(d \in \mathbb{R}, (x,y) \in X^2)$. For k in $M_1 \setminus \{1 - \Delta\}$ and l in $M_0 \setminus \{\Delta\}$ it holds that*

(1) If $\Theta \models_M r(x,y) \geq l$ then $\Theta \models r(x,y) \geq l - \Delta$
(2) If $\Theta \models_M r(x,y) \leq k$ then $\Theta \models r(x,y) \leq k + \Delta$

Proof. If $\Theta \models_M r(x,y) \geq l$, then by Proposition 5.5, $\Theta \cup \{r(x,y) \leq l-\Delta\}$ is not FI–satisfiable. Hence in every FI–interpretation of Θ, it holds that $r(x,y) > l - \Delta$, and in particular, $r(x,y) \geq l - \Delta$. The second implication is shown in the same way. $\qquad\square$

In the remainder of this section, we will investigate when weak entailment coincides with entailment, i.e., in which situations Proposition 5.5 also holds for (regular) entailment. Clearly $\Theta \cup \{\phi_1 \vee \phi_2 \vee \cdots \vee \phi_n\} \models \gamma$ iff $\Theta \cup \{\phi_1\} \models \gamma$ and $\Theta \cup \{\phi_2\} \models \gamma$ and ... and $\Theta \cup \{\phi_n\} \models \gamma$. Therefore, we can restrict ourselves to the case where Θ only contains atomic FI–formulas.

As we discussed in Section 5.3.1, for each set of FI–formulas Θ, we can find a set of linear constraints Ψ which is P–satisfiable iff Θ is FI–satisfiable. If Ψ does not contain any disjunctive linear constraints, we can represent Ψ as a graph G whose nodes correspond to variables like x_l^- or x_l^+ ($l \in M_0$). If Ψ contains a linear constraint $x + d \leq y$, we add an edge from the node corresponding with x to the node corresponding with y which is labeled with $(\leq, d)$. Similarly, if Ψ contains a linear constraint $x + d < y$, we add an edge labeled with $(<, d)$. The sum of two labels $(\leq, d_1)$ and $(\leq, d_2)$ is defined as $(\leq, d_1 + d_2)$, while the sum of $(<, d_1)$ and $(\leq, d_2)$, $(\leq, d_1)$ and $(<, d_2)$, or $(<, d_1)$ and $(<, d_2)$, is defined as $(<, d_1 + d_2)$. A cycle for which the edge labels sum up to $(\leq, d)$, with $d > 0$, or to $(<, d')$, with $d' \geq 0$, is called a forbidden cycle. It holds that Ψ is P–satisfiable iff there are no forbidden cycles in G [Kautz and Ladkin (1991)]. If Ψ does contain disjunctive linear constraints, every choice of the disjuncts leads to a different graph representation, and Ψ is P–satisfiable as soon as one of these graphs is free of forbidden cycles.

In the following, nodes corresponding to variables like x_l^- will be called beginning nodes, while nodes corresponding to variables like x_l^+ will be called ending nodes. Furthermore, we will sometimes assume that $\Delta = \frac{1}{2p}$ for some $p \in \mathbb{N} \setminus \{0\}$. Nodes like x_l^- or x_l^+ will then be called white nodes if $l \in \{2\Delta, 4\Delta, \ldots, 1\}$ and black nodes otherwise. Finally, for $l \in M \setminus \{0, \Delta\}$ and $k \in M_1$, $x_{l-\Delta}^-$ (resp. $x_{k+\Delta}^+$) will be called the left neighbour of x_l^- (resp. x_k^+), while $x_{k+\Delta}^-$ (resp. $x_{l-\Delta}^+$) will be called the right neighbour of x_k^- (resp. x_l^+).

Graphs representing linear constraints derived from a set of FI–formulas exhibit some interesting properties. In particular, the following two lemmas will be useful in reducing entailment checking to FI–satisfiability checking, or, equivalently, weak entailment checking.

Lemma 5.1. *Let $\Delta = \frac{1}{2p}$ for some $p \in \mathbb{N} \setminus \{0\}$, and let Θ be a (finite) set of FI–formulas. Let Ψ be the corresponding set of linear constraints and let G be the graph representation corresponding to a particular choice of disjuncts for the disjunctive constraints in Ψ. Furthermore, assume that there is a path in G from v to u in which each edge either corresponds to a linear* *constraint of the form (5.17)–(5.19), or is the result of an FI–formula in Θ of the form $bb_d^{\ll}(x,y) \leq k$, $ee_d^{\ll}(x,y) \leq k$, $be_d^{\ll}(x,y) \leq k$, or $eb_d^{\ll}(x,y) \geq l$ for some k in $\{0, 2\Delta, 4\Delta, \ldots, 1-2\Delta\}$ and l in $\{2\Delta, 4\Delta, \ldots, 1\}$). Assume, moreover, that:*

(1) v is a black beginning node and u is a white beginning node, or
(2) v is a white ending node and u is a black ending node, or
(3) v is a white ending node and u is a white beginning node, or
(4) v is a black beginning node and u is a black ending node.

It holds that there is a path in G from v to the left neighbour of u, as well as a path from the right neighbour of v to u. Moreover, for both paths, the edge labels sum up to the same value as for the original path.

Proof. As an example, we show that there is a path from v to the left neighbour of u when v is a black beginning node and u is a white beginning node. Let $v_0 = v, v_1, v_2, \ldots, v_n = u$ be a path in G from v to u. If an edge from v_j to v_{j+1} in G corresponds to a linear constraint that is the result of an FI–formula of the form $bb_d^{\ll}(x,y) \leq k$, with $k \in \{0, 2\Delta, 4\Delta, \ldots, 1-2\Delta\}$, then v_j and v_{j+1} are either both white beginning nodes, or both black beginning nodes. If this edge is the result of an FI–formula of the form $ee_d^{\ll}(x,y) \leq k$, v_j and v_{j+1} are both white ending nodes or both black ending nodes. Finally, if the edge from v_j to v_{j+1} is the result of an FI–formula of the form $be_d^{\ll}(x,y) \leq k$, or an FI–formula of the form $eb_d^{\ll}(x,y) \geq l$, with $l \in \{2\Delta, 4\Delta, \ldots, 1\}$, either v_j is a white ending node and v_{j+1} a black beginning node, or v_j is a black ending node and v_{j+1} a white beginning node. The only remaining possibility is that the edge from v_j to v_{j+1} corresponds to a linear constraint of the form (5.17)–(5.19).

First assume that none of the edges on the path from v to u corresponds to a linear constraint of the form (5.17)–(5.19). Then all of the nodes $v_1, \ldots, v_{n-1}$ need to be beginning nodes, as none of the remaining types of edges starts at a beginning node and ends at an ending node. This means that all edges $(v_0, v_1), (v_1, v_2), \ldots, (v_{n-1}, v_n)$ would correspond to a linear constraint that is the result of an FI–formula of the form $bb_d^{\ll}(x,y) \leq k$. Thus, from the fact that v is a black node, we establish that $v_1, v_2, \ldots, v_n$ are all black nodes. This, however, is not possible since $u = v_n$ is a white beginning node.

Hence, at least one of the edges corresponds to a linear constraint of the form (5.17)–(5.19). Let (v_s, v_{s+1}) be the last of these edges. If (v_s, v_{s+1}) corresponds to an edge of the form (5.17), v_{s+1} is a white ending node.

Then all edges between v_{s+1} and v_n correspond to FI–formulas of the form $ee_d^{\ll}(x,y) \leq k$, $be_d^{\ll}(x,y) \leq k$, or $eb_d^{\ll}(x,y) \geq l$. This would imply that the nodes $v_{s+2}, v_{s+3}, \ldots, v_n$ are all white ending nodes or black beginning nodes. This, however, is not possible since $u = v_n$ is a white beginning node. Therefore, (v_s, v_{s+1}) has to correspond to either (5.18) or (5.19). In both cases, v_{s+1} is the right neighbour of v_s, and the path $v_0, v_1, \ldots, v_s, v'_{s+2}, v'_{s+3}, \ldots, v'_n$, where v'_i denotes the left neighbour of v_i, is a path from v to the left neighbour v'_n of u. Moreover, the edge labels of $v'_{s+2}, v'_{s+3}, \ldots, v'_n$ are the same as those of $v_{s+2}, v_{s+3}, \ldots, v_n$ (i.e., $(\leq, 0)$), and the edge label of (v_s, v_{s+1}) is $(\leq, 0)$, which adds nothing to the sum of the edge labels on the original path.   □

We define the right(resp. left) neighbour of an edge from v to u as the edge from the right (resp. left) neighbour of v to the right (resp. left) neighbour of u.

Lemma 5.2. *Let* $\Delta = \frac{1}{2p}$ *for some p in* $\mathbb{N} \setminus \{0\}$, *and let* Θ *and* Ψ *be defined as before. Moreover, assume that all upper and lower bounds in* Θ *are taken from* $\{0, 2\Delta, 4\Delta, \ldots, 1\}$. *Let* $\mathcal{I}$ *be a P–model of* Ψ, *and let* G_1 *be the corresponding graph representation of* Ψ *without forbidden cycles. Let the graph* G_2 *be constructed from* G_1 *by replacing*

(1) edges resulting from an FI–formula of the form $bb_d^{\ll}(x,y) \geq l$ *by their right neighbour if they start from a black beginning node;*

(2) edges resulting from an FI–formula of the form $ee_d^{\ll}(x,y) \geq l$ *by their right neighbour if they start from a white ending node;*

(3) edges resulting from an FI–formula of the form $be_d^{\ll}(x,y) \geq l$ *or* $eb_d^{\ll}(x,y) \leq k$ *by their right neighbour if they start from a black beginning node.*

It holds that G_2 *does not contain any forbidden cycles.*

Proof.   Assume that G_2 contains a forbidden cycle $v_1, v_2, \ldots, v_n, v_1$, and let (v_r, v_{r+1}) be an edge in G_2 that does not occur in G_1. Then (v_r, v_{r+1}) is the right neighbour of the edge (v'_r, v'_{r+1}) from G_1.

Moreover, first assume that v_r is a white beginning node and v_{r+1} is a black beginning node. Suppose that the edge from v_r to v_{r+1} is the only edge in the cycle that corresponds to an FI–formula of the form $bb_d^{\ll}(x,y) \geq l$, $ee_d^{\ll}(x,y) \geq l$, $be_d^{\ll}(x,y) \geq l$ or $eb_d^{\ll}(x,y) \leq k$. This means that the path $v_{r+1}, v_{r+2}, \ldots, v_n, v_1, \ldots, v_r$ in G_2 also exists in G_1. Indeed, none of the constraints on the edges of this path fulfills the conditions for replacement in

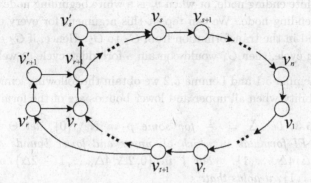

Fig. 5.8   The forbidden cycle in G_2 is independent from the fact that the edge (v'_r, v'_{r+1}) in G_1 was replaced by (v_r, v_{r+1}).

the construction process of G_2 from G_1. Furthermore, all of the constraints on the edges of this path fulfill the conditions of Lemma 5.1. Hence, we establish that in G_1 there is a path from v_{r+1} to v'_r whose edge labels sum up to the same value as the edge labels of the path $v_{r+1}, v_{r+2}, \ldots, v_{r-1}, v_r$. This would mean that G_1 contains the forbidden cycle consisting of the path from v_{r+1} to v'_r, the edge from v'_r to v'_{r+1} and the edge from v'_{r+1} to v_{r+1}. Note that the latter edge exists since v'_{r+1} is the left neighbour of v_{r+1}.

Therefore, at least two edges in the forbidden cycle have to correspond to an FI–formula of the form $bb_d^\lll(x,y) \geq l$, $ee_d^\lll(x,y) \geq l$, $be_d^\lll(x,y) \geq l$ or $eb_d^\lll(x,y) \leq k$. Let the edge from v_s to v_{s+1} be the first such edge in the forbidden cyle after v_{r+1}, and let the edge from v_t to v_{t+1} be the last such edge in the forbidden cycle before v_r (where $r + 1 = s$ or $t + 1 = r$ are also allowed). Figure 5.8 depicts the forbidden cycle. It holds that v_s is either a white beginning node or a black ending node, because of the way we transformed G_1 to G_2. In both cases, we can establish by Lemma 5.1 that there is a path from v_{r+1} to the left neighbour v'_s of v_s whose edge labels sum up to the same value as those of the path from v_{r+1} to v_s. In the same way, we have by construction of G_2 that v_{t+1} is either a black beginning node or a white ending node. From Lemma 5.1, we obtain that there is a path from v_{t+1} to v'_r, whose edge labels sum up to the same value as those of the path from v_{t+1} to v_r.

Thus we have established that the forbidden cycle in G_2 is independent from the fact that the edge (v'_r, v'_{r+1}) in G_1 was replaced by (v_r, v_{r+1}). In a similar way, we can show this result when v_r is a black ending node and

v_{r+1} is a white ending node, or when v_r is a white beginning node and v_{r+1} is a white ending node. We can repeat this argument for every edge that was changed in the transformation from G_1 to G_2. Hence, if G_2 contained a forbidden cycle, then G_1 would contain a forbidden cycle as well. □

From Lemma 5.1 and Lemma 5.2 we obtain the following lemma about FI–satisfiability when all upper and lower bounds are of the form $2i\Delta$.

Lemma 5.3. *Let* $\Delta = \frac{1}{2p}$ *for some* p *in* $\mathbb{N} \setminus \{0\}$, *let* Θ *be a set of atomic FI–formulas in which all upper and lower bounds are taken from* $\{0, 2\Delta, 4\Delta, \ldots, 1\}$. *For* l *in* $\{0, 2\Delta, 4\Delta, \ldots, 1 - 2\Delta\}$ *and* k *in* $\{2\Delta, 4\Delta, \ldots, 1\}$, *it holds that:*

(1) $\Theta \cup \{bb_d^{\lll}(x, y) \geq l + \Delta\}$ *is FI–satisfiable iff* $\Theta \cup \{bb_d^{\lll}(x, y) \geq l + 2\Delta\}$ *is FI–satisfiable;*

(2) $\Theta \cup \{ee_d^{\lll}(x, y) \geq l + \Delta\}$ *is FI–satisfiable iff* $\Theta \cup \{ee_d^{\lll}(x, y) \geq l + 2\Delta\}$ *is FI–satisfiable;*

(3) $\Theta \cup \{be_d^{\lll}(x, y) \geq l + \Delta\}$ *is FI–satisfiable iff* $\Theta \cup \{be_d^{\lll}(x, y) \geq l + 2\Delta\}$ *is FI–satisfiable;*

(4) $\Theta \cup \{eb_d^{\lll}(x, y) \leq k - \Delta\}$ *is FI–satisfiable iff* $\Theta \cup \{eb_d^{\lll}(x, y) \leq k - 2\Delta\}$ *is FI–satisfiable.*

Proof. As an example, we show that $\Theta \cup \{bb_d^{\lll}(x, y) \geq l + \Delta\}$ is FI–satisfiable iff $\Theta \cup \{bb_d^{\lll}(x, y) \geq l + 2\Delta\}$ is FI–satisfiable. If Θ is not FI–satisfiable, or x or y does not occur in the FI–formulas in Θ, the proof is trivial. Therefore, assume that Θ is FI–satisfiable and contains both FI–formulas involving x and FI–formulas involving y. If $\Theta \cup \{bb_d^{\lll}(x, y) \geq l + \Delta\}$ is not FI–satisfiable, then clearly $\Theta \cup \{bb_d^{\lll}(x, y) \geq l + 2\Delta\}$ is not FI–satisfiable either. Hence, we only need to show that if $\Theta \cup \{bb_d^{\lll}(x, y) \geq l + 2\Delta\}$ is not FI–satisfiable, $\Theta \cup \{bb_d^{\lll}(x, y) \geq l + \Delta\}$ cannot be FI–satisfiable.

Let Ψ be the set of linear constraints corresponding to the FI–formulas in Θ, and let $\mathcal{I}$ be a P–model of Ψ. The linear constraint corresponding to $bb_d^{\lll}(x, y) \geq l + \Delta$ is given by:

$$x_{l+\Delta}^- < y_\Delta^- - d \vee x_{l+2\Delta}^- < y_{2\Delta}^- - d \vee \cdots \vee x_1^- < y_{1-l}^- - d \qquad (5.67)$$

while the linear constraint corresponding to $bb_d^{\lll}(x, y) \geq l + 2\Delta$ is given by

$$x_{l+2\Delta}^- < y_\Delta^- - d \vee x_{l+3\Delta}^- < y_{2\Delta}^- - d \vee \cdots \vee x_1^- < y_{1-l-\Delta}^- - d \qquad (5.68)$$

If $\Theta \cup \{bb_d^{\lll}(x, y) \geq l + 2\Delta\}$ is not FI–satisfiable, a forbidden cycle emerges when adding an edge corresponding to any of the disjuncts of (5.68) to the graph representation of Θ which corresponds with $\mathcal{I}$. This means that any P–model of Θ will correspond to a choice of disjuncts that leads to a graph representation G of Θ in which there is a path from y_{Δ}^{-} to $x_{l+2\Delta}^{-}$, a path from $y_{2\Delta}^{-}$ to $x_{l+3\Delta}^{-}$, etc. Moreover, the edge labels of the path from $y_{(i+1)\Delta}^{-}$ to $x_{l+(2+i)\Delta}^{-}$ sum up to a value $(d_i, \leq)$ or $(d_i, <)$ such that $d_i + d \geq 0$ $(i \in \{0, 1, 2, \ldots, \frac{1-l}{\Delta} - 2\})$.

We now transform the graph G to a graph G' by applying the transformation from Lemma 5.2. The changing of edges in this transformation corresponds to choosing different disjuncts for the disjunctive linear constraints in Ψ. As this transformation cannot introduce forbidden cycles, the graph G' corresponds to a P–model of Ψ. Therefore G' contains a path from $y_{(i+1)\Delta}^{-}$ to $x_{l+(2+i)\Delta}^{-}$ for every i in $\{0, 1, 2, \ldots, \frac{1-l}{\Delta} - 2\}$. Let $y_{\Delta}^{-} = v_0, v_1, v_2, \ldots, v_n = x_{l+2\Delta}^{-}$ be a path from y_{Δ}^{-} to $x_{l+2\Delta}^{-}$.

If this path contains no edges that correspond to an FI–formula of the form $bb_{d'}^{\lll}(x', y') \geq l'$, $ee_{d'}^{\lll}(x', y') \geq l'$, $be_{d'}^{\lll}(x', y') \geq l'$ or $eb_{d'}^{\lll}(x', y') \leq k'$, we can apply Lemma 5.1 to establish that there is a path in G' from y_{Δ}^{-} to $x_{l+\Delta}^{-}$, the left neighbour of v_n, and a path from $y_{2\Delta}^{-}$, the right neighbour of y_{Δ}^{-}, to $x_{l+2\Delta}^{-}$. As none of the edges in these paths are changed in the transformation from G to G', these paths also occur in G.

Next, assume that the path from v_0 to v_n contains at least one edge which corresponds to an FI–formula of the form $bb_{d'}^{\lll}(x', y') \geq l'$, $ee_{d'}^{\lll}(x', y') \geq l'$, $be_{d'}^{\lll}(x', y') \geq l'$ or $eb_{d'}^{\lll}(x', y') \leq k'$. Let (v_s, v_{s+1}) and (v_r, v_{r+1}) be the first and last of these edges respectively. Then v_s is either a white beginning node or a black ending node, because of the nature of the transformation from G to G'. The path between v_0 and v_s therefore satisfies the conditions of Lemma 5.1. Thus we find that G' contains a path from $y_{2\Delta}^{-}$, the right neighbour of y_{Δ}^{-}, to $x_{l+2\Delta}^{-}$. Similarly, v_{r+1} is either a black beginning node, or a white ending node. By Lemma 5.1 we find that G' contains a path from y_{Δ}^{-} to $x_{l+\Delta}^{-}$, the left neighbour of v_n.

In the same way, we find from the fact that G' contains a path from $y_{3\Delta}^{-}$ to $x_{l+4\Delta}^{-}$ that G' also contains a path from $y_{3\Delta}^{-}$ to $x_{l+3\Delta}^{-}$ and from $y_{4\Delta}^{-}$ to $x_{l+4\Delta}^{-}$, etc. Adding an edge to G' corresponding to any of the disjuncts in (5.67) therefore leads to a forbidden cycle in G'. Using Lemma 5.2, we can conclude from this that adding an edge to G corresponding to any of the disjuncts in (5.67) would lead to a forbidden cycle as well. Hence, in any P–model of Θ, it holds that neither $x_{l+\Delta}^{-} < y_{\Delta}^{-} - d$, $x_{l+2\Delta}^{-} < y_{2\Delta}^{-} - d, \ldots$, or $x_1^{-} < y_{1-l}^{-} - d$ can be satisfied, or, in other words, that $\Theta \cup \{bb_d^{\lll}(x, y) \geq l + \Delta\}$ is not FI–satisfiable. $\square$

Finally, we arrive at the following characterization of entailment in terms of FI–satisfiability for FI–formulas of the form $bb_d^{\ll}(x,y) \leq k$, $ee_d^{\ll}(x,y) \leq k$, $be_d^{\ll}(x,y) \leq k$, and $eb_d^{\ll}(x,y) \geq l$.

Proposition 5.7. *Let Θ be a set of atomic FI–formulas. It holds for k in M_1 and l in M_0 that*

(1) $\Theta \models bb_d^{\ll}(x,y) \leq k$ iff $\Theta \cup \{bb_d^{\ll}(x,y) \geq k+\Delta\}$ is not FI–satisfiable;
(2) $\Theta \models ee_d^{\ll}(x,y) \leq k$ iff $\Theta \cup \{ee_d^{\ll}(x,y) \geq k+\Delta\}$ is not FI–satisfiable;
(3) $\Theta \models be_d^{\ll}(x,y) \leq k$ iff $\Theta \cup \{be_d^{\ll}(x,y) \geq k+\Delta\}$ is not FI–satisfiable;
(4) $\Theta \models eb_d^{\ll}(x,y) \geq l$ iff $\Theta \cup \{eb_d^{\ll}(x,y) \leq l-\Delta\}$ is not FI–satisfiable.

Proof. As an example, we show that $\Theta \models bb_d^{\ll}(x,y) \leq k$ iff $\Theta \cup \{bb_d^{\ll}(x,y) \geq k+\Delta\}$ is not FI–satisfiable. Clearly, if $\Theta \cup \{bb_d^{\ll}(x,y) \geq k+\Delta\}$ is FI–satisfiable, then $\Theta \not\models bb_d^{\ll}(x,y) \leq k$. Therefore, we only need to show that if there is an FI–model of Θ which does not satisfy $bb_d^{\ll}(x,y) \leq k$, it holds that $\Theta \cup \{bb_d^{\ll}(x,y) \geq k+\Delta\}$ is FI–satisfiable.

Let $\mathcal{I}$ be an FI–model of Θ, and assume that $bb_d^{\ll}(x^{\mathcal{I}},y^{\mathcal{I}}) > k$. There exists an n in $\mathbb{N}$ such that $bb_d^{\ll}(x^{\mathcal{I}},y^{\mathcal{I}}) \geq k + \frac{\Delta}{2^n}$. Obviously, we have that $\Theta \cup \{bb_d^{\ll}(x,y) \geq k + \frac{\Delta}{2^n}\}$ is FI–satisfiable. By letting $\frac{\Delta}{2^n}$ play the role of Δ, we obtain using Lemma 5.3 that $\Theta \cup \{bb_d^{\ll}(x,y) \geq k + \frac{\Delta}{2^{n-1}}\}$ is FI–satisfiable. Again applying Lemma 5.3 reveals that also $\Theta \cup \{bb_d^{\ll}(x,y) \geq k + \frac{\Delta}{2^{n-2}}\}$ is FI–satisfiable. By repeating this argument n times, we find that $\Theta \cup \{bb_d^{\ll}(x,y) \geq k + \Delta\}$ is FI–satisfiable. $\square$

To find a characterization of entailment for FI–formulas of the form $bb_d^{\ll}(x,y) \geq l$, $ee_d^{\ll}(x,y) \geq l$, $be_d^{\ll}(x,y) \geq l$, and $eb_d^{\ll}(x,y) \leq k$, we restrict ourselves to the case where Θ only contains FI–formulas from $\mathcal{F}_X^t$.

Lemma 5.4. *Let $\Delta = \frac{1}{2p}$ for some $p \in \mathbb{N} \setminus \{0\}$, let Θ be a set of FI–formulas from $\mathcal{F}_X^t$ in which all upper and lower bounds are taken from $\{0, 2\Delta, 4\Delta, \ldots, 1\}$. For l in $\{0, 2\Delta, 4\Delta, \ldots, 1 - 2\Delta\}$ and k in $\{2\Delta, 4\Delta, \ldots, 1\}$, it holds that:*

(1) $\Theta \cup \{be_d^{\ll}(x,y) \leq k-\Delta\}$ is FI–satisfiable iff $\Theta \cup \{be_d^{\ll}(x,y) \leq k-2\Delta\}$ is FI–satisfiable;
(2) $\Theta \cup \{eb_d^{\ll}(x,y) \geq l+\Delta\}$ is FI–satisfiable iff $\Theta \cup \{eb_d^{\ll}(x,y) \geq l+2\Delta\}$ is FI–satisfiable.

Moreover, for k in $\{4\Delta, 6\Delta, \ldots, 1\}$, it holds that

(1) $\Theta \cup \{bb_d^{\ll}(x,y) \leq k-\Delta\}$ is FI–satisfiable iff $\Theta \cup \{bb_d^{\ll}(x,y) \leq k-2\Delta\}$ is FI–satisfiable;

(2) $\Theta \cup \{ee_d^{\lll}(x,y) \leq k - \Delta\}$ *is FI–satisfiable iff* $\Theta \cup \{ee_d^{\lll}(x,y) \leq k - 2\Delta\}$ *is FI–satisfiable.*

Proof. As an example, we show that for $k \in \{4\Delta, 6\Delta, \ldots, 1\}$, $\Theta \cup \{bb_d^{\lll}(x,y) \leq k - \Delta\}$ is FI–satisfiable iff $\Theta \cup \{bb_d^{\lll}(x,y) \leq k - 2\Delta\}$ is FI–satisfiable. Clearly, if $\Theta \cup \{bb_d^{\lll}(x,y) \leq k - 2\Delta\}$ is FI–satisfiable, then also $\Theta \cup \{bb_d^{\lll}(x,y) \leq k - \Delta\}$ is FI–satisfiable. Conversely, we show that if $\Theta \cup \{bb_d^{\lll}(x,y) \leq k - 2\Delta\}$ is not FI–satisfiable, then also $\Theta \cup \{bb_d^{\lll}(x,y) \geq k - \Delta\}$ is not FI–satisfiable.

Let Ψ be the set of linear constraints corresponding to Θ. The linear constraints corresponding to $bb_d^{\lll}(x,y) \leq k - 2\Delta$ are given by:

$$\{y_\Delta^- \leq x_{k-\Delta}^- + d, y_{2\Delta}^- \leq x_k^- + d, \ldots, y_{1-k+2\Delta}^- \leq x_1^- + d\} \tag{5.69}$$

while the linear constraints corresponding to $bb_d^{\lll}(x,y) \leq k - \Delta$ are given by

$$\{y_\Delta^- \leq x_k^- + d, y_{2\Delta}^- \leq x_{k+\Delta}^- + d, \ldots, y_{1-k+\Delta}^- \leq x_1^- + d\} \tag{5.70}$$

Assume that $\Theta \cup \{bb_d^{\lll}(x,y) \leq k - 2\Delta\}$ is not FI–satisfiable. This means that the graph G corresponding to the linear constraints in Ψ contains a path from $x_{k-\Delta}^-$ to y_Δ^-, or a path from x_k^- to $y_{2\Delta}^-$, or $\ldots$, or a path from x_1^- to $y_{1-k+2\Delta}^-$. Moreover, the edge labels in this path sum up to $(<, d')$ where $d' + d \geq 0$, or $(\leq, d'')$ where $d'' + d > 0$, i.e., adding the edges corresponding to (5.69) would introduce a forbidden cycle in the graph. Note that there is only one graph G corresponding to Ψ, as Ψ contains no disjunctive linear constraints.

Let $v_1, v_2, \ldots, v_n$ be a path from $x_{k+(i-1)\Delta}^-$ to $y_{(1+i)\Delta}^-$, for some i in $\{0, 1, \ldots, 1 + \frac{1-k}{\Delta}\}$, where v_1 and v_n are both white beginning nodes or both black beginning nodes. First assume that this path contains no edges corresponding to an FI–formula of the form $bb_{d'}^{\lll}(x',y') \geq 1$, $ee_{d'}^{\lll}(x',y') \geq 1$, $be_{d'}^{\lll}(x',y') \geq 1$ or $eb_{d'}^{\lll}(x',y') \leq 0$. Note that edges corresponding to FI–formulas of the form $ee_d^{\lll}(x,y) \leq k$, $be_d^{\lll}(x,y) \leq k$, and $eb_d^{\lll}(x,y) \geq l$ always start at an ending node. Hence, either the path from v_1 to v_n contains no edges of the form $ee_d^{\lll}(x,y) \leq k$, $be_d^{\lll}(x,y) \leq k$, and $eb_d^{\lll}(x,y) \geq l$, or this path contains at least one edge corresponding to (5.17). In the former case, however, it is not possible to obtain a path from a node $a_{k_1}^-$ to a node $b_{k_2}^-$ if $k_1 > k_2$. Hence, since $k > 2\Delta$, the path from v_1 to v_n needs to contain at least one edge of the form (5.17). Assume that v_1 and v_n are white beginning nodes, and let the edge from v_i to v_{i+1} be the last edge of the form (5.17). Then v_{i+1} is a white ending node, and by Lemma 5.1

there exists a path from v_{i+1} to the left neighbour of v_n. Hence, there is a path from $x_{k+(i-1)\Delta}^-$ to $y_{i\Delta}^-$. In particular, we obtain that adding the edges corresponding to (5.70) would introduce a forbidden cycle, in other words, that $\Theta \cup \{bb_d^\lll(x,y) \geq k - \Delta\}$ cannot be FI–satisfiable. Next, assume that v_1 and v_n are black beginning nodes and let the edge from v_j to v_{j+1} be the first edge of the form (5.17). Using Lemma 5.1, we now find that there must exist a path from the right neighbour of v_1 to v_j, and again, that $\Theta \cup \{bb_d^\lll(x,y) \geq k - \Delta\}$ is not FI–satisfiable.

Finally, assume that the path from v_1 to v_n contains at least one edge corresponding to an FI–formula of the form $bb_{d'}^\lll(x',y') \geq 1$, $ee_{d'}^\lll(x',y') \geq 1$, $be_{d'}^\lll(x',y') \geq 1$ or $eb_{d'}^\lll(x',y') \leq 0$. Let the edge from v_i to v_{i+1} and the edge from v_j to v_{j+1} be the first and the last of these edges respectively. Then v_{j+1} is either a black beginning node or a white ending node and v_i is either a white beginning node or a black ending node. Using Lemma 5.1, we find that there must exist a path from v_1 to the left neighbour of v_n if v_1 and v_n are white beginning nodes, and a path from the right neighbour of v_1 to v_n if v_1 and v_n are black beginning nodes. In either case, we find that adding the edges corresponding to (5.70) would introduce a forbidden cycle. $\square$

Note that the FI–satisfiability of $\Theta \cup \{bb_d^\lll(x,y) \leq \Delta\}$ does not necessarily imply that $\Theta \cup \{bb_d^\lll(x,y) \leq 0\}$ is FI–satisfiable. For example, for $d' + d > 0$, it holds that $\{bb_{d'}^\lll(y,x) \leq 0, bb_d^\lll(x,y) \leq \Delta\}$ is FI–satisfiable, while $\{bb_{d'}^\lll(y,x) \leq 0, bb_d^\lll(x,y) \leq 0\}$ is not. Similarly, we have that $\{ee_{d'}^\lll(y,x) \leq 0, ee_d^\lll(x,y) \leq \Delta\}$ is FI–satisfiable and $\{ee_{d'}^\lll(y,x) \leq 0, e_d^\lll(x,y) \leq 0\}$ is not.

Proposition 5.8. *Let Θ be a set of atomic FI–formulas from $\mathcal{F}_X^t$. For k in M_1 and l in M_0, it holds that*

(1) $\Theta \models be_d^\lll(x,y) \geq l$ iff $\Theta \cup \{be_d^\lll(x,y) \leq l - \Delta\}$ is not FI–satisfiable;
(2) $\Theta \models eb_d^\lll(x,y) \leq k$ iff $\Theta \cup \{eb_d^\lll(x,y) \geq k + \Delta\}$ is not FI–satisfiable.

Moreover, for l in $M_0 \setminus \{\Delta\}$, it holds that

(1) $\Theta \models bb_d^\lll(x,y) \geq l$ iff $\Theta \cup \{bb_d^\lll(x,y) \leq l - \Delta\}$ is not FI–satisfiable;
(2) $\Theta \models ee_d^\lll(x,y) \geq l$ iff $\Theta \cup \{ee_d^\lll(x,y) \leq l - \Delta\}$ is not FI–satisfiable.

Proof. The proof is entirely analogous to the proof of Proposition 5.7, using Lemma 5.4 instead of Lemma 5.3. $\square$

Proposition 5.8 does not hold in general when Θ contains atomic FI–formulas from $\mathcal{F}_X \setminus \mathcal{F}_X^t$. As a counterexample, let $\Delta = 0.25$ and

$\Theta = \{bb^{\ll}(a,e) \geq 0.75, bb^{\ll}(d,g) \geq 0.75, bb^{\ll}(e,f) \geq 1, bb^{\ll}(b,c) \geq 1, bb^{\ll}(b,a) \leq 0.5, bb^{\ll}(d,c) \leq 0.5, bb^{\ll}(g,f) \leq 0.5, bb^{\ll}(d,e) \leq 0.75\}$. It holds that $\Theta \cup \{bb^{\ll}(a,g) \leq 0.375\}$ is FI–satisfiable, implying that $\Theta \not\models bb^{\ll}(a,g) \geq 0.5$, whereas $\Theta \cup \{bb^{\ll}(a,g) \leq 0.25\}$ is not FI–satisfiable.

Note that Proposition 5.8 provides no characterization of entailment for $bb_d^{\ll}(x,y) \geq \Delta$ or $ee_d^{\ll}(x,y) \geq \Delta$. However, to check entailment for $bb_d^{\ll}(x,y) \geq \Delta$ or $ee_d^{\ll}(x,y) \geq \Delta$, we can always redefine the set M as $\{0, \frac{\Delta}{2}, \Delta, \ldots, 1 - \frac{\Delta}{2}, 1\}$, i.e., we let $\frac{\Delta}{2}$ play the role of Δ. Also note that from Proposition 5.7 and 5.8, it follows that the tractability of $\mathcal{F}_X^t$ w.r.t. FI–satisfiability carries over to entailment checking. Indeed, if Θ only contains FI–formulas from $\mathcal{F}_X^t$, $\Theta \models \gamma$ can be checked by checking the FI–satisfiability of a set of FI–formulas which contains at most one FI–formula which is not in $\mathcal{F}_X^t$. Although this one FI–formula may correspond to a disjunctive linear constraint, the number of disjuncts is bounded by $|M|$. Therefore, FI–satisfiability can be checked in polynomial time, using $O(|M|)$ P–satisfiability checks of sets of linear constraints without disjuncts.

In addition to entailment checking, it may also be of interest to know what the strongest upper bound or lower bound is for the value of $bb_d^{\ll}(x,y)$, $ee_d^{\ll}(x,y)$, $be_d^{\ll}(x,y)$ or $eb_d^{\ll}(x,y)$, given that a set of FI–formulas Θ is satisfied. As a corollary of Proposition 5.7, we find that the strongest upper bound of $bb_d^{\ll}(x,y)$, $ee_d^{\ll}(x,y)$ and $be_d^{\ll}(x,y)$, as well as the strongest lower bound of $eb_d^{\ll}(x,y)$, is always a value from M:

Corollary 5.1. *Let Θ be a set of atomic FI–formulas. It holds that ($d \in \mathbb{R}$, $(x,y) \in X^2$)*

$$\inf\{k|k \in [0,1] \wedge \Theta \models bb_d^{\ll}(x,y) \leq k\}$$
$$= \min\{k|k \in M \wedge \Theta \models bb_d^{\ll}(x,y) \leq k\}$$
$$\inf\{k|k \in [0,1] \wedge \Theta \models ee_d^{\ll}(x,y) \leq k\}$$
$$= \min\{k|k \in M \wedge \Theta \models ee_d^{\ll}(x,y) \leq k\}$$
$$\inf\{k|k \in [0,1] \wedge \Theta \models be_d^{\ll}(x,y) \leq k\}$$
$$= \min\{k|k \in M \wedge \Theta \models be_d^{\ll}(x,y) \leq k\}$$
$$\sup\{k|k \in [0,1] \wedge \Theta \models eb_d^{\ll}(x,y) \geq k\}$$
$$= \max\{k|k \in M \wedge \Theta \models eb_d^{\ll}(x,y) \geq k\}$$

In the same way, as a corollary of Proposition 5.8, we can establish the strongest lower bound of $bb_d^{\ll}(x,y)$, $ee_d^{\ll}(x,y)$ and $be_d^{\ll}(x,y)$, as well as the strongest upper bound of $eb_d^{\ll}(x,y)$, given that a set of atomic FI–formulas from $\mathcal{F}_X^t$ is satisfied.

Corollary 5.2. *Let Θ be a set of atomic FI–formulas from $\mathcal{F}_X^t$. It holds that $(d \in \mathbb{R}, (x, y) \in X^2)$*

$$\sup\{k | k \in [0, 1] \wedge \Theta \models be_d^{\lll}(x, y) \geq k\}$$
$$= \max\{k | k \in M \wedge \Theta \models be_d^{\lll}(x, y) \geq k\}$$
$$\inf\{k | k \in [0, 1] \wedge \Theta \models eb_d^{\lll}(x, y) \leq k\}$$
$$= \min\{k | k \in M \wedge \Theta \models eb_d^{\lll}(x, y) \leq k\}$$

If $\Theta \models bb_d^{\lll}(x, y) \geq \Delta$ or $\Theta \cup \{bb_d^{\lll}(x, y) \leq 0\}$ is FI–satisfiable, resp.
$\Theta \models ee_d^{\lll}(x, y) \geq \Delta$ or $\Theta \cup \{ee_d^{\lll}(x, y) \leq 0\}$ is FI–satisfiable, it holds that

$$\sup\{k | k \in [0, 1] \wedge \Theta \models bb_d^{\lll}(x, y) \geq k\}$$
$$= \max\{k | k \in M \wedge \Theta \models bb_d^{\lll}(x, y) \geq k\}$$
$$\sup\{k | k \in [0, 1] \wedge \Theta \models ee_d^{\lll}(x, y) \geq k\}$$
$$= \max\{k | k \in M \wedge \Theta \models ee_d^{\lll}(x, y) \geq k\}$$

Finally, if $\Theta \models bb_d^{\lll}(x, y) \geq \Delta$ while $\Theta \cup \{bb_d^{\lll}(x, y) \leq 0\}$ is not FI–satisfiable, resp. $\Theta \models ee_d^{\lll}(x, y) \geq \Delta$ while $\Theta \cup \{ee_d^{\lll}(x, y) \leq 0\}$ is not FI–satisfiable, it holds that in any FI–model $\mathcal{I}$ of Θ

$$bb_d^{\lll}(x^{\mathcal{I}}, y^{\mathcal{I}}) > 0$$
$$ee_d^{\lll}(x^{\mathcal{I}}, y^{\mathcal{I}}) > 0$$

while for any $k > 0$, there exists an FI–model $\mathcal{I}$ of Θ in which

$$bb_d^{\lll}(x^{\mathcal{I}}, y^{\mathcal{I}}) < k$$
$$ee_d^{\lll}(x^{\mathcal{I}}, y^{\mathcal{I}}) < k$$

In other words, in this last case, the strongest lower bound implied by Θ is a strict lower bound.

As becomes clear from Corollary 5.1 and 5.2, finding the strongest upper and lower bounds on $bb_d^{\lll}(x, y)$, $ee_d^{\lll}(x, y)$, $be_d^{\lll}(x, y)$, or $eb_d^{\lll}(x, y)$ implied by Θ can be done by $O(log(|M|))$ FI–satisfiability checks, using binary search.

5.3.4 *Implementation of a Fuzzy Temporal Reasoner*

In Section 5.3.1, we have shown how checking the FI–satisfiability of a set Θ of FI–formulas can be reduced to checking the P–satisfiability of a set Ψ of linear constraints. These linear constraints are disjunctions of atomic linear constraints of the form

$$x \leq y - d \qquad\qquad x < y - d \qquad\qquad (5.71)$$

If Ψ contains no disjunctions, i.e., if all constraints in Ψ are atomic constraints of the form (5.71), checking the satisfiability of Ψ boils down to checking the corresponding graph for forbidden cycles. This, in turn, can be done in $O(n^3)$ time (n being the number of variables in Ψ), using Floyd–Warshall's all–pairs shortest–path algorithm [Floyd (1962); Warshall (1962)]. Instead of adding distances, however, edge labels like $(d, <)$ and $(d, \leq)$ are added, as defined as in Section 5.3.3. Finding a solution, i.e., a P–model of Ψ can be done in $O(n^3)$ time using Algorithm 2 from [Gerevini and Cristani (1997)]; we omit the details. On the other hand, if Ψ does contain disjunctive linear constraints, backtracking is needed to verify there is at least one choice of disjuncts, for every disjunction, which leads to a graph without forbidden cycles.

We will focus on reasoning about purely qualitative fuzzy temporal information (i.e., $d = 0$), because, as we will see in the next chapter, this is what we need most frequently in applications which are based on temporal information from unstructured texts. Atomic linear constraints then take the form of $x \leq y$ or $x < y$. To find a solution, a variant of topological sort can be used which runs in $O(n^2)$ time [van Beek (1992)].

5.3.4.1 *Optimized backtracking*

Let $\Psi = \Psi_1 \cup \Psi_2$ where Ψ_1 only contains atomic linear constraints, i.e., expressions of the form $x \leq y$ or $x < y$, and Ψ_2 only contains disjunctive linear constraints. Our backtracking algorithm proceeds by choosing, in each step, one disjunctive linear constraint $\phi_1 \vee \phi_2 \vee \cdots \vee \phi_k$ from Ψ_2. Next, we verify whether there is an i in $\{1, 2, \ldots, k\}$ such that $\Psi_1 \cup \{\phi_i\} \cup (\Psi_2 \setminus \{\phi_1 \vee \cdots \vee \phi_k\})$ is satisfiable. When $\Psi_2 = \emptyset$, we can check the satisfiability of Ψ_1 using a variant of topological sort. The backtracking process is described in Function `Satisfiable`.

It is well–known that naive backtracking approaches like Function `Satisfiable` can be optimized significantly. Following [Tsamardinos and Pollack (2003)], we implemented forward checking, conflict–directed backjumping, semantic branching, removal of subsumed variables and no–good recording to this end. We briefly sketch each of these techniques; for further details, we refer to [Tsamardinos and Pollack (2003)].

Forward checking One of the most well–known optimizations of backtracking algorithms is called forward checking. In our algorithm, this means that we verify, for all disjunctive constraints in $\Psi_2 \setminus \{\phi_1 \vee \phi_2 \vee \cdots \vee \phi_k\}$, which disjuncts are consistent with $\Psi_1 \cup \{\phi_i\}$. In this way, we can eliminate

---

Function Satisfiable

Input: Set Ψ_1 of atomic linear constraints of the form $x \leq y$ or $x < y$; set Ψ_2 of disjunctive linear constraints of the form $x_1 \leq y_1 \vee \cdots \vee x_k < y_k$.

Output: *false* if $\Psi_1 \cup \Psi_2$ is satisfiable; *true* otherwise.

1 if $\Psi_2 = \emptyset$ then
2   return hasSolution(Ψ_1)
3 else
4   Select a disjunctive linear constraint $\phi_1 \vee \phi_2 \vee \ldots \phi_k$ from Ψ_2
5   for $i \leftarrow 1$ to k do
6          $\Psi_1^i \leftarrow \Psi_1 \cup \{\phi_i\}$
7          $\Psi_2^i \leftarrow \Psi_2 \setminus \{\phi_1 \vee \phi_2 \vee \cdots \vee \phi_k\}$
8   if *Satisfiable(Ψ_1^i, Ψ_2^i)* then
9   return *true*
10   return *false*

---

many disjuncts, thereby reducing the branching factor of the search tree considerably, i.e., the average value of k in Function Satisfiable. Moreover, if there exists at least one disjunctive constraint in Ψ_2 whose disjuncts are all inconsistent with $\Psi_1 \cup \{\phi_i\}$, we know that Ψ is not satisfiable and we can end the backtracking process, thus pruning the search tree. Finally, by eliminating disjuncts, some disjunctive linear constraints can become atomic linear constraints (i.e., if all but one disjuncts are inconsistent with $\Psi_1 \cup \{\phi_i\}$). Such constraints can be removed from Ψ_2 and added to Ψ_1.

Conflict–directed backjumping The backtracking process can be visualized by a search tree in which each node corresponds to a disjunctive linear constraint. This is illustrated in Figure 5.9. For a disjunctive linear constraint $\phi^1 = \phi_1^1 \vee \cdots \vee \phi_{k_1-1}^1 \vee \phi_{k_1}^1$, we can choose between k_1 disjuncts. Accordingly, the node corresponding to ϕ^1 has k_1 child nodes. In the backtracking process, we may, for example, first choose to examine the disjunct ϕ_1^1. Next, the constraint $\phi^2 = \phi_1^2 \vee \cdots \vee \phi_{k_1-1}^2 \vee \phi_{k_2}^2$ is considered, and we may choose to examine the disjunct ϕ_1^2 first. Now assume that for all disjuncts of the next constraint ϕ^3, the forward checking procedure detects an inconsistency. This implies that the combination of disjuncts that was chosen so far can never lead to a solution. In the standard backtracking algorithm, we then continue by examining disjunct ϕ_2^2, instead of ϕ_1^2. If this fails, we may continue with $\phi_3^2, \ldots, \phi_{k_2}^2$. If all disjuncts fail, we again move

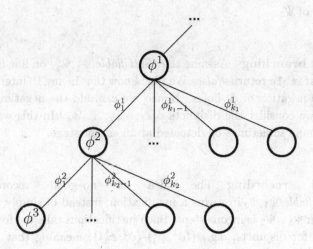

Fig. 5.9   Backtracking process.

one level up in the search tree and consider the next disjunct of ϕ^1, viz., ϕ_2^1. However, rather than always moving one level up, we can immediately move up two levels in the search tree if we can somehow establish that the inconsistencies detected after examining ϕ^3 are all independent of disjunct ϕ_1^2. In this way, we do not need to examine the disjuncts $\phi_2^2, \ldots, \phi_{k_2}^2$. Similarly, if we can establish that the inconsistencies are independent of the fact that ϕ_1^1 was chosen, we can move up another level in the search tree. This technique is called conflict–directed backjumping and can lead to significant improvement when inconsistencies are caused by choices that were made much earlier in the backtracking process.

Recall that inconsistencies occur when the forward checking procedure has eliminated every disjunct ϕ_i^j of a particular disjunctive linear constraint ϕ^j. To establish which disjuncts are responsible for an inconsistency, we keep track of which of the earlier chosen disjuncts were used to justify the elimination of each disjunct ϕ_i^j.

Removing subsumed variables   When the next disjunctive constraint $\phi = \phi_1 \vee \phi_2 \vee \cdots \vee \phi_k$ from Ψ_2 is selected, it is possible that one of the disjuncts ϕ_i is already satisfied. For example, assume that ϕ_i corresponds to $x < z$, and that Ψ_1 already contains the atomic constraints $x < y$ and $y \leq z$. Clearly, the constraint $x < z$ will be satisfied in any P–interpretation of Ψ_1 already. In consequence, there is no need to consider any of the other disjuncts of ϕ and we can immediately proceed with the next disjunctive constraint of Ψ_2.

Semantic branching   Assume that *Satisfiable(Ψ_1^i, Ψ_2^i)* on line 8 of Function `Satisfiable` returns *false*. We then know that in any P–interpretation of Ψ_1, the negation of ϕ_i holds. Hence, we can add the negation of ϕ_i to Ψ_1 when we consider the disjuncts $\phi_{i+1}, \phi_{i+2}, \ldots, \phi_k$. In this way, inconsistencies may sometimes be detected at an earlier stage.

No–good recording   The idea of no–good recording is that *Satisfiable(Ψ_1, Ψ_2)* returns a justification, instead of simply returning *false*, when $\Psi_1 \cup \Psi_2$ is inconsistent. Such justifications take the form of sets of choices for disjuncts, e.g., $\{(\phi^1, \phi_3^1), (\phi^5, \phi_8^5)\}$, meaning that whenever disjunct ϕ_3^1 is chosen in the disjunctive constraint ϕ^1, as well as disjunct ϕ_8^5 in the disjunctive constraint ϕ^5, every choice of disjuncts in the remaining disjunctive constraints will necessarily lead to an inconsistency. Obviously such justifications can be used to prune the search tree. For example, if disjunct ϕ_3^1 has already been chosen, earlier in the backtracking process, we know that disjunct ϕ_8^5 does not need to be considered when examining constraint ϕ^5. When an inconsistency is detected by the forward checking procedure, the set of disjuncts that are responsible for this inconsistency can be used as justification. Note that this same set of disjuncts is also used to implement conflict–directed backjumping. If *Satisfiable(Ψ_1, Ψ_2)* needs to report failure because *Satisfiable(Ψ_1^i, Ψ_2^i)* reported inconsistency for every i, the justifications returned by *Satisfiable(Ψ_1^i, Ψ_2^i)* can easily be used to construct a justification of *Satisfiable(Ψ_1, Ψ_2)*; we omit the details.

Constraint and disjunct selection   Finally, performance of the backtracking process can be influenced by the order in which the disjunctive constraints in Ψ_2 are considered, and for each disjunctive constraint ϕ, the order in which the different disjuncts of ϕ are examined. In particular, at line 4 of Procedure `Satisfiable`, we can choose the disjunctive constraint with the fewest disjuncts. This will typically reduce the average branching factor of the search tree. The order in which the disjuncts of the chosen constraint are examined is based on how constrained their variables are. For example, disjunct $x \leq y$ will be examined before $u \leq v$ when Ψ_1 contains more constraints involving x or y than constraints involving u or v.

5.3.4.2 *Experimental evaluation*

To perform an experimental evaluation of the various optimizations, we randomly generate sets of (atomic) FI–formulas Θ as follows. Let the parameters n and Δ represent the number of variables in Θ ($|X| = n$) and the precision which is used to encode the various lower bounds respectively, and let p be a constant in $]0, 1]$. Note that there are $n(n - 1)$ pairs of variables (x, y) in X^2 satisfying $x \neq y$, and for each of these pairs, an upper and lower bound for $bb^{\ll}(x, y)$, $ee^{\ll}(x, y)$, $be^{\ll}(x, y)$ and $eb^{\ll}(x, y)$ can be specified. Hence, at most $8n(n - 1)$ atomic FI–formulas can be specified to constrain the possible fuzzy time spans corresponding to each of the n variables.

When randomly generating constraints, we need to ensure that none of these sets are trivially inconsistent. For example, if Θ contains both $bb^{\ll}(x, y) \geq \lambda_1$ and $bb^{\ll}(x, y) \leq \lambda_2$, we should make sure that $\lambda_1 \leq \lambda_2$. As before, we only consider upper and lower bounds involving $bb^{\ll}$, $ee^{\ll}$, $be^{\ll}$ and $eb^{\ll}$. Specifically, for each pair of variables (x, y) in X^2, we randomly select two values r_1 and r_2 from M (using a uniform distribution). With a probability p we add the formula $bb^{\ll}(x, y) \geq \min(r_1, r_2)$, and with probability $1 - p$ we specify no lower bound for $bb^{\ll}(x, y)$ at all. Similarly, with probability p we add the formula $bb^{\ll}(x, y) \leq \max(r_1, r_2)$ and with probability $1 - p$ we specify no upper bound for $bb^{\ll}(x, y)$. For $ee^{\ll}(x, y)$, $be^{\ll}(x, y)$ and $eb^{\ll}(x, y)$, we proceed in the same manner. Thus we obtain a set Θ in which approximately $8n(n - 1)p$ FI–formulas are specified.

To quantify the relative effectiveness of each of the optimizations, we generated 1000 sets of atomic FI–formulas for different values of Δ, keeping $n = 5$ and $p = 0.1$ fixed. The average and maximal execution time[6] that was needed to check the FI–satisfiability of each of these sets is depicted in Figure 5.10 for four different cases: using no optimizations, using only forward checking (FC), using both forward checking and conflict–directed backjumping (FC+CDB) and using all the optimizations described above. This figure reveals that forward checking significantly reduces both the maximal and average execution time. Moreover, additionally applying conflict–directed backjumping further reduces the maximal execution time, and, for small values of Δ (i.e., large values of $\frac{1}{\Delta}$), also the average execution time. However, additionally applying the other optimizations, viz. removing sub-

---

[6]All algorithms were implemented in Java and executed on a 2.80 GHz Pentium 4 system running Windows XP, SP2. The JVM was allowed to use 400 MB of internal memory.

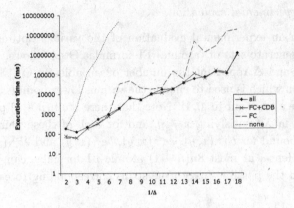

(a) Maximal execution time

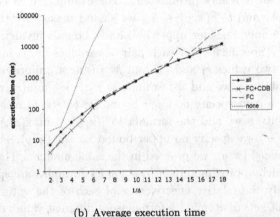

(b) Average execution time

Fig. 5.10   Maximal and average execution time needed to detect inconsistencies for $n = 5$, $p = 0.1$ and varying values of Δ.

sumed variables, semantic branching and no–good recording, has no clear impact on the execution time.

5.4   Efficient Reasoning about Fuzzy Time Spans

Even after optimizing the backtracking process, the computational cost of (complete) reasoning about FI–formulas is prohibitively high for many practical applications. Therefore, in this section we derive polynomial–time algorithms which are sound, but incomplete, i.e., which will detect some, but not all inconsistencies. Despite the incompleteness of such an algorithm, it may be that inconsistencies remain only undetected in some pathological cases. In the majority of the applications, it is not critical that every inconsistency is detected, as long as *most* inconsistencies can be detected. For simplicity, we will not consider metric constraints below (i.e., $d = 0$).

In the following, let $C(x, y)$ denote the set of formulas from Θ involving the variables x and y, and let $X = \{x_1, x_2, \ldots, x_n\}$. Without loss of generality, we can assume that Θ only contains lower bounds; e.g., an upper bound like $eb^{\preccurlyeq}(x_i, x_j) \leq 0.7$ can be replaced by the equivalent FI–formula $be^{\ll}(x_j, x_i) \geq 0.3$. Moreover, we can assume that Θ contains exactly one lower bound for each of the fuzzy temporal relations $bb^{\ll}, bb^{\preccurlyeq}, ee^{\ll}, ee^{\preccurlyeq}, be^{\ll}, be^{\preccurlyeq}, eb^{\ll}, eb^{\preccurlyeq}$ and each pair of variables (x, y) from X^2. Typically, many of these lower bounds will be 0, which means that we have no information at all about the corresponding fuzzy temporal relation for the corresponding pair of variables. Note that $C(x, y)$ is completely specified by 16 values from $[0, 1]$, corresponding to 8 lower bounds for the fuzzy temporal relations applied to (x, y) and 8 lower bounds for the fuzzy temporal relations applied to (y, x). For the ease of presentation, we will therefore represent $C(x, y)$ as two lists of 8 values. Specifically, we write

$$C(x, y) = \langle [\alpha_1, \beta_1, \gamma_1, \delta_1, \alpha_1', \beta_1', \gamma_1', \delta_1'], [\alpha_2, \beta_2, \gamma_2, \delta_2, \alpha_2', \beta_2', \gamma_2', \delta_2'] \rangle \quad (5.72)$$

to denote the following set of lower bounds

$$
\begin{array}{llll}
be^{\preccurlyeq}(x, y) \geq \alpha_1 & be^{\ll}(x, y) \geq \alpha_1' & be^{\preccurlyeq}(y, x) \geq \alpha_2 & be^{\ll}(y, x) \geq \alpha_2' \\
bb^{\preccurlyeq}(x, y) \geq \beta_1 & bb^{\ll}(x, y) \geq \beta_1' & bb^{\preccurlyeq}(y, x) \geq \beta_2 & bb^{\ll}(y, x) \geq \beta_2' \\
ee^{\preccurlyeq}(x, y) \geq \gamma_1 & ee^{\ll}(x, y) \geq \gamma_1' & ee^{\preccurlyeq}(y, x) \geq \gamma_2 & ee^{\ll}(y, x) \geq \gamma_2' \\
eb^{\preccurlyeq}(x, y) \geq \delta_1 & eb^{\ll}(x, y) \geq \delta_1' & eb^{\preccurlyeq}(y, x) \geq \delta_2 & eb^{\ll}(y, x) \geq \delta_2'
\end{array}
$$

We will furthermore write $C_1(x, y)$ (resp. $C_2(x, y)$) to denote the subset of $C(x, y)$ containing the lower bounds for the fuzzy temporal relations applied to (x, y) (resp. (y, x)). Both $C_1(x, y)$ and $C_2(x, y)$ can be represented by a list of 8 values; for the set $C(x, y)$ defined in (5.72), we write

$$C_1(x, y) = [\alpha_1, \beta_1, \gamma_1, \delta_1, \alpha_1', \beta_1', \gamma_1', \delta_1']$$
$$C_2(x, y) = [\alpha_2, \beta_2, \gamma_2, \delta_2, \alpha_2', \beta_2', \gamma_2', \delta_2']$$

Note that $C_1(x, y) = C_2(y, x)$ and $C_2(x, y) = C_1(y, x)$.

For (x, y) in X^2, $C(x, y)$ acts as a constraint on the possible values of x and y. The idea of our algorithm is to incrementally refine these constraints, i.e., increase some of the corresponding lower bounds, based on known properties of the fuzzy temporal relations. A first way to do this is by utilizing information about the ordering of relatedness measures (Proposition 3.1). For example, if $\alpha_1 = 0.4$ and $\beta_1 = 0.6$, we could change the value of α_1 to 0.6 since whenever $bb^\preccurlyeq(x,y) \geq 0.6$, we also have that $be^\preccurlyeq(x,y) \geq 0.6$. Procedure `Normalise` shows how the dependencies from Proposition 3.1 can be used for updating the various lower bounds conveyed by $C(x,y)$.

Procedure `Normalise`

    Data: $C(x,y) =$
$$\langle [\alpha_1, \beta_1, \gamma_1, \delta_1, \alpha_1', \beta_1', \gamma_1', \delta_1'], [\alpha_2, \beta_2, \gamma_2, \delta_2, \alpha_2', \beta_2', \gamma_2', \delta_2'] \rangle$$
    Result: If possible, the lower bounds in $C(x,y)$ are increased by
         using the dependencies from Proposition 3.1.

1 **for** i *in* $\{1,2\}$ **do**
2    $\beta_i' \leftarrow \max(\beta_i', \delta_i')$
3    $\gamma_i' \leftarrow \max(\gamma_i', \delta_i')$
4    $\alpha_i' \leftarrow \max(\alpha_i', \beta_i', \gamma_i')$
5    $\delta_i \leftarrow \max(\delta_i', \delta_i)$
6    $\beta_i \leftarrow \max(\beta_i', \beta_i, \delta_i)$
7    $\gamma_i \leftarrow \max(\gamma_i', \gamma_i, \delta_i)$
8    $\alpha_i \leftarrow \max(\alpha_i', \alpha_i, \beta_i, \gamma_i)$

Example 5.3. Let $C(x,y)$ be given by

$C(x,y) = \langle [0.3, 0.6, 0.2, 0.3, 0.6, 0.3, 0.5, 0.4], [0.7, 0.5, 0.4, 0.3, 0.5, 0.1, 0.6, 0.2] \rangle$

Applying `Normalise` to $C(x,y)$ yields

$C(x,y) = \langle [0.6, 0.6, 0.5, 0.4, 0.6, 0.4, 0.5, 0.4], [0.7, 0.5, 0.6, 0.3, 0.6, 0.2, 0.6, 0.2] \rangle$

If $C(x,y)$ does not change by applying `Normalise`, $C(x,y)$ is called normalised. Note that after applying `Normalise` once, $C(x,y)$ is always normalised.

Another way of deriving stronger lower bounds is by using the transitivity rules for relatedness measures, viz. the rules from Table 3.1. Specifically, given $C_1(x,y)$ and $C_1(y,z)$, we can draw some conclusions concerning the lower bounds in $C_1(x,z)$. Function `Compose` takes as input the lists of lower bounds $C_1(x,y)$ and $C_1(y,z)$ and returns a list S of lower bounds for $be^\preccurlyeq(x,z)$, $bb^\preccurlyeq(x,z)$, ..., $eb^\ll(x,z)$. We can then refine the lower bounds in $C_1(x, z)$ by including all constraints from S. Let $C_1(x, y)$ be defined as before and let S be defined as

$$S = [\alpha, \beta, \gamma, \delta, \alpha', \beta', \gamma', \delta']$$

We write $C_1(x, y) \cup S$ to denote the union of the lower bounds in $C_1(x, y)$ and S, i.e.,

$$C_1(x, y) \cup S = [\max(\alpha_1, \alpha), \max(\beta_1, \beta), \max(\gamma_1, \gamma), \max(\delta_1, \delta), \quad (5.73)$$

$$\max(\alpha'_1, \alpha'), \max(\beta'_1, \beta'), \max(\gamma'_1, \gamma'), \max(\delta'_1, \delta')] \quad (5.74)$$

Finally, we need a way to detect inconsistent constraints. Function

---

Function Compose

Input: $C_1(x, y) = [\alpha_1, \beta_1, \gamma_1, \delta_1, \alpha'_1, \beta'_1, \gamma'_1, \delta'_1]$,
$\quad\quad\quad C_1(y, z) = [\alpha_2, \beta_2, \gamma_2, \delta_2, \alpha'_2, \beta'_2, \gamma'_2, \delta'_2]$

Output: A set S of lower bounds for $be^{\preccurlyeq}(x, z)$, $bb^{\preccurlyeq}(x, z)$, ...,
$\quad\quad\quad eb^{\ll}(x, z)$; $S = [\alpha, \beta, \gamma, \delta, \alpha', \beta', \gamma', \delta']$

1   $\alpha \leftarrow \max(T_W(\alpha_1, \gamma_2), T_W(\beta_1, \alpha_2))$
2   $\beta \leftarrow \max(T_W(\alpha_1, \delta_2), T_W(\beta_1, \beta_2))$
3   $\gamma \leftarrow \max(T_W(\gamma_1, \gamma_2), T_W(\delta_1, \alpha_2))$
4   $\delta \leftarrow \max(T_W(\gamma_1, \delta_2), T_W(\delta_1, \beta_2))$
5   $\alpha' \leftarrow \max(T_W(\alpha'_1, \gamma_2), T_W(\beta'_1, \alpha_2), T_W(\alpha_1, \gamma'_2), T_W(\beta_1, \alpha'_2))$
6   $\beta' \leftarrow \max(T_W(\alpha'_1, \delta_2), T_W(\beta'_1, \beta_2), T_W(\alpha_1, \delta'_2), T_W(\beta_1, \beta'_2))$
7   $\gamma' \leftarrow \max(T_W(\gamma'_1, \gamma_2), T_W(\delta'_1, \alpha_2), T_W(\gamma_1, \gamma'_2), T_W(\delta_1, \alpha'_2))$
8   $\delta' \leftarrow \max(T_W(\gamma'_1, \delta_2), T_W(\delta'_1, \beta_2), T_W(\gamma_1, \delta'_2), T_W(\delta_1, \beta'_2))$

Consistent finds inconsistencies by checking whether the dependencies (4.3)–(4.6) are violated. For example, regardless of the fuzzy time interval that is assigned to x and y, it holds that $be^{\preccurlyeq}(x, y) = 1 - eb^{\ll}(y, x)$. Hence, for $C(x, y)$ defined in (5.72), if $\alpha_1 > 1 - \delta'_2$, this constraint can never be satisfied.

Procedure **Closure** is the resulting procedure for finding inconsistencies, similar in spirit to Allen's algorithm. Lines 1–5 ensure that all constraints are initially normalised, and that no inconsistencies can be detected. Subsequently, constraints are composed using the function **Compose** until no lower bound can be strengthened anymore. Each time a lower bound is increased, the consistency of the corresponding constraint is checked. Note that $C_1(x_{i_0}, x_{k_0}) \subset S$ iff $C_1(x_{i_0}, x_{k_0}) \cup S \neq C_1(x_{i_0}, x_{k_0})$, where $C_1(x_{i_0}, x_{k_0}) \cup S$ is defined as in (5.73). If the constraint $C_1(x_{i_0}, x_{k_0})$ is changed, some triplets need to be reconsidered. Therefore, on line 14 the set *todo* is updated.

Function Consistent

Input: $C(x, y) =$
$$\langle [\alpha_1, \beta_1, \gamma_1, \delta_1, \alpha_1', \beta_1', \gamma_1', \delta_1'], [\alpha_2, \beta_2, \gamma_2, \delta_2, \alpha_2', \beta_2', \gamma_2', \delta_2'] \rangle$$

Output: *false* if it is known that the FI–formulas in $C(x, y)$ cannot be satisfied by assigning a fuzzy time interval to x and y; *true* otherwise.

1 **if** $\alpha_1 > 1 - \delta_2' \vee \beta_1 > 1 - \beta_2' \vee \gamma_1 > 1 - \gamma_2' \vee \delta_1 > 1 - \alpha_2'$
   $\vee \alpha_1' > 1 - \delta_2 \vee \beta_1' > 1 - \beta_2 \vee \gamma_1' > 1 - \gamma_2 \vee \delta_1' > 1 - \alpha_2$ **then**

2   **return** *false*

3 **else**

4   **return** *false*

Procedure Closure

1 **for** $i \leftarrow 1$ **to** n **do**

2   **for** $j \leftarrow i + 1$ **to** n **do**

3   Normalise($C(x_i, x_j)$)

4   **if** $\neg$Consistent($C(x_i, x_j)$) **then**

5   **return** inconsistency found

6 $todo \leftarrow \{(i, j, k) | 1 \leq i, j, k \leq n \wedge i \neq j \neq k\}$

7 **while** $todo \neq \emptyset$ **do**

8   Select and remove a triplet (i_0, j_0, k_0) from $todo$

9    $S \leftarrow C_1(x_{i_0}, x_{k_0}) \cup$Compose($C_1(x_{i_0}, x_{j_0}), C_1(x_{j_0}, x_{k_0})$)

10   **if** $C_1(x_{i_0}, x_{k_0}) \subset S$ **then**

11       $C_1(x_{i_0}, x_{k_0}) \leftarrow S$

12   Normalise($C(x_{i_0}, x_{k_0})$)

13   **if** Consistent(S) **then**

14          $todo \leftarrow todo \cup \{(i_0, k_0, l) | 1 \leq l \leq n \wedge l \neq i_0 \neq k_0\}$

15                $\cup \{(l, i_0, k_0) | 1 \leq l \leq n \wedge l \neq i_0 \neq k_0\}$

16   **else**

17   **return** inconsistency found

To analyse the time complexity of this procedure, we assume that all lower bounds are initially taken from the finite set $M = \{0, \Delta, 2\Delta, \ldots, 1\}$. As long as all lower bounds are finitely representable, this assumption can always be met. It is easy to see that the lower bounds returned by Function Compose and the lower bounds resulting from Procedure Normalise are then contained in M as well. As a consequence, each constraint $C(x, y)$ can at most be changed $O(|M|)$ times. As, moreover, there are $O(n^2)$ such constraints, and each change adds $O(n)$ elements to the set *todo*, Procedure **Closure** takes $O(|M|n^3)$ time to complete.

5.4.1 2–Consistency

If for every pair of variables (x, y) from X^2, $C(x, y)$ is a consistent constraint, then Θ is called 2–consistent or arc–consistent. Clearly, if Θ is not 2–consistent, Θ cannot be consistent, hence we can sometimes detect inconsistencies by only checking 2–consistency. In particular, we would like to improve Function **Consistent** such that it returns only *true* if the input is indeed a consistent constraint $C(x, y)$. First we establish a number of dependencies between fuzzy temporal relations, and, subsequently, we show that the consistency of $C(x, y)$ can always be decided by checking whether these dependencies, as well as the dependencies implied by (4.3)–(4.6), are violated. At the same time, the new dependencies will allow us to improve Procedure **Normalise**.

Lemma 5.5. *Let A and B be fuzzy time intervals. It holds that*

$$be^{\ll}(A, B) \geq T_W(be^{\preceq}(A, B), \min(bb^{\preceq}(A, B), ee^{\preceq}(A, B)), 1 - eb^{\preceq}(A, B)) \tag{5.75}$$

Proof. Let m_a and m_b be arbitrary modal values of A and B respectively. If $m_a < m_b$, we find that $be^{\ll}(A, B) \geq T_W(A(m_a), B(m_b), L^{\ll}(m_a, m_b)) = 1$, hence (5.75) is trivially true.

Next, if $m_a > m_b$, we find $eb^{\preceq}(A, B) \leq I_W(A(m_a), I_W(B(m_b), L^{\preceq}(m_a, m_b))) = 0$, hence (5.75) degenerates to

$$be^{\ll}(A, B) \geq T_W(be^{\preceq}(A, B), \min(bb^{\preceq}(A, B), ee^{\preceq}(A, B))) \tag{5.76}$$

We furthermore obtain

$$bb^{\preceq}(A, B) = \inf_{q \in \mathbb{R}} I_W(B(q), \sup_{p \in \mathbb{R}} T_W(A(p), L^{\preceq}(p, q)))$$

$$\leq I_W(B(m_b), \sup_{p \in \mathbb{R}} T_W(A(p), L^{\preceq}(p, m_b)))$$

$$= \sup_{p \in \mathbb{R}} T_W(A(p), L^{\preceq}(p, m_b))$$

As A is increasing for values smaller than m_a, and $m_b < m_a$, we find that

$$\sup_{p \in \mathbb{R}} T_W(A(p), L^{\preceq}(p, m_b)) = T_W(A(m_b), L^{\preceq}(m_b, m_b)) = A(m_b)$$

In a similar way, we find $ee^{\prec}(A, B) \leq B(m_a)$.

Since A, B and $L^{\prec}$ are upper semi–continuous, it holds that the suprema in the definition of $be^{\prec}$ are attained. In particular, it holds for some p_0 and q_0 satisfying $p_0 \leq q_0$ that

$$be^{\prec}(A, B) = \sup_{p \in \mathbb{R}} T_W(A(p), \sup_{q \in \mathbb{R}} T_W(B(q), L^{\prec}(p, q)))$$

$$= T_W(A(p_0), B(q_0), L^{\prec}(p_0, q_0))$$

$$= T_W(A(p_0), B(q_0))$$

We can assume without loss of generality that $p_0, q_0 \in [m_b, m_a]$, because A and B are both increasing for values smaller than m_b and decreasing for values greater than m_a. Moreover, as A is increasing and B is decreasing over $[m_b, m_a]$, we can assume that $p_0 = q_0$. Since $m_b < m_a$ either $p_0 > m_b$ or $p_0 < m_a$. If $p_0 > m_b$, we find

$$be^{\ll}(A, B) = \sup_{p \in \mathbb{R}} T_W(A(p), \sup_{q \in \mathbb{R}} T_W(B(q), L^{\ll}(p, q)))$$

$$\geq T_W(A(m_b), B(p_0))$$

$$\geq T_W(bb^{\prec}(A, B), B(p_0))$$

$$\geq T_W(bb^{\prec}(A, B), T_W(A(p_0), B(p_0)))$$

$$= T_W(bb^{\prec}(A, B), be^{\prec}(A, B))$$

Similarly, if $p_0 < m_a$, we find $be^{\ll}(A, B) \geq T_W(ee^{\prec}(A, B), be^{\prec}(A, B))$. In both cases, (5.76) is satisfied.

Finally, assume $m_a = m_b = m$. Then $be^{\prec}(A, B) \geq T_W(A(m), B(m), L^{\prec}(m, m)) = 1$, hence (5.75) degenerates to

$$be^{\ll}(A, B) \geq T_W(\min(bb^{\prec}(A, B), ee^{\prec}(A, B)), 1 - eb^{\prec}(A, B)) \qquad (5.77)$$

We obtain

$$be^{\ll}(A, B) = \sup_{p \in \mathbb{R}} T_W(A(p), \sup_{q \in \mathbb{R}} T_W(B(q), L^{\ll}(p, q)))$$

$$\geq \sup_{p \in \mathbb{R}} T_W(A(p), L^{\ll}(p, m))$$

$$= \sup_{p < m} A(p)$$

$$= \lim_{\varepsilon \xrightarrow{>} 0} A(m - \varepsilon)$$

and

$$bb^{\prec}(A, B) = \inf_{q \in \mathbb{R}} I_W(B(q), \sup_{p \in \mathbb{R}} T_W(A(p), L^{\prec}(p, q)))$$

$$\leq \lim_{\substack{\varepsilon \to 0 \\ >}} I_W(B(m - \varepsilon), \sup_{p \in \mathbb{R}} T_W(A(p), L^{\prec}(p, m - \varepsilon)))$$

$$= \lim_{\substack{\varepsilon \to 0 \\ >}} I_W(B(m - \varepsilon), A(m - \varepsilon))$$

$$= I_W(\lim_{\substack{\varepsilon \to 0 \\ >}} B(m - \varepsilon), \lim_{\substack{\varepsilon \to 0 \\ >}} A(m - \varepsilon))$$

$$\leq I_W(\lim_{\substack{\varepsilon \to 0 \\ >}} B(m - \varepsilon), be^{\ll}(A, B))$$

Using the residuation principle (2.21), we obtain

$$bb^{\prec}(A, B) \leq I_W(\lim_{\substack{\varepsilon \to 0 \\ >}} B(m - \varepsilon), be^{\ll}(A, B))$$

$$\Leftrightarrow T_W(bb^{\prec}(A, B), \lim_{\substack{\varepsilon \to 0 \\ >}} B(m - \varepsilon)) \leq be^{\ll}(A, B)$$

$$\Leftrightarrow \lim_{\substack{\varepsilon \to 0 \\ >}} B(m - \varepsilon) \leq I_W(bb^{\prec}(A, B), be^{\ll}(A, B))$$

Similarly, we find $\lim_{\substack{\varepsilon \to 0 \\ >}} A(m + \varepsilon) \leq I_W(ee^{\prec}(A, B), be^{\ll}(A, B))$. From this, we establish

$$eb^{\prec}(A, B)$$

$$= \inf_{p \in \mathbb{R}} I_W(A(p), \inf_{q \in \mathbb{R}} I_W(B(q), L^{\prec}(p, q)))$$

$$= \inf_{p \in \mathbb{R}} I_W(A(p), \inf_{q < p}(1 - B(q)))$$

$$= \min(\inf_{p \leq m} I_W(A(p), \inf_{q < p}(1 - B(q))), \inf_{p > m} I_W(A(p), \inf_{q < p}(1 - B(q))))$$

$$= \min(I_W(A(m), \inf_{q < m}(1 - B(q))), \inf_{p > m} I_W(A(p), (1 - B(m))))$$

$$= \min(I_W(1, \inf_{q < m}(1 - B(q))), \inf_{p > m} I_W(A(p), 0))$$

$$= \min(\inf_{q < m}(1 - B(q)), \inf_{p > m}(1 - A(p)))$$

$$= \min(\lim_{\substack{\varepsilon \to 0 \\ >}}(1 - B(m - \varepsilon)), \lim_{\substack{\varepsilon \to 0 \\ >}}(1 - A(m + \varepsilon)))$$

$$= 1 - \max(\lim_{\substack{\varepsilon \to 0 \\ >}} B(m - \varepsilon), \lim_{\substack{\varepsilon \to 0 \\ >}} A(m + \varepsilon))$$

$$\geq 1 - \max(I_W(bb^{\prec}(A, B), be^{\ll}(A, B)), I_W(ee^{\prec}(A, B), be^{\ll}(A, B)))$$

$$= 1 - I_W(\min(bb^{\prec}(A, B), ee^{\prec}(A, B)), be^{\ll}(A, B))$$

Finally, using the residuation principle (2.21) yields

$$eb^{\preccurlyeq}(A, B) \geq 1 - I_W(\min(bb^{\preccurlyeq}(A, B), ee^{\preccurlyeq}(A, B)), be^{\ll}(A, B))$$
$$\Leftrightarrow 1 - eb^{\preccurlyeq}(A, B) \leq I_W(\min(bb^{\preccurlyeq}(A, B), ee^{\preccurlyeq}(A, B)), be^{\ll}(A, B))$$
$$\Leftrightarrow T_W(1 - eb^{\preccurlyeq}(A, B), \min(bb^{\preccurlyeq}(A, B), ee^{\preccurlyeq}(A, B))) \leq be^{\ll}(A, B) \qquad \square$$

Using (4.3)–(4.6), we obtain the following corollary.

Corollary 5.3. *Let A and B be fuzzy time intervals. It holds that*

$$be^{\ll}(A, B) \leq S_W(1 - eb^{\preccurlyeq}(A, B), eb^{\ll}(A, B), \max(bb^{\ll}(A, B), ee^{\ll}(A, B)))$$

Proof. By Lemma 5.5, it holds that

$$be^{\ll}(B, A) \geq T_W(be^{\preccurlyeq}(B, A), \min(bb^{\preccurlyeq}(B, A), ee^{\preccurlyeq}(B, A)), 1 - eb^{\preccurlyeq}(B, A))$$

which is equivalent to

$$1 - eb^{\preccurlyeq}(A, B)$$
$$\geq T_W(1 - eb^{\ll}(A, B), 1 - \max(bb^{\ll}(A, B), ee^{\ll}(A, B)), be^{\ll}(A, B))$$

Using the residuation principle (2.21), (2.34) and (2.13), we find

$$be^{\ll}(A, B)$$
$$\leq I_W(T_W(1 - eb^{\ll}(A, B), 1 - \max(bb^{\ll}(A, B), ee^{\ll}(A, B))),$$
$$\quad 1 - eb^{\preccurlyeq}(A, B))$$
$$= S_W(1 - T_W(1 - eb^{\ll}(A, B), 1 - \max(bb^{\ll}(A, B), ee^{\ll}(A, B))),$$
$$\quad 1 - eb^{\preccurlyeq}(A, B))$$
$$= S_W(eb^{\ll}(A, B), \max(bb^{\ll}(A, B), ee^{\ll}(A, B)), 1 - eb^{\preccurlyeq}(A, B)) \qquad \square$$

Lemma 5.6. *Let A and B be fuzzy time intervals. It holds that*

$$bb^{\ll}(A, B) \leq T_W(bb^{\preccurlyeq}(A, B), \max(be^{\ll}(A, B), 1 - eb^{\preccurlyeq}(A, B))) \qquad (5.78)$$
$$ee^{\ll}(A, B) \leq T_W(ee^{\preccurlyeq}(A, B), \max(be^{\ll}(A, B), 1 - eb^{\preccurlyeq}(A, B))) \qquad (5.79)$$

Proof. As an example, we show (5.78). The proof of (5.79) is entirely analogous. Let m_a and m_b be arbitrary modal values of A and B respectively. If $m_a > m_b$, we find that $eb^{\preccurlyeq}(A, B) \leq I_W(A(m_a), I_W(B(m_b), L^{\preccurlyeq}(m_a, m_b))) = 0$. Hence, (5.78) degenerates to $bb^{\ll}(A, B) \leq bb^{\preccurlyeq}(A, B)$ which is always satisfied by Proposition 3.1. If $m_a < m_b$, we find that

$$be^{\ll}(A, B) \geq T_W(A(m_a), T_W(B(m_b), L^{\ll}(m_a, m_b))) = 1$$

Hence, (5.78) again degenerates to $bb^{\ll}(A, B) \leq bb^{\preccurlyeq}(A, B)$.

Finally, assume that $m_a = m_b = m$. Using the fact that A and B are increasing (resp. decreasing) for values smaller (resp. greater) than m, we find

$$
\begin{aligned}
&bb^{\preccurlyeq}(A, B) \\
&= \inf_{q \in \mathbb{R}} I_W(B(q), \sup_{p \in \mathbb{R}} T_W(A(p), L^{\preccurlyeq}(p, q))) \\
&= \min(\inf_{q < m} I_W(B(q), \sup_{p \in \mathbb{R}} T_W(A(p), L^{\preccurlyeq}(p, q))), \\
&\qquad \inf_{q \geq m} I_W(B(q), \sup_{p \in \mathbb{R}} T_W(A(p), L^{\preccurlyeq}(p, q)))) \\
&= \min(\inf_{q < m} I_W(B(q), T_W(A(q), L^{\preccurlyeq}(q, q))), \\
&\qquad \inf_{q \geq m} I_W(B(q), T_W(A(m), L^{\preccurlyeq}(m, q)))) \\
&= \min(\inf_{q < m} I_W(B(q), A(q)), 1) \\
&= \inf_{q < m} I_W(B(q), A(q))
\end{aligned}
$$

Since the support of A and B is bounded, there will always exist a $q_0 < m$ for which $1 - B(q_0) + A(q_0) \leq 1$, hence

$$bb^{\preccurlyeq}(A, B) = \inf_{q < m}(1 - B(q) + A(q)) \tag{5.80}$$

In the same way, we can show that

$$bb^{\ll}(A, B) = \sup_{p < m}(A(p) - B(p)) \tag{5.81}$$

Note that (5.78) is equivalent to

$$
\begin{aligned}
bb^{\ll}(A, B) &> T_W(bb^{\preccurlyeq}(A, B), be^{\ll}(A, B)) \\
&\Rightarrow bb^{\ll}(A, B) \leq T_W(bb^{\preccurlyeq}(A, B), 1 - eb^{\preccurlyeq}(A, B))
\end{aligned}
$$

which is in turn equivalent to

$$
\begin{aligned}
bb^{\ll}(A, B) &> T_W(bb^{\preccurlyeq}(A, B), be^{\ll}(A, B)) \\
&\Rightarrow bb^{\ll}(A, B) \leq bb^{\preccurlyeq}(A, B) - eb^{\preccurlyeq}(A, B)
\end{aligned}
$$

We will show that $bb^{\ll}(A, B) \leq bb^{\preccurlyeq}(A, B) - eb^{\preccurlyeq}(A, B)$ is satisfied under the assumption $bb^{\ll}(A, B) > T_W(bb^{\preccurlyeq}(A, B), be^{\ll}(A, B))$. It holds that

$$
\begin{aligned}
eb^{\preccurlyeq}(A, B) &= \inf_{p \in \mathbb{R}} I_W(A(p), \inf_{q \in \mathbb{R}} I_W(B(q), L^{\preccurlyeq}(p, q))) \\
&\leq I_W(A(m), \inf_{q \in \mathbb{R}} I_W(B(q), L^{\preccurlyeq}(m, q))) \\
&= \inf_{q \in \mathbb{R}} I_W(B(q), L^{\preccurlyeq}(m, q)) \\
&= \inf_{q < m} I_W(B(q), 0) \\
&= 1 - \sup_{q < m} B(q)
\end{aligned}
$$

Hence, it is sufficient to show that $1 - \sup_{q<m} B(q) \leq bb^{\preccurlyeq}(A, B) - bb^{\ll}(A, B)$ or, equivalently,

$$(\forall \varepsilon > 0)(\exists q_0 < m)(B(q_0) \geq 1 - bb^{\preccurlyeq}(A, B) + bb^{\ll}(A, B) - \varepsilon) \qquad (5.82)$$

Let $\varepsilon > 0$; we show that there indeed exists a q_0 satisfying $q_0 < m$ and $B(q_0) \geq 1 - bb^{\preccurlyeq}(A, B) + bb^{\ll}(A, B) - \varepsilon$.

First note that

$$
\begin{aligned}
be^{\ll}(A, B) &= \sup_{p \in \mathbb{R}} T_W(A(p), \sup_{q \in \mathbb{R}} T_W(B(q), L^{\ll}(p, q))) \\
&\geq \sup_{p \in \mathbb{R}} T_W(A(p), T_W(B(m), L^{\ll}(p, m))) \\
&= \sup_{p < m} A(p)
\end{aligned}
$$

Hence

$$(\forall p < m)(be^{\ll}(A, B) \geq A(p)) \qquad (5.83)$$

From (5.81) we find that

$$(\forall \varepsilon' > 0)(\exists p < m)(A(p) - B(p) > bb^{\ll}(A, B) - \varepsilon')$$

Let $\varepsilon_1 > 0$ be such that $\varepsilon_1 \leq \min(\frac{\varepsilon}{2}, bb^{\ll}(A, B) - bb^{\preccurlyeq}(A, B) - be^{\ll}(A, B) + 1)$. Note that the assumption that $bb^{\ll}(A, B) > T_W(bb^{\preccurlyeq}(A, B), be^{\ll}(A, B))$ implies that $bb^{\ll}(A, B) > bb^{\preccurlyeq}(A, B) + be^{\ll}(A, B) - 1$ and thus that $bb^{\ll}(A, B) - bb^{\preccurlyeq}(A, B) - be^{\ll}(A, B) + 1 > 0$. There exists a $p_0 < m$ such that $A(p_0) - B(p_0) > bb^{\ll}(A, B) - \varepsilon_1$. By definition of ε_1, we have that

$$
\begin{aligned}
B(p_0) &< A(p_0) - bb^{\ll}(A, B) + \varepsilon_1 \\
&\leq A(p_0) - bb^{\ll}(A, B) + bb^{\ll}(A, B) - bb^{\preccurlyeq}(A, B) - be^{\ll}(A, B) + 1 \\
&= A(p_0) - bb^{\preccurlyeq}(A, B) - be^{\ll}(A, B) + 1
\end{aligned}
$$

and using (5.83)

$$B(p_0) < 1 - bb^{\preccurlyeq}(A, B) \tag{5.84}$$

From (5.80) we find that

$$(\forall \varepsilon' > 0)(\exists q < m)(1 - B(q) + A(q) < bb^{\preccurlyeq}(A, B) + \varepsilon')$$

Let $\varepsilon_2 > 0$ be such that $\varepsilon_2 \leq \min(\frac{\varepsilon}{2}, 1 - bb^{\preccurlyeq}(A, B) - B(p_0))$. Note that $1 - bb^{\preccurlyeq}(A, B) - B(p_0) > 0$ by (5.84). There exists a $q_1 < m$ such that $1 - B(q_1) + A(q_1) < bb^{\preccurlyeq}(A, B) + \varepsilon_2$. By definition of ε_2, we have that

$$
\begin{aligned}
B(q_1) &> 1 + A(q_1) - bb^{\preccurlyeq}(A, B) - \varepsilon_2 \\
&\geq 1 + A(q_1) - bb^{\preccurlyeq}(A, B) - 1 + bb^{\preccurlyeq}(A, B) + B(p_0) \\
&= A(q_1) + B(p_0) \\
&\geq B(p_0)
\end{aligned}
$$

From $B(q_1) > B(p_0)$, we know that $p_0 < q_1$ and $A(p_0) \leq A(q_1)$.

Finally, we obtain using $A(p_0) \leq A(q_1)$, and the definition of p_0, q_1, ε_1 and ε_2 that

$$
\begin{aligned}
B(q_1) &> 1 + A(q_1) - bb^{\preccurlyeq}(A, B) - \varepsilon_2 \\
&\geq 1 + A(p_0) - bb^{\preccurlyeq}(A, B) - \varepsilon_2 \\
&> 1 + B(p_0) + bb^{\lll}(A, B) - \varepsilon_1 - bb^{\preccurlyeq}(A, B) - \varepsilon_2 \\
&\geq 1 + B(p_0) + bb^{\lll}(A, B) - \frac{\varepsilon}{2} - bb^{\preccurlyeq}(A, B) - \frac{\varepsilon}{2} \\
&= 1 + B(p_0) + bb^{\lll}(A, B) - bb^{\preccurlyeq}(A, B) - \varepsilon \\
&\geq 1 + bb^{\lll}(A, B) - bb^{\preccurlyeq}(A, B) - \varepsilon
\end{aligned}
$$

Hence, (5.82) is satisfied for $q_0 = q_1$. $\qquad\qquad\square$

For crisp intervals $A = [a^-, a^+]$ and $B = [b^-, b^+]$, (5.78) corresponds to the trivial observation that if $a^- < b^-$ then $a^- \leq b^-$ and ($a^- < b^+$ or $b^- < a^+$).

Lemma 5.7. *Let A and B be fuzzy time intervals. It holds that*

$$eb^{\lll}(A, B) > 0 \Rightarrow be^{\lll}(A, B) = 1 \tag{5.85}$$

Proof. Let m_a and m_b be arbitrary modal values of A and B respectively. If $m_a < m_b$, we find

$$
\begin{aligned}
be^{\lll}(A, B) &= \sup_{p \in \mathbb{R}} T_W(A(p), \sup_{q \in \mathbb{R}} T_W(B(q), L^{\lll}(p, q))) \\
&\geq T_W(A(m_a), T_W(B(m_b), L^{\lll}(m_a, m_b))) \\
&= 1
\end{aligned}
$$

If, on the other hand, $m_a \geq m_b$, we obtain

$$eb^{\ll}(A, B) = \inf_{p \in \mathbb{R}} I_W(A(p), \inf_{q \in \mathbb{R}} I_W(B(q), L^{\ll}(p, q)))$$
$$\leq I_W(A(m_a), I_W(B(m_b), L^{\ll}(m_a, m_b)))$$
$$= 0$$

Hence, it holds that $eb^{\ll}(A, B) = 0 \lor be^{\ll}(A, B) = 1$, which is equivalent to (5.85). $\square$

Lemma 5.7 becomes trivial when A and B are crisp intervals: $a^+ < b^- \Rightarrow a^- < b^+$. Using (4.5) and (4.6), we obtain the following corollary.

Corollary 5.4. *Let A and B be fuzzy time intervals. It holds that*

$$eb^{\prec}(A, B) > 0 \Rightarrow be^{\prec}(A, B) = 1 \qquad (5.86)$$

Proof. By Lemma 5.7, we know that

$$eb^{\ll}(A, B) > 0 \Rightarrow be^{\ll}(A, B) = 1$$

Hence, we also have

$$1 - be^{\prec}(A, B) > 0 \Rightarrow 1 - eb^{\prec}(A, B) = 1$$
$$\Leftrightarrow be^{\prec}(A, B) < 1 \Rightarrow eb^{\prec}(A, B) = 0$$
$$\Leftrightarrow \neg(eb^{\prec}(A, B) = 0) \Rightarrow \neg(be^{\prec}(A, B) < 1)$$
$$\Leftrightarrow eb^{\prec}(A, B) > 0 \Rightarrow be^{\prec}(A, B) = 1$$

$\square$

The following proposition states that the dependencies introduced in this section, in addition to the dependencies implied by (4.3)–(4.6), are sufficient for checking the consistency of $C(x, y)$. Note that this means that we have discovered all dependencies, i.e., every other dependency between the fuzzy temporal relations applied to the same variables x and y will be entailed by the aforementioned dependencies.

Proposition 5.9. *Let $\alpha, \beta, \gamma, \delta, \alpha', \beta', \gamma', \delta' \in [0, 1]$. There exist fuzzy time intervals A and B such that $be^{\prec}(A, B) = \alpha$, $bb^{\prec}(A, B) = \beta$, $ee^{\prec}(A, B) = \gamma$, $eb^{\prec}(A, B) = \delta$, $be^{\ll}(A, B) = \alpha'$, $bb^{\ll}(A, B) = \beta'$, $ee^{\ll}(A, B) = \gamma'$ and $eb^{\ll}(A, B) = \delta'$ iff*

$$\alpha \geq \beta \geq \delta \tag{5.87}$$
$$\alpha \geq \gamma \geq \delta \tag{5.88}$$
$$\alpha \geq \alpha' \tag{5.89}$$
$$\gamma \geq \gamma' \tag{5.90}$$
$$\alpha' \geq T_W(\alpha, \min(\beta, \gamma), 1 - \delta) \tag{5.91}$$
$$\beta' \leq T_W(\beta, \max(\alpha', 1 - \delta)) \tag{5.92}$$
$$\alpha' = 1 \vee \delta' = 0 \tag{5.93}$$
$$\alpha' \geq \beta' \geq \delta' \tag{5.94}$$
$$\alpha' \geq \gamma' \geq \delta' \tag{5.95}$$
$$\beta \geq \beta' \tag{5.96}$$
$$\delta \geq \delta' \tag{5.97}$$
$$\alpha' \leq S_W(1 - \delta, \delta', \max(\beta', \gamma')) \tag{5.98}$$
$$\gamma' \leq T_W(\gamma, \max(\alpha', 1 - \delta)) \tag{5.99}$$
$$\alpha = 1 \vee \delta = 0 \tag{5.100}$$

Proof. The proof is presented in Appendix A. $\square$

Given the lower bounds in $C(x, y)$, Proposition 5.9 can be used to specify a system of (disjunctions of) linear inequalities Σ which has a solution iff $C(x, y)$ is consistent. Function `Consistent-revised` shows how this can be done. The variables $a, b, \ldots, d'$ correspond to the unknown values of $be^{\prec}(x, y), bb^{\prec}(x, y), \ldots, eb^{\ll}(x, y)$. The inequalities on lines 1–2 ensure that any solution of Σ satisfies the lower bounds in $C(x, y)$. Note that the lower bounds in $C_2(x, y)$ are converted into upper bounds using (4.3)–(4.6). The dependencies from Proposition 3.1 (i.e., (5.87)–(5.90) and (5.94)–(5.97)) are imposed by the inequalities on line 3. Line 4 corresponds to (5.91) and (5.98). To see this, consider for example (5.91):

$$\alpha' \geq T_W(\alpha, \min(\beta, \gamma), 1 - \delta)$$
$$\Leftrightarrow \alpha' \geq \max(0, \alpha + T_W(\min(\beta, \gamma), 1 - \delta) - 1)$$
$$\Leftrightarrow \alpha' \geq \max(0, \alpha + \max(0, \min(\beta, \gamma) - \delta) - 1)$$
$$\Leftrightarrow \alpha' \geq 0 \wedge \alpha' \geq \alpha - 1 \wedge \alpha' \geq \alpha + \min(\beta, \gamma) - \delta - 1$$

As $\alpha' \geq 0$ and $\alpha' \geq \alpha - 1$ are trivially satisfied, the last expression is equivalent to $\alpha' \geq \alpha + \min(\beta, \gamma) - \delta - 1$. In the same way, line 5 corresponds to (5.92) and (5.99) and line 6 corresponds to (5.93) and (5.100). Checking whether a system of linear inequalities has a solution can be done using a linear programming solver. Since the number of variables and inequalities in Σ is constant, checking whether Σ has a solution can be done in constant time. Note that, as Σ contains disjunctions, more than one system of linear inequalities may need to be checked.

Function `Consistent-revised`

Input: $C(x, y) =$
$$\langle [\alpha_1, \beta_1, \gamma_1, \delta_1, \alpha_1', \beta_1', \gamma_1', \delta_1'], [\alpha_2, \beta_2, \gamma_2, \delta_2, \alpha_2', \beta_2', \gamma_2', \delta_2'] \rangle$$

Output: *false* if $C(x, y)$ cannot be satisfied by assigning a fuzzy
time interval to x and y; *true* otherwise

1   $\Sigma \leftarrow \{ \alpha_1 \le a \le 1 - \delta_2', \beta_1 \le b \le 1 - \beta_2', \gamma_1 \le c \le 1 - \gamma_2', \delta_1 \le d \le 1 - \alpha_2',$

2      $\alpha_1' \le a' \le 1 - \delta_2, \beta_1' \le b' \le 1 - \beta_2, \gamma_1' \le c' \le 1 - \gamma_2, \delta_1' \le d' \le$
    $1 - \alpha_2,$

3      $a \ge b \ge d, a \ge c \ge d, a' \ge b' \ge d', a' \ge c' \ge d', a \ge a', b \ge$
    $b', c \ge c', d \ge d',$

4      $(a' \ge a + b - d - 1 \lor a' \ge a + c - d - 1), (a' \le$
    $1 - d + d' + b' \lor a' \le 1 - d + d' + c'),$

5      $(b' \le b + a' - 1 \lor b' \le b - d), (c' \le c + a' - 1 \lor c' \le c - d),$

6      $(a \ge 1 \lor d \le 0), (a' \ge 1 \lor d' \le 0) \}$

7 **if** Σ *has a solution* **then**

8   **return** *true*

9 **else**

10   **return** *false*

The same dependencies can also be used to improve Procedure `Normalise`, yielding Procedure `Normalise-revised`. Consider, for example, the dependency from Lemma 5.5. Using (4.6) we establish

$$be^{\ll}(A, B) \ge T_W(be^{\prec}(A, B), \min(bb^{\prec}(A, B), ee^{\prec}(A, B)), 1 - eb^{\prec}(A, B))$$
$$\Leftrightarrow be^{\ll}(A, B) \ge T_W(be^{\prec}(A, B), \min(bb^{\prec}(A, B), ee^{\prec}(A, B)), be^{\ll}(B, A))$$

which gives rise to line 8 in Procedure `Normalise-revised`. Hence, given the lower bounds for $be^{\prec}(A, B)$, $bb^{\prec}(A, B)$, $ee^{\prec}(A, B)$ and $be^{\ll}(B, A)$, we can infer a lower bound for $be^{\ll}(A, B)$. Furthermore, by applying (2.21), (2.33) and (4.6) we find

$$be^{\ll}(A, B) \ge T_W(be^{\prec}(A, B), \min(bb^{\prec}(A, B), ee^{\prec}(A, B)), be^{\ll}(B, A))$$
$$\Leftrightarrow I_W(be^{\ll}(B, A), be^{\ll}(A, B))$$
$$\ge T_W(be^{\prec}(A, B), \min(bb^{\prec}(A, B), ee^{\prec}(A, B)))$$

$$\Leftrightarrow I_W(1 - be^{\ll}(A, B), 1 - be^{\ll}(B, A))$$
$$\geq T_W(be^{\preccurlyeq}(A, B), \min(bb^{\preccurlyeq}(A, B), ee^{\preccurlyeq}(A, B)))$$
$$\Leftrightarrow 1 - be^{\ll}(B, A)$$
$$\geq T_W(be^{\preccurlyeq}(A, B), \min(bb^{\preccurlyeq}(A, B), ee^{\preccurlyeq}(A, B)), 1 - be^{\ll}(A, B))$$
$$\Leftrightarrow eb^{\preccurlyeq}(A, B) \geq T_W(be^{\preccurlyeq}(A, B), \min(bb^{\preccurlyeq}(A, B), ee^{\preccurlyeq}(A, B)), eb^{\preccurlyeq}(B, A))$$

which may allow to find a stronger lower bound for $eb^{\preccurlyeq}(A, B)$, as expressed in line 9. Similarly, we obtain

$$eb^{\preccurlyeq}(A, B) \geq T_W(be^{\preccurlyeq}(A, B), \min(bb^{\preccurlyeq}(A, B), ee^{\preccurlyeq}(A, B)), eb^{\preccurlyeq}(B, A))$$
$$\Leftrightarrow eb^{\ll}(B, A) \geq T_W(be^{\ll}(B, A), \min(bb^{\preccurlyeq}(A, B), ee^{\preccurlyeq}(A, B)), eb^{\preccurlyeq}(B, A))$$

corresponding to line 10 in Procedure Normalise-revised. In the same way, lines 11–12 are valid updates due to Lemma 5.6. Finally, note that lines 4–5 correspond to Lemma 5.7 and lines 6–7 correspond to Corollary 5.4.

Procedure Normalise-revised

Data: $C(x, y) =$
$$\langle [\alpha_1, \beta_1, \gamma_1, \delta_1, \alpha'_1, \beta'_1, \gamma'_1, \alpha'_1], [\alpha_2, \beta_2, \gamma_2, \delta_2, \alpha'_2, \beta'_2, \gamma'_2, \alpha'_2] \rangle$$

Result: If possible, the lower bounds in $C(x, y)$ are increased.

```
1  Normalise(C(x, y))
2  while changes occur do
3      for i in {1, 2} do
4          if δᵢ > 0 then
5              αᵢ = 1
6          if δ'ᵢ > 0 then
7              α'ᵢ = 1
8          α'ᵢ ← max(α'ᵢ, T_W(αᵢ, min(βᵢ, γᵢ), α'₁₋ᵢ))
9          δᵢ ← max(δᵢ, T_W(αᵢ, min(βᵢ, γᵢ), δ₁₋ᵢ))
10         δ'₁₋ᵢ ← max(δ'₁₋ᵢ, T_W(α'₁₋ᵢ, min(βᵢ, γᵢ), δ₁₋ᵢ))
11         βᵢ ← max(βᵢ, S_W(β'ᵢ, min(δᵢ, δ₁₋ᵢ)))
12         γᵢ ← max(γᵢ, S_W(γ'ᵢ, min(δᵢ, δ₁₋ᵢ)))
```

5.4.2 *Transitivity of Fuzzy Temporal Relations*

To further improve on Procedure Closure, in this section we investigate some transitivity properties which are stronger than those from Table 3.1.

To keep the problem manageable, we omit the fuzzy temporal relations $be^{\ll}$, $bb^{\ll}$, $ee^{\ll}$ and $eb^{\ll}$ from the following discussion. Note that these fuzzy temporal relations are somewhat less useful for applications like multi–document summarization or temporal question answering, as a natural language statement expressing that the end of A occurred before B, for example, does not always mean that the end of A is strictly before the beginning of B, i.e., it may still be possible that the end of A coincides with the beginning of B.

We want to derive the strongest lower bounds possible for $be^{\preccurlyeq}(x,z)$, $bb^{\preccurlyeq}(x,z)$, $ee^{\preccurlyeq}(x,z)$ and $eb^{\preccurlyeq}(x,z)$ given only lower bounds for $be^{\preccurlyeq}(x,y)$, $bb^{\preccurlyeq}(x,y)$, $ee^{\preccurlyeq}(x,y)$, $eb^{\preccurlyeq}(x,y)$, $be^{\preccurlyeq}(y,z)$, $bb^{\preccurlyeq}(y,z)$, $ee^{\preccurlyeq}(y,z)$ and $eb^{\preccurlyeq}(y,z)$ for some variable y. First, in the following three lemmas, we investigate some transitivity properties which may sometimes yield stronger conclusions than the transitivity rules from Table 3.1.

Lemma 5.8. *Let A, B and C be fuzzy time intervals. It holds that*

$$bb^{\preccurlyeq}(A,C) \geq \min(be^{\preccurlyeq}(A,B) + T_W(ee^{\preccurlyeq}(A,B), eb^{\preccurlyeq}(B,C)), eb^{\preccurlyeq}(B,C),$$
$$bb^{\preccurlyeq}(A,B) + T_W(eb^{\preccurlyeq}(B,C), be^{\preccurlyeq}(A,B))) \qquad (5.101)$$

$$ee^{\preccurlyeq}(A,C) \geq \min(T_W(eb^{\preccurlyeq}(A,B), bb^{\preccurlyeq}(B,C)) + be^{\preccurlyeq}(B,C), eb^{\preccurlyeq}(A,B),$$
$$T_W(eb^{\preccurlyeq}(A,B), be^{\preccurlyeq}(B,C)) + ee^{\preccurlyeq}(B,C)) \qquad (5.102)$$

Proof. As an example, we show (5.101). The proof of (5.102) is entirely analogous. When $be^{\preccurlyeq}(A,B) = 1$, the right–hand side of (5.101) becomes

$$\min(1 + T_W(ee^{\preccurlyeq}(A,B), eb^{\preccurlyeq}(B,C)), eb^{\preccurlyeq}(B,C),$$
$$bb^{\preccurlyeq}(A,B) + T_W(eb^{\preccurlyeq}(B,C), 1))$$
$$= \min(eb^{\preccurlyeq}(B,C), bb^{\preccurlyeq}(A,B) + eb^{\preccurlyeq}(B,C))$$
$$= eb^{\preccurlyeq}(B,C)$$
$$= T_W(1, eb^{\preccurlyeq}(B,C))$$
$$= T_W(be^{\preccurlyeq}(A,B), eb^{\preccurlyeq}(B,C))$$

which proves (5.101), since we know from the transitivity table for relatedness measures that $bb^{\preccurlyeq}(A,C) \geq T_W(be^{\preccurlyeq}(A,B), eb^{\preccurlyeq}(B,C))$ holds. Hence, we can assume that $be^{\preccurlyeq}(A,B) < 1$.

Let m_a and m_b be modal values of A and B respectively. From $be^{\preccurlyeq}(A,B) < 1$ we know that $m_a > m_b$. Indeed, if $m_a \leq m_b$, we would find that

$$be^{\preccurlyeq}(A,B) \geq T_W(A(m_a), T_W(B(m_b), L^{\preccurlyeq}(m_a, m_b))) = 1$$

Using the fact that A is increasing for values smaller than m_b (since $m_b < m_a$), we obtain

$$
\begin{aligned}
bb^{\preceq}(A,B) &= \inf_{q\in\mathbb{R}} I_W(B(q), \sup_{p\in\mathbb{R}} T_W(A(p), L^{\preceq}(p,q))) \\
&\leq I_W(B(m_b), \sup_{p\in\mathbb{R}} T_W(A(p), L^{\preceq}(p,m_b))) \\
&= \sup_{p\in\mathbb{R}} T_W(A(p), L^{\preceq}(p,m_b)) \\
&= T_W(A(m_b), L^{\preceq}(m_b,m_b)) \\
&= A(m_b)
\end{aligned}
$$

Similarly, we obtain $ee^{\preceq}(A,B) \leq B(m_a)$.

Furthermore, due to the fact that A is increasing and B is decreasing in $[m_b, m_a]$, we have

$$
\begin{aligned}
be^{\preceq}(A,B) &= \sup_{p\in\mathbb{R}} T_W(A(p), \sup_{q\in\mathbb{R}} T_W(B(q), L^{\preceq}(p,q))) \\
&= \sup_{p\in[m_b,m_a]} T_W(A(p), \sup_{q\in[m_b,m_a]} T_W(B(q), L^{\preceq}(p,q))) \\
&= \sup_{p\in[m_b,m_a]} T_W(A(p), T_W(B(p), L^{\preceq}(p,p))) \\
&= \sup_{p\in[m_b,m_a]} T_W(A(p), B(p))
\end{aligned}
$$

Because A and B are upper semi–continuous, the supremum in this last expression is attained for some p_0 in $[m_b, m_a]$, i.e., $be^{\preceq}(A,B) = T_W(A(p_0), B(p_0))$.

From the definition of $eb^{\preceq}(B,C)$, we find

$$
\begin{aligned}
&(\forall p,q \in \mathbb{R})(eb^{\preceq}(B,C) \leq I_W(B(p), I_W(C(q), L^{\preceq}(p,q)))) \\
&\Rightarrow (\forall p,q \in \mathbb{R})(p > q \Rightarrow eb^{\preceq}(B,C) \leq I_W(B(p), I_W(C(q), 0))) \\
&\Leftrightarrow (\forall p,q \in \mathbb{R})(p > q \Rightarrow eb^{\preceq}(B,C) \leq I_W(B(p), 1 - C(q)))
\end{aligned}
$$

and using the residuation principle (2.21)

$$
\Leftrightarrow (\forall p,q \in \mathbb{R})(p > q \Rightarrow T_W(eb^{\preceq}(B,C), B(p)) \leq 1 - C(q)) \qquad (5.103)
$$

We find

$$bb^{\preccurlyeq}(A,C) = \inf_{q \in \mathbb{R}} I_W(C(q), \sup_{p \in \mathbb{R}} T_W(A(p), L^{\preccurlyeq}(p,q)))$$

$$= \min(\inf_{q < m_b} I_W(C(q), \sup_{p \in \mathbb{R}} T_W(A(p), L^{\preccurlyeq}(p,q))),$$

$$\inf_{q \in [m_b, p_0[} I_W(C(q), \sup_{p \in \mathbb{R}} T_W(A(p), L^{\preccurlyeq}(p,q))),$$

$$\inf_{q \in [p_0, m_a[} I_W(C(q), \sup_{p \in \mathbb{R}} T_W(A(p), L^{\preccurlyeq}(p,q))),$$

$$\inf_{q \geq m_a} I_W(C(q), \sup_{p \in \mathbb{R}} T_W(A(p), L^{\preccurlyeq}(p,q))))$$

Examining each of these four cases individually, we obtain using (5.103)

$$\inf_{q < m_b} I_W(C(q), \sup_{p \in \mathbb{R}} T_W(A(p), L^{\preccurlyeq}(p,q))) \geq \inf_{q < m_b} 1 - C(q)$$

$$\geq \inf_{q < m_b} T_W(eb^{\preccurlyeq}(B,C), B(m_b))$$

$$= eb^{\preccurlyeq}(B,C)$$

Using (5.103), the fact that $B(p_0) \geq T_W(A(p_0), B(p_0)) = be^{\preccurlyeq}(A,B)$ and the fact that $A(m_b) \geq bb^{\preccurlyeq}(A,B)$, we obtain

$$\inf_{q \in [m_b, p_0[} I_W(C(q), \sup_{p \in \mathbb{R}} T_W(A(p), L^{\preccurlyeq}(p,q)))$$

$$\geq \inf_{q \in [m_b, p_0[} I_W(C(q), A(q))$$

$$= \inf_{q \in [m_b, p_0[} \min(1, 1 - C(q) + A(q))$$

$$\geq \inf_{q \in [m_b, p_0[} \min(1, T_W(eb^{\preccurlyeq}(B,C), B(p_0)) + A(q))$$

$$\geq \min(1, T_W(eb^{\preccurlyeq}(B,C), B(p_0)) + A(m_b))$$

$$\geq \min(1, T_W(eb^{\preccurlyeq}(B,C), be^{\preccurlyeq}(A,B)) + bb^{\preccurlyeq}(A,B))$$

In the same fashion, we establish

$$\inf_{q \in [p_0, m_a[} I_W(C(q), \sup_{p \in \mathbb{R}} T_W(A(p), L^{\preccurlyeq}(p,q)))$$

$$\geq \min(1, T_W(eb^{\preccurlyeq}(B,C), ee^{\preccurlyeq}(A,B)) + be^{\preccurlyeq}(A,B))$$

Finally, we have

$$\inf_{q \geq m_a} I_W(C(q), \sup_{p \in \mathbb{R}} T_W(A(p), L^{\preccurlyeq}(p,q)))$$

$$\geq \inf_{q \geq m_a} I_W(C(q), T_W(A(m_a), L^{\preccurlyeq}(m_a,q)))$$

$$= \inf_{q \geq m_a} I_W(C(q), 1)$$

$$= 1 \qquad\qquad\qquad \square$$

Lemma 5.9. *Let A, B and C be fuzzy time intervals. It holds that*

$$T_W(be^{\preccurlyeq}(A,B), eb^{\preccurlyeq}(B,C)) > 0 \Rightarrow be^{\preccurlyeq}(A,C) \geq be^{\preccurlyeq}(A,B) \qquad (5.104)$$

$$T_W(be^{\preccurlyeq}(B,C), eb^{\preccurlyeq}(A,B)) > 0 \Rightarrow be^{\preccurlyeq}(A,C) \geq be^{\preccurlyeq}(B,C) \qquad (5.105)$$

Proof. As an example, we show (5.104). The proof of (5.105) is entirely analogous. Assume that the antecedent $T_W(be^{\preccurlyeq}(A,B), eb^{\preccurlyeq}(B,C)) > 0$ holds. Since A and B are upper semi–continuous, it holds that the suprema in the definition of $be^{\preccurlyeq}(A,B)$ are attained, i.e., there exists a x_0 and y_0 in $\mathbb{R}$ such that $x_0 \leq y_0$ and $T_W(A(x_0), B(y_0)) = be^{\preccurlyeq}(A,B)$.

Let m_c be a modal value of C. It holds that

$$
\begin{aligned}
eb^{\preccurlyeq}(B,C) &\leq I_W(B(y_0), I_W(C(m_c), L^{\preccurlyeq}(y_0, m_c))) \\
&= I_W(B(y_0), I_W(1, L^{\preccurlyeq}(y_0, m_c))) \\
&= I_W(B(y_0), L^{\preccurlyeq}(y_0, m_c))
\end{aligned}
$$

Since $B(y_0) \geq T_W(A(x_0), B(y_0)) = be^{\preccurlyeq}(A,B)$ and the fact that I_W is decreasing in its first argument, we obtain $eb^{\preccurlyeq}(B,C) \leq I_W(be^{\preccurlyeq}(A,B), L^{\preccurlyeq}(y_0, m_c))$ which is, by (2.21), equivalent to

$$T_W(eb^{\preccurlyeq}(B,C), be^{\preccurlyeq}(A,B)) \leq L^{\preccurlyeq}(y_0, m_c)$$

Hence, from our assumption that $T_W(be^{\preccurlyeq}(A,B), eb^{\preccurlyeq}(B,C)) > 0$, we find that $L^{\preccurlyeq}(y_0, m_c) > 0$, or, $y_0 \leq m_c$. Since, $x_0 \leq y_0$, we also have that $x_0 \leq m_c$. This observation leads to

$$be^{\preccurlyeq}(A,C) \geq T_W(A(x_0), T_W(C(m_c), L^{\preccurlyeq}(x_0, m_c))) = A(x_0) \geq be^{\preccurlyeq}(A,B) \; \square$$

If $T_W(be^{\preccurlyeq}(A,B), eb^{\preccurlyeq}(B,C)) > 0$ then $be^{\preccurlyeq}(B,C) = 1$ by Corollary 5.4, hence

$$be^{\preccurlyeq}(A,B) = \min(be^{\preccurlyeq}(A,B), be^{\preccurlyeq}(B,C)) \qquad (5.106)$$

In the same way, we have that (5.106) holds when $T_W(be^{\preccurlyeq}(B,C), eb^{\preccurlyeq}(A,B)) > 0$. This leads to the following corollary:

Corollary 5.5. *Let A, B and C be fuzzy time intervals. It holds that*

$$T_W(be^{\preccurlyeq}(A,B), eb^{\preccurlyeq}(B,C)) > 0 \vee T_W(be^{\preccurlyeq}(B,C), eb^{\preccurlyeq}(A,B)) > 0$$
$$\Rightarrow be^{\preccurlyeq}(A,C) \geq \min(be^{\preccurlyeq}(A,B), be^{\preccurlyeq}(B,C))$$

Lemma 5.10. *Let A, B and C be fuzzy time intervals. It holds that*

$$eb^{\preccurlyeq}(A,C) \geq \min(eb^{\preccurlyeq}(A,B), eb^{\preccurlyeq}(B,C))$$

Proof. It holds by definition of $eb^{\preceq}$ that

$$(\forall q \in \mathbb{R})(eb^{\preceq}(B,C) \leq I_W(B(q), \inf_{r \in \mathbb{R}} I_W(C(r), L^{\preceq}(q,r))))$$

or, using the residuation principle

$$(\forall q \in \mathbb{R})(T_W(eb^{\preceq}(B,C), B(q)) \leq \inf_{r \in \mathbb{R}} I_W(C(r), L^{\preceq}(q,r))) \qquad (5.107)$$

Let m_b be a modal value of B. Using (5.107), we find

$$\inf_{p \leq m_b} I_W(A(p), \inf_{r \in \mathbb{R}} I_W(C(r), L^{\preceq}(p,r)))$$

$$\geq \inf_{p \leq m_b} I_W(A(p), \inf_{r \in \mathbb{R}} I_W(C(r), L^{\preceq}(m_b, r)))$$

$$\geq \inf_{p \leq m_b} I_W(A(p), T_W(eb^{\preceq}(B,C), B(m_b)))$$

$$= \inf_{p \leq m_b} I_W(A(p), eb^{\preceq}(B,C))$$

$$\geq eb^{\preceq}(B,C)$$

and similarly $\inf_{p > m_b} I_W(A(p), \inf_{r \in \mathbb{R}} I_W(C(r), L^{\preceq}(p,r))) \geq eb^{\preceq}(A,B)$. This leads to

$$eb^{\preceq}(A,C)$$

$$= \inf_{p \in \mathbb{R}} I_W(A(p), \inf_{r \in \mathbb{R}} I_W(C(r), L^{\preceq}(p,r)))$$

$$= \min(\inf_{p \leq m_b} I_W(A(p), \inf_{r \in \mathbb{R}} I_W(C(r), L^{\preceq}(p,r))),$$

$$\inf_{p > m_b} I_W(A(p), \inf_{r \in \mathbb{R}} I_W(C(r), L^{\preceq}(p,r))))$$

$$\geq \min(eb^{\preceq}(B,C), eb^{\preceq}(A,B))$$

$\square$

Note that if A, B and C are crisp intervals, the three previous lemmas become trivial.

The next proposition shows that the transitivity rules from Lemma 5.8–5.10, together with those from Table 3.1, are the strongest transitivity rules possible given only a lower bound for $be^{\preceq}(x,y)$, $bb^{\preceq}(x,y)$, $ee^{\preceq}(x,y)$, $eb^{\preceq}(x,y)$, $be^{\preceq}(y,z)$, $bb^{\preceq}(y,z)$, $ee^{\preceq}(y,z)$ and $eb^{\preceq}(y,z)$ for some variable y. In particular, this proposition states that if one of the lower bounds on $be^{\preceq}(x,z)$, $bb^{\preceq}(x,z)$, $ee^{\preceq}(x,z)$ and $eb^{\preceq}(x,z)$ that are obtained from applying these transitivity rules would be further increased, there always exist fuzzy sets A, B and C corresponding to the variables x, y and z such that this lower bound is violated.

Proposition 5.10. *Let* $\alpha_1, \alpha_2, \beta_1, \beta_2, \gamma_1, \gamma_2, \delta_1, \delta_2 \in [0,1]$ *such that*

$$\alpha_1 \geq \beta_1 \geq \delta_1 \qquad\qquad \alpha_1 \geq \gamma_1 \geq \delta_1 \qquad (5.108)$$
$$\alpha_2 \geq \beta_2 \geq \delta_2 \qquad\qquad \alpha_2 \geq \gamma_2 \geq \delta_2 \qquad (5.109)$$
$$\alpha_1 = 1 \vee \delta_1 = 0 \qquad\qquad \alpha_2 = 1 \vee \delta_2 = 0 \qquad (5.110)$$

In other words, $\alpha_1, \alpha_2, \beta_1, \beta_2, \gamma_1, \gamma_2, \delta_1, \delta_2$ *satisfy the conditions from Proposition 5.9 involving only these values.*

Furthermore, let $\alpha_3, \beta_3, \gamma_3$ *and* δ_3 *be defined as*

$$\alpha_3 = \begin{cases} 1 & \text{if } T_W(\gamma_1, \delta_2) > 0 \text{ or } T_W(\delta_1, \beta_2) > 0 \\ \min(\alpha_1, \alpha_2) & \text{if } T_W(\gamma_1, \delta_2) = T_W(\delta_1, \beta_2) = 0 \text{ and} \\ & (T_W(\alpha_1, \delta_2) > 0 \text{ or } T_W(\delta_1, \alpha_2) > 0) \\ \max(T_W(\beta_1, \alpha_2), T_W(\alpha_1, \gamma_2)) & \text{otherwise} \end{cases}$$

$$\beta_3 = \max(T_W(\beta_1, \beta_2), \min(\alpha_1 + T_W(\delta_2, \gamma_1), \delta_2, \beta_1 + T_W(\delta_2, \alpha_1)))$$
$$\gamma_3 = \max(T_W(\gamma_1, \gamma_2), \min(\alpha_2 + T_W(\delta_1, \beta_2), \delta_1, \gamma_2 + T_W(\delta_1, \alpha_2)))$$
$$\delta_3 = \max(T_W(\delta_1, \beta_2), T_W(\gamma_1, \delta_2), \min(\delta_1, \delta_2))$$

There exist fuzzy time intervals A, B and C satisfying $be^{\preccurlyeq}(A, C) = \alpha_3$ *and*

$$be^{\preccurlyeq}(A, B) \geq \alpha_1 \qquad (5.111)$$
$$bb^{\preccurlyeq}(A, B) \geq \beta_1 \qquad (5.112)$$
$$ee^{\preccurlyeq}(A, B) \geq \gamma_1 \qquad (5.113)$$
$$eb^{\preccurlyeq}(A, B) \geq \delta_1 \qquad (5.114)$$
$$be^{\preccurlyeq}(B, C) \geq \alpha_2 \qquad (5.115)$$
$$bb^{\preccurlyeq}(B, C) \geq \beta_2 \qquad (5.116)$$
$$ee^{\preccurlyeq}(B, C) \geq \gamma_2 \qquad (5.117)$$
$$eb^{\preccurlyeq}(B, C) \geq \delta_2 \qquad (5.118)$$

Similarly, there exist fuzzy time intervals A, B and C which satisfy $bb^{\preccurlyeq}(A, C) = \beta_3$ *and* (5.111)–(5.118). *There furthermore exist fuzzy time intervals A, B and C which satisfy* $ee^{\preccurlyeq}(A, C) = \gamma_3$ *and* (5.111)–(5.118). *Finally, there exist fuzzy time intervals A, B and C which satisfy* $eb^{\preccurlyeq}(A, C) = \delta_3$ *and* (5.111)–(5.118).

Proof. The proof is presented in Appendix B. $\qquad\qquad\qquad\square$

When A, B and C satisfy (5.111)–(5.118), we already know that they satisfy $be^{\preccurlyeq}(A, C) \geq \alpha_3$, $bb^{\preccurlyeq}(A, C) \geq \beta_3$, $ee^{\preccurlyeq}(A, C) \geq \gamma_3$ and $eb^{\preccurlyeq}(A, C) \geq \delta_3$ from Lemma 5.8–5.10 and the transitivity rules from Table 3.1. The fact that

$be^\preccurlyeq(A,C) = 1$ when $T_W(\gamma_1, \delta_2) > 0$ or $T_W(\delta_1, \beta_2) > 0$ follows from the fact that $eb^\preccurlyeq(A,C) > 0$ in this case, using Corollary 5.4. Based on Proposition 5.10 we can improve Function `Compose` to Function `Compose-revised`.

Function `Compose-revised`

Input: $C_1(x,y) = [\alpha_1, \beta_1, \gamma_1, \delta_1, \alpha_1', \beta_1', \gamma_1', \delta_1']$,
  $C_1(y,z) = [\alpha_2, \beta_2, \gamma_2, \delta_2, \alpha_2', \beta_2', \gamma_2', \delta_2']$

Output: A set S of lower bounds for $be^\preccurlyeq(x,z)$, $bb^\preccurlyeq(x,z)$, ...,
  $eb^\preccurlyeq(x,z)$; $S = [\alpha, \beta, \gamma, \delta, \alpha', \beta', \gamma', \delta']$

if $T_W(\gamma_1, \delta_2) > 0 \lor T_W(\delta_1, \beta_2) > 0$ **then**
  $\alpha \leftarrow 1$

else if $T_W(\alpha_1, \delta_2) > 0 \lor T_W(\delta_1, \alpha_2) > 0$ **then**
  $\alpha \leftarrow \min(\alpha_1, \alpha_2)$

else
  $\alpha \leftarrow \max(T_W(\beta_1, \alpha_2), T_W(\alpha_1, \gamma_2))$

$\beta \leftarrow \max(T_W(\beta_1, \beta_2), \min(\alpha_1 + T_W(\delta_2, \gamma_1), \delta_2, \beta_1 + T_W(\delta_2, \alpha_1)))$
$\gamma \leftarrow \max(T_W(\gamma_1, \gamma_2), \min(\alpha_2 + T_W(\delta_1, \beta_2), \delta_1, \gamma_2 + T_W(\delta_1, \alpha_2)))$
$\delta \leftarrow \max(T_W(\delta_1, \beta_2), T_W(\gamma_1, \delta_2), \min(\delta_1, \delta_2))$
$\alpha' \leftarrow \max(T_W(\alpha_1', \gamma_2), T_W(\beta_1', \alpha_2), T_W(\alpha_1, \gamma_2'), T_W(\beta_1, \alpha_2'))$
$\beta' \leftarrow \max(T_W(\alpha_1', \delta_2), T_W(\beta_1', \beta_2), T_W(\alpha_1, \delta_2'), T_W(\beta_1, \beta_2'))$
$\gamma' \leftarrow \max(T_W(\gamma_1', \gamma_2), T_W(\delta_1', \alpha_2), T_W(\gamma_1, \gamma_2'), T_W(\delta_1, \alpha_2'))$
$\delta' \leftarrow \max(T_W(\gamma_1', \delta_2), T_W(\delta_1', \beta_2), T_W(\gamma_1, \delta_2'), T_W(\delta_1, \beta_2'))$

5.4.3   *Experimental Results*

In this section, we compare the performance of `Complete`, i.e., the optimized complete algorithm from Section 5.3.4, as well as the procedure `Closure` and its following variants:

(1) `Closure-rev1` uses `Normalise-revised` and `Consistent-revised` instead of `Normalise` and `Consistent`.
(2) `Closure-rev2` uses `Compose-revised` instead of `Compose`.
(3) `Closure-rev3` uses `Normalise-revised`, `Consistent-revised` and `Compose-revised` instead of `Normalise`, `Consistent` and `Compose`.

In a first experiment, we keep $n = 5$ and $p = 0.1$ fixed, and analyse the behaviour of the algorithms for varying values of Δ. For each Δ in $\{\frac{1}{18}, \frac{1}{17}, \frac{1}{16}, \ldots, \frac{1}{2}\}$, we generated 1000 sets of constraints using the method described in Section 5.3.4.2. Table 5.1 shows how many of these sets are

Table 5.1 Number of inconsistencies detected for $n = 5$, $p = 0.1$ and varying values of Δ (©2009 IEEE).

$\frac{1}{\Delta}$	2	3	4	5	6	7	8	9	10	11	12	13	14	15	16	17	18
Complete	219	275	289	319	328	357	399	401	419	417	438	398	422	427	444	455	448
Closure	171	187	181	219	193	196	230	221	227	229	251	221	257	241	252	232	229
Closure-rev1	209	260	275	295	299	319	369	359	382	378	397	372	372	395	402	414	407
Closure-rev2	198	211	208	222	224	232	274	257	285	279	302	258	309	277	303	285	276
Closure-rev3	217	275	289	317	326	352	396	398	419	415	436	397	420	422	443	453	442

Table 5.2 Number of inconsistencies detected for $p = 0.1$, $\Delta = 0.1$ and a varying number of variables n (©2009 IEEE).

n	3	4	5	6	7	8	9	10	11	12	13	14	15	16	17	18	19
Complete	120	243	419	588	759	865	932	979	992	998	1000	1000	1000	1000	1000	1000	1000
Closure	78	130	237	334	476	523	651	748	828	882	926	945	965	988	993	996	998
Closure-rev1	118	225	382	542	698	804	888	945	980	990	996	1000	1000	1000	1000	1000	1000
Closure-rev2	82	145	285	412	573	675	811	912	940	981	998	996	1000	1000	1000	1000	1000
Closure-rev3	120	241	419	586	756	860	927	976	991	997	1000	1000	1000	1000	1000	1000	1000

Table 5.3 Number of inconsistencies detected for $n = 5$, $\Delta = 0.1$ and a varying value of p (©2009 IEEE).

p	0.04	0.08	0.12	0.16	0.20	0.24	0.28	0.32	0.34	0.36	0.40	0.44	0.48	0.52	0.56	0.60
Complete	44	290	534	753	882	951	984	989	999	1000	1000	1000	1000	1000	1000	1000
Closure	21	170	303	495	633	755	844	909	954	974	989	991	993	997	999	1000
Closure-rev1	40	260	488	691	847	925	972	983	997	998	999	1000	1000	999	1000	1000
Closure-rev2	25	198	375	580	721	839	922	957	978	994	996	998	998	999	1000	1000
Closure-rev3	44	287	531	747	881	949	981	988	999	1000	1000	1000	1000	1000	1000	1000

found to be inconsistent for each of the reasoning procedures. Table 5.1 reveals that many inconsistencies are not detected by Procedure Closure, especially for small values of Δ; e.g., for $\Delta = \frac{1}{18}$, only 51% of the inconsistent sets are identified. Both Closure-rev1 and Closure-rev2 improve on Closure significantly. Procedure Closure-rev3, which combines the improvements used in Closure-rev1 and Closure-rev2, provides even better results: inconsistencies are detected in all but a few cases.

Figure 5.11 depicts the execution time needed on average for each of the 1000 sets of constraints, while Figure 5.12 depicts the maximal execu-

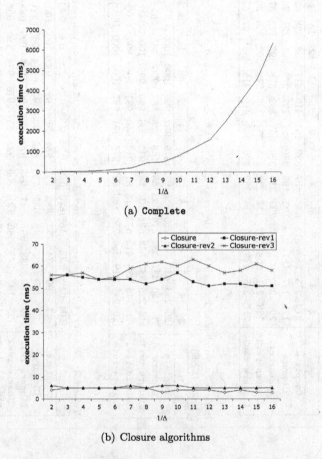

(a) **Complete**

(b) Closure algorithms

Fig. 5.11   Average execution time needed to detect inconsistencies for $n = 5$, $p = 0.1$ and varying values of Δ (©2009 IEEE).

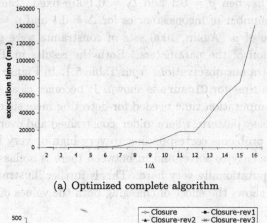

(a) Optimized complete algorithm

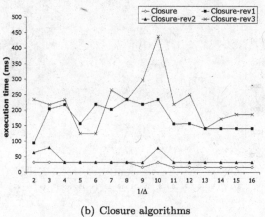

(b) Closure algorithms

Fig. 5.12 Maximal execution time needed to detect inconsistencies for $n = 5$, $p = 0.1$ and varying values of Δ (©2009 IEEE).

tion time that was needed to check the consistency of a set of constraints. From these figures, it becomes clear that the execution time of Closure, Closure-rev1, Closure-rev2, and Closure-rev3 is, in practice, largely independent of the value of Δ, whereas the execution time of Complete depends heavily on this value. These results furthermore suggest that Complete may be useful in practice, as long as the size of M is relatively small (e.g., $\Delta = \frac{1}{3}$ or $\Delta = \frac{1}{4}$). For smaller values of Δ (i.e., when M is larger), the execution time of Closure and its variants is significantly less than that of Complete.

Table 5.2 displays the number of inconsistencies that are found for various values of n when $p = 0.1$ and $\Delta = 0.1$ are fixed. Similarly, Table 5.3 shows the number of inconsistencies for $\Delta = 0.1$ and $n = 5$ fixed, and a varying value of p. Again, 1000 sets of constraints were generated for each combination of the parameters. Both the results in Table 5.2 and Table 5.3 confirm our observations from Table 5.1. In Figure 5.13, the average execution time for **Closure** is shown. It becomes clear from this figure that the computation time needed for detecting inconsistencies follows an easy–hard–easy pattern, where under–constrained and over–constrained problems, i.e., problems corresponding to very high or very low values of p and/or n, are easy to solve, and in between there is a class of problems which are computationally very hard. This is further illustrated in Figure 5.14(a), which shows the effect of changing both the values of p and n.

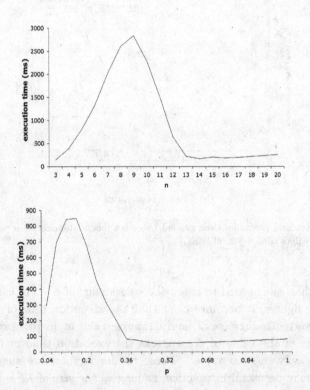

Fig. 5.13   Average execution time needed by **Complete** to detect inconsistencies for (a) $p = 0.1$, $\Delta = 0.1$ and a varying value of n, and for (b) $\Delta = 0.1$, $n = 5$ and a varying value of p (©2009 IEEE).

Closure-rev3 is much more efficient than Complete, as can be seen in Figure 5.14(b). When considering maximal execution time, this difference is even more pronounced: for the sets of constraints that were used for the results in Figure 5.13, the maximal execution time for Complete was over 448 seconds ($p = 0.04$, $n = 14$), while for Closure-rev3 this was less than 10 seconds ($p = 0.08$, $n = 12$). Hence, Closure-rev3 seems to be a good compromise between completeness and scalability. However, although most inconsistencies can be detected using Closure-rev3, there will always be inconsistent sets of constraints for which this procedure fails. One ex-

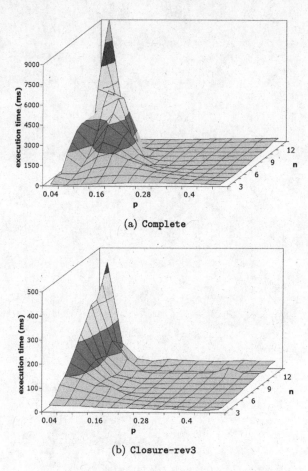

(a) Complete

(b) Closure-rev3

Fig. 5.14   Average execution time needed to detect inconsistencies for $\Delta = 0.1$ and a varying value of p and n (©2009 IEEE).

ample involving only three variables is $\Theta = \{ee^{\preccurlyeq}(y,z) \geq 0.2, eb^{\preccurlyeq}(x,z) \geq 0.1, eb^{\ll}(x,y) \geq 0.3, ee^{\ll}(z,x) \geq 0.8\}$.

Chapter 6

Event–based Information Retrieval

6.1 Introduction

As time is paramount in our perception of the world, much of the information users are looking for is subject to temporal constraints. Users may, for instance, be interested in pictures of the New York skyline before and after September 11, 2001, in facts and figures about the 1986 FIFA World Cup, or in news stories about the first manned moon landing. Accordingly, there is a growing interest in information retrieval (IR) systems that exhibit some form of temporal awareness. We will refer to such systems as event–based, or temporally aware IR systems. For example, in the question answering (QA) community, there has recently been considerable attention devoted to answering temporally restricted questions such as *How many paintings did Piet Mondriaan make during his Amsterdam years* and *In what city did the Olympic Winter Games take place before Salt Lake City*[1] [Harabagiu and Bejan (2005); Moldovan *et al.* (2005); Pustejovksy *et al.* (2005); Saquete *et al.* (2004); Vallin *et al.* (2005)]. In the context of multi–document summarization, temporal information has, among others, been employed to obtain a chronological ordering of sentences from different documents [Mani *et al.* (2003); Okazaki *et al.* (2004); Barzilay *et al.* (2002)], to summarize relevant information about events from a stream of news stories [Allan *et al.* (2001, 1998)], and to automatically generate overview timelines containing the most important events from a news corpus [Chieu and Lee (2004); Prabowo *et al.* (2007); Swan and Allan (2000)]. Finally, in the context of historical digital libraries, some efforts have been made towards temporally aware query interfaces, allowing users to find documents about certain time periods or events [Allen (2004); Mckay and Cunningham (2000); Moldovan

---

[1]Questions taken from the 2006 CLEF English–Dutch question set

et al. (2005); Smith (2002)].

Nonetheless, the capabilities of current IR systems to handle events and temporal information are still quite limited. This is in marked contrast to geographic IR systems and local search services like Google Maps[2] or Yahoo! local[3], which can rely on a vast amount of structured, geographical background knowledge, predominantly in the form of gazetteers. The key problem in transferring results from the field of geographic IR, being conceptually very similar to event–based retrieval, is the fact that no reasonably comprehensive, structured repositories of temporal information are available. A possible solution, adopted by Web 2.0 applications like Upcoming[4] is to rely on user communities to obtain such repositories. While this may be a reasonable approach, especially for local events (e.g. concerts, temporary exhibitions, . . .) as in the case of Upcoming, a significant increase in coverage can be expected by (additionally) trying to extract temporal information about events from large document collections. However, existing techniques for recognizing and grounding events in documents are very much focused on news stories, relying heavily on the fact that news stories tend to have an explicit time stamp and on language characteristics of the news genre. On the other hand, many types of events are outside the scope of news collections, e.g., historical and local events, necessitating the use of different techniques in different types of collections.

When moving outside the realm of news stories, explicit temporal information becomes rare. Quantitative temporal information, i.e., dates and time spans of events, can often not be found, and linguistic techniques to obtain qualitative temporal relations, e.g., based on the tense and aspect of verbs, are likely to fail. Therefore, in this chapter, we investigate alternative techniques for acquiring temporal information about events from web documents. The main idea is to extract a knowledge base containing (fuzzy) time spans, if possible, and qualitative relations between those events for which explicit time spans could not be found. For well-known events, quantitative information can usually be found relatively easily. However, the time spans of such events are not always well–defined, resulting in a wide array of possible beginning and ending dates, each of which are justified to some extent. To cope with this, we demonstrate how fuzzy time spans for such vague events can automatically be constructed based on such candidate beginning and ending dates. For lesser–known events, reliable quantitative

---

[2] http://maps.google.com
[3] http://local.yahoo.com
[4] http://upcoming.yahoo.com

information can usually not be found, but, as will become clear below, qualitative information — in particular before and during relations — can often be used as an appropriate surrogate. After (fuzzy) time spans and qualitative relations have been mined from the web, fuzzy temporal reasoning is used to detect and repair inconsistencies in the extracted information, resulting in a consistent, and therefore more reliable, knowledge base. The knowledge base thus obtained can subsequently be used in the retrieval process to deduce whether a given event satisfies the temporal constraints specified in the user's query. Note how in this way, most of the processing is performed off–line, whereas the actual user query can be executed very efficiently.

Our focus is on the automatic acquisition of (fuzzy) temporal information from the web, given a collection of events of interest. A related, but largely orthogonal problem is finding occurrences of (significant) events in texts and recognizing which occurrences refer to the same event. Especially for events that are not named, this problem is highly non–trivial, often requiring deep linguistic processing. For example, [Harabagiu and Bejan (2005)] is concerned with techniques to establish that *Iraq invases Kuwait* corresponds to the same event as *Hussein's annexation of Kuwait*. To avoid such problems in the present analysis, we focus on named events which are easy to recognize in texts, in particular military conflicts such as the Battle of the Bulge or the Vietnam War. The techniques being introduced, however, are entirely domain–independent. Moreover, as we are only interested in its temporal dimension, we use the term event in a rather informal way. As a consequence, the same approach can also be used for states (e.g., Nicolas Sarkozy is president of France) and time periods (e.g., the Age of Enlightenment).

The main research questions which we address are the following. How feasible is it to construct a knowledge base of temporal information from the web? To what extent does qualitative temporal information help in an IR setting? What is the role of temporal reasoning, and of fuzzy temporal reasoning in particular?

6.2 Temporal Information Extraction

There is a large body of work on extracting temporal information from news stories. For example, [Mani and Wilson (2000)] is concerned with resolving temporal expressions such as *today*, *last week*, or *in April*. Problems include the disambiguation between specific and non–specific (e.g., February is usually cold) temporal expressions, and deciding which temporal expressions should be resolved w.r.t. the document time stamp and which should be resolved w.r.t. other reference dates. In [Filatova and Hovy (2001)], an attempt is made to automatically assign time stamps (intervals or points) to every event–clause in a news story, while [Lapata and Lascarides (2006)] deals with learning which temporal relations may hold between the main and subordinate clauses of a sentence, starting from sentences where a temporal marker (e.g., before, while, until, . . .) makes this relation explicit.

To facilitate machine learning approaches to temporal information extraction, the TimeML markup language has been conceived [Pustejovksy *et al.* (2005)], which allows to annotate events and time expressions with semantic information, as well as temporal relations between events and between events and time expressions. In [Boguraev and Ando (2005)], for instance, TimeBank, a TimeML annotated corpus, is used to train a system that recognizes events and temporal relations between them. In [Moldovan *et al.* (2005)], temporal reasoning is used to support question answering, based on temporal information extracted by a classifier which was trained on the TimeBank corpus. Most of the techniques described above, however, fail to work when other types of documents than news stories are considered. The TimeBank corpus, for instance, consists entirely of news stories. Moreover, many types of documents are not time–stamped. Historical documents, for example, often cover a large time span, making document time stamps of little use [Smith (2002)].

Another relevant line of research tries to identify phrases that describe events in collections of time–stamped documents by looking at the distribution of the time stamps of the documents in which these phrases occur. In particular, to verify that a phrase e corresponds to an event with time span T, [Swan and Allan (2000)] proposes to count the number of documents whose time stamp is respectively during and outside T, and for each of these two groups, the number of documents which contain e and the number of documents which do not. Based on these frequency counts, a χ^2 test is used to test whether e occurs significantly more during T than outside T. In [Chieu and Lee (2004)], a similar approach is adopted, although events are represented as complete sentences, rather than phrases, and the log–likelihood ratio is used, rather than χ^2. A similar solution to this problem, based on naive scan methods, is suggested in [Rattenbury *et al.* (2007)], where Flickr[5] tags are used rather than time–stamped documents. Finally, in [Smith (2002)], co-occurrences of dates and place names in historical documents are used to identify significant events.

These statistical techniques can be used to identify time segments (e.g., days, weeks, months or years) during which an event is talked about, and thus to provide an approximate location in time. However, they are not suitable to identify exact temporal boundaries of events. To find exact beginning and ending dates of events, surface patterns such as *<EVENT> began on <DATE>* can be used. The use of patterns to find appropriate entities is a standard technique in QA systems [Etzioni *et al.* (2004); Ravichandran and Hovy (2002); Soubbotin and Soubbotin (2001)].

6.3   Extracting Time spans

6.3.1   *Crisp Time Spans*

The beginning and ending dates of well–known events can usually be extracted from web documents relatively easily. When there is a high number of documents that contain information about an event, it is likely that at least some of these documents explicitly mention its temporal boundaries. For example, if we want to know when the Battle of Britain took place, we can submit queries such as "the Battle of Britain began on", "the Battle of Britain took place from" or "the Battle of Britain ended on" to a search engine. From the search results, we can then extract the corresponding beginning and ending dates. Specifically, we use the following patterns (regular expression) to this end:

(1) <event> (started|began) (in|on|around) <date>
(2) <event> lasted from <date> (until|to|till) <date>
(3) <event> ended (in|on|around) <date>
(4) <event> lasted (until|to|till) <date>

where <date> is a regular expression for some common date–formats, including vague dates such as "the early 1940s". In our experiments, we only use the snippets returned by Google to extract these dates. In this way, beginning and ending dates can be found very efficiently, without the need to retrieve full documents corresponding to the search results. For example, submitting "the Battle of Britain began on" as a query to Google, among

---

[5]http://www.flickr.com

others the following snippet is returned:

> The 114 days of the Battle of Britain began on July 10, 1940. It was
> the first day of intensive daylight bombing of Britain by the German
> Luftwaffe. ...

which matches the first pattern, yielding July 10, 1940 as a candidate
beginning date. From one snippet, however, we cannot obtain a reliable
beginning date: web pages frequently contain incorrect information and,
moreover, the use of patterns may lead to misinterpretations. For instance,
among the top results from Google, we also find the following snippet:

> The second phase of the Battle of Britain began on August 24, 1940,
> when the Luftwaffe attempted to destroy the seven key fighter stations
> surrounding ...

again matching the first pattern and thereby erroneously suggesting that
August 24, 1940 is the beginning of the Battle of Britain. One possible
solution would be to apply more advanced linguistic techniques. A natural language parser, for instance, could identify that *The second phase
of the Battle of Britain* is the subject of *began*, rather than *the Battle of
Britain*. However, the use of parsers in this context has a number of important disadvantages. First, it makes the extraction of time spans much
more time–consuming. Not only is sentence parsing in itself slow, it requires that the full documents be retrieved : snippet boundaries usually
do not correspond to sentence boundaries, which are needed for accurate
parsing. Furthermore, much information on web pages is conveyed in incomplete sentence fragments, ungrammatical sentences or sentences that
are too long for parsing. As an alternative, we therefore rely on redundancy. For well–known events, our patterns will match a large number of
snippets, corresponding to a large number of candidate beginning dates and
ending dates. If there is sufficient agreement among these dates, we can be
quite confident that the corresponding time span is indeed correct. Some of
the time spans we obtained in this way are presented in Table 6.1. To each
time span, we can attach a confidence score between 0 and 1, based on the
number of sources (web documents) by which it is confirmed. Specifically,
we define the confidence score $c_t(e)$ of the time span of a given event e as

$$c_t(e) = \min(1 - \frac{1}{1+n^-}, 1 - \frac{1}{1+n^+})$$

where n^- and n^+ are the number of times the beginning and ending dates
were found respectively. For example, the beginning date of the Siege of

Table 6.1   Crisp time spans of 20th century military conflicts (dd/mm/yyyy)

Name	Begin	End	Conf
Battle of Tsushima	14/05/1905	28/05/1905	0.91
Siege of Antwerp	29/09/1914	10/10/1914	0.91
Battle of Jutland	31/05/1916	01/06/1916	0.89
3rd Battle of Ypres	31/07/1917	06/11/1917	0.90
Battle of Saipan	15/06/1944	09/07/1944	0.50
Ardennes Campaign	16/12/1944	25/01/1945	0.67
Battle of Iwo Jima	19/02/1945	16/03/1945	0.89

Antwerp was found in 19 different documents, while its ending date was found in 10 documents, resulting in a confidence score of

$$\min(1 - \frac{1}{20}, 1 - \frac{1}{11}) = \frac{10}{11} \tag{6.1}$$

6.3.2   Fuzzy Time Spans

As illustrated above, when only one possible beginning date and one possible ending date is found, crisp time spans can easily be constructed. For most events, however, a number of different beginning and ending dates are found. Although this can be due to misinterpretation of some sentences, or incorrect information in some web documents, most frequently, different dates are found because people disagree about the exact beginning and ending dates of the event under consideration. While the concept of a battle may seem to be well–defined at first glance, defining its exact onset is often difficult. Does a battle start from the moment that troops are moving in position? From the moment the first shot is fired, or the first bomb is dropped? Usually, the official time span of a battle reflects the period during which fighting is most intense, but this again is ill–defined, and to a large extent arbitrary. As a consequence, historians tend to disagree about the most appropriate time span of events such as battles, e.g.[6]:

> British historians date the battle from 10 July to 31 October 1940, which represented the most intense period of daylight bombing. German historians usually place the beginning of the battle in mid-August 1940 and end it in May 1941, ...

The result is that different beginnings and endings for the Battle of Britain can be found. Among the top results returned by Google, for instance, we also find

---

[6]http://en.wikipedia.org/wiki/Battle_of_Britain, accessed October 24, 2007.

The Battle of Britain began on 30 June 1940. Reichsmarschall Hermann Göering, head of the Luftwaffe, ordered his force to draw the RAF into battle by . . .

and

The Battle of Britain began on August 1940. After the French collapsed under the Blitzkrieg and surrendered in June, the Germans were not exactly sure what . . .

To cope with this vagueness, we will represent the time span of such vague events using fuzzy time spans. In many applications, experts are used to define membership functions of fuzzy sets. For example, [Nagypál and Motik (2003)] presents an application using fuzzy time spans to delineate historical events, where fuzzy time spans are manually constructed by experts (i.e., historians). Clearly, an approach based on experts is not sufficiently scalable to support event–based IR. An alternative technique, called polling, is proposed in [Hersh and Caramazza (1976)]. The main idea is to ask a group of people whether a particular vague concept C applies to a particular object o. The membership value of o in the fuzzy set modelling C is then defined as the fraction of test subjects who answered affirmatively. An overview of alternative techniques to construct membership functions can be found in [Bilgiç and Türksen (1999)].

To define fuzzy time spans, we use a related technique, employing the different beginnings and endings found on web pages as a substitute for test subjects. Specifically, for an event e, we construct two fuzzy sets B^e and E^e in $\mathbb{R}$. The fuzzy set B^e is an increasing fuzzy set, which models for t in $\mathbb{R}$ the degree to which t is after the beginning of event e, whereas E^e is a decreasing fuzzy set modelling the degree to which t is before the ending of e. The fuzzy time span for e is then defined as $B^e \cap E^e$. Let $b_1, b_2, \ldots, b_n$ be the possible beginnings for event e that were extracted from the Google results ($b_i \in \mathbb{R}$) and let $f(b_i)$ be the number of times b_i was found as a possible beginning. Similarly, let $e_1, e_2, \ldots, e_m$ be the possible endings for x ($e_i \in \mathbb{R}$) and let $g(e_i)$ be the number of occurrences of e_i as a possible ending.

The basic idea is that $B^e(t)$ should reflect the percentage of people that considers t to be after the beginning of e. In the same way, $E^e(t)$ should reflect the percentage of people that considers t to be before the ending of e. This leads to the following definition:

$$B^e(t) = \frac{\sum_{b_i \leq t} f(b_i)}{\sum_{i=1}^{n} f(b_i)} \qquad (6.2)$$

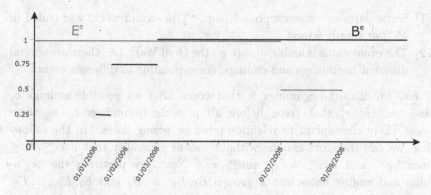

Fig. 6.1 Constructing a fuzzy interval from the beginning dates 01/01/2008 (1x), 15/01/2008 (2x), 01/03/2008 (1x), and the ending dates 30/06/2008 (3x) and 31/08/2008 (3x) (date format: dd/mm/yyyy).

$$E^e(t) = \frac{\sum_{e_i \geq t} g(e_i)}{\sum_{i=1}^{m} g(e_i)} \tag{6.3}$$

for all t in $\mathbb{R}$. For example, assuming that January 1, 2008 and March 1, 2008 are found once as the beginning date for e, and January 15, 2008 is found twice, the fuzzy set B^e depicted in Figure 6.1 is obtained. Similarly, the fuzzy set E^e is obtained when the ending dates June 30, 2008 and August 31, 2008 are found the same number of times, e.g., three times. When $b_i \leq e_j$ for all i in $\{1, 2, \ldots, n\}$ and all j in $\{1, 2, \ldots, m\}$, $B^e \cap E^e$ is a fuzzy time interval, corresponding to the vague temporal extent of e.

This solution still suffers from two important shortcomings. First, the assumption that $b_i \leq e_j$ for all i and j might not be satisfied, in which case the extracted information is inconsistent. This would result in a fuzzy set $B^e \cap E^e$ which is not normalised, and therefore not a fuzzy time interval. Second, we have assumed that beginnings and endings are always specified as exact dates. In practice, however, we frequently find beginnings and endings expressed as intervals ("World War II began in September 1939"), or even using vague descriptions ("World War II began in the *late* 1930s"). Both issues are addressed in the following paragraphs.

6.3.2.1 *Inconsistent dates*

There are two reasons why $b_i > e_j$ may hold for some i in $\{1, 2, \ldots, n\}$ and j in $\{1, 2, \ldots, m\}$:

(1) Some dates are misinterpreted (e.g., "The second world war ended in 45") or simply wrong.
(2) The event name is ambiguous (e.g., the Civil War), i.e., there are several different beginnings and endings, corresponding to different events.

First, we discard beginnings b_i that come after all possible endings e_j and endings e_j that come before all possible beginnings b_i, as these most likely correspond to misinterpreted or wrong dates. In the following, we can therefore assume without loss of generality that $\max_{i=1}^{n} b_i \leq \max_{j=1}^{m} e_j$ and $\min_{i=1}^{n} b_i \leq \min_{j=1}^{m} e_j$. Next, we partition the beginning and ending dates into k groups $B_1, B_2, \ldots, B_k$ and $E_1, E_2, \ldots, E_k$, respectively, such that $\max B_i < \min B_{i+1}$, $\max E_i < \min E_{i+1}$ and $\max E_i \leq \min B_{i+1}$ for all i in $\{1, \ldots, k-1\}$, and $\max B_j < \min E_j$ for all j in $\{1, \ldots, k\}$. For example, let the set of possible beginning and ending dates be given by $\{01/01/2008, 01/02/2008, 01/03/2008, 01/04/2008\}$ and $\{15/01/2008, 01/03/2008, 01/05/2008\}$; we find $k = 3$ and

$$B_1 = \{01/01/2008\} \quad B_2 = \{01/02/2008\} \quad B_3 = \{01/03/2008, 01/04/2008\}$$
$$E_1 = \{15/01/2008\} \quad E_2 = \{01/03/2008\} \quad E_3 = \{01/05/2008\}$$

In other words, we group possible beginnings (resp. endings) that cannot be separated by a possible ending (resp. beginning). Note that some of the B_i's or E_j's may contain only incorrect dates. We can assume, however, that a high number of occurrences of correct dates will be found on the web, and only few occurrences of incorrect dates. Therefore, we discard groups of dates that do not correspond to a sufficiently high number of occurrences. In particular, let α be a small constant in $]0, 1[$. For all i in $\{1, 2, \ldots, k\}$, if

$$\sum_{b \in B_i} f(b) < \alpha \max_{1 \leq j \leq k} \sum_{b \in B_j} f(b)$$

we discard the group B_i and join E_{i-1} and E_i together (or discard E_i if it is the first group). Analogously, if

$$\sum_{e \in E_i} g(e) < \alpha \max_{1 \leq j \leq k} \sum_{e \in E_j} g(e)$$

we discard the group E_i and join B_i and B_{i+1} together (or discard B_i if it is the last group). Let $B'_1, \ldots, B'_{k'}$ and $E'_1, \ldots, E'_{k'}$ be the resulting groups of dates. If $k' = 1$, we can define B^e and E^e as in (6.2) and (6.3), using only the dates from B'_1 and E'_1. On the other hand, if $k' > 1$, we assume that the event name under consideration is ambiguous. In the experiments below, our solution is not to assign a fuzzy time span in this case. Alternatively, we can choose a (B_i', E_j') with $i \leq j$ and define B^e and E^e as before, using only the dates from B_i' and E_j'.

6.3.2.2 *Underspecified dates*

Underspecified (September 1939) and vague (the late 1939s) expressions are used to refer to the beginning and ending of an event for two different reasons:

(1) The event began or ended on a particular date which is not completely specified (incompleteness).
(2) The event began or ended gradually during the period denoted by the underspecified or vague date (vagueness).

The first case occurs when the exact date is unknown to the author of the text, or not relevant in that context. The second case corresponds to situations in which the author is aware of the fact that temporal boundaries of the event are ill–defined. In the preceding discussion, we have mainly considered situations in which vagueness arises because of disagreement between different people (historians). For events such as the Cold War, this clearly is a simplification, since most people would consider its beginning as an inherently gradual process. Note, however, that the location in time of this gradual beginning can still be the subject of disagreement.

Both underspecified and vague time expressions can naturally be represented as (fuzzy) intervals. Let $\beta_1, \beta_2, \ldots, \beta_s$ be the fuzzy intervals corresponding to the possible underspecified or vague beginnings of event e, and let $\epsilon_1, \epsilon_2, \ldots, \epsilon_r$ be the fuzzy intervals corresponding to the underspecified or vague endings. Let $f(\beta_i)$ be the number of occurrences of β_i as a possible beginning and let $g(\epsilon_j)$ be the number of occurrences of ϵ_j as a possible ending. Finally, let $b_1, b_2, \ldots, b_n$ and $e_1, e_2, \ldots, e_m$ be the possible (completely specified) beginning and ending dates, as before. For each β_i, we need to decide whether it should be interpreted as incomplete information, or as the result of vague temporal boundaries (and similar for each ϵ_j). In the former case, we expect that in addition to the underspecified or vague beginning β_i, there also is some b_l referring to the same date. Therefore, if $\beta_i(b_l) > 0$ for some b_l, we assume that the former case holds; otherwise, we assume that the latter case holds (i.e., the event began gradually). In particular, we define the sets I_1, I_2, F_1 and F_2 as follows:

$$I_1 = \{\beta | \beta \in \{\beta_1, \ldots, \beta_s\} \text{ and } (\exists i \in \{1, \ldots, n\})(\beta(b_i) > 0)\}$$

$$I_2 = \{\beta_1, \ldots, \beta_s\} \setminus I_1$$
$$F_1 = \{\epsilon | \epsilon \in \{\epsilon_1, \ldots, \epsilon_r\} \text{ and } (\exists i \in \{1, \ldots, m\})(\epsilon(e_i) > 0)\}$$
$$F_2 = \{\epsilon_1, \ldots, \epsilon_r\} \setminus F_1$$

i.e., I_1 (resp. F_1) is the set of beginnings (resp. endings) for which the first interpretation is assumed (incompleteness), whereas I_2 (resp. F_2) is the set of beginnings (resp. endings) for which the second interpretation is assumed (vagueness). Furthermore, for a fuzzy interval A, we define the fuzzy sets A^- and A^+ in $\mathbb{R}$ as

$$A^-(t) = \frac{\int_{-\infty}^{t} A(x)\, dx}{\int_{-\infty}^{+\infty} A(x)\, dx} \qquad A^+(t) = \frac{\int_{t}^{+\infty} A(x)\, dx}{\int_{-\infty}^{+\infty} A(x)\, dx}$$

for all t in $\mathbb{R}$. If A represents a (vague) time period, $A^-(t)$ (resp. $A^+(t)$) expresses the fraction of A which is before (resp. after) t. The fuzzy sets B^e and E^e are then defined for t in $\mathbb{R}$ as

$$B^e(t) = \frac{\sum_{\beta \in I_2} f(\beta)\beta^-(t) + \sum_{b_i \leq t} f(b_i) + \sum_{\beta \in I_1} f(\beta) \frac{\sum_{b_i \leq t} \beta(b_i) f(b_i)}{\sum_{j=1}^{n} \beta(b_j) f(b_j)}}{\sum_{i=1}^{n} f(b_i) + \sum_{i=1}^{s} f(\beta_i)} \tag{6.4}$$

$$E^e(t) = \frac{\sum_{\epsilon \in F_2} g(\epsilon)\epsilon^+(t) + \sum_{e_i \geq t} g(e_i) + \sum_{\epsilon \in F_1} g(\epsilon) \frac{\sum_{e_i \geq t} \epsilon(e_i) g(e_i)}{\sum_{j=1}^{m} \epsilon(e_j) g(e_j)}}{\sum_{i=1}^{m} g(e_i) + \sum_{i=1}^{r} g(\epsilon_i)} \tag{6.5}$$

The first term in the numerator of (6.4) represents the influence of under-specified and vague dates for which the second interpretation is assumed. The contribution of a vague or underspecified date β to the membership degree of t is proportional to the number of times it was found (i.e., $f(\beta)$) and the fraction of the corresponding fuzzy interval that is before t. For example, if "January 2008" was found 5 times and t denotes 15/01/2008, the corresponding contribution would be $5 \cdot 0.5 = 2.5$. The second term represents the influence of exact dates and is similar in spirit to (6.2). Finally, the third term represents the influence of vague and underspecified dates for which the first interpretation is assumed. For sufficiently large t, $\sum_{b_i \leq t} \beta(b_i) f(b_i) = \sum_{j=1}^{n} \beta(b_j) f(b_j)$ and the total contribution of a term β in I_1 is $f(\beta)$. In general, in this third term, the impact of exact beginning dates b_i that are compatible with an underspecified or vague date β (i.e., such that $\beta(b_i) > 0$ holds) is increased. This increase is proportional to the number of occurrences $f(b_i)$ and to the degree of compatibility $\beta(b_i)$. The interpretation of (6.5) is entirely analogous. As an example, Figure 6.2 depicts the fuzzy set B^e which is obtained when January 2008 is found

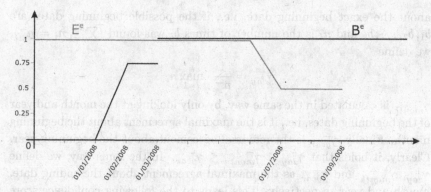

Fig. 6.2 Constructing a fuzzy interval from the beginning dates January 2008 (3x), 01/03/2008 (1x), and the ending dates June 2008 (3x) and 31/08/2008 (3x).

three times as the beginning date and 01/03/2008 once, as well as the fuzzy set E^e which is obtained when both June 2008 and 31/08/2008 are found three times as the ending date; note that in this example $I_1 = F_1 = \emptyset$.

6.3.2.3 Confidence scores

As for crisp time spans, we can attach a confidence score to fuzzy time spans depending on n^- and n^+, the (total) number of times a beginning date and an ending date were found. In addition, however, our confidence in a fuzzy time span may also be affected by the fact that there are different beginning and/or ending dates. The more disagreement about the beginning and ending dates, the higher the number of supporting web documents (i.e., the values of n^- and n^+) has to be to obtain a reliable fuzzy time span. For example, if we find five occurrences of the same beginning date, and there are no other candidates, we can be quite confident that this beginning date is correct. In the same way, if we find five times 01/01/2008 and five times 01/02/2008 as the beginning date, it is likely that both dates are correct to some extent. On the other hand, if we find five or ten different beginning dates, our confidence in each individual date is quite low. Moreover, if different beginning dates are found, our confidence in the resulting fuzzy time span depends on how close those different dates are to each other: if we find five beginning dates which are all in February 2008, we can be more confident than if there is one beginning date in 1876, one beginning date in 1946, one beginning date in 1986, etc. Therefore, to estimate the level of agreement we look at how often the same date, the same month and the same year are mentioned. Specifically, γ_{day}^- is the maximal agreement about the exact beginning date, i.e., if the possible beginning dates are $b_1, b_2, \ldots, b_k$ and n_i is the number of times b_i was found ($\sum_{i=1}^{k} n_i = n^-$), we define

$$\gamma_{day}^- = \frac{1}{n^-} \cdot \max_{i=1}^{k} n_i$$

γ_{month}^- is calculated in the same way, by only looking at the month and year of the beginning dates, i.e., it is the maximal agreement about the beginning month. Finally, γ_{year}^- is the maximal agreement about the beginning year. Clearly, it holds that $\gamma_{day}^- \leq \gamma_{month}^- \leq \gamma_{year}^-$. In the same way, we define γ_{day}^+, γ_{month}^+ and γ_{year}^+ as the maximal agreement about the ending date, month and year respectively. This leads to the following confidence score for the fuzzy time span of an event e:

$$c_t(e) = \min(1 - \frac{1}{1 + n^- w_{begin}}, 1 - \frac{1}{1 + n^+ w_{end}}) \tag{6.6}$$

where

$$w_{begin} = 0.25(1 + \gamma_{day}^- + \gamma_{month}^- + \gamma_{year}^-)$$
$$w_{end} = 0.25(1 + \gamma_{day}^+ + \gamma_{month}^+ + \gamma_{year}^+)$$

Note that if there is only one beginning date and one ending date, the time span of the event under consideration is in fact crisp. Accordingly, it holds in this case that $w_{begin} = w_{end} = 1$ and (6.6) degenerates to (6.1).

Figure 6.3 illustrates the fuzzy time span we obtained for the Battle of Britain. The fuzzy time span of the Battle of Britain clearly reflects the two most commonly used beginnings (mid August and July 10, 1940). A similar observation can be made w.r.t. the ending, although October 31, 1940 is mentioned much more often as the ending of the Battle of Britain than May 1941, and thereby has a much greater influence on the membership degrees. Figure 6.4 depicts the fuzzy time spans we found for World War I, World War II, the Vietnam War and the Cold War. Note that despite the lack of agreement about when, for instance, the Cold War began, its fuzzy time span still receives a high confidence score due to a very high number of supporting documents (166 beginning date and 80 ending date occurrences).

6.4   Extracting Qualitative Relations

For many lesser–known events, it is likely that no web document explicitly mentions a beginning or ending date, causing the approach outlined in

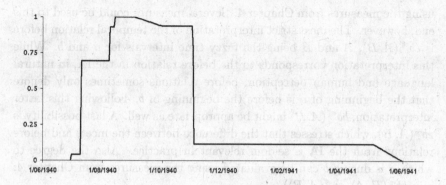

Fig. 6.3 Fuzzy time span of the Battle of Britain (conf. 0.98)

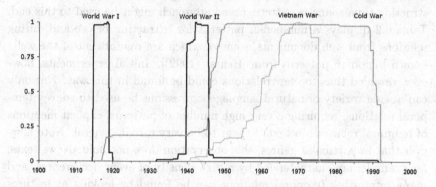

Fig. 6.4 Fuzzy time spans of World War I (conf. 0.99), World War II (conf. 0.99), the Vietnam War (conf. 0.97) and the Cold War (conf. 0.97).

Section 6.3 to fail. For example, explicit mentions of ending dates for battles are particularly rare. Moreover, beginning and ending dates are often presented in tables, or other (textual or non–textual) forms which are very hard to recognize by automated methods. However, the actual time spans are usually not required in an IR setting: all we need to establish is whether or not an event satisfies a given temporal constraint. For example, to assess whether information about the Battle of Britain is relevant to a query asking for information about "battles during World War II", we need to find out whether a during relation holds between the Battle of Britain and World War II. One way to accomplish this is by comparing the (fuzzy) time spans of both events. For example, if the time spans of event a and event b are available, we can calculate the degree to which a is before b

using the measures from Chapter 4. Several measures could be used to this end, however. The most strict interpretation of the temporal relation before is $eb^{\ll}(A, B)$, A and B being the fuzzy time intervals for a and b. While this interpretation corresponds to the before relation in the IA, in natural language and human perception, before relations sometimes only denote that the beginning of a is before the beginning of b. Following this latter interpretation, $bb^{\ll}(A, B)$ might be appropriate as well. A last possibility is $eb^{\prec}(A, B)$, which stresses that the difference between the meets and before relations from the IA is seldom relevant in practice. Also the degree to which a is during b can be evaluated using the measures from Chapter 4: $\min(bb^{\prec}(B, A), ee^{\prec}(A, B))$.

However, we can also try to find evidence for temporal relations directly, without the need for time spans. By analogy with our approach for constructing time spans, a pattern–based approach might be used to this end. Table 6.2 displays a number of patterns for extracting before and during relations from web documents, some of which are reminiscent of the well-known hyponym patterns from [Hearst (1992)]. Initial experiments, however, revealed that too few relations could be found in this way. Not only can a wide variety of natural language expressions be used to convey temporal relations, requiring a very high number of patterns, explicit mentions of temporal relations in texts appear to be very rare in general. Note however that in particular genres, this observation does not hold. News texts, for example, are characterized by a high density of event occurrences, and many interesting temporal relations can be found by looking at features such as verb tense and certain temporal prepositions. Accordingly, much of

Table 6.2   Patterns for qualitative temporal relations between events.

Before patterns	During patterns
$\langle event_1 \rangle$ gave way to $\langle event_2 \rangle$	$\langle event_1 \rangle$ took place during $\langle event_2 \rangle$
$\langle event_2 \rangle$ was a result of $\langle event_1 \rangle$	$\langle event_1 \rangle$ happened during $\langle event_2 \rangle$
$\langle event_1 \rangle$ was succeeded by $\langle event_2 \rangle$	$\langle event_2 \rangle$ escalated during $\langle event_1 \rangle$
$\langle event_2 \rangle$ happened after $\langle event_1 \rangle$	$\langle event_2 \rangle$ changed after $\langle event_1 \rangle$
$\langle event_2 \rangle$ occurred after $\langle event_1 \rangle$	$\langle event_2 \rangle$ continued after $\langle event_1 \rangle$
$\langle event_2 \rangle$ took place after $\langle event_1 \rangle$	$\langle event_1 \rangle$ and other events during $\langle event_2 \rangle$
$\langle event_2 \rangle$ began after $\langle event_1 \rangle$	$\langle event_1 \rangle$, a turning point in $\langle event_2 \rangle$
$\langle event_2 \rangle$, which followed $\langle event_1 \rangle$	$\langle event_1 \rangle$ was a pivotal point in $\langle event_2 \rangle$
$\langle event_2 \rangle$, which succeeded $\langle event_1 \rangle$	$\langle event_1 \rangle$ and its place in $\langle event_2 \rangle$
$\langle event_2 \rangle$ was inspired by $\langle event_1 \rangle$	$\langle event_1 \rangle$ and other events from $\langle event_2 \rangle$
$\langle event_1 \rangle$ and the ensuing $\langle event_2 \rangle$	$\langle event_2 \rangle$ events such as $\langle event_1 \rangle$
$\langle event_1 \rangle$ and the following $\langle event_2 \rangle$	$\langle event_2 \rangle$ changed after $\langle event_1 \rangle$
during $\langle event_1 \rangle$ and later during $\langle event_2 \rangle$	$\langle event_2 \rangle$ escalated during $\langle event_1 \rangle$

the literature on mining temporal relations from texts has focused on the news genre (e.g., [Allan *et al.* (1998, 2001); Barzilay *et al.* (2002); Filatova and Hovy (2001); Mani *et al.* (2003)]). In this section, we will focus on two heuristic techniques which are more widely applicable and less tied to one particular genre. Our techniques are redundancy–based, however, requiring that the events under consideration are talked about in a sufficiently large number of different documents. As such, they are complementary to existing, more linguistically oriented approaches.

6.4.1 *Co–occurring Dates*

A first heuristic technique is inspired by research in question answering systems [Brill *et al.* (2002); Kwok *et al.* (2001); Monz and de Rijke (2002)]. Various authors have discovered that the answer to a question can often be found by simply looking at entities of an appropriate semantic type which occur near words or phrases from the question. For example, to answer a question such as *Who was the first man in space?*, a named entity tagger can be used to find names of persons in sentences containing the phrase "first man in space", or with lower confidence, the words "first", "man" and "space". By counting which name occurs most often in such sentences, a surprisingly high accuracy can often be achieved.

Moving to event time spans, we can expect that dates which often occur near an event name are strongly related to the event and typically correspond to its beginning or ending date, or the date of an important sub–event. In particular, for each event name, we retrieve the first 50 documents returned by Yahoo!, using the event name as query. Subsequently, we extract from these documents all dates which occur within 200 characters from the event name. In this way, a high number of dates is typically found for each event, most of which are related to it. However, it is usually not possible to construct a reliable (fuzzy) time span from these dates. For example, for the Battle of Britain we find the dates presented in Table 6.3. In this case, the dates that were found are all during the Battle of Britain to some extent, although the most common beginning and ending dates are missing. The results for World War II in Table 6.4 include both common beginning (01/09/1939) and ending dates (08/05/1945 and 02/09/1945), although some incorrect dates are found as well (22/06/0194, 23/09/2002 and 30/05/2004). Finally, for the Invasion of Normandy (Table 6.5) only the correct beginning and ending dates are found.

Table 6.3   Dates found in web documents within 200 characters from the Battle of Britain

Date	Freq.	Date	Freq.
14/07/1940	3	04/09/1940	2
31/07/1940	3	07/09/1940	4
24/08/1940	2	09/09/1940	2
31/08/1940	5	30/09/1940	5
03/09/1940	2		

Table 6.4   Dates found in web documents within 200 characters from World War II

Date	Freq.	Date	Freq.
22/06/0194	1	07/05/1945	3
01/09/1939	6	08/05/1945	2
22/06/1941	2	02/09/1945	8
06/01/1942	1	23/09/2002	3
06/06/1944	1	30/05/2004	5

Table 6.5   Dates found in web documents within 200 characters from the Invasion of Normandy

Date	Freq.	Date	Freq.
06/06/1944	15	25/06/1944	6

Hence, while the dates that are found using this technique are useful to gain information about the approximate temporal location of events, we cannot rely on them to derive actual time spans. However, using the dates found by this method, we can derive useful information about the likelihood that some temporal relation holds between two given events. Initially, we assume that all temporal relations are crisp: either a is before b or not, either a is during b or not.

6.4.1.1   *Before*

First, consider the temporal relation *before* between two events a and b. Let the dates that were found for event a be given by $D^a = \{d_1^a, d_2^a, \ldots, d_n^a\}$, and let f_i^a be the number of times date d_i^a was found. Similarly, let $D^b = \{d_1^b, d_2^b, \ldots, d_m^b\}$ be the dates that were found for event b, and let f_i^b be the corresponding frequency. Typically, we will require that $n \geq 5$ and $m \geq 5$ to ensure significance. Every pair of dates (d_i^a, d_j^b) such that $d_i^a < d_j^b$ (i.e., date d_i^a comes strictly before date d_j^b in time) serves as evidence for $before(a, b)$, whereas every pair of dates (d_i^a, d_j^b) such that $d_i^a \geq d_j^b$ serves as evidence against $before(a, b)$:

$$pos^{bef}(a, b) = \sum_{\substack{i=1}}^{n} \sum_{\substack{j=1 \\ d_i^a < d_j^b}}^{m} f_i^a \cdot f_j^b$$

$$neg^{bef}(a, b) = \sum_{\substack{i=1}}^{n} \sum_{\substack{j=1 \\ d_i^a \geq d_j^b}}^{m} f_i^a \cdot f_j^b$$

As soon as $pos^{bef}(a, b)$ is greater than $neg^{bef}(a, b)$, or equivalently $\frac{pos^{bef}(a,b)}{pos^{bef}(a,b)+neg^{bef}(a,b)} > 0.5$, there is reason to believe that $before(a, b)$ holds. This leads to the following confidence score

$$c_1^{bef}(a, b) = 2 \cdot \max(0, \frac{pos^{bef}(a, b)}{pos^{bef}(a, b) + neg^{bef}(a, b)} - 0.5) \qquad (6.7)$$

provided that $n \neq 0$ and $m \neq 0$, and therefore $pos^{bef}(a, b) + neg^{bef}(a, b) > 0$; otherwise, we define $c_1^{bef}(a, b) = 0$. Note that a factor 2 is introduced to obtain a confidence score in $[0, 1]$. It is easy to see that $c_1^{bef}(a, b) = 1$ iff all dates in D^a are strictly before all dates in D^b, and $c_1^{bef}(a, b) = 0$ iff $pos^{bef}(a, b) \leq neg^{bef}(a, b)$.

If a fuzzy time interval is available for both event a and event b, the measures from Chapter 4 could be used, as explained above. Next, if a fuzzy time interval A is known for event a, but no fuzzy time interval is known for b, we can count positive and negative evidence by looking at how many dates were found for b that are after a. Note that a crisp date d is a special case of a fuzzy time interval, hence we can use the measure $eb^{\ll}$ to define $pos^{bef}(a, b)$ and $neg^{bef}(a, b)$. We obtain

$$pos^{bef}(a, b) = \sum_{j=1}^{m} eb^{\ll}(A, d_j^b) \cdot f_j^b$$

$$neg^{bef}(a, b) = \sum_{j=1}^{m} (1 - eb^{\ll}(A, d_j^b)) \cdot f_j^b = \sum_{j=1}^{m} be^{\preccurlyeq}(d_j^b, A) \cdot f_j^b$$

and $c_1^{bef}(a, b)$ is again given by (6.7). Finally, if a fuzzy time interval is available for event b, but not for event a, we can proceed in an entirely similar way.

6.4.1.2 *During*

To estimate the likelihood that event a happened during event b, written $during(a, b)$, we proceed in a similar way. The main idea is that triples of dates (d_i^a, d_j^b, d_k^b) satisfying $d_j^b \leq d_i^a \leq d_k^b$ serve as evidence for $during(a, b)$, whereas triples satisfying $d_i^a < d_j^b < d_k^b$ or $d_j^b < d_k^b < d_i^a$ serve as evidence against $during(a, b)$:

$$pos^{dur}(a, b) = \sum_{i=1}^{n} \sum_{\substack{j=1 \\ d_j^b \leq d_i^a}}^{m} \sum_{\substack{k=1 \\ d_i^a \leq d_k^b \\ d_j^b < d_k^b}}^{m} f_i^a \cdot f_j^b \cdot f_k^b$$

$$neg^{dur}(a, b) = \sum_{i=1}^{n} \sum_{\substack{j=1 \\ d_i^a < d_j^b}}^{m} \sum_{\substack{k=1 \\ d_j^b < d_k^b}}^{m} f_i^a \cdot f_j^b \cdot f_k^b + \sum_{i=1}^{n} \sum_{\substack{k=1 \\ d_k^b < d_i^a}}^{m} \sum_{\substack{j=1 \\ d_j^b < d_k^b}}^{m} f_i^a \cdot f_j^b \cdot f_k^b$$

The corresponding confidence score is analogously defined as (6.7):

$$c_1^{dur}(a, b) = 2 \cdot \max(0, \frac{pos^{dur}(a, b)}{pos^{dur}(a, b) + neg^{dur}(a, b)} - 0.5) \qquad (6.8)$$

provided that $n \neq 0$ and $m \geq 2$; $c_1^{dur}(a, b) = 0$ otherwise. It holds that $c_1^{dur}(a, b) = 1$ if $m = 2$ and for all d_i^a in D^a either $d_1^b \leq d_i^a \leq d_2^b$ or $d_2^b \leq d_i^a \leq d_1^b$. The intuition behind this confidence score is further clarified in the next example.

Example 6.1. First, let $D^a = \{18/01/2008, 21/01/2008\}$ and $D^b = \{10/01/2008, 30/01/2008\}$, and assume that all dates were found 5 times, i.e., $f_1^a = f_2^a = f_1^b = f_2^b = 5$. As only two dates were found for event b, it is likely that these correspond to the beginning and ending date of b. Furthermore, since all dates in D^a are between these two dates, it is very plausible that $during(a, b)$ holds. We find

$$pos^{dur}(a, b) = f_1^a \cdot f_1^b \cdot f_2^b + f_2^a \cdot f_1^b \cdot f_2^b = 5 \cdot 5 \cdot 5 + 5 \cdot 5 \cdot 5 = 250$$
$$neg^{dur}(a, b) = 0$$

and

$$c_1^{dur}(a, b) = 2 \cdot \max(0, \frac{250}{250} - 0.5) = 1$$

As another example, let $D^a = \{18/01/2008, 21/01/2008\}$ and $D^b = \{10/01/2008, 12/01/2008, 24/01/2008, 30/01/2008\}$, and again assume that all dates were found 5 times. In this case, it is less clear which of the dates in D^b correspond to the beginning and ending dates of b. It might be that $10/01/2008$ is the beginning date and $30/01/2008$ is the ending date, in which case $12/01/2008$ and $24/01/2008$ would probably correspond to important turning points of event b, but it might also be the case that, for instance, 24/01/2008 is the beginning date and 30/01/2008 is the ending date while 10/01/2008 and 12/01/2008 correspond to preceding events which have led to b. Therefore, our confidence in $during(a, b)$ should be less than in the first example. We obtain

$$pos^{dur}(a, b) = f_1^a \cdot f_1^b \cdot f_3^b + f_1^a \cdot f_1^b \cdot f_4^b + f_1^a \cdot f_2^b \cdot f_3^b + f_1^a \cdot f_2^b \cdot f_4^b$$
$$+ f_2^a \cdot f_1^b \cdot f_3^b + f_2^a \cdot f_1^b \cdot f_4^b + f_2^a \cdot f_2^b \cdot f_3^b + f_2^a \cdot f_2^b \cdot f_4^b$$
$$= 1000$$

$$neg^{dur}(a, b) = f_1^a \cdot f_1^b \cdot f_2^b + f_2^a \cdot f_1^b \cdot f_2^b + f_1^a \cdot f_3^b \cdot f_4^b + f_2^a \cdot f_3^b \cdot f_4^b = 500$$

and

$$c_1^{dur}(a, b) = 2 \cdot \max(0, \frac{1000}{1500} - 0.5) = \frac{1}{3}$$

Finally, let $D^a = \{11/01/2008\}$ and $D^b = \{10/01/2008, 12/01/2008, 24/01/2008, 30/01/2008\}$, and assume all dates were found 5 times. We find

$$pos^{dur}(a, b) = f_1^a \cdot f_1^b \cdot f_2^b + f_1^a \cdot f_1^b \cdot f_3^b + f_1^a \cdot f_1^b \cdot f_4^b = 375$$
$$neg^{dur}(a, b) = f_1^a \cdot f_2^b \cdot f_3^b + f_1^a \cdot f_2^b \cdot f_4^b + f_1^a \cdot f_3^b \cdot f_4^b = 375$$

and

$$c_1^{dur}(a, b) = 2 \cdot \max(0, \frac{375}{750} - 0.5) = 0$$

Hence, a high value of $c_1^{dur}(a, b)$ is only possible if b has clearly marked beginning and ending dates, i.e., if there are only two different dates which occur often near b.

If a fuzzy time interval is available for both event a and event b, the measures from Chapter 4 could again be. Next, if a fuzzy time interval B is available for event b, but no fuzzy time interval is known for event a, we find

$$pos^{dur}(a, b) = \sum_{i=1}^{n} \min(bb^{\preccurlyeq}(B, d_i^a), ee^{\preccurlyeq}(d_i^a, B)) \cdot f_i^a = \sum_{i=1}^{n} B(d_i^a) \cdot f_i^a$$

$$neg^{dur}(a, b) = \sum_{i=1}^{n} (1 - B(d_i^a)) \cdot f_i^a$$

and $c_1^{dur}(a, b)$ is given by (6.8). Finally, the case where a fuzzy time interval is available for a but not for b could be treated in the same way. Note, however, that it is unlikely that $during(a, b)$ when only for a a fuzzy time span can be found. Indeed, if $during(a, b)$ we could expect that more information about b can be found than about a. Therefore, we will not consider this situation in the remainder of this chapter.

6.4.2   Document Structure

Our second heuristic is based on the structure of event occurrences in web documents. Specifically, let n_1 be the number of times we find (the first occurrence of) a before (the first occurrence of) b in sections of web documents, lists on web pages, and in titles of sections within the same level; let n_2 be the number of times we find b before a. Furthermore, let m_1 be the number of times event a occurs in the body of a section whose title refers to event b and let m_2 be the number of times event b occurs in the body of a section whose title refers to event a. As will be discussed in detail below, the values of n_1, n_2, m_1 and m_2 can be used to check whether $before(a, b)$ and $during(a, b)$ are likely to hold. To obtain these values, we retrieve relevant documents using the Yahoo! search engine. However, if we use a query such as "Battle of Britain", all top ranked documents will be specifically about this battle, which heavily biases the resulting values. Therefore, we omit all documents whose title refers to the Battle of Britain. To this end, the query we actually use is given by

```
"Battle of Britain" -intitle:Britain
```

which excludes documents whose title contains the word "Britain" from the search results. In general, we use the -intitle option to exclude the longest word from the event name which does not refer to a type of military conflict (e.g., war, battle, campaign, offensive, . . .).

6.4.2.1   Before

There are many reasons why the order of occurrence of events in a narrative may be different from their chronological ordering. News stories, for instance, tend to start with the most recent events, after which they might go into detail about relevant background information from the past. Nonetheless, linguistic analyses have demonstrated that the event order in news stories is — albeit not completely — to a large extent chronological (e.g., [Schokkenbroek (1999)]). Similarly, although historical documents have a tendency to digress, thereby linking events from the main linear narrative to earlier or later events [Smith (2002)], we can still expect the order of occurrence to be chronological more often than not. By looking at the relative order of occurrence of two events a and b, we may therefore be able to derive information about the likelihood of $before(a, b)$. In particular, n_1 being significantly higher than n_2 is a strong indication of $before(a, b)$. To test whether the difference between n_1 and n_2 is greater than could be expected by chance, we employ a binomial test:

$$p_2^{bef}(a,b) = \sum_{k=n_1}^{n_1+n_2} \binom{n_1+n_2}{k} 0.5^k (1-0.5)^{n_1+n_2-k}$$

If the difference is deemed significant, e.g., $p_2^{bef}(a,b) < 0.05$, we assume that $before(a,b)$ holds. In that case, we assign a confidence score which is similar in spirit to (6.7) and (6.8)

$$c_2^{bef}(a,b) = 2\max(0, \frac{n_1}{n_1+n_2} - 0.5)$$

Note that the scores $p_2^{bef}(a,b)$ and $c_2^{bef}(a,b)$ have a slightly different focus. For example, if $n_1 = 1$ and $n_2 = 0$, $c_2^{bef}(a,b) = 1$ although no reliable conclusion can be derived. Accordingly, we have that $p_2^{bef}(a,b) = 0.5$, i.e., the probability that the observed situation arises by chance is 50%. On the other hand, both when $n_1 = 9$ and $n_2 = 1$, or $n_1 = 537$ and $n_2 = 463$, it holds that $p_2^{bef}(a,b) \approx 0.01$, whereas $c_2^{bef}(a,b) = 0.8$ in the former case and $c_2^{bef}(a,b) = 0.074$ in the latter. In our experiments, we mainly use $c_2^{bef}(a,b)$ when a score is required that is comparable to c_1^{bef}, and $p_2^{bef}(a,b)$ otherwise.

6.4.2.2 *During*

Instances of during relations can be found in a similar way, by looking at section titles containing the name of an event. For instance, if the title of a section refers to World War II and its body contains a reference to the Battle of Britain, there is some reason to believe that the Battle of Britain happened during World War II. Note, however, that also the opposite might occur: a section about the Battle of Britain referring to World War II in its body. In other words, if m_1 is sufficiently high, it is very likely that either $during(a,b)$ or $during(b,a)$ holds. In many cases, $during(b,a)$ can be excluded a priori using background information. For example, knowing that battles can be part of a war but not vice versa, we can exclude the case that World War II is a part of the Battle of Britain. Our confidence in $during(a,b)$ can then be expressed by any increasing function of $m_1 + m_2$ in $[0,1]$, e.g.:

$$c_2^{dur}(a,b) = \frac{m_1+m_2}{4+m_1+m_2}$$

For example, if $m_1+m_2 = 1$, we have $c_2^{dur}(a,b) = 0.2$, while for $m_1+m_2 = 2$ and $m_1+m_2 = 4$, we find $c_2^{dur}(a,b) \approx 0.33$ and $c_2^{dur}(a,b) = 0.5$ respectively.

In general, however, neither $during(a, b)$ nor $during(b, a)$ can be excluded a priori, and therefore, a high value of $m_1 + m_2$ is not sufficient to conclude $during(a, b)$. To decide whether $during(a, b)$ holds, in this case, we compare the values of m_1 and m_2. In particular, when $during(a, b)$ is the case, it is likely that m_1 is significantly higher than m_2. For example, we can expect to find more section titles referring to World War II than section titles referring to the Battle of Britain. Again, we use a binomial test to determine the significance:

$$p_2^{dur}(a, b) = \sum_{k=m_1}^{m_1+m_2} \binom{m_1 + m_2}{k} 0.5^k (1 - 0.5)^{m_1+m_2-k}$$

The corresponding confidence score is given by

$$c_2'^{dur}(a, b) = 2 \max(0, \frac{m_1}{m_1 + m_2} - 0.5)$$

6.5 Fuzzy Temporal Reasoning

6.5.1 *Constructing a Knowledge Base*

The previously described heuristic techniques result in a large amount of temporal information. While we can expect most of this information to be reliable, some incorrect information will inevitably be derived. In part this can be explained by the heuristic nature of the techniques involved, although other causes apply as well (e.g., using the web as a source for data acquisition). An even more fundamental problem is related to the vagueness of event boundaries. As an example, consider the vague boundaries of World War II from Figure 6.4. Depending on the point of view taken, the Japanese Invasion of China (1937) is either before or during World War II. Accordingly, the techniques outlined above yield conflicting information:

$$c_1^{bef}(invChina, WW2) = 0.74$$
$$c_2^{dur}(invChina, WW2) = 0.5$$

where $invChina$ and $WW2$ are used as abbreviations of the Japanese Invasion of China and World War II respectively. The most appropriate solution, in this case, is not to ignore either $before(invChina, WW2)$ or $during(invChina, WW2)$, but to model that both relations are satisfied to a certain degree between 0 and 1. Therefore, we apply fuzzy temporal reasoning to find an interpretation of the available information which is FI–satisfiable. By imposing FI–satisfiability, we can expect that incorrect information will be detected and removed from the knowledge base, and, moreover, partially correct information (e.g., conflicts which arise because of vagueness) will be weakened but not completely removed. In particular, a variation of Procedure `Closure-rev3` from the previous chapter will be used; detected inconsistencies will be repaired based on the confidence scores of each relation.

Rather than constructing one large knowledge base containing information about every war of interest, a separate knowledge base is constructed for each war, ensuring the scalability of the presented techniques. Specifically, we have constructed a knowledge base for the 25 wars from Table 6.6. To construct a knowledge base for a war, we first construct a set of related events and subsequently try to establish temporal relations between these events. To this end, in the specific case of World War II, for instance, the following five queries are sent to Google:

(1) `allintitle:World War II`
(2) `"World War II"`
(3) `"World War II" events`
(4) `"World War II" battle`
(5) `"World War II" timeline`

The first query asks for documents which have the terms "World" "War" and "II" in their title, while the second asks for documents containing the exact phrase "World War II". The last three queries ask for documents that additionally contain the terms "events", "battle" or "timeline", which tends to increase the likelihood of finding relevant event names in the returned web documents. Next, these five queries are also sent to Yahoo!, replacing the first query by `intitle:World War II` to conform to its syntax. For each query, at most 1000 documents were retrieved, which leads to a maximum of 10000 documents. In practice, however, there often is overlap between the result lists of the different queries. The actual number of documents retrieved for each war is shown in the second column of Table 6.6.

In a second step, a part–of–speech (POS) tagger is used to extract noun phrases (NPs) occurring in these web documents[7]. From these NPs, we subsequently selected those that likely refer to a military conflict using a number of simple heuristic rules. A simple NP, which does not contain any prepositions, is selected if it satisfies the following requirements:

---

[7]We used the POS–tagger from the Stanford NLP Group, available from http://nlp.stanford.edu/.

Table 6.6 For every war, a separate knowledge base was constructed by retrieving a number of web documents (2nd column) from which events of interest were extracted. Next, a number of before and during relations was identified (3rd and 4th column), as well as a number of (fuzzy) time spans (5th column). Evaluation is based on a number of battles which are known to have taken place during the respective wars (6th column).

Name	# Documents	# Before	# During	# Time Spans	# Battles
American Civil War (1861–1865)	3904	3938	420	34	338
American Revolutionary War (1775–1783)	3359	7329	762	44	132
Chinese Civil War (1927–1950)	1247	7179	264	41	51
Continuation War (1941–1944)	3545	6233	833	39	8
Falklands War (1982)	1262	6314	372	42	29
Finnish War (1808–1809)	1281	6252	566	42	10
First Boer War (1880–1881)	1087	5826	520	53	4
First Chechen War (1994–1996)	1260	2653	89	25	6
Gulf War (1990–1991)	4489	7694	189	42	7
Korean War (1950–1953)	4357	8841	150	49	26
Napoleonic Wars (1803–1815)	1326	4881	380	39	191
Philippine–American War (1899–1902)	1209	5551	261	44	16
Polish September Campaign (1939)	974	3393	442	25	28
Polish–Soviet War (1919–1921)	1209	3848	395	31	15
Russo–Japanese War (1904–1905)	1281	4772	410	40	17
Second Boer War (1899–1902)	1246	3827	225	41	15
Second Chechen War (1999–2007)	1261	2612	88	26	15
Second Sino-Japanese War (1937–1945)	1072	5113	514	29	64
Spanish Civil War (1936–1939)	4260	8592	461	57	24
Spanish–American War (1898)	1224	2516	194	32	21
Vietnam War (1959–1975)	4513	9185	341	47	115
War of the Pacific (1879–1884)	1305	4040	254	34	10
World War I (1914–1919)	3723	8652	517	56	198
World War II (1939–1945)	4073	8876	673	47	329
Yom Kippur War (1973)	3730	7243	350	42	4

(1) it contains a capitalized word different from "The";

(2) it contains a reference to some kind of military conflict, i.e., a word such as battle, siege, attack, offensive, war, operation, campaign, ...;

(3) it does not start with a number of selected words, including a, an, his, her, this, most, some, every, any, ...

Examples of noun phrases satisfying these requirements are "World War II", "the Pearl Harbor attack" or "Operation Desert Storm"; examples of noun phrases which violate at least one requirement are "operation desert storm", "D-day" and "most World War II battles". In addition to simple NPs, also noun phrases of the form "$\langle NP_1 \rangle$ IN $\langle NP_2 \rangle$" are allowed, where $\langle NP_1 \rangle$ and $\langle NP_2 \rangle$ are simple noun phrases and IN denotes an arbitrary preposition, provided the following requirements are satisfied:

(1) $\langle NP_2 \rangle$ contains a capitalized word different from "The";

(2) $\langle NP_1 \rangle$ contains a reference to some kind of military conflict;

(3) $\langle NP_2 \rangle$ does not contain a reference to some kind of military conflict;

(4) $\langle NP_1 \rangle$ does not start with a number of selected words.

Examples of noun phrases satisfying these requirements are "the Battle of the Bulge", "the Attack on Pearl Harbor" and "the Battle for Leyte Gulf". Next, the number of occurrences of each event are counted, ignoring case, as well as a possible starting "the", e.g. "The Battle of the Bulge" and "battle of the Bulge" would be treated as the same event name. As an example, Table 6.7 displays the most frequently occurring event names in the set of documents that was retrieved for World War II. This table contains many famous World War II battles and operations, although many other military conflicts are found as well (e.g., the Vietnam War, World War I, ...). Note that not all names actually refer to events: national world war ii memorial, defense dept., war information, ...However, it is unlikely that temporal relations will be found involving these names. Therefore, we can expect that most of these non–events will be excluded from the final knowledge base.

Our aim is to obtain a reliable knowledge base, containing temporal information about the most important World War II events (and similar for the other 24 knowledge bases). The focus in the construction process is therefore more on accuracy (precision) than on completeness (recall). To ensure that sufficient information about each event in the knowledge base can be found, the construction of the knowledge base is restricted to the 250 most frequently occurring event names. Note that this has an additional

Table 6.7   The 102 most frequently occurring event names in documents about World War II.

Name	Freq.	Name	Freq.	Name	Freq.
world war ii	12032	national world war ii memorial	99	revolutionary war	54
second world war	1300	operation market garden	97	german attack	54
world war	1175	world war 2 t-shirts and gifts	94	invasion of normandy	53
cold war	682	operation barbarossa	92	world war ii timeline	53
world war i	530	operation overlord	87	american battle monuments commission	53
world war 2	501	battle of the coral sea	87	russian revolution	51
battle of the bulge	482	war department	86	operation sealion	51
battle of britain	430	battle of normandy	84	japanese attack	50
world war two	429	pearl harbor attack	80	soviet offensive	50
civil war	417	operation torch	79	battle of france	49
war on germany	349	winter war	78	world war ii casualties	47
battle of midway	336	north african campaign	77	second battle of el alamein	46
vietnam war	305	battle of kursk	75	world war ii era	46
war ii	285	battle of leyte gulf	74	battle of guadalcanal	46
pacific war	277	world war ii history	73	world war iii	45
korean war	276	world war ii world war ii	73	invasion of france	43
first world war	251	phony war	70	world war ii combat	41
attack on pearl harbor	223	german invasion of poland	67	french revolution	41
war on japan	217	italian campaign	67	doolittle raid	41
great war	185	american civil war	65	japanese war crimes	41
battle of the atlantic	167	european war	64	persian gulf war	40
spanish civil war	146	bombing of pearl harbor	64	german war machine	39
world war i.	137	d-day invasion	63	german invasion of the soviet union	39
total war	133	great patriotic war	63	invasion of russia	38
world war ii memorial	128	spanish-american war	61	world war iv	38
normandy invasion	127	siege of leningrad	61	world war one	37
iraq war	122	german offensive	61	war bonds	37
war on the united states	120	world war ii online	60	battle of berlin	36
japanese attack on pearl harbor	118	air war	59	battle of okinawa	36
battle of stalingrad	115	battle of iwo jima	57	first battle of el alamein	35
american revolution	106	war information	56	operation bagration	35
defense dept.	105	invasion of sicily	55	invasion of italy	35
invasion of poland	102	world war ii posters	55	battle of the river plate	34
gulf war	102	german invasion	54	war front	33

advantage of efficiency. For each of these events, we try to construct a (fuzzy) time interval from the web, as described in Section 6.3. If the confidence score $c_t(e)$ of the fuzzy time interval of an event e is at least 0.9, it is added to the knowledge base; such events e will be referred to as grounded events. Furthermore, for each of the 250×250 event–pairs, we check whether a before or during relation is likely to hold, using the two heuristic techniques from Section 6.4. In particular, a before or during relation is added to the knowledge base if the evidence found by at least one of both techniques is deemed significant and the corresponding confidence score is at least 0.8. In that case, a new confidence score is assigned to the relation which is a weighted sum of the confidence scores assigned by both techniques. For example, if a before relation is added to the knowledge base between events e_1 and e_2, the corresponding confidence score is given by

$$c^{bef}(e_1, e_2) = 0.5 \cdot c_1^{*bef}(e_1, e_2) + 0.5 \cdot c_2^{*bef}(e_1, e_2) \qquad (6.9)$$

where

$$c_1^{*bef}(e_1, e_2) = \begin{cases} c_1^{bef}(e_1, e_2) & \text{If at least 5 date instances are found} \\ & \qquad \text{for } e_1 \text{ and } e_2 \\ 0 & \text{otherwise} \end{cases}$$

$$c_2^{*bef}(e_1, e_2) = \begin{cases} c_2^{bef}(e_1, e_2) & \text{If } p_2^{bef}(e_1, e_2) < 0.05 \\ 0 & \text{otherwise} \end{cases}$$

Note that in this way, a higher confidence is given to relations that are found by both techniques. Table 6.6 summarizes the number of before and during relations which are thus added to each of the knowledge bases, as well as the number of fuzzy time intervals. Note that the number of grounded events is typically between 25 and 50, i.e., between 10% and 20%. Furthermore, note that the number of before relations that is found is much greater than the number of during relations.

6.5.2 *Reasoning*

The purpose of fuzzy temporal reasoning in this context is twofold: inferring new information and increasing the reliability of the knowledge base by detecting and repairing inconsistencies. Note that inferring new fuzzy temporal relations and detecting inconsistencies was the focus of Chapter 5, where among others Procedure `Closure-rev3` was introduced as a means for efficient temporal reasoning. Here, we will utilize a variant of Procedure `Closure-rev3`, which is called Procedure `Closure-rev4` and uses the notations from Chapter 5 (e.g., C_1). A first deviation from Procedure `Closure-rev3` is that the closure process in Procedure `Closure-rev4` is not halted the moment an inconsistency is detected. Instead, all consequences which do not rely on inconsistent premises are derived. The second difference is that inconsistencies can now occur between temporal relations and groundings (i.e., fuzzy time intervals), in addition to inconsistencies amongst different temporal relations. To cope with this, reference to a function `Grounding-consistent` has been added which returns *true* iff the corresponding temporal relation is compatible with the available groundings. In particular, this function always returns *true* when either the first or the second argument refers to an ungrounded event. When both x_i and x_j correspond to grounded events, the exact temporal relationship between these events can easily be calculated. `Grounding-consistent`(x_i, x_j) then returns *true* if the derived temporal relation between x_i and x_j is compatible with this exact temporal relationship. For example, let X_i and X_j be the fuzzy time intervals of events x_i and x_j, and let $C_1(x_i, x_j)$ be given by

$$C_1(x_i, x_j) = [0.4, 0.4, 0, 0.2, 0.4, 0.4, 0, 0.2]$$

which entails, among others, the restriction that $eb^{\ll}(X_i, X_j)$ should be at least 0.2. Therefore, if X_i and X_j satisfy $eb^{\ll}(X_i, X_j) = 0.1$, for instance, `Grounding-consistent`(x_i, x_j) is false. In general, if $C_1(x_i, x_j)$ is given by

$$C_1(x_i, x_j) = [\alpha, \beta, \gamma, \delta, \alpha', \beta', \gamma', \delta']$$

and X_i and X_j are the groundings (fuzzy time intervals) of x_i and x_j, it holds that

$$
\begin{aligned}
\text{`Grounding-consistent`}(x_i, x_j) \equiv\ & be^{\prec}(X_i, X_j) \geq \alpha \wedge bb^{\prec}(X_i, X_j) \geq \beta \\
& \wedge\, ee^{\prec}(X_i, X_j) \geq \gamma \wedge eb^{\prec}(X_i, X_j) \geq \delta \\
& \wedge\, be^{\ll}(X_i, X_j) \geq \alpha' \wedge bb^{\ll}(X_i, X_j) \geq \beta' \\
& \wedge\, ee^{\ll}(X_i, X_j) \geq \gamma' \wedge eb^{\ll}(X_i, X_j) \geq \delta'
\end{aligned}
$$

After Procedure `Closure-rev4` has finished, an attempt is made to repair the detected inconsistencies. An inconsistency detected by Procedure `Consistent-revised` can be repaired by weakening one or more of the premises which have been used to arrive at this inconsistency. Initially, when *before*(e_1, e_2) is added to the knowledge base, this is represented as the temporal relation $\langle [1, 1, 1, 1, 1, 1, 1, 1], [0, 0, 0, 0, 0, 0, 0, 0] \rangle$ (using the notations from Chapter 5). In other words, it is imposed that the fuzzy time intervals E_1 and E_2 of e_1 and e_2 (which may or may not be known) should satisfy $eb^{\ll}(E_1, E_2) \geq 1$. This is a rather strict interpretation of

---

Procedure `Closure-rev4`

---

1    $todo \leftarrow \{(i,j,k) | 1 \le i,j,k \le n \wedge i \ne j \ne k\}$

2   **while** $todo \ne \emptyset$ **do**

3   Select and remove a triplet (i_0, j_0, k_0) from $todo$

4   **if** `Consistent-revised`$(C_1(x_{i_0}, x_{j_0}))$ *and*
      `Consistent-revised`$(C_1(x_{j_0}, x_{k_0}))$ *and*
      `Grounding-consistent`(x_{i_0}, x_{j_0}) *and*
      `Grounding-consistent`(x_{j_0}, x_{k_0}) **then**

5          $S \leftarrow C_1(x_{i_0}, x_{k_0}) \cup$
         `Compose-revised`$(C_1(x_{i_0}, x_{j_0}), C_1(x_{j_0}, x_{k_0}))$

6   **if** $C_1(x_{i_0}, x_{k_0}) \subset S$ **then**

7             $C_1(x_{i_0}, x_{k_0}) \leftarrow S$

8   `Normalise-revised`$(C(x_{i_0}, x_{k_0}))$

9             $todo \leftarrow todo \cup \{(i_0, k_0, l) | 1 \le l \le n \wedge l \ne i_0 \ne k_0\}$

10             $\cup \{(l, i_0, k_0) | 1 \le l \le n \wedge l \ne i_0 \ne k_0\}$

$before(e_1, e_2)$ which can be weakened in various ways. In particular, for a fixed $\Delta = \frac{1}{\rho}$ (for some ρ in $\mathbb{N} \setminus \{0\}$), we consider the following chain of representations (in decreasing order of strength):

$$\langle [1,1,1,1,1,1,1,1], [0,0,0,0,0,0,0,0] \rangle$$
$$\langle [1,1,1,1-\Delta, 1-\Delta, 1-\Delta, 1-\Delta, 1-\Delta], [0,0,0,0,0,0,0,0] \rangle$$

$$\cdots$$

$$\langle [1,1,1,\Delta,\Delta,\Delta,\Delta,\Delta], [0,0,0,0,0,0,0,0] \rangle$$
$$\langle [1,1,1,0,0,0,0,0], [0,0,0,0,0,0,0,0] \rangle \quad (6.10)$$
$$\langle [1-\Delta, 1-\Delta, 1-\Delta, 0,0,0,0,0], [0,0,0,0,0,0,0,0] \rangle$$

$$\cdots$$

$$\langle [\Delta,\Delta,\Delta,0,0,0,0,0], [0,0,0,0,0,0,0,0] \rangle$$
$$\langle [0,0,0,0,0,0,0,0], [0,0,0,0,0,0,0,0] \rangle$$

Similarly, $during(e_1, e_2)$ is initially represented as a constraint $bb^{\preccurlyeq}(E_2, E_1) \ge 1 \wedge ee^{\preccurlyeq}(E_1, E_2) \ge 1$ on the (possibly unknown) fuzzy time intervals of e_1 and e_2. Again, this representation can be gradually weakened:

$$\langle [1,0,1,0,0,0,0,0], [1,1,0,0,0,0,0,0] \rangle$$
$$\langle [1-\Delta, 0, 1-\Delta, 0,0,0,0,0], [1-\Delta, 1-\Delta, 0,0,0,0,0,0] \rangle$$

$$\cdots \quad (6.11)$$

$$\langle [\Delta, 0, \Delta, 0,0,0,0,0], [\Delta, \Delta, 0,0,0,0,0,0] \rangle$$
$$\langle [0,0,0,0,0,0,0,0], [0,0,0,0,0,0,0,0] \rangle$$

In our experiments, we use $\Delta = 0.25$, which balances expressivity and efficiency: smaller values of Δ lead to increased flexibility, but require more computation time. In principle, an inconsistency detected by Function `Grounding-consistent` can be repaired in two ways: by discarding at least one grounding or by weakening the representation of one or more temporal relations. In practice, however, we only apply the latter technique, i.e., inconsistencies are always repaired by weakening the representation of temporal relations. The main motivation is that the fuzzy time intervals are much more reliable than the temporal relations, the latter being the result of inherently fallible heuristic techniques. To avoid over–sensitivity to small variations in the membership functions of fuzzy time intervals, inconsistencies with groundings are only repaired if the amount by which the inconsistent lower bound is too high, is at least $\frac{\Delta}{2}$. In other words, the actual definition of Function `Grounding-consistent` is given by

$$\texttt{Grounding-consistent}(x_i, x_j)$$

$$\equiv be^{\preccurlyeq}(X_i, X_j) \geq \alpha - \frac{\Delta}{2} \wedge bb^{\preccurlyeq}(X_i, X_j) \geq \beta - \frac{\Delta}{2}$$

$$\wedge ee^{\preccurlyeq}(X_i, X_j) \geq \gamma - \frac{\Delta}{2} \wedge eb^{\preccurlyeq}(X_i, X_j) \geq \delta - \frac{\Delta}{2}$$

$$\wedge be^{\preccurlyeq\!\!\!\preccurlyeq}(X_i, X_j) \geq \alpha' - \frac{\Delta}{2} \wedge bb^{\preccurlyeq\!\!\!\preccurlyeq}(X_i, X_j) \geq \beta' - \frac{\Delta}{2}$$

$$\wedge ee^{\preccurlyeq\!\!\!\preccurlyeq}(X_i, X_j) \geq \gamma' - \frac{\Delta}{2} \wedge eb^{\preccurlyeq\!\!\!\preccurlyeq}(X_i, X_j) \geq \delta' - \frac{\Delta}{2}$$

Initially, before Procedure `Closure-rev4` is applied, every temporal relation in the knowledge base corresponds to the representation of an assertion of the form $before(e_1, e_2)$ or $during(e_1, e_2)$, as discovered by the techniques from Section 6.4. We will refer to these temporal relations as the initial relations. After applying Procedure `Closure-rev4`, a number of inconsistent temporal relations may have been derived. Each of these inconsistencies, however, can be traced back to its premises, i.e., a particular set of initial relations. By sufficiently weakening one or more of these premises, the cause of each inconsistency can be eliminated. To this end, for each inconsistent relation, one or more of its premises are weakened, and all previous updates to the knowledge base that were based on one of the weakened initial relations, are made undone. Finally, Procedure `Closure-rev4` is applied a second time. If inconsistencies still occur, some initial relations are further weakened, and the whole process is repeated until no inconsistencies can be discovered anymore.

Thus, the process of inconsistency repairing is reduced to choosing which premises to weaken. To make this choice, the confidence scores, defined as in (6.9), play a central role. The lower the confidence score of a relation, the higher the chance that it is either incorrect, or that disagreement about its correctness exists due to vagueness. In addition to confidence scores, we can base our decision on the number of inconsistencies a certain premise participates in. If a given initial relation r is (partially) incorrect, it is likely that more than one inconsistency will be derived from it. In other words, the number of times w^- that a relation r occurs as the premise of an inconsistent relation provides useful information about the likelihood of its correctness. There also is a second reason why a high value of w^- serves as an indication that r should be weakened. In general, we are interested in finding a satisfiable knowledge base containing as much information as possible. A high value of w^- suggests that a lot of conflicts will be solved by only weakening r. If we decide not to weaken r, several other relations may have to be weakened to obtain the same effect, resulting in a less informative knowledge base.

Whereas inconsistent relations can provide evidence against the correctness of a particular initial relation, we can sometimes also establish evidence in favor. In particular, if a consistent relation r is derived between two grounded events e_i and e_j, we can be certain that it is correct (assuming the groundings are always correct). Hence, the number of times w^+ a relation r occurs as the premise of such a correct relation provides information about the likelihood of its correctness as well. In particular, an initial relation of the form $before(e_1, e_2)$ is given a score $s^{bef}(e_1, e_2)$ defined by

$$s^{bef}(e_1, e_2) = \frac{1 + w^+}{1 + w^+ + w^-} c^{bef}(e_1, e_2)$$

In the same way, an initial relation of the form $during(e_1, e_2)$ is given a score $s^{dur}(e_1, e_2)$ defined by

$$s^{dur}(e_1, e_2) = \frac{1 + w^+}{1 + w^+ + w^-} c^{dur}(e_1, e_2)$$

Among all the premises of an inconsistent relation r, the relation with the lowest score s_{min} is weakened. Furthermore, to increase the robustness of the approach, all premises of r whose score is close to s_{min} are weakened as well. Specifically, we weaken all premises whose score is less than $s_{min} + 0.1$. When a relation is weakened, its representation is changed to the next representation in the chain ((6.10) or (6.11)).

Table 6.8 displays the events that are considered to be during World War II, to some extent, after all inconsistencies in the corresponding knowledge base have been repaired. Comparing this table to Table 6.7, it is clear that almost no non–event names occur in the knowledge base. The only exceptions are "world war ii commemorative series" and "world war ii letters", which do not refer to events at all, and "world war ii world war ii" and "war ii", which are the result of incorrect HTML parsing or POS tagging. Note that the knowledge base contains most significant World War II events, and, moreover, does not contain any real errors, such as battles from World War I or other, non–contemporary wars. Furthermore, the degree to which each of the during relations hold (also shown in Table 6.8) provides useful information. In particular, low membership degrees (0.25) often occur with vague and ambiguous events such as "german offensive", "war on finland", "war on bulgaria".

6.5.3   Event Retrieval

To perform event–based IR, we typically need to find those objects (e.g., documents, people, events) that satisfy a given temporal constraint. This temporal constraint can contain explicit time references. A user may, for instance, be interested in documents from a historical digital library about painters from the 18th century, while question answering systems need to deal with questions such as "Who was prime minister in Belgium in the 1950s". Taking document retrieval as an example, an obvious strategy is to assign a time stamp to all documents in the indexed collection (off line), based on the dates which occur in it, and compare this time stamp to the time references in the temporal constraint [Alonso *et al.* (2007); Mckay and Cunningham (2000)]. Another possibility, however, is that the temporal constraint itself already refers to an event instead of a date: pictures of Ghent during World War II, documents about Russian literature in the Cold War Period, etc. It is this latter case in which we are primarily interested. By far the most frequently occurring temporal relation in such constraints is the during relation. Therefore, we will focus the discussion on how to decide whether or not an event e happened during some large–scale event such as World War II, although other types of temporal relations can be treated in a similar way (e.g., before and after relations). In particular, the task which we address is to rank a set of events according to our confidence that they are during, e.g., World War II.

The result of the fuzzy temporal reasoning phase is a highly reliable, FI–satisfiable knowledge base for every war of interest. While these knowledge bases are likely to contain the most significant military conflicts of the

Table 6.8 Events during World War II after repairing all inconsistencies in the corresponding knowledge base.

Name	Deg.	Name	Deg.	Name	Deg.
north african campaign	1.0	japanese invasion	0.75	war on britain and france	0.75
operation market-garden	1.0	phoney war	0.75	normandy invasion	1.0
operation barbarossa	0.75	dieppe raid	0.75	d-day invasion	1.0
battle of the atlantic	0.75	attack on pearl harbor	1.0	battle of el alamein	1.0
battle of the philippine sea	1.0	allied invasion of normandy	1.0	invasion of france	0.75
german invasion of the soviet union	0.25	allied strategic bombing	1.0	invasion of sicily	1.0
doolittle raid	1.0	operation torch	1.0	battle of moscow	0.75
italian campaign	1.0	ardennes offensive	0.75	battle of monte cassino	0.75
winter war	0.75	invasion of italy	1.0	war on germany and italy	1.0
world war ii	1.0	allied invasion	1.0	invasion of britain	0.75
coral sea battle	0.25	battle of berlin	1.0	battle of coral sea	0.75
battle of france	0.25	world war ii world war ii	1.0	battle of stalingrad	1.0
great patriotic war	0.75	battle of normandy	1.0	european war	0.75
world war 2	0.75	battle of the coral sea	1.0	operation dragoon	1.0
second battle of kharkov	1.0	invasion of the soviet union	0.75	battle for okinawa	0.75
battle of midway	1.0	guadalcanal campaign	1.0	second battle of el alamein	1.0
german offensive	0.25	hurtgen forest battle	1.0	invasion of poland	0.75
german war effort	1.0	allied war effort	1.0	continuation war	0.75
war on finland	0.25	war on japan	0.75	battle of kursk	1.0
climactic battle	1.0	war on the soviet union	1.0	attack on poland	0.75
operation dynamo	0.75	pearl harbor attack	0.75	world war two	0.75
battle of iwo jima	1.0	battle of the bulge	1.0	world war ii letters	1.0
first battle of el alamein	1.0	invasion of normandy	1.0	operation overlord	1.0
second world war	0.75	siege of leningrad	1.0	battle of okinawa	0.75
pacific war	0.75	battle for stalingrad	0.75	operation compass	0.75
japanese attack on pearl harbor	1.0	1945 world war ii	1.0	japanese attack	0.75
war on bulgaria	0.25	naval battle of guadalcanal	0.25	war ii	0.75
world war ii commemorative series	0.75	bombing of pearl harbor	0.75	battle of guadalcanal	1.0
invasion of midway island	0.75	battle of britain	0.75		

corresponding wars, many others will be missing. Looking at the events from Table 6.8, for instance, we see many large–scale events (e.g., phoney war, italian campaign, operation barbarossa) and some famous battles (e.g., battle of midway, battle of iwo jima, battle of the bulge), but most of the hundreds of World War II battles are missing. However, as explained below, even if an event e is missing, the knowledge base can play a key role in deciding whether or not e happened during World War II. For example, consider the Battle of Crete. Using the techniques from Section 6.4, the following scores can be used to decide whether $during(battleCrete, WW2)$ holds:

$$c_1^{dur}(battleCrete, WW2) \qquad c_2^{dur}(battleCrete, WW2)$$

If both scores are 0, it may be that $during(battleCrete, WW2)$ is false, but it is also possible that nothing can be established about the temporal relation between the Battle of Crete and World War II using the techniques from Section 6.4. In the latter case, the knowledge base that was constructed for World War II can often solve the dilemma. For example, knowing that the Battle of Britain and the Normandy Invasion are during World War II, we can derive that $during(battleCrete, WW2)$ if we can establish that both $before(battleBritain, battleCrete)$ and $before(battleCrete, normandyInvasion)$ are the case. To this end, the following scores can be used (abbreviating $battleBritain$, $battleCrete$ and $normandyInvastion$)

$$c_1^{bef}(bBritain, bCrete) \cdot c_1^{bef}(bCrete, normandyInv)$$
$$(1 - p_2^{bef}(bBritain, bCrete)) \cdot (1 - p_2^{bef}(bCrete, normandyInv))$$

Similarly, knowing from the knowledge base that Operation Barbarossa is during World War II (to a large extent), it is sufficient to derive that the Battle of Kiev happened during Operation Barbarossa to conclude $during(battleKiev, WW2)$. In general, to check whether $during(e_1, e_2)$ holds, we can

(1) try to establish directly that $during(e_1, e_2)$ holds using the techniques from Section 6.4;
(2) try to establish that e_1 took place during an event e, which is contained in the knowledge base and is known to be during e_2 to a large degree;
(3) try to establish that e_1 took place between the events e and e', both being contained in the knowledge base and known to be during e_2 to a large degree.

The latter two strategies can be implemented using the following scores:

$$c_3^{dur}(e_1, e_2; \lambda) = \max\{c_1^{dur}(e_1, e) | \Theta \models during(e_1, e_2) \geq \lambda\}$$

$$c_4^{dur}(e_1, e_2; \lambda) = \max\{c_2^{dur}(e_1, e) | \Theta \models during(e_1, e_2) \geq \lambda\}$$

$$c_5^{dur}(e_1, e_2; \lambda) = \max\{c_1^{bef}(e_1, e) \cdot c_1^{bef}(e, e_2) |$$
$$\Theta \models \{before(e_1, e) \geq \lambda, before(e, e_2) \geq \lambda\}\}$$

$$c_6^{dur}(e_1, e_2; \lambda) = \max\{(1 - p_2^{bef}(e_1, e)) \cdot (1 - p_2^{bef}(e, e_2)) |$$
$$\Theta \models \{before(e_1, e) \geq \lambda, before(e, e_2) \geq \lambda\}\}$$

where Θ is the knowledge base corresponding to event e_2 and $\lambda \in [0, 1]$. Using these additional scores when both $c_1^{dur}(e_1, e_2) = 0$ and $c_2^{dur}(e_1, e_2) = 0$ helps to disambiguate between situations where $during(e_1, e_2)$ is false and situations in which $during(e_1, e_2)$ could not be established due to a lack of information. Another way of tackling this problem is to check if either $before(e_1, e_2)$ or $before(e_2, e_1)$ can be derived, in which case we can conclude that $during(e_1, e_2)$ is false. The following scores can be used to this end, some of which again use the knowledge base Θ:

$$c_1^{ndur}(e_1, e_2) = 1 - \max(c_1^{bef}(e_1, e_2), c_1^{bef}(e_2, e_1))$$

$$c_2^{ndur}(e_1, e_2) = 1 - \max(1 - p_2^{bef}(e_1, e_2), 1 - p_2^{bef}(e_2, e_1))$$

$$c_3^{ndur}(e_1, e_2; \lambda) = 1 - \max(\{c_1^{bef}(e_1, e) | \Theta \models before(e, e_2) \geq \lambda\}$$
$$\cup \{c_1^{bef}(e, e_1) | \Theta \models before(e_2, e) \geq \lambda\})$$

$$c_4^{ndur}(e_1, e_2; \lambda) = 1 - \max(\{1 - p_2^{bef}(e_1, e) | \Theta \models before(e, e_2) \geq \lambda\}$$
$$\cup \{1 - p_2^{bef}(e, e_1) | \Theta \models before(e_2, e) \geq \lambda\})$$

$$c_5^{ndur}(e_1, e_2; \lambda) = 1 - \max(\{c_1^{dur}(e_1, e) | \Theta \models before(e, e_2) \geq \lambda\}$$
$$\cup \{c_1^{dur}(e_1, e) | \Theta \models before(e_2, e) \geq \lambda\})$$

$$c_6^{ndur}(e_1, e_2; \lambda) = 1 - \max(\{c_2^{dur}(e_1, e) | \Theta \models before(e, e_2) \geq \lambda\}$$
$$\cup \{c_2^{dur}(e_1, e) | \Theta \models before(e_2, e) \geq \lambda\})$$

Thus, to find events that are during, e.g., World War II, a large number of scores are at hand, which need to be combined to produce a meaningful ranking of events. Ideally, the events about which we are confident they are during World War II are ranked first, followed by the events about which nothing could be derived, and finally, the events about which we are confident they are not during World War II. First note that in the scenario we are envisioning, scores $c_3^{dur}(e_1, e_2; \lambda)$, $c_5^{dur}(e_1, e_2; \lambda)$, $c_3^{ndur}(e_1, e_2; \lambda)$ and $c_5^{ndur}(e_1, e_2; \lambda)$ are of no use. The reason is that these scores are based on available dates for event e_1. If enough dates are available for e_1, however, the relationship between e_1 and e_2 could also be identified directly, using c_1^{dur} and c_1^{ndur}. This holds because event e_2 always is a large–scale event, for which we have a fuzzy time span at our disposal (i.e., the 25 wars from Table 6.6).

To combine the remaining scores, a statistical classifier could be trained which decides if an event e should be ranked before or after an event e', given the scores for both events. This, however, requires that a sufficient amount of training and test data is available. Other approaches, such as most voting mechanisms, rely on weights that are manually assigned to each scoring function. After initial experimentation with such techniques, we found that the performance of the overall system heavily depended on these weights, where different weights led to optimal performance for different events. As the robustness of the resulting systems is therefore questionable, we will rely on a simpler strategy, focusing on the principle, rather than trying to find an optimal way of combining the different scores. In particular, for each scoring function c, we define a classifier C for events e and e' as

$$C(e, e') = \begin{cases} 1 & \text{if } c(e, e_2) > c(e', e_2) \\ -1 & \text{if } c(e, e_2) < c(e', e_2) \\ 0 & \text{otherwise} \end{cases}$$

assuming that we are interested in events during e_2. Next, these classifiers are ranked according to their reliability. For example, assume that the classifiers C_1, C_2 and C_3 are used, and that C_1 is deemed more reliable than C_2, which is in turn deemed more reliable than C_3. In this case, event e is ranked before event e' if

$$C_1(e, e') > 0$$

or, if

$$C_1(e, e') = 0 \text{ and } C_2(e, e') > 0$$

or, if

$$C_1(e, e') = 0 \text{ and } C_2(e, e') = 0 \text{ and } C_3(e, e') > 0$$

If also $C_3(e, e') = 0$, the relative ranking of e and e' is arbitrary. We will denote this system by $[c_1, c_2, c_3]$, where c_i is the scoring function corresponding to classifier C_i. Note that this approach only relies on a meaningful ranking of classifiers according to their reliability, and no parameter tuning is required. Therefore, we can expect that the performance of the overall system is less sensitive to the actual events to be classified than, for instance, approaches based on (weighted) voting.

6.6 Experimental Results

Generating a ground truth for a query asking for battles that took place during a given war is particularly difficult, because the time spans of most battles are not available in a structured form. Note that this was in fact the main motivation for the work described in this chapter. Moreover, due to the vagueness of the temporal boundaries of World War II, even with a time span for each battle, it may not always be clear which battles to consider relevant. To cope with this, we extracted lists of military conflicts, mostly battles, that are considered to be during various wars according to Wikipedia[8]. The number of battles that were thus found for each war is shown in the last column of Table 6.6. To evaluate and compare the effectiveness of different techniques, we consider the battles found in Wikipedia for World War II to be relevant, and the battles found for non-overlapping wars, such as World War I, the Vietnam War or the Korean War to be irrelevant.

In particular, we have compared the performance of five different systems. The first system, $B1$ (Baseline 1), only uses (fuzzy) time spans and qualitative relations that have been obtained by comparing dates, i.e.

$$B1 = [c_1^{dur}]$$

Similarly, $B2$ (Baseline 2) only uses qualitative relations that have been obtained by looking at document structure:

$$B2 = [c_2{}^{dur}]$$

Next, $B3$ (Baseline 3) combines both strategies as follows:

$$B3 = [c_2^{*dur}, c_1^{dur}, c_2^{dur}]$$

where

$$c_2^{*dur} = \begin{cases} c_2{}^{dur} & \text{if } m_1 + m_2 \geq k \\ 0 & \text{otherwise} \end{cases}$$

Note that m_1 and m_2 have been defined in Section 6.4.2. An optimal performance was found for $k = 2$. This means that when $m_1 + m_2 \geq 2$, Baseline 2 is more reliable than Baseline 1, whereas Baseline 1 is more reliable when $m_1 + m_2 = 1$. The system $F1$ (Fuzzy Reasoning 1) uses the

[8]http://en.wikipedia.org/wiki/Category:Battles_by_war, accessed October 29, 2007

knowledge base to obtain a conclusion when the two heuristic techniques fail:

$$F1 = [c_2^{*dur}, c_1^{dur}, c_6^{dur}(.,.;1), c_4^{dur}(.,.;1), c_2^{dur}, c_6^{dur}(.,.;0.75), c_4^{dur}(.,.;0.75),$$
$$c_6^{dur}(.,.;0.5), c_4^{dur}(.,.;0.5), c_6^{dur}(.,.;0.25), c_4^{dur}(.,.;0.25)]$$

where in particular C_2^{*dur}, C_1^{dur}, $C_6^{dur}(.,.;1)$ and $C_4^{dur}(.,.;1)$ are considered to be the most reliable classifiers. Finally, $F2$ (Fuzzy Reasoning 2) additionally considers negative information:

$$F2 = [c_2^{*dur}, c_1^{dur}, c_6^{dur}(.,.;1), c_4^{dur}(.,.;1), c_2^{dur}, c_6^{ndur}(.,.;1), c_2^{ndur}, c_1^{ndur},$$
$$c_4^{ndur}(.,.;1), c_6^{ndur}(.,.;0.5), c_4^{ndur}(.,.;0.5), c_6^{dur}(.,.;0.75),$$
$$c_4^{dur}(.,.;0.75), c_6^{dur}(.,.;0.5), c_4^{dur}(.,.;0.5), c_6^{dur}(.,.;0.25), c_4^{dur}(.,.;0.25)]$$

For each war W in Table 6.6, the five systems produced a ranking of all the military conflicts from Wikipedia. Ideally, all conflicts that took place during W are found at the top of this ranking, followed by the other events. We evaluated the performance of each system in terms of precision and recall. In general, the precision and recall of a set of elements A are defined as

$$precision(A) = \frac{|A \cap R|}{|A|} \qquad recall(A) = \frac{|A \cap R|}{|R|}$$

where R is the set of all relevant elements. In this context, R is the set of military conflicts found in Wikipedia for war W. To evaluate the quality of the event rankings, the precision at particular cut–off points in the ranking can be calculated. The precision at position k, written $P@k$, is defined as the precision of the first k elements in the ranking. The quality of a given ranking can then be quantified by the average precision (AP), i.e., the average of the precision at the list positions of all relevant elements; if there are n relevant elements, which occur in the ranking at positions $k_1, k_2, \ldots, k_n$, AP is given by

$$\frac{1}{n} \sum_{i=1}^{n} P@k_i$$

The average precision of the rankings for all 25 wars is shown in Table 6.9. In the second column (Rand), the expected average precision of a random ordering is shown, calculated by dividing the number of relevant events (i.e., the events found in Wikipedia for the given war) by the total number of events (i.e., the events found in Wikipedia for any of the 25 wars). The last row displays the mean average precision (MAP), which is defined as the mean of the average precisions over all 25 wars.

Table 6.9   Comparison of the different systems in terms of average precision.

Name	Rand	$B1$	$B2$	$B3$	$F1$	$F2$
American Civil War	0.190	0.865	0.285	0.872	0.895	0.919
American Revolutionary War	0.070	0.851	0.078	0.819	0.841	0.849
Chinese Civil War	0.040	0.551	0.623	0.837	0.918	0.963
Continuation War	0.006	0.420	0.131	0.451	0.452	0.476
Falklands War	0.006	0.431	0.917	0.994	1	1
Finnish War	0.006	0.013	0.013	0.013	0.012	0.020
First Boer War	0.002	1	0.002	1	1	1
First Chechen War	0.003	0.503	0.183	0.838	0.834	0.848
Gulf War	0.004	0.470	0.016	0.461	0.453	0.460
Korean War	0.010	0.413	0.871	0.932	0.934	0.936
Napoleonic Wars	0.110	0.068	0.125	0.068	0.068	0.065
Philippine–American War	0.009	0.763	0.754	0.816	0.913	0.920
Polish September Campaign	0.020	0.277	0.307	0.505	0.738	0.775
Polish–Soviet War	0.009	0.410	0.787	0.853	0.915	0.934
Russo–Japanese War	0.009	0.658	0.770	0.943	0.943	0.944
Second Boer War	0.008	0.737	0.534	0.779	0.941	0.933
Second Chechen War	0.008	0.191	0.541	0.663	0.701	0.748
Second Sino–Japanese War	0.050	0.395	0.610	0.794	0.889	0.894
Spanish Civil War	0.010	0.676	0.595	0.877	1	1
Spanish–American War	0.010	0.582	0.148	0.514	0.481	0.512
Vietnam War	0.060	0.796	0.849	0.967	0.980	0.980
War of the Pacific	0.005	0.305	0.007	0.305	0.488	0.585
World War I	0.110	0.801	0.739	0.919	0.937	0.939
World War II	0.210	0.690	0.796	0.909	0.945	0.948
Yom Kippur War	0.002	0.510	1	1	1	1
MAP	0.039	0.535	0.467	0.725	0.771	0.786

Both $B1$ and $B2$ achieve a decent performance which is significantly better than the performance of a random ranking. Especially the performance of $B2$ is somewhat surprising: while $B1$ is based on the fuzzy time spans of all 25 wars in addition to co–occurring dates for all events, in $B2$ only document structure is taken into account. A particularly interesting observation is that the performance of $B1$ is largely complementary to the performance of $B2$. For example, while $B1$ performs significantly better than $B2$ for the American Revolutionary War or the First Boer War, the opposite is true for the Falklands War or the Yom Kippur War. This is further illustrated by the results for $B3$, which improve greatly on the results of both $B1$ and $B2$. Next, as the results for $F1$ reveal, applying fuzzy temporal reasoning has a clearly positive impact, which is substantial in several cases (e.g., Polish September Campaign, Second Boer War, War of the Pacific). Finally, the results of $F2$ show that introducing negative information (not during) consistently leads to (slightly) better performance.

To gain a better understanding of why $B3$, $F1$ and $F2$ yield increasingly better results, Figure 6.5 depicts a number of Precision–Recall graphs. Such a graph displays the precision that can be achieved for a particular recall level. Specifically, if the relevant elements in a ranking are located at positions k_1, k_2, ..., k_n, the precision corresponding to recall level $\frac{i}{n}$ is given by $P@k_i$. The Precision–Recall graph is obtained by calculating the precision corresponding to all recall levels $\frac{1}{n}$, $\frac{2}{n}$, ..., 1. Note that the more this graph is located to the top and to the right, the better the performance of the corresponding system. Looking at Figure 6.5(a–c), we can see that $B1$ and $B2$ display an almost perfect behaviour at small recall levels, but precision very quickly drops to almost 0 from a particular point. This means that these systems are very strong in terms of precision: if evidence is found that e is during W, this is a reliable indication of $during(e, W)$. Their drawback, however, is a limited strength in terms of recall: for a large number of relevant events, no evidence can be found. By adding more sophisticated techniques, evidence for $during(e, W)$ can be found for a larger group of events e. This observation essentially justifies the cascading of classifiers. First, we try to rank events according to classifiers with high precision and low recall; if this fails, increasingly less reliable classifiers are tried, characterized by an increasingly lower precision and higher recall. Figure 6.5(d) depicts the result of averaging the Precision–Recall graphs over all 25 wars. This again shows that $B3$ is consistently better than both $B1$ and $B2$, that $F1$ is consistently better than $B3$ and that $F2$ is consistently better than $F1$. However, neither of $B1$ and $B2$ is better than the other: $B1$ displays the best performance for recall levels up to 0.5 (on average), while $B2$ displays the best performance for higher recall levels.

The experimental results demonstrate that by mining qualitative temporal relations from the web, in addition to (fuzzy) time intervals, accurate rankings of events can be obtained. While we have exclusively dealt with military conflicts, the domain–independent nature of the introduced techniques suggests that the same strategy can be used in other domains as well, although the relative impact of co–occurring dates and document structure might vary. For example, military conflicts are often described in documents adopting a style reminiscent of encyclopedia articles, exhibiting a tendency to mention dates wherever possible. While a similar tendency might be expected for other types of historical events, it is not clear to what extent contemporary events follow the same pattern. In particular, when moving to news events, a significant contribution of linguistic techniques can be expected to arrive at meaningful temporal relations.

In addition to using linguistic techniques, the overall framework can be

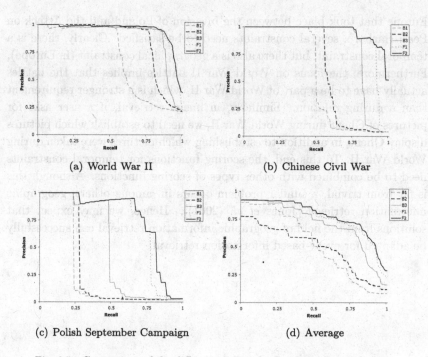

(a) World War II (b) Chinese Civil War

(c) Polish September Campaign (d) Average

Fig. 6.5   Comparison of the different systems by Precision–Recall graphs.

improved along various lines. First, more documents can be retrieved to support the two heuristic techniques. Currently, only 50 documents are used to find co–occurring dates. While this is sufficient for some events, for other events, too few of the 50 documents are relevant. For some events, for example, a substantial fraction of the documents is concerned with films, books or computer games about the corresponding war or battle. The dates found in these documents typically refer to the release date of the movie, publishing date of the book, etc. A document classifier, detecting if a page is actually about the military conflict might therefore be beneficial. Further improvements can be made in the way the different scoring functions are combined. While the cascading strategy displays a good performance, training a statistical classifier might lead to even better results. To ensure the robustness of such a system, however, a much larger evaluation corpus would be needed.

In practical applications, a ranking of events is seldom the end result desired by a user. Typically, a temporally restricted query also contains a non–temporal part. If a user asks for a list of "World War II battles in

Europe that took place between the Invasion of Poland and the Attack on Pearl Harbor", several constraints need to be satisfied. Clearly, there is a temporal constraint, but there also is a geographical constraint (in Europe). Furthermore, the focus on World War II battles implies that the battles actually have to be a part of World War II, which is a stronger requirement than a during relation. Similarly, in image retrieval, if a user asks for pictures of Ghent during World War II, we need to establish which pictures display Ghent, in addition to establishing which pictures were taken during World War II. To this end, the scoring functions for temporal constraints need to be combined with other types of scoring functions. Although this is far from trivial, a similar problem occurs in, among others, geographic information retrieval [Jones *et al.* (2001)]. Hence, we may expect that solutions from the field of geographic information retrieval can successfully be adapted for event-based information retrieval.

Chapter 7

Representing Fuzzy Spatial Information

7.1 Introduction

Although political regions, such as countries, states, or provinces, have officially defined — and therefore crisp — boundaries, many of the places people refer to in everyday communication (i.e., vernacular places), do not (e.g., [Bennett (2001); Bittner and Stell (2002); Erwig and Schneider (1997); Fisher (2000); Montello *et al.* (2003); Varzi (2001a); Waters and Evans (2003)]). Even the names of political regions are often used in a way that is not in perfect accordance with their official definitions; a typical example are city neighbourhoods, whose official boundaries, if they exist, are merely intended for administrative purposes (e.g., electoral divisions). Boundaries of regions may be vague for various reasons. For example, [Waters and Evans (2003)] distinguishes between four different characteristics, all of which may be concurrently present:

Continuousness occurs when the boundaries rely on a continuous variable (e.g., mountains — elevation).

Aggregation occurs when the boundaries are obtained by aggregating the values of different variables (e.g., soil types — particle sizes in different samples).

Averaging occurs when the actual boundaries vary in time (e.g., rivers, shorelines).

Ambiguity occurs when linguistic terms are used to define regions (e.g., the *high* crime area).

Vernacular place names occur at very different scales (Ghent's city centre, the Highlands, the Middle East). Moreover, a variety of techniques can be used to capture their spatial semantics. Approaches based on supervaluation semantics (e.g., [Bennett (2001); Kulik (2001); Varzi (2001a)]), for instance, associate a set of possible crisp *precisifications* with a vague language concept, and reason about assertions that are true in every precisification, in some precisification, etc., typically using first–order logic. They are mainly motivated by philosophical considerations about the nature of vagueness, and tend to be less suitable as workable, computational models. Particularly popular are techniques which represent a vague region as a pair of crisp sets (e.g., [Bittner and Stell (2002); Clementini and Di Felice (1997); Cohn and Gotts (1996)]). The main idea is that a vague region can be approximated by defining a set of locations $\underline{a}$ which are definitely in the vague region, as well as a set of locations $\overline{a}$ which are in the vague region to some extent (where $\underline{a} \subseteq \overline{a}$); the complement of $\overline{a}$ is then the set of locations which are definitely not in the vague region. The resulting models are very efficient, and theoretical results (e.g., reasoning procedures) can usually be obtained relatively easily from existing results for crisp regions. Note that vague regions are in this case formally equivalent to flou sets [Gentilhomme (1968)] of locations. Finally, fuzzy set theory is frequently employed to model vague regions (e.g., [Fisher (2000); Goodchild *et al.* (1998); Hill *et al.* (1999); Li and Li (2004); Liu and Shi (2006)]). Although the resulting models may be somewhat less efficient than models based on pairs of crisp regions, their increased flexibility is often needed to accurately capture vague boundaries. Moreover, a pair $(\underline{a}, \overline{a})$ of crisp regions with $\underline{a} \subseteq \overline{a}$ can be seen as a special case of a fuzzy set, e.g., by assigning all points in $\underline{a}$ membership degree 1, all points in $\overline{a} \setminus \underline{a}$ membership degree 0.5, and all other points membership degree 0. In this chapter, we will therefore focus on modelling techniques based on fuzzy set theory.

When some of the regions involved are vague, spatial relations can be vague as well. For instance, it is not clear whether the Alps are included in, overlapping with, or disjoint from Southern Europe, as each of these relations seems defensible to some extent. Moreover, in contrast to most temporal relations, many spatial relations are inherently vague, even when restricted to well–defined, crisp places. A typical example are natural language relations expressing nearness such as within walking distance, across the street from, a few steps away from, a short walk to, etc. Given that a hotel is located *within walking distance* of the Gent Sint–Pieters train station, for instance, we can reasonably assume that it is definitely closer than, say, 5 kilometre from the station. Furthermore, hotels within 1 kilometre are definitely within walking distance, but what about hotels that are 2 kilometre from the station, or 3 kilometre? Clearly, there is a gradual

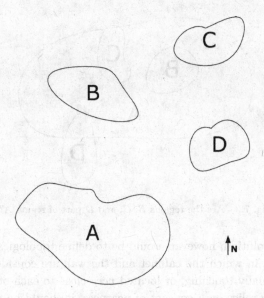

Fig. 7.1   Are the regions B, C, and D north of region A?

transition from distances that are definitely compatible with a concept such
as *within walking distance* to distances that are definitely not compatible.
Another example are relations expressing cardinal directions (north, south,
east, west) or relative orientation (left, right, in front of). For example,
considering the regions from Figure 7.1, we clearly have that B is north of
A, but what about regions C and D? Rather than north of A, D might be
considered northeast of A, whereas C is neither clearly north nor northeast
of A. Again the transition from being north of A to not being north of
A is gradual, rather than abrupt. A last example, which will be the main
focus of this and the following chapter, are topological relations such as
containment, adjacency, overlap, disjointness, etc. While topological relations between vague regions are clearly vague, topological relations between
crisp regions are generally considered to be crisp, as they are traditionally
defined by precise mathematical techniques (e.g., using point–set topology).
However, such a strict interpretation does not always correspond very well
to the way topological relations are used in natural language. For example,
it is commonplace to say that a cabinet is located against a wall even if
there is a gap of a few millimetres between the cabinet and the wall. In
traditional frameworks for modelling topological relations, the cabinet and
the wall would be considered disjoint, irrespective of the size of the gap. A

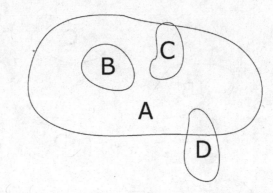

Fig. 7.2   Are the regions B, C, and D part of region A?

more natural solution, however, would be to define topological relations as fuzzy relations in which the cabinet and the wall are considered adjacent if they are actually touching, or located *very close* to each other. Because adjacency then relies on a concept of nearness, it should be modelled as a vague relation. For containment, a similar observation can be made; consider, for instance, the regions depicted in Figure 7.2. Clearly, B is a part of A, and D is not. However, while C is in principle not a part of A, we could intuitively think of C as being a part of A to a large extent, because *most* of C is contained in A.

In this chapter, we investigate how vague spatial relations can be modelled using the framework of relatedness measures from Chapter 3. Next, we focus more closely on topological information by developing a' fuzzification of the Region Connection Calculus, a well–known framework for representing topological relations. After demonstrating various properties of this general framework, we reveal its relationship with the fuzzy spatial relations based on relatedness measures.

7.2   Spatial Relations

7.2.1   *Crisp Spatial Relations*

There is an increasing interest in formalisms that describe properties of space in a qualitative way, especially involving topological (e.g., A is adjacent to B, A is contained in B), directional (e.g., A is located north of B), distance (e.g., A is located far from B) and size (e.g., A is larger than B, A is small) information. In the context of geographical information systems

(GISs), for instance, qualitative relations are useful to express and process spatial queries, while route planners and GPS systems benefit from using qualitative descriptions as they are often easier to understand by humans than quantitative descriptions (e.g., compare *turn right immediately after the bridge* with *turn right in 673 metres*). Moreover, sometimes only qualitative information is known about a place of interest, e.g., because only a textual description is available. For example, [Wieczorek *et al.* (2004)] discusses the problem of georeferencing (i.e., finding the location of) places described in scientific reports of where and when a specimen was discovered. Another important area in which qualitative spatial relations can play an important role is geographical information retrieval (GIR) [Abdelmoty *et al.* (2006)]. The goal of a geographical information retrieval system is to pinpoint information in a large document collection that is both relevant to a general query, and to a given geographical context (e.g., web pages about movie theatres near Ghent, Belgium). On one hand, this could be achieved by finding addresses, transforming these addresses to geographical coordinates, and comparing these coordinates with available (structured) information. However, there is also a lot of relevant geographical information available in the form of qualitative relations, either extracted from natural language texts (e.g., from the web), or a priori available from geo-ontologies [Abdelmoty *et al.* (2006)]. We will discuss the use of spatial relations for GIR in more detail in Chapter 9.

Topological information plays a paramount role in the way spatial configurations are perceived, and has, accordingly, received a lot of attention in the literature. Two formalisms are particularly prevalent: the 9–intersection model [Egenhofer and Franzosa (1991)] and the Region Connection Calculus (RCC) [Randell *et al.* (1992)]. The former distinguishes between eight topological relations that can hold between regions A and B. Regions are represented as closed sets in a topological space, and relations are defined by intersecting the interior, boundary and exterior of A with the interior, boundary and exterior of B, and looking at which of these 9 intersections yields the empty set. The RCC essentially models the same eight topological relations, using a first–order theory, however, without explicit reference to topological spaces. As it is more tailored towards spatial reasoning, we will rely on this framework, rather than the 9–intersection model, in this and the following chapter.

In the RCC, spatial relations are defined using a primitive reflexive and symmetric relation C which models the notion of connection between regions. For example, we may think of regions as sets of points, and define C

Table 7.1   Definition of topological relations in the RCC; a and b denote regions, i.e., elements of the universe U of regions.

Name	Relation	Definition
Disconnected From	$DC(a, b)$	$\neg C(a, b)$
Part Of	$P(a, b)$	$(\forall c \in U)(C(c, a) \Rightarrow C(c, b))$
Proper Part Of	$PP(a, b)$	$P(a, b) \wedge \neg P(b, a)$
Equal To	$EQ(a, b)$	$P(a, b) \wedge P(b, a)$
Overlaps With	$O(a, b)$	$(\exists c \in U)(P(c, a) \wedge P(c, b))$
Discrete From	$DR(a, b)$	$\neg O(a, b)$
Partially Overlaps With	$PO(a, b)$	$O(a, b) \wedge \neg P(a, b) \wedge \neg P(b, a)$
Externally Connected To	$EC(a, b)$	$C(a, b) \wedge \neg O(a, b)$
Non–Tangential Part Of	$NTP(a, b)$	$P(a, b) \wedge \neg(\exists c \in U)(EC(c, a) \wedge EC(c, b))$
Tangential PP	$TPP(a, b)$	$PP(a, b) \wedge \neg NTP(a, b)$
Non–Tangential PP	$NTPP(a, b)$	$\neg P(b, a) \wedge NTP(a, b)$

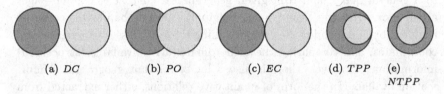

(a) *DC*   (b) *PO*   (c) *EC*   (d) *TPP*   (e)
                                                                        NTPP

Fig. 7.3   Intuitive meaning of some RCC relations.

such that for two regions a and b, $C(a, b)$ holds iff a and b have a point in common[1]. Other topological relations are defined in terms of the relation C, as shown in Table 7.1. Usually, in the RCC, regions are assumed to be regular closed sets, and two regions are said to be connected if they share at least one point [Gotts (1996)]. In this interpretation, P corresponds to the classical subset relation, while O holds between two regions if their interiors share at least one point. This intended interpretation of the RCC is illustrated in Figure 7.3. Another possibility is to define regions as regular open sets, and to define two regions to be connected if their closures share at least one point. In this case, for example, O holds between two regions if they share at least one point. However, it is important to keep in mind that the RCC does not impose a particular representation of regions, nor a particular interpretation of connection. The only restriction imposed by

---

[1] Throughout this chapter, we will use upper case letters like $A, B, C, \ldots$ to denote specific regions, and lower case letters like $a, b, c, \ldots$ to denote variables that take values from the universe U of regions.

the RCC is that the relation C is reflexive and symmetric. For example, in [Ralha and Ralha (2003)] the RCC relations are used to dynamically structure information from distributed hypermedia systems such as the web. In this context, regions are represented as vectors of attributes describing information units (e.g., paragraphs in a document), and two regions are connected if the degree of similarity of the corresponding information units exceeds a given threshold. Another interpretation of connection is introduced in [Aiello and Ottens (2007)] in the context of image processing, where regions are defined as black–and–white images and C is defined using dilations. Dilations are morphological operators that are often used in image processing for segmentation of images, boundary detection, etc. Using this interpretation of C, the RCC relations can be used for processing black–and–white images.

Note how all RCC relations are defined without referring to points, i.e., by taking regions, rather than points, as primitive spatial objects. This characteristic effectively makes the RCC the spatial counterpart of the Interval Algebra, which uses times spans, rather than instants, as primitive temporal objects. Often, applications only refer to the eight relations EQ, EC, DC, PO, $NTPP$, TPP, $NTPP^{-1}$ and TPP^{-1}, which can be shown to be jointly exhaustive and pairwise disjoint, i.e., between any two regions, exactly one of these relations holds. The RCC restricted to these eight relations is called RCC–8. Similarly, the RCC restricted to the relations EQ, DR, PO, PP and PP^{-1} is called RCC–5.

Also directional information, and the interaction between direction and distance has been extensively studied. Representing cardinal directions between points is relatively straightforward. In Figure 7.4, three common techniques are displayed to define cardinal directions w.r.t. a reference point p [Abdelmoty (1995); Frank (1996); Goyal (2000); Hong (1994)]. In the cone–based model (Fig. 7.4(a) and 7.4(b)), the cardinal direction between a point q and the reference point p is defined based on the angle between the line pq and a fixed line, called a meridian, thus partitioning space in 4 or 8 direction intervals. On the other hand, in the projection–based model (Fig. 7.4(c)), North–East (NE), North–West (NW), South–East (SE) and South–West (SW) are represented as regions, whereas North (N), East (E), South (S) and West (W) are represented as lines. Some qualitative frameworks combine cardinal directions with qualitative distance relations [Clementini *et al.* (1997); Frank (1996); Hong (1994)]. The main idea is to define a finite number of non–overlapping distance intervals, corresponding to linguistic terms like very near, near, far, etc., and to encode in a composition table

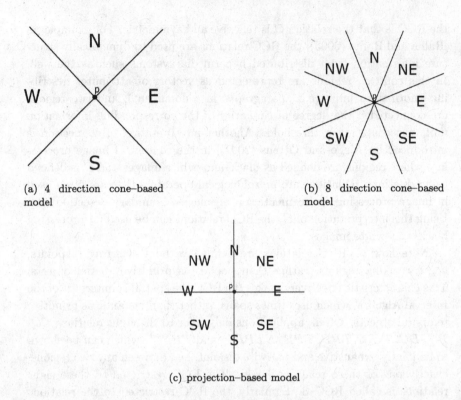

(a) 4 direction cone–based model

(b) 8 direction cone–based model

(c) projection–based model

Fig. 7.4   Cardinal directions from a reference point p.

how these distance classes interact with cardinal directions. For example, knowing that p is very far north of q and r is near and south of p, we can establish that r is north of q and either far or very far of q.

Various techniques to model cardinal directions between regions, instead of points, have been proposed. Most of these techniques approximate each region by its minimal bounding box, and model qualitative relations between these bounding boxes, typically inspired by Allen's Interval Algebra [Guesgen (1989); Papadias and Sellis (1994); Sharma (1996)]. While computationally very efficient, relying only on minimal bounding boxes is often not enough to accurately model cardinal directions between regions. Therefore, also the actual shapes of the regions are taken into account in more recent models [Goyal (2000); Skiadopoulos and Koubarakis (2004)]. As an example, consider the reference region A in Figure 7.5. To model the cardinal direction between regions A and B, space is partitioned into regions corresponding to N, NE, E, etc., based on the minimal bounding

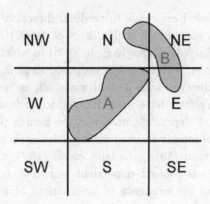

Fig. 7.5   Cardinal directions from a reference region A.

box of A. The cardinal direction of A and B is then represented as the enumeration of all regions overlapping with B. For instance, in the example from Figure 7.5, the relation between A and B would be represented as N;NE;E, i.e., B is considered partially north, partially north–east and partially east of A.

Finally, also other combinations of qualitative relations have been considered, including topology and direction [Sharma (1996); Li (2007)], and topology and size [Gerevini and Renz (2002)].

7.2.2 *Fuzzification of Spatial Relations*

Many spatial relations from natural language are inherently vague, even when the objects involved are crisp regions or points. In [Dutta (1991)], a general framework based on fuzzy restrictions and the compositional rule of inference is proposed to cope with vague distance and direction information between points, such as "*p* is located about 3 kilometres north of *q*". Both distance and direction constraints are modelled as triangular fuzzy sets, but their interaction is, unfortunately, not considered in the proposed reasoning algorithm. Nearness of places is also considered in [Guesgen and Albrecht (2000)], where the degree of nearness of two places is either defined as the reciprocal of their Euclidean distance, or assumed to be known in advance, i.e., a complete enumeration of the nearness of every pair of places is specified. Fuzzy spatial relations between crisp regions have been considered in [Vazirgiannis (2000)], where for example the degree of adjacency between two regions is defined based on the fraction of their boundary that is actually shared. A graded approach to cardinal direction relations between crisp regions is also considered in [Kulik *et al.* (2002)]. However, rather than modelling an absolute degree (e.g., in $[0,1]$) to which some region B is north of some region A, a technique is proposed to rank objects according to how compatible they are with a constraint such as "north of A".

A lot of research efforts have been directed towards understanding and modelling the context–dependent nature of the human perception of nearness. Early work has mainly focused on cognitive aspects of nearness (e.g. [Lundberg and Eckman (1973); Sadalla *et al.* (1980)]), showing, among others, that nearness is context–dependent and that cognitive distortions can occur because of the existence of landmarks. More recently, several computational models for nearness have been suggested, to some extent based on results from cognitive geography. For example, [Worboys (2001)] discusses three possible approaches to represent nearness: a three–valued approach, a four–valued approach, and a fuzzy approach. In the three-valued approach, the nearness of two places can either be true, false, or undecided. By analysing the results of a questionnaire, the authors conclude that nearness is neither symmetric nor transitive, although some weakened asymmetry and transitivity properties seem to hold. An analysis based on a four–valued logic aims at finding out whether situations in which the nearness of two places is undecided result from too much information (e.g. a is both near and not near to b; truth glut hypothesis) or too little (e.g. a is neither near b nor not near b; truth gap hypothesis). The results from the questionnaire provide some evidence towards the truth gap hypothesis. Finally, the fuzzy approach allows to differentiate between degrees of nearness. The degree of nearness of two places is based on the percentage of the participants that considered these places to be near. In [Gahegan (1995)], the effect of scale factors on the perceived degree of nearness is taken into account. Other context dependencies are discussed, but not implemented into the model; in particular, the attractiveness of objects (e.g., 1 km from a shop may be far, but 1 km from a toxic waste dump very near) and reachability. Finally, [Robinson (2000)] deals with the construction of fuzzy sets for concepts such as near and far, by asking the user a series of questions of the form *Do you consider x to be far from y*, which have to be answered by either yes or no (x and y are cities, and users are given a map to answer the questions). The goal is to allow for flexible querying in GIS systems, by using membership definitions of vague nearness relations that correspond to the interpretation of these concepts by the user.

In addition to modelling vague spatial relations such as nearness, considerable work has been done on generalizing spatial relations to cope with vague regions. Most models of topological relations between vague regions extend either the RCC or the 9–intersection model by treating a vague region a as a pair of two crisp regions: one region $\underline{a}$ which consists of the points that definitely belong to the vague region, and one region $\overline{a}$ whose complement consists of the points that definitely do not belong to the vague region. The region defined by $\overline{a} \setminus \underline{a}$ (provided $\underline{a}$ is a proper part of $\overline{a}$) consists of the points for which it is hard to tell whether they are in the vague region or not. A well–known example is the Egg–Yolk calculus [Cohn and Gotts (1996)], which is based on the RCC. In [Clementini and Di Felice (1997)], a similar approach, based on the notion of a thick boundary, is proposed as an extension of the 9–intersection model. Both models cause a significant increase in the number of possible relations: 601 and 44 relations respectively. For example, instead of specifying that two regions a and b overlap, we may specify that $\overline{a}$ and $\underline{b}$ overlap (but not $\underline{a}$ and $\underline{b}$), or that $\overline{a}$ and $\overline{b}$ overlap, or that $\underline{a}$ and $\underline{b}$ overlap, etc. where $\underline{a}$ and $\overline{a}$ (respectively $\underline{b}$ and $\overline{b}$) represent the yolk and the egg of a (respectively b). Another possibility, which is adopted in [Roy and Stell (2001)], is to stay with the spatial relations of the RCC, but to use three–valued relations instead of classical two–valued relations.

Other approaches have been concerned with defining (fuzzy) spatial relations between vague regions represented as fuzzy sets. For example, in [Zhan (1998)] and [Schneider (2001)], generalizations of the 9–intersection model based on α–levels of fuzzy sets are suggested. In [Tang and Kainz (2002)], a generalization of the 9–intersection model is introduced using concepts from fuzzy topology, yielding a set of 44 crisp spatial relations. Another generalization of the 9–intersection model, using similar fuzzy topological concepts, is proposed in [Liu and Shi (2006)], again obtaining 44 relations between fuzzy sets. On the other hand, [Li and Li (2004)] uses the RCC as a starting point to define crisp spatial relations between fuzzy sets. However, this approach can only be used when the membership values of the fuzzy sets are taken from a finite universe. The total number of relations is dependent on the cardinality of the finite set of membership values. In [Guesgen (2002)] degrees of appropriateness are assigned to RCC relations, modelling possibilistic uncertainty. These degrees could be interpreted as encoding, for instance, preferences or possibilistic uncertainty. In [Palshikar (2004)], definitions of fuzzy topological relations between vague regions in a discrete space (e.g., fuzzy sets of grid cells) are provided. Finally, [Du *et al.* (2005a)] and [Du *et al.* (2005b)] discuss fuzzy topological

relations with the goal of modelling position uncertainty of region boundaries.

All of the aforementioned approaches have in common that certain assumptions are made on how vague regions are represented. Moreover, they
are mainly applicable to geographical contexts, and can usually not be used
in situations where, for example, RCC relations are used in a metaphorical
way. The generality and much of the elegance of the RCC is lost in this
way. A different possibility is to generalize the RCC relations directly, without making any assumptions on how regions should be represented. This
idea has already been pursued, to some extent, in [Esterline *et al.* (1997)],
where the starting point is to define connection as an arbitrary symmetric
fuzzy relation C in the universe U of regions, satisfying a weak reflexivity
property, namely $C(a, a) > 0.5$ for every region a in U. The fuzzy relation
P (part of), for example, is defined by

$$P(a, b) = \inf_{z \in U} I_{S_M}(C(z, a), C(z, b)) \tag{7.1}$$

where a and b are regions in U. However, many properties of the original
RCC relations are lost in this approach. For example, in correspondence
with the reflexivity of P in the RCC, it would be desirable that $P(a, a) = 1$
for any region a in U. Unfortunately, this is, in general, not the case when
(7.1) is used to define P, due to the choice of I_{S_M} to generalize logical
implication. Similarly, many interesting transitivity properties are also lost,
which makes the fuzzy relations unsuitable for spatial reasoning.

Besides topological relations, also other spatial relations between vague
regions have been investigated. For example, [Cicerone and Felice (2000)]
introduces a framework for modelling cardinal directions between vague
regions with a broad boundary, i.e., vague regions represented as pairs of
crisp regions. In [Sun and Li (2005)], fuzzy morphology is applied to define
cardinal directions between fuzzy sets. Finally, the use of fuzzy morphology
to define spatial relations between fuzzy sets has also been addressed in
[Bloch (2006)].

7.3   Definitions Based on Relatedness Measures

In Chapter 4 we used relatedness measures to define fuzzy temporal relations between fuzzy time spans based on fuzzy point relations. In this
section, we show how the same technique can be applied for fuzzy spatial
relations. First, we introduce fuzzy spatial relations between points, ex-

pressing vague distance information, as well as cardinal directions. Next, in Section 7.3.2, we show how these fuzzy point relations can be combined with relatedness measures to model nearness and cardinal directions between vague regions, as well as some topological relations and size constraints. Finally, in Section 7.3.3, we show how the sup–T composition of fuzzy spatial relations, which is needed to perform fuzzy spatial reasoning, can be evaluated or approximated in an efficient way.

7.3.1 *Fuzzy Spatial Relations between Points*

Fuzzy spatial relations between points can be defined in a similar spirit as the fuzzy temporal relations $L^{\preceq}_{(\alpha,\beta)}$ and $L^{\ll}_{(\alpha,\beta)}$ between time instants. In particular, we define the degree $N_{(\alpha,\beta)}(p,q)$ to which two points p and q in $\mathbb{R}^2$ are near each other as $(\alpha,\beta \geq 0)$

$$N_{(\alpha,\beta)}(p,q) = \begin{cases} 1 & \text{if } d(p,q) \leq \alpha \\ 0 & \text{if } d(p,q) > \alpha + \beta \\ \frac{\alpha+\beta-d(p,q)}{\beta} & \text{otherwise } (\beta \neq 0) \end{cases}$$

where d represents the Euclidean distance in $\mathbb{R}^2$. Note how $N_{(\alpha,\beta)}(p,q)$ can be regarded as the degree to which the distance between p and q is at most about α. The parameter β defines how flexible "about α" is interpreted. The degree $F_{(\alpha,\beta)}(p,q)$ to which p is far from q is defined as $(\alpha,\beta \geq 0)$

$$F_{(\alpha,\beta)}(p,q) = 1 - N_{(\alpha,\beta)}(p,q)$$

It is easy to see that

$$F_{(\alpha,\beta)}(p,q) = \begin{cases} 1 & \text{if } d(p,q) > \alpha + \beta \\ 0 & \text{if } d(p,q) \leq \alpha \\ \frac{d(p,q)-\alpha}{\beta} & \text{otherwise } (\beta \neq 0) \end{cases}$$

$F_{(\alpha,\beta)}(p,q)$ can be interpreted as the degree to which the distance between p and q is more than about $\alpha + \beta$, where β again controls the flexibility in the interpretation of "about $\alpha + \beta$". The relationship between $N_{(\alpha,\beta)}(p,q)$ and $F_{(\alpha,\beta)}(p,q)$ on one hand, and $d(p,q)$ on the other is depicted in Figure 7.6. Finally, to model the cardinal direction between a reference point p and a point q, we use the (positive) angle θ_{pq} between the Y–axis (i.e., a meridian) and the line pq, i.e., the azimuth of q w.r.t. p. For example, if q is completely north, east, south, or west of p, θ_{pq} is 0, $\frac{\pi}{2}$, π, or $\frac{3\pi}{2}$ respectively.

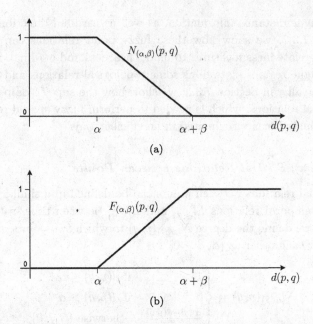

Fig. 7.6   Relationship between the degree to which two points p and q are near or far from each other and their distance $d(p, q)$.

In general, if p and q are specified by their coordinates (p_x, p_y) and (q_x, q_y), θ_{pq} is given by (assuming $p \neq q$)

$$
\theta_{pq} = \begin{cases}
\frac{\pi}{2} - \arctan(\frac{q_y - p_y}{q_x - p_x}) & \text{if } q_x > p_x \\
\frac{3\pi}{2} - \arctan(\frac{q_y - p_y}{q_x - p_x}) & \text{if } q_x < p_x \\
0 & \text{if } q_x = p_x \text{ and } q_y > p_y \\
\pi & \text{if } q_x = p_x \text{ and } q_y < p_y
\end{cases}
\tag{7.2}
$$

This relationship between θ_{pq} and the position of q w.r.t. p is further illustrated in Figure 7.7. The following lemma provides an alternative definition of θ_{pq} that will be of particular use in the proofs of propositions throughout this chapter.

Lemma 7.1. *Let $\theta \in [0, 2\pi[$, $d > 0$, $p = (p_x, p_y)$ and $q = (q_x, q_y)$ such that*

$$
q_x = p_x + d\cos(\frac{\pi}{2} - \theta)
$$

$$
q_y = p_y + d\sin(\frac{\pi}{2} - \theta)
$$

It holds that $\theta_{pq} = \theta$.

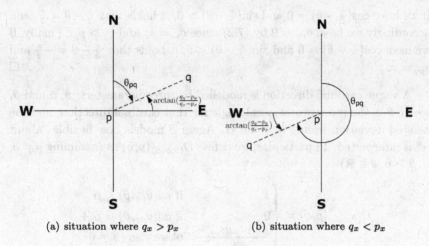

(a) situation where $q_x > p_x$ (b) situation where $q_x < p_x$

Fig. 7.7   Direction of q w.r.t. reference point p.

Proof. First assume that $\cos(\frac{\pi}{2} - \theta) > 0$, i.e., $\frac{\pi}{2} - \theta \in]-\frac{\pi}{2}, \frac{\pi}{2}[$ or $\theta \in]0, \pi[$. In particular, this implies that $\arctan(\tan(\frac{\pi}{2} - \theta)) = \frac{\pi}{2} - \theta$. From (7.2), we thus obtain (note that $q_x > p_x$)

$$
\begin{aligned}
\theta_{pq} &= \frac{\pi}{2} - \arctan\left(\frac{q_y - p_y}{q_x - p_x}\right) \\
&= \frac{\pi}{2} - \arctan\left(\frac{d\sin(\frac{\pi}{2} - \theta)}{d\cos(\frac{\pi}{2} - \theta)}\right) \\
&= \frac{\pi}{2} - \arctan(\tan(\frac{\pi}{2} - \theta)) \\
&= \frac{\pi}{2} - (\frac{\pi}{2} - \theta) \\
&= \theta
\end{aligned}
$$

Next, if $\cos(\frac{\pi}{2} - \theta) < 0$, it holds that $\frac{\pi}{2} - \theta \in]-\frac{3\pi}{2}, -\frac{\pi}{2}[$ or $\theta \in]\pi, 2\pi[$. This entails that $\arctan(\tan(\frac{\pi}{2} - \theta)) = \arctan(\tan(\frac{3\pi}{2} - \theta)) = \frac{3\pi}{2} - \theta$, yielding (note that $q_x < p_x$)

$$
\begin{aligned}
\theta_{pq} &= \frac{3\pi}{2} - \arctan\left(\frac{q_y - p_y}{q_x - p_x}\right) \\
&= \frac{3\pi}{2} - \arctan\left(\frac{d\sin(\frac{\pi}{2} - \theta)}{d\cos(\frac{\pi}{2} - \theta)}\right) \\
&= \frac{3\pi}{2} - \arctan(\tan(\frac{\pi}{2} - \theta)) \\
&= \frac{3\pi}{2} - (\frac{3\pi}{2} - \theta) \\
&= \theta
\end{aligned}
$$

If we have $\cos(\frac{\pi}{2} - \theta) = 0$ and $\sin(\frac{\pi}{2} - \theta) > 0$, it holds that $\frac{\pi}{2} - \theta = \frac{\pi}{2}$, and accordingly we have $\theta_{pq} = 0$ by (7.2) since $q_x = p_x$ and $q_y > p_y$. Finally, if we have $\cos(\frac{\pi}{2} - \theta) = 0$ and $\sin(\frac{\pi}{2} - \theta) < 0$, it holds that $\frac{\pi}{2} - \theta = -\frac{\pi}{2}$ and $\theta_{pq} = \pi$. $\qquad\qquad\qquad\qquad\qquad\qquad\qquad\qquad\qquad\qquad\qquad\qquad\quad$ $\square$

A vague cardinal direction is modelled by three parameters: θ, α and β, where θ is the most prototypical angle for that cardinal direction, and the allowed deviation from θ is about α. Again β models how flexible "about α" is interpreted. In particular, we define $D_{(\theta,\alpha,\beta)}(p,q)$ as (assuming $p \neq q$, $\alpha, \beta \geq 0$, $\theta \in \mathbb{R}$)

$$D_{(\theta,\alpha,\beta)}(p,q) = \begin{cases} 1 & \text{if } ad(\theta_{pq}, \theta) \leq \alpha \\ 0 & \text{if } ad(\theta_{pq}, \theta) > \alpha + \beta \\ \frac{\alpha + \beta - ad(\theta_{pq}, \theta)}{\beta} & \text{otherwise } (\beta \neq 0) \end{cases}$$

where ad represents the unsigned angular difference, i.e., for θ_1 and θ_2 in $\mathbb{R}$, we define

$$ad(\theta_1, \theta_2) = \min(norm(\theta_2 - \theta_1), 2\pi - norm(\theta_2 - \theta_1))$$

where $norm(\theta) = \theta + 2k\pi$ for k the unique integer satisfying $\theta + 2k\pi \in [0, 2\pi[$. Note that $ad(\theta_1, \theta_2) \in [0, \pi]$. For example, east could be modelled by the fuzzy relation $D_{(\frac{\pi}{2}, \frac{\pi}{8}, \frac{\pi}{4})}$. The fuzzy set of points which are east of a reference point p, using this interpretation, is displayed in Figure 7.8. In this figure, membership degrees $D_{(\frac{\pi}{2}, \frac{\pi}{8}, \frac{\pi}{4})}(p,q)$ for various points q are depicted using grayscale colors, black being membership degree 1 and white being 0. Note that this approach allows for a refinement of the traditional cone–based model (see Figure 7.4(b)).

7.3.2   *Fuzzy Spatial Relations between Vague Regions*

To extend the fuzzy spatial relations from Section 7.3.1 to fuzzy spatial relations between vague regions, represented as fuzzy sets in $\mathbb{R}^2$, the relatedness measures from Chapter 3 can be used in various ways. Let A and B be fuzzy sets in $\mathbb{R}^2$. The degree to which B is north of A, for example, could be modelled as

$$North^1_{(\alpha,\beta)}(A,B) = (A \circ_T D_{(0,\alpha,\beta)}) \rhd_{I_T} B$$

expressing that B is north of A to the extent that every point in B is north of at least one point in A. For example, consider the (crisp) regions A,

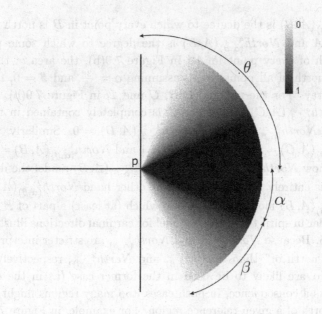

Fig. 7.8 Fuzzy set $D_{(\frac{\pi}{2}, \frac{\pi}{8}, \frac{\pi}{4})}(p, .)$ of points which are east of p.

B, C and D depicted in Figure 7.9(a). For the simplicity of the example, crisp regions are used and $\beta = 0$ is assumed. The area of the plane which is north of at least one point in A, assuming $\alpha = \frac{\pi}{4}$, is shown in light–gray. Since only C is completely contained in this gray area, it holds that $North^1_{(\alpha,\beta)}(A, C) = 1$ and $North^1_{(\alpha,\beta)}(A, B) = North^1_{(\alpha,\beta)}(A, D) = 0$. In addition to varying the values of α and β, also different relatedness measures can be utilized to obtain stricter or more tolerant interpretations of being "north of". A more tolerant alternative, for example, is

$$North^2_{(\alpha,\beta)}(A, B) = A \circ_T D_{(0,\alpha,\beta)} \circ_T B$$

expressing that B is north of A to the degree that some point in B is north of some point in A. Since in Figure 7.9(a), C and D are overlapping with the gray area, $North^2_{(\alpha,\beta)}(A, C) = North^2_{(\alpha,\beta)}(A, D) = 1$ while still $North^2_{(\alpha,\beta)}(A, B) = 0$. When $North^1_{(\alpha,\beta)}$ or $North^2_{(\alpha,\beta)}$ is used, B is considered north of A to the degree that (part of) B is north of at least one point in A. Another alternative is to require that (part of) B is north of every point in A, which leads to the following definitions:

$$North^3_{(\alpha,\beta)}(A, B) = A \triangleleft_{I_T} D_{(0,\alpha,\beta)} \triangleright_{I_T} B$$

$$North^4_{(\alpha,\beta)}(A, B) = (A \triangleleft_{I_T} D_{(0,\alpha,\beta)}) \circ_T B$$

$North^3_{(\alpha,\beta)}(A,B)$ is the degree to which every point in B is north of every point in A and $North^4_{(\alpha,\beta)}(A,B)$ is the degree to which some point in B is north of every point in A. In Figure 7.9(b), the area of the plane which is north of all points in A, assuming $\alpha = \frac{3\pi}{8}$ and $\beta = 0$, is shown in light–gray. For the regions A, B, C and D in Figure 7.9(b), it holds that $North^3_{(\alpha,\beta)}(A,C) = 1$, since C is completely contained in the gray area, and $North^3_{(\alpha,\beta)}(A,B) = North^3_{(\alpha,\beta)}(A,D) = 0$. Similarly, we have $North^4_{(\alpha,\beta)}(A,C) = North^4_{(\alpha,\beta)}(A,D) = 1$ and $North^4_{(\alpha,\beta)}(A,B) = 0$.

Note how $North^1_{(\alpha,\beta)}(A,B)$ and $North^3_{(\alpha,\beta)}(A,B)$ model the degree to which B is entirely north of A. On the other hand $North^2_{(\alpha,\beta)}(A,B)$ and $North^4_{(\alpha,\beta)}(A,B)$ model the degree to which (at least) a part of B is north of A, similar in spirit to the crisp model for cardinal directions illustrated in Figure 7.5. Because $North^3_{(\alpha,\beta)}$ and $North^4_{(\alpha,\beta)}$ are stricter interpretations of being "north of" than $North^1_{(\alpha,\beta)}$ and $North^2_{(\alpha,\beta)}$, respectively, larger values of α are likely to be used in the former case (as in the example above). As a consequence, in both cases, too many regions might be considered north of a given reference region. For example, in Figure 7.9(a), it holds that $North^2(A,D) = 1$, while D is intuitively not north of A at all. Similarly, in Figure 7.9(b), the fact that $North^4(A,D) = 1$ appears somewhat counterintuitive. By intersecting the corresponding fuzzy relations, the best of both worlds may be achieved:

$$North^{13}_{(\alpha_1,\beta_1,\alpha_2,\beta_2)}(A,B) = (North^1_{(\alpha_1,\beta_1)} \cap North^3_{(\alpha_2,\beta_2)})(A,B)$$

$$North^{24}_{(\alpha_1,\beta_1,\alpha_2,\beta_2)}(A,B) = (North^2_{(\alpha_1,\beta_1)} \cap North^4_{(\alpha_2,\beta_2)})(A,B)$$

where typically $\alpha_1 \leq \alpha_2$. The result is illustrated in Figure 7.9(c). Assuming $\alpha_1 = \frac{\pi}{4}$, $\alpha_2 = \frac{3\pi}{8}$ and $\beta_1 = \beta_2 = 0$, the gray area consists of the points that are north of some point in A w.r.t. α_1 and north of all points in A w.r.t. α_2. It holds that

$$North^{13}_{(\alpha_1,\beta_1,\alpha_2,\beta_2)}(A,B) = North^{24}_{(\alpha_1,\beta_1,\alpha_2,\beta_2)}(A,B) = 0$$

$$North^{13}_{(\alpha_1,\beta_1,\alpha_2,\beta_2)}(A,C) = North^{24}_{(\alpha_1,\beta_1,\alpha_2,\beta_2)}(A,C) = 0$$

$$North^1_{(\alpha_1,\beta_1)}(A,B) = North^2_{(\alpha_1,\beta_1)}(A,B) = 1$$

$$North^3_{(\alpha_2,\beta_2)}(A,C) = North^4_{(\alpha_2,\beta_2)}(A,C) = 1$$

Other cardinal directions, such as east or southwest, can be modelled in entirely the same fashion.

Nearness between vague regions can be expressed in a similar way. In particular, we define the degree $Near_{(\alpha,\beta)}(A,B)$ to which A is near B as

$$Near_{(\alpha,\beta)}(A,B) = A \circ_T N_{(\alpha,\beta)} \circ_T B$$

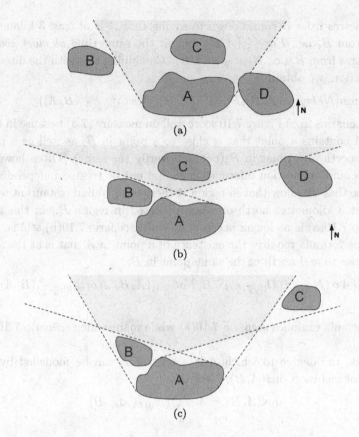

Fig. 7.9   Various interpretations of "north of A".

In other words, A is considered near B to the degree that some point in A is close to some point in B. The degree to which A is far from B can be modelled as

$$Far_{(\alpha,\beta)}(A, B) = A \lhd_{I_T} F_{(\alpha,\beta)} \rhd_{I_T} B$$

If $T = T_W$, it holds by Proposition 3.9 that

$$
\begin{aligned}
Far_{(\alpha,\beta)}(A, B) &= A \lhd_{I_T} F_{(\alpha,\beta)} \rhd_{I_T} B \\
&= A \lhd_{I_T} coN_{(\alpha,\beta)} \rhd_{I_T} B \\
&= 1 - Near_{(\alpha,\beta)}(A, B)
\end{aligned}
$$

Sometimes both orientation and distance information is provided, which can be modelled using the measures introduced above. Suppose that we know that A is about 3 kilometres north of B. Claiming that A is *about*

3 kilometres from B comes down to saying that A is *at least* 3 kilometres away from B, i.e., $Far_{(2,1)}(A, B)$, but at the same time *at most about* 3 kilometres from B, i.e., $Near_{(3,1)}(A, B)$. Combining this with the direction information, we obtain

$$\min(Near_{(3,1)}(A, B), Far_{(2,1)}(A, B), North^2_{(0, \frac{\pi}{8}, \frac{\pi}{4})}(B, A)) \qquad (7.3)$$

Both scenarios from Figure 7.10 score well on measure (7.3) because in both cases A contains a point that is close to a point in B, as well as a point that is north of a point in B (not necessarily the same). Often however, distance and orientation information should not be treated independently. Suppose that we know that in region A there is an Italian restaurant which is about 3 kilometres north of a hotel located in region B. In this case, scenario 7.10(a) is no longer acceptable, while scenario 7.10(b) still is. The following formula requires the existence of a point in A that is at the same time close to and north of the same point in B:

$$\min(A \circ (N_{(3,1)} \cap D_{(0, \frac{\pi}{8}, \frac{\pi}{4})}) \circ B, Far_{(2,1)}(A, B), North^1_{(0, \frac{\pi}{8}, \frac{\pi}{4})}(B, A))$$

$$(7.4)$$

This formula excludes scenario 7.10(a) while maintaining scenario 7.10(b).

Next, the degree to which A is a part of B can be modelled by the degree of inclusion $incl(A, B)$. Note that

$$incl(A, B) = A \lhd_{I_T} (N_{(0,0)} \lhd_{I_T} B)$$

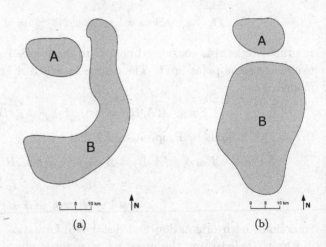

Fig. 7.10 Two scenarios in which A is close to B, and north of B.

Additional information about where A is located inside B may be available. We may know that A is close to B's boundary, that A is in the heart of B, in the south–western corner, in the northern part, etc. Again, relatedness measures can be used to model such fuzzy spatial relations. For example, the degree to which A is located in the northern part of B can be defined by

$$\min(incl(A, B), A \circ_T (N_{(\alpha,\beta)} \cap D_{(0, \frac{\pi}{8}, \frac{\pi}{4})}) \circ_T coB)$$

For appropriate α and β, this is the degree to which A is a part of B, and some point outside B is both close to and north of some point in A. Alternatively, we can model the degree to which A is in the northern part of B as the degree to which all points that are both close to and south of A are in B:

$$\min(incl(A, B), A \lhd_{I_T} ((N_{(\alpha,\beta)} \cap D_{(\pi, \frac{\pi}{8}, \frac{\pi}{4})}) \lhd_{I_T} B))$$

Similarly, the degree to which A is located in the heart of B can be modelled by the degree to which all points close to A are located in B:

$$\min(incl(A, B), A \lhd_{I_T} (N_{(\alpha,\beta)} \lhd_{I_T} B))$$

From Proposition 3.8, we moreover find

$$\min(incl(A, B), A \lhd_{I_T} (N_{(\alpha,\beta)} \lhd_{I_T} B)) = A \lhd_{I_T} (N_{(\alpha,\beta)} \lhd_{I_T} B)$$

since $N_{(0,0)} \subseteq N_{(\alpha,\beta)}$ for $\alpha, \beta \geq 0$.

Finally, size constraints can be modelled using $N_{(\alpha,\beta)}$ and $F_{(\alpha,\beta)}$. For example, we define the degree to which A is small as

$$Small_{(\alpha,\beta)}(A) = A \lhd_{I_T} N_{(\alpha,\beta)} \rhd_{I_T} A$$

In other words, the degree to which A is small is defined as the degree to which every point in A is close to every other point in A. Analogously, the degree to which A is large can be defined as the degree to which every point in A is far from at least one other point in A:

$$Large^1_{(\alpha,\beta)}(A) = A \lhd_{I_T} (F_{(\alpha,\beta)} \circ_T A)$$

Alternatively, the degree to which A is large can be defined as the degree to which some point in A is far from at least one other point in A:

$$Large^2_{(\alpha,\beta)}(A) = A \circ_T F_{(\alpha,\beta)} \circ_T A$$

Note that for $T = T_W$, by Proposition 3.9, it holds that

$$Large^2_{(\alpha,\beta)}(A) = 1 - Small_{(\alpha,\beta)}(A)$$

As the discussion above shows, relatedness measures offer a flexible and very expressive means to define fuzzy spatial relations between regions. One impediment for practical applications, however, is that appropriate values of various parameters have to be found. Knowing that a region is small, for example, does not always translate straightforwardly to suitable values of the parameters α and β in the definition of $Small_{(\alpha,\beta)}$. To cope with this, different techniques can be used for different spatial relations. In [Pan *et al.* (2006)], a technique to learn typical durations of events is proposed. Similar ideas might be used to learn typical sizes of places of a given semantic type (e.g., city neighbourhood, park, cemetery), resulting in values of the parameters α and β in the definition of $Small_{(\alpha,\beta)}$ for each semantic type. The parameters in the definitions of cardinal directions may be defined as such, implying that north, for instance, is always interpreted in the same way (e.g., $North^1_{(\frac{\pi}{8},\frac{\pi}{4})}$). In Chapter 9 we will show how suitable values of α and β can be found to interpret natural language nearness relations such as "within walking distance" as $Near_{(\alpha,\beta)}$. In addition to such data–driven techniques to model natural language information, available, incomplete quantitative information may be used. For example, on the web, we may find a number of places that are located in a given neighbourhood. Although this may not be enough information to actually construct good boundaries for this neighbourhood, it will probably tell us something about its approximate size. Similarly, many gazetteers contain approximate information about the location of a region, typically in the form of centroids (i.e., a central point) or minimal bounding boxes (i.e., the minimal rectangle which encompasses the region and whose sides are parallel to the axes). Minimal bounding boxes are useful to derive imprecise size information, while both centroids and minimal bounding boxes may be used to derive imprecise cardinal directions and distance relations.

7.3.3   *Composing Fuzzy Spatial Relations*

When using the fuzzy spatial relations from Section 7.3.2, the transitivity table for relatedness measures (Table 3.1) plays a key role in deriving new information from information that is explicitly given. For example, knowing that $Near_{(10,5)}(A,B) = 0.7$, $Small_{(1,1)}(B) = 0.9$ and $Near_{(5,20)}(B,C) = 0.8$, what can we say about the nearness of A and C? From Table 3.1, we find

$$T(0.7, 0.9, 0.8)$$

$$= T(Near_{(10,5)}(A, B), Small_{(1,1)}(B), Near_{(5,20)}(B, C))$$
$$= T(A \circ_T N_{(10,5)} \circ_T B, B \lhd_{I_T} N_{(1,1)} \rhd_{I_T} B, B \circ_T N_{(5,20)} \circ_T C)$$
$$\leq T(A \circ_T ((N_{(10,5)} \circ_T N_{(1,1)}) \rhd_{I_T} B), B \circ_T N_{(5,20)} \circ_T C)$$
$$\leq A \circ_T (N_{(10,5)} \circ_T N_{(1,1)} \circ_T N_{(5,20)}) \circ_T C$$

Hence, to obtain a lower bound of the degree to which A is near C, we need to evaluate the sup–T composition of fuzzy spatial point relations. This can be accomplished by applying Proposition 7.1 below. First, we show the following lemma.

Lemma 7.2. *For all a, b and c in $\mathbb{R}^2$, it holds that ($\alpha_1, \alpha_2, \beta_1, \beta_2 \geq 0$)*

$$T_W(N_{(\alpha_1,\beta_1)}(a, b), N_{(\alpha_2,\beta_2)}(b, c)) \leq N_{(\alpha_1+\alpha_2,\max(\beta_1,\beta_2))}(a, c) \qquad (7.5)$$

Proof. If $d(a, b) > \alpha_1 + \beta_1$, $d(b, c) > \alpha_2 + \beta_2$ or $d(a, c) \leq \alpha_1 + \alpha_2$, (7.5) is trivially satisfied. Therefore, assume $d(a, b) \leq \alpha_1 + \beta_1$, $d(b, c) \leq \alpha_2 + \beta_2$ and $d(a, c) > \alpha_1 + \alpha_2$. If $d(a, b) \leq \alpha_1$ and $d(b, c) \leq \alpha_2$, we have because of the triangle inequality that $d(a, c) \leq d(a, b) + d(b, c) \leq \alpha_1 + \alpha_2$, and thus $N_{(\alpha_1+\alpha_2,\max(\beta_1,\beta_2))}(a, c) = 1$ and (7.5).

If $d(a, b) \leq \alpha_1$ and $\alpha_2 < d(b, c) \leq \alpha_2 + \beta_2$ we find $d(a, c) \leq d(a, b) + d(b, c) \leq \alpha_1 + \alpha_2 + \beta_2 \leq \alpha_1 + \alpha_2 + \max(\beta_1, \beta_2)$. We obtain (note that $\alpha_2 < \alpha_2 + \beta_2$ entails $\beta_2 > 0$)

$$T_W(N_{(\alpha_1,\beta_1)}(a, b), N_{(\alpha_2,\beta_2)}(b, c)) \leq N_{(\alpha_1+\alpha_2,\max(\beta_1,\beta_2))}(a, c)$$
$$\Leftrightarrow N_{(\alpha_2,\beta_2)}(b, c) \leq N_{(\alpha_1+\alpha_2,\max(\beta_1,\beta_2))}(a, c)$$
$$\Leftrightarrow \frac{\alpha_2 + \beta_2 - d(b, c)}{\beta_2} \leq \frac{\alpha_1 + \alpha_2 + \max(\beta_1, \beta_2) - d(a, c)}{\max(\beta_1, \beta_2)}$$
$$\Leftrightarrow \frac{\alpha_2 + \beta_2 - d(b, c)}{\beta_2} \leq 1 + \frac{\alpha_1 + \alpha_2 - d(a, c)}{\max(\beta_1, \beta_2)}$$

Using the assumption $d(a, c) > \alpha_1 + \alpha_2$, we find

$$\Leftarrow \frac{\alpha_2 + \beta_2 - d(b, c)}{\beta_2} \leq 1 + \frac{\alpha_1 + \alpha_2 - d(a, c)}{\beta_2}$$
$$\Leftrightarrow \frac{\alpha_2 + \beta_2 - d(b, c)}{\beta_2} \leq \frac{\alpha_1 + \alpha_2 + \beta_2 - d(a, c)}{\beta_2}$$
$$\Leftrightarrow -d(b, c) \leq \alpha_1 - d(a, c)$$
$$\Leftrightarrow d(a, c) \leq \alpha_1 + d(b, c)$$

The latter expression is satisfied because of the triangle inequality and the assumption $d(a, b) \leq \alpha_1$. The proof for the case where $d(b, c) \leq \alpha_2$ and $\alpha_1 < d(a, b) \leq \alpha_1 + \beta_1$ is entirely analogous. Finally, assume $\alpha_1 < d(a, b) \leq$

$\alpha_1 + \beta_1$ and $\alpha_2 < d(b,c) \leq \alpha_2 + \beta_2$. We find using the triangle inequality (note that $\beta_1 > 0$ and $\beta_2 > 0$)

$$T_W(N_{(\alpha_1,\beta_1)}(a,b), N_{(\alpha_2,\beta_2)}(b,c))$$
$$\leq T_W(N_{(\alpha_1,\max(\beta_1,\beta_2))}(a,b), N_{(\alpha_2,\max(\beta_1,\beta_2))}(b,c))$$
$$= \max(0, \frac{\alpha_1 + \max(\beta_1,\beta_2) - d(a,b)}{\max(\beta_1,\beta_2)} + \frac{\alpha_2 + \max(\beta_1,\beta_2) - d(b,c)}{\max(\beta_1,\beta_2)} - 1)$$
$$= \max(0, \frac{\alpha_1 + \alpha_2 + \max(\beta_1,\beta_2) - d(a,b) - d(b,c)}{\max(\beta_1,\beta_2)})$$
$$\leq \max(0, \frac{\alpha_1 + \alpha_2 + \max(\beta_1,\beta_2) - d(a,c)}{\max(\beta_1,\beta_2)})$$
$$= N_{(\alpha_1+\alpha_2,\max(\beta_1,\beta_2))}(a,c) \qquad \qquad \square$$

Proposition 7.1. *It holds that $(\alpha_1, \alpha_2, \beta_1, \beta_2 \geq 0)$*

$$N_{(\alpha_1,\beta_1)} \circ_{T_W} N_{(\alpha_2,\beta_2)} = N_{(\alpha_1+\alpha_2,\max(\beta_1,\beta_2))} \qquad (7.6)$$

Proof.   By Lemma 7.2 we already know

$$N_{(\alpha_1,\beta_1)} \circ_{T_W} N_{(\alpha_2,\beta_2)} \subseteq N_{(\alpha_1+\alpha_2,\max(\beta_1,\beta_2))} \qquad (7.7)$$

We show that the converse also holds for $\beta_1 \leq \beta_2$; the proof for $\beta_1 > \beta_2$ is completely analogous. Let a and c be arbitrary elements from $\mathbb{R}^2$. If $d(a,c) \leq \alpha_1$, it holds that

$$(N_{(\alpha_1,\beta_1)} \circ_{T_W} N_{(\alpha_2,\beta_2)})(a,c) = \sup_{b \in \mathbb{R}^2} T_W(N_{(\alpha_1,\beta_1)}(a,b), N_{(\alpha_2,\beta_2)}(b,c))$$
$$\geq \sup_{b \in \mathbb{R}^2} T_W(N_{(\alpha_1,\beta_1)}(a,c), N_{(\alpha_2,\beta_2)}(c,c))$$
$$= N_{(\alpha_1,\beta_1)}(a,c)$$
$$= 1$$
$$\geq N_{(\alpha_1+\alpha_2,\max(\beta_1,\beta_2))}(a,c)$$

Next, assume $d(a,c) > \alpha_1$ and $\beta_2 > 0$. We obtain

$$(N_{(\alpha_1,\beta_1)} \circ_{T_W} N_{(\alpha_2,\beta_2)})(a,c)$$
$$= \sup_{b \in \mathbb{R}^2} T_W(N_{(\alpha_1,\beta_1)}(a,b), N_{(\alpha_2,\beta_2)}(b,c))$$
$$\geq T_W(N_{(\alpha_1,\beta_1)}(a, a + \alpha_1 \frac{\vec{ac}}{\|\vec{ac}\|}), N_{(\alpha_2,\beta_2)}(a + \alpha_1 \frac{\vec{ac}}{\|\vec{ac}\|}, c))$$
$$= N_{(\alpha_2,\beta_2)}(a + \alpha_1 \frac{\vec{ac}}{\|\vec{ac}\|}, c)$$

$$= \min(1, \max(0, \frac{\alpha_2 + \beta_2 - d(a + \alpha_1 \frac{\overrightarrow{ac}}{\|\overrightarrow{ac}\|}, c)}{\beta_2}))$$

$$= \min(1, \max(0, \frac{\alpha_1 + \alpha_2 + \beta_2 - d(a, c)}{\beta_2}))$$

$$= N_{(\alpha_1 + \alpha_2, \beta_2)}(a, c)$$

Finally, for $d(a, c) > \alpha_1$ and $\beta_2 = 0$, we find

$$(N_{(\alpha_1, \beta_1)} \circ_{T_W} N_{(\alpha_2, 0)})(a, c)$$

$$= \sup_{b \in \mathbb{R}^2} T_W(N_{(\alpha_1, \beta_1)}(a, b), N_{(\alpha_2, 0)}(b, c))$$

$$\geq T_W(N_{(\alpha_1, \beta_1)}(a, a + \alpha_1 \frac{\overrightarrow{ac}}{\|\overrightarrow{ac}\|}), N_{(\alpha_2, 0)}(a + \alpha_1 \frac{\overrightarrow{ac}}{\|\overrightarrow{ac}\|}, c))$$

$$= N_{(\alpha_2, 0)}(a + \alpha_1 \frac{\overrightarrow{ac}}{\|\overrightarrow{ac}\|}, c)$$

If $d(a + \alpha_1 \frac{\overrightarrow{ac}}{\|\overrightarrow{ac}\|}, c) \leq \alpha_2$, we immediately have $N_{(\alpha_2, 0)}(a + \alpha_1 \frac{\overrightarrow{ac}}{\|\overrightarrow{ac}\|}, c) = 1 \geq N_{(\alpha_1 + \alpha_2, \beta_2)}(a, c)$. If, on the other hand, $d(a + \alpha_1 \frac{\overrightarrow{ac}}{\|\overrightarrow{ac}\|}, c) > \alpha_2$, it holds that $N_{(\alpha_1 + \alpha_2, 0)}(a, c) = 0$, i.e., $d(a, c) > \alpha_1 + \alpha_2$. Indeed, from $d(a, c) > \alpha_1$, we have $d(a + \alpha_1 \frac{\overrightarrow{ac}}{\|\overrightarrow{ac}\|}, c) = d(a, c) - \alpha_1$, which together with $d(a + \alpha_1 \frac{\overrightarrow{ac}}{\|\overrightarrow{ac}\|}, c) > \alpha_2$ yields $d(a, c) = \alpha_1 + d(a + \alpha_1 \frac{\overrightarrow{ac}}{\|\overrightarrow{ac}\|}, c) > \alpha_1 + \alpha_2$. $\square$

Going back to our example, Proposition 7.1 reveals that (choosing $T = T_W$)

$$T_W(0.7, 0.9, 0.8) \leq A \circ_{T_W} (N_{(10,5)} \circ_{T_W} N_{(1,1)} \circ_{T_W} N_{(5,20)}) \circ_{T_W} C$$

$$= A \circ_{T_W} N_{(16,20)} \circ_{T_W} C$$

$$= Near_{(16,20)}(A, C)$$

As already pointed out above, sometimes orientation information is provided together with distance information. Taking both into account simultaneously allows to infer stronger information. For example, knowing that two regions A and C are near a university district B, we can establish more about the nearness of A and C if we additionally know that they are both at the same side of B (e.g., both north of B). As illustrated in (7.4), modelling combined distance and orientation can be achieved by using the intersection of $N_{(\alpha_1, \beta_1)}$ and $D_{(\theta_2, \alpha_2, \beta_2)}$ in the relatedness measures. This gives rise to the need for evaluating sup–T compositions of the form ($\alpha_1, \alpha_2, \alpha_3, \alpha_4, \beta_1, \beta_2, \beta_3, \beta_4 \geq 0$, θ_2, θ_4 in $[0, 2\pi[$)

$$(N_{(\alpha_1, \beta_1)} \cap D_{(\theta_2, \alpha_2, \beta_2)}) \circ (N_{(\alpha_3, \beta_3)} \cap D_{(\theta_4, \alpha_4, \beta_4)}) \tag{7.8}$$

Unfortunately, this sup–T composition cannot be evaluated as easily as in Proposition 7.1, because of the complex interactions of orientation and nearness. Moreover, calculating the exact sup–T composition relies on heavy geometrical computations and is usually not feasible in applications. To cope with this, we present an upper bound for this sup–T composition which can be evaluated in constant time, assuming $T = T_W$. Although the presented results rely on our choice for the Łukasiewicz t–norm, they can easily be extended to cope with other t–norms such as the minimum. First, we extend the definition of angular difference ad to intervals. Let $\theta_1, \theta_2, \theta_3, \theta_4$ be in $\mathbb{R}$ such that $\theta_1 \leq \theta_2$ and $\theta_3 \leq \theta_4$. We define

$$ad^*([\theta_1, \theta_2], [\theta_3, \theta_4]) = \min_{\theta \in [\theta_1, \theta_2]} \min_{\theta' \in [\theta_3, \theta_4]} ad(\theta, \theta')$$

It holds that $ad^*([\theta_1, \theta_2], [\theta_3, \theta_4]) = 0$ if $[\theta_1, \theta_2]$ and $[\theta_3 + 2k\pi, \theta_4 + 2k\pi]$ overlap for some k in $\mathbb{Z}$, and $ad^*([\theta_1, \theta_2], [\theta_3, \theta_4]) = \min(ad(\theta_2, \theta_3), ad(\theta_4, \theta_1))$ otherwise. Before showing how nearness information between points a and c can be derived from nearness and orientation information between a and b and between b and c, we show two technical lemmas.

Lemma 7.3. *Let $a \in [-2, 2]$ and let f be defined for x and y in $\mathbb{R}$ by*

$$f(x, y) = x^2 + y^2 + axy$$

The maximum of $f(x, y)$ subject to $(x, y) \in [0, d_1] \times [0, d_2]$ ($d_1 \geq 0$, $d_2 \geq 0$) is attained in either (d_1, d_2), $(d_1, 0)$ or $(0, d_2)$.

Proof. It holds that $\frac{\partial^2}{\partial x^2} f(x, y) = \frac{\partial^2}{\partial y^2} f(x, y) = 2$ for any x and y in $\mathbb{R}$, hence the partial mappings of f are convex quadratic functions. As a consequence, f does not have any maxima in $\mathbb{R}^2$ (local or global). The maximum value for (x, y) in $[0, d_1] \times [0, d_2]$ is therefore attained in (d_1, d_2), $(d_1, 0)$, $(0, d_2)$ or $(0, 0)$. Moreover, since $f(0, 0) = 0$ and $f(x, y) \geq x^2 + y^2 - 2xy = (x - y)^2 \geq 0$, it holds that the maximum value is attained in (d_1, d_2), $(d_1, 0)$ or $(0, d_2)$. $\qquad\qquad\square$

Lemma 7.4. *Let x be in $[0, \pi]$; it holds that*

$$\cos u_0 - (x - u_0) \sin u_0 \leq \cos x \leq \cos u_1 - (x - u_1) \sin u_1$$

where

$$u_0 = 2.331122370$$
$$u_1 = 0.8104702832$$

Proof.   The tangent line f to the cosine function in a point $(u, \cos u)$ is defined by

$$f_u(x) = \cos u - (x - u)\sin u$$

for every x in $\mathbb{R}$. For u in $[\frac{\pi}{2}, \pi]$, f_u is a lower approximation of $\cos$ over $[0, \pi]$, provided $f_u(0) \leq 1$. Similarly, for u in $[0, \frac{\pi}{2}]$, f_u is an upper approximation of $\cos$ over $[0, \pi]$, provided $f_u(\pi) \geq -1$. In particular, it holds that $f_{u_0}(0) = 1$ and $f_{u_1}(\pi) = -1$, the values of u_0 and u_1 being found numerically using Maple 9.5. Figure 7.11 depicts the functions $\cos$, f_{u_0} and f_{u_1}.   □

Proposition 7.2. *Let a and c be in $\mathbb{R}^2$, $\alpha_1, \alpha_2, \alpha_3, \alpha_4 \geq 0$, $\beta_1, \beta_2, \beta_3, \beta_4 \geq 0$ and θ_2 and θ_4 in $[0, 2\pi[$. It holds that*

$$\sup_{b \in \mathbb{R}^2} T_W ((N_{(\alpha_1,\beta_1)} \cap D_{(\theta_2,\alpha_2,\beta_2)})(a,b), (N_{(\alpha_3,\beta_3)} \cap D_{(\theta_4,\alpha_4,\beta_4)})(b,c)) \quad (7.9)$$

$$\leq (N_{(\alpha_1,\beta_1)} \cup N_{(\alpha_3,\beta_3)} \cup (N_{(\alpha_1+\alpha_3,\beta_3)} \cap N_{(\alpha,\beta)})$$

$$\cup (N_{(\alpha_1+\alpha_3,\beta_1)} \cap N_{(\alpha,\beta')}))(a,c)$$

where

$$\alpha = \sqrt{\alpha_1^2 + \alpha_3^2 - 2\alpha_1\alpha_3(t_0 + t_1)} \qquad (7.10)$$

$$\beta = \sqrt{\alpha_1^2 + (\alpha_3 + \beta_3)^2 - 2\alpha_1(\alpha_3 + \beta_3)t_0} - \alpha \qquad (7.11)$$

$$\beta' = \sqrt{(\alpha_1 + \beta_1)^2 + \alpha_3^2 - 2(\alpha_1 + \beta_1)\alpha_3 t_0} - \alpha \qquad (7.12)$$

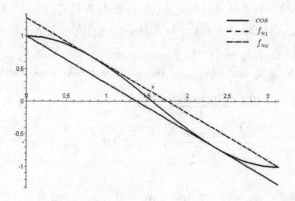

Fig. 7.11   Upper and lower approximation of the cosine function.

and

$$t_0 = \cos u_0 + \sin u_0 (ad^*([\theta_2 - \alpha_2, \theta_2 + \alpha_2], [\theta_4 - \alpha_4, \theta_4 + \alpha_4])$$
$$- \max(\beta_2, \beta_4) - \pi + u_0)$$
$$t_1 = \max(\beta_2, \beta_4) \sin u_0$$

Proof. To prove this result, we will show that for every λ in $]0, 1]$, it holds that

$$\sup_{b \in \mathbb{R}^2} T_W((N_{(\alpha_1, \beta_1)} \cap D_{(\theta_2, \alpha_2, \beta_2)})(a, b), (N_{(\alpha_3, \beta_3)} \cap D_{(\theta_4, \alpha_4, \beta_4)})(b, c)) \geq \lambda$$

$$\Rightarrow (N_{(\alpha_1, \beta_1)} \cup N_{(\alpha_3, \beta_3)} \cup (N_{(\alpha_1 + \alpha_3, \beta_3)} \cap N_{(\alpha, \beta)})$$
$$\cup (N_{(\alpha_1 + \alpha_3, \beta_1)} \cap N_{(\alpha, \beta')}))(a, c) \geq \lambda$$

Since $N_{(\alpha_1, \beta_1)}$, $D_{(\theta_2, \alpha_2, \beta_2)}$, $N_{(\alpha_3, \beta_3)}$ and $D_{(\theta_4, \alpha_4, \beta_4)}$ are upper semi-continuous, the supremum in the left–hand side of (7.9) is attained. Hence, for $\lambda \in]0, 1]$, we find that

$$\sup_{b \in \mathbb{R}^2} T_W((N_{(\alpha_1, \beta_1)} \cap D_{(\theta_2, \alpha_2, \beta_2)})(a, b), (N_{(\alpha_3, \beta_3)} \cap D_{(\theta_4, \alpha_4, \beta_4)})(b, c)) \geq \lambda$$

$$\Leftrightarrow (\exists b \in \mathbb{R}^2)(T_W((N_{(\alpha_1, \beta_1)} \cap D_{(\theta_2, \alpha_2, \beta_2)})(a, b),$$
$$(N_{(\alpha_3, \beta_3)} \cap D_{(\theta_4, \alpha_4, \beta_4)})(b, c)) \geq \lambda)$$

$$\Leftrightarrow (\exists b \in \mathbb{R}^2)(\exists \lambda_1, \lambda_2 \in [0, 1])(N_{(\alpha_1, \beta_1)}(a, b) \geq \lambda_1 \wedge D_{(\theta_2, \alpha_2, \beta_2)}(a, b) \geq \lambda_1$$
$$\wedge N_{(\alpha_3, \beta_3)}(b, c) \geq \lambda_2 \wedge D_{(\theta_4, \alpha_4, \beta_4)}(b, c) \geq \lambda_2 \wedge T_W(\lambda_1, \lambda_2) = \lambda)$$

Under our assumption that $\lambda \in]0, 1]$, $T_W(\lambda_1, \lambda_2) = \lambda$ is equivalent to $\lambda_2 = \lambda + 1 - \lambda_1$. Furthermore, $T_W(\lambda_1, \lambda_2) = \lambda$ implies $\lambda_1 \geq \lambda$, hence

$$\Leftrightarrow (\exists b \in \mathbb{R}^2)(\exists \lambda_1 \in [\lambda, 1])(N_{(\alpha_1, \beta_1)}(a, b) \geq \lambda_1 \wedge D_{(\theta_2, \alpha_2, \beta_2)}(a, b) \geq \lambda_1$$
$$\wedge N_{(\alpha_3, \beta_3)}(b, c) \geq \lambda + 1 - \lambda_1 \wedge D_{(\theta_4, \alpha_4, \beta_4)}(b, c) \geq \lambda + 1 - \lambda_1)$$

Let b be in $\mathbb{R}^2$ and λ_1 in $[\lambda, 1]$. First assume $\beta_2 \neq 0$ and $\beta_4 \neq 0$. From $D_{(\theta_2, \alpha_2, \beta_2)}(a, b) \geq \lambda_1$ and $D_{(\theta_4, \alpha_4, \beta_4)}(b, c) \geq \lambda + 1 - \lambda_1$ we know that

$$\frac{\alpha_2 + \beta_2 - ad(\theta_{ab}, \theta_2)}{\beta_2} \geq \lambda_1$$

$$\frac{\alpha_4 + \beta_4 - ad(\theta_{bc}, \theta_4)}{\beta_4} \geq \lambda + 1 - \lambda_1$$

and hence

$$ad(\theta_{ab}, \theta_2) \leq \alpha_2 + (1 - \lambda_1)\beta_2 \leq \alpha_2 + (1 - \lambda_1)\max(\beta_2, \beta_4) \qquad (7.13)$$
$$ad(\theta_{bc}, \theta_4) \leq \alpha_4 + (\lambda_1 - \lambda)\beta_4 \leq \alpha_4 + (\lambda_1 - \lambda)\max(\beta_2, \beta_4) \qquad (7.14)$$

Next, consider the case that $\beta_2 = 0$. From $D_{(\theta_2, \alpha_2, \beta_2)}(a, b) \geq \lambda_1 \geq \lambda > 0$, we find that $ad(\Theta_{ab}, \theta_2) \leq \alpha$, and in particular, we again have (7.13). Similarly, if $\beta_4 = 0$, we again find (7.14). In other words, for some k_1 and k_2 in $\mathbb{Z}$, we always have

$$\theta_{ab} + 2k_1\pi \in [\theta_2 - \alpha_2 - (1 - \lambda_1)\max(\beta_2, \beta_4), \theta_2 + \alpha_2 + (1 - \lambda_1)\max(\beta_2, \beta_4)]$$

$$\theta_{bc} + 2k_1\pi \in [\theta_4 - \alpha_4 - (\lambda_1 - \lambda)\max(\beta_2, \beta_4), \theta_4 + \alpha_4 + (\lambda_1 - \lambda)\max(\beta_2, \beta_4)]$$

The first interval is of the form $[p_1 + \lambda_1 \max(\beta_2, \beta_4), p_2 - \lambda_1 \max(\beta_2, \beta_4)]$ while the second is of the form $[q_1 - \lambda_1 \max(\beta_2, \beta_4), q_2 + \lambda_1 \max(\beta_2, \beta_4)]$, with λ_1 not occurring in p_1, p_2, q_1 or q_2. Hence, the angular difference between both intervals is independent of λ_1, i.e.

$$ad^*([\theta_2 - \alpha_2 - (1 - \lambda_1)\max(\beta_2, \beta_4), \theta_2 + \alpha_2 + (1 - \lambda_1)\max(\beta_2, \beta_4)],$$
$$[\theta_4 - \alpha_4 - (\lambda_1 - \lambda)\max(\beta_2, \beta_4), \theta_4 + \alpha_4 + (\lambda_1 - \lambda)\max(\beta_2, \beta_4)])$$
$$= ad^*([\theta_2 - \alpha_2, \theta_2 + \alpha_2], [\theta_4 - \alpha_4 - (1 - \lambda)\max(\beta_2, \beta_4),$$
$$\theta_4 + \alpha_4 + (1 - \lambda)\max(\beta_2, \beta_4)])$$

For each λ in $[0, 1]$, we use γ_λ as a shorthand for the latter expression. We can conclude that the angle between the lines ab and bc is at least γ_λ. Note that γ_λ is equal to

$$\max(0, ad^*([\theta_2 - \alpha_2, \theta_2 + \alpha_2], [\theta_4 - \alpha_4, \theta_4 + \alpha_4]) - (1 - \lambda)\max(\beta_2, \beta_4))$$

From $N_{(\alpha_1, \beta_1)}(a, b) \geq \lambda_1$ and $N_{(\alpha_3, \beta_3)}(b, c) \geq \lambda + 1 - \lambda_1$ we find for $\beta_1 \neq 0$ and $\beta_2 \neq 0$

$$\frac{\alpha_1 + \beta_1 - d(a, b)}{\beta_1} \geq \lambda_1$$

$$\frac{\alpha_3 + \beta_3 - d(b, c)}{\beta_3} \geq \lambda + 1 - \lambda_1$$

Furthermore, if $\beta_1 = 0$ we find $d(a, b) \leq \alpha_1$ and if $\beta_3 = 0$ we find $d(b, c) \leq \alpha_3$. In other words, we always have

$$d(a, b) \leq \alpha_1 + (1 - \lambda_1)\beta_1 \qquad (7.15)$$

$$d(b, c) \leq \alpha_3 + (\lambda_1 - \lambda)\beta_3 \qquad (7.16)$$

From the law of cosines, we know that (see Figure 7.12 for an illustration)

$$d(a, c)^2 = d(a, b)^2 + d(b, c)^2 - 2d(a, b)d(b, c)\cos(\pi - ad(\theta_{ab}, \theta_{bc}))$$

Since $ad(\theta_{ab}, \theta_{bc}) \geq \gamma_\lambda$, $\gamma_\lambda \in [0, \pi]$ and $ad(\theta_{ab}, \theta_{bc}) \in [0, \pi]$, we have $\cos(\pi - ad(\theta_{ab}, \theta_{bc})) \geq \cos(\pi - \gamma_\lambda)$, and thus

$$d(a, c)^2 \leq d(a, b)^2 + d(b, c)^2 - 2d(a, b)d(b, c)\cos(\pi - \gamma_\lambda) \qquad (7.17)$$

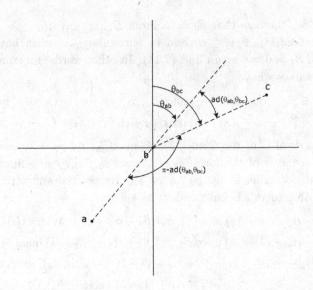

Fig. 7.12 Using the cosine law, we derive the distance between a and c from $d(a,b)$, $d(b,c)$ and the angle between the lines ab and bc.

Taking into account the constraints (7.15) and (7.16), we know from Lemma 7.3 that the right–hand side of (7.17) is maximized for either $d(a,b) = \alpha_1 + (1 - \lambda_1)\beta_1$ and $d(b,c) = \alpha_3 + (\lambda_1 - \lambda)\beta_3$, for $d(a,b) = \alpha_1 + (1 - \lambda_1)\beta_1$ and $d(b,c) = 0$, or for $d(a,b) = 0$ and $d(b,c) = \alpha_3 + (\lambda_1 - \lambda)\beta_3$. Therefore, we have that

$$\begin{aligned}
d(a,c)^2 &\leq \max((\alpha_1 + (1 - \lambda_1)\beta_1)^2, (\alpha_3 + (\lambda_1 - \lambda)\beta_3)^2, \\
&\quad (\alpha_1 + (1 - \lambda_1)\beta_1)^2 + (\alpha_3 + (\lambda_1 - \lambda)\beta_3)^2 \\
&\quad - 2(\alpha_1 + (1 - \lambda_1)\beta_1)(\alpha_3 + (\lambda_1 - \lambda)\beta_3)\cos(\pi - \gamma_\lambda)) \\
&\leq \max((\alpha_1 + (1 - \lambda)\beta_1)^2, (\alpha_3 + (1 - \lambda)\beta_3)^2, \\
&\quad (\alpha_1 + (1 - \lambda_1)\beta_1)^2 + (\alpha_3 + (\lambda_1 - \lambda)\beta_3)^2 \\
&\quad - 2(\alpha_1 + (1 - \lambda_1)\beta_1)(\alpha_3 + (\lambda_1 - \lambda)\beta_3)\cos(\pi - \gamma_\lambda))
\end{aligned}$$

To find an upper bound of $d(a,c)$ which is independent of the actual value of λ_1, we calculate which λ_1 in $[\lambda, 1]$ maximizes $f(\lambda_1)$, where

$$\begin{aligned}
f(\lambda_1) &= (\alpha_1 + (1 - \lambda_1)\beta_1)^2 + (\alpha_3 + (\lambda_1 - \lambda)\beta_3)^2 \\
&\quad - 2(\alpha_1 + (1 - \lambda_1)\beta_1)(\alpha_3 + (\lambda_1 - \lambda)\beta_3)\cos(\pi - \gamma_\lambda)
\end{aligned}$$

The first– and second–order derivative of f are given by

$$f'(\lambda_1) = 2(\beta_1^2 + \beta_3^2 + 2\beta_1\beta_3 \cos(\pi - \gamma_\lambda))\lambda_1$$
$$- 2(\alpha_1 + \beta_1)(\beta_1 + \beta_3 \cos(\pi - \gamma_\lambda))$$
$$+ 2(\alpha_3 - \lambda\beta_3)(\beta_3 + \beta_1 \cos(\pi - \gamma_\lambda))$$
$$f''(\lambda_1) = 2(\beta_1^2 + \beta_3^2 + 2\beta_1\beta_3 \cos(\pi - \gamma_\lambda))$$

Note that $f''(\lambda_1) \geq 0$. Indeed, we find from $\cos(\pi - \gamma_\lambda) \geq -1$

$$\beta_1^2 + \beta_2^2 + 2\beta_1\beta_3 \cos(\pi - \gamma_\lambda) \geq \beta_1^2 + \beta_3^2 - 2\beta_1\beta_3 = (\beta_1 - \beta_3)^2 \geq 0$$

As a consequence, f is a convex function whose maximum in $[\lambda, 1]$ is attained in either λ or 1. Hence, we obtain

$$f(\lambda_1) \leq \max(\alpha_1^2 + (\alpha_3 + (1-\lambda)\beta_3)^2 - 2\alpha_1(\alpha_3 + (1-\lambda)\beta_3) \cos(\pi - \gamma_\lambda),$$
$$(\alpha_1 + (1-\lambda)\beta_1)^2 + \alpha_3^2 - 2(\alpha_1 + (1-\lambda)\beta_1)\alpha_3 \cos(\pi - \gamma_\lambda))$$

We furthermore find using Lemma 7.4

$\cos(\pi - \gamma_\lambda)$

$= \max(-1, \cos(\pi - \gamma_\lambda))$

$\geq \max(-1, \cos u_0 - (\pi - \gamma_\lambda - u_0) \sin u_0)$

$= \max(-1, \gamma_\lambda \sin u_0 + \cos u_0 - (\pi - u_0) \sin u_0)$

$= \max(-1, \max(0, ad^*([\theta_2 - \alpha_2, \theta_2 + \alpha_2], [\theta_4 - \alpha_4, \theta_4 + \alpha_4])$
$\qquad\qquad - (1 - \lambda) \max(\beta_2, \beta_4)) \sin u_0 + \cos u_0 - (\pi - u_0) \sin u_0)$

$= \max(-1, \cos u_0 - (\pi - u_0) \sin u_0, \lambda \max(\beta_2, \beta_4) \sin u_0$
$\qquad + (ad^*([\theta_2 - \alpha_2, \theta_2 + \alpha_2], [\theta_4 - \alpha_4, \theta_4 + \alpha_4])$
$\qquad - \max(\beta_2, \beta_4) - \pi + u_0) \sin u_0 + \cos u_0)$

$= \max(-1, -1.276433706, \lambda \max(\beta_2, \beta_4) \sin u_0$
$\qquad + (ad^*([\theta_2 - \alpha_2, \theta_2 + \alpha_2], [\theta_4 - \alpha_4, \theta_4 + \alpha_4])$
$\qquad - \max(\beta_2, \beta_4) - \pi + u_0) \sin u_0 + \cos u_0)$

$= \max(-1, \lambda \max(\beta_2, \beta_4) \sin u_0$
$\qquad + (ad^*([\theta_2 - \alpha_2, \theta_2 + \alpha_2], [\theta_4 - \alpha_4, \theta_4 + \alpha_4])$
$\qquad - \max(\beta_2, \beta_4) - \pi + u_0) \sin u_0 + \cos u_0)$

$= \max(-1, t_0 + t_1\lambda)$

We find

$$\alpha_1^2 + (\alpha_3 + (1-\lambda)\beta_3)^2 - 2\alpha_1(\alpha_3 + (1-\lambda)\beta_3) \cos(\pi - \gamma_\lambda)$$
$$\leq \alpha_1^2 + (\alpha_3 + (1-\lambda)\beta_3)^2 - 2\alpha_1(\alpha_3 + (1-\lambda)\beta_3) \max(-1, t_0 + t_1\lambda)$$
$$= \min(\alpha_1^2 + (\alpha_3 + (1-\lambda)\beta_3)^2 + 2\alpha_1(\alpha_3 + (1-\lambda)\beta_3),$$
$$\alpha_1^2 + (\alpha_3 + (1-\lambda)\beta_3)^2 - 2\alpha_1(\alpha_3 + (1-\lambda)\beta_3)(t_0 + t_1\lambda))$$

It holds that

$$\alpha_1^2 + (\alpha_3 + (1-\lambda)\beta_3)^2 + 2\alpha_1(\alpha_3 + (1-\lambda)\beta_3) = (\alpha_1 + \alpha_3 + (1-\lambda)\beta_3)^2$$

Moreover, it can be verified that

$$\alpha_1^2 + (\alpha_3 + (1-\lambda)\beta_3)^2 - 2\alpha_1(\alpha_3 + (1-\lambda)\beta_3)(t_0 + t_1\lambda)$$
$$= (\alpha + (1-\lambda)\beta)^2 + \beta_3\lambda(\lambda-1)(\beta_3 + 2\alpha_1 t_1)$$
$$\leq (\alpha + (1-\lambda)\beta)^2$$

where α and β are defined by (7.10) and (7.11). The last step follows from the fact that $\beta_3\lambda(\lambda-1)(\beta_3 + 2\alpha_1 t_1) \leq 0$ since $\lambda - 1 \leq 0$, $\alpha_1, \beta_3 \geq 0$ and $t_1 = 0.7246113541 \cdot \max(\beta_2, \beta_4) \geq 0$.

Similarly, we find that

$$(\alpha_1 + (1-\lambda)\beta_1)^2 + \alpha_3^2 - 2(\alpha_1 + (1-\lambda)\beta_1)\alpha_3 \cos(\pi - \gamma_\lambda)$$
$$\leq \min((\alpha_1 + \alpha_3 + (1-\lambda)\beta_1)^2, (\alpha + (1-\lambda)\beta')^2)$$

Thus we have shown that

$$d(a,c) \leq \max(\alpha_1 + (1-\lambda)\beta_1, \alpha_3 + (1-\lambda)\beta_3, \min(\alpha_1 + \alpha_3 + (1-\lambda)\beta_3,$$
$$\alpha + (1-\lambda)\beta), \min(\alpha_1 + \alpha_3 + (1-\lambda)\beta_1, \alpha + (1-\lambda)\beta'))$$

In other words

$$d(a,c) \leq \alpha_1 + (1-\lambda)\beta_1 \vee d(a,c) \leq \alpha_3 + (1-\lambda)\beta_3$$
$$\vee \, (d(a,c) \leq \alpha_1 + \alpha_3 + (1-\lambda)\beta_3 \wedge d(a,c) \leq \alpha + (1-\lambda)\beta)$$
$$\vee \, (d(a,c) \leq \alpha_1 + \alpha_3 + (1-\lambda)\beta_1 \wedge d(a,c) \leq \alpha + (1-\lambda)\beta')$$

which is equivalent to

$$N_{(\alpha_1,\beta_1)}(a,c) \geq \lambda \vee N_{(\alpha_3,\beta_3)}(a,c) \geq \lambda$$
$$\vee \, (N_{(\alpha_1+\alpha_3,\beta_3)}(a,c) \geq \lambda \wedge N_{(\alpha,\beta)}(a,c) \geq \lambda)$$
$$\vee \, (N_{(\alpha_1+\alpha_3,\beta_1)}(a,c) \geq \lambda \wedge N_{(\alpha,\beta')}(a,c) \geq \lambda)$$

or

$$(N_{(\alpha_1,\beta_1)} \cup N_{(\alpha_3,\beta_3)} \cup (N_{(\alpha_1+\alpha_3,\beta_3)} \cap N_{(\alpha,\beta)})$$
$$\cup \, (N_{(\alpha_1+\alpha_3,\beta_1)} \cap N_{(\alpha,\beta')}))(a,c) \geq \lambda \qquad \square$$

The sup–T composition of a fuzzy relation $(N_{(\alpha_1,\beta_1)} \cap D_{(\theta_2,\alpha_2,\beta_2)})$ and a fuzzy relation $(N_{(\alpha_3,\beta_3)} \cap D_{(\theta_4,\alpha_4,\beta_4)})$ is a fuzzy relation R in $\mathbb{R}^2 \times \mathbb{R}^2$. The membership value of this fuzzy relation R in (a,c) depends on the distance of a and c and the cardinal direction of c w.r.t. a. Hence R can be seen as a fuzzy constraint on the possible distances and relative cardinal directions of two points. Let R_d be the induced fuzzy distance constraint, i.e.

$$R_d(a,c) = \sup_{p \in \mathbb{R}^2} \sup_{\substack{q \in \mathbb{R}^2 \\ d(p,q)=d(a,c)}} R(p,q)$$

for all a and c in $\mathbb{R}^2$. Proposition 7.2 allows us to find an upper bound for this distance constraint R_d. In Figure 7.13 the actual value of $R_d(a,c)$, in function of $d(a,c)$, is compared with the value of this upper bound, showing that the latter is a very close approximation of the former. Note that the approximation provided by Proposition 7.2 can be evaluated in constant time. On the other hand, calculating the exact value of $R_d(a,c)$ may be very difficult (if not impossible) and time–consuming.

In Proposition 7.3 below, we establish an upper bound for the induced fuzzy direction constraint. However, this upper bound does not depend on nearness information. As, moreover, for all a and c in $\mathbb{R}^2$, it holds that

$$\left(N_{(\alpha_1,\beta_1)} \cap D_{(\theta_2,\alpha_2,\beta_2)}\right) \circ_{T_W} \left(N_{(\alpha_3,\beta_3)} \cap D_{(\theta_4,\alpha_4,\beta_4)}\right)(a,c)$$
$$\leq D_{(\theta_2,\alpha_2,\beta_2)} \circ_{T_W} D_{(\theta_4,\alpha_4,\beta_4)}(a,c)$$

we only need to provide an upper bound for the latter expression. Again, we first show a number of technical lemmas.

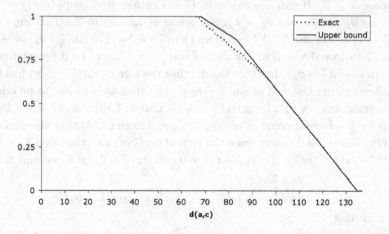

Fig. 7.13   Fuzzy distance constraint induced by the sup–T composition of $N_{(60,15)} \cap D_{(\pi,\frac{\pi}{16},\pi)}$ and $N_{(15,60)} \cap D_{(\frac{\pi}{2},\frac{\pi}{16},\frac{\pi}{16})}$, as well as the upper bound resulting from Proposition 7.2.

Lemma 7.5. *Let $a = (a_x, a_y)$ be in $\mathbb{R}^2$, and let θ_1 and θ_2 be in $\mathbb{R}$. Furthermore, let L be the half–line containing the points $d^u = (d_x^u, d_y^u)$ satisfying*

$$d_x^u = a_x + \cos(\frac{\pi}{2} - \theta_1) + u \cdot \cos(\frac{\pi}{2} - \theta_2)$$

$$d_y^u = a_y + \sin(\frac{\pi}{2} - \theta_1) + u \cdot \sin(\frac{\pi}{2} - \theta_2)$$

for some $u \geq 0$. It holds that $a \in L$ iff $\theta_1 = \theta_2 + k\pi$ for some odd integer k.

Proof.   First, assume $\theta_1 = \theta_2 + k\pi$ for some odd integer k. It holds that

$$
\begin{aligned}
d_x^1 &= a_x + \cos(\frac{\pi}{2} - \theta_1) + \cos(\frac{\pi}{2} - \theta_2) \\
&= a_x + \cos(\frac{\pi}{2} - \theta_2 - k\pi) + \cos(\frac{\pi}{2} - \theta_2) \\
&= a_x + \cos(\frac{\pi}{2} - \theta_2 - \pi) + \cos(\frac{\pi}{2} - \theta_2) \\
&= a_x - \cos(\frac{\pi}{2} - \theta_2) + \cos(\frac{\pi}{2} - \theta_2) \\
&= a_x
\end{aligned}
$$

and similarly, we have $d_y^1 = a_y$. Conversely, assume $a \in L$. This is the case exactly when

$$\cos(\frac{\pi}{2} - \theta_1) + u \cdot \cos(\frac{\pi}{2} - \theta_2) = 0 \tag{7.18}$$

$$\sin(\frac{\pi}{2} - \theta_1) + u \cdot \sin(\frac{\pi}{2} - \theta_2) = 0 \tag{7.19}$$

for some $u \geq 0$. If $\cos(\frac{\pi}{2} - \theta_2) = 0$, (7.18) entails that $\cos(\frac{\pi}{2} - \theta_1) = 0$, implying $\theta_1 = k_1\pi$ and $\theta_2 = k_2\pi$ for some k_1 and k_2 in $\mathbb{Z}$. This implies $\sin(\frac{\pi}{2} - \theta_1) = 1$ or $\sin(\frac{\pi}{2} - \theta_1) = -1$, and $\sin(\frac{\pi}{2} - \theta_2) = 1$ or $\sin(\frac{\pi}{2} - \theta_2) = -1$. From (7.19), we derive that the sign of $\sin(\frac{\pi}{2} - \theta_1)$ has to be different from the sign of $\sin(\frac{\pi}{2} - \theta_2)$. In other words, that the sign of $\sin(\frac{\pi}{2} - k_1\pi)$ has to be different from the sign of $\sin(\frac{\pi}{2} - k_2\pi)$, i.e., that $k_1 - k_2$ has to be odd. In the same way, we find from $\sin(\frac{\pi}{2} - \theta_2) = 0$ and (7.19) that $\theta_1 = \frac{\pi}{2} - k_1\pi$ and $\theta_2 = \frac{\pi}{2} - k_2\pi$ for some k_1 and k_2 in $\mathbb{Z}$, and from (7.18) that the sign of $\cos(k_1\pi)$ has to be different from the sign of $\cos(k_2\pi)$ and thus that $k_1 - k_2$ has to be odd. Finally, if $\cos(\frac{\pi}{2} - \theta_2) \neq 0$ and $\sin(\frac{\pi}{2} - \theta_2) \neq 0$, we find that

$$u = -\frac{\cos(\frac{\pi}{2} - \theta_1)}{\cos(\frac{\pi}{2} - \theta_2)} \qquad\qquad u = -\frac{\sin(\frac{\pi}{2} - \theta_1)}{\sin(\frac{\pi}{2} - \theta_2)}$$

which implies

$$\cos(\frac{\pi}{2} - \theta_1)\sin(\frac{\pi}{2} - \theta_2) - \sin(\frac{\pi}{2} - \theta_1)\cos(\frac{\pi}{2} - \theta_2) = 0$$

$$\Leftrightarrow \sin(\theta_1 - \theta_2) = 0$$

which is satisfied exactly when $\theta_1 = \theta_2 + k\pi$ for some k in $\mathbb{Z}$. Again (7.19) implies that the sign of $\sin(\frac{\pi}{2} - \theta_1)$ is opposite to the sign of $\sin(\frac{\pi}{2} - \theta_2)$, which implies that k has to be odd. □

Lemma 7.6. *Let $a = (a_x, a_y)$ be in $\mathbb{R}^2$, and let θ_1 and θ_2 be in $[0, 2\pi[$. Furthermore, let L be the half-line containing the points $d^u = (d_x^u, d_y^u)$ satisfying*

$$d_x^u = a_x + \cos(\frac{\pi}{2} - \theta_1) + u \cdot \cos(\frac{\pi}{2} - \theta_2)$$
$$d_y^u = a_y + \sin(\frac{\pi}{2} - \theta_1) + u \cdot \sin(\frac{\pi}{2} - \theta_2)$$

for some $u \geq 0$. If $a_x = p_x$ and $a_y < p_y$ for some p on L then one of the following holds: (1) $\theta_2 - \theta_1 \in]-2\pi, -\pi[\cup]\pi, 2\pi[$, (2) $\theta_1 = \theta_2 = 0$, (3) $\theta_1 = 0$ and $\theta_2 = \pi$, or (4) $\theta_1 = \pi$ and $\theta_2 = 0$.

Proof. The relationship between L, θ_1 and θ_2 is illustrated in Figure 7.14. Note that Figure 7.14(b) satisfies the condition of the lemma because there is a point $p = (p_x, p_y)$ on L with $a_x = p_x$ and $a_y < p_y$. Figure 7.14(a) on the other hand does not satisfy the condition of the lemma because for the only p on L with $a_x = p_x$, it holds that $a_y > p_y$.

Let $\theta_1 \leq \theta_2$ and assume there is some point $p = (p_x, p_y)$ on L that satisfies $a_x = p_x$ and $a_y < p_y$. This is the case when

$$\cos(\frac{\pi}{2} - \theta_1) + u \cdot \cos(\frac{\pi}{2} - \theta_2) = 0 \qquad (7.20)$$
$$\sin(\frac{\pi}{2} - \theta_1) + u \cdot \sin(\frac{\pi}{2} - \theta_2) > 0 \qquad (7.21)$$

From (7.20), we know that the sign of $\cos(\frac{\pi}{2} - \theta_1)$ is opposite to the sign of $\cos(\frac{\pi}{2} - \theta_2)$. From θ_1 and θ_2 in $[0, 2\pi[$ and $\theta_1 \leq \theta_2$, this can only be the case when $\cos(\frac{\pi}{2} - \theta_1) \geq 0$ and $\cos(\frac{\pi}{2} - \theta_2) \leq 0$.

If $\cos(\frac{\pi}{2} - \theta_2) = 0$, (7.20) implies $\cos(\frac{\pi}{2} - \theta_1) = 0$ and $\theta_1 = k_1\pi$, $\theta_2 = k_2\pi$ for some k_1 and k_2 in $\mathbb{Z}$. From (7.21), we know that either $\sin(\frac{\pi}{2} - k_1\pi) = 1$ or $\sin(\frac{\pi}{2} - k_2\pi) = 1$, in other words, that at least one of k_1, k_2 is even. Considering that $\theta_1 \leq \theta_2$ and $\theta_1, \theta_2 \in [0, 2\pi[$, we have that $\theta_1 = 0$, and $\theta_2 = 0$ or $\theta_2 = \pi$.

If $\cos(\frac{\pi}{2} - \theta_2) < 0$, we find from (7.20) and (7.21)

$$\sin(\frac{\pi}{2} - \theta_1) - \frac{\cos(\frac{\pi}{2} - \theta_1)}{\cos(\frac{\pi}{2} - \theta_2)} \cdot \sin(\frac{\pi}{2} - \theta_2) > 0$$

and by $\cos(\frac{\pi}{2} - \theta_2) < 0$

$$\sin(\frac{\pi}{2} - \theta_1)\cos(\frac{\pi}{2} - \theta_2) - \cos(\frac{\pi}{2} - \theta_1)\sin(\frac{\pi}{2} - \theta_2) < 0$$

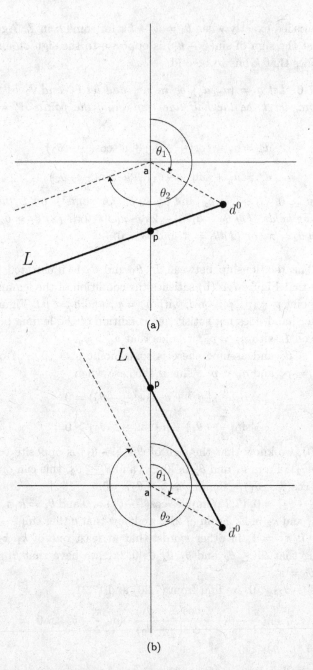

(a)

(b)

Fig. 7.14   Relationship between the half–line L and the cardinal directions θ_1 and θ_2 when (a) $\theta_2 - \theta_1 \in \,]0, \pi[$ and (b) $\theta_2 - \theta_1 \in \,]\pi, 2\pi[$.

i.e.,

$$\sin(\theta_2 - \theta_1) < 0$$

Since $\theta_1 \leq \theta_2$ and $\theta_1, \theta_2 \in [0, 2\pi[$, the latter expression entails $\theta_2 - \theta_1 \in]\pi, 2\pi[$.

Conversely, if $\theta_1 > \theta_2$, then the sign of $\cos(\frac{\pi}{2} - \theta_1)$ can only be opposite to the sign of $\cos(\frac{\pi}{2} - \theta_2)$ if $\cos(\frac{\pi}{2} - \theta_1) \leq 0$ and $\cos(\frac{\pi}{2} - \theta_2) \geq 0$. If $\cos(\frac{\pi}{2} - \theta_2) = 0$, we again find that $\sin(\frac{\pi}{2} - k_1\pi) = 1$ or $\sin(\frac{\pi}{2} - k_2\pi) = 1$ for some $k_1, k_2 \in \mathbb{Z}$, and that at least one of k_1, k_2 is even. Considering $\theta_1 > \theta_2$ and $\theta_1, \theta_2 \in [0, 2\pi[$, this is only possible if $\theta_2 = 0$ and $\theta_1 = \pi$.

If $\cos(\frac{\pi}{2} - \theta_2) > 0$, we find from (7.20) and (7.21)

$$\sin(\theta_2 - \theta_1) > 0$$

which entails $\theta_2 - \theta_1 \in]-2\pi, -\pi[$, considering $\theta_1 > \theta_2$ and $\theta_1, \theta_2 \in [0, 2\pi[$.

Next, we provide a characterization of the set of cardinal directions between a and all points of L. In Figure 7.14(a), for example, this set is $[\theta_1, \theta_2[$, while in Figure 7.14(b) this set is $]\theta_2, 0[\cup [0, \theta_1]$. We generalize this in the following lemma.

Lemma 7.7. *Let* $a = (a_x, a_y)$ *be a point in* $\mathbb{R}^2$, *and let* θ_1 *and* θ_2 *be in* $[0, 2\pi[$. *Furthermore, let* L *be the half–line containing the points* $d^u = (d_x^u, d_y^u)$ *satisfying*

$$d_x^u = a_x + \cos(\frac{\pi}{2} - \theta_1) + u \cdot \cos(\frac{\pi}{2} - \theta_2)$$
$$d_y^u = a_y + \sin(\frac{\pi}{2} - \theta_1) + u \cdot \sin(\frac{\pi}{2} - \theta_2)$$

for some $u \geq 0$. *Let* D *be the set of possible cardinal directions of the points on* L *w.r.t.* a:

$$A = \{\theta_{ad} | d \in L\} \tag{7.22}$$

It holds that

$$A = \begin{cases} [\theta_1, \theta_2[& \text{if } \theta_2 - \theta_1 \in]0, \pi[\\ ]\theta_2, \theta_1] & \text{if } \theta_2 - \theta_1 \in]-\pi, 0[\\ [\theta_1, 2\pi[\cup [0, \theta_2[& \text{if } \theta_2 - \theta_1 \in]-2\pi, -\pi[\\ ]\theta_2, 2\pi[\cup [0, \theta_1] & \text{if } \theta_2 - \theta_1 \in]\pi, 2\pi[\\ \{\theta_1\} & \text{if } \theta_2 - \theta_1 = 0 \\ \{\theta_1, \theta_2\} & \text{if } \theta_2 - \theta_1 \in \{-\pi, \pi\} \end{cases}$$

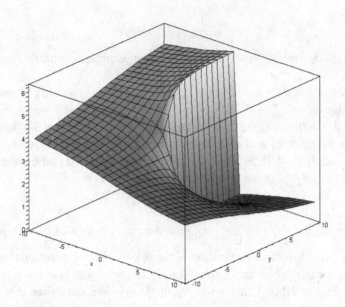

Fig. 7.15   Cardinal direction of a point (x, y) w.r.t. the point $(0, 0)$.

Proof.   Assume $\theta_2 - \theta_1 \in\ ]0, \pi[$. Let f be the function that maps a pair of points (p, q) to their cardinal direction θ_{pq} in $[0, 2\pi[$, f being undefined for $p = q$. Figure 7.15 depicts the value of $f(p, q)$, where $p = (0, 0)$ and $q = (x, y)$. From Lemma 7.1, we immediately obtain $f(a, d^0) = \theta_1$. Next, we show that $\lim_{u \to +\infty} f(a, d^u) = \theta_2$. Note that $\theta_2 - \theta_1 \in\ ]0, \pi[$ entails $a \neq d^u$ for every $u \geq 0$ by Lemma 7.5. Hence, using (7.2), $f(a, d^u)$ is given by

$$\begin{cases} \frac{\pi}{2} - \arctan(\frac{\sin(\frac{\pi}{2} - \theta_1) + u\sin(\frac{\pi}{2} - \theta_2)}{\cos(\frac{\pi}{2} - \theta_1) + u\cos(\frac{\pi}{2} - \theta_2)}) & \text{if } \cos(\frac{\pi}{2} - \theta_1) + u\cos(\frac{\pi}{2} - \theta_2) > 0 \\ \frac{3\pi}{2} - \arctan(\frac{\sin(\frac{\pi}{2} - \theta_1) + u\sin(\frac{\pi}{2} - \theta_2)}{\cos(\frac{\pi}{2} - \theta_1) + u\cos(\frac{\pi}{2} - \theta_2)}) & \text{if } \cos(\frac{\pi}{2} - \theta_1) + u\cos(\frac{\pi}{2} - \theta_2) < 0 \\ 0 & \text{if } \cos(\frac{\pi}{2} - \theta_1) + u\cos(\frac{\pi}{2} - \theta_2) = 0 \\ & \text{and } \sin(\frac{\pi}{2} - \theta_1) + u\sin(\frac{\pi}{2} - \theta_2) > 0 \\ \pi & \text{otherwise} \end{cases}$$

(1) First, consider the case where $\cos(\frac{\pi}{2} - \theta_2) \neq 0$ and $\sin(\frac{\pi}{2} - \theta_2) \neq 0$. For sufficiently large u, it then holds that $\cos(\frac{\pi}{2} - \theta_1) + u \cdot \cos(\frac{\pi}{2} - \theta_2) \neq 0$, hence, to determine $\lim_{u \to +\infty} f(a, d^u)$, we are only dealing with the first or the second case in the definition of $f(a, d^u)$. More in particular, for

large u, the contribution of $\cos(\frac{\pi}{2}-\theta_1)$ can be neglected: if $\cos(\frac{\pi}{2}-\theta_2) > 0$ then for $u \to +\infty$, $f(a, d^u)$ behaves as in the first part of its definition, while if $\cos(\frac{\pi}{2}-\theta_2) < 0$, only the second part comes into play. In either case, we need to determine

$$\lim_{u \to +\infty} \frac{\sin(\frac{\pi}{2} - \theta_1) + u \cdot \sin(\frac{\pi}{2} - \theta_2)}{\cos(\frac{\pi}{2} - \theta_1) + u \cdot \cos(\frac{\pi}{2} - \theta_2)} = \frac{\sin(\frac{\pi}{2} - \theta_2)}{\cos(\frac{\pi}{2} - \theta_2)}$$

This entails that $\lim_{u \to +\infty} f(a, d^u) = f(a, p_2)$ where $p_2 = (a_x + \cos(\frac{\pi}{2} - \theta_2), a_y + \sin(\frac{\pi}{2} - \theta_2))$. By Lemma 7.1, this leads to $\lim_{u \to +\infty} f(a, d^u) = \theta_2$.

(2) Next, if $\cos(\frac{\pi}{2} - \theta_2) = 0$, we have $\theta_2 = 0$ or $\theta_2 = \pi$. The case where $\theta_2 = 0$ is not possible, however, as $\theta_2 - \theta_1 \in\,]0, \pi[$ and $\theta_1 \in [0, 2\pi[$. From $\theta_2 = \pi$ we derive $\sin(\frac{\pi}{2} - \theta_2) < 0$, and $\theta_1 \in\,]0, \pi[$, which in turn implies $\cos(\frac{\pi}{2} - \theta_1) > 0$. We obtain

$$\lim_{u \to +\infty} \frac{\sin(\frac{\pi}{2} - \theta_1) + u \cdot \sin(\frac{\pi}{2} - \theta_2)}{\cos(\frac{\pi}{2} - \theta_1) + u \cdot \cos(\frac{\pi}{2} - \theta_2)}$$

$$= \lim_{u \to +\infty} \frac{\sin(\frac{\pi}{2} - \theta_1) + u \cdot \sin(\frac{\pi}{2} - \theta_2)}{\cos(\frac{\pi}{2} - \theta_1)}$$

$$= -\infty$$

Using the fact that $\cos(\frac{\pi}{2} - \theta_1) + u \cdot \cos(\frac{\pi}{2} - \theta_2) = \cos(\frac{\pi}{2} - \theta_1) > 0$, we find by the definition of f

$$\lim_{u \to +\infty} f(a, d^u) = \frac{\pi}{2} - \lim_{x \to -\infty} \arctan(x) = \pi$$

Hence, again we have that $\lim_{u \to +\infty} f(a, d^u) = \theta_2$.

(3) Finally, if $\sin(\frac{\pi}{2} - \theta_2) = 0$, we have $\theta_2 = \frac{\pi}{2}$ or $\theta_2 = \frac{3\pi}{2}$. For example, if $\theta_2 = \frac{\pi}{2}$ (the case $\theta_2 = \frac{3\pi}{2}$ is entirely analogous), it holds that $\cos(\frac{\pi}{2} - \theta_2) > 0$. For sufficiently large u, we therefore have that $\cos(\frac{\pi}{2} - \theta_1) + u \cdot \cos(\frac{\pi}{2} - \theta_2) > 0$, hence

$$\lim_{u \to +\infty} \frac{\sin(\frac{\pi}{2} - \theta_1) + u \cdot \sin(\frac{\pi}{2} - \theta_2)}{\cos(\frac{\pi}{2} - \theta_1) + u \cdot \cos(\frac{\pi}{2} - \theta_2)}$$

$$= \lim_{u \to +\infty} \frac{\sin(\frac{\pi}{2} - \theta_1)}{\cos(\frac{\pi}{2} - \theta_1) + u \cdot \cos(\frac{\pi}{2} - \theta_2)}$$

$$= 0$$

By definition of f, we find

$$\lim_{u \to +\infty} f(a, d^u) = \frac{\pi}{2} - \lim_{x \to 0} \arctan x = \frac{\pi}{2}$$

Hence, in each case, we have that $\lim_{u\to+\infty} f(a, d^u) = \theta_2$. Furthermore, it holds that f is continuous in (p, q) unless $p = q$, or $p_x = q_x$ and $p_y < q_y$. Since $\theta_2 - \theta_1 \in]0, \pi[$, we know from Lemma 7.6 that no point p on L satisfies $a_x = p_x$ and $a_y < p_y$, while Lemma 7.5 implies that no point p on L satisfies $a = p$. Hence, for every $u \geq 0$, f is continuous in (a, d^u). From the intermediate value theorem, we can therefore infer that for every θ in $[\theta_1, \theta_2[$, there is a $u \geq 0$ such that $f(a, d^u) = \theta$. Moreover, since $f(a, d^u)$ is a strictly monotonically increasing or decreasing function of u, it holds that for $\theta \notin [\theta_1, \theta_2[$, there can be no $u \geq 0$ such that $f(a, d^u) = \theta$, i.e., $A = [\theta_1, \theta_2[$.

In entirely the same fashion, it is possible to show that $A =]\theta_2, \theta_1]$ if $\theta_2 - \theta_1 \in]-\pi, 0[$. To show that $A = [\theta_1, 2\pi[\cup [0, \theta_2[$ if $\theta_2 - \theta_1 \in]-2\pi, -\pi[$, a proof can be given which is analogous to the proof of the first case using an alternative definition of cardinal direction by which south is cardinal direction 0, west $\frac{\pi}{2}$, etc. The alternative cardinal directions θ'_1 and θ'_2 corresponding to θ_1 and θ_2 are then given by $\theta'_1 = \theta_1 - \pi$ and $\theta'_2 = \theta_2 + \pi$, where we used the fact that $\theta_1 \in [\pi, 2\pi[$ and $\theta_2 \in [0, \pi[$ when $\theta_2 - \theta_1 \in]-2\pi, -\pi[$. Hence, it holds that $\theta'_2 - \theta'_1 \in]0, \pi[$. Similarly, the fourth case can be shown analogously to the second case. Finally, the result for $\theta_2 - \theta_1 \in \{-\pi, 0, \pi\}$ is trivial. $\qquad\square$

Intuitively, Lemma 7.7 states that when the positive angle between θ_1 and θ_2 is strictly less than π, all cardinal directions between θ_1 and θ_2 (clockwise) are contained in A, whereas when the positive angle between θ_1 and θ_2 is strictly greater than π, the cardinal directions between θ_2 and θ_1 (clockwise) are contained in A. To formalise this intuitive interpretation, we introduce the notion of positive angular difference *pad* for θ_1 and θ_2 in $\mathbb{R}$ as

$$pad(\theta_1, \theta_2) = norm(\theta_2 - \theta_1)$$

Next, let *clockwise* be defined for θ_1 and θ_2 in $\mathbb{R}$ as

$clockwise(\theta_1, \theta_2)$

$$= \begin{cases} [norm(\theta_1), norm(\theta_2)] & \text{if } norm(\theta_1) \leq norm(\theta_2) \\ [norm(\theta_1), 2\pi[\cup [0, norm(\theta_2)] & \text{otherwise} \end{cases}$$

Lemma 7.7 can then be rephrased as

$$A = \begin{cases} clockwise(\theta_1, \theta_2) \setminus \{\theta_2\} & \text{if } pad(\theta_1, \theta_2) < \pi \\ clockwise(\theta_2, \theta_1) \setminus \{\theta_2\} & \text{if } pad(\theta_1, \theta_2) > \pi \\ \{\theta_1, \theta_2\} & \text{if } pad(\theta_1, \theta_2) = \pi \end{cases}$$

Lemma 7.8. *For $\theta_1, \theta_2 \in \mathbb{R}$ and $\theta \geq 0$ it holds that*

$$pad(\theta_1 + \theta, \theta_2) \geq pad(\theta_1, \theta_2) - \theta \qquad (7.23)$$

$$pad(\theta_1, \theta_2 - \theta) \geq pad(\theta_1, \theta_2) - \theta \qquad (7.24)$$

Proof. As an example, we show (7.23). Let k in $\mathbb{Z}$ be such that

$$norm(\theta_2 - \theta_1) = \theta_2 - \theta_1 + 2k\pi$$

If $\theta_2 - \theta_1 + 2k\pi - \theta \geq 0$, we have

$$pad(\theta_1 + \theta, \theta_2) = norm(\theta_2 - \theta_1 - \theta) = \theta_2 - \theta_1 + 2k\pi - \theta = pad(\theta_1, \theta_2) - \theta$$

On the other hand, if $\theta_2 - \theta_1 + 2k\pi - \theta < 0$, we have

$$pad(\theta_1, \theta_2) - \theta = \theta_2 - \theta_1 + 2k\pi - \theta < 0 \leq pad(\theta_1 + \theta, \theta_2) \qquad \square$$

The next proposition provides an upper approximation for the sup–T composition of two cardinal directions.

Proposition 7.3. *Let a and c be in $\mathbb{R}^2$, $\alpha_1, \alpha_2 \geq 0$, $\beta_1, \beta_2 \geq 0$ and θ_1 and θ_2 in $[0, 2\pi[$. It holds that*

$$\sup_{b \in \mathbb{R}^2} T_W(D_{(\theta_1, \alpha_1, \beta_1)}(a, b), D_{(\theta_2, \alpha_2, \beta_2)}(b, c)) \leq (R_1 \cup R_2 \cup R_3 \cup R_4)(a, c)$$

$$(7.25)$$

where

$$R_1(a, c) = D_{(\theta_1, \alpha_1, \beta_1)}(a, c)$$

$$R_2(a, c) = D_{(\theta_2, \alpha_2, \beta_2)}(a, c)$$

$$R_3(a, c) = \begin{cases} D_{(\theta', \alpha', 0)}(a, c) & \text{if } pad(\theta_1 + \alpha_1, \theta_2 - \alpha_2) < \pi + \max(\beta_1, \beta_2) \\ 0 & \text{otherwise} \end{cases}$$

$$R_4(a, c) = \begin{cases} D_{(\theta'', \alpha'', 0)}(a, c) & \text{if } pad(\theta_2 + \alpha_2, \theta_1 - \alpha_1) < \pi + \max(\beta_1, \beta_2) \\ 0 & \text{otherwise} \end{cases}$$

and

$$\alpha' = \frac{pad(\theta_1 + \alpha_1, \theta_2 - \alpha_2)}{2} \qquad \alpha'' = \frac{pad(\theta_2 + \alpha_2, \theta_1 - \alpha_1)}{2}$$

$$\theta' = norm(\theta_1 + \alpha_1 + \alpha') \qquad \theta'' = norm(\theta_2 + \alpha_2 + \alpha'')$$

Proof. To prove this result, we will show that for every λ in $]0, 1]$ and every b in $\mathbb{R}^2$, it holds that

$$T_W(D_{(\theta_1, \alpha_1, \beta_1)}(a, b), D_{(\theta_2, \alpha_2, \beta_2)}(b, c)) \geq \lambda \Rightarrow (R_1 \cup R_2 \cup R_3 \cup R_4)(a, c) \geq \lambda$$

$$(7.26)$$

which implies that for every λ in $]0,1]$

$$\sup_{b\in\mathbb{R}^2} T_W\big(D_{(\theta_1,\alpha_1,\beta_1)}(a,b), D_{(\theta_2,\alpha_2,\beta_2)}(b,c)\big) \geq \lambda$$

$$\Rightarrow (R_1 \cup R_2 \cup R_3 \cup R_4)(a,c) \geq \lambda$$

which, in turn, implies (7.25).

As in the proof of Proposition 7.2, we obtain for every b in $\mathbb{R}^2$

$$T_W\big(D_{(\theta_1,\alpha_1,\beta_1)}(a,b), D_{(\theta_2,\alpha_2,\beta_2)}(b,c)\big) \geq \lambda$$

$$\Leftrightarrow (\exists \lambda_1 \in [\lambda,1])\big(D_{(\theta_1,\alpha_1,\beta_1)}(a,b) \geq \lambda_1 \wedge D_{(\theta_2,\alpha_2,\beta_2)}(b,c) \geq \lambda+1-\lambda_1\big)$$

Let λ_1 be in $[\lambda,1]$ such that $D_{(\theta_1,\alpha_1,\beta_1)}(a,b) \geq \lambda_1$ and $D_{(\theta_2,\alpha_2,\beta_2)}(b,c) \geq \lambda+1-\lambda_1$. Furthermore, as in the proof of Proposition 7.2, we find that this is the case exactly when $\theta_{ab}+2k_1\pi \in [\gamma_1,\gamma_2]$ and $\theta_{bc}+2k_2\pi \in [\gamma_3,\gamma_4]$ for some k_1 and k_2 in $\mathbb{Z}$, where

$$[\gamma_1,\gamma_2] = [\theta_1-\alpha_1-(1-\lambda_1)\beta_1, \theta_1+\alpha_1+(1-\lambda_1)\beta_1]$$

$$[\gamma_3,\gamma_4] = [\theta_2-\alpha_2-(\lambda_1-\lambda)\beta_2, \theta_2+\alpha_2+(\lambda_1-\lambda)\beta_2]$$

Note that, since θ_{ab} and θ_{bc} are in $[0,2\pi[$, it holds that

$$\theta_{ab} \in clockwise(\gamma_1,\gamma_2) \qquad \theta_{bc} \in clockwise(\gamma_3,\gamma_4)$$

Hence, to prove (7.26), it is sufficient to show $(R_1 \cup R_2 \cup R_3 \cup R_4)(a,c) \geq \lambda$ under the assumption that there exists a λ_1 in $[\lambda,1]$ with $\theta_{ab} \in clockwise(\gamma_1,\gamma_2)$ and $\theta_{bc} \in clockwise(\gamma_3,\gamma_4)$. Let $a = (a_x,a_y)$, $b = (b_x,b_y)$ and $c = (c_x,c_y)$. The coordinates of b can be written relative to the coordinates of reference point a as:

$$b_x = a_x + d(a,b)\cos(\frac{\pi}{2}-\theta_{ab})$$

$$b_y = a_y + d(a,b)\sin(\frac{\pi}{2}-\theta_{ab})$$

Similarly, the coordinates of c can be written relative to the coordinates of b as:

$$c_x = b_x + d(b,c)\cos(\frac{\pi}{2}-\theta_{bc})$$

$$c_y = b_y + d(b,c)\sin(\frac{\pi}{2}-\theta_{bc})$$

Together this yields

$$c_x = a_x + d(a,b)\cos(\frac{\pi}{2}-\theta_{ab}) + d(b,c)\cos(\frac{\pi}{2}-\theta_{bc})$$

$$c_y = a_y + d(a,b)\sin(\frac{\pi}{2}-\theta_{ab}) + d(b,c)\sin(\frac{\pi}{2}-\theta_{bc})$$

If $d(a,b) = 0$, it holds that $(c_x, c_y) = (a_x + d(b,c)\cos(\frac{\pi}{2} - \theta_{bc}), a_y + d(b,c)\sin(\frac{\pi}{2} - \theta_{bc}))$. By Lemma 7.1 this entails $\theta_{ac} = \theta_{bc}$. Hence, because of our assumption that $\theta_{bc} \in clockwise(\gamma_3, \gamma_4)$:

$$\theta_{ac} \in clockwise(\theta_2 - \alpha_2 - (\lambda_1 - \lambda)\beta_2, \theta_2 + \alpha_2 + (\lambda_1 - \lambda)\beta_2) \qquad (7.27)$$

Note that, since $\lambda_1 \leq 1$, this entails that

$$\theta_{ac} \in clockwise(\theta_2 - \alpha_2 - (1 - \lambda)\beta_2, \theta_2 + \alpha_2 + (1 - \lambda)\beta_2) \qquad (7.28)$$

Hence, it holds that

$$ad(\theta_{ac}, \theta_2) \leq \alpha_2 + (1 - \lambda)\beta_2$$

and therefore $D_{(\theta_2, \alpha_2, \beta_2)}(a, c) \geq \lambda$ and $R_2(a, c) \geq \lambda$. Hence, for $d(a,b) = 0$, (7.26) is always satisfied. Similarly, if $d(b,c) = 0$, it holds that $\theta_{ac} = \theta_{ab}$, hence

$$\theta_{ac} \in clockwise(\theta_1 - \alpha_1 - (1 - \lambda_1)\beta_1, \theta_1 + \alpha_1 + (1 - \lambda_1)\beta_1)$$

Since $\lambda_1 \geq \lambda$, we obtain

$$\theta_{ac} \in clockwise(\theta_1 - \alpha_1 - (1 - \lambda)\beta_1, \theta_1 + \alpha_1 + (1 - \lambda)\beta_1)$$

Similarly as in the previous case, we obtain that $R_1(a, c) \geq \lambda$; hence, (7.26) is always satisfied for $d(b,c) = 0$. Finally, let $d(a,b) > 0$ and let the point $c' = (c'_x, c'_y)$ be defined by

$$c'_x = a_x + \cos(\frac{\pi}{2} - \theta_{ab}) + \frac{d(b,c)}{d(a,b)}\cos(\frac{\pi}{2} - \theta_{bc}) \qquad (7.29)$$

$$c'_y = a_y + \sin(\frac{\pi}{2} - \theta_{ab}) + \frac{d(b,c)}{d(a,b)}\sin(\frac{\pi}{2} - \theta_{bc}) \qquad (7.30)$$

Clearly it holds that $\theta_{ac} = \theta_{ac'}$, since $\frac{c'_y - a_y}{c'_x - a_x} = \frac{c_y - a_y}{c_x - a_x}$ and the sign of $c'_x - a_x$ and $c'_y - a_y$ is the same as the sign of $c_x - a_x$ and $c_y - a_y$, respectively. Note that c' is a point on the half–line defined in Lemma 7.7, with $\theta_1 = \theta_{ab}$ and $\theta_2 = \theta_{bc}$. Therefore, Lemma 7.7 can be applied to obtain information on the cardinal direction $\theta_{ac'}$, which, as explained above, is equal to θ_{ac}. First, note that if $\theta_{ac} \in clockwise(\gamma_1, \gamma_2)$ or $\theta_{ac} \in clockwise(\gamma_3, \gamma_4)$, we have, as before, that $R_1(a, c) \geq \lambda$ or $R_2(a, c) \geq \lambda$. This is in particular the case when $\theta_{ac} = \theta_{ab}$ or $\theta_{ac} = \theta_{bc}$ since θ_{ab} is in $clockwise(\gamma_1, \gamma_2)$ and θ_{bc} is in $clockwise(\gamma_3, \gamma_4)$. Next, assume that θ_{ac} is in $clockwise(\theta_{ab}, \theta_{bc})$, but not in $clockwise(\gamma_1, \gamma_2)$ or in $clockwise(\gamma_3, \gamma_4)$, which in particular entails $\theta_{ac} \neq \theta_{ab}$ and $\theta_{ac} \neq \theta_{bc}$. Using Lemma 7.7, we derive from $\theta_{ac} \in clockwise(\theta_{ab}, \theta_{bc})$, $\theta_{ac} \neq \theta_{ab}$ and $\theta_{ac} \neq \theta_{bc}$ that $pad(\theta_{ab}, \theta_{bc}) < \pi$.

Note that γ_2 and γ_3 are in $clockwise(\theta_{ab}, \theta_{bc})$ and, moreover γ_2 comes before γ_3 (i.e., $pad(\theta_{ab}, \gamma_2) < pad(\theta_{ab}, \gamma_3)$). Indeed, if this were not the case, then $clockwise(\theta_{ab}, \theta_{bc}) \subseteq clockwise(\gamma_1, \gamma_2) \cup clockwise(\gamma_3, \gamma_4)$ would hold, which is in violation with the assumption that $\theta_{ac} \notin clockwise(\gamma_1, \gamma_2)$ and $\theta_{ac} \notin clockwise(\gamma_3, \gamma_4)$ while $\theta_{ac} \in clockwise(\theta_{ab}, \theta_{bc})$. We therefore also find $\theta_{ac} \in clockwise(\gamma_2, \gamma_3)$ and $pad(\gamma_2, \gamma_3) < pad(\theta_{ab}, \theta_{bc}) < \pi$. Furthermore, we have by Lemma 7.8

$$pad(\gamma_2, \gamma_3) = pad(\theta_1 + \alpha_1 + (1 - \lambda_1)\beta_1, \theta_2 - \alpha_2 - (\lambda_1 - \lambda)\beta_2)$$
$$\geq pad(\theta_1 + \alpha_1, \theta_2 - \alpha_2) - (1 - \lambda_1)\beta_1 - (\lambda_1 - \lambda)\beta_2$$

which implies

$$pad(\theta_1 + \alpha_1, \theta_2 - \alpha_2) \leq pad(\gamma_2, \gamma_3) + (1 - \lambda_1)\beta_1 + (\lambda_1 - \lambda)\beta_2$$
$$< \pi + (1 - \lambda_1)\beta_1 + (\lambda_1 - \lambda)\beta_2$$

We obtain

$$pad(\theta_1 + \alpha_1, \theta_2 - \alpha_2) < \pi + (1 - \lambda_1)\beta_1 + (\lambda_1 - \lambda)\beta_2$$
$$\leq \pi + (1 - \lambda_1)\max(\beta_1, \beta_2) + (\lambda_1 - \lambda)\max(\beta_1, \beta_2)$$
$$= \pi + (1 - \lambda)\max(\beta_1, \beta_2)$$
$$\leq \pi + \max(\beta_1, \beta_2)$$

Hence, if θ_{ac} is in $clockwise(\theta_{ab}, \theta_{bc})$, but not in $clockwise(\gamma_1, \gamma_2)$ or in $clockwise(\gamma_3, \gamma_4)$, it holds that $R_3(a, c) = D_{(\theta', \alpha', 0)}(a, c)$. From $\theta_{ac} \in clockwise(\gamma_2, \gamma_3)$, we furthermore derive that

$$\theta_{ac} \in clockwise(\theta_1 + \alpha_1, \theta_2 - \alpha_2)$$

and therefore $D_{(\theta', \alpha', 0)}(a, c) = 1 \geq \lambda$. Similarly, if θ_{ac} is in $clockwise(\theta_{bc}, \theta_{ab})$ and not in $clockwise(\gamma_1, \gamma_2)$ or in $clockwise(\gamma_3, \gamma_4)$, it holds that $R_4(a, c) = 1 \geq \lambda$. $\square$

By using Proposition 7.2 and 7.3, an upper bound can be derived for the sup–T composition of fuzzy spatial relations which express nearness and cardinal direction. Figures 7.16 and 7.17 show examples of the exact composition of such relations, as well as of the calculated upper bounds. The center of each picture is the reference point a. Both in Figure 7.16 and 7.17 we are interested in points c that are near and east of a point b which, in turn, is near and south of a. The compatibility of locations c with this information is displayed. In Figure 7.17 the compatible area is much larger because the parameters of the fuzzy spatial relations are higher, which allows for more tolerance. Both the examples in Figure 7.16(a) and 7.17(a) clearly illustrate the complex interactions of nearness and cardinal direction: the compatibility of a location c with the given information is a non–trivial function of both its orientation and distance to the reference point a. It is not feasible to use the exact sup–T composition in applications, as this would require heavy geometrical computations, and, typically, information about a large number of regions is known. Using the two propositions above, the sup–T composition can be approximated in constant time. Moreover, since this approximation is guaranteed to be an upper bound, the resulting reasoning procedure is sound, although not necessarily complete.

7.4 Fuzzifying the RCC

In the remainder of this chapter, we will focus on fuzzy topological relations, and more in particular, a generalization of the RCC. As pointed out in the introduction of this chapter, there are several reasons why topological relations are sometimes more naturally represented as graded relations. For example, while the relations EC and DC are mutually exclusive, in practical applications it is often difficult, or even undesirable, to differentiate between situations where two regions are very close to each other, but disconnected, and situations where two regions are connected. Therefore, a gradual approach might be more desirable in which two regions can be simultaneously externally connected and disconnected to a certain extent, depending on how close they are to each other. In this way, vagueness is introduced in the definition of topological relations. Also when the regions involved are vague, it is often more natural to model topological relations as graded relations.

Using relatedness measures, it is possible to model such fuzzy topological relations. For example, the degree $C^1_{(\alpha,\beta)}(A, B)$ to which two fuzzy sets A and B in $\mathbb{R}^2$ are connected could be expressed by

$$C^1_{(\alpha,\beta)}(A, B) = A \circ_T N_{(\alpha,\beta)} \circ_T B \qquad (7.31)$$

Similarly, the degree $NTPP^1_{(\alpha,\beta)}(A, B)$ to which A is a non–tangential proper part of B could be given by

$$NTPP^1_{(\alpha,\beta)}(A, B) = A \lhd (N_{(\alpha,\beta)} \lhd B)$$

One shortcoming of this technique is that it is confined to the particular interpretation where regions are fuzzy sets in a Euclidean space and connection is modelled in terms of nearness. In this section, we introduce a generalization of the RCC based on an arbitrary reflexive and symmetric

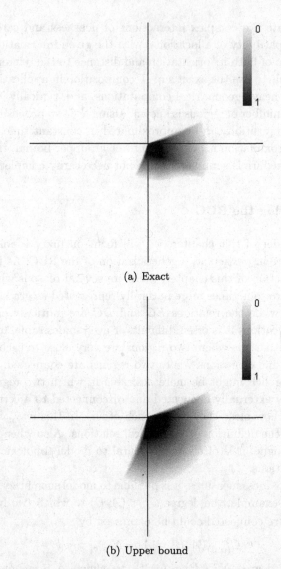

(a) Exact

(b) Upper bound

Fig. 7.16 Sup–T composition of $N_{(15,30)} \cap D_{(\pi, \frac{\pi}{16}, \frac{\pi}{16})}$ and $N_{(15,60)} \cap D_{(\frac{\pi}{2}, \frac{\pi}{16}, \frac{\pi}{16})}$ and the corresponding upper bound.

fuzzy relation C. In the spirit of the RCC, we do not impose any constraints on how regions are represented, or how connection should be interpreted. Therefore, our fuzzy relations can be used in contexts where space is used in a metaphorical way (e.g., regions as information units or images), as

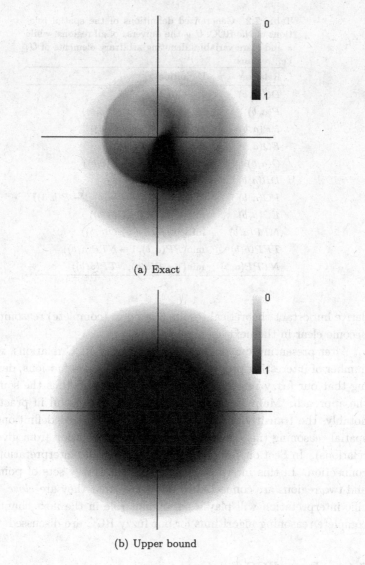

(a) Exact

(b) Upper bound

Fig. 7.17 Sup–T composition of $N_{(60,15)} \cap D_{(\pi, \frac{\pi}{16}, \pi)}$ and $N_{(15,60)} \cap D_{(\frac{\pi}{2}, \frac{\pi}{16}, \pi)}$ and the corresponding upper bound.

well as in, for example, geographical applications. Moreover, since we do not impose any specific interpretation of connection, our definitions are not tied to any particular source of vagueness. An additional — and perhaps even more important — advantage of this approach, is that it allows us to

Table 7.2   Generalized definitions of the spatial relations of the RCC. U is the universe of all regions, while a and b are variables denoting arbitrary elements of U, i.e., regions.

Relation	Definition
$DC(a,b)$	$1 - C(a,b)$
$P(a,b)$	$\inf_{c \in U} I_T(C(c,a), C(c,b))$
$PP(a,b)$	$\min(P(a,b), 1 - P(b,a))$
$EQ(a,b)$	$\min(P(a,b), P(b,a))$
$O(a,b)$	$\sup_{c \in U} T(P(c,a), P(c,b))$
$DR(a,b)$	$1 - O(a,b)$
$PO(a,b)$	$\min(O(a,b), 1 - P(a,b), 1 - P(b,a))$
$EC(a,b)$	$\min(C(a,b), 1 - O(a,b))$
$NTP(a,b)$	$\inf_{c \in U} I_T(C(c,a), O(c,b))$
$TPP(a,b)$	$\min(PP(a,b), 1 - NTP(a,b))$
$NTPP(a,b)$	$\min(1 - P(b,a), NTP(a,b))$

derive important theoretical results related to (complete) reasoning, as will become clear in the next chapter.

After presenting our definitions of the fuzzy RCC relations, we show a number of interesting properties of our generalized definitions, demonstrating that our fuzzy relations behave intuitively, and thus the soundness of the approach. Many of these properties are also useful in practice; most notably, the transitivity properties of our generalized definitions support spatial reasoning (i.e., the inference of new information from given spatial relations). In Section 7.5, we focus on one specific interpretation of fuzzy connection. In this interpretation, regions are fuzzy sets of points in $\mathbb{R}^n$, and two regions are connected to the degree that they are *close*. This specific interpretation will play a paramount role in the next chapter, where complete reasoning algorithms for our fuzzy RCC are discussed.

7.4.1   *Fuzzy RCC Relations*

In the following, we assume that T is a left–continuous t–norm and C a reflexive and symmetric fuzzy relation in U, where for two regions a and b, $C(a,b)$ expresses the degree to which a and b are connected. Table 7.2 proposes our generalization of the spatial relations of the RCC, expressing the degree $P(a,b)$ to which a is a part of b, the degree $O(a,b)$ to which a overlaps with b, etc. Most of these expressions are straightforward generalizations of the definitions in Table 7.1, where logical operators are generalized using their corresponding fuzzy logic operators, and universal and existential quantification is generalized using the infimum and supremum respectively. Note, however, that logical conjunction is sometimes modelled by min (e.g., in $EQ(a, b)$) and sometimes by T (e.g., in $O(a, b)$). This is because in the former case, the joint satisfaction of two independent constraints is evaluated, hence idempotency is desirable (recall that min is the only idempotent t–norm). However, in the latter case, this idempotency is not required, and other choices of T than the minimum should not be excluded a priori.

It is well–known that fuzzifying two formulas that are equivalent in binary logic does not necessarily yield two equivalent formulas in fuzzy logic. Hence, it may be desirable to generalize formulas that are equivalent to the original definitions of some of the RCC relations, rather than the original definitions themselves. This is the case for NTP, where our definitions are simpler to manipulate than the definitions resulting from a straightforward generalization, and, moreover, yield a generalization that satisfies more interesting properties. When C is a crisp relation, our definitions coincide with the original definitions of the RCC. To see why this is also true for NTP, we consider the following lemma.

Lemma 7.9.

$$P(a, b) \land \neg(\exists c \in U)(EC(c, a) \land EC(c, b)) \equiv (\forall c \in U)(C(c, a) \Rightarrow O(c, b))$$
(7.32)

Proof. First, we prove

$$P(a, b) \land \neg(\exists c \in U)(EC(c, a) \land EC(c, b)) \Rightarrow (\forall c \in U)(C(c, a) \Rightarrow O(c, b))$$

or, equivalently,

$$P(a, b) \Rightarrow (\neg(\exists c \in U)(EC(c, a) \land EC(c, b)) \Rightarrow (\forall c \in U)(C(c, a) \Rightarrow O(c, b)))$$

Assuming $P(a, b)$, i.e., $C(c, a) \Rightarrow C(c, b)$ for all u in U, we obtain:

$$\neg(\exists c \in U)(EC(c, a) \land EC(c, b))$$
$$\equiv (\forall c \in U)(\neg EC(c, a) \lor \neg EC(c, b))$$
$$\equiv (\forall c \in U)(\neg C(c, a) \lor O(c, a) \lor \neg C(c, b) \lor O(c, b))$$

From $C(c, a) \Rightarrow C(c, b)$, we obtain $\neg C(c, a) \lor \neg C(c, b) \equiv \neg C(c, a)$. Moreover, we can show that, under the assumption that $P(a, b)$, it holds that

$O(c, a) \Rightarrow O(c, b)$, and hence $O(c, a) \vee O(c, b) \equiv O(c, b)$. Thus we find

$$(\forall c \in U)(\neg C(c, a) \vee O(c, a) \vee \neg C(c, b) \vee O(c, b))$$
$$\equiv (\forall c \in U)(\neg C(c, a) \vee O(c, b))$$
$$\equiv (\forall c \in U)(C(c, a) \Rightarrow O(c, b))$$

Conversely, we immediately have that $(\forall c \in U)(C(c, a) \Rightarrow O(c, b)) \Rightarrow P(a, b)$, since $O(u, v) \Rightarrow C(u, v)$ for all u and v in U. Finally, we show that also $(\forall c \in U)(C(c, a) \Rightarrow O(c, b)) \Rightarrow \neg(\exists c \in U)(EC(c, a) \wedge EC(c, b))$

$$(\forall c \in U)(C(c, a) \Rightarrow O(c, b))$$
$$\equiv (\forall c \in U)(\neg C(c, a) \vee O(c, b))$$
$$\Rightarrow (\forall c \in U)(\neg C(c, a) \vee O(c, a) \vee \neg C(c, b) \vee O(c, b))$$
$$\equiv (\forall c \in U)(\neg EC(c, a) \vee \neg EC(c, b))$$
$$\equiv \neg(\exists c \in U)(EC(c, a) \wedge EC(c, b)) \qquad \square$$

Note that the right–hand side of (7.32) is the alternative definition of NTP which we have used for our generalization.

7.4.2   *Properties*

Next, we show some properties of our generalized RCC relations which are desirable in practice. They also serve as a justification of some of the decisions we made regarding the definitions of the fuzzy spatial relations, e.g., the use of residual implicators, and the somewhat peculiar definitions of TPP and $NTPP$. The first proposition shows that the (ir)reflexivity of the original RCC relations carries over to our generalization.

Proposition 7.4. *The fuzzy relations P, O and EQ are reflexive, while the fuzzy relations DC, PP, DR, PO, EC, TPP and $NTPP$ are irreflexive.*

Proof.   Using (2.23), we find

$$P(a, a) = \inf_{z \in U} I_T(C(z, a), C(z, a)) = \inf_{z \in U} 1 = 1$$

For the fuzzy relation O, we obtain

$$O(a, a) = \sup_{z \in U} T(P(z, a), P(z, a)) \geq T(P(a, a), P(a, a)) = T(1, 1) = 1$$

The reflexivity of EQ immediately follows from the reflexivity of P, while the irreflexivity of DC follows from the reflexivity of C. The irreflexivity of PP, PO, TPP, and $NTPP$ follows from the reflexivity of P, and the irreflexivity of DR and EC follows from the reflexivity of O. $\qquad \square$

The relations of the RCC are not independent of each other. For example, if $TPP(a, b)$ holds, then also $PP(a, b)$. The following proposition generalizes such dependencies.

Proposition 7.5.

1. $PO(a, b) \leq O(a, b)$
2. $NTPP(a, b) \leq PP(a, b)$
3. $EQ(a, b) \leq P(a, b)$
4. $O(a, b) \leq C(a, b)$
5. $EC(a, b) \leq DR(a, b)$
6. $NTP(a, b) \leq P(a, b)$
7. $TPP(a, b) \leq PP(a, b)$
8. $PP(a, b) \leq P(a, b)$
9. $P(a, b) \leq O(a, b)$
10. $EC(a, b) \leq C(a, b)$
11. $DC(a, b) \leq DR(a, b)$

Proof. First, we show that $O(a, b) \leq C(a, b)$:

$$O(a, b) = \sup_{z \in U} T(P(z, a), P(z, b))$$

$$= \sup_{z \in U} T(\inf_{u \in U} I_T(C(u, z), C(u, a)), \inf_{u \in U} I_T(C(u, z), C(u, b)))$$

$$\leq \sup_{z \in U} T(I_T(C(z, z), C(z, a)), I_T(C(a, z), C(a, b)))$$

$$= \sup_{z \in U} T(I_T(1, C(z, a)), I_T(C(a, z), C(a, b)))$$

By (2.22), the symmetry of C, and (2.25), we obtain

$$= \sup_{z \in U} T(C(z, a), I_T(C(a, z), C(a, b)))$$

$$= \sup_{z \in U} T(C(z, a), I_T(C(z, a), C(a, b)))$$

$$\leq C(a, b)$$

As a corollary, we also have $DC(a, b) \leq DR(a, b)$, $NTP(a, b) \leq P(a, b)$ and $NTPP(a, b) \leq PP(a, b)$.

Next, we show that $P(a, b) \leq O(a, b)$:

$$O(a, b) = \sup_{z \in U} T(P(z, a), P(z, b))$$

$$\geq T(P(a, a), P(a, b))$$

$$= T(1, P(a, b))$$

$$= P(a, b)$$

where we made use of the reflexivity of P. The remaining inequalities follow straightforwardly from the definition of the minimum. $\square$

In the original RCC, if $PP(a,b)$ holds, then we know that either $TPP(a,b)$ or $NTPP(a,b)$. The following proposition presents a generalization of this and similar observations.

Proposition 7.6.

$$S_W(TPP(a,b), NTPP(a,b)) \geq PP(a,b) \tag{7.33}$$

$$S_W(PP(a,b), EQ(a,b)) \geq P(a,b) \tag{7.34}$$

$$S_W(PO(a,b), P(a,b), PP^{-1}(a,b)) \geq O(a,b) \tag{7.35}$$

$$S_W(O(a,b), EC(a,b)) \geq C(a,b) \tag{7.36}$$

$$S_W(EC(a,b), DC(a,b)) \geq DR(a,b) \tag{7.37}$$

$$S_W(C(a,b), DC(a,b)) = 1 \tag{7.38}$$

$$S_W(O(a,b), DR(a,b)) = 1 \tag{7.39}$$

Proof.   As an example, we show (7.33). We obtain

$S_W(TPP(a,b), NTPP(a,b))$

$= S_W(\min(PP(a,b), 1 - NTP(a,b)), \min(1 - P(b,a), NTP(a,b)))$

$\geq S_W(\min(PP(a,b), 1 - NTP(a,b)), \min(1 - P(b,a), P(a,b), NTP(a,b)))$

$= S_W(\min(PP(a,b), 1 - NTP(a,b)), \min(PP(a,b), NTP(a,b)))$

By (2.15), and the fact that $S_W(x, 1-x) = 1$ for every x in $[0,1]$, we obtain

$\geq \min(PP(a,b), S_W(NTP(a,b), 1 - NTP(a,b)))$

$= \min(PP(a,b), 1)$

$= PP(a,b)$

$\square$

Note that the Łukasiewicz t–conorm is used in the previous proposition, regardless of the choice for T in the definitions of the fuzzy spatial relations. Note that t–conorms such as S_M or S_P cannot be used since they do not satisfy the law of the excluded middle, i.e., for x in $[0,1]$, it does not hold that $S_M(1-x,x) = 1$ or $S_P(1-x,x) = 1$ in general.

The RCC–8 and RCC–5 subsets of RCC relations have the important property that they are jointly exhaustive and pairwise disjoint (JEPD), i.e., for any two regions, exactly one of the RCC–8 relations holds, and exactly one of the RCC–5 relations. In the following propositions, we show that a generalization of this property remains valid for our definitions. Again the Łukasiewicz connectives are used in these properties to express the joint exhaustivity and the mutual exclusiveness.

Proposition 7.7. *Let R and Q be two of the fuzzy relations DC, EQ, EC, PO, TPP, NTPP, TPP^{-1} and $NTPP^{-1}$. If $R \neq Q$, it holds that*

$$T_W(R(a,b), Q(a,b)) = 0$$

Proof. As an example, we show that $T_W(EC(a,b), DC(a,b)) = 0$:

$$\begin{aligned}
T_W(EC(a,b), DC(a,b)) &= T_W(\min(1 - O(a,b), C(a,b)), 1 - C(a,b)) \\
&\leq T_W(C(a,b), 1 - C(a,b)) \\
&= 0
\end{aligned}$$

where we used the fact that $T_W(x, 1 - x) = 0$ for every x in $[0,1]$. $\square$

Note that Proposition 7.7 does not hold in general for t–norms such as T_M and T_P. For example, let a, b and c be regions for which $NTP(a,b) = 0.6$, $P(a,b) = 0.8$ and $P(b,a) = 0$. It holds that

$$NTPP(a,b) = \min(1 - 0, 0.6) = 0.6$$
$$TPP(a,b) = \min(0.8, 1 - 0, 1 - 0.6) = 0.4$$

Hence we find

$$T_M(NTPP(a,b), TPP(a,b)) = 0.4 > 0$$
$$T_P(NTPP(a,b), TPP(a,b)) = 0.24 > 0$$

Proposition 7.8.

$$\begin{aligned}
S_W(&DC(a,b), EQ(a,b), EC(a,b), PO(a,b), \\
&TPP(a,b), NTPP(a,b), TPP^{-1}(a,b), NTPP^{-1}(a,b)) = 1
\end{aligned}$$

Proof.

$$\begin{aligned}
S_W(&DC(a,b), EQ(a,b), EC(a,b), PO(a,b), \\
&TPP(a,b), NTPP(a,b), TPP^{-1}(a,b), NTPP^{-1}(a,b)) \\
&\geq S_W(DC(a,b), EQ(a,b), EC(a,b), PO(a,b), PP(a,b), PP^{-1}(a,b)) \\
&\geq S_W(DC(a,b), EC(a,b), PO(a,b), P(a,b), PP^{-1}(a,b)) \\
&\geq S_W(DC(a,b), EC(a,b), O(a,b)) \\
&\geq S_W(DC(a,b), C(a,b)) \\
&= S_W(1 - C(a,b), C(a,b)) \\
&= 1
\end{aligned}$$

Where we used (7.33), (7.34), (7.35), (7.36), the definition of DC, and the fact that $S_W(1 - x, x) = 1$ for all x in $[0,1]$. $\square$

Analogously, we can show the following two propositions about the generalized RCC–5 relations.

Proposition 7.9. *Let R and Q be two of the fuzzy relations DR, EQ, PO, PP and PP^{-1}. If $R \neq Q$, it holds that*

$$T_W(R(a,b), Q(a,b)) = 0$$

Proposition 7.10.

$$S_W(DR(a,b), EQ(a,b), PO(a,b), PP(a,b), PP^{-1}(a,b)) = 1$$

7.4.3   *Transitivity*

To facilitate spatial reasoning with the RCC–8 relations, a composition table (or transitivity table) has been introduced in [Cui *et al.* (1993)], similar in spirit to Allen's transitivity table for temporal relations (Table 4.2). The purpose of such a table is to specify, for each pair R, S of RCC–8 relations, the union of all RCC–8 relations F for which $F \cap (R \circ S) \neq \emptyset$, where the composition $R \circ S$ is defined for a and c in U as

$$(R \circ S)(a,c) \equiv (\exists b \in U)(R(a,b) \wedge S(b,c))$$

In other words, the composition table specifies which RCC–8 relations may hold between the regions a and c, given that $R(a,b)$ and $S(b,c)$ for some region b in U.

For example, as can be seen from Table 7.3, when $DC(a,b)$ and $EC(b,c)$ holds, either $DC(a,c)$, $EC(a,c)$, $PO(a,c)$, $TPP(a,c)$, or $NTPP(a,c)$ must hold. Therefore, the RCC–8 composition table contains $\{DC, EC, PO, TPP, NTPP\}$ in the entry on the row corresponding to DC and the column corresponding to EC. However, from the fact that the RCC–8 relations are JEPD, we easily obtain that the relations DC, EC, $PO, TPP, NTPP$ and P^{-1} are also JEPD; hence we have that

$$DC \cup EC \cup PO \cup TPP \cup NTPP = coP^{-1}$$

Therefore, the entry in the composition table could equivalently be coP^{-1} instead of the entry $\{DC, EC, PO, TPP, NTPP\}$. Similarly, all unions of RCC relations in the RCC–8 composition table can equivalently be formulated as intersections of C, P, P^{-1}, O, NTP, NTP^{-1}, DC, $\neg P$, $\neg P^{-1}$, DR, $\neg NTP$, and $\neg NTP^{-1}$. A more or less similar observation was made in [Bennett (1998)]. The resulting composition table is shown in Table 7.4. To show that Table 7.4 is indeed equivalent to Table 7.3, we need the following lemma.

Table 7.3 Original RCC–8 composition table (where EQ is omitted) [Cui et al. (1993)]. Table entries that contain more than one RCC–8 relation correspond to the *union* of the given relations; 1 denotes the union of all RCC–8 relations, i.e., the universal relation in the universe of regions U.

	DC	EC	PO	TPP	$NTPP$	TPP^{-1}	$NTPP^{-1}$
DC	1	$DC,EC,$ $PO,TPP,$ $NTPP$	$DC,EC,$ $PO,TPP,$ $NTPP$	$DC,EC,$ $PO,TPP,$ $NTPP$	$DC,EC,$ $PO,TPP,$ $NTPP$	DC	DC
EC	$DC,EC,$ $PO,TPP^{-1},$ $NTPP^{-1}$	$DC,EC,$ $PO,TPP,$ TPP^{-1},EQ	$DC,EC,$ $PO,TPP,$ $NTPP$	$EC,PO,$ $TPP,$ $NTPP$	$PO,TPP,$ $NTPP$	DC,EC	DC
PO	$DC,EC,$ $PO,TPP^{-1},$ $NTPP^{-1}$	$DC,EC,$ $PO,TPP^{-1},$ $NTPP^{-1}$	1	$PO,TPP,$ $NTPP$	$PO,TPP,$ $NTPP$	$DC,EC,$ $PO,TPP^{-1},$ $NTPP^{-1}$	$DC,EC,$ $PO,TPP^{-1},$ $NTPP^{-1}$
TPP	DC	DC,EC	$DC,EC,$ $PO,TPP,$ $NTPP$	$TPP,$ $NTPP$	$NTPP$	$DC,EC,$ $PO,TPP,$ TPP^{-1},EQ	$DC,EC,$ $PO,TPP^{-1},$ $NTPP^{-1}$
$NTPP$	DC	DC	$DC,EC,$ $PO,TPP,$ $NTPP$	$NTPP$	$NTPP$	$DC,EC,$ $PO,TPP,$ $NTPP$	1
TPP^{-1}	$DC,EC,$ $PO,TPP^{-1},$ $NTPP^{-1}$	$EC,PO,$ $TPP^{-1},$ $NTPP^{-1}$	$PO,$ $TPP^{-1},$ $NTPP^{-1}$	$PO,EQ,$ $TPP,$ TPP^{-1}	$PO,TPP,$ $NTPP$	$TPP^{-1},$ $NTPP^{-1}$	$NTPP^{-1}$
$NTPP^{-1}$	$DC,EC,$ $PO,TPP^{-1},$ $NTPP^{-1}$	$PO,TPP^{-1},$ $NTPP^{-1}$	$PO,$ $TPP^{-1},$ $NTPP^{-1}$	$PO,$ $TPP^{-1},$ $NTPP^{-1}$	$PO,TPP^{-1},$ $TPP,NTPP,$ $NTPP^{-1},EQ$	$NTPP^{-1}$	$NTPP^{-1}$

Table 7.4   Alternative formulation of the RCC–8 composition table (where EQ is omitted).   Table entries containing more than one relation correspond to the *intersection* of the given relations; 1 denotes the universal relation in the universe of regions U.

	DC	EC	PO	TPP	$NTPP$	TPP^{-1}	$NTPP^{-1}$
DC	1	coP^{-1}	coP^{-1}	coP^{-1}	coP^{-1}	DC	DC
EC	coP	$coNTP, coNTP^{-1}$	coP^{-1}	C, coP^{-1}	O, coP^{-1}	DR	DC
PO	coP	coP	1	O, coP^{-1}	O, coP^{-1}	coP	coP
TPP	DC	DR	coP^{-1}	P, coP^{-1}	NTP, coP^{-1}	$coNTP, coNTP^{-1}$	coP
$NTPP$	DC	DC	coP^{-1}	NTP, coP^{-1}	NTP, coP^{-1}	coP^{-1}	1
TPP^{-1}	coP	C, coP	O, coP	$O, coNTP, coNTP^{-1}$	O, coP^{-1}	P^{-1}, coP	NTP^{-1}, coP
$NTPP^{-1}$	coP	O, coP	O, coP	O, coP	O	NTP^{-1}, coP	NTP^{-1}, coP

Lemma 7.10.

$$(\exists z \in U)(EC(z,b)) \Rightarrow (NTP(a,b) \equiv NTPP(a,b))$$

Proof. *Assume that for some z it holds that $EC(z,b)$, i.e., $C(z,b)$ and $\neg O(z,b)$. To show that, under this assumption, $NTP(a,b) \equiv NTPP(a,b)$, we only need to show that $NTP(a,b) \Rightarrow \neg P(b,a)$. To this end, we show that $\neg P(b,a)$ holds under the assumption $NTP(a,b)$*

$$\neg P(b,a) \equiv \neg(\forall c \in U)(C(c,b) \Rightarrow C(c,a))$$
$$\equiv (\exists c \in U)(C(c,b) \wedge \neg C(c,a))$$

Using our alternative definition of $NTP(a,b)$, we find that $C(c,a) \Rightarrow O(c,b)$ holds, and hence also $\neg O(c,b) \Rightarrow \neg C(c,a)$. We obtain

$$\Leftarrow (\exists c \in U)(C(c,b) \wedge \neg O(c,b))$$
$$\Leftarrow (C(z,b) \wedge \neg O(z,b))$$

The latter right hand side corresponds to our initial assumption $EC(z,b)$, which concludes the proof. ☐

Proposition 7.11. *The unions of the RCC–8 relations in the entries of Table 7.3 are equal to the corresponding intersections of the RCC relations in Table 7.4.*

Proof. Above we have already shown that $coP^{-1} = DC \cup EC \cup PO \cup TPP \cup NTPP$. Most equalities can analogously be obtained using the fact that, beside the RCC–8 and RCC–5 relations, the following sets of RCC relations are also JEPD (which easily follows from the fact that the RCC–8 and RCC–5 relations are JEPD):

$$\{DC, EC, PO, TPP, NTPP, P^{-1}\}$$
$$\{DC, EC, PO, TPP^{-1}, NTPP^{-1}, P\}$$
$$\{DR, PO, TPP, NTPP, P^{-1}\}$$
$$\{DR, PO, TPP^{-1}, NTPP^{-1}, P\}$$
$$\{DR, PO, TPP, NTPP, TPP^{-1}, NTPP^{-1}, EQ\}$$

To show the equality corresponding to the entry on the second row, second column, we need to show that

$$(EC(a,b) \wedge EC(b,c) \Rightarrow (DC \cup EC \cup PO \cup TPP \cup TPP^{-1} \cup EQ)(a,c))$$
$$\equiv (EC(a,b) \wedge EC(b,c) \Rightarrow \neg NTP(a,c) \wedge \neg NTP^{-1}(a,c))$$

or, equivalently, using the fact that the RCC–8 relations are JEPD

$$(EC(a,b) \land EC(b,c) \Rightarrow \neg NTPP(a,c) \land \neg NTPP^{-1}(a,c))$$
$$\equiv (EC(a,b) \land EC(b,c) \Rightarrow \neg NTP(a,c) \land \neg NTP^{-1}(a,c))$$

which is equivalent to showing

$$(NTPP(a,c) \land \neg NTPP^{-1}(a,c)) \equiv (\neg NTP(a,c) \land \neg NTP^{-1}(a,c))$$

under the assumption that $EC(a,b)$ and $EC(b,c)$ hold. This assumption implies that $(\exists z \in U)(EC(z,a))$ and $(\exists z \in U)(EC(z,c))$. Using Lemma 7.10, we conclude from this that

$$NTP(c,a) \equiv NTPP(c,a)$$
$$NTP(a,c) \equiv NTPP(a,c)$$

Finally, the equivalences corresponding to the entry on the fourth row, sixth column and the entry on the sixth row, fourth column, can be proven entirely analogously.   □

Generalizations of Table 7.4 and Table 7.3, using our generalized RCC relations, are not equivalent anymore. However, we still have

$$1 - P^{-1}(a,c) \leq S_W(DC(a,c), EC(a,c), PO(a,c), TPP(a,c), NTPP(a,c)) \tag{7.40}$$

Indeed, using Proposition 7.6 and the symmetry of DR and PO, we find

$$S_W(DC(a,c), EC(a,c), PO(a,c), TPP(a,c), NTPP(a,c), P^{-1}(a,c))$$
$$\geq S_W(DR(a,c), PO(a,c), PP(a,c), P^{-1}(a,c))$$
$$\geq S_W(DR(a,c), O(a,c))$$
$$= 1$$

which is equivalent to (7.40).

Transitivity properties of fuzzy relations generally take the form of inequalities of the form $T(R(a,b), S(b,c)) \leq Q(a,c)$ where R, S and Q are fuzzy relations in a suitable universe. As a consequence of (7.40),

$$T(DC(a,b), EC(b,c)) \leq 1 - P^{-1}(a,c)$$

is a stronger statement than

$$T(DC(a,b), EC(b,c))$$
$$\leq S_W(DC(a,c), EC(a,c), PO(a,c), TPP(a,c), NTPP(a,c))$$

Therefore, our aim is to generalize Table 7.4 rather than Table 7.3. However, as the entries of this table are formulated in terms of C, DC, O, DR

etc., we will provide a generalized transitivity table (shown in Table 7.5) where rows and columns correspond to fuzzy relations such as $C, DC, O,$ or DR, rather than generalized RCC–8 relations. Below, we will introduce a spatial reasoning algorithm which can, among others, be used to reason about generalized RCC–8 relations using the generalized transitivity rules from Table 7.5. As we will show, a direct generalization of Table 7.4 can easily be obtained using this spatial reasoning algorithm.

To show the correctness of Table 7.5, we need the following lemma.

Lemma 7.11. *Let a and b be arbitrary regions from U. It holds that*

$$P(a,b) = \inf_{z \in U} I_T(P(z,a), P(z,b)) \tag{7.41}$$

$$P(a,b) \leq \inf_{z \in U} I_T(O(z,a), O(z,b)) \tag{7.42}$$

$$P(a,b) = \inf_{z \in U} I_T(P(b,z), P(a,z)) \tag{7.43}$$

$$P(a,b) = \inf_{z \in U} I_T(NTP(z,a), NTP(z,b)) \tag{7.44}$$

$$P(a,b) = \inf_{z \in U} I_T(NTP(b,z), NTP(a,z)) \tag{7.45}$$

$$NTP(a,b) = \inf_{z \in U} I_T(P(z,a), NTP(z,b)) \tag{7.46}$$

$$NTP(a,b) = \inf_{z \in U} I_T(P(b,z), NTP(a,z)) \tag{7.47}$$

$$O(a,b) = \inf_{z \in U} I_T(P(a,z), O(b,z)) \tag{7.48}$$

Proof. As an example, we show (7.41). Using (2.20), we find

$$\inf_{z \in U} I_T(P(z,a), P(z,b))$$

$$= \inf_{z \in U} I_T(\inf_{u \in U} I_T(C(u,z), C(u,a)), \inf_{u \in U} I_T(C(u,z), C(u,b)))$$

$$= \inf_{z \in U} \inf_{u \in U} I_T(\inf_{u' \in U} I_T(C(u',z), C(u',a)), I_T(C(u,z), C(u,b)))$$

$$\geq \inf_{z \in U} \inf_{u \in U} I_T(I_T(C(u,z), C(u,a)), I_T(C(u,z), C(u,b)))$$

and by (2.26) and (2.25)

$$= \inf_{z \in U} \inf_{u \in U} I_T(T(C(u,z), I_T(C(u,z), C(u,a))), C(u,b))$$

$$\geq \inf_{z \in U} \inf_{u \in U} I_T(C(u,a), C(u,b))$$

$$= \inf_{u \in U} I_T(C(u,a), C(u,b))$$

$$= P(a,b)$$

which already shows that $P(a, b) \leq \inf_{z \in U} I_T(P(z, a), P(z, b))$. Conversely we find, using the reflexivity of P, and (2.22)

$$\inf_{z \in U} I_T(P(z, a), P(z, b)) \leq I_T(P(a, a), P(a, b)) = I_T(1, P(a, b)) = P(a, b) \quad \square$$

Proposition 7.12. *Let R and S be two generalized RCC–8 relations, and let Q be the fuzzy relation in the entry of Table 7.5 on the row corresponding to R and the column corresponding to S. Furthermore, assume that the t–norm T used in the generalized definitions of the RCC relations satisfies $T_W \leq T$. For every region a, b, and c, it holds that*

$$T_W(R(a, b), S(b, c)) \leq Q(a, c) \tag{7.49}$$

For example, the entry on the second row, first column should be interpreted as

$$T_W(DC(a, b), C(b, c)) \leq (coP^{-1})(a, c) \tag{7.50}$$

Proof.   As an example, we show how to prove that

$$T_W((coP^{-1})(a, b), P(b, c)) \leq (coP^{-1})(a, c)$$

Using (7.43), we find

$$
\begin{aligned}
T_W((coP^{-1})(a, b), P(b, c)) &= T_W(1 - P(b, a), P(b, c)) \\
&= T_W(1 - P(b, a), \inf_{z \in U} I_T(P(c, z), P(b, z))) \\
&\leq T_W(1 - P(b, a), I_T(P(c, a), P(b, a)))
\end{aligned}
$$

Using the fact that $T_W \leq T$ and Lemma 2.6, we obtain

$$
\begin{aligned}
&\leq T_W(1 - P(b, a), I_W(P(c, a), P(b, a))) \\
&= T_W(1 - P(b, a), \min(1, 1 - P(c, a) + P(b, a))) \\
&= T_W(1 - P(b, a), \min(1, 1 - (1 - P(b, a)) + (1 - P(c, a)))) \\
&= T_W(1 - P(b, a), I_W(1 - P(b, a), 1 - P(c, a)))
\end{aligned}
$$

And by (2.25)

$$\leq 1 - P(c, a) = (coP^{-1})(a, c) \quad \square$$

Recall that T_M and T_P are greater than T_W, i.e., the generalized transitivity rules hold when T_W, T_P, or T_W is used in the definition of the generalized RCC relations. Note that when the Łukasiewicz t–norm in (7.49) is replaced by T_M or T_P, the corresponding proposition is not valid anymore, even when

T_M or T_P is used in the definition of the generalized RCC relations. To see this, consider the following counterexample.

Example 7.1. Let $U = \{a, b, c\}$, i.e., U only consists of three regions. Using the reflexivity of C, (2.23), and (2.22), we obtain

$$P(c, a) = \min(I_T(C(a, c), C(a, a)), I_T(C(b, c), C(b, a)), I_T(C(c, c), C(c, a)))$$
$$= \min(I_T(C(a, c), 1), I_T(C(b, c), C(b, a)), I_T(1, C(c, a)))$$
$$= \min(1, I_T(C(b, c), C(b, a)), C(c, a))$$
$$= \min(I_T(C(b, c), C(b, a)), C(c, a))$$

Furthermore, assume that C satisfies $C(c, a) = 0.9$, $C(b, c) = 0.2$, and $C(b, a) = 0.4$. When T_M and I_M are used in the definition of the generalized RCC relations, we obtain (using the symmetry of C):

$$(coP^{-1})(a, c) = 1 - P(c, a) = 1 - \min(1, 0.9) = 1 - 0.9 = 0.1$$
$$T_M(DC(a, b), C(b, c)) = \min(1 - C(a, b), C(b, c)) = \min(0.6, 0.2) = 0.2$$

Hence

$$T_M(DC(a, b), C(b, c)) > (coP^{-1})(a, c)$$

Similarly, when T_P and I_P are used in the definition of the generalized RCC relations, we have

$$(coP^{-1})(a, c) = 1 - P(c, a) = 1 - \min(1, 0.9) = 1 - 0.9 = 0.1$$
$$T_P(DC(a, b), C(b, c)) = (1 - C(a, b))C(b, c) = 0.6 \cdot 0.2 = 0.12$$

and thus

$$T_P(DC(a, b), C(b, c)) > (coP^{-1})(a, c)$$

Many of the generalized RCC relations from Table 7.2 are defined as the minimum of some of the fuzzy relations from Table 7.5. To derive transitivity rules for these fuzzy relations, based on the transitivity rules from Table 7.5, we can use the fact that (x, y, and z in $[0, 1]$)

$$T_W(\min(x, y), z) \leq \min(T_W(x, z), T_W(y, z)) \tag{7.51}$$

which tells us how the minimum from the definition of the generalized RCC–8 relations interacts with the Łukasiewicz t–norm from the transitivity rules.

Table 7.5   Transitivity table for the generalized RCC relations. Note that the transitivity rules summarized in this table only hold when the t-norm T in the definition of the fuzzy relations satisfies $T_w \leq T$.

	C	DC	P	P^{-1}	coP	coP^{-1}	O	DR	NTP	NTP^{-1}	$coNTP$	$coNTP^{-1}$
C	C	coP	C	C	1	1	1	$coNTP$	O	1	1	1
DC	coP^{-1}	1	coP^{-1}	DC	1	1	coP^{-1}	1	coP^{-1}	DC	1	1
P	1	DC	P	1	1	coP^{-1}	1	DR	NTP	1	$coNTP$	1
P^{-1}	C	coP	O	P^{-1}	coP	1	O	coP	O	NTP^{-1}	$coNTP$	$coNTP^{-1}$
coP	1	1	1	coP	1	1	1	1	1	coP	1	1
coP^{-1}	1	1	coP^{-1}	1	1	1	1	coP	coP^{-1}	1	1	1
O	1	coP	O	1	1	coP^{-1}	O	coP	O	1	1	1
DR	$coNTP^{-1}$	1	coP^{-1}	DR	1	1	coP^{-1}	1	coP^{-1}	DC	1	coP^{-1}
NTP	1	DC	NTP	1	1	coP^{-1}	NTP	DC	NTP	1	coP	1
NTP^{-1}	O	coP	O	NTP^{-1}	coP	1	O	coP	O	NTP^{-1}	coP	coP^{-1}
$coNTP$	1	1	1	$coNTP$	1	1	1	coP	1	coP	1	1
$coNTP^{-1}$	1	1	$coNTP^{-1}$	1	1	1	1	1	coP^{-1}	1	1	1

Note that (7.51) is a special case of (2.6). For example, using (7.51) we obtain, for regions a, b and c in U,

$$T_W(DC(a,b), EC(b,c))$$
$$= T_W(DC(a,b), \min(C(b,c), DR(b,c)))$$
$$\leq \min(T_W(DC(a,b), C(b,c)), T_W(DC(a,b), DR(b,c)))$$

From Table 7.5 we have

$$\leq \min((coP^{-1})(a,c), 1)$$
$$= (coP^{-1})(a,c)$$

This corresponds to the RCC-8 transitivity rule that from $DC(a,b)$ and $EC(b,c)$, it follows that $coP^{-1}(a,c)$ (see Table 7.4). In general, we can apply the following algorithm:

(1) Assume two fuzzy spatial relations R and Q are given that can be written as

$$R = \min(r_1, \ldots, r_n)$$
$$Q = \min(q_1, \ldots, q_m)$$

where r_i and q_j ($1 \leq i \leq n$, $1 \leq j \leq m$) are C, DC, P, P^{-1}, coP, coP^{-1}, O, DR, NTP, NTP^{-1}, $coNTP$ or $coNTP^{-1}$. This applies, among others, to all RCC–8 and RCC–5 relations.

(2) Repeatedly applying (7.51) yields

$$T_W(R(a,b), Q(b,c)) = T_W(\min_{i=1}^{n} r_i(a,b), \min_{j=1}^{m} q_j(b,c))$$
$$\leq \min_{i=1}^{n} \min_{j=1}^{m} T_W(r_i(a,b), q_j(b,c))$$

(3) For each i and each j, use Table 7.5 to obtain a conclusion of the form

$$T_W(r_i(a,b), q_j(b,c)) \leq t_{ij}(a,c) \tag{7.52}$$

Hence we obtain

$$T_W(R(a,b), Q(b,c)) \leq \min_{i=1}^{n} \min_{j=1}^{m} t_{ij}(a,c) \tag{7.53}$$

(4) Use Proposition 7.5 to obtain a minimal subset A of $\{t_{ij} | 1 \leq i \leq n, 1 \leq j \leq m\}$ for which it holds that

$$\min_{i=1}^{n} \min_{j=1}^{m} t_{ij}(a,c) = \min_{t \in A} t(a,c) \tag{7.54}$$

(5) We conclude

$$T_W(R(a,b), Q(b,c)) \leq \min_{t \in A} t(a,c) \qquad (7.55)$$

Finally we show that applying this algorithm is a sound generalization of applying RCC–8 transitivity rules.

Proposition 7.13. *If C is a crisp relation, the deductions made for the RCC–8 relations using the spatial reasoning algorithm above are equivalent to the deductions made using the composition table introduced in [Cui et al. (1993)] (i.e., Table 7.3).*

Proof. Each entry of the RCC–8 composition table (Table 7.3) corresponds to a transitivity rule of the form $R(a,b) \wedge S(b,c) \Rightarrow Q(a,c)$, where R and S are RCC–8 relations and Q is the union of some RCC–8 relations. We need to show that a conclusion equivalent to $Q(a,c)$ is obtained by our algorithm when $R(a,b)$ and $S(b,c)$ are known to hold. As an example, we show this for the entry on the second row, second column. Applying our spatial reasoning algorithm, we obtain

$$\begin{aligned}
T_W&(EC(a,b), EC(b,c)) \\
&= T_W(\min(C(a,b), 1 - O(a,b)), \min(C(b,c), 1 - O(b,c))) \\
&= T_W(\min(C(a,b), DR(a,b)), \min(C(b,c), DR(b,c))) \\
&\leq \min(T_W(C(a,b), C(b,c)), T_W(C(a,b), DR(b,c)), \\
&\qquad\quad T_W(DR(a,b), C(b,c)), T_W(DR(a,b), DR(b,c))) \\
&\leq \min(1, 1 - NTP(a,c), 1 - NTP^{-1}(a,c), 1) \\
&= \min(1 - NTP(a,c), 1 - NTP^{-1}(a,c))
\end{aligned}$$

If C is a crisp relation, then EC and NTP are crisp relations as well. Hence, we have established that from $EC(a,b)$ and $EC(b,c)$ it follows that $\neg NTP(a,c)$ and $\neg NTP^{-1}(a,c)$, which is equivalent to $DC(a,c) \vee EC(a,c) \vee PO(a,c) \vee TPP(a,c) \vee TPP^{-1}(a,c) \vee EQ(a,c)$ by Proposition 7.11. $\qquad \square$

Note how in the proof of Proposition 7.13, a generalization is obtained of the transitivity rule $EC(a,b) \wedge EC(b,c) \Rightarrow \neg NTP(a,c) \wedge \neg NTP^{-1}(a,c)$, which corresponds to the entry on the second row, second column of Table 7.4. In general, we can show that applying the algorithm above to generalized RCC–8 relations is always equivalent to a generalization of the corresponding transitivity rule from Table 7.4.

Proposition 7.13 demonstrates that the transitivity rules from Table 7.5 behave intuitively when applied to crisp spatial information. It furthermore provides a means to deduce new information from given assertions about fuzzy topological relations. However, it does not provide any guarantees on the completeness of the inferences made. A detailed discussion of such issues is provided in the next chapter.

7.5 Interpretation of Fuzzy RCC Relations

The definitions of RCC relations like P and O, involving quantifiers that range over arbitrary regions, are difficult to evaluate. Furthermore, it is often unclear how a specific interpretation of C influences the semantics of relations like P and O. In other words, the generality of the framework — achieved by treating regions as primitive objects, independent of a particular representation — may actually be undesirable in practical applications. Therefore, more intuitive characterizations of the RCC relations, corresponding to a particular interpretation of C and certain assumptions on how regions are defined, are generally used in applications. For example, the standard semantics of C are specified in terms of mathematical topology. Recall that a subset τ of the power set 2^X of a non–empty set X is called a topology on X iff

(1) $\emptyset \in \tau$ and $X \in \tau$
(2) $A \in \tau \wedge B \in \tau \Rightarrow A \cap B \in \tau$
(3) $(\forall i \in I)(A_i \in \tau) \Rightarrow \bigcup_{i \in I} A_i \in \tau$

A subset A of X is called open iff $A \in \tau$ and closed if its complement $X \setminus A$ is open. The interior $i(A)$ of A is the largest open set that is contained in A, while the closure $cl(A)$ of A is the smallest closed set that contains A. Finally, A is called regular open iff $i(cl(A)) = A$ and regular closed iff $cl(i(A)) = A$. Often, in the RCC, regions are assumed to be regular closed sets, and two regions are said to be connected if they share at least one point [Gotts (1996)]. In this interpretation, P corresponds to the subset relation, while O holds between two regions if their interiors share at least one point. Another possibility is to define regions as regular open sets, and to define two regions to be connected if their closures share at least one point. In this case, for example, O holds between two regions if they share at least one point.

Our generalization inherits the generality of the RCC, likewise calling for explicit definitions of the fuzzy topological relations corresponding with specific representations of regions and interpretations of C. To this end, we provide in this section, explicit definitions of the fuzzy spatial relations for the particular case where connection is defined in terms of nearness between fuzzy sets. These definitions pave the way for practical applications in which the notion of connection is graded rather than black–and–white. They furthermore reveal a correspondence between fuzzy RCC relations and fuzzy spatial relations based on relatedness measures.

7.5.1   *Resemblance Relations*

The fuzzy relation $N_{(\alpha,\beta)}$, introduced in Section 7.3.1, can be used to model nearness between points. A more general way to model nearness between points is to use models for approximate equality. In particular, fuzzy T–equivalence relations seem to be an appropriate candidate, at first glance. Recall that a fuzzy T–equivalence relation (w.r.t. a t–norm T) in a universe X is a reflexive, symmetric fuzzy relation R in X that satisfies T–transitivity, that is

$$T(R(x,y), R(y,z)) \leq R(x,z)$$

for all x, y, and z in X. However, using fuzzy T–equivalence relations imposes rather strict limitations on the interpretation of approximate equality, and therefore nearness. Problems occur in situations where we want to define two points to be close to degree 1, even if their distance is strictly positive. For example, consider a two–dimensional Euclidean space, and assume that, whenever the distance between two points is less than or equal to 0.1, we call these points close to degree 1. If we have three points a, b, and c such that $d(a,b) = 0.1$, $d(b,c) = 0.1$ and $d(a,c) = 0.2$ (i.e., a, b, and c are on a line), then a and b are close to degree 1, b and c are close to degree 1, by definition. If we impose T–transitivity on the nearness relation, a and c have to be close to degree 1 as well. Since it is natural to define nearness (in a given context) only in terms of the distance between two points, this means that any two points whose distance is less than 0.2, are close to degree 1. Repeating this argument, we obtain that any two points whose distance is less than 0.4, 0.8, 1.6, etc. are close to degree 1.

To avoid such problems, we will use the more general notion of a resemblance relation [De Cock and Kerre (2003a,b)]. Recall that a mapping d from X^2 to $[0, +\infty[$ is called a pseudometric on X iff $d(x,x) = 0$, $d(x,y) = d(y,x)$ and $d(x,y) + d(y,z) \geq d(x,z)$ for all x, y and z in X. A fuzzy relation R in X is called a resemblance relation w.r.t. a pseudometric

d on X iff for all x, y, z and u in X

$$R(x, x) = 1 \tag{7.56}$$

$$d(x, y) \leq d(z, u) \Rightarrow R(x, y) \geq R(z, u) \tag{7.57}$$

Note that (7.57) implies that any resemblance relation is also symmetric. However, the third property of fuzzy T–equivalence relations, T–transitivity, does not hold anymore in general.

For example, for $\alpha, \beta \geq 0$, the fuzzy relation $N_{(\alpha,\beta)}$ is a resemblance relation in $\mathbb{R}^2$. The fact that $N_{(\alpha,\beta)}$ satisfies (7.57) can be seen from the fact that the graph in Figure 7.6(a) is decreasing. If $\alpha > 0$, $N_{(\alpha,\beta)}$ is not T–transitive for any t–norm T. To see this, let a, b, and c be collinear points such that $d(a, b) = d(b, c) = \alpha$ and $d(a, c) = 2\alpha$. It holds that $T(N_{(\alpha,\beta)}(a, b), N_{(\alpha,\beta)}(b, c)) = T(1, 1) = 1$, while $N_{(\alpha,\beta)}(a, c) < 1$.

The following lemma will be useful to derive specific definitions of the generalized RCC relations below.

Lemma 7.12. *Let $(X, \|.\|)$ be a normed vector space, d the induced metric (i.e., $d(x, y) = \|y - x\|$ for all x and y in X), and R a resemblance relation w.r.t. d. It holds that the fuzzy relation E in X defined for all x and z in X by*

$$E(x, z) = \inf_{y \in X} I_T(R(x, y), R(y, z)) \tag{7.58}$$

is a fuzzy T–equivalence relation in U.

Proof. The reflexivity of E follows immediately from the symmetry of R and (2.23). To show the symmetry of E, we use the fact that, since R satisfies (7.57), there must exist a function f from $[0, +\infty[$ to $[0, 1]$ such that $R(x, y) = f(d(x, y))$ for every x and y in X. We obtain

$$
\begin{aligned}
E(x, z) &= \inf_{y \in X} I_T(R(x, y), R(y, z)) \\
&= \inf_{y_0 \in X} I_T(R(x, x + z - y_0), R(x + z - y_0, z)) \\
&= \inf_{y_0 \in X} I_T(f(d(x, x + z - y_0)), f(d(x + z - y_0, z))) \\
&= \inf_{y_0 \in X} I_T(f(\|x + z - y_0 - x\|), f(\|z - (x + z - y_0)\|)) \\
&= \inf_{y_0 \in X} I_T(f(\|z - y_0\|), f(\|y_0 - x\|)) \\
&= \inf_{y_0 \in X} I_T(f(d(z, y_0)), f(d(y_0, x))) \\
&= \inf_{y_0 \in X} I_T(R(z, y_0), R(y_0, x)) \\
&= E(z, x)
\end{aligned}
$$

Finally, the T–transitivity of E follows from (2.6), the symmetry of R, and (2.28):

$$T(E(a,b), E(b,c)) = T(\inf_{y \in X} I_T(R(a,y), R(y,b)), \inf_{y \in X} I_T(R(b,y), R(y,c)))$$

$$\leq \inf_{y \in X} T(I_T(R(a,y), R(y,b)), \inf_{y' \in X} I_T(R(b,y'), R(y',c)))$$

$$\leq \inf_{y \in X} T(I_T(R(a,y), R(y,b)), I_T(R(b,y), R(y,c)))$$

$$= \inf_{y \in X} T(I_T(R(a,y), R(y,b)), I_T(R(y,b), R(y,c)))$$

$$\leq \inf_{y \in X} I_T(R(a,y), R(y,c))$$

$$= E(a,c) \qquad \qquad \square$$

Corollary 7.1. *For x, y, and z in X, it holds that*

$$I_T(R(x,y), R(y,z)) \geq E(x,z) \tag{7.59}$$

$$T(E(x,y), R(y,z)) \leq R(x,z) \tag{7.60}$$

$$I_T(E(x,z), R(y,z)) \geq R(x,y) \tag{7.61}$$

where we used (2.21) to obtain (7.60) and (7.61).

The previous lemma does not hold in general for an arbitrary reflexive and symmetric fuzzy relation R, as is illustrated by the following counterexample.

Example 7.2. Assume that R is defined as

$$R(x,y) = \begin{cases} 0 & \text{if } (x = b \wedge y \neq b \wedge y \neq a) \text{ or } (x \neq b \wedge x \neq a \wedge y = b) \\ 1 & \text{otherwise} \end{cases}$$

where $a, b \in X$, and $a \neq b$. Obviously, R is reflexive and symmetric. However,

$$E(a,b) = \inf_{y \in X} I_T(R(a,y), R(y,b)) \leq I_T(R(a,c), R(c,b)) = I_T(1,0) = 0$$

where $c \neq a$ and $c \neq b$, while

$$E(b,a)$$

$$= \inf_{y \in X} I_T(R(b,y), R(y,a))$$

$$= \min(\inf_{y \neq a,b} I_T(R(b,y), R(y,a)), I_T(R(b,b), R(b,a)), I_T(R(b,a), R(a,a)))$$

$$= \min(\inf_{y \neq a,b} I_T(0, R(y,a)), I_T(1,1), I_T(1,1))$$

$$= 1$$

hence E is not symmetric, in general, when R does not satisfy (7.57).

Note that while T–transitivity is not required, and not even desirable for resemblance relations such as $N_{(\alpha,\beta)}$, the T–transitivity of the fuzzy relation E defined in (7.58) will be needed to derive our characterization of the generalized RCC relations. This is the reason why we only consider resemblance relations to model nearness between points, rather than arbitrary symmetric and reflexive fuzzy relations. Also the following lemma will be useful.

Lemma 7.13. *Let E be defined as in Lemma 7.12, and let A be a fuzzy set in X. It holds that*

$$E{\uparrow}(R{\uparrow}A) = E{\downarrow}(R{\uparrow}A) = R{\uparrow}A$$
$$E{\uparrow}(R{\downarrow}A) = E{\downarrow}(R{\downarrow}A) = R{\downarrow}A$$

Proof. As an example, we show that $E{\downarrow}(R{\uparrow}A) = R{\uparrow}A$. We obtain, due to the reflexivity of E and (2.22),

$$(E{\downarrow}(R{\uparrow}A))(x) = \inf_{y\in X} I_T(E(y,x), \sup_{z\in X} T(R(z,y), A(z)))$$
$$\leq I_T(E(x,x), \sup_{z\in X} T(R(z,x), A(z)))$$
$$= \sup_{z\in X} T(R(z,x), A(z))$$
$$= (R{\uparrow}A)(x)$$

Conversely, using (2.18), (2.24), the symmetry of E and R, and (7.61), we find for x in X

$$(E{\downarrow}(R{\uparrow}A))(x) = \inf_{y\in X} I_T(E(y,x), \sup_{z\in X} T(R(z,y), A(z)))$$
$$\geq \inf_{y\in X} \sup_{z\in X} I_T(E(y,x), T(R(z,y), A(z)))$$
$$\geq \inf_{y\in X} \sup_{z\in X} T(I_T(E(y,x), R(z,y)), A(z))$$
$$\geq \inf_{y\in X} \sup_{z\in X} T(R(z,x), A(z))$$
$$= \sup_{z\in X} T(R(z,x), A(z))$$
$$= (R{\uparrow}A)(x)$$
$\square$

In the following, regions are defined as normalized fuzzy sets in the universe X. Henceforth, we will assume that this universe X is equipped with a norm $\|.\|$, that d is the induced metric, and that R is a resemblance relation w.r.t. d. Direct and superdirect images under a fuzzy relation (not necessarily involving a resemblance relation) have proven useful in many contexts. When R is a resemblance relation, however, we can give a specific interpretation to $R{\uparrow}A$, $R{\downarrow}A$, $R{\downarrow}{\uparrow}A$, and $R{\uparrow}{\downarrow}A$. This is illustrated in Figure 7.18 for a normalized fuzzy set A in $\mathbb{R}$, and $R = N_{(\alpha,\beta)}$. Note that we use $\mathbb{R}$ for the ease of depicting the membership functions, while in practice, of course, fuzzy sets in $\mathbb{R}^2$ and $\mathbb{R}^3$ are more commonly used to represent regions. Intuitively, $R{\uparrow}A$ is a fuzzy set that contains all the points that are close to some point of the region A (w.r.t. R), while $R{\downarrow}A$ contains the points that are located in A, but not close to the boundary of A, i.e., the points that are located in the heart of the region. The membership functions of $R{\uparrow}{\downarrow}A$ and $R{\downarrow}{\uparrow}A$ are more similar to the membership function of A than those of $R{\uparrow}A$ and $R{\downarrow}A$. In fact, $R{\downarrow}{\uparrow}A$ and $R{\uparrow}{\downarrow}A$ only differ from A in that steep parts of the membership function of A have become more gentle (depending on the parameter β). For $R{\downarrow}{\uparrow}A$ and $R{\uparrow}{\downarrow}A$ this causes an increase and a decrease in membership degrees respectively.

7.5.2   Semantics of the Fuzzy RCC Relations

We define connection of two regions as nearness w.r.t. a resemblance relation R.

Definition 7.1. For normalized fuzzy sets A and B in X, we define the degree $C(A, B)$ to which A and B are connected as

$$C(A, B) = A \circ_T R \circ_T B \qquad (7.62)$$

Note that the fuzzy relation $C^1_{(\alpha,\beta)}$, defined in (7.31), is a special case of this definition of connection.

Depending on the context, there may be (at least) two different reasons for introducing nearness in the definition of C. First, we may want to express that small distances should be ignored. Intuitively, C expresses the degree to which A and B have a point in common. However, if A and B have no point in common, but some point of A is very close to some point of B, we still want to have that A is connected to B (to some degree). In other words, the resemblance relation in the definition of C is used to model indiscernibility of locations in this case. The second reason is that we may want to express (vague) distance information. For example, two city neighbourhoods are called connected if they are within walking distance of each other, or within a three kilometre radius, etc.

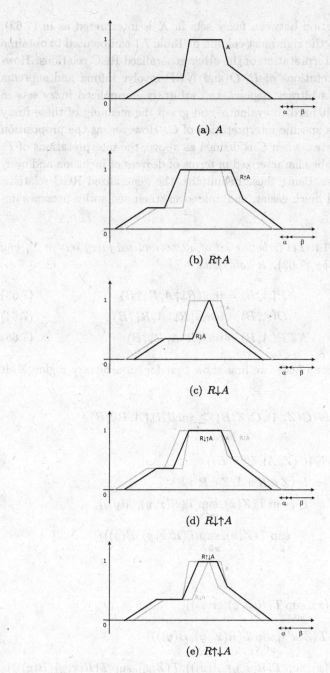

(a) A

(b) $R{\uparrow}A$

(c) $R{\downarrow}A$

(d) $R{\downarrow}{\uparrow}A$

(e) $R{\uparrow}{\downarrow}A$

Fig. 7.18 Effect of taking the direct and superdirect image of a fuzzy set A under a resemblance relation $R = N_{(\alpha,\beta)}$.

When connection between fuzzy sets in X is interpreted as in (7.62), the definitions in the rightmost column of Table 7.1 can be used to obtain a corresponding interpretation of the other generalized RCC relations. However, the interpretations of P, O and NTP involve infima and suprema that range over arbitrary regions, i.e., arbitrary normalized fuzzy sets in X. This makes it hard to evaluate, and grasp the meaning of these fuzzy relations under a specific interpretation of C. However, as the proposition below demonstrates, when C is defined as above, the interpretations of P, O and NTP can be characterized in terms of degrees of inclusion and overlap of fuzzy sets. Using these definitions, the generalized RCC relations can be evaluated much easier, and, moreover, their semantics becomes immediately clear.

Proposition 7.14. *Let U be the set of all normalized fuzzy sets in X, and let C be defined by (7.62). It holds that*

$$P(A, B) = incl(R{\downarrow}{\uparrow}A, R{\downarrow}{\uparrow}B) \tag{7.63}$$

$$O(A, B) = overl(R{\downarrow}{\uparrow}A, R{\downarrow}{\uparrow}B) \tag{7.64}$$

$$NTP(A, B) = incl(R{\uparrow}A, R{\downarrow}{\uparrow}B) \tag{7.65}$$

Proof. To prove (7.63), we first show that for an arbitrary region Z, it holds that

$$I_T(C(Z, A), C(Z, B)) \geq incl(R{\downarrow}{\uparrow}A, R{\downarrow}{\uparrow}B)$$

$$
\begin{aligned}
&I_T(C(Z, A), C(Z, B)) \\
&= I_T(Z \circ R \circ A, Z \circ R \circ B) \\
&= I_T(\sup_{x \in X} T(Z(x), \sup_{y \in X} T(R(x, y), A(y))), \\
&\qquad \sup_{x \in X} T(Z(x), \sup_{y \in X} T(R(x, y), B(y))))
\end{aligned}
$$

and by (2.19)

$$
\begin{aligned}
&= \inf_{x \in X} I_T(T(Z(x), \sup_{y \in X} T(R(x, y), A(y))), \\
&\qquad \sup_{x' \in X} T(Z(x'), \sup_{y \in X} T(R(x', y), B(y)))) \\
&\geq \inf_{x \in X} I_T(T(Z(x), \sup_{y \in X} T(R(x, y), A(y))), T(Z(x), \sup_{y \in X} T(R(x, y), B(y))))
\end{aligned}
$$

Finally, by (2.29), (2.23), and (2.65) we obtain

$$\geq \inf_{x \in X} T(I_T(Z(x), Z(x)), I_T(\sup_{y \in X} T(R(x,y), A(y)), \sup_{y \in X} T(R(x,y), B(y))))$$

$$= \inf_{x \in X} I_T(\sup_{y \in X} T(R(x,y), A(y)), \sup_{y \in X} T(R(x,y), B(y)))$$

$$= incl(R{\uparrow}A, R{\uparrow}B)$$

$$= incl(R{\downarrow}{\uparrow}A, R{\downarrow}{\uparrow}B)$$

By the definition of infimum as the greatest lower bound, we conclude that

$$P(A,B) = \inf_{Z \in U} I_T(C(Z,A), C(Z,B)) \geq incl(R{\downarrow}{\uparrow}A, R{\downarrow}{\uparrow}B) \qquad (7.66)$$

Conversely, we find

$$P(A,B) = \inf_{Z \in U} I_T(C(Z,A), C(Z,B))$$

$$= \inf_{Z \in U} I_T(\sup_{x \in X} T(Z(x), \sup_{y \in X} T(R(x,y), A(y))),$$

$$\sup_{x \in X} T(Z(x), \sup_{y \in X} T(R(x,y), B(y))))$$

For every z in X, we define the normalized fuzzy set S_z for x in X as

$$S_z(x) = \begin{cases} 1 & \text{if } x = z \\ 0 & \text{otherwise} \end{cases}$$

In other words, S_z corresponds to the crisp singleton set $\{z\}$. By monotonicity of the infimum, we find

$$\leq \inf_{z \in X} I_T(\sup_{x \in X} T(S_z(x), \sup_{y \in X} T(R(x,y), A(y))),$$

$$\sup_{x \in X} T(S_z(x), \sup_{y \in X} T(R(x,y), B(y))))$$

$$= \inf_{z \in X} I_T(\sup_{y \in X} T(R(z,y), A(y)), \sup_{y \in X} T(R(z,y), B(y)))$$

$$= incl(R{\uparrow}A, R{\uparrow}B)$$

Applying (2.65) to this last expression completes the proof of (7.63).

To prove (7.64), we first show that for an arbitrary region Z, it holds that

$$T(P(Z,A), P(Z,B)) \leq overl(R{\downarrow}{\uparrow}A, R{\downarrow}{\uparrow}B)$$

As we have defined regions as normalized fuzzy sets, there must exist an m in X for which $Z(m) = 1$. We obtain by (7.63) and (2.65)

$$
\begin{aligned}
T(P&(Z, A), P(Z, B)) \\
&= T(incl(R{\downarrow}{\uparrow}Z, R{\downarrow}{\uparrow}A), incl(R{\downarrow}{\uparrow}Z, R{\downarrow}{\uparrow}B)) \\
&= T(incl(R{\uparrow}Z, R{\uparrow}A), incl(R{\uparrow}Z, R{\uparrow}B)) \\
&= T(\inf_{x \in X} I_T(\sup_{y \in X} T(R(x,y), Z(y)), (R{\uparrow}A)(x)), \\
&\qquad \inf_{x \in X} I_T(\sup_{y \in X} T(R(x,y), Z(y)), (R{\uparrow}B)(x))) \\
&\leq T(\inf_{x \in X} I_T(T(R(x,m), Z(m)), (R{\uparrow}A)(x)), \\
&\qquad \inf_{x \in X} I_T(T(R(x,m), Z(m)), (R{\uparrow}B)(x))) \\
&= T(\inf_{x \in X} I_T(R(x,m), (R{\uparrow}A)(x)), \inf_{x \in X} I_T(R(x,m), (R{\uparrow}B)(x))) \\
&\leq \sup_{y \in X} T(\inf_{x \in X} I_T(R(x,y), (R{\uparrow}A)(x)), \inf_{x \in X} I_T(R(x,y), (R{\uparrow}B)(x))) \\
&= overl(R{\downarrow}{\uparrow}A, R{\downarrow}{\uparrow}B)
\end{aligned}
$$

By the definition of the supremum as least upper bound, we conclude from this

$$
O(A, B) = \sup_{z \in U} T(P(Z, A), P(Z, B)) \leq overl(R{\downarrow}{\uparrow}A, R{\downarrow}{\uparrow}B)
$$

Conversely, we find by (7.63)

$$
\begin{aligned}
O(A, B) &= \sup_{Z \in U} T(P(Z, A), P(Z, B)) \\
&= \sup_{Z \in U} T(\inf_{x \in X} I_T(\sup_{y \in X} T(R(x,y), Z(y)), (R{\uparrow}A)(x)), \\
&\qquad \inf_{x \in X} I_T(\sup_{y \in X} T(R(x,y), Z(y)), (R{\uparrow}B)(x))) \\
&\geq \sup_{z \in X} T(\inf_{x \in X} I_T(\sup_{y \in X} T(R(x,y), S_z(y)), (R{\uparrow}A)(x)), \\
&\qquad \inf_{x \in X} I_T(\sup_{y \in X} T(R(x,y), S_z(y)), (R{\uparrow}B)(x))) \\
&= \sup_{z \in X} T(\inf_{x \in X} I_T(R(x,z), (R{\uparrow}A)(x)), \inf_{x \in X} I_T(R(x,z), (R{\uparrow}B)(x))) \\
&= overl(R{\downarrow}{\uparrow}A, R{\downarrow}{\uparrow}B)
\end{aligned}
$$

where the fuzzy set S_z is defined as before. This proves (7.64).

Finally, we prove (7.65). Let Z be an arbitrary region. We obtain by (7.64)

$$I_T(C(Z, A), O(Z, B))$$

$$= I_T(\sup_{x \in X} T(Z(x), \sup_{y \in X} T(A(y), R(x, y))), \sup_{x \in X} T((R{\downarrow}{\uparrow}Z)(x), (R{\downarrow}{\uparrow}B)(x)))$$

By (2.19), we find

$$= \inf_{x \in X} I_T(T(Z(x), \sup_{y \in X} T(A(y), R(x, y))), \sup_{x' \in X} T((R{\downarrow}{\uparrow}Z)(x'), (R{\downarrow}{\uparrow}B)(x')))$$

$$\geq \inf_{x \in X} I_T(T(Z(x), \sup_{y \in X} T(A(y), R(x, y))), T((R{\downarrow}{\uparrow}Z)(x), (R{\downarrow}{\uparrow}B)(x)))$$

and by Lemma 2.17 and (2.26)

$$\geq \inf_{x \in X} I_T(T((R{\downarrow}{\uparrow}Z)(x), \sup_{y \in X} T(A(y), R(x, y))), T((R{\downarrow}{\uparrow}Z)(x), (R{\downarrow}{\uparrow}B)(x)))$$

$$= \inf_{x \in X} I_T(\sup_{y \in X} T(A(y), R(x, y)), I_T((R{\downarrow}{\uparrow}Z)(x), T((R{\downarrow}{\uparrow}Z)(x), (R{\downarrow}{\uparrow}B)(x))))$$

Finally, using (2.24) and (2.23), we find

$$\geq \inf_{x \in X} I_T(\sup_{y \in X} T(A(y), R(x, y)), T(I_T((R{\downarrow}{\uparrow}Z)(x), (R{\downarrow}{\uparrow}Z)(x)), (R{\downarrow}{\uparrow}B)(x)))$$

$$= \inf_{x \in X} I_T(\sup_{y \in X} T(A(y), R(x, y)), (R{\downarrow}{\uparrow}B)(x))$$

$$= incl(R{\uparrow}A, R{\downarrow}{\uparrow}B)$$

From the definition of infimum as the greatest lower bound, we conclude from this

$$NTP(A, B) = \inf_{Z \in U} I_T(C(Z, A), O(Z, B)) \geq incl(R{\uparrow}A, R{\downarrow}{\uparrow}B)$$

Conversely, we find by (7.64)

$$NTP(A, B)$$

$$= \inf_{Z \in U} I_T(C(Z, A), O(Z, B))$$

$$= \inf_{Z \in U} I_T(C(Z, A), \sup_{x \in X} T((R{\downarrow}{\uparrow}Z)(x), (R{\downarrow}{\uparrow}B)(x)))$$

$$\leq \inf_{z \in X} I_T(C(S_z, A), \sup_{x \in X} T((R{\downarrow}{\uparrow}S_z)(x), (R{\downarrow}{\uparrow}B)(x)))$$

$$= \inf_{z \in X} I_T(C(S_z, A), \sup_{x \in X} T(\inf_{y \in X} I_T(R(x, y), \sup_{v \in X} T(R(y, v), S_z(v))),$$

$$(R{\downarrow}{\uparrow}B)(x)))$$

$$= \inf_{z \in X} I_T(C(S_z, A), \sup_{x \in X} T(\inf_{y \in X} I_T(R(x, y), R(y, z)), (R{\downarrow}{\uparrow}B)(x)))$$

and by Lemma 7.12, Lemma 7.13, and the symmetry of C

$$= \inf_{z \in X} I_T(C(S_z, A), \sup_{x \in X} T(E(x, z), (R{\downarrow}{\uparrow}B)(x)))$$

$$= \inf_{z \in X} I_T(C(A, S_z), (R{\downarrow}{\uparrow}B)(z))$$

$$= \inf_{z \in X} I_T(\sup_{x \in X} T(A(x), \sup_{y \in X} T(R(x, y), S_z(y))), (R{\downarrow}{\uparrow}B)(z))$$

$$= \inf_{z \in X} I_T(\sup_{x \in X} T(A(x), R(x, z)), (R{\downarrow}{\uparrow}B)(z))$$

$$= \inf_{z \in X} I_T((R{\uparrow}A)(z), (R{\downarrow}{\uparrow}B)(z))$$

$$= incl(R{\uparrow}A, R{\downarrow}{\uparrow}B)$$

which concludes the proof of (7.65).   □

Note that P and O correspond to the usual degree of inclusion and the degree of overlap between the R–closures of the fuzzy sets, while $NTP(A, B)$ is the degree to which every point that is close to a point from A, is contained in the R–closure of B. In other words, $NTP(A, B)$ is the degree to which A is a part of B that is not located close to the boundary of B. When $R = N_{(\alpha, \beta)}$ is used to model nearness, the parameter α can be used to specify, for example, how close two regions should be considered to be connected. This is illustrated in the following example.

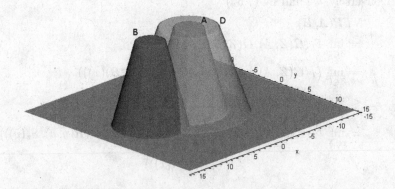

Fig. 7.19   Normalised fuzzy sets A, B, and C in $\mathbb{R}^2$, representing regions.

Example 7.3. Consider the normalized fuzzy sets A, B, and D in $\mathbb{R}^2$, defined for (x, y) in $\mathbb{R}^2$ as

$$A(x, y) = \min(1, \max(0, \frac{5 - \sqrt{x^2 + y^2}}{3}))$$

$$B(x, y) = \min(1, \max(0, \frac{5 - \sqrt{(x-7)^2 + y^2}}{3}))$$

$$D(x, y) = \min(1, \max(0, \frac{8 - \sqrt{x^2 + y^2}}{4}))$$

These fuzzy sets are shown in Figure 7.19. Using $N_{(1,0)}$ to model nearness and the Łukasiewicz connectives T_W and I_W in the definition of C, it can be shown that

$$O(A, B) = T_W(A(3.5, 0), B(3.5, 0)) = T_W(0.5, 0.5) = 0$$

$$O(D, B) = T_W(D(5, 0), B(5, 0)) = T_W(\frac{3}{4}, 1) = \frac{3}{4}$$

$$C(A, B) = T_W(A(4, 0), B(5, 0)) = T_W(\frac{1}{3}, 1) = \frac{1}{3}$$

$$NTP(A, D) = I_W(A(2, 0), D(3, 0)) = I_W(1, 1) = 1$$

It can indeed be seen from Figure 7.19 that there is quite some overlap between D and B. On the other hand, the degree of overlap between A and B is too small for $O(A, B) > 0$ to hold. While $O(A, B)$ and $O(D, B)$ are independent of the parameter α, we can obtain different values for $C(A, B)$ and $NTP(A, D)$ by changing α. For example, choosing $\alpha = 2$ yields

$$C(A, B) = T_W(A(3, 0), B(5, 0)) = T_W(\frac{2}{3}, 1) = \frac{2}{3}$$

$$NTP(A, D) = I_W(A(2, 0), D(4, 0)) = I_W(1, 1) = 1$$

while $\alpha = 3$ leads to

$$C(A, B) = T_W(A(2, 0), B(5, 0)) = T_W(1, 1) = 1$$

$$NTP(A, D) = I_W(A(2, 0), D(5, 0)) = I_W(1, \frac{3}{4}) = \frac{3}{4}$$

Note how increasing the value of α makes the fuzzy relation C more tolerant, and the fuzzy relation NTP less tolerant. For example, A is located somewhat away from the boundary of D, hence $NTP(A, D) = 1$ when α is sufficiently small ($\alpha \leq 2$). However, when α becomes too large (e.g., $\alpha = 3$), A is considered to be too close to the boundary of D for $NTP(A, D) = 1$ to hold.

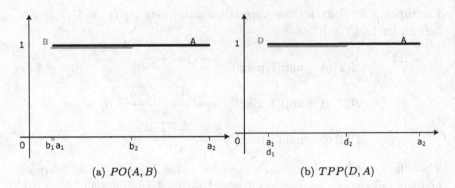

(a) $PO(A, B)$ (b) $TPP(D, A)$

Fig. 7.20   In the usual RCC semantics we have the counterintuitive fact that $PO(A, B)$ and $\neg TPP(B, A)$, while $TPP(D, A)$ and $\neg PO(A, D)$.

The next example illustrates how appropriate values of the parameter β in $N_{(\alpha, \beta)}$ lead to a gradual transition between generalized RCC relations like PO and TPP.

Example 7.4. Consider the regions A, B, and D shown in Figure 7.20, corresponding to the crisp intervals $[a_1, a_2]$, $[b_1, b_2]$, and $[d_1, d_2]$ respectively. Using the original RCC relations, we have that $PO(A, B)$, $\neg TPP(B, A)$, $TPP(D, A)$, and $\neg PO(A, D)$. Nonetheless, the situations depicted in Figure 7.20(a) and 7.20(b) are very similar, as the distance between a_1 and b_1 is very small. In many application domains it would be desirable that the spatial relations behave similarly in similar situations. Using our fuzzy relations, this can be achieved because the transition between TPP and PO is gradual for $\beta > 0$. Assume, for example, that $R = N_{(\alpha, \beta)}$ is used, where $\alpha = 5(a_1 - b_1)$, and $\beta = 2(a_1 - b_1)$. It holds that

$$TPP(B, A)$$
$$= \min(PP(B, A), 1 - NTP(B, A))$$
$$= \min(incl(R{\downarrow}{\uparrow}B, R{\downarrow}{\uparrow}A), 1 - incl(R{\downarrow}{\uparrow}A, R{\downarrow}{\uparrow}B),$$
$$1 - incl(R{\uparrow}B, R{\downarrow}{\uparrow}A))$$

When, for example, the Łukasiewicz connectives T_W and I_W are used, we can show that

$$incl(R{\downarrow}{\uparrow}B, R{\downarrow}{\uparrow}A) = 0.5$$
$$incl(R{\downarrow}{\uparrow}A, R{\downarrow}{\uparrow}B) = 0$$
$$incl(R{\uparrow}B, R{\downarrow}{\uparrow}A) = 0$$

Hence, we obtain $TPP(B, A) = 0.5$. In the same way, we can establish that $PO(A, B) = 0.5$, $TPP(D, A) = 1$, and $PO(A, D) = 0$. In this way, we express that although A and B partially overlap to some extent, we could still consider B to be a tangential proper part of A as well. Higher values of β correspond to a higher value of $TPP(B, A)$ and a lower value of $PO(A, B)$, i.e., the higher the value of β, the more similar the situation in Figure 7.20(a) is considered to be to the situation in Figure 7.20(b). For example, when $\beta = 3(a_1 - b_1)$ we have that $TPP(B, A) = 0.66$ and $PO(A, B) = 0.33$. When $\beta \leq a_1 - b_1$ we have that $TPP(B, A) = 0$ and $PO(A, B) = 1$. In other words, the parameter β can be used to control how smooth the transition between, for example, PO and TPP should be.

Finally, we provide two special cases of Proposition 7.14, corrresponding to situations where the fuzzy sets involved are R–closed, and situations where the resemblance relation R is T–transitive. When A and B are R–closed (i.e., when the membership functions of A and B contain no *steep* parts or discontinuities), we immediately obtain

$$P(A, B) = incl(A, B) \tag{7.67}$$

$$O(A, B) = overl(A, B) \tag{7.68}$$

$$NTP(A, B) = incl(R{\uparrow}A, B) \tag{7.69}$$

If the resemblance relation R is T–transitive, then some of the RCC relations cannot be distinguished anymore.

Proposition 7.15. *If R is T–transitive (i.e., R is a fuzzy T–equivalence relation), it holds that*

$$C(A, B) = O(A, B)$$

Proof. Using Proposition 7.14 and Lemma 2.15, we obtain

$$O(A, B) = overl(R{\downarrow}{\uparrow}A, R{\downarrow}{\uparrow}B)$$

$$= overl(R{\uparrow}A, R{\uparrow}B)$$

$$= \sup_{x \in X} T(\sup_{y \in X} T(R(y, x), A(y)), \sup_{y \in X} T(R(y, x), B(y)))$$

Using the associativity and symmetry of T, (2.7), and the symmetry of R, we find

$$= \sup_{x \in X} \sup_{y \in X} \sup_{y' \in X} T(T(R(y, x), A(y)), T(R(y', x), B(y')))$$

$$= \sup_{x \in X} \sup_{y \in X} \sup_{y' \in X} T(A(y), T(T(R(y, x), R(x, y')), B(y')))$$

$$= \sup_{y \in X} T(A(y), \sup_{y' \in X} T(\sup_{x \in X} T(R(y, x), R(x, y')), B(y')))$$

and finally, using the T–transitivity of R

$$\leq \sup_{y \in X} T(A(y), \sup_{y' \in X} T(\sup_{x \in X} R(y, y'), B(y')))$$

$$= \sup_{y \in X} T(A(y), \sup_{y' \in X} T(R(y, y'), B(y')))$$

$$= A \circ R \circ B$$

$$= C(A, B)$$

Conversely, we find, using the reflexivity of R

$$C(A, B) = \sup_{y \in X} T(A(y), \sup_{y' \in X} T(R(y, y'), B(y')))$$

$$= \sup_{y \in X} T(A(y), \sup_{y' \in X} T(T(R(y, y'), R(y', y')), B(y')))$$

$$\leq \sup_{y \in X} T(A(y), \sup_{y' \in X} T(\sup_{x \in X} T(R(y, x), R(x, y')), B(y')))$$

$$= O(A, B)$$

□

This again shows that fuzzy T–equivalence relations are not appropriate to model nearness in this context.

Chapter 8

Reasoning about Fuzzy Spatial Information

8.1 Introduction

As in the temporal domain, a large proportion of the spatial information conveyed in natural language text is of a qualitative nature. We may learn, for instance, that a certain geographic region is adjacent to, contained in or overlapping with another. In contrast to the temporal domain, however, there usually is an abundance of quantitative information available as well, e.g., in the form of geographical coordinates. One reason is that addresses of places which are located in a given region can be extracted from web documents relatively easily. Subsequently, these addresses can be translated to their geographical coordinates through a process called geocoding. Suppose, for example, that we want to model the spatial extent of two geographical regions A and B. From web documents, we may extract a number of places in each of these regions, as illustrated in Figure 8.1(a). In this figure, circles correspond to locations in region A, whereas triangles correspond to locations in region B. In addition to geographical coordinates of places, official boundaries for political regions (countries, provinces, cities, electoral divisions, etc.) are typically available from gazetteers. To some extent, this changes the nature of the reasoning tasks of interest in practical applications. However, through a number of use cases, we will demonstrate below that fuzzy spatial reasoning is nonetheless of paramount importance in building vague spatial models from the web. Note that although we will only focus on (fuzzy) topological relations in this chapter, many of the arguments given apply to other types of spatial relations as well.

Use case 1: building quantitative geographical models While, at first glance, the availability of quantitative information may seem to make any processing of topological spatial information redundant, the opposite is in fact true, i.e., topological information is often required because of given quantitative information, to convert it into reliable geographical models. Note that qualitative relations are used in this case to help build quantitative models, rather than as a surrogate for them. Consider again the regions A and B from Figure 8.1(a). Given only this quantitative information, what exactly would be a plausible boundary of region A? Knowing that A and B are adjacent, the boundary in Figure 8.1(b) would be a good candidate. On the other hand, if A were overlapping with B, the boundary in Figure 8.1(c) is more likely to be (approximately) correct. Hence, the actual boundaries that result from quantitative information about the location of a region depend on its topological relation with other regions. Moreover, as many geographical regions are vague, also the topological relations between them are only vaguely defined. Consider, for example, the following statements about the location of the Chiado and Baixa neighbourhoods in Lisbon, Portugal:

(1) The Elevador de Santa Justa is an impressive steel lift built in 1900 to link the Baixa district to the Chiado.[1]
(2) Shops in the Baixa tend to be pricier than elsewhere, though. Chiado, the adjacent neighbourhood, has ...[2]
(3) Baixa, or downtown Lisbon, is the heart of the city.[3]
(4) Located in the heart of the historic Chiado quarter, in downtown Lisbon, Chiado Residence ...[4]

In the RCC, we can encode the topological information from these statements as

$$DC(Baixa, Chiado) \tag{8.1}$$

$$EC(Baixa, Chiado) \tag{8.2}$$

$$EQ(downtown\ Lisbon, Baixa) \tag{8.3}$$

$$O(Chiado, downtown\ Lisbon) \tag{8.4}$$

Note that this encoding into RCC was done manually here. Automating this process is definitely not trivial, but it is outside the scope of the current discussion. While all four statements are true to some extent, the

---

[1]http://www.telegraph.co.uk/travel/main.jhtml?xml=/travel/2006/03/01/etmykind01.xml, accessed April 13, 2007.

[2]http://www.thisistravel.co.uk/travel/guides/city.htmlLisbon-what-to-buy_article.html?in_article_id=17537&in_page_id=1, accessed April 20, 2007.

[3]http://www.golisbon.com/sight-seeing/baixa.html, accessed April 13, 2007

[4]http://www.chiadoresidence.com/location.htm, accessed April 13, 2007.

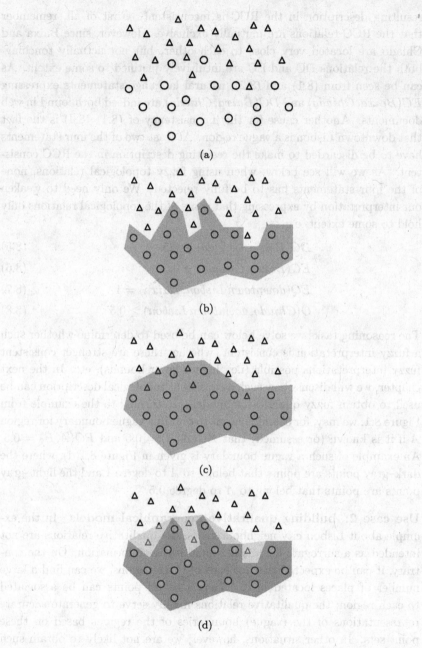

Fig. 8.1 Locations in region *A* (circles) and region *B* (triangles), and some possible resulting boundaries for *A*.

resulting description in the RCC is inconsistent. First of all, remember that the RCC relations are mutually exclusive. However, since Baixa and Chiado are located very close to each other, but not actually touching, both the relations DC and EC are intuitively justified to some extent. As can be seen from (8.1) and (8.2), natural language statements expressing $EC(Baixa, Chiado)$ and $DC(Baixa, Chiado)$ are indeed both found in web documents. Another cause for the inconsistency of (8.1)–(8.4) is the fact that downtown Lisbon is a vague region. At least two of the four statements have to be discarded to make the resulting description in the RCC consistent. As we will see below, when using fuzzy topological relations, none of the four statements has to be fully rejected. We only need to weaken our interpretation by expressing that some of the topological relations only hold to some extent, e.g.

$$DC(Baixa, Chiado) \geq 0.5 \qquad (8.5)$$

$$EC(Baixa, Chiado) \geq 0.5 \qquad (8.6)$$

$$EQ(downtown\ Lisbon, Baixa) = 1 \qquad (8.7)$$

$$O(Chiado, downtown\ Lisbon) \geq 0.5 \qquad (8.8)$$

The reasoning tasks we solve below can be used to determine whether such a fuzzy interpretation is consistent, whether there are stronger consistent fuzzy interpretations possible (i.e., higher lower bounds), etc. In the next chapter, we will discuss how such a consistent topological description can be used to obtain fuzzy quantitative models. Returning to the example from Figure 8.1, we may, for example, want to obtain a vague boundary for region A if it is known (or assumed) that $EC(A, B) = 0.5$ and $PO(A, B) = 0.5$. An example of such a vague boundary is given in Figure 8.1(d), where the dark–gray points are points that belong to A to degree 1 and the light–gray points are points that belong to A to degree 0.5.

Use case 2: building qualitative geographical models In the example about Lisbon city neighbourhoods, the qualitative relations are not intended as a surrogate for missing quantitative information. On the contrary, it can be expected that for each of these regions, we can find a large number of places located in it. Thus a set of points can be associated to each region; the qualitative relations mainly serve to generate accurate representations of the (vague) boundaries of the regions based on these point sets. In other situations, however, we are not likely to obtain such point sets and qualitative descriptions are all that is available. For example, when the region to be modelled is not a city neighbourhood, but a

park, forest, cultural heritage site or university campus, we will probably
not find many addresses or places contained in it. To illustrate this point,
assume we want to acquire a spatial model of Stanley Park in Vancouver,
B.C., Canada. Such a model may, for instance, be of interest in geographical information retrieval systems and question answering systems to help
people locate tourist attractions such as the Vancouver Aquarium, Second
Beach or Ceperley Meadows. Information about the spatial configuration
of Stanley Park attractions and landmarks can be obtained by extracting
spatial relations from texts:

(1) English Bay is awesome, and all the beaches around Stanley Park are
    nice too (I really like Second Beach). [5]
(2) There are two beaches (called Third and Second) right in Stanley Park
    [6]
(3) Second Beach is technically in Stanley Park.[7]
(4) An 8.8 kilometre (5.5 mile) seawall path circles the park, which is used
    [8]
(5) The seawall in Vancouver, Canada is a stone wall that was constructed
    around the perimeter of Stanley Park ... [9]

The spatial information conveyed in these statements can be translated
into RCC formulas and, as before, the resulting description is inconsistent.
In particular, the first statement seems to indicate that Second Beach is
adjacent to Stanley Park, whereas the second expresses that Second Beach
is in fact contained in Stanley Park. Hence, there seems to be some vagueness about the exact boundaries of Stanley Park, i.e., about whether the
boundaries encompass Second Beach or not. This is further exemplified in
the third statement which conveys that Second Beach is located in Stanley
Park, but, at the same time, not really considered to be a part of it. Similarly, it is unclear whether the Seawall is adjacent to or contained in Stanley
Park, i.e., both TPP and EC hold between the Seawall and Stanley Park to
some extent. Again, the fuzzy topological reasoning algorithms introduced
below could be applied to find a consistent fuzzy model. Finally, note that,
in addition to topological information, also direction and nearness informa-

---

[5]http://www.nextbody.com/forums/archive/index.php/t-4178.html, accessed December 18, 2007.

[6]http://www.whyvancouver.com/beaches.html, accessed December 18, 2007.

[7]http://members.virtualtourist.com/m/tt/8079/, accessed December 18, 2007.

[8]http://en.wikipedia.org/wiki/Stanley_Park, accessed December 18, 2007.

[9]http://en.wikipedia.org/wiki/Seawall_%28Vancouver%29, accessed December 18,
2007.

tion are likely to play a central role in building spatial representations of regions such as Stanley Park.

Use case 3: building non–geographical spatial models   Spatial reasoning and information processing do not only occur in geography. For example, a significant fraction of the information in biomedical ontologies is topological, and accordingly, the issue of spatial reasoning in this context has received a lot of attention (e.g., [Donnelly *et al.* (2006); Schulz *et al.* (2006); Smith *et al.* (2005)]). Along similar lines, spatial relations occur in descriptions of various spatial scenes, e.g., specifications of multimedia documents [M. Vazirgiannis (1998)], eye witness reports of a traffic accident, textual descriptions about the rooms' arrangement in a house, etc. Usually, spatial relations are initially expressed in a crisp way, but vagueness is introduced when descriptions of the same scene, either in structured form (e.g., ontologies) or textual form, from various sources are merged [Worboys and Clementini (2001)]. In this case, fuzzy spatial reasoning could be used to integrate conflicting spatial descriptions of a given scene. It is important to note here that this process does not only apply to the three–dimensional physical scenes found in reality or their two–dimensional abstractions, which we have used in our examples so far, but also to conceptual spaces of arbitrary dimension.

Conceptual spaces have been developed in [Gärdenfors (2000)] as a powerful means to define the semantics of concepts. As opposed to symbolic approaches such as description logics, concepts are given precise definitions as convex regions in a (typically) Euclidean space, whose dimensions correspond to qualities of the objects under consideration. As a simple example, consider the concepts *Tall Person* and *Short Person*, which can be modelled as intervals of the real line, representing compatible height ranges. Naturally, regions in conceptual spaces that correspond to vague concepts are characterized by vague boundaries, e.g., concepts such as *Tall Person* and *Short Person* could be modelled by fuzzy intervals, rather than crisp intervals.

In [Gärdenfors and Williams (2001)], a technique is proposed to construct the actual regions corresponding to concepts, based on prototypes (i.e., typical instances of the concept). It is assumed that the numerical values for each of the quality dimensions are known for these prototypes (e.g., the heights of a number of tall people, and the heights of a number of short people). Techniques from computational geometry (Voronoi tesselations) are then used to convert this prototype information to actual regions. Interestingly, very similar techniques have already been used to obtain boundaries for geographic regions [Alani (2001)]. It is proposed in [Gärdenfors and Williams (2001)] to use the RCC to reason about the concept definitions (i.e., regions in the conceptual space of interest) that are acquired in this way.

By generalizing this idea to regions with fuzzy boundaries, reasoning in our fuzzy RCC could be used to address challenging problems related to the modelling of vague concepts. Consider, for example, the well–known Wine Ontology[10]. In this ontology, many wine–related concepts are defined, e.g., *Dry Wine, Table Wine, Late Harvest Wine*, etc., as well as relations between these concepts. When thinking of concepts as regions in a conceptual space, such relations typically correspond to topological spatial relations. For example, the information that *Wine* is a subclass of *Potable Liquid* implies a relation PP between the corresponding regions, whereas the constraint that the properties *Dry, Off-Dry* and *Sweet* are mutually exclusive implies $DR(Dry, Off\text{-}Dry)$, $DR(Dry, Sweet)$ and $DR(Off\text{-}Dry, Sweet)$. Moreover, assuming that some prototypes are available for each concept, region boundaries could be generated from which relations such as TPP, $NTPP$ and EC between concepts could, in turn, be derived. However, whereas the wine ontology in itself is consistent, it is well–known that merging it with other knowledge bases about wine easily leads to inconsistencies [Ovchinnikova *et al.* (2007)]. For example, many subclass relations are, in fact, not valid for certain particular cases: *Port* is defined as a subclass of *Red Wine*, while in reality there are some white port wines as well; the Wine Ontology claims that wines are made from at least one type of grape, which is clearly not the case for apple wine or rice wine; concepts such as *Dry Wine* are to some extent subjective, and different ontologies might use slightly different definitions (e.g., based on sugar content only, based on sugar content relative to acidity, based on taste, etc.). Using fuzzy topological reasoning, we may obtain consistent interpretations claiming that, for example, *Apple Wine* is a subclass of *Wine* to degree 0.3, and that *Wine* is a subclass of *MadeFromGrapes* to degree 0.7.

In all of the scenarios above, fuzzy topological reasoning is used to obtain a consistent interpretation of conflicting information. The main reasoning task of interest therefore remains to check the satisfiability of a knowledge base such as $\{NTPP(a, b) \geq 0.7, P(b, c) \leq 0.4, EC(a, c) \leq 0.5\}$, similar

---

[10]http://www.w3.org/TR/owl-guide/wine.rdf

in spirit to the FI–satisfiability problem we discussed in Chapter 5. After reviewing some related work, we will formalize this reasoning task and present a solution based on linear programming. This solution can also be used to solve a number of related tasks such as entailment checking or finding the best truth–value bound. In Section 8.4, we show how reasoning in our fuzzy RCC can be reduced to reasoning in the original RCC. In addition to yielding importing practical advantages (e.g., implementation of optimized reasoners), this reduction is useful to leverage theoretical results of the RCC to our fuzzy RCC. As a specific example, we reveal an interesting relationship between our fuzzy RCC and the well–known Egg–Yolk approach to topological vagueness. Finally, we prove that any satisfiable knowledge base in our fuzzy RCC can be interpreted in terms of fuzzy sets and nearness, in any dimension.

8.2 Spatial Reasoning

Reasoning about topological information encoded in RCC–8 has been well studied. Most reasoning tasks of interest are NP–complete [Renz and Nebel (1999)]. In consequence, and inspired by results about reasoning in the IA (interval algebra), considerable work has been devoted to finding tractable subfragments of RCC–8, i.e., subsets of the 2^8 relations that can be expressed in RCC–8 for which reasoning is tractable [Grigni *et al.* (1995); Nebel (1994); Renz (1999); Renz and Nebel (1999)]. In [Nebel (1994)], it was shown that reasoning in RCC–8 is tractable, provided only base relations are used (i.e., no disjunctive information such as $(TPP \cup EC)(a,b)$). Of special interest are subsets of RCC–8 relations that are maximally tractable, i.e., such that every proper superset of RCC–8 relations would result in NP–completeness. A first maximal tractable subfragment, containing 146 relations, was identified in [Renz and Nebel (1999)]. Two additional maximal tractable subfragments were identified in [Renz (1999)], containing 158 and 160 relations. In [Renz (1999)] it was moreover shown that these three subfragments are the only maximal tractable subfragments of RCC–8 that contain all eight base relations. Recall that in the IA, there was only one maximal tractable subfragment, the ORD–Horn subfragment, containing all 13 basic Allen relations. In all three subfragments of RCC–8, satisfiability can be decided using an $O(n^3)$ path–consistency algorithm, similar to Allen's algorithm for temporal reasoning. Finally, experimental results in [Renz and Nebel (2001)] indicate that using these maximal tractable subfragments for reasoning in RCC–8 has a significant impact on computation time: almost all problem instances up to 500 regions could be solved in a very efficient way (mostly less than 1 minute on a Sun Ultra 1 machine with 128MB of internal memory).

Usually, a knowledge base of RCC–8 relations is called satisfiable (or consistent) if it can be realized in some topological space, i.e., if all variables can be interpreted by regions in some topological space such that all imposed relations hold [Renz and Nebel (1999)]. In practice, however, it might be interesting to know whether a set of RCC–8 formulas can be realized by (regular closed) subsets of, for example, $\mathbb{R}^2$ or $\mathbb{Z}^2$ and, if so, which additional constraints on these subsets might be imposed (e.g., convexity, internal connectedness, etc.). In [Renz (2002)], it was shown that any satisfiable set of RCC–8 formulas can be realized in $\mathbb{R}^n$ for every n in $\mathbb{N} \setminus \{0\}$. In other words, satisfiability and realizability in $\mathbb{R}^n$ are equivalent. For $n \geq 3$, this result also holds when regions are constrained to be internally connected, and even if they are constrained to be polytopes. Unfortunately, for $n = 2$ and $n = 1$ this result does not hold in general. Furthermore, until recently, it was not even known if the problem of checking whether a knowledge base of RCC–8 relations can be realized by internally connected two–dimensional regions is in NP, or even decidable. In particular, this problem can be related to the problem of recognizing a special class of graphs called string graphs [Grigni *et al.* (1995); Kratochvíl (1991)]. In [Schaefer *et al.* (2003)], it was shown that recognizing string graphs, and therefore deciding whether an RCC–8 knowledge base is realizable by internally connected regions in $\mathbb{R}^2$, is indeed in NP. Note that checking whether a knowledge base of RCC–8 relations can be realized by internally connected one–dimensional regions essentially corresponds to an undirected variant of the satisfiability problem in the IA, and is therefore in NP. In [Li (2006)], it was shown that any satisfiable set of RCC–8 formulas can also be realized by subsets of $\mathbb{Z}^2$ (i.e., the digital plane).

Several generalizations of RCC–8 and the 9–intersection model [Egenhofer and Franzosa (1991)] have been defined with the aim of specifying vague topological information. Recall from the previous chapter, for instance, that a vague region is modelled in the Egg–Yolk calculus [Cohn and Gotts (1996)] as a pair of crisp regions (a_1, a_2), and topological relations between vague regions (a_1, a_2) and (b_1, b_2) are represented as topological relations between these crisp regions. Since a_1, a_2, b_1 and b_2 are RCC regions, algorithms for reasoning in RCC–8 can be used to reason in the Egg–Yolk calculus as well. As pointed out in the previous chapter, there are also many approaches to spatial vagueness in which topological relations are defined as fuzzy relations, allowing to capture gradual boundaries in a more natural way. To the best of our knowledge, however, no complete reasoning procedures or complexity results have been investigated for such fuzzy topological relations.

Many spatial relations from natural language are inherently vague, even when the objects involved are crisp regions or points. In [Dutta (1991)], a general framework based on fuzzy restrictions and the compositional rule of inference is proposed to cope with vague distance and direction information between points, such as "*p* is located about 3 kilometres north of *q*". Both distance and direction constraints are modelled as triangular fuzzy sets, but their interaction is, unfortunately, not considered in the proposed reasoning algorithm. Nearness of places is also considered in [Guesgen and Albrecht (2000)], where the degree of nearness of two places is either defined as the reciprocal of their Euclidean distance, or assumed to be known in advance, i.e., a complete enumeration of the nearness of every pair of places is specified. Fuzzy spatial relations between crisp regions have been considered in [Vazirgiannis (2000)], where for example the degree of adjacency between two regions is defined based on the fraction of their boundary that is actually shared. A graded approach to cardinal direction relations between crisp regions is also considered in [Kulik *et al.* (2002)]. However, rather than modelling an absolute degree (e.g., in [0, 1]) to which some region B is north of some region A, a technique is proposed to rank objects according to how compatible they are with a constraint such as "north of A".

8.3   Satisfiability of Fuzzy Topological Information

8.3.1   *Definitions*

In the introduction, we mentioned that the main reasoning task of interest is checking the satisfiability of a knowledge base such as $A = \{NTPP(a, b) \geq 0.7, P(b, c) \leq 0.4, EC(a, c) \leq 0.5\}$. An important question here is what exactly we mean by satisfiability. Clearly, for A to be satisfiable, it should be possible to map the variables a, b, c to particular objects $a^{\mathcal{I}}$, $b^{\mathcal{I}}$, $c^{\mathcal{I}}$ from some interpretation domain D, and the relation C to some reflexive and symmetric fuzzy relation $C^{\mathcal{I}}$ in D such that all formulas in A hold, i.e., such that $NTPP^{\mathcal{I}}(a^{\mathcal{I}}, b^{\mathcal{I}}) \geq 0.7$, $P^{\mathcal{I}}(b^{\mathcal{I}}, c^{\mathcal{I}}) \leq 0.4$ and $EC^{\mathcal{I}}(a^{\mathcal{I}}, c^{\mathcal{I}}) \leq 0.5$ (where $NTPP^{\mathcal{I}}$, $P^{\mathcal{I}}$ and $EC^{\mathcal{I}}$ are defined in terms of $C^{\mathcal{I}}$). However, should we impose additional restrictions on this interpretation domain D?

For fuzzy temporal reasoning, we specifically required an interpretation in which variables were mapped to fuzzy intervals. By analogy, we might require here that variables be mapped to regions in some fuzzy topological space, or normalised sets in $\mathbb{R}^n$ for some n, possibly constrained by additional requirements like upper semi–continuity. As we will see below, however, all these definitions of satisfiability are equivalent. Formally, we are therefore interested in the satisfiability of sets of fuzzy RCC formulas, defined as follows.

Definition 8.1 (atomic fuzzy RCC formula). *An atomic fuzzy RCC formula is a formula of the form* $R(a, b) \leq \lambda$ *or* $R(a, b) \geq \lambda$, *where* R *is either* C *or one of the fuzzy topological relations from Table 7.2 (P, O, ..., NTPP), $\lambda \in [0, 1]$, and a and b are elements from the universe of regions* U.

Definition 8.2 (fuzzy RCC formula). *A fuzzy RCC formula is a formula of the form* $f_1 \vee f_2 \vee \cdots \vee f_m$, *where* f_i *is an atomic fuzzy RCC formula* $(1 \leq i \leq m)$.

By analogy, we will also refer to expressions such as $NTPP(a, b) \vee \neg PO(b, d)$ as (crisp) RCC formulas.

Definition 8.3 (Interpretation). *An interpretation* $\mathcal{I}$ *is a mapping from the universe of regions* U *to some interpretation domain* D, *and from* C *to a reflexive and symmetric fuzzy relation* $C^{\mathcal{I}}$ *in* D.

Since all fuzzy topological relations are defined in terms of C, we can extend the interpretation of C to interpretations of the other fuzzy topological relations; e.g., for all u and v in U, we define

$$P^{\mathcal{I}}(u^{\mathcal{I}}, v^{\mathcal{I}}) = \inf_{w \in U} I_T(C^{\mathcal{I}}(w^{\mathcal{I}}, u^{\mathcal{I}}), C^{\mathcal{I}}(w^{\mathcal{I}}, v^{\mathcal{I}}))$$

For example, let D be the universe of normalised fuzzy sets in $\mathbb{R}^n$ with a bounded support. Let $R_{(\alpha, \beta)}$ be the fuzzy relation in $\mathbb{R}^n$ defined for all p and q in $\mathbb{R}^n$ by $(\alpha, \beta \geq 0)$

$$R_{(\alpha, \beta)}(p, q) = \begin{cases} 1 & \text{if } d(p, q) \leq \alpha \\ 0 & \text{if } d(p, q) > \alpha + \beta \\ \frac{\alpha + \beta - d(p, q)}{\beta} & \text{otherwise } (\beta \neq 0) \end{cases} \qquad (8.9)$$

where d is the Euclidean distance in $\mathbb{R}^n$. Note that for $n = 2$, $R_{(\alpha, \beta)}$ is the degree of nearness $N_{(\alpha, \beta)}$ defined in the previous chapter. Furthermore let $C_{(\alpha,\beta)}$, $P_{(\alpha,\beta)}$, $O_{(\alpha,\beta)}$ $NTP_{(\alpha,\beta)}$ be defined as in (7.62)–(7.65), using $R = R_{(\alpha,\beta)}$, i.e., for all normalised fuzzy sets A and B in $\mathbb{R}^n$, we have

$$C_{(\alpha,\beta)}(A,B) = A \circ_T R_{(\alpha,\beta)} \circ_T B$$

$$P_{(\alpha,\beta)}(A,B) = incl(R_{(\alpha,\beta)}{\downarrow}{\uparrow}A, R_{(\alpha,\beta)}{\downarrow}{\uparrow}B)$$

$$O_{(\alpha,\beta)}(A,B) = overl(R_{(\alpha,\beta)}{\downarrow}{\uparrow}A, R_{(\alpha,\beta)}{\downarrow}{\uparrow}B)$$

$$NTP_{(\alpha,\beta)}(A,B) = incl(R_{(\alpha,\beta)}{\uparrow}A, R_{(\alpha,\beta)}{\downarrow}{\uparrow}B)$$

Below, we will sometimes use expressions like R_α, C_α and P_α to denote the fuzzy relations $R_{(\alpha,0)}$, $C_{(\alpha,0)}$ and $P_{(\alpha,0)}$ respectively. If $C^{\mathcal{I}} = C_{(\alpha,\beta)}$, we know from Proposition 7.14 that $P^{\mathcal{I}} = P_{(\alpha,\beta)}$, $O^{\mathcal{I}} = O_{(\alpha,\beta)}$, and $NTP^{\mathcal{I}} = NTP_{(\alpha,\beta)}$. We will refer to interpretations of this type as $(n; \alpha, \beta)$–interpretations.

Definition 8.4 (satisfiability). *An interpretation $\mathcal{I}$ satisfies an atomic fuzzy RCC formula of the form $R(a,b) \leq \lambda$ (resp. $R(a,b) \geq \lambda$) iff $R^{\mathcal{I}}(a^{\mathcal{I}}, b^{\mathcal{I}}) \leq \lambda$ (resp. $R^{\mathcal{I}}(a^{\mathcal{I}}, b^{\mathcal{I}}) \geq \lambda$) holds. Furthermore, $\mathcal{I}$ satisfies a fuzzy RCC formula $f_1 \vee f_2 \vee \cdots \vee f_m$ iff it satisfies at least one of the atomic fuzzy RCC formulas $f_1, f_2, \ldots, f_m$. Finally, $\mathcal{I}$ satisfies a set of fuzzy RCC formulas Θ, written $\mathcal{I} \models \Theta$, iff it satisfies every fuzzy RCC formula in Θ. If such an interpretation $\mathcal{I}$ satisfying Θ exists, Θ is called satisfiable (or consistent) and $\mathcal{I}$ is called a model of Θ. An $(n; \alpha, \beta)$–interpretation which satisfies Θ is called an $(n; \alpha, \beta)$–model of Θ.*

Below, we will also talk about interpretations and models of sets of crisp RCC formulas. When there is cause for confusion, we will talk about F–satisfiability, F–interpretations and F–models to refer to the concepts introduced above, and about C–satisfiability, C–interpretations and C–models to refer to the corresponding concepts for crisp RCC formulas. The standard way to define C–interpretations is to map variables to regular closed subsets in $\mathbb{R}^n$ and to interpret C such that two regular closed subsets A and B are connected iff $A \cap B \neq \emptyset$. Below we will refer to such C–interpretations as standard interpretations, and denote the corresponding topological relations in $\mathbb{R}^n$ by C^n, P^n, O^n, etc. Note that P^n corresponds to the subset relation, and $O^n(A,B)$ iff $i(A) \cap i(B) \neq \emptyset$, where $i(A)$ denotes the interior of A.

While it can be convenient in applications to use fuzzy RCC formulas such as $EC(a,b) \geq 0.5$, every set Θ of fuzzy RCC formulas can equivalently be written as a set Θ' of fuzzy RCC formulas which only involve the fuzzy topological relations C, P, O and NTP. As an example, consider the fuzzy

RCC formula $EC(a, b) \geq 0.4 \vee DC(a, b) \leq 0.3$. Using the definitions from Table 7.2, we find

$$EC(a, b) \geq 0.4 \vee DC(a, b) \leq 0.3$$
$$\Leftrightarrow (C(a, b) \geq 0.4 \wedge 1 - O(a, b) \geq 0.4) \vee 1 - C(a, b) \leq 0.3$$
$$\Leftrightarrow (C(a, b) \geq 0.4 \wedge O(a, b) \leq 0.6) \vee C(a, b) \geq 0.7$$
$$\Leftrightarrow (C(a, b) \geq 0.4 \vee C(a, b) \geq 0.7)$$
$$\wedge (O(a, b) \leq 0.6 \vee C(a, b) \geq 0.7)$$
$$\Leftrightarrow C(a, b) \geq 0.4 \wedge (O(a, b) \leq 0.6 \vee C(a, b) \geq 0.7)$$

Thus, if $EC(a, b) \geq 0.4 \vee DC(a, b) \leq 0.3$ occurs in Θ, we could replace it by $\{C(a, b) \geq 0.4, O(a, b) \leq 0.6 \vee C(a, b) \geq 0.7\}$. For this reason, the following discussion will predominantly be restricted to sets of fuzzy RCC formulas involving only C, P, O and NTP.

Note that in general, such a set does not completely specify, for every pair of variables, the degree to which each of the fuzzy topological relations C, P, O and NTP should hold. For example, consider the set $A = \{C(a, b) \geq 0.5, O(b, a) \leq 0.7\}$, which is satisfied by an interpretation $\mathcal{I}$ if $C^{\mathcal{I}}(a^{\mathcal{I}}, b^{\mathcal{I}}) = 0.5$ and $O^{\mathcal{I}}(b^{\mathcal{I}}, a^{\mathcal{I}}) = 0.6$, but also, among others, if $C^{\mathcal{I}}(a^{\mathcal{I}}, b^{\mathcal{I}}) = O^{\mathcal{I}}(b^{\mathcal{I}}, a^{\mathcal{I}}) = 0.5$ or $C^{\mathcal{I}}(a^{\mathcal{I}}, b^{\mathcal{I}}) = O^{\mathcal{I}}(b^{\mathcal{I}}, a^{\mathcal{I}}) = 0.6$. Formally, we have that every model of, for instance, $A_1 = \{C(a, b) \geq 0.6, C(b, a) \leq 0.6, O(a, b) \geq 0.6, O(b, a) \leq 0.6\}$ is also a model of A, hence A_1 could be regarded as a refinement of the information in A.

Definition 8.5 (refinement). *Let Θ_1 and Θ_2 be sets of fuzzy RCC formulas. Θ_2 is called a refinement of Θ_1 iff every model of Θ_2 is also a model of Θ_1. If both Θ_1 is a refinement of Θ_2 and Θ_2 is a refinement of Θ_1, Θ_1 and Θ_2 are called equivalent.*

In practice, we can repeatedly refine a set of fuzzy RCC formulas until the exact degree to which C, P, O and NTP should hold between every pair of variables is specified. We will refer to such sets as normalised sets of fuzzy RCC relations.

Definition 8.6 (normalised). *Let Θ be a set of fuzzy RCC formulas, and let V be the set of regions that are used in the formulas from Θ ($V \subseteq U$). Θ is called normalised iff*

(1) for each fuzzy topological relation R in $\{C, P, O, NTP\}$ and all regions a and b in V, Θ contains a formula of the form $R(a, b) \leq 0$ or $R(a, b) \geq 1$,

or both formulas of the form $R(a, b) \leq \lambda$ and $R(a, b) \geq \lambda$ for a given λ in $]0, 1[$;

(2) Θ contains no other formulas.

The first condition in the definition above guarantees that the membership degree of each of the fuzzy topological relations is uniquely determined for each pair of regions in V, while the second condition prevents the inclusion of superfluous additional information. Clearly, every satisfiable set of fuzzy RCC formulas Θ can be refined to a normalised set. Furthermore, Θ is satisfiable iff there exists at least one refinement which is satisfiable.

8.3.2   *Satisfiability*

8.3.2.1   *Normalised sets*

First, we show how the satisfiability of a normalised set of fuzzy RCC formulas can be checked. A normalised set of fuzzy RCC formulas is completely characterized by four matrices, containing the membership degrees of the fuzzy topological relations C, P, O and NTP for each pair of regions in V. For example $(V = \{a, b, c\})$:

$$
C = \begin{matrix} & a & b & c \\ a & \\ b & \\ c & \end{matrix}\begin{pmatrix} 1 & 0.6 & 0.8 \\ 0.6 & 1 & 0.6 \\ 0.8 & 0.6 & 1 \end{pmatrix} \qquad P = \begin{matrix} & a & b & c \\ a & \\ b & \\ c & \end{matrix}\begin{pmatrix} 1 & 0.6 & 0 \\ 0 & 1 & 0 \\ 0.8 & 0.4 & 1 \end{pmatrix} \qquad (8.10)
$$

$$
O = \begin{matrix} & a & b & c \\ a & \\ b & \\ c & \end{matrix}\begin{pmatrix} 1 & 0.6 & 0.8 \\ 0.6 & 1 & 0.4 \\ 0.8 & 0.4 & 1 \end{pmatrix} \qquad NTP = \begin{matrix} & a & b & c \\ a & \\ b & \\ c & \end{matrix}\begin{pmatrix} 0 & 0.6 & 0 \\ 0 & 0 & 0 \\ 0.4 & 0.4 & 0.6 \end{pmatrix} \qquad (8.11)
$$

There are a number of necessary conditions for satisfiability that follow straightforwardly from the properties of the fuzzy topological relations which were investigated in Chapter 7. For example, from Proposition 7.5, we already know that for every u and v in V, it needs to hold that

$$NTP(u, v) \leq P(u, v) \leq O(u, v) \leq C(u, v) \qquad (8.12)$$

For normalised sets, (8.12) translates into restrictions on the corresponding matrix representation. In particular, this implies that the elements of the matrix for NTP should be smaller than the corresponding elements of the matrix for P, which should in turn be smaller than the elements of the matrix for O, which should be smaller than the elements of the matrix for C. It is easy to verify that this is indeed the case in the example (8.10)–(8.11). Next, by definition C is a symmetric fuzzy relation, from which we can easily derive that O is a symmetric fuzzy relation as well. This means that for every u and v in V, we have

$$C(u,v) = C(v,u) \tag{8.13}$$
$$O(u,v) = O(v,u) \tag{8.14}$$

In terms of the matrix representation, this means that the matrices for C and O should be symmetric matrices. From Proposition 7.4, we furthermore know that for every u in V, it needs to hold that

$$P(u,u) = O(u,u) = C(u,u) = 1 \tag{8.15}$$

implying that the elements on the diagonal of the matrices for C, O and P should all be 1. The requirements (8.12)–(8.15) can easily be checked by performing $O(|V|^2)$ simple arithmetic comparisons. Clearly, if any of these requirements is violated, the corresponding set of fuzzy RCC formulas is not satisfiable. Finally, a set of additional requirements follows from the transitivity rules in Table 7.5. One such rule is that for every u, v and w in V, it needs to hold that

$$T(P(u,v), P(v,w)) \leq P(u,w) \tag{8.16}$$

From the matrices above, we find for $u = c$, $v = a$ and $w = b$

$$P(c,a) = 0.8 \qquad P(a,b) = 0.6 \qquad P(c,b) = 0.4$$

If $T = T_W$, we obtain $T_W(P(c,a), P(a,b)) = T_W(0.8, 0.6) = 0.4$, hence (8.16) is satisfied. If T is the minimum, on the other hand, we find $\min(P(c,a), P(a,b)) = 0.6 > 0.4$, violating (8.16). In total there are 144 entries in Table 7.5. However, 84 of these entries are 1, corresponding to transitivity rules that are trivially satisfied (e.g., $T(C(u,v), O(v,w)) \leq 1$). This means that at most 60 transitivity rules need to be checked. Moreover, most of these transitivity rules are the dual of another rule. For example, in Table 7.5, there are two entries corresponding to the rules

$$T(P(u,v), P(v,w)) \leq P(u,w) \tag{8.17}$$
$$T(P^{-1}(u,v), P^{-1}(v,w)) \leq P^{-1}(u,w) \tag{8.18}$$

Clearly, if (8.17) holds for all u, v and w in V, then (8.18) will be satisfied as well. In consequence, the number of remaining transitivity rules can almost be halved: only the following 31 rules need to be checked.

$$T(C(u,v), DC(v,w)) \leq coP(u,w)$$

$$T(C(u,v), P(v,w)) \leq C(u,w)$$

$$T(C(u,v), DR(v,w)) \leq coNTP(u,w)$$

$$T(C(u,v), NTP(v,w)) \leq O(u,w)$$

$$T(DC(u,v), P(v,w)) \leq coP^{-1}(u,w)$$

$$T(DC(u,v), P^{-1}(v,w)) \leq DC(u,w)$$

$$T(DC(u,v), O(v,w)) \leq coP^{-1}(u,w)$$

$$T(DC(u,v), NTP(v,w)) \leq coP^{-1}(u,w)$$

$$T(DC(u,v), NTP^{-1}(v,w)) \leq DC(u,w)$$

$$T(P(u,v), P(v,w)) \leq P(u,w)$$

$$T(P(u,v), coP^{-1}(v,w)) \leq coP^{-1}(u,w)$$

$$T(P(u,v), DR(v,w)) \leq DR(u,w)$$

$$T(P(u,v), coNTP^{-1}(v,w)) \leq coNTP^{-1}(u,w)$$

$$T(P(u,v), NTP(v,w)) \leq NTP(u,w)$$

$$T(DR(u,v), NTP^{-1}(v,w)) \leq DC(u,w)$$

$$T(DR(u,v), NTP(v,w)) \leq coP^{-1}(u,w)$$

$$T(P^{-1}(u,v), NTP^{-1}(v,w)) \leq NTP^{-1}(u,w)$$

$$T(P^{-1}(u,v), NTP(v,w)) \leq O(u,w)$$

$$T(P^{-1}(u,v), coNTP(v,w)) \leq coNTP(u,w)$$

$$T(P^{-1}(u,v), P(v,w)) \leq O(u,w)$$

$$T(coP^{-1}(u,v), NTP(v,w)) \leq coP^{-1}(u,w)$$

$$T(P^{-1}(u,v), DR(v,w)) \leq coP(u,w)$$

$$T(coP(u,v), NTP^{-1}(v,w)) \leq coP(u,w)$$

$$T(P^{-1}(u,v), coP(v,w)) \leq coP(u,w)$$

$$T(NTP(u,v), NTP(v,w)) \leq NTP(u,w)$$

$$T(P^{-1}(u,v), O(v,w)) \leq O(u,w)$$

$$T(NTP(u,v), coNTP^{-1}(v,w)) \leq coP^{-1}(u,w)$$

$$T(O(u,v), DR(v,w)) \leq coP(u,w)$$

$$T(NTP^{-1}(u,v), NTP(v,w)) \leq O(u,w)$$

$$T(O(u,v), NTP(v,w)) \leq O(u,w)$$

$$T(NTP^{-1}(u,v), coNTP(v,w)) \leq coP(u,w)$$

Each of these transitivity rules has to be checked for all $|V|^3$ triples of variables from Θ. In summary, the properties of the fuzzy topological relations which we introduced in the previous chapter lead to a number of necessary conditions for satisfiability, which can be checked in $O(|V|^3)$ time. As the next proposition reveals, these necessary conditions are also sufficient, provided Θ does not contain a fuzzy RCC formula of the form $NTP(v,v) \geq 1$.

Proposition 8.1. *Let Θ be a normalised, finite set of fuzzy RCC formulas, $T = T_W$ and let V be the set of variables occurring in Θ ($|V| = n$). Assume, moreover, that Θ does not contain fuzzy RCC formulas of the form $NTP(v,v) \geq 1$. If Θ satisfies (8.12)–(8.15), as well as the 31 transitivity rules above, for all u, v and w in V, it holds that Θ has an $(n; \alpha, 0)$–model for every $\alpha > 0$.*

Proof. Here we only provide a brief sketch; the complete proof is presented in Appendix C. In particular, we can prove that there exists a mapping f from V to normalised, bounded fuzzy sets in $\mathbb{R}^n$ such that for every pair (a, b) of variables from V, it holds that

$$C_\alpha(f(a), f(b)) = \lambda_{ab}^C \tag{8.19}$$
$$O_\alpha(f(a), f(b)) = \lambda_{ab}^O \tag{8.20}$$
$$P_\alpha(f(a), f(b)) = \lambda_{ab}^P \tag{8.21}$$
$$NTP_\alpha(f(a), f(b)) = \lambda_{ab}^{NTP} \tag{8.22}$$

where λ_{ab}^C, for example, is the value of $C(a, b)$ that is imposed by Θ. In other words, we assume that Θ contains the formulas $C(a, b) \leq \lambda_{ab}^C$ and $C(a, b) \geq \lambda_{ab}^C$, and similar for O, P and NTP. Note that n, the dimension of the Euclidean space under consideration, corresponds to the number of variables in Θ. Rather than specifying f directly, however, we first define a mapping f^I which assigns to each variable in V an n–dimensional sphere that is sufficiently far away from the spheres of all the other variables in V. Next, building on f^I, we specify a mapping f^C such that (8.19) is satisfied for all a and b in V, but not necessarily (8.20)–(8.22). To this end, $f^C(a)$ is defined as the union of $f^I(a)$ and a number of fuzzy subsets of $\mathbb{R}^n$ that are within distance α of some of the other spheres. The support of these fuzzy subsets are again n–dimensional spheres; the membership value of the points in their support is determined by the values λ_{ab}^C. Next, adopting a similar strategy, f^C is extended to a mapping f^O satisfying both (8.19) and (8.20), which is in turn extended to a mapping f^P satisfying

(8.19)–(8.21). Finally, we inductively define a mapping f^i for each i in $\mathbb{N}$. Using the assumption that Θ does not contain any formulas of the form $NTP(v, v) \geq 1$, we show that for some m_0 in $\mathbb{N}$, it holds that $f^n(a) = f^{m_0}(a)$ for all $n \geq m_0$ and all a in V. The proof is completed by showing that for $f = f^{m_0}$, (8.19)–(8.22) are all satisfied, i.e., f^{m_0} corresponds to an $(n; \alpha, 0)$–model of Θ. $\qquad\square$

Corollary 8.1. *Under the assumptions of Proposition 8.1, it holds that Θ is consistent iff (8.12)–(8.15) and the 31 transitivity rules above are satisfied for all u, v and w in V.*

The condition that Θ does not contain any fuzzy RCC formulas of the form $NTP(v, v) \geq 1$ is not a limitation, as such formulas can only be satisfied by very counterintuitive interpretations. For example, in $(n; \alpha, \beta)$–interpretations $\mathcal{I}$ where $\alpha > 0$ (i.e., two different points can still be considered fully connected), $NTP(v, v) \geq 1$ can only be satisfied if $v^{\mathcal{I}} = \mathbb{R}^n$. Moreover, recall that NTP is normally not considered in the RCC at all. We introduced it mainly as a shorthand to define and generalize the RCC–8 relations $NTPP$ and TPP. In applications, we will typically start from a set Θ_0 of fuzzy RCC formulas which does not involve any (disjuncts of) fuzzy RCC formulas of the form $NTP(u, v) \geq \lambda$ or $NTP(u, v) \leq \lambda$ at all. Proposition 8.1 is then applied to different refinements Θ of Θ_0 to check whether at least one such refinement is satisfiable. It turns out that, if Θ_0 is satisfiable and does not contain fuzzy RCC formulas involving NTP, there always exists a normalised set of fuzzy RCC formulas Θ which is a refinement of Θ_0 and does not contain any formulas of the form $NTP(v, v) \geq 1$.

Definition 8.7 (Standard). *A set of fuzzy RCC formulas is called standard if it does not contain (a disjunct of) a fuzzy RCC formula of the form $NTP(u, v) \geq \lambda$ or $NTP(u, v) \leq \lambda$ ($u, v \in U$ and $\lambda \in [0, 1]$). Similarly, a set of crisp RCC formulas is called standard if it does not contain (a disjunct of) an RCC formula of the form $NTP(u, v)$ or $\neg NTP(u, v)$.*

Note that standard sets can still contain fuzzy RCC formulas of the form $NTPP(u, v) \geq \lambda$, $NTPP(u, v) \leq \lambda$, $TPP(u, v) \geq \lambda$ and $TPP(u, v) \leq \lambda$. The following proposition reveals that the additional constraint from Proposition 8.1 that formulas of the form $NTP(v, v) \geq 1$ do not occur, does not have to be considered in satisfiability checking procedures, provided only standard sets are allowed. In other words, to check the satisfiability of a standard set of fuzzy RCC formulas Θ, we only need to check whether the necessary conditions we identified above are satisfied in at least one refinement of Θ.

Proposition 8.2. *Let Θ_0 be a standard, finite set of fuzzy RCC formulas and let $T = T_W$. If Θ_0 can be refined to a normalised set of fuzzy RCC formulas Θ_1 which satisfies (8.12)–(8.15), as well as the transitivity rules for fuzzy topological relations, it holds that Θ_0 is satisfiable.*

Proof. Let $V = \{v_1, v_2, \ldots, v_k\}$ be the set of variables occurring in Θ_0 and let Θ_1 be defined for every v_i and v_j in V by

$$C(v_i, v_j) \geq \lambda_{ij}^C \qquad\qquad C(v_i, v_j) \leq \lambda_{ij}^C$$
$$P(v_i, v_j) \geq \lambda_{ij}^P \qquad\qquad P(v_i, v_j) \leq \lambda_{ij}^P$$
$$O(v_i, v_j) \geq \lambda_{ij}^O \qquad\qquad O(v_i, v_j) \leq \lambda_{ij}^O$$
$$NTP(v_i, v_j) \geq \lambda_{ij}^{NTP} \qquad\qquad NTP(v_i, v_j) \leq \lambda_{ij}^{NTP}$$

for some λ_{ij}^C, λ_{ij}^P, λ_{ij}^O and λ_{ij}^{NTP} in $[0,1]$. Let M be the set of all these membership degrees, i.e.

$$M = \bigcup_{1 \leq i,j \leq k} \{\lambda_{ij}^C, \lambda_{ij}^P, \lambda_{ij}^O, \lambda_{ij}^{NTP}\}$$

and let $\delta > 0$ be such that δ is strictly less than

$$\min\{\min(T_W(\lambda_1, \lambda_2), 1 - T_W(\lambda_1, \lambda_2)) | \lambda_1, \lambda_2 \in M \text{ and } 0 < T_W(\lambda_1, \lambda_2) < 1\}$$

provided $M \supset \{0, 1\}$; if $M = \{0, 1\}$, on the other hand, δ can be an arbitrary value from $]0, 1[$. Note that a suitable δ can always be found, since Θ_0, and therefore also Θ_1 and M are finite. Furthermore, by assumption, we have that $\lambda_{ii}^P = 1$ for all i in $\{1, 2, \ldots, k\}$, hence it holds that $1 \in M$. This implies that for every m in $M \setminus \{0, 1\}$

$$\delta < \min(m, 1 - m) \tag{8.23}$$

To prove this proposition, we will construct a normalised set of fuzzy RCC formulas Θ which satisfies the assumptions of Proposition 8.1, and is, moreover, a refinement of Θ_0. In particular, Θ contains the following formulas

$$C(v_i, v_j) \geq \lambda_{ij}^C \qquad\qquad C(v_i, v_j) \leq \lambda_{ij}^C$$
$$P(v_i, v_j) \geq \lambda_{ij}^P \qquad\qquad P(v_i, v_j) \leq \lambda_{ij}^P$$
$$O(v_i, v_j) \geq \lambda_{ij}^O \qquad\qquad O(v_i, v_j) \leq \lambda_{ij}^O$$
$$NTP(v_i, v_j) \geq \gamma_{ij}^{NTP} \qquad\qquad NTP(v_i, v_j) \leq \gamma_{ij}^{NTP}$$

for every v_i and v_j in V, where

$$\gamma_{ij}^{NTP} = \begin{cases} 1 - \delta & \text{if } \lambda_{ij}^{NTP} = 1 \text{ and } \lambda_{ji}^{P} = 1 \\ \lambda_{ij}^{NTP} & \text{otherwise} \end{cases}$$

Note that $\gamma_{ij}^{NTP} \leq \lambda_{ij}^{NTP}$ always holds. To complete the proof, we need to show that $\gamma_{ii}^{NTP} < 1$ for all i in $\{1, 2, \ldots, k\}$, that Θ is a refinement of Θ_0, and that Θ satisfies (8.12)–(8.15) as well as the transitivity rules for fuzzy topological relations.

By assumption, we know that $\lambda_{ii}^{P} = 1$ for all i in $\{1, 2, \ldots, k\}$. If $\lambda_{ii}^{NTP} = 1$, we therefore have $\gamma_{ii}^{NTP} = 1 - \delta < 1$ and if $\lambda_{ii}^{NTP} < 1$, we have $\gamma_{ii}^{NTP} = \lambda_{ii}^{NTP} < 1$. Next, if Θ were not a refinement of Θ_0, there would have to be a (disjunct of a) formula in Θ_0 of one of the following forms

$$NTPP(v_i, v_j) \geq \lambda \tag{8.24}$$

$$NTPP(v_i, v_j) \leq \lambda \tag{8.25}$$

$$TPP(v_i, v_j) \geq \lambda \tag{8.26}$$

$$TPP(v_i, v_j) \leq \lambda \tag{8.27}$$

which is violated in models of Θ. Indeed, there would have to exist a model $\mathcal{I}$ of Θ which is not a model of Θ_0. Since every model of Θ_1 is a model of Θ_0, this means that some fuzzy RCC formula in Θ_0 is violated because of the fact that $NTP^{\mathcal{I}}(v_i^{\mathcal{I}}, v_j^{\mathcal{I}})$ is γ_{ij}^{NTP} instead of λ_{ij}^{NTP} for some i and j in $\{1, 2, \ldots, k\}$. However, (8.25) can certainly not be violated by $\mathcal{I}$ as for all v_i and v_j, the value of $NTPP^{\mathcal{I}}(v_i^{\mathcal{I}}, v_j^{\mathcal{I}})$ is not greater in models of Θ than in models of Θ_1. Neither can (8.26) be violated, for the same reason. Furthermore, (8.24) could only be violated by $\mathcal{I}$ if $\gamma_{ij}^{NTP} \neq \lambda_{ij}^{NTP}$, but this implies $\lambda_{ji}^{P} = 1$ and therefore $P^{\mathcal{I}}(v_j^{\mathcal{I}}, v_i^{\mathcal{I}}) = 1$, and hence $NTPP^{\mathcal{I}}(v_i^{\mathcal{I}}, v_j^{\mathcal{I}}) = 0$, in any model of Θ_1. As the value of $NTPP^{\mathcal{I}}(v_i^{\mathcal{I}}, v_j^{\mathcal{I}})$ is not greater in models of Θ than in models of Θ_1, this implies that $NTPP^{\mathcal{I}}(v_i^{\mathcal{I}}, v_j^{\mathcal{I}}) = 0$. Hence, as the value of $NTPP^{\mathcal{I}}(v_i^{\mathcal{I}}, v_j^{\mathcal{I}})$ is the same in models of Θ_1 and in models of Θ, (8.24) cannot be violated. In entirely the same way, we have that (8.27) can never be violated.

As Θ_1 satisfies requirements (8.12)–(8.15), we immediately find that Θ satisfies requirements (8.13)–(8.15) and, moreover

$$\lambda_{ij}^{NTP} \leq \lambda_{ij}^{P} \leq \lambda_{ij}^{O} \leq \lambda_{ij}^{C}$$

for all i and j in $\{1, 2, \ldots, k\}$. Since $\gamma_{ij}^{NTP} \leq \lambda_{ij}^{NTP}$, we also have $\gamma_{ij}^{NTP} \leq \lambda_{ij}^{P}$. In other words, Θ also satisfies (8.12).

Finally, we show that Θ satisfies each of the transitivity rules for fuzzy topological relations, and in particular, each of the 31 transitivity rules introduced above. Note that we only need to check the transitivity rules involving NTP; we know that the others are satisfied from the fact that Θ_1 satisfies all transitivity rules. Moreover, most of the remaining transitivity rules are satisfied because $\gamma_{ij}^{NTP} \leq \lambda_{ij}^{NTP}$. For this reason, we only need to show that Θ satisfies the following transitivity rules.

$$T_W(P(v_i, v_j), NTP(v_j, v_l)) \leq NTP(v_i, v_l) \tag{8.28}$$

$$T_W(NTP(v_i, v_j), NTP(v_j, v_l)) \leq NTP(v_i, v_l) \tag{8.29}$$

$$T_W(P^{-1}(v_i, v_j), NTP^{-1}(v_j, v_l)) \leq NTP^{-1}(v_i, v_l) \tag{8.30}$$

$$T_W(P(v_i, v_j), coNTP^{-1}(v_j, v_l)) \leq coNTP^{-1}(v_i, v_l) \tag{8.31}$$

$$T_W(P^{-1}(v_i, v_j), coNTP(v_j, v_l)) \leq coNTP(v_i, v_l) \tag{8.32}$$

$$T_W(NTP(v_i, v_j), coNTP^{-1}(v_j, v_l)) \leq coP^{-1}(v_i, v_l) \tag{8.33}$$

$$T_W(NTP^{-1}(v_i, v_j), coNTP(v_j, v_l)) \leq coP(v_i, v_l) \tag{8.34}$$

First, assume that (8.28) were violated, i.e.

$$T_W(\lambda_{ij}^P, \gamma_{jl}^{NTP}) > \gamma_{il}^{NTP} \tag{8.35}$$

Since $T_W(\lambda_{ij}^P, \lambda_{jl}^{NTP}) \leq \lambda_{il}^{NTP}$, this is only possible if $\gamma_{il}^{NTP} < \lambda_{il}^{NTP}$, which implies $\lambda_{il}^{NTP} = \lambda_{li}^P = 1$ and $\gamma_{il}^{NTP} = 1 - \delta$. By definition of δ, $\gamma_{il}^{NTP} = 1 - \delta$ entails, together with assumption (8.35), that $T_W(\lambda_{ij}^P, \gamma_{jl}^{NTP}) = 1$ and, in other words, $\lambda_{ij}^P = \gamma_{jl}^{NTP} = 1$. From $\lambda_{jl}^{NTP} \geq \gamma_{jl}^{NTP}$, we furthermore establish $\lambda_{jl}^{NTP} = 1$. Since Θ_1 satisfies all transitivity rules, we know that

$$\lambda_{lj}^P \geq T_W(\lambda_{li}^P, \lambda_{ij}^P) = 1$$

From $\lambda_{lj}^P = 1$ and $\lambda_{jl}^{NTP} = 1$, we finally obtain $\gamma_{jl}^{NTP} = 1 - \delta$, a contradiction. Hence (8.28) is always satisfied. Moreover, since $\gamma_{ij}^{NTP} \leq \lambda_{ij}^{NTP} \leq \lambda_{ij}^P$, this implies that (8.29) is always satisfied as well. In entirely the same fashion, we can show that (8.30) can never be violated by Θ.

Next, assume that (8.31) were violated, i.e.

$$T_W(\lambda_{ij}^P, 1 - \gamma_{lj}^{NTP}) > 1 - \gamma_{li}^{NTP}$$

This is only possible if $\gamma_{lj}^{NTP} < \lambda_{lj}^{NTP}$, in other words, if $\lambda_{lj}^{NTP} = \lambda_{jl}^P = 1$ and $\gamma_{lj}^{NTP} = 1 - \delta$. Hence, we have $1 - \gamma_{li}^{NTP} < T_W(\lambda_{ij}^P, 1 - \gamma_{lj}^{NTP}) \leq \delta$, which implies $\gamma_{li}^{NTP} = 1$ by (8.23), and thus $\lambda_{li}^{NTP} = 1$. This yields $T_W(\lambda_{ij}^P, \delta) > 0$, which, in turn, entails $\lambda_{ij}^P = 1$, again using (8.23). Because Θ_1 satisfies all transitivity rules, we know that

$$T_W(\lambda_{ij}^P, \lambda_{jl}^P) \leq \lambda_{il}^P$$

As $\lambda_{ij}^P = \lambda_{jl}^P = 1$, we therefore have $\lambda_{il}^P = 1$. As moreover $\lambda_{li}^{NTP} = 1$, we find that $\gamma_{li}^{NTP} = 1 - \delta$, a contradiction. The proof for (8.32) is entirely analogous.

Finally, assume that (8.33) were violated, i.e.

$$T_W(\gamma_{ij}^{NTP}, 1 - \gamma_{lj}^{NTP}) > 1 - \lambda_{li}^P$$

Note that this can only be the case if $\gamma_{lj}^{NTP} < \lambda_{lj}^{NTP}$, or, in other words, $\lambda_{lj}^{NTP} = \lambda_{jl}^P = 1$ and $\gamma_{lj}^{NTP} = 1 - \delta$. From $T_W(\gamma_{ij}^{NTP}, \delta) > 0$, we find $\gamma_{ij}^{NTP} = 1$ using (8.23), and thus $\lambda_{ij}^{NTP} = 1$. Furthermore, we have from $1 - \lambda_{li}^P < T_W(\gamma_{ij}^{NTP}, 1 - \gamma_{lj}^{NTP}) = \delta$ that $\lambda_{li}^P = 1$, again using (8.23). However, from $\lambda_{jl}^P = 1$ and $\lambda_{li}^P = 1$, we find $\lambda_{ji}^P = 1$, which together with $\lambda_{ij}^{NTP} = 1$ implies $\gamma_{ij}^{NTP} = 1 - \delta$, a contradiction. The proof of (8.34) is entirely analogous. $\qquad\square$

Corollary 8.2. *Let $T = T_W$. It holds that a standard, finite set of fuzzy RCC formulas Θ is satisfiable iff it can be refined to a normalised set Θ' which does not violate the transitivity rules for fuzzy topological relations nor the requirements (8.12)–(8.15).*

8.3.2.2   Standard sets of fuzzy RCC formulas

Let Θ be a standard set of fuzzy RCC formulas involving variables from a set $V = \{v_1, \ldots, v_n\}$. As explained above, we can rewrite the fuzzy RCC formulas in Θ such that only disjunctions of fuzzy RCC formulas involving $C, P, O,$ and NTP occur, thus obtaining a set Θ'. Clearly, Θ' is equivalent to Θ, hence every refinement of Θ' is also a refinement of Θ. Note that although Θ' is not a standard set of fuzzy RCC formulas, we can still apply Proposition 8.2 and Corollary 8.2, because Θ' is equivalent to a standard set.

To decide whether Θ', and therefore Θ, is satisfiable, we need to find membership degrees for $C(v_i, v_j)$, $P(v_i, v_j)$, $O(v_i, v_j)$, and $NTP(v_i, v_j)$, for each pair of regions (v_i, v_j) in V^2, such that the transitivity rules and the requirements (8.12)–(8.15) are satisfied, as well as the inequalities imposed by the fuzzy RCC formulas in Θ'; or show that no such membership degrees exist. As we will show next, these requirements on the membership degrees can be formulated as a system of (disjunctions of) linear inequalities Σ, where both the number of variables and the number of inequalities is polynomial in the size of Θ. This means that the satisfiability of Θ' can be decided using a linear programming solver and backtracking (if Θ' contains disjunctions). In the following, let x_{ij}^C, x_{ij}^P, x_{ij}^O and x_{ij}^{NTP} be variables, corresponding to the values of $C(v_i, v_j)$, $P(v_i, v_j)$, $O(v_i, v_j)$, and $NTP(v_i, v_j)$ respectively. For every variable x_{ij}^R (where R is C, P, O or NTP), we add to Σ the constraint

$$0 \leq x_{ij}^R \leq 1$$

This ensures that every solution of Σ can be interpreted as a normalised set of fuzzy RCC formulas Θ^Σ, containing exactly the formulas

$$R(v_i, v_j) \geq x_{ij}^R \qquad\qquad R(v_i, v_j) \leq x_{ij}^R$$

assuming for simplicity $x_{ij}^R \in]0, 1[$. Next, the fuzzy RCC formulas in Θ' can all be written as disjunctions of linear inequalities involving these variables. For example, if Θ' contains the fuzzy RCC formula $NTP(v_1, v_2) \geq 0.4 \vee O(v_3, v_4) \leq 0.7$, we add the following constraint to Σ

$$x_{12}^{NTP} \geq 0.4 \vee x_{34}^O \leq 0.7$$

This ensures that if Σ has a solution, Θ^Σ is a refinement of Θ'. To ensure that Θ^Σ is satisfiable, we add linear inequalities corresponding to (8.12)–(8.15):

$$x_{ij}^{NTP} \leq x_{ij}^P \leq x_{ij}^O \leq x_{ij}^C \qquad x_{ij}^C = x_{ji}^C \qquad x_{ij}^O = x_{ji}^O \qquad x_{ii}^P \geq 1$$

Finally, to guarantee that solutions of Σ do not violate the transitivity rules, we add an additional inequality for each of the 31 transitivity rules identified above and each triplet (v_i, v_j, v_k) in V^3. For example, because of the first of these transitivity rules, we know that

$$T_W(C(v_i, v_j), DC(v_j, v_k)) \leq coP(v_i, v_k)$$

which is equivalent to

$$(C(v_i, v_j) + 1 - C(v_j, v_k) - 1 \leq 1 - P(v_i, v_k)) \wedge 0 \leq 1 - P(v_i, v_k)$$

or

$$(C(v_i, v_j) - C(v_j, v_k) \leq 1 - P(v_i, v_k)) \wedge P(v_i, v_k) \leq 1$$

Hence, we add the following inequality to Σ

$$x_{ij}^C - x_{jk}^C \leq 1 - x_{ik}^P$$

Note that $x_{ik}^P \leq 1$ is already in Σ and does, therefore, not have to be considered here anymore.

Thus we have constructed a system Σ of disjunctions of linear inequalities such that, if Σ has a solution, the corresponding normalised set of fuzzy

RCC formulas Θ^Σ satisfies the assumptions from Proposition 8.2, implying that Θ and Θ' are satisfiable. If Σ does not contain any disjunctions, deciding whether Σ has a solution can be done in polynomial time using a linear programming solver [Karmarkar (1984)] (assuming that the number of bits required to represent each of the lower and upper bounds in Θ is bounded by a constant). For example, let Θ' be defined as

$$\Theta' = \{C(b,c) \geq 0.6, P(c,a) \geq 0.8, O(a,c) \geq 0.4,$$
$$O(b,a) \leq 0.6, O(b,c) \leq 0.5, NTP(a,b) \geq 0.6, \quad (8.36)$$
$$NTP(c,c) \geq 0.6\}$$

Solving the corresponding system of linear inequalities Σ using the lp_solve[11] linear programming solver yields the consistent, normalised set of fuzzy RCC formulas defined by (8.10)–(8.11). If Θ' contains disjunctions, we can use a backtracking algorithm to determine whether any choice of the disjuncts leads to a system of linear inequalities that has a solution.

8.3.2.3 *Computational complexity*

The construction above entails that the problem of checking the satisfiability of a set of fuzzy RCC formulas is in NP. We show that this problem is also NP–hard. Note that by restricting the fuzzy relations C_α, O_α, P_α and NTP_α to crisp sets, crisp spatial relations are obtained. The next lemma reveals that these crisp spatial relations correspond to interpretations of the RCC.

Lemma 8.1. *Let $\mathcal{I}$ be defined such that for every u in U, $u^\mathcal{I}$ is a crisp, non-empty, bounded subset of $\mathbb{R}^n$ for some n in $\mathbb{N} \setminus \{0\}$. It holds that*

$$P_\alpha(u^\mathcal{I}, v^\mathcal{I}) \equiv (\forall w \in U)(C_\alpha(w^\mathcal{I}, u^\mathcal{I}) \Rightarrow C_\alpha(w^\mathcal{I}, v^\mathcal{I}))$$
$$O_\alpha(u^\mathcal{I}, v^\mathcal{I}) \equiv (\exists w \in U)(P_\alpha(w^\mathcal{I}, u^\mathcal{I}) \wedge P_\alpha(w^\mathcal{I}, v^\mathcal{I}))$$
$$NTP_\alpha(u^\mathcal{I}, v^\mathcal{I}) \equiv (\forall w \in U)(C_\alpha(w^\mathcal{I}, u^\mathcal{I}) \Rightarrow O(w^\mathcal{I}, v^\mathcal{I}))$$

Proof. By definition, we have

$$P_\alpha(u^\mathcal{I}, v^\mathcal{I}) = incl(R_\alpha{\downarrow}{\uparrow}u^\mathcal{I}, R_\alpha{\downarrow}{\uparrow}v^\mathcal{I})$$
$$O_\alpha(u^\mathcal{I}, v^\mathcal{I}) = overl(R_\alpha{\downarrow}{\uparrow}u^\mathcal{I}, R_\alpha{\downarrow}{\uparrow}v^\mathcal{I})$$
$$NTP_\alpha(u^\mathcal{I}, v^\mathcal{I}) = incl(R_\alpha{\uparrow}u^\mathcal{I}, R_\alpha{\downarrow}{\uparrow}v^\mathcal{I})$$

---

[11]http://sourceforge.net/projects/lpsolve

and by Proposition 7.14 that

$$P_\alpha(u^\mathcal{I}, v^\mathcal{I}) = \inf_{w \in U} I_T(C_\alpha(w^\mathcal{I}, u^\mathcal{I}), C_\alpha(w^\mathcal{I}, v^\mathcal{I}))$$

$$O_\alpha(u^\mathcal{I}, v^\mathcal{I}) = \sup_{w \in U} T(P_\alpha(w^\mathcal{I}, u^\mathcal{I}), P_\alpha(w^\mathcal{I}, v^\mathcal{I}))$$

$$NTP_\alpha(u^\mathcal{I}, v^\mathcal{I}) = \inf_{w \in U} I_T(C_\alpha(w^\mathcal{I}, u^\mathcal{I}), O(w^\mathcal{I}, v^\mathcal{I}))$$

By assumption, $u^\mathcal{I}$, $v^\mathcal{I}$ and $w^\mathcal{I}$ are crisp sets. Hence, for example, also $C_\alpha(w^\mathcal{I}, u^\mathcal{I})$ and $C_\alpha(w^\mathcal{I}, v^\mathcal{I})$ take crisp values. Therefore, we have that $\inf_{w \in U} I_T(C_\alpha(w^\mathcal{I}, u^\mathcal{I}), C_\alpha(w^\mathcal{I}, v^\mathcal{I})) = 1$ iff

$$(\forall w \in U)(C_\alpha(w^\mathcal{I}, u^\mathcal{I}) \Rightarrow C_\alpha(w^\mathcal{I}, v^\mathcal{I}))$$

and $\inf_{w \in U} I_T(C_\alpha(w^\mathcal{I}, u^\mathcal{I}), C_\alpha(w^\mathcal{I}, v^\mathcal{I})) = 0$ otherwise. The expressions for $O_\alpha(u^\mathcal{I}, v^\mathcal{I})$ and $NTP_\alpha(u^\mathcal{I}, v^\mathcal{I})$ follow in entirely the same manner. $\square$

It follows from Proposition 8.1 that every standard, C–satisfiable set Θ of RCC formulas can be interpreted by an $(n; \alpha, 0)$–model. Indeed, crisp RCC formulas such as $NTPP(v_1, v_2) \vee \neg EC(v_1, v_3)$ can be interpreted as fuzzy RCC formulas with upper and lower bounds in $\{0, 1\}$, i.e., $NTPP(v_1, v_2) \geq 1 \vee EC(v_1, v_3) \leq 0$. Moreover, since all upper and lower bounds come from $\{0, 1\}$, it follows from the construction process in the proof of Proposition 8.1 that the fuzzy RCC formulas can be interpreted by crisp sets. This leads to the following corollary.

Corollary 8.3. *Every finite, standard, C–satisfiable set of RCC formulas can be interpreted by an $(n; \alpha, 0)$–model in which every variable is interpreted as a crisp, non–empty, bounded subset of $\mathbb{R}^n$.*

Moreover, from [Renz (2002)] we already know that every C–satisfiable set of RCC formulas can be interpreted by a standard RCC model in any dimension. Thus, we also have the next corollary.

Corollary 8.4. *Let Θ be a set of RCC formulas. If Θ has an $(n; \alpha, 0)$–model, Θ also has a standard model in $\mathbb{R}^m$ for every m in $\mathbb{N} \setminus \{0\}$.*

In particular, we have that checking the C–satisfiability of a set of RCC formulas can be reduced to checking the F–satisfiability of a set of fuzzy RCC formulas. Since the former problem is known to be NP–hard [Renz and Nebel (1999)], we thus find that also the latter problem is NP–hard. Hence, we have the following proposition.

Proposition 8.3. *Checking the F–satisfiability of a set of fuzzy RCC formulas is NP–complete $(T = T_W)$.*

Note that the F–satisfiability problem for fuzzy RCC formulas is in the same complexity class as the C–satisfiability problem in RCC-5 and RCC-8.

8.3.3   *Other Reasoning Tasks*

Besides satisfiability checking, also other interesting reasoning tasks, such as entailment checking, finding the best truth-value bound, and inconsistency repairing, can be cast into systems of linear inequalities.

8.3.3.1   *Entailment*

Definition 8.8. Let Θ be a set of fuzzy RCC formulas and γ a fuzzy RCC formula; Θ is said to entail γ, written $\Theta \models \gamma$, if γ is satisfied in every model of Θ.

Without loss of generality, we can assume that Θ only contains (disjunctions of) formulas involving C, O, P and NTP. Furthermore, note that

$$\Theta \cup \{f_1 \vee f_2 \vee \cdots \vee f_m\} \models \gamma \Leftrightarrow (\Theta \cup \{f_1\} \models \gamma) \wedge \cdots \wedge (\Theta \cup \{f_m\} \models \gamma) \tag{8.37}$$

As a consequence, it is sufficient to show how $\Theta \models \gamma$ can be checked for the case where Θ does not contain any disjunctions. In other words, we can assume that all formulas in Θ are of the form $R(u, v) \geq \lambda$ and $R(u, v) \leq \lambda$ where R can be C, O, P or NTP. Let Σ furthermore be the corresponding system of linear inequalities, having a solution iff Θ is satisfiable. We can now extend Σ to a system of linear inequalities Σ_γ such that Σ_γ does not have a solution iff $\Theta \models \gamma$. First assume that γ does not contain disjunctions, e.g., $\gamma \equiv P(u, v) \geq 0.7$. Clearly, it holds that $\Theta \models \gamma$ iff $\Theta \cup \{\neg\gamma\}$ is not satisfiable, i.e., iff $\Theta_\gamma = \Theta \cup \{P(v_i, v_j) < 0.7\}$ is not satisfiable. If v_i or v_j do not occur in Θ, then Θ_γ is satisfiable iff Θ is satisfiable, i.e., we can take $\Sigma_\gamma = \Sigma$. Typically, v_i and v_j will already occur in Θ however. In that case, we can take

$$\Sigma_\gamma = \Sigma \cup \{x_{ij}^P < 0.7\}$$

As before, we can show that Σ_γ has a solution iff Θ_γ is satisfiable. Note that we do not have to add additional inequalities corresponding to (8.12)–(8.15) and the transitivity rules, since these are already contained in Σ (as v_i and v_j occur in Θ as well).

Note that Σ_γ contains a strict inequality, and can therefore not directly be solved using a linear programming solver. However, we can equivalently write Σ_γ as $\Sigma'_\gamma = \Sigma \cup \{x_{ij}^P \leq 0.7, x_{ij}^P \neq 0.7\}$. In [Jonsson and Bäckström (1998)], techniques for solving systems of linear inequalities with additional disequalities are introduced. Clearly, if $\Sigma \cup \{x_{ij}^P \leq 0.7\}$ does not have a solution, then neither has Σ'_γ. Therefore, assume that $\Sigma \cup \{x_{ij}^P \leq 0.7\}$ does have a solution. To find whether also Σ'_γ has a solution, we can make use of the fact that linear programming solvers can find the solution of a system of linear inequalities which minimizes or maximizes a given objective function. In particular, we can thus find the minimal and maximal values of the objective function x_{ij}^P, given the system of inequalities $\Sigma \cup \{x_{ij}^P \leq 0.7\}$. It holds that Σ'_γ does not have a solution iff both this minimal and maximal value is 0.7.

Example 8.1. As an example, consider again the set Θ' from (8.36), and suppose we want to check whether $\Theta' \models \gamma$ for $\gamma \equiv C(a, c) \geq 0.9$. We have

$$\Sigma'_\gamma = \Sigma \cup \{x_{ac}^C \leq 0.9, x_{ac}^C \neq 0.9\}$$

where x_{ac}^C is the variable in Σ corresponding to the value of $C(a, c)$. Maximizing the objective function x_{ac}^C subject to the constraints in $\Sigma \cup \{x_{ac}^C \leq 0.9\}$, we obtain $x_{ac}^C = 0.9$, whereas we obtain $x_{ac}^C = 0.8$ when minimizing x_{ac}^C. Since $0.8 \neq 0.9$, we have that Σ'_γ has a solution, and therefore, that $\Theta' \not\models C(a, c) \geq 0.9$. For $\gamma \equiv C(a, c) \geq 0.8$, we obtain

$$\Sigma'_\gamma = \Sigma \cup \{x_{ac}^C \leq 0.8, x_{ac}^C \neq 0.8\}$$

Both when minimizing x_{ac}^C and maximizing x_{ac}^C, subject to $\Sigma \cup \{x_{ac}^C \leq 0.8\}$, we obtain $x_{ac}^C = 0.8$. Therefore Σ'_γ does not have a solution, and $\Theta' \models C(a, c) \geq 0.8$.

If γ is the disjunction of more than one atomic fuzzy RCC formula, we can proceed in a similar way. For example, let $\gamma = NTP(v_1, v_2) \leq 0.7 \vee P(v_3, v_4) \geq 0.5 \vee O(v_1, v_4) \geq 0.9$. For each disjunct, we now have to add a strict inequality to Σ, corresponding to its negation. We obtain

$$\Sigma_\gamma = \Sigma \cup \{x_{12}^{NTP} > 0.7, x_{34}^P < 0.5, x_{14}^O < 0.9\}$$

or, using disequalities

$$\Sigma'_\gamma = \Sigma \cup \{x_{12}^{NTP} \geq 0.7, x_{34}^P \leq 0.5, x_{14}^O \leq 0.9, x_{12}^{NTP} \neq 0.7,$$
$$x_{34}^P \neq 0.5, x_{14}^O \neq 0.9\}$$

To solve, Σ'_γ, we can apply the following lemma.

Lemma 8.2. *Let Σ be a system of linear inequalities, and let $\{\gamma_1, \ldots, \gamma_k\}$ be a set of linear disequalities. It holds that $\Sigma \cup \{\gamma_1, \ldots, \gamma_k\}$ has a solution iff $\Sigma \cup \{\gamma_1\}, \Sigma \cup \{\gamma_2\}, \ldots, \Sigma \cup \{\gamma_k\}$ all have a solution.*

Proof. This lemma follows straightforwardly from Lemma 17 in [Jonsson and Bäckström (1998)]. ☐

8.3.3.2   *Best Truth–Value Bound*

The notion of the best truth value bound was originally introduced in [Straccia (2001)] in the context of fuzzy description logics. Here it consists of finding the strongest possible lower and upper bound for the values of $C(a, b)$, $P(a, b)$, $O(a, b)$, or $NTP(a, b)$, given that a set Θ of fuzzy RCC formulas is satisfied. Formally, we want to find the values of $lub_R(a, b; \Theta)$ and $glb_R(a, b; \Theta)$ for R either C, P, O, or NTP:

Definition 8.9. Let R be one of the fuzzy topological relations C, P, O, or NTP. Moreover, let Θ be a set of fuzzy RCC formulas. For regions a and b, $lub_R(a, b; \Theta)$ and $glb_R(a, b; \Theta)$ are defined as

$$lub_R(a, b; \Theta) = \inf\{\lambda | \lambda \in [0, 1] \wedge \Theta \models R(a, b) \leq \lambda\}$$
$$glb_R(a, b; \Theta) = \sup\{\lambda | \lambda \in [0, 1] \wedge \Theta \models R(a, b) \geq \lambda\}$$

Finding the best truth–value bounds can be done very analogously to entailment checking. Let Θ be a set of fuzzy RCC formulas. Moreover, let V, Θ and Σ be defined as before, i.e., Σ is a system of linear inequalities which has a solution iff Θ is consistent and V is the set of variables occurring in Θ. If $a \notin V$ or $b \notin V$, we immediately find that $lub_C(a, b; \Theta) = 1$, as the possible values of $C(a, b)$ are not constrained by the formulas in Θ. Therefore, assume that $a, b \in V$. A linear programming solver can be used to find a solution of Σ that maximizes $C(a, b)$. This maximal value of $C(a, b)$ is equal to $lub_C(a, b; \Theta)$. In the same way, the solution of Σ which minimizes $C(a, b)$ yields the value of $glb_C(a, b; \Theta)$. For R equal to P, O, or NTP, the values of $lub_R(a, b; \Theta)$ and $glb_R(a, b; \Theta)$ can be found in entirely the same way.

For example, again considering the set Θ' defined by (8.36), we find that $lub_C(a, c; \Theta') = 0.9$ and $glb_C(a, c; \Theta') = 0.8$. This means that for any model $\mathcal{I}$ of Θ', it holds that

$$C^{\mathcal{I}}(a^{\mathcal{I}}, c^{\mathcal{I}}) \in [0.8, 0.9]$$

8.3.3.3   *Inconsistency repairing*

In real-world applications, available topological information is often inconsistent. For example, although none of the four assertions (8.1)–(8.4) is clearly wrong, the resulting set is inconsistent because some assertions are only partially true. To remedy such inconsistencies, we weaken the interpretation of the available topological information. For example, (8.1)–(8.4) could be interpreted as

$$DC(Baixa, Chiado) \geq \lambda_1 \qquad (8.38)$$

$$EC(Baixa, Chiado) \geq \lambda_2 \qquad (8.39)$$

$$EQ(downtown\,Lisbon, Baixa) \geq \lambda_3 \qquad (8.40)$$

$$O(Chiado, downtown\,Lisbon) \geq \lambda_4 \qquad (8.41)$$

where $\lambda_1, \lambda_2, \lambda_3, \lambda_4 \in [0, 1]$. Usually, we want the interpretation to be as strong as possible, i.e., we want to choose $\lambda_1, \lambda_2, \lambda_3$, and λ_4 such that increasing one of these values leads to inconsistency. This can again be formulated as a linear programming problem. First, we rewrite (8.38)–(8.41) as a set Θ' of fuzzy RCC relations containing only (disjunctions of) atomic fuzzy RCC formulas involving C, P, O, or NTP:

$$C(Baixa, Chiado) \leq 1 - \lambda_1 \qquad (8.42)$$

$$C(Baixa, Chiado) \geq \lambda_2 \qquad (8.43)$$

$$O(Baixa, Chiado) \leq 1 - \lambda_2 \qquad (8.44)$$

$$P(downtown\,Lisbon, Baixa) \geq \lambda_3 \qquad (8.45)$$

$$P(Baixa, downtown\,Lisbon) \geq \lambda_3 \qquad (8.46)$$

$$O(Chiado, downtown\,Lisbon) \geq \lambda_4 \qquad (8.47)$$

We now consider the corresponding system of inequalities Σ. As before, each solution of Σ corresponds to a model of (8.38)–(8.41). Unlike before, however, the membership degrees λ_1, λ_2, λ_3 and λ_4 are additional variables, rather than constants. By specifying $\lambda_1 + \lambda_2 + \lambda_3 + \lambda_4$ as the objective function (to be maximized), we obtain an interpretation that cannot be strengthened without introducing inconsistencies. Using lp_solve, we find $\lambda_1 = \lambda_2 = \lambda_3 = 0.5$ and $\lambda_4 = 1$. If a priori information is available about the reliability of each of the statements, this idea can be further extended by using weights in the objective function. For example, if the first and last statement are assumed to be somewhat less reliable, $0.5\lambda_1 + 0.8\lambda_2 + 0.8\lambda_3 + 0.5\lambda_4$ could be used as the objective function, yielding $\lambda_1 = \lambda_2 = \lambda_4 = 0.5$ and $\lambda_3 = 1$.

8.4 Properties

In this section, we provide a number of additional, important properties of our approach to fuzzy topological reasoning. We start by demonstrating how reasoning in the fuzzy RCC can be reduced to reasoning in the original RCC. On one hand, this allows to use optimized RCC reasoners for reasoning in the fuzzy RCC, adopting for example the heuristic strategies introduced in [Renz and Nebel (2001)]. On the other hand, this reduction is particularly useful to leverage theoretical properties of the RCC to corresponding properties of the fuzzy RCC. Illustrating this point, we reveal a relationship between our framework and the Egg–Yolk calculus in Section 8.4.2. Finally, in Section 8.4.3 we show that any standard, satisfiable set Θ of fuzzy RCC formulas can be interpreted using fuzzy sets and nearness in any dimension, thus generalizing the observation from Proposition 8.1 that Θ can be realized in one particular dimension n. In particular, this implies that we can always find models in two–dimensional and three–dimensional Euclidean space.

8.4.1   *Reduction to the RCC*

In Chapter 5, we reduced fuzzy temporal reasoning to reasoning about linear constraints, starting from the observation that whenever a set of FI–formulas is FI–satisfiable, it can be satisfied by FI–models in which each fuzzy time interval only takes a finite number of different membership degrees. For fuzzy topological reasoning, we can pursue a similar strategy, thereby reducing fuzzy topological reasoning to reasoning about RCC formulas. By analogy to fuzzy temporal reasoning, the cornerstone is the observation that a satisfiable set of fuzzy RCC formulas can always be satisfied by models taking only finitely different membership degrees.

Let $\Delta \in \,]0,1[$ such that $\Delta = \frac{1}{\rho}$ for a certain ρ in $\mathbb{N} \setminus \{0\}$. Furthermore let M_Δ and $M_{\frac{\Delta}{2}}$ be defined as

$$M_\Delta = \{0, \Delta, 2\Delta, \dots, 1-\Delta, 1\}$$
$$M_{\frac{\Delta}{2}} = \{0, \frac{\Delta}{2}, \Delta, \dots, 1 - \frac{\Delta}{2}, 1\}$$

Henceforth, we will always assume that all the upper and lower bounds in the set of fuzzy RCC formulas Θ are taken from M_Δ. While being a theoretical restriction, this has no practical consequences as computers only deal with finite precision anyway. Below, we show that if Θ is satisfiable, it has an $(n; \alpha, 0)$–model in which only membership degrees from $M_{\frac{\Delta}{2}}$ are used. First, we introduce the following lemma.

Lemma 8.3. *Let a, a' and b in $[0,1]$, and ε in $]0,1]$ such that $a < a' + \varepsilon$.*

It holds that

$$T_W(a, b) < T_W(a', b) + \varepsilon$$

Proof. If $T_W(a, b) > 0$, we have

$$
\begin{aligned}
T_W(a, b) &= a + b - 1 \\
&< a' + b - 1 + \varepsilon \\
&\leq \max(a' + b - 1, 0) + \varepsilon \\
&= T_W(a', b) + \varepsilon
\end{aligned}
$$

If $T_W(a', b) = 0$, we have

$$T_W(a, b) = 0 < \varepsilon \leq T_W(a', b) + \varepsilon$$

□

Proposition 8.4. *Let $T = T_W$ and let Θ be a standard, satisfiable set of fuzzy RCC formulas whose upper and lower bounds are all in M_Δ. Furthermore, let V be the set of variables occurring in Θ and $|V| = n$. There exists a model of Θ mapping every variable v occurring in Θ to a normalised, bounded fuzzy set in $\mathbb{R}^n$ which only takes membership degrees from $M_{\frac{\Delta}{2}}$.*

Proof. From Proposition 8.1 and Proposition 8.2, we already know that Θ has an $(n; \alpha, 0)$–model $\mathcal{I}'$. To prove the proposition, we show how we can modify $\mathcal{I}'$ to an $(n; \alpha, 0)$–model $\mathcal{I}$ which satisfies the additional requirement that all membership degrees come from $M_{\frac{\Delta}{2}}$. In particular for v in V and p in $\mathbb{R}^n$, $\mathcal{I}$ is defined as

$$
v^{\mathcal{I}}(p) = \begin{cases} v^{\mathcal{I}'}(p) & \text{if } v^{\mathcal{I}'}(p) \in M_{\frac{\Delta}{2}} \setminus M_\Delta \\ k\Delta & \text{if } k\Delta - \frac{\Delta}{2} < v^{\mathcal{I}'}(p) < k\Delta + \frac{\Delta}{2}, \text{ for a given } k \text{ in } \mathbb{N} \end{cases}
$$

Note that $v^{\mathcal{I}}(p) < v^{\mathcal{I}'}(p) + \frac{\Delta}{2}$ always holds. Clearly, $\mathcal{I}$ is an $(n; \alpha, 0)$–interpretation mapping every variable from v to a normalised bounded fuzzy set taking only membership degrees from $M_{\frac{\Delta}{2}}$. Hence, we only need to show that $\mathcal{I}$ satisfies all formulas from Θ. In particular, we will show that every atomic fuzzy RCC formula with an upper or lower bound in M_Δ that is satisfied by $\mathcal{I}'$, is also satisfied by $\mathcal{I}$. This implies that also disjunctive fuzzy RCC formulas remain satisfied; indeed, it follows that all disjuncts that are satisfied by $\mathcal{I}'$ are satisfied by $\mathcal{I}$.

Consider atomic fuzzy RCC formulas of the form $C(a, b) \leq \lambda$ and $C(a, b) \geq \lambda$. We will first show that for each (p_0, q_0) in $\mathbb{R}^n \times \mathbb{R}^n$ and each λ_0 in M_Δ, it holds that

$$T_W(a^{\mathcal{I}'}(p_0), R_\alpha(p_0, q_0), b^{\mathcal{I}'}(q_0)) \leq \lambda_0$$
$$\Rightarrow T_W(a^{\mathcal{I}}(p_0), R_\alpha(p_0, q_0), b^{\mathcal{I}}(q_0)) \leq \lambda_0 \qquad (8.48)$$
$$T_W(a^{\mathcal{I}'}(p_0), R_\alpha(p_0, q_0), b^{\mathcal{I}'}(q_0)) \geq \lambda_0$$
$$\Rightarrow T_W(a^{\mathcal{I}}(p_0), R_\alpha(p_0, q_0), b^{\mathcal{I}}(q_0)) \geq \lambda_0 \qquad (8.49)$$

Since $a^{\mathcal{I}}(p_0)$ and $b^{\mathcal{I}}(q_0)$ are in $M_{\frac{\Delta}{2}}$, we also have $T_W(a^{\mathcal{I}}(p_0), R_\alpha(p_0, q_0),$ $b^{\mathcal{I}}(q_0)) \in M_{\frac{\Delta}{2}}$. First assume that also the stronger statement $T_W(a^{\mathcal{I}}(p_0),$ $R_\alpha(p_0, q_0), b^{\mathcal{I}}(q_0)) \in M_\Delta$ is satisfied. As $a^{\mathcal{I}}(p_0) < a^{\mathcal{I}'}(p_0) + \frac{\Delta}{2}$ and $b^{\mathcal{I}}(q_0) <$ $b^{\mathcal{I}'}(q_0) + \frac{\Delta}{2}$, we find using Lemma 8.3

$$T_W(a^{\mathcal{I}}(p_0), R_\alpha(p_0, q_0), b^{\mathcal{I}}(q_0)) < T_W(a^{\mathcal{I}'}(p_0), R_\alpha(p_0, q_0), b^{\mathcal{I}'}(q_0)) + \frac{\Delta}{2}$$
$$< T_W(a^{\mathcal{I}'}(p_0), R_\alpha(p_0, q_0), b^{\mathcal{I}'}(q_0)) + \Delta$$

Using the assumption $T_W(a^{\mathcal{I}}(p_0), R_\alpha(p_0, q_0), b^{\mathcal{I}}(q_0)) \in M_\Delta$, and the fact that Δ and λ_0 are in M_Δ, we find

$$T_W(a^{\mathcal{I}'}(p_0), R_\alpha(p_0, q_0), b^{\mathcal{I}'}(q_0)) \leq \lambda_0$$
$$\Rightarrow T_W(a^{\mathcal{I}}(p_0), R_\alpha(p_0, q_0), b^{\mathcal{I}}(q_0)) - \Delta < \lambda_0$$
$$\Rightarrow T_W(a^{\mathcal{I}}(p_0), R_\alpha(p_0, q_0), b^{\mathcal{I}}(q_0)) \leq \lambda_0$$

showing (8.48). In entirely the same fashion, we find that

$$T_W(a^{\mathcal{I}}(p_0), R_\alpha(p_0, q_0), b^{\mathcal{I}}(q_0)) > T_W(a^{\mathcal{I}'}(p_0), R_\alpha(p_0, q_0), b^{\mathcal{I}'}(q_0)) - \Delta$$

from which we obtain (8.49).

Next, assume $T_W(a^{\mathcal{I}}(p_0), R_\alpha(p_0, q_0), b^{\mathcal{I}}(q_0)) \in M_{\frac{\Delta}{2}} \setminus M_\Delta$. This means that either $a^{\mathcal{I}}(p_0) \in M_{\frac{\Delta}{2}} \setminus M_\Delta$ and $b^{\mathcal{I}}(q_0) \in M_\Delta$, or $a^{\mathcal{I}}(p_0) \in M_\Delta$ and $b^{\mathcal{I}}(q_0) \in M_{\frac{\Delta}{2}} \setminus M_\Delta$. Assume, for instance, the former case (the proof for the latter case is entirely analogous). From $a^{\mathcal{I}}(p_0) \in M_{\frac{\Delta}{2}} \setminus M_\Delta$, we have by construction $a^{\mathcal{I}}(p_0) = a^{\mathcal{I}'}(p_0)$. From $b^{\mathcal{I}}(q_0) < b^{\mathcal{I}'}(q_0) + \frac{\Delta}{2}$, we obtain using Lemma 8.3

$$T_W(a^{\mathcal{I}}(p_0), R_\alpha(p_0, q_0), b^{\mathcal{I}}(q_0)) = T_W(a^{\mathcal{I}'}(p_0), R_\alpha(p_0, q_0), b^{\mathcal{I}}(q_0))$$
$$< T_W(a^{\mathcal{I}'}(p_0), R_\alpha(p_0, q_0), b^{\mathcal{I}'}(q_0)) + \frac{\Delta}{2}$$

Using $T_W(a^{\mathcal{I}}(p_0), R_\alpha(p_0, q_0), b^{\mathcal{I}}(q_0)) \in M_{\frac{\Delta}{2}}$, this leads to

$$T_W(a^{\mathcal{I}'}(p_0), R_\alpha(p_0, q_0), b^{\mathcal{I}'}(q_0)) \leq \lambda_0$$
$$\Rightarrow T_W(a^{\mathcal{I}}(p_0), R_\alpha(p_0, q_0), b^{\mathcal{I}}(q_0)) - \frac{\Delta}{2} < \lambda_0$$
$$\Rightarrow T_W(a^{\mathcal{I}}(p_0), R_\alpha(p_0, q_0), b^{\mathcal{I}}(q_0)) \leq \lambda_0$$

showing (8.48). In entirely the same fashion, we find that

$$T_W(a^{\mathcal{I}}(p_0), R_\alpha(p_0, q_0), b^{\mathcal{I}}(q_0)) > T_W(a^{\mathcal{I}'}(p_0), R_\alpha(p_0, q_0), b^{\mathcal{I}'}(q_0)) - \frac{\Delta}{2}$$

from which we obtain (8.49).

Hence, we have that (8.48) and (8.49) are always satisfied. To complete the proof, we show that this implies for every λ in M_Δ

$$C_\alpha(a^{\mathcal{I}'}, b^{\mathcal{I}'}) \leq \lambda \Rightarrow C_\alpha(a^{\mathcal{I}}, b^{\mathcal{I}}) \leq \lambda \tag{8.50}$$

$$C_\alpha(a^{\mathcal{I}'}, b^{\mathcal{I}'}) \geq \lambda \Rightarrow C_\alpha(a^{\mathcal{I}}, b^{\mathcal{I}}) \geq \lambda \tag{8.51}$$

If $C_\alpha(a^{\mathcal{I}'}, b^{\mathcal{I}'}) \leq \lambda$, we have for every (p, q) in $\mathbb{R}^n \times \mathbb{R}^n$

$$T_W(a^{\mathcal{I}'}(p), R_\alpha(p, q), b^{\mathcal{I}'}(q)) \leq \lambda$$

which implies by (8.48)

$$T_W(a^{\mathcal{I}}(p), R_\alpha(p, q), b^{\mathcal{I}}(q)) \leq \lambda$$

From the monotonicity of the supremum (Lemma 2.7) we have (8.50), i.e.

$$C_\alpha(a^{\mathcal{I}}, b^{\mathcal{I}}) = \sup_{p,q \in \mathbb{R}^n} T_W(a^{\mathcal{I}}(p), R_\alpha(p, q), b^{\mathcal{I}}(q)) \leq \lambda$$

Finally, assume $C_\alpha(a^{\mathcal{I}'}, b^{\mathcal{I}'}) \geq \lambda$. Because $a^{\mathcal{I}'}$ and $b^{\mathcal{I}'}$ only take a finite number of different membership degrees, the supremum in $C_\alpha(a^{\mathcal{I}'}, b^{\mathcal{I}'})$ is attained in some (p_0, q_0) in $\mathbb{R}^n \times \mathbb{R}^n$ implying

$$T_W(a^{\mathcal{I}'}(p_0), R_\alpha(p_0, q_0), b^{\mathcal{I}'}(q_0)) \geq \lambda$$

or, by (8.49)

$$T_W(a^{\mathcal{I}}(p_0), R_\alpha(p_0, q_0), b^{\mathcal{I}}(q_0)) \geq \lambda$$

We conclude

$$C_\alpha(a^{\mathcal{I}}, b^{\mathcal{I}}) = \sup_{p,q \in \mathbb{R}^n} T_W(a^{\mathcal{I}}(p), R_\alpha(p, q), b^{\mathcal{I}}(q))$$
$$\geq T_W(a^{\mathcal{I}}(p_0), R_\alpha(p_0, q_0), b^{\mathcal{I}}(q_0))$$
$$\geq \lambda$$

The proof for fuzzy RCC formulas involving P, O or NTP is analogous.$\square$

Note that from the construction process in the proof of Proposition 8.1, we know that when Θ is a normalised set in which all bounds are taken from M_Δ, Θ has a model in which all membership degrees are taken from M_Δ, which is a stronger result than what is expressed in the proposition above. An arbitrary set of fuzzy RCC formulas Θ therefore also has a model in which all membership degrees are taken from M_Δ, provided Θ can be refined using only bounds from M_Δ. Whether or not such a particular model can always be found when Θ satisfies the conditions of Proposition 8.4 is currently still an open problem.

As Proposition 8.5 below shows, when the fuzzy topological relations C_α, O_α, P_α and NTP_α are applied to fuzzy sets which only take membership degrees from a finite set, their value can be found by checking whether a finite number of crisp spatial relations are satisfied. First we show three technical lemmas.

Lemma 8.4. *Let λ be in $]0, 1]$ and let A be a fuzzy set in $\mathbb{R}^n$. It holds that*

$$(R_\alpha \downarrow_{I_W} A)_\lambda = R_\alpha \downarrow (A_\lambda)$$

Proof.   Assume $p \in (R_\alpha \downarrow_{I_W} A)_\lambda$, i.e.

$$\inf_{q \in \mathbb{R}^n} I_W(R_\alpha(p, q), A(q)) \geq \lambda$$

This means that for every q satisfying $(p, q) \in R_\alpha$, it holds that $A(q) \geq \lambda$, or equivalently $q \in A_\lambda$, i.e.

$$(p, q) \in R_\alpha \Rightarrow q \in A_\lambda \tag{8.52}$$

which entails

$$p \in R_\alpha \downarrow (A_\lambda)$$

Conversely, assume $p \in R_\alpha \downarrow (A_\lambda)$. This implies for every q in $\mathbb{R}^n$

$$(p, q) \in R_\alpha \Rightarrow q \in A_\lambda$$

or

$$(p, q) \in R_\alpha \Rightarrow A(q) \geq \lambda$$

implying

$$I_W(R_\alpha(p, q), A_\lambda(q)) \geq \lambda$$

Hence, by definition of the infimum as greatest lower bound, we have

$$\inf_{q \in \mathbb{R}^n} I_W(R_\alpha(p, q), A_\lambda(q)) \geq \lambda$$

which means $p \in (R_\alpha \downarrow_{I_W} A)_\lambda$. $\square$

Lemma 8.5. *Let λ be in $]0, 1]$ and let A be a fuzzy set in $\mathbb{R}^n$ which only takes a finite number of different membership degrees. It holds that*

$$(R_\alpha \uparrow_{T_W} A)_\lambda = R_\alpha \uparrow (A_\lambda)$$

Proof. Assume $p \in (R_\alpha \uparrow_{T_W} A)_\lambda$, i.e.

$$\sup_{q \in \mathbb{R}^n} T_W(R_\alpha(p, q), A(q)) \geq \lambda$$

Since A only takes a finite number of different membership degrees, this supremum is attained. Hence, there is a q_0 such that $d(p, q_0) \leq \alpha$ and $A(q_0) \geq \lambda$. In other words

$$(\exists q \in \mathbb{R}^n)((p, q) \in R_\alpha \wedge q \in A_\lambda)$$

or $p \in R_\alpha \uparrow (A_\lambda)$. Conversely, assume $p \in R_\alpha \uparrow (A_\lambda)$. This means that for some q_0, $d(p, q_0) \leq \alpha$ and $A(q_0) \geq \lambda$, hence, $T_W(R_\alpha(p, q_0), A(q_0)) \geq \lambda$. In particular, this entails

$$\sup_{q \in \mathbb{R}^n} T_W(R_\alpha(p, q), A(q)) \geq \lambda$$

or $p \in (R_\alpha \uparrow_{T_W} A)_\lambda$. □

Note that the condition that A only takes a finite number of different membership degrees is not redundant. For example, assume $n = 1$ and let A be defined for q in $\mathbb{R}$ by

$$A(q) = \begin{cases} \frac{\lambda q}{\alpha} & \text{if } q \in [0, \alpha[\\ 0 & \text{otherwise} \end{cases}$$

for a given λ in $]0, 1]$ and $\alpha > 0$. Then $A(q) < \lambda$ for all q in $\mathbb{R}$ and $\lim_{q \to \atop >} \alpha A(q) = \lambda$. This means

$$(R_\alpha \uparrow_{T_W} A)(0) = \sup_{q \in \mathbb{R}} T_W(R_\alpha(0, q), A(q)) = \sup\{\frac{\lambda q}{\alpha} | q \in [0, \alpha[\} = \lambda$$

and $0 \in (R_\alpha \uparrow_{T_W} A)_\lambda$. On the other hand, we have $A_\lambda = \emptyset$, implying $R_\alpha \uparrow (A_\lambda) = \emptyset$ and in particular $0 \notin R_\alpha \uparrow (A_\lambda)$.

Lemma 8.6. *Let A and B be crisp, non–empty, bounded subsets of $\mathbb{R}^n$. It holds that $NTP_\alpha(A, B) \equiv NTPP_\alpha(A, B)$ $(\alpha > 0)$.*

Proof. We need to show that $NTP_\alpha(A, B) \Rightarrow \neg P_\alpha(B, A)$. Assume that both $NTP_\alpha(A, B)$ and $P_\alpha(B, A)$ hold. From $NTP_\alpha(A, B)$ we know $R_\alpha \uparrow A \subseteq R_\alpha \downarrow \uparrow B$, while $P_\alpha(B, A)$ entails $R_\alpha \downarrow \uparrow B \subseteq R_\alpha \downarrow \uparrow A$. Together, this yields $R_\alpha \uparrow A \subseteq R_\alpha \downarrow \uparrow A$. Since $\alpha > 0$, this is only possible if $A = \emptyset$ or $A = \mathbb{R}^n$, which have both been excluded by assumption. □

Proposition 8.5. *Let A and B be normalised, bounded fuzzy sets in $\mathbb{R}^n$ which only take membership degrees from $M_{\frac{\Delta}{2}}$, let λ be in $M_{\frac{\Delta}{2}} \setminus \{0\}$ and let λ' be in $M_{\frac{\Delta}{2}} \setminus \{1\}$. It holds that $(\alpha > 0)$*

$$C_\alpha(A, B) \geq \lambda \Leftrightarrow C_\alpha(A_1, B_\lambda) \vee C_\alpha(A_{1-\frac{\Delta}{2}}, B_{\lambda+\frac{\Delta}{2}})$$
$$\vee \cdots \vee C_\alpha(A_\lambda, B_1) \tag{8.53}$$

$$C_\alpha(A, B) \leq \lambda' \Leftrightarrow DC_\alpha(A_1, B_{\lambda'+\frac{\Delta}{2}}) \wedge DC_\alpha(A_{1-\frac{\Delta}{2}}, B_{\lambda'+\Delta})$$
$$\wedge \cdots \wedge DC_\alpha(A_{\lambda'+\frac{\Delta}{2}}, B_1) \tag{8.54}$$

$$O_\alpha(A, B) \geq \lambda \Leftrightarrow O_\alpha(A_1, B_\lambda) \vee O_\alpha(A_{1-\frac{\Delta}{2}}, B_{\lambda+\frac{\Delta}{2}})$$
$$\vee \cdots \vee O_\alpha(A_\lambda, B_1) \tag{8.55}$$

$$O_\alpha(A, B) \leq \lambda' \Leftrightarrow DR_\alpha(A_1, B_{\lambda'+\frac{\Delta}{2}}) \wedge DR_\alpha(A_{1-\frac{\Delta}{2}}, B_{\lambda'+\Delta})$$
$$\wedge \cdots \wedge DR_\alpha(A_{\lambda'+\frac{\Delta}{2}}, B_1) \tag{8.56}$$

$$P_\alpha(A, B) \geq \lambda \Leftrightarrow P_\alpha(A_1, B_\lambda) \wedge P_\alpha(A_{1-\frac{\Delta}{2}}, B_{\lambda-\frac{\Delta}{2}})$$
$$\wedge \cdots \wedge P_\alpha(A_{1-\lambda+\frac{\Delta}{2}}, B_{\frac{\Delta}{2}}) \tag{8.57}$$

$$P_\alpha(A, B) \leq \lambda' \Leftrightarrow \neg P_\alpha(A_1, B_{\lambda'+\frac{\Delta}{2}}) \vee \neg P_\alpha(A_{1-\frac{\Delta}{2}}, B_{\lambda'})$$
$$\vee \cdots \vee \neg P_\alpha(A_{1-\lambda'}, B_{\frac{\Delta}{2}}) \tag{8.58}$$

$$NTP_\alpha(A, B) \geq \lambda \Leftrightarrow NTPP_\alpha(A_1, B_\lambda) \wedge NTPP_\alpha(A_{1-\frac{\Delta}{2}}, B_{\lambda-\frac{\Delta}{2}})$$
$$\wedge \cdots \wedge NTPP_\alpha(A_{1-\lambda+\frac{\Delta}{2}}, B_{\frac{\Delta}{2}}) \tag{8.59}$$

$$NTP_\alpha(A, B) \leq \lambda' \Leftrightarrow \neg NTPP_\alpha(A_1, B_{\lambda'+\frac{\Delta}{2}}) \vee \neg NTPP_\alpha(A_{1-\frac{\Delta}{2}}, B_{\lambda'})$$
$$\vee \cdots \vee \neg NTPP_\alpha(A_{1-\lambda'}, B_{\frac{\Delta}{2}}) \tag{8.60}$$

Proof.   To show the first equivalence, we find

$$C_\alpha(A, B) \geq \lambda \Leftrightarrow \sup_{p,q \in \mathbb{R}^n} T_W(A(p), R_\alpha(p, q), B(q)) \geq \lambda$$

Since A and B only take a finite number of different membership degrees the supremum is attained and

$$C_\alpha(A, B) \geq \lambda \Leftrightarrow (\exists p, q \in \mathbb{R}^n)(T_W(A(p), R_\alpha(p, q), B(q)) \geq \lambda)$$
$$\Leftrightarrow (\exists p, q \in \mathbb{R}^n)(d(p, q) \leq \alpha \wedge T_W(A(p), R_\alpha(p, q), B(q)) \geq \lambda)$$
$$\Leftrightarrow (\exists p, q \in \mathbb{R}^n)(d(p, q) \leq \alpha \wedge T_W(A(p), B(q)) \geq \lambda)$$

Since A and B only take membership degrees from $M_{\frac{\Delta}{2}}$, we can enumerate the possible values of $A(p)$ and $B(q)$ for which $T_W(A(p), B(q)) \geq \lambda$:

$$\Leftrightarrow (\exists p, q \in \mathbb{R}^n)(d(p,q) \leq \alpha \wedge ((A(p) \geq 1 \wedge B(q) \geq \lambda)$$
$$\vee (A(p) \geq 1 - \frac{\Delta}{2} \wedge B(q) \geq \lambda + \frac{\Delta}{2})$$
$$\vee \cdots \vee (A(p) \geq \lambda \wedge B(q) \geq 1)))$$

$$\Leftrightarrow (\exists p, q \in \mathbb{R}^n)(d(p,q) \leq \alpha \wedge ((p \in A_1 \wedge q \in B_\lambda)$$
$$\vee (p \in A_{1-\frac{\Delta}{2}} \wedge q \in B_{\lambda+\frac{\Delta}{2}})$$
$$\vee \cdots \vee (p \in A_\lambda \wedge q \in B_1)))$$

$$\Leftrightarrow (\exists p, q \in \mathbb{R}^n)((d(p,q) \leq \alpha \wedge p \in A_1 \wedge q \in B_\lambda)$$
$$\vee (d(p,q) \leq \alpha \wedge p \in A_{1-\frac{\Delta}{2}} \wedge q \in B_{\lambda+\frac{\Delta}{2}})$$
$$\vee \cdots \vee (d(p,q) \leq \alpha \wedge p \in A_\lambda \wedge q \in B_1))$$

$$\Leftrightarrow (\exists p, q \in \mathbb{R}^n)(d(p,q) \leq \alpha \wedge p \in A_1 \wedge q \in B_\lambda)$$
$$\vee (\exists p, q \in \mathbb{R}^n)(d(p,q) \leq \alpha \wedge p \in A_{1-\frac{\Delta}{2}} \wedge q \in B_{\lambda+\frac{\Delta}{2}})$$
$$\vee \cdots \vee (\exists p, q \in \mathbb{R}^n)(d(p,q) \leq \alpha \wedge p \in A_\lambda \wedge q \in B_1)$$

$$\Leftrightarrow C_\alpha(A_1, B_\lambda) \vee C_\alpha(A_{1-\frac{\Delta}{2}}, B_{\lambda+\frac{\Delta}{2}}) \vee \cdots \vee C_\alpha(A_\lambda, B_1)$$

Next, (8.54) follows easily from (8.53):

$$C_\alpha(A, B) \leq \lambda' \Leftrightarrow \neg(C_\alpha(A, B) > \lambda')$$

Since A and B only take values from $M_{\frac{\Delta}{2}}$, $C_\alpha(A, B)$ can only take values from $M_{\frac{\Delta}{2}}$ either. Hence

$$C_\alpha(A, B) \leq \lambda' \Leftrightarrow \neg(C_\alpha(A, B) \geq \lambda' + \frac{\Delta}{2})$$

and by (8.53)

$$C_\alpha(A, B) \leq \lambda'$$
$$\Leftrightarrow \neg(C_\alpha(A_1, B_{\lambda'+\frac{\Delta}{2}}) \vee C_\alpha(A_{1-\frac{\Delta}{2}}, B_{\lambda'+\Delta}) \vee \cdots \vee C_\alpha(A_{\lambda'+\frac{\Delta}{2}}, B_1))$$
$$\Leftrightarrow DC_\alpha(A_1, B_{\lambda'+\frac{\Delta}{2}}) \wedge DC_\alpha(A_{1-\frac{\Delta}{2}}, B_{\lambda'+\Delta}) \wedge \cdots \wedge DC_\alpha(A_{\lambda'+\frac{\Delta}{2}}, B_1)$$

To show (8.55), we find using Lemma 8.4 and Lemma 8.5

$$O_\alpha(A, B) \geq \lambda \Leftrightarrow \sup_{p \in \mathbb{R}^n} T_W(R_\alpha{\downarrow}{\uparrow}A(p), R_\alpha{\downarrow}{\uparrow}B(p)) \geq \lambda$$
$$\Leftrightarrow (\exists p \in \mathbb{R}^n)(T_W(R_\alpha{\downarrow}{\uparrow}A(p), R_\alpha{\downarrow}{\uparrow}B(p)) \geq \lambda)$$
$$\Leftrightarrow (\exists p \in \mathbb{R}^n)((R_\alpha{\downarrow}{\uparrow}A(p) \geq 1 \wedge R_\alpha{\downarrow}{\uparrow}B(p) \geq \lambda)$$
$$\vee (R_\alpha{\downarrow}{\uparrow}A(p) \geq 1 - \frac{\Delta}{2} \wedge R_\alpha{\downarrow}{\uparrow}B(p) \geq \lambda + \frac{\Delta}{2})$$

$$\vee \cdots \vee (R_\alpha \downarrow \uparrow A(p) \geq \lambda \wedge R_\alpha \downarrow \uparrow B(p) \geq 1))$$

$$\Leftrightarrow (\exists p \in \mathbb{R}^n)((p \in (R_\alpha \downarrow \uparrow A)_1 \wedge p \in (R_\alpha \downarrow \uparrow B)_\lambda)$$

$$\vee (p \in (R_\alpha \downarrow \uparrow A)_{1-\frac{\Delta}{2}} \wedge p \in (R_\alpha \downarrow \uparrow B)_{\lambda+\frac{\Delta}{2}})$$

$$\vee \cdots \vee (p \in (R_\alpha \downarrow \uparrow A)_\lambda \wedge p \in (R_\alpha \downarrow \uparrow B)_1))$$

$$\Leftrightarrow (\exists p \in \mathbb{R}^n)((p \in (R_\alpha \downarrow \uparrow A_1) \wedge p \in (R_\alpha \downarrow \uparrow B_\lambda))$$

$$\vee (p \in (R_\alpha \downarrow \uparrow A_{1-\frac{\Delta}{2}}) \wedge p \in (R_\alpha \downarrow \uparrow B_{\lambda+\frac{\Delta}{2}}))$$

$$\vee \cdots \vee (p \in (R_\alpha \downarrow \uparrow A_\lambda) \wedge p \in (R_\alpha \downarrow \uparrow B_1)))$$

$$\Leftrightarrow (\exists p \in \mathbb{R}^n)(p \in (R_\alpha \downarrow \uparrow A_1) \wedge p \in (R_\alpha \downarrow \uparrow B_\lambda))$$

$$\vee (\exists p \in \mathbb{R}^n)(p \in (R_\alpha \downarrow \uparrow A_{1-\frac{\Delta}{2}}) \wedge p \in (R_\alpha \downarrow \uparrow B_{\lambda+\frac{\Delta}{2}}))$$

$$\vee \cdots \vee (\exists p \in \mathbb{R}^n)(p \in (R_\alpha \downarrow \uparrow A_\lambda) \wedge p \in (R_\alpha \downarrow \uparrow B_1))$$

$$\Leftrightarrow O_\alpha(A_1, B_\lambda) \vee O_\alpha(A_{1-\frac{\Delta}{2}}, B_{\lambda+\frac{\Delta}{2}}) \vee \cdots \vee O_\alpha(A_\lambda, B_1)$$

Furthermore, (8.56) follows from (8.55) in the same way that (8.54) follows from (8.53). Next, to show (8.58), we obtain, again employing Lemma 8.4 and Lemma 8.5

$$P_\alpha(A, B) \leq \lambda'$$

$$\Leftrightarrow \inf_{p \in \mathbb{R}^n} I_W(R_\alpha \downarrow \uparrow A(p), R_\alpha \downarrow \uparrow B(p)) \leq \lambda'$$

$$\Leftrightarrow (\exists p \in \mathbb{R}^n)(I_W(R_\alpha \downarrow \uparrow A(p), R_\alpha \downarrow \uparrow B(p)) \leq \lambda')$$

$$\Leftrightarrow (\exists p \in \mathbb{R}^n)((R_\alpha \downarrow \uparrow A(p) \geq 1 \wedge R_\alpha \downarrow \uparrow B(p) \leq \lambda')$$

$$\vee (R_\alpha \downarrow \uparrow A(p) \geq 1 - \frac{\Delta}{2} \wedge R_\alpha \downarrow \uparrow B(p) \leq \lambda' - \frac{\Delta}{2})$$

$$\vee \cdots \vee (R_\alpha \downarrow \uparrow A(p) \geq 1 - \lambda' \wedge R_\alpha \downarrow \uparrow B(p) \leq 0))$$

$$\Leftrightarrow (\exists p \in \mathbb{R}^n)((R_\alpha \downarrow \uparrow A(p) \geq 1 \wedge \neg (R_\alpha \downarrow \uparrow B(p) > \lambda'))$$

$$\vee (R_\alpha \downarrow \uparrow A(p) \geq 1 - \frac{\Delta}{2} \wedge \neg (R_\alpha \downarrow \uparrow B(p) > \lambda' - \frac{\Delta}{2}))$$

$$\vee \cdots \vee (R_\alpha \downarrow \uparrow A(p) \geq 1 - \lambda' \wedge \neg (R_\alpha \downarrow \uparrow B(p) > 0)))$$

$$\Leftrightarrow (\exists p \in \mathbb{R}^n)((R_\alpha \downarrow \uparrow A(p) \geq 1 \wedge \neg (R_\alpha \downarrow \uparrow B(p) \geq \lambda' + \frac{\Delta}{2}))$$

$$\vee (R_\alpha \downarrow \uparrow A(p) \geq 1 - \frac{\Delta}{2} \wedge \neg (R_\alpha \downarrow \uparrow B(p) \geq \lambda'))$$

$$\vee \cdots \vee (R_\alpha \downarrow \uparrow A(p) \geq 1 - \lambda' \wedge \neg (R_\alpha \downarrow \uparrow B(p) \geq \frac{\Delta}{2})))$$

$$\Leftrightarrow (\exists p \in \mathbb{R}^n)((p \in (R_\alpha \downarrow \uparrow A)_1 \wedge p \notin (R_\alpha \downarrow \uparrow B)_{\lambda'+\frac{\Delta}{2}})$$

$$\vee (p \in (R_\alpha \downarrow \uparrow A)_{1-\frac{\Delta}{2}} \wedge p \notin (R_\alpha \downarrow \uparrow B)_{\lambda'})$$

$$\vee \cdots \vee (p \in (R_\alpha\!\downarrow\!\uparrow\! A)_{1-\lambda'} \wedge p \notin (R_\alpha\!\downarrow\!\uparrow\! B)_{\frac{\Delta}{2}}))$$

$$\Leftrightarrow (\exists p \in \mathbb{R}^n)((p \in (R_\alpha\!\downarrow\!\uparrow\! A_1) \wedge p \notin (R_\alpha\!\downarrow\!\uparrow\! B_{\lambda'+\frac{\Delta}{2}}))$$

$$\vee (p \in (R_\alpha\!\downarrow\!\uparrow\! A_{1-\frac{\Delta}{2}}) \wedge p \notin (R_\alpha\!\downarrow\!\uparrow\! B_{\lambda'}))$$

$$\vee \cdots \vee (p \in (R_\alpha\!\downarrow\!\uparrow\! A_{1-\lambda'}) \wedge p \notin (R_\alpha\!\downarrow\!\uparrow\! B_{\frac{\Delta}{2}})))$$

$$\Leftrightarrow (\exists p \in \mathbb{R}^n)(p \in (R_\alpha\!\downarrow\!\uparrow\! A_1) \wedge p \notin (R_\alpha\!\downarrow\!\uparrow\! B_{\lambda'+\frac{\Delta}{2}}))$$

$$\vee (\exists p \in \mathbb{R}^n)(p \in (R_\alpha\!\downarrow\!\uparrow\! A_{1-\frac{\Delta}{2}}) \wedge p \notin (R_\alpha\!\downarrow\!\uparrow\! B_{\lambda'}))$$

$$\vee \cdots \vee (\exists p \in \mathbb{R}^n)(p \in (R_\alpha\!\downarrow\!\uparrow\! A_{1-\lambda'}) \wedge p \notin (R_\alpha\!\downarrow\!\uparrow\! B_{\frac{\Delta}{2}}))$$

$$\Leftrightarrow \neg(\forall p \in \mathbb{R}^n)(p \notin (R_\alpha\!\downarrow\!\uparrow\! A_1) \vee p \in (R_\alpha\!\downarrow\!\uparrow\! B_{\lambda'+\frac{\Delta}{2}}))$$

$$\vee \neg(\forall p \in \mathbb{R}^n)(p \notin (R_\alpha\!\downarrow\!\uparrow\! A_{1-\frac{\Delta}{2}}) \vee p \in (R_\alpha\!\downarrow\!\uparrow\! B_{\lambda'}))$$

$$\vee \cdots \vee \neg(\forall p \in \mathbb{R}^n)(p \notin (R_\alpha\!\downarrow\!\uparrow\! A_{1-\lambda'}) \vee p \in (R_\alpha\!\downarrow\!\uparrow\! B_{\frac{\Delta}{2}}))$$

$$\Leftrightarrow \neg(\forall p \in \mathbb{R}^n)(p \in (R_\alpha\!\downarrow\!\uparrow\! A_1) \Rightarrow p \in (R_\alpha\!\downarrow\!\uparrow\! B_{\lambda'+\frac{\Delta}{2}}))$$

$$\vee \neg(\forall p \in \mathbb{R}^n)(p \in (R_\alpha\!\downarrow\!\uparrow\! A_{1-\frac{\Delta}{2}}) \Rightarrow p \in (R_\alpha\!\downarrow\!\uparrow\! B_{\lambda'}))$$

$$\vee \cdots \vee \neg(\forall p \in \mathbb{R}^n)(p \in (R_\alpha\!\downarrow\!\uparrow\! A_{1-\lambda'}) \Rightarrow p \in (R_\alpha\!\downarrow\!\uparrow\! B_{\frac{\Delta}{2}}))$$

$$\Leftrightarrow \neg P_\alpha(A_1, B_{\lambda'+\frac{\Delta}{2}}) \vee \neg P_\alpha(A_{1-\frac{\Delta}{2}}, B_{\lambda'}) \vee \cdots \vee \neg P_\alpha(A_{1-\lambda'}, B_{\frac{\Delta}{2}})$$

and (8.57) follows from (8.58) in the same way that (8.54) follows from (8.53). To show (8.60) we find entirely analogously as for (8.58) that

$$NTP_\alpha(A, B) \leq \lambda' \Leftrightarrow \neg NTP_\alpha(A_1, B_{\lambda'+\frac{\Delta}{2}}) \vee \neg NTP_\alpha(A_{1-\frac{\Delta}{2}}, B_{\lambda'})$$

$$\vee \cdots \vee \neg NTP_\alpha(A_{1-\lambda'}, B_{\frac{\Delta}{2}})$$

from which (8.60) follows by Lemma 8.6. Finally, (8.59) follows from (8.60) in the same way that (8.54) follows from (8.53). $\square$

Recall from Lemma 8.1 that C_α, O_α, P_α and NTP_α can be used to define C–interpretations of RCC formulas. This observation suggests how we can reason about fuzzy RCC formulas by translating them first to crisp RCC formulas, thereby applying Proposition 8.5. In particular, we can relate the regions from the crisp RCC formulas to α–level sets of the regions from the fuzzy RCC formulas. Let Θ be a standard set of fuzzy RCC formulas, and let V be the set of variables (regions) occurring in Θ. We construct a set of RCC formulas Γ over the set of variables V', containing for each v in V, the variables $v_{\frac{\Delta}{2}}$, v_Δ, ..., v_1. In particular, we add the following RCC formulas to Γ, for each v in V

$$\{P(v_{\frac{\Delta}{2}}, v_\Delta), P(v_\Delta, v_{\Delta+\frac{\Delta}{2}}), \dots, P(v_{1-\frac{\Delta}{2}}, v_1)\} \tag{8.61}$$

This ensures that we can associate F–interpretations of Θ with C–interpretations of Γ and vice versa. In particular, given a C–interpretation $\mathcal{I}'$ of Γ which maps every v in V' to a non–empty, bounded region in $\mathbb{R}^n$, we can define an F–interpretation $\mathcal{I}$ of Θ as

$$v^{\mathcal{I}}(p) = \begin{cases} \max\{\lambda | \lambda \in M_{\frac{\Delta}{2}} \setminus \{0\} \wedge p \in v_\lambda^{\mathcal{I}'}\} & \text{if } p \in v_{\frac{\Delta}{2}}^{\mathcal{I}'} \\ 0 & \text{otherwise} \end{cases} \tag{8.62}$$

for all v in V and p in $\mathbb{R}^n$. Conversely, we can define a C–interpretation $\mathcal{I}'$ of Γ, given an F–interpretation $\mathcal{I}$ of Θ which maps every variable to a normalised, bounded fuzzy set in $\mathbb{R}^n$ taking only membership degrees from $M_{\frac{\Delta}{2}}$:

$$p \in v_\lambda^{\mathcal{I}'} \equiv p \in \{q | q \in \mathbb{R}^n \wedge v^{\mathcal{I}}(q) \geq \lambda\} \tag{8.63}$$

for $\lambda \in M_{\frac{\Delta}{2}} \setminus \{0\}$. In addition to (8.61), we also add (sets of) RCC formulas to Γ corresponding with each of the fuzzy RCC formulas in Θ. For example, if Θ contains the fuzzy RCC formula $EC(a,b) \geq 0.5 \vee P(c,d) \leq 0$, being equivalent to $(C(a,b) \geq 0.5 \wedge O(a,b) \leq 0.5) \vee P(c,d) \leq 0$, we obtain the following expression by Proposition 8.5 (assuming $\Delta = 0.5$)

$$((C(a_1, b_{0.5}) \vee C(a_{0.75}, b_{0.75}) \vee C(a_{0.5}, b_1)) \wedge \neg O(a_1, b_{0.75}) \wedge \neg O(a_{0.75}, b_1))$$
$$\vee \neg P(c_1, d_{0.25}) \vee \neg P(c_{0.75}, d_{0.5}) \vee \neg P(c_{0.5}, d_{0.75}) \vee \neg P(c_{0.25}, d_1)$$

which corresponds to the following set of RCC formulas

$$\{(C(a_1, b_{0.5}) \vee C(a_{0.75}, b_{0.75}) \vee C(a_{0.5}, b_1) \vee \neg P(c_1, d_{0.25}) \vee \neg P(c_{0.75}, d_{0.5})$$
$$\vee \neg P(c_{0.5}, d_{0.75}) \vee \neg P(c_{0.25}, d_1), \neg O(a_1, b_{0.75}) \vee \neg P(c_1, d_{0.25})$$
$$\vee \neg P(c_{0.75}, d_{0.5}) \vee \neg P(c_{0.5}, d_{0.75}) \vee \neg P(c_{0.25}, d_1), \neg O(a_{0.75}, b_1)$$
$$\vee \neg P(c_1, d_{0.25}) \vee \neg P(c_{0.75}, d_{0.5}) \vee \neg P(c_{0.5}, d_{0.75}) \vee \neg P(c_{0.25}, d_1)\}$$

If $\mathcal{I}'$ is a C–model of Γ and $\mathcal{I}$ is the F–interpretation of Θ defined by (8.62), we know from Proposition 8.5 that $\mathcal{I}$ will be an F–model of Θ, and vice versa, if $\mathcal{I}$ is an F–model of Θ, we know that the C–interpretation $\mathcal{I}'$ of Γ, defined by (8.63), will be a C–model of Γ. Note that if Θ is F–satisfiable, there always exists an F–model of Θ which maps variables to normalised, bounded fuzzy sets in $\mathbb{R}^n$ (Proposition 8.1 and Proposition 8.2), and if Γ is C–satisfiable, there always exists a C–model of Γ which maps variables to non–empty, bounded sets in $\mathbb{R}^n$ [Renz (2002)]. We thus have the following corollary of Proposition 8.5.

Corollary 8.5. *Let Θ be a standard set of fuzzy RCC formulas and let Γ be the corresponding set of (crisp) RCC formulas, obtained through the construction process outlined above. It holds that Θ is F–satisfiable iff Γ is C–satisfiable.*

8.4.2 *Relationship with the Egg–Yolk Calculus*

Until now, we have mainly considered interpretations of fuzzy topological relations in terms of fuzzy sets and nearness, i.e., $(n; \alpha, \beta)$–interpretations. On the other hand, as our generalization of the RCC is not explicitly tied to this type of interpretations, it seems that it should also encompass other models of vague topological information. In this section, we demonstrate that this is indeed the case by revealing a relationship between our approach and the Egg–Yolk calculus, the latter being neither based on nearness nor on fuzzy sets.

In the most general form of the Egg–Yolk calculus, a vague region A is represented as k nested (crisp) sets $(A^1, A^2, \ldots, A^k)$, where A^1 contains the points that definitely belong to the vague region, and $co(A^k)$ contains the points that definitely do not $(A^1 \subseteq A^2 \subseteq \cdots \subseteq A^k)$. In other words, the sets A^1, A^2, A^3, $\ldots$, A^k are increasingly more tolerant boundaries for the vague region. Without loss of generality, we can assume that A^i is a non–empty, bounded, regular closed subset of $\mathbb{R}^n$, for some n in $\mathbb{N} \setminus \{0\}$. Note that typically $k = 2$, in which case A^1 is called the yolk and A^2 is called the white of vague region A. We will refer to k nested sets that represent a vague region, as an Egg–Yolk region. Egg–Yolk relations, i.e., topological relations between two Egg–Yolk regions A and B, are defined by expressing which are the possible RCC relations that may hold between the corresponding nested sets $(A^1, A^2, \ldots, A^k)$ and $(B^1, B^2, \ldots, B^k)$. For example, to express that A is a part of B, we may require

$$P(A^1, B^1) \wedge P(A^2, B^2) \wedge \cdots \wedge P(A^k, B^k) \qquad (8.64)$$

or, adopting a stricter interpretation, that $P(A^k, B^1)$. On the other hand, we may also define fuzzy topological relations between Egg–Yolk regions, imposing, for instance, that A and B are connected to degree 1 if A^1 and B^1 are connected, and to some lower degree if A^1 and B^1 are not connected but A^i and B^j are connected for some i and j in $\{1, 2, \ldots, k\}$.

The k nested sets $(A^1, A^2, \ldots, A^k)$ can naturally be regarded as the α–level sets of a fuzzy set A, i.e., $A^1 = A_1$, $A^2 = A_{\frac{k-1}{k}}$, $\ldots$, $A^k = A_{\frac{1}{k}}$. Thus, given an $(n; \alpha, 0)$–interpretation $\mathcal{I}_0$ of a set of fuzzy RCC formulas Θ taking only membership degrees from $M_{\frac{1}{k}}$, we can straightforwardly construct a new interpretation $\mathcal{I}$ in which each variable v is interpreted as an Egg–Yolk region $v^{\mathcal{I}} = (v^1, \ldots, v^k)$, where

$$v^i = (v^{\mathcal{I}_0})_{\frac{k-i+1}{k}} \qquad (8.65)$$

Moreover, if we define $C^{\mathcal{I}}$ such that (assuming $\max \emptyset = 0$)

$$C^{\mathcal{I}}(u^{\mathcal{I}}, v^{\mathcal{I}}) = C^{\mathcal{I}}((u^1, \ldots, u^k), (v^1, \ldots, v^k))$$

$$= \max\{\frac{k+1-i}{k} | i \in \{1, \ldots, k\} \wedge (C_\alpha(u^1, v^i) \vee C_\alpha(u^2, v^{i-1})$$

$$\vee \cdots \vee C_\alpha(u^i, v^1))\} \qquad (8.66)$$

it holds by Proposition 8.5 that for all regions u and v

$$C^{\mathcal{I}_0}(u^{\mathcal{I}_0}, v^{\mathcal{I}_0}) = C^{\mathcal{I}}(u^{\mathcal{I}}, v^{\mathcal{I}}) \qquad (8.67)$$

Indeed, since $u^{\mathcal{I}_0}$ and $v^{\mathcal{I}_0}$ are, by assumption, fuzzy sets taking only membership degrees from $M_{\frac{1}{k}}$, we know that $C^{\mathcal{I}_0}(u^{\mathcal{I}_0}, v^{\mathcal{I}_0}) = C_\alpha(u^{\mathcal{I}_0}, v^{\mathcal{I}_0}) \in M_{\frac{1}{k}}$. Assuming $C^{\mathcal{I}_0}(u^{\mathcal{I}_0}, v^{\mathcal{I}_0}) > 0$, this means that the value of $C^{\mathcal{I}_0}(u^{\mathcal{I}_0}, v^{\mathcal{I}_0})$ is the largest element λ from $M_{\frac{1}{k}}$ such that $C^{\mathcal{I}_0}(u^{\mathcal{I}_0}, v^{\mathcal{I}_0}) \geq \lambda$ holds, or equivalently by Proposition 8.5, such that

$$C_\alpha((u^{\mathcal{I}_0})_1, (v^{\mathcal{I}_0})_\lambda) \vee C_\alpha((u^{\mathcal{I}_0})_{1-\frac{1}{k}}, (v^{\mathcal{I}_0})_{\lambda+\frac{1}{k}}) \vee \cdots \vee C_\alpha((u^{\mathcal{I}_0})_\lambda, (v^{\mathcal{I}_0})_1)$$

For $\lambda \in M_{\frac{1}{k}}$, it holds that $\lambda = \frac{k-i+1}{k}$ for some i in $\{1, \ldots, k\}$. Thus we find that $C^{\mathcal{I}_0}(u^{\mathcal{I}_0}, v^{\mathcal{I}_0}) = \frac{k-i+1}{k}$ where i is the smallest element in $\{1, \ldots, k\}$ satisfying

$$C_\alpha((u^{\mathcal{I}_0})_1, (v^{\mathcal{I}_0})_{\frac{k-i+1}{k}}) \vee C_\alpha((u^{\mathcal{I}_0})_{1-\frac{1}{k}}, (v^{\mathcal{I}_0})_{\frac{k-i+2}{k}})$$

$$\vee \cdots \vee C_\alpha((u^{\mathcal{I}_0})_{\frac{k-i+1}{k}}, (v^{\mathcal{I}_0})_1)$$

By the correspondence (8.65), we therefore have that $C^{\mathcal{I}_0}(u^{\mathcal{I}_0}, v^{\mathcal{I}_0}) = \frac{k-i+1}{k}$, where i is the smallest value in $\{1, \ldots, k\}$ such that

$$C_\alpha(u^1, v^i) \vee C_\alpha(u^2, v^{i-1}) \vee \cdots \vee C_\alpha(u^i, v^1)$$

in other words (8.67). If $C^{\mathcal{I}_0}(u^{\mathcal{I}_0}, v^{\mathcal{I}_0}) = 0$, then $DC_\alpha(u^1, v^i)$, $DC_\alpha(u^2, v^{i-1})$, $\ldots$, $DC_\alpha(u^i, v^1)$ will hold for all i in $\{1, \ldots, k\}$, and we therefore find (8.67) again.

Note that (8.67) entails that $\mathcal{I}_0$ is an F–model of Θ iff $\mathcal{I}$ is an F–model of Θ, and, moreover, that

$$P^{\mathcal{I}_0}(u^{\mathcal{I}_0}, v^{\mathcal{I}_0}) = P^{\mathcal{I}}(u^{\mathcal{I}}, v^{\mathcal{I}})$$

$$O^{\mathcal{I}_0}(u^{\mathcal{I}_0}, v^{\mathcal{I}_0}) = O^{\mathcal{I}}(u^{\mathcal{I}}, v^{\mathcal{I}})$$

$$NTP^{\mathcal{I}_0}(u^{\mathcal{I}_0}, v^{\mathcal{I}_0}) = NTP^{\mathcal{I}}(u^{\mathcal{I}}, v^{\mathcal{I}})$$

Following a similar line of reasoning as for $C^{\mathcal{I}}$, we thus obtain from Proposition 8.5 that (assuming $\max \emptyset = 0$)

$$P^{\mathcal{I}}(u^{\mathcal{I}}, v^{\mathcal{I}}) = P^{\mathcal{I}}((u^1, \ldots, u^k), (v^1, \ldots, v^k))$$

$$= \max\{\frac{k+1-i}{k} | i \in \{1, \ldots, k\} \wedge P_\alpha(u^1, v^i) \wedge P_\alpha(u^2, v^{i+1})$$

$$\wedge \cdots \wedge P_\alpha(u^{k+1-i}, v^k)\}$$

$$O^{\mathcal{I}}(u^{\mathcal{I}}, v^{\mathcal{I}}) = O^{\mathcal{I}}((u^1, \ldots, u^k), (v^1, \ldots, v^k))$$

$$= \max\{\frac{k+1-i}{k} | i \in \{1, \ldots, k\} \wedge (O_\alpha(u^1, v^i) \vee O_\alpha(u^2, v^{i-1})$$

$$\vee \cdots \vee O_\alpha(u^i, v^1))\}$$

$$NTP^{\mathcal{I}}(u^{\mathcal{I}}, v^{\mathcal{I}}) = NTP^{\mathcal{I}}((u^1, \ldots, u^k), (v^1, \ldots, v^k))$$

$$= \max\{\frac{k+1-i}{k} | i \in \{1, \ldots, k\} \wedge NTPP_\alpha(u^1, v^i)$$

$$\wedge \cdots \wedge NTPP_\alpha(u^{k+1-i}, v^k)\}$$

Although $\mathcal{I}$ maps variables to Egg–Yolk regions, the fuzzy topological relations between them are still defined using nearness, in contrast to typical Egg–Yolk interpretations, where spatial relations are defined in terms of standard RCC relations such as C^n, O^n, P^n and NTP^n. Recall, for example, that for A and B two subsets of $\mathbb{R}^n$, $C^n(A, B) \equiv A \cap B \neq \emptyset$.

Definition 8.10. Let Θ be a set of fuzzy RCC formulas and let V be the set of regions used. An F–interpretation $\mathcal{I}$ of Θ is called an Egg–Yolk interpretation of Θ w.r.t. (k, n) if it maps every v in V to an Egg–Yolk region, and C is interpreted for Egg–Yolk regions $(u^1, \ldots, u^k)$ and $(v^1, \ldots, v^k)$ by $(k, n \in \mathbb{N} \setminus \{0\}, \max \emptyset = 0)$:

$$C^{\mathcal{I}}((u^1, \ldots, u^k), (v^1, \ldots, v^k))$$

$$= \max\{\frac{k+1-i}{k} | i \in \{1, \ldots, k\} \wedge (C^n(u^1, v^i) \vee C^n(u^2, v^{i-1})$$

$$\vee \cdots \vee C^n(u^i, v^1))\} \qquad (8.68)$$

An Egg–Yolk interpretation which is also a model of Θ is called an Egg–Yolk model of Θ.

Let $\mathcal{I}$ be defined as in (8.66). If $\mathcal{I}$ is an F–model of a standard set of fuzzy RCC formulas Θ, then Θ must also have an Egg–Yolk model $\mathcal{I}'$. Indeed, identifying Egg–Yolk regions with their corresponding fuzzy sets, we can use the construction process from Corollary 8.5 to obtain a set of RCC formulas Γ which is C–satisfiable iff Θ is F–satisfiable. The variables occurring in Γ correspond to the different nested sets of the Egg–Yolk regions (or equivalently, to the α–level sets of the corresponding fuzzy sets), and $\mathcal{I}$ naturally corresponds to an $(n; \alpha, 0)$–model of Γ. Specifically, the variables occurring in Γ are mapped to the crisp regions u^1, u^2, ..., u^k, where $(u^1, \ldots, u^k)$ is the Egg–Yolk region corresponding to the interpretation of region u under $\mathcal{I}$, i.e., $u^{\mathcal{I}} = (u^1, \ldots, u^k)$. From Corollary (8.4), we know that Γ must also have a standard model. In this standard model, the variables from Γ are mapped to crisp regions, which can again be interpreted as the nested sets of Egg–Yolk regions. Specifically, this leads to an Egg–Yolk interpretation $\mathcal{I}'$ where $u^{\mathcal{I}'} = (u'^1, \ldots, u'^k)$, i.e., the variable from Γ which was initially mapped to crisp region u^i is in the new interpretation mapped to another crisp region u'^i. Because $\mathcal{I}'$ moreover corresponds to a standard model of Γ, we have that $C^n(u'^i, v'^j) \equiv C_\alpha(u^i, v^j)$ for all regions u and v occurring in Θ and all i and j in $\{1, 2, \ldots, k\}$. In other words, interpreting connection as in (8.68), $\mathcal{I}'$ corresponds to an Egg–Yolk model of Θ. Together with Proposition 8.4, this leads to the following proposition.

Proposition 8.6. *Let Θ be an F–satisfiable standard set of fuzzy RCC formulas in which all upper and lower bounds are taken from $\{0, \frac{2}{k}, \frac{4}{k}, \ldots, 1\}$ for some $k \in \mathbb{N} \setminus \{0\}$ ($T = T_W$). It holds that Θ has an Egg–Yolk model w.r.t. (k, n) for every n in $\mathbb{N} \setminus \{0\}$.*

Note that because of the construction process above, it holds that

$$C_\alpha(u^i, v^j) \equiv C^n(u'^i, v'^j)$$

$$P_\alpha(u^i, v^j) \equiv P^n(u'^i, v'^j)$$

$$O_\alpha(u^i, v^j) \equiv O^n(u'^i, v'^j)$$

$$NTP_\alpha(u^i, v^j) \equiv NTP^n(u'^i, v'^j)$$

for all variables u and v occurring in Θ, and all i and j in $\{1, 2, \ldots, k\}$. Since, moreover, $C^{\mathcal{I}}(u^{\mathcal{I}}, v^{\mathcal{I}}) = C^{\mathcal{I}'}(u^{\mathcal{I}'}, v^{\mathcal{I}'})$ for all regions u and v, it holds that $(\max \emptyset = 0)$

$$P^{\mathcal{I}'}((u'^1, \ldots, u'^k), (v'^1, \ldots, v'^k))$$

$$= \max\{\frac{k+1-i}{k} | i \in \{1, \ldots, k\} \wedge P^n(u'^1, v'^i) \wedge P^n(u'^2, v'^{i+1})$$

$$\wedge \cdots \wedge P^n(u'^{k+1-i}, v'^k)\}$$

$$O^{\mathcal{I}'}((u'^1, \ldots, u^k), (v'^1, \ldots, v'^k))$$

$$= \max\{\frac{k+1-i}{k} | i \in \{1, \ldots, k\} \wedge (O^n(u'^1, v'^i) \vee O^n(u'^2, v'^{i-1})$$

$$\vee \cdots \vee O^n(u'^i, v'^1))\}$$

$$NTP^{\mathcal{I}'}((u'^1, \ldots, u'^k), (v'^1, \ldots, v'^k))$$

$$= \max\{\frac{k+1-i}{k} | i \in \{1, \ldots, k\} \wedge NTPP^n(u'^1, v'^i)$$

$$\wedge \cdots \wedge NTPP^n(u'^{k+1-i}, v'^k)\}$$

Note that $P^{\mathcal{I}'}(u^{\mathcal{I}'}, v^{\mathcal{I}'}) = 1$ corresponds to the notion of containment between Egg–Yolk regions expressed in (8.64). For $i < k$, $P^{\mathcal{I}'}(u^{\mathcal{I}'}, v^{\mathcal{I}'}) = \frac{i}{k}$ corresponds to a more flexible notion of containment. In other words, a fuzzy topological relation R corresponds to a list of Egg–Yolk relations $(R^1, R^2, \ldots, R^k)$, where $R^i(u, v)$ corresponds to $R(u, v) \geq \frac{k+1-i}{k}$. For example, if $k = 2$, $O(u, v) = 1$ means that the yolk of u overlaps with the yolk of v, while $O(u, v) \geq 0.5$ means that either the yolk of u overlaps with the white of v, or the white of u overlaps with the yolk of v. Similarly, $P(u, v) = 1$ means that the yolk of u is contained in the yolk of v, and the white of u is contained in the white of v, whereas $P(u, v) \geq 0.5$ means that the yolk of u is contained in the white of v. We conclude this section with an example illustrating the relationship between $(n; \alpha, 0)$–interpretations and Egg–Yolk interpretations.

Example 8.2.

Let Θ be the normalised set of fuzzy RCC formulas, defined by the following four matrices:

$$C = \begin{array}{c} \\ a \\ b \end{array} \begin{array}{cc} a & b \\ \begin{pmatrix} 1 & 0.75 \\ 0.75 & 1 \end{pmatrix} \end{array} \qquad P = \begin{array}{c} \\ a \\ b \end{array} \begin{array}{cc} a & b \\ \begin{pmatrix} 1 & 0 \\ 0.5 & 1 \end{pmatrix} \end{array}$$

$$O = \begin{array}{c} \\ a \\ b \end{array} \begin{array}{cc} a & b \\ \begin{pmatrix} 1 & 0.5 \\ 0.5 & 1 \end{pmatrix} \end{array} \qquad NTP = \begin{array}{c} \\ a \\ b \end{array} \begin{array}{cc} a & b \\ \begin{pmatrix} 1 & 0 \\ 0.25 & 1 \end{pmatrix} \end{array}$$

This set Θ is satisfied by the $(1; 20, 0)$–interpretation $\mathcal{I}$ which maps the variables a and b to the fuzzy sets A and B in $\mathbb{R}$ from Figure 8.2(a), i.e., $a^{\mathcal{I}} = A$ and $b^{\mathcal{I}} = B$. Since Θ is normalised and contains only upper

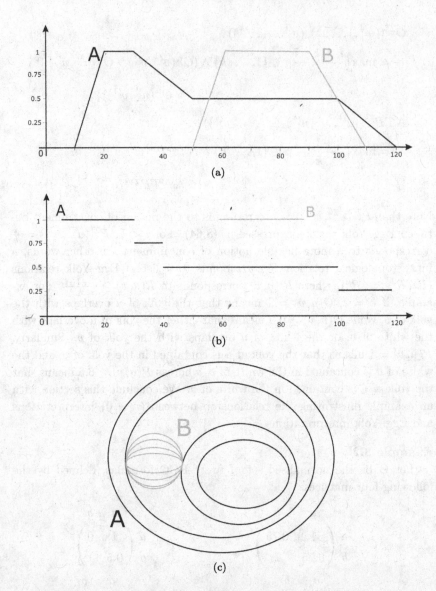

Fig. 8.2   An $(n; \alpha, 0)$–model can naturally be linked to an Egg–Yolk model.

and lower bounds from $M_{0.25} = \{0, 0.25, 0.5, 0.75, 1\}$, there also exists an $(n; \alpha, 0)$–model which only uses membership degrees from $M_{0.25}$. Such a model is shown in Figure 8.2(b) for $n = 1$ and $\alpha = 20$. Furthermore, this model is closely related to a model $\mathcal{I}'$ in which regions are interpreted as

Egg–Yolk regions and $C^{\mathcal{I}'}$ is given by (8.66):

$$a^{\mathcal{I}'} = ([5, 30], [5, 40], [5, 100], [5, 120])$$
$$b^{\mathcal{I}'} = ([60, 90], [60, 90], [60, 90], [60, 90])$$

Note that under interpretation $\mathcal{I}'$, for example, $[5, 40]$ and $[60, 90]$ are connected, because $d(40, 60) = |60 - 40| \leq 20$. In other words, because connection is interpreted in terms of nearness, the intervals need not actually have a point in common to be connected.

Finally, it is also possible to construct an Egg–Yolk model $\mathcal{I}''$ in which C is interpreted as in (8.68); for example

$$a^{\mathcal{I}''} = ([100, 120], [90, 130], [60, 140], [50, 150])$$
$$b^{\mathcal{I}''} = ([60, 90], [60, 90], [60, 90], [60, 90])$$

As Egg–Yolk models are not interpreted in terms of nearness, two intervals need to have a point in common to be connected, e.g., $[60, 90]$ and $[90, 130]$. Note that Proposition 8.6 guarantees the existence of an Egg–Yolk model in any dimension. In Figure 8.2(c), for instance, a model is depicted in $\mathbb{R}^2$.

8.4.3 *Realizability in Any Dimension*

From the previous discussion, we already know that standard, satisfiable sets of fuzzy RCC formulas Θ have an Egg–Yolk model in any dimension (provided the upper and lower bounds are finitely representable), and an $(n; \alpha, 0)$–model in at least one particular dimension n. In this section, we prove that an $(m; \alpha, 0)$–model of Θ can be found in any dimension m as well. Specifically, we show that an $(1; \alpha, 0)$–model can always be found, and, subsequently, that this $(1; \alpha, 0)$–model can be converted into an $(m; \alpha, 0)$–model for any m in $\mathbb{N} \setminus \{0\}$.

Lemma 8.7. *Let* $A = [a_1, a_2] \cup [a_3, a_4] \cup \cdots \cup [a_{2n-1}, a_{2n}]$ *such that* $a_1 < a_2 < a_3 < \cdots < a_{2n}$. *For sufficiently small* $\gamma > 0$, *it holds that* $R_\gamma{\downarrow}A = [a_1 + \gamma, a_2 - \gamma] \cup [a_3 + \gamma, a_4 - \gamma] \cup \cdots \cup [a_{2n-1} + \gamma, a_{2n} - \gamma]$.

Proof. Let $\gamma > 0$ be chosen such that

$$\gamma < \min_{i=1}^{n} \frac{a_{2i} - a_{2i-1}}{2}$$

We then find for each p in $\mathbb{R}$

$p \in R_\gamma{\downarrow}A$

$\equiv (\forall q \in \mathbb{R})((p,q) \in R_\gamma \Rightarrow q \in A)$

$\equiv (\forall q \in \mathbb{R})(d(p,q) \leq \gamma \Rightarrow q \in A)$

$\equiv p \in [a_1 + \gamma, a_2 - \gamma] \cup [a_3 + \gamma, a_4 - \gamma] \cup \cdots \cup [a_{2n-1} + \gamma, a_{2n} - \gamma]$

$\square$

Lemma 8.8. *Let* $A = [a_1, a_2] \cup [a_3, a_4] \cup \cdots \cup [a_{2n-1}, a_{2n}]$ *such that* $a_1 < a_2 < a_3 < \cdots < a_{2n}$. *For sufficiently small* $\gamma > 0$, *it holds that* $R_\gamma{\uparrow}A = [a_1 - \gamma, a_2 + \gamma] \cup [a_3 - \gamma, a_4 + \gamma] \cup \cdots \cup [a_{2n-1} - \gamma, a_{2n} + \gamma]$ *and* $a_1 - \gamma < a_2 + \gamma < a_3 - \gamma < \cdots < a_{2n} + \gamma$.

Proof. Let $\gamma > 0$ be chosen such that

$$\gamma < \min_{i=2}^{n} \frac{a_{2i-1} - a_{2i-2}}{2}$$

We then find for each p in $\mathbb{R}$

$p \in R_\gamma{\uparrow}A$

$\equiv (\exists q \in \mathbb{R})(R_\gamma(p,q) \wedge q \in A)$

$\equiv (\exists q \in \mathbb{R})(d(p,q) \leq \gamma \wedge q \in A)$

$\equiv p \in [a_1 - \gamma, a_2 + \gamma] \cup [a_3 - \gamma, a_4 + \gamma] \cup \cdots \cup [a_{2n-1} - \gamma, a_{2n} + \gamma]$

$\square$

Corollary 8.6. *If A is the union of a finite number of closed, non-degenerate intervals, it holds that $R_\gamma{\downarrow}{\uparrow}A = A$ for any sufficiently small $\gamma > 0$.*

Proposition 8.7. *Let Θ be an F-satisfiable standard set of fuzzy RCC formulas whose upper and lower bounds are finitely representable. It holds that Θ has an $(1; \alpha, 0)$-model for some $\alpha > 0$.*

Proof. Since Θ is satisfiable, there exists an Egg–Yolk model in any dimension, and, in particular, an Egg–Yolk model $\mathcal{I}$ in $\mathbb{R}$. Let V be the set of variables used in Θ. For every v in V, $v^{\mathcal{I}}$ corresponds to an Egg–Yolk region $(v^1, v^2, \ldots, v^k)$ whose k nested sets each are the union of a finite number of closed, non–degenerate intervals in $\mathbb{R}$. Next, we show that there exists a model $\mathcal{I}'$ which also maps variables to Egg–Yolk regions, but which interprets C as in (8.66). From Section 8.4.2, we then know that $\mathcal{I}'$ corresponds to an $(1; \alpha, 0)$–model in which each variable v in V is interpreted as a fuzzy set taking only membership degrees from $M_{\frac{1}{k}}$, its α–level sets corresponding to the k nested sets of the Egg–Yolk region $v^{\mathcal{I}'}$. In particular, we define $\mathcal{I}'$ for v in V as the Egg–Yolk region whose i^{th} component v'^i is given by

$$v'^i = R_\gamma \downarrow v^i$$

for a given $\gamma > 0$. We show that $\mathcal{I}'$ is a model of Θ, provided γ and the parameter $\alpha > 0$ from (8.66) are taken sufficiently small. In particular, we show that when A and B are the union of a finite number of closed, non–degenerate intervals in $\mathbb{R}$, it holds that

$$C^1(A, B) \Leftrightarrow C_\alpha(R_\gamma \downarrow A, R_\gamma \downarrow B)$$
$$P^1(A, B) \Leftrightarrow P_\alpha(R_\gamma \downarrow A, R_\gamma \downarrow B)$$
$$O^1(A, B) \Leftrightarrow O_\alpha(R_\gamma \downarrow A, R_\gamma \downarrow B)$$
$$NTP^1(A, B) \Leftrightarrow NTP_\alpha(R_\gamma \downarrow A, R_\gamma \downarrow B)$$

from which the proposition follows. Note that when γ is sufficiently small, $R_\gamma \downarrow A$ and $R_\gamma \downarrow B$ are the union of a finite number of closed, non–degenerate intervals in $\mathbb{R}$ by Lemma 8.7. First, consider

$$C^1(A, B) \Rightarrow C_\alpha(R_\gamma \downarrow A, R_\gamma \downarrow B) \tag{8.69}$$

If $C^1(A, B)$, we know that there is some p in $A \cap B$. From Lemma 8.7 we furthermore know that there is some q_1 in $R_\gamma \downarrow A$ and some q_2 in $R_\gamma \downarrow B$ such that $d(p, q_1) \leq \gamma$ and $d(p, q_2) \leq \gamma$, and also $d(q_1, q_2) \leq 2\gamma$. Hence, (8.69) holds as soon as $\gamma \leq \frac{\alpha}{2}$. We show the implication in the opposite direction by contraposition, i.e.:

$$DC^1(A, B) \Rightarrow DC_\alpha(R_\gamma \downarrow A, R_\gamma \downarrow B) \tag{8.70}$$

If $DC^1(A, B)$, we know that $d = \inf_{p \in A, q \in B} d(p, q) > 0$. Therefore, it suffices to choose $\alpha < d$ to have $DC_\alpha(A, B)$, which entails $DC_\alpha(R_\gamma \downarrow A, R_\gamma \downarrow B)$ since $R_\gamma \downarrow A \subseteq A$ and $R_\gamma \downarrow B \subseteq B$.

Next, we consider

$$O^1(A, B) \Rightarrow O_\alpha(R_\gamma \downarrow A, R_\gamma \downarrow B) \tag{8.71}$$

From $O^1(A, B)$ we know that there is some p in $i(A) \cap i(B)$. Since $p \in i(A) \cap i(B)$ we know that all points in a sufficiently small neighbourhood of p are also located in A and in B, in other words, that for sufficiently small γ, we have $p \in R_\gamma \downarrow A \cap R_\gamma \downarrow B$, which implies $p \in R_\alpha \downarrow \uparrow (R_\gamma \downarrow A) \cap R_\alpha \downarrow \uparrow (R_\gamma \downarrow B)$

and (8.71). Again, we show the implication in the opposite direction by contraposition:

$$DR^1(A, B) \Rightarrow DR_\alpha(R_\gamma{\downarrow}A, R_\gamma{\downarrow}B) \qquad (8.72)$$

From $DR^1(A, B)$, we know that for any p in $\mathbb{R}$ either $p \notin i(A)$ or $p \notin i(B)$. We obtain

$$(\forall p \in \mathbb{R})(p \notin i(A) \lor p \notin i(B))$$
$$\Leftrightarrow (\forall p \in \mathbb{R})(\neg(\exists \varepsilon > 0)(\forall q \in \mathbb{R})(d(p, q) \le \varepsilon \Rightarrow q \in A)$$
$$\lor \neg(\exists \varepsilon > 0)(\forall q \in \mathbb{R})(d(p, q) \le \varepsilon \Rightarrow q \in B))$$
$$\Leftrightarrow (\forall p \in \mathbb{R})((\forall \varepsilon > 0)(p \notin R_\varepsilon{\downarrow}A) \lor (\forall \varepsilon > 0)(p \notin R_\varepsilon{\downarrow}B))$$
$$\Rightarrow (\forall p \in \mathbb{R})(p \notin R_\gamma{\downarrow}A \lor p \notin R_\gamma{\downarrow}B)$$

By Corollary 8.6, we can assume that $R_\gamma{\downarrow}A = R_\alpha{\downarrow}{\uparrow}(R_\gamma{\downarrow}A)$ and $R_\gamma{\downarrow}B = R_\alpha{\downarrow}{\uparrow}(R_\gamma{\downarrow}B)$. Furthermore, note that this does not imply that the value of α depends on the value of γ. Indeed, from the proof of Lemma 8.7 and 8.8, it is clear that any value of α for which $A = R_\alpha{\downarrow}{\uparrow}A$ also satisfies $R_\gamma{\downarrow}A = R_\alpha{\downarrow}{\uparrow}(R_\gamma{\downarrow}A)$, the former expression being independent of γ. Hence, we have

$$(\forall p \in \mathbb{R})(p \notin R_\alpha{\downarrow}{\uparrow}(R_\gamma{\downarrow}A) \lor p \notin R_\alpha{\downarrow}{\uparrow}(R_\gamma{\downarrow}B))$$

or, in other words, $DR_\alpha(R_\gamma{\downarrow}A, R_\gamma{\downarrow}B)$.

To show

$$P^1(A, B) \Rightarrow P_\alpha(R_\gamma{\downarrow}A, R_\gamma{\downarrow}B) \qquad (8.73)$$

we find from $P^1(A, B)$ that $A \subseteq B$, and therefore also $R_\alpha{\downarrow}{\uparrow}(R_\gamma{\downarrow}A) \subseteq R_\alpha{\downarrow}{\uparrow}(R_\gamma{\downarrow}B)$, or, $P_\alpha(R_\gamma{\downarrow}A, R_\gamma{\downarrow}B)$. To show the implication in the opposite direction, we find from $\neg P^1(A, B)$ that there is a p in $\mathbb{R}$ such that $p \in i(A)$ and $p \notin B$. This implies that all points in a sufficiently small neighbourhood of p are in A, or, $p \in R_\gamma{\downarrow}A$, provided γ is sufficiently small. From $p \notin B$ we also have $p \notin R_\gamma{\downarrow}B$. Finally, from Corollary 8.6, we can assume $R_\gamma{\downarrow}A = R_\alpha{\downarrow}{\uparrow}(R_\gamma{\downarrow}A)$ and $R_\gamma{\downarrow}B = R_\alpha{\downarrow}{\uparrow}(R_\gamma{\downarrow}B)$, and thus $\neg P_\alpha(R_\gamma{\downarrow}A, R_\gamma{\downarrow}B)$.

Finally, we consider NTP:

$$NTP^1(A, B) \Rightarrow NTP_\alpha(R_\gamma{\downarrow}A, R_\gamma{\downarrow}B) \qquad (8.74)$$

From $NTP^1(A, B)$, we know that $A \subseteq i(B)$. Furthermore, as A (resp. B), is the union of a finite number of closed, non–degenerate intervals $A_1, A_2, \ldots, A_s$ (resp. $B_1, B_2, \ldots, B_t$), for each $A_i = [a_i^-, a_i^+]$ there exists a $B_j = [b_j^-, b_j^+]$ such that $[a_i^-, a_i^+] \subseteq]b_j^-, b_j^+[$. This implies that for sufficiently small γ, we also have $[a_i^- + \gamma, a_i^+ - \gamma] \subseteq]b_j^- + \gamma, b_j^+ - \gamma[$, which in turn implies that $[a_i^- + \gamma - \alpha, a_i^+ - \gamma + \alpha] \subseteq [b_j^- + \gamma, b_j^+ - \gamma]$ if $\alpha < \min(b_j^+ - \gamma - a_i^+ + \gamma, a_i^- + \gamma - b_j^- - \gamma) = \min(b_j^+ - a_i^+, a_i^- - b_j^-)$. Using Lemma 8.7, this implies in particular that $R_\alpha\uparrow(R_\gamma\downarrow A) \subseteq R_\gamma\downarrow B$. Finally, from Corollary 8.6, we know that for sufficiently small α, $R_\gamma\downarrow B = R_\alpha\downarrow\uparrow(R_\gamma\downarrow B)$, and thus $NTP_\alpha(R_\gamma\downarrow A, R_\gamma\downarrow B)$. To show the implication in the opposite direction, we find from $\neg NTP^1(a, b)$ that $\neg(A \subseteq i(B))$, which for sufficiently small α and γ implies $\neg(R_\alpha\uparrow(R_\gamma\downarrow A) \subseteq i(R_\alpha\uparrow(R_\gamma\downarrow B)))$ by Lemma 8.7 and Lemma 8.8. In other words, there must exist a p in $\mathbb{R}$ such that $p \in R_\alpha\uparrow(R_\gamma\downarrow A)$ and $p \notin i(R_\alpha\uparrow(R_\gamma\downarrow B))$. This means that

$$(\forall \varepsilon > 0)(\exists q \in \mathbb{R})(d(p, q) \leq \varepsilon \wedge q \notin R_\alpha\uparrow(R_\gamma\downarrow B))$$

and in particular

$$(\exists q \in \mathbb{R})(d(p, q) \leq \alpha \wedge q \notin R_\alpha\uparrow(R_\gamma\downarrow B))$$

or

$$\neg(\forall q \in \mathbb{R})(d(p, q) \leq \alpha \Rightarrow q \in R_\alpha\uparrow(R_\gamma\downarrow B))$$

and therefore $p \notin R_\alpha\downarrow\uparrow(R_\gamma\downarrow B)$, while $p \in R_\alpha\uparrow(R_\gamma\downarrow A)$, which means that $\neg NTP_\alpha(R_\gamma\downarrow A, R_\gamma\downarrow B)$. $\qquad\square$

Note that the $(1; \alpha, 0)$–model $\mathcal{I}'$ constructed in the proof above maps every variable v to a fuzzy set taking only membership degrees from $M_{\frac{1}{k}}$. This fuzzy set is characterized by the k corresponding α–level sets which are all the union of a finite number of closed, non–degenerate intervals. In particular, let the $\frac{i}{k}$–level set of the fuzzy set $v^{\mathcal{I}'}$ be given by

$$[v_{i1}^-, v_{i1}^+] \cup [v_{i2}^-, v_{i2}^+] \cup [v_{in_i}^-, v_{in_i}^+]$$

We now define a new interpretation $\mathcal{I}''$ in which v is mapped to the fuzzy set taking only membership degrees from $M_{\frac{1}{k}}$, whose $\frac{i}{k}$–level set is given by

$$[\frac{v_{i1}^- \alpha'}{\alpha}, \frac{v_{i1}^+ \alpha'}{\alpha}] \cup [\frac{v_{i2}^- \alpha'}{\alpha}, \frac{v_{i2}^+ \alpha'}{\alpha}] \cup [\frac{v_{in_i}^- \alpha'}{\alpha}, \frac{v_{in_i}^+ \alpha'}{\alpha}]$$

Note that for p and q in $\mathbb{R}$, it holds that $d(\frac{p\alpha'}{\alpha}, \frac{q\alpha'}{\alpha}) = |\frac{p\alpha'}{\alpha} - \frac{q\alpha'}{\alpha}| = \frac{\alpha'}{\alpha}|p - q| = \frac{\alpha'}{\alpha}d(p, q)$. Therefore, for all regions u and v, $C_\alpha(u^{\mathcal{I}'}, v^{\mathcal{I}'})$ implies $C_{\alpha'}(u^{\mathcal{I}''}, v^{\mathcal{I}''})$. Hence, as $\mathcal{I}'$ is an $(1; \alpha, 0)$–model of Θ, it holds that $\mathcal{I}''$ is an $(1; \alpha', 0)$–model of Θ. We therefore have the following corollary.

Corollary 8.7. *Let Θ be an F–satisfiable standard set of fuzzy RCC formulas whose upper and lower bounds are finitely representable. It holds that Θ has an $(1; \alpha, 0)$–model for every $\alpha > 0$.*

Intuitively, it seems obvious that when a set of fuzzy RCC formulas can
be realized in one dimension, it can be realized in all higher dimensions as
well. The next proposition reveals that this is indeed the case. The key
observation is that the role of closed, non–degenerate intervals in $\mathbb{R}$ can be
generalized by m–dimensional hypercubes. In particular, given an interval
$[a, b]$ $(a < b)$, we define the associated hypercube as the hypercube with
center $(\frac{a+b}{2}, 0, 0, \ldots, 0)$ whose edges have length $b - a$ and are all parallel
to one of the axes. As an example, the hypercubes H and G corresponding
to the intervals $[80, 120]$ and $[80, 200]$ are depicted in Figure 8.3 for $m = 3$.

Lemma 8.9. *Let $a < b$, $c < d$ and let H and G be the m–dimensional
hypercubes associated with $[a, b]$ and $[c, d]$. It holds that*

$$\inf_{p \in [a,b], q \in [c,d]} d(p, q) = \inf_{p \in H, q \in Q} d(p, q)$$

*where the notation d is both used to refer to the Euclidean distance in $\mathbb{R}$
and $\mathbb{R}^m$.*

Proof.   Clearly, for every p in $[a, b]$ and q in $[c, d]$, it holds that

$$d(p, q) = d((p, 0, 0, \ldots, 0), (q, 0, 0, \ldots, 0))$$

and moreover $(p, 0, 0, \ldots, 0) \in H$ and $(q, 0, 0, \ldots, 0) \in G$. Hence, we already
have

$$\inf_{p \in [a,b], q \in [c,d]} d(p, q) \geq \inf_{p \in H, q \in Q} d(p, q)$$

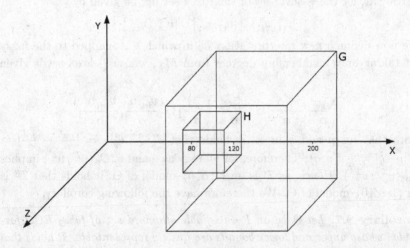

Fig. 8.3   Hypercubes H and G corresponding to the intervals $[80, 120]$ and $[80, 200]$.

On the other hand, let $(p_1, p_2, \ldots, p_m) \in H$ and $(q_1, q_2, \ldots, q_m) \in G$. We have that

$$d((p_1, p_2, \ldots, p_m), (q_1, q_2, \ldots, q_m))$$
$$= \sqrt{d(p_1, q_1)^2 + d(p_2, q_2)^2 + \cdots + d(p_m, q_m)^2}$$
$$\geq d(p_1, q_1)$$

and moreover $p_1 \in [a, b]$ and $q_1 \in [c, d]$, hence

$$\inf_{p \in [a,b], q \in [c,d]} d(p, q) \leq \inf_{p \in H, q \in Q} d(p, q) \qquad \square$$

Lemma 8.10. *Let $\mathcal{I}$ be an $(m; \alpha, 0)$–model of a set of fuzzy RCC formulas Θ $(\alpha > 0)$ and let V be the set of variables occurring in Θ. Furthermore, let $\mathcal{I}'$ be the $(m; \alpha, 0)$–interpretation defined for v in V as*

$$v^{\mathcal{I}'} = R_\alpha \downarrow \uparrow v^{\mathcal{I}}$$

Then $\mathcal{I}'$ is a model of Θ.

Proof. First note that for every fuzzy set in $\mathbb{R}^m$, it holds that

$$C_\alpha(A, B) = C_\alpha(R_\alpha \downarrow \uparrow A, R_\alpha \downarrow \uparrow B)$$

Indeed, we have by (2.7) and (2.49)

$$C_\alpha(R_\alpha \downarrow \uparrow A, R_\alpha \downarrow \uparrow B)$$
$$= \sup_{p, q \in \mathbb{R}^m} T_W((R_\alpha \downarrow \uparrow A)(p), R_\alpha(p, q), (R_\alpha \downarrow \uparrow B)(q))$$
$$= \sup_{q \in \mathbb{R}^m} T_W(\sup_{p \in \mathbb{R}^m} T_W((R_\alpha \downarrow \uparrow A)(p), R_\alpha(p, q)), (R_\alpha \downarrow \uparrow B)(q))$$
$$= \sup_{q \in \mathbb{R}^m} T_W((R_\alpha \uparrow \downarrow \uparrow A)(q), (R_\alpha \downarrow \uparrow B)(q))$$
$$= \sup_{q \in \mathbb{R}^m} T_W((R_\alpha \uparrow A)(q), (R_\alpha \downarrow \uparrow B)(q))$$
$$= \sup_{q \in \mathbb{R}^m} T_W(\sup_{p \in \mathbb{R}^m} T_W(R_\alpha(p, q), A(p)), (R_\alpha \downarrow \uparrow B)(q))$$
$$= \sup_{p \in \mathbb{R}^m} T_W(A(p), \sup_{q \in \mathbb{R}^m} T_W(R_\alpha(p, q), (R_\alpha \downarrow \uparrow B)(q)))$$
$$= \sup_{p \in \mathbb{R}^m} T_W(A(p), (R_\alpha \uparrow \downarrow \uparrow B)(p))$$
$$= \sup_{p \in \mathbb{R}^m} T_W(A(p), (R_\alpha \uparrow B)(p))$$
$$= \sup_{p \in \mathbb{R}^m} T_W(A(p), \sup_{q \in \mathbb{R}^m} T_W(R_\alpha(p, q), B(q)))$$
$$= C_\alpha(A, B)$$

From (2.52), we immediately find

$$O_\alpha(A, B) = O_\alpha(R_\alpha{\downarrow}{\uparrow}A, R_\alpha{\downarrow}{\uparrow}B)$$
$$P_\alpha(A, B) = P_\alpha(R_\alpha{\downarrow}{\uparrow}A, R_\alpha{\downarrow}{\uparrow}B)$$

Finally, from (2.49) and (2.52), we have

$$NTP_\alpha(A, B) = NTP_\alpha(R_\alpha{\downarrow}{\uparrow}A, R_\alpha{\downarrow}{\uparrow}B) \qquad \square$$

Lemma 8.11. *Let H be an m-dimensional hypercube and $\alpha > 0$. It holds that*

$$R_\alpha{\downarrow}{\uparrow}H = H$$

Proof. From Lemma 2.17, we already know

$$R_\alpha{\downarrow}{\uparrow}H \supseteq H$$

If $R_\alpha{\downarrow}{\uparrow}H \supset H$, there would be a p in $\mathbb{R}^m$ such that $p \in R_\alpha{\downarrow}{\uparrow}H$ but $p \notin H$. From $p \notin H$ we derive that there is a q in $\mathbb{R}^m$ such that $d(p, q) = \alpha$ and $d(q, h) > \alpha$ for every h in H. However, since $p \in R_\alpha{\downarrow}{\uparrow}H$ we have $q \in R_\alpha{\uparrow}H$, or $d(q, h) \leq \alpha$ for some h in H, a contradiction. $\qquad \square$

Lemma 8.12. *Let $\alpha > 0$, $a < b$, $c < d$ and let H and G be the m-dimensional hypercubes associated with $[a, b]$ and $[c, d]$. It holds that*

$$[a - \alpha, b + \alpha] \subseteq [c, d] \Leftrightarrow R_\alpha{\uparrow}H \subseteq G$$

Proof. First, we show

$$[a - \alpha, b + \alpha] \subseteq [c, d] \Rightarrow R_\alpha{\uparrow}H \subseteq G$$

Assume that $[a - \alpha, b + \alpha] \subseteq [c, d]$ and that for some $p = (p_1, \ldots, p_m)$ in $\mathbb{R}^m$, it holds that $p \in R_\alpha{\uparrow}H$. From $p \in R_\alpha{\uparrow}H$, we know that for some $h = (h_1, \ldots, h_m)$ in H, it holds that $d(p, h) \leq \alpha$, and therefore $|p_1 - h_1| \leq \alpha$, implying $p_1 \in [a - \alpha, b + \alpha]$ and in particular $p_1 \in [c, d]$. From $p \in R_\alpha{\uparrow}H$ we derive $d(p, p') \leq \frac{b-a}{2} + \alpha$, where $p' = (p_1, 0, 0, \ldots, 0)$. Furthermore, from $[a - \alpha, b + \alpha] \subseteq [c, d]$, we have $\frac{b-a}{2} + \alpha = \frac{b+\alpha-(a-\alpha)}{2} \leq \frac{d-c}{2}$, which entails $p \in G$.

The implication in the opposite direction follows trivially from the fact that for every p in $[a - \alpha, b + \alpha]$, it holds that $(p, 0, 0, \ldots, 0)$ is in $R_\alpha{\uparrow}H$ and therefore in G, if $R_\alpha{\uparrow}H \subseteq G$, and that for every point in G, the first coordinate is in $[c, d]$. $\qquad \square$

Proposition 8.8. *Let Θ be an F-satisfiable standard set of fuzzy RCC formulas whose upper and lower bounds are finitely representable. It holds that Θ has an $(m; \alpha, 0)$-model for every $\alpha > 0$ and every m in $\mathbb{N} \setminus \{0\}$.*

Proof. For an arbitrary $\alpha > 0$, we know from the discussion above that Θ has an $(1; \alpha, 0)$–model $\mathcal{I}$ in which each variable v is mapped to a fuzzy set in $\mathbb{R}$, taking only membership degrees from $M_{\frac{1}{k}}$. Moreover, this fuzzy set is characterized by k α–level sets, which are all the union of a finite number of closed, non–degenerate intervals. In particular, let the $\frac{i}{k}$–level set of $v^{\mathcal{I}}$ be given by

$$[v_{i1}^-, v_{i1}^+] \cup [v_{i2}^-, v_{i2}^+] \cup [v_{in_i}^-, v_{n_i}^+]$$

Without loss of generality, we can assume that $R_\alpha\!\downarrow\!\uparrow v^{\mathcal{I}} = v^{\mathcal{I}}$. Indeed, if this were not the case, we could transform $\mathcal{I}$ as in Lemma 8.10, yielding $R_\alpha\!\downarrow\!\uparrow v^{\mathcal{I}} = v^{\mathcal{I}}$ by (2.52).

We can now define an $(m, \alpha, 0)$–interpretation $\mathcal{I}'$ mapping the variable v to the fuzzy set in $\mathbb{R}^m$ which takes only membership degrees from $M_{\frac{1}{k}}$ and whose $\frac{i}{k}$–level set is defined by the union of a finite number of m–dimensional hypercubes

$$H_1^i \cup H_2^i \cup \ldots, H_{n_i}^i$$

where H_j^i is the hypercube associated with $[v_{ij}^-, v_{ij}^+]$. First, we show that $C_\alpha(v^{\mathcal{I}}, u^{\mathcal{I}}) = C_\alpha(v^{\mathcal{I}'}, u^{\mathcal{I}'})$. Since $v^{\mathcal{I}}$ and $u^{\mathcal{I}}$ only take membership degrees from $M_{\frac{1}{k}}$, we know that there is a p and q in $\mathbb{R}$ such that $d(p, q) \leq \alpha$ and

$$C_\alpha(v^{\mathcal{I}}, u^{\mathcal{I}}) = T(v^{\mathcal{I}}(p), u^{\mathcal{I}}(q))$$

From Lemma 8.9, we know that there are p' and q' in $\mathbb{R}^m$ such that $d(p', q') \leq \alpha$ and

$$T(v^{\mathcal{I}}(p), u^{\mathcal{I}}(q)) = T(v^{\mathcal{I}'}(p'), u^{\mathcal{I}'}(q')) \tag{8.75}$$

which already implies $C_\alpha(v^{\mathcal{I}}, u^{\mathcal{I}}) \leq C_\alpha(v^{\mathcal{I}'}, u^{\mathcal{I}'})$.

We also have the converse: there are p' and q' in $\mathbb{R}^m$ satisfying $d(p', q')$ and

$$C_\alpha(v^{\mathcal{I}'}, u^{\mathcal{I}'}) = T(v^{\mathcal{I}'}(p'), u^{\mathcal{I}'}(q'))$$

and by Lemma 8.9 we know that there are p and q in $\mathbb{R}$ satisfying (8.75). We can conclude

$$C_\alpha(v^{\mathcal{I}}, u^{\mathcal{I}}) = C_\alpha(v^{\mathcal{I}'}, u^{\mathcal{I}'}) \tag{8.76}$$

Note that from $R_\alpha\!\downarrow\!\uparrow v^{\mathcal{I}} = v^{\mathcal{I}}$, we easily find $R_\alpha\!\downarrow\!\uparrow v^{\mathcal{I}'} = v^{\mathcal{I}'}$ using Lemma 8.11. This leads to

$$O_\alpha(v^{\mathcal{I}}, u^{\mathcal{I}}) = overl(v^{\mathcal{I}}, u^{\mathcal{I}})$$
$$O_\alpha(v^{\mathcal{I}'}, u^{\mathcal{I}'}) = overl(v^{\mathcal{I}'}, u^{\mathcal{I}'})$$

and $O_\alpha(v^\mathcal{I}, u^\mathcal{I}) = O_\alpha(v^{\mathcal{I}'}, u^{\mathcal{I}'})$ follows in the same way as (8.76). Furthermore, $P_\alpha(v^\mathcal{I}, u^\mathcal{I}) = P_\alpha(v^{\mathcal{I}'}, u^{\mathcal{I}'})$ follows from the fact that $[a, b] \subseteq [c, d]$ iff $H \subseteq G$, where H and G are the associated hypercubes of $[a, b]$ and $[c, d]$ respectively. Finally, $NTP_\alpha(v^\mathcal{I}, u^\mathcal{I}) = NTP_\alpha(v^{\mathcal{I}'}, u^{\mathcal{I}'})$ follows from Lemma 8.12. $\qquad\qquad\square$

Let Θ be a finite, standard set of fuzzy RCC formulas whose upper and lower bounds are finitely representable. We have established that the following statements are all equivalent (Γ being the set of crisp RCC formulas from Corollary 8.5).

(1) Θ is F–satisfiable;
(2) Γ is C–satisfiable;
(3) Θ can be refined to a normalised set of fuzzy RCC formulas satisfying (8.12)–(8.15), as well as the transitivity rules for fuzzy topological relations;
(4) Θ has an Egg–Yolk model in at least one dimension;
(5) Θ has an Egg–Yolk model in any dimension;
(6) Θ has an $(m; \alpha, 0)$–model for at least one $\alpha > 0$ and one m in $\mathbb{N} \setminus \{0\}$;
(7) Θ has an $(m; \alpha, 0)$–model for any $\alpha > 0$ and any m in $\mathbb{N} \setminus \{0\}$.

Chapter 9

Geographic Information Retrieval

9.1 Introduction

The geographical scope of a web page often influences its relevancy. Unfortunately, the keyword–centered paradigm of most search engines is not very well suited to accommodate for geographical constraints. One reason is the high ambiguity of geographic names. The gazetteer of the US Census Bureau, for example, contains 86 entries for the place name Springfield, in the US alone[1]. Similarly, the names of most well-known European cities occur in the US as well: Paris is a city in two Canadian states, and at least 15 US states[2]. As a result of this ambiguity in place names, simply adding the term "Paris" to the query terms, for example, will not provide satisfactory results, especially when results about one of the lesser–known places in the US is desired. Adding the corresponding US state might help precision in this case, but this will generally lead to a drop in recall. A second, related problem is that traditional search engines cannot cope with spatial relations such as nearness and containment. When searching for information about French wine, for example, web pages about Bordeaux wine are clearly relevant, even if they do not contain the terms France or French. Similarly, when looking for job opportunities around Ghent, we are typically also interested in opportunities in nearby cities. In this latter case, however, relevant web pages are not likely to contain the term Ghent at all. The solution provided by geographic information retrieval (GIR) systems [Bucher *et al.* (2005); Gey *et al.* (2006); Jones *et al.* (2002); Larson and Frontiera (2004)] is to identify and store the geographic scope

---

[1]See http://www.census.gov/cgi-bin/gazetteer/, accessed February 8, 2008.
[2]See http://en.wikipedia.org/wiki/Paris_%28disambiguation%29, accessed February 8, 2008.

of each web document (at indexing time), and compare it (at query time) with the geographic context of the query, which can either be identified by place names occurring in the query, the location of the user, or explicitly represented geographical constraints. To identify the geographic scope of a web document, typically place names in the document are identified and disambiguated. Subsequently, a gazetteer is used to assign geographical coordinates to each of these place names. In addition, the geographic scope can be further analysed by looking at telephone numbers, zip codes, street names, and IP addresses. We will refer to this kind of systems as geographic document retrieval systems. Local search services, such as Google Maps[3], Yahoo! local[4] and MSN search local[5], are a different kind of GIR systems, which allow users to search for a particular business satisfying an explicitly specified geographic constraint. A user may, for example, be interested in restaurants, hotels, grocery stores, dentists, etc., that are located close to some specified address. Currently, such queries are evaluated against a fixed list of businesses. This allows local search services to display a high degree of accuracy, and to interact with users through a very convenient interface: query results are presented in an intuitive way, including maps that show the locations of the retrieved businesses, driving directions, user reviews, etc. Hence, it should come as no surprise that local search services have become increasingly popular.

However, local search services work in a way that is very different from traditional search engines, which use crawlers that continuously search the web for new information. The sole use of a static, structured knowledge base gives rise to a number of important limitations. First of all, it restricts the coverage of the system, as many businesses will not be contained in the knowledge base, even if there are websites that contain useful information about their location. Moreover, it limits the covered information to the kind that is traditionally contained in the well-known yellow pages, while it is exactly the inclusion of more dynamic, ephemeral information that would bring local search services to their full potential [Himmelstein (2005)]. Similarly, geographic document retrieval systems rely on a static gazetteer which is typically restricted to officially defined place names. A second, related limitation of current GIR systems is their limited flexibility for specifying geographical constraints. Rather than asking for *restaurants near 219 4th Ave N, Seattle*, a user might want to know about *restaurants*

---

[3]http://maps.google.com/
[4]http://local.yahoo.com
[5]http://search.msn.com/local/

near the Space Needle, or about *restaurants in Seattle's Queen Anne neigh-bourhood*. Unfortunately, most gazetteers contain very limited information about landmarks, and non–political regions such as neighbourhoods and districts. Moreover, even if a neighbourhood name is covered in a gazetteer, its location is usually approximated only by a centroid or a minimal bounding box. The main reason for this is that the boundaries of most regions are ill-defined. For example, the absence of region boundaries in the well–known GNIS gazetteer is motivated as follows[6]:

> Regions are application driven and highly susceptible to perception. Sometimes, people might agree on the core of a region, but agreement deteriorates rapidly outward from that core.

As a consequence, current local search services provide almost no support for geographical restrictions involving neighbourhood names.

A promising solution to the aforementioned problems is to augment the available structured information with information extracted from the web. On one hand, this could be information extracted from semi-structured data. Many lists of hotels, restaurants, attractions, etc. are available on the web. Usually, it is quite easy to extract from such lists, the relevant names and corresponding addresses, either by writing a wrapper manually, or by using automated wrapper induction techniques [Eikvil (1999); Kushmerick (2000)]. However, most information on the web is still in unstructured form, i.e., free natural language text. Because it may be very hard to find the address of a particular business or landmark in (unstructured) web documents, we can sometimes only rely on hints in natural language sentences about their location. We may know, for example, that some hotel is located in Belltown, within walking distance from Pike Place Market, and a few blocks away from the Space Needle. While we cannot derive the exact location of the hotel from this, we may be able to approximate its location accurately enough to estimate the relevance w.r.t. a given query. Similarly, by relying on cues from web documents, we might be able to derive reasonable fuzzy footprints, i.e., fuzzy sets of locations modelling the spatial extent of a region. Particularly for an information retrieval task, fuzzy footprints are more suitable than regions with crisp boundaries, since the membership degrees allow to rank the results based on the extent to which they satisfy the geographical constraint. First, businesses in the core of the neighbourhood are returned as everybody would agree that these businesses satisfy the geographical constraint. Next, businesses with

---

[6]http://geonames.usgs.gov/faqs.html#25, accessed January 18, 2007.

a decreasing degree of membership are returned, i.e., businesses for which there might be an increasing amount of disagreement.

The focus in this chapter is on the automated acquisition of geographic knowledge from the web. In particular, our aim is to explore the role of fuzzy spatial relations, fuzzy footprints, and fuzzy spatial reasoning in this context. After an overview of related work in Section 9.2, Section 9.3 introduces and validates techniques for using nearness information from natural language to approximate the location of places. Next, in Section 9.4 we focus on a related problem: extracting fuzzy footprints for city neighbourhoods. After identifying the key challenges, we show how reliable fuzzy footprints can be obtained from very noisy input data. To obtain these fuzzy footprints, however, information about the topological relationships that hold between different neighbourhoods is employed. In practice, this topological information might not be available. This calls for techniques in which topological relations between city neighbourhoods are harvested automatically from the web. Using the city of Cardiff as a case study, we show how, by analogy with Chapter 6, redundancy–based techniques can be utilized to acquire topological relations and how fuzzy spatial reasoning can be used to increase the reliability of the extracted information.

9.2   Acquisition of Geographical Knowledge

Although the concept of nearness is well–studied, to the best of our knowledge, the automatic construction of a computational representation for natural language nearness relations like *within walking distance*, has not yet been addressed. However, [Yao and Thill (2005)] addresses the inverse problem of predicting which natural language nearness relation is most appropriate (e.g. very near, near, normal, etc.), given the exact distance and context variables. The context variables allow the statistical model to deal with factors such as scale, the type of activity, etc. While the results seem promising, the proposed technique can only be applied to this inverse problem, and not to find the (fuzzy) range of possible distances, given a natural language nearness relation. Also the application of nearness information in GIR has, until now, been rather limited. One problem in practical applications is that cognitively adequate approaches to model nearness do not only rely on the distance between two places, but also on certain context factors. For example, the presence of important landmarks can substantially influence the degree to which people consider two places to be near. Therefore, in [Tezuka and Tanaka (2005)], techniques to extract the names of cognitively significant landmarks from the web are introduced. One advantage of the suggested techniques is that they allow to determine the significance of a landmark in a quantitative way. Alternatively, a data mining technique for finding significant place names is proposed in [Duckham and Worboys (2001)], also with the aim of bridging the gap between computational and cognitive approaches to nearness. In [Tezuka *et al.* (2001)], it is proposed to limit the range of places that are near a certain landmark, based on the popularity of the landmark. In particular, the paper claims that the more popular a particular landmark is, the larger the area considered to be near that landmark will be. The use of nearness relations in natural language to improve geographical information retrieval, was also addressed in [Delboni *et al.* (2007)]. The aim of their work is to improve the geographical awareness of traditional search engines, by using information about landmarks and nearness relations for query expansion. The working hypothesis is that nearness relations such as *near, close, in front of,* etc. all have a similar meaning. Hence, a user interested in *hotels near the Space Needle,* is also interested in *hotels close to the Space Needle.* Using this technique, they show a significant improvement in terms of precision and recall of geographically relevant web pages, compared to traditional search engines (Google was used in their experiments). The main advantages of their approach is that no gazetteers are needed, and that the proposed query expansion strategy can be applied to any traditional keyword-based search engine with minimal effort.

Next, the acquisition of representations of the spatial extent of vague geographic regions has received considerable attention. In [Montello *et al.* (2003)], a user study was conducted which indicates that neighbourhoods like *downtown* are indeed perceived as vague by most people. Moreover, when comparing the interpretations of the same neighbourhood by different people, a fair amount of agreement was witnessed, although two people seldom agree on the exact (vague) boundaries. The results of this study are important as they indicate that constructing a fuzzy set to represent the spatial extent of a neighbourhood is indeed meaningful. In [Harada and Sadahiro (2005)], a statistical model is described that predicts the probability that a user would use a particular neighbourhood name R to describe the location of a particular shop s. This model provides some evidence that this probability depends on the distance between s and the center c of R, and on the density of shops on the path between c and s. A few automatic procedures to construct representations of vague regions already exist. In some approaches, a single crisp boundary is constructed to represent a vague region, assuming that the vagueness of the boundary is not important for the intended application. In [Reinbacher *et al.* (2005)], for example, an algorithm is discussed to find a reasonable polygon for a vague region R, based on a set of points that are assumed to lie in the region, and a set of points that are assumed to lie outside the region. These sets are extracted automatically from web pages containing phrases like x *is located in* R. Another way of obtaining such a polygon is proposed in [Arampatzis *et al.* (2006)], pursuing a similar strategy. A graded approach is introduced in [Purves *et al.* (2005)], using an interpolation technique to obtain a representation similar to fuzzy footprints from a weighted set of points that are assumed to lie in the region. This set of points is obtained by querying Google for pages about the region and assuming that every place on these pages is located in the region. In this way, many false positives are obtained, i.e., places that are incorrectly assumed to lie in the region. To make the approach more robust to such errors in the input, the points are weighted based on their frequency of occurrence [Clough *et al.* (2005)]. These weights, however, reflect the importance of a particular place, rather than a degree of membership in the corresponding region. All of the aforementioned approaches deal only with large-scale regions such as the Alpes, Western Europe, etc. To our knowledge, the automatic construction of (fuzzy) footprints for city neighbourhoods has not yet been considered. As for large-scale regions, official boundaries for city neighbourhoods are usually nonexistent. Moreover, various user studies (e.g., [Sastry *et al.* (2002); Cho (2003)]) have shown that in cases where official definitions do exist, these definitions rarely correspond to residents' perception of the neighbourhood boundaries.

9.3   Location Approximation and Local Search

9.3.1   *Collecting Data*

This section primarily deals with the use of natural language nearness relations to estimate the approximate location of a place. One way of obtaining such nearness information is by processing free natural language text. This, however, requires the recognition of hotel names, landmarks, etc. in texts, as well as disambiguating all place name occurrences. To abstract away from these, largely orthogonal tasks, we mainly focus on data extracted from semi-structured documents to construct a suitable knowledge base of spatial information. One example is *Hotel-Rates.com*[7], which contains a list of hotels for most reasonably large cities in the world. We extract the information in these lists by manually defining rules that are based on the structure of the corresponding HTML documents, a technique which is known as screen scraping. Although this technique is very useful for the kind of experiments described in this chapter, more advanced techniques would be required to implement a fully fledged local search service. One possibility is to use automated wrapper induction techniques, which try to discover the rules that would be used for screen scraping automatically (see [Eikvil (1999)] for an overview).

Furthermore, for each hotel in the lists, a pointer to a document about the hotel is provided. These documents contain a natural language description of the hotel, as well as semi–structured information about the surrounding neighbourhood and nearby attractions. To analyse the natural language description, we first parse all relevant sentences using the Stanford Parser[8]. Then we extract spatial relations using patterns such as

```
located within walking distance of <NP>
located in the heart of <NP>
```

For example, in a sentence like *The hotel is located within walking distance of the University of Washington campus, and . . .*, the parser would correctly identify *the University of Washington campus* as a noun phrase (NP). Because this sentence therefore matches the pattern, we assume that the nearness relation *within walking distance* holds between the hotel that is described on the web page, and the University of Washington campus. We use a large set of patterns, covering almost 20 named nearness relations: within walking distance from, in the heart of, in the midst of, next to, near, next door from, close to, within close proximity of, within easy reach of, in the center of, opposite from, in front of, in the vicinity of, adjacent to, a few steps from, a short walk to, across the street from, a few metres from, a few blocks from. In addition, we also use phrases expressing a number of kilometers, miles, blocks, metres, and yards. From the semi-structured information, we extract additional nearness relations, as well as information about the surrounding neighbourhood (when available). For most hotels, for example, nearness information is provided in the following form:

```
Seattle Public Library - across the street <br>
Ranier Square - 2.0 blocks <br>
```

---

[7]http://www.hotel-rates.com/
[8]http://nlp.stanford.edu/downloads/lex-parser.shtml

```
Victoria Ferry - 14.0 blocks <br>
Pioneer Square - 7.0 blocks <br>
Seattle Aquarium - 9.0 blocks <br>
Pike Place Market - 7.0 blocks <br>
Seattle Waterfront - 5.0 blocks <br>
5th Avenue Theater - 2.0 blocks <br>
Seattle Art Museum - 5.0 blocks
```

Due to the occurrence of HTML tags, such nearness relations can easily be extracted. On average, this process resulted in 11.27 natural language hints per hotel. In a similar way, we extract spatial information from *channels.nl*[9] and from *openlist*[10]. From *openlist*, we also extract lists of restaurants and lists of touristic attractions, as well as some useful nearness relation available in semi-structured form. In particular, for most hotels, a list of nearby restaurants and attractions is provided, as well as a number of alternative (close) hotels that could be considered. Furthermore, *openlist* also contains lists of places that are located in a particular neighbourhood of the city. We use these lists to add information about the surrounding neighbourhood of places to our knowledge base.

In total we extracted information about 56 US cities. The process outlined above, gives us a list of over 60000 place names (7819 hotels, 47152 restaurants, and 8504 touristic attractions) with corresponding addresses, as well as spatial relations between some of the hotels and some of the attractions and restaurants. We use the geocoding service of the Google Maps API[11] to translate the addresses to geographical coordinates.

In addition to using nearness information, we will also utilize information about the spatial extent of neighbourhoods. To this end, we need a list of places that are assumed to lie in each neighbourhood of interest. Apart from the information that is already in our knowledge base, we use information coming from two sources for this: Yahoo! local, and *restaurants.com*[12]. To extract relevant places from Yahoo! local, we submit a query with the name of the neighbourhood as a keyword, and the name of the city as the geographical restriction. From the list of places that is returned, we keep the places whose name contains the name of the neighbourhood (e.g. *Belltown pizza* is probably located in Belltown), as well as places from whose description we can find out that they are located in the neighbourhood, using a pattern-based approach. The information on *restaurants.com* is

---

[9]http://www.channels.nl/
[10]http://www.openlist.com/
[11]http://www.google.com/apis/maps/
[12]http://www.restaurants.com

semi-structured; we use screen scraping to extract the names and addresses of restaurants that are located in a particular neighbourhood, as well as a list of neighbourhood names for the city under consideration.

9.3.2 Representing Vague Geographical Information

9.3.2.1 Fuzzy nearness relations

A lot of useful geographical information in natural language takes the form of vague assertions about the nearness of two places. A question which naturally arises from this is: what can we say about the possible locations of an unknown place x, knowing only the location of a and the fact that a is, e.g., at walking distance from x? Our knowledge about the location of x is clearly vague, i.e., there exists a set of locations that are definitely compatible with this knowledge, there exists a set of locations that are definitely not compatible, and there exists a third set, consisting of borderline cases, which are neither fully compatible, nor fully incompatible. As in Chapter 7, we will use fuzzy relations to model nearness. In particular, a natural language nearness relation will be modelled by a fuzzy relation depending on four parameters: two parameters corresponding to a flexible upper bound and two parameters corresponding to a flexible lower bound.

Definition 9.1. Let α, β, γ, δ be non-negative real numbers such that $\alpha \leq \beta \leq \gamma \leq \delta$. The fuzzy relation $R_{(\alpha,\beta,\gamma,\delta)}$ in the universe of locations is defined for locations x and y as:

$$R_{(\alpha,\beta,\gamma,\delta)}(x,y) = \begin{cases} \frac{d(x,y)-\alpha}{\beta-\alpha} & \text{if } \alpha < d(x,y) < \beta \\ 1 & \text{if } \beta \leq d(x,y) \leq \gamma \\ \frac{\delta-d(x,y)}{\delta-\gamma} & \text{if } \gamma < d(x,y) < \delta \\ 0 & \text{otherwise} \end{cases} \tag{9.1}$$

where d is the straight-line distance[13].

Note that, using the notations from Chapter 7, it holds that $R_{(\alpha,\beta,\gamma,\delta)} = F_{(\alpha,\beta-\alpha)} \cap N_{(\gamma,\delta-\gamma)}$ (assuming $\beta - \alpha > 0$). By representing a natural language nearness relation such as *within walking distance* as a fuzzy relation $R_{(\alpha,\beta,\gamma,\delta)}$, we specify a fuzzy lower bound and fuzzy upper bound on the

---

[13]One can think of this straight-line distance as the Euclidean distance. However, in practice usually the circle distance (i.e., the length of the shortest path between two points on the surface of a sphere) would be used instead, since locations are typically expressed as longitude and latitude coordinates.

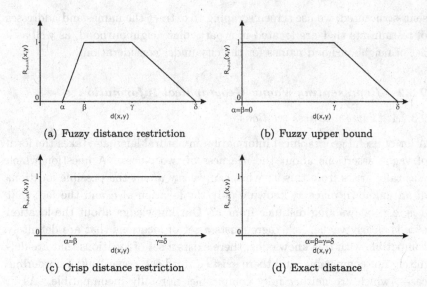

(a) Fuzzy distance restriction   (b) Fuzzy upper bound

(c) Crisp distance restriction   (d) Exact distance

Fig. 9.1   A nearness relation is represented as a fuzzy restriction on the distance between the two places x and y it applies to.

possible distances between places that are said to be within walking distance from each other. This is illustrated in Figure 9.1(a). If only an upper bound is required, we can choose $\alpha = \beta = 0$, as shown in Figure 9.1(b). Figures 9.1(c) and 9.1(d) illustrate that also crisp restrictions, such as *between 2 and 4 kilometers* and *exactly 1.5 kilometers*, can be represented within this framework. The use of trapezoidally shaped fuzzy sets to define nearness relations, offers many advantages. First of all, processing trapezoidally shaped fuzzy sets is computationally much more efficient than processing arbitrary fuzzy sets or relations (e.g., Proposition 7.1). Furthermore, trapezoidally shaped fuzzy sets are defined using only four parameters, which have an intuitive meaning. Finally, the use of fuzzy sets with a relatively simple shape is important for the robustness of the approach. Since we use the web to obtain input data, we usually have a large amount of data available to construct an appropriate representation of a particular nearness relation. However, using the web also implies that individual samples of our input data may not be very reliable. Using trapezoidally shaped fuzzy sets allows to sufficiently abstract away from individual input samples.

This stands in contrast to approaches like [Robinson (2000)], in which interpretations of nearness relations are constructed by directly asking ques-

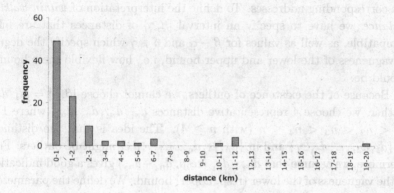

Fig. 9.2 Frequency of distances between places that are said to be within walking distance of each other.

tions to human users. In such approaches, relatively little data is usually available, which is, however, very reliable. Therefore, it may be useful to use fuzzy sets with a more complex shape, which fit the actual input data more accurately, and to use prior knowledge about the human users to make decisions in the case of inconsistencies between different users.

9.3.2.2 *Representing named nearness relations*

A lot of information about the nearness of places is expressed in texts using named natural language relations such as *within walking distance*. To represent such information within the framework outlined above, we need to find appropriate values of the parameters α, β, γ, and δ, for each frequently occurring named nearness relation. To find these values, we start with a set $S = \{(p_1, q_1), (p_2, q_2), \ldots, (p_n, q_n)\}$ of pairs of places that are said to be within walking distance of each other, and for which we know the exact distance. In particular, let d_i be the (straight-line) distance between p_i and q_i. Without loss of generality, we can assume that $d_1 \leq d_2 \leq \cdots \leq d_n$. Figure 9.2 shows how often the distance between places from our knowledge base that are said to be within walking distance of each other is between 0 and 1 kilometer, between 1 and 2 kilometer, etc. As can be seen from this figure, the set S contains outliers, e.g., places that are more than 10 km away from each other, but are still said to be within walking distance. This can, for example, be due to errors in the phase of extracting information from web pages, the use of ambiguous place names, or incorrect geocoding of the corresponding addresses. To define the interpretation of *within walking distance*, we have to specify an interval $[\beta, \gamma]$ of distances that are fully compatible, as well as values for $\beta - \alpha$ and $\delta - \gamma$ which specify the degree of vagueness of the lower and upper bound, i.e., how flexible these bounds should be.

Because of the existence of outliers, we cannot choose $[\beta, \gamma] = [d_1, d_n]$. Rather, we choose 4 representative distances $d_{n_1}, d_{n_2}, d_{n_3}, d_{n_4}$, where $1 \leq n_1 < n_2 < n_3 < n_4 \leq n$ (with $n \geq 4$). The idea is that the distances in $\{d_1, d_2, \ldots, d_{n_1-1}\}$ and in $\{d_{n_4+1}, d_{n_4+2}, \ldots, d_n\}$ might be outliers. Furthermore, we assume that $d_{n_2} - d_{n_1}$ (resp. $d_{n_4} - d_{n_3}$) gives a good indication of the vagueness of the lower (resp. upper) bound. We define the parameters α, β, γ, and δ, i.e., the interpretation of *within walking distance* as:

$$\alpha = d_{n_1} - a_1(d_{n_2} - d_{n_1}) \tag{9.2}$$

$$\beta = d_{n_1} - a_2(d_{n_2} - d_{n_1}) \tag{9.3}$$

$$\gamma = d_{n_4} + a_3(d_{n_4} - d_{n_3}) \tag{9.4}$$

$$\delta = d_{n_4} + a_4(d_{n_4} - d_{n_3}) \tag{9.5}$$

where $a_1 \geq a_2 \geq 0$ and $a_4 \geq a_3 \geq 0$. Large values of the parameters a_i correspond to a tolerant interpretation of the nearness relation, while small values of a_i correspond to a strict interpretation. For example, choosing $a_2 = a_3 = 0$ means that only the distances in $[d_{n_1}, d_{n_4}]$ are considered to be fully compatible with the nearness relation under consideration. Such an interpretation would probably be too strict for many applications. On the other hand, if these parameter values would be chosen too large, the resulting fuzzy relations would be too tolerant, and would therefore convey too little information. Optimal values of a_1, a_2, a_3, and a_4 depend on the kind of data that is used. We use $a_2 = a_3 = 1$ and $a_1 = a_4 = 3$, as initial experiments revealed that these values provide an appropriate trade-off between flexibility and informativity for the kind of data discussed here. Also the optimal value of the parameters n_1, n_2, n_3, n_4 might depend on the kind of data that is used; we used $n_1 = \frac{n}{5}$, $n_2 = \frac{2n}{5}$, $n_3 = \frac{3n}{5}$ and $n_4 = \frac{4n}{5}$ (assuming n is a multiple of 5, for simplicity). This choice of parameters leads to the interpretations in Table 9.1. For example, knowing that x is within walking distance of y, all distances between 0.05 and 2.55 kilometer are equally possible candidates for the straight-line distance (see the first row of Table 9.1). Moreover, all distances between 0 and 4.09 kilometer are all possible to some extent. Note that when $\alpha \leq 0$ and $\beta \leq 0$, no lower bound on the possible distances is imposed. As could be expected, nearness relations such as *near* and *close* convey less information than *within walking distance* or *across the street*, i.e., a wider range of distances is compatible. For example, all distances between 0 to 15.51 kilometer are fully compatible with the concept *Close*. However, the upper bound of *adjacent* is somewhat surprising, as one could expect that the meaning of *adjacent* would be quite similar to the meaning of *across the street*. For example, all distances up to 12.36 kilometer are compatible to some extent with the concept *adjacent*, while only distances up to 1.27 kilometer are considered compatible to some extent with *across the street*. A closer look at the data, reveals that adjacent is often used w.r.t. places whose spatial extent is not negligible (e.g., parks or famous streets). However, like in most gazetteers, we have represented the location of, for example, a park, as a point, and used the distance to this point rather than to the boundary of the park. Solutions to this problem are far from obvious, since the boundaries of parks are usually not available, and automated methods to extract footprints from the web are not suitable for places like parks.

Nearness relations can not only be found in texts, we can also extract information about nearness from semi-structured information sources. In particular, from *openlist* we extract for each hotel a list of nearby attractions and restaurants, and a list of alternative hotels that could be considered. We treat this information in the same way as natural language nearness relations; the results are also shown in Table 9.1. Although these relations are clearly much more general than, for example, *within walking distance*, they can still be very useful, as we have a very high number of such relations at our disposal.

In the previous discussion, we have neglected the fact that the meaning of nearness relations can be dependent on the context in which they are used. Mostly this is justified because all relations actually occur in more or less the same context. For example, scale factors should not be taken into account because the scale is always similar, i.e., that of a large US city. Another issue is the asymmetry of nearness relations. For example, if we would extract a list of nearby hotels from the web page of a famous touristic attraction, we would have to interpret this in a different way than if we would extract a list of nearby attractions from the web page of a hotel. Again, this is not a problem when using the relations from our knowledge base, since they always express nearness from the point of view of the hotel. One factor that may be relevant, however, is the influence of the popularity of touristic attractions. As pointed out in [Tezuka *et al.* (2001)], the interpretation of *near a famous place* may be less specific than *near a rather unknown place*, because, for example, hotel owners want to

Table 9.1 Interpretations for some frequently occurring named nearness relations (distances in km).

Nearness relation	Frequency	d_{n_1}	d_{n_2}	d_{n_3}	d_{n_4}	α	β	γ	δ
Within walking distance	114	0.38	0.70	1.00	1.77	-0.59	0.05	2.55	4.09
Across the street	36	0.09	0.21	0.29	0.54	-0.27	-0.03	0.78	1.27
Near	39	0.45	1.20	2.07	9.21	-1.78	-0.29	16.34	30.60
Close	24	0.87	2.44	3.57	9.54	-3.84	-0.70	15.51	27.44
Adjacent	52	0.18	0.32	0.79	3.68	-0.24	0.04	6.57	12.36
Nearby (openlist.com)	12419	0.96	1.66	2.44	3.36	-1.11	0.27	4.29	6.15
Alternates (openlist.com)	4151	1.13	2.73	5.74	11.59	-3.67	-0.46	17.44	29.14

Table 9.2 Refined interpretations for some frequently occurring named nearness relations (distances in km). Popular places are defined as places that occur at least 5 times as the object of a nearness relation in our knowledge base.

Nearness relation		Freq.	d_{n_1}	d_{n_2}	d_{n_3}	d_{n_4}	α_0	β_0	γ_0	δ_0
Within walking distance	not popular	27	0.27	0.35	0.73	1.43	0.03	0.19	2.14	3.55
	popular	87	0.50	0.81	1.02	1.77	-0.42	0.19	2.52	4.03
Across the street	not popular	11	0.08	0.15	0.28	0.36	-0.11	0.01	0.43	0.57
	popular	25	0.17	0.22	0.30	0.56	0.03	0.12	0.83	1.36
Near	not popular	15	0.73	1.69	2.32	12.27	-2.15	-0.23	22.22	42.12
	popular	24	0.37	0.87	2.00	7.86	-1.13	-0.12	13.73	25.45
Close	not popular	4	0	0.17	3.57	11.20	-0.17	-0.52	18.82	34.07
	popular	20	1.41	3.31	3.95	9.54	-4.27	-0.47	15.14	26.33
Adjacent	not popular	20	0.10	0.44	0.79	9.39	-0.91	-0.23	17.99	35.19
	popular	32	0.18	0.28	0.98	3.68	-0.08	0.09	6.38	11.78
Nearby (openlist.com)	not popular	554	1.88	2.85	3.71	4.62	-1.01	0.92	5.54	7.36
	popular	11865	0.94	1.61	2.38	3.27	-1.08	0.26	4.15	5.92
Alternates (openlist.com)	not popular	481	0.54	1.34	3.19	6.76	-1.85	-0.25	10.33	17.48
	popular	3670	1.25	2.97	6.28	12.24	-3.91	-0.47	18.20	30.13

suggest that their hotel is close to famous places. To assess whether this claim holds for the kind of information in our knowledge base, we refined the interpretations from Table 9.1 to those in Table 9.2. The idea is that we calculate two sets of parameters for each nearness relation: one using only popular places, and one using only unpopular places, where a place is defined as popular if it occurs at least 5 times as the object of a nearness relation in our knowledge base. Table 9.2 clearly shows that *within walking distance, across the street,* and the alternatives given by openlist.com, are in accordance with this claim from [Tezuka *et al.* (2001)]. However, the other relations display the exact opposite behaviour, i.e., the interpretation of nearness seems to be more narrow for popular places. One possible explanation for this could be that famous places tend to be in the city centre, where hotels, restaurants, and touristic attractions are more close to each other than in the outskirts. In some experiments, we will use these refined interpretations, except for *close*, because there are too few occurrences of this relation in our knowledge base to find reliable parameters.

9.3.2.3 *Representing quantified nearness relations*

While there is already an abundance of nearness information on web pages that uses named relations, there may be even more information that expresses nearness in terms of a specific number of kilometers, miles, blocks, etc. Although a statement like *the hotel is located at 3 kilometers from the Space Needle* might seem to convey an exact distance at first glance, the intended distance restriction is vague. First of all, *at 3 kilometers* should probably be understood as *at approximately 3 kilometers*, since overspecific information, such as *at 3.124 kilometers*, is generally avoided in texts. Next, it may happen that the writer of this information does not know the exact distance, and simply writes 3 kilometers as an approximation of the real distance. Finally, it is not clear whether the 3 kilometer restriction applies to the straight-line distance, or to the actual travelling distance. This is further complicated by the fact that we have no information about the actual travelling distance. Even using a route planner would not solve all problems, since, for example, the walking distance may differ from the travelling distance by car (e.g., due to one way streets).

However, the actual travelling distance usually differs from the straight-line distance by at most a factor $\sqrt{2}$. To see this, consider a city block street layout as in Figure 9.3(a). The length of the shortest path from place a to place b is $\sqrt{2}d(a,b)$ kilometers, where $d(a,b)$ is the straight-line distance in

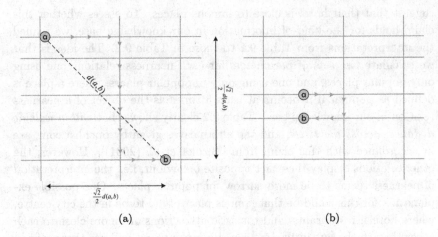

(a)   (b)

Fig. 9.3   We assume that the actual travelling distance from a to b differs from the straight-line distance $d(a,b)$ by at most a factor $\sqrt{2}$.

kilometers. The situation in Figure 9.3(a) reflects the worst possible street layout (i.e., the street layout that results in the longest distance) which still has the property that there is a path for which the distance to b is decreased in every step. Especially when the straight-line distance between a and b is very small, a situation like in Figure 9.3(b) can occur, where all paths to b pass at some point c where the straight-line distance to b is greater than from a. To cope with this, we will treat small distances in a different way, as is explained below. To find appropriate values of the parameters α, β, γ, and δ for a nearness relation such as *3 kilometers from* we assume that $\alpha = 3\alpha_0$, $\beta = 3\beta_0$, $\gamma = 3\gamma_0$, $\delta = 3\delta_0$, where the parameters α_0, β_0, γ_0, and δ_0 are the same for all nearness relations of the form r *kilometers from* $(r \in]0, +\infty[)$. To determine the values of α_0, β_0, γ_0, and δ_0, we proceed as for named nearness relations, using the distances $d_1, d_2, \ldots, d_n$ that are obtained by dividing the straight-line distance of every two places that are said to be *at r kilometers* from each other, by r. In other words, rather than modelling *r kilometers from*, we model *1 kilometer from*, and multiply the parameters that are obtained by r. The resulting parameters, modelling in fact *1 kilometer from*, *1 mile from*, and *1 block from*, are shown in Table 9.3. Note that the ranges of possible distances entail the ranges that could be expected from the argument above, i.e., $[\frac{1}{\sqrt{2}}, 1] = [0.707, 1]$ for kilometer, and $[\frac{1.6093}{\sqrt{2}}, 1.6093] = [1.138, 1.6093]$ for mile. Also, the ranges are quite vague, resulting from the fact that the distances mentioned in texts are often approximations and the fact that, for example, hotel owners are not always fully honest about the true location of their hotel. Furthermore, note that the range of possible distances for *1 block from* is more vague than those for *1 kilometer from* or *1 mile from*. This is due to the fact that a block is an inherently vague unit, unlike a kilometer or a mile.

Another reason for the deviation from the ranges $[0.707, 1]$ and $[1.138, 1.6093]$ are the simplifications we made w.r.t. reachability, i.e., the difference between the straight-line distance and the actual travelling distance. As we argued above, we can expect this to be particularly true for small distances. Our proposed solution is to use different sets of parameters for small distances. The results of this are shown in Table 9.4, which confirm our idea that small distances behave in a different way. For example, all distances in the range $[0.152, 1.449]$ are fully compatible with the nearness relation *0.1 km from*, while the distances in $[0.70, 2.78]$ and $[4.8, 11.6]$ are fully compatible with the nearness relations *1 km from* and *10 km from* respectively.

9.3.2.4 *Representing neighbourhoods*

Semi-structured and unstructured information usually contains a lot of information about the neighbourhood in which a particular place is located. Like information about the nearness to other places, information about the surrounding neighbourhood of a place could be very useful to find an approximation of its location. However, this requires a representation of the spatial extent, i.e., a footprint, of city neighbourhoods. As the boundaries of such neighbourhoods are typically vague, gazetteers contain either no information at all about neighbourhoods, or provide only a centroid (i.e., the coordinates of a single place that is considered to be the centre of the neighbourhood). To be able to use neighbourhood information, we will therefore try to find information about the boundaries of neighbourhoods automatically.

Recall that our knowledge base contains, for each neighbourhood of interest, a set $L = \{l_1, l_2, \ldots, l_m\}$ of places that are assumed to lie in the neighbourhood. We will use this information to construct a fuzzy footprint, i.e., a fuzzy set F in the universe of locations, such that $F(x)$ expresses the degree to which a location x is contained in the neighbourhood. Let l^* be the medoid of the set L, i.e., the place of L for which the sum of the distances to the other places is minimal:

Table 9.3 Interpretations for some frequently occurring quantified nearness relations (distances in km, $r \in [0, +\infty[$, $k \in \mathbb{N} \setminus \{0\}$).

Nearness relation	Frequency	d_{n_1}	d_{n_2}	d_{n_3}	d_{n_4}	α_0	β_0	γ_0	δ_0
r kilometer(s)	785	0.64	0.81	0.96	1.20	0.13	0.47	1.43	1.90
r mile(s)	3063	1.00	1.24	1.47	1.80	0.27	0.75	2.13	2.79
k block(s)	672	0.10	0.14	0.22	0.81	-0.02	0.06	1.39	2.57

Table 9.4 Refined interpretations for some frequently occurring quantified nearness relations (distances in km).

Nearness relation		Frequency	d_{n_1}	d_{n_2}	d_{n_3}	d_{n_4}	α_0	β_0	γ_0	δ_0
r kilometer(s)	$r \in [0, 0.5]$	26	2.13	2.74	4.73	9.61	0.31	1.52	14.49	24.26
	$r \in [0.5, 1]$	54	0.88	1.07	1.39	2.08	0.32	0.70	2.78	4.18
	$r \in [1, 5]$	269	0.61	0.78	0.98	1.22	0.12	0.45	1.45	1.91
	$r \in [5, +\infty[$	436	0.63	0.79	0.92	1.04	0.17	0.48	1.16	1.41
r mile(s)	$r \in [0, 0.5]$	260	1.47	1.86	2.86	6.46	0.28	1.07	10.06	17.26
	$r \in [0.5, 1]$	476	1.07	1.37	1.64	2.09	0.16	0.77	2.53	3.42
	$r \in [1, 5]$	1030	1.00	1.21	1.47	1.78	0.38	0.79	2.09	2.71
	$r \in [5, +\infty[$	1297	0.89	1.17	1.36	1.56	0.05	0.61	1.76	2.15
k block(s)	$k = 1$	97	0.17	0.29	1.01	5.10	-0.21	0.04	9.18	17.34
	$k = 2$	113	0.12	0.21	0.30	1.74	-0.11	0.04	3.18	6.06
	$k = 3$	95	0.11	0.15	0.23	1.53	-0.01	0.07	2.83	5.44
	$k > 3$	367	0.09	0.11	0.16	0.32	0.01	0.06	0.49	0.82

$$l^* = \underset{l_1 \in L}{\arg\min} \sum_{l_2 \in L \setminus \{l_1\}} d(l_1, l_2) \tag{9.6}$$

Without loss of generality, we can assume that $d(l^*, l_1) \leq d(l^*, l_2) \leq \cdots \leq d(l^*, l_m)$. Our main idea to find a fuzzy footprint is very similar to the way we constructed the interpretations for the nearness relations. In particular, we assume that at most 40% of the locations in L are noisy (i.e., incorrectly classified as lying in the neighbourhood), and that the difference $d(l^*, l_{\frac{3m}{5}}) - d(l^*, l_{\frac{2m}{5}})$ gives a good indication of the vagueness of the boundaries of the neighbourhood (where we assume that m is a multiple of 5, for simplicity). For locations l in L, we define F as:

$$F(l) = \begin{cases} 1 & \text{if } d(l^*, l) \leq \lambda \\ 0 & \text{if } d(l^*, l) \geq \rho \\ \frac{\rho - d(l^*, l)}{\rho - \lambda} & \text{otherwise} \end{cases} \tag{9.7}$$

where

$$\lambda = d(l^*, l_{\frac{3m}{5}}) \tag{9.8}$$

$$\rho = d(l^*, l_{\frac{3m}{5}}) + 4(d(l^*, l_{\frac{3m}{5}}) - d(l^*, l_{\frac{2m}{5}})) \tag{9.9}$$

Note that (at least) 60% of the locations in L are assumed to lie in the neighbourhood to degree 1. The definition of F for locations l that are not contained in L, is based on the convex hull of particular subsets of L. For $k \in]0, 1]$, we define the set M_k of locations as the convex hull of the locations l of L for which $F(l) \geq k$. Finally, for an arbitrary location l (i.e., l not necessarily in L), we define F as:

$$F(l) = \sup\{k | k \in]0, 1] \text{ and } l \in M_k\} \tag{9.10}$$

For example, assume that $L = \{l_1, l_2, l_3, l_4, l_5, l_6\}$, $l_1 = l^*$, and that $F(l_1) = F(l_2) = F(l_3) = 1$, $F(l_4) = 0.9$, $F(l_5) = 0.8$, and $F(l_6) = 0.7$. The resulting definitions of the sets M_1, $M_{0.8}$, and $M_{0.7}$ are shown in Figure 9.4. For any location l, $F(l) = 1$ provided $l \in M_1$, while $F(l) = 0.9$ iff $l \in M_{0.9} \setminus M_1$, $F(l) = 0.8$ iff $l \in M_{0.8} \setminus M_{0.9}$, $F(l) = 0.7$ iff $l \in M_{0.7} \setminus M_{0.8}$, and $F(l) = 0$ otherwise.

9.3.3 *Location Approximation*

In Section 9.3.2, we explained how natural language hints such as x *is located within walking distance from* a, and x *is located in* N could be interpreted. If a is a place with a known location, and N a neighbourhood

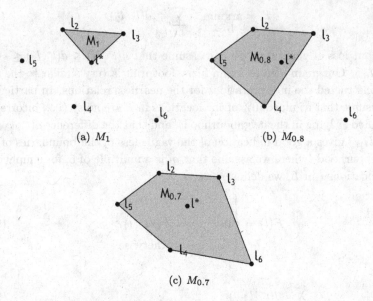

Fig. 9.4   Definition of the sets M_1, $M_{0.8}$, and $M_{0.7}$

with a known fuzzy footprint, these hints can be translated to fuzzy sets, defining which places are compatible, and to what extent. In this section, we will show how the location of x can be estimated, using only natural language hints that relate x to places with a known location or fuzzy footprint.

Because we cannot assume that all information about x is consistent, we will first identify the locations that are consistent with as much of our information as possible. Let A_1, A_2, ..., A_n be the fuzzy sets of locations that were obtained by interpreting all natural language hints about the location of x. For information about the surrounding neighbourhood like x *is located in N*, this is the fuzzy footprint of the region N defined in Section 9.3.2.4. For nearness information like x *is located within walking distance from a*, this is the fuzzy set A_i defined for all locations l by $A_i(l) = R_{(\alpha,\beta,\gamma,\delta)}(l, a)$, where the parameters $(\alpha, \beta, \gamma, \delta)$ are those that correspond to our interpretation of *within walking distance*. We define the score of a location l as:

$$score(l) = \sum_{i=1}^{n} A_i(l) \tag{9.11}$$

This score reflects how compatible the location is with the available knowledge. Note how the use of fuzzy sets provides the flexibility that is needed when combining different constraints. Assume for example that there are only two fuzzy sets A_1 and A_2. If there exist locations l such that $A_1(l) = 1$ and $A_2(l) = 1$, we will prefer such locations. In this case our information about x is maximally consistent. When such locations do not exist, we will prefer locations that maximize $A_1(l) + A_2(l) < 2$. Using crisp sets, we would either not have found any location that is consistent with both A_1 and A_2 in the second case, or we would not have been able to differentiate between optimal and sub-optimal locations in the first case.

Let S be the set of locations l whose score is maximal (i.e., such that there are no locations with a higher score). This set of locations identifies a region in the real plane, which is usually not convex, and may consist of several disconnected parts. As the estimation l_0 of the location of x, we will choose a central location from the set S. In particular, we consider a set of, e.g., 100 points that are uniformly chosen in the region identified by S. We define l_0 as the medoid of this set, as defined in (9.6).

In the following, we will use four different techniques to estimate the location of a place, three based on the procedure outlined above, and one baseline:

(i) Fuzzy-1: We use the aforementioned procedure, where neither named nearness relations nor quantified nearness relations are interpreted using the refined interpretations, i.e., nearness relations are interpreted like in Table 9.1 and 9.3.

(ii) Fuzzy-2: Same as Fuzzy-1, but the refined interpretations are used for quantified nearness relations, i.e., nearness relations are interpreted like in Table 9.1 and 9.4.

(iii) Fuzzy-3: Same as Fuzzy-2, but the refined interpretations are also used for named nearness relations, i.e., nearness relations are interpreted like in Table 9.2 and 9.4.

As a baseline technique, we estimate the location of x without interpreting the nearness relations, and without using fuzzy footprints for neighbourhoods. The idea is that every natural language hint is mapped to a single location. Information like x *is located within walking distance of y* is mapped to the location of y, and information like x *is located in R* is mapped to a central location of the region R. Let $Y = \{y_1, y_2, \ldots, y_n\}$ be the set of locations that are obtained in this way. As an estimation of the location of x, the baseline system will choose the centre of gravity l_0 of Y, i.e.:

$$l_0 = \frac{1}{n} \sum_{y \in Y} y \qquad (9.12)$$

where locations are assumed to be represented as vectors of coordinates. The purpose of using this baseline system is to evaluate how much the performance of the systems Fuzzy-1, Fuzzy-2, and Fuzzy-3 is affected by the actual interpretation of the nearness relations and the representation of neighbourhoods.

9.3.4   *Experimental Results*

9.3.4.1   *Location approximation*

As a first evaluation of the four systems, we tried to estimate the location of hotels and touristic attractions in a number of cities, using natural language hints and the locations of the other places. In other words, to estimate the location of a hotel or an attraction, we assume that the locations of all other hotels and attractions, as well as the restaurants in our knowledge base, are known. To obtain a fair evaluation, the parameters used for the interpretation of the nearness relations were determined without using the locations in Seattle for the experiments involving Seattle locations, and similar for the other cities. Thus a different set of parameters was used for each city.

Table 9.5 displays the median of the straight-line distance between the estimated location of hotels and touristic attractions, and the actual location. We used the median instead of the average, because the average is too much influenced by outliers to be useful here. A first observation is that the baseline system actually performs quite well. Nonetheless, the results in Table 9.5 clearly show that a significant improvement over the baseline was achieved by the systems Fuzzy-1, Fuzzy-2, and Fuzzy-3, which was also confirmed by a Wilcoxon signed ranks test ($p < 0.001$). This suggests that the increased complexity due to the interpretation of nearness relations, and the use of fuzzy footprints is justified for the task of location approximation. However, refining the interpretations of the nearness relations does not seem to improve the performance, i.e., the overall performance of Fuzzy-1 is not worse — even slightly better — than the performance of Fuzzy-2 and Fuzzy-3 (Wilcoxon signed ranks, $p < 0.001$).

Table 9.5   Median of the straight-line distance (in km) between the actual locations of hotels and touristic attractions, and the approximated location.

	Hotels				Attractions			
	Baseline	Fuzzy-1	Fuzzy-2	Fuzzy-3	Baseline	Fuzzy-1	Fuzzy-2	Fuzzy-3
Atlanta	3.34	1.89	1.97	1.97	4.34	1.74	1.74	1.73
Boston	1.33	1.01	0.97	0.97	1.51	0.91	1.39	1.50
Chicago	1.98	0.67	0.72	0.69	2.19	0.83	1.24	1.42
Las Vegas	2.21	1.35	1.62	1.44	2.94	1.42	1.74	1.89
Los Angeles	2.16	1.53	1.54	1.55	2.47	1.75	1.79	1.81
Miami	2.10	1.51	1.46	1.57	4.06	3.10	3.73	3.28
Minneapolis	3.84	1.55	1.53	1.52	2.02	1.98	1.98	2.51
New York	1.36	0.74	0.75	0.73	1.04	0.85	0.73	0.73
Philadelphia	1.51	1.34	1.43	1.40	2.32	1.19	1.18	1.33
Sacramento	3.44	2.34	2.07	2.50	2.59	1.23	1.35	1.73
San Francisco	1.02	0.46	0.48	0.45	1.47	0.64	0.75	0.58
Seattle	2.08	0.98	1.07	1.08	2.27	1.27	1.45	1.53

Table 9.6   Average Spearman rank correlation between the hotel rankings obtained using the estimated locations, and using the exact locations.

	Baseline	Fuzzy-1	Fuzzy-2	Fuzzy-3
Atlanta	0.53	0.73	0.73	0.74
Boston	0.57	0.63	0.63	0.63
Chicago	0.34	0.75	0.76	0.75
Las Vegas	0.44	0.60	0.58	0.59
Los Angeles	0.76	0.87	0.87	0.86
Miami	0.62	0.71	0.70	0.70
Minneapolis	0.50	0.73	0.73	0.70
New York	0.57	0.72	0.73	0.73
Philadelphia	0.56	0.68	0.66	0.65
Sacramento	0.51	0.69	0.67	0.66
San Francisco	0.26	0.59	0.61	0.62
Seattle	0.59	0.83	0.81	0.80

9.3.4.2   *Local search*

In a local search setting, the system has to provide a ranking of, for example, hotels, that are near a given landmark. Ideally, the hotels in such a ranking are ordered by increasing distance from the landmark, i.e., the first hotel in the list returned by the local search service is the hotel that is closest to the landmark, the second hotel is the second closest hotel, etc. To assess how well our system performs at the task of finding such a ranking, we used the Spearman rank coefficient, which is well-suited to measure the correlation between different rankings of search results [Bar-Ilan (2005)]. The rankings we used in this experiment were obtained using the estimated locations of the hotels, and the exact locations of the touristic attractions. For each attraction a in each of the cities, we considered a query *hotels near a*, and calculated the Spearman rank coefficient between the ranking obtained with the estimated hotel locations, and the optimal ranking, i.e., the ranking obtained using the exact locations. Note that only the rankings are evaluated, and not the position at which to cut off the list of businesses returned. Therefore, the results are independent of the particular nearness relation that is used in the query. The results are shown in Table 9.6. The Spearman rank coefficient is always between -1 and 1, where 1 means a perfect correlation (i.e., the rankings are identical), 0 means no correlation at all, and -1 means a perfect negative correlation. The conclusions are similar as for Table 9.5: the behaviour of Fuzzy-1, Fuzzy-2, and Fuzzy-3 are very similar, and outperform the baseline system.

One disadvantage of using the Spearman rank coefficient is that the

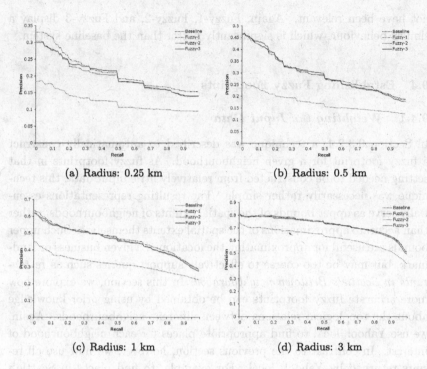

(a) Radius: 0.25 km

(b) Radius: 0.5 km

(c) Radius: 1 km

(d) Radius: 3 km

Fig. 9.5   Precision–recall curves for a query like *hotels near a*, where hotels are considered relevant to the query iff they are located at most 0.25 km, 0.5 km, 1 km, or 3 km away from *a*.

meaning of the results is not very intuitive: how useful is a ranking whose correlation coefficient w.r.t. the optimal ranking is 0.75? A more intuitive way of evaluating the rankings is in terms of the well-known precision and recall measures. However, this requires that we know which hotels are relevant to a query like *hotels near a*. In the experiments, we assumed that a hotel is relevant to the query iff its location is within a fixed radius of *a*. Figure 9.5 shows the precision–recall curves for 4 different radiuses. The queries we considered were again *hotels near a* for each touristic attraction *a* in each of the cities. The values shown in Figure 9.5 are averaged over all these queries. For example, when a 3 km radius is used, the precision at a recall level of 0.5 is about 0.75 for Fuzzy-1, Fuzzy-2, and Fuzzy-3. This means that if a user would go through the list of returned hotels until she has seen half of the relevant hotels, 25% of the hotels she looked at would not have been relevant. Again, Fuzzy-1, Fuzzy-2, and Fuzzy-3 display a similar behaviour, which is significantly better than the baseline system.

9.4   Establishing Fuzzy Footprints

9.4.1   *Weighting the Input Data*

In Section 9.3.2.4, a technique was described to automatically construct a fuzzy footprint for a given neighbourhood. As fuzzy footprints in that setting needed to be constructed from relatively little input data, this technique was necessarily rather simple. The resulting representations essentially serve as upper bounds of the spatial extents of neighbourhoods, rather than accurate approximations of the spatial extents themselves. Such upper bounds are useful for approximating the location of a given business or landmark, but may be too coarse to effectively support queries such as *restaurants in Seattle's Belltown neighbourhood*. In this section, we explore how more accurate fuzzy footprints can be obtained by using prior knowledge about the topological relations between different neighbourhoods. Again, we use Yahoo! local to find appropriate places for each neighbourhood of interest. In contrast to the previous section, however, we now use all results returned by Yahoo! local. For example, to find places in Seattle's Belltown neighbourhood, we would send a query with *Seattle* as the geographic restriction and *Belltown* as the actual query, as before. What is returned is a list of businesses in Seattle that contain the word *Belltown* in the name of the business, in the accompanying natural language description of the business, in a user review, or in one of the other fields describing the business. Thus, we usually obtain a relatively high number of places. However, not all of these places are actually located in the neighbourhood. To increase the robustness of the algorithm, we attach weights to each of the places, expressing our confidence that they are actually located in the neighbourhood. Let $p_1, p_2, \ldots, p_k$ be the list of places that was returned for some neighbourhood of interest L. Our confidence in each of these places is based on two different assumptions:

(1) The position of a place in the list that was returned by Yahoo! local is a good indication of the probability that the place is actually located in the neighbourhood.
(2) The further a place is from the center of a neighbourhood, the less likely it is located in this neighbourhood.

The first assumption is inspired by the fact that the ordering of the businesses in the list returned by Yahoo! local, is based on the importance of the query terms (i.e., the neighbourhood name) in their descriptions. For example, the places with the highest ranks are places whose name contains the name of the neighbourhood. We can be quite confident that these places are indeed located in the neighbourhood; e.g., *Belltown Pizza* is probably located in the Belltown neighbourhood. On the other hand, places that are further down the list often contain the neighbourhood name, for example, only in some user review. Our confidence a_i in the fact that p_i is indeed located in L, based on the first assumption, is defined by:

$$a_i = \begin{cases} 1 & \text{if } L \text{ occurs in the name of } p_i \\ \max(0.3, 1 - \frac{i}{k}) & \text{otherwise} \end{cases}$$

Note that our confidence in the correctness of a place is at least 0.3. This ensures that even the places towards the end of the list will have some — albeit limited — impact on the final result.

The idea behind the second assumption is that, although quite a few of the places returned by Yahoo! local may not be located in the corresponding neighbourhood, we can still identify the center of the neighbourhood in a very accurate way. To model this notion of center, we use the medoid m of the set $\{p_1, p_2, \ldots, p_k\}$, as defined by (9.6). Our confidence b_i in the fact that p_i is indeed located in L, based on the second assumption, is defined as a decreasing function of the distance between p_i and m:

$$b_i = \begin{cases} 1 & \text{if } d(p_i, m) \leq \alpha \\ \frac{\alpha + \beta - d(p_i, m)}{\beta} & \text{if } \alpha < d(p_i, m) < \alpha + \beta \\ 0 & \text{if } d(p_i, m) \geq \alpha + \beta \end{cases}$$

Note how the values of α and β reflect how tolerant we are w.r.t. our second assumption. We can, for example, define these values based on how close to the medoid *most* of the places are located. In particular, let $\pi_1, \pi_2, \ldots, \pi_k$ be a permutation of $1, 2, \ldots, k$ such that $d(p_{\pi_1}, m) \leq d(p_{\pi_2}, m) \leq \cdots \leq d(p_{\pi_k}, m)$. We assume that at least 60% of the places are correct, i.e., located in the neighbourhood L. This is reflected in the following definition of α (assuming, for simplicity, that k is a multiple of 5):

$$\alpha = d(p_{\pi_{0.6k}}, m) \tag{9.13}$$

The value of β will determine how tolerant we are for the remaining places. The idea is that the difference $d(p_{\pi_{0.6k}}, m) - d(p_{\pi_{0.4k}}, m)$ gives a good indication of how tightly the neighbourhood is clustered around the center m.

This leads to the following definition of β:

$$\beta = 4(d(p_{\pi_{0.6k}}, m) - d(p_{\pi_{0.4k}}, m))$$

Finally, our overall confidence c_i in the correctness of a place p_i is defined as the product of a_i and b_i:

$$c_i = a_i b_i$$

9.4.2   Defining Neighbourhoods

Neighbourhood boundaries are generally considered to be inherently fuzzy [Sastry *et al.* (2002)]. However, apart from their gradual nature, neighbourhood boundaries are also ill-defined because of a lack of agreement between different people. Several studies have shown, for example, that the perception of the boundaries of a neighbourhood is influenced by factors such as age, gender, length of residence, socio-economic class, etc. (e.g., [Cho (2003)]). Hence, the degree of membership of a place in a fuzzy footprint should reflect how much people agree that this place is part of the neighbourhood.

A related problem is that the definition of neighbourhood boundaries is context-dependent. For example, in some contexts, Seattle's Belltown neighbourhood is considered to be a part of Downtown Seattle, while in other contexts it is assumed that the two neighbourhoods are bordering on each other. We cope with this by defining a neighbourhood relative to some list of neighbourhoods $\mathcal{L} = \{L_1, L_2, \ldots, L_n\}$. In the first context, $\mathcal{L}$ will contain both Downtown and Belltown, while in the second context, Belltown will be excluded from $\mathcal{L}$. Intuitively, the list $\mathcal{L}$ defines a partitioning of a city into a set of neighbourhoods, i.e., such that the spatial extent of the city is equal to the union of the spatial extents of the neighbourhoods in $\mathcal{L}$, and such that the spatial extents of the neighbourhoods are pairwise disjoint. However, we also allow *default regions* like Central Seattle, whose spatial extent, in this context, would cover all places in Central Seattle that are not contained in any of the other neighbourhoods. In this way, our approach can also be used when a complete enumeration of every neighbourhood is not available.

For convenience, we use L_i both to refer to the name of a neighbourhood, and to the fuzzy footprint describing its spatial extent. To construct this fuzzy footprint, we use the places $p_1^i, p_2^i, \ldots, p_{k_i}^i$ extracted from Yahoo! local, and their confidence scores $c_1^i, c_2^i, \ldots, c_{k_i}^i$, where all the places p_j^i are assumed to be located in L_i. Such a set of places has been obtained for

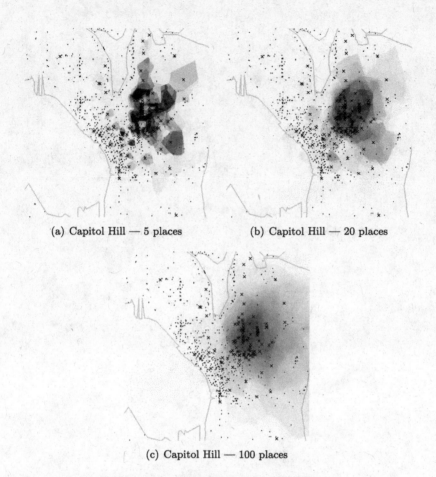

(a) Capitol Hill — 5 places   (b) Capitol Hill — 20 places

(c) Capitol Hill — 100 places

Fig. 9.6 Definitions of the fuzzy footprints for Seattle's Capitol Hill neighbourhood for varying definitions of the set N_x of places nearby x. In (a) the set N_x consists of the 5 places closest to x, while in (b) and (c), 20 places and 100 places are used respectively. Darker regions correspond to a higher degree of membership.

every neighbourhood in $\mathcal{L}$. Let $\mathcal{P}$ be the set of all these places, and let $\mathcal{P}_i = \{p_1^i, p_2^i, \ldots, p_{k_i}^i\}$ be the set of places corresponding to neighbourhood L_i; note that $\mathcal{P} = \bigcup_{i=1}^{n} \mathcal{P}_i$.

The main idea to define the membership degree $L_i(x)$ of an arbitrary location x (i.e., not necessarily corresponding to a place in $\mathcal{P}$) in the neighbourhood L_i, is to use the fraction of nearby places that are assumed to lie in L_i, i.e., included in the set $\mathcal{P}_i$. This idea is closely related to a

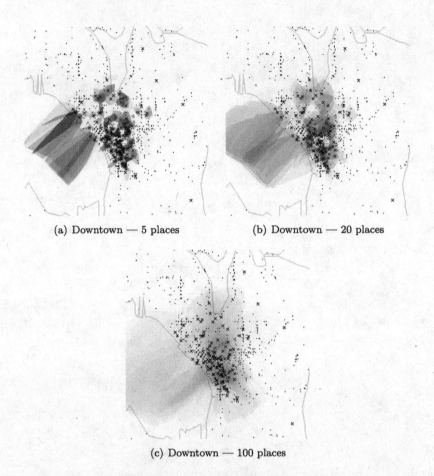

(a) Downtown — 5 places   (b) Downtown — 20 places

(c) Downtown — 100 places

Fig. 9.7   Definitions of the fuzzy footprints for Downtown Seattle when the closest (a) 5 places, (b) 20 places, and (c) 100 places are contained in N_x. Darker regions correspond to a higher degree of membership.

voting model for fuzzy sets, where the degree of membership of an object in a fuzzy set modelling a certain vague property, reflects the percentage of people that would answer positive when asked whether or not this object satisfies the property. However, rather than treating all nearby places (votes) in the same way, the impact of each place is weighted based on its confidence score and its distance to x:

$$L_i(x) = \frac{\sum_{x_0 \in N_x} f_i(x_0) g(x, x_0)}{\sum_{x_0 \in N_x} \max_{j=1}^n f_j(x_0) g(x, x_0)} \qquad (9.14)$$

where f_j is defined for a place x_0 as $(j \in \{1, 2, \ldots, n\})$

$$f_j(x_0) = \begin{cases} c_s^j & \text{if } x_0 = p_s^j \text{ for some } s \in \{1, 2, \ldots, k_j\} \\ 0 & \text{otherwise} \end{cases}$$

The value $f_j(x_0)$ is equal to our confidence that x_0 is located in L_j, provided $x_0 \in \mathcal{P}_j$, i.e., provided x_0 is contained in the list of businesses returned by Yahoo! local for the neighbourhood L_j; otherwise, $f_j(x_0) = 0$. The function g should be a decreasing function of the distance between x and x_0. We used the function g defined for two locations x and x_0 as

$$g(x, x_0) = \frac{1}{1 + d(x, x_0)}$$

Finally, the set N_x is the set of places that are considered to be nearby x $(N_x \subseteq \mathcal{P})$.

9.4.3 *Analyzing the Fuzzy Footprints*

The impact of using different definitions of N_x is illustrated in Figures 9.6 and 9.7. In Figure 9.6 (resp. 9.7), the crosses correspond to the places from $\mathcal{P}$ that are assumed to lie in the Capitol Hill (resp. Downtown) neighbourhood of Seattle, while the dots correspond to the places that are assumed to lie in one of the other neighbourhoods. The empty area in the lower left corner corresponds to the sea. Both figures display the same places, although the crosses from one figure will correspond to dots in the other figure.

When N_x only contains the 5 places of $\mathcal{P}$ that are closest to x, the resulting fuzzy footprint is very sensitive to the actual input, i.e., to the businesses that were returned by Yahoo! local. When increasing the number of places that are considered, the resulting fuzzy footprint becomes smoother, and less sensitive to individual places in the input. In the remainder of this section, we will assume that N_x contains the 100 places that are closest to x. Note that when other sources would be available which would allow to find large sets of places for each neighbourhood in a more accurate way, optimal performance might be achieved by looking at a lower number of nearby places.

Note that, as can be seen from Figure 9.7, a large part of the area that is covered by the fuzzy footprint of Downtown is actually located in the sea. Although this is clearly incorrect, it is of no importance in the context of local search, since there are no businesses located in the sea (otherwise no parts of the sea would have been covered by the fuzzy footprints in the first place). In contexts where this would be a problem, this can easily be solved by intersecting the fuzzy footprints with a detailed footprint of Seattle, based on the official boundaries, which can be found in the Tiger gazetteer[14].

Dark regions in the representation of Capitol Hill in Figure 9.6 correspond to light regions in the representation of Downtown in Figure 9.7, and vice versa. This is particularly noticeable in Figures 9.6(a) and 9.7(a). More generally, we find for any location x that

$$\sum_{i=1}^{n} L_i(x) = \sum_{i=1}^{n} \frac{\sum_{x_0 \in N_x} f_i(x_0)g(x,x_0)}{\sum_{x_0 \in N_x} \max_{j=1}^{n} f_j(x_0)g(x,x_0)}$$

$$= \frac{\sum_{x_0 \in N_x} \sum_{i=1}^{n} f_i(x_0)g(x,x_0)}{\sum_{x_0 \in N_x} \max_{j=1}^{n} f_j(x_0)g(x,x_0)}$$

We can furthermore assume that $f_i(x_0) > 0$ for exactly one i, i.e., $\sum_{i=1}^{n} f_i(x_0)g(x,x_0) = \max_{j=1}^{n} f_j(x_0)g(x,x_0)$, which leads to

$$\sum_{i=1}^{n} L_i(x) = 1$$

In other words, the fuzzy footprints $L_1, L_2, \ldots, L_n$ define a fuzzy partition of the city under consideration. This is important because it ensures that our intended intuitive meaning of $\mathcal{L}$ as an exhaustive and mutual exclusive set of neighbourhoods is reflected in the definition of the fuzzy footprints.

Figure 9.8 illustrates our ability to deal with the context-dependency of neighbourhood boundaries. In particular, the definition of Downtown Seattle is shown in two different contexts. In the first context, Belltown is assumed to be a neighbourhood next to Downtown, i.e., Belltown, as well as Downtown, is included in the list of neighbourhoods $\mathcal{L}$. The resulting fuzzy footprints for Belltown and Downtown are shown in Figures 9.8(a) and 9.8(b). In the second context, Belltown is not included in the list of neighbourhoods $\mathcal{L}$, and is thus implicitly assumed to be a part of Downtown. The fuzzy footprint for Downtown in this second context is shown in Figure 9.8(c). Note that the places and fuzzy footprints in Figure 9.8 are shown at a smaller scale than those in Figures 9.6 and 9.7.

9.4.4   *Experimental Results*

As there are no official boundaries for most city neighbourhoods, it is difficult to evaluate the quality of our fuzzy footprints directly. Instead, we will

---

[14]http://www.census.gov/geo/tiger99/tl_1999.html

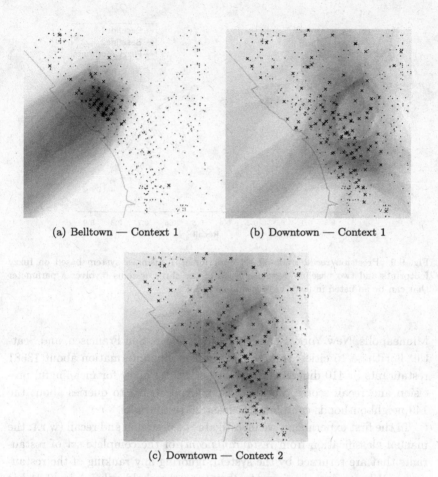

(a) Belltown — Context 1   (b) Downtown — Context 1

(c) Downtown — Context 2

Fig. 9.8 In (a), a fuzzy footprint of the Belltown neighbourhood in Seattle is shown, where darker regions correspond to a higher degree of membership. Figures (b) and (c) show a fuzzy footprint of Downtown Seattle in two different contexts, viz. when Belltown is included in the list of neighbourhoods $\mathcal{L}$ (Context 1), and when it is not (Context 2).

analyse the impact of using the fuzzy footprints in a local search context. To this end, we will compare the results of a query of the form *restaurants in <neighbourhood>*, obtained using our fuzzy footprints, against a manual classification of restaurants by neighbourhood. We extracted such a manual classification from *restaurants.com*[15] for 15 US cities: Atlanta, Austin, Baltimore, Boston, Cambridge, Chicago, Las Vegas, Los Angeles, Miami,

---

[15]http://www.restaurants.com

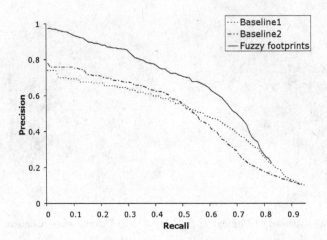

Fig. 9.9   Precision/recall trade-off for experiment 1, using a system based on fuzzy footprints and two baseline systems. Each of the three systems involves a parameter that can be adjusted in favor of precision or recall.

Minneapolis, New York, Philadelphia, San Diego, San Francisco, and Seattle. For these 15 cities, *restaurants.com* contains information about 13681 restaurants in 410 different neighbourhoods. To allow for meaningful precision and recall scores, we limited our experiments to queries about the 149 neighbourhoods containing at least 25 restaurants.

In the first experiment, we investigate the precision and recall (w.r.t. the manual classification from *restaurants.com*) of the complete set of restaurants that are returned by the system, ignoring any ranking of the restaurants. When using the fuzzy footprints, a threshold value λ in $]0,1]$ has to be chosen to decide which restaurants to return. The set of restaurants that is returned is then equal to the set of restaurants whose degree of membership in the fuzzy footprint for the neighbourhood imposed by the query is at least λ. Clearly this threshold parameter can be used to tune the performance of the system towards better precision or better recall. Figure 9.9 shows the resulting precision/recall trade-off, and compares our approach with two baseline techniques.

Both baseline systems return all restaurants that are located within a certain radius of the medoid of the neighbourhood, as defined in (9.6). For the first baseline, this radius is a constant r. By increasing or decreasing the value of r, the precision/recall trade-off can be adjusted. The second baseline system returns all restaurants within a radius of $r_0\alpha$, where α is defined in (9.13), and r_0 is a constant. The idea here is that the value of α gives a good indication of the size of the neighbourhood, and should thus be useful to determine an appropriate radius. As can be seen from Figure 9.9, neither of the two baselines is better than the other. When high precision is needed, the first baseline performs better than the second, while for higher recall values, the second baseline outperforms the first.

Clearly, the system using our fuzzy footprints constitutes a significant improvement over both baseline systems. For low recall values, the precision is almost 1, from which we can conclude that the fuzzy footprints correctly identify the core of the neighbourhoods. Towards the higher recall values, the gain in performance over the baseline systems somewhat decreases. This can be explained by the fact that to obtain a high recall, some restaurants may have to be included for which there might be disagreement about which neighbourhood they belong to. As the assignment of a single neighbourhood to such restaurants is, to some extent, arbitrary, it becomes harder to make a more intelligent decision than simply returning every restaurant within a certain radius. In fact, a similar behaviour could be expected when comparing different human assignments.

Using the fuzzy footprints, it is not possible to obtain a recall value that is, on average, more than 0.83 for the 149 queries considered. This means that on average, 17% of the restaurants that are located in a neighbourhood have membership degree 0 in the corresponding fuzzy footprint. The main reason for this is that for some lesser known neighbourhoods, too few businesses are returned by Yahoo! local. As a consequence, some of the fuzzy footprints are completely incorrect, and cover (almost) none of the restaurants that are actually located in the neighbourhood. In other words, the problem lies mainly in the data acquisition phase, rather than in the construction of the fuzzy footprints. Note that the precision values corresponding to the lower recall values are not affected by this, because the membership degrees of restaurants in the fuzzy footprints of these problematic neighbourhoods are all very low. If the threshold λ is set to be sufficiently high, then no restaurants at all will be returned for these neighbourhoods.

The evaluation task in the first experiment can be seen as a two–stage process. First, the restaurants have to be ranked, based on how likely it is that they should be included in the result set, and then a choice has to be made about how many restaurants to return, i.e., at which point to cut off the ranked list of restaurants. Note that the two baseline systems in our first experiment only differ in the second stage of this process; both use

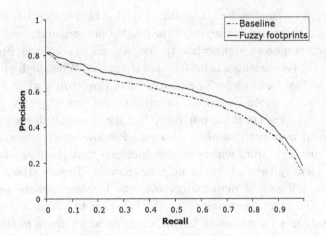

Fig. 9.10   Averaged precision/recall graph for experiment 2, using a system based on fuzzy footprints and a baseline system.

the distance of the restaurants to the medoid of the neighbourhood as the ranking criterium. In a second experiment, we only looked at the ranking of the restaurants. In the system based on fuzzy footprints, the degree of membership of a restaurant in the fuzzy footprint of the neighbourhood is used to rank the restaurants. The distance between each of the restaurants and the medoid is used to break ties, and, in particular, to rank the restaurants that have membership degree 0. In the baseline system, the restaurants are ranked according to their distance to the medoid. For each of the 149 queries, the precision at different recall levels, and at different list cutoffs, was calculated. The resulting precision/recall graph is shown in Figure 9.10.

This figure shows that using fuzzy footprints results in a better ranking of the restaurants. However, the improvement over the baseline system is less apparent than in the first experiment. At very low recall points, the precision of the fuzzy footprint approach and the baseline is even (almost) identical. This is because in both systems the top restaurants in the list are usually the same, i.e., the restaurants in the immediate vicinity of the medoid of the neighbourhood. Similar conclusions can be drawn from the results in Table 9.7, which compares the precision at different (fixed) list cutoffs for both rankings.

For the task of ranking the restaurants, only the relative order of the membership degrees is important. The second stage of the process from

Table 9.7 Precision at fixed list cutoffs for the fuzzy footprint approach and
the baseline system in experiment 2.
$P@n$ denotes the precision of the first
n restaurants in the list.

	Baseline	Fuzzy footprints
$P@1$	0.660	0.654
$P@2$	0.629	0.673
$P@3$	0.648	0.667
$P@4$	0.657	0.684
$P@5$	0.657	0.679
$P@10$	0.648	0.677
$P@20$	0.618	0.653
$P@30$	0.578	0.623
$P@40$	0.535	0.585
$P@50$	0.499	0.546

experiment 1, on the other hand, is based on the actual values of the
membership degrees. Although the second experiment demonstrates that
the ordering of the restaurants imposed by the membership degrees of the
fuzzy footprints is useful, it also shows that a significant gain in precision
is achieved by choosing the right cutoff position, based on the absolute
membership degrees of the fuzzy footprints.

9.5 Modelling the Neighbourhoods of Cardiff: A Case Study

Section 9.4 clearly indicated that reasonable fuzzy footprints can be obtained for city neighbourhoods, starting from very noisy input data. Some
issues remain unresolved, however. Most important, we started from a list
of neighbourhood names which we assumed to form a partitioning of the
city under consideration. In practice, on the other hand, we may not always have such a list at our disposal. Furthermore, even when the list
is available, it will typically only contain neighbourhood names within a
certain level of granularity. Going back to the example of Seattle, for instance, neighbourhoods can be grouped to the larger areas of Central City,
North End and South End. Conversely, neighbourhoods such as Downtown Seattle can be subdivided into smaller regions: International District,
First Hill, Pioneer Square, Central Waterfront, ...[16]. For some neighbour-

---

[16]http://en.wikipedia.org/wiki/Seattle_neighborhoods#Districts_and_
neighborhoods, accessed February 12, 2008.

hoods, alternative names might moreover exist; e.g., Pill Hill and First Hill in Seattle. Similarly, new, informal neighbourhood names are often introduced. An example is Frelard, which is sometimes used to denote the region on the boundary between Ballard and Fremont in Seattle. A second issue is that the quality of the fuzzy footprints largely depends on the popularity of the neighbourhood. While very accurate representations of Downtown Seattle can be acquired, modelling a residential neighbourhood towards the outskirts of Seattle, such as Wedgwood for example, may be a lot more challenging. A promising solution is to make more extensive use of qualitative relations to cope with sparseness of exact quantitative point locations.

To address both issues, we discuss in this section how topological information about neighbourhoods may be extracted from the web, in particular containment and adjacency relations. We furthermore show how fuzzy spatial reasoning helps to increase the reliability of the extracted relations. As a case study we focus on the city of Cardiff in Wales, UK.

9.5.1   *Containment Relations*

Containment relations are omnipresent in web documents, but unfortunately, they are most frequently implicit. By far the richest source of containment relations are addresses of the following kind

```
Monthermer Road 67, Cathays, Cardiff, Wales, UK
```

Typically, such addresses mention increasingly larger regions; e.g., from the address above we can derive that Monthermer Road 67 is located in Cathays, which is a part of Cardiff, which is in Wales, which is in the UK. Web documents contain a wealth of addresses, although parsing addresses is often complicated by occurrences of HTML tags. For example, in the following address, different constituents are placed on different lines.

```
<p>Aberdare Hall<br /> Corbett Road<br /> Cathays<br /> Cardiff
<br /> Wales
```

Therefore, we do not only need to look at commas when parsing addresses, but also at the HTML tag `<br />`. This is, however, not the only possibility. We also find examples such as

```
Department of Geology<br> National Museums &amp;
Galleries of Wales<br>Cathays Park<br> Cardiff
```

where **
** is used to separate different constituents, and

```
<b>St Cuthbert's R.C Primary School</b><br />Letton Road,
<br />Butetown, <br />Cardiff, <br />
```

where **,
** is used. In addition to addresses, implicit containment relations are sometimes found in URLs, e.g.:

```
action="/gallery/Europe/United_Kingdom/Wales/Cardiff/Roath/"
```

Again, we witness a series of containment relations, although now the largest region is mentioned first (Europe), followed each time by a smaller subregion. Finally, implicit containment relations are often formulated in ad hoc ways:

```
<a href="place.php?place=914">
Cardiff - Cathays - Alexandra Gardens</a>
```

The only constant in all these examples is that regions are ordered from largest to smallest, or from smallest to largest, and between each region name, the same separating string occurs. Knowing that region R_2 is part of region R_1, we can therefore expect to find parts R_3 of R_2 by looking for occurrences of the pattern $R_3 \# R_2 \# R_1$ or $R_1 \# R_2 \# R_3$, where $\#$ is a recurring, but otherwise arbitrary string (e.g., **
**). This heuristic can be useful to identify those regions from a set $\mathcal{R}$ of region names that are located in R_2, but, being a heuristic, it is bound to fail occasionally, e.g.:

```
<meta name="keywords" content="Holiday Inn Cardiff City Centre,
Wales, Cardiff, Europe, Hotel Offers">
```

which would lead us to conclude that Europe is a part of Cardiff. Moreover, if we have no prior knowledge at all about the regions that can possibly be located in R_2, it is not always easy to correctly parse the name of R_3. Consider, for example, the following HTML fragment:

```
<P align=left><FONT color=#000080 size=1>Icon courtesy
of St. Martin Church, Roath, Cardiff, Wales</FONT>
```

How do we decide that "St. Martin Church" is part of Roath, rather than "Icon courtesy of St. Martin Church"? One possibility is to change the patterns to $\# R_3 \# R_2 \# R_1$ and $R_1 \# R_2 \# R_3 \#$", in which case fewer matches will be found, but for each match, we should be able to correctly identify R_3. Another, more heuristic solution is to rely on capitalization, which will result in more containment relations, but with a lower accuracy.

As a first experiment, we tried to identify the names of the neighbourhoods of Cardiff. To this end, we retrieved the first 500 documents returned by Google and Yahoo! for the queries "Cardiff * South Glamorgan", "Cardiff * Glamorgan", "Cardiff * Wales", "Cardiff * UK", "South Glamorgan * Cardiff", "Glamorgan * Cardiff", "Wales * Cardiff" and "UK * Cardiff". For example, the first query "Cardiff * South Glamorgan" requests documents in which the term Cardiff occurs within a few words before the phrase "South Glamorgan". Note that South Glamorgan is the county of Wales in which Cardiff is located. Next, we scanned these web documents for matches of the patterns $\#R_3\#R_2\#R_1$ and $R_1\#R_2\#R_3\#$", where R_2 is Cardiff and R_1 is one of South Glamorgan, Glamorgan, Wales or UK. The strings matching R_3 are possibly neighbourhoods of Cardiff, but they need, in fact, not be place names at all. To filter out matches that do not correspond to places, two techniques are used. The first technique is based on some manually defined rules: the first and last word need to be capitalized, the place name has to be within 2 and 30 characters, and special characters such as $<$ or (are not allowed. The second technique is based on the observation that if R_3 is a place name, then Google should at least find some results for the queries "located in R_3", "located in the R_3", "situated in R_3" or "situated in the R_3". If the four queries together yield less than 5 results, R_3 is filtered. Table 9.8 displays the resulting neighbourhood candidates, together with the number of times they were found. Most names in the first column are actual neighbourhoods in Cardiff. Notable exceptions are the large–scale regions South Glamorgan and Wales, and Swansea (which is about 60 km from Cardiff). Furthermore, note that although more errors occur for regions that have been found fewer times, even some of the regions that have only been found once are correct (e.g., Adamsdown and Danescourt). Hence, there is need for an additional filter of neighbourhood names, but it cannot rely on the frequency information.

In Table 9.8, two types of errors occur: place names that are not contained in Cardiff (e.g., Wales, Swansea, Edinburgh), and strings that do not correspond to place names at all (e.g., Women, The, Shopping, Bar). In both cases, the names are not likely to co–occur with the term "Cardiff" very often. To assess whether R is likely to be a region in Cardiff, we use Google to estimate the number of web documents q_1 containing R, as well the number of web documents q_2 containing both R and Cardiff. If $\frac{q_2}{q_1} > 0.75$, we can be quite confident that R is indeed in Cardiff. The converse, however, is not necessarily true. For example, while "City Centre" corresponds to a neighbourhood in Cardiff, most documents containing

Table 9.8 Region names matching the pattern #R3#R2#R1 or R1#R2#R3#", where R2 is Cardiff and R1 is one of South Glamorgan, Glamorgan, Wales or UK.

Name	Freq	Name	Freq	Name	Freq	Name	Freq	Name	Freq
South Glamorgan	236	Grangetown	15	High Street Arcade	6	Government	3	UK	1
Cardiff University	109	Rhiwbina	15	Band	5	Old St Mellons	2	Gwent	1
Roath	81	Heath	15	St.-Mellons	4	Welsh	2	Llandough	1
Cardiff Bay	73	Women	14	Docks	4	Central Cardiff	2	St	1
Rumney	71	Penarth	13	Mermaid Quay	4	Wisbech	2	Work	1
Canton	62	Riverside	13	City Centre	4	Food	2	Northern Ireland	1
Cathays	61	Fairwater	12	Old-St.-Mellons	4	Caerau	2	Best	1
Llanishen	57	Cowbridge Road East	11	Castleton	4	County Hall	2	Italian	1
Cardiff	56	Cathays Park	10	Pontyclun	4	Butetown	2	International	1
Llandaff	45	Gabalfa	10	Llandaff-North	4	Arena	2	UNITED KINGDOM	1
Llanedeyrn	44	Lisvane	10	Europe	4	School	2	Adamsdown	1
Whitchurch	39	Leckwith	10	Taffs-Well	4	Scotland	2	British	1
Pentwyn	35	Pontprennau	10	Dyffryn	4	Cardiff Castle	2	Angel	1
Tongwynlais	34	Barry	10	Map	4	Broadway	2	Porth	1
St. Mellons	31	Newport	9	St.-Nicholas	4	Edinburgh	2	St Mary	1
Heath Park	31	Glamorgan	9	Caerphilly	4	Castle Arcade	2	Accommodation	1
Atlantic Wharf	30	Marshfield	9	Marriott	4	Carmarthenshire	2	Indian	1
Llandaff North	30	The Hayes	9	St.-Fagans	4	Bar	2	Rhondda	1
Cardiff Gate	30	Pontcanna	8	St Fagans	3	United Kingdom	2	Design	1
Culverhouse Cross	26	South Wales	8	Park	3	Education	2	Brecon Beacons	1
Cardiff Gate Business Park	21	Rhoose	8	Holiday	3	Walworth	2	Manchester	1
Wales	20	University Hospital of Wales	8	Hilton	3	Vale of Glamorgan	2	Pontypridd	1
Taffs Well	19	Roath Park	7	Future	3	French	1	Cowbridge	1
St Mellons	19	Splott	7	Brighton	3	Brighton	1	Peter	1
Thornhill	19	Kingsway	7	Hotel	3	Online	1	St. Georges	1
Llanrumney	19	Thistle	7	Premier	3	Brecon	1	Danescourt	1
Radyr	18	Stadium	6	Bridgend	3	Llantwit Major	1	Region	1
Birchgrove	17	Ocean Park	6	House	3	The Point	1	Lincoln	1
Penylan	17	Shopping	6	Lakeside	3	Vale	1		
Ely	16	Old St. Mellons	6	St. Mary's Street	3	American	1		
Swansea	15			Health	3	Queens Arcade	1		
				Road	3				

"City Centre" will not contain "Cardiff".

Another way of identifying place names in Cardiff is by geocoding addresses involving these names and looking at the spatial distribution of the resulting coordinates. For example, to find locations in Cathays, we can look for occurrences of patterns such as

$<$*streetname*$>$ $<$*nr*$>$, Cathays, Cardiff

where $<$*streetname*$>$ is the name of a street in Cardiff. In particular let $\mathcal{P}$ be the set of points (coordinates) that are thus found for a region R. Let p_0 be the medoid of $\mathcal{P}$ (as defined in (9.6)), r_1 the median of $d(p_0, p)$ over all p in $\mathcal{P}$, and r_2 the median deviation, i.e., the median of the value $|d(p_0, p) - r_1|$ over all p in $\mathcal{P}$. Below, we assume that $d(p, q)$ corresponds to the distance between p and q in kilometers. The more the points of $\mathcal{P}$ are clustered together over a relatively small area, the higher the chance that R is indeed a neighbourhood. Assuming that $r_1 + r_2$ is a reasonable approximation of the radius of R, this suggests that the likelihood of R being a neighbourhood is inversely proportional to $(r_1 + r_2)^2$. Moreover, the more addresses found involving both a Cardiff street name and the region name R, i.e., the higher the number of points in $\mathcal{P}$, the higher the chance that R is a neighbourhood, suggesting that the likelihood that R is a neighbourhood is proportional to $|\mathcal{P}|$. Specifically, if $r_1 + r_2 > 0$ and $\frac{|\mathcal{P}|}{(r_1 + r_2)^2} > 1$, we assume that R is a neighbourhood, but again the converse does not hold, i.e., there may be neighbourhoods in Cardiff for which no addresses are found. This leads to the following filter for the names of Table 9.8: if either $\frac{q_2}{q_1} > 0.75$ or $\frac{|\mathcal{P}|}{(r_1 + r_2)^2} > 1$, R is considered to be a neighbourhood name. In other words, if none of the two techniques finds evidence that R is a neighbourhood in Cardiff, we assume that R is either outside Cardiff or not a place name. The resulting neighbourhood names (ignoring case) are provided in Table 9.9, showing the remarkable effectiveness of the additional filtering technique.

In addition to identifying the neighbourhoods of a city, the technique introduced can also be exploited to find parts of a neighbourhood, including smaller–scale regions, squares, buildings, parks, etc. The most reliable conclusions can be drawn when a containment relation is found between two of the earlier identified neighbourhood names. From the following HTML fragments, for example, we can correctly derive that Atlantic Wharf is part of the Cardiff Bay neighbourhood, which is, in turn, sometimes seen as a part of Butetown.

Table 9.9   Neighbourhoods in Cardiff after additional filtering.

cardiff university	llanrumney	roath park
roath	radyr	splott
cardiff bay	birchgrove	old st. mellons
rumney	penylan	high street arcade
canton	ely	st.-mellons
cathays	grangetown	docks
llanishen	rhiwbina	mermaid quay
cardiff	heath	old-st.-mellons
llandaff	penarth	llandaff-north
llanedeyrn	riverside	taffs-well
whitchurch	fairwater	st.-fagans
pentwyn	cowbridge road east	st fagans
tongwynlais	cathays park	lakeside
st. mellons	gabalfa	old st mellons
heath park	lisvane	central cardiff
atlantic wharf	leckwith	caerau
llandaff north	pontprennau	butetown
cardiff gate	barry	cardiff castle
culverhouse cross	marshfield	llantwit major
cardiff gate business park	the hayes	adamsdown
taffs well	pontcanna	pontypridd
st mellons	rhoose	danescourt
thornhill	university hospital of wales	

```
Atlantic Wharf,Cardiff Bay,Cardiff,

<br>Cardiff Bay, Butetown, Cardiff, CF10
```

Unfortunately, the technique also fails in some cases. For example, we could erroneously assume that Cardiff Bay is contained in Llantwit Major (which is a town outside Cardiff) because of the following fragment:

```
<span class="main"><br> Cardiff<br> Llantwit Major<br>
Cardiff Bay<br>
```

Hence, again an additional filtering step is required. The error in the example above, for example, could easily be detected by collecting and comparing addresses of places in Cardiff Bay and Llantwit Major, which would reveal that the respective addresses are too far apart for a containment relation to be possible. In general, errors will be detected in a subsequent fuzzy spatial reasoning step, where inconsistencies between different relations as well as inconsistencies with available quantitative information will be identified.

Often we are also interested in finding new parts of a neighbourhood, i.e., places that were not identified earlier. Typically, a high number of such places can be found, e.g.:

```
<a href="place.php?place=866">Cardiff - Cathays - Sophia Gardens
 - The National Sports Centre for Wales</a>
```

As before, errors are introduced in this extraction phase: sometimes the names that occur as arguments of the relations are not place names at all, sometimes they are too ambiguous (e.g., Hotel), and sometimes they are unique place names but the spatial relation itself is incorrect. Unlike the previous cases, however, errors are more difficult to recognize, as less information can typically be found about buildings and small–scale regions than about neighbourhoods or cities. To reliably extract places that occur within neighbourhoods, more accurate extraction techniques may need to be used (leading to a lower recall), or additional relations should be collected (e.g., orientation and nearness relations to support or refute the extracted containment relations).

9.5.2 Adjacency Relations

If explicit mentions of containment relations in texts are already rare, this even holds more for adjacency relations. One exception is when people state that something is located in the border zone between two neighbourhoods. From the following sentence, for example, we can establish that Cathays and Roath are adjacent neighbourhoods[17]:

4 Double Bedroom house located on the border of Cathays and Roath.

Although this kind of information is often expressed, many variations on the exact phrasing are possible, e.g.[18]:

Small 1 bedroom flat in the Cathays/Roath area.

In general, people use adjacent neighbourhoods often in the same context. To assess the likelihood that two regions R_1 and R_2 are adjacent, we therefore count the number of times we find occurrences of "R_1 / R_2", "R_1 & R_2" and "R_1 and R_2". We furthermore provide a higher weight when this phrase is followed by words such as neighbourhood, area, etc. Specifically, an occurrence of "Cathays and Roath" is given weight 1, while "the Cathays and Roath area" would be given weight 2.

---

[17]http://2let2students.co.uk/CMS2/index.php?option=com_hotproperty&task= view&id=299&Itemid=114, accessed February 13, 2008.

[18]http://www.nestoria.co.uk/cathays/flat/rent, accessed February 13, 2008.

Unfortunately, this technique requires a prohibitively high number of search engine requests. For example, considering the 68 neighbourhoods from Table 9.9, at least $68 \times 67 \times 3 = 13668$ search engine requests would be needed (assuming we submit the queries 'R_1 / R_2", "R_1 & R_2" and "R_1 and R_2" to Google or Yahoo!). Therefore, rather than considering all pairs of regions R_1 and R_2, an initial filtering step is performed. As for containment relations, two complementary techniques are used: one based on co–occurrence and one based on addresses. For the first technique, we use the documents that were already collected for R_1 and R_2 to find containment relations. In these documents, we count the number of times f that R_1 and R_2 occur within 100 characters of each other. If $f > 5$, we apply the method described above to assess the likelihood that R_1 and R_2 are adjacent. For the second heuristic, let $\mathcal{P}^1$ and $\mathcal{P}^2$ be the coordinates of locations that were found to be in R_1 and R_2 respectively, and let p_0^1 and p_0^2 be the corresponding medoids. Furthermore, let r_1^1 and r_1^2 be the median distances from p_0^1 and p_0^2, and let r_2^1 and r_2^2 be the median deviations from these median distances. If a sufficiently high number of coordinates was found for R_1 and R_2, the distance between p_0^1 and p_0^2 should be small compared to the values of r_1^1, r_2^1, r_1^2, r_2^2. In particular, we assume that $r_1^1 + 2r_2^1$ and $r_1^2 + 2r_2^2$ are reasonable approximations of the radius of R_1 and R_2 respectively. Therefore, if $d(p_0^1, p_0^2) < 0.2 + r_1^1 + r_1^2 + 2(r_2^1 + r_2^2)$ (assuming $d(p_0^1, p_0^2)$ is the distance in kilometer between p_0^1 and p_0^2), we consider R_1 and R_2 as a pair of possibly adjacent neighbourhoods and apply the aforementioned method.

Table 9.10 contains the containment and adjacency relations that were obtained using the redundancy–based techniques explained above, involving Cardiff University, Cathays and Cardiff Bay. A general observation we can make about these results is that adjacency relations seem to be more reliable than containment relations, although errors are found for both types of relations. To each of the relations, a confidence score is attached based on the number of times the relation was found. These confidence scores, which are also displayed in Table 9.10, provide useful information about the likelihood that a relation is correct.

9.5.3 *Fuzzy Spatial Reasoning*

After the neighbourhoods of Cardiff are identified and additional containment and adjacency relations are collected, a fuzzy spatial reasoner can be employed. As in temporal information retrieval (Chapter 6), the main pur-

Table 9.10   Topological relations found for three neighbourhoods of Cardiff using redundancy–based techniques.

Region	Relation	Confidence
cardiff university	P(cardiff university,cathays park)	0.41
	P(cardiff university,university hospital of wales)	0.42
	P(cardiff university,heath park)	0.68
	P(cardiff university,whitchurch)	0.45
	EC(cardiff university,university hospital of wales)	0.16
cathays	P(culverhouse cross,cathays)	0.16
	P(roath,cathays)	0.35
	P(gabalfa,cathays)	0.16
	P(cardiff castle,cathays)	0.12
	P(adamsdown,cathays)	0.125
	P(cathays park,cathays)	0.29
	P(penylan,cathays)	0.16
	P(cathays,central cardiff)	0.18
	P(cathays,cardiff castle)	0.12
	P(cathays,roath)	0.12
	EC(cathays,roath)	0.81
	EC(cathays,cardiff bay)	0.09
	EC(cathays,gabalfa)	0.09
	EC(cathays,canton)	0.23
	EC(cathays,pontcanna)	0.09
	EC(cathays,adamsdown)	0.23
	EC(cathays,cathays park)	0.68
	EC(cathays,penylan)	0.16
	EC(cathays,heath)	0.58
cardiff bay	P(cardiff bay,llantwit major)	0.12
	P(llanedeyrn,cardiff bay)	0.12
	P(grangetown,cardiff bay)	0.20
	P(cardiff castle,cardiff bay)	0.29
	P(atlantic wharf,cardiff bay)	0.41
	P(cardiff gate,cardiff bay)	0.16
	P(mermaid quay,cardiff bay)	0.53
	P(caerau,cardiff bay)	0.20
	P(cardiff bay,grangetown)	0.08
	P(cardiff bay,butetown)	0.32
	P(cardiff bay,atlantic wharf)	0.12
	P(cardiff bay,mermaid quay)	0.29
	P(cardiff bay,splott)	0.08
	EC(cardiff bay,ely)	0.09
	EC(cardiff bay,butetown)	0.54
	EC(cardiff bay,grangetown)	0.52
	EC(cardiff bay,penarth)	0.66
	EC(cardiff bay,cardiff castle)	0.16
	EC(cardiff bay,atlantic wharf)	0.41
	EC(cardiff bay,mermaid quay)	0.28
	EC(cardiff bay,docks)	0.58
	EC(cardiff bay,cathays)	0.09
	EC(cardiff bay,st fagans)	0.09
	EC(cardiff bay,cathays park)	0.16
	EC(cardiff bay,canton)	0.16
	EC(cardiff bay,splott)	0.16

pose of using a reasoner is to identify new relations by applying transitivity rules, and detect and repair inconsistencies. Again, we can expect that incorrect information will be completely removed from the initial knowledge base, whereas spatial relations involved in conflicts due to vagueness are only partially removed. The exact algorithm we use is similar in spirit to the algorithm used in Chapter 6 for fuzzy temporal reasoning, replacing temporal relations by spatial relations, and applying the corresponding transitivity rules for propagating fuzzy spatial information. Initially a containment relation between R_1 and R_2 is interpreted as $P(R_1, R_2) = 1$, while an adjacency relation is interpreted as $EC(R_1, R_2) = 1$. To each of the fuzzy spatial relations in the initial knowledge base, a confidence score is attached which is based on the number of different sources that indicate the relationship. When conflicts are detected, these confidence scores are used to decide which fuzzy spatial relations to weaken.

In addition to containment and adjacency relations, we add a number of relations of the form $DC(R_1, R_2) = 1$, based on available coordinates. Let $\mathcal{P}^1$ and $\mathcal{P}^2$ be sets of coordinates of places in R_1 and R_2, and let p_0^1, p_0^2, r_1^1, r_1^2, r_2^1 and r_2^2 be defined from $\mathcal{P}^1$ and $\mathcal{P}^2$ as before. Assuming that $r_1^1 + 2r_2^1$ and $r_1^2 + 2r_2^2$ are good estimations of the radius of R_1 and R_2, if $d(p_0^1, p_0^2)$ is much larger than $r_1^1 + r_1^2 + 2(r_2^1 + r_2^2)$, we can expect that R_1 is disconnected from R_2. Specifically, if $|\mathcal{P}^1| > 5$, $|\mathcal{P}^2| > 5$ and $d(p_0^1, p_0^2) > 0.5 + r_1^1 + r_1^2 + 2(r_2^1 + r_2^2)$, we add $DC(R_1, R_2) = 1$ to the initial knowledge base. The confidence score attached to this relation then depends on the value of $d(p_0^1, p_0^2)$.

A portion of the knowledge base that was obtained after fuzzy spatial reasoning is shown in Figure 9.11. For the ease of presentation, only containment and adjacency relations are displayed, and fuzzy spatial relations that follow straightforwardly from others have been omitted. For example, from the fact that $P(UHW, HP) = 1$ and $P(HP, H) \geq 0.75$, we immediately find that also $P(UHW, H) \geq 0.75$ holds, where UHW, HP and H are abbreviations for the University Hospital of Wales, Heath Park and Heath respectively. Note that values such as 0.5 and 0.75 correspond to lower bounds for the corresponding fuzzy spatial relations. A first observation from the results in Figure 9.11 is that most fuzzy spatial relations are adjacency relations (EC), which could be expected since most of the place names in Table 9.9 are indeed non–overlapping neighbourhoods. Some notable exceptions occur, however, such as the University Hospital of Wales, Roath Park, Cardiff University, etc., but, accordingly, in most of these cases, containment relations have been found. Another observation is

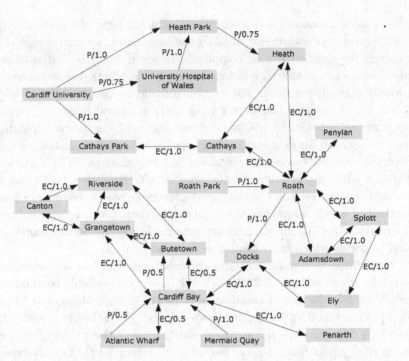

Fig. 9.11   Fuzzy spatial relations between neighbourhoods of Cardiff.

that most of the fuzzy spatial relations hold to degree 1. This results from
the fact that only a small number of inconsistencies were detected, which
has two causes: a large fraction of the extracted relations are correct, and
about some regions too little information is available to find inconsistencies.
For example, $P(Roath, Docks) = 1$ is one of the few clearly wrong results.
Since little information about the Docks area is available, however, this did
not result in any conflicts and the error was not detected by the reasoning
algorithm. Another error was introduced by the reasoning algorithm due to
the ambiguity of the place name Cardiff University, part of which is located
in Cathays Park. On the other hand, the University Hospital is located in
Heath Park, which led to the conclusion that Heath Park and Cathays Park
are overlapping (to degree 1).

Another interesting case is the relationship between Cardiff Bay and
Butetown. Cardiff Bay is located towards the outskirts of an area that
used to be called Tiger Bay and is more recently called Butetown, suggesting a containment relation. However, people living in or near the recently

redeveloped and wealthy Cardiff Bay tend to consider their neighbourhood as disjoint from the much poorer Butetown region. Hence, both a containment relation and an adjacency relation are justified between Cardiff Bay and Butetown, to some extent. Accordingly, both fuzzy spatial relations have received a lower bound of 0.5 in the knowledge base. Similarly, as the exact boundaries of Cardiff Bay are ill–defined, both a containment relation and an adjacency relation are justified, to some extent, between Atlantic Wharf and Cardiff Bay.

Formally evaluating the correctness of the resulting knowledge base is difficult, if not impossible, as the spatial relationships between different neighbourhoods are often inherently ill–defined. For example, we might impose that Cathays Park and Roath Park should be contained in Cathays and Roath, respectively, whereas our knowledge base considers Cathays Park as being adjacent to Cathays. In Wikipedia, on the other hand, Cathays Park is assumed to be within Cathays[19], but Roath Park is assumed to be adjacent to Roath[20]. While a containment relation might be the most intuitive, both scenarios are defensible, e.g., reserving the term Roath for the residential area, excluding the nearby park. The scale of our case study, being restricted to one city, should furthermore be taken into account when drawing conclusions.

Nonetheless, there are a number of clear observations that can be made. First, it appears that harvesting qualitative spatial relations from the web is feasible and that a reasonable accuracy can be obtained. We cannot, however, expect the resulting description to be complete, i.e., there will always be pairs of regions whose topological relationship remains unknown. For popular neighbourhoods in the city centre, many topological relations are typically found (e.g., Roath, Cardiff Bay, . . .), while this is less likely to be the case for residential neighbourhoods towards the outskirts of the city, which are often only mentioned in a very small number of web documents. Next, incorrect topological relations do not as easily lead to inconsistencies as incorrect temporal relations. For example, when only adjacency relations are found, inconsistencies can never occur. This difference with temporal information is crucial, as sufficient topological relations can only be found by heuristic techniques, relying on the subsequent reasoning step to detect errors. In the experiments described above, we partially solved this problem by adding DC relations based on available quantitative information. Thus, the chances that an error in the knowledge base leads to an inconsis-

---

[19]http://en.wikipedia.org/wiki/Cathays, accessed February 13, 2008.
[20]http://en.wikipedia.org/wiki/Roath, accessed February 13, 2008.

tency are increased, resulting in fewer unrepaired errors. Along the same lines, a significant increase in performance can be expected when topological relations would be combined with orientation and nearness information, resulting in more inferences and more detected inconsistencies. A related issue is the disambiguation of place names. If an accurate decision procedure can be constructed that identifies which names refer unambiguously to a particular place, a much larger number of places could be added to the knowledge base, e.g., monuments, landmarks, hotels, etc, again leading to more reliable conclusions. Furthermore, nearness and orientation information between places may be easier to find than between neighbourhoods. Finally, it should be possible to use quantitative information more thoroughly, for instance, using the boundaries of administrative subdivisions of a city, or using detailed gazetteers containing the exact location of streets.

Automatically acquiring detailed geographical models of cities from the web, involving the place names used in everyday communication, clearly is a challenging problem. In this chapter, we explored important ideas, related to modelling nearness, constructing fuzzy footprints of neighbourhoods and mining topological relations. To arrive at really successful solutions, all these ideas will have to be combined, and other avenues will have to be explored. We have, however, provided the formal groundwork, identified the key challenges and outlined a promising solution.

Conclusions

The primary aim of our work was to introduce a computational framework for the representation of vague temporal and spatial information. In an introductory chapter, the need for such a framework was motivated from an information retrieval (IR) perspective. We stressed how temporal and spatial concepts are bound to play an increasingly central role in IR, as the use of semantics gains importance. The inability of existing methods to cope with the vagueness that pervades these concepts was furthermore discussed, leading to the following three main research questions:

(1) How can temporal and spatial relations be defined between vague events and regions, respectively, being at the same time intuitive and well–behaved in terms of elementary properties (transitivity, reflexivity, symmetry, etc.)?

(2) How can classical reasoning tasks such as satisfiability checking be appropriately generalized? Can effective solutions to these tasks be found? How does adding vagueness affect computational complexity, from a theoretical point of view, and the actual computation time, in practice?

(3) How can the overall framework help information retrieval tasks? Is vagueness in this context as paramount as we expected? Do the proposed algorithms sufficiently scale to large knowledge bases to be useful?

Moreover, the study of both temporal and spatial information gives rise to a number of additional questions. Allen's Interval Algebra (IA) for temporal reasoning bears close similarities with the Region Connection Calculus (RCC) for spatial reasoning. Are these similarities preserved when generalizing to cope with vagueness? Can the same techniques be used to solve

459

the corresponding reasoning tasks?

The second chapter familiarized the reader with a number of important notions from the theory of fuzzy sets. The advantages of using fuzzy sets to represent vague concepts were briefly explored, and compared against alternative theories. In the remainder of the book, fuzzy sets of real numbers were used to model the time spans of vague events, while fuzzy sets of locations — typically points in $\mathbb{R}^2$ or $\mathbb{R}^3$ — were used to model the spatial extent of vague regions. In the same way, temporal and spatial relations between such fuzzy sets were modelled as fuzzy relations, using, respectively, fuzzy relations between time points and locations as a stepping stone. Before focusing on time and space, however, this general process of leveraging fuzzy relations between objects to fuzzy relations between fuzzy sets of these objects was studied in more detail. To this end, we introduced the general notion of relatedness measures in Chapter 3, building on fuzzy relational calculus as the formal groundwork. We compared the behaviour of different relatedness measures in terms of (ir)reflexivity, (a)symmetry, interaction with union, intersection, complement, etc. Of special interest are the transitivity properties of relatedness measures, which were summarized in Table 3.1.

The following three chapters were concerned with the notion of time, each addressing one of the three aforementioned research questions. In Chapter 4, we applied the relatedness measures to define fuzzy temporal relations between vague events, thus inheriting many useful properties. We showed how this approach naturally leads to a generalization of the IA in which all important properties of the original algebra are preserved. For example, the thirteen base relations of the IA are jointly exhaustive and pairwise disjoint (JEPD). Likewise, the thirteen corresponding fuzzy temporal relations were shown to be JEPD w.r.t. the Łukasiewicz connectives. Generalizations of (a)symmetry and (ir)reflexivity properties were furthermore proved to hold, as well as a transitivity table (Table 4.6) that constitutes a sound generalization of the transitivity table Allen introduced in 1983 for crisp temporal reasoning. Although most theoretical results from Chapter 4 are independent of this choice, we advocated the use of the Łukasiewicz connectives in the definition of the fuzzy temporal relations. For this specific choice of connectives, we subsequently investigated how the fuzzy temporal relations can be evaluated in practice. Due to occurrences of suprema and infima, it is often difficult to find the exact degree to which some fuzzy temporal relation holds between two particular fuzzy time spans, whereas acquiring good approximations may be time–consuming. However, we showed how the exact values can be found very efficiently when using the Łukasiewicz connectives in combination with piecewise linear membership functions.

Next, in Chapter 5 we studied reasoning tasks for fuzzy temporal relations. Reasoning in the IA is typically based on enforcing path–consistency in combination with (optimized) backtracking algorithms. This essentially reduces temporal reasoning to a repeated application of transitivity rules. Intuitively, we might expect that a similar situation should occur with fuzzy temporal reasoning, simply replacing Allen's transitivity table with our generalization. It turns out, however, that this is not the case and more subtle effects need to be taken into account. To decide whether a knowledge base Θ of fuzzy temporal relations is satisfiable (or consistent), we provided a reduction to crisp temporal reasoning. Specifically, we revealed how a knowledge base Γ of crisp temporal relations can be constructed in polynomial time, such that Γ is satisfiable iff Θ is satisfiable. The cornerstone in this reduction is a proposition which asserts the existence of an interpretation involving only fuzzy time spans that take a finite number of different membership degrees, provided all upper and lower bounds imposed by Θ are finitely representable (Proposition 5.1). In particular, this proposition allowed us to identify a fuzzy temporal relation between two fuzzy time spans with a finite number of crisp temporal relations between the α–level sets of the fuzzy time spans. Subsequently, we studied the computational complexity of fuzzy temporal reasoning. The most important conclusion is that satisfiability checking in this context is NP–complete. Hence, from a theoretical perspective, adding vagueness to temporal reasoning does not increase the computational complexity. We furthermore identified a maximal tractable subset of fuzzy temporal relations, generalizing among others the well–known ORD–Horn subfragment of the IA. In most knowledge representation frameworks, including the IA, tasks such as entailment checking can be straightforwardly reduced to satisfiability checking. We showed how this result does not carry over to fuzzy temporal reasoning, since the set of considered formulas is not closed under negation. Nevertheless, we revealed that the correspondence between entailment checking and satisfiability checking is preserved in all but a few cases.

In many application scenarios, completeness of the reasoning algorithms is not critical, whereas high demands are placed on the actual execution time. The central focus in the second part of Chapter 5 was therefore on the derivation of efficient algorithms which are sound, but not necessarily complete. We briefly explored existing optimizations for disjunctive temporal reasoning problems, maintaining completeness, and found that, while a significant speed–up can be achieved for fuzzy temporal reasoning, the overall execution time remains prohibitively high for our intended application, viz. IR. At the other end of the spectrum, we considered a direct generalization of Allen's path–consistency algorithm, resulting in a very efficient, but incomplete algorithm, requiring $O(n^3)$ time (n being the number of variables). Unfortunately, this latter algorithm fails to detect inconsistencies too frequently. Our main aim was to construct an $O(n^3)$ algorithm which is "less incomplete", i.e., which detects inconsistencies in all but a few pathological cases. To this end, we took a closer look at the propagation of fuzzy temporal relations (Proposition 5.10), as well as at the subtle dependencies between different fuzzy temporal relations, resulting in a characterization of 2–consistency (Proposition 5.9). Through a number of experiments with synthetic datasets, we demonstrated the practical significance of both propositions, yielding an "almost complete" $O(n^3)$ algorithm. An important observation is the strong influence of the number of different upper and lower bounds used. In general, we assumed that all bounds in the knowledge base are taken from the finite set $\{0, \Delta, 2\Delta, \ldots, 1\}$. For $\Delta = 1$, fuzzy temporal reasoning degenerates to crisp temporal reasoning, whereas values like $\Delta = 0.5$ or $\Delta = 0.25$ seem to provide an interesting trade–off between expressive power and actual execution time.

Chapter 6 explored the applicability of our framework for information retrieval tasks. In particular, we were concerned with extracting fuzzy time spans of events from the web, with extracting qualitative temporal relations using redundancy–based heuristics, and with the use of fuzzy temporal reasoning to detect and repair inconsistencies in the collected knowledge base. We found that reliable fuzzy time spans can be obtained using relatively simple techniques, provided the event under consideration is large–scale, and well–known (e.g., World War II, the Renaissance, the Great Depression,...). For lesser–known events, we proposed to harvest qualitative relations and use these as a surrogate for missing time spans. Notwithstanding that explicit mentions of temporal relations in texts can be rare, our redundancy–based heuristics resulted in a high number of surprisingly accurate relations. Experimental results moreover demonstrated that fuzzy temporal reasoning has a substantial positive impact on retrieval effectiveness. In addition, the proposed methodology suggests a number of promising avenues for future work. For example, the acquisition of a highly reliable knowledge base of fuzzy temporal relations enables the use of more advanced user interfaces; e.g., timelines containing the most important events of interest could be adopted as a flexible means to browse through a document collection, photograph collection, or through digital libraries in general.

The last three chapters addressed our three research questions for spatial information, following the same pattern as Chapters 4–6. In Chapter 7, we investigated various ways of defining fuzzy spatial relations. Starting again from the notion of relatedness measure, we introduced fuzzy spatial relations modelling nearness and cardinal direction between vague regions, as well as flexible size constraints and several refinements of containment. These definitions depend on fuzzy relations between points in space, whose transitivity properties determine the transitivity rules of the fuzzy spatial relations. In contrast to the temporal domain, where transitivity between fuzzy time point relations was found to be relatively straightforward, the transitivity properties of fuzzy point relations in the spatial domain are inherently complex. In particular, we stressed the non–trivial ways in which nearness and orientation information interacts, making analytical solutions often impossible. To cope with this, we introduced approximate solutions, which yields sound, but incomplete inferencing (Propositions 7.2 and 7.3). In the second part of Chapter 7, we focused on topological relations such as overlap, containment and adjacency. Rather than providing specific definitions of topological relations, for instance using relatedness measures, we introduced a generalization of the RCC which aims at capturing vagueness about topological relations in general. Our fuzzy RCC relations are independent of a particular representation of regions (e.g., in a topological space, two–dimensional Euclidean space, ...), of a particular interpretation of connection — being the primitive relation from which all topological relations are derived — and of a particular source of vagueness. To demonstrate that our fuzzy topological relations are well–behaved, we showed a number of important properties, related to the JEPD nature of particular subsets of RCC relations (generalizations of the RCC–8 and RCC–5 base relations), reflexivity, symmetry and transitivity (Table 7.5). Finally, we considered the particular case where regions are represented as fuzzy sets in $\mathbb{R}^n$ and connection is defined in terms of nearness. This particular case stresses two common sources of vagueness in topological relations: the regions involved may be vague, and objects that are very close, but not actually touching, are often perceived as adjacent (and therefore connected). We revealed an important correspondence between the fuzzy RCC relations, under this particular interpretation, and the fuzzy spatial relations defined by relatedness measures (Proposition 7.14).

The reasoning tasks associated with our fuzzy RCC were discussed in Chapter 8. The most important result from this chapter is that satisfiability checking in the fuzzy RCC essentially corresponds to verifying that no transitivity, reflexivity and symmetry rules are violated (Proposition 8.1). This stands in marked contrast with the temporal domain, where additional effects, which are not captured by transitivity rules, played a key role. We furthermore proved that any satisfiable knowledge base of fuzzy RCC relations can be realized by interpreting regions as fuzzy sets in $\mathbb{R}^n$, for an arbitrary n in $\mathbb{N} \setminus \{0\}$, and by interpreting connection in terms of nearness. For practical reasoning, we showed how satisfiability checking can be reduced to solving systems of linear inequalities and backtracking. Each system of linear inequalities can be solved in polynomial time using a linear programming solver, leading to an overall NP–complete time complexity. Related reasoning tasks such as entailment checking and inconsistency repairing can moreover be solved in a similar way. Thus, as for temporal reasoning, we find that adding vagueness does not alter the computational complexity of topological reasoning. Next, we proved how reasoning in the fuzzy RCC can be reduced to reasoning in the original RCC, using a similar technique as for fuzzy temporal reasoning in Chapter 5. Specifically, we showed that an interpretation is guaranteed to exist which only involves fuzzy sets taking a finite number of different membership degrees (Proposition 8.4). However, here the purpose is primarily theoretical: by the reduction, important theoretical results from the RCC can be leveraged to our fuzzy RCC. As an important example, it allowed us to show the aforementioned result of realizability in any dimension n. The reduction to the RCC furthermore allowed us to establish a close relationship with the Egg–Yolk calculus for topological reasoning under vagueness. Among others, this led to an alternative interpretation of connection as a fuzzy relation, thus supporting our claim of generality.

In the final chapter, we considered a number of applications of fuzzy spatial relations in geographic information retrieval (GIR). A first task was concerned with location approximation. Using only some natural language cues about the location of a place p (e.g., p is within walking distance of q, p is located in vague region R), we tried to approximate the geographical coordinates of p as accurately as possible. To this end, we represented natural language nearness relations such as "within walking distance" as fuzzy relations, adopting a data–driven approach to fill in some necessary parameters. A similar technique was introduced to approximate the spatial extent of a vague region. As both techniques rely on noisy input data, the main point of departure was the robustness of the resulting models (e.g., avoiding over–fitting of the input data). Experimental results revealed a significant improvement over baseline systems, suggesting that natural language cues are indeed useful in finding approximate locations. Next, we focused more closely on approximating the spatial extent of city neighbourhoods. We highlighted the context–dependent nature of neighbourhood boundaries, and the resulting need for information about the topological relations that hold between different neighbourhoods. A technique was introduced which uses this topological information to obtain fuzzy footprints of city neigh-bourhoods, i.e., fuzzy sets of locations representing their spatial extent. In a number of experiments, we demonstrated that reliable fuzzy footprints can generally be found, provided that the needed topological information is available. For practical applications, however, two important issues remain: the required topological information may not be available, and the quality of the footprints largely depends on the popularity of the neighbourhood. Moreover, the techniques discussed rely on knowledge about places located in each neighbourhood, and can therefore not easily be extended to cope with other types of regions, e.g., the spatial configuration of different parts of a park. These issues were finally addressed in a case study about the city of Cardiff. We discussed how, by analogy with temporal relations, topo-logical relations may be extracted from the web using redundancy–based heuristics, and how fuzzy spatial reasoning may subsequently be used to im-prove the reliability of the collected information. However, for lesser–known regions, often too little information can be found to allow for meaningful inferences. This calls for a more general spatial reasoning framework, in which not only fuzzy topological relations are considered, but inferences are also made regarding nearness and orientation information.

In conclusion, we have introduced a novel framework for reasoning with vague information about time and space, which is not only attractive from a theoretical perspective — many interesting properties are preserved in the generalization from traditional techniques while maintaining their com-putational complexity — but has, moreover, demonstrated a clear applica-tion potential. While applications beyond IR can be conceived, temporal and geographic constraints in IR pose a particularly interesting challenge. The fusion of soft computing (fuzzy sets), artificial intelligence (temporal and spatial reasoning) and information retrieval is relatively unique, but nonetheless — we believe — paramount in any successful solution.

Appendix A

Proof of Proposition 5.9

From Proposition 3.1, Lemma 5.5, Corollary 5.3, Lemma 5.6, Lemma 5.7 and Corollary 5.4, we already know that for all fuzzy time intervals A and B the constraints (5.87)–(5.100) on $\alpha, \beta, \gamma, \delta, \alpha', \beta', \gamma', \delta'$ are satisfied. To show the converse, we provide a constructive proof, showing that whenever these constraints are satisfied, corresponding fuzzy time intervals A and B can be found. The proof proceeds by case analysis.

(1) First assume that $\delta > 0$, $\delta' > 0$ and $\gamma' \geq \beta'$. Let $p_1 < p_2 < p_3 < p_4 < p_5 < p_6$ be real numbers, and let A and B be defined as

$$A = \{[p_2, p_3[/I_W(\beta, \beta'), p_3/1,]p_3, p_4]/I_W(\delta, \delta'),]p_4, p_5]/1 - \gamma',$$
$$]p_5, p_6]/1 - \gamma\}$$
$$B = \{[p_1, p_3[/1 - \beta, [p_3, p_5[/1 - \delta', p_5/1\}$$

First, we verify that A and B are indeed fuzzy time intervals. In particular, it has to hold that $I_W(\beta, \beta') \leq 1$, $1 - \gamma \leq 1 - \gamma' \leq I_W(\delta, \delta') \leq 1$ and $1 - \beta \leq 1 - \delta' \leq 1$. Most of these inequalities are trivial or follow straightforwardly from (5.87)–(5.90) and (5.94)–(5.97). To see why $1 - \gamma' \leq I_W(\delta, \delta')$, first note that $\alpha' = 1$ due to our assumption that $\delta' > 0$ and (5.93). From (5.98) we therefore find that

$$1 \leq S_W(1 - \delta, \delta', \max(\beta', \gamma'))$$

hence

$$1 \leq 1 - \delta + \delta' + \max(\beta', \gamma')$$

Using our assumption that $\gamma' \geq \beta'$ yields

$$1 - \gamma' \leq 1 - \delta + \delta'$$

467

from which we find $1 - \gamma' \leq I_W(\delta, \delta')$. Next, we show that the fuzzy temporal relations evaluate to the required values $\alpha, \beta, \ldots, \delta'$ for A and B. Using Lemma 4.13, we find

$$
\begin{aligned}
be^{\ll}(A, B) &= \max(T_W(A(p_3), B(p_5)), T_W(A(p_3), B(p_6))) \\
&= \max(T_W(1, 1), T_W(1, 0)) \\
&= 1
\end{aligned}
$$

Recall that $\alpha' = 1$ because of (5.93) and our assumption that $\delta' > 0$. Using Proposition 3.1, we immediately find

$$
be^{\prec}(A, B) \geq be^{\ll}(A, B) = 1
$$

Note that $\alpha = 1$ because of (5.100) and our assumption that $\delta > 0$. Next, we find

$$
\begin{aligned}
bb^{\prec}(A, B) &= \min(I_W(B(p_1), A(p_1)), I_W(B(p_2), A(p_2)), \\
&\qquad I_W(B(p_3), A(p_3))) \\
&= \min(I_W(1 - \beta, 0), I_W(1 - \beta, I_W(\beta, \beta')), I_W(1 - \delta', 1)) \\
&= \min(I_W(1 - \beta, 0), I_W(1 - \beta, I_W(\beta, \beta'))) \\
&= I_W(1 - \beta, 0) \\
&= \beta
\end{aligned}
$$

Using (2.31), (5.96) and (5.94), we find (still using Lemma 4.13)

$$
\begin{aligned}
bb^{\ll}(A, B) &= \max(T_W(A(p_1), 1 - B(p_1)), T_W(A(p_2), 1 - B(p_2)), \\
&\qquad T_W(A(p_3), 1 - B(p_3))) \\
&= \max(T_W(0, \beta), T_W(I_W(\beta, \beta'), \beta), T_W(1, \delta')) \\
&= \max(T_W(I_W(\beta, \beta'), \beta), \delta') \\
&= \max(\min(\beta, \beta'), \delta') \\
&= \beta'
\end{aligned}
$$

Next, we find

$$
\begin{aligned}
ee^{\prec}(A, B) &= \min(I_W(A(p_5), B(p_5)), I_W(A(p_6), B(p_6))) \\
&= \min(I_W(1 - \gamma', 1), I_W(1 - \gamma, 0)) \\
&= \min(1, \gamma) \\
&= \gamma
\end{aligned}
$$

and

$$ee^{\ll}(A, B) = \max(T_W(B(p_5), 1 - A(p_5)), T_W(B(p_6), 1 - A(p_6)))$$
$$= \max(T_W(1, \gamma'), T_W(0, \gamma))$$
$$= \max(\gamma', 0)$$
$$= \gamma'$$

Using (5.97), (5.87) and (5.88) and the fact that $1 - \gamma' \leq I_W(\delta, \delta')$, we find

$$eb^{\preccurlyeq}(A, B)$$
$$= \min(1 - T_W(A(p_3), B(p_2)), 1 - T_W(A(p_4), B(p_3)),$$
$$\qquad 1 - T_W(A(p_5), B(p_4)), 1 - T_W(A(p_6), B(p_5)))$$
$$= \min(1 - T_W(1, 1 - \beta), 1 - T_W(I_W(\delta, \delta'), 1 - \delta'),$$
$$\qquad 1 - T_W(1 - \gamma', 1 - \delta'), 1 - T_W(1 - \gamma, 1))$$
$$= \min(\beta, 1 - T_W(I_W(\delta, \delta'), 1 - \delta'), \gamma)$$

and by (2.33) and (2.31)

$$= \min(\beta, 1 - T_W(I_W(1 - \delta', 1 - \delta), 1 - \delta'), \gamma)$$
$$= \min(\beta, 1 - \min(1 - \delta', 1 - \delta), \gamma)$$
$$= \min(\beta, \delta, \gamma)$$
$$= \delta$$

Finally, by (5.94) and (5.95), we establish

$$eb^{\ll}(A, B)$$
$$= \min(1 - T_W(A(p_3), B(p_1)), 1 - T_W(A(p_3), B(p_2)),$$
$$\qquad 1 - T_W(A(p_3), B(p_3)), 1 - T_W(A(p_4), B(p_4)),$$
$$\qquad 1 - T_W(A(p_5), B(p_5)))$$
$$= \min(1 - T_W(1, 1 - \beta), 1 - T_W(1, 1 - \delta'), 1 - T_W(I_W(\delta, \delta'), 1 - \delta'),$$
$$\qquad 1 - T_W(1 - \gamma', 1))$$
$$= \min(\beta, \delta', \gamma')$$
$$= \delta'$$

(2) If $\delta > 0$, $\delta' > 0$ and $\beta' > \gamma'$, A and B are defined as

$$A = \{p_2/1,]p_2, p_4]/1 - \delta',]p_4, p_6]/1 - \gamma\}$$
$$B = \{[p_1, p_2[/1 - \beta, [p_2, p_3[/1 - \beta', [p_3, p_4[/I_W(\delta, \delta'), p_4/1,$$
$$\qquad]p_4, p_5]/I_W(\gamma, \gamma')\}$$

To show the convexity of A and B, it is sufficient to show that $1 - \beta' \leq I_W(\delta, \delta')$, because $1 - \gamma \leq 1 - \delta'$ and $1 - \beta \leq 1 - \beta'$ follow trivially from (5.87)–(5.100). As in the previous case, we find from $\alpha' = 1$ and (5.98) that

$$1 \leq 1 - \delta + \delta' + \max(\beta', \gamma')$$

Using our assumption that $\beta' > \gamma'$, however, we now find

$$1 - \beta' \leq 1 - \delta + \delta'$$

and thus $1 - \beta' \leq I_W(\delta, \delta')$.

Next, we obtain from $\alpha' = 1$

$$
\begin{aligned}
be^{\ll}&(A, B) \\
&= \max(T_W(A(p_2), B(p_4)), T_W(A(p_2), B(p_5)), T_W(A(p_2), B(p_6))) \\
&= T_W(A(p_2), B(p_4)) \\
&= 1 \\
&= \alpha'
\end{aligned}
$$

and from $\alpha = 1$

$$be^{\preceq}(A, B) \geq be^{\ll}(A, B) = 1 = \alpha$$

We furthermore find

$$
\begin{aligned}
bb^{\preceq}(A, B) &= \min(I_W(B(p_1), A(p_1)), I_W(B(p_2), A(p_2))) \\
&= \min(I_W(1 - \beta, 0), I_W(1 - \beta', 1)) \\
&= I_W(1 - \beta, 0) \\
&= \beta
\end{aligned}
$$

$$
\begin{aligned}
bb^{\ll}(A, B) &= \max(T_W(1 - B(p_1), A(p_1)), T_W(1 - B(p_2), A(p_2))) \\
&= \min(T_W(\beta, 0), T_W(\beta', 1)) \\
&= \beta'
\end{aligned}
$$

$$
\begin{aligned}
ee^{\preceq}&(A, B) \\
&= \min(I_W(A(p_4), B(p_4)), I_W(A(p_5), B(p_5)), I_W(A(p_6), B(p_6))) \\
&= \min(I_W(1 - \delta', 1), I_W(1 - \gamma, I_W(\gamma, \gamma')), I_W(1 - \gamma, 0)) \\
&= \min(I_W(1 - \gamma, I_W(\gamma, \gamma')), I_W(1 - \gamma, 0)) \\
&= \min(I_W(1 - \gamma, I_W(\gamma, \gamma')), \gamma) \\
&= \min(1, \gamma + I_W(\gamma, \gamma'), \gamma) \\
&= \gamma
\end{aligned}
$$

Using (2.31), (5.90) and (5.95), we obtain

$$ee^{\ll}(A, B) = \max(T_W(1 - A(p_4), B(p_4)), T_W(1 - A(p_5), B(p_5)),$$
$$T_W(1 - A(p_6), B(p_6)))$$
$$= \max(T_W(\delta', 1), T_W(\gamma, I_W(\gamma, \gamma')), T_W(\gamma, 0))$$
$$= \max(T_W(\delta', 1), T_W(\gamma, I_W(\gamma, \gamma')))$$
$$= \max(\delta', \min(\gamma, \gamma'))$$
$$= \gamma'$$

We find by (2.35), (2.33), (2.31) and (5.97)

$$eb^{\preccurlyeq}(A, B)$$
$$= \min(1 - T_W(A(p_2), B(p_1)), 1 - T_W(A(p_3), B(p_2)),$$
$$1 - T_W(A(p_4), B(p_3)), 1 - T_W(A(p_5), B(p_4)),$$
$$1 - T_W(A(p_6), B(p_4)))$$
$$= \min(1 - T_W(1, 1 - \beta), 1 - T_W(1 - \delta', 1 - \beta'),$$
$$1 - T_W(1 - \delta', I_W(\delta, \delta')), 1 - T_W(1 - \gamma, 1),$$
$$1 - T_W(1 - \gamma, 1))$$
$$= \min(\beta, I_W(1 - \delta', \beta'), 1 - T_W(1 - \delta', I_W(1 - \delta', 1 - \delta)), \gamma)$$
$$= \min(\beta, I_W(1 - \delta', \beta'), 1 - \min(1 - \delta', 1 - \delta), \gamma)$$
$$= \min(\beta, I_W(1 - \delta', \beta'), \delta, \gamma)$$

From $1 - \beta' \leq I_W(\delta, \delta')$ we find $\delta \leq I_W(1 - \beta', \delta')$ by twice applying (2.21). Together with (5.87)–(5.88), we can conclude $\min(\beta, I_W(1 - \delta', \beta'), \delta, \gamma) = \delta$.

Finally, using (2.33), (2.31), (5.96), (5.97) and (5.94), we find

$$eb^{\ll}(A, B)$$
$$= \min(1 - T_W(B(p_1), A(p_2)), 1 - T_W(B(p_2), A(p_2)),$$
$$1 - T_W(B(p_3), A(p_3)), 1 - T_W(B(p_4), A(p_4)))$$
$$= \min(1 - T_W(1 - \beta, 1), 1 - T_W(1 - \beta', 1), 1 - T_W(I_W(\delta, \delta'), 1 - \delta'),$$
$$1 - T_W(1, 1 - \delta'))$$
$$= \min(\beta, \beta', 1 - T_W(I_W(1 - \delta', 1 - \delta), 1 - \delta'), \delta')$$
$$= \min(\beta, \beta', 1 - \min(1 - \delta', 1 - \delta), \delta')$$
$$= \delta'$$

(3) If $\delta = 0$ and $\beta < \gamma$, A and B are defined as
$$A = \{[p_1, p_2[/\beta', [p_2, p_3[/\beta, [p_3, p_4[/I_W(\alpha, \alpha'), p_4/1,]p_4, p_5]/I_W(\gamma, \gamma')\}$$
$$B = \{p_2/1,]p_2, p_4]/\alpha,]p_4, p_6]/\gamma'\}$$

To show the convexity of A and B, we only need to show $\beta \leq I_W(\alpha, \alpha')$, which is equivalent to $\alpha' \geq T_W(\beta, \alpha)$ by (2.21). By the assumptions $\beta < \gamma$ and $\delta = 0$, this is equivalent to (5.91). Next, we find using (5.96) and (5.87)

$$be^{\preccurlyeq}(A, B)$$
$$= \max(T_W(A(p_1), B(p_2)), T_W(A(p_2), B(p_2)), T_W(A(p_3), B(p_3)),$$
$$\qquad T_W(A(p_4), B(p_4)))$$
$$= \max(T_W(\beta', 1), T_W(\beta, 1), T_W(I_W(\alpha, \alpha'), \alpha), T_W(1, \alpha))$$
$$= \max(\beta', \beta, \min(\alpha, \alpha'), \alpha)$$
$$= \alpha$$

From $\alpha' \geq T_W(\beta, \alpha)$, (5.94), (5.95) and (5.89), we establish

$$be^{\ll}(A, B)$$
$$= \max(T_W(B(p_2), A(p_1)), T_W(B(p_3), A(p_2)), T_W(B(p_4), A(p_3)),$$
$$\qquad T_W(B(p_5), A(p_4)), T_W(B(p_6), A(p_4)))$$
$$= \max(T_W(1, \beta'), T_W(\alpha, \beta), T_W(\alpha, I_W(\alpha, \alpha')), T_W(\gamma', 1), T_W(\gamma', 1))$$
$$= \max(\beta', T_W(\alpha, \beta), \min(\alpha, \alpha'), \gamma')$$
$$= \max(T_W(\alpha, \beta), \alpha')$$
$$= \alpha'$$

Next, we find

$$bb^{\preccurlyeq}(A, B) = \min(I_W(B(p_1), A(p_1)), I_W(B(p_2), A(p_2)))$$
$$= \min(I_W(0, \beta'), I_W(1, \beta))$$
$$= \beta$$

$$bb^{\ll}(A, B) = \max(T_W(1 - B(p_1), A(p_1)), T_W(1 - B(p_2), A(p_2)))$$
$$= \min(T_W(1, \beta'), T_W(0, \beta))$$
$$= \beta'$$

Using (2.31), (5.90) and (5.88), we have

$$ee^{\preccurlyeq}(A, B)$$
$$= \min(I_W(A(p_4), B(p_4)), I_W(A(p_5), B(p_5)), I_W(A(p_6), B(p_6)))$$
$$= \min(I_W(1, \alpha), I_W(I_W(\gamma, \gamma'), \gamma'), I_W(0, \gamma'))$$
$$= \min(\alpha, 1 - T_W(I_W(1 - \gamma', 1 - \gamma), 1 - \gamma'))$$
$$= \min(\alpha, 1 - \min(1 - \gamma, 1 - \gamma'))$$
$$= \gamma$$

We furthermore have

$$ee^{\ll}(A,B) = \max(T_W(1-A(p_4), B(p_4)), T_W(1-A(p_5), B(p_5)),$$
$$T_W(1-A(p_6), B(p_6)))$$
$$= \max(T_W(0,\alpha), T_W(1-I_W(\gamma,\gamma'),\gamma'), T_W(1,\gamma'))$$
$$= T_W(1,\gamma')$$
$$= \gamma'$$

Using the assumption $\delta = 0$, we obtain

$$eb^{\preceq}(A,B) = \min(1-T_W(A(p_4), B(p_2)), 1-T_W(A(p_5), B(p_2)),$$
$$1-T_W(A(p_6), B(p_2)))$$
$$\leq 1-T_W(A(p_4), B(p_2))$$
$$= 1-T_W(1,1)$$
$$= 0$$
$$= \delta$$

From (5.97), we find $\delta' = 0$. Using Proposition 3.1 we have

$$eb^{\ll}(A,B) \leq eb^{\preceq}(A,B) = 0 = \delta'$$

(4) If $\delta = 0$ and $\beta \geq \gamma$, A and B are defined as

$$A = \{[p_1, p_3[/\beta', [p_3, p_5[/\alpha, p_5/1\}$$
$$B = \{[p_2, p_3[/I_W(\beta,\beta'), p_3/1,]p_3, p_4]/I_W(\alpha,\alpha'),]p_4, p_5]/\gamma,]p_5, p_6]/\gamma'\}$$

To show the convexity of A and B, it is sufficient to show $\gamma \leq I_W(\alpha,\alpha')$, which is equivalent to $\alpha' \geq T_W(\gamma,\alpha)$ by (2.21). By the assumptions $\beta \geq \gamma$ and $\delta = 0$, this is equivalent to (5.91). The other inequalities that need to hold follow trivially from (5.87)–(5.100).
Using (2.31) and (5.88) we find

$$be^{\preceq}(A,B)$$
$$= \max(T_W(A(p_1), B(p_3)), T_W(A(p_2), B(p_3)), T_W(A(p_3), B(p_3)),$$
$$T_W(A(p_4), B(p_4)), T_W(A(p_5), B(p_5)))$$
$$= \max(T_W(A(p_3), B(p_3)), T_W(A(p_4), B(p_4)), T_W(A(p_5), B(p_5)))$$
$$= \max(T_W(\alpha, 1), T_W(\alpha, I_W(\alpha,\alpha')), T_W(1,\gamma))$$
$$= \max(\alpha, \min(\alpha,\alpha'), \gamma)$$
$$= \alpha$$

By (2.31), (5.89), (5.94) and (5.95), we find

$$be^{\ll}(A, B)$$
$$= \max(T_W(B(p_3), A(p_2)), T_W(B(p_4), A(p_3)), T_W(B(p_5), A(p_4)),$$
$$\qquad T_W(B(p_6), A(p_5)))$$
$$= \max(T_W(1, \beta'), T_W(I_W(\alpha, \alpha'), \alpha), T_W(\gamma, \alpha), T_W(\gamma', 1))$$
$$= \max(\beta', \min(\alpha, \alpha'), T_W(\gamma, \alpha), \gamma')$$
$$= \max(\alpha', T_W(\gamma, \alpha))$$

From $\alpha' \geq T_W(\gamma, \alpha)$, as shown above, we find that the latter expression equals α'.

Using (2.33), (2.35), (2.31), (5.96) and (5.87), we obtain

$$bb^{\preccurlyeq}(A, B)$$
$$= \min(I_W(B(p_1), A(p_1)), I_W(B(p_2), A(p_2)), I_W(B(p_3), A(p_3)))$$
$$= \min(I_W(0, \beta'), I_W(I_W(\beta, \beta'), \beta'), I_W(1, \alpha))$$
$$= \min(1 - T_W(I_W(1 - \beta', 1 - \beta), 1 - \beta'), \alpha)$$
$$= \min(1 - \min(1 - \beta, 1 - \beta'), \alpha)$$
$$= \min(\beta, \alpha)$$
$$= \beta$$

We furthermore have

$$bb^{\ll}(A, B) = \max(T_W(1 - B(p_1), A(p_1)), T_W(1 - B(p_2), A(p_2)),$$
$$\qquad T_W(1 - B(p_3), A(p_3)))$$
$$= \max(T_W(1, \beta'), T_W(1 - I_W(\beta, \beta'), \beta'), T_W(0, \alpha))$$
$$= \max(\beta', T_W(1 - I_W(\beta, \beta'), \beta'))$$
$$= \beta'$$

$$ee^{\preccurlyeq}(A, B) = \min(I_W(A(p_5), B(p_5)), I_W(A(p_6), B(p_6)))$$
$$= \min(I_W(1, \gamma), I_W(0, \gamma'))$$
$$= \gamma$$

$$ee^{\ll}(A, B) = \max(T_W(1 - A(p_5), B(p_5)), T_W(1 - A(p_6), B(p_6)))$$
$$= \max(T_W(0, \gamma), T_W(1, \gamma'))$$
$$= \gamma'$$

Using the assumption $\delta = 0$

$$eb^{\preccurlyeq}(A, B) \leq 1 - T_W(A(p_5), B(p_3)) = 0 = \delta$$

From (5.97), we find $\delta' = 0$. Using Proposition 3.1 we have

$$eb^{\ll}(A, B) \leq eb^{\preccurlyeq}(A, B) = 0 = \delta'$$

(5) If $\delta > 0$, $\delta' = 0$, $\alpha' \geq 1 - \delta$ and $\alpha' > S_W(1 - \delta, \beta')$, A and B are defined as

$$A = \{[p_2, p_3[/I_W(\delta, \beta'), p_3/1,]p_3, p_5]/T_W(\alpha', 1 - \gamma')\}$$
$$B = \{[p_1, p_2[/1 - \beta, [p_2, p_3[/1 - \delta, p_3/1,]p_3, p_4]/\alpha',$$
$$]p_4, p_5]/T_W(\gamma, 1 - \gamma', \alpha')\}$$

The convexity of A and B follows immediately from (5.87)–(5.100). Using the assumption $\delta > 0$ and (5.100), we find $\alpha = 1$:

$$be^{\preccurlyeq}(A, B) \geq T_W(A(p_3), B(p_3)) = 1 = \alpha$$

From (2.36), (2.34) and the assumption $S_W(1 - \delta, \beta') < \alpha'$, we obtain

$$
\begin{aligned}
be&^{\ll}(A, B) \\
&= \max(T_W(B(p_3), A(p_2)), T_W(B(p_4), A(p_3)), T_W(B(p_5), A(p_3))) \\
&= \max(T_W(1, I_W(\delta, \beta')), T_W(\alpha', 1), T_W(T_W(\gamma, 1 - \gamma', \alpha'), 1)) \\
&= \max(I_W(\delta, \beta'), \alpha', T_W(\gamma, 1 - \gamma', \alpha')) \\
&= \max(I_W(\delta, \beta'), \alpha') \\
&= \max(S_W(1 - \delta, \beta'), \alpha') \\
&= \alpha'
\end{aligned}
$$

and by (2.36), we have

$$
\begin{aligned}
bb&^{\preccurlyeq}(A, B) \\
&= \min(I_W(B(p_1), A(p_1)), I_W(B(p_2), A(p_2)), I_W(B(p_3), A(p_3))) \\
&= \min(I_W(1 - \beta, 0), I_W(1 - \delta, I_W(\delta, \beta')), I_W(1, 1)) \\
&= \min(\beta, I_W(T_W(1 - \delta, \delta), \beta')) \\
&= \min(\beta, I_W(0, \beta')) \\
&= \beta
\end{aligned}
$$

From the assumption $S_W(1 - \delta, \beta') < \alpha'$, we have $S_W(1 - \delta, \beta') < 1$, and therefore $1 - \delta + \beta' < 1$ or $\beta' < \delta$. Together with (2.31), this yields

$$bb^{\ll}(A, B) = \max(T_W(1 - B(p_1), A(p_1)), T_W(1 - B(p_2), A(p_2)),$$
$$T_W(1 - B(p_3), A(p_3)))$$
$$= \max(T_W(\beta, 0), T_W(\delta, I_W(\delta, \beta')), T_W(0, 1))$$
$$= T_W(\delta, I_W(\delta, \beta'))$$
$$= \min(\delta, \beta')$$
$$= \beta'$$

We find using (2.35) and (2.31)

$$ee^{\preccurlyeq}(A, B)$$
$$= \min(I_W(A(p_3), B(p_3)), I_W(A(p_4), B(p_4)), I_W(A(p_5), B(p_5)))$$
$$= \min(I_W(1, 1), I_W(T_W(\alpha', 1 - \gamma'), \alpha'), I_W(T_W(\alpha', 1 - \gamma'),$$
$$T_W(\gamma, 1 - \gamma', \alpha')))$$
$$= I_W(T_W(\alpha', 1 - \gamma'), T_W(\gamma, 1 - \gamma', \alpha'))$$
$$= 1 - T_W(T_W(\alpha', 1 - \gamma'), I_W(T_W(\alpha', 1 - \gamma'), 1 - \gamma))$$
$$= 1 - \min(T_W(\alpha', 1 - \gamma'), 1 - \gamma)$$

$1 - \gamma \leq T_W(\alpha', 1 - \gamma')$, and therefore $ee^{\preccurlyeq}(A, B) = \gamma$, follows using (5.95) and $\alpha' \geq 1 - \delta \geq 1 - \gamma$ (by the assumption $\alpha' \geq 1 - \delta$ and (5.88))

$$1 - \gamma \leq T_W(\alpha', 1 - \gamma') \Leftrightarrow 1 - \gamma \leq \alpha' - \gamma'$$
$$\Leftrightarrow \gamma' \leq \alpha' + \gamma - 1$$
$$\Leftrightarrow \gamma' \leq T_W(\alpha', \gamma)$$

The latter equivalence holds due to (5.99) and the assumption $\alpha' \geq 1 - \delta$.

Using (2.36), (2.35), (2.31) and (5.95), we obtain

$$ee^{\ll}(A, B) = \max(T_W(1 - A(p_3), B(p_3)), T_W(1 - A(p_4), B(p_4)),$$
$$T_W(1 - A(p_5), B(p_5)))$$
$$= \max(T_W(0, 1), T_W(1 - T_W(\alpha', 1 - \gamma'), \alpha'),$$
$$T_W(1 - T_W(\alpha', 1 - \gamma'), T_W(\gamma, 1 - \gamma', \alpha')))$$
$$= T_W(1 - T_W(\alpha', 1 - \gamma'), \alpha')$$
$$= T_W(I_W(\alpha', \gamma'), \alpha')$$
$$= \min(\alpha', \gamma')$$
$$= \gamma'$$

Using (2.35), we find

$$eb^{\preccurlyeq}(A, B) = \min(1 - T_W(A(p_3), B(p_2)), 1 - T_W(A(p_4), B(p_3)),$$
$$1 - T_W(A(p_5), B(p_3)))$$
$$= \min(1 - T_W(A(p_3), B(p_2)), 1 - T_W(A(p_4), B(p_3)))$$
$$= \min(1 - T_W(1, 1 - \delta), 1 - T_W(T_W(\alpha', 1 - \gamma'), 1))$$
$$= \min(\delta, I_W(\alpha', \gamma'))$$

To establish $eb^{\preccurlyeq}(A, B) = \delta$, we need to show $\delta \leq I_W(\alpha', \gamma')$. From (5.98), we find that $\beta' < \gamma'$, since otherwise $\alpha' \leq S_W(1 - \delta, \delta', \beta') = S_W(1 - \delta, \beta')$ would hold, contradicting the assumption $\alpha' > S_W(1 - \delta, \beta')$. This furthermore implies $\alpha' \leq S_W(1 - \delta, \gamma')$. Using (2.21), this yields

$$\alpha' \leq S_W(1 - \delta, \gamma') \Leftrightarrow \alpha' \leq I_W(\delta, \gamma')$$
$$\Leftrightarrow T_W(\delta, \alpha') \leq \gamma'$$
$$\Leftrightarrow \delta \leq I_W(\alpha', \gamma')$$

Finally, we find

$$eb^{\preccurlyeq}(A, B) \leq 1 - T_W(B(p_3), A(p_3)) = 1 - T_W(1, 1) = 0 = \delta'$$

(6) If $\delta > 0$, $\delta' = 0$, $\alpha' \geq 1 - \delta$ and $\alpha' > S_W(1 - \delta, \gamma')$, A and B are defined as

$$A = \{[p_1, p_2[/T_W(\beta, 1 - \beta', \alpha'), [p_2, p_3[/\alpha', p_3/1,]p_3, p_4]/1 - \delta,$$
$$]p_4, p_5]/1 - \gamma\}$$
$$B = \{[p_1, p_3[/T_W(\alpha', 1 - \beta'), p_3/1,]p_3, p_4]/I_W(\delta, \gamma')\}$$

The convexity of A and B follows immediately from (5.87)–(5.100). We obtain

$$be^{\preccurlyeq}(A, B) \geq T_W(A(p_3), B(p_3)) = 1 = \alpha$$

and using the assumption $S_W(1 - \delta, \gamma') < \alpha'$

$$be^{\preccurlyeq}(A, B)$$
$$= \max(T_W(B(p_3), A(p_2)), T_W(B(p_4), A(p_3)), T_W(B(p_5), A(p_3)))$$
$$= \max(T_W(1, \alpha'), T_W(I_W(\delta, \gamma'), 1), T_W(0, 1))$$
$$= \max(\alpha', I_W(\delta, \gamma'))$$
$$= \max(\alpha', S_W(1 - \delta, \gamma'))$$
$$= \alpha'$$

From (2.35) and (2.31), we obtain

$bb^\preccurlyeq(A, B)$

$= \min(I_W(B(p_1), A(p_1)), I_W(B(p_2), A(p_2)), I_W(B(p_3), A(p_3)))$

$= \min(I_W(T_W(\alpha', 1 - \beta'), T_W(\beta, 1 - \beta', \alpha')),$

$\qquad I_W(T_W(\alpha', 1 - \beta'), \alpha'), I_W(1, 1))$

$= I_W(T_W(\alpha', 1 - \beta'), T_W(\beta, 1 - \beta', \alpha'))$

$= 1 - T_W(T_W(\alpha', 1 - \beta'), I_W(T_W(\alpha', 1 - \beta'), 1 - \beta))$

$= 1 - \min(T_W(\alpha', 1 - \beta'), 1 - \beta)$

To prove $bb^\preccurlyeq(A, B) = \beta$, we show $1 - \beta \leq T_W(\alpha', 1 - \beta')$. Using (5.94) and the fact that $\alpha' \geq 1 - \delta \geq 1 - \beta$ (by the assumption $\alpha' \geq 1 - \delta$ and (5.87)), we find

$$1 - \beta \leq T_W(\alpha', 1 - \beta') \Leftrightarrow 1 - \beta \leq \alpha' - \beta'$$
$$\Leftrightarrow \beta' \leq \alpha' + \beta - 1$$
$$\Leftrightarrow \beta' \leq T_W(\alpha', \beta)$$

The latter expression is satisfied by (5.92) and the assumption that $\alpha' \geq 1 - \delta$.

Next, we find using (2.35), (2.31) and (5.94)

$bb^\ll(A, B) = \max(T_W(1 - B(p_1), A(p_1)), T_W(1 - B(p_2), A(p_2)),$

$\qquad T_W(1 - B(p_3), A(p_3)))$

$= \max(T_W(1 - T_W(\alpha', 1 - \beta'), T_W(\beta, 1 - \beta', \alpha')),$

$\qquad T_W(1 - T_W(\alpha', 1 - \beta'), \alpha'), T_W(0, 1))$

$= T_W(1 - T_W(\alpha', 1 - \beta'), \alpha')$

$= T_W(I_W(\alpha', \beta'), \alpha')$

$= \min(\beta', \alpha')$

$= \beta'$

and using (2.26) and (2.36)

$ee^\preccurlyeq(A, B)$

$= \min(I_W(A(p_3), B(p_3)), I_W(A(p_4), B(p_4)), I_W(A(p_5), B(p_5)))$

$= \min(I_W(1, 1), I_W(1 - \delta, I_W(\delta, \gamma')), I_W(1 - \gamma, 0))$

$= \min(I_W(1 - \delta, I_W(\delta, \gamma')), I_W(1 - \gamma, 0))$

$= \min(I_W(T_W(1 - \delta, \delta), \gamma'), I_W(1 - \gamma, 0))$

$= \min(I_W(0, \gamma'), I_W(1 - \gamma, 0))$

$$= I_W(1 - \gamma, 0)$$
$$= \gamma$$

Note that the assumption $S_W(1 - \delta, \gamma') < \alpha'$ implies $S_W(1 - \delta, \gamma') < 1$ and therefore $1 - \delta + \gamma' < 1$, or $\gamma' < \delta$. Together with (2.31) this yields

$$ee^{\ll}(A, B) = \max(T_W(1 - A(p_3), B(p_3)), T_W(1 - A(p_4), B(p_4)),$$
$$T_W(1 - A(p_5), B(p_5)))$$
$$= \max(T_W(0, 1), T_W(\delta, I_W(\delta, \gamma')), T_W(\gamma, 0))$$
$$= T_W(\delta, I_W(\delta, \gamma'))$$
$$= \min(\delta, \gamma')$$
$$= \gamma'$$

Next, using (2.35) we find

$$eb^{\preccurlyeq}(A, B) = \min(1 - T_W(A(p_3), B(p_2)), 1 - T_W(A(p_4), B(p_3)),$$
$$1 - T_W(A(p_5), B(p_3)))$$
$$= \min(1 - T_W(A(p_3), B(p_2)), 1 - T_W(A(p_4), B(p_3)))$$
$$= \min(1 - T_W(1, T_W(\alpha', 1 - \beta')), 1 - T_W(1 - \delta, 1))$$
$$= \min(1 - T_W(\alpha', 1 - \beta'), \delta)$$
$$= \min(I_W(\alpha', \beta'), \delta)$$

Hence, $eb^{\preccurlyeq}(A, B) = \delta$ follows from $\delta \leq I_W(\alpha', \beta')$; using (2.21) and (2.34), we find

$$\delta \leq I_W(\alpha', \beta') \Leftrightarrow T_W(\delta, \alpha') \leq \beta'$$
$$\Leftrightarrow \alpha' \leq I_W(\delta, \beta')$$
$$\Leftrightarrow \alpha' \leq S_W(1 - \delta, \beta')$$

where the latter expression follows from (5.98). Indeed, (5.98) implies $\beta' > \gamma'$, since otherwise $\alpha' \leq S_W(1 - \delta, \delta', \gamma') = S_W(1 - \delta, \gamma')$ would hold, contradicting the assumption $\alpha' > S_W(1 - \delta, \gamma')$. Hence, we also have $\alpha' \leq S_W(1 - \delta, \beta')$ by (5.98).
Finally, we find

$$eb^{\ll}(A, B) \leq 1 - T_W(B(p_3), A(p_3)) = 1 - T_W(1, 1) = 0 = \delta'$$

(7) If $\delta > 0$, $\delta' = 0$, $\alpha' \geq 1 - \delta$, $\alpha' \leq S_W(1 - \delta, \min(\beta', \gamma'))$, A and B are defined as

$$A = \{[p_2, p_3 / I_W(\beta, \beta'), [p_3, p_4 / \alpha', p_4 / 1,]p_4, p_6] / 1 - \gamma\}$$
$$B = \{[p_1, p_3 / 1 - \beta, [p_3, p_4 / 1 - \delta, p_4 / 1,]p_4, p_5] / I_W(\gamma, \gamma')\}$$

To prove that B is convex, we show $\alpha' \geq I_W(\gamma, \gamma')$. Using (5.90) and $\alpha' \geq 1 - \delta \geq 1 - \gamma$ (by the assumption $\alpha' \geq 1 - \delta$ and (5.88)), we find

$$\alpha' \geq I_W(\gamma, \gamma') \Leftrightarrow \alpha' \geq 1 - \gamma + \gamma'$$
$$\Leftrightarrow \alpha' + \gamma - 1 \geq \gamma'$$
$$\Leftrightarrow T_W(\alpha', \gamma) \geq \gamma'$$

The latter expression is satisfied by (5.99) and the assumption $\alpha' \geq 1 - \delta$. In the same way, we can show $\alpha' \geq I_W(\beta, \beta')$, which is needed to establish the convexity of A. Finally, $1 - \beta \leq 1 - \delta$ follows from (5.87). We find

$$be^{\preccurlyeq}(A, B) \geq T_W(A(p_4), B(p_4)) = 1 = \alpha$$

Using the fact that $\alpha' \geq I_W(\gamma, \gamma')$, as shown above, we find

$$be^{\ll}(A, B)$$
$$= \max(T_W(B(p_4), A(p_3)), T_W(B(p_5), A(p_4)), T_W(B(p_6), A(p_4)))$$
$$= \max(T_W(B(p_4), A(p_3)), T_W(B(p_5), A(p_4)))$$
$$= \max(T_W(1, \alpha'), T_W(I_W(\gamma, \gamma'), 1))$$
$$= \max(\alpha', I_W(\gamma, \gamma'))$$
$$= \alpha'$$

From the assumption $1 - \delta \leq \alpha'$ we find $I_W(1 - \delta, \alpha') = 1$ by (2.23). This yields

$$bb^{\preccurlyeq}(A, B)$$
$$= \min(I_W(B(p_1), A(p_1)), I_W(B(p_2), A(p_2)), I_W(B(p_3), A(p_3)),$$
$$\qquad I_W(B(p_4), A(p_4)))$$
$$= \min(I_W(1 - \beta, 0), I_W(1 - \beta, I_W(\beta, \beta')), I_W(1 - \delta, \alpha'), I_W(1, 1))$$
$$= \min(I_W(1 - \beta, 0), I_W(1 - \delta, \alpha'))$$
$$= \min(\beta, 1)$$
$$= \beta$$

We find (2.31) and (5.96)

$$bb^{\ll}(A, B) = \max(T_W(1 - B(p_1), A(p_1)), T_W(1 - B(p_2), A(p_2)),$$
$$\qquad T_W(1 - B(p_3), A(p_3)), T_W(1 - B(p_4), A(p_4)))$$
$$= \max(T_W(\beta, 0), T_W(\beta, I_W(\beta, \beta')), T_W(\delta, \alpha'), T_W(0, 1))$$
$$= \max(T_W(\beta, I_W(\beta, \beta')), T_W(\delta, \alpha'))$$
$$= \max(\min(\beta, \beta'), T_W(\delta, \alpha'))$$
$$= \max(\beta', T_W(\delta, \alpha'))$$

Next we prove $\beta' \geq T_W(\delta, \alpha')$, thereby showing $bb^{\ll}(A, B) = \beta'$. If $\beta' \geq \delta$, then we clearly have $\beta' \geq T_W(\delta, \alpha')$. On the other hand, if $\beta' < \delta$, we find $S_W(1-\delta, \beta') = 1-\delta+\beta'$. Together with the assumption $\alpha' \leq S_W(1 - \delta, \min(\beta', \gamma'))$ we find

$$\alpha' \leq S_W(1 - \delta, \min(\beta', \gamma')) \Rightarrow \alpha' \leq S_W(1 - \delta, \beta')$$
$$\Leftrightarrow \alpha' \leq 1 - \delta + \beta'$$
$$\Leftrightarrow \alpha' + \delta - 1 \leq \beta'$$
$$\Leftrightarrow \max(0, \alpha' + \delta - 1) \leq \beta'$$
$$\Leftrightarrow T_W(\alpha', \delta) \leq \beta'$$

Next, we find

$$ee^{\prec}(A, B)$$
$$= \min(I_W(A(p_4), B(p_4)), I_W(A(p_5), B(p_5)), I_W(A(p_6), B(p_6)))$$
$$= \min(I_W(1, 1), I_W(1 - \gamma, I_W(\gamma, \gamma')), I_W(1 - \gamma, 0))$$
$$= I_W(1 - \gamma, 0)$$
$$= \gamma$$

Using (2.31) and (5.90), we obtain

$$ee^{\ll}(A, B) = \max(T_W(1 - A(p_4), B(p_4)), T_W(1 - A(p_5), B(p_5)),$$
$$T_W(1 - A(p_6), B(p_6)))$$
$$= \max(T_W(0, 1), T_W(\gamma, I_W(\gamma, \gamma')), T_W(\gamma, 0))$$
$$= T_W(\gamma, I_W(\gamma, \gamma'))$$
$$= \min(\gamma, \gamma')$$
$$= \gamma'$$

and using (5.88)

$$eb^{\prec}(A, B) = \min(1 - T_W(A(p_4), B(p_3)), 1 - T_W(A(p_5), B(p_4)),$$
$$1 - T_W(A(p_6), B(p_4)))$$
$$= \min(1 - T_W(A(p_4), B(p_3)), 1 - T_W(A(p_5), B(p_4)))$$
$$= \min(1 - T_W(1, 1 - \delta), 1 - T_W(1 - \gamma, 1))$$
$$= \min(\delta, \gamma)$$
$$= \delta$$

Finally, we find

$$eb^{\ll}(A, B) \leq 1 - T_W(B(p_4), A(p_4)) = 1 - T_W(1, 1) = 0 = \delta'$$

(8) If $\delta > 0$, $\delta' = 0$, $\alpha' < 1 - \delta$ and $\beta \leq \gamma$, A and B are defined as
$$A = \{[p_1, p_2[/\beta', [p_2, p_3[/T_W(\beta, 1 - \delta), [p_3, p_4[/\alpha', p_4/1,$$
$$]p_4, p_5]/I_W(\gamma, \gamma')\}$$
$$B = \{[p_2, p_4[/1 - \delta, p_4/1,]p_4, p_6]/\gamma'\}$$

To prove the convexity of A, we show $\beta' \leq T_W(\beta, 1-\delta) \leq \alpha'$. From the assumption that $\alpha' < 1-\delta$ and (5.92) we already have $\beta' \leq T_W(\beta, 1-\delta)$, while $T_W(\beta, 1 - \delta) \leq \alpha'$ follows from (5.91) and the fact that $\alpha = 1$. We find
$$be^{\preccurlyeq}(A, B) \geq T_W(A(p_4), B(p_4)) = 1 = \alpha$$
From (5.95) we obtain
$$be^{\ll}(A, B)$$
$$= \max(T_W(B(p_4), A(p_3)), T_W(B(p_5), A(p_4)), T_W(B(p_6), A(p_4)))$$
$$= \max(T_W(B(p_4), A(p_3)), T_W(B(p_5), A(p_4)))$$
$$= \max(T_W(1, \alpha'), T_W(\gamma', 1))$$
$$= \max(\alpha', \gamma')$$
$$= \alpha'$$
By (2.35), (2.31) and (5.87) we find
$$bb^{\preccurlyeq}(A, B)$$
$$= \min(I_W(B(p_1), A(p_1)), I_W(B(p_2), A(p_2)), I_W(B(p_3), A(p_3)),$$
$$I_W(B(p_4), A(p_4)))$$
$$= \min(I_W(0, \beta'), I_W(1 - \delta, T_W(\beta, 1 - \delta)), I_W(1 - \delta, \alpha'), I_W(1, 1))$$
$$= I_W(1 - \delta, T_W(\beta, 1 - \delta))$$
$$= 1 - T_W(1 - \delta, I_W(1 - \delta, 1 - \beta))$$
$$= 1 - \min(1 - \delta, 1 - \beta)$$
$$= \max(\delta, \beta)$$
$$= \beta$$
Using (2.36) we obtain $T_W(\delta, T_W(\beta, 1 - \delta)) \leq T_W(\delta, 1 - \delta) = 0$, and, additionally using the assumption $\alpha' < 1-\delta$, $T_W(\delta, \alpha') \leq T_W(\delta, 1-\delta) = 0$. This yields
$$bb^{\ll}(A, B) = \max(T_W(1 - B(p_1), A(p_1)), T_W(1 - B(p_2), A(p_2)),$$
$$T_W(1 - B(p_3), A(p_3)), T_W(1 - B(p_4), A(p_4)))$$
$$= \max(T_W(1, \beta'), T_W(\delta, T_W(\beta, 1 - \delta)), T_W(\delta, \alpha'), T_W(0, 1))$$
$$= \max(\beta', T_W(\delta, \alpha'))$$
$$= \beta'$$

From (2.35), (2.31) and (5.90)

$$ee^{\preccurlyeq}(A,B)$$
$$= \min(I_W(A(p_4), B(p_4)), I_W(A(p_5), B(p_5)), I_W(A(p_6), B(p_6)))$$
$$= \min(I_W(1,1), I_W(I_W(\gamma, \gamma'), \gamma'), I_W(0, \gamma'))$$
$$= I_W(I_W(\gamma, \gamma'), \gamma')$$
$$= 1 - T_W(I_W(\gamma, \gamma'), 1 - \gamma')$$
$$= 1 - T_W(I_W(1 - \gamma', 1 - \gamma), 1 - \gamma')$$
$$= 1 - \min(1 - \gamma', 1 - \gamma)$$
$$= \max(\gamma', \gamma)$$
$$= \gamma$$

Using (2.35) and (2.36) we have

$$ee^{\ll}(A,B) = \max(T_W(1 - A(p_4), B(p_4)), T_W(1 - A(p_5), B(p_5)),$$
$$T_W(1 - A(p_6), B(p_6)))$$
$$= \max(T_W(0,1), T_W(1 - I_W(\gamma, \gamma'), \gamma'), T_W(1, \gamma'))$$
$$= \max(T_W(T_W(\gamma, 1 - \gamma'), \gamma'), T_W(1, \gamma'))$$
$$= T_W(1, \gamma')$$
$$= \gamma'$$

$$eb^{\preccurlyeq}(A,B) = \min(1 - T_W(A(p_4), B(p_3)), 1 - T_W(A(p_5), B(p_4)),$$
$$1 - T_W(A(p_6), B(p_4)))$$
$$= \min(1 - T_W(A(p_4), B(p_3)), 1 - T_W(A(p_5), B(p_4)))$$
$$= \min(1 - T_W(1, 1 - \delta), 1 - T_W(I_W(\gamma, \gamma'), 1))$$
$$= \min(\delta, 1 - I_W(\gamma, \gamma'))$$

To show $\delta \leq 1 - I_W(\gamma, \gamma')$ we find using (5.90) and (5.88)

$$\delta \leq 1 - I_W(\gamma, \gamma') \Leftrightarrow \delta \leq \gamma - \gamma'$$
$$\Leftrightarrow 1 - \delta + \gamma - 1 \geq \gamma'$$
$$\Leftrightarrow T_W(1 - \delta, \gamma) \geq \gamma'$$

The latter expression is satisfied due to (5.99) and the assumption $\alpha' < 1 - \delta$. Finally, we find

$$eb^{\ll}(A,B) \leq 1 - T_W(B(p_4), A(p_4)) = 1 - T_W(1,1) = 0 = \delta'$$

(9) If $\delta > 0$, $\delta' = 0$, $\alpha' < 1 - \delta$ and $\beta > \gamma$, A and B are defined as

$$A = \{[p_1, p_3[/\beta', p_3/1,]p_3, p_5]/1 - \delta\}$$

$$B = \{[p_2, p_3[/I_W(\beta, \beta'), p_3/1,]p_3, p_4]/\alpha',]p_4, p_5]/T_W(\gamma, 1 - \delta),$$
$$]p_5, p_6]/\gamma'\}$$

To prove the convexity of B, we show $\gamma' \leq T_W(\gamma, 1 - \delta) \leq \alpha'$. From (5.99) and the assumption $\alpha' < 1 - \delta$ we already have $\gamma' \leq T_W(\gamma, 1 - \delta)$, while $T_W(\gamma, 1 - \delta) \leq \alpha'$ follows from (5.91) and the fact that $\alpha = 1$. We find

$$be^{\preccurlyeq}(A, B) \geq T_W(A(p_3), B(p_3)) = 1 = \alpha$$

From (5.94) we find

$$be^{\ll}(A, B)$$
$$= \max(T_W(B(p_3), A(p_2)), T_W(B(p_4), A(p_3)), T_W(B(p_5), A(p_3)),$$
$$\quad T_W(B(p_6), A(p_3)))$$
$$= \max(T_W(B(p_3), A(p_2)), T_W(B(p_4), A(p_3)))$$
$$= \max(T_W(1, \beta'), T_W(\alpha', 1))$$
$$= \max(\beta', \alpha')$$
$$= \alpha'$$

Using (2.35), (2.33) and (2.31) we find

$$bb^{\preccurlyeq}(A, B)$$
$$= \min(I_W(B(p_1), A(p_1)), I_W(B(p_2), A(p_2)), I_W(B(p_3), A(p_3)))$$
$$= \min(I_W(0, \beta'), I_W(I_W(\beta, \beta'), \beta'), I_W(1, 1))$$
$$= I_W(I_W(\beta, \beta'), \beta')$$
$$= 1 - T_W(I_W(\beta, \beta'), 1 - \beta')$$
$$= 1 - T_W(I_W(1 - \beta', 1 - \beta), 1 - \beta')$$
$$= 1 - \min(1 - \beta, 1 - \beta')$$
$$= \beta$$

and using (2.35) and (2.36) we obtain

$$bb^{\ll}(A, B) = \max(T_W(1 - B(p_1), A(p_1)), T_W(1 - B(p_2), A(p_2)),$$
$$\quad T_W(1 - B(p_3), A(p_3)))$$
$$= \max(T_W(1, \beta'), T_W(1 - I_W(\beta, \beta'), \beta'), T_W(0, 1))$$
$$= \max(\beta', T_W(1 - I_W(\beta, \beta'), \beta'))$$
$$= \max(\beta', T_W(T_W(\beta, 1 - \beta'), \beta'))$$
$$= \beta'$$

From (5.91), (2.35), (2.31) and (5.88), we find

$$ee^{\preccurlyeq}(A, B)$$

$$= \min(I_W(A(p_3), B(p_3)), I_W(A(p_4), B(p_4)), I_W(A(p_5), B(p_5)),$$
$$\qquad I_W(A(p_6), B(p_6)))$$

$$= \min(I_W(1, 1), I_W(1 - \delta, \alpha'), I_W(1 - \delta, T_W(\gamma, 1 - \delta)), I_W(0, \gamma'))$$

$$= \min(I_W(1 - \delta, \alpha'), I_W(1 - \delta, T_W(\gamma, 1 - \delta)))$$

$$= I_W(1 - \delta, T_W(\gamma, 1 - \delta))$$

$$= 1 - T_W(1 - \delta, I_W(\gamma, \delta))$$

$$= 1 - T_W(1 - \delta, I_W(1 - \delta, 1 - \gamma))$$

$$= 1 - \min(1 - \delta, 1 - \gamma)$$

$$= \gamma$$

Note that $T_W(\delta, \alpha') \leq T_W(\delta, 1 - \delta) = 0$ due to (2.36) and the assumption that $\alpha' < 1 - \delta$. Together with (2.36) this yields

$$ee^{\preccurlyeq}(A, B) = \max(T_W(1 - A(p_3), B(p_3)), T_W(1 - A(p_4), B(p_4)),$$
$$\qquad T_W(1 - A(p_5), B(p_5)), T_W(1 - A(p_6), B(p_6)))$$

$$= \max(T_W(0, 1), T_W(\delta, \alpha'), T_W(\delta, T_W(\gamma, 1 - \delta)), T_W(1, \gamma'))$$

$$= \max(T_W(\delta, \alpha'), T_W(1, \gamma'))$$

$$= \max(T_W(\delta, \alpha'), \gamma')$$

$$= \max(0, \gamma')$$

$$= \gamma'$$

We furthermore have

$$eb^{\preccurlyeq}(A, B) = \min(1 - T_W(A(p_3), B(p_2)), 1 - T_W(A(p_4), B(p_3)),$$
$$\qquad 1 - T_W(A(p_5), B(p_3)), 1 - T_W(A(p_6), B(p_3)))$$

$$= \min(1 - T_W(A(p_3), B(p_2)), 1 - T_W(A(p_4), B(p_3)))$$

$$= \min(1 - T_W(1, I_W(\beta, \beta')), 1 - T_W(1 - \delta, 1))$$

$$= \min(1 - I_W(\beta, \beta'), \delta)$$

To show $\delta \leq 1 - I_W(\beta, \beta')$, we find using (5.96) and (5.87)

$$\delta \leq 1 - I_W(\beta, \beta') \Leftrightarrow \delta \leq \beta - \beta'$$
$$\Leftrightarrow 1 - \delta + \beta - 1 \geq \beta'$$
$$\Leftrightarrow T_W(1 - \delta, \beta) \geq \beta'$$

where the latter inequality holds because of (5.92). Finally, we obtain

$$eb^{\preccurlyeq}(A, B) \leq 1 - T_W(B(p_3), A(p_3)) = 1 - T_W(1, 1) = 0 = \delta'$$

Appendix B

Proof of Proposition 5.10

The proof proceeds by a case analysis on the values of δ_1 ($\delta_1 = 0$ or $\delta_1 > 0$) and δ_2 ($\delta_2 = 0$ or $\delta_2 > 0$). To show this proposition, for each case, we present a constructive proof by defining fuzzy time intervals A, B and C that satisfy the restrictions (5.111)–(5.118) and the restriction that $be^\preccurlyeq(A,C) = \alpha_3$. In addition, we define fuzzy time intervals satisfying (5.111)–(5.118) and the restriction that $bb^\preccurlyeq(A,C) = \beta_3$, and similar for the restrictions $ee^\preccurlyeq(A,C) = \gamma_3$ and $eb^\preccurlyeq(A,C) = \delta_3$.

B.1 $\delta_1 = \delta_2 = 0$

B.1.1   *Restrictions for $be^\preccurlyeq(A,C)$ and $eb^\preccurlyeq(A,C)$*

First we show that the restrictions on $be^\preccurlyeq(A,C)$ and $eb^\preccurlyeq(A,C)$ can always be satisfied. In particular, let A, B and C be defined as follows

$$A = \{[p_1, p_4[/T_W(\beta_1, \alpha_2), [p_4, p_7[/\beta_1, p_7/1\}$$
$$B = \{[p_2, p_5[/\alpha_2, p_5/1,]p_5, p_8]/\alpha_1\}$$
$$C = \{p_3/1,]p_3, p_6]/\gamma_2,]p_6, p_9]/T_W(\alpha_1, \gamma_2)\}$$

where $p_1 < p_2 < \cdots < p_9$ are real numbers. Clearly, A, B and C are fuzzy time intervals. First, we verify that (5.111)–(5.118) are satisfied. We find

$$be^\preccurlyeq(A,B) \geq T_W(A(p_7), B(p_7)) = \alpha_1$$

Using Lemma 4.13 we obtain

$bb^\preccurlyeq(A,B)$
$$= \min(I_W(B(p_1), A(p_1)), I_W(B(p_2), A(p_2)), I_W(B(p_4), A(p_4)),$$
$$I_W(B(p_5), A(p_5)))$$

$$= \min(I_W(0, T_W(\beta_1, \alpha_2)), I_W(\alpha_2, T_W(\beta_1, \alpha_2)), I_W(\alpha_2, \beta_1), I_W(1, \beta_1))$$
$$= \min(I_W(\alpha_2, T_W(\beta_1, \alpha_2)), I_W(1, \beta_1))$$
$$= \min(I_W(\alpha_2, T_W(\beta_1, \alpha_2)), \beta_1)$$

Using (2.35), (2.33) and (2.31) we find

$$= \min(I_W(\alpha_2, 1 - I_W(\beta_1, 1 - \alpha_2)), \beta_1)$$
$$= \min(1 - T_W(\alpha_2, I_W(\beta_1, 1 - \alpha_2)), \beta_1)$$
$$= \min(1 - T_W(\alpha_2, I_W(\alpha_2, 1 - \beta_1)), \beta_1)$$
$$= \min(1 - \min(\alpha_2, 1 - \beta_1), \beta_1)$$
$$= \min(\max(1 - \alpha_1, \beta_1), \beta_1)$$
$$= \beta_1$$

Next, we find (still using Lemma 4.13)

$$ee^{\preccurlyeq}(A, B) = \min(I_W(A(p_7), B(p_7)), I_W(A(p_8), B(p_8)))$$
$$= \min(I_W(1, \alpha_1), I_W(0, \alpha_1))$$
$$= \alpha_1$$
$$\geq \gamma_1$$

and

$$eb^{\preccurlyeq}(A, B) \leq 1 - T_W(A(p_7), B(p_5)) = 1 - T_W(1, 1) = 0$$

$$be^{\preccurlyeq}(B, C) \geq T_W(B(p_3), C(p_3)) = \alpha_2$$

$$bb^{\preccurlyeq}(B, C) = \min(I_W(C(p_2), B(p_2)), I_W(C(p_3), B(p_3)))$$
$$= \min(I_W(0, \alpha_2), I_W(1, \alpha_2))$$
$$= \alpha_2$$
$$\geq \beta_2$$

$$ee^{\preccurlyeq}(B, C)$$
$$= \min(I_W(B(p_5), C(p_5)), I_W(B(p_6), C(p_6)), I_W(B(p_8), C(p_8)),$$
$$\qquad I_W(B(p_9), C(p_9)))$$
$$= \min(I_W(1, \gamma_2), I_W(\alpha_1, \gamma_2), I_W(\alpha_1, T_W(\alpha_1, \gamma_2)), I_W(0, T_W(\alpha_1, \gamma_2)))$$
$$= \min(\gamma_2, I_W(\alpha_1, T_W(\alpha_1, \gamma_2)))$$

and using (2.35) and (2.31)

$$\begin{aligned}
&= \min(\gamma_2, I_W(\alpha_1, 1 - I_W(\alpha_1, 1 - \gamma_2))) \\
&= \min(\gamma_2, 1 - T_W(\alpha_1, I_W(\alpha_1, 1 - \gamma_2))) \\
&= \min(\gamma_2, 1 - \min(\alpha_1, 1 - \gamma_2)) \\
&= \min(\gamma_2, \max(1 - \alpha_1, \gamma_2)) \\
&= \gamma_2
\end{aligned}$$

$$eb^{\preccurlyeq}(B, C) \le 1 - T_W(B(p_5), C(p_3)) = 1 - T_W(1, 1) = 0$$

Next, we show that A and C satisfy the restrictions for $be^{\preccurlyeq}(A, C)$ and $eb^{\preccurlyeq}(A, C)$. By Lemma 4.13, we have

$$\begin{aligned}
be^{\preccurlyeq}(A, C) &= \max(T_W(A(p_1), C(p_3)), T_W(A(p_3), C(p_3)), T_W(A(p_4), C(p_4)), \\
&\qquad T_W(A(p_6), C(p_6)), T_W(A(p_7), C(p_7))) \\
&= \max(T_W(T_W(\beta_1, \alpha_2), 1), T_W(\beta_1, \gamma_2), T_W(1, T_W(\alpha_1, \gamma_2))) \\
&= \max(T_W(\beta_1, \alpha_2), T_W(\beta_1, \gamma_2), T_W(\alpha_1, \gamma_2)) \\
&= \max(T_W(\beta_1, \alpha_2), T_W(\alpha_1, \gamma_2))
\end{aligned}$$

which equals α_3 since $T_W(\alpha_1, \delta_2) = T_W(\alpha_1, 0) = 0$ and $T_W(\delta_1, \alpha_2) = T_W(0, \alpha_2) = 0$. Using Lemma 4.13, we obtain

$$eb^{\preccurlyeq}(A, C) \le 1 - T_W(A(p_7), C(p_3)) = 0$$

B.1.2 *Restrictions for $bb^{\preccurlyeq}(A, C)$ and $ee^{\preccurlyeq}(A, C)$*

To show that the restrictions for $bb^{\preccurlyeq}(A, C)$ and $ee^{\preccurlyeq}(A, C)$ can be satisfied as well, we define A, B and C as follows

$$\begin{aligned}
A &= \{[p_1, p_4[/T_W(\beta_1, \beta_2), [p_4, p_8[/\beta_1, [p_8, p_{10}[/\alpha_1, [p_{10}, p_{12}]/1\} \\
B &= \{[p_2, p_6[/\beta_2, [p_6, p_9[/1,]p_9, p_{13}]/\gamma_1\} \\
C &= \{[p_3, p_5]/1,]p_5, p_7]/\alpha_2,]p_7, p_{11}]/\gamma_2,]p_{11}, p_{14}]/T_W(\gamma_1, \gamma_2)\}
\end{aligned}$$

where $p_1 < p_2 < \cdots < p_{14}$ are real numbers. Again we first verify that (5.111)–(5.118) are satisfied. We obtain

$$be^{\preccurlyeq}(A, B) \ge T_W(A(p_8), B(p_8)) = T_W(\alpha_1, 1) = \alpha_1$$

Using (2.35) and (2.31), we find

$bb^{\preccurlyeq}(A, B)$

$= \min(I_W(B(p_1), A(p_1)), I_W(B(p_2), A(p_2)), I_W(B(p_4), A(p_4)),$
$\qquad I_W(B(p_6), A(p_6)))$

$= \min(I_W(0, T_W(\beta_1, \beta_2)), I_W(\beta_2, T_W(\beta_1, \beta_2)), I_W(\beta_2, \beta_1), I_W(1, \beta_1))$

$= \min(I_W(\beta_2, T_W(\beta_1, \beta_2)), \beta_1)$

$= \min(I_W(\beta_2, 1 - I_W(\beta_1, 1 - \beta_2)), \beta_1)$

$= \min(1 - T_W(\beta_2, I_W(\beta_1, 1 - \beta_2)), \beta_1)$

$= \min(1 - \min(\beta_2, 1 - \beta_1), \beta_1)$

$= \min(\max(1 - \beta_2, \beta_1), \beta_1)$

$= \beta_1$

$$ee^{\preccurlyeq}(A, B) = \min(I_W(A(p_{12}), B(p_{12})), I_W(A(p_{13}), B(p_{13})))$$
$$= \min(I_W(1, \gamma_1), I_W(0, \gamma_1))$$
$$= \gamma_1$$

$$eb^{\preccurlyeq}(A, B) \leq 1 - T_W(A(p_{10}), B(p_9)) = 1 - T_W(1, 1) = 0$$

$$be^{\preccurlyeq}(B, C) \geq T_W(B(p_6), C(p_6)) = \alpha_2$$

$$bb^{\preccurlyeq}(B, C) = \min(I_W(C(p_2), B(p_2)), I_W(C(p_3), B(p_3)))$$
$$= \min(I_W(0, \beta_2), I_W(1, \beta_2))$$
$$= \beta_2$$

Using (2.35) and (2.31), we find

$ee^{\preccurlyeq}(B, C)$

$= \min(I_W(B(p_9), C(p_9)), I_W(B(p_{11}), C(p_{11})), I_W(B(p_{13}), C(p_{13})),$
$\qquad I_W(B(p_{14}), C(p_{14})))$

$= \min(I_W(1, \gamma_2), I_W(\gamma_1, \gamma_2), I_W(\gamma_1, T_W(\gamma_1, \gamma_2)), I_W(0, T_W(\gamma_1, \gamma_2)))$

$= \min(\gamma_2, I_W(\gamma_1, T_W(\gamma_1, \gamma_2)))$

$= \min(\gamma_2, I_W(\gamma_1, 1 - I_W(\gamma_1, 1 - \gamma_2)))$

$$= \min(\gamma_2, 1 - T_W(\gamma_1, I_W(\gamma_1, 1 - \gamma_2)))$$
$$= \min(\gamma_2, 1 - \min(\gamma_1, 1 - \gamma_2))$$
$$= \min(\gamma_2, \max(1 - \gamma_1, \gamma_2))$$
$$= \gamma_2$$

$$eb^{\preccurlyeq}(B, C) \leq 1 - T_W(B(p_6), C(p_5)) = 1 - T_W(1, 1) = 0$$

Thus we already have that (5.111)–(5.118) are satisfied. To show that the restriction for $bb^{\preccurlyeq}(A, C)$ is satisfied, we obtain

$$
\begin{aligned}
bb^{\preccurlyeq}(A, C) &= \min(I_W(C(p_1), A(p_1)), I_W(C(p_3), A(p_3))) \\
&= \min(I_W(0, T_W(\beta_1, \beta_2)), I_W(1, T_W(\beta_1, \beta_2))) \\
&= T_W(\beta_1, \beta_2) \\
&= \max(T_W(\beta_1, \beta_2), 0) \\
&= \max(T_W(\beta_1, \beta_2), \min(\alpha_1 + T_W(\delta_2, \gamma_1), 0, \beta_1 + T_W(\delta_2, \alpha_1))) \\
&= \max(T_W(\beta_1, \beta_2), \min(\alpha_1 + T_W(\delta_2, \gamma_1), \delta_2, \beta_1 + T_W(\delta_2, \alpha_1)))
\end{aligned}
$$

and for $ee^{\preccurlyeq}(A, C)$

$$
\begin{aligned}
ee^{\preccurlyeq}(A, C) &= \min(I_W(A(p_{12}), C(p_{12})), I_W(A(p_{14}), C(p_{14}))) \\
&= \min(I_W(1, T_W(\gamma_1, \gamma_2)), I_W(0, T_W(\gamma_1, \gamma_2))) \\
&= T_W(\gamma_1, \gamma_2) \\
&= \max(T_W(\gamma_1, \gamma_2), \min(\alpha_2 + T_W(\delta_1, \beta_2), \delta_1, \gamma_2 + T_W(\delta_1, \alpha_2)))
\end{aligned}
$$

B.2 $\delta_1 = 0, \delta_2 > 0$

B.2.1   *Restriction for* $be^{\preccurlyeq}(A, C)$

First we show that the restriction for $be^{\preccurlyeq}(A, C)$ can be satisfied when $\delta_1 = 0$ and $\delta_2 > 0$. We separately consider the cases where $1 - \delta_2 \geq \alpha_1$ and $1 - \delta_2 < \alpha_1$.

B.2.1.1   *Assuming* $1 - \delta_2 \geq \alpha_1$

Let A, B and C be defined as

$$A = \{[p_1, p_6[/\beta_1, p_6/1\}$$
$$B = \{p_2/1,]p_2, p_4]/1 - \delta_2,]p_4, p_7]/\alpha_1\}$$
$$C = \{p_3/1,]p_3, p_5]/\gamma_2,]p_5, p_8]/T_W(\alpha_1, \gamma_2)\}$$

where $p_1 < p_2 < \cdots < p_8$ are real numbers. Clearly, A, B and C are fuzzy time intervals, considering the assumption $1 - \delta_2 \geq \alpha_1$. We find

$$be^{\preccurlyeq}(A, B)$$
$$= \max(T_W(A(p_1), B(p_2)), T_W(A(p_2), B(p_2)), T_W(A(p_4), B(p_4)),$$
$$\quad T_W(A(p_6), B(p_6)))$$
$$= \max(T_W(\beta_1, 1), T_W(\beta_1, 1), T_W(\beta_1, 1 - \delta_2), T_W(1, \alpha_1))$$
$$= \max(T_W(\beta_1, 1), T_W(1, \alpha_1))$$
$$= \max(\beta_1, \alpha_1)$$
$$\geq \alpha_1$$

$$bb^{\preccurlyeq}(A, B) = \min(I_W(B(p_1), A(p_1)), I_W(B(p_2), A(p_2)))$$
$$= \min(I_W(0, \beta_1), I_W(1, \beta_1))$$
$$= I_W(1, \beta_1)$$
$$= \beta_1$$

$$ee^{\preccurlyeq}(A, B) = \min(I_W(A(p_6), B(p_6)), I_W(A(p_7), B(p_7)))$$
$$= \min(I_W(1, \alpha_1), I_W(0, \alpha_1))$$
$$= \alpha_1$$
$$\geq \gamma_1$$

$$eb^{\preccurlyeq}(A, B) = \min(1 - T_W(A(p_6), B(p_2)), 1 - T_W(A(p_7), B(p_2)))$$
$$= \min(1 - T_W(1, 1), 1 - T_W(0, 1))$$
$$= 0$$
$$= \delta_1$$

$$be^{\preccurlyeq}(B, C) \geq T_W(B(p_2), C(p_3)) = T_W(1, 1) = 1 = \alpha_2$$

where $\alpha_2 = 1$ because of our assumption that $\delta_2 > 0$.

$$bb^{\preccurlyeq}(B, C) = I_W(C(p_2), B(p_2)) = 1 \geq \beta_2$$

$ee^{\preccurlyeq}(B, C)$

$= \min(I_W(B(p_3), C(p_3)), I_W(B(p_4), C(p_4)), I_W(B(p_5), C(p_5)),$
$\qquad I_W(B(p_7), C(p_7)), I_W(B(p_8), C(p_8)))$

$= \min(I_W(1 - \delta_2, 1), I_W(1 - \delta_2, \gamma_2), I_W(\alpha_1, \gamma_2), I_W(\alpha_1, T_W(\alpha_1, \gamma_2)),$
$\qquad I_W(0, T_W(\alpha_1, \gamma_2)))$

$= \min(I_W(1 - \delta_2, \gamma_2), I_W(\alpha_1, T_W(\alpha_1, \gamma_2)))$

Using (2.35) and (2.31), we find

$\qquad = \min(I_W(1 - \delta_2, \gamma_2), I_W(\alpha_1, 1 - I_W(\alpha_1, 1 - \gamma_2)))$

$\qquad = \min(I_W(1 - \delta_2, \gamma_2), 1 - T_W(\alpha_1, I_W(\alpha_1, 1 - \gamma_2)))$

$\qquad = \min(I_W(1 - \delta_2, \gamma_2), 1 - \min(\alpha_1, 1 - \gamma_2))$

$\qquad = \min(I_W(1 - \delta_2, \gamma_2), \max(1 - \alpha_1, \gamma_2))$

$\qquad \geq \min(I_W(1 - \delta_2, \gamma_2), \gamma_2)$

$\qquad = \gamma_2$

$eb^{\preccurlyeq}(B, C) = \min(1 - T_W(B(p_2), C(p_1)), 1 - T_W(B(p_3), C(p_2)),$
$\qquad\qquad 1 - T_W(B(p_4), C(p_3)), 1 - T_W(B(p_5), C(p_3)),$
$\qquad\qquad 1 - T_W(B(p_7), C(p_3)), 1 - T_W(B(p_8), C(p_3)))$

$\qquad = \min(1 - T_W(B(p_2), C(p_1)), 1 - T_W(B(p_3), C(p_2)),$
$\qquad\qquad 1 - T_W(B(p_4), C(p_3)))$

$\qquad = \min(1 - T_W(1, 0), 1 - T_W(1 - \delta_2, 0), 1 - T_W(1 - \delta_2, 1))$

$\qquad = \delta_2$

We already have that (5.111)–(5.118) are satisfied. To show that the restriction for $be^{\preccurlyeq}(A, C)$ is satisfied, we find

$be^{\preccurlyeq}(A, C)$

$= \max(T_W(A(p_1), C(p_3)), T_W(A(p_3), C(p_3)), T_W(A(p_5), C(p_5)),$
$\qquad T_W(A(p_6), C(p_6)))$

$= \max(T_W(\beta_1, 1), T_W(\beta_1, 1), T_W(\beta_1, \gamma_2), T_W(1, T_W(\alpha_1, \gamma_2)))$

$= \max(\beta_1, T_W(\beta_1, \gamma_2), T_W(\alpha_1, \gamma_2))$

$= \max(\beta_1, T_W(\alpha_1, \gamma_2))$

From $\delta_2 > 0$, we find $\alpha_2 = 1$, hence

$\qquad = \max(T_W(\beta_1, \alpha_2), T_W(\alpha_1, \gamma_2))$

$\qquad = \alpha_3$

B.2.1.2   *Assuming $1 - \delta_2 < \alpha_1$ and $1 - \delta_2 < \gamma_1$*

In this case, it holds that $T_W(\gamma_1, \delta_2) > 0$. For any A, B and C satisfying (5.111)–(5.118), it will then hold that

$$eb^{\preccurlyeq}(A,C) \geq T_W(ee^{\preccurlyeq}(A,B), eb^{\preccurlyeq}(B,C)) \geq T_W(\gamma_1, \delta_2) > 0$$

and, hence, $be^{\preccurlyeq}(A,C) = 1 = \alpha_3$ by Corollary 5.4.

B.2.1.3   *Assuming $1 - \delta_2 < \alpha_1$ and $1 - \delta_2 \geq \gamma_1$*

If $1 - \delta_2 < \alpha_1$ and $1 - \delta_2 \geq \gamma_1$, we show that the restriction for $be^{\preccurlyeq}(A,C)$ is satisfied by

$$A = \{[p_1, p_4[/\alpha_1, p_4/1\}$$
$$B = \{p_2/1,]p_2, p_5]/\gamma_1\}$$
$$C = \{p_3/1,]p_3, p_5]/T_W(\gamma_1, \gamma_2)\}$$

where $p_1 < p_2 < \cdots < p_5$ are real numbers. A, B and C are clearly convex. We obtain

$$\begin{aligned}
be^{\preccurlyeq}(A,B) &= \max(T_W(A(p_1), B(p_2)), T_W(A(p_2), B(p_2)), T_W(A(p_4), B(p_4))) \\
&= \max(T_W(\alpha_1, 1), T_W(\alpha_1, 1), T_W(1, \gamma_1)) \\
&= \max(\alpha_1, \gamma_1) \\
&= \alpha_1
\end{aligned}$$

$$\begin{aligned}
bb^{\preccurlyeq}(A,B) &= \min(I_W(B(p_1), A(p_1)), I_W(B(p_2), A(p_2))) \\
&= \min(I_W(0, \alpha_1), I_W(1, \alpha_1)) \\
&= \alpha_1 \\
&\geq \beta_1
\end{aligned}$$

$$\begin{aligned}
ee^{\preccurlyeq}(A,B) &= \min(I_W(A(p_4), B(p_4)), I_W(A(p_5), B(p_5))) \\
&= \min(I_W(1, \gamma_1), I_W(0, \gamma_1)) \\
&= \gamma_1
\end{aligned}$$

$$\begin{aligned}
eb^{\preccurlyeq}(A,B) &= \min(1 - T_W(A(p_4), B(p_2)), 1 - T_W(A(p_5), B(p_2))) \\
&= \min(1 - T_W(1, 1), 1 - T_W(0, 1)) \\
&= 0 \\
&= \delta_1
\end{aligned}$$

$$be^{\preceq}(B,C) = T_W(B(p_2), C(p_3)) = 1$$

$$bb^{\preceq}(B,C)) = I_W(C(p_2), B(p_2)) = I_W(0,1) = 1 \geq \beta_2$$

By (2.35) and (2.31), we find

$$
\begin{aligned}
ee^{\preceq}(B,C) &= \min(I_W(B(p_3), C(p_3)), I_W(B(p_4), C(p_4))) \\
&= \min(I_W(\gamma_1, 1), I_W(\gamma_1, T_W(\gamma_1, \gamma_2))) \\
&= I_W(\gamma_1, T_W(\gamma_1, \gamma_2)) \\
&= I_W(\gamma_1, 1 - I_W(\gamma_1, 1 - \gamma_2)) \\
&= 1 - T_W(\gamma_1, I_W(\gamma_1, 1 - \gamma_2)) \\
&= 1 - \min(\gamma_1, 1 - \gamma_2) \\
&= \max(1 - \gamma_1, \gamma_2) \\
&\geq \gamma_2
\end{aligned}
$$

Using the assumption $1 - \delta_2 \geq \gamma_1$, we find

$$
\begin{aligned}
&eb^{\preceq}(B,C) \\
&= \min(1 - T_W(B(p_2), C(p_1)), 1 - T_W(B(p_3), C(p_2)), \\
&\qquad 1 - T_W(B(p_5), C(p_3))) \\
&= \min(1 - T_W(1,0), 1 - T_W(\gamma_1, 0), 1 - T_W(\gamma_1, 1)) \\
&= 1 - \gamma_1 \\
&\geq \delta_2
\end{aligned}
$$

Hence, (5.111)–(5.118) are satisfied. For $be^{\preceq}(A,C)$, we obtain

$$
\begin{aligned}
be^{\preceq}(A,C) &= \max(T_W(A(p_1), C(p_3)), T_W(A(p_3), C(p_3)), \\
&\qquad T_W(A(p_4), C(p_4))) \\
&= \max(T_W(\alpha_1, 1), T_W(\alpha_1, 1), T_W(1, T_W(\gamma_1, \gamma_2))) \\
&= \alpha_1
\end{aligned}
$$

By assumption, $\delta_2 > 0$ implies $\alpha_2 = 1$. Thus we obtain

$$
\begin{aligned}
&= \min(\alpha_1, \alpha_2) \\
&= \alpha_3
\end{aligned}
$$

B.2.2 Restrictions for $bb^{\preceq}(A,C)$ and $ee^{\preceq}(A,C)$

We consider two different cases.

B.2.2.1 *Assuming $\beta_1 + T_W(\alpha_1, \delta_2) \geq \alpha_1 + T_W(\gamma_1, \delta_2)$*

We show that the restrictions for $bb^{\preccurlyeq}(A, C)$ and $ee^{\preccurlyeq}(A, C)$ are satisfied by

$$A = \{[p_1, p_3[/T_W(\beta_1, \beta_2, 1 - \delta_2), [p_3, p_5[/\alpha_1, p_5/1,]p_5, p_7]/1 - T_W(\gamma_1, \gamma_2)\}$$
$$B = \{[p_1, p_3[/T_W(\beta_2, 1 - \delta_2), p_3/1,]p_3, p_5]/\gamma_1,]p_5, p_7]/\min(\gamma_1, 1 - \gamma_2)\}$$
$$C = \{[p_2, p_4[/1 - \delta_2, [p_4, p_6[/1 - T_W(\delta_2, \gamma_1), p_6/1\}$$

where $p_1 < p_2 < \cdots < p_7$ are real numbers. A, B and C are clearly convex.
We obtain

$$
\begin{aligned}
be^{\preccurlyeq}(A, B) &= \max(T_W(A(p_1), B(p_3)), T_W(A(p_3), B(p_3)), T_W(A(p_5), B(p_5))) \\
&= \max(T_W(T_W(\beta_1, \beta_2, 1 - \delta_2), 1), T_W(\alpha_1, 1), T_W(1, \gamma_1)) \\
&\geq \alpha_1
\end{aligned}
$$

From (2.35) and (2.31) we find

$$
\begin{aligned}
&bb^{\preccurlyeq}(A, B) \\
&= \min(I_W(B(p_1), A(p_1)), I_W(B(p_3), A(p_3))) \\
&= \min(I_W(T_W(\beta_2, 1 - \delta_2), T_W(\beta_1, \beta_2, 1 - \delta_2)), I_W(1, \alpha_1)) \\
&= \min(I_W(T_W(\beta_2, 1 - \delta_2), 1 - I_W(T_W(\beta_2, 1 - \delta_2), 1 - \beta_1), I_W(1, \alpha_1)) \\
&= \min(1 - T_W(T_W(\beta_2, 1 - \delta_2), I_W(T_W(\beta_2, 1 - \delta_2), 1 - \beta_1), \alpha_1) \\
&= \min(1 - \min(T_W(\beta_2, 1 - \delta_2), 1 - \beta_1), \alpha_1) \\
&= \min(\max(1 - T_W(\beta_2, 1 - \delta_2), \beta_1), \alpha_1) \\
&\geq \beta_1
\end{aligned}
$$

$$
\begin{aligned}
ee^{\preccurlyeq}(A, B) &= \min(I_W(A(p_5), B(p_5)), I_W(A(p_7), B(p_7))) \\
&= \min(I_W(1, \gamma_1), I_W(1 - T_W(\gamma_1, \gamma_2), \min(\gamma_1, 1 - \gamma_2))) \\
&= \min(\gamma_1, I_W(1 - T_W(\gamma_1, \gamma_2), \min(\gamma_1, 1 - \gamma_2)))
\end{aligned}
$$

If $\gamma_1 \leq 1 - \gamma_2$ we find

$$I_W(1 - T_W(\gamma_1, \gamma_2), \min(\gamma_1, 1 - \gamma_2)) = I_W(1 - T_W(\gamma_1, \gamma_2), \gamma_1) \geq \gamma_1$$

Conversely, if $\gamma_1 > 1 - \gamma_2$ we find using (2.33), (2.35) and (2.31)

$$
\begin{aligned}
I_W(1 - T_W(\gamma_1, \gamma_2), \min(\gamma_1, 1 - \gamma_2)) &= I_W(1 - T_W(\gamma_1, \gamma_2), 1 - \gamma_2) \\
&= I_W(\gamma_2, T_W(\gamma_1, \gamma_2)) \\
&= I_W(\gamma_2, 1 - I_W(\gamma_1, 1 - \gamma_2)) \\
&= 1 - T_W(\gamma_2, I_W(\gamma_2, 1 - \gamma_1)) \\
&= 1 - \min(\gamma_2, 1 - \gamma_1) \\
&= \max(1 - \gamma_2, \gamma_1) \\
&= \gamma_1
\end{aligned}
$$

$$
eb^{\preccurlyeq}(A, B) \leq 1 - T_W(A(p_5), B(p_3)) = 1 - T_W(1, 1) = 0 = \delta_1
$$

$$
be^{\preccurlyeq}(B, C) \geq T_W(B(p_3), C(p_6)) = 1 = \alpha_2
$$

Using (2.35) and (2.31), we obtain

$$
\begin{aligned}
bb^{\preccurlyeq}(B, C) &= \min(I_W(C(p_1), B(p_1)), I_W(C(p_2), B(p_2)), I_W(C(p_3), B(p_3))) \\
&= \min(I_W(0, T_W(\beta_2, 1 - \delta_2)), I_W(1 - \delta_2, T_W(\beta_2, 1 - \delta_2)), \\
&\qquad I_W(1 - \delta_2, 1)) \\
&= I_W(1 - \delta_2, T_W(\beta_2, 1 - \delta_2)) \\
&= I_W(1 - \delta_2, 1 - I_W(1 - \delta_2, 1 - \beta_2)) \\
&= 1 - T_W(1 - \delta_2, I_W(1 - \delta_2, 1 - \beta_2)) \\
&= 1 - \min(1 - \delta_2, 1 - \beta_2) \\
&= \beta_2
\end{aligned}
$$

$$
\begin{aligned}
ee^{\preccurlyeq}(B, C) &= \min(I_W(B(p_6), C(p_6)), I_W(B(p_7), C(p_7))) \\
&= \min(I_W(\min(\gamma_1, 1 - \gamma_2), 1), I_W(\min(\gamma_1, 1 - \gamma_2), 0)) \\
&= I_W(\min(\gamma_1, 1 - \gamma_2), 0) \\
&\geq I_W(1 - \gamma_2, 0) \\
&= \gamma_2
\end{aligned}
$$

By (2.35) and (2.31), we have

$eb^{\preceq}(B,C)$
$= \min(1 - T_W(B(p_3), C(p_2)), 1 - T_W(B(p_4), C(p_3)), 1 - T_W(B(p_5), C(p_4)),$
$\qquad 1 - T_W(B(p_6), C(p_5)), 1 - T_W(B(p_7), C(p_6)))$
$= \min(1 - T_W(1, 1 - \delta_2), 1 - T_W(\gamma_1, 1 - \delta_2), 1 - T_W(\gamma_1, 1 - T_W(\delta_2, \gamma_1)),$
$\qquad 1 - T_W(\min(\gamma_1, 1 - \gamma_2), 1 - T_W(\delta_2, \gamma_1)), 1 - T_W(\min(\gamma_1, 1 - \gamma_2), 1))$
$= \min(\delta_2, 1 - T_W(\gamma_1, 1 - T_W(\delta_2, \gamma_1)), 1 - \min(\gamma_1, 1 - \gamma_2))$
$= \min(\delta_2, 1 - T_W(\gamma_1, I_W(\gamma_1, 1 - \delta_2)), \max(\gamma_2, 1 - \gamma_1))$
$= \min(\delta_2, 1 - \min(\gamma_1, 1 - \delta_2), \max(\gamma_2, 1 - \gamma_1))$
$= \min(\delta_2, \max(1 - \gamma_1, \delta_2), \max(\gamma_2, 1 - \gamma_1))$
$= \delta_2$

This shows that (5.111)–(5.118) are satisfied. Again using (2.35) and (2.31), we find

$bb^{\preceq}(A,C)$
$= \min(I_W(C(p_1), A(p_1)), I_W(C(p_2), A(p_2)), I_W(C(p_3), A(p_3)),$
$\qquad I_W(C(p_4), A(p_4)), I_W(C(p_5), A(p_5)))$
$= \min(I_W(0, T_W(\beta_1, \beta_2, 1 - \delta_2)), I_W(1 - \delta_2, T_W(\beta_1, \beta_2, 1 - \delta_2)),$
$\qquad I_W(1 - \delta_2, \alpha_1), I_W(1 - T_W(\delta_2, \gamma_1), \alpha_1), I_W(1 - T_W(\delta_2, \gamma_1), 1))$
$= \min(I_W(1 - \delta_2, T_W(\beta_1, \beta_2, 1 - \delta_2)), I_W(1 - T_W(\delta_2, \gamma_1), \alpha_1))$
$= \min(I_W(1 - \delta_2, 1 - I_W(1 - \delta_2, 1 - T_W(\beta_1, \beta_2))),$
$\qquad I_W(1 - T_W(\delta_2, \gamma_1), \alpha_1))$
$= \min(1 - T_W(1 - \delta_2, I_W(1 - \delta_2, 1 - T_W(\beta_1, \beta_2))),$
$\qquad I_W(1 - T_W(\delta_2, \gamma_1), \alpha_1))$
$= \min(1 - T_W(1 - \delta_2, I_W(1 - \delta_2, 1 - T_W(\beta_1, \beta_2))),$
$\qquad \min(1, T_W(\delta_2, \gamma_1) + \alpha_1))$
$= \min(1 - \min(1 - \delta_2, 1 - T_W(\beta_1, \beta_2)), T_W(\delta_2, \gamma_1) + \alpha_1)$
$= \min(\max(\delta_2, T_W(\beta_1, \beta_2)), T_W(\delta_2, \gamma_1) + \alpha_1)$
$\leq \min(\max(\delta_2, T_W(\beta_1, \beta_2)), \max(T_W(\delta_2, \gamma_1) + \alpha_1, T_W(\beta_1, \beta_2)))$
$= \max(T_W(\beta_1, \beta_2), \min(\delta_2, T_W(\delta_2, \gamma_1) + \alpha_1))$

and using the assumption $\beta_1 + T_W(\alpha_1, \delta_2) \geq \alpha_1 + T_W(\gamma_1, \delta_2)$, we obtain

$\qquad \leq \max(T_W(\beta_1, \beta_2), \min(\delta_2, \beta_1 + T_W(\alpha_1, \delta_2), T_W(\delta_2, \gamma_1) + \alpha_1))$

Finally, we find

$$ee^{\preceq}(A,C) = \min(I_W(A(p_6), C(p_6)), I_W(A(p_7), C(p_7)))$$
$$= \min(I_W(1 - T_W(\gamma_1, \gamma_2), 1), I_W(1 - T_W(\gamma_1, \gamma_2), 0))$$
$$= T_W(\gamma_1, \gamma_2)$$

B.2.2.2 *Assuming* $\beta_1 + T_W(\alpha_1, \delta_2) < \alpha_1 + T_W(\gamma_1, \delta_2)$

We show that the restrictions for $bb^{\preceq}(A,C)$ and $ee^{\preceq}(A,C)$ are satisfied by

$$A = \{[p_1, p_3[/T_W(\beta_1, \beta_2, 1 - \delta_2), [p_3, p_5[/\beta_1, p_5/1,]p_5, p_7]/1 - T_W(\gamma_1, \gamma_2)\}$$
$$B = \{[p_1, p_3[/T_W(\beta_2, 1 - \delta_2), p_3/1,]p_3, p_5]/\alpha_1,]p_5, p_7]/\min(\gamma_1, 1 - \gamma_2)\}$$
$$C = \{[p_2, p_4[/1 - \delta_2, [p_4, p_6[/1 - T_W(\delta_2, \alpha_1), p_6/1\}$$

where $p_1 < p_2 < \cdots < p_7$ are real numbers. A, B and C are clearly convex.
We obtain

$$be^{\preceq}(A,B)$$
$$= \max(T_W(A(p_1), B(p_3)), T_W(A(p_3), B(p_3)), T_W(A(p_5), B(p_5)))$$
$$= \max(T_W(T_W(\beta_1, \beta_2, 1 - \delta_2), 1), T_W(\beta_1, 1), T_W(1, \alpha_1))$$
$$= \max(T_W(\beta_1, \beta_2, 1 - \delta_2), \beta_1, \alpha_1)$$
$$= \alpha_1$$

From (2.35) and (2.31) we find

$$bb^{\preceq}(A,B)$$
$$= \min(I_W(B(p_1), A(p_1)), I_W(B(p_3), A(p_3)))$$
$$= \min(I_W(T_W(\beta_2, 1 - \delta_2), T_W(\beta_1, \beta_2, 1 - \delta_2)), I_W(1, \beta_1))$$
$$= \min(I_W(T_W(\beta_2, 1 - \delta_2), 1 - I_W(T_W(\beta_2, 1 - \delta_2), 1 - \beta_1)), I_W(1, \beta_1))$$
$$= \min(1 - T_W(T_W(\beta_2, 1 - \delta_2), I_W(T_W(\beta_2, 1 - \delta_2), 1 - \beta_1)), \beta_1)$$
$$= \min(1 - \min(T_W(\beta_2, 1 - \delta_2), 1 - \beta_1), \beta_1)$$
$$= \min(\max(1 - T_W(\beta_2, 1 - \delta_2), \beta_1), \beta_1)$$
$$= \beta_1$$

$$ee^{\preceq}(A,B) = \min(I_W(A(p_5), B(p_5)), I_W(A(p_7), B(p_7)))$$
$$= \min(I_W(1, \alpha_1), I_W(1 - T_W(\gamma_1, \gamma_2), \min(\gamma_1, 1 - \gamma_2)))$$
$$= \min(\alpha_1, I_W(1 - T_W(\gamma_1, \gamma_2), \min(\gamma_1, 1 - \gamma_2)))$$

If $\gamma_1 \leq 1 - \gamma_2$ we find

$$\min(\alpha_1, I_W(1 - T_W(\gamma_1, \gamma_2), \min(\gamma_1, 1 - \gamma_2)))$$
$$= \min(\alpha_1, I_W(1 - T_W(\gamma_1, \gamma_2), \gamma_1))$$
$$\geq \min(\alpha_1, \gamma_1)$$
$$= \gamma_1$$

Conversely, if $\gamma_1 > 1 - \gamma_2$ we find using (2.33), (2.35) and (2.31)

$$\min(\alpha_1, I_W(1 - T_W(\gamma_1, \gamma_2), \min(\gamma_1, 1 - \gamma_2)))$$
$$= \min(\alpha_1, I_W(1 - T_W(\gamma_1, \gamma_2), 1 - \gamma_2))$$
$$= \min(\alpha_1, I_W(\gamma_2, T_W(\gamma_1, \gamma_2)))$$
$$= \min(\alpha_1, I_W(\gamma_2, 1 - I_W(\gamma_1, 1 - \gamma_2)))$$
$$= \min(\alpha_1, 1 - T_W(\gamma_2, I_W(\gamma_2, 1 - \gamma_1)))$$
$$= \min(\alpha_1, 1 - \min(\gamma_2, 1 - \gamma_1))$$
$$\geq \min(\alpha_1, \gamma_1)$$
$$= \gamma_1$$

$$eb^{\preccurlyeq}(A, B) \leq 1 - T_W(A(p_5), B(p_3)) = 1 - T_W(1, 1) = 0$$

$$be^{\preccurlyeq}(B, C) \geq T_W(B(p_3), C(p_6)) = 1$$

Using (2.35) and (2.31), we find

$$bb^{\preccurlyeq}(B, C)$$
$$= \min(I_W(C(p_1), B(p_1)), I_W(C(p_2), B(p_2)), I_W(C(p_3), B(p_3)))$$
$$= \min(I_W(0, T_W(\beta_2, 1 - \delta_2)), I_W(1 - \delta_2, T_W(\beta_2, 1 - \delta_2)), I_W(1 - \delta_2, 1))$$
$$= I_W(1 - \delta_2, T_W(\beta_2, 1 - \delta_2))$$
$$= I_W(1 - \delta_2, 1 - I_W(1 - \delta_2, 1 - \beta_2))$$
$$= 1 - T_W(1 - \delta_2, I_W(1 - \delta_2, 1 - \beta_2))$$
$$= 1 - \min(1 - \delta_2, 1 - \beta_2)$$
$$= \max(\delta_2, \beta_2)$$
$$= \beta_2$$

$$ee^{\preceq}(B,C) = \min(I_W(B(p_6),C(p_6)),I_W(B(p_7),C(p_7)))$$
$$= \min(I_W(\min(\gamma_1,1-\gamma_2),1),I_W(\min(\gamma_1,1-\gamma_2),0))$$
$$= I_W(\min(\gamma_1,1-\gamma_2),0)$$
$$= 1-\min(\gamma_1,1-\gamma_2)$$
$$= \max(1-\gamma_1,\gamma_2)$$
$$\geq \gamma_2$$

Using (2.35) and (2.31), we obtain

$$eb^{\preceq}(B,C)$$
$$= \min(1-T_W(B(p_3),C(p_2)),1-T_W(B(p_4),C(p_3)),$$
$$\quad 1-T_W(B(p_5),C(p_4)),1-T_W(B(p_6),C(p_5)),$$
$$\quad 1-T_W(B(p_7),C(p_6)))$$
$$= \min(1-T_W(1,1-\delta_2),1-T_W(\alpha_1,1-\delta_2),1-T_W(\alpha_1,1-T_W(\delta_2,\alpha_1)),$$
$$\quad 1-T_W(\min(\gamma_1,1-\gamma_2),1-T_W(\delta_2,\alpha_1)),$$
$$\quad 1-T_W(\min(\gamma_1,1-\gamma_2),1))$$
$$= \min(1-T_W(1,1-\delta_2),1-T_W(\alpha_1,1-T_W(\delta_2,\alpha_1)),$$
$$\quad 1-T_W(\min(\gamma_1,1-\gamma_2),1))$$
$$= \min(\delta_2,1-T_W(\alpha_1,I_W(\alpha_1,1-\delta_2)),\max(1-\gamma_1,\gamma_2))$$
$$= \min(\delta_2,1-T_W(\alpha_1,I_W(\alpha_1,1-\delta_2)))$$
$$= \min(\delta_2,1-\min(\alpha_1,1-\delta_2))$$
$$= \min(\delta_2,\max(1-\alpha_1,\delta_2))$$
$$= \delta_2$$

Hence, (5.111)–(5.118) are satisfied. Using (2.35) and (2.31), we obtain

$$bb^{\preceq}(A,C)$$
$$= \min(I_W(C(p_1),A(p_1)),I_W(C(p_2),A(p_2)),I_W(C(p_3),A(p_3)),$$
$$\quad I_W(C(p_4),A(p_4)),I_W(C(p_5),A(p_5)))$$
$$= \min(I_W(0,T_W(\beta_1,\beta_2,1-\delta_2)),I_W(1-\delta_2,T_W(\beta_1,\beta_2,1-\delta_2)),$$
$$\quad I_W(1-\delta_2,\beta_1),I_W(1-T_W(\delta_2,\alpha_1),\beta_1),I_W(1-T_W(\delta_2,\alpha_1),1))$$
$$= \min(I_W(1-\delta_2,T_W(\beta_1,\beta_2,1-\delta_2)),I_W(1-T_W(\delta_2,\alpha_1),\beta_1))$$
$$= \min(I_W(1-\delta_2,1-I_W(1-\delta_2,1-T_W(\beta_1,\beta_2))),$$
$$\quad I_W(1-T_W(\delta_2,\alpha_1),\beta_1))$$

$$= \min(1 - T_W(1 - \delta_2, I_W(1 - \delta_2, 1 - T_W(\beta_1, \beta_2))),$$
$$\quad I_W(1 - T_W(\delta_2, \alpha_1), \beta_1))$$
$$= \min(1 - T_W(1 - \delta_2, I_W(1 - \delta_2, 1 - T_W(\beta_1, \beta_2))),$$
$$\quad \min(1, T_W(\delta_2, \alpha_1) + \beta_1))$$
$$= \min(1 - \min(1 - \delta_2, 1 - T_W(\beta_1, \beta_2)), T_W(\delta_2, \alpha_1) + \beta_1)$$
$$= \min(\max(\delta_2, T_W(\beta_1, \beta_2)), T_W(\delta_2, \alpha_1) + \beta_1)$$
$$\leq \min(\max(\delta_2, T_W(\beta_1, \beta_2)), \max(T_W(\delta_2, \alpha_1) + \beta_1, T_W(\beta_1, \beta_2)))$$
$$= \max(T_W(\beta_1, \beta_2), \min(\delta_2, T_W(\delta_2, \alpha_1) + \beta_1))$$

Using the assumption $\beta_1 + T_W(\alpha_1, \delta_2) < \alpha_1 + T_W(\gamma_1, \delta_2)$, we find
$$= \max(T_W(\beta_1, \beta_2), \min(\delta_2, T_W(\delta_2, \alpha_1) + \beta_1, \alpha_1 + T_W(\gamma_1, \delta_2)))$$

Finally, we obtain
$$ee^{\preccurlyeq}(A, C) = \min(I_W(A(p_6), C(p_6)), I_W(A(p_7), C(p_7)))$$
$$= \min(I_W(1 - T_W(\gamma_1, \gamma_2), 1), I_W(1 - T_W(\gamma_1, \gamma_2), 0))$$
$$= T_W(\gamma_1, \gamma_2)$$

B.2.3   *Restriction for* $eb^{\preccurlyeq}(A, C)$

We show that the restriction for $eb^{\preccurlyeq}$ is satisfied by
$$A = \{[p_1, p_3[/\beta_1, [p_3, p_5[/\alpha_1, p_5/1]\}$$
$$B = \{[p_1, p_3[/\beta_2, p_3/1,]p_3, p_6]/\gamma_1\}$$
$$C = \{[p_2, p_4[/1 - \delta_2, [p_4, p_7[/1 - T_W(\gamma_1, \delta_2), p_7/1]\}$$

where $p_1 < p_2 < \cdots < p_7$ are real numbers. Note that A, B and C are convex.

We obtain
$$be^{\preccurlyeq}(A, B) = \max(T_W(A(p_1), B(p_3)), T_W(A(p_3), B(p_3)), T_W(A(p_5), B(p_5)))$$
$$= \max(T_W(\beta_1, 1), T_W(\alpha_1, 1), T_W(1, \gamma_1))$$
$$= \max(\beta_1, \alpha_1, \gamma_1)$$
$$= \alpha_1$$

$$bb^{\preccurlyeq}(A, B) = \min(I_W(B(p_1), A(p_1)), I_W(B(p_3), A(p_3)))$$
$$= \min(I_W(\beta_2, \beta_1), I_W(1, \alpha_1))$$
$$= \min(I_W(\beta_2, \beta_1), \alpha_1)$$
$$\geq \min(\beta_1, \alpha_1)$$
$$\geq \beta_1$$

$$ee^{\preccurlyeq}(A,B) = \min(I_W(A(p_5), B(p_5)), I_W(A(p_6), B(p_6)))$$
$$= \min(I_W(1, \gamma_1), I_W(0, \gamma_1))$$
$$= \gamma_1$$

$$eb^{\preccurlyeq}(A,B) \geq 0 = \delta_1$$

$be^{\preccurlyeq}(B,C)$
$$= \max(T_W(B(p_1), C(p_7)), T_W(B(p_2), C(p_7)), T_W(B(p_3), C(p_7)))$$
$$= \max(T_W(\beta_2, 1), T_W(\beta_2, 1), T_W(1, 1))$$
$$= 1$$

$bb^{\preccurlyeq}(B,C)$
$$= \min(I_W(C(p_1), B(p_1)), I_W(C(p_2), B(p_2)), I_W(C(p_3), B(p_3)))$$
$$= \min(I_W(0, \beta_2), I_W(1 - \delta_2, \beta_2), I_W(1 - \delta_2, 1))$$
$$= I_W(1 - \delta_2, \beta_2)$$
$$\geq \beta_2$$

$$ee^{\preccurlyeq}(B,C) = I_W(B(p_7), C(p_7)) = I_W(0,1) = 1 \geq \gamma_2$$

By (2.35) and (2.31), we find

$eb^{\preccurlyeq}(B,C)$
$$= \min(1 - T_W(B(p_3), C(p_2)), 1 - T_W(B(p_4), C(p_3)),$$
$$1 - T_W(B(p_6), C(p_4)), 1 - T_W(B(p_7), C(p_6)))$$
$$= \min(1 - T_W(1, 1 - \delta_2), 1 - T_W(\gamma_1, 1 - \delta_2), 1 - T_W(\gamma_1,$$
$$1 - T_W(\gamma_1, \delta_2)), 1 - T_W(0, 1 - T_W(\gamma_1, \delta_2)))$$
$$= \min(\delta_2, 1 - T_W(\gamma_1, 1 - T_W(\gamma_1, \delta_2)))$$
$$= \min(\delta_2, 1 - T_W(\gamma_1, I_W(\gamma_1, 1 - \delta_2)))$$
$$= \min(\delta_2, 1 - \min(\gamma_1, 1 - \delta_2))$$
$$= \min(\delta_2, \max(1 - \gamma_1, \delta_2))$$
$$= \delta_2$$

We already have that (5.111)–(5.118) are satisfied. To show that the restriction on $eb^\preceq(A, C)$ is also satisfied, we find

$$eb^\preceq(A, C)$$
$$= \min(1 - T_W(A(p_5), C(p_4)), 1 - T_W(A(p_7), C(p_5)))$$
$$= \min(1 - T_W(1, 1 - T_W(\gamma_1, \delta_2)), 1 - T_W(0, 1 - T_W(\gamma_1, \delta_2)))$$
$$= T_W(\gamma_1, \delta_2)$$

B.3 $\delta_1 > 0$, $\delta_2 = 0$

B.3.1   *Restriction for* $be^\preceq(A, C)$

To show that the restriction for $be^\preceq(A, C)$ can be satisfied, we consider three different cases

B.3.1.1   *Assuming* $1 - \delta_1 \geq \alpha_2$

If $1 - \delta_1 \geq \alpha_2$, we show that the restriction is satisfied by

$$A = \{[p_1, p_3[/T_W(\beta_1, \alpha_2), [p_3, p_5[/\beta_1, p_5/1\}$$
$$B = \{[p_1, p_4[/\alpha_2, [p_4, p_6[/1 - \delta_1, p_6/1\}$$
$$C = \{p_2/1,]p_2, p_7]/\gamma_2\}$$

where $p_1 < p_2 < \cdots < p_7$ are real numbers. Note that A, B and C are convex, considering the assumption $1 - \delta_1 \geq \alpha_2$.

$$be^\preceq(A, B) \geq T_W(A(p_5), B(p_6)) = 1 = \alpha_1$$

Using (2.35) and (2.31), we obtain

$$bb^\preceq(A, B)$$
$$= \min(I_W(B(p_1), A(p_1)), I_W(B(p_3), A(p_3)), I_W(B(p_4), A(p_4)),$$
$$\qquad I_W(B(p_5), A(p_5)))$$
$$= \min(I_W(\alpha_2, T_W(\beta_1, \alpha_2)), I_W(\alpha_2, \beta_1), I_W(1 - \delta_1, \beta_1), I_W(1 - \delta_1, 1))$$
$$= \min(I_W(\alpha_2, T_W(\beta_1, \alpha_2)), I_W(1 - \delta_1, \beta_1))$$
$$= \min(I_W(\alpha_2, 1 - I_W(\alpha_2, 1 - \beta_1)), I_W(1 - \delta_1, \beta_1))$$
$$= \min(1 - T_W(\alpha_2, I_W(\alpha_2, 1 - \beta_1)), I_W(1 - \delta_1, \beta_1))$$
$$= \min(1 - \min(\alpha_2, 1 - \beta_1), I_W(1 - \delta_1, \beta_1))$$
$$= \min(\max(1 - \alpha_2, \beta_1), I_W(1 - \delta_1, \beta_1))$$
$$\geq \beta_1$$

$$ee^{\preccurlyeq}(A, B) = I_W(A(p_6), B(p_6)) = I_W(0, 1) = 1 \geq \gamma_1$$

$$\begin{aligned}
eb^{\preccurlyeq}(A, B) &= \min(1 - T_W(A(p_5), B(p_4)), 1 - T_W(A(p_6), B(p_5))) \\
&= \min(1 - T_W(1, 1 - \delta_1), 1 - T_W(0, 1 - \delta_1)) \\
&= \delta_1
\end{aligned}$$

$$\begin{aligned}
&be^{\preccurlyeq}(B, C) \\
&= \max(T_W(B(p_1), C(p_2)), T_W(B(p_2), C(p_2)), T_W(B(p_4), C(p_4)), \\
&\qquad T_W(B(p_6), C(p_6))) \\
&= \max(T_W(B(p_2), C(p_2)), T_W(B(p_4), C(p_4)), T_W(B(p_6), C(p_6))) \\
&= \max(T_W(\alpha_2, 1), T_W(1 - \delta_1, \gamma_2), T_W(1, \gamma_2)) \\
&= \max(\alpha_2, \gamma_2) \\
&= \alpha_2
\end{aligned}$$

$$\begin{aligned}
bb^{\preccurlyeq}(B, C) &= \min(I_W(C(p_1), B(p_1)), I_W(C(p_2), B(p_2))) \\
&= \min(I_W(0, \alpha_2), I_W(1, \alpha_2)) \\
&= \alpha_2 \\
&\geq \beta_2
\end{aligned}$$

$$\begin{aligned}
ee^{\preccurlyeq}(B, C) &= \min(I_W(B(p_6), C(p_6)), I_W(B(p_7), C(p_7))) \\
&= \min(I_W(1, \gamma_2), I_W(0, \gamma_2)) \\
&= \gamma_2
\end{aligned}$$

$$eb^{\preccurlyeq}(B, C) \geq 0 = \delta_2$$

Hence, we have that (5.111)–(5.118) are satisfied. Finally, we find

$$\begin{aligned}
&be^{\preccurlyeq}(A, C) \\
&= \max(T_W(A(p_1), C(p_2)), T_W(A(p_2), C(p_2)), T_W(A(p_3), C(p_3)), \\
&\qquad T_W(A(p_5), C(p_5))) \\
&= \max(T_W(T_W(\beta_1, \alpha_2), 1), T_W(T_W(\beta_1, \alpha_2), 1), T_W(\beta_1, \gamma_2), T_W(1, \gamma_2)) \\
&= \max(T_W(\beta_1, \alpha_2), T_W(\beta_1, \alpha_2), T_W(\beta_1, \gamma_2), \gamma_2) \\
&= \max(T_W(\beta_1, \alpha_2), \gamma_2)
\end{aligned}$$

From $\delta_1 > 0$, we find $\alpha_1 = 1$, hence

$$= \max(T_W(\beta_1, \alpha_2), T_W(\alpha_1, \gamma_2))$$
$$= \alpha_3$$

B.3.1.2   *Assuming $1 - \delta_1 < \alpha_1$ and $1 - \delta_1 < \beta_2$*

In this case, it holds that $T_W(\delta_1, \beta_2) > 0$. For any A, B and C satisfying (5.111)–(5.118), it will then hold that

$$eb^{\preccurlyeq}(A, C) \geq T_W(eb^{\preccurlyeq}(A, B), bb^{\preccurlyeq}(B, C)) \geq T_W(\delta_1, \beta_2) > 0$$

and, hence, $be^{\preccurlyeq}(A, C) = 1 = \alpha_3$ by Corollary 5.4.

$1 - \delta_1 < \alpha_1$ and $1 - \delta_1 \geq \beta_2$ We show that the restriction for $be^{\preccurlyeq}(A, C)$ is satisfied for

$$A = \{[p_1, p_3[/T_W(\beta_1, \beta_2), p_3/1]\}$$
$$B = \{[p_1, p_4[/\beta_2, p_4/1]\}$$
$$C = \{p_2/1,]p_2, p_5]/\alpha_2\}$$

where $p_1 < p_2 < \cdots < p_5$ are real numbers. Note that A, B and C are convex.

$$be^{\preccurlyeq}(A, B) \geq T_W(A(p_3), B(p_4)) = 1 = \alpha_1$$

Using (2.35) and (2.31) we find

$$bb^{\preccurlyeq}(A, B) = \min(I_W(B(p_1), A(p_1)), I_W(B(p_3), A(p_3)))$$
$$= \min(I_W(\beta_2, T_W(\beta_1, \beta_2)), I_W(\beta_2, 1))$$
$$= I_W(\beta_2, T_W(\beta_1, \beta_2))$$
$$= I_W(\beta_2, 1 - I_W(\beta_2, 1 - \beta_1))$$
$$= 1 - T_W(\beta_2, I_W(\beta_2, 1 - \beta_1))$$
$$= 1 - \min(\beta_2, 1 - \beta_1)$$
$$\geq \beta_1$$

$$ee^{\preccurlyeq}(A, B) = I_W(A(p_4), B(p_4)) = 1 \geq \gamma_1$$

Using the assumption $1 - \delta_1 \geq \beta_2$, we find

$$eb^{\preccurlyeq}(A, B) = \min(1 - T_W(A(p_3), B(p_2)), 1 - T_W(A(p_4), B(p_3)))$$
$$= \min(1 - T_W(1, \beta_2), 1 - T_W(0, \beta_2))$$
$$= 1 - \beta_2$$
$$\geq \delta_1$$

$$be^{\preccurlyeq}(B,C) = \max(T_W(B(p_1),C(p_2)),T_W(B(p_2),C(p_2)),T_W(B(p_4),C(p_4)))$$
$$= \max(T_W(\beta_2,1),T_W(\beta_2,1),T_W(1,\alpha_2))$$
$$= \max(\beta_2,\alpha_2)$$
$$= \alpha_2$$

$$bb^{\preccurlyeq}(B,C) = \min(I_W(C(p_1),B(p_1)),I_W(C(p_2),B(p_2)))$$
$$= \min(I_W(0,\beta_2),I_W(1,\beta_2))$$
$$= \beta_2$$

$$ee^{\preccurlyeq}(B,C) = \min(I_W(B(p_4),C(p_4)),I_W(B(p_5),C(p_5)))$$
$$= \min(I_W(1,\alpha_2),I_W(0,\alpha_2))$$
$$= \alpha_2$$
$$\geq \gamma_2$$

$$eb^{\preccurlyeq}(B,C) \geq 0 = \delta_2$$

Hence, we have that (5.111)–(5.118) are satisfied. Finally, we obtain

$$be^{\preccurlyeq}(A,C) = \max(T_W(A(p_1),C(p_2)),T_W(A(p_2),C(p_2)),T_W(A(p_3),C(p_3)))$$
$$= \max(T_W(T_W(\beta_1,\beta_2),1),T_W(T_W(\beta_1,\beta_2),1),T_W(1,\alpha_2))$$
$$= \max(T_W(\beta_1,\beta_2),\alpha_2)$$
$$= \alpha_2$$

From $\delta_1 > 0$ we know that $\alpha_1 = 1$, hence

$$\alpha_2 = \min(\alpha_1,\alpha_2) = \alpha_3$$

B.3.2 Restrictions for $bb^{\preccurlyeq}(A,C)$ and $ee^{\preccurlyeq}(A,C)$

B.3.2.1 Assuming $\alpha_2 + T_W(\delta_1,\beta_2) \geq \gamma_2 + T_W(\delta_1,\alpha_2)$

Assuming $\alpha_2 + T_W(\delta_1,\beta_2) \geq \gamma_2 + T_W(\delta_1,\alpha_2)$, we show that the restrictions for $bb^{\preccurlyeq}(A,C)$ and $ee^{\preccurlyeq}(A,C)$ are satisfied by

$A = \{p_2/1,]p_2,p_4]/1 - T_W(\delta_1,\alpha_2),]p_4,p_7]/1 - \delta_1\}$

$B = \{[p_1,p_3[/\min(1 - \beta_1,\beta_2), [p_3,p_5[/\alpha_2,p_5/1,]p_5,p_8]/T_W(\gamma_1,1 - \delta_1)\}$

$C = \{[p_1,p_3[/1 - T_W(\beta_1,\beta_2),p_3/1,]p_3,p_6]/\gamma_2,]p_6,p_8]/T_W(\gamma_1,\gamma_2,1 - \delta_1)\}$

where $p_1 < p_2 < \cdots < p_8$ are real numbers. Clearly, A, B and C are fuzzy time intervals. We find

$$be^{\preccurlyeq}(A, B) \geq T_W(A(p_2), B(p_5)) = 1 = \alpha_1$$

where $\alpha_1 = 1$ follows from $\delta_1 > 0$.

$$
\begin{aligned}
bb^{\preccurlyeq}(A, B) &= \min(I_W(B(p_1), A(p_1)), I_W(B(p_2), A(p_2))) \\
&= \min(I_W(\min(1 - \beta_1, \beta_2), 0), I_W(\min(1 - \beta_1, \beta_2), 1)) \\
&= I_W(\min(1 - \beta_1, \beta_2), 0) \\
&= 1 - \min(1 - \beta_1, \beta_2) \\
&= \max(\beta_1, 1 - \beta_2) \\
&\geq \beta_1
\end{aligned}
$$

Using (2.35), (2.31) and $\delta_1 \leq \gamma_1$

$$
\begin{aligned}
&ee^{\preccurlyeq}(A, B) \\
&= \min(I_W(A(p_5), B(p_5)), I_W(A(p_7), B(p_7)), I_W(A(p_8), B(p_8))) \\
&= \min(I_W(1 - \delta_1, 1), I_W(1 - \delta_1, T_W(\gamma_1, 1 - \delta_1)), I_W(0, T_W(\gamma_1, 1 - \delta_1))) \\
&= I_W(1 - \delta_1, T_W(\gamma_1, 1 - \delta_1)) \\
&= I_W(1 - \delta_1, 1 - I_W(1 - \delta_1, 1 - \gamma_1)) \\
&= 1 - T_W(1 - \delta_1, I_W(1 - \delta_1, 1 - \gamma_1)) \\
&= 1 - \min(1 - \delta_1, 1 - \gamma_1) \\
&= \max(\delta_1, \gamma_1) \\
&= \gamma_1
\end{aligned}
$$

and by (2.35), (2.31) and $\delta_1 \leq \beta_1$

$$
\begin{aligned}
&eb^{\preccurlyeq}(A, B) \\
&= \min(1 - T_W(A(p_2), B(p_1)), 1 - T_W(A(p_3), B(p_2)), \\
&\qquad 1 - T_W(A(p_4), B(p_3)), 1 - T_W(A(p_5), B(p_4)), \\
&\qquad 1 - T_W(A(p_7), B(p_5)), 1 - T_W(A(p_8), B(p_5))) \\
&= \min(1 - T_W(1, \min(1 - \beta_1, \beta_2)), \\
&\qquad 1 - T_W(1 - T_W(\delta_1, \alpha_2), \min(1 - \beta_1, \beta_2)), \\
&\qquad 1 - T_W(1 - T_W(\delta_1, \alpha_2), \alpha_2), \\
&\qquad 1 - T_W(1 - \delta_1, \alpha_2), 1 - T_W(1 - \delta_1, 1), 1 - T_W(0, 1)) \\
&= \min(1 - T_W(1, \min(1 - \beta_1, \beta_2)), 1 - T_W(1 - T_W(\delta_1, \alpha_2), \alpha_2), \delta_1) \\
&= \min(\max(\beta_1, 1 - \beta_2)), 1 - T_W(I_W(\alpha_2, 1 - \delta_1), \alpha_2), \delta_1)
\end{aligned}
$$

$$= \min(\max(\beta_1, 1 - \beta_2)), 1 - \min(\alpha_2, 1 - \delta_1), \delta_1)$$
$$= \min(\max(\beta_1, 1 - \beta_2)), \max(1 - \alpha_2, \delta_1), \delta_1)$$
$$= \delta_1$$

From $\gamma_2 \leq \alpha_2$, we find

$$be^{\preccurlyeq}(B, C)$$
$$= \max(T_W(B(p_1), C(p_3)), T_W(B(p_3), C(p_3)), T_W(B(p_5), C(p_5)))$$
$$= \max(T_W(B(p_3), C(p_3)), T_W(B(p_5), C(p_5)))$$
$$= \max(T_W(\alpha_2, 1), T_W(1, \gamma_2))$$
$$= \max(\alpha_2, \gamma_2)$$
$$= \alpha_2$$

Next, we find

$$bb^{\preccurlyeq}(B, C) = \min(I_W(1 - T_W(\beta_1, \beta_2), \min(1 - \beta_1, \beta_2)), I_W(1, \alpha_2))$$
$$= \min(I_W(1 - T_W(\beta_1, \beta_2), \min(1 - \beta_1, \beta_2)), \alpha_2)$$

If $\beta_2 \leq 1 - \beta_1$ we find

$$I_W(1 - T_W(\beta_1, \beta_2), \min(1 - \beta_1, \beta_2)) = I_W(1 - T_W(\beta_1, \beta_2), \beta_2)$$
$$\geq \beta_2$$

Conversely, if $\beta_2 > 1 - \beta_1$ we find using (2.33), (2.35) and (2.31)

$$I_W(1 - T_W(\beta_1, \beta_2), \min(1 - \beta_1, \beta_2)) = I_W(1 - T_W(\beta_1, \beta_2), 1 - \beta_1)$$
$$= I_W(\beta_1, T_W(\beta_1, \beta_2))$$
$$= I_W(\beta_1, 1 - I_W(\beta_1, 1 - \beta_2))$$
$$= 1 - T_W(\beta_1, I_W(\beta_1, 1 - \beta_2))$$
$$= 1 - \min(\beta_1, 1 - \beta_2)$$
$$= \max(1 - \beta_1, \beta_2)$$
$$\geq \beta_2$$

From (2.35) and (2.31), we have

$$ee^{\preccurlyeq}(B, C)$$
$$= \min(I_W(B(p_5), C(p_5)), I_W(B(p_6), C(p_6)), I_W(B(p_8), C(p_8)))$$
$$= \min(I_W(1, \gamma_2), I_W(T_W(\gamma_1, 1 - \delta_1), \gamma_2), I_W(T_W(\gamma_1, 1 - \delta_1),$$
$$T_W(\gamma_1, \gamma_2, 1 - \delta_1)))$$
$$= \min(\gamma_2, I_W(T_W(\gamma_1, 1 - \delta_1), T_W(\gamma_1, \gamma_2, 1 - \delta_1)))$$

$$= \min(\gamma_2, I_W(T_W(\gamma_1, 1 - \delta_1), 1 - I_W(T_W(\gamma_1, 1 - \delta_1), 1 - \gamma_2)))$$
$$= \min(\gamma_2, 1 - T_W(T_W(\gamma_1, 1 - \delta_1), I_W(T_W(\gamma_1, 1 - \delta_1), 1 - \gamma_2)))$$
$$= \min(\gamma_2, 1 - \min(T_W(\gamma_1, 1 - \delta_1), 1 - \gamma_2))$$
$$= \min(\gamma_2, \max(1 - T_W(\gamma_1, 1 - \delta_1), \gamma_2))$$
$$= \gamma_2$$

$$eb^{\preccurlyeq}(B, C) \geq 0 = \delta_2$$

This already shows that (5.111)–(5.118) are satisfied. For $bb^{\preccurlyeq}(A, C)$, we find

$$bb^{\preccurlyeq}(A, C) = \min(I_W(C(p_1), A(p_1)), I_W(C(p_2), A(p_2)))$$
$$= \min(I_W(1 - T_W(\beta_1, \beta_2), 0), I_W(1 - T_W(\beta_1, \beta_2), 1))$$
$$= T_W(\beta_1, \beta_2)$$

Finally, using (2.35) and (2.31), we find

$$ee^{\preccurlyeq}(A, C)$$
$$= \min(I_W(A(p_3), C(p_3)), I_W(A(p_4), C(p_4)), I_W(A(p_6), C(p_6)),$$
$$\qquad I_W(A(p_7), C(p_7)), I_W(A(p_8), C(p_8)))$$
$$= \min(I_W(1 - T_W(\delta_1, \alpha_2), 1), I_W(1 - T_W(\delta_1, \alpha_2), \gamma_2), I_W(1 - \delta_1, \gamma_2),$$
$$\qquad I_W(1 - \delta_1, T_W(\gamma_1, \gamma_2, 1 - \delta_1)), I_W(0, T_W(\gamma_1, \gamma_2, 1 - \delta_1)))$$
$$= \min(I_W(1 - T_W(\delta_1, \alpha_2), \gamma_2), I_W(1 - \delta_1, \gamma_2),$$
$$\qquad I_W(1 - \delta_1, T_W(\gamma_1, \gamma_2, 1 - \delta_1)))$$
$$= \min(I_W(1 - T_W(\delta_1, \alpha_2), \gamma_2),$$
$$\qquad I_W(1 - \delta_1, T_W(\gamma_1, \gamma_2, 1 - \delta_1)))$$
$$= \min(I_W(1 - T_W(\delta_1, \alpha_2), \gamma_2),$$
$$\qquad I_W(1 - \delta_1, 1 - I_W(1 - \delta_1, 1 - T_W(\gamma_1, \gamma_2))))$$
$$= \min(I_W(1 - T_W(\delta_1, \alpha_2), \gamma_2), 1 - T_W(1 - \delta_1, I_W(1 - \delta_1, 1 - T_W(\gamma_1, \gamma_2))))$$
$$= \min(T_W(\delta_1, \alpha_2) + \gamma_2, 1 - T_W(1 - \delta_1, I_W(1 - \delta_1, 1 - T_W(\gamma_1, \gamma_2))))$$
$$= \min(T_W(\delta_1, \alpha_2) + \gamma_2, 1 - \min(1 - \delta_1, 1 - T_W(\gamma_1, \gamma_2)))$$
$$= \min(T_W(\delta_1, \alpha_2) + \gamma_2, \max(\delta_1, T_W(\gamma_1, \gamma_2)))$$
$$\leq \min(\max(T_W(\delta_1, \alpha_2) + \gamma_2, T_W(\gamma_1, \gamma_2)), \max(\delta_1, T_W(\gamma_1, \gamma_2)))$$
$$= \max(T_W(\gamma_1, \gamma_2), \min(T_W(\delta_1, \alpha_2) + \gamma_2, \delta_1))$$

B.3.2.2 *Assuming $\alpha_2 + T_W(\delta_1, \beta_2) < \gamma_2 + T_W(\delta_1, \alpha_2)$*

If $\alpha_2 + T_W(\delta_1, \beta_2) < \gamma_2 + T_W(\delta_1, \alpha_2)$, the restrictions for $bb^{\preccurlyeq}(A, C)$ and $ee^{\preccurlyeq}(A, C)$ are satisfied by

$$A = \{p_2/1,]p_2, p_4]/1 - T_W(\delta_1, \beta_2),]p_4, p_7]/1 - \delta_1\}$$
$$B = \{[p_1, p_3[/\min(1 - \beta_1, \beta_2), [p_3, p_4[/\beta_2, p_4/1,]p_4, p_8]/T_W(\gamma_1, 1 - \delta_1)\}$$
$$C = \{[p_1, p_3[/1 - T_W(\beta_1, \beta_2), p_3/1,]p_3, p_4]/\alpha_2,]p_4, p_6]/\gamma_2,$$
$$]p_6, p_8]/T_W(\gamma_1, \gamma_2, 1 - \delta_1)\}$$

where $p_1 < p_2 < \cdots < p_8$ are real numbers. Clearly, A, B and C are fuzzy time intervals. We find

$$be^{\preccurlyeq}(A, B) \geq T_W(A(p_2), B(p_4)) = 1 = \alpha_1$$

where $\alpha_1 = 1$ follows from $\delta_1 > 0$. Next, we obtain

$$
\begin{aligned}
bb^{\preccurlyeq}(A, B) &= \min(I_W(B(p_1), A(p_1)), I_W(B(p_2), A(p_2))) \\
&= \min(I_W(\min(1 - \beta_1, \beta_2), 0), I_W(\min(1 - \beta_1, \beta_2), 1)) \\
&= I_W(\min(1 - \beta_1, \beta_2), 0) \\
&= 1 - \min(1 - \beta_1, \beta_2) \\
&= \max(\beta_1, 1 - \beta_2) \\
&\geq \beta_1
\end{aligned}
$$

Using (2.35), (2.31) and $\delta_1 \leq \gamma_1$, we find

$$
\begin{aligned}
ee&^{\preccurlyeq}(A, B) \\
&= \min(I_W(A(p_4), B(p_4)), I_W(A(p_7), B(p_7)), I_W(A(p_8), B(p_8))) \\
&= \min(I_W(1 - T_W(\delta_1, \beta_2), 1), I_W(1 - \delta_1, T_W(\gamma_1, 1 - \delta_1)), \\
&\qquad I_W(0, T_W(\gamma_1, 1 - \delta_1))) \\
&= I_W(1 - \delta_1, T_W(\gamma_1, 1 - \delta_1)) \\
&= I_W(1 - \delta_1, 1 - I_W(1 - \delta_1, 1 - \gamma_1)) \\
&= 1 - T_W(1 - \delta_1, I_W(1 - \delta_1, 1 - \gamma_1)) \\
&= \max(\delta_1, \gamma_1) \\
&= \gamma_1
\end{aligned}
$$

From (2.35), (2.31) and $\delta_1 \leq \beta_1$, we find

$$
\begin{aligned}
&eb^{\preccurlyeq}(A, B) \\
&= \min(1 - T_W(A(p_2), B(p_1)), 1 - T_W(A(p_3), B(p_2)), \\
&\qquad 1 - T_W(A(p_4), B(p_3)), 1 - T_W(A(p_7), B(p_4)), \\
&\qquad 1 - T_W(A(p_8), B(p_4))) \\
&= \min(1 - T_W(1, \min(1 - \beta_1, \beta_2)), \\
&\qquad 1 - T_W(1 - T_W(\delta_1, \beta_2), \min(1 - \beta_1, \beta_2)), \\
&\qquad 1 - T_W(1 - T_W(\delta_1, \beta_2), \beta_2), 1 - T_W(1 - \delta_1, 1), 1 - T_W(0, 1)) \\
&= \min(1 - T_W(1, \min(1 - \beta_1, \beta_2)), 1 - T_W(1 - T_W(\delta_1, \beta_2), \beta_2), \delta_1) \\
&= \min(\max(\beta_1, 1 - \beta_2), 1 - T_W(I_W(\beta_2, 1 - \delta_1), \beta_2), \delta_1) \\
&= \min(\max(\beta_1, 1 - \beta_2), 1 - \min(\beta_2, 1 - \delta_1), \delta_1) \\
&= \min(\max(\beta_1, 1 - \beta_2), \max(1 - \beta_2, \delta_1), \delta_1) \\
&= \delta_1
\end{aligned}
$$

and by $\beta_2 \leq \alpha_2$

$$
\begin{aligned}
be^{\preccurlyeq}(B, C) &= \max(T_W(B(p_1), C(p_3)), T_W(B(p_3), C(p_3)), T_W(B(p_4), C(p_4))) \\
&= \max(T_W(B(p_3), C(p_3)), T_W(B(p_4), C(p_4))) \\
&= \max(T_W(\beta_2, 1), T_W(1, \alpha_2)) \\
&= \max(\beta_2, \alpha_2) \\
&= \alpha_2
\end{aligned}
$$

Next, we obtain

$$
\begin{aligned}
bb^{\preccurlyeq}(B, C) &= \min(I_W(C(p_1), B(p_1)), I_W(C(p_3), B(p_3))) \\
&= \min(I_W(1 - T_W(\beta_1, \beta_2), \min(1 - \beta_1, \beta_2)), I_W(1, \beta_2)) \\
&= \min(I_W(1 - T_W(\beta_1, \beta_2), \min(1 - \beta_1, \beta_2)), \beta_2)
\end{aligned}
$$

If $\beta_2 \leq 1 - \beta_1$, we find

$$
I_W(1 - T_W(\beta_1, \beta_2), \min(1 - \beta_1, \beta_2)) = I_W(1 - T_W(\beta_1, \beta_2), \beta_2) \geq \beta_2
$$

Conversely, if $\beta_2 > 1 - \beta_1$, we find by (2.33), (2.35) and (2.31)

$$
\begin{aligned}
I_W(1 - T_W(\beta_1, \beta_2), \min(1 - \beta_1, \beta_2)) &= I_W(1 - T_W(\beta_1, \beta_2), 1 - \beta_1) \\
&= I_W(\beta_1, T_W(\beta_1, \beta_2)) \\
&= 1 - T_W(\beta_1, I_W(\beta_1, 1 - \beta_2)) \\
&= 1 - \min(\beta_1, 1 - \beta_2) \\
&\geq \beta_2
\end{aligned}
$$

Furthermore, from (2.35), (2.31) and $\gamma_2 \leq \alpha_2$, we find

$$ee^{\preceq}(B,C)$$
$$= \min(I_W(B(p_4), C(p_4)), I_W(B(p_6), C(p_6)), I_W(B(p_8), C(p_8)))$$
$$= \min(I_W(1, \alpha_2), I_W(T_W(\gamma_1, 1 - \delta_1), \gamma_2),$$
$$\qquad I_W(T_W(\gamma_1, 1 - \delta_1), T_W(\gamma_1, \gamma_2, 1 - \delta_1)))$$
$$= \min(\alpha_2, I_W(T_W(\gamma_1, 1 - \delta_1), T_W(\gamma_1, \gamma_2, 1 - \delta_1)))$$
$$= \min(\alpha_2, I_W(T_W(\gamma_1, 1 - \delta_1), 1 - I_W(T_W(\gamma_1, 1 - \delta_1), 1 - \gamma_2)))$$
$$= \min(\alpha_2, 1 - T_W(T_W(\gamma_1, 1 - \delta_1), I_W(T_W(\gamma_1, 1 - \delta_1), 1 - \gamma_2)))$$
$$= \min(\alpha_2, 1 - \min(T_W(\gamma_1, 1 - \delta_1), 1 - \gamma_2))$$
$$\geq \min(\alpha_2, \gamma_2)$$
$$= \gamma_2$$

We immediately have

$$eb^{\preceq}(B,C) \geq 0 = \delta_2$$

This already shows that (5.111)–(5.118) are satisfied. We furthermore have

$$bb^{\preceq}(A,C) = \min(I_W(C(p_1), A(p_1)), I_W(C(p_2), A(p_2)))$$
$$= \min(I_W(1 - T_W(\beta_1, \beta_2), 0), I_W(1 - T_W(\beta_1, \beta_2), 1))$$
$$= T_W(\beta_1, \beta_2)$$

Finally, we find using (2.35) and (2.31)

$$ee^{\preceq}(A,C)$$
$$= \min(I_W(A(p_3), C(p_3)), I_W(A(p_4), C(p_4)), I_W(A(p_6), C(p_6)),$$
$$\qquad I_W(A(p_7), C(p_7)), I_W(A(p_8), C(p_8)))$$
$$= \min(I_W(1 - T_W(\delta_1, \beta_2), 1), I_W(1 - T_W(\delta_1, \beta_2), \alpha_2), I_W(1 - \delta_1, \gamma_2),$$
$$\qquad I_W(1 - \delta_1, T_W(\gamma_1, \gamma_2, 1 - \delta_1)), I_W(0, T_W(\gamma_1, \gamma_2, 1 - \delta_1)))$$
$$= \min(I_W(1 - T_W(\delta_1, \beta_2), \alpha_2), I_W(1 - \delta_1, T_W(\gamma_1, \gamma_2, 1 - \delta_1)))$$
$$= \min(I_W(1 - T_W(\delta_1, \beta_2), \alpha_2),$$
$$\qquad I_W(1 - \delta_1, 1 - I_W(1 - \delta_1, 1 - T_W(\gamma_1, \gamma_2))))$$
$$= \min(I_W(1 - T_W(\delta_1, \beta_2), \alpha_2),$$
$$\qquad 1 - T_W(1 - \delta_1, I_W(1 - \delta_1, 1 - T_W(\gamma_1, \gamma_2))))$$
$$= \min(I_W(1 - T_W(\delta_1, \beta_2), \alpha_2), 1 - \min(1 - \delta_1, 1 - T_W(\gamma_1, \gamma_2)))$$
$$= \min(I_W(1 - T_W(\delta_1, \beta_2), \alpha_2), \max(\delta_1, T_W(\gamma_1, \gamma_2)))$$
$$= \min(T_W(\delta_1, \beta_2) + \alpha_2, \max(\delta_1, T_W(\gamma_1, \gamma_2)))$$

$$\leq \min(\max(T_W(\delta_1, \beta_2) + \alpha_2, T_W(\gamma_1, \gamma_2)), \max(\delta_1, T_W(\gamma_1, \gamma_2)))$$
$$= \max(T_W(\gamma_1, \gamma_2), \min(T_W(\delta_1, \beta_2) + \alpha_2, \delta_1))$$

B.3.3   *Restriction for $eb^{\preccurlyeq}(A, C)$*

Finally, the restriction for $eb^{\preccurlyeq}(A, C)$ is satisfied by

$$A = \{p_1/1,]p_1, p_4]/1 - T_W(\delta_1, \beta_2),]p_4, p_6]/1 - \delta_1\}$$
$$B = \{[p_2, p_5[/\beta_2, p_5/1,]p_5, p_7]/\gamma_1\}$$
$$C = \{p_3/1,]p_3, p_5]/\alpha_2,]p_5, p_7]/\gamma_2\}$$

where $p_1 < p_2 < \cdots < p_7$ are real numbers. Clearly, A, B and C are fuzzy time intervals.

$$be^{\preccurlyeq}(A, B) = T_W(A(p_1), B(p_5)) = 1 = \alpha_1$$

where $\alpha_1 = 1$ follows from $\delta_1 > 0$. Next, we find

$$bb^{\preccurlyeq}(A, B) = I_W(B(p_1), A(p_1)) = I_W(0, 1) = 1 \geq \beta_1$$

and

$$ee^{\preccurlyeq}(A, B) = \min(I_W(A(p_5), B(p_5)), I_W(A(p_6), B(p_6)), I_W(A(p_7), B(p_7)))$$
$$= \min(I_W(1 - \delta_1, 1), I_W(1 - \delta_1, \gamma_1), I_W(0, \gamma_1))$$
$$= I_W(1 - \delta_1, \gamma_1)$$
$$\geq \gamma_1$$

Using (2.35) and (2.31), we find

$$eb^{\preccurlyeq}(A, B)$$
$$= \min(1 - T_W(A(p_1), B(p_0)), 1 - T_W(A(p_2), B(p_1)),$$
$$\qquad 1 - T_W(A(p_4), B(p_2)), 1 - T_W(A(p_5), B(p_4)),$$
$$\qquad 1 - T_W(A(p_6), B(p_5)), 1 - T_W(A(p_7), B(p_5)))$$
$$= \min(1 - T_W(1, 0), 1 - T_W(1 - T_W(\delta_1, \beta_2), 0),$$
$$\qquad 1 - T_W(1 - T_W(\delta_1, \beta_2), \beta_2), 1 - T_W(1 - \delta_1, \beta_2),$$
$$\qquad 1 - T_W(1 - \delta_1, 1), 1 - T_W(0, 1))$$
$$= \min(1 - T_W(1 - T_W(\delta_1, \beta_2), \beta_2), \delta_1)$$
$$= \min(1 - T_W(I_W(\beta_2, 1 - \delta_1), \beta_2), \delta_1)$$
$$= \min(1 - \min(\beta_2, 1 - \delta_1), \delta_1)$$
$$= \min(\max(1 - \beta_2, \delta_1), \delta_1)$$
$$= \delta_1$$

From $\beta_2 \leq \alpha_2$, we have

$$be^\preceq(B, C)$$
$$= \max(T_W(B(p_2), C(p_3)), T_W(B(p_3), C(p_3)), T_W(B(p_5), C(p_5)))$$
$$= \max(T_W(B(p_3), C(p_3)), T_W(B(p_5), C(p_5)))$$
$$= \max(T_W(\beta_2, 1), T_W(1, \alpha_2))$$
$$= \max(\beta_2, \alpha_2)$$
$$= \alpha_2$$

We immediately have

$$bb^\preceq(B, C) = \min(I_W(C(p_2), B(p_2)), I_W(C(p_3), B(p_3)))$$
$$= \min(I_W(0, \beta_2), I_W(1, \beta_2))$$
$$= \beta_2$$

and by $\gamma_2 \leq \alpha_2$

$$ee^\preceq(B, C) = \min(I_W(B(p_5), C(p_5)), I_W(B(p_7), C(p_7)))$$
$$= \min(I_W(1, \alpha_2), I_W(\gamma_1, \gamma_2))$$
$$\geq \min(\alpha_2, \gamma_2)$$
$$= \gamma_2$$

It holds that

$$eb^\preceq(B, C) \geq 0 = \delta_2$$

Thus, we have that (5.111)–(5.118) are satisfied. Finally, we obtain

$$eb^\preceq(A, C)$$
$$= \min(1 - T_W(A(p_1), C(p_0)), 1 - T_W(A(p_3), C(p_1)),$$
$$\quad 1 - T_W(A(p_4), C(p_3)), 1 - T_W(A(p_5), C(p_3)),$$
$$\quad 1 - T_W(A(p_6), C(p_3)), 1 - T_W(A(p_7), C(p_3)))$$
$$= \min(1 - T_W(1, 0), 1 - T_W(1 - T_W(\delta_1, \beta_2), 0),$$
$$\quad 1 - T_W(1 - T_W(\delta_1, \beta_2), 1), 1 - T_W(1 - \delta_1, 1),$$
$$\quad 1 - T_W(1 - \delta_1, 1), 1 - T_W(0, 1))$$
$$= \min(T_W(\delta_1, \beta_2), \delta_1, \delta_1)$$
$$= T_W(\delta_1, \beta_2)$$

B.4 $\quad \delta_1 > 0, \, \delta_2 > 0$

Finally, we consider the case where $\delta_1 > 0$ and $\delta_2 > 0$.

B.4.1 *Restrictions for* $bb^{\preceq}(A, C)$ *and* $ee^{\preceq}(A, C)$

The restrictions for $bb^{\preceq}(A, C)$ and $ee^{\preceq}(A, C)$ are satisfied by

$$A = \{p_2/1,]p_2, p_5]/1 - \max(\delta_1, T_W(\gamma_1, \gamma_2))\}$$
$$B = \{[p_1, p_3[/1 - \beta_1, p_3/1,]p_3, p_5]/1 - \gamma_2\}$$
$$C = \{[p_1, p_4[/1 - \max(\delta_2, T_W(\beta_1, \beta_2)), p_4/1\}$$

where $p_1 < p_2 < \cdots < p_5$ are real numbers. Clearly, A, B and C are convex, and therefore fuzzy time intervals. We find

$$be^{\preceq}(A, B) \geq T_W(A(p_2), B(p_3)) = 1 = \alpha_1$$

where $\alpha_1 = 1$ follows from $\delta_1 > 0$. and

$$
\begin{aligned}
bb^{\preceq}(A, B) &= \min(I_W(B(p_1), A(p_1)), I_W(B(p_2), A(p_2))) \\
&= \min(I_W(1 - \beta_1, 0), I_W(1 - \beta_1, 1)) \\
&= \beta_1
\end{aligned}
$$

Using (2.33), (2.35) and (2.31), we obtain

$$
\begin{aligned}
ee^{\preceq}&(A, B) \\
&= \min(I_W(A(p_3), B(p_3)), I_W(A(p_5), B(p_5))) \\
&= \min(I_W(1 - \max(\delta_1, T_W(\gamma_1, \gamma_2)), 1), \\
&\qquad I_W(1 - \max(\delta_1, T_W(\gamma_1, \gamma_2)), 1 - \gamma_2)) \\
&= I_W(1 - \max(\delta_1, T_W(\gamma_1, \gamma_2)), 1 - \gamma_2) \\
&\geq I_W(1 - T_W(\gamma_1, \gamma_2), 1 - \gamma_2) \\
&= I_W(\gamma_2, T_W(\gamma_1, \gamma_2)) \\
&= I_W(\gamma_2, 1 - I_W(\gamma_2, 1 - \gamma_1)) \\
&= 1 - T_W(\gamma_2, I_W(\gamma_2, 1 - \gamma_1)) \\
&= 1 - \min(\gamma_2, 1 - \gamma_1) \\
&= \max(1 - \gamma_2, \gamma_1) \\
&\geq \gamma_1
\end{aligned}
$$

Using $\delta_1 \leq \beta_1$, we find

$$
\begin{aligned}
eb^{\preceq}&(A, B) \\
&= \min(1 - T_W(A(p_2), B(p_1)), 1 - T_W(A(p_3), B(p_2)), \\
&\qquad 1 - T_W(A(p_5), B(p_3))) \\
&= \min(1 - T_W(1, 1 - \beta_1), 1 - T_W(1 - \max(\delta_1, T_W(\gamma_1, \gamma_2)), 1 - \beta_1), \\
&\qquad 1 - T_W(1 - \max(\delta_1, T_W(\gamma_1, \gamma_2)), 1)) \\
&= \min(\beta_1, \max(\delta_1, T_W(\gamma_1, \gamma_2))) \\
&\geq \delta_1
\end{aligned}
$$

From $\delta_2 > 0$, we have $\alpha_2 = 1$, hence

$$be^{\preceq}(B, C) \geq T_W(B(p_3), C(p_4)) = 1 = \alpha_2$$

Next, we have using (2.33), (2.35) and (2.31)

$$
\begin{aligned}
bb^{\preceq}(B, C) &= \min(I_W(C(p_1), B(p_1)), I_W(C(p_3), B(p_3))) \\
&= \min(I_W(1 - \max(\delta_2, T_W(\beta_1, \beta_2)), 1 - \beta_1), \\
&\qquad I_W(1 - \max(\delta_2, T_W(\beta_1, \beta_2)), 1)) \\
&= I_W(1 - \max(\delta_2, T_W(\beta_1, \beta_2)), 1 - \beta_1) \\
&\geq I_W(1 - T_W(\beta_1, \beta_2), 1 - \beta_1) \\
&= I_W(\beta_1, T_W(\beta_1, \beta_2)) \\
&= I_W(\beta_1, 1 - I_W(\beta_1, 1 - \beta_2)) \\
&= 1 - T_W(\beta_1, I_W(\beta_1, 1 - \beta_2)) \\
&= 1 - \min(\beta_1, 1 - \beta_2) \\
&\geq \beta_2
\end{aligned}
$$

We furthermore obtain

$$
\begin{aligned}
ee^{\preceq}(B, C) &= \min(I_W(B(p_4), C(p_4)), I_W(B(p_5), C(p_5))) \\
&= \min(I_W(1 - \gamma_2, 1), I_W(1 - \gamma_2, 0)) \\
&= \gamma_2
\end{aligned}
$$

and using $\delta_2 \leq \gamma_2$

$$
\begin{aligned}
&eb^{\preceq}(B, C) \\
&= \min(1 - T_W(B(p_3), C(p_1)), 1 - T_W(B(p_4), C(p_3)), \\
&\qquad 1 - T_W(B(p_5), C(p_4))) \\
&= \min(1 - T_W(1, 1 - \max(\delta_2, T_W(\beta_1, \beta_2))), \\
&\qquad 1 - T_W(1 - \gamma_2, 1 - \max(\delta_2, T_W(\beta_1, \beta_2))), 1 - T_W(1 - \gamma_2, 1)) \\
&= \min(\max(\delta_2, T_W(\beta_1, \beta_2)), \gamma_2) \\
&\geq \delta_2
\end{aligned}
$$

Thus, we have that (5.111)–(5.118) are satisfied. Next, we find

$$
\begin{aligned}
&bb^{\preceq}(A, C) \\
&= \min(I_W(C(p_1), A(p_1)), I_W(C(p_2), A(p_2))) \\
&= \min(I_W(1 - \max(\delta_2, T_W(\beta_1, \beta_2)), 0), I_W(1 - \max(\delta_2, T_W(\beta_1, \beta_2)), 1)) \\
&= I_W(1 - \max(\delta_2, T_W(\beta_1, \beta_2)), 0) \\
&= \max(\delta_2, T_W(\beta_1, \beta_2))
\end{aligned}
$$

From $\delta_1 > 0$ and $\delta_2 > 0$, we know that $\alpha_1 = \alpha_2 = 1$. Hence, it holds that $\beta_1 + T_W(\delta_2, \alpha_1) = \beta_1 + \delta_2 \geq \delta_2$ and $\alpha_1 + T_W(\delta_2, \gamma_1) \geq 1 \geq \delta_2$. Thus we find

$$\max(\delta_2, T_W(\beta_1, \beta_2))$$
$$= \max(T_W(\beta_1, \beta_2), \min(\alpha_1 + T_W(\delta_2, \gamma_1), \delta_2, \beta_1 + T_W(\delta_2, \alpha_1)))$$

In the same way, we have

$$ee^{\preccurlyeq}(A, C)$$
$$= \min(I_W(A(p_4), C(p_4)), I_W(A(p_5), C(p_5)))$$
$$= \min(I_W(1 - \max(\delta_1, T_W(\gamma_1, \gamma_2)), 1), I_W(1 - \max(\delta_1, T_W(\gamma_1, \gamma_2)), 0))$$
$$= \max(\delta_1, T_W(\gamma_1, \gamma_2))$$
$$= \max(T_W(\gamma_1, \gamma_2), \min(\alpha_2 + T_W(\delta_1, \beta_2), \delta_1, \gamma_2 + T_W(\delta_1, \alpha_2)))$$

B.4.2 Restrictions for $be^{\preccurlyeq}(A, C)$ and $eb^{\preccurlyeq}(A, C)$

Finally, the restrictions for $be^{\preccurlyeq}(A, C)$ and $eb^{\preccurlyeq}(A, C)$ are satisfied by

$$A = \{[p_1, p_3]/1,]p_3, p_6]/1 - \max(\delta_1, T_W(\gamma_1, \delta_2))\}$$
$$B = \{[p_1, p_4[/\min(1 - \delta_1, \beta_2), p_4/1,]p_4, p_7]/\min(1 - \delta_2, \gamma_1)\}$$
$$C = \{[p_2, p_5[/1 - \max(\delta_2, T_W(\delta_1, \beta_2)), [p_5, p_7]/1\}$$

where $p_1 < p_2 < \cdots < p_7$ are real numbers. Clearly, A, B and C are convex.

$$be^{\preccurlyeq}(A, B) \geq T_W(A(p_2), B(p_4)) = 1 = \alpha_1$$

where $\alpha_1 = 1$ follows from $\delta_1 > 0$.

$$bb^{\preccurlyeq}(A, B) = I_W(B(p_1), A(p_1)) = I_W(\min(1 - \delta_1, \beta_2), 1) = 1 \geq \beta_1$$

Next, we find

$$ee^{\preccurlyeq}(A, B)$$
$$= \min(I_W(A(p_4), B(p_4)), I_W(A(p_6), B(p_6)), I_W(A(p_7), B(p_7)))$$
$$= \min(I_W(1 - \max(\delta_1, T_W(\gamma_1, \delta_2)), 1),$$
$$\qquad I_W(1 - \max(\delta_1, T_W(\gamma_1, \delta_2)), \min(1 - \delta_2, \gamma_1)),$$
$$\qquad I_W(0, \min(1 - \delta_2, \gamma_1)))$$
$$= I_W(1 - \max(\delta_1, T_W(\gamma_1, \delta_2)), \min(1 - \delta_2, \gamma_1))$$

If $\gamma_1 \le 1 - \delta_2$, we find

$$I_W(1 - \max(\delta_1, T_W(\gamma_1, \delta_2)), \min(1 - \delta_2, \gamma_1))$$
$$= I_W(1 - \max(\delta_1, T_W(\gamma_1, \delta_2)), \gamma_1)$$
$$\ge \gamma_1$$

Conversely, assume $\gamma_1 > 1 - \delta_2$. If $\delta_1 \ge T_W(\gamma_1, \delta_2)$, we know by (2.21) that $\gamma_1 \le I_W(\delta_2, \delta_1)$. Using (2.33), we then find

$$I_W(1 - \max(\delta_1, T_W(\gamma_1, \delta_2)), \min(1 - \delta_2, \gamma_1))$$
$$= I_W(1 - \delta_1, 1 - \delta_2)$$
$$= I_W(\delta_2, \delta_1)$$
$$\ge \gamma_1$$

If, on the other hand, $\delta_1 < T_W(\gamma_1, \delta_2)$, we find by (2.33), (2.35) and (2.31)

$$I_W(1 - \max(\delta_1, T_W(\gamma_1, \delta_2)), \min(1 - \delta_2, \gamma_1))$$
$$= I_W(1 - T_W(\gamma_1, \delta_2), 1 - \delta_2)$$
$$= I_W(\delta_2, T_W(\gamma_1, \delta_2))$$
$$= I_W(\delta_2, 1 - I_W(\delta_2, 1 - \gamma_1))$$
$$= 1 - T_W(\delta_2, I_W(\delta_2, 1 - \gamma_1))$$
$$= 1 - \min(\delta_2, 1 - \gamma_1)$$
$$= \max(1 - \delta_2, \gamma_1)$$
$$\ge \gamma_1$$

Next, we find

$$eb^{\preccurlyeq}(A, B)$$
$$= \min(1 - T_W(A(p_3), B(p_1)), 1 - T_W(A(p_4), B(p_3)),$$
$$\quad 1 - T_W(A(p_6), B(p_4)), 1 - T_W(A(p_7), B(p_4)))$$
$$= \min(1 - T_W(1, \min(1 - \delta_1, \beta_2)),$$
$$\quad 1 - T_W(1 - \max(\delta_1, T_W(\gamma_1, \delta_2)), \min(1 - \delta_1, \beta_2)),$$
$$\quad 1 - T_W(1 - \max(\delta_1, T_W(\gamma_1, \delta_2)), 1), 1 - T_W(0, 1))$$
$$= \min(1 - \min(1 - \delta_1, \beta_2), \max(\delta_1, T_W(\gamma_1, \delta_2)))$$
$$= \min(\max(\delta_1, 1 - \beta_2), \max(\delta_1, T_W(\gamma_1, \delta_2)))$$
$$\ge \delta_1$$

and

$$be^{\preccurlyeq}(B, C) \ge T_W(B(p_4), C(p_7)) = 1 = \alpha_2$$

where $\alpha_2 = 1$ follows from $\delta_2 > 0$. It holds that

$$bb^{\preceq}(B,C)$$
$$= \min(I_W(C(p_1), B(p_1)), I_W(C(p_2), B(p_2)), I_W(C(p_4), B(p_4)))$$
$$= \min(I_W(0, \min(1 - \delta_1, \beta_2)),$$
$$I_W(1 - \max(\delta_2, T_W(\delta_1, \beta_2)), \min(1 - \delta_1, \beta_2)),$$
$$I_W(1 - \max(\delta_2, T_W(\delta_1, \beta_2)), 1))$$
$$= I_W(1 - \max(\delta_2, T_W(\delta_1, \beta_2)), \min(1 - \delta_1, \beta_2))$$

If $\beta_2 \leq 1 - \delta_1$, we find

$$I_W(1 - \max(\delta_2, T_W(\delta_1, \beta_2)), \min(1 - \delta_1, \beta_2))$$
$$= I_W(1 - \max(\delta_2, T_W(\delta_1, \beta_2)), \beta_2)$$
$$\geq \beta_2$$

Conversely, assume $\beta_2 > 1 - \delta_1$. If $\delta_2 \geq T_W(\delta_1, \beta_2)$, we know from (2.21) that $I_W(\delta_1, \delta_2) \geq \beta_2$. Using (2.33), we then find

$$I_W(1 - \max(\delta_2, T_W(\delta_1, \beta_2)), \min(1 - \delta_1, \beta_2)) = I_W(1 - \delta_2, 1 - \delta_1))$$
$$= I_W(\delta_1, \delta_2)$$
$$\geq \beta_2$$

If, on the other hand, $\delta_2 < T_W(\delta_1, \beta_2)$, we find using (2.33), (2.35) and (2.31)

$$I_W(1 - \max(\delta_2, T_W(\delta_1, \beta_2)), \min(1 - \delta_1, \beta_2))$$
$$= I_W(1 - T_W(\delta_1, \beta_2), 1 - \delta_1)$$
$$= I_W(\delta_1, T_W(\delta_1, \beta_2))$$
$$= I_W(\delta_1, 1 - I_W(\delta_1, 1 - \beta_2))$$
$$= 1 - T_W(\delta_1, I_W(\delta_1, 1 - \beta_2))$$
$$= 1 - \min(\delta_1, 1 - \beta_2)$$
$$\geq \beta_2$$

Next, we find

$$ee^{\preceq}(B,C) = I_W(B(p_7), C(p_7)) = I_W(\min(1 - \delta_2, \gamma_1), 1) = 1 \geq \gamma_2$$

and

$$eb^{\preccurlyeq}(B,C)$$
$$= \min(1 - T_W(B(p_4), C(p_3)), 1 - T_W(B(p_5), C(p_4)),$$
$$\qquad 1 - T_W(B(p_7), C(p_5)))$$
$$= \min(1 - T_W(1, 1 - \max(\delta_2, T_W(\delta_1, \beta_2))), 1 - T_W(\min(1 - \delta_2, \gamma_1),$$
$$\qquad 1 - \max(\delta_2, T_W(\delta_1, \beta_2))), 1 - T_W(\min(1 - \delta_2, \gamma_1), 1))$$
$$= \min(\max(\delta_2, T_W(\delta_1, \beta_2)), 1 - \min(1 - \delta_2, \gamma_1))$$
$$= \min(\max(\delta_2, T_W(\delta_1, \beta_2)), \max(\delta_2, 1 - \gamma_1))$$
$$\geq \delta_2$$

Hence, it holds that (5.111)–(5.118) are satisfied. It furthermore holds that

$$be^{\preccurlyeq}(A,C) = T_W(A(p_1), C(p_5)) = 1$$

From $\delta_1 > 0$ and $\delta_2 > 0$, we know $\alpha_1 = \alpha_2 = 1$, hence $T_W(\alpha_1, \delta_2) = \delta_2 > 0$ and $T_W(\delta_1, \alpha_2) = \delta_1 > 0$. Therefore, one of the first two cases in the definition of α_3 applies. Since $\min(\alpha_1, \alpha_2) = 1$, we conclude $\alpha_3 = 1$. Finally, we have

$$eb^{\preccurlyeq}(A,C)$$
$$= \min(1 - T_W(A(p_3), C(p_2)), 1 - T_W(A(p_5), C(p_3)),$$
$$\qquad 1 - T_W(A(p_6), C(p_5)), 1 - T_W(A(p_7), C(p_5)))$$
$$= \min(1 - T_W(1, 1 - \max(\delta_2, T_W(\delta_1, \beta_2))),$$
$$\qquad 1 - T_W(1 - \max(\delta_1, T_W(\gamma_1, \delta_2)), 1 - \max(\delta_2, T_W(\delta_1, \beta_2))),$$
$$\qquad 1 - T_W(1 - \max(\delta_1, T_W(\gamma_1, \delta_2)), 1), 1 - T_W(0, 1))$$
$$= \min(\max(\delta_2, T_W(\delta_1, \beta_2)), \max(\delta_1, T_W(\gamma_1, \delta_2)))$$
$$\leq \min(\max(\delta_2, T_W(\delta_1, \beta_2), T_W(\gamma_1, \delta_2)),$$
$$\qquad \max(\delta_1, T_W(\delta_1, \beta_2), T_W(\gamma_1, \delta_2)))$$
$$= \max(T_W(\delta_1, \beta_2), T_W(\gamma_1, \delta_2), \min(\delta_1, \delta_2))$$

Appendix C

Proof of Proposition 8.1

In the following, we assume $\alpha > 0$ and $\alpha_0 > 0$, where α_0 is a sufficiently large constant ($\alpha \ll \alpha_0$). Moreover, let Θ be a normalised set of RCC formulas over a set of variables V satisfying requirements (8.12)–(8.15) and the transitivity rules for fuzzy topological relations. For every pair of variables (a, b) in V^2, the values of $C^{\mathcal{I}}(a^{\mathcal{I}}, a^{\mathcal{I}})$, $P^{\mathcal{I}}(a^{\mathcal{I}}, a^{\mathcal{I}})$, $O^{\mathcal{I}}(a^{\mathcal{I}}, a^{\mathcal{I}})$ and $NTP^{\mathcal{I}}(a^{\mathcal{I}}, a^{\mathcal{I}})$ are then identical in any model $\mathcal{I}$ of Θ. Below, we will refer to these values as λ_{ab}^C, λ_{ab}^P, λ_{ab}^O and λ_{ab}^{NTP}. In other words, we assume that for every (a, b) in V^2, Θ contains the fuzzy RCC formulas

$$C(a,b) \geq \lambda_{ab}^C \quad C(a,b) \leq \lambda_{ab}^C \quad P(a,b) \geq \lambda_{ab}^P \quad P(a,b) \leq \lambda_{ab}^P$$
$$O(a,b) \geq \lambda_{ab}^O \quad O(a,b) \leq \lambda_{ab}^O \quad NTP(a,b) \geq \lambda_{ab}^{NTP} \quad NTP(a,b) \leq \lambda_{ab}^{NTP}$$

where, by assumption, $\lambda_{aa}^{NTP} < 1$ for every a in V. We will prove that there exists a mapping f from V to the set of normalised, bounded fuzzy sets in $\mathbb{R}^n$ such that

$$C_\alpha(f(a), f(b)) = \lambda_{ab}^C \tag{C.1}$$
$$O_\alpha(f(a), f(b)) = \lambda_{ab}^O \tag{C.2}$$
$$P_\alpha(f(a), f(b)) = \lambda_{ab}^P \tag{C.3}$$
$$NTP_\alpha(f(a), f(b)) = \lambda_{ab}^{NTP} \tag{C.4}$$

for all (a, b) in V^2, in other words, that f defines an $(n; \alpha, 0)$ interpretation which satisfies Θ. In particular, we choose $n = |V|$, i.e., the dimension of the Euclidean space is the same as the number of different variables in Θ. Furthermore, we can always define a total ordering on the elements of V; we write $V = \{v_1, v_2, \ldots, v_n\}$. For the ease of presentation, we will write λ_{ij}^C instead of $\lambda_{v_i v_j}^C$, λ_{ij}^O instead of $\lambda_{v_i v_j}^O$, etc.

C.1   Lemmas

Before presenting the actual proof of Proposition 8.1, we first show a number of technical lemmas. For each point a in $\mathbb{R}^n$, we let P_a and L_a be the fuzzy sets in $\mathbb{R}^n$ defined as

$$P_a(p) = R_{\alpha_0}(a, p)$$
$$L_a(p) = R_{\alpha}(a, p)$$

for all p in $\mathbb{R}^n$. Note that P_a and L_a are n–dimensional spheres in $\mathbb{R}^n$ with center a and radius α_0 and α respectively. Moreover, for λ in $[0, 1]$, we let L_a^λ and P_a^λ be the fuzzy sets in $\mathbb{R}^n$ defined as

$$L_a^\lambda(p) = T(\lambda, L_a(p))$$
$$P_a^\lambda(p) = T(\lambda, P_a(p))$$

for all p in $\mathbb{R}^n$.

Lemma C.1. *Let T be a left–continuous t–norm , I_T its residual implicator, and let λ be in $[0, 1]$. It holds that*

$$R_\alpha{\downarrow}_{I_T}{\uparrow}_T P_a^\lambda = P_a^\lambda \tag{C.5}$$
$$R_\alpha{\downarrow}_{I_T}{\uparrow}_T L_a^\lambda = L_a^\lambda \tag{C.6}$$

Proof. As an example, we show (C.5); the proof of (C.6) is entirely analogous. Because R_α is a crisp relation, for every point p that is at the same time in the support of $R_\alpha{\downarrow}_{I_T}{\uparrow}_T P_a^\lambda$ and in the support of P_a^λ, it holds that

$$(R_\alpha{\downarrow}_{I_T}{\uparrow}_T P_a^\lambda)(p) = (P_a^\lambda)(p)$$

Hence, it suffices to show that

$$supp(R_\alpha{\downarrow}_{I_T}{\uparrow}_T P_a^\lambda) = supp(P_a^\lambda)$$

Clearly $supp(P_a^\lambda)$ is the set of points which are within distance α_0 of a, i.e., $supp(P_a^\lambda) = P_a$. Furthermore, the support of $R_\alpha{\uparrow}_T P_a^\lambda$ consists of the points p that are within distance α of some point p from $supp(P_a^\lambda)$. In other words, $supp(R_\alpha{\uparrow}_T P_a^\lambda)$ is an n–dimensional sphere with center a and radius $\alpha_0 + \alpha$. Finally, the support of $R_\alpha{\downarrow}_{I_T}{\uparrow}_T P_a^\lambda$ consists of the points q satisfying

$$(\forall p \in \mathbb{R}^n)(d(p, q) \leq \alpha \Rightarrow p \in supp(R_\alpha{\uparrow}_T P_a^\lambda))$$

or

$$(\forall p \in \mathbb{R}^n)(d(p, q) \leq \alpha \Rightarrow d(p, a) \leq \alpha_0 + \alpha)$$

The latter expression is equivalent to $d(q, a) \leq \alpha_0$, or $q \in P_a$. $\square$

Lemma C.2. *Let T be a left–continuous t–norm and I_T its residual implicator and let A, B and D be fuzzy sets in $\mathbb{R}^n$ such that $d(p,q) > 2\alpha$ for every p in $supp(D)$ and every q in $supp(B)$. It holds that*

$$O_\alpha(A \cup B, D) = O_\alpha(A, D)$$

Proof. It is easy to see that $O_\alpha(A \cup B, D) \geq O_\alpha(A, D)$. We show by contradiction that $O_\alpha(A \cup B, D) \leq O_\alpha(A, D)$ must hold as well. Assume that $O_\alpha(A \cup B, D) > O_\alpha(A, D)$ were the case. For some p_0 in $\mathbb{R}^n$, we then have by the monotonicity of the supremum (Lemma 2.7)

$$T_W(R_\alpha{\downarrow}_{I_T}{\uparrow}_T(A \cup B)(p_0), R_\alpha{\downarrow}_{I_T}{\uparrow}_T D(p_0))$$
$$> T_W(R_\alpha{\downarrow}_{I_T}{\uparrow}_T A(p_0), R_\alpha{\downarrow}_{I_T}{\uparrow}_T D(p_0))$$

which is only possible if

$$R_\alpha{\downarrow}_{I_T}{\uparrow}_T(A \cup B)(p_0) \tag{C.7}$$
$$> R_\alpha{\downarrow}_{I_T}{\uparrow}_T A(p_0) \tag{C.8}$$

and

$$R_\alpha{\downarrow}_{I_T}{\uparrow}_T D(p_0) > 0 \tag{C.9}$$

From (C.7), we have

$$\inf_{q \in \mathbb{R}^n} I_T(R_\alpha(p_0, q), \sup_{r \in \mathbb{R}^n} T(R_\alpha(q, r), (A \cup B)(r)))$$
$$> \inf_{q \in \mathbb{R}^n} I_T(R_\alpha(p_0, q), \sup_{r \in \mathbb{R}^n} T(R_\alpha(q, r), A(r)))$$

From the monotonicity of the infimum (Lemma 2.7), we derive that there must be some q_0 in $\mathbb{R}^n$ such that

$$I_T(R_\alpha(p_0, q_0), \sup_{r \in \mathbb{R}^n} T(R_\alpha(q_0, r), (A \cup B)(r)))$$
$$> I_T(R_\alpha(p_0, q_0), \sup_{r \in \mathbb{R}^n} T(R_\alpha(q_0, r), A(r)))$$

implying $R_\alpha(p_0, q_0) \neq 0$ and therefore $d(p_0, q_0) \leq \alpha$ and $R_\alpha(p_0, q_0) = 1$. In particular, we obtain using (2.22)

$$I_T(R_\alpha(p, q_0), \sup_{r \in \mathbb{R}^n} T(R_\alpha(q_0, r), (A \cup B)(r)))$$

$$> I_T(R_\alpha(p, q_0), \sup_{r \in \mathbb{R}^n} T(R_\alpha(q_0, r), A(r)))$$

$$\Leftrightarrow I_T(1, \sup_{r \in \mathbb{R}^n} T(R_\alpha(q_0, r), (A \cup B)(r))) > I_T(1, \sup_{r \in \mathbb{R}^n} T(R_\alpha(q_0, r), A(r)))$$

$$\Leftrightarrow \sup_{r \in \mathbb{R}^n} T(R_\alpha(q_0, r), (A \cup B)(r)) > \sup_{r \in \mathbb{R}^n} T(R_\alpha(q_0, r), A(r))$$

$$\Leftrightarrow \sup_{r \in \mathbb{R}^n} T(R_\alpha(q_0, r), \max(A(r), B(r))) > \sup_{r \in \mathbb{R}^n} T(R_\alpha(q_0, r), A(r))$$

$$\Leftrightarrow \max(\sup_{r \in \mathbb{R}^n} T(R_\alpha(q_0, r), A(r)), \sup_{r \in \mathbb{R}^n} T(R_\alpha(q_0, r), B(r)))$$

$$> \sup_{r \in \mathbb{R}^n} T(R_\alpha(q_0, r), A(r))$$

$$\Leftrightarrow \sup_{r \in \mathbb{R}^n} T(R_\alpha(q_0, r), B(r)) > \sup_{r \in \mathbb{R}^n} T(R_\alpha(q_0, r), A(r))$$

Hence, from Lemma 2.7, we know that for some r_0 in $\mathbb{R}^n$, it holds that

$$T(R_\alpha(q_0, r_0), B(r_0)) > T(R_\alpha(q_0, r_0), A(r_0)) \tag{C.10}$$

implying $R_\alpha(q_0, r_0) > 0$ and thus $d(q_0, r_0) \leq \alpha$. On the other hand, we find using $R_\alpha(p_0, q_0) = 1$

$$R_\alpha \downarrow_{I_T} \uparrow_T D(p_0) \leq I_T(R_\alpha(p_0, q_0), \sup_{r \in \mathbb{R}^n} T(R_\alpha(q_0, r), D(r)))$$

$$= \sup_{r \in \mathbb{R}^n} T(R_\alpha(q_0, r), D(r))$$

Using (C.9), we can infer that $\sup_{r \in \mathbb{R}^n} T(R_\alpha(q_0, r), D(r)) > 0$, and

$$T(R_\alpha(q_0, r_1), D(r_1)) > 0 \tag{C.11}$$

for some r_1 in $\mathbb{R}^n$. This entails $R_\alpha(q_0, r_1) = 1$, or $d(q_0, r_1) \leq \alpha$. From $d(q_0, r_1) \leq \alpha$ and $d(q_0, r_0) \leq \alpha$, we find $d(r_0, r_1) \leq 2\alpha$ using the triangle inequality. However, from (C.10) and (C.11), we find $B(r_0) > 0$ and $D(r_1) > 0$, which violates the assumption that $d(p, q) > 2\alpha$ for every p in $supp(D)$ and every q in $supp(B)$. $\quad\square$

Corollary C.1. *Let T be a left–continuous t–norm and I_T its residual implicator and let B and D be fuzzy sets in $\mathbb{R}^n$ such that $d(p, q) > 2\alpha$ for every p in $supp(D)$ and every q in $supp(B)$. It holds that*

$$O_\alpha(B, D) = 0$$

Lemma C.3. *Let A, B and D be fuzzy sets in a universe X such that*
$$\sup_{x \in X} A(x) > \max(\sup_{x \in X} B(x), \sup_{x \in X} D(x))$$
It holds that $A(x_0) > B(x_0)$ and $A(x_0) > D(x_0)$ for some x_0 in X.

Proof. It holds that
$$\max(\sup_{x \in X} B(x), \sup_{x \in X} D(x)) = \sup_{x \in X} \max(B(x), D(x))$$
From Lemma 2.7 we therefore find that
$$A(x_0) > \max(B(x_0), D(x_0))$$
for some x_0 in X, in other words, $A(x_0) > B(x_0)$ and $A(x_0) > D(x_0)$ $\quad\square$

Lemma C.4. *Let T be a left–continuous t–norm and I_T its residual implicator and let A, B, D and E be fuzzy sets in $\mathbb{R}^n$ such that $d(p,q) > 4\alpha$ for every p in $supp(A)$ and every q in $supp(B)$. It holds that*
$$O_\alpha(A \cup B \cup E, D) = \max(O_\alpha(A \cup E, D), O_\alpha(B \cup E, D))$$

Proof. Clearly, we have that $O_\alpha(A \cup B \cup E, D) \geq O_\alpha(A \cup E, D)$ and $O_\alpha(A \cup B \cup E, D) \geq O_\alpha(B \cup E, D)$, hence
$$O_\alpha(A \cup B \cup E, D) \geq \max(O_\alpha(A \cup E, D), O_\alpha(B \cup E, D))$$
We show by contradiction that also $O_\alpha(A \cup B \cup E, D) \leq \max(O_\alpha(A \cup E, D), O_\alpha(B \cup E, D))$ needs to hold. Therefore, assume $O_\alpha(A \cup B \cup E, D) > \max(O_\alpha(A \cup E, D), O_\alpha(B \cup E, D))$. By Lemma C.3, we know that for some p_0 in $\mathbb{R}^n$

$$(R_\alpha\downarrow_{I_T}\uparrow_T(A \cup B \cup E))(p_0) > (R_\alpha\downarrow_{I_T}\uparrow_T(A \cup E))(p_0) \qquad (C.12)$$

$$(R_\alpha\downarrow_{I_T}\uparrow_T(A \cup B \cup E))(p_0) > (R_\alpha\downarrow_{I_T}\uparrow_T(B \cup E))(p_0) \qquad (C.13)$$

For every q_0 in $\mathbb{R}^n$ such that $d(p_0, q_0) \leq \alpha$, we find from (C.12) using (2.22) and (2.54)

$$(R_\alpha\downarrow_{I_T}\uparrow_T(A \cup B \cup E))(p_0) > (R_\alpha\downarrow_{I_T}\uparrow_T(A \cup E))(p_0)$$

$$\Rightarrow (R_\alpha\downarrow_{I_T}\uparrow_T(A \cup B \cup E))(p_0) > 0$$

$$\Leftrightarrow \inf_{q \in \mathbb{R}^n} I_T(R_\alpha(p_0, q), (R_\alpha\uparrow_T(A \cup B \cup E))(q)) > 0$$

$$\Rightarrow I_T(R_\alpha(p_0, q_0), (R_\alpha\uparrow_T(A \cup B \cup E))(q_0)) > 0$$

$$\Leftrightarrow I_T(1, (R_\alpha\uparrow_T(A \cup B \cup E))(q_0)) > 0$$

$$\Leftrightarrow (R_\alpha\uparrow_T(A \cup B \cup E))(q_0) > 0$$

$$\Leftrightarrow \max((R_\alpha\uparrow_T A)(q_0), (R_\alpha\uparrow_T B)(q_0), (R_\alpha\uparrow_T E)(q_0)) > 0$$

$$\Leftrightarrow \max(\sup_{r \in \mathbb{R}^n} T(R_\alpha(q_0, r), A(r)), \sup_{r \in \mathbb{R}^n} T(R_\alpha(q_0, r), B(r)),$$

$$\sup_{r \in \mathbb{R}^n} T(R_\alpha(q_0, r), E(r))) > 0$$

Hence, for every q_0 in $\mathbb{R}^n$ such that $d(p_0, q_0) \leq \alpha$, there exists some r_0 in $supp(A)$, $supp(B)$ or $supp(E)$ such that $d(q_0, r_0) \leq \alpha$.

Let X be the set of all points q for which $d(p_0, q) \leq \alpha$. For every q in X, we know from the derivation above that q is either within distance α of some point in $supp(A)$, $supp(B)$ or $supp(E)$. Hence, we can write $X = X_a \cup X_b \cup X_e$ such that X_a (resp. X_b, X_e) contains all points from X within distance α of $supp(A)$ (resp. $supp(B)$, $supp(E)$). Note that either $X_a \cap X = \emptyset$ or $X_b \cap X = \emptyset$. Indeed, if $r_1 \in X_a \cap X$ and $r_2 \in X_b \cap X$ for some $r_1, r_2 \in \mathbb{R}^n$, we would find using the triangle inequality that $d(p_a, p_b) \leq d(p_a, r_1) + d(r_1, p_0) + d(p_0, r_2) + d(r_2, p_b) \leq 4\alpha$ for some p_a in $supp(A)$ and some p_b in $supp(B)$. Therefore, either $X = X_a \cup X_e$ or $X = X_b \cup X_e$. Hence, we have either

$$(R_\alpha \!\uparrow_T (A \cup B \cup E))(q) = (R_\alpha \!\uparrow_T (A \cup E))(q)$$

for every q in X, or

$$(R_\alpha \!\uparrow_T (A \cup B \cup E))(q) = (R_\alpha \!\uparrow_T (B \cup E))(q)$$

for every q in X, which implies that either

$$(R_\alpha \!\downarrow_{I_T} \!\uparrow_T (A \cup B \cup E))(p_0) = (R_\alpha \!\downarrow_{I_T} \!\uparrow_T (A \cup E))(p_0)$$

or

$$(R_\alpha \!\downarrow_{I_T} \!\uparrow_T (A \cup B \cup E))(p_0) = (R_\alpha \!\downarrow_{I_T} \!\uparrow_T (B \cup E))(p_0)$$

which contradicts either (C.12) or (C.13).   □

Lemma C.5. *Let T be a left–continuous t–norm and I_T its residual implicator and let A, B, A' and B' be fuzzy sets in $\mathbb{R}^n$. If*

$$\sup_{p \in \mathbb{R}^n} T((R_\alpha \!\downarrow_{I_T} \!\uparrow_T A)(p), (R_\alpha \!\downarrow_{I_T} \!\uparrow_T B)(p))$$

$$< \sup_{p \in \mathbb{R}^n} T((R_\alpha \!\downarrow_{I_T} \!\uparrow_T (A \cup A'))(p), (R_\alpha \!\downarrow_{I_T} \!\uparrow_T (B \cup B'))(p))$$

then it holds that

$$\sup_{p \in \mathbb{R}^n} T((R_\alpha \!\downarrow_{I_T} \!\uparrow_T (A \cup A'))(p), (R_\alpha \!\downarrow_{I_T} \!\uparrow_T (B \cup B'))(p))$$

$$\leq \max(hgt(A'), hgt(B'))$$

Proof. From the monotonicity of the supremum (Lemma 2.7), we know that there exists a p_0 in $\mathbb{R}^n$ such that

$$T((R_\alpha \!\downarrow_{I_T} \!\uparrow_T (A \cup A'))(p_0), (R_\alpha \!\downarrow_{I_T} \!\uparrow_T (B \cup B'))(p_0))$$
$$> T((R_\alpha \!\downarrow_{I_T} \!\uparrow_T A)(p_0), (R_\alpha \!\downarrow_{I_T} \!\uparrow_T B)(p_0))$$

This entails that either

$$(R_\alpha\downarrow_{I_T}\uparrow_T(A\cup A'))(p_0) > (R_\alpha\downarrow_{I_T}\uparrow_T A)(p_0) \tag{C.14}$$

or

$$(R_\alpha\downarrow_{I_T}\uparrow_T(B\cup B'))(p_0) > (R_\alpha\downarrow_{I_T}\uparrow_T B)(p_0) \tag{C.15}$$

Assume, for example, (C.14); the proof for the case where (C.15) holds is entirely analogous. From the monotonicity of the infimum (Lemma 2.7), we know that there exists a q_0 in $\mathbb{R}^n$ such that

$$I_T(R_\alpha(p_0,q_0),(R_\alpha\uparrow_T(A\cup A'))(q_0)) > I_T(R_\alpha(p_0,q_0),(R_\alpha\uparrow_T A)(q_0))$$

This is only possible if $R_\alpha(p_0,q_0) > 0$, i.e., $d(p_0,q_0) \leq \alpha$ and $R_\alpha(p_0,q_0) = 1$. From (2.22), we thus have

$$(R_\alpha\uparrow_T(A\cup A'))(q_0) > (R_\alpha\uparrow_T A)(q_0)$$

and by (2.54)

$$\max((R_\alpha\uparrow_T A)(q_0),(R_\alpha\uparrow_T A')(q_0)) > (R_\alpha\uparrow_T A)(q_0)$$

or equivalently

$$(R_\alpha\uparrow_T A')(q_0) > (R_\alpha\uparrow_T A)(q_0) \tag{C.16}$$

We conclude using $R_\alpha(p_0,q_0) = 1$ and (2.54)

$$
\begin{aligned}
(R_\alpha\downarrow_{I_T}\uparrow_T(A\cup A'))(p_0) &= \inf_{q\in\mathbb{R}^n} I_T(R_\alpha(p_0,q),(R_\alpha\uparrow_T(A\cup A'))(q))\\
&\leq I_T(R_\alpha(p_0,q_0),(R_\alpha\uparrow_T(A\cup A'))(q_0))\\
&= (R_\alpha\uparrow_T(A\cup A'))(q_0)\\
&= \max((R_\alpha\uparrow_T A)(q_0),(R_\alpha\uparrow_T A')(q_0))\\
&= (R_\alpha\uparrow_T A')(q_0)\\
&= \sup_{r\in\mathbb{R}} T(R_\alpha(q_0,r),A'(r))\\
&\leq \sup_{r\in\mathbb{R}} A'(r)\\
&= hgt(A')
\end{aligned}
$$

$\square$

Lemma C.6. *Let T be a left–continuous t–norm and I_T its residual implicator. Furthermore, let A_i and B_j be fuzzy sets in $\mathbb{R}^n$, for all i in $\{1,2,\ldots,m\}$ and j in $\{1,2,\ldots,m'\}$, such that*

$$A_i(p) = T(\lambda_i, R_{\alpha_i}(a_i,p))$$
$$B_j(p) = T(\lambda'_j, R_{\alpha'_j}(b_j,p))$$

for every p in $\mathbb{R}^n$, where $\lambda_i, \lambda'_j \in [0,1]$, a_i and b_j in $\mathbb{R}^n$, $\alpha_i \geq \alpha$ and $\alpha'_j \geq \alpha$ (*i* in $\{1, 2, \ldots, m\}$ and j in $\{1, 2, \ldots, m'\}$). If the points $a_1, a_2, \ldots, a_m, b_1, b_2, \ldots, b_{m'}$ are collinear, it holds that

$$O_\alpha(\bigcup_{i=1}^{m} A_i, \bigcup_{j=1}^{m'} B_j) = \max_{i=1}^{m} \max_{j=1}^{m'} O_\alpha(A_i, B_j) \tag{C.17}$$

Proof.   Without loss of generality, we can assume $\lambda_i > 0$ and $\lambda'_j > 0$ for all i in $\{1, 2, \ldots, m\}$ and j in $\{1, 2, \ldots, m'\}$. First, assume that $a_1 = a_2 = \cdots = a_m = b_1 = b_2 = \cdots = b_{m'} = a$ for a certain a in $\mathbb{R}^n$. We find

$$O_\alpha(\bigcup_{i=1}^{m} A_i, \bigcup_{j=1}^{m'} B_j) = \sup_{p \in \mathbb{R}^n} T((R_\alpha \downarrow_{I_T} \uparrow_T \bigcup_{i=1}^{m} A_i)(p), (R_\alpha \downarrow_{I_T} \uparrow_T \bigcup_{j=1}^{m'} B_j)(p))$$

Clearly, for each i, $(R_\alpha \downarrow_{I_T} \uparrow_T \bigcup_{i=1}^{m} A_i)$ and $(R_\alpha \downarrow_{I_T} \uparrow_T \bigcup_{j=1}^{m'} B_j)$ attain their maximal value λ_i and λ'_i, respectively, in a; hence

$$= T((R_\alpha \downarrow_{I_T} \uparrow_T \bigcup_{i=1}^{m} A_i)(a), (R_\alpha \downarrow_{I_T} \uparrow_T \bigcup_{j=1}^{m'} B_j)(a))$$

$$= T(\max_{i=1}^{m} \lambda_i, \max_{j=1}^{m'} \lambda'_j)$$

$$= \max_{i=1}^{m} \max_{j=1}^{m'} T(\lambda_i, \lambda'_j)$$

$$= \max_{i=1}^{m} \max_{j=1}^{m'} T((R_\alpha \downarrow_{I_T} \uparrow_T A_i)(a), (R_\alpha \downarrow_{I_T} \uparrow_T B_j)(a))$$

$$= \max_{i=1}^{m} \max_{j=1}^{m'} \sup_{p \in \mathbb{R}^n} T((R_\alpha \downarrow_{I_T} \uparrow_T A_i)(p), (R_\alpha \downarrow_{I_T} \uparrow_T B_j)(p))$$

$$= \max_{i=1}^{m} \max_{j=1}^{m'} O_\alpha(A_i, B_j)$$

Next, assume that not all points a_i and b_j are equal. The set of points $\{a_1, \ldots, a_m, b_1, \ldots, b_{m'}\}$ then defines a line L. Moreover, the set of points p on this line for which $A_i(p) > 0$ corresponds to a closed line segment $[a_i^-, a_i^+]$, where $d(a_i^-, a_i^+) = 2\alpha_i \geq 2\alpha$. In the same way, the points p on L for which $B_j(p) > 0$ correspond to a closed line segment $[b_j^-, b_j^+]$ with $d(b_j^-, b_j^+) \geq 2\alpha$.

Note that from (2.58), we already know

$$O_\alpha(\bigcup_{i=1}^m A_i, \bigcup_{j=1}^{m'} B_j) = \sup_{p \in \mathbb{R}^n} T((R_\alpha \downarrow_{I_T} \uparrow_T \bigcup_{i=1}^m A_i)(p), (R_\alpha \downarrow_{I_T} \uparrow_T \bigcup_{j=1}^{m'} B_j)(p))$$

$$\geq \sup_{p \in \mathbb{R}^n} T((\bigcup_{i=1}^m R_\alpha \downarrow_{I_T} \uparrow_T A_i)(p), (\bigcup_{j=1}^{m'} R_\alpha \downarrow_{I_T} \uparrow_T B_j)(p))$$

$$= \sup_{p \in \mathbb{R}^n} \max_{i=1}^m \max_{j=1}^{m'} T((R_\alpha \downarrow_{I_T} \uparrow_T A_i)(p), (R_\alpha \downarrow_{I_T} \uparrow_T B_j)(p))$$

$$= \max_{i=1}^m \max_{j=1}^{m'} \sup_{p \in \mathbb{R}^n} T((R_\alpha \downarrow_{I_T} \uparrow_T A_i)(p), (R_\alpha \downarrow_{I_T} \uparrow_T B_j)(p))$$

$$= \max_{i=1}^m \max_{j=1}^{m'} O_\alpha(A_i, B_j)$$

Hence, we only need to show

$$O_\alpha(\bigcup_{i=1}^m A_i, \bigcup_{j=1}^{m'} B_j) \leq \max_{i=1}^m \max_{j=1}^{m'} O_\alpha(A_i, B_j)$$

Note that if $O_\alpha(\bigcup_{i=1}^m A_i, \bigcup_{j=1}^{m'} B_j) = 0$ this is trivial. Therefore, assume that $O_\alpha(\bigcup_{i=1}^m A_i, \bigcup_{j=1}^{m'} B_j) > 0$. Since the fuzzy sets A_i and B_j only take a finite number of different membership degrees, there exists a p_0 in $\mathbb{R}^n$ such that

$$O_\alpha(\bigcup_{i=1}^m A_i, \bigcup_{j=1}^{m'} B_j) = T((R_\alpha \downarrow_{I_T} \uparrow_T \bigcup_{i=1}^m A_i)(p_0), (R_\alpha \downarrow_{I_T} \uparrow_T \bigcup_{j=1}^{m'} B_j)(p_0))$$

$$(\text{C.18})$$

Without loss of generality, we can assume that p_0 is on L. Indeed, if p_0 were not on L, there always exists a p_0' on L whose distance to each of the a_i and b_j is not greater than that of p_0, implying that the membership degree of p_0' in $(R_\alpha \downarrow_{I_T} \uparrow_T \bigcup_{i=1}^m A_i)$ and $(R_\alpha \downarrow_{I_T} \uparrow_T \bigcup_{j=1}^{m'} B_j)$ is at least as high as that of p_0. Furthermore, by Lemma 2.17 and (2.54) we have that

$$(R_\alpha \downarrow_{I_T} \uparrow_T \bigcup_{i=1}^m A_i)(p_0) \leq (R_\alpha \uparrow_T \bigcup_{i=1}^m A_i)(p_0) = \max_{i=1}^m (R_\alpha \uparrow_T A_i)(p_0)$$

For a given s in $\{1, 2, \ldots, m\}$, we have

$$\max_{i=1}^m (R_\alpha \uparrow_T A_i)(p_0) = (R_\alpha \uparrow_T A_s)(p_0) = \sup_{r \in \mathbb{R}^n} T(R_\alpha(p_0, r), A_s(r))$$

Moreover, the supremum in the latter expression is attained for some r_0 in $\mathbb{R}^n$ satisfying $d(r_0, p_0) \leq \alpha$, i.e.

$$\sup_{r \in \mathbb{R}^n} T(R_\alpha(p_0, r), A_s(r)) = A_s(r_0)$$

Hence we have established that for some r_0 in $\mathbb{R}^n$ satisfying $d(r_0, p_0) \leq \alpha$ and a given s in $\{1, 2, \ldots, m\}$

$$(R_\alpha \downarrow_{I_T} \uparrow_T \bigcup_{i=1}^{m} A_i)(p_0) \leq A_s(r_0)$$

Since p_0 and a_s are on L, we can assume without loss of generality that r_0 is on L as well. Furthermore, if the supremum is attained in several points r on L, we choose as r_0 the one closest to the middle of the line segment $[a_s^-, a_s^+]$. Similarly, we find that for some r_1 in $\mathbb{R}^n$ satisfying $d(r_1, p_0) \leq \alpha$ and a given t in $\{1, 2, \ldots, m'\}$

$$(R_\alpha \downarrow_{I_T} \uparrow_T \bigcup_{j=1}^{m'} B_j)(p_0) \leq B_t(r_1)$$

We can assume that r_1 is on L, and, moreover, that r_1 is chosen as close as possible to the middle of the line segment $[b_t^-, b_t^+]$. From (C.18) and our earlier assumption that $O_\alpha(\bigcup_{i=1}^{m} A_i, \bigcup_{j=1}^{m'} B_j) > 0$, we moreover find $A_s(r_0) > 0$ and $B_t(r_1) > 0$, in other words, $A_s(r_0) = \lambda_s$ and $B_t(r_1) = \lambda_t'$.

Using $d(r_1, p_0) \leq \alpha$, we find

$$(R_\alpha \downarrow_{I_T} \uparrow_T \bigcup_{i=1}^{m} A_i)(p_0) = \inf_{q \in \mathbb{R}^n} I_T(R_\alpha(p_0, q), (R_\alpha \uparrow_T \bigcup_{i=1}^{m} A_i)(q))$$

$$\leq I_T(R_\alpha(p_0, r_1), (R_\alpha \uparrow_T \bigcup_{i=1}^{m} A_i)(r_1))$$

$$= (R_\alpha \uparrow_T \bigcup_{i=1}^{m} A_i)(r_1)$$

For a given k in $\{1, 2, \ldots, m\}$ and a given r_2 in $\mathbb{R}^n$ satisfying $d(r_1, r_2) \leq \alpha$, we have that

$$(R_\alpha \uparrow_T \bigcup_{i=1}^{m} A_i)(r_1) = A_k(r_2)$$

In the same way, it holds for a given l in $\{1, 2, \ldots, m'\}$ and r_3 in $\mathbb{R}^n$ satisfying $d(r_0, r_3) \leq \alpha$ that

$$(R_\alpha \downarrow_{I_T} \uparrow_T \bigcup_{j=1}^{m'} B_j)(p_0) \leq B_l(r_3)$$

Without loss of generality, we can assume that r_2 and r_3 are on L, that r_2 is chosen as close as possible to the middle of the line segment $[a_k^-, a_k^+]$, and that r_3 is chosen as close as possible to the middle of the line segment $[b_l^-, b_l^+]$. Moreover, from (C.18) and $O_\alpha(\bigcup_{i=1}^m A_i, \bigcup_{j=1}^{m'} B_j) > 0$, we find $A_k(r_2) > 0$ and $B_l(r_3) > 0$, in other words, $A_k(r_2) = \lambda_k$ and $B_l(r_3) = \lambda_l'$.

To complete the proof, we perform a case analysis on the values of $A_k(p_0)$, $B_t(p_0)$, $A_s(p_0)$ and $B_l(p_0)$. First assume that $A_k(p_0) = 0$ and $B_t(p_0) = 0$. Since r_2 is on L and $A_k(r_2) > 0$, we know that r_2 is on the line segment $[a_k^-, a_k^+]$. Similarly, since r_1 is on L and $B_t(r_1) > 0$, we know that r_1 is on the line segment $[b_t^-, b_t^+]$. Furthermore, since $A_k(p_0) = B_t(p_0) = 0$, we know that p_0 is on L, but not on either of the line segments $[a_k^-, a_k^+]$ and $[b_t^-, b_t^+]$. The fact that $d(r_1, p_0) \leq \alpha$, $d(r_1, r_2) \leq \alpha$, $d(a_k^-, a_k^+) \geq 2\alpha$ and $d(b_t^-, b_t^+) \geq 2\alpha$ then implies that the line segments $[a_k^-, a_k^+]$ and $[b_t^-, b_t^+]$ are overlapping. Indeed, assume for example that $[a_k^-, a_k^+]$ and $[b_t^-, b_t^+]$ were not overlapping and $[a_k^-, a_k^+]$ came entirely before $[b_t^-, b_t^+]$ (i.e., $d(a_k^+, b_t^-) > 0$ and $d(a_k^-, b_t^-) > d(a_k^+, b_t^-)$); this situation is depicted in Figure C.1. From $d(r_1, r_2) \leq \alpha$ and $d(r_1, p_0) \leq \alpha$, we derive that $d(r_2, p_0) \leq 2\alpha$. Since $r_2 \in [a_k^-, a_k^+]$, $d(b_t^-, b_t^+) \geq 2\alpha$ and the assumption that $[a_k^-, a_k^+]$ comes before $[b_t^-, b_t^+]$, we obtain that p_0 comes before b_t^+. Similarly, using $r_1 \in [b_t^-, b_t^+]$ and $d(a_k^-, a_k^+) \geq 2\alpha$, the assumption that $[a_k^-, a_k^+]$ comes before $[b_t^-, b_t^+]$ entails that p_0 comes after a_k^-. In other words, as $p_0 \notin [a_k^-, a_k^+]$ and $p_0 \notin [b_t^-, b_t^+]$, we have that p_0 is located between a_k^+ and b_t^-. However, r_1 was chosen as close as possible the the middle of $[b_t^-, b_t^+]$, subject to $d(r_1, p_0) \leq \alpha$. Since $p_0 \notin [b_t^-, b_t^+]$ and $d(b_t^-, b_t^+) \geq 2\alpha$, this implies $d(p_0, r_1) = \alpha$. This means in particular that all points r satisfying $d(r, r_1) \leq \alpha$ cannot be in $[a_k^-, a_k^+]$, which violates the fact that $d(r_1, r_2) \leq \alpha$. In the same way, we obtain a contradiction if $[b_t^-, b_t^+]$ came entirely before $[a_k^-, a_k^+]$. From this observation, we find for some point p_1 on both $[a_k^-, a_k^+]$ and $[b_t^-, b_t^+]$

$$\max_{i=1}^m \max_{j=1}^{m'} O_\alpha(A_i, B_j) \geq O_\alpha(A_k, B_t)$$

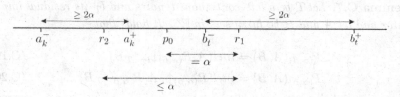

Fig. C.1 Assuming that $[a_k^-, a_k^+]$ and $[b_t^-, b_t^+]$ are not overlapping leads to an inconsistency.

$$= \sup_{p \in \mathbb{R}^n} T((R_\alpha \downarrow_{I_T} \uparrow_T A_k)(p), (R_\alpha \downarrow_{I_T} \uparrow_T B_t)(p))$$

$$\geq T((R_\alpha \downarrow_{I_T} \uparrow_T A_k)(p_1), (R_\alpha \downarrow_{I_T} \uparrow_T B_t)(p_1))$$

$$= T(\lambda_k, \lambda'_t)$$

$$= T(A_k(r_2), B_t(r_1))$$

$$\geq T((R_\alpha \downarrow_{I_T} \uparrow_T \bigcup_{i=1}^m A_i)(p_0), (R_\alpha \downarrow_{I_T} \uparrow_T \bigcup_{j=1}^{m'} B_j)(p_0))$$

$$= O_\alpha(\bigcup_{i=1}^m A_i, \bigcup_{j=1}^{m'} B_j)$$

In entirely the same fashion, we can show (C.17) when $A_s(p_0) = 0$ and $B_l(p_0) = 0$. Hence, we only need to consider the case where $A_k(p_0) > 0$ or $B_t(p_0) > 0$, and $A_s(p_0) > 0$ and $B_l(p_0) > 0$. If $A_k(p_0) > 0$ and $B_l(p_0) > 0$, we have that $p_0 \in [a_k^-, a_k^+]$ and $p_0 \in [b_l^-, b_l^+]$ and thus that $[a_k^-, a_k^+]$ and $[b_l^-, b_l^+]$ are overlapping, yielding (C.17) as in the first case. In entirely the same way, we can show (C.17) when $A_k(p_0) > 0$ and $B_t(p_0) > 0$, when $A_s(p_0) > 0$ and $B_l(p_0) > 0$, or when $A_s(p_0) > 0$ and $B_t(p_0) > 0$. Next, assume $A_k(p_0) > 0$, $A_s(p_0) > 0$, $B_t(p_0) = 0$ and $B_l(p_0) = 0$. Since $A_s(p_0) > 0$ and p_0 on L, we know that p_0 is on the line segment $[a_s^-, a_s^+]$. Since we have chosen r_0 as the point closest to the middle of $[a_s^-, a_s^+]$, subject to $d(p_0, r_0) \leq \alpha$, we find from $p_0 \in [a_s^-, a_s^+]$ and $d(a_s^-, a_s^+) \geq 2\alpha$ that $d(a_s^-, r_0) \geq \alpha$ and $d(a_s^+, r_0) \geq \alpha$. From $d(r_0, r_3) \leq \alpha$ we can conclude that r_3 is on the line segment $[a_s^-, a_s^+]$ as well. Since, moreover, r_3 is on line segment $[b_l^-, b_l^+]$ (as $B_l(r_3) > 0$ and r_3 on L), we obtain that $[a_s^-, a_s^+]$ and $[b_l^-, b_l^+]$ are overlapping. Thus we can show (C.17) in the same way as in the previous cases. Finally, in the case where $A_k(p_0) = 0$, $A_s(p_0) = 0$, $B_t(p_0) > 0$ and $B_l(p_0) > 0$, we can analogously show that $[a_k^-, a_k^+]$ and $[b_t^-, b_t^+]$ are overlapping. $\square$

Lemma C.7. *Let T be a left–continuous t–norm and I_T its residual implicator and let A and B be fuzzy sets in $\mathbb{R}^n$. It holds that*

$$P_{(\alpha,\beta)}(A, B) = incl(A, R_{(\alpha,\beta)} \downarrow_{I_T} \uparrow_T B) \tag{C.19}$$

$$P_{(\alpha,\beta)}(A, B) = incl(R_{(\alpha,\beta)} \uparrow_T A, R_{(\alpha,\beta)} \uparrow_T B) \tag{C.20}$$

Proof. These alternative definitions of $P_{(\alpha,\beta)}$ follow immediately from (2.64) and (2.65). $\square$

Lemma C.8. *Let T be a left-continuous t-norm and I_T its residual implicator. For all a and b in $[0,1]$, it holds that*

$$b > I_T(a,0) \Rightarrow T(a,b) > 0$$

Proof. By contraposition we need to show $T(a,b) \leq 0 \Rightarrow b \leq I_T(a,0)$, which holds because of (2.21). $\square$

Lemma C.9. *If T is a continuous Archimedean t-norm, it holds that*

$$0 < T(a,b) \wedge T(a,b) = T(a,b') \Rightarrow b = b' \qquad \text{(C.21)}$$

Proof. Assume $b < b'$ and $0 < T(a,b)$, and let f be defined as in Lemma 2.1. We show by contradiction that $T(a,b) \neq T(a,b')$. Note that $T(a,b') > 0$, since $b < b'$ and $T(a,b) > 0$. Since f is strictly decreasing, it holds that $f(b) > f(b')$ and $f(a) + f(b) > f(a) + f(b')$. Moreover, as f^{-1} is strictly decreasing as well, we have

$$f^{-1}(f(a) + f(b)) < f^{-1}(f(a) + f(b'))$$

On the other hand, we find from $T(a,b) > 0$ and $T(a,b') > 0$ that

$$f^{(-1)}(f(a) + f(b)) = f^{-1}(f(a) + f(b))$$
$$f^{(-1)}(f(a) + f(b')) = f^{-1}(f(a) + f(b'))$$

and therefore

$$f^{(-1)}(f(a) + f(b)) < f^{(-1)}(f(a) + f(b'))$$

or $T(a,b) < T(a,b')$. In entirely the same way, we can show that $T(a,b) \neq T(a,b')$ when $0 < T(a,b)$ and $b > b'$. We conclude that

$$0 < T(a,b) \wedge b \neq b' \Rightarrow T(a,b) \neq T(a,b')$$

which is equivalent to (C.21) by shunting and contraposition. $\square$

Lemma C.10. *If T is a continuous Archimedean t-norm, it holds that*

$$T(a,b) = a \Leftrightarrow b = 1 \vee a = 0$$

for all a and b in $[0,1]$.

Proof. Clearly we have $T(a,b) = a$ when $b = 1$ or $a = 0$. Conversely, we show that $a > 0 \Rightarrow b = 1$ when $T(a,b) = a$. Assume $a > 0$ and $T(a,b) = a$. From Lemma C.9 and $T(a,b) = a = T(a,1)$, we immediately have $b = 1$. $\square$

C.2   Connection

Rather than constructing the function f at once, we first construct a function f^C from V to the class of fuzzy sets in $\mathbb{R}^n$, satisfying (C.1) but not necessarily (C.2)–(C.4). Subsequently, we will define a function f^O satisfying (C.1) and (C.2), but not necessarily (C.3) and (C.4), etc. Henceforth, we always assume that T is a left–continuous t–norm and I_T its residual implicator.

Let ρ be a sufficiently large, positive real number and let f^I be the function from V to the set of normalised, bounded fuzzy sets in $\mathbb{R}^n$, defined for each v_i in V by

$$f^I(v_i) = P_{a_i}$$

where a_i is the point in $\mathbb{R}^n$ whose coordinates are all 0, except for the ith coordinate which is ρ. For example, $f^I(v_1) = (\rho, 0, 0, \ldots, 0)$. Note that in this way, an n–dimensional sphere with radius α_0 is considered. As ρ is sufficiently large, each sphere $f^I(v_i)$ is far apart from all the other spheres $f^I(v_j)$ with $j \neq i$. To achieve the required degree of connectedness, the regions corresponding to variables v_i and v_j should be connected to degree λ_{ij}^C (see (C.1)). We therefore enlarge region $f^I(v_i)$ by adding fuzzy sets in $\mathbb{R}^n$ that are sufficiently close to the centers of $f^I(v_j)$ with $j \neq i$. Specifically, from f^I, we define the function f^C for each v_i in V and p in $\mathbb{R}^n$ as

$$f^C(v_i)(p) = \max(f^I(v_i)(p), \max_{\substack{1 \leq j \leq n \\ j \neq i}} T(\lambda_{ij}^C, L_{b_{ij}}(p))) \qquad (C.22)$$

where $b_{ij} = a_j + (2\alpha + \alpha_0)\frac{\overrightarrow{a_j a_i}}{\|\overrightarrow{a_j a_i}\|}$. The construction of the points a_i and b_{ij} for the case $n = 3$ is depicted in Figure C.2. In particular, b_{ij} is on the line from a_i to a_j at a distance of $2\alpha + \alpha_0$ from a_j. Hence, the sphere $L_{b_{ij}}$ with radius α has a center that is relatively close to a_j.

For $i \neq j$, the distance between a_i and a_j is $\sqrt{2}\rho$, hence, by taking ρ sufficiently large, we can assume that $d(a_i, a_j)$ is sufficiently large, and in particular

$$d(a_i, a_j) > 2\alpha_0 + 4\alpha \qquad (C.23)$$

Moreover, the distance between b_{il} and a_l and the distance between b_{jm} and a_m, is fixed ($2\alpha + \alpha_0$). Hence, by taking ρ sufficiently large, we can also assume that $d(b_{il}, b_{jm})$ is sufficiently large for $l \neq m$, and in particular

$$d(b_{il}, b_{jm}) > 8\alpha \qquad (C.24)$$

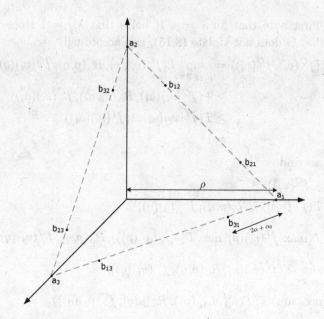

Fig. C.2   Construction of the points a_i and b_{ij} $(1 \leq i, j \leq 3, i \neq j)$.

Note that the actual value of ρ depends on the value of α_0 in this way. Furthermore, by increasing the value of α_0, the distance between b_{il} and b_{jl} increases as well (assuming $i \neq j$). Hence, by taking α_0 sufficiently large, we can assume for $i \neq j$ that

$$d(b_{il}, b_{jl}) > 8\alpha \tag{C.25}$$

Finally, note that for $i \neq m$

$$
\begin{aligned}
d(a_i, b_{jm}) &= d(a_i, a_m + (2\alpha + \alpha_0)\frac{\overrightarrow{a_m a_j}}{\|\overrightarrow{a_m a_j}\|}) \\
&\geq d(a_i, a_m) - (2\alpha + \alpha_0) \\
&= \sqrt{2}\rho - (2\alpha + \alpha_0)
\end{aligned}
$$

Hence, by taking ρ sufficiently large, we can assume that

$$d(a_i, b_{jm}) > 8\alpha + \alpha_0 \tag{C.26}$$

The following lemma demonstrates that f^C indeed satisfies (C.1).

Lemma C.11. *For all v_i and v_j in V, it holds that*

$$C_\alpha(f^C(v_i), f^C(v_j)) = \lambda_{ij}^C$$

Proof. First note that for $i = j$, it holds that $\lambda_{ij}^C = 1$ since we have assumed that Θ does not violate (8.15), and accordingly

$$C_\alpha(f^C(v_i), f^C(v_i)) = \sup_{p,q \in \mathbb{R}^n} T(f^C(v_i)(p), R_\alpha(p,q), f^C(v_i)(q))$$

$$\geq T(f^C(v_i)(a_i), R_\alpha(a_i, a_i), f^C(v_i)(a_i))$$

$$\geq T(f^I(v_i)(a_i), 1, f^I(v_i)(a_i))$$

$$= 1$$

For $i \neq j$ we find

$$C_\alpha(f^C(v_i), f^C(v_j))$$

$$= \sup_{p,q \in \mathbb{R}^n} T(f^C(v_i)(p), R_\alpha(p,q), f^C(v_j)(q))$$

$$= \sup_{p,q \in \mathbb{R}^n} T(\max(f^I(v_i)(p), \max_{l \neq i} T(\lambda_{il}^C, L_{b_{il}}(p))), R_\alpha(p,q), f^C(v_j)(q))$$

$$= \max(\sup_{p,q \in \mathbb{R}^n} T(f^I(v_i)(p), R_\alpha(p,q), f^C(v_j)(q)),$$

$$\max_{l \neq i} \sup_{p,q \in \mathbb{R}^n} T(T(\lambda_{il}^C, L_{b_{il}}(p)), R_\alpha(p,q), f^C(v_j)(q)))$$

$$= \max(\sup_{p,q \in \mathbb{R}^n} T(f^I(v_i)(p), R_\alpha(p,q), \max(f^I(v_j)(q), \max_{m \neq j} T(\lambda_{jm}^C, L_{b_{jm}}(q)))),$$

$$\max_{l \neq i} \sup_{p,q \in \mathbb{R}^n} T(T(\lambda_{il}^C, L_{b_{il}}(p)), R_\alpha(p,q),$$

$$\max(f^I(v_j)(q), \max_{m \neq j} T(\lambda_{jm}^C, L_{b_{jm}}(q)))))$$

$$= \max(\sup_{p,q \in \mathbb{R}^n} T(f^I(v_i)(p), R_\alpha(p,q), f^I(v_j)(q)),$$

$$\max_{m \neq j} \sup_{p,q \in \mathbb{R}^n} T(f^I(v_i)(p), R_\alpha(p,q), T(\lambda_{jm}^C, L_{b_{jm}}(q))),$$

$$\max_{l \neq i} \sup_{p,q \in \mathbb{R}^n} T(T(\lambda_{il}^C, L_{b_{il}}(p)), R_\alpha(p,q), f^I(v_j)(q)),$$

$$\max_{l \neq i} \max_{m \neq j} \sup_{p,q \in \mathbb{R}^n} T(T(\lambda_{il}^C, L_{b_{il}}(p)), R_\alpha(p,q), T(\lambda_{jm}^C, L_{b_{jm}}(q))))$$

For every p in the $supp(P_{a_i})$ and every q in $supp(P_{a_j})$ it holds that $d(p, a_i) \leq \alpha_0$ and $d(q, a_j) \leq \alpha_0$. Using (C.23), this implies $d(p,q) > 4\alpha > \alpha$. Thus, we find

$$\sup_{p,q \in \mathbb{R}^n} T(f^I(v_i)(p), R_\alpha(p,q), f^I(v_j)(q))$$

$$= \sup_{p,q \in \mathbb{R}^n} T(P_{a_i}(p), R_\alpha(p,q), P_{a_j}(q))$$

$$= 0$$

In a similar way, using (C.24) and (C.25) we find

$$\sup_{p,q \in \mathbb{R}^n} T(L_{b_{il}}(p), R_\alpha(p,q), L_{b_{jm}}(q)) = 0$$

which yields

$$\max_{l \neq i} \max_{m \neq j} \sup_{p,q \in \mathbb{R}^n} T(T(\lambda_{il}^C, L_{b_{il}}(p)), R_\alpha(p,q), T(\lambda_{jm}^C, L_{b_{jm}}(q)))$$

$$\leq \max_{l \neq i} \max_{m \neq j} \sup_{p,q \in \mathbb{R}^n} T(L_{b_{il}}(p), R_\alpha(p,q), L_{b_{jm}}(q)) \quad .$$

$$= 0$$

Next, using (C.26) we have that for every p in $supp(P_{a_i})$ and every q in $supp(L_{b_{jm}})$, it holds that $d(p,q) > 7\alpha > \alpha$. Thus, we find

$$\sup_{p,q \in \mathbb{R}^n} T(f^I(v_i)(p), R_\alpha(p,q), T(\lambda_{jm}^C, L_{b_{jm}}(q))) = 0$$

provided $i \neq m$. As a consequence, we find

$$\max_{m \neq j} \sup_{p,q \in \mathbb{R}^n} T(f^I(v_i)(p), R_\alpha(p,q), T(\lambda_{jm}^C, L_{b_{jm}}(q)))$$

$$= \sup_{p,q \in \mathbb{R}^n} T(f^I(v_i)(p), R_\alpha(p,q), T(\lambda_{ji}^C, L_{b_{ji}}(q)))$$

and in entirely the same way, we obtain

$$\max_{l \neq i} \sup_{p,q \in \mathbb{R}^n} T(T(\lambda_{il}^C, L_{b_{il}}(p)), R_\alpha(p,q), f^I(v_j)(q))$$

$$= \sup_{p,q \in \mathbb{R}^n} T(T(\lambda_{ij}^C, L_{b_{ij}}(p)), R_\alpha(p,q), f^I(v_j)(q))$$

This yields

$$C_\alpha(f^C(v_i), f^C(v_j))$$

$$= \max(0, \sup_{p,q \in \mathbb{R}^n} T(f^I(v_i)(p), R_\alpha(p,q), T(\lambda_{ji}^C, L_{b_{ji}}(q))),$$

$$\sup_{p,q \in \mathbb{R}^n} T(T(\lambda_{ij}^C, L_{b_{ij}}(p)), R_\alpha(p,q), f^I(v_j)(q)), 0)$$

$$= \max(T(\lambda_{ji}^C, \sup_{p,q \in \mathbb{R}^n} T(f^I(v_i)(p), R_\alpha(p,q), L_{b_{ji}}(q))),$$

$$T(\lambda_{ij}^C, \sup_{p,q \in \mathbb{R}^n} T(L_{b_{ij}}(p), R_\alpha(p,q), f^I(v_j)(q))))$$

We furthermore have

$$\sup_{p,q\in\mathbb{R}^n} T(L_{b_{ij}}(p), R_\alpha(p,q), f^I(v_j)(q))$$

$$\geq T(L_{b_{ij}}(b_{ij} - \alpha\frac{\overrightarrow{a_j a_i}}{\|\overrightarrow{a_j a_i}\|}), R_\alpha(b_{ij} - \alpha\frac{\overrightarrow{a_j a_i}}{\|\overrightarrow{a_j a_i}\|}, a_j + \alpha_0\frac{\overrightarrow{a_j a_i}}{\|\overrightarrow{a_j a_i}\|}),$$

$$f^I(v_j)(a_j + \alpha_0\frac{\overrightarrow{a_j a_i}}{\|\overrightarrow{a_j a_i}\|}))$$

$$= R_\alpha(b_{ij} - \alpha\frac{\overrightarrow{a_j a_i}}{\|\overrightarrow{a_j a_i}\|}, a_j + \alpha_0\frac{\overrightarrow{a_j a_i}}{\|\overrightarrow{a_j a_i}\|})$$

$$= R_\alpha(a_j + (2\alpha + \alpha_0)\frac{\overrightarrow{a_j a_i}}{\|\overrightarrow{a_j a_i}\|} - \alpha\frac{\overrightarrow{a_j a_i}}{\|\overrightarrow{a_j a_i}\|}, a_j + \alpha_0\frac{\overrightarrow{a_j a_i}}{\|\overrightarrow{a_j a_i}\|})$$

$$= R_\alpha(a_j + (\alpha + \alpha_0)\frac{\overrightarrow{a_j a_i}}{\|\overrightarrow{a_j a_i}\|}, a_j + \alpha_0\frac{\overrightarrow{a_j a_i}}{\|\overrightarrow{a_j a_i}\|})$$

$$= 1$$

Since Θ satisfies requirement (8.13), we know that $\lambda_{ij}^C = \lambda_{ji}^C$. Using this observation, we can conclude

$$C_\alpha(f^C(v_i), f^C(v_j))$$
$$= \max(T(\lambda_{ij}^C, \sup_{p,q\in\mathbb{R}^n} T(f^I(v_i)(p), R_\alpha(p,q), L_{b_{ji}}(q))), \lambda_{ij}^C)$$
$$= \lambda_{ij}^C$$

where the last step follows from $T \leq T_M$ for every t–norm T. □

C.3 Overlap

Next, we define a function f^O satisfying both (C.1) and (C.2). Specifically, for each v_i in V and p in $\mathbb{R}^n$, we define

$$f^O(v_i)(p) = \max(f^C(v_i)(p), \max_{\substack{1\leq j\leq n \\ j\neq i}} T(\lambda_{ij}^O, L_{c_{ij}}(p))) \tag{C.27}$$

where $c_{ij} = a_j + (\alpha_0 + \alpha)\frac{\overrightarrow{a_j a_i}}{\|\overrightarrow{a_j a_i}\|}$. The construction of the points c_{ij} for the case $n = 3$ is depicted in Figure C.3.

Following a similar line of reasoning as for (C.23)–(C.26), we find that, by taking α_0 and ρ sufficiently large, we can assume for $l \neq m$

$$d(c_{il}, c_{jm}) > 8\alpha \tag{C.28}$$

$$d(b_{il}, c_{jm}) > 8\alpha \tag{C.29}$$

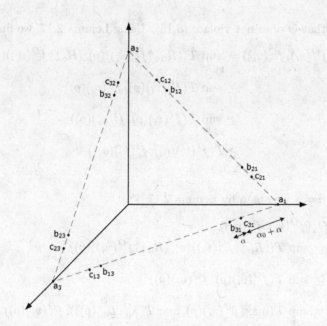

Fig. C.3   Construction of the points a_i, b_{ij} and c_{ij} $(1 \le i, j \le 3, i \ne j)$.

and for $i \ne j$

$$d(c_{il}, c_{jl}) > 8\alpha \qquad \text{(C.30)}$$
$$d(b_{il}, c_{jl}) > 8\alpha \qquad \text{(C.31)}$$

and, finally, for $i \ne m$

$$d(a_i, c_{jm}) > 8\alpha + \alpha_0 \qquad \text{(C.32)}$$

In the following two lemmas, we prove that f^O satisfies, respectively, (C.2) and (C.1).

Lemma C.12. *For all v_i and v_j in V, it holds that*

$$O_\alpha(f^O(v_i), f^O(v_j)) = \lambda_{ij}^O$$

Proof.   First note that for $i = j$, it holds that $\lambda_{ij}^O = 1$ since we have assumed that Θ does not violate (8.15). Using Lemma 2.17, we find

$$
\begin{aligned}
O_\alpha(f^O(v_i), f^O(v_i)) &= \sup_{p \in \mathbb{R}^n} T((R_\alpha\downarrow\uparrow f^O(v_i))(p), (R_\alpha\downarrow\uparrow f^O(v_i))(p)) \\
&\geq \sup_{p \in \mathbb{R}^n} T(f^O(v_i)(p), f^O(v_i)(p)) \\
&\geq \sup_{p \in \mathbb{R}^n} T(f^I(v_i)(p), f^I(v_i)(p)) \\
&\geq T(f^I(v_i)(a_i), f^I(v_i)(a_i)) \\
&= 1
\end{aligned}
$$

Next, for $i \neq j$ we obain by Lemma 2.17

$$
\begin{aligned}
&O_\alpha(f^O(v_i), f^O(v_j)) \\
&= \sup_{p \in \mathbb{R}^n} T((R_\alpha\downarrow\uparrow f^O(v_i))(p), (R_\alpha\downarrow\uparrow f^O(v_j))(p)) \\
&\geq \sup_{p \in \mathbb{R}^n} T(f^O(v_i)(p), f^O(v_j)(p)) \\
&= \sup_{p \in \mathbb{R}^n} T(\max(f^C(v_i)(p), \max_{l \neq i} T(\lambda_{il}^O, L_{c_{il}}(p))), f^O(v_j)(p)) \\
&\geq \sup_{p \in \mathbb{R}^n} T(\max_{l \neq i} T(\lambda_{il}^O, L_{c_{il}}(p)), f^O(v_j)(p)) \\
&\geq \sup_{p \in \mathbb{R}^n} T(\max_{l \neq i} T(\lambda_{il}^O, L_{c_{il}}(p)), f^C(v_j)(p)) \\
&\geq \sup_{p \in \mathbb{R}^n} T(T(\lambda_{ij}^O, L_{c_{ij}}(p)), f^C(v_j)(p)) \\
&= T(\lambda_{ij}^O, \sup_{p \in \mathbb{R}^n} T(L_{c_{ij}}(p), f^C(v_j)(p)))
\end{aligned}
$$

We furthermore find

$$
\begin{aligned}
&\sup_{p \in \mathbb{R}^n} T(L_{c_{ij}}(p), f^C(v_j)(p)) \\
&\geq \sup_{p \in \mathbb{R}^n} T(L_{c_{ij}}(p), f^I(v_j)(p)) \\
&= \sup_{p \in \mathbb{R}^n} T(R_\alpha(c_{ij}, p), R_{\alpha_0}(a_j, p)) \\
&\geq T(R_\alpha(c_{ij}, c_{ij} - \alpha \frac{\overrightarrow{a_j a_i}}{\|\overrightarrow{a_j a_i}\|}), R_{\alpha_0}(a_j, c_{ij} - \alpha \frac{\overrightarrow{a_j a_i}}{\|\overrightarrow{a_j a_i}\|})) \\
&= R_{\alpha_0}(a_j, c_{ij} - \alpha \frac{\overrightarrow{a_j a_i}}{\|\overrightarrow{a_j a_i}\|}) \\
&= R_{\alpha_0}(a_j, a_j + (\alpha_0 + \alpha) \frac{\overrightarrow{a_j a_i}}{\|\overrightarrow{a_j a_i}\|} - \alpha \frac{\overrightarrow{a_j a_i}}{\|\overrightarrow{a_j a_i}\|})
\end{aligned}
$$

$$= R_{\alpha_0}(a_j, a_j + \alpha_0 \frac{\overrightarrow{a_j a_i}}{\|\overrightarrow{a_j a_i}\|})$$

$$= 1$$

Hence, we already have

$$O_\alpha(f^O(v_i), f^O(v_j)) \geq \lambda_{ij}^O$$

Conversely, we show $O_\alpha(f^O(v_i), f^O(v_j)) \leq \lambda_{ij}^O$. Note that

$$f^O(v_i)(p) = \max(f^C(v_i)(p), \max_{l \neq i} T(\lambda_{il}^O, L_{c_{il}}(p)))$$

$$= \max(f^C(v_i)(p), T(\lambda_{ij}^O, L_{c_{ij}}(p)), \max_{l \neq i,j} T(\lambda_{il}^O, L_{c_{il}}(p)))$$

$$= (f^C(v_i) \cup L_{c_{ij}}^{\lambda_{ij}^O} \cup \bigcup_{l \neq i,j} L_{c_{il}}^{\lambda_{il}^O})(p)$$

and similarly

$$f^O(v_j)(p) = (f^C(v_j) \cup L_{c_{ji}}^{\lambda_{ji}^O} \cup \bigcup_{m \neq i,j} L_{c_{jm}}^{\lambda_{jm}^O})(p)$$

Using (C.28)–(C.32) and Lemma C.2, we obtain

$$O_\alpha(f^C(v_i) \cup \bigcup_{l \neq i,j} L_{c_{il}}^{\lambda_{il}^O}, f^C(v_j) \cup \bigcup_{m \neq i,j} L_{c_{jm}}^{\lambda_{jm}^O})$$

$$= O_\alpha(f^C(v_i) \cup \bigcup_{l \neq i,j} L_{c_{il}}^{\lambda_{il}^O}, f^C(v_j))$$

$$= O_\alpha(f^C(v_i), f^C(v_j))$$

From Lemma C.4, (C.26) and (C.24) we find

$$O_\alpha(f^C(v_i), f^C(v_j))$$

$$= O_\alpha(f^I(v_i) \cup \bigcup_{l \neq i} L_{b_{il}}^{\lambda_{il}^C}, f^I(v_j) \cup \bigcup_{m \neq j} L_{b_{jm}}^{\lambda_{jm}^C})$$

$$= \max_{l \neq i} \max_{m \neq j} \max(O_\alpha(f^I(v_i), f^I(v_j)), O_\alpha(f^I(v_i), L_{b_{jm}}^{\lambda_{jm}^C}), O_\alpha(L_{b_{il}}^{\lambda_{il}^C}, f^I(v_j)),$$

$$O_\alpha(L_{b_{il}}^{\lambda_{il}^C}, L_{b_{jm}}^{\lambda_{jm}^C}))$$

$$\leq \max_{l \neq i} \max_{m \neq j} \max(O_\alpha(f^I(v_i), f^I(v_j)), O_\alpha(f^I(v_i), L_{b_{jm}}), O_\alpha(L_{b_{il}}, f^I(v_j)),$$

$$O_\alpha(L_{b_{il}}^{\lambda_{il}^C}, L_{b_{jm}}))$$

Using Lemma C.1, we find

$$O_\alpha(f^I(v_i), f^I(v_j)) = \sup_{p \in \mathbb{R}^n} T((R_\alpha{\downarrow}{\uparrow}f^I(v_i))(p), (R_\alpha{\downarrow}{\uparrow}f^I(v_j))(p))$$

$$= \sup_{p \in \mathbb{R}^n} T((R_\alpha{\downarrow}{\uparrow}P_{v_i})(p), (R_\alpha{\downarrow}{\uparrow}P_{v_j})(p))$$

$$= \sup_{p \in \mathbb{R}^n} T(P_{v_i}(p), P_{v_j}(p))$$

From (C.23), we find $\sup_{p \in \mathbb{R}^n} T(P_{v_i}(p), P_{v_j}(p)) = 0$. In the same way, we can show

$$O_\alpha(f^I(v_i), L_{b_{jm}}) = 0$$
$$O_\alpha(L_{b_{il}}, f^I(v_j)) = 0$$
$$O_\alpha(L_{b_{il}}^{\lambda_{il}^C}, L_{b_{jm}}) = 0$$

Hence, we have shown

$$O_\alpha(f^C(v_i) \cup \bigcup_{l \neq i,j} L_{c_{il}}^{\lambda_{il}^O}, f^C(v_j) \cup \bigcup_{m \neq i,j} L_{c_{jm}}^{\lambda_{jm}^O}) = 0$$

If $O_\alpha(f^O(v_i), f^O(v_j)) = 0$, then $O_\alpha(f^O(v_i), f^O(v_j)) \leq \lambda_{ij}^O$ is trivially satisfied. Therefore, assume $O_\alpha(f^O(v_i), f^O(v_j)) > 0$. From Lemma C.5 and the fact that $\lambda_{ij}^O = \lambda_{ji}^O$ we find

$$O_\alpha(f^O(v_i), f^O(v_j)) \leq \max(\sup_{p \in \mathbb{R}^n} T(\lambda_{ij}^O, L_{c_{ij}}(p)), \sup_{p \in \mathbb{R}^n} T(\lambda_{ji}^O, L_{c_{ji}}(p)))$$

$$\leq \max(\lambda_{ij}^O, \lambda_{ji}^O)$$

$$= \lambda_{ij}^O$$

$\square$

Note that in the proof above, it is shown that

$$\sup_{p \in \mathbb{R}^n} T(f^O(v_i)(p), f^O(v_j)(p)) \geq \lambda_{ij}^O$$

Since $f^O(v_i) \subseteq R_\alpha{\downarrow}{\uparrow}f^O(v_i)$, we also have

$$\sup_{p \in \mathbb{R}^n} T(f^O(v_i)(p), f^O(v_j)(p)) \leq \lambda_{ij}^O$$

In other words, we have the following corollary

Corollary C.2. *For all v_i and v_j in V, it holds that*

$$O_\alpha(f^O(v_i), f^O(v_j)) = \sup_{p \in \mathbb{R}^n} T(f^O(v_i)(p), f^O(v_j)(p))$$

Lemma C.13. *For all v_i and v_j in V, it holds that*

$$C_\alpha(f^O(v_i), f^O(v_j)) = \lambda_{ij}^C$$

Proof. Since $f^O(v_i) \supseteq f^C(v_i)$ and $f^O(v_j) \supseteq f^C(v_j)$, it holds that $C_\alpha(f^O(v_i), f^O(v_j)) \geq C_\alpha(f^C(v_i), f^C(v_j))$. From Lemma C.11, we know $C_\alpha(f^C(v_i), f^C(v_j)) = \lambda_{ij}^C$. Hence, we only need to show that $C_\alpha(f^O(v_i), f^O(v_j)) \leq \lambda_{ij}^C$. Using a similar line of reasoning as in Lemma C.11, we obtain

$$
\begin{aligned}
& C_\alpha(f^O(v_i), f^O(v_j)) \\
&= \sup_{p,q \in \mathbb{R}^n} T(\max(f^C(v_i)(p), \max_{l \neq i} T(\lambda_{il}^O, L_{c_{il}}(p))), R_\alpha(p,q), \\
&\qquad\qquad \max(f^C(v_j)(q), \max_{k \neq j} T(\lambda_{jk}^O, L_{c_{jk}}(q)))) \\
&= \max(\sup_{p,q \in \mathbb{R}^n} T(f^C(v_i)(p), R_\alpha(p,q), f^C(v_j)(q)), \\
&\qquad \max_{l \neq i} \sup_{p,q \in \mathbb{R}^n} T(T(\lambda_{il}^O, L_{c_{il}}(p)), R_\alpha(p,q), f^C(v_j)(q)), \\
&\qquad \max_{k \neq j} \sup_{p,q \in \mathbb{R}^n} T(f^C(v_i)(p), R_\alpha(p,q), T(\lambda_{jk}^O, L_{c_{jk}}(q))), \\
&\qquad \max_{l \neq i} \max_{k \neq j} \sup_{p,q \in \mathbb{R}^n} T(T(\lambda_{il}^O, L_{c_{il}}(p)), R_\alpha(p,q), T(\lambda_{jk}^O, L_{c_{jk}}(q)))) \\
&= \max(\sup_{p,q \in \mathbb{R}^n} T(f^C(v_i)(p), R_\alpha(p,q), f^C(v_j)(q)), \\
&\qquad \sup_{p,q \in \mathbb{R}^n} T(T(\lambda_{ij}^O, L_{c_{ij}}(p)), R_\alpha(p,q), f^O(v_j)(q)), \\
&\qquad \sup_{p,q \in \mathbb{R}^n} T(f^C(v_i)(p), R_\alpha(p,q), T(\lambda_{ji}^O, L_{c_{ji}}(q))), 0)
\end{aligned}
$$

Using Lemma C.11, we find

$$
\begin{aligned}
&= \max(\lambda_{ij}^C, \sup_{p,q \in \mathbb{R}^n} T(f^C(v_i)(p), R_\alpha(p,q), T(\lambda_{ji}^O, L_{c_{ji}}(q))), \\
&\qquad \sup_{p,q \in \mathbb{R}^n} T(T(\lambda_{ij}^O, L_{c_{ij}}(p)), R_\alpha(p,q), f^C(v_j)(q))) \\
&\leq \max(\lambda_{ij}^C, \lambda_{ji}^O, \lambda_{ij}^O)
\end{aligned}
$$

From our assumption that Θ satisfies (8.12) and (8.14) we know

$$\max(\lambda_{ij}^C, \lambda_{ji}^O, \lambda_{ij}^O) = \lambda_{ij}^C$$

$\square$

C.4   Part of

We define the function f^P for each v_i in V and p in $\mathbb{R}^n$ as

$$f^P(v_i)(p) = \max_{l=1}^{n} T(\lambda_{li}^P, f^O(v_l)(p)) \qquad (C.33)$$

Note that $f^P(v_i) \supseteq f^O(v_i)$ for all v_i in V. Indeed, from the fact that Θ satisfies (8.15), we know that $\lambda_{ii}^P = 1$ for all i in $\{1, 2, \ldots, n\}$. Below, we prove that f^P satisfies (C.1), (C.2) and (C.3).

Lemma C.14. *For all v_i and v_j in V, it holds that*

$$P_\alpha(f^O(v_i), f^P(v_j)) = \lambda_{ij}^P$$

Proof.   From (C.19), Lemma 2.17, (2.24) and (2.23), we find

$$
\begin{aligned}
P_\alpha(f^O(v_i), f^P(v_j)) &= \inf_{p \in \mathbb{R}^n} I_T(f^O(v_i)(p), (R_\alpha{\downarrow}{\uparrow} f^P(v_j))(p)) \\
&\geq \inf_{p \in \mathbb{R}^n} I_T(f^O(v_i)(p), f^P(v_j)(p)) \\
&= \inf_{p \in \mathbb{R}^n} I_T(f^O(v_i)(p), \max_{l=1}^{n} T(\lambda_{lj}^P, f^O(v_l)(p))) \\
&\geq \inf_{p \in \mathbb{R}^n} I_T(f^O(v_i)(p), T(\lambda_{ij}^P, f^O(v_i)(p))) \\
&\geq \inf_{p \in \mathbb{R}^n} T(\lambda_{ij}^P, I_T(f^O(v_i)(p), f^O(v_i)(p))) \\
&= \inf_{p \in \mathbb{R}^n} T(\lambda_{ij}^P, 1) \\
&= \lambda_{ij}^P
\end{aligned}
$$

Conversely, we show $P_\alpha(f^O(v_i), f^P(v_j)) \leq \lambda_{ij}^P$. Using Lemma 2.17, we find for all i in $\{1, 2, \ldots, n\}$

$$(R_\alpha{\uparrow} f^O(v_i))(a_i) \geq f^O(v_i)(a_i) \geq f^I(v_i)(a_i) = 1$$

Furthermore, for $i \neq j$, we will show that

$$(R_\alpha{\uparrow} f^O(v_j))(a_i) = 0$$

In particular, we need to show that for every p in $supp(f^O(v_j))$, it holds that $d(p, a_i) > \alpha$. Note that when $p \in supp(f^O(v_j))$, it holds that $d(p, a_j) \leq \alpha_0$ or for some k in $\{1, 2, \ldots, n\}$, $d(p, b_{jk}) \leq \alpha$ or $d(p, c_{jk}) \leq \alpha$. If $d(p, a_j) \leq \alpha_0$, $d(p, a_i) > \alpha$ follows from (C.23). Furthermore, if $k \neq i$, $d(p, b_{jk}) \leq \alpha$ and $d(p, c_{jk}) \leq \alpha$ each imply $d(p, a_i) > \alpha$ because of (C.26) and (C.32). Finally, $d(p, b_{ji}) \leq \alpha$ and $d(p, c_{ji}) \leq \alpha$ each imply $d(p, a_i) > \alpha$ because

$d(b_{ji}, a_i) = 2\alpha + \alpha_0$ and $d(c_{ji}, a_i) = \alpha + \alpha_0$. Thus, we obtain using (C.19) and (2.22)

$$P_\alpha(f^O(v_i), f^P(v_j))$$
$$= \inf_{p \in \mathbb{R}^n} I_T(f^O(v_i)(p), (R_\alpha{\downarrow}{\uparrow} f^P(v_j))(p))$$
$$= \inf_{p \in \mathbb{R}^n} I_T(f^O(v_i)(p), \inf_{q \in \mathbb{R}^n} I_T(R_\alpha(p,q),$$
$$\sup_{r \in \mathbb{R}^n} T(R_\alpha(q,r), \max_{l=1}^n T(\lambda_{lj}^P, f^O(v_l)(r)))))$$
$$\leq I_T(f^O(v_i)(a_i), \inf_{q \in \mathbb{R}^n} I_T(R_\alpha(a_i, q),$$
$$\sup_{r \in \mathbb{R}^n} T(R_\alpha(q,r), \max_{l=1}^n T(\lambda_{lj}^P, f^O(v_l)(r)))))$$
$$\leq I_T(f^O(v_i)(a_i), I_T(R_\alpha(a_i, a_i), \sup_{r \in \mathbb{R}^n} T(R_\alpha(a_i, r), \max_{l=1}^n T(\lambda_{lj}^P, f^O(v_l)(r)))))$$
$$= I_T(f^O(v_i)(a_i), \sup_{r \in \mathbb{R}^n} T(R_\alpha(a_i, r), \max_{l=1}^n T(\lambda_{lj}^P, f^O(v_l)(r))))$$
$$= I_T(f^O(v_i)(a_i), \max_{l=1}^n T(\lambda_{lj}^P, \sup_{r \in \mathbb{R}^n} T(R_\alpha(a_i, r), f^O(v_l)(r))))$$
$$= I_T(f^O(v_i)(a_i), \max_{l=1}^n T(\lambda_{lj}^P, (R_\alpha{\uparrow} f^O(v_l))(a_i)))$$
$$= I_T(f^O(v_i)(a_i), T(\lambda_{ij}^P, (R_\alpha{\uparrow} f^O(v_i))(a_i)))$$
$$= I_T(f^O(v_i)(a_i), T(\lambda_{ij}^P, 1))$$
$$= I_T(1, T(\lambda_{ij}^P, 1))$$
$$= \lambda_{ij}^P$$

$\square$

The lemma below shows that f^P satisfies (C.1) for a certain class of t–norms, and in particular for $T = T_W$.

Lemma C.15. *If T is a continuous Archimedean t–norm, it holds for all v_i and v_j in V that*

$$P_\alpha(f^P(v_i), f^P(v_j)) = \lambda_{ij}^P$$

Proof. From Lemma C.14, we already know that $P_\alpha(f^O(v_i), f^P(v_j)) = \lambda_{ij}^P$. Since $f^P(v_i) \supseteq f^O(v_i)$ this entails

$$P_\alpha(f^P(v_i), f^P(v_j)) \leq \lambda_{ij}^P$$

We show by contradiction that also $P_\alpha(f^P(v_i), f^P(v_j)) \geq \lambda_{ij}^P$. Assume $P_\alpha(f^P(v_i), f^P(v_j)) < \lambda_{ij}^P$. As the fuzzy sets $f^P(v_i)$ and $f^P(v_j)$ only take a finite number of different membership degrees, the infimum in the definition of $P_\alpha(f^P(v_i), f^P(v_j))$ is attained in some point p_0 in $\mathbb{R}^n$; using (C.19), we find

$$P_\alpha(f^P(v_i), f^P(v_j)) = \inf_{p \in \mathbb{R}^n} I_T(f^P(v_i)(p), (R_\alpha{\downarrow}{\uparrow}f^P(v_j))(p))$$
$$= I_T(f^P(v_i)(p_0), (R_\alpha{\downarrow}{\uparrow}f^P(v_j))(p_0))$$

and using our assumption that $P_\alpha(f^P(v_i), f^P(v_j)) < \lambda_{ij}^P$, we have in particular

$$I_T(f^P(v_i)(p_0), (R_\alpha{\downarrow}{\uparrow}f^P(v_j))(p_0)) < 1$$

which implies, by (2.23)

$$(R_\alpha{\downarrow}{\uparrow}f^P(v_j))(p_0) < f^P(v_i)(p_0) \tag{C.34}$$

Furthermore, for some k in $\{1, 2, \ldots, n\}$, it holds that

$$f^P(v_i)(p_0) = \max_{l=1}^n T(\lambda_{li}^P, f^O(v_l)(p_0)) = T(\lambda_{ki}^P, f^O(v_k)(p_0)) \tag{C.35}$$

which together with (C.34) yields

$$(R_\alpha{\downarrow}{\uparrow}f^P(v_j))(p_0) < T(\lambda_{ki}^P, f^O(v_k)(p_0))$$

From the residuation principle (2.21), we find

$$(R_\alpha{\downarrow}{\uparrow}f^P(v_j))(p_0) < T(\lambda_{ki}^P, f^O(v_k)(p_0))$$
$$\Leftrightarrow \neg(T(\lambda_{ki}^P, f^O(v_k)(p_0)) \leq (R_\alpha{\downarrow}{\uparrow}f^P(v_j))(p_0))$$
$$\Leftrightarrow \neg(\lambda_{ki}^P \leq I_T(f^O(v_k)(p_0), (R_\alpha{\downarrow}{\uparrow}f^P(v_j))(p_0)))$$
$$\Leftrightarrow \lambda_{ki}^P > I_T(f^O(v_k)(p_0), (R_\alpha{\downarrow}{\uparrow}f^P(v_j))(p_0))$$

From this observation we obtain by (C.35), (2.26), (2.31) (using the continuity of T), (C.19) and Lemma C.14

$$T(\lambda_{ki}^P, P_\alpha(f^P(v_i), f^P(v_j)))$$
$$= T(\lambda_{ki}^P, I_T(f^P(v_i)(p_0), (R_\alpha{\downarrow}{\uparrow}f^P(v_j))(p_0)))$$
$$= T(\lambda_{ki}^P, I_T(T(\lambda_{ki}^P, f^O(v_k)(p_0)), (R_\alpha{\downarrow}{\uparrow}f^P(v_j))(p_0)))$$
$$= T(\lambda_{ki}^P, I_T(\lambda_{ki}^P, I_T(f^O(v_k)(p_0), (R_\alpha{\downarrow}{\uparrow}f^P(v_j))(p_0))))$$
$$= \min(\lambda_{ki}^P, I_T(f^O(v_k)(p_0), (R_\alpha{\downarrow}{\uparrow}f^P(v_j))(p_0)))$$
$$= I_T(f^O(v_k)(p_0), (R_\alpha{\downarrow}{\uparrow}f^P(v_j))(p_0))$$
$$\geq \inf_{p \in \mathbb{R}^n} I_T(f^O(v_k)(p), (R_\alpha{\downarrow}{\uparrow}f^P(v_j))(p))$$
$$= P_\alpha(f^O(v_k), f^P(v_j))$$
$$= \lambda_{kj}^P$$

If $\lambda_{kj}^P > 0$, this implies $T(\lambda_{ki}^P, P_\alpha(f^P(v_i), f^P(v_j))) > 0$. Together with our assumption that $P_\alpha(f^P(v_i), f^P(v_j)) < \lambda_{ij}^P$, this yields

$$T(\lambda_{ki}^P, P_\alpha(f^P(v_i), f^P(v_j))) < T(\lambda_{ki}^P, \lambda_{ij}^P)$$

by Lemma C.9 (using the fact that T is a continuous Archimedean t–norm). Together with $T(\lambda_{ki}^P, P_\alpha(f^P(v_i), f^P(v_j))) \geq \lambda_{kj}^P$, we obtain

$$\lambda_{kj}^P < T(\lambda_{ki}^P, \lambda_{ij}^P)$$

On the other hand, as we assumed that Θ does not violate any of the transitivity rules from Table 7.5, we know that

$$\lambda_{kj}^P \geq T(\lambda_{ki}^P, \lambda_{ij}^P) \tag{C.36}$$

From this contradiction, we derive $\lambda_{kj}^P = 0$. However, we have

$$P_\alpha(f^P(v_i), f^P(v_j)) = I_T(\lambda_{ki}^P, I_T(f^O(v_k)(p_0), (R_\alpha{\downarrow}{\uparrow}f^P(v_j))(p_0)))$$

which yields by (C.19) and Lemma C.14

$$\begin{aligned} P_\alpha(f^P(v_i), f^P(v_j)) &\geq I_T(\lambda_{ki}^P, \inf_{p \in \mathbb{R}^n} I_T(f^O(v_k)(p), (R_\alpha{\downarrow}{\uparrow}f^P(v_j))(p))) \\ &= I_T(\lambda_{ki}^P, P_\alpha(f^O(v_k), f^P(v_j))) \\ &= I_T(\lambda_{ki}^P, \lambda_{kj}^P) \end{aligned}$$

From $\lambda_{kj}^P = 0$ and $\lambda_{ij}^P > P_\alpha(f^P(v_i), f^P(v_j)) \geq I_T(\lambda_{ki}^P, \lambda_{kj}^P)$, we find by Lemma C.8 that $T(\lambda_{ki}^P, \lambda_{ij}^P) > 0$. Using (C.36), this implies $\lambda_{kj}^P > 0$. From this contradiction, we conclude that the assumption $P_\alpha(f^P(v_i), f^P(v_j)) < \lambda_{ij}^P$ can never be satisfied. $\qquad\square$

The next lemma shows that f^P also satisfies (C.1).

Lemma C.16. *For all v_i and v_j in V, it holds that*

$$C_\alpha(f^P(v_i), f^P(v_j)) = \lambda_{ij}^C$$

Proof. From Lemma C.13 we know that $C_\alpha(f^O(v_i), f^O(v_j)) = \lambda_{ij}^C$. Since $f^P(v_i) \supseteq f^O(v_i)$ and $f^P(v_j) \supseteq f^O(v_j)$, we already have

$$C_\alpha(f^P(v_i), f^P(v_j)) \geq \lambda_{ij}^C$$

Conversely, we show that also $C_\alpha(f^P(v_i), f^P(v_j)) \leq \lambda_{ij}^C$. Because the fuzzy sets $f^P(v_i)$ and $f^P(v_j)$ only take a finite number of different membership degrees, the suprema in the definition of $C_\alpha(f^P(v_i), f^P(v_j))$ are attained for a certain (p_0, q_0) in $\mathbb{R}^n \times \mathbb{R}^n$:

$$\begin{aligned} \sup_{p,q \in \mathbb{R}^n} &\ T(f^P(v_i)(p), R_\alpha(p,q), f^P(v_j)(q)) \\ &= T(f^P(v_i)(p_0), R_\alpha(p_0, q_0), f^P(v_j)(q_0)) \end{aligned}$$

For certain k and m in $\{1, 2, \ldots, n\}$, it holds that

$$f^P(v_i)(p_0) = \max_{l=1}^{n} T(\lambda_{li}^P, f^O(v_l)(p_0)) = T(\lambda_{ki}^P, f^O(v_k)(p_0))$$

$$f^P(v_j)(q_0) = \max_{l=1}^{n} T(\lambda_{lj}^P, f^O(v_l)(q_0)) = T(\lambda_{mj}^P, f^O(v_m)(q_0))$$

This yields, using Lemma C.13

$$
\begin{aligned}
&C_\alpha(f^P(v_i), f^P(v_j)) \\
&= T(f^P(v_i)(p_0), R_\alpha(p_0, q_0), f^P(v_j)(q_0)) \\
&= T(T(\lambda_{ki}^P, f^O(v_k)(p_0)), R_\alpha(p_0, q_0), T(\lambda_{mj}^P, f^O(v_m)(q_0))) \\
&= T(T(\lambda_{ki}^P, \lambda_{mj}^P), T(f^O(v_k)(p_0), R_\alpha(p_0, q_0), f^O(v_m)(q_0))) \\
&\leq T(T(\lambda_{ki}^P, \lambda_{mj}^P), \sup_{p,q \in \mathbb{R}^n} T(f^O(v_k)(p), R_\alpha(p, q), f^O(v_m)(q))) \\
&= T(T(\lambda_{ki}^P, \lambda_{mj}^P), C_\alpha(f^O(v_k), f^O(v_m))) \\
&= T(\lambda_{ki}^P, \lambda_{mj}^P, \lambda_{km}^C)
\end{aligned}
$$

Because Θ satisfies (8.13) and does not violate any of the transitivity rules from Table 7.5, we have

$$T(\lambda_{km}^C, \lambda_{ki}^P) = T(\lambda_{mk}^C, \lambda_{ki}^P) \leq \lambda_{mi}^C$$
$$T(\lambda_{mi}^C, \lambda_{mj}^P) = T(\lambda_{im}^C, \lambda_{mj}^P) \leq \lambda_{ij}^C$$

We thus obtain

$$T(\lambda_{ki}^P, \lambda_{mj}^P, \lambda_{km}^C) \leq T(\lambda_{mi}^C, \lambda_{mj}^P) \leq \lambda_{ij}^C \qquad \square$$

Lemma C.17. *For all v_i in V, it holds that*

$$f^P(v_i) = \bigcup_{l=1}^{n} (P_{a_l}^{\lambda_{li}^P} \cup \bigcup_{m \neq l} (L_{b_{lm}}^{T(\lambda_{li}^P, \lambda_{lm}^C)} \cup L_{c_{lm}}^{T(\lambda_{li}^P, \lambda_{lm}^O)}))$$

Proof. For p in $\mathbb{R}^n$, we find

$$
\begin{aligned}
f^P(v_i)(p) &= \max_{l=1}^{n} T(\lambda_{li}^P, f^O(v_l)(p)) \\
&= \max_{l=1}^{n} T(\lambda_{li}^P, \max(f^C(v_l)(p), \max_{m \neq l} T(\lambda_{lm}^O, L_{c_{lm}}(p)))) \\
&= \max_{l=1}^{n} T(\lambda_{li}^P, \max(f^I(v_l)(p), \max_{m \neq l} T(\lambda_{lm}^C, L_{b_{lm}}(p)), \\
&\qquad\qquad\qquad \max_{m \neq l} T(\lambda_{lm}^O, L_{c_{lm}}(p)))) \\
&= \max_{l=1}^{n} \max(T(\lambda_{li}^P, f^I(v_l)(p)), \max_{m \neq l} T(\lambda_{li}^P, \lambda_{lm}^C, L_{b_{lm}}(p)),
\end{aligned}
$$

$$\max_{m\neq l} T(\lambda_{li}^P, \lambda_{lm}^O, L_{c_{lm}}(p)))$$

$$= \max_{l=1}^n \max(T(\lambda_{li}^P, P_{a_l}(p)), \max_{m\neq l} T(\lambda_{li}^P, \lambda_{lm}^C, L_{b_{lm}}(p)),$$

$$\max_{m\neq l} T(\lambda_{li}^P, \lambda_{lm}^O, L_{c_{lm}}(p)))$$

$$= \bigcup_{l=1}^n (P_{a_l}^{\lambda_{li}^P} \cup \bigcup_{m\neq l} (L_{b_{lm}}^{T(\lambda_{li}^P, \lambda_{lm}^C)} \cup L_{c_{lm}}^{T(\lambda_{li}^P, \lambda_{lm}^O)}))(p) \qquad \square$$

Lemma C.18. *For all v_i and v_j in V, it holds that*

$$O_\alpha(f^P(v_i), f^P(v_j)) = \sup_{p\in\mathbb{R}^n} T(f^P(v_i)(p), f^P(v_j)(p))$$

Proof. The supremum in $O_\alpha(f^P(v_i), f^P(v_j))$ is attained for a certain p_0 in $\mathbb{R}^n$:

$$O_\alpha(f^P(v_i), f^P(v_j)) = T((R_\alpha\downarrow\uparrow f^P(v_i))(p_0), (R_\alpha\downarrow\uparrow f^P(v_j))(p_0))$$

By Lemma C.17 we know

$$f^P(v_i) = \bigcup_{l=1}^n (P_{a_l}^{\lambda_{li}^P} \cup \bigcup_{m\neq l} (L_{b_{lm}}^{T(\lambda_{li}^P, \lambda_{lm}^C)} \cup L_{c_{lm}}^{T(\lambda_{li}^P, \lambda_{lm}^O)}))$$

$$f^P(v_j) = \bigcup_{l=1}^n (P_{a_l}^{\lambda_{lj}^P} \cup \bigcup_{m\neq l} (L_{b_{lm}}^{T(\lambda_{lj}^P, \lambda_{lm}^C)} \cup L_{c_{lm}}^{T(\lambda_{lj}^P, \lambda_{lm}^O)}))$$

From Lemma C.4, we find using (C.23)–(C.26) and (C.28)–(C.32)

$$O_\alpha(f^P(v_i), f^P(v_j))$$

$$= \max_{1\leq l_1, l_2\leq n} O_\alpha(P_{a_{l_1}}^{\lambda_{l_1i}^P} \cup \bigcup_{m\neq l_1} (L_{b_{l_1m}}^{T(\lambda_{l_1i}^P, \lambda_{l_1m}^C)} \cup L_{c_{l_1m}}^{T(\lambda_{l_1i}^P, \lambda_{l_1m}^O)}),$$

$$P_{a_{l_2}}^{\lambda_{l_2j}^P} \cup \bigcup_{m\neq l_2} (L_{b_{l_2m}}^{T(\lambda_{l_2j}^P, \lambda_{l_2m}^C)} \cup L_{c_{l_2m}}^{T(\lambda_{l_2j}^P, \lambda_{l_2m}^O)}))$$

From Corollary C.1, we find for $l_1 \neq l_2$

$$O_\alpha(P_{a_{l_1}}^{\lambda_{l_1i}^P} \cup \bigcup_{m\neq l_1} (L_{b_{l_1m}}^{T(\lambda_{l_1i}^P, \lambda_{l_1m}^C)} \cup L_{c_{l_1m}}^{T(\lambda_{l_1i}^P, \lambda_{l_1m}^O)}),$$

$$P_{a_{l_2}}^{\lambda_{l_2j}^P} \cup \bigcup_{m\neq l_2} (L_{b_{l_2m}}^{T(\lambda_{l_2j}^P, \lambda_{l_2m}^C)} \cup L_{c_{l_2m}}^{T(\lambda_{l_2j}^P, \lambda_{l_2m}^O)}))$$

$$= 0$$

again using (C.23)–(C.26) and (C.28)–(C.32). In other words

$$O_\alpha(f^P(v_i), f^P(v_j))$$
$$= \max_{l=1}^{n} O_\alpha(P_{a_l}^{\lambda_{li}^P} \cup \bigcup_{m \neq l} (L_{b_{lm}}^{T(\lambda_{li}^P, \lambda_{lm}^C)} \cup L_{c_{lm}}^{T(\lambda_{li}^P, \lambda_{lm}^O)}),$$
$$P_{a_l}^{\lambda_{lj}^P} \cup \bigcup_{m \neq l} (L_{b_{lm}}^{T(\lambda_{lj}^P, \lambda_{lm}^C)} \cup L_{c_{lm}}^{T(\lambda_{lj}^P, \lambda_{lm}^O)}))$$

Applying Lemma C.4 once more, we find

$$O_\alpha(f^P(v_i), f^P(v_j))$$
$$= \max_{l=1}^{n} \max_{m_1 \neq l} \max_{m_2 \neq l} O_\alpha(P_{a_l}^{\lambda_{li}^P} \cup L_{b_{lm_1}}^{T(\lambda_{li}^P, \lambda_{lm_1}^C)} \cup L_{c_{lm_1}}^{T(\lambda_{li}^P, \lambda_{lm_1}^O)},$$
$$P_{a_l}^{\lambda_{lj}^P} \cup L_{b_{lm_2}}^{T(\lambda_{lj}^P, \lambda_{lm_2}^C)} \cup L_{c_{lm_2}}^{T(\lambda_{lj}^P, \lambda_{lm_2}^O)})$$

and in particular

$$O_\alpha(f^P(v_i), f^P(v_j)) \tag{C.37}$$
$$= \max_{l=1}^{n} \max_{m_1 \neq l} \max_{m_2 \neq l} T((R_\alpha \downarrow \uparrow (P_{a_l}^{\lambda_{li}^P} \cup L_{b_{lm_1}}^{T(\lambda_{li}^P, \lambda_{lm_1}^C)} \cup L_{c_{lm_1}}^{T(\lambda_{li}^P, \lambda_{lm_1}^O)}))(p_0),$$
$$(R_\alpha \downarrow \uparrow (P_{a_l}^{\lambda_{lj}^P} \cup L_{b_{lm_2}}^{T(\lambda_{lj}^P, \lambda_{lm_2}^C)} \cup L_{c_{lm_2}}^{T(\lambda_{lj}^P, \lambda_{lm_2}^O)}))(p_0))$$

Moreover, note that

$$O_\alpha(f^P(v_i), f^P(v_j)) \tag{C.38}$$
$$\geq \max_{l=1}^{n} \max_{m \neq l} T((R_\alpha \downarrow \uparrow (P_{a_l}^{\lambda_{li}^P} \cup L_{b_{lm}}^{T(\lambda_{li}^P, \lambda_{lm}^C)} \cup L_{c_{lm}}^{T(\lambda_{li}^P, \lambda_{lm}^O)}))(p_0),$$
$$(R_\alpha \downarrow \uparrow (P_{a_l}^{\lambda_{lj}^P} \cup L_{b_{lm}}^{T(\lambda_{lj}^P, \lambda_{lm}^C)} \cup L_{c_{lm}}^{T(\lambda_{lj}^P, \lambda_{lm}^O)}))(p_0))$$

Assume that the latter inequality were a strict inequality. This would imply that for some m_1

$$(R_\alpha \downarrow \uparrow (P_{a_l}^{\lambda_{li}^P} \cup L_{b_{lm_1}}^{T(\lambda_{li}^P, \lambda_{lm_1}^C)} \cup L_{c_{lm_1}}^{T(\lambda_{li}^P, \lambda_{lm_1}^O)}))(p_0) > (R_\alpha \downarrow \uparrow P_{a_l}^{\lambda_{li}^P})(p_0) \quad \text{(C.39)}$$

Indeed, if this were not the case, we could choose $m_1 = m_2$ in (C.37) and the inequality in (C.38) would be an equality. Similarly, we would have for some $m_2 \neq m_1$

$$(R_\alpha \downarrow \uparrow (P_{a_l}^{\lambda_{lj}^P} \cup L_{b_{lm_2}}^{T(\lambda_{lj}^P, \lambda_{lm_2}^C)} \cup L_{c_{lm_2}}^{T(\lambda_{lj}^P, \lambda_{lm_2}^O)}))(p_0) > (R_\alpha \downarrow \uparrow P_{a_l}^{\lambda_{lj}^P})(p_0) \quad \text{(C.40)}$$

From (C.39), we derive that for some point q_0 in $supp(L_{b_{lm_1}}^{T(\lambda_{li}^P, \lambda_{lm_1}^C)} \cup L_{c_{lm_1}}^{T(\lambda_{li}^P, \lambda_{lm_1}^O)})$, it holds that $d(p_0, q_0) \leq 2\alpha$. Similarly, we derive from (C.40) that for some point r_0 in $supp(L_{b_l m_2}^{T(\lambda_{lj}^P, \lambda_{lm_2}^C)} \cup L_{c_l m_2}^{T(\lambda_{lj}^P, \lambda_{lm_2}^O)})$, it holds that $d(p_0, r_0) \leq 2\alpha$, and due to the triangle inequality $d(q_0, r_0) \leq 4\alpha$. From (C.23)–(C.26) and (C.28)–(C.32), we know that this is only possible if $m_1 = m_2$, a contradiction. Hence, we have shown

$$O_\alpha(f^P(v_i), f^P(v_j)) = \max_{l=1}^n \max_{m \neq l} O_\alpha(P_{a_l}^{\lambda_{li}^P} \cup L_{b_l m}^{T(\lambda_{li}^P, \lambda_{lm}^C)} \cup L_{c_l m}^{T(\lambda_{li}^P, \lambda_{lm}^O)},$$
$$P_{a_l}^{\lambda_{lj}^P} \cup L_{b_l m}^{T(\lambda_{lj}^P, \lambda_{lm}^C)} \cup L_{c_l m}^{T(\lambda_{lj}^P, \lambda_{lm}^O)})$$

By Lemma C.6, we find

$$O_\alpha(f^P(v_i), f^P(v_j))$$
$$= \max_{l=1}^n \max_{m \neq l} \max(O_\alpha(P_{a_l}^{\lambda_{li}^P}, P_{a_l}^{\lambda_{lj}^P}), O_\alpha(P_{a_l}^{\lambda_{li}^P}, L_{b_l m}^{T(\lambda_{lj}^P, \lambda_{lm}^C)}),$$
$$O_\alpha(P_{a_l}^{\lambda_{li}^P}, L_{c_l m}^{T(\lambda_{lj}^P, \lambda_{lm}^O)}), O_\alpha(L_{b_l m}^{T(\lambda_{lj}^P, \lambda_{lm}^C)}, P_{a_l}^{\lambda_{lj}^P}),$$
$$O_\alpha(L_{b_l m}^{T(\lambda_{lj}^P, \lambda_{lm}^C)}, L_{b_l m}^{T(\lambda_{lj}^P, \lambda_{lm}^C)}), O_\alpha(L_{b_l m}^{T(\lambda_{lj}^P, \lambda_{lm}^C)}, L_{c_l m}^{T(\lambda_{lj}^P, \lambda_{lm}^O)}),$$
$$O_\alpha(L_{c_l m}^{T(\lambda_{li}^P, \lambda_{lm}^O)}, P_{a_l}^{\lambda_{lj}^P}), O_\alpha(L_{c_l m}^{T(\lambda_{li}^P, \lambda_{lm}^O)}, L_{b_l m}^{T(\lambda_{lj}^P, \lambda_{lm}^C)})$$
$$O_\alpha(L_{c_l m}^{T(\lambda_{li}^P, \lambda_{lm}^O)}, L_{c_l m}^{T(\lambda_{lj}^P, \lambda_{lm}^O)}))$$

and by Lemma C.1

$$O_\alpha(f^P(v_i), f^P(v_j))$$
$$= \max_{l=1}^n \max_{m \neq l} \max(\sup_{p \in \mathbb{R}^n} T(P_{a_l}^{\lambda_{li}^P}(p), P_{a_l}^{\lambda_{lj}^P}(p)), \sup_{p \in \mathbb{R}} T(P_{a_l}^{\lambda_{li}^P}(p), L_{b_l m}^{T(\lambda_{lj}^P, \lambda_{lm}^C)}(p)),$$
$$\sup_{p \in \mathbb{R}^n} T(P_{a_l}^{\lambda_{li}^P}(p), L_{c_l m}^{T(\lambda_{lj}^P, \lambda_{lm}^O)}(p)),$$
$$\sup_{p \in \mathbb{R}} T(L_{b_l m}^{T(\lambda_{lj}^P, \lambda_{lm}^C)}(p), P_{a_l}^{\lambda_{lj}^P}(p)),$$
$$\sup_{p \in \mathbb{R}^n} T(L_{b_l m}^{T(\lambda_{lj}^P, \lambda_{lm}^C)}(p), L_{b_l m}^{T(\lambda_{lj}^P, \lambda_{lm}^C)}(p)),$$
$$\sup_{p \in \mathbb{R}} T(L_{b_l m}^{T(\lambda_{lj}^P, \lambda_{lm}^C)}(p), L_{c_l m}^{T(\lambda_{lj}^P, \lambda_{lm}^O)}(p)),$$
$$\sup_{p \in \mathbb{R}^n} T(L_{c_l m}^{T(\lambda_{li}^P, \lambda_{lm}^O)}(p), P_{a_l}^{\lambda_{lj}^P}(p)),$$
$$\sup_{p \in \mathbb{R}} T(L_{c_l m}^{T(\lambda_{li}^P, \lambda_{lm}^O)}(p), L_{b_l m}^{T(\lambda_{lj}^P, \lambda_{lm}^C)}(p)),$$

$$\sup_{p\in\mathbb{R}^n} T(L_{c_{lm}}^{T(\lambda_{li}^P,\lambda_{lm}^O)}(p), L_{c_{lm}}^{T(\lambda_{lj}^P,\lambda_{lm}^O)}(p))),$$

$$= \max_{l=1}^{n}\max_{m\neq l}\sup_{p\in\mathbb{R}^n} T((P_{a_l}^{\lambda_{li}^P}\cup L_{b_{lm}}^{T(\lambda_{li}^P,\lambda_{lm}^C)}\cup L_{c_{lm}}^{T(\lambda_{li}^P,\lambda_{lm}^O)})(p),$$

$$(P_{a_l}^{\lambda_{lj}^P}\cup L_{b_{lm}}^{T(\lambda_{lj}^P,\lambda_{lm}^C)}\cup L_{c_{lm}}^{T(\lambda_{lj}^P,\lambda_{lm}^O)})(p))$$

In other words

$$O_\alpha(f^P(v_i), f^P(v_j)) = \sup_{p\in\mathbb{R}^n} T(f^P(v_i)(p), f^P(v_j)(p)) \qquad\qquad \square$$

Lemma C.19. *For all v_i and v_j in V, it holds that*

$$O_\alpha(f^P(v_i), f^P(v_j)) = \lambda_{ij}^O$$

Proof. From Lemma C.12, we know that $O_\alpha(f^O(v_i), f^O(v_j)) = \lambda_{ij}^O$. Therefore, since $f^P(v_i) \supseteq f^O(v_i)$ and $f^P(v_j) \supseteq f^O(v_j)$ we already have

$$O_\alpha(f^P(v_i), f^P(v_j)) \geq \lambda_{ij}^O$$

Conversely, we find by Lemma C.18

$$O_\alpha(f^P(v_i), f^P(v_j)) = \sup_{p\in\mathbb{R}^n} T(f^P(v_i)(p), f^P(v_j)(p))$$

Since the fuzzy sets $f^P(v_i)$ and $f^P(v_j)$ only take a finite number of different membership degrees, the supremum in the right–hand side is attained for some p_0 in $\mathbb{R}^n$:

$$\sup_{p\in\mathbb{R}^n} T(f^P(v_i)(p), f^P(v_j)(p)) = T(f^P(v_i)(p_0), f^P(v_j)(p_0))$$

For certain k and m in $\{1, 2, \ldots, n\}$, it moreover holds that

$$f^P(v_i)(p_0) = \max_{l=1}^{n} T(\lambda_{li}^P, f^O(v_l)(p_0)) = T(\lambda_{ki}^P, f^O(v_k)(p_0))$$

$$f^P(v_j)(p_0) = \max_{l=1}^{n} T(\lambda_{lj}^P, f^O(v_l)(p_0)) = T(\lambda_{mj}^P, f^O(v_m)(p_0))$$

We thus obtain

$$O_\alpha(f^P(v_i), f^P(v_j)) = T(f^P(v_i)(p_0), f^P(v_j)(p_0))$$
$$= T(\lambda_{ki}^P, f^O(v_k)(p_0), \lambda_{mj}^P, f^O(v_m)(p_0))$$
$$\leq T(\lambda_{ki}^P, \lambda_{mj}^P, \sup_{p\in\mathbb{R}^n} T(f^O(v_k)(p), f^O(v_m)(p)))$$

and using Corollary C.2 and Lemma C.12

$$= T(\lambda_{ki}^P, \lambda_{mj}^P, O_\alpha(f^O(v_k), f^O(v_m)))$$
$$= T(\lambda_{ki}^P, \lambda_{mj}^P, \lambda_{km}^O)$$

Because Θ satisfies (8.14), as well as the transitivity rules from Table 7.5, we know that

$$T(\lambda^O_{km}, \lambda^P_{ki}) = T(\lambda^O_{mk}, \lambda^P_{ki}) \leq \lambda^O_{mi}$$
$$T(\lambda^O_{mi}, \lambda^P_{mj}) = T(\lambda^O_{im}, \lambda^P_{mj}) \leq \lambda^O_{ij}$$

This yields

$$T(\lambda^P_{ki}, \lambda^P_{mj}, \lambda^O_{km}) \leq T(\lambda^O_{mi}, \lambda^P_{mj}) \leq \lambda^O_{ij} \qquad \square$$

C.5 Non–Tangential Part of

For m in $\mathbb{N} \setminus \{0\}$, the function f^m is defined as

$$f^m(v_i)(p) = \max(f^{m-1}(v_i)(p), \max_{l=1}^n T(\lambda^{NTP}_{li}, (R_\alpha \uparrow f^{m-1}(v_l))(p)))$$

for all p in $\mathbb{R}^n$ and v_i in V. Furthermore, we define $f^0 = f^P$.

Lemma C.20. *Let T be a nilpotent t–norm. There exists an m in $\mathbb{N}$ such that $f^m = f^l$ for every $l \geq m$ $(l \in \mathbb{N})$.*

Proof. We show this result by contradiction. Assume that for every m in $\mathbb{N}$ there is a v_k in V such that $f^{m+1}(v_k) \supset f^m(v_k)$. For every m, this means that there is a v_k in V and a p_0 in $\mathbb{R}^n$ such that

$$f^m(v_k)(p_0) < f^{m+1}(v_k)(p_0)$$

$$\Leftrightarrow f^m(v_k)(p_0) < \max(f^m(v_k)(p_0), \max_{j=1}^n T(\lambda^{NTP}_{jk}, (R_\alpha \uparrow f^m(v_j))(p_0)))$$

$$\Leftrightarrow f^m(v_k)(p_0) < \max_{j=1}^n T(\lambda^{NTP}_{jk}, (R_\alpha \uparrow f^m(v_j))(p_0))$$

For some j_0 in $\{1, 2, \ldots, n\}$ we have

$$f^m(v_k)(p_0) < T(\lambda^{NTP}_{j_0 k}, (R_\alpha \uparrow f^m(v_{j_0}))(p_0)) \qquad (C.41)$$

Assuming $m \geq 1$, this implies

$$(R_\alpha \uparrow f^m(v_{j_0}))(p_0) > (R_\alpha \uparrow f^{m-1}(v_{j_0}))(p_0) \qquad (C.42)$$

Indeed, if this were not the case, i.e., if $(R_\alpha \uparrow f^m(v_{j_0}))(p_0) = (R_\alpha \uparrow f^{m-1}(v_{j_0}))(p_0)$, we would obtain

$$f^m(v_k)(p_0) \geq T(\lambda^{NTP}_{j_0 k}, (R_\alpha \uparrow f^{m-1}(v_{j_0}))(p_0))$$
$$= T(\lambda^{NTP}_{j_0 k}, (R_\alpha \uparrow f^m(v_{j_0}))(p_0))$$

contradicting (C.41).

Since $f^m(v_{i_0}))$ only takes a finite number of different membership degrees, we find for a certain p_1 satisfying $d(p_0, p_1) \leq \alpha$

$$(R_\alpha \uparrow f^m(v_{j_0}))(p_0) = \sup_{q \in \mathbb{R}^n} T(R_\alpha(p_0, q), f^m(v_{j_0})(q))$$

$$= T(R_\alpha(p_0, p_1), f^m(v_{j_0})(p_1))$$

$$= f^m(v_{j_0})(p_1)$$

From (C.42), we find

$$f^m(v_{j_0})(p_1) = (R_\alpha \uparrow f^m(v_{j_0}))(p_0)$$

$$> (R_\alpha \uparrow f^{m-1}(v_{j_0}))(p_0)$$

$$= \sup_{q \in \mathbb{R}^n} T(R_\alpha(p_0, q), f^{m-1}(v_{j_0})(q))$$

$$\geq f^{m-1}(v_{j_0})(p_1)$$

Therefore, we have

$$f^m(v_{j_0})(p_1) = \max(f^{m-1}(v_{j_0})(p_1), \max_{j=1}^n T(\lambda_{jj_0}^{NTP}, (R_\alpha \uparrow f^{m-1}(v_j))(p_1)))$$

$$= \max_{j=1}^n T(\lambda_{jj_0}^{NTP}, (R_\alpha \uparrow f^{m-1}(v_j))(p_1))$$

and for a certain j_1 in $\{1, 2, \ldots, n\}$

$$f^m(v_{j_0})(p_1) = T(\lambda_{j_1 j_0}^{NTP}, (R_\alpha \uparrow f^{m-1}(v_{j_1}))(p_1))$$

We have shown

$$(R_\alpha \uparrow f^m(v_{j_0}))(p_0) = T(\lambda_{j_1 j_0}^{NTP}, (R_\alpha \uparrow f^{m-1}(v_{j_1}))(p_1))$$

This yields together with (C.41)

$$f^m(v_k)(p_0) < T(\lambda_{j_0 k}^{NTP}, (R_\alpha \uparrow f^m(v_{j_0}))(p_0)) \qquad \text{(C.43)}$$

$$= T(\lambda_{j_0 k}^{NTP}, \lambda_{j_1 j_0}^{NTP}, (R_\alpha \uparrow f^{m-1}(v_{j_1}))(p_1))$$

Assuming $m \geq 2$, this implies

$$(R_\alpha \uparrow f^{m-1}(v_{j_1}))(p_1) > (R_\alpha \uparrow f^{m-2}(v_{j_1}))(p_1)$$

Indeed, if $(R_\alpha \uparrow f^{m-1}(v_{j_1}))(p_1) \leq (R_\alpha \uparrow f^{m-2}(v_{j_1}))(p_1)$ were the case, we would obtain

$$T(\lambda_{j_0 k}^{NTP}, \lambda_{j_1 j_0}^{NTP}, (R_\alpha \uparrow f^{m-1}(v_{j_1}))(p_1))$$

$$\leq T(\lambda_{j_0 k}^{NTP}, \lambda_{j_1 j_0}^{NTP}, (R_\alpha \uparrow f^{m-2}(v_{j_1}))(p_1))$$

$$\leq T(\lambda_{j_0 k}^{NTP}, f^{m-1}(v_{j_0})(p_1))$$

$$= T(\lambda_{j_0 k}^{NTP}, T(R_\alpha(p_0, p_1), f^{m-1}(v_{j_0})(p_1)))$$

$$\leq T(\lambda_{j_0 k}^{NTP}, \sup_{q \in \mathbb{R}^n} T(R_\alpha(p_0, q), f^{m-1}(v_{j_0})(q)))$$

$$= T(\lambda_{j_0 k}^{NTP}, (R_\alpha \uparrow f^{m-1}(v_{j_0}))(p_0))$$

$$\leq f^m(v_k)(p_0)$$

contradicting (C.43). By repeatedly applying the same argument, we obtain for some v_{j_m} in V and p_m in $\mathbb{R}^n$

$$f^m(v_k)(p_0) < T(\lambda_{j_0 k}^{NTP}, \lambda_{j_1 j_0}^{NTP}, \ldots, \lambda_{j_m j_{m-1}}^{NTP}, (R_\alpha \uparrow f^0(v_{j_m}))(p_m)) \quad \text{(C.44)}$$

Note that m can be chosen arbitrarily large. In particular, if we choose m such that $m > n$, there exists a cycle, i.e., there is an s and a t in $\{0, 1, \ldots, m\}$ such that $v_{j_s} = v_{j_t}$. On the other hand, (C.44) can only be satisfied if the right–hand side is strictly positive, hence

$$T(\lambda_{j_0 k}^{NTP}, \lambda_{j_1 j_0}^{NTP}, \ldots, \lambda_{j_m j_{m-1}}^{NTP}) > 0 \quad \text{(C.45)}$$

Moreover, since Θ satisfies all transitivity rules from Table 7.5 and Θ does not contain any fuzzy RCC formulas of the form $NTP(v, v) \geq 1$, we have that

$$0 < T(\lambda_{j_0 k}^{NTP}, \lambda_{j_1 j_0}^{NTP}, \ldots, \lambda_{j_m j_{m-1}}^{NTP}) \leq \lambda_{j_t j_t}^{NTP} \leq \sup_{i=1}^{n} \lambda_{ii}^{NTP} < 1$$

As T is a nilpotent t–norm, there exists an n_0 in $\mathbb{N}$ such that

$$T(\underbrace{\sup_{i=1}^{n} \lambda_{ii}^{NTP}, \sup_{i=1}^{n} \lambda_{ii}^{NTP}, \ldots, \sup_{i=1}^{n} \lambda_{ii}^{NTP}}_{n_0}) = 0$$

By choosing $m > n_0 \cdot n$, at least n_0 cycles will exist, and therefore

$$T(\lambda_{j_0 k}^{NTP}, \lambda_{j_1 j_0}^{NTP}, \ldots, \lambda_{j_m j_{m-1}}^{NTP}) \leq T(\underbrace{\sup_{i=1}^{n} \lambda_{ii}^{NTP}, \sup_{i=1}^{n} \lambda_{ii}^{NTP}, \ldots, \sup_{i=1}^{n} \lambda_{ii}^{NTP}}_{n_0}) = 0$$

contradicting (C.45). Therefore, we have that for some m in $\mathbb{N}$, it holds that $f^{m+1} = f^m$. For any v_k in V and p in $\mathbb{R}^n$, we then also find

$$
\begin{aligned}
f^{m+2}(v_k)(p) &= \max(f^{m+1}(v_k)(p), \max_{j=1}^{n} T(\lambda_{jk}^{NTP}, (R_\alpha \uparrow f^{m+1}(v_j))(p))) \\
&= \max(f^m(v_k)(p), \max_{j=1}^{n} T(\lambda_{jk}^{NTP}, (R_\alpha \uparrow f^m(v_j))(p))) \\
&= f^{m+1}(v_k)(p)
\end{aligned}
$$

By induction, it follows that $f^l = f^m$ for every $l \geq m$. $\qquad \square$

Henceforth, let T be a continuous, Archimedean, nilpotent t–norm and let m_0 in $\mathbb{N}$ be such that $f^{m_0} = f^{m_0+1}$. Note in the proof above that such an m_0 can be found which only depends on the size of Θ, the value of $\sup_{i=1}^{n} \lambda_{ii}^{NTP}$ and the t–norm being used. Hence, without loss of generality, we can assume that

$$\alpha_0 > (m_0 + 2)\alpha \quad \text{(C.46)}$$

Next, for i in $\{1, 2, \ldots, n\}$, we define the point p_i as

$$p_i = a_i + (\alpha + \alpha_0)\frac{\overrightarrow{a_j a_i}}{\|\overrightarrow{a_j a_i}\|}$$

where j is an arbitrary element of $\{1, \ldots, i-1, i+1, \ldots, n\}$. Figure C.4 illustrates the construction of the points p_i for $n = 3$. Clearly, it holds that

$$d(p_i, a_i) = \alpha + \alpha_0 \qquad (C.47)$$

Furthermore, for $l \neq i$

$$d(p_i, b_{li}) > d(p_i, a_i) = \alpha + \alpha_0$$
$$d(p_i, c_{li}) > d(p_i, a_i) = \alpha + \alpha_0$$

Using (C.46), we obtain in particular that

$$d(p_i, b_{li}) > (m_0 + 1)\alpha \qquad (C.48)$$
$$d(p_i, c_{li}) > (m_0 + 1)\alpha \qquad (C.49)$$

Moreover, by taking ρ sufficiently large, we can assume that for $l \neq i$ and $k \neq l$

$$d(p_i, a_l) > m_0\alpha + \alpha_0 \qquad (C.50)$$
$$d(p_i, b_{kl}) > (m_0 + 1)\alpha \qquad (C.51)$$
$$d(p_i, c_{kl}) > (m_0 + 1)\alpha \qquad (C.52)$$

Moreover, we will also need to strengthen the assumptions (C.23)–(C.26) and (C.28)–(C.32). In particular, we can assume without loss of generality that $(i \neq j)$

$$d(a_i, a_j) > (2m_0 + 4)\alpha + 2\alpha_0 \qquad (C.53)$$
$$d(b_{li}, b_{lj}) > (2m_0 + 6)\alpha \qquad (C.54)$$
$$d(b_{il}, b_{jk}) > (2m_0 + 6)\alpha \qquad (C.55)$$
$$d(c_{li}, c_{lj}) > (2m_0 + 6)\alpha \qquad (C.56)$$
$$d(c_{il}, c_{jk}) > (2m_0 + 6)\alpha \qquad (C.57)$$
$$d(b_{li}, c_{lj}) > (2m_0 + 6)\alpha \qquad (C.58)$$
$$d(b_{il}, c_{jk}) > (2m_0 + 6)\alpha \qquad (C.59)$$
$$d(a_i, b_{ji}) > (2m_0 + 6)\alpha \qquad (C.60)$$
$$d(a_i, c_{ji}) > (2m_0 + 6)\alpha \qquad (C.61)$$
$$d(a_i, b_{lj}) > (2m_0 + 5)\alpha + \alpha_0 \qquad (C.62)$$
$$d(a_i, c_{lj}) > (2m_0 + 5)\alpha + \alpha_0 \qquad (C.63)$$

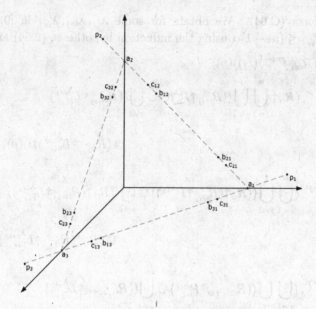

Fig. C.4 Construction of the points p_i ($1 \leq i \leq 3$).

Lemma C.21. *For every m in $\mathbb{N}$ and v_k in V there is a t in $\mathbb{N}$ such that*

$$f^m(v_k) = \bigcup_{i=1}^{n} \bigcup_{j=1}^{t}((R_{\alpha_{ij}} \uparrow P_{a_i}^{\lambda_{ij}}) \cup \bigcup_{s \neq i}((R_{\alpha_{isj}} \uparrow L_{b_{is}}^{\lambda_{isj}}) \cup (R_{\alpha'_{isj}} \uparrow L_{c_{is}}^{\lambda'_{isj}})))$$

$$(C.64)$$

for some $\lambda_{ij}, \lambda_{isj}, \lambda'_{isj}$ in $[0,1]$ and $0 \leq \alpha_{ij}, \alpha_{isj}, \alpha'_{isj} \leq m\alpha$.

Proof. The case $m = 0$ follows trivially from Lemma C.17 (for $t = 1$, $\alpha_{ij} = \alpha_{isj} = \alpha'_{isj} = 0$). We show by induction that this lemma also holds for $m > 0$; let $m > 0$ and assume that the lemma holds for $m-1$ (induction hypothesis). By definition, we have for all p in $\mathbb{R}^n$

$$f^m(v_k)(p) = \max(f^{m-1}(v_k)(p), \max_{l=1}^{n} T(\lambda_{lk}^{NTP}, (R_\alpha \uparrow f^{m-1}(v_l))(p)))$$

By the induction hypothesis, $f^{m-1}(v_k)$ is already of the form (C.64). Therefore, it is sufficient to show that for every l in $\{1, 2, \ldots, n\}$ the fuzzy set A_l in $\mathbb{R}^n$ defined for all p in $\mathbb{R}^n$ by

$$A_l(p) = T(\lambda_{lk}^{NTP}, (R_\alpha \uparrow f^{m-1}(v_l))(p))$$

is of the form (C.64). We obtain for some $\lambda_{ij}, \lambda_{isj}, \lambda'_{isj}$ in $[0,1]$, $0 \leq \alpha_{ij}, \alpha_{isj}, \alpha'_{isj} \leq (m-1)\alpha$ using the induction hypothesis, (2.54) and (2.7)

$$T(\lambda_{lk}^{NTP}, (R_\alpha\uparrow f^{m-1}(v_l))(p))$$

$$= T(\lambda_{lk}^{NTP}, (R_\alpha\uparrow \bigcup_{i=1}^{n}\bigcup_{j=1}^{t}((R_{\alpha_{ij}}\uparrow P_{a_i}^{\lambda_{ij}}) \cup \bigcup_{s\neq i}((R_{\alpha_{isj}}\uparrow L_{b_{is}}^{\lambda_{isj}})$$

$$\cup (R_{\alpha'_{isj}}\uparrow L_{c_{is}}^{\lambda'_{isj}})))))(p))$$

$$= T(\lambda_{lk}^{NTP}, (\bigcup_{i=1}^{n}\bigcup_{j=1}^{t}((R_\alpha\uparrow(R_{\alpha_{ij}}\uparrow P_{a_i}^{\lambda_{ij}})) \cup \bigcup_{s\neq i}((R_\alpha\uparrow(R_{\alpha_{isj}}\uparrow L_{b_{is}}^{\lambda_{isj}}))$$

$$\cup (R_\alpha\uparrow(R_{\alpha'_{isj}}\uparrow L_{c_{is}}^{\lambda'_{istj}})))))(p))$$

$$= T(\lambda_{lk}^{NTP}, (\bigcup_{i=1}^{n}\bigcup_{j=1}^{t}((R_{\alpha_{ij}+\alpha}\uparrow P_{a_i}^{\lambda_{ij}}) \cup \bigcup_{s\neq i}((R_{\alpha_{isj}+\alpha}\uparrow L_{b_{is}}^{\lambda_{isj}})$$

$$\cup (R_{\alpha'_{isj}+\alpha}\uparrow L_{c_{is}}^{\lambda'_{isj}}))))(p))$$

$$= (\bigcup_{i=1}^{n}\bigcup_{j=1}^{t}((R_{\alpha_{ij}+\alpha}\uparrow P_{a_i}^{T(\lambda_{lk}^{NTP},\lambda_{ij})}) \cup \bigcup_{s\neq i}((R_{\alpha_{isj}+\alpha}\uparrow L_{b_{is}}^{T(\lambda_{lk}^{NTP},\lambda_{isj})})$$

$$\cup (R_{\alpha'_{isj}+\alpha}\uparrow L_{c_{is}}^{T(\lambda_{lk}^{NTP},\lambda'_{isj})}))))(p) \qquad \square$$

Lemma C.22. *It holds that*

$$NTP_\alpha(f^{m_0}(v_i), f^{m_0}(v_j)) = \lambda_{ij}^{NTP}$$

for all v_i and v_j in V.

Proof. By definition of f^{m_0+1}, we find for every p in $\mathbb{R}^n$

$$f^{m_0+1}(v_j)(p) = \max(f^{m_0}(v_j)(p), \max_{l=1}^{n} T(\lambda_{lj}^{NTP}, (R_\alpha\uparrow f^{m_0}(v_l))(p)))$$

Using $f^{m_0+1} = f^{m_0}$, we find in particular $f^{m_0+1}(v_j)(p) = f^{m_0}(v_j)(p)$, leading to

$$f^{m_0}(v_j)(p) \geq \max_{l=1}^{n} T(\lambda_{lj}^{NTP}, (R_\alpha\uparrow f^{m_0}(v_l))(p))$$

$$\geq T(\lambda_{ij}^{NTP}, (R_\alpha\uparrow f^{m_0}(v_i))(p))$$

and by (2.21)

$$I_T((R_\alpha \uparrow f^{m_0}(v_i))(p), f^{m_0}(v_j)(p)) \geq \lambda_{ij}^{NTP}$$

As this inequality holds for every p in $\mathbb{R}^n$, we have by definition of the infimum

$$\inf_{p \in \mathbb{R}^n} I_T((R_\alpha \uparrow f^{m_0}(v_i))(p), f^{m_0}(v_j)(p)) \geq \lambda_{ij}^{NTP}$$

From Lemma 2.17, we moreover have $f^{m_0}(v_j)(p) \leq (R_\alpha \downarrow \uparrow f^{m_0}(v_j))(p)$, yielding

$$NTP_\alpha(f^{m_0}(v_i), f^{m_0}(v_j)) = \inf_{p \in \mathbb{R}^n} I_T((R_\alpha \uparrow f^{m_0}(v_i))(p), (R_\alpha \downarrow \uparrow f^{m_0}(v_j))(p))$$

$$\geq \inf_{p \in \mathbb{R}^n} I_T((R_\alpha \uparrow f^{m_0}(v_i))(p), f^{m_0}(v_j)(p))$$

$$\geq \lambda_{ij}^{NTP}$$

Next, we show that also $NTP_\alpha(f^{m_0}(v_i), f^{m_0}(v_j)) \leq \lambda_{ij}^{NTP}$. From (C.47), we find

$$(R_\alpha \uparrow f^m(v_i))(p_i) \geq (R_\alpha \uparrow f^O(v_i))(p_i) \geq (R_\alpha \uparrow f^I(v_i))(p_i) = 1 \qquad \text{(C.65)}$$

for every m in $\mathbb{N}$. By (C.48)–(C.52), we moreover find for $k \neq i$

$$(R_\alpha \uparrow^{m_0} f^O(v_k))(p_i) = \cdots = (R_\alpha \uparrow\uparrow f^O(v_k))(p_i) = (R_\alpha \uparrow f^O(v_k))(p_i) = 0 \qquad \text{(C.66)}$$

We obtain for $k \neq i$, using (2.7), (C.66) and (C.65)

$$(R_\alpha \uparrow f^O(v_k))(p_i) = (R_\alpha \uparrow f^P(v_k))(p_i)$$

$$= \sup_{p \in \mathbb{R}^n} T(R_\alpha(p_i, p), f^P(v_k)(p))$$

$$= \sup_{p \in \mathbb{R}^n} T(R_\alpha(p_i, p), \max_{l=1}^n T(\lambda_{lk}^P, f^O(v_l)(p)))$$

$$= \max_{l=1}^n T(\lambda_{lk}^P, \sup_{p \in \mathbb{R}^n} T(R_\alpha(p_i, p), f^O(v_l)(p)))$$

$$= \max_{l=1}^n T(\lambda_{lk}^P, (R_\alpha \uparrow f^O(v_l))(p_i))$$

$$= T(\lambda_{ik}^P, (R_\alpha \uparrow f^O(v_i))(p_i))$$

$$= \lambda_{ik}^P$$

In entirely the same fashion, we find

$$(R_\alpha \uparrow^2 f^O(v_k))(p_i) = \cdots = (R_\alpha \uparrow^{m_0} f^O(v_k))(p_i) = \lambda_{ik}^P$$

Using (2.7), this leads to

$$(R_\alpha \uparrow f^1(v_k))(p_i)$$

$$= \sup_{p \in \mathbb{R}^n} T(R_\alpha(p_i, p), f^1(v_k)(p))$$

$$= \sup_{p \in \mathbb{R}^n} T(R_\alpha(p_i, p), \max(f^0(v_k)(p), \max_{l=1}^n T(\lambda_{lk}^{NTP}, (R_\alpha \uparrow f^0(v_l))(p))))$$

$$= \max(\sup_{p \in \mathbb{R}^n} T(R_\alpha(p_i, p), f^0(v_k)(p)),$$

$$\max_{l=1}^n T(\lambda_{lk}^{NTP}, \sup_{p \in \mathbb{R}^n} T(R_\alpha(p_i, p), (R_\alpha \uparrow f^0(v_l))(p))))$$

$$= \max((R_\alpha \uparrow f^0(v_k))(p_i), \max_{l=1}^n T(\lambda_{lk}^{NTP}, (R_\alpha \uparrow\uparrow f^0(v_l))(p_i)))$$

$$= \max(\lambda_{ik}^P, \max_{l=1}^n T(\lambda_{lk}^{NTP}, \lambda_{il}^P))$$

Because Θ satisfies the transitivity rules from Table 7.5 as well as requirement (8.12), we know that for every l in $\{1, 2, \ldots, n\}$

$$T(\lambda_{il}^P, \lambda_{lk}^{NTP}) \le \lambda_{ik}^{NTP} \le \lambda_{ik}^P \qquad (C.67)$$

Hence, we have

$$(R_\alpha \uparrow f^1(v_k))(p_i) = \lambda_{ik}^P$$

and in entirely the same way, we find

$$(R_\alpha \uparrow^2 f^1(v_k))(p_i) = \cdots = (R_\alpha \uparrow^{m_0-1} f^1(v_k))(p_i) = \lambda_{ik}^P$$

By repeating the same argument, we obtain

$$(R_\alpha \uparrow f^2(v_k))(p_i) = \cdots = (R_\alpha \uparrow^{m_0-2} f^2(v_k))(p_i) = \lambda_{ik}^P$$

$$(R_\alpha \uparrow f^3(v_k))(p_i) = \cdots = (R_\alpha \uparrow^{m_0-3} f^2(v_k))(p_i) = \lambda_{ik}^P$$

$$\cdots$$

$$(R_\alpha \uparrow f^{m_0-1}(v_k))(p_i) = \lambda_{ik}^P$$

In particular, this yields, using (C.65) and (C.67)

$$f^{m_0}(v_j)(p_i)$$

$$= \max(f^{m_0-1}(v_j)(p_i), \max_{l=1}^n T(\lambda_{lj}^{NTP}, (R_\alpha \uparrow f^{m_0-1}(v_l))(p_i)))$$

$$= \max(f^{m_0-1}(v_j)(p_i), T(\lambda_{ij}^{NTP}, (R_\alpha \uparrow f^{m_0-1}(v_i))(p_i)),$$

$$\max_{l \ne i} T(\lambda_{lj}^{NTP}, (R_\alpha \uparrow f^{m_0-1}(v_l))(p_i)))$$

$$= \max(f^{m_0-1}(v_j)(p_i), \lambda_{ij}^{NTP}, \max_{l \ne i} T(\lambda_{lj}^{NTP}, \lambda_{il}^P))$$

$$= \max(f^{m_0-1}(v_j)(p_i), \lambda_{ij}^{NTP})$$

and in the same way

$$f^{m_0-1}(v_j)(p_i) = \max(f^{m_0-2}(v_j)(p_i), \lambda_{ij}^{NTP})$$

$$\cdots$$

$$f^1(v_j)(p_i) = \max(f^0(v_j)(p_i), \lambda_{ij}^{NTP})$$

As $f^0(v_j)(p_i) = 0$, this means

$$f^{m_0}(v_j)(p_i) = \lambda_{ij}^{NTP}$$

Finally, we find using (C.65)

$$NTP_\alpha(f^{m_0}(v_i), f^{m_0}(v_j))$$
$$= \inf_{p \in \mathbb{R}^n} I_T((R_\alpha \uparrow f^{m_0}(v_i))(p), (R_\alpha \downarrow \uparrow f^{m_0}(v_j))(p))$$
$$\leq I_T((R_\alpha \uparrow f^{m_0}(v_i))(p_i), (R_\alpha \downarrow \uparrow f^{m_0}(v_j))(p_i))$$
$$= (R_\alpha \downarrow \uparrow f^{m_0}(v_j))(p_i)$$
$$= \inf_{q \in \mathbb{R}^n} I_T(R_\alpha(p_i, q), \sup_{r \in \mathbb{R}^n} T(R_\alpha(q, r), f^{m_0}(v_j)(r)))$$
$$\leq I_T(R_\alpha(p_i, p_i + \alpha \frac{\vec{a_i p_i}}{\|\vec{a_i p_i}\|}), \sup_{r \in \mathbb{R}^n} T(R_\alpha(p_i + \alpha \frac{\vec{a_i p_i}}{\|\vec{a_i p_i}\|}, r), f^{m_0}(v_j)(r)))$$
$$= \sup_{r \in \mathbb{R}^n} T(R_\alpha(p_i + \alpha \frac{\vec{a_i p_i}}{\|\vec{a_i p_i}\|}, r), f^{m_0}(v_j)(r))$$

From (C.48)–(C.52) and Lemma C.21, we know that all points in the support of $f^{m_0}(v_j)$ that are within distance α of $p_i + \alpha \frac{\vec{a_i p_i}}{\|\vec{a_i p_i}\|}$ are the points in the support of $\bigcup_{l=1}^t (R_{\alpha_l} \uparrow P_{a_i}^{\lambda_l})$ for some t in $\mathbb{N}$, $\alpha_l \leq m_0\alpha$ and λ^l in $[0,1]$. In particular, this is the set of points within a certain distance α_{l_0} of a_i $(1 \leq l_0 \leq t)$. This implies that

$$\sup_{r \in \mathbb{R}^n} T(R_\alpha(p_i + \alpha \frac{\vec{a_i p_i}}{\|\vec{a_i p_i}\|}, r), f^{m_0}(v_j)(r))$$
$$= T(R_\alpha(p_i + \alpha \frac{\vec{a_i p_i}}{\|\vec{a_i p_i}\|}, p_i), f^{m_0}(v_j)(p_i))$$

since p_i is the closest point to a_i which is within distance α of $p_i + \alpha \frac{\vec{a_i p_i}}{\|\vec{a_i p_i}\|}$. We conclude

$$T(R_\alpha(p_i + \alpha \frac{\vec{a_i p_i}}{\|\vec{a_i p_i}\|}, p_i), f^{m_0}(v_j)(p_i)) = f^{m_0}(v_j)(p_i) = \lambda_{ij}^{NTP}$$

$\square$

Lemma C.23. *For every $m \leq m_0$ in $\mathbb{N}$, and every v_i and v_j in V, it holds that*

$$\sup_{p,q \in \mathbb{R}^n} T(f^m(v_i)(p), R_{3\alpha}(p,q), f^m(v_j)(q))$$

$$= \sup_{p,q \in \mathbb{R}^n} T(f^m(v_i)(p), R_\alpha(p,q), f^m(v_j)(q))$$

Proof.   Since $R_{3\alpha} \supseteq R_\alpha$ we already have

$$\sup_{p,q \in \mathbb{R}^n} T(f^m(v_i)(p), R_{3\alpha}(p,q), f^m(v_j)(q))$$

$$\geq \sup_{p,q \in \mathbb{R}^n} T(f^m(v_i)(p), R_\alpha(p,q), f^m(v_j)(q))$$

Conversely, we have that the supremum in the left–hand side is attained for some p_0 and q_0 in $\mathbb{R}^n$ satisfying $d(p_0, q_0) \leq 3\alpha$:

$$\sup_{p,q \in \mathbb{R}^n} T(f^m(v_i)(p), R_{3\alpha}(p,q), f^m(v_j)(q)) = T(f^m(v_i)(p_0), f^m(v_j)(q_0))$$

From Lemma C.21, we know that for some $\lambda_1, \lambda_2, \lambda_3$ in $[0,1]$, $1 \leq i_1, s_1 \leq n$ and $0 \leq \alpha_1, \alpha_2, \alpha_3 \leq m\alpha$

$$f^m(v_i)(p_0) = ((R_{\alpha_1} \uparrow P_{a_{i_1}}^{\lambda_1}) \cup (R_{\alpha_2} \uparrow L_{b_{i_1 s_1}}^{\lambda_2}) \cup (R_{\alpha_3} \uparrow L_{c_{i_1 s_1}}^{\lambda_3}))(p_0)$$

and that for some $\lambda_4, \lambda_5, \lambda_6$ in $[0,1]$, $1 \leq i_2, s_2 \leq n$ and $0 \leq \alpha_4, \alpha_5, \alpha_6 \leq m\alpha$

$$f^m(v_j)(q_0) = ((R_{\alpha_4} \uparrow P_{a_{i_2}}^{\lambda_4}) \cup (R_{\alpha_5} \uparrow L_{b_{i_2 s_2}}^{\lambda_5}) \cup (R_{\alpha_6} \uparrow L_{c_{i_2 s_2}}^{\lambda_6}))(q_0)$$

Hence

$$T(f^m(v_i)(p_0), f^m(v_j)(q_0)) = \max(T((R_{\alpha_1} \uparrow P_{a_{i_1}}^{\lambda_1})(p_0), (R_{\alpha_4} \uparrow P_{a_{i_2}}^{\lambda_4})(q_0)),$$

$$T((R_{\alpha_1} \uparrow P_{a_{i_1}}^{\lambda_1})(p_0), (R_{\alpha_5} \uparrow L_{b_{i_2 s_2}}^{\lambda_5})(q_0)),$$

$$T((R_{\alpha_1} \uparrow P_{a_{i_1}}^{\lambda_1})(p_0), (R_{\alpha_6} \uparrow L_{c_{i_2 s_2}}^{\lambda_6})(q_0)),$$

$$T((R_{\alpha_2} \uparrow L_{b_{i_1 s_1}}^{\lambda_2})(p_0), (R_{\alpha_4} \uparrow P_{a_{i_2}}^{\lambda_4})(q_0)),$$

$$T((R_{\alpha_2} \uparrow L_{b_{i_1 s_1}}^{\lambda_2})(p_0), (R_{\alpha_5} \uparrow L_{b_{i_2 s_2}}^{\lambda_5})(q_0)),$$

$$T((R_{\alpha_2} \uparrow L_{b_{i_1 s_1}}^{\lambda_2})(p_0), (R_{\alpha_6} \uparrow L_{c_{i_2 s_2}}^{\lambda_6})(q_0)),$$

$$T((R_{\alpha_3} \uparrow L_{c_{i_1 s_1}}^{\lambda_3})(p_0), (R_{\alpha_4} \uparrow P_{a_{i_2}}^{\lambda_4})(q_0)),$$

$$T((R_{\alpha_3} \uparrow L_{c_{i_1 s_1}}^{\lambda_3})(p_0), (R_{\alpha_5} \uparrow L_{b_{i_2 s_2}}^{\lambda_5})(q_0)),$$

$$T((R_{\alpha_3} \uparrow L_{c_{i_1 s_1}}^{\lambda_3})(p_0), (R_{\alpha_6} \uparrow L_{c_{i_2 s_2}}^{\lambda_6})(q_0)))$$

To complete the proof, we show that points p_1 and q_1 in $\mathbb{R}^n$ can be found satisfying $d(p_1, q_1) \leq \alpha$ and

$$f^m(v_i)(p_0) \leq f^m(v_i)(p_1) \tag{C.68}$$

$$f^m(v_j)(q_0) \leq f^m(v_j)(q_1) \tag{C.69}$$

First assume that the maximum above is equal to its first argument, i.e.

$$f^m(v_i)(p_0) = (R_{\alpha_1} \uparrow P_{a_{i_1}}^{\lambda_1})(p_0)$$

$$f^m(v_j)(q_0) = (R_{\alpha_4} \uparrow P_{a_{i_2}}^{\lambda_4})(q_0)$$

When $i_1 \neq i_2$, none of the points in the support of $(R_{\alpha_1} \uparrow P_{a_{i_1}}^{\lambda_1})$ is within distance 3α of at least one point from the support of $(R_{\alpha_4} \uparrow P_{a_{i_2}}^{\lambda_4})$. Indeed, for all points p in the support of $(R_{\alpha_1} \uparrow P_{a_{i_1}}^{\lambda_1})$ it holds that $d(p, a_{i_1}) \leq \alpha_1 + \alpha_0 \leq m\alpha + \alpha_0$, while for all points q in the support of $(R_{\alpha_4} \uparrow P_{a_{i_2}}^{\lambda_4})$, it holds that $d(q, a_{i_2}) \leq \alpha_4 + \alpha_0 \leq m\alpha + \alpha_0$. Using (C.53) and the assumption $m \leq m_0$ this implies in particular $d(p, q) > 3\alpha$. Hence, either $(R_{\alpha_1} \uparrow P_{a_{i_1}}^{\lambda_1})(p_0) = 0$ or $(R_{\alpha_4} \uparrow P_{a_{i_2}}^{\lambda_4})(q_0) = 0$, and points p_1 and q_1 satisfying (C.68)–(C.69) clearly exist. When $i_1 = i_2$, the supports of $(R_{\alpha_1} \uparrow P_{a_{i_1}}^{\lambda_1})$ and $(R_{\alpha_4} \uparrow P_{a_{i_2}}^{\lambda_4})$ overlap; hence, we can assume

$$(R_{\alpha_1} \uparrow P_{a_{i_1}}^{\lambda_1})(p_0) = (R_{\alpha_1} \uparrow P_{a_{i_1}}^{\lambda_1})(a_{i_1}) = \lambda_1$$

$$(R_{\alpha_4} \uparrow P_{a_{i_2}}^{\lambda_4})(q_0) = (R_{\alpha_4} \uparrow P_{a_{i_2}}^{\lambda_4})(a_{i_2}) = \lambda_4$$

and (C.68)–(C.69) are satisfied for $p_1 = a_{i_1}$ and $q_1 = a_{i_2} = a_{i_1}$.

Next, assume that the maximum above is equal to its second argument, i.e.

$$f^m(v_i)(p_0) = (R_{\alpha_1} \uparrow P_{a_{i_1}}^{\lambda_1})(p_0)$$

$$f^m(v_j)(q_0) = (R_{\alpha_5} \uparrow L_{b_{i_2 s_2}}^{\lambda_5})(q_0)$$

If $i_1 \neq s_2$ we find $f^m(v_i)(p_0) = 0$ or $f^m(v_j)(q_0) = 0$ using (C.62). If $i_1 = s_2$, it holds for

$$p_1 = a_{i_1} + \alpha_0 \frac{\overrightarrow{a_{i_1} b_{i_2 s_2}}}{\|\overrightarrow{a_{i_1} b_{i_2 s_2}}\|}$$

$$q_1 = a_{i_1} + (\alpha_0 + \alpha) \frac{\overrightarrow{a_{i_1} b_{i_2 s_2}}}{\|\overrightarrow{a_{i_1} b_{i_2 s_2}}\|}$$

that p_1 is in the support of $P_{a_{i_1}}^{\lambda_1}$, q_1 is in the support of $L_{b_{i_2 s_2}}^{\lambda_5}$ and $d(p_1, q_1) \leq \alpha$. Moreover

$$f^m(v_i)(p_1) \geq (R_{\alpha_1} \uparrow P_{a_{i_1}}^{\lambda_1})(p_1) = \lambda_1 \geq (R_{\alpha_1} \uparrow P_{a_{i_1}}^{\lambda_1})(p_0)$$

$$f^m(v_j)(q_1) \geq (R_{\alpha_5} \uparrow L_{b_{i_2 s_2}}^{\lambda_5})(q_1) = \lambda_5 \geq (R_{\alpha_5} \uparrow L_{b_{i_2 s_2}}^{\lambda_5})(q_0)$$

The other seven cases, where the maximum above is equal to its third, fourth, ..., ninth argument, are entirely analogous. Hence, we always have that points p_1 and q_1 can be found, satisfying $d(p_1, q_1) \leq \alpha$ and

$$T(f^m(v_i)(p_1), f^m(v_j)(q_1)) \geq T(f^m(v_i)(p_0), f^m(v_j)(q_0))$$

We conclude

$$\sup_{p,q\in\mathbb{R}^n} T(f^m(v_i)(p), R_\alpha(p,q), f^m(v_j)(q))$$

$$\geq T(f^m(v_i)(p_1), f^m(v_j)(q_1))$$

$$\geq T(f^m(v_i)(p_0), f^m(v_j)(q_0))$$

$$= \sup_{p,q\in\mathbb{R}^n} T(f^m(v_i)(p), R_{3\alpha}(p,q), f^m(v_j)(q))$$

$\square$

As $R_\alpha \subseteq R_{2\alpha} \subseteq R_{3\alpha}$, we immediately have the following corollary.

Corollary C.3.

$$\sup_{p,q\in\mathbb{R}^n} T(f^m(v_i)(p), R_{2\alpha}(p,q), f^m(v_j)(q))$$

$$= \sup_{p,q\in\mathbb{R}^n} T(f^m(v_i)(p), R_\alpha(p,q), f^m(v_j)(q))$$

Lemma C.24. *For all v_i and v_j in V, it holds that*

$$C_\alpha(f^{m_0}(v_i), f^{m_0}(v_j)) = \lambda_{ij}^C$$

Proof. By Lemma C.16, we already have that $C_\alpha(f^0(v_i), f^0(v_j)) = \lambda_{ij}^C$ for every v_i and v_j in V. We will show by induction that for all m in $\{1, 2, \ldots, m_0\}$ and all v_i and v_j in V, it holds that $C_\alpha(f^m(v_i), f^m(v_j)) = \lambda_{ij}^C$. Let m be in $\{1, 2, \ldots, m_0\}$ and assume that $C_\alpha(f^{m-1}(v_i), f^{m-1}(v_j)) = \lambda_{ij}^C$ for all v_i and v_j in V (induction hypothesis). We obtain

$$C_\alpha(f^m(v_i), f^m(v_j))$$

$$= \sup_{p,q\in\mathbb{R}^n} T(f^m(v_i)(p), R_\alpha(p,q), f^m(v_j)(q))$$

$$= \sup_{p,q\in\mathbb{R}^n} T(\max(f^{m-1}(v_i)(p), \max_{l=1}^{n} T(\lambda_{li}^{NTP}, (R_\alpha\uparrow f^{m-1}(v_l))(p))), R_\alpha(p,q),$$

$$\max(f^{m-1}(v_j)(q), \max_{l=1}^{n} T(\lambda_{lj}^{NTP}, (R_\alpha\uparrow f^{m-1}(v_l))(q))))$$

$$= \max(\sup_{p,q\in\mathbb{R}^n} T(f^{m-1}(v_i)(p), R_\alpha(p,q), f^{m-1}(v_j)(q)),$$

$$\max_{l=1}^{n} \sup_{p,q\in\mathbb{R}^n} T(\lambda_{li}^{NTP}, (R_\alpha\uparrow f^{m-1}(v_l))(p), R_\alpha(p,q), f^{m-1}(v_j)(q)),$$

$$\max_{l=1}^{n} \sup_{p,q\in\mathbb{R}^n} T(f^{m-1}(v_i)(p), R_\alpha(p,q), \lambda_{lj}^{NTP}, (R_\alpha\uparrow f^{m-1}(v_l))(q)),$$

$$\max_{l_1=1}^{n}\max_{l_2=1}^{n} \sup_{p,q\in\mathbb{R}^n} T(\lambda_{l_1 i}^{NTP}, (R_\alpha\uparrow f^{m-1}(v_{l_1}))(p), R_\alpha(p,q), \lambda_{l_2 j}^{NTP},$$

$$(R_\alpha\uparrow f^{m-1}(v_{l_2}))(q)))$$

Note that because of the induction hypothesis

$$\sup_{p,q\in\mathbb{R}^n} T(f^{m-1}(v_i)(p), R_\alpha(p,q), f^{m-1}(v_j)(q)) \qquad \text{(C.70)}$$
$$= C_\alpha(f^{m-1}(v_i), f^{m-1}(v_j))$$
$$= \lambda_{ij}^C$$

Next, we find for each l in $\{1, 2, \ldots, n\}$, using (2.7), Corollary C.3 and the induction hypothesis

$$\sup_{p,q\in\mathbb{R}^n} T(\lambda_{li}^{NTP}, (R_\alpha{\uparrow}f^{m-1}(v_l))(p), R_\alpha(p,q), f^{m-1}(v_j)(q))$$
$$= T(\lambda_{li}^{NTP}, \sup_{q\in\mathbb{R}^n} T(\sup_{p\in\mathbb{R}^n} T((R_\alpha{\uparrow}f^{m-1}(v_l))(p), R_\alpha(p,q)), f^{m-1}(v_j)(q)))$$
$$= T(\lambda_{li}^{NTP}, \sup_{q\in\mathbb{R}^n} T((R_\alpha{\uparrow}{\uparrow}f^{m-1}(v_l))(p), f^{m-1}(v_j)(q)))$$
$$= T(\lambda_{li}^{NTP}, \sup_{q\in\mathbb{R}^n} T((R_{2\alpha}{\uparrow}f^{m-1}(v_l))(p), f^{m-1}(v_j)(q)))$$
$$= T(\lambda_{li}^{NTP}, \sup_{q\in\mathbb{R}^n} T(\sup_{p\in\mathbb{R}^n} T(f^{m-1}(v_l)(p), R_{2\alpha}(p,q)), f^{m-1}(v_j)(q)))$$
$$= T(\lambda_{li}^{NTP}, \sup_{p,q\in\mathbb{R}^n} T(f^{m-1}(v_l)(p), R_{2\alpha}(p,q), f^{m-1}(v_j)(q)))$$
$$= T(\lambda_{li}^{NTP}, \sup_{p,q\in\mathbb{R}^n} T(f^{m-1}(v_l)(p), R_\alpha(p,q), f^{m-1}(v_j)(q)))$$
$$= T(\lambda_{li}^{NTP}, C_\alpha(f^{m-1}(v_l), f^{m-1}(v_j)))$$
$$= T(\lambda_{li}^{NTP}, \lambda_{lj}^C)$$

Since Θ satisfies (8.12)–(8.14), as well as all transitivity rules from Table 7.5, we have that

$$T(\lambda_{lj}^C, \lambda_{li}^{NTP}) = T(\lambda_{jl}^C, \lambda_{li}^{NTP}) \le \lambda_{ji}^O = \lambda_{ij}^O \le \lambda_{ij}^C$$

and thus

$$\sup_{p,q\in\mathbb{R}^n} T(\lambda_{li}^{NTP}, (R_\alpha{\uparrow}f^{m-1}(v_l))(p), R_\alpha(p,q), f^{m-1}(v_j)(q)) \le \lambda_{ij}^C \qquad \text{(C.71)}$$

In entirely the same way, we have

$$\sup_{p,q\in\mathbb{R}^n} T(f^{m-1}(v_i)(p), R_\alpha(p,q), \lambda_{lj}^{NTP}, (R_\alpha{\uparrow}f^{m-1}(v_l))(q)) \le \lambda_{ij}^C \qquad \text{(C.72)}$$

for all l in $\{1, 2, \ldots, n\}$. Finally, we obtain for all l_1 and l_2 in $\{1, 2, \ldots, n\}$, using (2.7), Lemma C.23 and the induction hypothesis

$$\sup_{p,q \in \mathbb{R}^n} T(\lambda_{l_1 i}^{NTP}, (R_\alpha \uparrow f^{m-1}(v_{l_1}))(p), R_\alpha(p,q), \lambda_{l_2 j}^{NTP}, (R_\alpha \uparrow f^{m-1}(v_{l_2}))(q))$$

$$= T(T(\lambda_{l_1 i}^{NTP}, \lambda_{l_2 j}^{NTP}), \sup_{q \in \mathbb{R}^n} T(\sup_{p \in \mathbb{R}^n} T((R_\alpha \uparrow f^{m-1}(v_{l_1}))(p), R_\alpha(p,q)),$$
$$(R_\alpha \uparrow f^{m-1}(v_{l_2}))(q)))$$

$$= T(T(\lambda_{l_1 i}^{NTP}, \lambda_{l_2 j}^{NTP}), \sup_{q \in \mathbb{R}^n} T((R_\alpha \uparrow\uparrow f^{m-1}(v_{l_1}))(q),$$
$$(R_\alpha \uparrow f^{m-1}(v_{l_2}))(q)))$$

$$= T(T(\lambda_{l_1 i}^{NTP}, \lambda_{l_2 j}^{NTP}), \sup_{q \in \mathbb{R}^n} T((R_\alpha \uparrow\uparrow f^{m-1}(v_{l_1}))(q),$$
$$\sup_{r \in \mathbb{R}^n} T(R_\alpha(r,q), f^{m-1}(v_{l_2})(r))))$$

$$= T(T(\lambda_{l_1 i}^{NTP}, \lambda_{l_2 j}^{NTP}), \sup_{r \in \mathbb{R}^n} T(\sup_{q \in \mathbb{R}^n} T((R_\alpha \uparrow\uparrow f^{m-1}(v_{l_1}))(q), R_\alpha(r,q)),$$
$$f^{m-1}(v_{l_2})(r)))$$

$$= T(T(\lambda_{l_1 i}^{NTP}, \lambda_{l_2 j}^{NTP}), \sup_{r \in \mathbb{R}^n} T((R_\alpha \uparrow\uparrow\uparrow f^{m-1}(v_{l_1}))(r), f^{m-1}(v_{l_2})(r)))$$

$$= T(T(\lambda_{l_1 i}^{NTP}, \lambda_{l_2 j}^{NTP}), \sup_{r \in \mathbb{R}^n} T((R_{3\alpha} \uparrow f^{m-1}(v_{l_1}))(r), f^{m-1}(v_{l_2})(r)))$$

$$= T(T(\lambda_{l_1 i}^{NTP}, \lambda_{l_2 j}^{NTP}), \sup_{r,p \in \mathbb{R}^n} T(f^{m-1}(v_{l_1})(p), R_{3\alpha}(p,r),$$
$$f^{m-1}(v_{l_2})(r)))$$

$$= T(T(\lambda_{l_1 i}^{NTP}, \lambda_{l_2 j}^{NTP}), \sup_{r,p \in \mathbb{R}^n} T(f^{m-1}(v_{l_1})(p), R_\alpha(p,r),$$
$$f^{m-1}(v_{l_2})(r)))$$

$$= T(T(\lambda_{l_1 i}^{NTP}, \lambda_{l_2 j}^{NTP}), C_\alpha(f^{m-1}(v_{l_1}), f^{m-1}(v_{l_2})))$$
$$= T(\lambda_{l_1 i}^{NTP}, \lambda_{l_2 j}^{NTP}, \lambda_{l_1 l_2}^{C})$$

Since Θ satisfies (8.12)–(8.14), as well as all transitivity rules from Table 7.5, we have that

$$T(\lambda_{l_1 i}^{NTP}, \lambda_{l_2 j}^{NTP}, \lambda_{l_1 l_2}^{C}) \le T(\lambda_{l_1 i}^{NTP}, \lambda_{l_1 j}^{O}) = T(\lambda_{l_1 i}^{NTP}, \lambda_{j l_1}^{O}) \le \lambda_{j i}^{O} \le \lambda_{j i}^{C} = \lambda_{ij}^{C}$$

and thus

$$\sup_{p,q \in \mathbb{R}^n} T(\lambda_{l_1 i}^{NTP}, (R_\alpha \uparrow f^{m-1}(v_{l_1}))(p), R_\alpha(p,q), \lambda_{l_2 j}^{NTP},$$
$$(R_\alpha \uparrow f^{m-1}(v_{l_2}))(q)) \le \lambda_{ij}^{C} \qquad (C.73)$$

From (C.70), (C.71), (C.72) and (C.73), we can conclude

$$C_\alpha(f^m(v_i), f^m(v_j)) = \lambda_{ij}^C$$

$\square$

Lemma C.25. *For all v_i and v_j in V, it holds that*

$$O_\alpha(f^m(v_i), f^m(v_j)) = \sup_{p \in \mathbb{R}^n} T(f^m(v_i)(p), f^m(v_j)(p))$$

for all m in $\{0, 1, \ldots, m_0\}$.

Proof. This lemma follows from Lemma C.6 in entirely the same way as Lemma C.18, using Lemma C.21 instead of Lemma C.17 and (C.53)–(C.63) instead of (C.23)–(C.26) and (C.28)–(C.32). $\square$

Lemma C.26. *For all v_i and v_j in V, it holds that*

$$O_\alpha(f^m(v_i), f^m(v_j)) = \lambda_{ij}^O$$

for all m in $\{0, 1, \ldots, m_0\}$.

Proof. By Lemma C.19, we already have that $O_\alpha(f^0(v_i), f^0(v_j)) = \lambda_{ij}^O$ for every v_i and v_j in V. We will show by induction that for all m in $\{1, 2, \ldots, m_0\}$ and all v_i and v_j in V, it holds that $O_\alpha(f^m(v_i), f^m(v_j)) = \lambda_{ij}^O$. Let m be in $\{1, 2, \ldots, m_0\}$ and assume that $O_\alpha(f^{m-1}(v_i), f^{m-1}(v_j)) = \lambda_{ij}^O$ for all v_i and v_j in V (induction hypothesis). We obtain using Lemma C.25

$$O_\alpha(f^m(v_i), f^m(v_j))$$

$$= \sup_{p \in \mathbb{R}^n} T(f^m(v_i)(p), f^m(v_j)(p))$$

$$= \sup_{p \in \mathbb{R}^n} T(\max(f^{m-1}(v_i)(p), \max_{l=1}^n T(\lambda_{li}^{NTP}, (R_\alpha \uparrow f^{m-1}(v_l))(p))),$$

$$\max(f^{m-1}(v_j)(p), \max_{l=1}^n T(\lambda_{lj}^{NTP}, (R_\alpha \uparrow f^{m-1}(v_l))(p))))$$

$$= \max(\sup_{p \in \mathbb{R}^n} T(f^{m-1}(v_i)(p), f^{m-1}(v_j)(p)),$$

$$\max_{l=1}^n \sup_{p \in \mathbb{R}^n} T(\lambda_{li}^{NTP}, (R_\alpha \uparrow f^{m-1}(v_l))(p), f^{m-1}(v_j)(p)),$$

$$\max_{l=1}^n \sup_{p \in \mathbb{R}^n} T(f^{m-1}(v_i)(p), \lambda_{lj}^{NTP}, (R_\alpha \uparrow f^{m-1}(v_l))(p)),$$

$$\max_{l_1=1}^n \max_{l_2=1}^n \sup_{p \in \mathbb{R}^n} T(\lambda_{l_1 i}^{NTP}, (R_\alpha \uparrow f^{m-1}(v_{l_1}))(p), \lambda_{l_2 j}^{NTP},$$

$$(R_\alpha \uparrow f^{m-1}(v_{l_2}))(p)))$$

By Lemma C.25 and the induction hypothesis, we have

$$\sup_{p\in\mathbb{R}^n} T(f^{m-1}(v_i)(p), f^{m-1}(v_j)(p)) = O_\alpha(f^{m-1}(v_i), f^{m-1}(v_j)) = \lambda_{ij}^O$$
(C.74)

Next, we find for each l in $\{1, 2, \ldots, n\}$, using (2.7) and Lemma C.24

$$\sup_{p\in\mathbb{R}^n} T(\lambda_{li}^{NTP}, (R_\alpha\uparrow f^{m-1}(v_l))(p), f^{m-1}(v_j)(p))$$

$$= T(\lambda_{li}^{NTP}, \sup_{p\in\mathbb{R}^n} T((R_\alpha\uparrow f^{m-1}(v_l))(p), f^{m-1}(v_j)(p)))$$

$$= T(\lambda_{li}^{NTP}, \sup_{p\in\mathbb{R}^n} T(\sup_{q\in\mathbb{R}^n} T(R_\alpha(p,q), f^{m-1}(v_l)(q)), f^{m-1}(v_j)(p)))$$

$$= T(\lambda_{li}^{NTP}, \sup_{p,q\in\mathbb{R}^n} T(f^{m-1}(v_j)(p), R_\alpha(p,q), f^{m-1}(v_l)(q)))$$

$$= T(\lambda_{li}^{NTP}, C_\alpha(f^{m-1}(v_j), f^{m-1}(v_l)))$$

$$= T(\lambda_{li}^{NTP}, \lambda_{jl}^C)$$

Moreover, since Θ satisfies (8.14) and the transitivity rules from Table 7.5, we have

$$T(\lambda_{li}^{NTP}, \lambda_{jl}^C) \leq \lambda_{ji}^O = \lambda_{ij}^O$$

and thus

$$\sup_{p\in\mathbb{R}^n} T(\lambda_{li}^{NTP}, (R_\alpha\uparrow f^{m-1}(v_l))(p), f^{m-1}(v_j)(p)) \leq \lambda_{ij}^O \qquad (C.75)$$

In the same way, we find for every l in $\{1, 2, \ldots, n\}$ that

$$\sup_{p\in\mathbb{R}^n} T(f^{m-1}(v_i)(p), \lambda_{lj}^{NTP}, (R_\alpha\uparrow f^{m-1}(v_l))(p)) \leq \lambda_{ij}^O \qquad (C.76)$$

Finally, for every l_1 and l_2 in $\{1, 2, \ldots, n\}$, we find using (2.7), Corollary C.3 and Lemma C.24

$$\sup_{p\in\mathbb{R}^n} T(\lambda_{l_1 i}^{NTP}, (R_\alpha\uparrow f^{m-1}(v_{l_1}))(p), \lambda_{l_2 j}^{NTP}, (R_\alpha\uparrow f^{m-1}(v_{l_2}))(p))$$

$$= T(T(\lambda_{l_1 i}^{NTP}, \lambda_{l_2 j}^{NTP}), \sup_{p\in\mathbb{R}^n} T((R_\alpha\uparrow f^{m-1}(v_{l_1}))(p), (R_\alpha\uparrow f^{m-1}(v_{l_2}))(p)))$$

$$= T(T(\lambda_{l_1 i}^{NTP}, \lambda_{l_2 j}^{NTP}), \sup_{p\in\mathbb{R}^n} T(\sup_{q\in\mathbb{R}^n} T(R_\alpha(p,q), f^{m-1}(v_{l_1})(q)),$$

$$\sup_{r\in\mathbb{R}^n} T(R_\alpha(p,r), f^{m-1}(v_{l_2})(r))))$$

$$= T(T(\lambda_{l_1 i}^{NTP}, \lambda_{l_2 j}^{NTP}), \sup_{q,r\in\mathbb{R}^n} T(f^{m-1}(v_{l_1})(q), \sup_{p\in\mathbb{R}^n} T(R_\alpha(p,q), R_\alpha(p,r)),$$

$$f^{m-1}(v_{l_2})(r)))$$

$$= T(T(\lambda_{l_1 i}^{NTP}, \lambda_{l_2 j}^{NTP}), \sup_{q,r \in \mathbb{R}^n} T(f^{m-1}(v_{l_1})(q), R_{2\alpha}(p,r), f^{m-1}(v_{l_2})(r)))$$

$$= T(T(\lambda_{l_1 i}^{NTP}, \lambda_{l_2 j}^{NTP}), \sup_{q,r \in \mathbb{R}^n} T(f^{m-1}(v_{l_1})(q), R_\alpha(p,r), f^{m-1}(v_{l_2})(r)))$$

$$= T(T(\lambda_{l_1 i}^{NTP}, \lambda_{l_2 j}^{NTP}), C_\alpha(f^{m-1}(v_{l_1}), f^{m-1}(v_{l_2})))$$

$$= T(\lambda_{l_1 i}^{NTP}, \lambda_{l_2 j}^{NTP}, \lambda_{l_1 l_2}^{C})$$

Since Θ satisfies (8.14) and the transitivity rules from Table 7.5, we have

$$T(\lambda_{l_1 i}^{NTP}, \lambda_{l_2 j}^{NTP}, \lambda_{l_1 l_2}^{C}) \leq T(\lambda_{l_1 i}^{NTP}, \lambda_{l_1 j}^{O}) = T(\lambda_{l_1 i}^{NTP}, \lambda_{j l_1}^{O}) \leq \lambda_{ji}^{O} = \lambda_{ij}^{O}$$

yielding

$$\sup_{p \in \mathbb{R}^n} T(\lambda_{l_1 i}^{NTP}, (R_\alpha \uparrow f^{m-1}(v_{l_1}))(p), \lambda_{l_2 j}^{NTP}, (R_\alpha \uparrow f^{m-1}(v_{l_2}))(p)) \leq \lambda_{ij}^{O}$$

$$(C.77)$$

From (C.74), (C.75), (C.76) and (C.77), we can conclude

$$O_\alpha(f^m(v_i), f^m(v_j)) = \lambda_{ij}^{O} \qquad \square$$

Lemma C.27. *For all i and j in $\{1, 2, \ldots, n\}$, it holds that*

$$f^m(v_i)(a_j) = \lambda_{ji}^{P}$$

for all m in $\{0, 1, \ldots, m_0\}$.

Proof. First, note that for $l \neq j$ it holds that $f^O(v_l)(a_j) = 0$ because of (C.23)–(C.26) and (C.28) and (C.31). Furthermore, $f^O(v_j)(a_j) \geq f^I(v_j)(a_j) = 1$. This leads to

$$f^0(v_i)(a_j) = f^P(v_i)(a_j)$$
$$= \max_{l=1}^{n} T(\lambda_{li}^{P}, f^O(v_l)(a_j))$$
$$= T(\lambda_{ji}^{P}, f^O(v_j)(a_j))$$
$$= \lambda_{ji}^{P}$$

For m in $\{1, 2, \ldots, m_0\}$, we show this lemma by induction. In particular, assume that $f^{m-1}(v_i)(a_j) = \lambda_{ji}^{P}$ for all i and j in $\{1, 2, \ldots, n\}$ (induction hypothesis). We obtain

$$f^m(v_i)(a_j) = \max(f^{m-1}(v_i)(a_j), \max_{l=1}^{n} T(\lambda_{li}^{NTP}, (R_\alpha \uparrow f^{m-1}(v_l))(a_j)))$$

$$= \max(\lambda_{ji}^{P}, \max_{l=1}^{n} T(\lambda_{li}^{NTP}, (R_\alpha \uparrow f^{m-1}(v_l))(a_j)))$$

To complete the proof, we show that for all l in $\{1, 2, \ldots, n\}$, it holds that

$$T(\lambda_{li}^{NTP}, (R_\alpha \uparrow f^{m-1}(v_l))(a_j)) \leq \lambda_{ji}^{P}$$

For $l = j$, we find, using the assumption that Θ satisfies (8.12)

$$T(\lambda_{ji}^{NTP}, (R_\alpha \uparrow f^{m-1}(v_j))(a_j)) \leq \lambda_{ji}^{NTP} \leq \lambda_{ji}^{P}$$

Next, assume that $l \neq j$. From Lemma C.21 and (C.53)–(C.63), it follows that $f^{m-1}(v_l)(p) = f^{m-1}(v_l)(a_j)$ for every p within distance α of a_j. We thus obtain from the induction hypothesis

$$T(\lambda_{li}^{NTP}, (R_\alpha \uparrow f^{m-1}(v_l))(a_j)) = T(\lambda_{li}^{NTP}, \sup_{p \in \mathbb{R}^n} T(R_\alpha(p, a_j), f^{m-1}(v_l)(p)))$$

$$= T(\lambda_{li}^{NTP}, \sup_{\substack{p \in \mathbb{R}^n \\ d(p, a_j) \leq \alpha}} f^{m-1}(v_l)(p))$$

$$= T(\lambda_{li}^{NTP}, f^{m-1}(v_l)(a_j))$$

$$= T(\lambda_{li}^{NTP}, \lambda_{jl}^{P})$$

Finally, since Θ satisfies (8.12), as well as the transitivity rules from Table 7.5, we have

$$T(\lambda_{jl}^{P}, \lambda_{li}^{NTP}) \leq \lambda_{ji}^{NTP} \leq \lambda_{ji}^{P} \qquad \square$$

Lemma C.28. *For all v_i and v_j in V, it holds that*

$$P_\alpha(f^m(v_i), f^m(v_j)) = \lambda_{ij}^{P}$$

for all m in $\{0, 1, \ldots, m_0\}$.

Proof. By Lemma C.15, we already have that $P_\alpha(f^0(v_i), f^0(v_j)) = \lambda_{ij}^{P}$ for every v_i and v_j in V. We will show by induction that for all m in $\{1, 2, \ldots, m_0\}$ and all v_i and v_j in V, it holds that $P_\alpha(f^m(v_i), f^m(v_j)) = \lambda_{ij}^{P}$. Let m be in $\{1, 2, \ldots, m_0\}$ and assume that $P_\alpha(f^{m-1}(v_i), f^{m-1}(v_j)) = \lambda_{ij}^{P}$ for all v_i and v_j in V (induction hypothesis). We obtain using (C.19)

$$P_\alpha(f^m(v_i), f^m(v_j))$$

$$= \inf_{p \in \mathbb{R}^n} I_T(f^m(v_i)(p), (R_\alpha \downarrow \uparrow f^m(v_j))(p))$$

$$= \inf_{p \in \mathbb{R}^n} I_T(\max(f^{m-1}(v_i)(p), \max_{l=1}^{n} T(\lambda_{li}^{NTP}, (R_\alpha \uparrow f^{m-1}(v_l))(p))),$$

$$(R_\alpha \downarrow \uparrow f^m(v_j))(p))$$

$$= \min(\inf_{p \in \mathbb{R}^n} I_T(f^{m-1}(v_i)(p), (R_\alpha \downarrow \uparrow f^m(v_j))(p)),$$

$$\min_{l=1}^{n} \inf_{p \in \mathbb{R}^n} I_T(T(\lambda_{li}^{NTP}, (R_\alpha \uparrow f^{m-1}(v_l))(p)), (R_\alpha \downarrow \uparrow f^m(v_j))(p)))$$

By $f^m(v_j) \supseteq f^{m-1}(v_j)$, (C.19) and the induction hypothesis, we have

$$\inf_{p \in \mathbb{R}^n} I_T(f^{m-1}(v_i)(p), (R_\alpha \downarrow \uparrow f^m(v_j))(p))$$

$$\geq \inf_{p \in \mathbb{R}^n} I_T(f^{m-1}(v_i)(p), (R_\alpha \downarrow \uparrow f^{m-1}(v_j))(p))$$

$$= P_\alpha(f^{m-1}(v_i), f^{m-1}(v_j))$$

$$= \lambda_{ij}^P$$

For each l in $\{1, 2, \ldots, n\}$, we have from Lemma 2.17, (2.29) and (2.23)

$$\inf_{p \in \mathbb{R}^n} I_T(T(\lambda_{li}^{NTP}, (R_\alpha \uparrow f^{m-1}(v_l))(p)), (R_\alpha \downarrow \uparrow f^m(v_j))(p))$$

$$\geq \inf_{p \in \mathbb{R}^n} I_T(T(\lambda_{li}^{NTP}, (R_\alpha \uparrow f^{m-1}(v_l))(p)), f^m(v_j)(p))$$

$$\geq \inf_{p \in \mathbb{R}^n} I_T(T(\lambda_{li}^{NTP}, (R_\alpha \uparrow f^{m-1}(v_l))(p)), T(\lambda_{lj}^{NTP}, (R_\alpha \uparrow f^{m-1}(v_l))(p)))$$

$$\geq \inf_{p \in \mathbb{R}^n} T(I_T(\lambda_{li}^{NTP}, \lambda_{lj}^{NTP}), I_T((R_\alpha \uparrow f^{m-1}(v_l))(p), (R_\alpha \uparrow f^{m-1}(v_l))(p)))$$

$$= \inf_{p \in \mathbb{R}^n} T(I_T(\lambda_{li}^{NTP}, \lambda_{lj}^{NTP}), 1)$$

$$= I_T(\lambda_{li}^{NTP}, \lambda_{lj}^{NTP})$$

Since Θ satisfies the transitivity rules from Table 7.5, we know that

$$T(\lambda_{li}^{NTP}, \lambda_{ij}^P) \leq \lambda_{lj}^{NTP}$$

or, by (2.21)

$$\lambda_{ij}^P \leq I_T(\lambda_{li}^{NTP}, \lambda_{lj}^{NTP})$$

Hence, we have shown

$$P_\alpha(f^m(v_i), f^m(v_j)) \geq \lambda_{ij}^P$$

Conversely, we obtain using (C.20), Lemma C.27

$$P_\alpha(f^m(v_i), f^m(v_j)) = \inf_{p \in \mathbb{R}^n} I_T((R_\alpha \uparrow f^m(v_i))(p), (R_\alpha \uparrow f^m(v_j))(p))$$

$$\leq I_T((R_\alpha \uparrow f^m(v_i))(a_i), (R_\alpha \uparrow f^m(v_j))(a_i))$$

$$= I_T(\lambda_{ii}^P, \lambda_{ij}^P)$$

As Θ satisfies (8.15), it holds that $\lambda_{ii}^P = 1$, hence by (2.22), we obtain

$$P_\alpha(f^m(v_i), f^m(v_j)) \leq \lambda_{ij}^P$$

$\square$

Bibliography

Abdelmoty, A. (1995). *Modelling and Reasoning in Spatial Databases: A Deductive Object–Oriented Approach*, Ph.D. thesis, Heriot-Watt University, Edinburgh.

Abdelmoty, A., Smart, P. and El-Geresy, B. (2006). Towards the practical use of qualitative spatial reasoning in geographic information retrieval, in *Proceedings of the 3rd IEEE Conference on Intelligent Systems*, pp. 71–76.

Adafre, S. and de Rijke, M. (2005). Discovering missing links in wikipedia, in *Proceedings of the 3rd International Workshop on Link Discovery*, pp. 90–97.

Aiello, M. and Ottens, B. (2007). The mathematical morpho–logical view on reasoning about space, in *Proceedings of the 20th International Joint Conference on Artificial Intelligence*, pp. 205–211.

A.K. Pujari, A. S. (1999). A new framework for reasoning about points, intervals and durations, in *Proceedings of the Sixteenth International Joint Conference on Artificial Intelligence*, pp. 1259–1267.

Alani, H. (2001). Voronoi-based region approximation for geographical information retrieval with gazetteers, *International Journal of Geographical Information Science* 15, 4, pp. 287–306.

Allan, J., Gupta, R. and Khandelwal, V. (2001). Temporal summaries of news topics, in *Proceedings of the 24th Annual International ACM SIGIR Conference on Research and Development in Information Retrieval*, pp. 10–18.

Allan, J., Papka, R. and Lavrenko, V. (1998). On-line new event detection and tracking, in *Proceedings of the 21st Annual International ACM SIGIR Conference on Research and Development in Information Retrieval*, pp. 37–45.

Allan, J., Wade, C. and Bolivar, A. (2003). Retrieval and novelty detection at the sentence level, in *Proceedings of the 26th Annual International ACM SIGIR Conference on Research and Development in Information Retrieval*, pp. 314–321.

Allen, J. (1983). Maintaining knowledge about temporal intervals, *Communications of the ACM* 26, 11, pp. 832–843.

Allen, R. (2004). A query interface for an event gazeteer, in *Proceedings of the 2004 Joint ACM/IEEE Conference on Digital Libraries*, pp. 72–73.

Alonso, O., Gertz, M. and Baeza-Yates, R. (2007). On the value of temporal information in information retrieval, *ACM SIGIR Forum* **41**, 2, pp. 35–41.

Arampatzis, A., van Kreveld, M., Reinbacher, I., Jones, C., Vaid, S., Clough, P., Joho, H. and Sanderson, M. (2006). Web-based delineation of imprecise regions, *Computers, Environment and Urban Systems* **30**, 4, pp. 436–459.

Badaloni, S. and Giacomin, M. (2006). The algebra IA^{fuz}: a framework for qualitative fuzzy temporal reasoning, *Artificial Intelligence* **170**, 10, pp. 872–908.

Balog, K., Bogers, T., Azzopardi, L., de Rijke, M. and van den Bosch, A. (2007). Broad expertise retrieval in sparse data environments, in *Proceedings of the 30th Annual International ACM SIGIR Conference on Research and Development in Information Retrieval*, pp. 551–558.

Bandler, W. and Kohout, L. (1980). Fuzzy relational products as a tool for analysis and synthesis of the behaviour of complex natural and artificial systems, in S. Wang and P. Chang (eds.), *Fuzzy Sets: Theory and Application to Policy Analysis and Information Systems* (Plenum Press, New York and London), pp. 341–367.

Bao, S., Wu, X., Fei, B., Xue, G., Su, Z. and Yu, Y. (2007). Optimizing web search using social annotations, in *Proceedings of the 16th International Conference on World Wide Web*, pp. 501–510.

Bar-Ilan, J. (2005). Comparing rankings of search results on the web, *Information Processing and Management: an International Journal* **41**, pp. 1511–1519.

Barro, S., Marín, R., Mira, J. and Patón, A. (1994). A model and a language for the fuzzy representation and handling of time, *Fuzzy Sets and Systems* **61**, 2, pp. 153–175.

Barzilay, R., Elhadad, M. and McKeown, K. (2002). Inferring strategies for sentence ordering in multidocument news summarization, *Journal of Artificial Intelligence Research* **17**, pp. 35–55.

Bellow, S. (1964). *Herzog* (Viking Press, New York).

Bennett, B. (1998). Determining consistency of topological relations, *Constraints* **3**, 2–3, pp. 213–225.

Bennett, B. (2001). What is a forest? On the vagueness of certain geographic concepts, *Topoi* **20**, 2, pp. 189–201.

Berners-Lee, T., Hendler, J. and Lassila, O. (2001). The semantic web, *Scientific American* **284**, 5, pp. 28–37.

Bilgiç, T. and Türksen, T. (1999). Measurement of membership functions: Theoretical and empirical work, in D. Dubois and H. Prade (eds.), *Handbook of Fuzzy Sets and Systems, Vol. 1* (Kluwer), pp. 195–232.

Billerbeck, B. and Zobel, J. (2004). Questioning query expansion: an examination of behaviour and parameters, in *Proceedings of the Australian Database Conference*, pp. 69–76.

Bittner, T. (2002). Approximate qualitative temporal reasoning, *Annals of Mathematics and Artificial Intelligence* **36**, 1–2, pp. 39–80.

Bittner, T. and Stell, J. (2002). Vagueness and rough location, *Geoinformatica* **6**, 2, pp. 99–121.

Bloch, I. (2006). Spatial reasoning under imprecision using fuzzy set theory, formal logics and mathematical morphology, *International Journal of Approximate Reasoning* **41**, 2, pp. 77–95.

Bodenhofer, U. (1999). A new approach to fuzzy orderings, *Tatra Mountains Mathematical Publications* **16**, pp. 21–29.

Bodenhofer, U. (2003). A unified framework of opening and closure operators with respect to arbitrary fuzzy relations, *Soft Computing* **7**, 4, pp. 220–227.

Boguraev, B. and Ando, R. (2005). TimeML–compliant text analysis for temporal reasoning, in *Proceedings of the International Joint Conference on Articifical Intelligence*, pp. 997–1003.

Borghini, A. and Varzi, A. (2006). Event location and vagueness, *Philosophical Studies* **128**, 2, pp. 313–336.

Bosch, A., Torres, M. and Marin, R. (2002). Reasoning with disjunctive fuzzy temporal constraint networks, in *Proceedings of the 9th International Symposium on Temporal Representation and Reasoning*, pp. 36–43.

Brill, E., Dumais, S. and Banko, M. (2002). An analysis of the AskMSR question-answering system, in *Proceedings of the ACL Conference on Empirical Methods in Natural Language Processing*, pp. 257–264.

Brin, S. and Page, L. (1998). The anatomy of a large–scale hypertextual web search engine, *Computer Networks and ISDN Systems* **30**, 1–7, pp. 107–117.

Bucher, B., Clough, P., Joho, H., Purves, R. and Syed, A. (2005). Geographic IR systems: requirements and evaluation, in *Proceedings of the 22nd International Cartographic Conference*.

Chan, S. (1978). Temporal delineation of international conflicts: Poisson results from the Vietnam War, 1963–1965, *International Studies Quarterly* **22**, 2, pp. 237–265.

Chen, J., Syau, Y.-R. and Ting, C.-J. (2004). Convexity and semicontinuity of fuzzy sets, *Fuzzy Sets and Systems* **143**, 3, pp. 459–469.

Chieu, H. and Lee, Y. (2004). Query based event extraction along a timeline, in *Proceedings of the 27th Annual International ACM SIGIR Conference on Research and development in information retrieval*, pp. 425–432.

Cho, C. (2003). *Study on the Effects of Resident–Perceived Neighborhood Boundaries on Public Services Accessibility & its Relation to Utilization: Using Geographic Information System, Focusing on the Case of Public Parks in Austin, Texas*, Ph.D. thesis, Texas A&M University.

Chu-Carroll, J. and Prager, J. (2007). An experimental study of the impact of information extraction accuracy on semantic search performance, in *Proceedings of the 16th ACM Conference on Information and Knowledge Management*, pp. 505–514.

Cicerone, S. and Felice, P. D. (2000). Cardinal relations between regions with a broad boundary, in *Proceedings of the 8th ACM International Symposium on Advances in Geographic Information Systems*, pp. 15–20.

Clementini, E. and Di Felice, P. (1997). Approximate topological relations, *International Journal of Approximate Reasoning* **16**, 2, pp. 173–204.

Clementini, E., Di Felice, P. and Hernández, D. (1997). Qualitative representation of positional information, *Artificial Intelligence* **95**, 2, pp. 317–356.

Clough, P., Joho, H., Jones, C. and Purves, R. (2005). Modelling vague places with knowledge from the web, *Unpublished, available at http://ext.dcs.dcs.shef.ac.uk/~u0015/darwinProjectProposals/SandersonMark/clough.pdf*.

Cohn, A. and Gotts, N. (1996). The 'egg-yolk' representation of regions with indeterminate boundaries, in *Geographic Objects with Indeterminate Boundaries (P.A. Burrough and A.U. Frank, eds.)* (Taylor and Francis Ltd.), pp. 171–187.

Collins, J. and Varzi, A. (2000). Unsharpenable vagueness, *Philosophical Topics* **28**, 1, pp. 1–10.

Craswell, N., Hawking, D. and Robertson, S. (2001). Effective site finding using link anchor information, in *Proceedings of the 24th Annual International ACM SIGIR Conference on Research and development in information retrieval*, pp. 250–257.

Cui, Z., Cohn, A. and Randell, D. (1993). Qualitative and topological relationships, in *Proceedings of the Third International Symposium on Advances in Spatial Databases*, pp. 296–315.

Dalli, A. (2006). System for spatio–temporal analysis of online news and blogs, in *Proceedings of the 15th International Conference on World Wide Web*, pp. 929–930.

Dang, H., Kelly, D. and Lin, J. (2007). Overview of the TREC 2007 question answering track, in *The Fifteenth Text REtrieval Conference Notebook*.

De Baets, B., De Meyer, H. and Naessens, H. (2001). A class of rational cardinality–based similarity measures, *Journal of Computational and Applied Mathematics* **132**, 1, pp. 51–69.

De Baets, B., De Meyer, H. and Naessens, H. (2002). On rational cardinality–based inclusion measures, *Fuzzy Sets and Systems* **128**, 2, pp. 169–183.

De Cock, M. (2002). *Een Grondige Studie van Linguïstische Wijzigers in de Vaagverzamelingenleer*, Ph.D. thesis, Ghent University.

De Cock, M. and Kerre, E. (2003a). On (un)suitable fuzzy relations to model approximate equality, *Fuzzy Sets and Systems* **133**, 2, pp. 137–153.

De Cock, M. and Kerre, E. (2003b). Why fuzzy $\mathcal{T}$-equivalence relations do not resolve the poincaré paradox, and related issues, *Fuzzy Sets and Systems* **133**, 2, pp. 181–192.

De Roure, D. and Hendler, J. (2004). E–science: the grid and the semantic web, *IEEE Intelligent Systems* **19**, 1, pp. 65–71.

Dechter, R., Meiri, I. and Pearl, J. (1991). Temporal constraint networks, *Artificial Intelligence* **49**, 1–3, pp. 61–95.

Delboni, T., Borges, K., Laender, A. and Jr., C. D. (2007). Semantic expansion of geographic web queries based on natural language positioning expressions, *Transactions in GIS* **11**, 3, pp. 377–397.

Donnelly, M., Bittner, T. and Rosse, C. (2006). A formal theory for spatial representations and reasoning in biomedical ontologies, *Artificial Intelligence in Medicine* **36**, pp. 1–27.

Douglas, J. (1933). The problem of Plateau, *Bulletin of the American Mathematical Society* **39**, pp. 227–251.

Drakengren, T. and Jonsson, P. (1997a). Eight maximal tractable subclasses of Allen's algebra with metric time, *Journal of Artificial Intelligence Research* **7**, pp. 25–45.

Drakengren, T. and Jonsson, P. (1997b). Twenty-one large tractable subclasses of Allen's algebra, *Artificial Intelligence* **93**, 1–2, pp. 297–319.

Du, S., Qin, Q., Wang, Q. and Li, B. (2005a). Fuzzy description of topological relations I: a unified fuzzy 9–intersection model, in *Advances in Natural Computation, LNCS 3612*, pp. 1261–1273.

Du, S., Wang, Q., Qin, Q. and Yang, Y. (2005b). Fuzzy description of topological relations II: computation methods and examples, in *Advances in Natural Computation, LNCS 3612*, pp. 1274–1279.

Dubois, D., Godo, L., Prade, H. and Esteva, F. (2005). An information–based discussion of vagueness, in H. Cohen and C. Lefebre (eds.), *Handbook of Categorization in Cognitive Science* (Elsevier), pp. 892–913.

Dubois, D., HadjAli, A. and Prade, H. (2003). Fuzziness and uncertainty in temporal reasoning, *Journal of Universal Computer Science* **9**, 9, pp. 1168–1194.

Dubois, D. and Prade, H. (1983). Ranking fuzzy numbers in the setting of possibility theory, *Information Sciences* **30**, 3, pp. 183–224.

Dubois, D. and Prade, H. (1989). Processing fuzzy temporal knowledge, *IEEE Transactions on Systems, Man, and Cybernetics* **19**, 4, pp. 729–744.

Dubois, D. and Prade, H. (1997). The place of fuzzy logic in AI, *Selected and Invited Papers from the Workshop on Fuzzy Logic in Artificial Intelligence, Lecture Notes in Computer Science* **1566**, pp. 9–21.

Dubois, D. and Prade, H. (2001). Possibility theory, probability theory and multiple–valued logics: a clarification, *Annals of Mathematics and Artificial Intelligence* **32**, pp. 35–66.

Duckham, M. and Worboys, M. (2001). Computational structure in three–valued nearness relations, in *Proceedings of the International Conference on Spatial Information Theory*, pp. 76–91.

Dutta, S. (1991). Approximate spatial reasoning: integrating qualitative and quantitative constraints, *International Journal of Approximate Reasoning* **5**, 3, pp. 307–330.

Egenhofer, M. and Franzosa, R. (1991). Point–set topological spatial relations, *International Journal of Geographical Information Systems* **5**, 2, pp. 161–174.

Eikvil, L. (1999). Information extraction from world wide web — a survey —, in *technical report*.

Elkan, C. (1994a). The paradoxical controversy over fuzzy logic, *IEEE Expert: Intelligent Systems and Their Applications* **9**, 4, pp. 47–49.

Elkan, C. (1994b). The paradoxical success of fuzzy logic, *IEEE Expert: Intelligent Systems and Their Applications* **9**, 4, pp. 3–8.

Erwig, M. and Schneider, M. (1997). Vague regions, in *Proceedings of the 5th International Symposium on Advances in Spatial Databases*, pp. 298–320.

Esterline, A., Dozier, G. and Homaifar, A. (1997). Fuzzy spatial reasoning, in *Proceedings of the 1997 International Fuzzy Systems Association Conference*, pp. 162–167.

Etzioni, O., Cafarella, M., Downey, D., Kok, S., Popescu, A.-M., Shaked, T., Soderland, S., Weld, D. and Yates, A. (2004). Web–scale information extraction in knowitall, in *Proceedings of the 13th International Conference on World Wide Web*, pp. 100–110.

Evans, D. and Zhai, C. (1996). Noun–phrase analysis in unrestricted text for information retrieval, in *Proceedings of the 34th Annual Meeting on Association for Computational Linguistics*, pp. 17–24.

Fensel, D., Decker, J. A. S., Erdmann, M., Schnurr, H.-P., Studer, R. and Witt, A. (2000). Lessons learned from applying AI to the web, *International Journal of Cooperative Information Systems* **9**, 4, pp. 361–382.

Filatova, E. and Hovy, E. (2001). Assigning time-stamps to event-clauses, in *Proceedings of the ACL-2001 Workshop on Temporal and Spatial Information Processing*, pp. 88–95.

Fine, K. (1975). Vagueness, truth and logic, *Synthese* **30**, pp. 265–300.

Fisher, P. (2000). Sorites paradox and vague geographies, *Fuzzy Sets and Systems* **113**, 1, pp. 7–18.

Floyd, R. (1962). Algorithm 97: Shortest path, *Communications of the ACM* **5**, 6, p. 345.

Fodor, J. and Roubens, M. (1994). *Fuzzy preference modelling and multicriteria decision support* (Kluwer Academic Publishers).

Frank, A. (1996). Qualitative spatial reasoning: Cardinal directions as an example, *International Journal of Geographic Information Systems* **10**, 3, pp. 269–290.

Freksa, C. (1992). Temporal reasoning based on semi–intervals, *Artificial Intelligence* **54**, 1–2, pp. 199–227.

Freksa, C. (1994). Fuzzy systems in AI, in R. Kruse, J. Gebhardt and R. Palm (eds.), *Fuzzy Systems in Computer Science* (Vieweg, Braunschweig/Wiesbaden), pp. 155–169.

Freksa, C. (1997). Spatial and temporal structures in cognitive processes, in *Foundations of Computer Science: Potential - Theory - Cognition, to Wilfried Brauer on the occasion of his sixtieth birthday*, pp. 379–387.

Gahegan, M. (1995). Proximity operators for qualitative spatial reasoning, in *Proceedings of the International Conference on Spatial Information Theory: A Theoretical Basis for GIS, LNCS 988*, pp. 31–44.

Gärdenfors, P. (2000). *Conceptual Spaces: The Geometry of Thought* (MIT Press).

Gärdenfors, P. and Williams, M.-A. (2001). Reasoning about categories in conceptual spaces, in *Proceedings of the Fourteenth International Joint Conference on Artificial Intelligence*, pp. 385–392.

Gentilhomme, Y. (1968). Les ensembles flous en linguistique, *Cahiers de Linguistique Théorique et Appliquée* **5**, pp. 47–65.

Gerevini, A. and Cristani, M. (1997). On finding a solution in temporal constraint satisfaction problems, in *Proceedings of the Fifteenth International Joint Conference on Artificial Intelligence*, pp. 1460–1465.

Gerevini, A. and Renz, J. (2002). Combining topological and size information for spatial reasoning, *Artificial Intelligence* **137**, pp. 1–42.

Gey, F., Larson, R., Sanderson, M., Bischoff, K., Mandl, T., Womser-Hacker, C., Santos, D. and Rocha, P. (2006). GeoCLEF 2006: the CLEF 2006 cross-language geographic information retrieval track overview, in *Working Notes for the CLEF 2006 Workshop*.

Glance, N., Hurst, M. and Tomokiyo, T. (2004). Blogpulse: automated trend discovery for weblogs, in *Proceedings of the WWW 2004 Workshop on the Weblogging Ecosystem*.

Goguen, J. (1967). L-fuzzy sets, *Journal of Mathematical Analysis and Applications* **18**, pp. 145–174.

Goodchild, M., Montello, D., Fohl, P. and Gottsegen, J. (1998). Fuzzy spatial queries in digital spatial data libraries, in *Proceedings of the IEEE World Congress on Computational Intelligence*, pp. 205–210.

Gotts, N. (1996). An axiomatic approach to topology for spatial information systems, in *Report 96.25, Research Report Series, School of Computer Studies, University of Leeds*.

Goyal, R. (2000). *Similarity Assessment for Cardinal Directions between Extended Spatial Objects*, Ph.D. thesis, University of Maine.

Grigni, M., Papadias, D. and Papadimitriou, C. (1995). Topological inference, in *Proceedings of the 14th International Joint Conference on Artificial Intelligence*, pp. 901–906.

Guesgen, H. (1989). Spatial reasoning based on Allen's temporal logic, in *Technical report TR-89-049, International Computer Science Institute, Berkley*.

Guesgen, H. (2002). From the egg–yolk to the scrambled–egg theory, in *Proceedings of the 15th International FLAIRS Conference*, pp. 476–480.

Guesgen, H. and Albrecht, J. (2000). Imprecise reasoning in geographic information systems, *Fuzzy Sets and Systems* **113**, 1, pp. 121–131.

Guesgen, H., Hertzberg, J. and Philpott, A. (1994). Towards implementing fuzzy Allen relations, in *Proceedings of the ECAI-94 Workshop on Spatial and Temporal Reasoning*, pp. 49–55.

Harabagiu, S. and Bejan, C. (2005). Question answering based on temporal inference, in *Proceedings of the AAAI-2005 Workshop on Inference for Textual Question Answering*.

Harada, Y. and Sadahiro, Y. (2005). A quantitative model of place names as a georeferencing system, in *Proceedings of GeoComputation*, URL http://igre.emich.edu/geocomputation2005/abstract_list/1200094.pdf.

Hearst, M. (1992). Automatic acquisition of hyponyms from large text corpora, in *Proceedings of the 14th conference on Computational linguistics*, pp. 539–545.

Hersh, H. M. and Caramazza, A. (1976). A fuzzy set approach to modifiers and vagueness in natural language, *Journal of Experimental Psychology* **105**, 3, pp. 254–276.

Hill, L., Frew, J. and Zheng, Q. (1999). Geographic names: the implementation of a gazetteer in a georeferenced digital library, *D-Lib Magazine* **5**, 1.

Himmelstein, M. (2005). Local search: the internet *is* the yellow pages, *Computer* **38**, pp. 26–34.

Hong, J. (1994). *Qualitative Distance and Direction Reasoning in Geographic Space*, Ph.D. thesis, University of Maine.

Hotho, A., Jäschke, R., Schmitz, C. and Stumme, G. (2006). Information retrieval in folksonomies: search and ranking, in *Proceedings of the European Semantic Web Conference*, pp. 411–426.

Hu, Y., Xin, G., Song, R., Hu, G., Shi, S., Cao, Y. and Li, H. (2005). Title extraction from bodies of HTML documents and its application to web page retrieval, in *Proceedings of the 28th Annual International ACM SIGIR Conference on Research and Development in Information Retrieval*, pp. 250–257.

Janssens, S. (2006). *Bell Inequalities for Cardinality–Based Similarity Measurement*, Ph.D. thesis, Ghent University.

Jijkoun, V., Mishne, G. and de Rijke, M. (2003). How frogs built the Berlin wall: A detailed error analysis of a question answering system for Dutch, in *Proceedings of the Cross Language Evaluation Forum (CLEF)*, pp. 523–534.

Jones, C., Alani, H. and Tudhope, D. (2001). Geographic information retrieval with ontologies of place, in *Proceedings of the International Conference on Spatial Information Theory: Foundations of Geographic Information Science*, pp. 322–335.

Jones, C., Purves, R., Ruas, A., Sanderson, M., Sester, M., van Kreveld, M. and Weibel, R. (2002). Spatial information retrieval and geographical ontologies: an overview of the SPIRIT project, in *Proceedings of the 25th annual international ACM SIGIR conference on Research and development in information retrieval*, pp. 389–390.

Jonsson, P. and Bäckström, C. (1998). A unifying approach to temporal constraint reasoning, *Artificial Intelligence* **102**, 1, pp. 143–155.

Karmarkar, N. (1984). A new polynomial-time algorithm for linear programming, *Combinatorica* **4**, 4, pp. 373–395.

Kautz, H. and Ladkin, P. (1991). Integrating metric and qualitative temporal reasoning, in *Proceedings of the Ninth National Conference on Artificial Intelligence (AAAI-91)*, pp. 241–246.

Keefe, R. (1998). Vagueness by numbers, *Mind* **107**, 427, pp. 565–580.

Keefe, R. (2003). Unsolved problems with numbers: reply to Smith, *Mind* **112**, 446, pp. 291–293.

Kerre, E. (1992). A walk through fuzzy relations and their applications to information retrieval, medical diagnosis and expert systems, in B. Ayyub, M. Gupta and L. Kanal (eds.), *Analysis and Management of Uncertainty: Theory and Applications* (Elsevier Science Publishers), pp. 141–151.

Kerre, E. (1993). *Introduction to the Basic Principles of Fuzzy Set Theory and Some of its Applications* (Communication and Cognition).

Kerre, E. and Van Schooten, A. (1988). A deeper look on fuzzy numbers from a theoretical as well as from a practical point of view, in M. Gupta and T. Yamakawa (eds.), *Fuzzy Logic in Knowledge–Based Systems, Decision and Control* (Elsevier Science Publishers), pp. 173–196.

Khatib, L., Morris, P., Morris, R. and Rossi, F. (2001). Temporal constraint reasoning with preferences, in *Proceedings of the Seventeenth International*

Joint Conference on Artificial Intelligence, pp. 322–327.

Kherfi, M., Ziou, D. and Bernardi, A. (2004). Image retrieval from the world wide web: issues, techniques, and systems, *ACM Computing Surveys* **36**, 1, pp. 35–67.

Klement, E., Mesiar, R. and Pap, E. (2002). *Triangular norms* (Kluwer Academic Publishers).

Ko, J., Si, L. and Nyberg, E. (2007). A probabilistic framework for answer selection in question answering, in *Proceedings of Human Language Technologies: The Annual Conference of the North American Chapter of the Association for Computational Linguistics (NAACL–HLT)*, pp. 524–531.

Koubarakis, M. (1992). Dense time and temporal constraints with ≠, in *Proceedings of the Third International Conference on Principles of Knowledge Representation and Reasoning*, pp. 24–35.

Koubarakis, M. (2001). Tractable disjunctions of linear constraints: basic results and applications to temporal reasoning, *Theoretical computer science* **266**, 1, pp. 311–339.

Kraaij, W. and Pohlmann, P. (1996). Viewing stemming as recall enhancement, in *Proceedings of the 19th annual international ACM SIGIR conference on Research and development in information retrieval*, pp. 40–48.

Kratochvíl, J. (1991). String graphs II: Recognizing string graphs is NP–hard, *Journal of Combinatorial Theory, Series B* **52**, 1, pp. 67–78.

Krokhin, A., Jeavons, P. and Jonsson, P. (2003). Reasoning about temporal relations: The tractable subalgebras of Allen's interval algebra, *Journal of the ACM* **50**, 5, pp. 591–640.

Kulik, L. (2001). A geometric theory of vague boundaries based on supervaluation, in *Proceedings of the International Conference on Spatial Information Theory: Foundations of Geographic Information Science*, pp. 44–59.

Kulik, L., Eschenbach, C., Habel, C. and Schmidtke, H. (2002). A graded approach to directions between extended objects, in *Proceedings of the Second International Conference on Geographic Information Science*, pp. 119–131.

Kumar, R., Novak, J., Raghavan, P. and Tomkins, A. (2005). On the bursty evolution of blogspace, *World Wide Web* **8**, 2, pp. 159–178.

Kurashima, T., Tezuka, T. and Tanaka, K. (2006). Mining and visualizing local experiences from blog entries, in *Proceedings of the 17th International Conference on Database and Expert Systems Applications*, pp. 213–222.

Kushmerick, N. (2000). Wrapper induction: efficiency and expressiveness, *Artificial Intelligence* **118**, pp. 15–68.

Kwok, C., Etzioni, O. and Weld, D. (2001). Scaling question answering to the Web, in *Proceedings of the 10th International Conference on World Wide Web*, pp. 150–161.

Ladkin, P. and Reinefeld, A. (1993). A symbolic approach to interval constraint problems, in *Artificial Intelligence and Symbolic Mathematical Computing, LNCS 737 (J. Calmet and J.A. Campbell, eds.)*, pp. 65–84.

Lapata, M. and Lascarides, A. (2006). Learning sentence–internal temporal relations, *Journal of Artificial Intelligence Research* **27**, pp. 85–117.

Larson, R. (1996). Geographic information retrieval and spatial browsing, in

L. Smith and M. Gluck (eds.), *Geographic Information Systems and Libraries: Patrons, Maps, and Spatial Information*, pp. 81–123.

Larson, R. and Frontiera, P. (2004). Geographic information retrieval (GIR): searching where and what, in *Proceedings of the 27th annual international ACM SIGIR conference on Research and development in information retrieval*, p. 600.

Lavrenko, V., Allan, J., DeGuzman, E., LaFlamme, D., Pollard, V. and Thomas, S. (2002). Relevance models for topic detection and tracking, in *Proceedings of the Second International Conference on Human Language Technology Research*, pp. 115–121.

Lefever, E., Fayruzov, T. and Hoste, V. (2007). A combined classification and clustering approach to web people disambiguation, in *Proceedings of the 4th International Workshop on Semantic Evaluations*, pp. 105–108.

Leidner, J., Sinclair, G. and Webber, B. (2003). Grounding spatial named entities for information extraction and question answering, in *Proceedings of the HTL-NAACL 2003 Workshop on Analysis of Geographic References*, pp. 31–38.

Li, S. (2006). On topological consistency and realization, *Constraints* **11**, 1, pp. 31–51.

Li, S. (2007). Combining topological and directional information for spatial reasoning, in *Proceedings of the 20th International Joint Conference on Artificial Intelligence*, pp. 435–440.

Li, Y. and Li, S. (2004). A fuzzy sets theoretic approach to approximate spatial reasoning, *IEEE Transactions on Fuzzy Systems* **12**, 6, pp. 745–754.

Lin, J. and Halavais, A. (2004). Mapping the blogosphere in America, in *Proceedings of the WWW 2004 Workshop on the Weblogging Ecosystem*.

Liu, K. and Shi, W. (2006). Computing the fuzzy topological relations of spatial objects based on induced fuzzy topology, *International Journal of Geographical Information Science* **20**, 8, pp. 857–883.

Lundberg, U. and Eckman, G. (1973). Subjective geographic distance: a multidimensional comparison, *Psychometrika* **38**, pp. 113–122.

M. Vazirgiannis, T. S., Y. Theodoridis (1998). Spatio-temporal composition and indexing for large multimedia applications, *Multimedia Systems* **6**, 4, pp. 284–298.

Macdonald, C. and Ounis, I. (2006). The TREC Blog06 collection: creating and analysing a blog test collection, in *DCS Technical Report TR-2006-224, Department of Computing Science, University of Glasgow*.

Mani, I., Schiffman, B. and Zhang, J. (2003). Inferring temporal ordering of events in news, in *Proceedings of the 2003 Conference of the North American Chapter of the Association for Computational Linguistics on Human Language Technology: companion volume of the Proceedings of HLT-NAACL 2003-short papers - Volume 2*, pp. 55–57.

Mani, I. and Wilson, G. (2000). Robust temporal processing of news, in *Proceedings of the 38th Annual Meeting of the ACL*, pp. 69–76.

Marín, R., Barro, S., Bosch, A. and Mira, J. (1994). Modelling the representation of time from a fuzzy perspective, *Cybernetics and Systems* **25**, 2, pp. 217–

231.

Mckay, D. and Cunningham, S. (2000). Mining dates from historical documents, in *technical report, Department of Computer Science, University of Waikato*.

Meiri, I. (1996). Combining qualitative and quantitative constraints in temporal reasoning, *Artificial Intelligence* **87**, 1, pp. 343–385.

Mihalcea, R. and Csomai, A. (2007). Wikify!: linking documents to encyclopedic knowledge, in *Proceedings of the Sixteenth ACM Conference on Information and Knowledge Management*, pp. 233–242.

Mihalcea, R. and Moldovan, D. (2001). Document indexing using named entities, *Studies in Informatics and Control* **10**, 1.

Milne, D., Witten, I. and Nichols, D. (2007). A knowledge–based search engine powered by wikipedia, in *Proceedings of the Sixteenth ACM Conference on Information and Knowledge Management*, pp. 445–454.

Moldovan, D., Clark, C. and Bowden, M. (2007). Lymba's PowerAnswer 4 in TREC 2007, in *The Fifteenth Text REtrieval Conference Notebook*.

Moldovan, D., Clark, C. and Harabagiu, S. (2005). Temporal context representation and reasoning, in *Proceedings of the 19th International Joint Conference on Artificial Intelligence*, pp. 1099–1104.

Montello, D., Goodchild, M., Gottsegen, J. and Fohl, P. (2003). Where's downtown?: behavioral methods for determining referents of vague spatial queries, *Spatial Cognition and Computation* **3**, 2-3, pp. 185–204.

Monz, C. and de Rijke, M. (2002). Tequesta: the University of Amsterdam's textual question answering system, in *Proceedings of the Tenth Text Retrieval Conference (TREC)*, pp. 519–528.

Nachtegael, M., De Cock, M., Van der Weken, D. and Kerre, E. (2002). Fuzzy relational images in computer science, **2561**, pp. 134–151.

Nagypál, G. and Motik, B. (2003). A fuzzy model for representing uncertain, subjective and vague temporal knowledge in ontologies, in *Proceedings of the International Conference on Ontologies, Databases and Applications of Semantics (ODBASE), LNCS 2888*, pp. 906–923.

Nebel, B. (1994). Computational properties of qualitative spatial reasoning: first results, in *Proceedings of the 19th German Conference on Artificial Intelligence*, pp. 233–244.

Nebel, B. (1997). Solving hard qualitative temporal reasoning problems: Evaluating the efficiency of using the ORD-Horn class, *Constraints* **1**, 3, pp. 175–190.

Nebel, B. and Bürckert, H.-J. (1995). Reasoning about temporal relations: a maximal tractable subset of Allen's interval algebra, *Journal of the ACM* **42**, 1, pp. 43–66.

Nie, Z., Ma, Y., Shi, S., Wen, J.-R. and W.-Y-Ma (2007). Web object retrieval, in *Proceedings of the 16th International Conference on World Wide Web*, pp. 81–89.

Novák, V., Perfilieva, I. and ckoř, J. M. (1999). *Mathematical Principles of Fuzzy Logic* (Kluwer Academic Publishers).

Ohlbach, H. (2004). Relations between fuzzy time intervals, in *Proceedings of the 11th International Symposium on Temporal Representation and Reasoning*, pp. 44–51.

Okazaki, N., Matsuo, Y. and Ishizuka, M. (2004). Improving chronological sentence ordering by precedence relation, in *Proceedings of the 20th International Conference on Computational Linguistics*.

Ovchinnikova, E., Wandmacher, T. and Kühnberger, K.-U. (2007). Solving terminological inconsistency problems in ontology design, *International Journal of Interoperability in Business Information Systems* **4**, pp. 65–80.

Page, L., Brin, S., Motwani, R. and Winograd, T. (1998). The PageRank citation ranking: bringing order to the web, in *technical report, Stanford Digital Library Technologies Project*.

Palshikar, G. (2004). Fuzzy region connection calculus in finite discrete space domains, *Applied Soft Computing* **4**, pp. 13–23.

Pan, F., Mulkar, R. and Hobbs, J. (2006). Learning event durations from event descriptions, in *Proceedings of the 21st International Conference on Computational Linguistics and the 44th annual meeting of the ACL*, pp. 393–400.

Papadias, D. and Sellis, T. (1994). Qualitative representation of spatial knowledge in two-dimensional space, *VLDB Journal* **3**, pp. 479–516.

Pianesi, F. and Varzi, A. (1996). Events, topology, and temporal relations, *The Monist* **79**, 1, pp. 89–116.

Prabowo, R., Thelwall, M. and Alexandrov, M. (2007). Generating overview timelines for major events in an RSS corpus, *Journal of Informatics* **1**, pp. 131–144.

Purves, R., Clough, P. and Joho, H. (2005). Identifying imprecise regions for geographic information retrieval using the web, in *Proceedings of the 13th Annual GIS Research UK Conference*.

Pustejovksy, J., Knippen, R., Littman, J. and Saurí, R. (2005). Temporal and event information in natural language text, *Language Resources and Evaluation* **39**, pp. 123–164.

Qiu, Y. and Frei, H. (1993). Concept based query expansion, in *Proceedings of the 16th Annual International ACM SIGIR Conference on Research and Development in Information Retrieval*, pp. 160–169.

Ralha, C. and Ralha, J. (2003). Intelligent mapping of hyperspace, in *Proceedings of the IEEE/WIC International Conference on Web Intelligence*, pp. 454–457.

Randell, D., Cui, Z. and Cohn, A. (1992). A spatial logic based on regions and connection, in *Proceedings of the 3rd International Conference on Knowledge Representation and Reasoning*, pp. 165–176.

Rattenbury, T., Good, N. and Naaman, M. (2007). Towards automatic extraction of event and place semantics from Flickr tags, in *Proceedings of the 30th Annual International ACM SIGIR Conference on Research and Development in Information Retrieval*, pp. 103–110.

Ravichandran, D. and Hovy, E. (2002). Learning surface text patterns for a question answering system, in *Proceedings of the 40th Annual Meeting of the ACL*, pp. 41–47.

Reinbacher, I., Benkert, M., van Kreveld, M., Mitchell, J. and Wolf, A. (2005). Delineating boundaries for imprecise regions, in *Proceedings of the 13th*

European Symposium on Algorithms, LNCS 3669, pp. 143–154.

Renz, J. (1999). Maximal tractable fragments of the Region Connection Calculus: A complete analysis, in *Proceedings of the 16th International Joint Conference on Artificial Intelligence*, pp. 448–454.

Renz, J. (2002). A canonical model of the Region Connection Calculus, *Journal of Applied Non-Classical Logics* 12, 3–4, pp. 469–494.

Renz, J. and Nebel, B. (1999). On the complexity of qualitative spatial reasoning: A maximal tractable fragment of the Region Connection Calculus, *Artificial Intelligence* 108, 1–2, pp. 69–123.

Renz, J. and Nebel, B. (2001). Efficient methods for qualitative spatial reasoning, *Journal of Artificial Intelligence Research* 15, pp. 289–318.

Robinson, V. (2000). Individual and multipersonal fuzzy spatial relations acquired using human-machine interaction, *Fuzzy Sets and Systems* 113, 1, pp. 133–145.

Roy, A. and Stell, J. (2001). Spatial relations between indeterminate regions, *International Journal of Approximate Reasoning* 27, 3, pp. 205–234.

Rui, Y., Huang, T. and Chang, S. (1999). Image retrieval: current techniques, promising directions and open issues, *Journal of Visual Communication and Image Representation* 10, 4, pp. 39–62.

Russell, B. (1923). Vagueness, *The Australasian Journal of Psychology and Philosophy* 1, pp. 84–92.

Sadalla, E., Burroughs, W. and Staplin, L. (1980). Reference points in spatial cognition, *Journal of Experimental Psychology: Human Learning and Memory* 6, pp. 516–528.

Sanderson, M. (2000). Retrieving with good sense, *Information Retrieval* 2, 1, pp. 49–69.

Saquete, E., Martínez-Barco, P., Muñoz, R. and Vicedo, J. (2004). Splitting complex temporal questions for question answering systems, in *Proceedings of the 42nd Annual Meeting of the ACL*.

Sastry, N., Pebley, A. and Zonta, M. (2002). Neighborhood definitions and the spatial dimension of daily life in Los Angeles, in *2002 annual meeting of the Population of Daily Life in Los Angeles, available at* http://www.rand.org/labor/DRU/DRU2400_8.pdf.

Schaefer, M., Sedgwick, E. and Stefankovic, D. (2003). Recognizing string graphs in NP, *Journal of Computer and System Sciences* 67, pp. 365–380.

Schneider, M. (2001). A design of topological predicates for complex crisp and fuzzy regions, in *Proceedings of the 20th International Conference on Conceptual Modeling, LNCS 2224*, pp. 103–116.

Schockaert, S. and De Cock, M. (2007). Neighborhood restrictions in geographic IR, in *Proceedings of the 30th Annual International ACM SIGIR Conference on Research and Development in Information Retrieval*, pp. 167–174.

Schockaert, S. and De Cock, M. (2008). Temporal reasoning about fuzzy intervals, *Artificial Intelligence* 172, pp. 1158–1193.

Schockaert, S. and De Cock, M. (2009). Efficient algorithms for fuzzy qualitative temporal reasoning, *IEEE Transactions on Fuzzy Systems* 17, 4, pp. 794–808.

Schockaert, S., De Cock, M., Cornelis, C. and Kerre, E. (2008a). Fuzzy region connection calculus: an interpretation based on closeness, *International Journal of Approximate Reasoning* **48**, pp. 332–347.

Schockaert, S., De Cock, M., Cornelis, C. and Kerre, E. (2008b). Fuzzy region connection calculus: representing vague topological information, *International Journal of Approximate Reasoning* **48**, pp. 314–331.

Schockaert, S., De Cock, M. and Kerre, E. (2005). Automatic acquisition of fuzzy footprints, in *Proceedings of the International Workshop on Semantic Based Geographic Information Systems, LNCS 3762*, pp. 1077–1086.

Schockaert, S., De Cock, M. and Kerre, E. (2006). An efficient characterization of fuzzy temporal interval relations, in *Proceedings of the IEEE World Congress on Computational Intelligence*, pp. 9026–9033.

Schockaert, S., De Cock, M. and Kerre, E. (2008c). Fuzzifying Allen's temporal interval relations, *IEEE Transactions on Fuzzy Systems* **16**, 2, pp. 517–533.

Schockaert, S., De Cock, M. and Kerre, E. (2008d). Location approximation for local search services using natural language hints, *International Journal of Geographical Information Science* **22**, 3, pp. 315–336.

Schockaert, S., De Cock, M. and Kerre, E. (2008e). Modelling nearness and cardinal direction between fuzzy regions, in *Proceedings of the IEEE World Congress on Computational Intelligence*, pp. 1548–1555.

Schockaert, S., De Cock, M. and Kerre, E. E. (2009). Spatial reasoning in a fuzzy region connection calculus, *Artificial Intelligence* **173**, 258-298.

Schockaert, S., De Cock, M. and Kerre, E. E. (to appear). Reasoning about fuzzy temporal information from the web: Towards retrieval of historical events, *Soft Computing* .

Schockaert, S., Smart, P. D., Abdelmoty, A. I. and Jones, C. B. (2008f). Mining topological relations from the web, in *Proceedings of the 19th International Workshop on Database and Expert Systems Applications*, pp. 652–656.

Schokkenbroek, C. (1999). News stories: structure, time and evaluation, *Time & Society* **8**, 1, pp. 59–98.

Schulz, S., Kumar, A. and Bittner, T. (2006). Biomedical ontologies: What part-of is and isn't, *Journal of Biomedical Informatics* **39**, pp. 350–361.

Shadbolt, N., Hall, W. and Berners-Lee, T. (2006). The semantic web revisited, *IEEE Intelligent Systems* **21**, pp. 96–101.

Sharma, J. (1996). *Integrated Spatial Reasoning in Geographic Information Systems: Combining Topology and Direction*, Ph.D. thesis, University of Maine.

Silva, M., Martins, B., Chaves, M., Afonso, A. and Cardoso, N. (2006). Adding geographic scopes to web resources, *Computers, Environment and Urban Systems* **30**, 4, pp. 378–399.

Sinha, D. and Dougherty, E. (1993). Fuzzification of set inclusion: theory and applications, *Fuzzy Sets and Systems* **55**, 1, pp. 15–42.

Skiadopoulos, S. and Koubarakis, M. (2004). Composing cardinal direction relations, *Artificial Intelligence* **152**, pp. 143–171.

Smeaton, A. and Berrut, C. (1996). Thresholding postings lists, query expansion by word–word distances and POS tagging of Spanish text, in *Proceedings of the 4th Text Retrieval Conference*.

Smeaton, A. F. (1999). Using NLP or NLP resources for information retrieval tasks, in T. Strzalkowski (ed.), *Natural language information retrieval* (Kluwer Academic Publishers), pp. 99–111.

Smith, B., Ceusters, W., Klagges, B., Köhler, J., Kumar, A., Lomax, J., Mungall, C., Neuhaus, F., Rector, A. and Rosse, C. (2005). Relations in biomedical ontologies, *Genome Biology* **6**, 5, p. R46.

Smith, D. (2002). Detecting and browsing events in unstructured text, in *Proceedings of the 25th Annual International ACM SIGIR Conference on Research and Development in Information Retrieval*, pp. 73–80.

Smith, N. (2003). Vagueness by numbers? No worries, *Mind* **112**, 446, pp. 283–290.

Smith, N. (2005). Vagueness as closeness, *Australasian Journal of Philosophy* **83**, 2, pp. 157–183.

Sontag, E. (1985). Real addition and the polynomial time hierarchy, *Information Processing Letters* **20**, 3, pp. 115–120.

Soubbotin, M. and Soubbotin, S. (2001). Patterns of potential answer expressions as clues to the right answer, in *Proceedings of the TREC-10 Conference*, pp. 175–182.

Sougata, M. (2005). Information retrieval and knowledge discovery utilising a biomedical semantic web, *Briefings in Bioinformatics* **6**, 3, pp. 252–262.

Stergiou, K. and Koubarakis, M. (2000). Backtracking algorithms for disjunctions of temporal constraints, *Artificial Intelligence* **120**, 1, pp. 81–117.

Straccia, U. (2001). Reasoning within fuzzy description logics, *Journal of Artificial Intelligence Research* **4**, pp. 137–166.

Sun, H. and Li, W. (2005). Modeling cardinal directional relations between fuzzy regions based on alpha-morphology, in *Location- and Context-Awareness, LNCS 3479*, pp. 169–179.

Swan, R. and Allan, J. (2000). Automatic generation of overview timelines, in *Proceedings of the 23rd Annual International ACM SIGIR Conference on Research and Development in Information Retrieval*, pp. 49–56.

Tang, X. and Kainz, W. (2002). Analysis of topological relations between fuzzy regions in a general fuzzy topological space, in *Proceedings of the Symposium on Geospatial Theory, Processing and Applications*, p. available at http://www.isprs.org/commission4/proceedings.

Tezuka, T., Lee, R., Takakura, H. and Kambayashi, Y. (2001). Models for conceptual geographical prepositions based on web resources, *Journal of Geographic Information and Decision Analysis* **5**, pp. 83–94.

Tezuka, T. and Tanaka, K. (2005). Landmark extraction: a web mining approach, in *Proceedings of the International Conference on Spatial Information Theory*, pp. 379–396.

Tsamardinos, I. and Pollack, M. E. (2003). Efficient solution techniques for disjunctive temporal reasoning problems, *Artificial Intelligence* **151**, 1–2, pp. 43–90.

Tsiporkova, E. and Zimmermann, H. (1998). Aggregation of compatibility and equality: a new class of similarity measures of fuzzy sets, in *Proceedings of the Seventh International Conference on Information Processing and Man-*

agement of Uncertainty in Knowledge–Based Systems, pp. 1769–1776.

Turunen, E. (1999). *Mathematics Behind Fuzzy Logic* (Physica–Verlag Heidelberg).

Valdés-Pérez, R. (1987). The satisfiability of temporal constraint networks, in *Proceedings of the Sixth National Conference on Artificial Intelligence*, pp. 256–260.

Vallin, A., Magnini, B., Giampiccolo, D., Aunimo, L., Ayache, C., Osenova, P., Peas, A., de Rijke, M., Sacaleanu, B., Santos, D. and Sutcliffe, R. (2005). Overview of the CLEF 2005 multilingual question answering track, in *Proceedings of CLEF 2005*.

van Beek, P. (1992). Reasoning about qualitative temporal information, *Artificial Intelligence* **58**, pp. 297–326.

van Beek, P. and Cohen, R. (1990). Exact and approximate reasoning about temporal relations, *Computational Intelligence* **6**, pp. 132–144.

Varzi, A. (2001a). Vagueness in geography, *Philosophy & Geography* **4**, 1, pp. 49–65.

Varzi, A. (2001b). Vagueness, logic, and ontology, *The Dialogue* **1**, pp. 135–154.

Vásconez, M. (2006). *Fuzziness and the Sorites Paradox: from Degrees to Contradictions*, Ph.D. thesis, Catholic University of Leuven.

Vazirgiannis, M. (2000). Uncertainty handling in spatial relationships, in *Proceedings of the 2000 ACM Symposium on Applied Computing*, pp. 494–500.

Vilain, M., Kautz, H. and van Beek, P. (1989). Constraint propagation algorithms for temporal reasoning: a revised report, in D. Weld and J. de Kleer (eds.), *Readings in Qualitative Reasoning about Physical Systems* (Morgan Kaufmann, San Mateo, CA), pp. 373–381.

von Ahn, L. and Dabbish, L. (2004). Labeling images with a computer game, in *Proceedings of the SIGCHI Conference on Human Factors in Computing Systems*, pp. 319–326.

Voorhees, E. (1999). Natural language processing and information retrieval, in M. Pazienza (ed.), *Information Extraction: Towards Scalable, Adaptable Systems* (SPringer-Verlag, London, UK), pp. 32–48.

Warshall, S. (1962). A theorem on Boolean matrices, *Journal of the ACM* **9**, 1, pp. 11–12.

Waters, T. and Evans, A. (2003). Tools for web–based GIS mapping of a "fuzzy" vernacular geography, in *Proceedings of the 7th International Conference on GeoComputation*, p. available at http://www.geocomputation.org/2003/.

Westerveld, T., Kraaij, W. and Hiemstra, D. (2002). Retrieving web pages using content, links, URLs and anchors, in *Proceedings of the 10th Text Retrieval Conference*.

Wieczorek, J., Guo, Q. and Hijmans, R. (2004). The point–radius method for georeferencing locality descriptions and calculating associated uncertainty, *International Journal of Geographical Information Science* **18**, 8, pp. 745–767.

Worboys, M. (2001). Nearness relations in environmental space, *International Journal of Geographical Information Science* **15**, pp. 633–651.

Worboys, M. and Clementini, E. (2001). Integration of imperfect spatial information, *Journal of Visual Languages and Computing* **12**, pp. 61–80.

Wu, F. and Weld, D. (2007). Autonomously semantifying wikipedia, in *Proceedings of the Sixteenth ACM Conference on Information and Knowledge Management*, pp. 41–50.

Yao, X. and Thill, J.-C. (2005). How far is too far? — A statistical approach to context–contingent proximity modeling, *Transactions in GIS* **9**, pp. 157–178.

Young, V. (1996). Fuzzy subsethood, *Fuzzy Sets and Systems* **77**, 3, pp. 371–384.

Zacks, J. and Tversky, B. (2001). Event structure in perception and conception, *Psychological Bulletin* **127**, 1, pp. 3–21.

Zadeh, L. (1965). Fuzzy sets, *Information and Control* **8**, 3, pp. 338–353.

Zadeh, L. (1973). Outline of a new approach to the analysis of complex systems and decision processes, *IEEE Transactions on System, Man and Cybernetics* **3**, 1, pp. 28–44.

Zadeh, L. (1978). Fuzzy sets as a basis for a theory of possibility, *Fuzzy Sets and Systems* **1**, pp. 3–28.

Zhan, F. (1998). Approximate analysis of binary topological relations between geographic regions with indeterminate boundaries, *Soft Computing* **2**, 2, pp. 28–34.

Zhao, J., Wroe, C., Goble, C., Stevens, R., Quan, D. and Greenwood, M. (2004). Using semantic web technologies for representing E–science provenance, in *Proceedings of the Third International Semantic Web Conference*, pp. 92–106.

Zwick, R., Carlstein, E. and Budescu, D. (1973). Measures of similarity among fuzzy concepts: a comparative analysis, *IEEE Transactions on System, Man and Cybernetics* **3**, 1, pp. 28–44.

Index

Allen relations, *see* interval algebra

fuzzy interval relations, 97
  2-consistency, 205
  complete reasoner, 194
  complexity, 160, 173
  definition, 100, 105
  entailment, 183
  experimental results, 198, 222
  incomplete reasoner, 200
  piecewise linear intervals, 122
  properties, 112
  satisfiability, 156, 168
  transitivity, 118, 215
fuzzy relation, 36
fuzzy set, 28, 41
fuzzy spatial relations
  approximate composition, 294
  definition, 288
  directional, 285
  nearness, 281, 284
  topological, 282, 317
    best truth-value bound, 379
    complexity, 376
    definition, 320
    entailment, 377
    models, 337
    properties, 322
    realizability, 398
    relation with Egg-Yolk
      calculus, 392
    relation with RCC, 382

    repairing inconsistency, 380
    satisfiability, 362
    transitivity, 326

implicator, 25
information retrieval, 1
  event-based, 12, 229, 262
    experimental results, 267
    extracting relations, 242
    extracting time spans, 233
    temporal reasoning, 252
  geographic, 12, 409
    experimental results, 430, 440
    extracting fuzzy footprints,
      434
    extracting topological
      relations, 446
    extraction of nearness
      relations, 417
    local search, 432
    location approximation, 414
    spatial reasoning, 453
interval algebra, 92
  complexity, 93, 157
  transitivity, 93

region connection calculus, 277
  complexity, 360
  definition, 277
relatedness measures, 49
resemblance relations, 338

semi-continuity, 33
spatial relations, 276
    directional, 279
    fuzzy, *see* fuzzy spatial relations
    topological, *see* region connection
            calculus
supervaluation semantics, 20, 44

t-conorm, 24
t-norm, 22
    Łukasiewicz, 101
temporal relations
    fuzzy, *see* fuzzy interval relations
    metric, 95
    possibilistic, 96
    rough, 97

vagueness, 17, 42
    events, 87
    regions, 273